Rick Steves.

BEST OF

EUROPE

Contents

Post-Pandemic Travels: Expect a Warm Welcome...and a Few Changes
Research for this guidebook was limited by the COVID-19 outbreak, and the long-term impact of the crisis on our recommended destinations is unclear. Some details in this book will change for post-pandemic travelers. Now more than ever, it's smart to reconfirm specifics as you plan and travel. As always, you can find major updates at RickSteves.com/update.

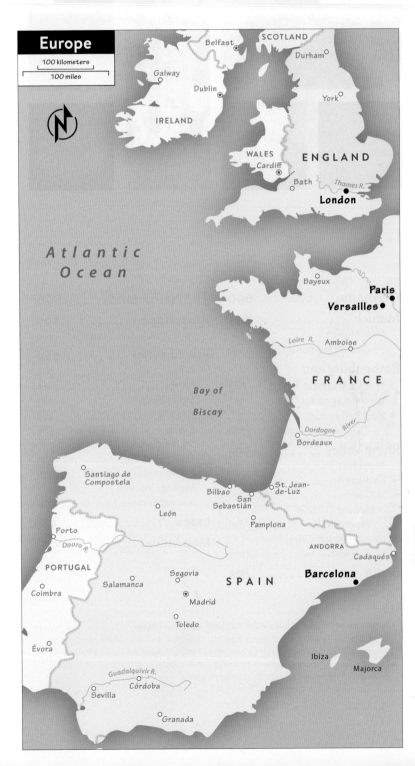

Introduction

Big Ben, the Eiffel Tower, and the Roman Colosseum. Yodeling in the Alps, biking down cobblestone paths, and taking a canal ride under the stars. Michelangelo's *David* and Rhine Valley castles. Sunny Riviera beaches, medieval German towns, and Spanish streets teeming with people after dark. Europe offers a rich smorgasbord of cultures: pasta and tapas, strudel and scones, Dutch pancakes and Swiss fondue, Parisian crêpes and Tuscan grapes. Follow your tastes and sample a little of everything for an unforgettable trip.

To wrestle Europe down to a manageable size, this selective book features its top destinations—from powerhouse cities to sleepy towns and cliff-hanging villages.

To help you assemble your dream trip, I've included advice on what to see and do in each destination, plus how to connect destinations by car or train. Whether you have a week or a month for your trip, this book will show you the best that Europe has to offer.

England
London, a thriving metropolis, teems with world-class museums, monuments, churches, parks, palaces, markets, theaters, pubs, and double-decker buses.

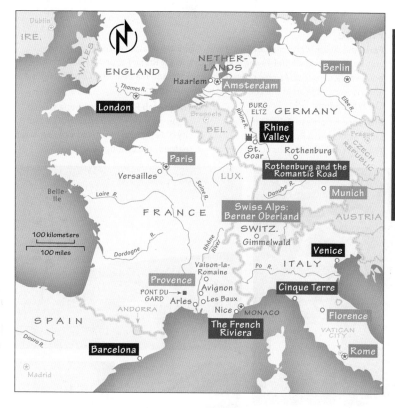

Spain

Barcelona is the center of Catalan culture, enlivened by people-friendly zones, a fun-to-explore old town, sandy beaches, and colorful works by native sons Gaudí, Picasso, and Miró.

France

Paris, the stylish world capital of food and culture, features the Eiffel Tower, grand boulevards, corner cafés, chic boutiques, and incomparable art at the Louvre and Orsay museums.

Provence is home to Arles (with Van Gogh sights and a Roman Arena), Avignon (with the famous bridge and brooding Palace of the Popes), the ancient Roman aqueduct of Pont du Gard, and the beautiful Côtes du Rhone wine road.

The French Riviera, a tempting stretch of sun-washed resorts, stars the elegant city of Nice, with its relaxed vibe, delicious seafood, and inviting beaches.

Italy

Rome is truly the Eternal City, studded with Roman remnants (Forum, Colosseum, Pantheon), floodlit-fountain squares, and the Vatican's Sistine Chapel.

Florence, the cradle of the Renaissance, offers the masterpiece-strewn Uffizi Gallery, Brunelleschi's dome-topped Duomo, Michelangelo's *David,* and Italy's best gelato.

The Cinque Terre consists of five idyllic Riviera hamlets along a rugged coastline, connected by hiking trails and dotted with vineyards and beaches.

Venice is a romantic island-city, powerful in medieval times and famous for St. Mark's Basilica, the Grand Canal, and singing gondoliers.

Germany

Munich is a bustling city with a traffic-free center, excellent museums, Baroque palaces, stately churches, rowdy beer halls, and the beautiful English Garden.

Rothenburg, a medieval, half-timbered town encircled by a walkable wall, is the highlight of the Romantic Road route, linking time-passed towns in the lovely countryside.

The Rhine Valley stars a mighty river steeped in legend, lined with storybook villages and imposing castles.

Berlin has thought-provoking museums, gleaming architecture, and trendy nightlife, plus evocative sections of the Wall that once divided the city and country.

Switzerland

The best chunk of the Swiss Alps is the **Berner Oberland,** featuring sky-high mountains, cliff-hanging villages, thundering waterfalls, scenic hikes, soaring lifts, and cogwheel train rides.

The Netherlands

Amsterdam is a progressive world capital with magnificent museums, dreamy canals, Golden-Age architecture, and a spirit of live and let live. Nearby Haarlem is a cozy, small-town home base alternative to big-city Amsterdam.

TRAVEL SMART

Approach Europe like a veteran traveler, even if it's your first trip. Design your itinerary, get a handle on your budget, make advance arrangements, and follow my travel strategies on the road. For advice on money, accommodations, transportation, and staying connected, see the Practicalities chapter. For cuisine tips, see each country's introduction.

Designing an Itinerary

Decide when to go. Peak season in much of Europe is June through September. For Spain and Italy, the best travel months are May, June, September, and October, which combine the convenience of peak season with pleasant weather (July and August can be sweltering along the Mediterranean). During peak season, it's best to reserve rooms well in advance, particularly in big cities. Throughout Europe, spring and fall generally have decent weather and lighter crowds. Winter can be cold and dreary, though big cities stay lively year-round.

As a general rule any time of year, the climate north of the Alps is mild, while south of the Alps it's like Arizona. If you wilt in the hot sun, avoid the Mediterranean in summer. If you want blue skies in the Swiss Alps and Britain, travel during the height of summer.

Choose your top destinations. The cosmopolitan cities of London and Paris are a must for anyone (and could merit a week apiece, if you have the time). Histo-

rians revel in Rome and romantics linger in Venice. If you'd like to storm some castles, explore the Rhine Valley. Art lovers are drawn to Florence's Renaissance treasures, and foodies savor France. Munich wins the award for the best beerhalls and oompah bands. For a mix of art, tapas, and irrepressible nightlife, experience Barcelona. Hikers make tracks to the Swiss Alps and Italy's Cinque Terre. To feel the pulse of 21st-century Germany, head to Berlin. Amsterdam, featuring Rembrandt, Anne Frank history, Van Gogh, and marijuana cafés, has something of interest for everyone. If medieval towns are your passion, walk the walls around Rothenburg. Beach baskers unroll their towels in the Cinque Terre, Barcelona, and the French Riviera. Photographers want to go everywhere.

Draft a rough itinerary. Figure out how many destinations you can comfortably fit in the time you have. Don't overdo it— few travelers wish they'd hurried more. Allow sufficient time per place. As a rough guideline, figure about three days for most major destinations and two days for smaller ones (take more time if you want to relax or explore). Any four or five of my recommended destinations (for example, London, Paris, the Rhine Valley, Swiss Alps, and Venice) would make a wonderful two-week trip. To reduce culture shock, start in London.

Staying in a home base—such as Arles, Munich, or Florence—and making day trips can be more time-efficient than changing locations and hotels. Minimize one-night stands; it can be worth taking a late-afternoon drive or train ride to get settled into a town for two nights.

Connect the dots. Link your destinations into a logical route. Determine which cities in Europe you'll fly into and out of. Begin your search for flights at Kayak.com. Even if you fly into a cheap flight hub like Frankfurt, you don't need to begin your trip there (there's a handy train station at the airport). For a gentler start to your trip, you could take a train to a nearby, smaller

town for your first stop (such as a Rhine village).

Decide if you'll be traveling through Europe by car, taking public transportation, or using a combination. Trains connect big cities easily and frequently. Regions that are rewarding to explore by car (such as Provence) have options for nondrivers, such as minibus tours, public transit, or taxis. A car is useless in cities.

Budget flights link many destinations. If your dream trip features Amsterdam, Rome, Berlin, and Barcelona, take planes instead of trains. To search for budget flights within Europe, try Skyscanner.com.

If you're on a tight budget, consider long-distance buses, which connect countries cheaply and slowly; Eurolines is one of several international companies.

Regardless of how you travel, allow plenty of time to get between destinations. To determine the approximate length of train journeys, see the train chart in the Practicalities chapter (also check schedules at Bahn.com). For driving distances, check Google Maps.

Plan your days. Fine-tune your trip; write out a day-by-day plan of where you'll be and what you want to see. To help you make the most of your time, I've suggested day plans for most destinations. But take sight closures into account: Avoid visiting a town on the one day a week that its must-see sights are closed. Check if any holidays or festivals will fall during your trip—these attract crowds and can close sights. For the latest, visit each country's national tourism website: VisitBritain.com, US.France.fr, Germany.travel.com, Italia.it, Holland.com, Spain.info, and MySwitzerland.com.

Give yourself some slack. Every trip, and every traveler, needs downtime for doing laundry, picnic shopping, relaxing, people-watching, and so on. Pace yourself. Assume you will return.

Ready, set... You've designed the perfect itinerary for the trip of a lifetime.

Trip Costs

Run a reality check on your dream trip. You'll have major transportation costs in addition to daily expenses.

Flight: A round-trip flight from the US to Europe can cost about $900 to $1,500 total, depending on where you fly from and when. Save time in Europe by flying into one city and out of another (e.g., into London and out of Rome).

Public Transportation: For a two-week

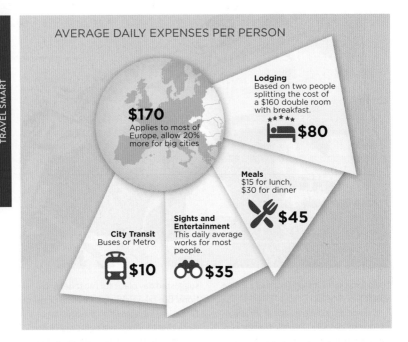

AVERAGE DAILY EXPENSES PER PERSON

$170
Applies to most of Europe, allow 20% more for big cities

Lodging
Based on two people splitting the cost of a $160 double room with breakfast.
$80

Meals
$15 for lunch, $30 for dinner
$45

City Transit
Buses or Metro
$10

Sights and Entertainment
This daily average works for most people.
$35

trip, allow about $350 for second-class trains and buses. Depending on your itinerary, you'll usually save money by buying train tickets as you go, but for a Europe-wide trip, a Eurail pass can be a good choice. Rail passes normally must be purchased outside of Europe; exceptions are German and Swiss passes, which can be purchased on site.

Keep in mind that many fast trains (such as France's TGV and the Eurostar linking London, Paris, and Amsterdam) require seat assignments, and advance booking is strongly recommended. In some cases, a short flight can be cheaper than taking the train.

Car Rental: Allow roughly $250 per week, not including tolls, gas, parking, and insurance. Rentals are cheapest if arranged from the US. Italy and Spain technically require drivers to carry an International Driving Permit ($20 at AAA. com).

Budget Tips: Cut your daily expenses by taking advantage of the deals you'll find throughout Europe and mentioned in this book.

City transit passes (for multiple rides or all-day use) decrease your cost per ride.

Avid sightseers buy combo-tickets or sightseeing passes that cover multiple museums. Or ask at sights if you're eligible for a discount, often available for youths (up to age 18), students (with proper I.D. cards, www.isic.org), families, and seniors, though some discounts apply only to citizens of the European Union.

Some businesses—especially hotels and walking-tour companies—offer discounts to my readers (look for the RS% symbol in the listings in this book).

Book your rooms directly with the hotel. Some hotels offer a discount if you pay in cash and/or stay three or more nights; check online or ask. And even seniors can sleep inexpensively in hostels (some have private double rooms). Or check Airbnb-type sites for deals.

It's no hardship to eat inexpensively in Europe. You can get tasty, affordable meals at cafeterias, local chain restaurants, and ethnic eateries. Groceries are everywhere; cultivate the art of picnicking in atmospheric settings.

When you splurge, choose an experience you'll always remember, such as a concert, gondola ride, or alpine lift. Minimize souvenir shopping. Focus instead on collecting vivid memories, wonderful stories, and new friends.

Before You Go

You'll have a smoother trip if you tackle a few things ahead of time. For more information on these topics, see the Practicalities chapter and check RickSteves.com, which has helpful travel tips and talks.

Make sure your travel documents are valid. If your passport is due to expire within six months of your ticketed date of return, you need to renew it. Allow up to six weeks to renew or get a passport (www.travel.state.gov). You may also need to register with the European Travel Information and Authorization System (ETIAS).

Arrange your transportation. Book your international flights. It's worth thinking about buying essential train tickets in advance, getting a rail pass, renting a car,

or booking cheap European flights. (You can wing it once you're there, but it may cost more.)

Book rooms well in advance, particularly if your trip falls during peak season or any major holidays or festivals.

Reserve or buy tickets in advance for major sights. You can reserve in advance for the Eiffel Tower in Paris, Florence's Uffizi Gallery, Barcelona's Sagrada Família, Amsterdam's Anne Frank House, and many more (specifics are included in this book). Some sights require reservations, such as the Borghese Gallery in Rome.

Consider travel insurance. Compare the cost of the insurance to the cost of your potential loss. Check whether your existing insurance (health, homeowners, or renters) covers you and your possessions overseas.

Call your bank. Alert your bank that you'll be using your debit and credit cards in Europe. Ask about transaction fees, and get the PIN number for your credit card. You won't need to bring along any European cash for your trip; instead, withdraw currency from cash machines while traveling.

Use your smartphone smartly. Sign up for an international service plan to reduce

Rick's Free Video Clips and Audio Tours

Rick Steves Classroom Europe, a powerful tool for teachers, is also useful for travelers. This video library contains over 400 short clips excerpted from my public television series. Enjoy these videos as you sort through options for your trip and to better understand what you'll see in Europe. Check it out at Classroom.RickSteves.com (just enter a topic to find everything I've filmed on a subject).

Rick Steves Audio Europe, a free app, makes it easy to download and listen to my audio tours offline as you travel. These audio tours (look for the 🎧) cover sights and neighborhoods in many of Europe's cities and towns. The app also offers insightful interviews from my public radio show with experts from Europe and around the globe. Find it in your app store or at RickSteves.com/AudioEurope.

your costs, or rely on Wi-Fi in Europe instead. Download any apps you'll want on the road, such as maps, translators, transit schedules, and Rick Steves Audio Europe (see sidebar).

Pack light. You'll walk with your luggage more than you think. I travel for weeks with a single carry-on bag and a daypack. Use the packing checklist in the Practicalities chapter as a guide.

Travel Strategies on the Road

If you have a positive attitude, equip yourself with good information, and expect to travel smart, you will.

Read—and reread—this book. To have an "A" trip, be an "A" student. As you study up on sights, note opening hours of sights, closed days, crowd-beating tips, and whether reservations are required or advisable. Check the latest at RickSteves. com/update.

Be your own tour guide. As you travel, get up-to-date info on sights, reserve tickets and tours, reconfirm hotels and travel arrangements, and check transit connections. Visit local tourist information offices. Upon arrival in a new town, lay the groundwork for a smooth departure; confirm the train, bus, or road you'll take when you leave.

Give local tours a spin. Your appreciation of a city or region and its history can increase dramatically if you take a walking tour or even hire a private guide. If you want to learn more about any aspect of Europe, experts are happy to teach you.

Outsmart thieves. Pickpockets abound in crowded places where tourists congregate. Treat commotions as smokescreens for theft. Keep your cash, credit cards, and passport secure in a money belt tucked under your clothes; carry only a day's spending money in your front pocket. Don't set valuable items down on counters or café tabletops where they can be quickly stolen or easily forgotten.

Minimize potential loss. Keep expensive gear to a minimum. Bring photocopies or take photos of important documents (passport and cards) to aid in replacement if they're lost or stolen. Back up photos and files frequently.

Guard your time and energy. Taking a taxi can be a good value if it saves you a long wait for a cheap bus or an exhausting walk across town. To avoid long lines at sights, follow my crowd-beating tips (such as making advance reservations or visiting sights early or late).

Be flexible. Even if you have a well-planned itinerary, expect changes, closures, sore feet, sweltering weather, and so on. Your Plan B could turn out to be even better.

Attempt the language. Many Europeans—especially those in the tourist trade and in big cities—speak English, but if you learn even just a few phrases of the local

Welcome to Rick Steves' Europe

Travel is intensified living—maximum thrills per minute and one of the last great sources of legal adventure. Travel is freedom. It's recess, and we need it.

I discovered a passion for European travel as a teen and have been sharing it ever since—through my bus tours, public television and radio shows, and travel guidebooks. Over the years, I've taught millions of travelers how to best enjoy Europe's blockbuster sights—and experience "Back Door" discoveries that most tourists miss.

This book offers a balanced mix of the best of Europe's exciting cities and small-town getaways. It's selective: There are dozens of walled towns in Europe, but I feature only the best ones. My self-guided museum tours and city walks give insight into the country's vibrant history and today's living, breathing culture.

I advocate traveling simply and smartly. Take advantage of my money- and time-saving tips on sightseeing, transportation, and more. Try local, character-istic alternatives to expensive hotels and restaurants. In many ways, spending more money only builds a thicker wall between you and what you traveled so far to see.

We visit Europe to experience it—to become temporary locals. Thoughtful travel engages us with the world, as we learn to appreciate other cultures and new ways to measure quality of life.

Judging from the positive feedback I receive from readers, this book will help you enjoy a fun, affordable, and rewarding vacation—whether it's your first trip or your tenth.

Happy travels!

Rick Steves

language, you'll get more smiles and make more friends. Practice the survival phrases near the end of this book, and even better, bring a phrase book.

Connect with the culture. Interacting with locals carbonates your experience. Enjoy the friendliness of the European people. Ask questions—most locals are happy to point you in their idea of the right direction. Set up your own quest for the best dessert, grandest viewpoint, funniest sign, or perfect sidewalk café. When an unexpected opportunity pops up, say "Yes!"

Hear the Swiss cowbells? Taste the beer-hall pretzel? Feel the magic of Venice? See the lights of the Eiffel Tower sparkling at night?

Your next stop. . .Europe!

England

Hilly England occupies the lower two-thirds of the island of Great Britain (with Scotland in the north). England is the size of Louisiana (about 50,000 square miles), with a population of just over 55 million. England's ethnic diversity sets it apart from the rest of the United Kingdom: Nearly one in three citizens is not associated with the Christian faith. The cradle of the Industrial Revolution, today's Britain has little heavy industry—its economic drivers are banking, insurance, and business services, plus energy production and agriculture.

London is England's—and Great Britain's—cosmopolitan capital. For the tourist, London offers a little of everything associated with Britain: castles, cathedrals, royalty, theater, and tea.

CUISINE SCENE AT A GLANCE

British cooking embraces international influences and good-quality ingredients. It's easy to eat well here. Even in London, plenty of inexpensive choices are available.

Pub grub is the most atmospheric budget option. You'll usually get reasonably priced (£8-15), hearty lunches and dinners under ancient timbers. Meals are usually served around 12:00-14:00 and 18:00-20:00. There's generally no table service. Order at the bar, then take a seat. Either they'll bring the food when it's ready, or you'll pick it up at the bar. Pay at the bar (sometimes when you order, sometimes after you eat). There's no need to tip unless it's a place with full table service. If you're on a tight budget, it's OK to share a meal.

Classier restaurants have some affordable deals. Lunch is usually cheaper than dinner; a top-end, £30-for-dinner restaurant often serves the same quality two courses as lunch deals for about half the price. Many restaurants have early-bird or pre-theater specials of two or three courses, often for significant savings, if you eat before 18:30 or 19:00; these deals may be offered daily or only on weekdays.

Global cuisine adds spice to England's cuisine. At Indian restaurants, an easy way to taste a variety of dishes is to order a *thali*—a sampler plate, generally served on a metal tray, with small servings of various specialties. Many Chinese and Thai places serve £6 meals and offer even cheaper takeaway boxes. Middle Eastern stands sell gyro sandwiches, falafel, and *shwarmas* (grilled meat in pita bread).

Chain restaurants abound, serving a variety of good-value meals, from sandwiches and salads (Pret à Manger, Le Pain Quotidien) and burgers (Byron) to sushi (Yo!, Wasabi, and Itsu), Indian (Masala Zone), Thai (Thai Square, Busaba Eathai), and more (Wagamama, Côte Brasserie, Ask, Pizza Express, Eat, and Loch Fyne Fish).

At **tearooms,** popular choices are a "cream tea," which consists of tea and a scone or two, or the pricier "afternoon tea," which comes with pastries and finger foods such as small, crust-less sandwiches. Two people can order one afternoon tea and one cream tea and share the afternoon tea's goodies.

Tipping: At pubs and places where you order at the counter, you don't have to tip. At restaurants and fancy pubs with waitstaff, it's not necessary to tip if a service charge is already included in the bill (common in London). Otherwise, it's appropriate to tip about 10-12 percent; you can add a bit more for finer dining or extra good service.

Other Budget Options: Fish-and-chips are a British classic; a takeaway box of fish-and-chips costs about £5-7. Grocery stores have inviting delis with good takeout food and sometimes sit-down eating. Good bets are the Marks & Spencer department stores, M&S Simply Food, and Sainsbury's Local.

London

A longtime tourist destination, London seems perpetually at your service, with an impressive slate of sights and entertainment. Blow through this urban jungle on the open deck of a double-decker bus and take a pinch-me-I'm-here walk through the West End. Hear the chimes of Big Ben and ogle the crown jewels at the Tower of London. Cruise the Thames River and take a spin on the London Eye. Hobnob with poets' tombstones in Westminster Abbey and rummage through civilization's attic at the British Museum.

London is also more than its museums and landmarks, it's a living, breathing, thriving organism...a coral reef of humanity. The city has changed dramatically in recent years: Many visitors are surprised to find how diverse and cosmopolitan it is. Chinese takeouts outnumber fish-and-chips shops. Eastern Europeans pull pints in British pubs, and Italians express your espresso. Outlying suburbs are home to huge communities of Indians and Pakistanis. This city of 10 million separate dreams is learning—sometimes fitfully—to live as a microcosm of its formerly vast empire.

LONDON IN 4 DAYS

Day 1: Get oriented by taking my Westminster Walk from Big Ben to Trafalgar Square (stop in Westminster Abbey and the Churchill War Rooms on the way). Grab lunch near Trafalgar Square (maybe at the café at St. Martin-in-the-Fields Church), then visit the nearby National Gallery or National Portrait Gallery.

On any evening: Have an early-bird dinner and take in a play in the West End or at Shakespeare's Globe. Choose from a concert, walking tour, or nighttime bus tour. Extend your sightseeing into the evening hours; some attractions stay open late. Settle in at a pub, or do some shopping at any of London's elegant department stores (generally open until 20:00 or 21:00). Stroll any of the main squares, fine parks, or the Jubilee Walkway for people-watching. Ride the London Eye Ferris wheel for grand city views.

Day 2: Early in the morning, take a double-decker hop-on, hop-off sightseeing bus tour from Victoria Station, and hop off for the Changing of the Guard at Buckingham Palace. After lunch, tour the British Museum and/or the nearby British Library.

Day 3: At the Tower of London, see the crown jewels and take the Beefeater tour. Then grab a picnic, catch a boat at Tower Pier, and have lunch on the Thames while cruising to Blackfriars Pier.

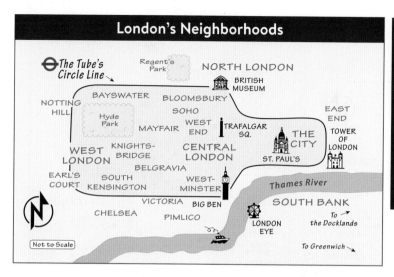

London's Neighborhoods

The Tube's Circle Line

NORTH LONDON

Regent's Park

BRITISH MUSEUM

NOTTING HILL

BAYSWATER

BLOOMSBURY

Hyde Park

SOHO

MAYFAIR

WEST END

TRAFALGAR SQ.

EAST END

WEST LONDON

KNIGHTS-BRIDGE

CENTRAL LONDON

THE CITY

TOWER OF LONDON

BELGRAVIA

ST. PAUL'S

EARL'S COURT

SOUTH KENSINGTON

WEST-MINSTER

Thames River

VICTORIA

BIG BEN

SOUTH BANK

CHELSEA

PIMLICO

LONDON EYE

To the Docklands

Not to Scale

To Greenwich

Tour St. Paul's Cathedral and climb its dome for views, then walk across Millennium Bridge to the South Bank to visit the Tate Modern, tour Shakespeare's Globe, or stroll the Jubilee Walkway.

Day 4: Take your pick of the Victoria and Albert Museum, Tate Britain, Imperial War Museum, or Houses of Parliament. Hit one of London's many lively open-air markets. Or cruise to Greenwich or Kew Gardens.

THE CROWN JEWELS

ORIENTATION

To grasp London more comfortably, see it as the old town in the city center without the modern, congested sprawl.

The Thames River (pron. "tems") runs roughly west to east through the city, with most sights on the North Bank. Mentally, maybe even physically, trim down your map to include only the area between the Tower of London (to the east), Hyde Park (west), Regent's Park (north), and the South Bank (south). This is roughly the area bordered by the Tube's Circle Line. This four-mile stretch between the Tower and Hyde Park (about a 1.5-hour walk) looks like a milk bottle on its side (see map), and holds most of the sights mentioned in this chapter.

The sprawling city becomes much more manageable if you think of it as a collection of neighborhoods.

Central London: This area contains the Westminster district, which includes Big Ben, Parliament, Westminster Abbey, Buckingham Palace, and Trafalgar Square, with its many major museums. The West End is the center of London's cultural life, with bustling squares: Piccadilly Circus and Leicester Square host cinemas, tour-

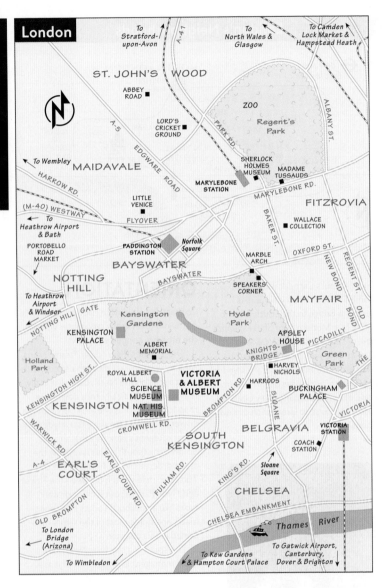

London

To Stratford-/upon-Avon

To North Wales & Glasgow

To Camden Lock Market & Hampstead Heath

ST. JOHN'S WOOD

ABBEY ROAD

ZOO

Regent's Park

ALBANY ST.

LORD'S CRICKET GROUND

PARK RD.

To Wembley

MAIDAVALE

EDGWARE ROAD

A-5

HARROW RD.

SHERLOCK HOLMES MUSEUM

MADAME TUSSAUDS

MARYLEBONE STATION

MARYLEBONE RD.

FITZROVIA

LITTLE VENICE

(M-40) WESTWAY

To Heathrow Airport & Bath

FLYOVER

BAKER ST.

WALLACE COLLECTION

OXFORD ST.

REGENT ST.

NEW BOND

PORTOBELLO ROAD MARKET

PADDINGTON STATION

Norfolk Square

MARBLE ARCH

BAYSWATER

BAYSWATER

NOTTING HILL

SPEAKERS' CORNER

MAYFAIR

OLD BOND

To Heathrow Airport & Windsor

NOTTING HILL GATE

Kensington Gardens

Hyde Park

KENSINGTON PALACE

ALBERT MEMORIAL

APSLEY HOUSE

PICCADILLY

KNIGHTS-BRIDGE

Green Park

THE

Holland Park

ROYAL ALBERT HALL

SCIENCE MUSEUM

VICTORIA & ALBERT MUSEUM

HARVEY NICHOLS

HARRODS

BUCKINGHAM PALACE

KENSINGTON HIGH ST.

NAT. HIS. MUSEUM

BROMPTON RD.

SLOANE

VICTORIA

CROMWELL RD.

KENSINGTON

SOUTH KENSINGTON

BELGRAVIA

VICTORIA STATION

WARWICK RD.

EARLS COURT RD.

FULHAM RD.

COACH STATION

A-4

EARL'S COURT

KING'S RD.

Sloane Square

OLD BROMPTON

CHELSEA

To London Bridge (Arizona)

CHELSEA EMBANKMENT

Thames River

To Wimbledon

To Kew Gardens & Hampton Court Palace

To Gatwick Airport, Canterbury, Dover & Brighton

ist traps, and nighttime glitz. Soho and Covent Garden are thriving people zones with theaters, restaurants, pubs, and boutiques. And Regent and Oxford streets are the city's main shopping zones.

North London: Neighborhoods in this part of town—including Bloomsbury, Fitzrovia, and Marylebone—contain such major sights as the British Museum and the overhyped Madame Tussauds Waxworks. Nearby, along busy Euston Road, is the British Library.

The City: Today's modern financial district, called simply "The City," was a walled town in Roman times. Gleaming skyscrapers are interspersed with histori-

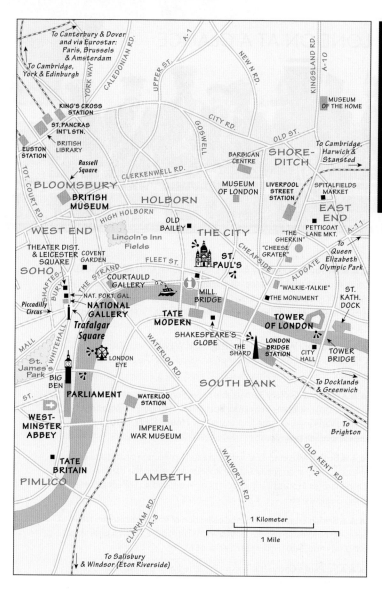

cal landmarks such as St. Paul's Cathedral and the Museum of London. The Tower of London and Tower Bridge lie at The City's eastern border.

East London: Just east of The City is the East End—the former stomping ground of Cockney ragamuffins and Jack the Ripper, and now an increasingly gen-trified neighborhood of hipsters, "pop-up" shops, and an emerging food scene.

The South Bank: The South Bank of the Thames River offers major sights (Tate Modern, Shakespeare's Globe, London Eye, Imperial War Museum) linked by a riverside walkway. Within this area, Southwark (SUTH-uck) stretches

LONDON AT A GLANCE

▲▲▲**Westminster Abbey** Britain's finest church and the site of royal coronations and burials since 1066. **Hours:** Abbey—Mon-Fri 9:30-16:30, Wed until 19:00, Sat 9:00-16:00 (Sept-April until 14:00); Diamond Jubilee Galleries—Mon-Fri 10:00-16:00, Sat 9:30-15:30; closed Sun except for worship. See page 37.

▲▲▲**Churchill War Rooms** Underground WWII headquarters of Churchill's war effort. **Hours:** Daily 9:30-18:00, July-Aug until 19:00. See page 46.

▲▲▲**National Gallery** Remarkable collection of European paintings (1250-1900), including Leonardo, Botticelli, Velázquez, Rembrandt, Turner, Van Gogh, and the Impressionists. **Hours:** Daily 10:00-18:00, Fri until 21:00. See page 46.

▲▲▲**British Museum** The world's greatest collection of artifacts of Western civilization, including the Rosetta Stone and the Parthenon's Elgin Marbles. **Hours:** Daily 10:00-17:30, Fri until 20:30 (select galleries only). See page 56.

▲▲▲**British Library** Fascinating collection of important literary treasures of the Western world. **Hours:** Mon-Thu 9:30-20:00, Fri until 18:00, Sat until 17:00, Sun 11:00-17:00. See page 61.

▲▲▲**St. Paul's Cathedral** The main cathedral of the Anglican Church, designed by Christopher Wren, with a climbable dome and daily evensong services. **Hours:** Mon-Sat 8:30-16:30, closed Sun except for worship. See page 65.

▲▲▲**Tower of London** Historic castle, palace, and prison housing the crown jewels and a witty band of Beefeaters. **Hours:** Tue-Sat 9:00-17:30, Sun-Mon from 10:00; Nov-Feb closes one hour earlier. See page 70.

▲▲▲**Victoria and Albert Museum** The best collection of decorative arts anywhere. **Hours:** Daily 10:00-17:45, Fri until 22:00 (select galleries only). See page 83.

▲▲**Houses of Parliament** Famous for Big Ben and occupied by the Houses of Lords and Commons. **Hours:** When Parliament is in session, generally open Oct-late July Mon-Thu, closed Fri-Sun and during recess late July-Sept. Guided tours offered year-round on Sat and most weekdays during recess. See page 41.

▲▲**Trafalgar Square** The heart of London, where Westminster, The City, and the West End meet. See page 46.

▲▲**National Portrait Gallery** A *Who's Who* of British history, featuring portraits of this nation's most important historical figures. **Hours:** Daily 10:00-18:00, Fri until 21:00. See page 51.

▲▲**Covent Garden** Vibrant people-watching zone with shops, cafés, and street musicians. See page 54.

▲▲**Changing of the Guard at Buckingham Palace** Hour-long spectacle at Britain's royal residence. **Hours:** May-July daily at 11:00, Aug-April Sun-Mon, Wed, and Fri. See page 55.

▲▲**London Eye** Enormous observation wheel, dominating—and offering commanding views over—London's skyline. **Hours:** Daily 10:00-20:30 or later, Sept-May 11:00-18:00. See page 76.

▲▲**Imperial War Museum** Exhibits examining military conflicts from the early 20th century to today. **Hours:** Daily 10:00-18:00. See page 76.

▲▲**Tate Modern** Works by Monet, Matisse, Dalí, Picasso, and Warhol displayed in a converted powerhouse complex. **Hours:** Daily 10:00-18:00, Fri-Sat until 22:00. See page 78.

▲▲**Shakespeare's Globe** Timbered, thatched-roof reconstruction of the Bard's original "wooden O." **Hours:** Theater complex, museum, and tours generally daily 9:00-17:30; April-Oct generally morning theater tours only. Plays are also staged here. See page 79.

▲▲**Tate Britain** Collection of British painting from the 16th century through modern times. **Hours:** Daily 10:00-18:00. See page 80.

▲▲**Natural History Museum** Packed with engaging exhibits and enthralled kids. **Hours:** Daily 10:00-18:00. See page 84.

from the Tate Modern to London Bridge. Pedestrian bridges connect the South Bank with The City and Trafalgar Square.

Rick's Tip: *You'll find pedestrian-focused maps around town—especially handy when exiting Tube stations. In this sprawling city—where predictable grid-planned streets are relatively rare—***it's smart to buy a good map.**

West London: This area contains neighborhoods such as Mayfair, Belgravia, Pimlico, Chelsea, South Kensington, and Notting Hill. It's home to London's wealthy and has many trendy shops and enticing restaurants. Here you'll find a range of museums (Victoria and Albert Museum, Tate Britain, and more), lively Victoria Station, and the vast green expanses of Hyde Park and Kensington Gardens.

Tourist Information

It's amazing how hard it can be to find unbiased sightseeing information and advice in London. You'll see "Tourist Information" offices advertised everywhere, but most are private agencies that make a big profit selling tours and advance sightseeing and/or theater tickets.

The **City of London Information Centre,** on the street just below St. Paul's Cathedral, is the only publicly funded—and impartial—"real" TI. It sells Oyster cards, London Passes, and advance "Fast Track" sightseeing tickets (all described later). It also stocks various free publications: *London Planner* (a monthly that lists all the sights, events, and hours), walking-tour brochures, the biweekly *Official London Theatre Guide,* a free Tube and bus map, and the *Guide to River Thames Boat Services.* The TI gives out a free map of The City and sells several citywide maps; ask if they have a free map with coupons for discounts on sights (Mon-Sat 9:30-17:30, Sun 10:00-16:00; Tube: St. Paul's, tel. 020/7606-3030, www.visitthecity.co.uk).

Visit London, which serves the greater London area, doesn't have an office you can visit in person—but does have an information-packed website (www.visitlondon.com).

Fast Track Tickets: To skip the ticket-buying queues at certain London sights, you can buy Fast Track tickets (sometimes called "priority pass" tickets) in advance—and they're typically cheaper than tickets sold right at the sight. These are smart for the Tower of London and Madame Tussauds Waxworks in high season. They're available through various sales outlets (including the City of London TI, souvenir stands, and faux TIs scattered throughout touristy areas).

Rick's Tip: *The Artful Dodger is alive and well in London.* **Beware of pickpockets,** *particularly on public transportation, among tourist crowds, and at street markets.*

London Pass: This pass, which covers many big sights and lets you skip some lines, is expensive but potentially worth the investment for extremely busy sightseers (£75/1 day, multi-day options available, sold at City of London TI, major train

stations, and airports, tel. 020/7293-0972, www.londonpass.com).

Helpful Hints

Laundry: Pimlico Launderette near Victoria Station has self-service and same-day full-service (daily 8:00-19:00, last wash at 17:30; 3 Westmoreland Terrace; tel. 020/7821-8692).

Rick's Tip: *Buying* **tickets online in advance** *is smart—you'll generally save a few pounds per sight and can skip the ticket-buying line once you arrive—though you may need to wait in a security line or pick up your ticket at the sight.*

Useful Apps: Mapway's free **Tube Map London Underground** and **Bus Times London** (www.mapway.com) apps show the easiest way to connect Tube stations and provide bus stops and route information. The handy **Citymapper** app for London covers every mode of public transit in the city. And **Time Out London**'s free app has reviews and listings for theater, museums, and movies.

Baggage Storage: Train stations have left-luggage counters, where each bag is scanned (just like at the airport); expect up to 45-minute waits (£12.50/24 hours per item, most stations open daily 7:00-23:00). You can also store bags at the airports (similar rates and hours, www.left-baggage.co.uk).

Tours
HOP-ON, HOP-OFF DOUBLE-DECKER BUS TOURS

London is full of hop-on, hop-off bus companies competing for your tourist pound. I've focused on the two companies I like the most: **Original** and **Big Bus.** Both offer essentially the same tours of the city's sightseeing highlights—an experience rated ▲▲▲.

Each company offers at least one route with live guides, and a second (sometimes different route) with recorded narration.

Buses run daily about every 10-15 minutes in summer and every 10-20 minutes in winter, starting at about 8:30. The last full loop usually leaves Victoria Station at around 20:00 in summer, and 17:00 in winter.

You can buy tickets online in advance, from drivers, or from staff at street kiosks (credit cards accepted at kiosks at major stops such as Victoria Station).

Original: City Sampler–£29, 24 hours–£34, RS%—£6 discount with this book, limit four discounts per book, they'll rip off the corner of this page, www.theoriginaltour.com.

Big Bus: £39 (cheaper online), tel. 020/7808-6753, www.bigbustours.com.

Rick's Tip: For an efficient intro to London, catch an 8:30 departure of a **hop-on, hop-off overview bus tour,** *riding most of the loop (which takes just over 1.5 hours, depending on traffic). Hop off just before 10:00 at Trafalgar Square (Cockspur Street, stop "S"), then walk briskly to Buckingham Palace to find a spot to watch the* **Changing of the Guard ceremony** *at 11:00.*

NIGHT BUS TOURS

Various companies offer a lower-priced, after-hours sightseeing circuit (1-2 hours). **Golden Tours** buses depart at 19:00 and 20:00 from their offices on Buckingham Palace Road (£28, tel. 020/7630-2028; www.goldentours.com). **See London By Night** buses offer live guides and frequent evening departures from Green Park (next to the Ritz Hotel); Oct-March at 19:30 and 21:20 only (£28.50, tel. 020/7183-4744, www.seelondonbynight.com).

WALKING TOURS

Top-notch local guides lead (sometimes big) groups on walking tours—worth ▲▲—through specific slices of London's past. **London Walks'** extensive daily schedule is online, as well as in a white brochure (most reliably found in the Café in the Crypt, below Trafalgar Square's St. Martin-in-the-Fields church). Their two-hour walks are led by top-quality professional guides (£12, cash only, private tours available, tel. 020/7624-3978, www.walks.com).

London Walks also offers day trips into the countryside (£20 plus £15-70 for transportation and admission costs, cash only: Stonehenge/Salisbury, Oxford/Cotswolds, Bath, and so on).

LOCAL GUIDES AND DRIVERS

Rates for London's registered Blue Badge guides are standard (about £165-200 for four hours and £270 or more for nine hours). I know and like these fine local guides: **Sean Kelleher** (tel. 020/8673-1624, mobile 07764-612-770, sean@seanlondonguide.com); **Britt Lonsdale** (£265/half-day, £365/day, tel. 020/7386-9907, mobile 07813-278-077, brittl@btinternet.com); **Joel Reid** (mobile 07887-955-720, joelyreid@gmail.com); **Tom Hooper** (mobile 07986-048-047, tomh1@btinternet.com); and **Gillian Chadwick** (£300/day, mobile 07889-976-598, gillychad@hotmail.co.uk). If you have a particular interest, London Walks (see earlier) can book one for your exact focus (£215/half-day).

Rick's Tip: If you're taking a bus tour mainly to get oriented, **save time and money** *by taking a night tour. You can munch a memorable picnic dinner while riding on the top deck.*

These guides have cars or a minibus for day trips, and also offer walking-only tours: **Janine Barton** (£390/half-day, £575/day, day tours outside

Thames Boat Piers

While Westminster Pier is the most popular, it's not the only dock in town. Consider all the options (listed from west to east, as the Thames flows).

Millbank Pier (North Bank): At the Tate Britain museum, used primarily by the Tate Boat ferry service (express connection to Tate Modern at Bankside Pier).

Westminster Pier (North Bank): Near the base of Big Ben, offers round-trip sightseeing cruises and lots of departures in both directions (though the Thames Clippers boats don't stop here). Nearby sights include Parliament and Westminster Abbey.

London Eye Pier (a.k.a. **Waterloo Pier,** South Bank): At the base of the London Eye; good, less-crowded alternative to Westminster, with many of the same cruise options (Waterloo Station is nearby).

Embankment Pier (North Bank): Near Covent Garden, Trafalgar Square, and Cleopatra's Needle (the obelisk on the Thames). This pier is used mostly for special boat trips, such as some RIB (rigid inflatable boats) and lunch and dinner cruises.

Festival Pier (South Bank): Next to the Royal Festival Hall, just downstream from the London Eye.

Blackfriars Pier (North Bank): In The City, not far from St. Paul's.

Bankside Pier (South Bank): Directly in front of the Tate Modern and Shakespeare's Globe.

London Bridge Pier (a.k.a. **London Bridge City Pier,** South Bank): Near the HMS Belfast.

Tower Pier (North Bank): At the Tower of London, at the east edge of The City and near the East End.

St. Katharine's Pier (North Bank): Just downstream from the Tower of London.

of London start at £625 depending on the distance, tel. 020/7402-4600, www. seeitinstyle.synthasite.com, jbsiis@aol. com); **Mike Dickson** (£345/half-day, £535/day, mobile 07769/905-811, michael. dickson5@btinternet.com); and **David Stubbs** (£375 for 1-3 people, £395 for 4-6 people, mobile 07775-888-534, www.londoncountrytours.co.uk, info@ londoncountrytours.co.uk).

CRUISE BOAT TOURS

London offers many made-for-tourist cruises, most on slow-moving, open-top boats accompanied by entertaining commentary (an experience worth ▲▲). Take a **short city-center cruise** by riding

a boat 30 minutes from Westminster Pier to Tower Pier (particularly handy if you're visiting the Tower of London anyway), or choose a **longer cruise** that includes a peek at the East End, riding from Westminster all the way to Greenwich (save time by taking the Tube back).

Each company runs cruises daily, about twice hourly, from morning until dark; many reduce frequency off-season. Boats come and go from various docks in the city center. The most popular places to embark are Westminster Pier (at the base of Westminster Bridge across the street from Big Ben) and London Eye Pier (also known as Waterloo Pier, across the river on the South Bank).

A one-way trip within the city center costs about £11. With a Travelcard, you get a 33 percent discount off most cruises; the Oyster card can often be used as payment but nets you a discount only on Thames Clippers.

The three dominant companies are **City Cruises** (handy 45-minute cruise from Westminster Pier to Tower Pier; www.citycruises.com), **Thames River Services** (fewer stops, classic boats, friendlier and more old-fashioned feel; www.thamesriverservices.co.uk), and **Circular Cruise** (full cruise takes about an hour, operated by Crown River Services, www.circularcruise.london).

Cruising Downstream, to Greenwich: Both **City Cruises** and **Thames River Services** head from Westminster Pier to Greenwich. The cruises are usually narrated by the captain, with most commentary given on the way to Greenwich. To maximize both efficiency and sightseeing, take a narrated cruise to Greenwich one way, and take the DLR back to avoid late-afternoon boat crowds.

Rick's Tip: *Zipping through London every 20-30 minutes, the* **Thames Clippers are designed for commuters.** *With no open deck and no commentary, they're* **not the best option for sightseeing.**

Cruising Upstream, to Kew Gardens: Thames River Boats leave for Kew Gardens from Westminster Pier (£15 one-way, £22 round-trip, discounts with Travelcard, 2-4/day depending on season, 1.5 hours, boats sail April-Oct, about half the trip is narrated, www.thamesriverboats.co.uk).

WESTMINSTER WALK

Just about every visitor to London strolls along historic Whitehall from Big Ben to Trafalgar Square. This walk is a whirlwind tour as well as a practical orientation to London. Most of the sights you'll see are described in more detail later in this chapter.

🎧 You can download a free, extended audio version of this walk.

Rick's Tip: Cars drive on the left side of the road—*confusing for foreign pedestrians and for foreign drivers. Always look right, look left, then look right again just to be sure.* **Jaywalking is treacherous** *when you're disoriented about which direction traffic is coming from.*

❍ Self-Guided Walk

Start halfway across ❶ **Westminster Bridge** for that "Wow, I'm really in London!" feeling. Get a close-up view of the **Houses of Parliament** and **Big Ben.** Downstream you'll see the **London Eye,** the city's giant Ferris wheel. Down the stairs to Westminster Pier are boats to the Tower of London and Greenwich (downstream) or Kew Gardens (upstream).

En route to Parliament Square, you'll pass a ❷ **statue of Boadicea,** the Celtic queen who unsuccessfully resisted Roman invaders in AD 60. Julius Caesar was the first Roman general to cross the Channel, but even he was weirded out by the island's strange inhabitants, who worshipped trees, sacrificed virgins, and went to war painted blue. Later, Romans subdued and civilized them, building roads and making this spot on the Thames—"Londinium"—a major urban center.

You'll find four red phone booths lining the north side of ❸ **Parliament Square** along Great George Street—great for a

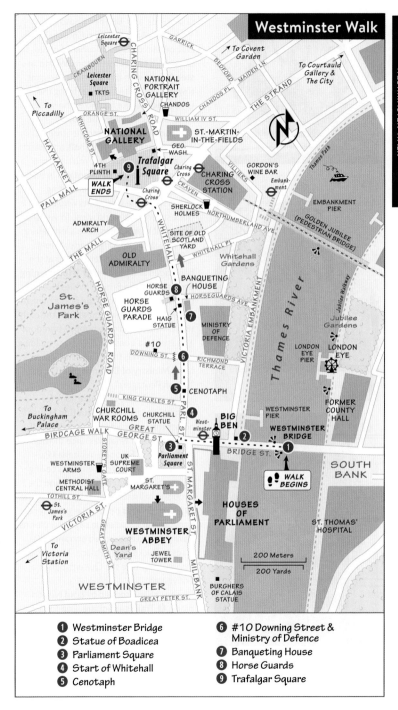

Westminster Walk

1. Westminster Bridge
2. Statue of Boadicea
3. Parliament Square
4. Start of Whitehall
5. Cenotaph
6. #10 Downing Street & Ministry of Defence
7. Banqueting House
8. Horse Guards
9. Trafalgar Square

A Boadicea statue

B Churchill statue in Parliament Square

C Horse Guards

phone-box-and-Big-Ben photo op.

Wave hello to Winston Churchill and Nelson Mandela in Parliament Square. To Churchill's right is the historic **Westminster Abbey,** with its two stubby, elegant towers. The white building (flying the Union Jack) at the far end of the square houses Britain's **Supreme Court.**

Head north up Parliament Street, which turns into ❹ **Whitehall,** and walk toward Trafalgar Square. You'll see the thought-provoking ❺ **Cenotaph** in the middle of the boulevard, reminding passersby of the many Brits who died in the last century's world wars. To visit the **Churchill War Rooms,** take a left before the Cenotaph, on King Charles Street.

Continuing on Whitehall, stop at the barricaded and guarded ❻ **#10 Downing Street** to see the British "White House," the traditional home of the prime minister since the position was created in the early 18th century. Break the bobby's boredom and ask him a question. The huge building across Whitehall from Downing Street is the **Ministry of Defence** (MOD), the "British Pentagon."

Nearing Trafalgar Square, look for the 17th-century ❼ **Banqueting House** across the street, which is just about all that remains of what was once the biggest palace in Europe—Whitehall Palace. If you visit, you can enjoy its ceiling paintings by Peter Paul Rubens, and the exquisite hall itself. Also take a look at the ❽ **Horse Guards** behind the gated fence. For 200 years, soldiers in cavalry uniforms have guarded this arched entrance that leads to Buckingham Palace. These elite troops constitute the Queen's personal bodyguard.

The column topped by Lord Nelson marks ❾ **Trafalgar Square,** London's central meeting point. The stately domed building on the far side of the square is the **National Gallery,** which is filled with the national collection of European paintings, and has a classy café in the Sainsbury Wing. To the right of the National Gal-

Trafalgar Square and St. Martin-in-the-Fields

lery is the 1722 **St. Martin-in-the-Fields Church** and its Café in the Crypt.

• *Our Westminster walk is over. But if you want to keep going, walk up Cockspur Street to Haymarket, then take a short left on Coventry Street to colorful* **Piccadilly Circus.** *Near here, you'll find several theaters and* **Leicester Square** *with its half-price TKTS booth for plays (see page 91). Walk through trendy* **Soho** *(north of Shaftesbury Avenue) for its fun pubs.*

SIGHTS

Central London
Westminster

These sights are listed in roughly geographical order from Westminster Abbey to Trafalgar Square, and are linked in my self-guided Westminster Walk (earlier) and 🎧 my free audio tour.

▲▲▲WESTMINSTER ABBEY

The greatest church in the English-speaking world, Westminster Abbey is where England's kings and queens have been crowned and buried since 1066. Like a stony refugee camp huddled outside St. Peter's Pearly Gates, Westminster Abbey has many stories to tell. To experience the church more vividly, take a live tour, or attend evensong or an organ concert.

Rick's Tip: Many of London's great **museums** *don't charge admission—though they do* **suggest a donation** *(typically £5). All such contributions are completely optional.*

Cost and Hours: £24, £5 more for timed-entry ticket to worthwhile Queen's Diamond Jubilee Galleries, family ticket available, cheaper online; Abbey—Mon-Fri 9:30-16:30, Wed until 19:00 (main church only), Sat 9:00-16:00 (Sept-April until 14:00), guided tours available; Queen's Galleries—Mon-Fri 10:00-16:00, Sat 9:30-15:30; Cloister—Mon-Sat 9:30-17:30; closed Sun to sightseers but open for services; last entry one hour before closing; Tube: Westminster or St. James's Park, tel. 020/7222-5152, www. westminster-abbey.org.

Rick's Tip: Westminster Abbey *is most crowded at midmorning and all day Saturdays and Mondays.* **Visit early, during lunch, or late.** *Weekdays after 14:30 are less congested; come late and stay for the 17:00 evensong. Skip the line by booking tickets in advance via the Abbey's website at www. westminster-abbey.org.*

Church Services and Music: Mon-Fri at 7:30 (prayer), 8:00 and 12:30 (communion), 17:00 evensong (on Wed it's spoken, not sung); Sat at 8:00 (communion), 9:00 (prayer), 15:00 (evensong; May-Aug it's at 17:00); Sun services generally come with more music: at 8:00 (communion), 10:00 (sung Matins), 11:15 (sung Eucharist), 15:00 (evensong), 18:30 (evening service). Services are free to anyone, though visitors who haven't paid church admission aren't allowed to linger afterward. Free organ recitals are usually held Sun at 17:45 (30 minutes).

Westminster Abbey Tour

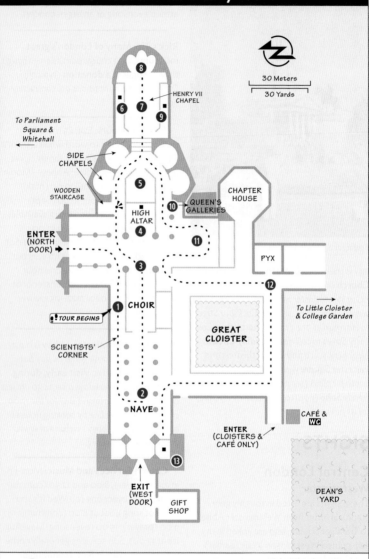

30 Meters
30 Yards

HENRY VII CHAPEL

To Parliament Square & Whitehall

SIDE CHAPELS

WOODEN STAIRCASE

CHAPTER HOUSE

QUEEN'S GALLERIES

HIGH ALTAR

ENTER (NORTH DOOR)

PYX

CHOIR

TOUR BEGINS

SCIENTISTS' CORNER

GREAT CLOISTER

To Little Cloister & College Garden

NAVE

ENTER (CLOISTERS & CAFÉ ONLY)

CAFÉ & WC

EXIT (WEST DOOR)

GIFT SHOP

DEAN'S YARD

1 Memorials
2 Nave
3 Choir
4 Coronation Spot
5 Shrine of Edward the Confessor
6 Tomb of Elizabeth I & Mary I
7 Chapel of King Henry VII

8 Royal Air Force Chapel
9 Tomb of Mary, Queen of Scots
10 Queen's Diamond Jubilee Galleries
11 Poets' Corner
12 Great Cloister
13 Coronation Chair

Tours: The included **multimedia guide** is excellent. Vergers (docents) give informative 90-minute **guided tours** (£7, schedule posted outside and inside entry, up to 5/day April-Sept, 2-4/day Oct-March).

⊙ SELF-GUIDED TOUR

• *Walk straight through the north transept. Follow the crowd flow to the right, passing through a number of...*

❶ **Memorials:** You'll pass statues on tombs, stained glass on walls, and plaques in the floor, all honoring illustrious Brits, both famous and not so famous.

• *Now enter the spacious nave and take it all in.*

❷ **Nave:** The Abbey's 10-story nave is the tallest in England. With saints in stained glass, heroes in carved stone, and the bodies of England's greatest citizens under the floor stones, Westminster Abbey is the religious heart of England.

The king who built the Abbey was Edward the Confessor. Find him in the stained glass windows on the left side of the nave (as you face the altar). He's in the third bay from the end (marked S: Edwardus rex...), dressed in white and blue,

with his crown, scepter, and ring.

On the floor near the west entrance of the Abbey is the flower-lined Grave of the Unknown Warrior, one ordinary WWI soldier buried in soil from France with lettering made from melted-down weapons from that war. Contemplate the 800,000 men from the British Empire who gave their lives. Their memory is so revered that, when Kate Middleton walked up the aisle on her wedding day, by tradition she had to step around the tomb.

• *Now walk straight up the nave toward the altar. This is the same route every future monarch walks on the way to being crowned. Midway up the nave, you pass through the colorful screen of an enclosure known as the...*

❸ **Choir:** These elaborately carved wood and gilded seats are where monks once chanted their services in the "quire"—as it's known in British church-speak. Today, it's where the Abbey's boys choir sings the evensong. Up ahead, the "high" (main) altar—which usually has a cross and candlesticks atop it—sits on the platform up the five stairs.

❹ **Coronation Spot:** The area immedi-

The west facade of Westminster Abbey

ately before the high altar is where every English coronation since 1066 has taken place. Royalty are also given funerals here, and it's where most of the last century's royal weddings have taken place, including the unions of Queen Elizabeth II and Prince Philip (1947) and Prince William and Kate Middleton (2011).

• *Now veer left and follow the crowd. Pause at the wooden staircase on your right. This is the royal tomb that started it all.*

❺ Shrine of Edward the Confessor: Step back and peek over the dark coffin of Edward I to see the tippy-top of the green-and-gold wedding-cake tomb of King Edward the Confessor—the man who built Westminster Abbey. It was finished just in time to bury Edward and to crown his foreign successor, William the Conqueror, in 1066. After Edward's death, people prayed at his tomb, and, after getting good results, he was made a saint. Edward's tall, central tomb (which unfortunately lost some of its luster when Henry VIII melted down the gold coffin case) is surrounded by the tombs of eight other kings and queens.

• *At the top of the stone staircase, veer left into the private burial chapel of Queen Elizabeth I.*

❻ Tomb of Queens Elizabeth I and Mary I: Although only one effigy is on the tomb (Elizabeth's), there are actually two queens buried beneath it, both daughters of Henry VIII (by different mothers). Bloody Mary—meek, pious, sickly, and Catholic—enforced Catholicism during

Tomb of Elizabeth I (and Mary I)

her short reign (1553-1558) by burning "heretics" at the stake.

Elizabeth—strong, clever, and Protestant—steered England on an Anglican course. She holds a royal orb symbolizing that she's queen of the whole globe. When 26-year-old Elizabeth was crowned in the Abbey, her right to rule was questioned (especially by her Catholic subjects) because she was considered the bastard seed of Henry VIII's unsanctioned marriage to Anne Boleyn. But Elizabeth's long reign (1559-1603) was one of the greatest in English history, a time when England ruled the seas and Shakespeare explored human emotions. When she died, thousands turned out for her funeral in the Abbey. Elizabeth's face on the tomb, modeled after her death mask, is considered a very accurate take on this hook-nosed, imperious "Virgin Queen" (she never married).

• *Continue into the ornate, flag-draped room up a few more stairs (directly behind the main altar).*

❼ Chapel of King Henry VII (the Lady Chapel): The light from the stained-glass windows; the colorful banners overhead; and the elaborate tracery in stone, wood, and glass give this room the festive air of a medieval tournament. The prestigious Knights of the Bath meet here, under the magnificent ceiling studded with gold pendants. The ceiling—of carved stone, not plaster (1519)—is the finest English Perpendicular Gothic and fan vaulting you'll see (unless you're going to King's College Chapel in Cambridge). The ceiling was sculpted on the floor in pieces, then jigsaw-puzzled into place. It capped the Gothic period and signaled the vitality of the coming Renaissance.

• *Go to the far end of the chapel and stand at the banister in front of the modern set of stained-glass windows.*

❽ Royal Air Force Chapel: Saints in robes and halos mingle with pilots in parachutes and bomber jackets. This tribute to WWII flyers is for those who earned their

angel wings in the Battle of Britain (July-Oct 1940). A bit of bomb damage has been preserved—the little glassed-over hole in the wall below the windows in the lower left-hand corner.

• *Exit the Chapel of Henry VII. Turn left into a side chapel with the tomb (the central one of three in the chapel).*

❾ Tomb of Mary, Queen of Scots: The beautiful, French-educated queen (1542-1587) was held under house arrest for 19 years by Queen Elizabeth I, who considered her a threat to her sovereignty. Elizabeth got wind of an assassination plot, suspected Mary was behind it, and had her first cousin (once removed) beheaded. When Elizabeth died childless, Mary's son—James VI, King of Scots—also became King James I of England and Ireland. James buried his mum here (with her head sewn back on) in the Abbey's most sumptuous tomb.

• *Exit Mary's chapel. Continue on, until you emerge in the south transept. Look for the doorway that leads to a stairway and elevator to the...*

❿ Queen's Diamond Jubilee Galleries: In 2018, the Abbey opened a space that had been closed off for 700 years—an internal gallery 70 feet above the main floor known as the triforium. This balcony—with stunning views over the nave—now houses a small museum of interesting objects related to the Abbey's construction, the monarchs who worshipped here, royal coronations, and more from its 1,000-year history. (Because of limited space, a timed-entry ticket is required.)

• *After touring the Queen's Galleries, return to the main floor. You're in...*

⓫ Poets' Corner: England's greatest artistic contributions are in the written word. Many writers (including Chaucer, Lewis Carroll, T. S. Eliot, and Charles Dickens) are honored with plaques and monuments; relatively few are actually buried here. Shakespeare is commemorated by a fine statue that stands near the end of the transept, overlooking the others.

Poets' Corner

• *Exit the church (temporarily) at the south door, which leads to the...*

⓬ Great Cloister: You're entering the inner sanctum of the Abbey's monastery. The buildings that adjoin the church housed the monks. Cloistered courtyards like this gave them a place to stroll in peace while meditating on God's creations.

• *Go back into the church for the last stop.*

⓭ Coronation Chair: A gold-painted oak chair waits here under a regal canopy for the next coronation. For every English coronation since 1308 (except two), it's been moved to its spot before the high altar to receive the royal buttocks. The chair's legs rest on lions, England's symbol.

▲▲HOUSES OF PARLIAMENT (PALACE OF WESTMINSTER)
This Neo-Gothic icon of London, the site of the royal residence from 1042 to 1547, is now the meeting place of the legislative branch of government. Like the US Capitol in Washington, DC, the complex is open to visitors, though the exterior may be under scaffolding for restoration. You can view parliamentary sessions in either the bickering House of Commons or the sleepy House of Lords. Or you can simply wander on your own (through a few closely monitored rooms) to appreciate the historic building itself.

The Palace of Westminster has been the center of political power in England for nearly a thousand years. In 1834, a horrendous fire gutted the Palace. It was

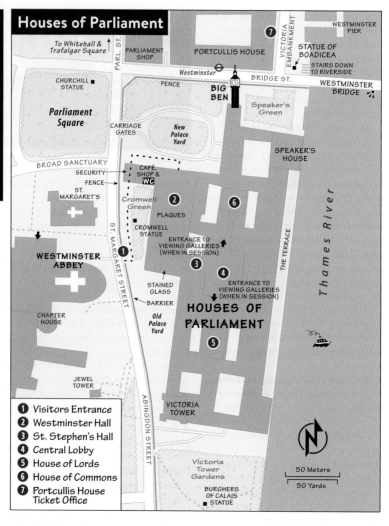

Houses of Parliament

- ❶ Visitors Entrance
- ❷ Westminster Hall
- ❸ St. Stephen's Hall
- ❹ Central Lobby
- ❺ House of Lords
- ❻ House of Commons
- ❼ Portcullis House Ticket Office

rebuilt in a retro, Neo-Gothic style that recalled England's medieval Christian roots—pointed arches, stained-glass windows, spires, and saint-like statues. At the same time, Britain was also retooling its government. Democracy was on the rise, the queen became a constitutional monarch, and Parliament emerged as the nation's ruling body. The Palace of Westminster became a symbol—a kind of cathedral—of democracy. A visit here offers a chance to tour a piece of living history and see the British government in action.

Cost and Hours: Free when Parliament is in session, otherwise must visit with a paid tour; nonticketed entry generally Oct-late July, House of Commons—Mon 14:30-22:30, Tue-Wed 11:30-19:30, Thu 9:30-17:30; House of Lords—Mon-Tue 14:30-22:00, Wed 15:00-22:00, Thu 11:00-19:30; last entry depends on debates; exact day-by-day schedule at www.parliament.uk.

Tours: Audioguide-£19.50, guided tour-£26.50, tours available Sat year-round 9:00-16:30 and most weekdays during recess (late July-Sept), 1.5 hours. Confirm the tour schedule and book ahead at www.parliament.uk or by calling 020/7219-4114. The ticket office also sells tour tickets, but there's no guarantee same-day spaces will be available (ticket office open Mon-Fri 10:00-16:00, Sat 9:00-16:30, closed Sun, in Portcullis House next to Westminster Tube Station, entrance on Victoria Embankment). For either a guided tour or an audioguide, arrive at the visitors entrance on Cromwell Green 20 minutes before your tour time to clear security.

Choosing a House: The House of Lords is less important politically, but they meet in a more ornate room, and the wait time is shorter (likely less than 30 minutes). The House of Commons is where major policy is made, but the room is sparse, and wait times are longer (30-60 minutes or more).

Rick's Tip: *For the* **public galleries** *in either House,* **lines are longest** *at the start of each session, particularly on Wednesdays. For the shortest wait, try to show up* **later in the afternoon** *(but don't push it, as things sometimes close down early).*

◑ SELF-GUIDED TOUR

Enter midway along the west side of the building (across the street from Westminster Abbey), where a tourist ramp leads to the ❶ **visitors entrance.** Line up for the airport-style security check. You'll be given a visitor badge. If you have questions, the attendants are helpful.

• *First, take in the cavernous...*

❷ **Westminster Hall:** This vast hall—covering 16,000 square feet—survived the 1834 fire, and is one of the oldest and most important buildings in England. England's vaunted legal system was invented in this hall, as this was the major court of the land for 700 years. King Charles I was tried and sentenced to death here. Guy Fawkes

The history of the Houses of Parliament spans more than 900 years.

Affording London's Sights

London is one of Europe's most expensive cities, but with its many free museums and affordable plays, it offers days of sightseeing thrills without requiring you to pinch your pennies (or your pounds).

Free Museums: Free sights include the British Museum, British Library, National Gallery, National Portrait Gallery, Tate Britain, Tate Modern, Imperial War Museum, Victoria and Albert Museum, Natural History Museum, and the Museum of London. Some of these museums request a donation of about £5, but whether you contribute is up to you.

Free Churches: Smaller churches let worshippers (and tourists) in free, although they may ask for a donation. The big sightseeing churches—Westminster Abbey and St. Paul's—charge higher admission fees, but offer free evensong services nearly daily (though you can't stick around afterward to sightsee). Westminster Abbey also offers free organ recitals most Sundays.

Other Freebies: London has plenty of free performances, such as lunch concerts at St. Martin-in-the-Fields. There's no charge to enjoy the pageantry of the Changing of the Guard, rants at Speakers' Corner in Hyde Park (on Sun afternoon), displays at Harrods, the people-watching scene at Covent Garden, and the colorful streets of the East End. It's free to view the legislature at work in the Houses of Parliament. You can get into the chapel at the Tower of London by attending Sunday services. And, Greenwich is an inexpensive outing.

Good-Value Tours: The London Walks tours with professional guides (£12) are one of the best deals you can get. Hop-on, hop-off big-bus tours, while expensive (around £30-40), provide a great overview and include free boat tours as well as city walks. (Or, for the price of a transit ticket, you could get similar views from the top of a double-decker public bus.) A one-hour Thames ride to Greenwich costs about £12 one-way, but most boats come with entertaining commentary.

Buy Tickets Online: Tickets for many popular and expensive sights can be purchased online in advance, which will usually save you a few pounds per ticket.

Theater: Compared with Broadway's prices, London's theater can be a bargain. Seek out the freestanding TKTS booth at Leicester Square to get discounts from 25 to 50 percent on good seats (and full-price tickets to the hottest shows with no service charges). Buying directly at the theater box office can score you a great deal on same-day tickets. A £5 "groundling" ticket for a play at Shakespeare's Globe is the best theater deal in town.

was condemned for plotting to blow up the Halls of Parliament in 1605.

• *Continue up the stairs, and enter...*

❸ **St. Stephen's Hall:** This long, beautifully lit room (which may be under renovation) was the original House of Commons. Members of Parliament (MPs) sat in church pews on either side of the

hall—the ruling faction on one side, the opposition on the other.

• *Continue into the...*

❹ **Central Lobby:** This ornate, octagonal, high-vaulted room is often called the "heart of British government," because it sits midway between the House of Commons (to the left) and the House of Lords (right). Video monitors list the schedule of meetings and events going on in this 1,100-room governmental hive. This is the best place to admire the Palace's interior decoration—carved wood, chandeliers, statues, and floor tiles.

• *This lobby marks the end of the public space where you can wander freely. From here, you'll visit the House of Lords or the House of Commons. If either house is in session, you'll go through a series of narrow halls and staircases to reach the upper viewing galleries.*

❺ **House of Lords:** When you're called, you'll walk to the Lords Chamber by way of the long Peers' Corridor—referring to the House's 800 unelected members, called "Peers." Paintings on the corridor walls depict the antiauthoritarian spirit brewing under the reign of Charles I. When you reach the House of Lords Chamber, you'll watch the proceedings from the upper-level visitors gallery. Debate may occur among the few Lords who show up at any given time, but these days, their role is largely advisory—they have no real power to pass laws on their own.

The Lords Chamber is church-like and impressive, with stained glass and intricately carved walls. At the far end is the Queen's gilded throne, where she sits once a year to give a speech to open Parliament. In front of the throne sits the woolsack—a cushion stuffed with wool. Here the Lord Speaker presides, with a ceremonial mace behind the backrest. To the Lord Speaker's right are the members of the ruling party (a.k.a. "government") and to his left are the members of the opposition (the Labour Party). Unaffiliated Crossbenchers sit in between.

❻ **House of Commons:** The Commons Chamber may be much less grandiose than the Lords', but this is where the sausage gets made. The House of Commons is as powerful as the Lords, prime minister, and Queen combined. When the prime minister visits, his ministers (or cabinet) join him on the front bench,

Big Ben

while lesser MPs (the "backbenchers") sit behind. It's often a fiery spectacle, as the prime minister defends his policies, while the opposition grumbles and harrumphs in displeasure. It's not unheard-of for MPs to get out of line and be escorted out by the Serjeant at Arms and his Parliamentary bouncers.

Nearby: Across the street from the Parliament building's St. Stephen's Gate, the **Jewel Tower** is a rare remnant of the old Palace of Westminster, used by kings until Henry VIII. The crude stone tower (1365-1366) was a guard tower in the palace wall, overlooking a moat. It contains an exhibit on the medieval Westminster Palace and the tower (£5.70, daily 10:00-18:00, shorter hours and closed Mon-Fri in off-season; tel. 020/7222-2219). Next to the tower is a quiet courtyard with picnic-friendly benches.

Big Ben, the 315-foot-high clock tower at the north end of the Palace of Westminster, is named for its 13-ton bell, Ben. Currently covered in scaffolding for renovation, the light above the clock is lit when Parliament is in session. The face of the clock is huge—you can actually see the minute hand moving (best view from half-way over Westminster Bridge).

▲▲▲CHURCHILL WAR ROOMS

This excellent sight offers a fascinating walk through the underground headquarters of the British government's WWII fight against the Nazis in the darkest days of the Battle of Britain. It has two parts: the war rooms themselves, and a top-notch museum dedicated to the man who steered the war from here, Winston Churchill. Allow 1-2 hours for your visit.

Cost and Hours: £22 for timed-entry ticket (buy online in advance), includes essential audioguide; daily 9:30-18:00, July-Aug until 19:00, last entry one hour before closing; on King Charles Street, 200 yards off Whitehall—follow signs, Tube: Westminster; tel. 020/7930-6961, www.iwm.org.uk/churchill-war-rooms.

Advance Tickets Recommended: While you can buy a ticket on-site, ticket-buying lines can be long (1-2 hours), so it's smart to buy a timed-entry ticket online in advance. You still may have to wait up to 30 minutes in the security line. Note: London Pass holders do not get to skip the line here—they wait along with ticket buyers.

Cabinet War Rooms: The 27-room, heavily fortified nerve center of the British war effort was used from 1939 to 1945. Churchill's room, the map room, and other rooms are just as they were in 1945. As you follow the one-way route, the audioguide explains each room and offers first-person accounts of wartime happenings here. While the rooms are spartan, you'll see how British gentility survived even as the city was bombarded—posted signs informed those working underground what the weather was like outside, and a cheery notice reminded them to turn off the lights to conserve electricity.

Churchill Museum: Don't bypass this museum, which occupies a large hall amid the war rooms. It dissects every aspect of the man behind the famous cigar, bowler hat, and V-for-victory sign. Artifacts, quotes, political cartoons, clear explanations, and interactive exhibits bring the colorful statesman to life. Many of the items on display—such as a European map divvied up in permanent marker, which Churchill brought to England from the postwar Potsdam Conference—drive home the remarkable span of history this man influenced.

On Trafalgar Square

Trafalgar Square, London's central square, worth ▲▲, is at the intersection of Westminster, The City, and the West End. It's the climax of most marches and demonstrations, and is a thrilling place to simply hang out. At the top of Trafalgar Square (north) sits the domed National Gallery with its grand staircase, and to the right, the steeple of St. Martin-in-the-Fields, built in 1722. In the center of the square, Lord Nelson stands atop his 185-foot-tall fluted granite column, gazing out toward Trafalgar, where he lost his life but defeated the French fleet. Part of this 1842 memorial is made from his victims' melted-down cannons. He's surrounded by spraying fountains, giant lions, and hordes of people (Tube: Charing Cross).

▲▲▲NATIONAL GALLERY

Displaying an unsurpassed collection of European paintings from 1250 to 1900—including works by Leonardo, Botticelli,

Churchill War Rooms

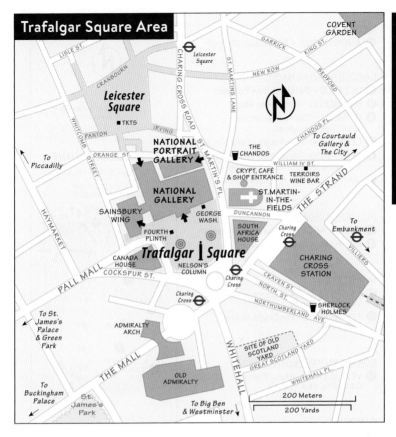

Trafalgar Square Area

Velázquez, Rembrandt, Turner, Van Gogh, and the Impressionists—this is one of Europe's great galleries. Use the map in this book to find specific examples of the art styles described here.

Cost and Hours: Free, £5 suggested donation, special exhibits extra; daily 10:00-18:00, Fri until 21:00, last entry to special exhibits 45 minutes before closing; floor plan-£2; on Trafalgar Square, Tube: Charing Cross or Leicester Square, tel. 020/7747-2885, www.nationalgallery.org.uk.

Tours: Free one-hour overview tours leave from the Sainsbury Wing info desk Mon-Fri at 14:00 (no tours Sat-Sun); excellent £5 audioguides—choose from one-hour highlights tour, several theme tours, or an option that lets you dial up info on any painting in the museum.

Eating: Consider splitting afternoon tea at the **$$$ National Dining Rooms,** on the first floor of the Sainsbury Wing. The **$$$ National Café,** located near the Getty Entrance, has a table-service restaurant and café. Seek out the **$ Espresso Bar,** near the Portico and Getty entrances, for sandwiches and pastries.

Visiting the Museum: Enter through the Sainsbury Entrance (facing Trafalgar Square), in the modern annex to the left of the classic building, and climb the stairs.

Medieval: In Room 51 (and nearby rooms), shiny gold paintings of saints, angels, Madonnas, and crucifixions float in an ethereal gold never-never land. Art

MEDIEVAL
1 ANONYMOUS – The Wilton Diptych

EARLY ITALIAN RENAISSANCE
2 UCCELLO – Battle of San Romano
3 BOTTICELLI – Venus and Mars
4 CRIVELLI – The Annunciation, with Saint Emidius
5 LEONARDO – The Virgin of the Rocks
6 LEONARDO – Virgin and Child with St. Anne and St. John the Baptist
7 VAN EYCK – The Arnolfini Portrait

HIGH RENAISSANCE
8 MICHELANGELO – The Entombment
9 RAPHAEL – Pope Julius II

MANNERISM
10 BRONZINO – An Allegory with Venus and Cupid
11 TINTORETTO – The Origin of the Milky Way

NORTHERN PROTESTANT ART
12 VERMEER – A Young Woman Standing at a Virginal

BAROQUE
13 RUBENS – The Judgment of Paris
14 REMBRANDT – Self-Portrait at the Age of 63
15 REMBRANDT – Belshazzar's Feast
16 VELÁZQUEZ – The Rokeby Venus
17 VAN DYCK – Equestrian Portrait of Charles I
18 CARAVAGGIO – The Supper at Emmaus

FRENCH ROCOCO
19 BOUCHER – Pan and Syrinx

BRITISH ROMANTIC ART
20 CONSTABLE – The Hay Wain
21 TURNER – The Fighting Téméraire

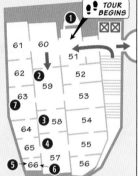

To Leicester Square ⊖ ↑
(5 min. walk)

SAINSBURY WING

ENTRANCE ON LEVEL 0

SELF-GUIDED TOUR
STARTS ON LEVEL 2

TOUR BEGINS

SAINSBURY
ENTRANCE

in the Middle Ages was religious, dominated by the Church. The illiterate faithful could meditate on an altarpiece and visualize heaven. It's as though they couldn't imagine saints and angels inhabiting the dreary world of rocks, trees, and sky they lived in. One of the finest medieval altarpieces, *The Wilton Diptych,* is tucked in the small alcove in Room 51.

Italian Renaissance: In painting, the Renaissance meant realism. Artists rediscovered the beauty of nature and the human body. In Room 63, find Van Eyck's *The Arnolfini Portrait* (1434), once thought to depict a wedding ceremony forced by the lady's swelling belly. Today it's understood as a portrait of a solemn, well-dressed, well-heeled couple, the

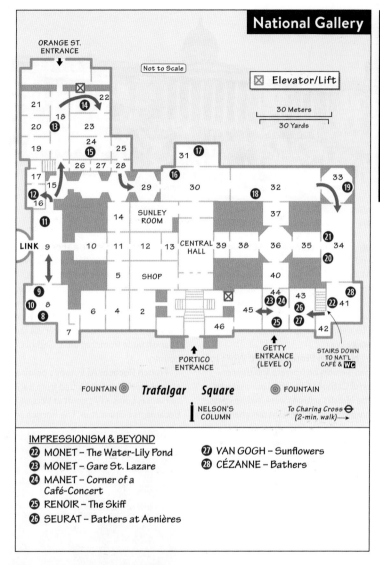

National Gallery

ORANGE ST. ENTRANCE

Not to Scale

⊠ Elevator/Lift

30 Meters
30 Yards

21 22 ⑭ 18 ⑬ 20 23 19 24 ⑮ 25 26 27 28 31 ⑰ ⑫ ⑯ 17 15 16 ⑪ 29 30 ⑱ 32 33 ⑲ 14 SUNLEY ROOM 37 ㉑ LINK 9 10 11 12 13 CENTRAL HALL 39 38 36 35 34 ⑳ 5 SHOP 40 ⑨ ⑩ 8 ⑧ 6 4 2 44 ㉓ ㉔ 43 ㉖ ㉒ ㉘ 41 45 ㉕ ㉗ 42 7 46

GETTY ENTRANCE (LEVEL 0)

STAIRS DOWN TO NAT'L CAFÉ & WC

PORTICO ENTRANCE

FOUNTAIN ◉ *Trafalgar Square* ◉ FOUNTAIN

NELSON'S COLUMN

To Charing Cross ⊖ (2-min. walk)→

IMPRESSIONISM & BEYOND

㉒ MONET – The Water-Lily Pond
㉓ MONET – Gare St. Lazare
㉔ MANET – Corner of a Café-Concert
㉕ RENOIR – The Skiff
㉖ SEURAT – Bathers at Asnières
㉗ VAN GOGH – Sunflowers
㉘ CÉZANNE – Bathers

Arnolfinis of Bruges, Belgium (the fashion of the day was to gather up the folds of one's extremely full-skirted dress).

Michelangelo's (unfinished) *The Entombment* is inspired by ancient statues of balanced, anatomically perfect, nude Greek gods. Renaissance balance and symmetry reign. Raphael's *Pope Julius II* gives a behind-the-scenes look at this complex leader. The pope's dress indicates wealth and success. But at the same time, he's a bent and broken man, with an expression that seems to say, "Is this all there is?"

Mannerism: Developed in reaction to the High Renaissance, Mannerism subverts the balanced, harmonious ideal of the previous era with exaggerated

The massive National Gallery is one of the world's great art museums.

proportions, asymmetrical compositions, and decorative color. In *The Origin of the Milky Way* by Venetian painter Tintoretto, the god Jupiter places his illegitimate son, baby Hercules, at his wife's breast. Juno says, "Wait a minute. That's not my baby!" Her milk spurts upward, becoming the Milky Way.

Northern Protestant Art: While Italy had wealthy aristocrats and the powerful Catholic Church to purchase art, the North's patrons were middle-class, hardworking, Protestant merchants. They wanted simple, cheap, no-nonsense pictures to decorate their homes and offices. Greek gods and Virgin Marys were out, hometown folks and hometown places were in—portraits, landscapes, still lifes, and slice-of-life scenes.

Look for Vermeer's *A Young Woman Standing at a Virginal.* By framing off such a small world to look at—from the blue chair in the foreground to the wall in back—Vermeer forces us to appreciate the tiniest details, the beauty of everyday things.

Baroque: While artists in Protestant and democratic Europe painted simple scenes, those in Catholic and aristocratic countries turned to the style called Baroque. Baroque art took what was flashy in Venetian art and made it flashier, what was gaudy and made it gaudier, what was dramatic and made it shocking.

In Velázquez's *The Rokeby Venus,* Venus lounges diagonally across the canvas, admiring herself, with flaring red, white, and gray fabrics to highlight her rosy white skin and inflame our passion. This work by the king's personal court painter is a rare Spanish nude from that ultra-Catholic country.

French Rococo: As Europe's political and economic center shifted from Italy to France, Louis XIV's court at Versailles became its cultural hub. The Rococo art

Van Eyck, The Arnolfini Portrait

of Louis' successors was as frilly, sensual, and suggestive as the decadent French court. We see their rosy-cheeked portraits and their fantasies: lords and ladies at play in classical gardens, where mortals and gods cavort together. One of the finest examples is the tiny *Pan and Syrinx* by Boucher.

British Romantic Art: The reserved British were more comfortable cavorting with nature than with the lofty gods. John Constable set up his easel out-of-doors, making quick sketches to capture the simple majesty of billowing clouds, spreading trees, and everyday rural life. The simple style of Constable's *The Hay Wain*—believe it or not—was considered shocking in its day.

Impressionism and Beyond: At the end of the 19th century, a new breed of artists burst out of the stuffy confines of the studio. They donned scarves and berets and set up their canvases in farmers' fields or carried their notebooks into crowded cafés, dashing off quick sketches in order to catch a momentary... impression. Check out Impressionist and Post-Impressionist masterpieces such as Van Gogh's *Sunflowers*.

Cézanne's *Bathers* are arranged in strict triangles. He uses the Impressionist technique of building a figure with dabs of paint (though his "dabs" are often larger-sized "cube" shapes) to make solid, 3-D geometrical figures in the style of the Renaissance. In the process, his cube shapes helped inspire a radical new style—Cubism—bringing art into the 20th century.

▲▲NATIONAL PORTRAIT GALLERY

A selective walk through this 500-year-long *Who's Who* of British history is quick and free, and puts faces on the story of England. The collection is well-described, not huge, and in historical sequence, from the 16th century on the second floor to today's royal family, usually housed on the ground floor. Some highlights: Henry VIII and wives; portraits of the "Virgin Queen" Elizabeth I, Sir Francis Drake, and Sir Walter Raleigh; the only real-life portrait of William Shakespeare; Oliver Cromwell and Charles I with his head on; portraits by Gainsborough and Reynolds; the Romantics (William Blake, Lord Byron, William Wordsworth, and company); Queen Victoria and her era; and the present royal family, including the late Princess Diana and the current Duchess of Cambridge—Kate.

Cost and Hours: Free, £5 suggested donation, special exhibits extra; daily 10:00-18:00, Fri until 21:00; excellent audioguide-£3, floor plan-£2; entry 100 yards off Trafalgar Square (around the corner from National Gallery, opposite Church of St. Martin-in-the-Fields), Tube: Charing Cross or Leicester Square, tel. 020/7306-0055, www.npg.org.uk.

▲ST. MARTIN-IN-THE-FIELDS

The church, built in the 1720s with a Gothic spire atop a Greek-type temple, is an oasis of peace on wild and noisy Trafalgar Square. St. Martin cared for the poor. "In the fields" was where the first church stood on this spot (in the 13th century), between Westminster and The City. Stepping inside, you still feel a compassion for

Princess Diana's portrait at the National Portrait Gallery

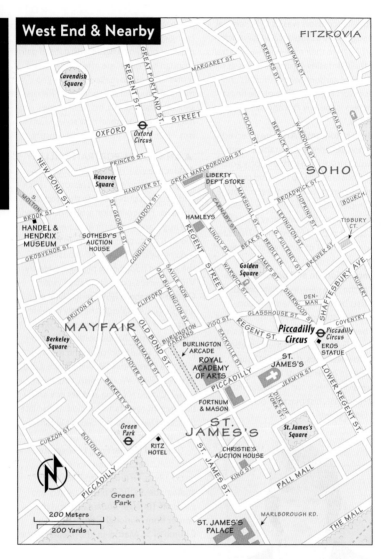

West End & Nearby

FITZROVIA

Cavendish
Square

MARGARET ST.

BERNERS ST.
NEWMAN ST.

GREAT PORTLAND ST.
REGENT ST.

OXFORD   STREET

Oxford
Circus

PRINCES ST.

NEW BOND ST.

MOLTON ST.

Hanover
Square

HANOVER ST.

GREAT MARLBOROUGH ST.

LIBERTY
DEP'T STORE

POLAND ST.
BERWICK ST.
WARDOUR ST.
DEAN ST.

SOHO

BROADWICK ST.
HOPKINS ST.

BOURCH.

ST. GEORGE'S ST.
MADDOX ST.

CARNABY ST.
MARSHALL ST.
LEVINGTON ST.

TISBURY
CT.

BROOK ST.

HANDEL &
HENDRIX
MUSEUM

SOTHEBY'S
AUCTION
HOUSE

GROSVENOR ST.

HAMLEYS

CONDUIT ST.

KINGLY ST.
REGENT STREET

BEAK ST.

BRIDLE LN.
G. PULTENEY ST.
JAMES ST.
BREWER ST.

Golden
Square

SHAFTESBURY AVE.

RUPERT

SAVILE ROW
OLD BURLINGTON ST.

CLIFFORD ST.

WARWICK ST.

SHERWOOD ST.

DEN-
MAN

COVENTRY

BRUTON ST.

MAYFAIR

OLD BOND ST.

GLASSHOUSE ST.

SHAFTESBURY AVE.

Berkeley
Square

ABLEMARLE ST.

BURLINGTON
GARDENS

VIGO ST.

REGENT ST.

Piccadilly
Circus

Piccadilly
Circus

BURLINGTON
ARCADE

SACKVILLE ST.

EROS
STATUE

DOVER ST.

ROYAL
ACADEMY
OF ARTS

PICCADILLY

ST.
JAMES'S

JERMYN ST.

LOWER REGENT ST.

BERKELEY ST.

FORTNUM
& MASON

DUKE OF
YORK ST.

CURZON ST.

BOLTON ST.

Green
Park

ST.
JAMES'S

St. James's
Square

RITZ
HOTEL

CHRISTIE'S
AUCTION HOUSE

ST. JAMES'S ST.

KING ST.

PALL MALL

PICCADILLY

Green
Park

200 Meters

200 Yards

MARLBOROUGH RD.

THE MALL

ST. JAMES'S
PALACE

the needs of the people in this neighborhood—the church serves the homeless and houses a Chinese community center. The modern east window—with grillwork bent into the shape of a warped cross—was installed in 2008 to replace one damaged in World War II.

A freestanding glass pavilion to the left of the church serves as the entrance to the church's underground areas. There you'll find the concert ticket office, a gift shop, brass-rubbing center, and the recommended support-the-church Café in the Crypt.

Cost and Hours: Free, donations welcome; Mon-Fri 8:30-18:00, Sat-Sun from 9:00, closed to visitors during services—listed at the entrance and on the website; Tube: Charing Cross, tel. 020/7766-1100, www.stmartin-in-the-fields.org.

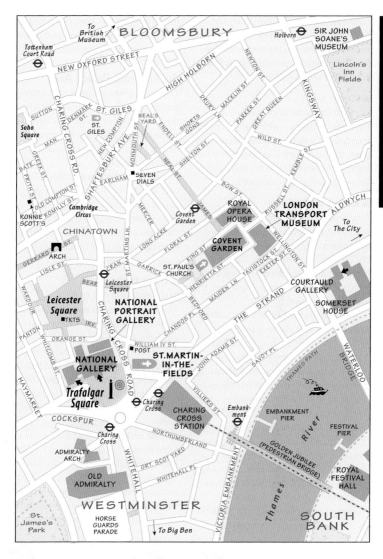

Rick's Tip: St. Martin-in-the-Fields *is famous for its* **concerts.** *Consider a free lunchtime concert (£3.50 suggested donation; Mon, Tue, and Fri at 13:00), an evening concert (£9-29, several nights a week at 19:30), or* **Wednesday night jazz** *(£8-15, at 20:00). See www.stmartin-in-the-fields.org for the schedule.*

The West End and Nearby
▲PICCADILLY CIRCUS

Although this square is slathered with neon billboards and tacky attractions (think of it as the Times Square of London), the surrounding streets are packed with great shopping opportunities. Nearby Shaftesbury Avenue and Leicester Square teem with fun-seekers, theaters, Chinese restaurants, and street singers. To the northeast is London's Chinatown and, beyond that, the funky Soho neighborhood. And curling to the northwest from Piccadilly Circus is genteel Regent Street, lined with exclusive shops.

▲SOHO

North of Piccadilly, once-seedy Soho has become trendy—with many recommended restaurants—and is well worth a gawk. It's the epicenter of London's thriving, colorful youth scene, a fun and funky *Sesame Street* of urban diversity.

▲▲COVENT GARDEN

This large square is filled with people and street performers—jugglers, sword swallowers, magicians, and guitar players. London's buskers (including those in the Tube) are auditioned, licensed, and assigned times and places where they are allowed to perform.

The square's centerpiece is a covered marketplace. A market has been here since medieval times, when it was the "convent" garden owned by Westminster Abbey. In the 1600s, it became a housing development with this courtyard as its center, done in the Palladian style by Inigo Jones. Today's fine iron-and-glass structure was built in 1830 to house the stalls of what became London's chief produce market. In 1973, its venerable arcades were converted to boutiques, cafés, and antique shops. A tourist market thrives here today.

Better Covent Garden lunch deals can be found by walking a block or two away from the eye of this touristic hurricane (check out the places north of the Tube station, along Endell and Neal Streets).

Buckingham Palace Area

The working headquarters of the British monarchy, Buckingham Palace is where the Queen carries out her official duties as the head of state. She and other members of the royal family also maintain apartments here.

Combo-Tickets: A £45 "Royal Day Out" combo-ticket covers the three palace sights that charge admission: the State Rooms, the Queen's Gallery, and the Royal Mews. You can also pay to enter each sight separately (prices listed later; www.royalcollection.org.uk).

▲STATE ROOMS AT BUCKINGHAM PALACE

This lavish home has been Britain's royal residence since 1837, when the newly ascended Queen Victoria moved in. When today's Queen is at home, the royal standard flies (a red, yellow, and blue flag); otherwise, the Union Jack flaps in the wind. The Queen opens her palace to the public—but only for a couple of months in summer, when she's out of town.

Cost and Hours: £25 timed-entry to State Rooms and throne room, includes audioguide; late July-Sept only, daily 9:30-19:30, Sept until 18:30, last entry 75 minutes before closing; limited to 8,000 visitors/day; Tube: Victoria, tel. 0303/123-7300—but Her Majesty rarely answers.

Piccadilly Circus

Covent Garden

The Changing of the Guard is all about pomp and ceremony.

QUEEN'S GALLERY AT BUCKINGHAM PALACE

A small sampling of Queen Elizabeth's personal collection of art is on display in five rooms in a wing adjoining the palace. The exhibits change two or three times a year and are lovingly described by the included audioguide. The gallery is small and security is tight (involving lines): Visit only if you're a patient art lover interested in the current exhibit.

Cost and Hours: £12, daily 10:00-17:30, from 9:30 late July-Sept, last entry 75 minutes before closing, tel. 0303/123-7301.

ROYAL MEWS

A visit to the Queen's working stables is likely to be disappointing unless you follow the included audioguide or the hourly guided tour (April-Oct only, 45 minutes), in which case it's fairly entertaining—especially if you're interested in horses and/or royalty. You'll see a few of the Queen's 30 horses, a fancy car, and a bunch of old carriages, finishing with the Gold State Coach (c. 1760, 4 tons, 4 mph).

Cost and Hours: £12; daily 10:00-17:00, off-season until 16:00; closed Sun in Feb, March, and Nov, plus all of Dec-Jan; last entry 45 minutes before closing, busiest immediately after Changing of the Guard, guided tours on the hour in summer, tel. 0303/123-7302.

Rick's Tip: *Want to go inside* **Buckingham Palace?** *It's* **open to the public only in late July through September,** *when the Queen is out of town.*

▲▲CHANGING OF THE GUARD AT BUCKINGHAM PALACE

This is the spectacle every London visitor has to see at least once: stone-faced, bearskin-hatted guards changing posts with much fanfare, accompanied by a brass band. The most famous part takes place right in front of Buckingham Palace most days at 11:00 (check www.householddivision.org.uk for schedule). Many tourists just show up and get lost in the crowds, but you can catch a satisfying glimpse from less crowded locations

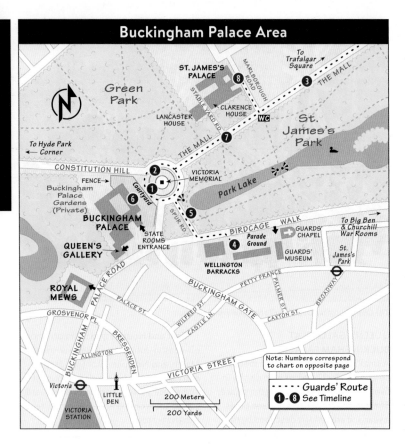

Buckingham Palace Area

Green Park

ST. JAMES'S PALACE ⑧

To Trafalgar Square

③ THE MALL

CLARENCE HOUSE

LANCASTER HOUSE

WC

St. James's Park

⑦

To Hyde Park Corner

CONSTITUTION HILL

FENCE→

Buckingham Palace Gardens (Private)

②
①
⑥

VICTORIA MEMORIAL

Courtyard

Park Lake

BUCKINGHAM PALACE

STATE ROOMS ENTRANCE

SPUR RD.

⑤

BIRDCAGE WALK

Parade Ground ④

GUARDS' CHAPEL

To Big Ben & Churchill War Rooms

QUEEN'S GALLERY

GUARDS' MUSEUM

St. James's Park

WELLINGTON BARRACKS

ROYAL MEWS

PALACE ROAD

PALACE ST.

BUCKINGHAM GATE

PETTY FRANCE

PALMER ST.

BROADWAY

GROSVENOR PL.

WILFRED ST.

CASTLE LN.

CAXTON ST.

BUCKINGHAM

BRESSENDEN

ALLINGTON

VICTORIA STREET

Note: Numbers correspond to chart on opposite page

Victoria ⊖

LITTLE BEN

VICTORIA STATION

200 Meters

200 Yards

- - - - Guards' Route
①-⑧ See Timeline

---

within a few hundred yards of the palace. To plan your sightseeing strategy (and understand what's going on), see the "Changing of the Guard Timeline."

Join a Tour: Local tour companies such as **Fun London Tours** more or less follow the guards' route but add in history and facts to their already entertaining march. These walks add color and good value to what can otherwise seem like a stressful mess of tourists (£17, Changing of the Guard tour starts at Piccadilly Circus at 9:40, must book online in advance, www.funlondontours.com).

North London

▲▲▲BRITISH MUSEUM

Simply put, this is the greatest chronicle of civilization...anywhere. A visit here is like taking a long hike through *Encyclopedia Britannica* National Park. The vast British Museum wraps around its Great Court (the huge entrance hall), with the most popular sections filling the ground floor: Egyptian, Assyrian, and ancient Greek, with the famous frieze sculptures from the Parthenon in Athens. The museum's stately Reading Room sometimes hosts special exhibits.

Cost and Hours: Free, £5 donation requested, special exhibits usually extra (and with timed ticket); daily 10:00-17:30, Fri until 20:30 (select galleries only), least

Changing of the Guard Timeline

When	What
10:00	Tourists gather by the ❶ fence outside Buckingham Palace and the ❷ Victoria Memorial.
10:45	Cavalry guards, headed up ❸ The Mall back from their Green Park barracks, pass Buckingham Palace en route to the Horse Guards (except on Sundays).
10:57	❹ The New Guard, led by a band, marches in a short procession from Wellington Barracks down ❺ Spur Road to Buckingham Palace.
11:00	Guards converge around the Victoria Memorial before entering the ❻ fenced courtyard of Buckingham Palace for the main Changing of the Guard ceremony. (Meanwhile, farther away along Whitehall, the Horse Guard changes guard—except on Sundays, when it's at 10:00.)
11:10	Relief guards leave from Buckingham Palace along The Mall to Clarence House, via ❼ Stable Yard Road.
11:25	The remaining Old Guard leaves St. James's Palace for Buckingham Palace.
11:37	Cavalry guards, headed down The Mall back to their Green Park barracks from Horse Guards, pass Buckingham Palace.
11:40	The entire Old Guard, led by a band, leaves Buckingham Palace and heads up Spur Road for Wellington Barracks, while a detachment of the New Guard leaves Buckingham Palace to march up The Mall to take over at ❽ St. James's Palace (arriving around 11:45).

crowded late on weekday afternoons, especially Fri; free guided tours offered, multimedia guide–£7; Great Russell Street, Tube: Tottenham Court Road, ticket desk tel. 020/7323-8181, www.britishmuseum.org.

Tours: Free 40-minute EyeOpener tours by volunteers focus on select rooms (daily 11:00-15:45, generally every 15 minutes). More in-depth 90-minute tours are offered Fri-Sun at 11:30 and 14:00. Ask about other specialty tours and lectures. The £7 multimedia guide offers dial-up audio commentary and video on 200 objects, as well as several substantial cerebral theme tours (must leave photo ID). There's also a fun family multimedia guide offering various themed routes.

🎧 Download my free British Museum audio tour.

Visiting the Museum: From the Great Court, doorways lead to all wings. To the left are the exhibits on Egypt, Assyria, and Greece—the highlights of your visit.

Egypt: Start with the Egyptian Gallery. Egypt was one of the world's first "civilizations"—a group of people with a government, religion, art, free time, and a written language. The Egypt we think of—pyramids, mummies, pharaohs, and guys who walk funny—lasted from 3000 to 1000 BC with hardly any change in the government, religion, or arts.

The first thing you'll see in the Egypt section is the **Rosetta Stone.** When this rock was unearthed in the Egyptian desert in 1799, it was a sensation in Europe. This black slab, dating from 196 BC, caused

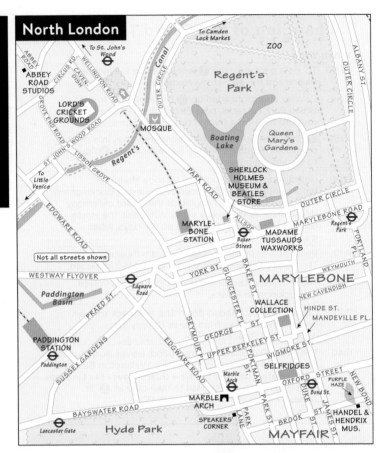

North London

To Camden Lock Market

ZOO

Regent's Park

To St. John's Wood

ABBEY ROAD STUDIOS

LORD'S CRICKET GROUNDS

MOSQUE

Boating Lake

Queen Mary's Gardens

To Little Venice

SHERLOCK HOLMES MUSEUM & BEATLES STORE

Not all streets shown

MARYLEBONE STATION

Baker Street

MADAME TUSSAUDS WAXWORKS

Regent's Park

WESTWAY FLYOVER

Edgware Road

YORK ST.

MARYLEBONE

Paddington Basin

PRAED ST.

WALLACE COLLECTION

HINDE ST.

MANDEVILLE PL.

NEW CAVENDISH

PADDINGTON STATION

Paddington

GEORGE

UPPER BERKELEY ST.

WIGMORE ST.

SELFRIDGES

OXFORD STREET

PURPLE HAZE

Marble Arch

Bond St.

MARBLE ARCH

BAYSWATER ROAD

Lancaster Gate

SPEAKERS' CORNER

Hyde Park

BROOK ST.

HANDEL & HENDRIX MUS.

MAYFAIR

a quantum leap in the study of ancient history. Finally, Egyptian writing could be decoded.

Next, wander past the many **statues,** including a seven-ton Ramesses, with the traditional features of a pharaoh (goatee, cloth headdress, and cobra diadem on his forehead). When Moses told the king of Egypt, "Let my people go!" this was the stony-faced look he got. You'll also see the Egyptian gods as animals—these include Amun, king of the gods, as a ram, and Horus, the god of the living, as a falcon.

At the end of the hall, climb the stairs or take the elevator to **mummy** land. Mummifying a body is much like following a recipe. First, disembowel it (but leave

A mummy case

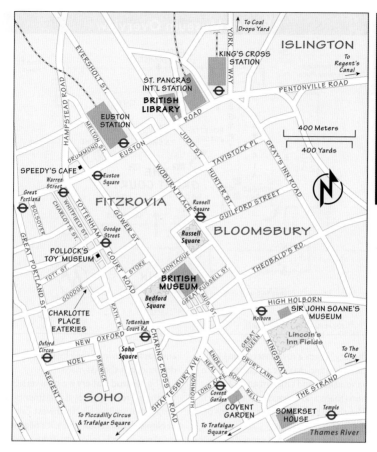

the heart inside), then pack the cavities with pitch, and dry it with natron, a natural form of sodium carbonate (and, I believe, the active ingredient in Twinkies). Then carefully bandage it head to toe with hundreds of yards of linen strips. Let it sit 2,000 years, and...*voilà!* The mummy was placed in a wooden coffin, which was put in a stone coffin, which was placed in a tomb. The result is that we now have Egyptian bodies that are as well preserved as Larry King. Many of the mummies here are from the time of the Roman occupation, when fine memorial portraits painted in wax became popular. X-ray photos in the display cases tell us more about these people.

Don't miss the animal mummies. Cats (near the entrance to Room 62) were popular pets. They were also considered incarnations of the cat-headed goddess Bastet. Worshipped in life as the sun god's allies, preserved in death, and memorialized with statues, cats were given the adulation they've come to expect ever since.

Assyria: Iraq has long been home to palace-building, iron-fisted rulers. The Assyrians conquered their southern neighbors and dominated the Middle East for 300 years (c. 900-600 BC). Their strength came from a superb army (chariots, mounted cavalry, and siege engines), a policy of terrorism against enemies ("I tied their heads to tree trunks all around

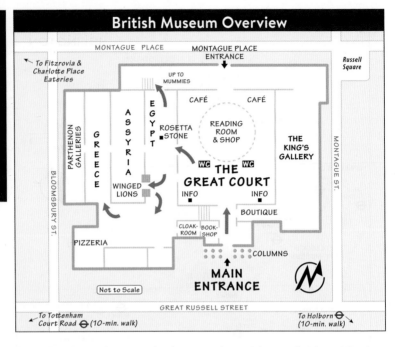

British Museum Overview

MONTAGUE PLACE

MONTAGUE PLACE ENTRANCE

Russell Square

To Fitzrovia & Charlotte Place Eateries

UP TO MUMMIES

CAFÉ   CAFÉ

E
G
Y
P
T

A
S
S
Y
R
I
A

ROSETTA STONE

READING ROOM & SHOP

THE KING'S GALLERY

PARTHENON GALLERIES

G
R
E
E
C
E

WC   **THE**   WC
GREAT COURT

WINGED LIONS

INFO   INFO

BOUTIQUE

BLOOMSBURY ST.

MONTAGUE ST.

CLOAK-ROOM   BOOK-SHOP

PIZZERIA

COLUMNS

Not to Scale

MAIN ENTRANCE

GREAT RUSSELL STREET

To Tottenham Court Road ⊖ (10-min. walk)

To Holborn ⊖ (10-min. walk)

the city," reads a royal inscription), ethnic cleansing and mass deportations of the vanquished, and efficient administration (roads and express postal service). They have been called the "Romans of the East."

Two human-headed winged stone lions guarded an Assyrian palace (11th-8th century BC). With the strength of a lion, the wings of an eagle, the brain of a man, and the beard of an ancient hipster, they protected the king from evil spirits and scared the heck out of foreign ambassadors and left-wing newspaper reporters. (What has five legs and flies? Take a close look. These winged quintupeds, which appear complete from both the front and the side, could guard both directions at once.)

Carved into the stone between the bearded lions' loins, you can see one of civilization's most impressive achievements—writing. This wedge-shaped **(cuneiform)** script is the world's first written language, invented 5,000 years ago by the Sumerians (of southern Iraq)

and passed down to their less-civilized descendants, the Assyrians.

The **Nimrud Gallery** is a mini version of the throne room and royal apartments of King Ashurnasirpal II's Northwest Palace at Nimrud (9th century BC). It's filled with royal propaganda reliefs, 30-ton marble bulls, and panels depicting wounded lions (lion-hunting was Assyria's sport of kings).

Greece: During its Golden Age (500-430 BC), Greece set the tone for all of Western civilization to follow. Democracy, theater, literature, mathematics, philosophy, science, gyros, art, and architecture as we know them, were virtually all invented by a single generation of Greeks in a small town of maybe 80,000 citizens.

Your walk through Greek history starts with pottery—from the earliest, with geometric patterns (8th century BC), to painted black silhouettes on the natural orange clay, and then a few crudely done red human figures on black backgrounds. Later, find a vase painted with frisky figures **(Wine Cooler Signed by Douris as**

Assyrian human-headed lions

A reconstructed Greek temple

Painter), which shows a culture really into partying, as well as an evolution into more realistic and three-dimensional figures.

The highlight is the **Parthenon Sculptures**—taken from the temple dedicated to Athena, the crowning glory of an enormous urban-renewal plan during Greece's Golden Age. While the building itself remains in Athens, many of the Parthenon's best sculptures are right here in the British Museum—the so-called Elgin Marbles, named for the shrewd British ambassador who had his men hammer, chisel, and saw them off the Parthenon in the early 1800s.

These much-wrangled-over bits of the Parthenon (from about 450 BC) are indeed impressive. The marble panels you see lining the walls of this large hall are part of the frieze that originally ran around the exterior of the Parthenon, under the eaves. The statues at either end of the hall once filled the Parthenon's triangular-shaped pediments and showed the birth of Athena. The relief panels known as metopes tell the story of the struggle between the forces of human civilization

and animal-like barbarism.

Rest of the Museum: Be sure to venture upstairs to see artifacts from Roman Britain that surpass anything you'll see at Hadrian's Wall or elsewhere in the country. Also look for the Sutton Hoo Ship Burial artifacts from a seventh-century royal burial on the east coast of England (Room 41). A rare Michelangelo cartoon (preliminary sketch) is in Room 90 (level 4).

▲▲▲BRITISH LIBRARY

Here, in just two rooms, are the literary treasures of Western civilization, from early Bibles to Shakespeare's *Hamlet* to Lewis Carroll's *Alice's Adventures in Wonderland* to the *Magna Carta*. The British Empire built its greatest monuments out of paper; it's through literature that England made her most lasting and significant contribution to civilization and the arts.

Cost and Hours: Free, £5 suggested donation, admission charged for special exhibits; Mon-Thu 9:30-20:00, Fri until 18:00, Sat until 17:00, Sun 11:00-17:00; 96 Euston Road, Tube: King's Cross St. Pancras or Euston, tel. 033/0333-1144, www.bl.uk.

Tours: Two £10 one-hour tours are offered daily—a Treasures Tour (generally at 11:00) and a building tour (generally at 14:00); book online or call 019/3754-6546. There are no audioguides for the permanent collection. Touch-screen computers in the permanent collection let you page virtually through some of the rare books.

🎧 Download my free British Library audio tour.

Visiting the Library: Everything that matters for your visit is in a tiny but exciting area variously called "The Sir John Ritblat Gallery," "Treasures of the British Library," or just "The Treasures." We'll concentrate on a handful of documents—literary and historical—that changed the course of history. Note that exhibits change often, and many of the museum's old, fragile manuscripts need to "rest" periodically in order to stay well-preserved.

Upon entering the Ritblat Gallery, start at the far side of the room with the display case showing historic ❶ **maps and views,** illustrating humans' shifting perspective of the world. Next, move into the area dedicated to ❷ **sacred texts and early Bibles,** including the Codex Sinaiticus (or the Codex Alexandrinus that may be on display instead). This bound book from around AD 350 is one of the oldest complete Bibles in existence—one of the first attempts to collect various books by different authors into one authoritative anthology. In the display cases called ❸ **Art of the Book,** you'll find various medieval-era books, some beautifully illustrated or "illuminated." The lettering is immaculate, but all are penned by hand. The most magnificent of these medieval British "monk-uscripts" is the **Lindisfarne Gospels,** from AD 698.

In the glass cases featuring early ❹ **printing,** you'll see the Gutenberg Bible—the first book printed in Europe using movable type (c. 1455). Suddenly, the Bible was available for anyone to read, fueling the Protestant Reformation.

Through a doorway is a small room with the ❺ **Magna Carta.** Though historians talk about *the* Magna Carta, several

The British Library is filled with treasures ranging from the Magna Carta to Beatles song sheets.

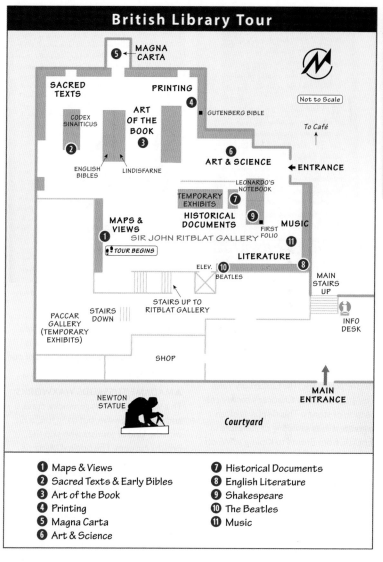

British Library Tour

- **5** MAGNA CARTA
- SACRED TEXTS
- PRINTING
- **4**
- ■ GUTENBERG BIBLE
- CODEX SINAITICUS
- ART OF THE BOOK **3**
- **2**
- Not to Scale
- To Café
- ENGLISH BIBLES
- LINDISFARNE
- **6** ART & SCIENCE
- ◄ ENTRANCE
- LEONARDO'S NOTEBOOK
- TEMPORARY EXHIBITS
- **7**
- **9**
- MAPS & VIEWS
- HISTORICAL DOCUMENTS
- FIRST FOLIO
- MUSIC
- **1**
- SIR JOHN RITBLAT GALLERY
- **11**
- ●! TOUR BEGINS
- LITERATURE
- **8**
- ELEV.
- **10**
- BEATLES
- MAIN STAIRS UP
- STAIRS UP TO RITBLAT GALLERY
- PACCAR GALLERY (TEMPORARY EXHIBITS)
- STAIRS DOWN
- INFO DESK
- SHOP
- NEWTON STATUE
- MAIN ENTRANCE
- Courtyard

- **1** Maps & Views
- **2** Sacred Texts & Early Bibles
- **3** Art of the Book
- **4** Printing
- **5** Magna Carta
- **6** Art & Science
- **7** Historical Documents
- **8** English Literature
- **9** Shakespeare
- **10** The Beatles
- **11** Music

different versions of the document exist, some of which are kept in this room. The basis for England's constitutional system of government, this "Great Charter" listing rules about mundane administrative issues was radical because of the simple fact that the king had agreed to abide by them as law.

Return to the main room to find display cases featuring trailblazing **6** **art and science** documents by early scientists such as Galileo, Isaac Newton, and many more. Pages from Leonardo da Vinci's notebook show his powerful curiosity, his genius for invention, and his famous backward and inside-out handwriting. Nearby are many more **7** **historical documents.** You may see letters by Henry VIII, Queen Elizabeth I,

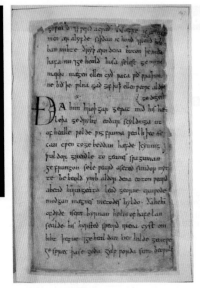

The only known manuscript of the epic saga Beowulf

Lewis Carroll's manuscript for Alice's Adventures in Wonderland

Darwin, Freud, Gandhi, and others.

Next, trace the evolution of ❽ **English literature.** Check out the AD 1000 manuscript of Beowulf, the first English literary masterpiece, and *The Canterbury Tales* (c. 1410), Geoffrey Chaucer's bawdy collection of stories. This display is often a greatest-hits sampling of literature in English, from Brontë to Kipling to Woolf to Joyce to Dickens. The most famous of England's writers—❾ **Shakespeare**— generally gets his own display case. Look for the First Folio—one of the 750 copies of 36 of the 37 known Shakespeare plays, published in 1623. If the First Folio is not out for viewing, the library should have other Shakespeare items on display.

Now fast-forward a few centuries to ❿ **The Beatles.** Look for photos of John Lennon, Paul McCartney, George Harrison, and Ringo Starr. Among the displays, you may find manuscripts of song lyrics written by Lennon and McCartney. In the ⓫ **music** section, there are manuscripts by Mozart, Beethoven, Chopin, and others (kind of an anticlimax after the Fab

Four, I know). George Frideric Handel's famous oratorio, the *Messiah* (1741), is often on display and marks the end of our tour. Hallelujah.

▲MADAME TUSSAUDS WAXWORKS

This waxtravaganza is gimmicky, crass, and crazy expensive, but dang fun...a hit with the kind of tourists who skip the British Museum. The original Madame Tussaud did wax casts of heads lopped off during the French Revolution (such as Marie-Antoinette's). She took her show on the road and ended up in London in 1835. Now it's all about singing with Lady Gaga, and partying with The Beatles. In addition to posing with all the eerily realistic wax dummies—from the Queen and Will and Kate to the Beckhams— you'll have the chance to learn how they created this waxy army; hop on a people-mover and cruise through a kid-pleasing "Spirit of London" time trip; and visit with Marvel superheroes. A nine-minute "4-D" show features a 3-D movie heightened by wind, "back ticklers," and other special effects.

The Beatles at Madame Tussauds

Rick's Tip: *To* skip **Madame Tussauds'** **ticket-buying line** *(which can be an hour or more), book a* **Priority Entrance** *ticket and reserve a time slot at least a day in advance. Or, pay royally for a Fast Track ticket in advance (available from souvenir shops or at the TI). The place is less crowded if you arrive after 15:00.*

Cost and Hours: £35, kids-£30 (free for kids under 3), up to 25 percent cheaper online; combo-deal with the London Eye. Very flexible hours (check online), but roughly July-Aug and school holidays daily 8:30-18:00, Sept-June Mon-Fri 10:00-16:00, Sat-Sun 9:00-17:00, these are last entry times—it stays open roughly two hours later; Marylebone Road, Tube: Baker Street, tel. 0871-894-3000, www.madametussauds.com.

The City

When Londoners say "The City," they mean the one-square-mile business center in East London that 2,000 years ago was Roman Londinium. The outline of the Roman city walls can still be seen in the arc of roads from Blackfriars Bridge to Tower Bridge. It's a fascinating district to wander on weekdays, but since almost nobody actually lives there, it's dull in the evening and on Saturday and Sunday.

You can 🎧 download my free audio tour of The City, which peels back the many layers of history in this oldest part of London.

▲▲▲ST. PAUL'S CATHEDRAL

Sir Christopher Wren's most famous church is the great St. Paul's, its elaborate interior capped by a 365-foot dome. Since World War II, St. Paul's has been Britain's symbol of resilience. Despite 57 nights of bombing, the Nazis failed to destroy the cathedral, thanks to St. Paul's volunteer fire watchmen, who stayed on the dome. Today you can climb the dome for a great city view. The crypt is a world of historic bones and memorials, including Admiral Nelson's tomb and interesting cathedral models.

Cost and Hours: £20, cheaper online,

includes church entry, dome climb, crypt, tour, and audioguide; Mon-Sat 8:30-16:30 (dome opens at 9:30), closed Sun except for worship; Tube: St. Paul's, tel. 020/7246-8350, www.stpauls.co.uk.

Avoiding Lines: Purchasing tickets in advance online saves a little time (and a little money); otherwise the wait can be 15-45 minutes in summer and on weekends. To avoid crowds in general, arrive first thing in the morning.

Rick's Tip: *If you come to St. Paul's 20 minutes early for evensong worship (under the dome), you may be able to grab a big wooden stall in the choir, next to the singers.*

Music and Church Services: Worship times are available on the church's website. Communion is generally Mon-Sat at 8:00 and 12:30. On Sunday, services are held at 8:00, 10:15 (Matins), 11:30 (sung Eucharist), 15:15 (evensong), and 18:00. The rest of the week, evensong is at 17:00 (Mon evensong is occasionally spoken, not sung). On some Sundays, there's a free organ recital at 16:45.

Tours: There are 1.5-hour **guided tours** Mon-Sat at 10:00, 11:00, 13:00, and 14:00 (call to confirm or ask at church). Free 15-minute **"highlights" tours** are offered throughout the day. The **audioguide** (included with admission) contains video clips that show the church in action.

🎧 Download my free St. Paul's Cathedral **audio tour.**

Visiting the Cathedral: Start at the far back of the **❶ nave,** behind the font. This big church feels big. At 515 feet long and 250 feet wide, it's Europe's fourth largest, after those in Rome (St. Peter's), Sevilla, and Milan. The spaciousness is accentuated by the relative lack of decoration. The simple, cream-colored ceiling and the clear glass in the windows light everything evenly. Wren wanted this: a simple, open church with nothing to hide. Unfortunately, only this entrance area keeps his original vision—the rest was encrusted with 19th-century Victorian ornamentation.

Ahead and on the left is the towering, black-and-white **❷ Wellington Monument.** Wren would have been appalled,

Majestic St. Paul's Cathedral is one of London's most iconic buildings.

St. Paul's Cathedral

ENTRANCE TO CRYPT
CAFÉ & **WC**

ENTER

To
St. Paul's ⊖

To →
One New Change
Terrace View

⑤

⑪

⑥ ⑩

DOME
③

CHOIR ④ HIGH
ALTAR ⑦

② ①

NAVE

PLAQUE

⑩

⑨ ⑪ ⑧

STAIRS

BISHOP'S
CHAIR

30 Meters
30 Yards

To
Millennium
Bridge

① Nave
② Wellington Monument
③ Dome
④ Choir & High Altar
⑤ HUNT–The Light of the World
⑥ MOORE–Mother and Child

⑦ American Memorial
(Jesus Chapel)
⑧ John Donne Statue
⑨ Nelson & Cornwallis Monuments
⑩ Climb the Dome (2 entrances)
⑪ Crypt Entrance (2 entrances)

but his church has become so central to England's soul that many national heroes are buried here (in the basement crypt).

The ❸ **dome** you see from here, painted with scenes from the life of St. Paul, is only the innermost of three. From the painted interior of the first dome, look up through the opening to see the light-filled lantern of the second dome. Finally, the whole thing is covered on the outside by the third and final dome, the shell of lead-covered wood that you see

from the street. Wren's ingenious three-in-one design was psychological as well as functional—he wanted a low, shallow inner dome so worshippers wouldn't feel diminished.

The ❹ **choir** area blocks your way, but you can see the altar at the far end under a golden canopy. Do a quick clockwise spin around the church. In the north transept (to your left as you face the altar), find the big painting ❺ *The Light of the World* (1904), by the Pre-Raphaelite William

The cathedral's interior is dazzling.

Views from St. Paul's dome are worth the climb.

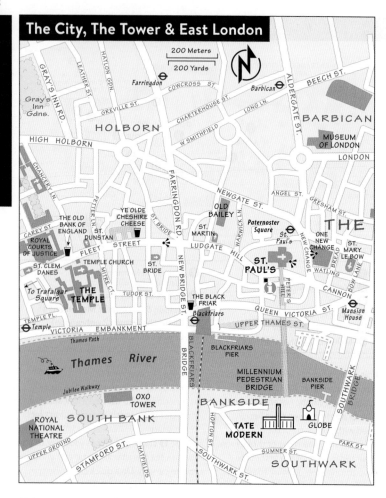

The City, The Tower & East London

Holman Hunt. Inspired by Hunt's own experience of finding Christ during a moment of spiritual crisis, the crowd-pleasing work was criticized by art highbrows for being "syrupy" and "simple"—even as it became the most famous painting in Victorian England.

Along the left side of the choir is the statue ❻ *Mother and Child* (1983), by the great modern sculptor Henry Moore. Typical of Moore's work, this Mary and Baby Jesus—inspired by the sight of British moms nursing babies in WWII bomb shelters—renders a traditional subject in an abstract, minimalist way.

The area behind the main altar, with three stained-glass windows, is the ❼ **American Memorial Chapel,** honoring the Americans who sacrificed their lives to save Britain in World War II. In brightly colored panes that arch around the big windows, spot the American eagle (center window, to the left of Christ), George Washington (right window, upper-right corner), and symbols of all 50 states (find your state seal). The Roll of Honor, a 500-page book under glass (immediately behind the altar), lists the names of

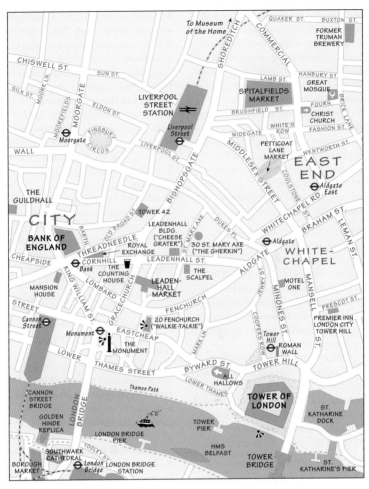

28,000 US servicemen and women based in Britain who gave their lives during the war.

Around the other side of the choir is a shrouded statue honoring ❽ **John Donne** (1573-1631), a passionate preacher in old St. Paul's, as well as a great poet ("never wonder for whom the bell tolls—it tolls for thee.") In the south transept are monuments to military greats ❾ **Horatio Nelson,** who fought Napoleon, and **Charles Cornwallis,** who was finished off by George Washington at Yorktown.

Climb the Dome: The 528-step climb is worthwhile. First you get to the Whispering Gallery (257 shallow steps, with views of the church interior). Whisper sweet nothings into the wall, and your partner (and anyone else) standing far away can hear you. For best effects, try whispering (not talking) with your mouth close to the wall, while your partner stands a few dozen yards away with his or her ear to the wall.

After another set of (steeper, narrower) stairs, you're at the Stone Gallery, with views of London. Finally, a long, tight metal staircase takes you to the very top of the cupola, the Golden Gallery, with stunning, unobstructed views of the city.

Crypt: The crypt is a world of historic bones and interesting cathedral models. Many legends are buried here—Horatio Nelson, who wore down Napoleon; the Duke of Wellington, who finished off Napoleon; and even Wren himself. Wren's actual tomb is marked by a simple black slab with no statue, though he considered this church to be his legacy. Back up in the nave, on the floor directly under the dome, is Christopher Wren's name and epitaph (written in Latin): "Reader, if you seek his monument, look around you."

▲MUSEUM OF LONDON

Scale models and costumes help you visualize everyday life in the city through history—from Neanderthals, to Romans, to Elizabethans, to Victorians, to Mods, to today. It's informative without being overwhelming, with enough whiz-bang multimedia displays to spice up otherwise humdrum artifacts.

Cost and Hours: Free, daily 10:00-18:00, last entry one hour before closing, see the day's events board for special talks and tours, café, lockers, 150 London Wall at Aldersgate Street, Tube: Barbican or St. Paul's plus a 5-minute walk, tel. 020/7001-9844, www.museumoflondon.org.uk.

▲▲▲TOWER OF LONDON

The Tower has served as a castle in wartime, a king's residence in peacetime,

and, most notoriously, as the prison and execution site of rebels. You can see the crown jewels, take a witty Beefeater tour, and ponder the executioner's block that dispensed with troublesome heirs to the throne and a couple of Henry VIII's wives.

Cost and Hours: £28.90, cheaper online, family ticket available; Tue-Sat 9:00-17:30, Sun-Mon from 10:00; Nov-Feb closes one hour earlier; free Beefeater tours available, skippable audioguide-£5, Tube: Tower Hill, tel. 0333-206-000, www.hrp.org.uk.

Advance Tickets: To avoid long ticket-buying lines, and save a few pounds, buy tickets in advance for a specific day on the Tower website (print at home or collect on-site at group ticket office—see map). Alternatively, buy a voucher on your way to the Tower at the Trader's Gate gift shop, down the steps from the Tower Hill Tube stop (look for the blue awning). The voucher is good any day and can be exchanged for a ticket at the group ticket office.

Visiting the Tower: Even an army the size of the ticket line couldn't storm this castle. The ❶ **entrance gate** where you'll show your ticket was just part of two concentric rings of complete defenses. When you're all set, go 50 yards straight ahead to the ❷ **traitors' gate.** This was the boat entrance to the Tower from the Thames. Turn left to pass underneath the archway into the inner courtyard. The big,

Tower of London

A Beefeater on duty

London's Best Views

For some viewpoints, you need to pay admission, and at the bars or restaurants, you'll need to buy a drink.

London Eye: Ride the giant Ferris wheel for stunning London views. See page 76.

St. Paul's Dome: You'll earn a striking, unobstructed view by climbing hundreds of steps to the cramped balcony of the church's cupola. See page 65.

One New Change: Get fine, free views of St. Paul's Cathedral and surroundings—nearly as good as those from St. Paul's Dome—from the rooftop terrace of the One New Change shopping mall just behind and east of the church.

Tate Modern: Head to the Tate Modern's annex—the Blavatnik Building—and ride the elevator to floor 10, where you'll enjoy sweeping views of the skyline (plus the Tate's own tower in the foreground). You can also ride to floor 6 of the main building. See page 78.

20 Fenchurch (a.k.a. "The Walkie-Talkie"): Get 360-degree views of London from the mostly enclosed Sky Garden. It's free but you'll need to make reservations in advance and bring photo ID (Mon-Fri 10:00-18:00, Sat-Sun 11:00-21:00, 20 Fenchurch Street, Tube: Monument, https://skygarden.london/sky-garden).

National Portrait Gallery: A mod top-floor restaurant peers over Trafalgar Square and the Westminster neighborhood. See page 51.

Waterstones Bookstore: Its hip, low-key, top-floor café/bar has reasonable prices and sweeping views of the London Eye, Big Ben, and the Houses of Parliament (Mon-Sat 9:00-22:00, Sun 12:00-18:30, on Sun bar closes one hour before bookstore, 203 Piccadilly, www.5thview.co.uk).

The Shard: The observation decks that cap this 1,020-foot-tall skyscraper offer London's most commanding views, but at an outrageously high price (£39—book online in advance, advance ticket includes free return ticket in case of bad weather, otherwise pay 25 percent more on-site; daily 10:00-22:00, shorter hours Oct-March; Tube: London Bridge—use London Bridge exit and follow signs, www.theviewfromtheshard.com).

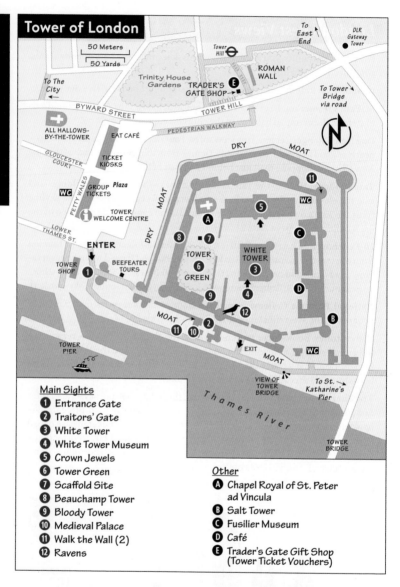

Tower of London

50 Meters
50 Yards

To East End
DLR Gateway Tower

Tower Hill

ROMAN WALL

To The City

TRADER'S GATE SHOP **E**

BYWARD STREET
TOWER HILL

To Tower Bridge via road

ALL HALLOWS-BY-THE-TOWER

EAT CAFÉ

PEDESTRIAN WALKWAY

GLOUCESTER COURT

TICKET KIOSKS

DRY   MOAT

N

WC

GROUP TICKETS

Plaza

PETTY WALES

11

TOWER WELCOME CENTRE

DRY   MOAT

5

WC

A

LOWER THAMES ST.

ENTER

8   **7**

C

TOWER SHOP **1**

BEEFEATER TOURS

TOWER GREEN **6**

WHITE TOWER **3**

4

D

9

MOAT

2

12

B

11 **10**

TOWER PIER

EXIT   MOAT

WC

VIEW OF TOWER BRIDGE

To St. Katharine's Pier

Thames River

TOWER BRIDGE

Main Sights

1 Entrance Gate
2 Traitors' Gate
3 White Tower
4 White Tower Museum
5 Crown Jewels
6 Tower Green
7 Scaffold Site
8 Beauchamp Tower
9 Bloody Tower
10 Medieval Palace
11 Walk the Wall (2)
12 Ravens

Other

A Chapel Royal of St. Peter ad Vincula
B Salt Tower
C Fusilier Museum
D Café
E Trader's Gate Gift Shop (Tower Ticket Vouchers)

white tower in the middle is the **3 White Tower,** the original structure that gave this castle complex its name. William the Conqueror built it more than 950 years ago to put 15 feet of stone between himself and those he conquered. The White Tower provided a gleaming reminder of the monarchy's absolute power. You could

be feasting on roast boar in the Banqueting Hall one night and chained to the walls of the prison the next.

Inside the White Tower is a **4 museum** with exhibits re-creating medieval life and the Tower's bloody history of torture and executions. The first suits of armor you see belonged to Henry VIII—on a horse,

Henry VIII (1491-1547)

The notorious king who single-handedly transformed England was a true Renaissance Man—six feet tall, handsome, charismatic, well-educated, and brilliant. He spoke English, Latin, French, and Spanish. A legendary athlete, he hunted, played tennis, and jousted with knights and kings. When 17-year-old Henry, the second monarch of the House of Tudor, was crowned king in Westminster Abbey, all of England rejoiced.

Henry left affairs of state in the hands of others, and filled his days with sports, war, dice, women, and the arts. But in 1529, Henry's personal life became a political atom bomb, and it changed the course of history. Henry wanted a divorce, partly because his wife had become too old to bear him a son, and partly because he'd fallen in love with Anne Boleyn. Henry begged the pope for an annulment, but—for political reasons—the pope refused. Henry went ahead and divorced his wife anyway, and he was excommunicated.

Henry's rejection of papal authority sparked the English Reformation. He forced monasteries to close, sold off some church land, and confiscated everything else for himself and the Crown. Meanwhile, the Catholic Church was reorganized into the (Anglican) Church of England, with Henry as its head. Though Henry himself basically adhered to Catholic doctrine, he discouraged the veneration of saints and relics, and commissioned an English translation of the Bible.

Henry famously had six wives. The issue was not his love life (which could have been satisfied by his numerous mistresses), but the politics of royal succession. To guarantee the Tudor family's dominance, he needed a male heir born by a recognized queen. Henry's first marriage, to Catherine of Aragon, had been arranged to cement an alliance with her parents, Ferdinand and Isabel of Spain. Catherine bore Henry a daughter, but no sons. Next came Anne Boleyn, who also gave birth to a daughter. After a turbulent few years with Anne and several miscarriages, a frustrated Henry had her beheaded at the Tower of London. His next wife, Jane Seymour, finally had a son (but Jane died soon after giving birth). A blind marriage with Anne of Cleves ended quickly when she proved to be both politically useless and ugly. Next, teen bride Catherine Howard ended up cheating on Henry, so she was executed. Henry finally found comfort—but no children—in his later years with his final wife, Catherine Parr.

Henry's last years were marked by paranoia, sudden rages, and despotism. He gave his perceived enemies the pink slip in his signature way—charged with treason and beheaded. Once-wealthy England was becoming depleted, thanks to Henry's expensive habits, which included making war on France, building and acquiring 50 palaces, and collecting fine tapestries and archery bows.

Henry forged a large legacy. He expanded the power of the monarchy, making himself the focus of a rising, modern nation-state. Simultaneously, he strengthened Parliament—largely because it agreed with his policies. He annexed Wales, and imposed English rule on Ireland (provoking centuries of resentment). He expanded the navy, paving the way for Britannia to soon rule the waves. And—thanks to Henry's marital woes—England would forever be a Protestant nation.

ENGLAND

Execution ax and block

slender in his youth (c. 1515), then more heavyset by 1540 (with his bigger-is-better codpiece). On the top floor are the Tower's actual execution ax and chopping block.

Across from the White Tower is the entrance to the ❺ **crown jewels.** The Sovereign's Scepter is encrusted with the world's largest cut diamond—the 530-carat Star of Africa, beefy as a quarter-pounder. The Crown of the Queen Mother (Elizabeth II's famous mum, who died in 2002) has the 106-carat Koh-I-

Noor diamond glittering on the front (considered unlucky for male rulers, it adorns the crown of the king's wife). The Imperial State Crown is what the Queen wears for official functions such as the State Opening of Parliament. Among its 3,733 jewels are Queen Elizabeth I's former earrings (the hanging pearls, top center), a stunning 13th-century ruby look-alike in the center, and Edward the Confessor's ring (the blue sapphire on top, in the center of the Maltese cross of diamonds).

Exiting the tower, turn right and walk past the White Tower, straight ahead to the grassy field called ❻ **Tower Green.** In medieval times, this was the "town square" for those who lived in the castle. Near the middle of Tower Green is a granite-paved square, the ❼ **Scaffold Site.** It was here that enemies of the Crown would kneel before the king for the final time. On the left as you face the chapel, is the ❽ **Beauchamp Tower** (pronounced "BEECH-um"), one of several places in the complex that housed Very Important Prisoners.

Down toward the river, at the bot-

The Tower Bridge has spanned the Thames since 1894.

tom corner of the green is the ❾ **Bloody Tower,** and beyond that the ❿ **Medieval Palace.** From the palace's throne room, continue up the stairs to ⓫ **walk the wall** for a fine view of the Tower Bridge. Between the White Tower and the Thames are cages housing the ⓬ **ravens.** According to tradition, the Tower and the British throne are only safe as long as ravens are present here. Other sights at the Tower include the Salt Tower and the Fusilier Museum.

TOWER BRIDGE

The iconic Tower Bridge (often mistakenly called London Bridge) was built in 1894 to accommodate the growing East End. While fully modern and hydraulically powered, the drawbridge was designed with a retro Neo-Gothic look. The bridge is most interesting when the drawbridge lifts to let ships pass, as it does a thousand times a year (best viewed from the Tower side of the Thames). For the bridge-lifting schedule, check the website or call.

You can tour the bridge at the **Tower Bridge Exhibition,** with a history display and a peek at the Victorian-era engine room that lifts the span. Included in your entrance is the chance to cross the bridge—138 feet above the road along a partially see-through glass walkway. As an exhibit, it's overpriced, though the adrenaline rush and spectacular city views from the walkway may help justify the cost.

Cost and Hours: £9.80, daily 10:00-18:00 in summer, 9:30-17:30 in winter, enter at northwest tower, Tube: Tower Hill, tel. 020/7403-3761, www.towerbridge.org.uk.

South Bank
▲JUBILEE WALKWAY

This riverside path is a popular pub-crawling pedestrian promenade that stretches all along the South Bank, offering grand views of the Houses of Parliament and St. Paul's. On a sunny day, this is the place to see Londoners out strolling. The Walkway hugs the river except just east of London Bridge, where it cuts inland for a couple of blocks. It has been expanded into a 60-mile "Greenway" circling the city, including the 2012 Olympics site.

The London Eye adds whimsical fun to London's stately skyline.

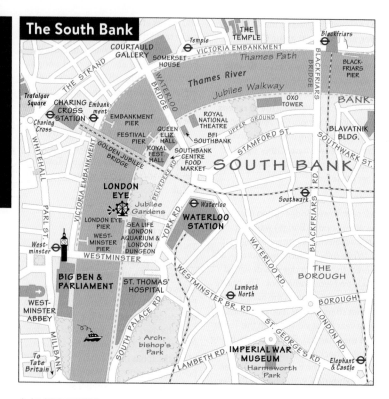

▲▲LONDON EYE

This giant Ferris wheel, towering above London opposite Big Ben, is one of the world's highest observational wheels and London's answer to the Eiffel Tower. Riding it is a memorable experience, even though London doesn't have much of a skyline, and the price is borderline outrageous. Whether you ride or not, the wheel is a sight to behold.

Twenty-eight people ride in each of its 32 air-conditioned capsules (representing the boroughs of London) for the 30-minute rotation (you go around only once). From the top of this 443-foot-high wheel—the second-highest public viewpoint in the city—even Big Ben looks small.

Cost and Hours: £30, cheaper online, family ticket and combo-ticket with Madame Tussauds and other attractions available; daily 10:00-20:30 or later, Sept-

May generally 11:00-18:00, check website for latest schedule, these are last-ascent times, Tube: Waterloo or Westminster. Thames boats come and go from London Eye Pier at the foot of the wheel.

Rick's Tip: *The* **London Eye** *is busiest between 11:00 and 17:00, especially on weekends year-round and every day in July and August.* **Book your ticket at** *www. londoneye.com, then print it at home, retrieve it from an onsite ticket machine (bring your payment card and confirmation code), or stand in the "Ticket Collection" line. Even if you buy in advance, you may wait to board (but it's not worth paying extra for a Fast Track ticket).*

▲▲IMPERIAL WAR MUSEUM

This impressive museum covers the wars and conflicts of the 20th and 21st centu-

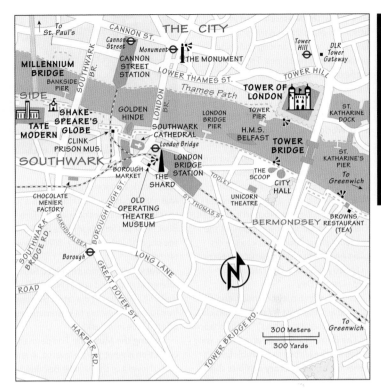

ries. You can walk chronologically through World War I, to the rise of fascism, World War II, the Cold War, the Troubles in Northern Ireland, the wars in Iraq and Afghanistan, and terrorism. Rather than glorify war, the museum explores the human side of the wartime experience and its effect on people back home. It raises thoughtful questions about one of civilization's more uncivilized, persistent traits. Allow plenty of time; lots of artifacts, interactive experiences, and multimedia exhibits can be engrossing.

Cost and Hours: Free, £5 suggested donation, special exhibits extra, daily 10:00-18:00, last entry one hour before closing, Tube: Lambeth North or Elephant and Castle; buses #3, #12, and #159 from Westminster area; tel. 020/7416-5000, www.iwm.org.uk.

Imperial War Museum

Imperial War Museum atrium

Visiting the Museum: Start in the atrium to grasp the massive scale of warfare as you wander among and under notable battle machines. The Spitfire plane overhead flew in the Battle of Britain. From here, the displays unfold chronologically as you work your way up from floor to floor. On level 0, enter **The First World War.** The highlight of the exhibit is a reconstructed trench, with a massive tank rearing overhead, where you're bombarded with the sounds of war. Climb the stairs for exhibits on **World War II.** A video clip shows the mesmerizing Adolf Hitler, who roused a defeated Germany to rearm for war again. At the museum shop, double back to see displays on Britain's fight against the Nazis in North Africa and Operation Overlord—i.e., D-Day.

Level 2, which may be under renovation, covers the **Post-War Years,** which began (as the plaque says) "In the shadow of The Bomb" (alongside an actual casing made for the Hiroshima bomb). Level 3 generally has **temporary exhibits** shedding light on why humans fight. The most powerful exhibit is on level 4—**The Holocaust.** Photos, video clips, and a few artifacts trace the sad story. A room-size model of the Auschwitz camp testifies to the scale of the slaughter and its banal orderliness. Crowning the museum on level 5, the **Lord Ashcroft Gallery** celebrates Britain's heroes who received the Victoria and George Crosses.

▲▲TATE MODERN

This striking museum fills a former power station across the river from St. Paul's with a powerhouse collection including Dalí, Picasso, Warhol, and much more.

Cost and Hours: Free, £5 suggested donation, fee for special exhibits; daily 10:00–18:00, Fri-Sat until 22:00, last entry to special exhibits 45 minutes before closing, especially crowded on weekend days (crowds thin out Fri and Sat evenings); view restaurant on top floor, across the Millennium Bridge from St. Paul's; Tube:

Tate Modern

Southwark, London Bridge, St. Paul's, Mansion House, or Blackfriars plus a 10- to 15-minute walk; or connect by Tate Boat museum ferry from Tate Britain—see page 116; tel. 020/7887-8888, www.tate.org.uk.

Tours: Free 45-minute guided tours are offered at 12:00 and 13:00 (Natalie Bell Building) and 14:00 (Blavatnik Building); free 10-minute gallery talks sometimes offered (see info desk).

Visiting the Museum: The permanent collection is generally on levels 2, 4, and part of level 3 of the Natalie Bell Building. Paintings are arranged according to theme, not artist. Paintings by Picasso, for example, might be scattered in different rooms on different levels. To help you get started, find the "Start Display" room on level 2—highlighting a range of artworks.

Since 1960, London has rivaled New York as a center for the visual arts. You'll find British artists displayed here—look for work by David Hockney, Henry Moore, and Barbara Hepworth. American art is also prominently represented—keep an eye out for abstract expressionist works by Mark Rothko and Jackson Pollock, and the pop art of Andy Warhol and Roy Lichtenstein. After you see the Old Masters of Modernism (Matisse, Picasso, Kandinsky, and so on), push your mental envelope with works by Pollock, Miró, Bacon, Picabia, Beuys, Twombly, and beyond.

You'll find temporary exhibits throughout the museum—some free, some requiring a special admission. Additionally, the main hall features a different monumental installation by a prominent artist each year. The museum's newer twisted-pyramid, 10-story Blavatnik Building also hosts changing themed exhibitions, performance art, experimental film, and interactive sculpture incorporating light and sound.

▲MILLENNIUM BRIDGE

The pedestrian bridge links St. Paul's Cathedral and the Tate Modern across the Thames. This is London's first new bridge in a century. When it opened, the $25 million bridge wiggled when people walked on it, so it promptly closed for repairs; 20 months and $8 million later, it reopened. Nicknamed the "blade of light" for its sleek minimalist design (370 yards long, four yards wide, stainless steel with teak planks), its clever aerodynamic handrails deflect wind over the heads of pedestrians.

▲▲SHAKESPEARE'S GLOBE

This replica of the original Globe Theatre was built, half-timbered and thatched, to appear as it was in Shakespeare's time. (This is the first thatched roof constructed in London since they were outlawed after the Great Fire of 1666.) It serves as a working theater by night and offers tours by day. The original Globe opened in 1599, debuting Shakespeare's play *Julius Caesar.* The Globe originally accommodated 2,200 seated and another 1,000 standing. Today, slightly smaller and leaving space for reasonable aisles,

the theater holds 800 seated and 600 groundlings.

Its promoters brag that the theater melds "the three A's"—actors, audience, and architecture—with each contributing to the play. The working theater hosts authentic performances of Shakespeare's plays with actors in period costumes, modern interpretations of his works, and some works by other playwrights. For details on attending a play, see page 92. The complex's smaller Sam Wanamaker Playhouse—an indoor, horseshoe-shaped Jacobean theater—allows the show to go on in the winter, when it's too cold for performances in the outdoor Globe. Seating fewer than 350, the playhouse is more intimate and sometimes uses authentic candle lighting for period performances. While the Globe mainly presents Shakespeare's works, the playhouse tends to focus on the works of his contemporaries (Jonson, Marlow, Fletcher) and some new plays.

Touring the Globe: Tours depart from the box office every half-hour and last for 40 minutes (£17, £10 for kids 5-15; during outdoor theater season—April-mid-Oct—last tours depart Mon at 17:00, Tue-Sat at 12:30, Sun at 11:30; off-season last tours Mon-Sat at 12:30, Sun at 17:00; Tube: Mansion House or London Bridge plus a 10-minute walk; or a short walk across the Millennium Bridge from St. Paul's Cathedral; tel. 020/7902-1400, www.shakespearesglobe.com).

Eating: The **$$$ Swan at the Globe** café offers a sit-down restaurant (for

Millennium Bridge

Shakespeare's Globe

lunch and dinner, reservations recommended, tel. 020/7928-9444, www.swanlondon.co.uk), a drinks-and-plates bar, and a sandwich-and-coffee cart (Mon-Fri 8:00-closing, depends on performance times, Sat-Sun from 10:00).

West London

▲▲TATE BRITAIN

One of Europe's great art houses, Tate Britain specializes in British painting from the 16th century through modern times. The museum has a good representation of William Blake's religious sketches, the Pre-Raphaelites' naturalistic and detailed art, Gainsborough's aristocratic ladies, and the best collection anywhere of J. M. W. Turner's swirling works.

Cost and Hours: Free, £4 suggested donation, fee for special exhibits; daily 10:00-18:00, last entry 45 minutes before closing; free tours generally daily; on the Thames River, south of Big Ben and north of Vauxhall Bridge, Tube: Pimlico, Tate Boat museum ferry goes directly to the museum from Tate Modern—see page 116; tel. 020/7887-8888, www.tate.org.uk.

Tours: Free guided tours are generally offered daily at 11:00 (the best overview tour), with specialty tours at 12:00, 14:00, and 15:00.

Visiting the Museum: Works from the early centuries are located in the west half of the building (to your left), and 20th-century art is in the east half. Also to the east, in the adjacent Clore Gallery, are the works of J. M. W. Turner, John Constable, and William Blake. The Tate rotates its vast collection of paintings, so it's difficult to predict exactly which works will be on display. Pick up a map as you enter (£1 suggested donation) or download the museum's helpful app for a room-by-room guide.

1700-1800—Art Blossoms: With peace at home (under three King Georges), a strong overseas economy, and a growing urban center in London, England's artistic life began to bloom.

As the English grew more sophisticated, so did their portraits. Painters branched out into other subjects, capturing slices of everyday life (find William Hogarth's unflinchingly honest portraits, and Thomas Gainsborough's elegant, educated women).

1800-1850—The Industrial Revolution: Newfangled inventions were everywhere, but along with technology came factories coating towns with soot, urban poverty, regimentation, and clock-punching. Many artists rebelled against "progress" and the modern world. They escaped the dirty cities to commune with nature. Or they found a new spirituality in intense human emotions, expressed in dramatic paintings of episodes from history. In rooms dedicated to the 1800s, you may see a number of big paintings devoted to the power of nature.

1837-1901—The Victorian Era: In the world's wealthiest nation, the prosperous middle class dictated taste in art. They admired paintings that were realistic (showcasing the artist's talent and work ethic), depicting slices of everyday life. Some paintings tug at the heartstrings, with scenes of parting couples, the grief of death, or the joy of families reuniting.

Overdosed with the gushy sentimentality of their day, a band of 20-year-old artists—including Sir John Everett Millais, Dante Gabriel Rossetti, and William Holman Hunt—said "Enough!" and dedicated themselves to creating less saccharine art

Victorian-era Lady of Shalott

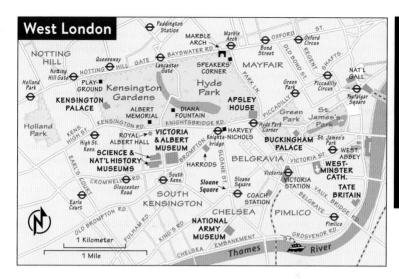

West London

(the Pre-Raphaelites). Like the Impressionists who followed them, they donned their scarves, barged out of the stuffy studio, and set up outdoors, painting trees, streams, and people, like scientists on a field trip. Still, they often captured nature with such a close-up clarity that it's downright unnatural.

British Impressionism: Realistic British art stood apart from the modernist trends in France, but some influences drifted across the Channel (Rooms 1890 and 1900). John Singer Sargent (American-born) studied with Parisian Impressionists, learning the thick, messy brushwork and play of light at twilight. James Tissot used Degas' snapshot technique to capture a crowded scene from an odd angle. And James McNeill Whistler (born in America, trained in Paris, lived in London) composed his paintings like music—see some of his paintings' titles.

1900-1950—World Wars: As two world wars whittled down the powerful British Empire, it still remained a major cultural force. British art mirrored many of the trends and "-isms" pioneered in Paris (Room 1930). You'll see Cubism like Picasso's, abstract art like Mondrian's, and so on. But British artists also continued

the British tradition of realistic paintings of people and landscapes.

If British painters were less than avant-garde, their sculptors were cutting edge. Henry Moore's statues—mostly female, mostly reclining—capture the human body in a few simple curves, with minimal changes to the rock itself. Francis Bacon has become Britain's best-known 20th-century painter, exemplifying the angst of the early post-WWII years. His deformed half-humans/half-animals express the existential human predicament of being caught in a world not of your own making, isolated and helpless to change it.

1950-2000—Modern World: No longer a world power, Britain in the Swinging '60s became a major exporter of pop culture. British art's traditional strengths—realism, portraits, landscapes, and slice-of-life scenes—were redone in the modern style. Look for works by David Hockney, Lucian Freud, Bridget Riley, and Gilbert and George.

Clore Gallery: Walking through J. M. W. Turner's life's work, you can watch Turner's style evolve from clear-eyed realism to hazy proto-Impressionism (1775-1851). You'll also see how Turner dabbled in different subjects: landscapes, seascapes, Roman ruins, snapshots of Venice, and so on. The corner room of the Clore Gallery is dedicated to John Constable (1776-1837), who painted the English landscape realistically, without idealizing it.

▲HYDE PARK AND SPEAKERS' CORNER

London's "Central Park," originally Henry VIII's hunting grounds, has more than 600 acres of lush greenery, Santander Cycles rental stations (described on page 116), the huge man-made Serpentine Lake (with rental boats and a lakeside swimming pool), the royal Kensington Palace (described next), and the ornate Neo-Gothic Albert Memorial across from the Royal Albert Hall (for more about the park, see www.royalparks.org.uk/parks/hyde-park). The western half of the park is known as Kensington Gardens. The park is huge—study a Tube map to choose the stop nearest to your destination.

On Sundays, from just after noon until early evening, **Speakers' Corner** offers soapbox oratory at its best (northeast corner of the park, Tube: Marble Arch). Characters climb their stepladders, wave their flags, pound emphatically on their sandwich boards, and share what they are convinced is their wisdom. Regulars have resident hecklers who know their lines and are always ready with a verbal jab or barb. "The grass roots of democracy" is actually a holdover from when the gallows stood here and the criminal was allowed to say just about anything he wanted to before he swung. I dare you to raise your voice and gather a crowd—it's easy to do.

The **Princess Diana Memorial Fountain** honors the "People's Princess," who once lived in nearby Kensington Palace. The low-key circular stream, great for cooling off your feet on a hot day, is in the south-central part of the park, near the Albert Memorial and Serpentine Gallery (Tube: Knightsbridge). A similarly named but different sight, the **Diana, Princess of Wales Memorial Playground,** in the park's northwest corner, is loads of fun for kids (Tube: Queensway).

KENSINGTON PALACE

For nearly 150 years (1689-1837), Kensington was the royal residence, before Buckingham Palace became the official home of the monarch. Sitting primly on its pleasant parkside grounds, the palace gives a barren yet regal glimpse into royal life—particularly that of Queen Victoria, who was born and raised here.

After Queen Victoria moved the monarchy to Buckingham Palace, lesser royals bedded down at Kensington. Princess Diana lived here both during and after her marriage to Prince Charles (1981-1997). More recently, Will and Kate moved in here. However—as many disappointed visitors discover—none of these more recent apartments are open to the public. The palace hosts a revolving series of temporary exhibits. To see what's on during your visit, check online.

Cost and Hours: £17.50; daily 10:00-18:00, Nov-Feb until 16:00, last entry one

Hyde Park

Kensington Palace

hour before closing; a long 10-minute stroll through Kensington Gardens from either High Street Kensington or Queensway Tube stations, tel. 0844-482-7788, www.hrp.org.uk.

Outside: Garden enthusiasts enjoy popping into the secluded Sunken Garden, 50 yards from the exit. Consider afternoon tea at the nearby Orangery (see page 107), built as a greenhouse for Queen Anne in 1704.

▲▲▲VICTORIA AND ALBERT MUSEUM

The world's top collection of decorative arts encompasses 2,000 years of art and design (ceramics, stained glass, fine furniture, clothing, jewelry, carpets, and more), displaying a surprisingly interesting and diverse assortment of crafts from the West, as well as from Asian and Islamic cultures. There's much to see, including Raphael's tapestry cartoons, Leonardo da Vinci's notebooks, the huge Islamic Ardabil Carpet (4,914 knots in every 10 square centimeters), a cast of Trajan's Column that depicts the emperor's conquests, and pop culture memorabilia, including the jumpsuit Mick Jagger wore for The Rolling Stones' 1972 world tour.

Cost and Hours: Free, £5 donation requested, fee for some special exhibits, daily 10:00-17:45, some galleries open Fri until 22:00, free tours daily, on Cromwell Road in South Kensington, Tube: South Kensington, from the Tube station a long tunnel leads directly to museum, tel. 020/7942-2000, www.vam.ac.uk.

Visiting the Museum: In the Grand Entrance lobby, look up into the rotunda to see the **Dale Chihuly chandelier,** epitomizing the spirit of the V&A's collection—beautiful manufactured objects that demonstrate technical skill and innovation, wedding the old with the new, and blurring the line between arts and crafts.

Now look up to the balcony (above the shop) and see the pointed arches of the **Hereford Screen,** a 35-by-35-foot, eight-ton rood screen (built for the Hereford Cathedral's sacred altar area). It looks medieval, but it was created with the most modern materials the Industrial Revolution could produce. George Gilbert Scott (1811-1878), who built the screen, redesigned much of London in the Neo-Gothic style, restoring old churches such as Westminster Abbey, renovating the Houses of Parliament, and building new structures like St. Pancras Station and the Albert Memorial—some 700 buildings in all.

Rick's Tip: *The Victoria and Albert Museum is huge and tricky to navigate. Spend £1 for the* **museum map** *available from the info desk.*

The V&A has (arguably) the best collection of Italian Renaissance sculpture outside Italy. One prime example is ***Samson Slaying a Philistine,*** by Giambologna (c. 1562), carved from a single block of marble, which shows the testy Israelite warrior rearing back, brandishing the jawbone of an ass, preparing to decapitate a man who'd insulted him.

The **Medieval and Renaissance Galleries** display 1,200 years of decorative arts, showing how the mix of pagan-Roman and medieval-Christian elements created modern Europe. In Room 8 is a glass case displaying the blue-and-gold, shoebox-sized **Becket Casket,** which contains the mortal remains (or relics) of St. Thomas Becket, who was brutally murdered. The enamel-and-metal workbox is a specialty of Limoges, France. In Room 10a, you'll run into the **Boar and Bear Hunt Tapestry.** Though most medieval art depicted the Madonna and saints, this colorful wool tapestry—woven in Belgium—provides a secular slice of life.

Two floors up, you'll see the tiny, pocket-size **notebook by Leonardo da Vinci** (Codex Forster III, 1490-1493), which dates from the years when he was living in Milan, shortly before undertaking his famous *Last Supper* fresco. The book's

Victoria and Albert Museum

contents are all over the map: meticulous sketches of the human head, diagrams illustrating nature's geometrical perfection, a horse's leg for a huge equestrian statue, and even drawings of the latest ballroom fashions. The adjacent computer lets you scroll through three of his notebooks and even flip his backwards handwriting to make it readable.

Back on level 0, enter Room 46b, and find **Michelangelo casts** and other replica statues. These plaster-cast versions of famous Renaissance statues allowed 19th-century art students who couldn't afford a rail pass to study the classics. In Room 42, you'll see **Islamic art,** reflecting both religious influences and a sophisticated secular culture. Many Islamic artists expressed themselves with beautiful but functional objects, such as the 630-square-foot Ardabil Carpet (1539-1540), which likely took a dozen workers years to complete. Also in the room are ceramics and glazed tile—all covered top to bottom in similarly complex patterns. The intricate interweaving, repetition, and unending lines suggest the complex, infinite nature of God (Allah).

In the hallway (technically "Room" 47b) is a glass case with a statue of **Shiva Nataraja,** one of the hundreds, if not thousands, of godlike incarnations of Hinduism's eternal being, Brahma. As long as Shiva keeps dancing, the universe will continue. In adjoining Room 41, a glass case in the center of the room contains

possessions of Emperor Shah Jahana, including a cameo portrait, thumb ring, and wine cup (made of white nephrite jade, 1657). Shah Jahan—or "King of the World"—ruled the largest empire of the day, covering northern India, Pakistan, and Afghanistan. At the far end of Room 41 is the huge wood-carved **Tipu's Tiger,** a life-size robotic toy, once owned by an oppressed Indian sultan. When you turned the crank, the Brit's left arm would flail, and both he and the tiger would roar through organ pipes. (The mechanism still works.)

The **Fashion Galleries** display centuries of English fashion, from ladies' underwear, hoop skirts, and rain gear to high-society evening wear, men's suits, and more. Across the hall are **Raphael's tapestry cartoons.** The V&A owns seven of these full-size designs (approximately 13 by 17 feet, done in tempera on paper, now mounted on canvas). The cartoons were sent to factories in Brussels, cut into strips (see the lines), and placed on the looms.

Upstairs, Room 57 is the heart of the **British Galleries,** which cover the era of Queen Elizabeth I. Find rare miniature portraits—a popular item of the day—including Hilliard's oft-reproduced *Young Man Among Roses* miniature, capturing the romance of a Shakespeare sonnet. Back in the Grand Entrance lobby, climb the staircase to level 2 to see **jewelry, theater artifacts, silver,** and more.

▲▲NATURAL HISTORY MUSEUM
Across the street from the Victoria and Albert, this mammoth museum covers everything from life ("creepy crawlies," human biology, our place in evolution, and awe-inspiring dinosaurs) to earth science (meteors, volcanoes, and earthquakes).

Cost and Hours: Free, £5 donation requested, fee for special exhibits, daily 10:00-18:00, helpful £1 map, long tunnel leads directly from South Kensington Tube station to museum (follow signs), tel. 020/7942-5000, exhibit info and reservations tel. 020/7942-5011, www.nhm.

ac.uk. Free visitor app available via the "Visit" section of the website.

Greenwich

This borough of London (worth ▲▲) is an easy, affordable boat trip or Docklands Light Railway (DLR) journey from downtown. Along with majestic, picnic-perfect parks are the stately trappings of Britain's proud nautical heritage and the Royal Observatory Greenwich, with a fine museum on how Greenwich Mean Time came to be, and a chance to straddle the eastern and western hemispheres at the prime meridian.

Getting There: Ride a boat to Greenwich for the scenery and commentary, and take the DLR back. Various tour boats—with commentary and open-deck seating (2/hour, 30-75 minutes)—and faster Thames Clippers (every 20-30 minutes, 20-55 minutes) depart from several piers in central London. Thames Clippers also connects Greenwich to the Docklands' Canary Wharf Pier (2-3/hour, 15 minutes).

By DLR, ride from the Bank-Monument Station to Cutty Sark Station in central Greenwich; it's one stop before the main—but less central—Greenwich Station (departs at least every 10 minutes, 20-minute ride, all in Zone 2). Or, catch bus #188 from Russell Square near the British Museum (about 45 minutes to Greenwich).

Eating: Greenwich's parks are picnic-perfect, especially around the National Maritime Museum and Royal Observatory. **$ Marks & Spencer Simply Food** sells ready-made lunches (55 Greenwich Church Street), and Greenwich Market offers an international variety of tasty food stalls (farmers market, arts and crafts, and food stands; daily 10:00-17:30; antiques Mon-Tue and Thu-Fri, www.greenwichmarketlondon.com). **$$$ The Old Brewery,** in the Discover Greenwich center, is a gastropub with classic British cuisine. **$$ The Trafalgar Tavern,** with a casual pub and pricier, elegant dining room, is a historical place for an overpriced meal. Up by the Royal Observatory, the elegant 1906 **$ Pavilion Café** offers tea, coffee, and counter-service food. At the bottom of Greenwich Park, **$$ White House Café** offers baked goodies and sandwiches.

▲▲CUTTY SARK

When first launched in 1869, the Scottish-built *Cutty Sark* was the last of the great China tea clippers and the queen of the seas. She was among the fastest clippers ever built, the culmination of centuries of ship design. With 32,000 square feet of sail—and favorable winds—she could travel 300 miles in a day. But as a new century dawned, steamers began to outmatch sailing ships for speed, and by the mid-1920s the *Cutty Sark* was the world's last operating clipper ship.

In 2012, the ship was restored and

Greenwich

Cutty Sark

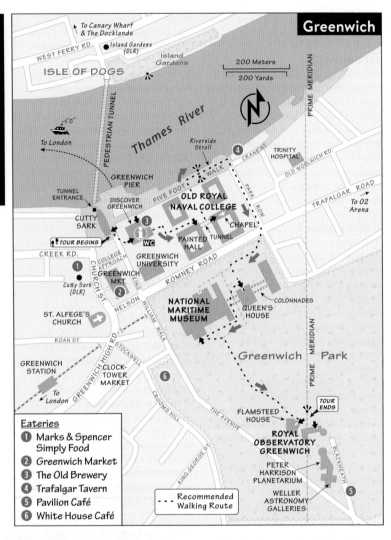

Greenwich

To Canary Wharf & The Docklands

WEST FERRY RD.

Island Gardens (DLR)

ISLE OF DOGS

Island Gardens

200 Meters
200 Yards

PRIME MERIDIAN

PEDESTRIAN TUNNEL

Thames River

To London

Riverside Stroll

TRINITY HOSPITAL

CRANE ST.

OLD WOOLWICH RD.

GREENWICH PIER

FIVE FOOT WALK

PARK ROW

TRAFALGAR ROAD

To O2 Arena

TUNNEL ENTRANCE

DISCOVER GREENWICH

OLD ROYAL NAVAL COLLEGE

CHAPEL

CUTTY SARK

TOUR BEGINS

PAINTED HALL

TUNNEL

GREENWICH UNIVERSITY

ROMNEY ROAD

CREEK RD.

COLLEGE APPROACH

CHURCH ST.

GREENWICH MKT.

NELSON RD.

KING WILLIAM WALK

Cutty Sark (DLR)

ST. ALFEGE'S CHURCH

NATIONAL MARITIME MUSEUM

COLONNADES

QUEEN'S HOUSE

ROAN ST.

GREENWICH STATION

To London

GREENWICH HIGH RD.

STOCKWELL

CLOCK-TOWER MARKET

Greenwich Park

PRIME MERIDIAN

CROOMS HILL

THE AVENUE

FLAMSTEED HOUSE

TOUR ENDS

KING GEORGE ST.

ROYAL OBSERVATORY GREENWICH

BLACKHEATH

PETER HARRISON PLANETARIUM

WELLER ASTRONOMY GALLERIES

Eateries

1. Marks & Spencer Simply Food
2. Greenwich Market
3. The Old Brewery
4. Trafalgar Tavern
5. Pavilion Café
6. White House Café

- - - Recommended Walking Route

reopened with a spectacular new glass-walled display space (though one critic groused that the ship now "looks like it has run aground in a giant greenhouse"). Displays explore the *Cutty Sark*'s 140-year history and the cargo she carried—everything from tea to wool to gunpowder—as she raced between London and ports all around the world.

Cost and Hours: £15, weekdays, £17 weekends, cheaper online, kids ages 4-15—£7.50, free for kids under age 4, family tickets available, combo-ticket with Royal Observatory—£26.25, kids combo-ticket—£17.60; daily 10:00-17:00; to skip the ticket-buying line reserve timed-entry tickets online or by phone, or show up around 13:00; unnecessary £6 guidebook, reservation tel. 020/8312-6608, www.rmg.co.uk.

OLD ROYAL NAVAL COLLEGE

Despite the name, these grand structures were built (1692) as a veterans' hospital to house disabled and retired sailors who'd served their country. In 1873, the hospital was transformed into one of the world's most prestigious universities for training naval officers. Today, the buildings host university students, music students, business conventions, concerts, and film crews drawn to the awe-inspiring space.

▲PAINTED HALL

Originally intended as a dining hall for pensioners, this sumptuously painted room was deemed too glorious (and, in the winter, too cold) for that purpose. So almost as soon as it was completed, it became simply a showcase for visitors. Impressive as it is, the admission is quite steep to see gigantic paintings by an artist you've never heard of, featuring second-rate royals. But those who appreciate artistic spectacles and picking out lavish details will find it worthwhile.

Cost and Hours: £12, daily 10:00-17:00, sometimes closed for private events, www.ornc.org. Ticket includes audioguide and a 45-minute guided tour of the Old Royal Naval College grounds, not including the Painted Hall (departs from Discover Greenwich at the top of each hour).

▲NATIONAL MARITIME MUSEUM

Great for anyone interested in the sea, this museum holds everything from a giant working paddlewheel to the uniform Admiral Horatio Nelson wore when he was killed at Trafalgar. A big glass roof tops three levels of slick, modern, kid-friendly exhibits about all things seafaring.

Cost and Hours: Free, daily 10:00-17:00, tel. 020/8858-4422, www.rmg.co.uk. The museum hosts frequent family-oriented events—ask at the desk.

▲▲ROYAL OBSERVATORY GREENWICH

Located on the prime meridian (0° longitude), this observatory is famous as the point from which all time and distances on earth are measured. A visit here gives you a taste of the sciences of astronomy, timekeeping, and seafaring—and how they all meld together—along with great views over Greenwich and the distant London skyline. In the courtyard, snap a selfie straddling the famous prime meridian line in the pavement. In the museum, there's the original 1600s-era observatory, the **Weller Astronomy Galleries,** and the state-of-the-art, **Peter Harrison Planetarium** (£10, shows about every 45 minutes during the observatory's opening times, no morning shows on school days, check schedule online).

Cost and Hours: £16, weekdays, £18 weekends, includes audioguide, combo-ticket with *Cutty Sark*—£26.25; daily 10:00-17:00; tel. 020/8858-4422, reservations tel. 020/8312-6608, www.rmg.co.uk.

Old Royal Naval College

Royal Observatory

Kew Gardens

Greater London

▲▲KEW GARDENS

For a fine riverside park and a palatial greenhouse jungle to swing through, take the Tube or the boat to every botanist's favorite escape. Garden lovers could spend days exploring Kew's 300 acres. For a quick visit, spend a fragrant hour wandering through three buildings: the Palm House, a humid Victorian world of iron, glass, and tropical plants that was built in 1844; a Waterlily House that Monet would swim for; and the Princess of Wales Conservatory, a meandering modern greenhouse with many different climate zones growing countless cacti, bug-munching carnivorous plants, and more. Check out the Xstrata Treetop Walkway, a 200-yard-long scenic steel walkway that puts you high in the canopy 60 feet above the ground.

Cost and Hours: £18, June-Aug £11 after 16:00, kids 4-16—£6, kids under 4—free; Mon-Thu 10:00-19:00, Fri-Sun until 20:00, closes earlier Sept-March—check schedule online, glasshouses close at 17:30 in high season—earlier off-season, free one-hour walking tours daily at 11:00 and 13:30, tel. 020/8332-5000, www.kew.org.

Getting There: By Tube, ride to Kew Gardens station, then cross the footbridge over the tracks, which drops you in a little community of plant-and-herb shops, a two-block walk from Victoria Gate (the main garden entrance). Boats also run to Kew Gardens from Westminster Pier (see page 34).

Eating: For a sun-dappled lunch or snack, walk 10 minutes from the Palm House to the **$$ Orangery Cafeteria** (Mon-Thu 10:00-17:30, Fri-Sun until 18:30, until 15:15 in winter, closes early for events).

EXPERIENCES

Shopping

Most stores are open Monday through Saturday from roughly 9:00 or 10:00 until 17:00 or 18:00, with a late night on Wednesday or Thursday (usually until 19:00 or 20:00). Many close on Sundays. Large department stores stay open later during the week (until about 21:00 Mon-Sat) with shorter hours on Sundays. If you're looking for bargains, visit one of the city's many street markets.

Shopping Streets

The best and most convenient shopping streets are in the West End and West London (roughly between Soho and Hyde Park). You'll find midrange shops

along **Oxford Street** (running east from Tube: Marble Arch), and fancier shops along **Regent Street** (stretching south from Tube: Oxford Circus to Piccadilly Circus) and **Knightsbridge** (where you'll find Harrods and Harvey Nichols; Tube: Knightsbridge). Other streets are more specialized, such as **Jermyn Street** for old-fashioned men's clothing (just south of Piccadilly) and **Charing** Cross Road for books. **Floral Street,** connecting Leicester Square to Covent Garden, is lined with boutiques.

Department Stores

Harrods is London's most famous and touristy department store, with more than four acres of retail space covering seven floors (Mon-Sat 10:00-21:00, Sun 11:30-18:00, Brompton Road, Tube: Knightsbridge, tel. 020/7730-1234, www.harrods.com).

Harvey Nichols was once Princess Diana's favorite and later Duchess Kate's. "Harvey Nick's" remains the department store *du jour* (Mon-Sat 10:00-20:00, Sun 11:30-18:00, near Harrods, 109 Knightsbridge, Tube: Knightsbridge, tel. 020/7235-5000, www.harveynichols.com).

Fortnum & Mason, the official department store of the Queen, embodies old-fashioned, British upper-class taste, with a storybook atmosphere. An elegant tea is served in their Diamond Jubilee Tea Salon (Mon-Sat 10:00-21:00, Sun 11:30-18:00, 181 Piccadilly, Tube: Green Park, tel. 020/7734-8040, www.fortnumandmason.com).

Liberty is a still-thriving 19th-century institution known for its artful displays and castle-like interior (Mon-Sat 10:00-20:00, Sun 11:30-18:00, Great Marlborough Street, Tube: Oxford Circus, tel. 020/7734-1234, www.liberty.co.uk).

Street Markets

Antique buffs and people-watchers love London's street markets. The best markets—which combine lively stalls and

a colorful neighborhood with cute and characteristic shops of their own—are Portobello Road and Camden Lock Market. Hagglers will enjoy the no-holds-barred bargaining.

IN NOTTING HILL

Portobello Road stretches for several blocks through the delightful, colorful, funky-yet-quaint Notting Hill neighborhood. Charming streets lined with pastel-painted houses and offbeat antique shops are enlivened on Fridays and Saturdays with 2,000 additional stalls (9:00-19:00), plus food, live music, and more (Tube: Notting Hill Gate, near recommended accommodations, tel. 020/7727-7684, www.portobelloroad.co.uk).

Rick's Tip: *Browse* **Portabello Road on Friday.** *Most stalls are open, with half the crowds of Saturday.*

IN CAMDEN TOWN

Camden Lock Market is a huge, trendy arts-and-crafts festival divided into three areas, each with its own vibe. The main market, set alongside the picturesque canal, features a mix of shops and stalls selling boutique crafts and artisanal foods. The market on the opposite side of Chalk Farm Road is edgier, with cheap ethnic food stalls, lots of canalside seating, and punk crafts. The Stables, a sprawling, incense-scented complex, is squeezed into tunnels under the old rail bridge just behind the main market (daily 10:00-19:00, busiest on weekends, tel. 020/3763-9999, www.camdenmarket.com).

IN THE EAST END

Spitalfields Market combines old brick buildings with sleek modern ones, all covered by a giant glass roof. Shops, stalls, and a rainbow of restaurant options are open every day (Mon-Fri 10:00-17:00, Sat from 11:00, Sun from 9:00; Tube: Liverpool Street; from the Tube stop, take Bishopsgate East exit, turn left, walk to Brushfield Street, and turn right; www.spitalfields.co.uk).

Petticoat Lane Market, a block from Spitalfields Market, sits on the otherwise dull Middlesex Street; adjoining Wentworth Street is grungier and more characteristic (Sun 9:00-14:00, sometimes later; smaller market Mon-Fri on Wentworth Street only; Middlesex Street and Wentworth Street, Tube: Liverpool Street).

The **Truman Markets,** housed in the former Truman Brewery on Brick Lane, are gritty and avant-garde. The markets are in full swing on Sundays (roughly 10:00-17:00), though you'll see some action on Saturdays (11:00-18:00). Surrounding shops and eateries are open all week (Tube: Liverpool Street or Aldgate East, www.vintage-market.co.uk).

Brick Lane is lined with Sunday market stands from about Buxton Street to Bethnal Green Road—about a 10-minute walk. Continuing another 10 minutes north, then turning right onto Columbia Road, takes you to **Columbia Road Flower Market** (Sun 8:00-15:00, www.columbiaroad.info). Halfway up Columbia Road, be sure to loop left up little Ezra Street, with characteristic eateries, boutiques, and antique vendors.

IN THE WEST END

The iron-and-glass **Covent Garden Market,** originally the garden for Westminster Abbey, hosts a mix of fun shops, eateries, and markets. Mondays are for antiques, while arts and crafts dominate the rest of the week. Produce stalls are open daily 10:30-18:00, and on Thursdays, a food market brightens up the square (Tube: Covent Garden, tel. 020/7395-1350, www.coventgardenlondonuk.com).

Jubilee Market features antiques on Mondays (5:00-17:00); a general market Tuesday through Friday (10:30-19:00); and arts and crafts on Saturdays and Sundays (10:00-18:00). It's located on the south side of Covent Garden (tel. 020/7379-4242, www.jubileemarket.co.uk).

Theater (a.k.a. "Theatre")

London's theater scene rivals Broadway's in quality and often beats it in price. Choose from 200 offerings—Shakespeare, musicals, comedies, thrillers, sex farces, cutting-edge fringe, revivals starring movie celebs, and more. London does it all well.

Rick's Tip: *Just like at home, London's theaters* **sell seats in a range of levels**—*but the Brits use different terms: stalls (ground floor), dress circle (first balcony), upper circle (second balcony), balcony (sky-high third balcony), and slips (cheap seats on the fringes). Discounted tickets are called "concessions" (abbreviated as "conc" or "s").*

West End Shows

Nearly all big-name shows are hosted in the theaters of the West End, clustering around Soho between Piccadilly and Covent Garden. With a centuries-old tradition of pleasing the masses, they present London theater at its grandest.

Well-known musicals may draw the biggest crowds, but the West End offers plenty of other crowd-pleasers, from revivals of classics to cutting-edge works by the hottest young playwrights. These productions tend to have shorter runs than famous musicals. Many productions star huge-name celebrities—London is a magnet for movie stars who want to stretch their acting chops.

The *Official London Theatre Guide*, a free booklet that's updated every two weeks, is a handy tool (find it at hotels, box offices, the City of London TI, and online at www.officiallondontheatre.co.uk). Check reviews at www.timeout.com/london.

Most performances are nightly except Sunday, usually with two or three matinees a week. The few shows that run on Sundays are mostly family fare (such as *The Lion King*).

TICKETS

Most shows have tickets available on short notice—likely at a discount. But if your time in London is limited—and you have your heart set on a particular show that's likely to sell out, you can buy peace of mind by booking tickets from home. For floor plans of the various theaters, see www.theatremonkey.com.

Advance Tickets: It's generally cheapest to buy your tickets directly from the theater, either through its website or by calling the theater box office. In most cases, a theater will reroute you to a third-party ticket vendor such as Ticketmaster (typically with a £3/ticket fee). You can have your tickets emailed to you or pick them up before show time at Will Call.

Rick's Tip: *The* **real TKTS booth** *(with its prominent sign) is a freestanding kiosk at the south edge of Leicester Square. Several dishonest outfits nearby advertise "official half-price tickets"—avoid these, where you'll pay closer to full price.*

Discount Tickets: The **TKTS Booth** at Leicester Square sells discounted tickets (25-50 percent off) for many shows (£3/ticket service charge, open Mon-Sat 10:00-19:00, Sun 11:00-16:30). You must buy in person at the kiosk, and the best deals are same-day only. The list of shows and prices is continually updated and posted outside the booth and on their website (www.tkts.co.uk). For the best choice and prices, come early in the day—the line starts forming even before the booth opens (it moves quickly).

Theater Box Office: Even if a show is "sold out," there's usually a way to get a seat. Many theaters offer various discounts or "concessions": same-day tickets, cheap returned tickets, standing-room, matinee, senior or student standby deals, and more. Start by check-

ing the show's website, then call the box office or simply drop by (many theaters are right in the tourist zone).

Same-day tickets (called **"day seats"**) can be an excellent deal. These generally go on sale *only in person* when the box office opens (typically at 10:00; people start lining up before then). These tickets (£20 or less) tend to be either in the nosebleed rows or with a restricted view. Another strategy is to show up at the box office shortly before show time (best on weekdays) and—before paying full price—ask about cheaper options. Last-minute return tickets are often sold at great prices as curtain time approaches.

For a helpful guide to "day seats"—including recent user reports on how early you need to show up—consult www.theatremonkey.com/dayseatfinder.htm; for tips on getting cheap and last-minute tickets, visit www.londontheatretickets.org and www.timeout.com/london/theatre.

Other Agencies: Although booking through a middleman such as your hotel or a ticket agency is quick and easy, prices are greatly inflated (legitimate resellers add up to a 25 percent booking fee). Ticket agencies and third-party websites are often just scalpers with an address. If you do buy from an agency, choose one who is a member of the Society of Ticket Agents and Retailers (look for the STAR logo—short for "secure tickets from authorized retailers").

Scalpers ("Touts"): You'll find scalpers hawking tickets outside theaters. Just like at home, those people may either be honest folk whose date just happened to cancel at the last minute...or unscrupulous thieves selling forgeries. London has many of the latter.

Beyond the West End

Tickets for lesser-known shows tend to be cheaper (figure £15-30), in part because most of the smaller theaters are government-subsidized. Read up on the latest

offerings online; Timeout.com is a great place to start. Major noncommercial theaters include the National Theatre, Barbican Centre, Royal Court Theatre, Menier Chocolate Factory, and Bridge Theatre. The Royal Shakespeare Company performs at various theaters around London.

SHAKESPEARE'S GLOBE

To see Shakespeare in a replica of the theater for which he wrote his plays, attend a play at the Globe. In this round, thatched-roof, open-air theater, the plays are performed much as Shakespeare intended—under the sky, with no amplification.

The play's the thing from late April through mid-October (usually Tue-Sat 14:00 and 19:30, Sun either 13:00 and/or 18:30, tickets can be sold out months in advance). You'll pay £5 to stand and £23-47 to sit, usually on a backless bench (only a few rows and the pricier Gentlemen's Rooms have seats with backs, £2 cushions and £4 add-on backrests a good investment; dress for the weather).

The £5 "groundling" or "yard" tickets—which are open to rain—are most fun. Scurry in early to stake out a spot on the stage's edge, where the most interaction with the actors occurs. You're a crude peasant. You can lean your elbows on the stage, munch a snack (yes, you can bring in food—but bag size is limited), or walk around. I've never enjoyed Shakespeare as much as here, performed as it was meant

A performance at Shakespeare's Globe

Evensong

One of my favorite experiences in Britain is to attend evensong at a great church. Evensong is an evening worship service that is typically sung rather than said (though some parts—including scripture readings, a few prayers, and a homily—are spoken). It follows the traditional Anglican service in the Book of Common Prayer, including prayers, scripture readings, canticles (sung responses), and hymns that are appropriate for the early evening—traditionally the end of the working day and before the evening meal. In major churches with resident choirs, a singing or chanting priest leads the service, and a choir—usually made up of both men's and boys' voices (to sing the lower and higher parts, respectively)—sings the responses. The choir usually sings a cappella, or is accompanied by an organ. Visitors are welcome and are given an order of service or a prayer book to help them follow along.

Impressive places for evensong include Westminster Abbey and St. Paul's. Evensong typically takes place in the small choir area, which is far more intimate than the main nave. It generally occurs daily between 17:00 and 18:00 (often two hours earlier on Sun)—check with individual churches for specifics. At smaller churches, evensong is sometimes spoken, not sung.

Note that evensong is not a performance—it's a somewhat somber worship service. If you enjoy worshipping in different churches, attending evensong can be a highlight. Most major churches also offer organ or choral concerts—look for posted schedules or ask at the information desk or gift shop.

to be in the "wooden O." If you can't get a ticket, take a guided tour of the theater and museum by day (see page 79).

The indoor Sam Wanamaker Playhouse allows Shakespearean-era plays and early-music concerts to be performed through the winter. Many of the productions in this intimate venue are one-offs and can be pricey.

To reserve tickets for plays at the Globe or Playhouse, drop by the box office (Mon-Sat 10:00-18:00, Sun until 17:00, open one hour later on performance days, New Globe Walk entrance, box office tel. 020/7401-9919, info tel. 020/7902-1400). You can also reserve online (www.shakespearesglobe.com, £2.50 booking fee). Try calling around noon the day of the performance to see if the box office expects any returned tickets. If so, they'll advise you to show up a little more than an hour before the show, when these tickets are sold (first-come, first-served).

The theater is on the South Bank, directly across the Thames over the Millennium Bridge from St. Paul's Cathedral (Tube: Mansion House or London Bridge).

Concerts at Churches

For easy, cheap, or free concerts in historic churches, attend a **lunch concert,** especially:

St. Bride's Church, with free half-hour lunch concerts twice a week at 13:15 (usually Tue and Fri—confirm in advance, church tel. 020/7427-0133, www.stbrides.com).

Temple Church, also in The City, with free organ recitals weekly (Wed at 13:15, www.templechurch.com).

St. James's at Piccadilly, with 50-minute concerts on Mon, Wed, and Fri at 13:10 (suggested £5 donation, info tel. 020/7734-4511, www.sjp.org.uk).

St. Martin-in-the-Fields, offering

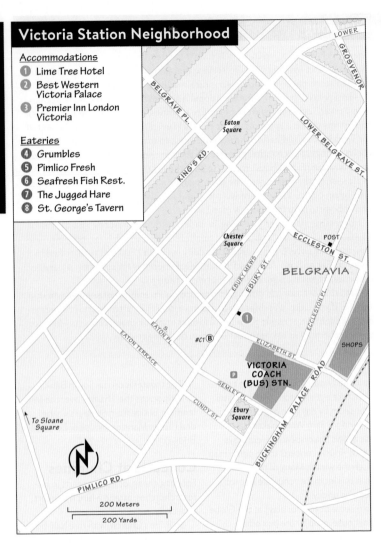

Victoria Station Neighborhood

Accommodations
1. Lime Tree Hotel
2. Best Western Victoria Palace
3. Premier Inn London Victoria

Eateries
4. Grumbles
5. Pimlico Fresh
6. Seafresh Fish Rest.
7. The Jugged Hare
8. St. George's Tavern

LOWER GROSVENOR

BELGRAVE PL.

Eaton Square

LOWER BELGRAVE ST.

KING'S RD.

Chester Square

ECCLESTON ST.

POST

BELGRAVIA

EBURY MEWS

EBURY ST.

ECCLESTON PL.

S. EATON PL.

EATON TERRACE

#C1 ⓑ

ELIZABETH ST.

SHOPS

VICTORIA COACH (BUS) STN.

SEMLEY PL.

CUNDY ST.

Ebury Square

BUCKINGHAM PALACE ROAD

To Sloane Square

PIMLICO RD.

200 Meters
200 Yards

concerts on Mon, Tue, and Fri at 13:00 (suggested £3.50 donation, church tel. 020/7766-1100, www.stmartin-in-the-fields.org).

St. Martin-in-the-Fields also hosts fine **evening concerts** by candlelight (£9-29, several nights a week at 19:30) and live jazz in its underground Café in the Crypt (£8-15, Wed at 20:00).

Evensong services are held at several churches, including St. Paul's Cathedral (see page 65) and Westminster Abbey (see page 37).

Free **organ recitals** are usually held on Sunday at 17:45 in Westminster Abbey (30 minutes, tel. 020/7222-5152). Many other churches have free concerts; ask for the *London Organ Concerts Guide* at the TI.

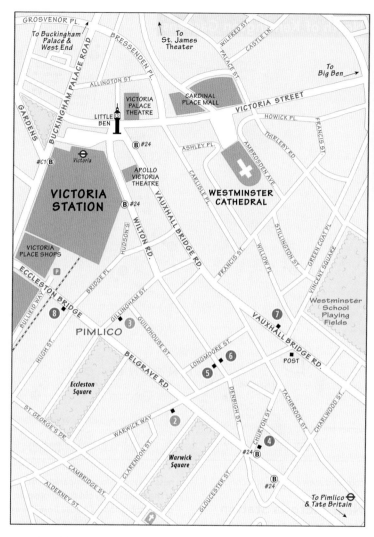

SLEEPING

London is an expensive city for lodging. Expect cheaper rooms to be relatively dumpy. Focus on choosing the right neighborhood, which is as important as selecting the right hotel. I rank accommodations from $ budget to $$$$ splurge. For the best deal, contact my family-run places directly by phone or email. Book well in advance for peak season or if your trip coincides with a major holiday or festival.

Looking for Hotel Deals Online: Given London's high hotel prices, it's worth searching for a deal. For more options, browse these accommodation discount sites: www.londontown.com (an informative site with a discount booking service), www.athomeinlondon.co.uk and www.londonbb.com (both list central B&Bs), www.lastminute.com, www.visitlondon.

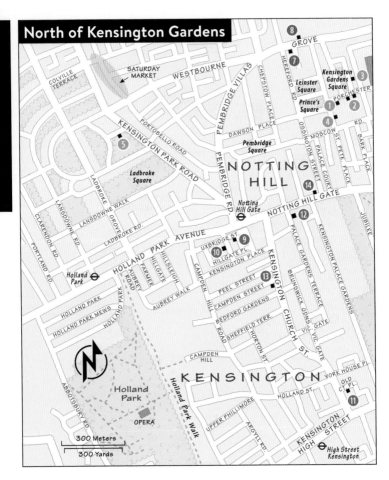

North of Kensington Gardens

com, and www.eurocheapo.com.

Near Victoria Station

The safe, surprisingly tidy streets behind Victoria Station teem with little, moderately-priced-for-London B&Bs.

$$$$ Lime Tree Hotel has 28 spacious, stylish, comfortable, thoughtfully decorated rooms, a helpful staff, a fun-loving breakfast room, and a delightful garden in back (135 Ebury Street, tel. 020/7730-8191, www.limetreehotel.co.uk, info@limetreehotel.co.uk, Charlotte and Matt, Laura manages the office).

$$ Best Western Victoria Palace offers modern, if slightly worn, business-class comfort compared with some of the other creaky old guesthouses in the neighborhood. Choose from the 43 rooms in the main building (at 60 Warwick Way), or pay about 20 percent less by booking a nearly identical room in one of the annexes, each a half-block away—an excellent value for this neighborhood if you skip breakfast (air-con, elevator in main building only, 17 Belgrave Road and 1 Warwick Way, reception at main building, tel. 020/7821-7113, www.bestwesternvictoriapalace.co.uk, info@bestwesternvictoriapalace.co.uk).

If considering chain hotels, there's also a fine **$$$ Premier Inn** in this area (82

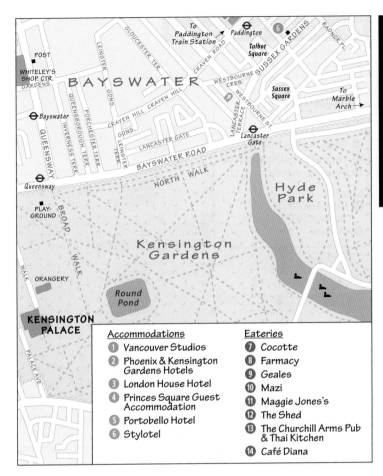

Accommodations
1. Vancouver Studios
2. Phoenix & Kensington Gardens Hotels
3. London House Hotel
4. Princes Square Guest Accommodation
5. Portobello Hotel
6. Stylotel

Eateries
7. Cocotte
8. Farmacy
9. Geales
10. Mazi
11. Maggie Jones's
12. The Shed
13. The Churchill Arms Pub & Thai Kitchen
14. Café Diana

Eccleston Square, www.premierinn.com).

North of Kensington Gardens

From the core of the tourist's London, vast Hyde Park spreads west, eventually becoming Kensington Gardens. Bayswater anchors the area; it's bordered by Notting Hill to the west and Paddington to the east. This area has quick bus and Tube access to downtown and, for London, is very cozy.

Bayswater and Notting Hill

$$$ **Vancouver Studios** has 45 modern, tastefully furnished rooms that come with fully equipped kitchenettes, or you can pay for a continental breakfast. It's nestled between Kensington Gardens Square and Prince's Square and has its own tranquil garden patio out back (laundry, 30 Prince's Square, tel. 020/7243-1270, www.vancouverstudios.co.uk, info@vancouverstudios.co.uk).

$$$ **Phoenix Hotel** offers spacious, stately public spaces and 125 modern-feeling rooms with classy decor. While the rates can vary wildly, it's a good choice if you can get a deal (elevator, 1 Kensington Gardens Square, tel. 020/7229-2494, www.phoenixhotel.co.uk,

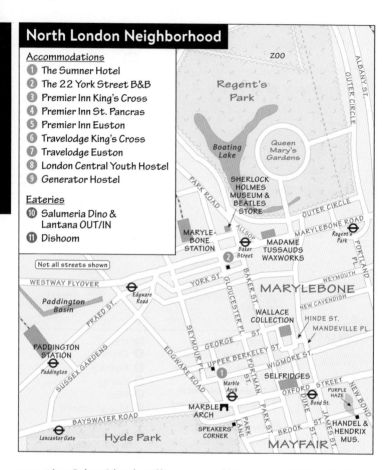

North London Neighborhood

Accommodations

1. The Sumner Hotel
2. The 22 York Street B&B
3. Premier Inn King's Cross
4. Premier Inn St. Pancras
5. Premier Inn Euston
6. Travelodge King's Cross
7. Travelodge Euston
8. London Central Youth Hostel
9. Generator Hostel

Eateries

10. Salumeria Dino & Lantana OUT/IN
11. Dishoom

Not all streets shown

reservations@phoenixhotel.co.uk).

$$$ London House Hotel has 103 spiffy, modern, cookie-cutter rooms at reasonable prices (family rooms, air-con, elevator, 81 Kensington Gardens Square, tel. 020/7243-1810, www. londonhousehotels.com, reservations@ londonhousehotels.com).

$$$ Princes Square Guest Accommodation is a crisp (if impersonal) place renting 50 businesslike rooms with pleasant, modern decor. It's well located, practical, and a very good value, especially if you can score a good rate (elevator, 23 Prince's Square, tel. 020/7229-9876, www.princessquarehotel.co.uk, info@ princessquarehotel.co.uk).

$$ Kensington Gardens Hotel, with the same owners as the Phoenix Hotel, laces 17 rooms together in a tall, skinny building (breakfast served at Phoenix Hotel, 9 Kensington Gardens Square, tel. 020/7243-7600, www. kensingtongardenshotel.co.uk, info@ kensingtongardenshotel.co.uk).

$$$$ Portobello Hotel is on a quiet residential street in the heart of Notting Hill. Its 21 rooms are funky yet elegant—both the style and location give it an urban-fresh feeling (elevator, 22 Stanley Gardens, tel. 020/7727-2777, www.portobellohotel.com, stay@ portobellohotel.com).

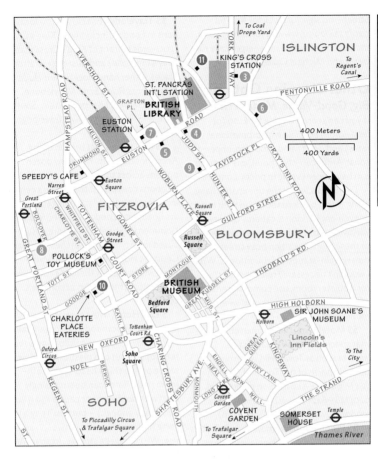

Near Paddington Station

$$ Stylotel feels like the stylish, super-modern, aluminum-clad big sister of the EasyHotel chain. While the 42 rooms can be cramped, the beds have space for luggage underneath (RS%, family rooms, air-con, elevator, 160 Sussex Gardens, tel. 020/7723-1026, www.stylotel.com, info@stylotel.com, Andreas).

North London

$$$$ The Sumner Hotel rents 19 rooms in a 19th-century Georgian townhouse sporting large contemporary rooms and a lounge with fancy modern Italian furniture. This swanky place packs in all the amenities and is conveniently located north of Hyde Park and near Oxford Street, a busy shopping destination—close to Selfridges and a Marks & Spencer (RS%, air-con, elevator, 54 Upper Berkeley Street, a block-and-a-half off Edgware Road, Tube: Marble Arch, tel. 020/7723-2244, www.thesumner.com, hotel@thesumner.com).

$$$ The 22 York Street B&B offers a casual alternative in the city center, with an inviting lounge and 10 traditional, hardwood, comfortable rooms, each named for a notable London landmark (near Marylebone/Baker Street: From Baker Street Tube station, walk 2 blocks down Baker Street and take a right to 22 York

Street—no sign, just look for #22; tel. 020/7224-2990, www.22yorkstreet.co.uk, mc@22yorkstreet.co.uk, energetically run by Liz and Michael Callis).

Other Sleeping Options
Big, Good-Value, Modern Hotels

If you can score a double for £100 (or less—often possible with promotional rates) and don't mind a modern, impersonal, American-style hotel, one of these can be a decent value in pricey London.

I've listed a few of the dominant chains, along with a quick rundown on their more convenient London locations. Quality can vary wildly so check online reviews. Some of these branches sit on busy streets in dreary train-station neighborhoods. While I wouldn't necessarily rule these out, ask for a quieter room, use common sense when exploring after dark, and wear a money belt.

$$ Motel One, the German chain that specializes in affordable style, has a branch at Tower Hill, a 10-minute walk north of the Tower of London (24 Minories—see map on page 68, tel. 020/7481-6420, www.motel-one.com, london-towerhill@motel-one.com).

$$ Premier Inn has more than 70 hotels in greater London. Convenient locations include a branch inside London County Hall (next to the London Eye), at Southwark/Borough Market (near Shakespeare's Globe, 34 Park Street), Southwark/Tate Modern (15 Great Suffolk Street), Kensington/Earl's Court (11 Knaresborough Place), Victoria (82 Eccleston Square), and Leicester Square (1 Leicester Place). In North London, several locations cluster between King's Cross St. Pancras and the British Museum: King's Cross, St. Pancras, and Euston. Avoid the Tower Bridge location, south of the bridge and a long walk from the Tube—but London City Tower Hill, north of the bridge on Prescot Street (see map on page 98)—works fine (www.premierinn.com).

$$ Travelodge has close to 70 locations in London, including at King's Cross (200 yards in front of King's Cross Station, Gray's Inn Road) and Euston (1 Grafton Place). Other handy locations include King's Cross Royal Scot, Marylebone, Covent Garden, Liverpool Street, Southwark, and Farringdon; www.travelodge.co.uk.

$$ Ibis, the budget branch of the AccorHotels group, has a few dozen options across the city, with a handful of locations convenient to London's center, including London Blackfriars (49 Blackfriars Road) and London City Shoreditch (5 Commercial Street). The more design-focused Ibis Styles has branches near Earl's Court (15 Hogarth Road) and Southwark, with a theater theme (43 Southwark Bridge Road; https://ibis.accorhotels.com).

$ EasyHotel, with several branches in good neighborhoods, offers generally tiny, super-efficient, no-frills rooms that feel popped out of a plastic mold, down to the prefab ship's head-type "bathroom pod." Rates can be surprisingly low (with doubles as cheap as £30 if you book early enough)—but you'll pay à la carte for expensive add-ons, such as TV use, Wi-Fi, luggage storage, fresh towels, and daily cleaning (breakfast, if available, comes from a vending machine). If you go with the base rate, it's like hosteling with privacy. But you get what you pay for (thin walls, flimsy construction, noisy fellow guests, and so on). They're only a good deal if you book far enough ahead to get a good price and skip the many extras. Locations include Victoria (34 Belgrave Road), South Kensington (14 Lexham Gardens), and Paddington (10 Norfolk Place); www.easyhotel.com.

$ Hub by Premier Inn—the budget chain's no-frills, pod-style division—offers extremely small rooms (just a little bigger than the bed) in convenient locations for low prices (from £69, www.premierinn.com/gb/en/hub.html).

Hostels

¢ **London Central Youth Hostel** is the flagship of London's hostels. Families and travelers of any age will feel welcome in this wonderful facility. You'll pay the same price for any bed—so try to grab one with a bathroom (families welcome to book an entire room, book long in advance; between Oxford Circus and Great Portland Street Tube stations at 104 Bolsover Street—see map on page 98, tel. 0345-371-9154, www.yha.org.uk, londoncentral@yha.org.uk).

¢ **Generator Hostel** is a brightly colored, hip hostel with a café and a DJ spinning the hits. It's in a renovated building tucked behind a busy street halfway between King's Cross and the British Museum (37 Tavistock Place—see map on page 98, Tube: Russell Square, tel. 020/7388-7666, http://staygenerator.com, ask.london@generatorhostels.com).

EATING

Whether it's dining well with the upper crust, sharing hearty pub fare with the blokes, or venturing to a fringe neighborhood to try the latest hotspot or street food at a market, eating out is an essential part of the London experience. The sheer variety of foods—from every corner of Britain's former empire and beyond—is astonishing.

Central London

Soho

With its status as *the* place where budding restaurateurs stake their claim on London's culinary map, Soho is a magnet for diners. Even if Soho isn't otherwise on your radar, make a point to dine here at least once.

$$$ Andrew Edmunds Restaurant is a tiny candlelit space where you'll want to hide your guidebook and not act like a tourist. This little place—with a loyal clientele—is the closest I've found to Parisian quality in a cozy restaurant in London. The extensive wine list, modern European cooking, and creative seasonal menu are worth the splurge (daily 12:30-15:30 & 17:30-22:45, these are last-order times, come early or call ahead, request ground floor rather than basement, 46 Lexington Street, tel. 020/7437-5708, www.andrewedmunds.com).

$$$ Temper Soho pleases well-heeled carnivores. From the nondescript office-block entrance, you'll descend to a cozy, stylish cellar filled with rich smoke from meat grilling on open fires. They carve off chunks for tacos and *parathas* (Indian-style flatbreads). The portions are small and pricey (order multiple courses), but meat lovers willing to pay leave satisfied (Mon-Sat 12:00-22:30, Sun until 21:00, 25 Broadwick Street, tel. 020/3879-3834).

$$$ Bocca di Lupo, a stylish and popular option, serves half and full portions of classic regional Italian food. Dressy but with a fun energy, it's a place where you'll be glad you made a reservation. The counter seating, on cushy stools with a view into the lively open kitchen, is particularly memorable, or you can take a table in the snug, casual back end (daily 12:30-15:00 & 17:15-23:00, 12 Archer Street, tel. 020/7734-2223, www.boccadilupo.com).

$$$ Kricket Soho serves upmarket Indian fare a few steps from Piccadilly Circus. Opt for the tight, stylish, unpretentious main floor (with counter seating surrounding an open kitchen) or the dining room in the cellar. The small-plates menu is an education in Indian cuisine beyond the corner curry house, with *kulchas* (miniature naan breads with toppings), *kheer* (rice pudding), and KFC—Keralan fried chicken (Mon-Sat 12:00-14:30 & 17:15-22:30, closed Sun, 12 Denman Street, tel. 020/7734-5612).

$$$$ Nopi is one of a handful of restaurants run by London celebrity chef Yotam Ottolenghi. The cellar features communal tables looking into the busy kitchen, and the cuisine is typical of Ottolenghi's mas-

Central London Restaurants

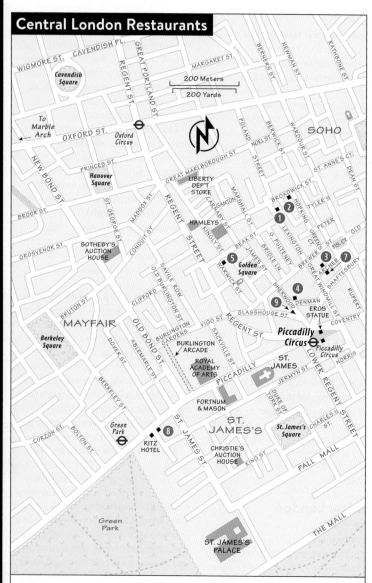

Eateries

1. Andrew Edmunds Restaurant
2. Temper Soho
3. Bocca di Lupo
4. Kricket Soho
5. Nopi
6. Hoppers
7. Gelupo Gelato
8. The Wolseley
9. Brasserie Zédel
10. Dishoom
11. Lamb & Flag Pub
12. Terroirs Wine Bar
13. St. Martin-in-the-Fields Café in the Crypt

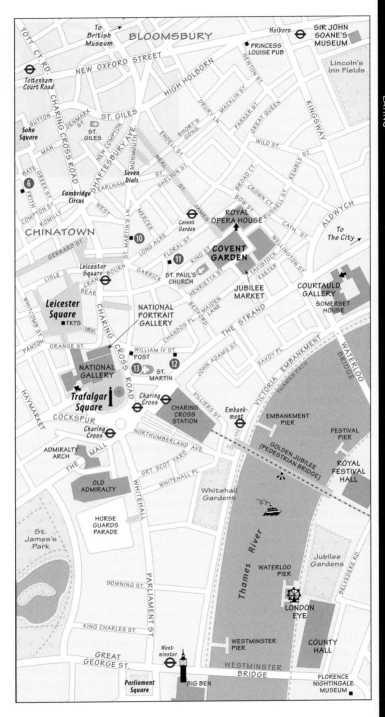

terful Eastern Mediterranean cooking, with an emphasis on seasonal produce. If you want to splurge in Soho, do it here (Mon-Sat 10:00-15:00 & 17:30-22:30, Sun until 16:00, 21 Warwick Street, tel. 020/7494-9584, www.ottolenghi.co.uk).

$$ Hoppers is an easy entry into Sri Lankan cuisine—reminiscent of Indian but with more tropical flourishes. You'll be glad the menu comes with a glossary of key terms—for example, hopper (a spongy yet firm rice-and-coconut pancake, shaped like a bowl), *kari* (Tamil for "curry"), and *roti* (flatbread). Be adventurous, and seek the waitstaff's advice (Mon-Sat 12:00-14:30 & 17:30-22:30, closed Sun, 49 Frith Street, tel. 020/3319-8110).

Gelato: Across the street from Bocca di Lupo (listed earlier) is its sister *gelateria,* **Gelupo,** with a wide array of ever-changing but always creative and delicious dessert favorites. Take away or enjoy their homey interior (daily 11:00-23:00, 7 Archer Street, tel. 020/7287-5555).

Near Piccadilly

$$$$ The Wolseley is the grand 1920s showroom of a long-defunct British car. The last Wolseley drove out with the Great Depression, but today this old-time bistro bustles with formal waiters serving traditional Austrian and French dishes in an elegant black-marble-and-chandeliers setting fit for its location next to the Ritz. Although the food can be unexceptional, prices are reasonable considering the grand presentation and setting. Reservations are a must (cheaper soup, salad, and sandwich "café menu" available in all areas of restaurant, daily 11:30-23:00, 160 Piccadilly, tel. 020/7499-6996, www.thewolseley.com). They're popular for their fancy cream tea or afternoon tea (see "Taking Tea in London" sidebar).

$$$ Brasserie Zédel is the former dining hall of the old Regent Palace Hotel, the biggest hotel in the world when built in 1915. Climbing down the stairs from street level, you're surprised by a gilded grand

hall that feels like a circa 1920 cruise ship, filled with a boisterous crowd enjoying big, rich French food—old-fashioned brasserie dishes. With vested waiters, fast service, and paper tablecloths, it's great for a group of friends. After 21:30, the lights dim, the candles are lit, and it gets more romantic with live jazz (nightly inexpensive *plats du jour,* daily 11:30-24:00, 20 Sherwood Street, tel. 020/7734-4888). Across the atrium is the hotel's original Bar Américain (which feels like the 1930s) and the Crazy Coqs venue—busy with "Live at Zédel" music, theater, comedy, and literary events (see www.brasseriezedel.com for schedule).

Near Covent Garden

$$$ Dishoom is London's hotspot for upscale Indian cuisine. The dishes seem familiar, but the flavors are a revelation. People line up early (starting around 17:00) for a seat, either on the bright, rollicking, brasserie-like ground floor or in the less appealing basement. Reservations are possible only until 17:45. With its oversized reputation, long lines of tourists, and multiple locations, it's easy to think it's overrated. But the food is simply phenomenal (daily 8:00-23:00, 12 Upper St. Martin's Lane, tel. 020/7420-9320, www.dishoom.com).

$$ Lamb and Flag Pub is a survivor—a spit-and-sawdust pub serving traditional grub (like meat pies) two blocks off Covent Garden, yet seemingly a world away. Here since 1772, this pub was a favorite of Charles Dickens and is now a hit with local workers. At lunch, it's all food. In the evening, the ground floor is for drinking and the food service is upstairs (long hours daily, 33 Rose Street, go up the narrow alley from Floral Street, tel. 020/7497-9504).

Near Trafalgar Square

$$$ Terroirs Wine Bar is an enticing place with a casual but classy ambience that exudes happiness. It's a few steps below street level, with a long zinc bar that has a kitchen view and two levels of tables. The fun menu is mostly Mediterranean and designed to share. The meat and cheese plates complement the fine wines available by the glass (Mon-Sat 12:00-23:00, small bites only from 15:00-17:30, closed Sun, reservations smart, two blocks from Trafalgar Square but tucked away at 5 William IV Street, tel. 020/7036-0660, www. terroirswinebar.com).

$$ St. Martin-in-the-Fields Café in the Crypt is just right for a tasty meal on a monk's budget—maybe even on a monk's tomb. You'll dine sitting on somebody's gravestone in an ancient crypt. Their enticing buffet line is kept stocked all day, serving breakfast, lunch, and dinner (hearty traditional desserts, free jugs of water). They also serve a restful £11 afternoon tea (daily 12:00-18:00). You'll find the café directly under St. Martin-in-the-Fields, facing Trafalgar Square—enter through the glass pavilion next to the church (generally daily 10:00-19:30, profits go to the church, Tube: Charing Cross, tel. 020/7766-1158). On Wednesday evenings you can dine to the music of a live jazz band at 20:00 (food available until 21:00, band plays until 22:00, £8-15 tickets). While here, check out the concert schedule for the busy church upstairs (or visit www.stmartin-in-the-fields.org).

West London
Victoria Station Area

$$ Grumbles brags it's been serving "good food and wine at non-scary prices since 1964." Offering a delicious mix of "modern eclectic French and traditional English," this unpretentious little place with cozy booths inside (on two levels) and a few nice sidewalk tables is the best spot to eat well in this otherwise workaday neighborhood. Their traditional dishes are their forte (early-bird specials, open daily 12:00-14:30 & 18:00-23:00, reservations wise, a half-block north of Belgrave Road at 35 Churton Street, tel. 020/7834-0149, www.grumblesrestaurant.co.uk).

$ Pimlico Fresh's breakfasts and lunches feature fresh, organic ingredients, served up with good coffee and/or fresh-squeezed juices. This place is heaven if you need a break from your hotel's bacon-eggs-beans routine (takeout lunches, vegetarian options, Mon-Fri 7:30-18:00—breakfast served until 15:00, Sat-Sun 8:30-18:00, 86 Wilton Road, tel. 020/7932-0030).

$$$ Seafresh Fish Restaurant is the neighborhood place for plaice—and classic and creative fish-and-chips cuisine. You can either step up to the cheaper **takeout counter,** or eat in—enjoying a white-fish ambience. Though Mario's father started this place in 1965, it feels like the chippy of the 21st century (Mon-Sat 12:00-15:00 & 17:00-22:30, closed Sun, 80 Wilton Road, tel. 020/7828-0747).

$$ The Jugged Hare, a 10-minute walk from Victoria Station, fills a lavish old bank building, with vaults replaced by kegs of beer and a kitchen. They have a traditional menu and a plush, vivid pub scene good for a meal or just a drink (food served Mon-Fri 11:00-21:00, Sat-Sun until 20:00, 172 Vauxhall Bridge Road, tel. 020/7828-1543).

$$ St. George's Tavern is the neighborhood's best pub for a full meal. They serve dinner from the same menu in three zones: on the sidewalk to catch the sun and enjoy some people-watching (mostly travelers with wheelie bags), in the ground-floor pub, and in a classier downstairs dining room with full table service. The scene is inviting for just a beer, too (food served daily 12:00-22:00, corner of Hugh Street and Belgrave Road, tel. 020/7630-1116).

North of Kensington Gardens
Bayswater and Notting Hill

$$ Cocotte is a "healthy rotisserie" restaurant specializing in delectable roast chicken, plus tempting sides and healthy salads (dine in or take away; daily 12:00-22:00, 95 Westbourne Grove, tel. 020/3220-0076).

$$$ Farmacy is focused on organic vegan fare...with a side of pretense. The menu includes earth bowls, meatless burgers and tacos, and superfood smoothies. With an all-natural, woodgrain vibe, it feels like a top-end health food store (daily 9:00-16:00 & 18:00-22:00, 74 Westbourne Grove, tel. 020/7221-0705).

$$$ Geales, which opened its doors in 1939 as a fish-and-chips shop, has been serving Notting Hill ever since. Today, while the menu is more varied, the emphasis is still on fish. The interior is casual, but the food is upscale. The crispy battered cod that put them on the map is still the best around (£15 two-course express menu for lunch and until 20:00 Tue-Fri; open Tue-Sun 12:00-15:00 & 18:00-22:00, closed Mon; reservations smart, 2 Farmer Street, just south of Notting Hill Gate Tube stop, tel. 020/7727-7528, www.geales.com).

$$$$ Mazi is a highly regarded Greek restaurant serving refined renditions of classic dishes, including Greek salad, grilled octopus, and *loukoumades* (doughnuts) in a contemporary, sophisticated setting. Since ordering several small plates can add up, the £15 two-course lunch is a good deal (daily 18:30-22:30, also Tue-Sun 12:00-15:00, 12 Hillgate Street, tel. 020/7229-3794).

Near Kensington Gardens

$$$$ Maggie Jones's has been feeding locals for over 50 years. Its countryside antique decor and candlelight make a visit a step back in time. It's a longer walk than most of my recommendations, but you'll get solid English cuisine. The portions are huge (especially the meat-and-fish pies, their specialty), and prices are a bargain at lunch. You're welcome to split your main course. The candlelit upstairs is the most romantic, while the basement is lively (daily 12:00-14:00 & 18:00-22:30, reservations recommended, 6 Old Court Place, east of Kensington Church Street, near High Street Kensington Tube stop, tel. 020/7937-6462, www.maggie-jones.co.uk).

$$$$ The Shed offers farm-to-table dishes in a rustic-chic setting. Owned by three brothers—a farmer, a chef, and a restaurateur—The Shed serves locally sourced modern English dishes. The portions are hearty, with big, meaty flavors—a change of pace from London's delicate high-end dining scene. It's tucked a block off busy Notting Hill Gate (Mon-Sat 18:00-24:00, also open for lunch Tue-Sat 12:00-15:00, closed Sun, reservations smart, 122 Palace Gardens Terrace, tel. 020/7229-4024, www.theshed-restaurant.com).

$$ The Churchill Arms Pub and Thai Kitchen is a combo establishment that's a hit in the neighborhood. It offers good beer and a thriving old-English ambience in front and hearty Thai dishes in an enclosed patio in the back. You can eat the Thai food in the tropical hideaway (table service) or in the atmospheric pub section (order at the counter). Bedecked with flowers on the exterior, it's festooned with Churchill memorabilia and chamber pots. Arrive by 18:00 or after 21:00 to avoid a line (food served daily 12:00-22:00, 119 Kensington Church Street, tel. 020/7727-4242 for the pub or 020/7792-1246 for restaurant, www.churchillarmskensington.co.uk).

$ Café Diana is a healthy little eatery

Taking Tea

While visiting London, consider partaking in this most British of traditions. While some tearooms—such as the finicky Fortnum & Mason—still require a jacket and tie, most others happily welcome tourists in jeans and sneakers (and cost, on average, £35-50). Most tearooms are usually open for lunch and close about 17:00.

Popular choices are a "cream tea," which consists of tea and a scone or two, or the pricier "afternoon tea," which comes with pastries and finger foods such as small, crustless sandwiches. It's perfectly acceptable for two people to order one afternoon tea and one cream tea and share the afternoon tea's goodies. At many places, you can spring an extra £10 or so to upgrade to a boozy "champagne tea."

Many museum restaurants offer a fine inexpensive tea service: For example, the **$$ Victoria and Albert Museum** café serves a classic cream tea in an elegant setting that won't break your budget.

$$$ The Wolseley serves a good afternoon tea between their meal service (generally served 15:00-18:30 daily, see full listing on page 104).

$$$$ Fortnum & Mason department store offers tea at several different restaurants. You can "Take Tea in the Parlour" for a reasonably priced experience (including ice cream and scones; Mon-Sat 10:00-19:30, Sun 11:30-17:00). The pièce de resistance is their Diamond Jubilee Tea Salon, named in honor of the Queen's 60th year on the throne. At royal prices, consider it dinner (Mon-Sat 12:00-19:00, Sun until 18:00, dress up a bit—no shorts, "children must be behaved," 181 Piccadilly, smart to reserve at least a week in advance, tel. 020/7734-8040, www.fortnumandmason.com).

$$$$ The Orangery at Kensington Palace may be closed for restoration when you visit. If so, you can take tea next door at the Kensington Palace Pavilion (daily 12:00-16:00, a 10-minute walk through Kensington Gardens from either Queensway or High Street Kensington Tube stations—see the map on page 96; tel. 020/3166-6113, www.hrp.org.uk).

serving sandwiches, salads, and Middle Eastern food. It's decorated with photos of Princess Diana, who used to drop by for pita sandwiches (daily 8:00-23:00, cash only, 5 Wellington Terrace, on Bayswater Road, opposite Kensington Palace Garden gates, where Di once lived, tel. 020/7792-9606, Abdul).

North London

To avoid the touristy crush right around the British Museum, head a few blocks west to the Fitzrovia area. Here, tiny Charlotte Place is lined with small eateries (including my first two listings);

nearby, the much bigger Charlotte Street has several more good options (Tube: Goodge Street). See the map on page 98 for locations.

$ Salumeria Dino serves up hearty £5 sandwiches, pasta, and Italian coffee. Dino, a native of Naples, has run his little shop for more than 30 years and has managed to create a classic-feeling Italian deli (cheap takeaway cappuccinos, Mon-Sat 7:30-18:00, closed Sun, 15 Charlotte Place, tel. 020/7580-3938).

$ Lantana OUT is an Australian coffee shop that sells modern soups, sandwiches, and salads at their takeaway window (£8 daily hot dish). **Lantana IN** is an adjacent sit-down café that serves pricier meals (both Mon-Fri 8:00-18:00, Sat-Sun 9:00-17:00, 13 Charlotte Place, tel. 020/7637-3347).

Near the British Library: Farther north, in the Coal Drops Yard development just behind King's Cross Station, is a branch of the renowned Indian restaurant **$$$ Dishoom** (see description for Covent Garden branch, earlier). Not only is the food excellent, but it's a fun excuse to explore this development—a repurposing of an old industrial site on Regent's Canal.

TRANSPORTATION

Getting Around London

To travel smart in a city this size, you must get comfortable with public transportation. London's excellent taxis, buses, and subway (Tube) system can take you anywhere you need to go—a blessing for travelers' precious vacation time, not to mention their feet.

For more information about public transit (bus and Tube), the best source is the helpful *Welcome to London* brochure, which includes both a Tube map and a handy schematic map of the best bus routes (available free at TIs, museums, and hotels).

For specific directions on how to get from point A to point B on London's transit, detailed transit maps, updated prices, and general information, check www.tfl.gov.uk, or call the info line at 0343-222-1234.

Tickets and Cards

For most tourists, the Oyster card transit pass is better than individual tickets. The transit system has nine zones, but almost all tourist sights are within Zones 1 and 2, so those are the prices I've listed. For more information, visit www.tfl.gov.uk/tickets.

Individual Tickets: Paper tickets for the Tube are ridiculously expensive (£5/

ride). At every Tube station, tickets are sold at easy-to-use self-service machines (hit "Adult Single" and enter your destination). Tickets are valid only on the day of purchase. But unless you're literally taking only one Tube ride your entire visit, you'll save money (and time) with an Oyster card.

Oyster Card: A pay-as-you-go Oyster card allows you to ride the Tube, buses, Docklands Light Railway (DLR), and Overground (suburban trains) for about half the rate of individual tickets. To use the card, simply touch it against the yellow card reader at the turnstile or entrance. It flashes green and the fare is automatically deducted. (You must also tap your card again to "touch out" as you exit the Tube, but not buses.)

Buy the card at any Tube station ticket machine, or look for nearby shops displaying the Oyster logo, where you can purchase a card or add credit without the wait. You'll pay £5 up front for the card, then load it with credit. One ride between Zones 1 and 2 during peak time costs £2.90; (£2.40 during off-peak). An automatic price cap guarantees you'll never pay more than £7.20 in one day for rides within Zones 1 and 2. If you think you'll take two or more rides in a day, £8 of credit will cover you, but it's smart to add a little more if you expect to travel outside the city center. If you're staying six or more days, consider adding a 7-Day Travelcard to your Oyster card (details below).

Oyster cards are not shareable among companions taking the same ride; all travelers need their own. If your balance gets

low, simply add credit—or "top up"—at a ticket machine, shop, or with the Transport for London (TFL) Oyster app (available on the App Store or Google Play). You can always see how much credit remains on your card with the app or by touching your card to the pad at any ticket machine. After your last ride you can have your unused balance up to £10 refunded by selecting "Pay as you go refund" on any ticket machine that gives change. For balances of more than £10, you can claim a refund online. The credit never expires—use it again on a future trip.

PASSES AND DISCOUNTS

7-Day Travelcard: Various Tube passes and deals are available but the only option of note is the 7-Day Travelcard. This is the best choice if you're staying six or more days and plan to use public transit a lot (£36.10 for Zones 1-2; £66 for Zones 1-6). For most travelers, the Zone 1-2 pass works best. Heathrow Airport is in Zone 6, but there's no need to buy the Zones 1-6 version if that's the only ride outside the city center you plan to take—instead you can pay a small supplement to cover the difference. You can add the 7-Day Travelcard to your Oyster card, or purchase the paper version at any National Rail train station.

Families: A paying adult can take up to four kids (ages 10 and under) for free on the Tube, DLR, Overground, and buses. Kids ages 11-15 get a discount. Explore other child and student discounts at www.tfl.gov.uk/tickets—or ask a Tube station employee.

River Cruises: A Travelcard gives you a 33 percent discount on most Thames cruises. The Oyster card gives you roughly a 10 percent discount on Thames Clippers (including the Tate Boat museum ferry).

By Tube

London's subway system is called the Tube or Underground (but never "subway," which, in Britain, refers to a pedestrian underpass). The Tube is one of this planet's great people-movers and usually the fastest long-distance transport in town (runs Mon-Sat about 5:00-24:00, Sun about 7:00-23:00; Central, Jubilee, Northern, Piccadilly, and Victoria lines also run Fri-Sat 24 hours). Two other commuter rail lines are tied into the network and use the same tickets: the Docklands Light Railway (called DLR) and the Overground.

Each line has a name (such as Circle, Northern, or Bakerloo) and two directions (indicated by the end-of-the-line stops). Find the line that will take you to your destination, and figure out roughly which direction (north, south, east, or west) you'll need to go to get there.

At the Tube station, with an Oyster card, touch it flat against the turnstile's yellow card reader, both when you enter and exit the station. With a paper ticket or paper Travelcard, feed it into the turnstile, reclaim it, and hang on to it—you'll need it later.

Find your train by following signs to your line and the (general) direction it's headed (such as Central Line: Eastbound). Since some tracks are shared by several lines, double-check before boarding: Make sure your destination is one of the stops listed on the sign at the platform. Also, check the electronic signboards that announce which train is next, and make sure the destination (the end-of-the-line stop) is the direction you want. Some trains, particularly on the Circle and District lines, split off for other directions, but each train has its final destination marked above its windshield and on the side of the cars.

Trains run about every 3-10 minutes. (A general rule of thumb is that it takes 30 minutes to travel six Tube stops (including walking time within stations), or roughly 5 minutes per stop. Check maps and signs for the most convenient exit.

The system can be fraught with construction delays and breakdowns. Pay

O Interchange stations

⬭ Internal interchange

O⸱⸱⸱O Under a 10 minute walk between stations

♿ Step-free from train to street

♿ Step-free from platform to street

† Services or access at these stations are subject to variation. To check before you travel, visit **tfl.gov.uk/plan-a-journey**

MAYOR OF LONDON

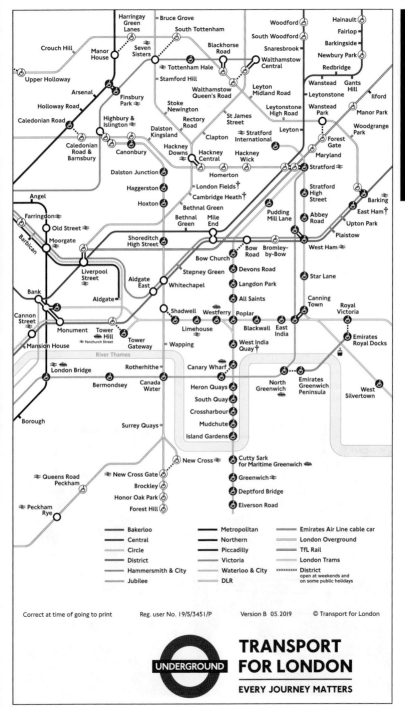

Bakerloo
Central
Circle
District
Hammersmith & City
Jubilee

Metropolitan
Northern
Piccadilly
Victoria
Waterloo & City
DLR

Emirates Air Line cable car
London Overground
TfL Rail
London Trams
District
open at weekends and
on some public holidays

Correct at time of going to print   Reg. user No. 19/S/3451/P   Version B 05.2019   © Transport for London

UNDERGROUND

TRANSPORT
FOR LONDON
EVERY JOURNEY MATTERS

attention to signs and announcements explaining necessary detours. Rush hours (8:00-10:00 and 16:00-19:00) can be packed and sweaty. If one train is stuffed—and another is coming in three minutes—it may be worth a wait to avoid the sardine routine. For help, check out the "Plan a Journey" feature at www.tfl. gov.uk.

TUBE ETIQUETTE

When your train arrives, stand off to the side and let riders exit before you board.

When the car is jam-packed, avoid using the hinged seats near the doors of some trains—they take up valuable standing space.

If you're blocking the door when the train stops, step out of the car and off to the side, let others off, then get back on.

Talk softly. Listen to how quietly Londoners communicate and follow their lead.

On escalators, stand on the right and pass on the left. But note that in some passageways or stairways, you might be directed to walk on the left (the direction Brits go when behind the wheel).

Discreet eating and drinking are fine; drinking alcohol and smoking are banned.

Be zipped up to thwart thieves.

Carefully check exit options before surfacing to street level. Signs point clearly to nearby sights—you'll save lots of walking by choosing the right exit.

By Bus

If you figure out the bus system, you'll swing like Tarzan through the urban jungle of London (see sidebar for a list of handy routes). Get in the habit of hopping buses for quick little straight shots, even just to get to a Tube stop. But during bump-and-grind rush hours (8:00-10:00 and 16:00-19:00), you'll usually go faster by Tube.

You can't buy single-trip tickets for buses, and you can't use cash to pay when boarding. Instead, you must have an Oyster card, a paper Travelcard, or a one-day Bus & Tram Pass (£5, can buy on day of travel only—not beforehand—from ticket machine in any Tube station). If you're using your Oyster card, any bus ride in downtown London costs £1.50 (capped at £4.50/day).

When your bus approaches, it's wise to hold your arm out to let the driver know you want on. Hop on and confirm your

destination with the driver (often friendly and helpful).

As you board, touch your Oyster card to the card reader, or show your paper Travelcard or Bus & Tram Pass to the driver. Unlike on the Tube, there's no need to show or tap your card when you hop off. On the older heritage "Routemaster" buses without card readers (used on the #15 route on summer weekends), you simply take a seat, and the conductor comes around to check cards and passes.

To alert the driver that you want to get off, press one of the red buttons (on the poles between the seats) before your stop.

By Taxi

London is the best taxi town in Europe. Big, black, carefully regulated cabs are everywhere—there are about 25,000 of them.

I've never met a crabby cabbie in London. They love to talk, and they know every nook and cranny in town. I ride in a taxi each day just to get my London questions answered. Drivers must pass a rigorous test on "The Knowledge" of London geography to earn their license.

If a cab's top light is on, just wave it down. Drivers flash lights when they see you wave. They have a tight turning radius, so you can hail cabs going in either direction. If waving doesn't work, ask someone where you can find a taxi stand. Telephoning a cab will get you one in a few minutes, but costs a little more (tel. 0871-871-8710).

Rides start at £3. The regular tariff #1 covers most of the day (Mon-Fri 5:00-20:00), tariff #2 is during "unsociable hours" (Mon-Fri 20:00-22:00 and Sat-Sun 5:00-22:00), and tariff #3 is for nighttime (22:00-5:00) and holidays. Rates go up about 20 percent with each higher tariff. Extra charges are explained in writing on the cab wall. All cabs accept credit and debit cards. Tip a cabbie by rounding up (maximum 10 percent).

Connecting downtown sights is quick and easy, and will cost you about £8-12 (for example, St. Paul's to the Tower of London, or between the two Tate museums). For a short ride, three adults in a cab generally travel at close to Tube prices—and groups of four or five adults should taxi everywhere. All cabs can carry five passengers, and some take six, for the same cost as a single traveler.

Don't worry about meter cheating. Licensed British cab meters come with a sealed computer chip and clock that ensures you'll get the correct tariff. The only way a cabbie can cheat you is by taking a needlessly long route. Don't, however, take a cab in bad traffic—especially to a destination efficiently served by the Tube.

By Uber

Uber faces legal challenges in London and may not be operating when you visit. If Uber is running, it can be much cheaper than a taxi and is a handy alternative if there's a long line for a taxi or if no cabs are available. Uber drivers generally don't know the city as well as regular cabbies, and they don't have the access to some fast lanes that taxis do. Still, if you like using Uber, it can work great here.

By Car

If you have a car, stow it—you don't want to drive in London. An £11.50 **congestion charge** is levied on any private car

Handy Bus Routes

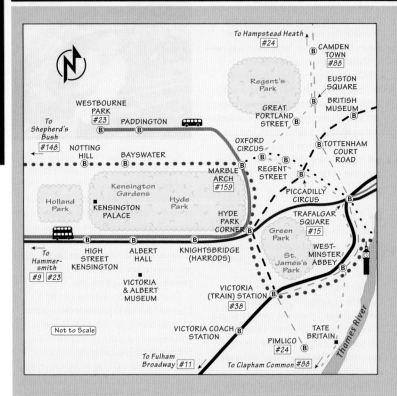

The best views are upstairs on a double-decker. Here are some of the most useful routes:

Route #9: High Street Kensington to Knightsbridge (Harrods) to Hyde Park Corner to Trafalgar Square to Aldwych (Somerset House).

Route #11: Victoria Station to Westminster Abbey to Trafalgar Square to St. Paul's and Liverpool Street Station and the East End.

Route #15: Trafalgar Square to St. Paul's to Tower of London (occasionally with heritage "Routemaster" old-style double-decker buses).

Route #159: Marble Arch to Oxford Circus to Piccadilly Circus to Trafalgar Square to Westminster and the Imperial War Museum. In addition, bus #139 also makes the corridor run between Marble Arch, Oxford Circus, Piccadilly Circus, and Trafalgar Square.

Route #23: Paddington Station to Marble Arch, Hyde Park Corner, Knightsbridge, Albert Hall, High Street Kensington, and on to Hammersmith.

Route #24: Pimlico to Victoria Station to Westminster Abbey to Trafalgar

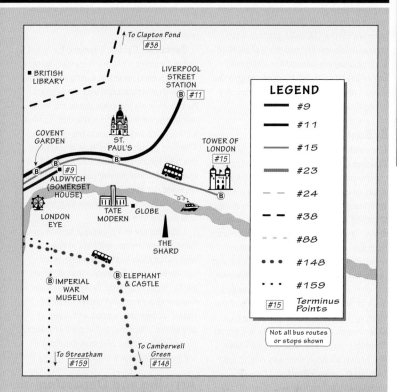

Square to Euston Square, then all the way north to Camden Town (Camden Lock Market) and Hampstead Heath.

Route #38: Victoria Station to Hyde Park Corner to Piccadilly Circus to British Museum.

Route #88: Tate Britain to Westminster Abbey to Trafalgar Square to Piccadilly Circus to Oxford Circus to Great Portland Street Station (Regent's Park), then north to Camden Town.

Route #148: Westminster Abbey to Victoria Station to Notting Hill and Bayswater (by way of the east end of Hyde Park and Marble Arch).

entering the city center during peak hours (Mon-Fri 7:00-18:00, no charge Sat-Sun and holidays). You can pay the fee either online or by phone (www.cclondon.com, from within the UK call 0343/222-2222, from outside the UK call 011-44-20/7649-9122, phones answered Mon-Fri 8:00-22:00, Sat 9:00-15:00, be ready to give the vehicle registration number and country of registration).

By Boat

The sleek, 220-seat catamarans used by **Thames Clippers** are designed for commuters rather than sightseers. Think of the boats as express buses on the river—they zip through London every 20-30 minutes, stopping at most of the major docks en route. They're fast: roughly 20-30 minutes from Embankment to Tower, 10 more minutes to Docklands/Canary Wharf, and 15 more minutes to Greenwich. However, the only outside access is on a crowded deck at the exhaust—choked back of the boat, where you're jostling for space to take photos. Any one-way ride in Central London (roughly London Eye to Tower Pier) costs £8.60; a one-way ride to East London (Canary Wharf and Greenwich) is £10, and a River Roamer all-day ticket costs £19.80 (discounts online and with Travelcard and Oyster card, www. thamesclippers.com).

The **Tate Boat** ferry service, which directly connects the Tate Britain (Millbank Pier) and the Tate Modern (Bankside Pier), is made for art lovers (£9 one-way, covered by River Roamer day ticket; buy ticket at kiosks or self-service machines before boarding or use Oyster card; for frequency and times, see www. tate.org.uk/visit/tate-boat).

By Bike

London operates a citywide bike-rental program similar to ones in other major European cities, and new bike lanes are still cropping up around town. Still, London isn't (yet) ideal for biking. Its network of designated bike lanes is far from complete, and the city's many one-way streets (not to mention the need to bike on the "wrong" side) can make biking here a bit more challenging.

Santander Cycles, intended for quick point-to-point trips, are fairly easy to rent. These cruisers have big, cushy seats, a bag rack with elastic straps, and three gears. Approximately 750 bike-rental stations are scattered throughout the city. To rent a bike, you'll pay an access fee (£2/day). The first 30 minutes are free; if you keep the bike for longer, you'll be charged £2 for every additional 30-minute period. Maps showing docking stations are available at major Tube stations, at www.tfl.gov.uk, and via the free app.

Helmets are not provided, so ride carefully. Stay to the far-left side of the road and watch closely at intersections for *left*-turning cars. Be aware that in most parks (including Hyde Park/Kensington Gardens) only certain paths are designated for bike use—you can't ride just anywhere. Maps posted at park entrances identify bike paths, and non-bike paths are generally clearly marked.

Arriving and Departing
By Plane

London has six airports; I've focused my coverage on the two most widely used—Heathrow and Gatwick—with a few tips for using the others (Stansted, Luton, London City, and Southend).

HEATHROW AIRPORT

For Heathrow's airport, flight, and transfer information, call the switchboard at 0844-335-1801, or visit the helpful website www. heathrow.com (code: LHR).

Heathrow's terminals are numbered T-2 through T-5. Each terminal is served by different airlines and alliances; for example, T-5 is exclusively for British Air and Iberia Air flights, while T-2 serves mostly Star Alliance flights, such as United and Lufthansa.

London's Airports

Luton

Luton

Stansted

Not to Scale

ST. PANCRAS

Southend

PADDINGTON

LIVERPOOL STREET

Reading

Windsor
#71 & 77

Rail Air Link

Southend

To Bath

Heathrow

Tube

VICTORIA

D.L.R.

London City

Guildford

Thames

VICTORIA COACH STN.

London

EUROSTAR

Gatwick

Ashford

To Paris, Amsterdam & Brussels

- - - - - Rail
═══ Eurostar Rail
──── Tube & D.L.R.
- - - - Bus

ALL BUSES ARE NATIONAL EXPRESS UNLESS NOTED

To Brighton

English Channel

You can walk between T-2 and T-3. From this central hub (called "Heathrow Central"), T-4 and T-5 split off in opposite directions (and are not walkable). The easiest way to travel between the T-2/T-3 cluster and either T-4 or T-5 is by Heathrow Express train (free to transfer between terminals, but tickets are required—hold onto your ticket even once you've passed through the turnstile—train departs every 15-20 minutes). You can also take a shuttle bus (free, serves all terminals), or the Tube (requires a ticket, serves all terminals).

If you're flying out of Heathrow, it's critical to confirm which terminal your flight will use (look at your ticket/boarding pass, check online, or call your airline in advance)—if it's T-4 or T-5, allow extra time. Taxi drivers generally know which terminal you'll need based on the airline, but bus drivers may not.

Services: Each terminal has an airport information desk (open long hours daily),

car-rental agencies, exchange bureaus, ATMs, a pharmacy, a VAT refund desk (tel. 0845-872-7627), and pay baggage storage (long hours daily, www.left-baggage.co.uk). Heathrow offers both free Wi-Fi and pay internet access points (in each terminal, check map for locations). You'll find a post office on the first floor of T-3 (departures area). Each terminal also has cheap eateries.

Heathrow's small **"TI"** (tourist info shop), even though it's a for-profit business, is worth a visit if you're nearby and want to pick up free information, including the London Planner visitors guide (long hours daily, 5-minute walk from T-3 in Tube station, follow signs to Underground; bypass queue for transit info to reach window for London questions).

Getting Between Heathrow and Downtown London: Options for traveling the 14 miles between Heathrow Airport and downtown London include Tube (about £6/person), bus (8-10/person),

express train with connecting Tube or taxi (£22-25, price does not include connecting Tube fare), or most expensive—taxi or car service. The one that works best for you will depend on your arrival terminal, your destination in central London, and your budget.

By Tube (Subway): The Tube takes you from any Heathrow terminal to downtown London in 50-60 minutes on the Piccadilly Line (6/hour, buy ticket at Tube station self-service machine). If you plan to use the Tube in London, it makes sense to buy a pay-as-you-go Oyster card (possibly adding a 7-Day Travelcard) at the airport's Tube station ticket machines. If you add a Travelcard that covers only Zones 1-2, you'll need to pay a small supplement for the initial trip from Heathrow (Zone 6) to downtown.

If you're taking the Tube from downtown London *to* the airport, note that Piccadilly Line trains don't stop at every terminal. Trains either stop at T-4, then T-2/T-3 (also called Heathrow Central), in that order; or T-2/T-3, then T-5. When leaving central London on the Tube, allow extra time if going to T-4 or T-5, and check the reader board in the station to make sure that the train goes to the right terminal before you board.

By Bus: Most buses depart from the outdoor common area called the Central Bus Station, a five-minute walk from the T-2/T-3 complex. To connect between T-4 or T-5 and the Central Bus Station, ride the free Heathrow Express train or the shuttle buses.

National Express has regular service from Heathrow's Central Bus Station to Victoria Coach Station in downtown London, near several of my recommended hotels. While slow, the bus is affordable and convenient for those staying near Victoria Station (£8-10, 1-2/hour, less frequent from Victoria Station to Heathrow, 45-75 minutes depending on time of day, tel. 0871-781-8181, www.nationalexpress.com). A less-frequent National Express bus goes from T-5 directly to Victoria Coach Station.

By Train: The **Heathrow Express** runs between Heathrow Airport and London's Paddington Station. At Paddington, you're in the thick of the Tube system, with easy access to any of my recommended neighborhoods.

The Heathrow Express is fast but pricey (£22-25 one-way, price depends on time of day, £37 round-trip, cheaper if purchased online in advance, covered by BritRail pass; 4/hour, Mon-Sat 5:00-24:00, Sun from 6:00, 15 minutes to downtown from Heathrow Central Station serving

T-2/T-3, 21 minutes from T-5; for T-4 take free transfer to Heathrow Central, tel. 0345-600-1515, www.heathrowexpress.co.uk).

A cheaper alternative to the Heathrow Express—the new **Crossrail Elizabeth line**—may not yet be operational by the time you visit, but when it opens, it will be faster (and more expensive) than the Tube; see www.tfl.gov.uk for updates.

By Car Service: Just Airports offers a private car service between five London airports and the city center (see website for price quote, tel. 020/8900-1666, www.justairports.com).

By Taxi or Uber: Taxis from the airport cost £45-75 to west and central London (one hour). For four people traveling together, this can be a reasonable option. Hotels can often line up a cab back to the airport for about £50. If running, Uber also offers London airport pickup and drop-off.

Gatwick Airport

Gatwick Airport is halfway between London and the south coast (code: LGW, tel. 0844-892-0322, www.gatwickairport.com). Gatwick has two terminals, North and South, which are easily connected by a free monorail (two-minute trip, runs 24 hours). Note that boarding passes say "Gatwick N" or "Gatwick S" to indicate your terminal. Gatwick Express trains (described next) stop only at Gatwick South.

Getting Between Gatwick and Downtown London: Gatwick Express trains are the best way into London from this airport. They shuttle conveniently between Gatwick South and London's **Victoria Station,** with many of my recommended hotels close by (£20 one-way, £35 round-trip, at least 10 percent cheaper if purchased online, Oyster cards accepted but no discount offered, 4/hour, 30 minutes, runs 5:00-24:00 daily, a few trains as early as 3:30, tel. 0845-850-1530, www.gatwickexpress.com). When going

to the airport, at Victoria Station note that Gatwick Express has its own ticket windows right by the platform (tracks 13 and 14). You'll also find easy-to-use ticket machines nearby.

A train also runs between Gatwick South and **St. Pancras International Station** (£12.10, 3-5/hour, 45-60 minutes, www.thetrainline.com)—useful for travelers taking the Eurostar train (to Paris, Amsterdam, or Brussels) or staying in the St. Pancras/King's Cross neighborhood.

While even slower, the **bus** is a cheap and handy option to the Victoria Station neighborhood. National Express runs a bus from Gatwick directly to Victoria Station (£10, at least hourly, 1.5 hours, tel. 0871-781-8181, www.nationalexpress.com); EasyBus has one that stops near the Earl's Court Tube stop (£4-10 depending on how far ahead you book, 2-3/hour, www.easybus.com).

London's Other Airports

Stansted Airport: From Stansted (code: STN, tel. 0844-335-1803, www.stanstedairport.com), **buses** connect the airport and London's Victoria Station neighborhood: National Express (£9-12, every 15 minutes, 2 hours, runs 24 hours a day, picks up and stops throughout London, ends at Victoria Coach Station or Liverpool Street Station, tel. 0871-781-8181, www.nationalexpress.com) and Airport Bus Express (£9, 2/hour, 1.5-2 hours). Or you can take the faster, pricier Stansted Express **train** (£19, cheaper if booked online, connects to London's Tube system at Tottenham Hale or Liverpool Street, 2-4/hour, 45 minutes, 4:30-23:00, www.stanstedexpress.com). Stansted is expensive by **cab;** figure £100-120 one-way from central London.

Luton Airport: For Luton (code: LTN, tel. 01582/405-100, www.london-luton.co.uk), the fastest way to get into London is by **train** to St. Pancras International Station (£14-17 one-way, 1-5/hour, 35-45 minutes—check schedule to avoid

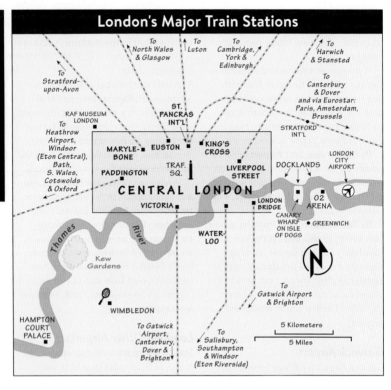

London's Major Train Stations

To North Wales & Glasgow

To Luton

To Cambridge, York & Edinburgh

To Harwich & Stansted

To Stratford-upon-Avon

To Canterbury & Dover and via Eurostar: Paris, Amsterdam, Brussels

RAF MUSEUM LONDON

ST. PANCRAS INT'L

STRATFORD INT'L

To Heathrow Airport, Windsor (Eton Central), Bath, S. Wales, Cotswolds & Oxford

MARYLE-BONE

EUSTON

KING'S CROSS

LONDON CITY AIRPORT

PADDINGTON

TRAF. SQ.

LIVERPOOL STREET

DOCKLANDS

CENTRAL LONDON

VICTORIA

LONDON BRIDGE

O2 ARENA

CANARY WHARF ON ISLE OF DOGS

GREENWICH

Thames River

WATER-LOO

Kew Gardens

HAMPTON COURT PALACE

WIMBLEDON

To Gatwick Airport & Brighton

To Gatwick Airport, Canterbury, Dover & Brighton

To Salisbury, Southampton & Windsor (Eton Riverside)

5 Kilometers

5 Miles

slower trains, tel. 0345-712-5678, www. eastmidlandstrains.co.uk); catch the 10-minute shuttle bus (every 10 minutes) from outside the terminal to the Luton Airport Parkway Station. When buying your train ticket to Luton, make sure you select "Luton Airport" as your destination rather than "Parkway Station" to ensure the shuttle fare is included.

The **National Express bus** A1 runs from Luton to Victoria Coach Station (£7-11 one-way, 2/hour, 1-1.5 hours, runs 24 hours, tel. 0871-781-8181, www. nationalexpress.com). The **Green Line express bus** #757 runs to Buckingham Palace Road, just south of Victoria Station, and stops en route near the Baker Street Tube station—best if you're staying near Paddington Station or in North London (£10 one-way, 2-4/hour, 1-1.5 hours, runs 24 hours, tel. 0344-800-4411, www. greenline.co.uk).

London City and Southend Airports: To get into the city center from London City Airport (code: LCY, tel. 020/7646-

0088, www.londoncityairport.com), take the Docklands Light Railway (DLR) to the Bank Tube station, which is one stop east of St. Paul's on the Central Line (less than £6 one-way, covered by Travelcard, a bit cheaper with an Oyster card, 20 minutes, www.tfl.gov.uk/dlr). Some EasyJet flights land farther out, at Southend Airport (code: SEN, tel. 01702/538-500, www.southendairport.com). Trains connect this airport to London's Liverpool Street Station (£16.20 one-way, 3-8/hour, 55 minutes, www.abelliogreateranglia.co.uk).

By Train

London has nine main stations:

Euston: Serves northwest England, North Wales, and Scotland.

St. Pancras International: Serves north and south England, plus the Eurostar to Paris, Amsterdam, or Brussels.

King's Cross: Serves northeast England and Scotland, including York and Edinburgh.

Liverpool Street: Serves east England, including Essex and Harwich.

London Bridge: Serves south England, including Brighton.

Waterloo: Serves south England, including Salisbury and Southampton.

Victoria: Serves Gatwick Airport, Canterbury, Dover, and Brighton.

Paddington: Serves south and southwest England, including Heathrow Airport, Windsor, Bath, Oxford, South Wales, and the Cotswolds.

Marylebone: Serves southwest and central England, including Stratford-upon-Avon.

Any train station has schedule information, can make reservations, and can sell tickets for any destination. Most stations offer a baggage-storage service (look for *left luggage* signs); because of long security lines, it can take a while to check or pick up your bag (www.left-baggage.co.uk). For more details on the services available at each station, see www.nationalrail.co.uk/stations. UK train info is available at www.traveline.org.uk.

TRAIN CONNECTIONS FROM LONDON

From Paddington Station to: Windsor (Windsor & Eton Central Station, 2/hour, 35 minutes, easy change at Slough), **Bath** (2/hour, 1.5 hours), **Oxford** (4/hour direct, 1 hour, more with transfer), **Moreton-in-Marsh** (hourly, 1.5 hours), **Penzance** (every 2 hours, 5 hours, more with change in Plymouth), **Cardiff** (2/hour, 2 hours).

From King's Cross Station: York (3/hour, 2 hours), **Durham** (hourly, 3 hours), **Edinburgh** (2/hour, 4.5 hours).

From Euston Station: Liverpool (hourly, 3 hours, transfer at Liverpool South Parkway), **Keswick/Lake District** (train to Penrith—hourly, 3.5 hours, then bus at Keswick).

From Marylebone Station: Stratford-upon-Avon (2/day direct, 2.5 hours; also 1-2/hour, 2 hours, transfer in Leamington Spa, Dorridge, or Birmingham Moor).

By Bus

Buses are slower but considerably cheaper than trains. Most depart from **Victoria Coach Station,** which is one long block south of Victoria Station, Tube: Victoria. Inside the station, you'll find basic eateries, kiosks, and a helpful information desk. For UK bus info, check www.traveline.info.

National Express buses go to: **Bath** (hourly, 3 hours), **Oxford** (2/hour, 2 hours), **Stratford-upon-Avon** (3/day, 3.5 hours), **Liverpool** (8/day direct, 5.5 hours, overnight available), **York** (3/day direct, 6 hours), **Durham** (3/day direct, 7 hours, train is better), **Edinburgh, Scotland** (2/day direct, 10 hours, go by train instead).

France

France is a place of gentle beauty. At 215,000 square miles (roughly 20 percent smaller than Texas), it is Western Europe's largest nation, with luxuriant forests, forever coastlines, and Europe's highest mountain ranges. You'll discover a dizzying array of artistic and architectural wonders—soaring cathedrals, chandeliered palaces, and museums filled with the cultural icons of the Western world.

Paris is the star of the show; Provence is small-town France at its best; and the French Riviera offers up beaches and an old-time elegance with a bit of glitz.

Wherever you visit in France, you'll enjoy *l'art de vivre*—the art of living. Experience the fine cuisine, velvety wines, and linger-long pastimes such as people-watching from sun-dappled cafés.

CUISINE SCENE AT A GLANCE

Know the terms for eating out: A menu is called *la carte* (which you use to order individual dishes á la carte). A *menu* is actually a multi-course, fixed-price meal. The daily special is a *plat du jour* (or just *plat*), a hearty, garnished hot plate for about €14-24. *Entrées* are appetizers. The main dish is the *plat principal*.

Cafés and brasseries are open long hours and serve food throughout the day. You're welcome to order just an omelet, salad, or bowl of soup, even for dinner.

Check the price list first, which by law must be posted prominently (if you don't see one, go elsewhere). There are two sets of prices: You'll pay more for the same drink if you're seated at a table *(salle)* than if you're seated or standing at the bar or counter *(comptoir)*.

Restaurants open for dinner around 19:00. Last seating is about 21:00 (22:00 in cities and Riviera towns). The table is yours for the night.

If a restaurant serves lunch, it generally begins at 12:00, with last orders taken at about 14:00. Lunches at restaurants are cheaper than dinners; to save money, make lunch your main meal.

If you're hungry when restaurants are closed (late afternoon), or if you want a light meal, head for a café, brasserie, deli, or bakery.

At restaurants, two people can split an *entrée* or a big salad and then each get a *plat principal*. It's considered inappropriate for two diners to share one main course.

Fixed-price *menus*, which include two or three courses, are generally a good value. With a three-course *menu* you'll choose a starter of soup, appetizer, or salad; select from several main courses with vegetables; and then finish up with a cheese course or dessert.

To order inexpensive wine with your meal, ask for table wine in a carafe (*pichet*; pee-shay), though finer restaurants usually offer wine only by the glass or bottle.

Tipping: Your server, who doesn't want to rush you, will rarely bring you the bill unless you request it. At cafés and restaurants, a 12-15 percent service charge is always included in the price of what you order, but you won't see it listed on your bill. Most locals never tip. If you feel the service was good, you could tip up to 5 percent extra in cash (credit-card receipts don't even have space to add a tip). But don't feel guilty if you don't leave a tip.

Budget Options: Try takeout delis, food stands, *crêperies*, and *boulangeries* (bakeries selling sandwiches, quiches, and tiny pizzas). You can assemble a picnic at various small shops, a one-stop *super-marché*, or an open-air morning market.

Paris

Paris has been a beacon of culture for centuries. As a world capital of art, fashion, food, literature, and ideas, it stands as a symbol of all the fine things human civilization can achieve, with a splash of romance and joie de vivre.

Paris offers sweeping boulevards, chatty crêpe stands, chic boutiques, and world-class art galleries. Sip decaf with deconstructionists at a sidewalk café, then step into an Impressionist painting in a tree-lined park. Pay homage to beloved Notre-Dame, recovering from a devastating fire. Master the Louvre and Orsay museums, and save some after-dark energy for this romantic city.

PARIS IN 3 DAYS

Day 1: Follow my Historic Paris Walk, featuring Ile de la Cité, Notre-Dame, the Latin Quarter, and Sainte-Chapelle. In the afternoon, tour the Louvre. Late in the day, enjoy the Place du Trocadéro scene and a twilight ride up the Eiffel Tower.

Day 2: Stroll the Champs-Elysées from the Arc de Triomphe (ascend for the view) to the Tuileries Garden, then tour the Orsay Museum.

Day 3: Head to Versailles. Catch RER/Train-C by 8:00 to arrive early. Tour the château's interior, then either visit the vast gardens, or return to Paris for more sightseeing.

On any evening: Take a nighttime tour by cruise boat, taxi/Uber, or bus. Or enjoy dinner on Ile St. Louis, then a floodlit walk by Notre-Dame. For a free skyline view, head to the rooftop of the neighboring Galeries Lafayette or Printemps department stores.

With extra time: Choose from Montmartre (Sacré-Cœur Basilica), the Army Museum and Napoleon's Tomb, the Rodin or Orangerie museums, the Marais neighborhood (Picasso Museum and Pompidou Center), or the Opéra Garnier (near the department stores).

ORIENTATION

Central Paris is circled by a ring road and split in half by the Seine River, which runs east-west. As you look downstream, the Right Bank (Rive Droite) is on your right, and the Left Bank (Rive Gauche) on your left. The bull's-eye on your map is Notre-Dame, on an island in the middle of the Seine.

Twenty arrondissements (administrative districts) spiral out from the center, like an escargot shell. If your hotel's zip code is 75007, you know (from the last two digits) that it's in the 7th arrondissement. The city is peppered with Métro stops, and most Parisians locate addresses by the closest stop. So in Parisian jargon, the Eiffel Tower is on la Rive Gauche (the Left Bank) in the 7ème (7th arrondissement), zip code 75007, Mo: Trocadéro (the nearest Métro stop).

The major sights cluster in convenient zones. Grouping your sightseeing, walks, dining, and shopping thoughtfully can save you lots of time and money.

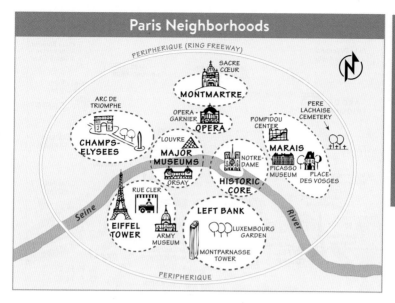

Paris Neighborhoods

Historic Core: This area centers on the Ile de la Cité ("Island of the City"), located in the middle of the Seine. On the Ile de la Cité, you'll find Paris' oldest sights, from Roman ruins to the medieval Notre-Dame and Sainte-Chapelle churches.

Major Museums Neighborhood: Located just west of the historic core, this is where you'll find the Louvre, Orsay, Orangerie, and Tuileries Garden.

Champs-Elysées: The greatest of the many grand, 19th-century boulevards on the Right Bank, the Champs-Elysées runs northwest from Place de la Concorde to the Arc de Triomphe.

Eiffel Tower Neighborhood: Dominated by the Eiffel Tower, this area also boasts the colorful Rue Cler, the Army Museum and Napoleon's Tomb, and the Rodin Museum.

Opéra Neighborhood: Surrounding the Opéra Garnier, this classy area on the Right Bank is home to a series of grand boulevards, monuments, and high-end shopping.

Left Bank: Anchored by the large Luxembourg Garden, the Left Bank is the traditional neighborhood of Paris' intellec-

tual, artistic, and café life.

Marais: Stretching eastward to Bastille along Rue de Rivoli/Rue St. Antoine, this neighborhood has lots of recommended restaurants and hotels, shops, the delightful Place des Vosges, and artistic sights such as the Pompidou Center and Picasso Museum.

Montmartre: This hill, topped by the bulbous white domes of Sacré-Cœur, hovers on the northern fringes of your Paris map.

Tourist Information

Paris' "TIs" can provide useful information but may have long lines. TIs sell Museum Passes and individual tickets to sights, but charge a small fee and may have longer lines than the museums.

The main TI is located at the **Hôtel de Ville** (daily 9:00-19:00, Nov-April from 10:00, 29 Rue de Rivoli—located on the north side of the Hôtel de Ville City Hall). Other TIs are at the **Carrousel du Louvre** shopping mall (just before the museum's security entrance, daily 10:00-20:00, 99 Rue de Rivoli) and at **Gare du Nord** (daily 8:00-18:00). In summer, TI kiosks may pop

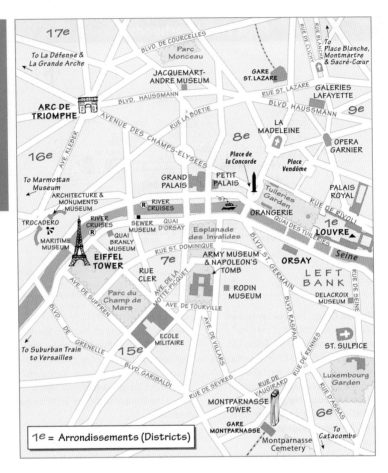

1e = Arrondissements (Districts)

up in the squares in front of Notre-Dame and Hôtel de Ville. Both **airports** have handy TIs with long hours.

Event Listings: The weekly *L'Officiel des Spectacles* (available at any newsstand) is in French only but has easy-to-decipher listings of the most up-to-date museum hours, art exhibits, concerts, festivals, plays, movies, and nightclubs. The *Paris Voice,* with snappy English-language reviews of concerts, plays, and current events, is available online-only at www.parisvoice.com.

Sightseeing Passes: In Paris there are two classes of sightseers—those with a **Paris Museum Pass,** and those who stand

in line. The pass admits you to many of Paris' most important sights, and it allows you to skip most ticket-buying lines (but not security lines)—which can save hours of waiting, especially in summer. Another benefit is that you can pop into lesser sights that otherwise might not be worth the expense. For more info, visit www.parismuseumpass.com.

Buy the pass in person upon arrival in Paris (it's not worth the cost or hassle to buy the pass online). The pass is sold at participating museums, monuments, TIs (small fee added)—including TIs at Paris airports—and some souvenir stores near major sights. Don't buy the pass at a major

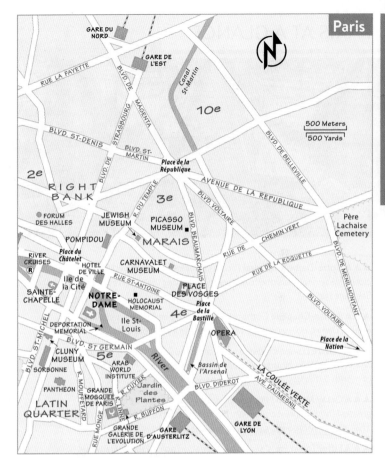

Paris

GARE DU NORD

GARE DE L'EST

Canal St-Martin

RUE LA FAYETTE

BLVD. DE MAGENTA

10e

500 Meters
500 Yards

BLVD. ST-DENIS

BLVD. DE STRASBOURG

BLVD. ST-MARTIN

BLVD. DE BELLEVILLE

2e

Place de la République

RIGHT BANK

3e

R. DU TEMPLE

AVENUE DE LA REPUBLIQUE

BLVD. VOLTAIRE

Père Lachaise Cemetery

FORUM DES HALLES

JEWISH MUSEUM

PICASSO MUSEUM

BLVD. BEAUMARCHAIS

CHEMIN VERT

BLVD. DE MÉNILMONTANT

POMPIDOU

MARAIS

RUE DE

RUE DE LA ROQUETTE

RIVER CRUISES
R

Place du Châtelet

HOTEL DE VILLE

CARNAVALET MUSEUM

RUE ST-ANTOINE

PLACE DES VOSGES

BLVD. VOLTAIRE

Ile de la Cité

SAINTE-CHAPELLE

NOTRE-DAME

HOLOCAUST MEMORIAL

Place de la Bastille

4e

DEPORTATION MEMORIAL

Ile St-Louis

OPERA

Place de la Nation

BLVD. ST-MICHEL

BLVD. ST GERMAIN

River

CLUNY MUSEUM

5e

ARAB WORLD INSTITUTE

Bassin de l'Arsenal

LA COULÉE VERTE

AVE. DAUMESNIL

SORBONNE

R. CUVIER

R. MOUFFETARD

PANTHEON

GRANDE MOSQUEE DE PARIS

Jardin des Plantes

BLVD. DIDEROT

LATIN QUARTER

R. LINNÉ

R. BUFFON

RUE MONGE

GRANDE GALERIE DE L'EVOLUTION

GARE D'AUSTERLITZ

GARE DE LYON

---

museum (such as the Louvre), where the supply can be spotty and lines long.

Avoid lines like these by making an advance reservation for the Eiffel Tower.

Rick's Tip: Don't buy the Paris Museum Pass for children and teens, *as most museums are free or discounted for those under age 18 (teenagers may need to show ID as proof of age). If parents have a Museum Pass, kids can usually skip the ticket lines as well. But a few places (Arc de Triomphe, Army Museum) require everyone—even passholders—to stand in line to collect free tickets for their children.*

Helpful Hints

Theft Alert: Paris is safe in terms of violent crime but is filled with thieves and

PARIS AT A GLANCE

▲▲▲**Notre-Dame Cathedral** Paris' most beloved church will likely be closed for several years due to restoration following the massive 2019 fire. See page 134.

▲▲▲**Sainte-Chapelle** Gothic cathedral with peerless stained glass. **Hours:** Daily 9:00-19:00, Oct-March until 17:00. See page 140.

▲▲▲**Louvre** Europe's oldest and greatest museum, starring *Mona Lisa* and *Venus de Milo*. **Hours:** Wed-Mon 9:00-18:00, Wed, Fri, and first Sat of month until 21:45, closed Tue. See page 146.

▲▲▲**Orsay Museum** Nineteenth-century art, including Europe's greatest Impressionist collection. **Hours:** Tue-Sun 9:30-18:00, Thu until 21:45, closed Mon. See page 153.

▲▲▲**Eiffel Tower** Paris' soaring exclamation point. **Hours:** Daily mid-June-Aug 9:00-24:45, Sept-mid-June 9:30-23:45. See page 160.

▲▲▲**Champs-Elysées** Paris' grand boulevard. See page 167.

▲▲▲**Versailles** The ultimate royal palace (Château), with a Hall of Mirrors, vast gardens, and a grand canal, plus a queen's playground (Trianon Palaces and Domaine de Marie-Antoinette). **Hours:** Château April-Oct Tue-Sun 9:00-18:30, Nov-March until 17:30; Trianon/Domaine April-Oct Tue-Sun 12:00-18:30, Nov-March until 17:30; gardens generally April-Oct daily 8:00-20:30, Nov-March until 18:00; entire complex closed Mon year-round except the Gardens. See page 208.

▲▲**Orangerie Museum** Monet's water lilies and modernist classics in a lovely setting. **Hours:** Wed-Mon 9:00-18:00, closed Tue. See page 158.

▲▲**Army Museum and Napoleon's Tomb** The emperor's imposing tomb, flanked by museums of France's wars. **Hours:** Daily 10:00-18:00, Nov-March until 17:00; tomb also open July-Aug until 19:00; tomb and Louis XIV-Napoleon I wing open April-Sept Tue until 21:00; Charles de Gaulle exhibit closed Mon year-round. See page 163.

▲▲**Rodin Museum** Works by the greatest sculptor since Michelangelo, with many statues in a peaceful garden. **Hours:** Tue-Sun 10:00-18:30, closed Mon. See page 164.

▲▲**Marmottan Museum** Art museum focusing on Monet. **Hours:** Tue-Sun 10:00-18:00, Thu until 21:00, closed Mon. See page 165.

▲▲**Cluny Museum** Medieval art with unicorn tapestries. **Hours:** Wed-Mon 9:15-17:45, closed Tue. See page 165.

▲▲**Arc de Triomphe** Triumphal arch marking the start of Champs-Elysées. **Hours:** Exterior always viewable; interior daily 10:00-23:00, Oct-March until 22:30. See page 169.

▲▲**Opéra Garnier** Grand belle époque theater with a modern ceiling by Chagall. **Hours:** Generally daily 10:00-16:30, mid-July-Aug until 18:00. See page 170.

▲▲**Picasso Museum** World's largest collection of Picasso's works. **Hours:** Tue-Fri 10:30-18:00, Sat-Sun from 9:30, closed Mon. See page 172.

▲▲**Pompidou Center** Modern art in colorful building with city views. **Hours:** Permanent collection open Wed-Mon 11:00-21:00, closed Tue. See page 173.

▲▲**Père Lachaise Cemetery** Final home of Paris' illustrious dead. **Hours:** Mon-Fri 8:00-18:00, Sat from 8:30, Sun from 9:00, until 17:30 in winter. See page 177.

▲▲**Sacré-Cœur Basilica and Montmartre** White basilica atop Montmartre with spectacular views. **Hours:** Daily 6:00-22:30; dome climb daily 9:30-19:00, Oct-April until 17:00. See page 178.

scammers who target tourists. Don't be paranoid; just be smart. Wherever there are crowds (especially of tourists) there are thieves at work. They thrive near famous monuments and on Métro and train lines that serve airports and high-profile tourist sights. It's smart to wear a money belt, put your wallet in your front pocket, loop your day bag over your shoulders, and keep a tight hold on your purse or shopping bag.

Muggings are rare, but they do occur. If you're out late, avoid dark riverfront embankments and any place with dim lighting and few pedestrians.

Tourist Scams: Be aware of the latest tricks, such as the "found ring" scam (a con artist pretends to find a "pure gold" ring on the ground and offers to sell it to you) or the "friendship bracelet" scam (a vendor asks you to help with a demo, makes a bracelet on your arm that seems like it can't easily be removed, and then asks you to pay for it). Don't be intimidated. They are removed with the pull of a string.

Distractions by a stranger—sometimes a "salesman," an "activist," or even someone posing as a deaf person—can all be tricks that function as a smokescreen for theft. As you try to wriggle away from the pushy stranger, an accomplice picks your pocket. For reports from my readers on the latest scams, go to https://community.ricksteves.com/travel-forum/tourist-scams.

Rick's Tip: *For many sights,* **you can buy advance tickets at the sight's website or through a third party** *(for a fee). Some require you to choose a specific time, including the Eiffel Tower, Louvre, and Catacombs. You can also buy advance tickets that allow you to skip ticket-buying lines for the Orsay and Sainte-Chapelle.*

Closed Days: The Orsay, Rodin, Marmottan, and Picasso museums are closed on Mondays, as are the Catacombs and the palace of Versailles (its gardens are open). Many other sights are closed on Tuesdays, including the Louvre, Orangerie, Cluny, and Pompidou museums.

Useful Apps: Gogo Paris reviews trendy places to eat, drink, relax, and sleep in Paris (www.gogocityguides.com/paris). The **RATP** app can help you plan Métro trips (see "Métro Resources" later in this chapter). 🎧 For my free audio tours of some of Paris' best neighborhoods and sights (Historic Paris and Rue Cler, Louvre and Orsay museums, Versailles Palace, and Père Lachaise Cemetery), get the free **Rick Steves Audio Europe** app.

Tobacco Stands *(Tabacs):* These little kiosks—usually just a counter inside a café—sell public-transit tickets, postage stamps (though not all sell international postage), and...oh yeah, cigarettes. To find a kiosk, just look for a *Tabac* sign and the red cylinder-shaped symbol above certain cafés.

Rick's Tip: **Parisian drivers are notorious for ignoring pedestrians**—*pay attention and don't assume you have the right of way, even in a crosswalk.*

Laundry: Two of my recommended sleeping neighborhoods include handy launderettes. In the Rue Cler, you'll find them on Rue Augereau, on Rue Amélie, and at the southeast corner of Rue Valadon and Rue de Grenelle. Launderettes are also scattered throughout the Marais, including on Impasse Guéménée and on Rue du Petit Musc.

Tours

Some tour companies offer a discount when you show this book (indicated in these listings with the abbreviation "RS%").

WALKING TOURS

Paris Walks offers a variety of thoughtful and entertaining two-hour walks, led by British and American guides (€15-20, generally 2/day—morning and afternoon,

Explore Paris by bike.

LOCAL GUIDES

For many, Paris merits hiring a Parisian as a guide (€230-280 half-day, €400-500 day). Try **Thierry Gauduchon** (mobile 06 19 07 30 77, tgauduchon@gmail.com); **Elisabeth Van Hest** (tel. 01 43 41 47 31, mobile 06 77 80 19 89, elisa.guide@gmail.com); **Sylvie Moreau** (tel. 01 74 30 27 46, mobile 06 87 02 80 67, sylvie.ja.moreau@gmail.com); or **Arnaud Servignat** (also does minivan tours of the countryside around Paris, mobile 06 68 80 29 05, www.french-guide.com, arnotour@icloud.com).

HOP-ON, HOP-OFF BUS TOURS

Several companies offer double-decker bus services connecting Paris' main sights, giving you an easy once-over of the city with a recorded commentary. Buses run from about 9:30-19:00 in high season. **L'OpenTour** has the most options with reasonably frequent service on four routes covering central Paris (1 day-€34, 2 days-€38, 3 days-€42, kids 4-11 pay €17 for 1, 2, or 3 days, tel. 01 42 66 56 56, www.paris.opentour.com). **Big Bus Paris** runs a fleet of buses around Paris on two routes (1 day-€34, 2 days-€38, kids 4-12-€17, €22 night tour, cheaper online, tel. 01 53 95 39 53, www.bigbustours.com), and **City Sightseeing Tours'** red buses run along two routes (11 stops each) and your ticket is valid for 24 or 48 hours from the time you buy it (1 day-€42, 2 days-€47, tickets valid for both routes, 3 buses/hour, 9 Avenue de l'Opèra, https://city-sightseeing.com).

BIKE TOURS

Bike About Tours offers easygoing tours of the eastern half of the city (Marais, Latin Quarter, and Ile de la Cité; RS%—10 percent discount, www.bikeabouttours.com).

Fat Tire Tours offers an extensive program of bike and walking tours (see earlier).

private tours available, check current offerings online, tel. 01 48 09 21 40, www.paris-walks.com, paris@paris-walks.com).

Context Travel offers "intellectual by design" walking tours geared for serious learners led by well-versed docents (book in advance—groups are limited to six participants; about €100/person, admission to sights extra, generally 3 hours, tel. 09 75 18 04 15, US tel. 800-691-6036, www.contexttravel.com, info@contexttravel.com).

Fat Tire Tours offers high-on-fun and casual walking tours. Their two-hour Classic Paris Walking Tour covers most major sights (usually Mon, Wed, and Fri at 10:00 or 15:00). Their "Skip the Line" tours get you into major sights, including Sainte-Chapelle, the Catacombs, Eiffel Tower, and Versailles. Reservations are required and can be made online, by phone, or in person at their office near the Eiffel Tower (€20-40/person for walking tours, €40-90/person for "Skip the Line" tours; RS%—€2 discount per person, 2-discount maximum; office generally open daily 9:00-18:00 or 19:00, shorter hours in winter, 24 Rue Edgar Faure, Mo: Dupleix, tel. 01 82 88 80 96, www.fattire-tours.com/paris).

HISTORIC PARIS WALK

Paris has been the cultural capital of Europe for centuries—as a Roman city, a bustling medieval metropolis, the birthplace of the Revolution, the bohemian haunt of the 1920s café scene, and now the glittering City of Light.

We'll start where the city did—on the Ile de la Cité—and make a foray onto the Left Bank. Along the way, we'll step into one of the city's greatest sights, Sainte-Chapelle.

The first two stops of the walk may be affected by reconstruction work on the Notre-Dame Cathedral, damaged in a 2019 fire. Be flexible, know there's a way around, and follow the route as well as you can.

Getting There: The closest Métro stops are Cité, Hôtel de Ville, and St. Michel, each a short walk away.

Length of This Walk: Allow three hours to do justice to this three-mile self-guided walk, beginning at Notre-Dame Cathedral and ending at Pont Neuf; follow the dotted line on the "Historic Paris Walk" map.

Tours: ⌒ Download a free Rick Steves audio version of this walk (see page 17.)

⊙ Self-Guided Walk

• *Begin in front of Notre-Dame Cathedral, the physical and historic bull's-eye of your Paris map.*

❶ *Notre-Dame Cathedral*

This beloved, famous church (worth ▲▲▲) is dedicated to "Our Lady" (Notre Dame), Mary. In April 2019, the church caught on fire—the roof fell in, though the structure remained intact. The church is closed to visitors for years during reconstruction and may have scaffolding and barricades when you visit.

Notre-Dame has long been the spiritual heart of Paris. Imagine the faith of the people who built this cathedral. They broke ground in 1163 with the hope

Notre-Dame, before the 2019 fire destroyed the roof and spire.

Notre-Dame's altarpiece survived the fire.

Notre-Dame's gargoyles have seen it all.

that someday their great-great-great-great-great-great grandchildren might attend the dedication Mass, which finally took place two centuries later, in 1345. Look up the 200-foot-tall bell towers. Masons supervised, but the people did much of the grunt work themselves for free—hauling the huge stones from distant quarries, and treading like rats on a wheel designed to lift the stones up, one by one. This kind of backbreaking manual labor created the real hunchbacks of Notre-Dame.

Circling the exterior of the church, notice many of the elements of Gothic: pointed arches, the lacy stone tracery of the windows, the gargoyles, and most distinctive of all, the flying buttresses at the back. These 50-foot stone "beams" sticking out of the church help support the structure, freeing up the walls to hold large windows. This is Gothic. Taller and filled with light, Notre-Dame was a major improvement over the earlier Romanesque style. Gothic architects were mas-

ters at playing architectural forces against each other to build loftier and brighter churches. The Gothic style was born here in Paris.

Along with a new roof, reconstruction will include a new spire—likely adorned by the former spire's 19th-century sculptures, which had been stored away and were spared by the fire.

Fortunately, Notre-Dame's famous gargoyles escaped the fate of the roof. Picture Quasimodo (the fictional hunchback) limping along the tower balconies among the gargoyles. These grotesque beasts represent souls caught between heaven and earth. Some also function as rainspouts (from the same French root word as "gargle") when there are no evil spirits to battle.

• *Behind Notre-Dame, cross the street and enter through the iron gate into the park at the tip of the island. (If this gate is closed, you can still enter the park 30 yards to the left.) Look for the stairs and head down to reach the...*

FRANCE

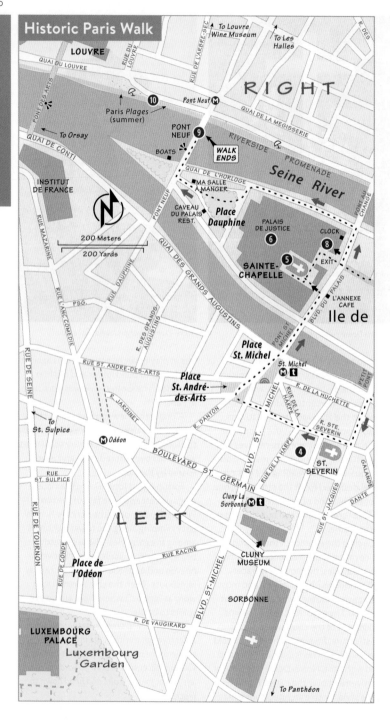

Historic Paris Walk

LOUVRE

QUAI DU LOUVRE

R. DU LOUVRE

R. DE L'ARBRE-SEC

To Louvre Wine Museum

To Les Halles

R. DES

RIGHT

PONT DES ARTS

QUAI DE CONTI

To Orsay

Paris Plages (summer)

10

Pont Neuf Ⓜ

QUAI DE LA MEGISSERIE

PONT NEUF

9

RIVERSIDE

PROMENADE

BOATS

WALK ENDS

Seine River

INSTITUT DE FRANCE

N

200 Meters
200 Yards

QUAI DE L'HORLOGE

MA SALLE À MANGER

CAVEAU DU PALAIS REST.

Place Dauphine

PALAIS DE JUSTICE

6

CLOCK

8

EXIT

PONTAU CHANGE

PONT NEUF

QUAI DES GRANDS AUGUSTINS

5

SAINTE-CHAPELLE

RUE MAZARINE

RUE DAUPHINE

R. DES GRANDS AUGUSTINS

BLVD. DU PALAIS

L'ANNEXE CAFE

Ile de

RUE DE SEINE

RUE L'ANC COMEDIE

PSG.

RUE ST. ANDRE-DES-ARTS

R. JARDINET

R. DANTON

Place St. Michel

Place St. André-des-Arts

PONT ST. MICHEL

St. Michel
Ⓜ ⓣ

PETIT PONT

BLVD. ST. MICHEL

RUE DE LA HARPE

R. DE LA HUCHETTE

R. STE. SEVERIN

GALANDE

To St. Sulpice

Ⓜ Odéon

BOULEVARD ST. GERMAIN

BLVD. ST. GERMAIN

4

ST. SEVERIN

DANTE

RUE ST. JACQUES

RUE ST. SULPICE

RUE DE TOURNON

RUE DE CONDE

Cluny La Sorbonne Ⓜ ⓣ

LEFT

Place de l'Odéon

RUE RACINE

CLUNY MUSEUM

BLVD. ST. MICHEL

SORBONNE

LUXEMBOURG PALACE

Luxembourg Garden

R. DE VAUGIRARD

To Panthéon

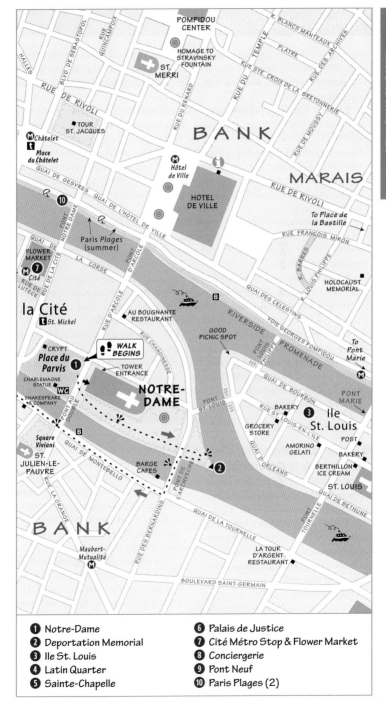

① Notre-Dame
② Deportation Memorial
③ Ile St. Louis
④ Latin Quarter
⑤ Sainte-Chapelle
⑥ Palais de Justice
⑦ Cité Métro Stop & Flower Market
⑧ Conciergerie
⑨ Pont Neuf
⑩ Paris Plages (2)

Affording Paris' Sights

Paris is an expensive city for tourists, with lots of pricey sights, but—fortunately—lots of freebies, too. Smart, budget-minded travelers begin by buying and getting the most out of a Paris Museum Pass, then considering these frugal sightseeing options.

Free (or Almost Free) Museums: Many of Paris' famous museums offer free entry on the first Sunday of the month, including the Orsay, Cluny, and Pompidou Center. These sights are free on the first Sunday of off-season months: the Louvre, Rodin Museum, and Arc de Triomphe (all Oct-March), and Versailles (Nov-March). Expect big crowds on free days. You can usually visit the Orsay Museum for free right when the ticket booth stops selling tickets. For just €4, the Rodin Museum garden lets you enjoy many of Rodin's finest works in a lovely outdoor setting.

Other Freebies: Many sights don't charge an entry fee, including the Notre-Dame Cathedral, Père Lachaise Cemetery, Deportation Memorial, Sacré-Cœur Basilica, and St. Sulpice Church (with organ recital). Paris' many glorious, entertaining parks are free.

Reduced Prices: Several sights offer a discount if you enter later in the day, including the Orsay, the Orangerie, and the Army Museum and Napoleon's Tomb (after 17:00 or 16:00 off-season). The Eiffel Tower costs less if you restrict your visit to the two lower levels—and even less if you use the stairs.

Good-Value Tours: At €15-20, Paris Walks' tours are a good value. The Seine River cruises (allow €15), best after dark, are also worthwhile.

Pricey...But Worth It? Certain big-ticket items—primarily the top of the Eiffel Tower, the Louvre, and Versailles—are expensive and crowded, but offer once-in-a-lifetime experiences. All together they amount to less than the cost of a ticket to Disneyland—only these are real.

❷ Deportation Memorial (Mémorial de la Déportation)

This ▲ memorial to the 200,000 French victims of the Nazi concentration camps (1940-1945) draws you into their experience. France was quickly overrun by Nazi Germany, and Paris spent the war years under Nazi occupation. Jews and dissidents were rounded up and deported—many never returned.

Cost and Hours: Free, Tue-Sun 10:00-19:00, Oct-March until 17:00, closed Mon year-round, may randomly close at other times, free 40-minute audioguide may be available; at the east tip of Ile de la Cité, behind Notre-Dame and near Ile St. Louis (Mo: Cité); tel. 01 46 33 87 56.

Visiting the Memorial: As you descend the steps, the city around you disappears. Surrounded by walls, you have become a prisoner. Your only freedom is your view of the sky and the tiny glimpse of the river below. Enter the dark, single-file chamber up ahead. Inside, the circular plaque in the floor reads, "They went to the end of the earth and did not return."

The hallway stretching in front of you is lined with 200,000 lighted crystals, one for each French citizen who died. Flickering at the far end is the eternal flame of hope. The tomb of the unknown deportee lies at your feet. Above, the inscription reads, "Dedicated to the living memory of the 200,000 French deportees shrouded by the night and the fog, exterminated in the Nazi concentration camps." The side

Deportation Memorial

Shakespeare and Company bookstore

rooms are filled with triangles—reminiscent of the identification patches inmates were forced to wear—each bearing the name of a concentration camp. Above the exit as you leave is the message you'll find at many other Holocaust sites: "Forgive, but never forget."

• *Back on street level, look across the river (north) to the island called...*

❸ Ile St. Louis

If Ile de la Cité is a tugboat laden with the history of Paris, it's towing this classy little residential dinghy, laden only with high-rent apartments, boutiques, characteristic restaurants, and famous ice cream shops. Ile St. Louis wasn't developed until much later than Ile de la Cité (17th century). What was a swampy mess is now harmonious Parisian architecture and one of Paris' most exclusive neighborhoods.

Ile St. Louis is a lovely place for an evening stroll. If you won't have time to come back later, consider taking a brief detour across the pedestrian bridge, Pont St. Louis, to explore this little island.

• *From the Deportation Memorial, cross the bridge to the Left Bank. Turn right and walk along the river until you reach the Pont au Double (the bridge leading to the facade of Notre-Dame). Carefully cross the street*

and continue on Quai de Montebello past a park until you see a cobbled lane on the left that leads to **Shakespeare and Company,** *an atmospheric reincarnation of the original 1920s bookshop and a good spot to page through books (37 Rue de la Bûcherie). Before returning to the island, walk a block behind Shakespeare and Company, and take a spin through...*

❹ The Latin Quarter

This area (worth ▲) has a touristy fame relating to its intriguing, artsy, bohemian character. This was perhaps Europe's leading university district in the Middle Ages, when Latin was the language of higher education. The neighborhood's main boulevards (St. Michel and St. Germain) are lined with cafés—once the haunts of great poets and philosophers, now the hangouts of tired tourists. Exploring a few blocks up or downriver from here gives you a better chance of feeling the pulse of what survives of Paris' classic Left Bank. For colorful wandering and café-sitting, afternoons and evenings are best.

Although it may look more like the Greek Quarter today (cheap gyros abound), this area is the Latin Quarter, named for the language you'd have heard on these streets if you walked them in

The Latin Quarter

the Middle Ages. The University of Paris (founded 1215), one of the leading educational institutions of medieval Europe, was (and still is) nearby. Walking along Rue St. Séverin, you can still see the shadow of the medieval sewer system. The street slopes into a central channel of bricks. In the days before plumbing and toilets, when people went to the river or neighborhood wells for their water, flushing meant throwing it out the window. At certain times of day, maids on the fourth floor would holler, *"Garde de l'eau!"* ("Watch out for the water!") and heave it into the streets, where it would eventually wash down into the Seine.

Consider a visit to the **Cluny Museum** for its medieval art and unicorn tapestries (see page 165). The **Sorbonne**—the University of Paris' humanities department— is also nearby; visitors can ogle at the famous dome, but aren't allowed to enter the building (two blocks south of the river on Boulevard St. Michel).

Don't miss **Place St. Michel.** This square is the traditional core of the Left Bank's artsy, liberal, hippie, bohemian district of poets, philosophers, winos, and *baba cools* (neo-hippies). In less commercial times, Place St. Michel was a gathering point for the city's malcontents and misfits. In 1830, 1848, and again in 1871, the citizens took the streets from the government troops, set up barricades *Les Miz*-style, and fought against royalist oppression. During World War II, the locals rose up against their Nazi oppressors (read the plaques under the dragons at the foot of the St. Michel fountain). Even today, whenever there's a student demonstration, it starts here.

• *From Place St. Michel, look across the river and find the prickly steeple of the Sainte-Chapelle church. Head toward it. Cross the river on Pont St. Michel and continue north along the Boulevard du Palais. On your left, you'll see the doorway to Sainte-Chapelle (usually with a line of people).*

❺ *Sainte-Chapelle*

This triumph of Gothic church architecture, worth ▲▲▲, is a cathedral of glass like no other. It was speedily built between 1242 and 1248 for King Louis IX—the only

Sainte-Chapelle is a cathedral of stained glass like no other.

French king who is now a saint—to house the supposed Crown of Thorns. Its architectural harmony is due to the fact that it was completed under the direction of one architect and in only six years—unheard of in Gothic times. By contrast, Notre-Dame took more than 200 years.

Cost and Hours: €10, €15 combo-ticket with Conciergerie, free for those under age 18, covered by Museum Pass, advance tickets sold on church website and at FNAC department stores; open daily 9:00-19:00, Oct-March until 17:00; audioguide-€3, 4 Boulevard du Palais, Mo: Cité, tel. 01 53 40 60 80, www.sainte-chapelle.fr. For info on upcoming church concerts, see page 183.

Avoiding Crowds: Security lines are shortest first thing in the morning (be in line by 9:00, or arrive at 10:00 after the early rush subsides) and on weekends (when the courts are closed). They're longest on Tuesday and daily 13:00-14:00 (when staff takes lunch). To avoid this line, it may be worth rearranging the order of the walk: See Sainte-Chapelle first, then walk over to Notre-Dame (5 minutes away). Or see Sainte-Chapelle at the end of the day—being the last person in the chapel is an experience you'll never forget.

Visiting the Church: Though the inside is beautiful, the exterior is basically functional. The muscular buttresses hold up the stone roof, so the walls are essentially there to display stained glass. The lacy spire is Neo-Gothic—added in the 19th century. Inside, the layout clearly shows an *ancien régime* approach to worship. The low-ceilinged basement was for staff and other common folk—worshipping under a sky filled with painted fleurs-de-lis, a symbol of the king. Royal Christians worshipped upstairs. The paint job, a 19th-century restoration, helps you imagine how grand this small, painted, jeweled chapel was. (Imagine Notre-Dame painted like this.) Each capital is playfully carved with a different plant's leaves.

Climb the spiral staircase to the Chapelle Haute. Fill the place with choral music, crank up the sunshine, face the top of the altar, really believe that the Crown

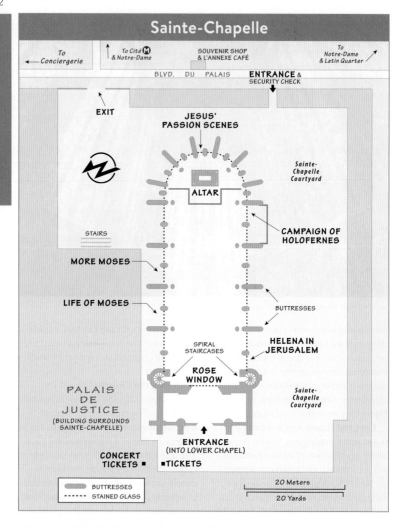

Sainte-Chapelle

of Thorns is there, and this becomes one awesome space.

Fiat lux. "Let there be light." From the first page of the Bible, it's clear: Light is divine. Light shines through stained glass like God's grace shining down to earth. Gothic architects used their new technology to turn dark stone buildings into lanterns of light. The glory of Gothic shines brighter here than in any other church.

The altar was raised up high to better display the Crown of Thorns, which cost King Louis more than three times as much as this church. Today, the relic is kept by the Notre-Dame Treasury (though it's occasionally brought out for display).

• *Exit Sainte-Chapelle. Back outside, as you walk around the church exterior, look down to see the foundation and take note of how much Paris has risen in the 750 years since Sainte-Chapelle was built. As you head toward the exit of the complex, you'll pass by the...*

❻ Palais de Justice

Sainte-Chapelle sits within a huge complex of buildings that has housed the local government since ancient Roman times. It was the site of the original Gothic palace of the early kings of France. The only surviving medieval parts are Sainte-Chapelle and the Conciergerie prison.

Most of the site is now covered by the giant Palais de Justice, built in 1776, home of the French Supreme Court. The motto *Liberté, Egalité, Fraternité* over the doors is a reminder that this was also the headquarters of the Revolutionary government. Here they doled out justice, condemning many to imprisonment in the Conciergerie downstairs—or to the guillotine.

• *Now pass through the big iron gate to the noisy Boulevard du Palais. Cross the street to the wide, pedestrian-only Rue de Lutèce and walk about halfway down.*

❼ Cité "Metropolitain" Métro Stop

Of the 141 original early-20th-century subway entrances, this is one of only a few survivors—now preserved as a national art treasure. (New York's Museum of Modern Art even exhibits one.) It marks Paris at its peak in 1900—on the cutting edge of Modernism, but with an eye for beauty. The curvy, plantlike ironwork is a textbook example of Art Nouveau, the style that rebelled against the erector-set squareness of the Industrial Age. Other similar Métro stations in Paris are Abbesses and Porte Dauphine.

The flower and plant market on Place Louis Lépine is a pleasant detour. On Sundays this square flutters with a busy bird market.

• *Pause here to admire the view. Sainte-Chapelle is a pearl in an ugly architectural oyster. Double back to the Palais de Justice, turn right onto Boulevard du Palais, and enter the Conciergerie (free with Museum Pass; pass holders can sidestep the ticket-buying line bottleneck).*

Cité Métro entrance

Conciergerie prison

❽ Conciergerie

Though barren inside, this former prison echoes with history. The Conciergerie was the last stop for the many victims of the guillotine, including France's last *ancien régime* queen, Marie-Antoinette. Before then, kings had used the building to torture and execute failed assassins. (One of its towers along the river was called "The Babbler," named for the pain-induced sounds that leaked from it.) When the Revolution (1789) toppled the king, the progressive Revolutionaries proudly unveiled a modern and more humane way to execute people—the guillotine. The Conciergerie was the epicenter of the Reign of Terror—the year-long period of the Revolution (1793-94) during which Revolutionary fervor spiraled out of control and thousands were killed. It was here at the Conciergerie that "enemies of the Revolution" were imprisoned, tried, sentenced, and marched off to Place de la Concorde for decapitation.

Cost and Hours: €9, €15 combo-ticket with Sainte-Chapelle, covered by Museum Pass, daily 9:30-18:00, videoguide-€6.50, 2 Boulevard du Palais, Mo: Cité, tel. 01 53 40 60 80, www.paris-conciergerie.fr.

Visiting the Conciergerie: Pick up a free map and breeze through the one-way, well-described circuit. You'll start in the spacious, low-ceilinged Hall of Men-at-Arms (Room 1), originally a guards' dining room warmed by four big fireplaces (look up the chimneys). During the Reign of Terror, this large hall served as a holding tank for the poorest prisoners. Then they were taken upstairs (in an area not open to visitors), where the Revolutionary tribunals grilled scared prisoners on their political correctness. Continue to the raised area at the far end of the room (Room 4, today's bookstore). This was the walkway of the executioner, who was known affectionately as "Monsieur de Paris."

Upstairs is a memorial room with the names of the 2,780 citizens condemned to death by the guillotine, including ex-King Louis XVI, Charlotte Corday (who murdered the Revolutionary writer Jean-Paul Marat in his bathtub), and—oh, the irony—Maximilien de Robespierre, the head rabble-rouser of the Revolution, who himself sent so many to the guillotine.

Just past the courtyard look up and notice the spikes still guarding from above.

Pont Neuf crosses the widest part of the Seine.

On October 16, 1793, Marie-Antoinette was awakened at 4:00 in the morning and led away. She walked the corridor, stepped onto the cart, and was slowly carried to Place de la Concorde, where she had her date with "Monsieur de Paris."

• *Back outside, turn left on Boulevard du Palais, then left again onto Quai de l'Horloge and walk along the river, past "The Babbler" tower.*

The bridge up ahead is the Pont Neuf, where we'll end this walk. At the first corner, veer left into a sleepy triangular square called Place Dauphine. It's amazing to find such coziness in the heart of Paris. From the equestrian statue of Henry IV, turn right onto Pont Neuf. Pause at the little nook halfway across.

❾ Pont Neuf and the Seine

This "new bridge" is now Paris' oldest. Built during Henry IV's reign (about 1600), its arches span the widest part of the river. Unlike other bridges, this one never had houses or buildings growing on it. The turrets were originally for vendors and street entertainers. In the days of Henry IV, who promised his peasants "a chicken in every pot every Sunday," this would have been a lively scene. From the bridge, look downstream (west) to see the next bridge, the pedestrian-only Pont des Arts. Ahead on the Right Bank is the long Louvre museum. Beyond that, on the Left Bank, is the Orsay.

• *Our walk is finished. From here, you can tour the Seine by boat (the departure point for Seine River cruises offered by Vedettes du Pont Neuf is through the park at the end of the island), continue to the Louvre, or head to the...*

❿ Riverside Promenades and Paris Plages

There's one traffic-free expanse on the Left Bank between the Eiffel Tower and the Orsay, and another on the Right Bank between the Louvre and the end of Ile St. Louis. Worth ▲▲, these areas are ideal for strolling, biking, having fun with the kids, dining (in pop-up drinking and eating establishments or at extravagant picnics complete with tablecloths and champagne)—or, simply dangling one's feet over the water and being in the moment. In balmy weather, the embankment takes on a special energy. Each summer, the Paris city government trucks in potted palm trees, hammocks,

Major Museums Neighborhood

● Bus #69 eastbound
❷ Bus #69 westbound

----- Bike Route

and lounge chairs to create colorful urban beaches—the Paris *Plages*.

Cost and Hours: Free, promenades always open, *Plages* run mid-July–mid-Aug daily 8:00–24:00, on Right Bank of Seine, just north of Ile de la Cité, between Pont des Arts and Pont de Sully.

SIGHTS

Major Museums Neighborhood

Paris' grandest park, the Tuileries Garden, was once the private property of kings and queens. Today it links the Louvre, Orangerie, and Orsay museums, all of which are within pleasant strolling distance of one another.

▲▲▲LOUVRE (MUSEE DU LOUVRE)

This is Europe's oldest, biggest, greatest, and second-most-crowded museum (after the Vatican). Housed in a

U-shaped, 16th-century palace (accentuated by a 20th-century glass pyramid), the Louvre is home to *Mona Lisa, Venus de Milo,* and hall after hall of Greek and Roman masterpieces, medieval jewels, Michelangelo statues, and paintings by the greatest artists from the Renaissance to the Romantics.

Touring the Louvre can be overwhelming, so be selective. Focus on the Denon wing, with Greek sculptures, Italian paintings (by Raphael and Leonardo), and, of course, French paintings (Neoclassical and Romantic), and the adjoining Sully wing, with Egyptian artifacts and more French paintings. For extra credit, tackle the Richelieu wing, displaying works from ancient Mesopotamia, as well as French, Dutch, and Northern art.

Cost: €15, includes special exhibits, free on first Sat of month after 18:00, covered by Museum Pass, timed-entry tickets available in advance at the website below.

The Louvre and its pyramid glows at night.

Hours: Wed-Mon 9:00-18:00, Wed, Fri, and first Sat of month until 21:45 (except on holidays), closed Tue, galleries start shutting 30 minutes before closing, last entry 45 minutes before closing.

Information: Tel. 01 40 20 53 17, recorded info tel. 01 40 20 51 51, www.louvre.fr.

Rick's Tip: Crowds can be miserable on Sun, Mon (the worst day), Wed, and in the morning. *Evening visits are quieter, and the glass pyramid glows after dark.*

Advance Tickets Recommended: Timed-entry tickets are available online in advance (enter at the pyramid up to 30 minutes before your allotted time)—see the Louvre website for details.

Under the Louvre's pyramid entrance

Using a Museum Pass: Even with a Museum Pass, it's advisable to make an advance reservation any time of year. However, buying a Museum Pass before arriving in Paris is not necessary—you can reserve online as late as the day of your visit, even in high season.

If you don't already have a Museum Pass, the "Museum Pass Tabac" (a.k.a. La Civette du Carrousel) sells them for no extra charge (cash only); it's just outside the Louvre entrance in the Carrousel du Louvre mall—follow *Museum Pass* signs inside the mall.

Buying Tickets On-Site: Inside the Louvre, tickets are sold in a side room under the pyramid—just line up for the next available self-service machine (PIN credit cards only) or ticket window.

Getting There: Métro stop Palais Royal-Musée du Louvre is the closest. From the station, you can either exit above ground to go in the pyramid entrance, or stay underground to use the Carrousel du Louvre entrance. Eastbound bus #69 stops along the Seine River; the best stop is labeled Quai François Mitterrand. Westbound #69 stops in front of the pyramid.

Getting In: There are two entrances. Everyone must pass through security at the entrances.

FRANCE

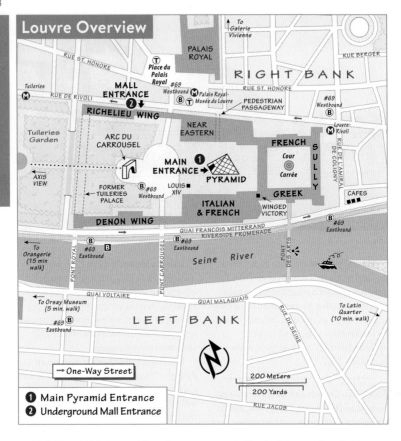

Louvre Overview

❶ Main Pyramid Entrance
❷ Underground Mall Entrance

→ One-Way Street

Main Pyramid Entrance: There is no grander entry than through the main entrance at the pyramid in the central courtyard. The security line here can be very long, but if you have a ticket or a pass, you can use the VIP line.

Underground Mall Entrance: The less crowded underground entrance is accessed through the Carrousel du Louvre shopping mall. Enter the mall at 99 Rue de Rivoli (the door with the shiny metal awning) or directly from the Métro stop Palais Royal-Musée du Louvre (stepping off the train, exit to *Musée du Louvre-Le Carrousel du Louvre*). Once inside the mall, continue toward the inverted pyramid next to the Louvre's security entrance. There's no priority

security line for Museum Pass holders here, but lines are generally shorter than the main pyramid entrance. (Don't follow signs to the *Passholders* entrance, which is at the pyramid, a long detour away.)

Once Inside: Once past security, everyone proceeds to the grand space beneath the glass pyramid with all the services. If you already have a ticket or Museum Pass, go directly to the galleries. Otherwise, you can buy a ticket (see "Buying Tickets On-Site," earlier).

Tours: Ninety-minute English-language **guided tours** leave twice daily from the *Accueil des Groupes* area, under the pyramid (normally at 11:00 and 14:00, plus 19:00 on Wed and Fri; possibly more often in summer; book in advance online; €12 plus admission, tour tel. 01 40 20 52 63).

🎧 Download my free Louvre Museum **audio tour.**

Baggage Check: It's free to store your bag in slick self-service lockers under the pyramid. Consider checking whatever you don't need—even if it's just a small bag—to make your visit more pleasant.

➲ SELF-GUIDED TOUR

With more than 30,000 works of art, the Louvre is a full inventory of Western civilization. To cover it all in one visit is impossible. Let's focus on the Louvre's specialties—Greek sculpture, Italian painting, and French painting.

• We'll start in the Sully wing, in Salle 16. To get there from the pyramid entrance, first enter the Denon wing, ascend several flights of escalators, and follow the crowds—then get out your map or ask for directions to the Venus de Milo.

THE GREEKS

Venus de Milo *(Aphrodite),* late 2nd century BC: This goddess of love created a sensation when she was discovered in 1820 on the Greek island of Melos. The Greeks pictured their gods in human form (meaning humans are godlike), telling us they had an optimistic view of the human race. Venus' well-proportioned body captures the balance and orderliness of the Greek universe. The twisting pose gives a balanced S-curve to her body (especially noticeable from the back view) that Golden Age Greeks and succeeding generations found beautiful. Most "Greek" statues are actually later Roman copies. This is a rare Greek original.

• Now head to Salle 6, behind Venus de Milo.

Parthenon Friezes, mid-5th century BC: These stone fragments once decorated the exterior of the greatest Athenian temple of the Greek Golden Age. The temple glorified the city's divine protector, Athena, and the superiority of the Athenians, who were feeling especially cocky, having just crushed their archrivals, the Persians. A model of the Parthenon shows

Venus de Milo

where the panels might have hung.

• About 50 yards away, find a grand staircase. Climb it to the first floor and the...

Winged Victory of Samothrace *(Victoire de Samothrace),* c. 190 BC: This woman with wings, poised on the prow of a ship, once stood on an island hilltop to commemorate a naval victory. Her clothes are windblown and sea-sprayed, clinging close enough to her body to win a wet T-shirt contest. Originally, her right arm was stretched high, celebrating the victory like a Super Bowl champion, waving a "we're number one" finger. This is the *Venus de Milo* gone Hellenistic, from the time after the culture of Athens was spread around the Mediterranean by Alexander the Great (c. 325 BC).

• Facing Winged Victory, *turn right (entering the Denon wing), and proceed to the large Salle 3.*

THE MEDIEVAL WORLD (1200-1500)

Cimabue, *The Madonna and Child in Majesty Surrounded by Angels (La Vierge et l'Enfant en Majesté Entourés de Six Anges),* c. 1280: During the Age of Faith (1200s),

almost every church in Europe had a painting like this one. Mary was a cult figure—even bigger than the late-20th-century Madonna—adored and prayed to by the faithful for bringing Baby Jesus into the world. These holy figures are laid flat on a gold background like cardboard cutouts, existing in a golden never-never land, as though the faithful couldn't imagine them as flesh-and-blood humans inhabiting our dark and sinful earth.

Giotto, *St. Francis of Assisi Receiving the Stigmata (Saint François d'Assise Recevant les Stigmates),* c. 1295-1300: Francis of Assisi (c. 1181-1226), a wandering Italian monk of renowned goodness, kneels on a rocky Italian hillside, pondering the pain of Christ's torture and execution. Suddenly, he looks up, startled, to see Christ himself, with six wings, hovering above. Christ shoots lasers from his wounds to the hands, feet, and side of the empathetic monk, marking him with the stigmata. Francis' humble love of man and nature inspired artists like Giotto to portray real human beings with real emotions, living in a physical world of beauty.

• *Room 3 spills into the long Grand Gallery. Find the following paintings in the Gallery, as you make your way to the* Mona Lisa *(midway down the gallery, in the adjoining Salle 6—just follow the signs and the people).*

Ⓐ Winged Victory of Samothrace

Ⓑ *Giotto,* St. Francis Receiving the Stigmata

Ⓒ *Leonardo da Vinci,* Mona Lisa

ITALIAN RENAISSANCE (1400-1600)

Leonardo da Vinci, *The Virgin and Child with St. Anne (La Vierge à l'Enfant Jésus avec Sainte-Anne),* c. 1510: Three generations—grandmother, mother, and child—are arranged in a pyramid, with Anne's face as the peak and the lamb as the lower right corner. It's as orderly as the geometrically perfect universe created by the Renaissance god. There's a psychological kidney punch in this happy painting. Jesus, the picture of childish joy, is innocently playing with a lamb—the symbol of his inevitable sacrificial death. The Louvre has the greatest collection of Leonardos in the world—five of them. Look for the neighboring *Virgin of the Rocks* and *John the Baptist.*

Raphael, *La Belle Jardinière,* c. 1507: Raphael perfected the style Leonardo pioneered. This configuration of Madonna, Child, and John the Baptist is also a balanced pyramid with hazy grace and beauty. The interplay of gestures and gazes gives the masterpiece both intimacy and cohesiveness, while Raphael's blended brushstrokes varnish the work with an iridescent smoothness. With Raphael, the Greek ideal of beauty—reborn in the Renaissance—reached its peak.

Leonardo da Vinci, *Mona Lisa,* a.k.a. *La Joconde,* 1503-1506: Leonardo was already an old man when François I invited him to France. Determined to pack light, he took only a few paintings with him. One was a portrait of Lisa del Giocondo, the wife of a wealthy Florentine merchant.

Mona may disappoint you. She's smaller than you'd expect, darker, engulfed in a huge room, and hidden behind a glaring pane of glass. The famous smile attracts you first, but try as you might, you can never quite see the corners of her mouth. The overall mood is one of balance and serenity, but there's also an element of mystery. *Mona's* smile and long-distance beauty are subtle and elusive, tempting but always just out of reach. *Mona* doesn't knock your socks off, but she winks at the patient viewer.

Paolo Veronese, *The Marriage at Cana (Les Noces de Cana),* 1562-1563: Venetian artists like Veronese painted the good life of rich, happy-go-lucky Venetian merchants. In a spacious setting of Renaissance architecture, colorful lords and ladies, decked out in their fanciest duds, feast on a great spread of food and drink. But believe it or not, this is a religious work showing the wedding celebration in which Jesus turned water into wine. With true Renaissance optimism, Venetians pictured Christ as a party animal, someone who loved the created world as much as they did.

• *Exit behind* Mona *into the Salle Denon (Room 76). Turn right for French Neo-*

ⓐ *Raphael,* La Belle Jardinière

ⓑ *Veronese,* The Marriage at Cana

ⓒ *Ingres,* La Grande Odalisque

ⓓ *Delacroix,* Liberty Leading the People

classicism (Salle Daru, David and Ingres); then backtrack through the Salle Denon for French Romanticism (Room 77, Géricault and Delacroix).

FRENCH PAINTING (1780-1850)

Jacques-Louis David, *The Coronation of Emperor Napoleon (Sacre de l'Empereur Napoléon),* 1806-1807: Napoleon holds aloft an imperial crown. This common-born son of immigrants is about to be crowned emperor of a "New Rome." He has just made his wife, Josephine, the empress, and she kneels at his feet. Seated behind Napoleon is the pope, who journeyed from Rome to place the imperial crown on his head. But Napoleon feels that no one is worthy of the task. At the last moment, he shrugs the pope aside.

Jean-Auguste-Dominique Ingres, *La Grande Odalisque,* 1814: Take *Venus de Milo,* turn her around, lay her down, and stick a hash pipe next to her, and you have the *Grande Odalisque.* Using clean, polished, sculptural lines, Ingres (ang-gruh) exaggerates the S-curve of a standing Greek nude. As in the *Venus de Milo,* rough folds of cloth set off her smooth skin. Ingres gave the face, too, a touch of *Venus'* idealized features, taking nature and improving on it. Ingres preserves *Venus'* backside for posterior—I mean, posterity.

Théodore Géricault, *The Raft of the Medusa (Le Radeau de la Méduse),* 1819: Clinging to a raft is a tangle of bodies and lunatics sprawled over each other. The scene writhes with agitated, ominous motion—the ripple of muscles, churning clouds, and choppy seas. The bodies rise up in a pyramid of hope, culminating in a flag wave. They signal frantically, trying to catch the attention of the tiny ship on the horizon, their last desperate hope... which did finally save them. Géricault uses rippling movement and powerful colors to catch us up in the excitement. (This painting was based on the actual sinking of the ship *Medusa* off the coast of Africa in 1816.)

Eugéne Delacroix, *Liberty Leading the*

Michelangelo's Slave *sculptures*

People (La Liberté Guidant le Peuple), 1831: The year is 1830. Parisians take to the streets to fight royalist oppressors. Leading them on through the smoke and over the dead and dying is the figure of Liberty, a strong woman waving the French flag. Does this symbol of victory look familiar? It's the *Winged Victory,* wingless and topless.

To stir our emotions, Delacroix uses only three major colors—the red, white, and blue of the French flag. France is the symbol of modern democracy, and this painting has long stirred its citizens' passion for liberty.

• *Exit the room at the far end (past the Café Mollien) and go downstairs, where you'll bump into...*

MORE ITALIAN RENAISSANCE

Michelangelo, *Slaves (Esclaves),* 1513-1515: These two statues by the earth's greatest sculptor are a bridge between the ancient and modern worlds. Michelangelo, like his fellow Renaissance artists, learned from the Greeks. The perfect anatomy, twisting poses, and idealized faces appear as if they could have been created 2,000 years earlier.

The *Dying Slave* twists listlessly against his T-shirt-like bonds, revealing his smooth skin. This is probably the most sensual nude that Michelangelo, the master of the male body, ever created. The *Rebellious Slave* fights against his bondage. His shoulders rotate one way, his head and leg turn the other. He even seems to be trying to release himself from the rock he's made of. Michelangelo said that his purpose was to carve away the marble to reveal the figures God put inside. This slave shows the agony of that process and the ecstasy of the result.

• Tour over! But, of course, there's so much more. After a break (or on a second visit), consider a stroll through a few rooms of the Richelieu wing, which contain some of the Louvre's most ancient pieces.

Rick's Tip: *Across from the Louvre (to the north) are the* **lovely courtyards of the stately Palais Royal** *(always open and free, entrance off Rue de Rivoli).* **Bring a picnic** *and create your own quiet break, or have a drink at one of the outdoor cafés at the courtyard's northern end.*

▲▲▲ORSAY MUSEUM (MUSEE D'ORSAY)

The Musée d'Orsay houses French art of the 1800s and early 1900s (specifically, 1848-1914), picking up where the Louvre's art collection leaves off. For us, that means Impressionism, the art of sun-dappled fields, bright colors, and crowded Parisian cafés. The Orsay houses the best general collection anywhere of Manet, Monet, Renoir, Degas, Van Gogh, Cézanne, and Gauguin.

Cost and Hours: €12, €9 Tue-Wed and Fri-Sun after 16:30 and Thu after 18:00, free on first Sun of month and often right when the ticket booth stops selling tickets (Tue-Wed and Fri-Sun at 17:00, Thu at 21:00; they won't let you in much after that), covered by Museum Pass, combo-ticket with Orangerie Museum

(€16) or Rodin Museum (€18). Museum open Tue-Sun 9:30-18:00, Thu until 21:45, closed Mon, last entry one hour before closing (45 minutes before on Thu), Impressionist galleries start shutting 45 minutes before closing, cafés and restaurant.

Information: Tel. 01 40 49 48 14, www.musee-orsay.fr.

Avoiding Lines: While everyone must wait to go through security, avoid the long ticket-buying lines with a Museum Pass, a combo-ticket, or by purchasing tickets in advance on the Orsay website; any of these entitle you to use a separate entrance. You can also buy tickets and Museum Passes (no mark-up; tickets valid 3 months) at the newspaper kiosk just outside the Orsay entrance (along Rue de la Légion d'Honneur).

Getting There: The museum, at 1 Rue de la Légion d'Honneur, sits above the RER/Train-C Musée d'Orsay stop; the nearest Métro stop is Solférino, three blocks southeast of the Orsay.

Getting In: As you face the entrance, pass and ticket holders enter on the right (Entrance C). Ticket purchasers enter on the left (Entrance A). Security checks slow down all entrances.

Rick's Tip: *If you're planning to* **get a combo-ticket for the Orsay Museum** *with either the Orangerie or the Rodin Museum, start at one of those museums instead, as they have shorter lines.*

Tours: Audioguides cost €5. English **guided tours** usually run daily at 11:30 (€6/1.5 hours, none on Sun, tours may also run at 14:30—inquire when you arrive).

🎧 Download my free Orsay Museum **audio tour.**

⊙ SELF-GUIDED TOUR

This former train station, the Gare d'Orsay, barely escaped the wrecking ball in the 1970s, when the French realized it'd be a great place to house the enormous collections of 19th-century art scattered throughout the city. The ground floor (level 0) houses early-19th-century art, mainly conservative art of the Academy and Salon, plus Realism. On the top floor is the core of the collection—the Impressionist rooms. If you're pressed for time, go directly there.

Remember that the museum rotates its large collection often, so find the latest arrangement on your current Orsay map, and be ready to go with the flow.

CONSERVATIVE ART

In the Orsay's first few rooms, you're surrounded by visions of idealized beauty—nude women in languid poses, Greek mythological figures, and anatomically perfect statues. This was the art adored by 19th-century French academics and the middle-class (*bourgeois*) public.

Jean-Auguste-Dominique **Ingres**' *The Source* (1856) is virtually a Greek statue on canvas. Like *Venus de Milo,* she's a balance of opposite motions. Alexandre **Cabanel** lays Ingres' *The Source* on her back. His *Birth of Venus* (1863) is a perfect fantasy, an orgasm of beauty.

REALISM

The French Realists rejected idealized classicism and began painting what they saw in the world around them. For Honoré **Daumier,** that meant looking at the stuffy bourgeois establishment that controlled the Academy and the Salon. In the 36 bustlets of *Celebrities of the Happy Medium* (1835), Daumier, trained as a political cartoonist, exaggerates each subject's most distinct characteristic to capture with vicious precision the pomposity and self-righteousness of these self-appointed arbiters of taste (most were members of the French parliament).

Jean-François **Millet**'s *The Gleaners* (1867) shows us three gleaners, the poor women who pick up the meager leftovers after a field has already been harvested for the wealthy. Here he captures the innate dignity of these stocky, tanned women who bend their backs quietly in a large field for their small reward. This is "Realism" in two senses. It's painted "realistically," not prettified. And it's the "real" world—not the fantasy world of Greek myth, but the harsh life of the working poor.

For a Realist's take on the traditional Venus, find Edouard **Manet**'s *Olympia*

The Orsay Museum occupies an early-20th-century railway station.

(1863). Compare this uncompromising nude with Cabanel's idealized, pastel, Vaseline-on-the-lens beauty in *The Birth of Venus*. In *Olympia*, the sharp outlines and harsh, contrasting colors are new and shocking. Manet replaced soft-core porn with hard-core art.

Gustave **Courbet**'s *The Painter's Studio* (1855) takes us backstage, showing us the gritty reality behind the creation of pretty pictures. We see Courbet himself in his studio, working diligently on a Realistic landscape, oblivious to the confusion around him. Milling around are ordinary citizens, not Greek heroes.

At the far end of the gallery, you'll find the Opéra Exhibit—a **glass floor** over a model of Paris with the 19th-century, green-domed Opéra Garnier at the center.

TOULOUSE-LAUTREC DETOUR

The Henri de **Toulouse-Lautrec** paintings in Room 10 rightly belong with the Post-Impressionist works on level 2, but since you're already here, enjoy his paintings incarnating the artist's love of nightlife and show business. Every night, Toulouse-Lautrec put on his bowler hat and visited the Moulin Rouge to draw the crowds, the can-can dancers, and the backstage action. He worked quickly, creating sketches in paint that serve as snapshots of a golden era. In *Jane Avril Dancing* (1891), he depicts the slim, graceful, elegant, and melancholy dancer, who stood out above the rabble. Her legs keep dancing while her mind is far away.

IMPRESSIONISM

The Impressionist collection is scattered randomly through Rooms 29-36 on the top floor. Look for masterworks by these artists:

Edouard **Manet**'s *Luncheon on the Grass* (*Le Déjeuner sur l'Herbe*, 1863) shocked Paris. It isn't the nudity, but the presence of the men in ordinary clothes that suddenly makes the nudes look naked.

You can see that a new revolutionary movement was starting to bud—Impres-

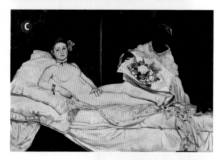

A *Cabanel, Birth of Venus*

B *Millet, The Gleaners*

C *Manet, Olympia*

D *Toulouse-Lautrec, Jane Avril Dancing*

Orsay Museum—Ground Floor

Orsay Museum ground floor map showing the Seine/River on the left (Riverside Promenade, Quai Voltaire, Quai Anatole France), with PONT ROYAL at top and SOLFERINO PEDESTRIAN BRIDGE at bottom. Streets include RUE DU BAC, RUE DE LILLE, RUE DE LA LEGION D'HONNEUR, RUE DE SOLFERINO. Features marked: ESCALATOR UP TO IMPRESSIONISM, CAFE, MANET, TOULOUSE-LAUTREC, CONSERVATIVE ART, REALISM, BOOKSTORE, BOOKS, VESTIAIRE (BAGGAGE CHECK), SECURITY, TICKET PURCHASERS, ENTRANCE, ADVANCE TICKET & PASS HOLDERS, Musee D'Orsay, Entrance Plaza, NEWSPAPER KIOSK. Numbered points 1–9 and START. Bus stops #69 Eastbound, #69 Westbound, Batobus Boat Stop. Notes: To Louvre via Tuileries Garden (10 Min. Walk / 15 Min. Walk), To Orangerie (10 Min. Walk), To M Solférino (15 Min. Walk) & Rodin Museum. "Not to Scale."

1 Main Gallery Statues
2 INGRES – The Source
3 CABANEL – The Birth of Venus
4 DAUMIER – Celebrities of the Happy Medium
5 MILLET – The Gleaners
6 MANET – Olympia
7 COURBET – The Painter's Studio
8 Opéra Exhibit
9 TOULOUSE-LAUTREC – Jane Avril Dancing

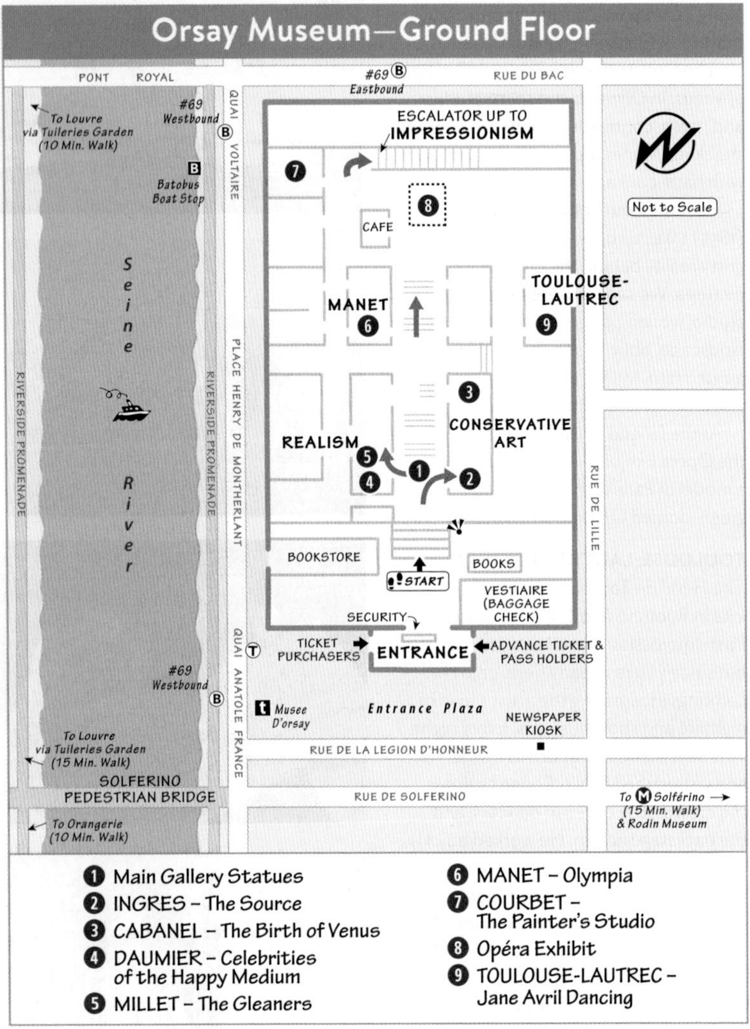

sionism. Notice the background: the messy brushwork of trees and leaves, the play of light on the pond, and the light that filters through the trees onto the woman who stoops in the haze. Also note the strong contrast of colors (white skin, black clothes, green grass).

Edgar **Degas** blends classical lines and Realist subjects with Impressionist color, spontaneity, and everyday scenes from urban Paris. He loved the unposed "snapshot" effect, catching his models off guard. Dance students, women at work, and café scenes are approached from odd angles that aren't always ideal but make the scenes seem more real. He gives us the backstage view of life. For instance, a dance rehearsal let Degas capture a behind-the-scenes look at bored, tired, restless dancers (*The Dance Class, La Classe de Danse,* c. 1873-1875). In the painting *In a Café* (*Dans un Café,* 1875-

POST-IMPRESSIONISM

Post-Impressionism—the style that employs Impressionism's bright colors while branching out in new directions—is scattered all around the museum. You'll get a taste of the style with Paul Cézanne on the top floor, with much more on level 2.

Paul **Cézanne** (say-zahn) brought Impressionism into the 20th century. After the color of Monet and the warmth of Renoir, Cézanne's rather impersonal canvases can be difficult to appreciate (see *The Card Players, Les Joueurs de Cartes*, 1890-1895). Where the Impressionists built a figure out of a mosaic of individual brushstrokes, Cézanne used blocks of paint to create a more solid, geometrical shape. These chunks are like little "cubes." It's no coincidence that his experiments in reducing forms to their geometric basics inspired the…Cubists. Because of his style (not the content), he is often called the first modern painter.

Like Michelangelo, Beethoven, and a select handful of others, Vincent **van Gogh** put so much of himself into his work that art and life became one. In the Orsay's collection of paintings (level 2), you'll see both Van Gogh's painting style and his life unfold, from his early days soaking up the Impressionist style (for example, see how he might build a bristling brown beard using thick strokes of red, yellow, and green side by side) to his richly creative but wildly unstable stint in the south of France (*Van Gogh's Room at Arles, La Chambre de Van Gogh à Arles*, 1889). Don't miss his final self-portrait (1889), showing a man engulfed in a confused background of brushstrokes that swirl and rave. Perhaps his troubled eyes know that in only a few months, he'll take a pistol and put a bullet through his chest.

Nearby are the paintings of Paul **Gauguin,** who got the travel bug early in childhood and grew up wanting to be a sailor. Instead, he became a stockbroker. At the age of 35, he got fed up with it all, quit his job, abandoned his wife (her stern

Degas, The Dance Class

1876), a weary lady of the evening meets morning with a last, lonely, nail-in-the-coffin drink in the glaring light of a four-in-the-morning café.

You'll see various paintings by Claude **Monet,** the father of Impressionism. In the 1860s, Monet (along with Renoir) began painting landscapes in the open air. He studied optics and pigments to know just the right colors he needed to reproduce the shimmering quality of reflected light. The key was to work quickly, when the light was just right, creating a fleeting "impression" of the scene.

Pierre-Auguste **Renoir** started out as a painter of landscapes, along with Monet, but later veered from the Impressionist's philosophy and painted images that were unabashedly "pretty." His best-known work is *Dance at the Moulin de la Galette* (*Bal du Moulin de la Galette*, 1876). On Sunday afternoons, working-class folk would dress up and head for the fields on Butte Montmartre (near Sacré-Cœur basilica) to dance, drink, and eat little crêpes (galettes) till dark. Renoir liked to go there to paint the common Parisians living and loving in the afternoon sun.

A *Renoir,* Dance at the Moulin de la Galette
B *Cézanne,* The Card Players
C *Van Gogh,* Van Gogh's Room at Arles
D *Gauguin,* Arearea

portrait bust may be nearby) and family, and took refuge in his art.

Gauguin traveled to the South Seas in search of the exotic, finally settling on Tahiti. His best-known works capture an idyllic Tahitian landscape peopled by exotic women engaged in simple tasks and making music (*Arearea,* 1892). The style is intentionally "primitive," collapsing the three-dimensional landscape into a two-dimensional pattern of bright colors. Gauguin wanted to communicate to his "civilized" colleagues back home that he'd found the paradise he'd always envisioned.

FRENCH SCULPTURE

The open-air mezzanine of level 2 is lined with statues. Stroll the mezzanine, enjoying the work of great French sculptors, including Auguste **Rodin.**

Born of working-class roots and largely self-taught, Rodin combined classical solidity with Impressionist surfaces to become one of the greatest sculptors since the Renaissance. Rodin's *St. John the Baptist Preaching* (bronze, 1881) captures the mystical visionary who was the precursor to Christ, the man who would announce the coming of the Messiah. Rodin's inspiration came in the form of a shaggy peasant—looking for work as a model—whose bearing caught the artist's eye. Coarse and hairy, with both feet planted firmly, if oddly, on the ground, this sculpture's rough, "unfinished" look reflects light in the same way the rough Impressionist brushwork does—making the statue come alive, never quite at rest in the viewer's eye.

Rodin's sculptures capture the groundbreaking spirit of much of the art in the Orsay Museum. With a stable base of 19th-century stone, he launched art into the 20th century.

▲▲ORANGERIE MUSEUM (MUSÉE DE L'ORANGERIE)

Located in the Tuileries Garden and drenched by natural light from skylights,

Monet's Water Lilies *at the Orangerie Museum*

the Orangerie (oh-rahn-zhuh-ree) is the closest you'll ever come to stepping right into an Impressionist painting. Start with the museum's claim to fame: Monet's *Water Lilies.* Then head downstairs to enjoy the manageable collection of select works by Utrillo, Cézanne, Renoir, Matisse, and Picasso.

Cost and Hours: €9, €6.50 after 17:00, free for those under age 18, €16 combo-ticket with Orsay Museum, €20 combo-ticket with Monet's Garden and House at Giverny, covered by Museum Pass; Wed-Mon 9:00-18:00, closed Tue; audioguide-€5, English guided tours usually Mon and Thu at 14:30 and Sat at 11:00, located in Tuileries Garden near Place de la Concorde (Mo: Concorde), 15-minute stroll from the Orsay, tel. 01 44 77 80 07, www.musee-orangerie.fr.

Visiting the Museum: On the main floor you'll find the main attraction, Monet's *Water Lilies (Nymphéas),* floating dreamily in oval rooms. These eight mammoth, curved panels immerse you in Monet's garden. We're looking at the pond in his garden at Giverny—dotted with water lilies, surrounded by foliage, and dappled by the reflections of the sky, clouds, and trees on the surface. But the true subject of these works is the play of reflected light off the surface of the pond.

Working at his home in Giverny, Monet built a special studio with skylights and wheeled easels to accommodate the canvases. For 12 years (1914-1926), Monet worked on these paintings obsessively. Monet completed all the planned canvases, but he didn't live to see them installed here. In 1927, the year after his death, these rooms were completed and the canvases put in place. Some call this the first "art installation"—art displayed in a space specially designed for it in order to enhance the viewer's experience.

In the underground gallery are select works of other Impressionist heavyweights well worth your time. The museum is small enough to enjoy in a short visit, but complete enough to show the bridge from Impressionism to Modernism. And it's all beautiful.

Eiffel Tower and Nearby

▲▲▲ EIFFEL TOWER
(LA TOUR EIFFEL)

Built on the 100th anniversary of the French Revolution (and in the spirit of the Industrial Revolution), the tower was the centerpiece of a World Expo designed simply to show off what people could build in 1889. For decades it was the tallest structure the world had ever known, and though it's since been eclipsed, it's still the most visited monument. Ride the elevators to the top of its 1,063 feet for expansive views that stretch 40 miles. Then descend to the two lower levels, where the views are arguably even better, since the monuments are more recognizable.

Cost and Hours: €25 to ride all the way to the top, €16 for just the two lower levels, €10 to climb the stairs to the first or second level, €19 to climb the stairs to the second level and take the elevator to the summit—must purchase summit elevator before entering tower, 50 percent cheaper for those under 25, 75 percent cheaper for those under 12, not covered by Museum Pass; open daily mid-June-Aug 9:00-24:45, Sept-mid-June 9:30-23:45, last ascent to top at 22:30 and to lower levels at 23:00 all year (elevator or stairs); cafés and great view restaurants, Mo: Bir-Hakeim or Trocadéro, RER/Train-C:

The Eiffel Tower stands more than 1,000 feet tall.

Eiffel Tower & Nearby

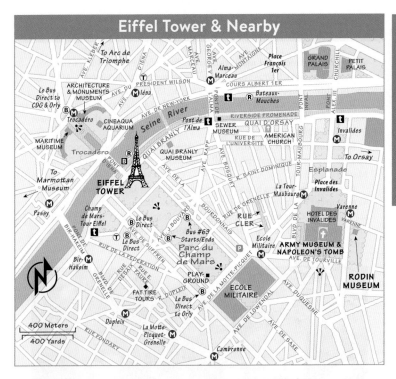

Champ de Mars-Tour Eiffel (all about a 10-minute walk away).

Information: Recorded information tel. 08 92 70 12 39, www.toureiffel.paris.

Reservations Smart: It's wise to make a reservation well in advance of your visit. At www.toureiffel.paris, you can book a time slot for your ascent; this allows you to skip the long initial entry line.

Online ticket sales open up 60 days before any given date (at 8:30 Paris time). Be sure of your date, as reservations are nonrefundable. To go all the way to the top, select "Lift entrance ticket with access to the summit" as your ticket type. You can either print your tickets (follow the specifications carefully) or download e-tickets to your phone. Note that email or text confirmations alone will not get you in; you must have a printed or electronic ticket showing the bar code.

If no slots are available, try buying a "Lift entrance ticket with access to 2nd floor"—the view from the second floor is arguably better anyway. Or, try the website again about a week before your visit—last-minute spots sometimes open up.

***

Rick's Tip: No reservation for the Eiffel Tower? *Get in line 30 minutes before it opens. Going late is the next-best bet (after 19:00 May-Aug). You can bypass some (but not all) lines if you have a reservation at either of the tower's view restaurants (Le Jules Verne or 58 Tour Eiffel).*

***

When to Go: For the best of all worlds, arrive with enough light to see the views, then stay as it gets dark to see the lights. The views are grand whether you ascend or not. At the top of the hour, a five-minute display features thousands of sparkling lights (best viewed from Place du Trocadéro or the grassy park below).

Open-Air Markets

Several traffic-free street markets overflow with flowers, produce, fish vendors, and butchers. Shops are open daily except Sunday afternoons, Monday, and lunchtime throughout the week (13:00 to 15:00 or 16:00).

Rue Cler—a wonderful place to sleep and dine as well as shop—is like a refined street market, serving an upscale neighborhood near the Eiffel Tower (Mo: Ecole Militaire).

Rue Montorgueil and **Rue Montmartre** are thriving, locally popular café-lined streets that run parallel just north of Les Halles (Mo: Etienne Marcel).

Rue Mouffetard is a happening market street by day and does double-duty as restaurant row at night. Hiding several blocks behind the Panthéon, it starts at Place Contrescarpe and ends below at St. Médard Church (Mo: Censier Daubenton). The upper stretch is pedestrian and touristic; the bottom stretch is purely Parisian.

Getting In: The perimeter of the tower is surrounded by glass walls for security purposes. So, while it's free to enter the area directly under the tower, you must first pass through an airport-like security check (allow 30 minutes or more at busy times). **If you have a reservation,** arrive at the tower 30 minutes before your entry time and look for either of the two entrances with green signs showing *Visiteurs avec Reservation* (Visitors with Reservation), where attendants scan your ticket and put you on the first available elevator. **Without a reservation,** follow signs for *Individuels* or *Visiteurs sans Tickets* (avoid lines selling tickets only for *Groupes*). The stairs entrance (usually a shorter line) is at the south pillar (next to Le Jules Verne restaurant entrance).

Security Check: Bags larger than 19" × 8" × 12" are not allowed, but there is no baggage check. All bags are subject to a security search. No knives, glass bottles, or cans are permitted.

BACKGROUND

The first visitor to the Paris World's Fair in 1889 walked beneath the "arch" formed by the newly built Eiffel Tower and entered the fairgrounds. This event celebrated both the centennial of the French Revolution and France's position as a global superpower. Bridge builder Gustave Eiffel (1832-1923) won the contest to build the fair's centerpiece by beating out rival proposals such as a giant guillotine.

The tower was nothing but a showpiece, with no functional purpose except to demonstrate to the world that France had the wealth, knowledge, and can-do spirit to erect a structure far taller than anything the world had ever seen. The original plan was to dismantle the tower as quickly as it was built after the celebration ended, but it was kept by popular demand.

The tower, including its antenna, stands 1,063 feet tall, or slightly higher than the 77-story Chrysler Building in New York. Its four support pillars straddle an area of 3.5 acres. Despite the tower's 7,300 tons of metal and 60 tons of paint, it is so well-engineered that it weighs no more per square inch at its base than a linebacker on tiptoes.

VISITING THE TOWER

There are three observation platforms, at roughly 200, 400, and 900 feet. If you want to see the entire tower, from top to bottom, then see it...from top to bottom.

There isn't a single elevator straight to the top (le sommet). To get there, you'll first ride an elevator (or hike up the stairs) to the second level. (For the hardy, there are 360 stairs to the first level and another 360 to the second). Once on the second level, immediately line up for the next elevator, to the top. Enjoy the views from the "summit," then ride back down to the second level. When you're ready, head to the first level via the stairs (no line and can take as little as five minutes) or take the elevator down. Explore the shops and exhibits on the first level. To leave, you can line up for the elevator, but it's quickest and most memorable

to take the stairs back down to earth.

For a final look, stroll across the river to Place du Trocadéro or to the end of the Champ de Mars and look back for great views. However impressive it may be by day, the tower is an awesome thing to behold at twilight, when it becomes engorged with light, and virile Paris lies back and lets night be on top. When darkness fully envelops the city, the tower seems to climax with a spectacular light show at the top of each hour...for five glorious minutes.

Near the Eiffel Tower

▲▲ARMY MUSEUM AND NAPOLEON'S TOMB (MUSEE DE L'ARMEE)

Napoleon's tomb rests beneath the golden dome of Les Invalides church. In addition to the tomb, the complex of Les Invalides—a former veterans' hospital built by Louis XIV—has various military collections, together called the Army Museum, Europe's greatest military museum. Visiting the different sections, you can watch the art of war unfold from

Army Museum and Napoleon's Tomb

Rodin's Burghers of Calais

Monet's Impression, Sunrise

stone axes to Axis powers.

Cost and Hours: €12, €9 after 17:00 (16:00 Nov-March), free for military personnel in uniform, free for kids but they must wait in line for ticket, covered by Museum Pass, extra fee for special exhibits and evening concerts; open daily 10:00-18:00, Nov-March until 17:00; Napoleon's Tomb also open July-Aug until 19:00; Napoleon's Tomb and Louis XIV-Napoleon I wing open April-Sept Tue until 21:00; Charles de Gaulle exhibit closed Mon year-round; videoguide-€6, cafeteria, tel. 08 10 11 33 99, www.musee-armee.fr.

Getting There: The Hôtel des Invalides is at 129 Rue de Grenelle, a 10-minute walk from Rue Cler (Mo: La Tour Maubourg, Varenne, or Invalides). You can also take bus #69 (from the Marais and Rue Cler), bus #87 (from Rue Cler and Luxembourg Garden area), or bus #63 from the St. Germain-des-Prés area.

Visiting the Museum: At the center of the complex, Napoleon Bonaparte lies majestically dead inside several coffins under a grand dome—a goose-bumping pilgrimage for historians. The dome overhead glitters with 26 pounds of thinly pounded gold leaf.

Your visit continues through an impressive range of museums filled with medieval armor, cannons and muskets, Louis XIV-era uniforms and weapons, and Napoleon's horse—stuffed and mounted.

The best section is dedicated to the two World Wars. Walk through displays well described in English on the trench warfare of World War I, the victory parades, France's horrendous losses, and the humiliating Treaty of Versailles that led to World War II.

The WWII rooms use black-and-white photos, maps, videos, and a few artifacts to trace Hitler's rise, the Blitzkrieg that overran France, America's entry into the war, D-Day, the concentration camps, the atomic bomb, the war in the Pacific, and the eventual Allied victory. There's special insight into France's role (the French Resistance), and how it was Charles de Gaulle that actually won the war.

▲▲RODIN MUSEUM (MUSEE RODIN)

This user-friendly museum with gardens is filled with passionate works by Auguste Rodin (1840-1917), the greatest sculptor since Michelangelo. You'll see *The Kiss, The Thinker, The Gates of Hell,* and many more, well displayed in the mansion where the sculptor lived and worked.

Cost and Hours: €10, includes museum and gardens, free for those under age 18, free on first Sun of the month Oct-March, €18 combo-ticket with Orsay Museum, both museum and garden covered by Museum Pass; Tue-Sun 10:00-18:30, closed Mon; audioguide-€6, mandatory baggage check, self-service café in garden, 77 Rue de Varenne, Mo: Varenne, tel. 01 44 18 61 10, www.musee-rodin.fr.

Visiting the Museum: Auguste Rodin (1840-1917) was a modern Michelangelo, sculpting human figures on an epic scale, revealing through their bodies his deepest thoughts and feelings. Like many of Michelangelo's unfinished works, Rodin's statues rise from the raw stone around them, driven by the life force. With missing limbs and scarred skin, these are prefab classics, making ugliness noble. Rodin's people are always moving restlessly. Even the famous *Thinker* is moving; while he's plopped down solidly, his mind is a million miles away.

Exhibits trace Rodin's artistic development, explain how his bronze statues were cast, and show some of the studies he created to work up to his masterpiece, the unfinished *Gates of Hell.* Learn about Rodin's tumultuous relationship with his apprentice and lover, Camille Claudel. Mull over what makes his sculptures some of the most evocative since the Renaissance. And stroll the beautiful gardens, packed with many of his greatest works (including *The Thinker*) and ideal for artistic reflection.

▲▲MARMOTTAN MUSEUM (MUSEE MARMOTTAN MONET)

In this private, intimate, and untouristy museum, you'll find the best collection anywhere of works by Impressionist headliner Claude Monet. Follow Monet's life through more than a hundred works, from simple sketches to the *Impression: Sunrise* painting that gave his artistic movement its start—and a name. The museum also displays some of the enjoyable large-scale canvases featuring the water lilies from his garden at Giverny.

Cost and Hours: €11, not covered by Museum Pass, €20 combo-ticket with Monet's garden and house at Giverny (lets you skip the line at Giverny); Tue-Sun 10:00-18:00, Thu until 21:00, closed Mon; audioguide-€3 (includes temporary exhibits), 2 Rue Louis-Boilly, Mo: La Muette, tel. 01 44 96 50 33, www.marmottan.fr.

Left Bank

Opposite Notre-Dame, on the left bank of the Seine, is the Latin Quarter. (For more about this neighborhood, see the "Historic Paris Walk," earlier).

▲▲CLUNY MUSEUM (MUSEE NATIONAL DU MOYEN AGE)

The Cluny is a treasure trove of Middle Ages (Moyen Age) art. Located on the side of a Roman bathhouse, it offers close-up looks at stained glass, Notre-Dame carvings, fine goldsmithing and jewelry, and rooms of tapestries. The highlights are several original stained-glass windows from Sainte-Chapelle and the exquisite series of six Lady and the Unicorn tapestries: A delicate, as-medieval-as-can-be noble lady introduces a delighted unicorn to the

Cluny Museum's Lady and the Unicorn tapestry

Luxembourg Garden

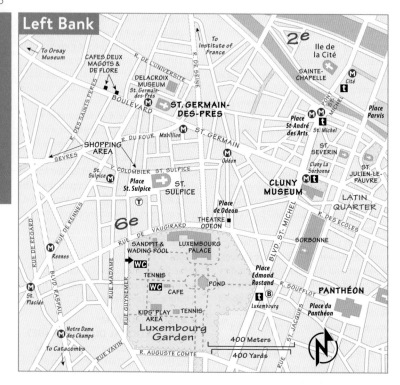

Left Bank

senses of taste, hearing, sight, smell, and touch. The museum is undergoing a multiyear renovation.

Cost and Hours: €8, includes audio-guide, free on first Sun of month, covered by Museum Pass (though pass holders pay €1 for audioguide); Wed-Mon 9:15-17:45, closed Tue; videoguide-€3; near corner of Boulevards St. Michel and St. Germain at 6 Place Paul Painlevé; Mo: Cluny-La Sorbonne, St. Michel, or Odéon; tel. 01 53 73 78 16, www.musee-moyenage.fr.

▲LUXEMBOURG GARDEN
(JARDIN DU LUXEMBOURG)
This lovely 60-acre garden is an Impressionist painting brought to life. Slip into a green chair pondside, enjoy the radiant flower beds, go jogging, play tennis or basketball, sail a toy sailboat, or take in a chess game or puppet show. Some of the park's prettiest (and quietest) sections lie around its perimeter.

Cost and Hours: Free, daily dawn until dusk, Mo: Odéon, RER/Train-B: Luxembourg.

▲CATACOMBS
Spiral down 60 feet below the street and walk a one-mile route through tunnels containing the anonymous bones of six million permanent Parisians. Lines to get in can be several hours long; it's essential to book online in advance. Once inside, allow an hour if you dawdle.

You'll descend 130 steps and land in a room with English posters describing 45 million years of ancient geology, then walk for 10 minutes through tunnels to reach the bones. Appreciate that some of these tunnels were originally built sans mortar. The sign, "Halt, this is the empire of the dead," announces your arrival at the bones. From here, shuffle along passageways of artfully arranged, skull-studded tibiae; admire 300-year-old sculptures

Looking down the Champs-Elysées from the Arc de Triomphe

cut into the walls of the catacombs; and see more cheery signs: "Happy is he who is forever faced with the hour of his death and prepares himself for the end every day." The highlight for me is the Crypt of the Passion (a.k.a. "the Barrel"), where bones are meticulously packed in a barrel shape hiding a support pillar.

Cost and Hours: €13, not covered by Museum Pass, Tue–Sun 10:00-20:30, closed Mon; purchase a timed-entry ticket online in advance at the website below or consider Fat Tire Tours' "Skip the Line" ticket (see page 133); otherwise arrive by 9:30 or after 18:00 to minimize wait; ticket booth closes at 19:30, come no later than 19:00 or risk not getting in; well-done audioguide-€5, pick up English visitors guide for explanations of key stops, tel. 01 43 22 47 63, www.catacombes.paris.fr.

Getting There: It's at 1 Place Denfert-Rochereau. Take the Métro to Denfert-Rochereau and follow *Sortie 1,* then find the lion in the big traffic circle; if he looked left rather than right, he'd stare right at the green entrance to the Catacombs.

Champs-Elysées and Nearby
▲▲▲CHAMPS-ELYSEES

This famous boulevard is Paris' backbone, with its greatest concentration of traffic (although it's delightfully traffic-free on the first Sunday of each month). From the Arc de Triomphe down Avenue des Champs-Elysées, all of France seems to converge on Place de la Concorde, the city's largest square. And though the Champs-Elysées has become as international as it is Parisian, a walk down the two-mile boulevard is still a must.

In 1667, Louis XIV opened the first section of the street, and it soon became *the* place to cruise in your carriage. (It still is

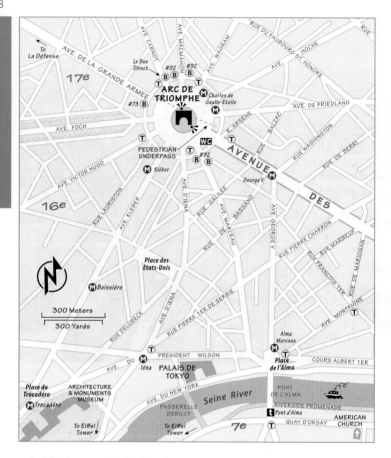

today.) By the 1920s, this boulevard was pure elegance—fancy residences, rich hotels, and cafés. Today it's home to big business, celebrity cafés, glitzy nightclubs, high-fashion shopping, and international people-watching. People gather here to celebrate Bastille Day (July 14), World Cup triumphs, and the finale of the Tour de France.

⊙ **Self-Guided Walk:** Start at the Arc de Triomphe (Mo: Charles de Gaulle-Etoile; if you're planning to tour the Arc, do it before starting this walk, described next) and head downhill on the left-hand side. The arrival of McDonald's (at #140) was an unthinkable horror, but these days dining chez MacDo has become typically

Parisian, and this branch is the most profitable McDonald's in the world.

The Lido (#116) is Paris' largest burlesque-type cabaret (and a multiplex cinema). Across the boulevard is the flagship store of leather-bag maker Louis Vuitton (#101). Fouquet's café (#99) is a popular spot for French celebrities, especially movie stars—note the names in the sidewalk in front. Enter if you dare for a €10 espresso. Ladurée café (#75) is also classy but has a welcoming and affordable takeout bakery.

Continuing on, you pass international-brand stores, such as Sephora, Disney, and the Gap. Car buffs should park themselves at the sleek café in the Renault store (#53, open noon-midnight). The car

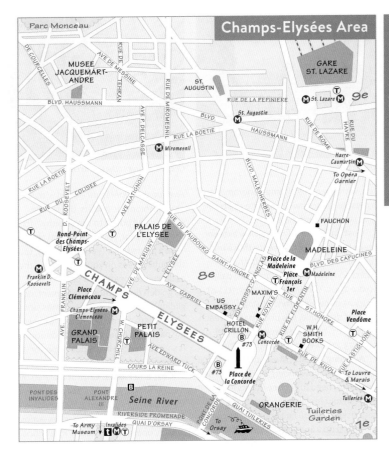

Champs-Elysées Area

exhibits change regularly, but a Formula One racecar made from 300,000 Legos is usually on display.

You can end your walk at the round Rond Point intersection (Mo: Franklin D. Roosevelt) or continue to obelisk-studded Place de la Concorde, Paris' largest square.

▲▲ARC DE TRIOMPHE

Napoleon had the magnificent Arc de Triomphe commissioned to commemorate his victory at the 1805 battle of Austerlitz. The foot of the arch is a stage on which the last two centuries of Parisian history have played out—from the funeral of Napoleon to the goose-stepping arrival of the Nazis to the triumphant return of Charles de Gaulle after the Allied libera-

tion. Examine the carvings on the pillars, featuring a mighty Napoleon and excitable Lady Liberty. Pay your respects at the Tomb of the Unknown Soldier. Then climb the 284 steps to the observation deck up

Arc de Triomphe

Opéra Garnier

Chagall ceiling at the Opéra Garnier

top, with sweeping skyline panoramas and a mesmerizing view down onto the traffic that swirls around the arch.

Cost and Hours: Free to view exterior; steps to rooftop-€12, free for those under age 18, free on first Sun of month Oct-March, covered by Museum Pass; daily 10:00-23:00, Oct-March until 22:30, last entry 45 minutes before closing; Place Charles de Gaulle, use underpass to reach arch, Mo: Charles de Gaulle-Etoile, tel. 01 55 37 73 77, www.paris-arc-de-triomphe.fr.

Avoiding Lines: A Museum Pass lets you bypass the slooow underground ticket line, unless you need to get free tickets for kids. You can tour much of the base of the Arc sans ticket, but you need one for the climb to the top (in a line you can't avoid). Lines disappear after 17:00—come for sunset.

Opéra Neighborhood

The glittering Garnier opera house anchors this neighborhood of broad boulevards and grand architecture. This area is also nirvana for high-end shoppers, with the opulent Galeries Lafayette and Printemps stores, and the sumptuous shops that line Place Vendôme and Place de la Madeleine. For a self-guided shopping stroll and a map of this area, see page 181.

▲▲OPERA GARNIER (OPERA NATIONAL DE PARIS—PALAIS GARNIER)

A gleaming grand theater of the belle époque, the Palais Garnier was built for Napoleon III and finished in 1875. From Avenue de l'Opéra, once lined with Paris' most fashionable haunts, the facade suggests "all power to the wealthy." To see the interior, you have several choices: Take a guided tour (your best look), tour the public areas on your own (using the audioguide), or attend a performance. Its golden decor (mostly gold paint, not gilding) features statues, columns, and chandeliers, all set off by colorful ceiling paintings. Note that the auditorium is sometimes off-limits due to performances and rehearsals.

Cost and Hours: €11, not covered by Museum Pass, generally daily 10:00-16:30, mid-July-Aug until 18:00, closes for rehearsals and performances—most reliably open 10:00-13:00; 8 Rue Scribe, Mo: Opéra, RER/Train-A: Auber, www.operadeparis.fr/en/visits/palais-garnier.

Tours: The €5 audioguide gives a good self-guided tour. Guided tours in English run July-Aug at 11:00 and 14:30 daily; Sept-June Wed, Sat, and Sun only; check website below for off-season tours and to confirm times year-round, arrive 30 minutes early for security screening (€15.50, includes entry, 1.5 hours, tel. 01 42 46 72 40 or 01 71 25 24 23, www.cultival.fr/en).

Rick's Tip: Across the street from the Opéra Garnier is the illustrious **Café de la Paix** *(on Place de l'Opéra). It's been a meeting spot for the local glitterati for generations. If you can afford the coffee, this spot offers a delightful break.*

Baron Georges-Eugène Haussmann

The elegantly uniform streets that make Paris so Parisian are the work of Baron Haussmann (1809-1891), who oversaw the modernization of the city in the mid-19th century. He cleared out the cramped, higgledy-piggledy, unhygienic medieval cityscape and replaced it with broad, straight boulevards lined with stately buildings and linked by modern train stations.

The quintessential view of Haussmann's work is from the pedestrian island immediately in front of the Opéra Garnier. You're surrounded by Paris circa 1870, when it was the capital of the world. Gaze down the surrounding boulevards to find the column of Place Vendôme in one direction, and the Louvre in another. Haussmann's uniform, cohesive buildings are all five stories tall, with angled, black slate roofs and formal facades. The balconies on the second and fifth floors match those of their neighbors, creating strong lines of perspective as the buildings stretch down the boulevard.

But there was more than aesthetics to the plan. In pre-Haussmann Paris, angry rioters would take to the narrow streets, setting up barricades to hold back government forces (as made famous in Victor Hugo's *Les Misérables*). With Haussmann's new design, government troops could circulate easily and fire cannons down the long, straight boulevards. A whiff of "grapeshot"—chains, nails, and other buckshot-type shrapnel—could clear out any revolutionaries in a hurry.

Marais Neighborhood and Nearby

Naturally, when in Paris you want to see the big sights—but to experience the city, you also need to visit a vital neighborhood. The Marais fits the bill, with trendy boutiques and art galleries, edgy cafés, narrow streets, leafy squares, Jewish bakeries, aristocratic mansions, and fun nightlife—and it's filled with real Parisians. It's the perfect setting to appreciate the flair of this great city.

Place des Vosges and West

▲▲PLACE DES VOSGES

Henry IV built this centerpiece of the Marais in 1605 and called it "Place Royale." As he'd hoped, it turned the Marais into Paris' most exclusive neighborhood. Walk to the center, where Louis XIII, on horseback, gestures, "Look at this wonderful square my dad built." Study the architecture: nine pavilions (houses) per side. The two highest—at the front and back—were for the king and queen (but were never used). Warm red brickwork—some real, some fake—is topped with sloped slate roofs, chimneys, and another quaint relic of a bygone era: TV antennas.

The insightful writer **Victor Hugo** lived at #6 from 1832 to 1848. (It's at the southeast corner of the square, marked by the French flag.) This was when he wrote much of his most important work, including his biggest hit, *Les Misérables*. Inside this free museum you'll wander through eight plush rooms, enjoy a fine view of the square, and find good WCs (free, Tue-Sun 10:00-18:00, closed Mon; tel. 01 42 72 10 16, http://maisonsvictorhugo.paris.fr).

Sample the flashy art galleries ringing the square (the best ones are behind Louis). Ponder a daring new piece for that blank wall at home. Or consider a pleasant break at one of the recommended eateries on the square.

Relaxing at the Place des Vosges

Picasso Museum

▲▲PICASSO MUSEUM (MUSEE PICASSO)

Whatever you think about Picasso the man, as an artist he was unmatched in the 20th century for his daring and productivity. The Picasso Museum has the world's largest collection of his work—some 400 paintings, sculptures, sketches, and ceramics—spread across five levels of this mansion in the Marais. A visit here walks you through the full range of this complex man's life and art.

Cost and Hours: €12.50, covered by Museum Pass, free on first Sun of month and for those under age 18 with ID; open Tue-Fri 10:30-18:00, Sat-Sun from 9:30, closed Mon, last entry 45 minutes before closing; audioguide-€5, 5 Rue de Thorigny, Mo: St. Sébastien-Froissart, St-Paul, or Chemin Vert, tel. 01 42 71 25 21, www.museepicassoparis.fr.

Visiting the Museum: The museum's fine audioguide is updated with each change to the exhibit. Floors 1 and 2 are the core of the museum with selections from its permanent collection. Floor 3 always features paintings from Picasso's personal collection—works of his that he never sold, and paintings by contemporaries (such as Miró, Matisse, Cézanne, and Braque) who inspired him.

Early Years and Early Cubism: In 1900, Picasso set out to make his mark in Paris. The brash Spaniard quickly became a poor, homesick foreigner, absorbing the styles of many painters while searching for his own artist's voice. When his best friend committed suicide, Picasso plunged into a **Blue Period,** painting emaciated beggars, hard-eyed pimps, and himself, bundled up against the cold, with eyes all cried out (*Autoportrait*, 1901).

In 1904, Picasso got a steady girlfriend, and suddenly saw the world through rose-colored glasses (the **Rose Period,** though the museum has very few works from this time). With his next-door neighbor, Georges Braque, Picasso invented Cubism, a fragmented, "cube"-shaped style. He'd fracture a figure (such as the musician in *Man with a Mandolin,* 1911) into a barely recognizable jumble of facets. Picasso sketched reality from every angle, then pasted it all together, a composite of different views.

Cubist Experiments: Modern art was being born. The first stage had been so-called Analytic Cubism: breaking the world down into small facets, to "analyze" the subject from every angle. Now it was time to "synthesize" it back together with the real world (Synthetic Cubism). Picasso created "constructions" that were essentially still-life paintings (a 2-D illusion) augmented with glued-on, real-life materials—wood, paper, rope, or chair caning (the real 3-D world). In a few short years, Picasso had turned painting in the direction it would go for the next 50 years.

During the gray and sad years of World War II, Picasso stayed in Paris. His beloved mother had died, and he endured an endless, bitter divorce while juggling his two longtime, feuding mistresses—as well as the occasional fling.

Later Years: At war's end, Picasso left Paris and all that emotional baggage behind, finding fun in the sun in the south of France. Sixty-five-year-old Pablo Picasso was reborn, enjoying worldwide fame. Picasso's Riviera works set the tone for the rest of his life—sunny, light-hearted, childlike, experimenting in new media, and using motifs of the sea, Greek mythology (fauns, centaurs), and animals (birds, goats, and pregnant baboons). Picasso was fertile to the end, still painting with bright thick colors at age 91.

▲▲POMPIDOU CENTER (CENTRE POMPIDOU)

One of Europe's greatest collections of far-out modern art is housed in the Musée National d'Art Moderne, on the fourth and fifth floors of this colorful exoskeletal building. Created ahead of its time, the modern and contemporary art in this collection is still waiting for the world to catch up.

The Pompidou Center and the square that fronts it are lively, with lots of people, street theater, and activity inside and out—a perpetual street fair. Kids of any age enjoy the fun, colorful fountain (an homage to composer Igor Stravinsky) next to the Pompidou Center.

Cost and Hours: €14, free on first Sun of month, Museum Pass covers permanent collection and escalators to sixth-floor panoramic views (plus occasional special exhibits); permanent collection open Wed-Mon 11:00-21:00, closed Tue, ticket counters close at 20:00; rest of the building open until 22:00 (Thu until 23:00); arrive after 17:00 to avoid crowds (mainly for special exhibits); free "Centre Pompidou" app, café on mezzanine, pricey view restaurant on level 6, Mo: Rambuteau or Hôtel de Ville, tel. 01 44 78 12 33, www.centrepompidou.fr.

Visiting the Museum: The Pompidou's "permanent" collection...isn't. But while

Ⓐ *Pompidou Center*

Ⓑ *Otto Dix,* Portrait of Journalist Sylvia von Harden

Ⓒ *Joan Miró,* Le Catalan

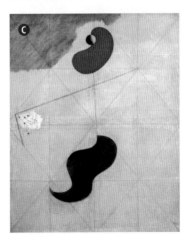

Marais Neighborhood & Nearby

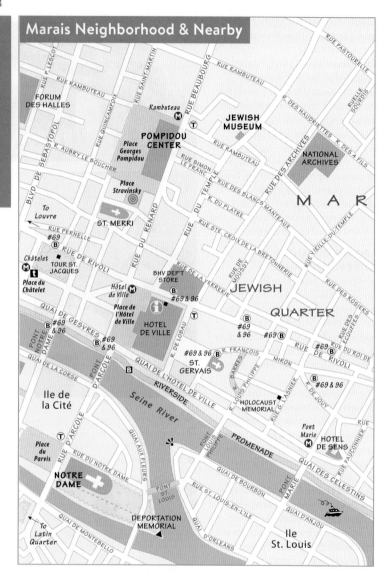

the paintings (and other pieces) change, the museum generally keeps the artists and various styles in a set order. You'll find this general scheme: ground floor—all services; basement—always photography exhibits and always free; floors 1 and 6—temporary exhibits (galleries 1-4); floors 4 and 5—the museum (what you're likely

here for). The museum starts on floor 5 with a one-way route, with the collection displayed in chronological order filling rooms in numerical order. It's that easy.

Use the museum's floor plans (posted on the wall) to find specific artists. See the classics—Picasso, Matisse, etc.—but be sure to leave time to browse the

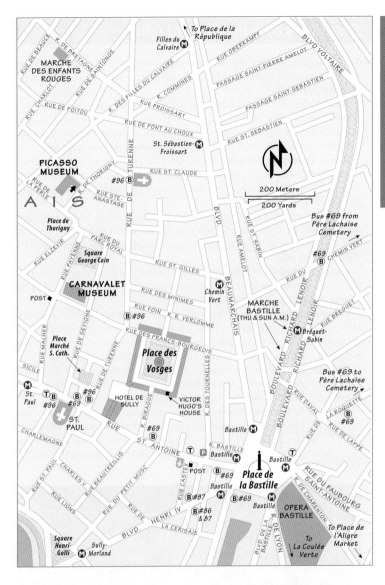

thought-provoking and fun art of more recent artists.

As you tour the Pompidou, remember that most of the artists, including foreigners, spent their formative years in Paris. In the 1910s, funky Montmartre was the mecca of Modernism—the era of Picasso, Braque, and Matisse. In the 1920s, the center shifted to the grand cafés of Montparnasse, where painters mingled with American expats such as Ernest Hemingway and Gertrude Stein. During World War II, it was Jean-Paul Sartre's Existentialist scene around St. Germain-des-Prés. After World War II, the global art focus moved to New York, but by the late 20th

Best Views over the City of Light

The brilliance of the City of Light is best appreciated by rising above it all. Many of the viewpoints listed here are free or covered by the Museum Pass; otherwise, expect to pay €8-20.

Eiffel Tower: It's hard to find a grander view of Paris than from the tower's second level (for most, it's better than from the top level). Go around sunset and stay after dark to see the tower illuminated; or go in the early morning to avoid the midday haze and crowds (not covered by Museum Pass, see page 160).

Arc de Triomphe: Without a doubt, this is the perfect place to see the glamorous Champs-Elysées (if you can manage the 284 steps). It's great during the day, but even greater at night, when the boulevard positively glitters (covered by Museum Pass, see page 169).

Steps of Sacré-Cœur: Join the party on Paris' only hilltop. Walk uphill, then hunker down on Sacré-Cœur's steps to enjoy the sunset and territorial views over Paris. Stay in Montmartre for dinner, then see the view again after dark (free, see page 178).

Galeries Lafayette or **Printemps:** Take the escalator to the top floor of either department store (they sit side by side) for a stunning overlook of the old Opéra district (free, see page 181).

Pompidou Center: Take the escalator up and admire the beautiful cityscape along with the exciting modern art (the sixth floor is the top, but the fifth-floor outdoor terrace is more enjoyable). There may be better views over Paris, but this is the best one from a museum (covered by Museum Pass, see page 173).

Place du Trocadéro: This square, a 20-minute walk from the Eiffel Tower, is *the* place to see the tower. Come for a look at Monsieur Eiffel's festive creation day or night (when the tower is lit up), before or after your tower visit.

Arab World Institute: This building near Ile St. Louis has 180-degree views over the river from its roof terrace (free for views, Tue-Sun 10:00-18:00, closed Mon; for terrace view don't wait in special exhibit line—ask for entrance for *"la terrasse"*; 1 Rue des Fossés Saint-Bernard, Place Mohammed V, Mo: Jussieu, tel. 01 40 51 38 38, www.imarabe.org).

Père Lachaise Cemetery

century, Paris had reemerged as a cultural touchstone for the world of modern art.

Rick's Tip: *The sixth floor of the Pompidou has **stunning views of the Paris city-scape.** Your Pompidou ticket or Museum Pass gets you there, or you can buy the €5 View of Paris ticket (good for the sixth floor only; doesn't include museum entry).*

East of Place des Vosges
▲▲PERE LACHAISE CEMETERY (CIMETIERE DU PERE LACHAISE)
Littered with the tombstones of many of the city's most illustrious dead, this is your best one-stop look at Paris' fascinating, romantic past residents. More like a small city, the cemetery is big and confusing, but it holds the graves of Frédéric Chopin, Molière, Edith Piaf, Oscar Wilde, Gertrude Stein, Jim Morrison, Héloïse and Abélard, and many more.

Cost and Hours: Free, Mon-Fri 8:00-18:00, Sat from 8:30, Sun from 9:00, until 17:30 in winter; two blocks from Mo: Gambetta (do not go to Mo: Père

Lachaise) and two blocks from bus #69's last stop; tel. 01 55 25 82 10, searchable map available at unofficial website: www. pere-lachaise.com.

Visiting the Cemetery: Enclosed by a massive wall and lined with 5,000 trees, the peaceful, car-free lanes and dirt paths of Père Lachaise cemetery encourage parklike meandering. Named for Father *(Père)* La Chaise, whose job was listening to Louis XIV's sins, the cemetery is relatively new, having opened in 1804 to accommodate Paris' expansion. Today, this 100-acre city of the dead (pop. 70,000) still accepts new residents, but real estate prices are sky high (a 21-square-foot plot costs more than €11,000).

This cemetery, with thousands of graves and tombs crammed every which way, has only a few pedestrian pathways to help you navigate. The map available from a nearby florist can also help guide you. I recommend taking a one-way tour through the cemetery, starting from the convenient Métro/bus stops at Place Gambetta, connecting a handful of graves from some of this necropolis' best-known residents, and taking a last bow at either the Père Lachaise or Philippe Auguste Métro stops, or a nearby bus #69 stop.

🎧 Download my free Père Lachaise Cemetery audio tour.

Rick's Tip: *To* **beat the crowds at Montmartre,** *come on a weekday or early on weekend mornings.*

Montmartre

Paris' highest hill, topped by Sacré-Cœur Basilica and rated ▲▲, is best known as the home of cabaret nightlife and bohemian artists. Struggling painters, poets, dreamers, and drunkards came here for cheap rent, untaxed booze, rustic landscapes, and views of the underwear of high-kicking cancan girls at the Moulin Rouge. These days, the hill is equal parts charm and kitsch—still vaguely village-like but mobbed with tourists and pickpockets on sunny weekends. Come for a bit of history, a getaway from Paris' noisy boulevards, and the view.

▲SACRE-CŒUR

You'll spot Sacré-Cœur, the Byzantine-looking white basilica atop Montmartre, from most viewpoints in Paris. Though only 130 years old, it's impressive and iconic, with a climbable dome, and marks Paris' highest natural point (430 feet). The church was finished only a century ago by Parisians humiliated by German invaders. Roman Catholics built it as a kind of penance for how the surrounding neighborhood sowed rebelliousness and division. Many French people were disgusted that in 1871 their government actually shot its own citizens, the Communards, who held out here on Montmartre after the French leadership surrendered to the Prussians.

Cost and Hours: Church-free, daily 6:00-22:30; dome-€6, not covered by Museum Pass, daily 8:30-20:00, Oct-

April until 17:00; modest dress required, tel. 01 53 41 89 00, www.sacre-coeur-montmartre.com.

Getting There: You can take the Métro to the Anvers stop (to avoid the stairs up to Sacré-Cœur, use one more Métro ticket and ride up on the funicular). Alternatively, from Place Pigalle, you can take bus #40, which drops you right by Sacré-Cœur (Funiculaire stop, costs one Métro ticket, 4/hour). A taxi from near the Seine saves time and avoids sweat (about €20, €25 at night).

Visiting the Church: The Sacré-Cœur (Sacred Heart) Basilica's exterior, with its onion domes and bleached-bone pallor, looks ancient, but it was finished only a century ago by Parisians humiliated by German invaders. The five-domed, Roman-Byzantine-looking basilica took 44 years to build (1875-1919). It stands on a foundation of 83 pillars sunk 130

Sacré-Cœur

feet deep, necessary because the ground beneath was honeycombed with gypsum mines. The exterior is laced with gypsum, which whitens with age.

Take a clockwise spin around the crowded interior to see impressive mosaics, a statue of St. Thérèse, a scale model of the church, and three stained-glass windows dedicated to Joan of Arc. Pause near the Stations of the Cross mosaic to give St. Peter's bronze foot a rub. For an unobstructed panoramic view of Paris, climb 260 feet (300 steps) up the tight and claustrophobic spiral stairs to the top of the dome.

EXPERIENCES

Seine Cruises

Several companies run one-hour boat cruises on the Seine. For a fun experience, cruise at twilight or after dark. The first three companies are convenient to Rue Cler hotels, and run daily year-round (April-Oct 10:00-22:30, 2-3/hour; Nov-March shorter hours, runs hourly). Check their websites for discounts.

Bateaux-Mouches departs from Pont de l'Alma's right bank and has the biggest open-top, double-decker boats (higher up means better views). But this company caters to tour groups, making their boats jammed and noisy (€13.50, kids 4-12-€6, tel. 01 42 25 96 10, www.bateaux-mouches.fr). **Vedettes de Paris** boats also anchor below the Eiffel Tower and offer better outdoor seating on most of their boats (€15 standard one-hour cruise, €12 one-way, €16 round-trip with stop at Notre-Dame, www.vedettesdeparis.fr). **Vedettes du Pont Neuf** offers essentially the same one-hour tour as the other companies with smaller boats; it starts and ends at Pont Neuf. The boats feature a live guide whose delivery (in English and French) may be as stiff as a recorded narration (€14, kids 4-12-€7, tip requested, nearly 2/hour, daily 10:30-22:30, tel. 01 46 33 98 38, www.vedettesdupontneuf.com).

Bus Restaurants

Dine to soft jazz as you glide along Paris' most famous boulevards and around its greatest monuments on an elegant double-decker bus restaurant. Dining is on the upper deck well above cars below, affording great views and glimpses into Parisian apartments. Buses are designed from scratch for this purpose with a kitchen, drink holders, big windows, toilets, and more. They move slowly, making drinking and dining a breeze. Two companies offer these tours: **Bus Toqué** (€56 for lunch, €90 for dinner, mobile 06 21 40 20 41, www.bustoque.fr) and **Bustronome** (tel. 09 54 44 45 55, www.bustronome.com).

Shopping

Wandering among elegant boutiques provides a break from the heavy halls of the Louvre, and, if you approach it right, a little cultural enlightenment. Even if you don't intend to buy anything, budget some time for window shopping, or, as the French call it, *faire du lèche-vitrines* ("window licking").

Before you enter a Parisian store, remember the following points:

In small stores, always say, *"Bonjour, Madame* or *Mademoiselle* or *Monsieur"* when entering. And remember to say *"Au revoir, Madame* or *Mademoiselle* or *Monsieur"* when leaving.

The customer is not always right. In fact, figure the clerk is doing you a favor by waiting on you.

Except in department stores, it's not normal for the customer to handle clothing. Ask first before you pick up an item: *"Je peux?"* (zhuh puh), meaning, "Can I?"

Saturday afternoons are *très* busy, but stores are generally closed on Sunday. Exceptions include the Galeries Lafayette store near the Opéra Garnier, the Carrousel du Louvre (underground shopping mall at the Louvre with a Printemps department store), and some shops near Sèvres-Babylone, along the Champs-Elysées, and in the Marais.

Don't feel obliged to buy. If a shop-keeper offers assistance, say, *"Je regarde, merci."* (Just looking, thank you.)

For information on VAT refunds and customs regulations, see the Practicalities chapter.

Department Stores (Les Grands Magasins)

Parisian department stores begin with their showy perfume and purse sections, almost always central on the ground floor. Helpful information desks are usually located at the main entrances near the perfume section (with floor plans in English). Stores generally have affordable restaurants (some with view terraces) and a good selection of fairly priced souvenirs and toys. Opening hours are customarily Monday through Saturday from 10:00 to 19:00 or 20:00. The major stores are open on Sundays and later on Thursdays, and all are jammed on Saturdays. You'll find both Galeries Lafayette and Printemps stores in several neighborhoods. The most convenient and most elegant sit side by side behind the Opéra Garnier, complementing that monument's similar, classy ambience (Mo: Chaussée d'Antin-La Fayette, Havre-Caumartin, or Opéra).

Boutique Strolls

Most shops are closed on Sunday, which is the perfect day to head for the **Marais,** where many shops remain open on Sunday (and close on Saturday) and most of the neighborhood is off-limits to cars. For eclectic, avant-garde boutiques, peruse the artsy shops between Place des Vosges and the Pompidou Center.

◯ PLACE DE LA MADELEINE TO PLACE DE L'OPERA

The ritzy streets connecting several high-priced squares—Place de la Madeleine, Place de la Concorde, Place Vendôme, and Place de l'Opéra—form a miracle mile of gourmet food shops, glittering jewelry stores, posh hotels, exclusive clothing

Sampling perfume

boutiques, and people who spend more on clothes in one day than I do in a year. To trace this route, see the "Opéra Neighborhood" map.

Start at Eglise de la Madeleine (Mo: Madeleine). In the northeast corner at #24 is the black-and-white awning of **Fauchon.** Founded on this location in 1886, this bastion of over-the-top edibles became famous around the world, catering to the refined tastes of the rich and famous. **Hédiard** (#21, northwest corner of the square) is older than Fauchon, and it's weathered the tourist mobs a bit better, though it may be closed for renovation during your visit. Hédiard's small red containers—of mustards, jams, coffee, candies, and tea—make great souvenirs.

Step inside tiny **La Maison des Truffe** (#19) to get a whiff of the product—truffles, those prized, dank, and dirty cousins of mushrooms. Check out the tiny jars in the display case. The venerable **Mariage Frères** (#17) shop demonstrates how good tea can smell and how beautifully it can be displayed. At **Caviar Kaspia** (#16), you can add caviar, eel, and vodka to your truffle collection.

Continue along, past **Marquise de Sévigné** chocolates (#11) and Fauchon's new razzle-dazzle hotel, then cross to the island in the middle of **Boulevard Malesherbes.** When the street officially opened in 1863, it ushered in the Golden Age of this neighborhood. Continue across Boulevard Malesherbes. Straight

Place de la Madeleine Shopping Walk

ahead is **Patrick Roger Chocolates** (#3), famous for its chocolates, and even more so for M. Roger's huge, whimsical, 150-pound chocolate sculptures of animals and fanciful creatures.

Turning right down **Rue Royale,** there's Dior, Chanel, and Gucci. At Rue St. Honoré, turn left and cross Rue Royale, pausing in the middle for a great view both ways. Check out **Ladurée** (#16) for an out-of-this-world pastry break in the busy 19th-century tea salon, or to just pick up some world-famous macarons. Continue east down **Rue St. Honoré.** The street is a three-block parade of chic boutiques—L'Oréal cosmetics, Jimmy Choo shoes, Valentino, and so on. Looking for a €1,000 handbag? This is your spot.

Find the shortcut on the left at #362 or turn left on Rue de Castiglione to reach **Place Vendôme.** This octagonal square is *très* elegant—enclosed by symmetrical Mansart buildings around a 150-foot

column. On the left side is the original Hôtel Ritz, opened in 1898. The square is also known for its upper-crust jewelry and designer stores—Van Cleef & Arpels, Dior, Chanel, Cartier, and others (if you have to ask how much...).

Leave Place Vendôme by continuing straight, up **Rue de la Paix**—strolling by still more jewelry, high-priced watches, and crystal—and enter **Place de l'Opéra:** You're in the middle of Right Bank glamour. Here you'll find the Opéra Garnier (described under Sights). If you're shopping until you're dropping, the Galeries Lafayette and Printemps department stores are located a few blocks up Rue Halévy.

SEVRES-BABYLONE TO ST. SULPICE

This Left Bank shopping area lets you sample smart clothing boutiques and clever window displays—and be tempted by tasty treats—while enjoying one of Paris' more attractive and boutique-filled neighborhoods (see "Left Bank" map, earlier).

Start at the Sèvres-Babylone Métro stop (take the Métro). You'll find the **Bon Marché,** Paris' oldest department store. Continue along Rue de Sèvres, working your way to Place St. Sulpice and making detours left and right as the spirit moves you. You'll pass some of Paris' smartest boutiques and coolest cafés, such as **Hermès** (at #17), and **Au Sauvignon Café** (at #10). Make a short detour up Rue du Cherche-Midi and find Paris' most celebrated bread—beautiful round loaves with designer crust—at the low-key **Poilâne** at #8. At the end of your walk, spill into Place St. Sulpice, with its big, twin-tower church. **Café de la Mairie** is a great spot to sip a *café crème,* admire the lovely square, and consider your next move. If you'd like more shopping options, you're in the heart of boutique shopping. As for me, stick a *fourchette* in me—I'm done.

Nightlife

Paris is brilliant after dark. Save energy from your day's sightseeing and experience the City of Light lit. Whether it's a concert at Sainte-Chapelle, a boat ride on the Seine, a walk in Montmartre, a hike up the Arc de Triomphe, or a late-night café, you'll see Paris at its best.

Jazz and Blues Clubs

With a lively mix of American, French, and international musicians, Paris has been an internationally acclaimed jazz capital since World War II. You'll pay €12-25 to enter a jazz club (may include one drink; if not, expect to pay €5-10 per drink; beer is cheapest). See *L'Officiel des Spectacles* under "Concerts" for listings, or, even better, the *Paris Voice* website. You can also check each club's website (all have English versions), or drop by the clubs to check out the calendars posted on their front doors. Music starts after 21:00 in most clubs. Some offer dinner concerts from about 20:30 on. Here are several good bets:

Caveau de la Huchette: This fun, characteristic old jazz/dance club fills an ancient Latin Quarter cellar with live jazz and frenzied dancing every night (admission about €15, €10 for those under 25, drinks from €7, daily from 21:30, no reservations needed, buy tickets at the door, 5 Rue de la Huchette, Mo: St. Michel, tel. 01 43 26 65 05, www.caveaudelahuchette.fr).

Other Venues: For a spot teeming with late-night activity and jazz, go to the two-block-long Rue des Lombards, at Boulevard Sébastopol, midway between the river and the Pompidou Center (Mo: Châtelet). **Au Duc des Lombards** is one of the most popular and respected jazz clubs in Paris, with concerts nightly in a great, plush, 110-seat theater-like setting (€30-55, €60-90 with dinner, buy online and arrive early for best seats, reasonable drink prices, shows usually at 19:30 and 21:30, 42 Rue des Lombards, tel. 01 42 33 22 88, www.ducdeslombards.fr). **Le Sunside** is just a block away. The club offers two little stages (ground floor and downstairs): "Le Sunset" stage tends toward contemporary world jazz; "le Sunside" stage features more traditional and acoustic jazz (concerts €20-30, a few are free; 60 Rue des Lombards, tel. 01 40 26 46 60, www.sunset-sunside.com).

Paris churches host frequent concerts.

Extend your sightseeing into the night.

Classical Concerts

For classical music on any night, consult *L'Officiel des Spectacles* magazine (check "Classique" under "Concerts" for listings), and look for posters at tourist-oriented churches. From March through November, these churches regularly host concerts: St. Sulpice, St. Germain-des-Prés, La Madeleine, St. Eustache, St. Julien-le-Pauvre, and Sainte-Chapelle.

Sainte-Chapelle: Enjoy the pleasure of hearing Mozart, Bach, or Vivaldi, surrounded by 800 years of stained glass (unheated—bring a sweater). The acoustical quality is surprisingly good. There are usually two concerts per evening, at about 19:00 and 20:30; specify which one you want when you buy or reserve your ticket. VIP tickets get you a seat in rows 3-10 (about €55), Prestige tickets cover the next 10 rows (€45), and Normal tickets are the last five rows (€35). Seats are unassigned within each section, so arrive at least 30 minutes early to get through the security line and snare a good view.

You can book at the box office, by phone, or online. Several companies sell tickets online. The small box office (with schedules and tickets) is to the left of the chapel entrance gate (8 Boulevard du Palais, Mo: Cité), or call 01 42 77 65 65 or 06 67 30 65 65 for schedules and reservations. You can leave your message in English—just speak clearly and spell your name. You can check schedules and buy your ticket at www.euromusicproductions.fr or www.ticketac.com).

Other Venues: Look also for daytime concerts in parks, such as the Luxembourg Garden. Even the Galeries Lafayette department store offers concerts. Many of these concerts are free (*entrée libre*), such as the Sunday atelier concert sponsored by the American Church (generally Sept-June at 17:00 but not every week and not in Dec, 65 Quai d'Orsay, Mo: Invalides, RER/Train-C: Pont de l'Alma, tel. 01 40 62 05 00, www.acparis.org). The Army Museum offers inexpensive afternoon and evening classical music concerts all year round (for programs—in French only—see www.musee-armee.fr). There are also concerts at the Louvre's auditorium (www.louvre.fr/en/auditorium-louvre/music).

Night Walks

Go for an evening walk to best appreciate the City of Light. Break for ice cream, pause at a café, and enjoy the sidewalk entertainers as you join the post-dinner Parisian parade. (Avoid poorly lit areas and stick to main thoroughfares.)

Trocadéro and Eiffel Tower: Worth ▲▲▲, this is one of Paris' most spectacular views at night. Take the Métro to the Trocadéro stop and join the party on Place du Trocadéro for a magnificent view of the glowing Eiffel Tower. It's a festival of hawkers, gawkers, drummers, and entertainers.

Champs-Elysées and the Arc de Triomphe: The ▲▲ Avenue des Champs-Elysées is best after dark. Start at the Arc de Triomphe (open late), then stroll down Paris' glittering grand promenade.

Ile St. Louis and Notre-Dame: This ▲▲ stroll features floodlit views of Notre-Dame and a taste of the Latin Quarter. Find your way to the east end of Rue St. Louis-en-l'Ile, stopping for dinner—or at least a Berthillon ice cream (at #31) or Amorino Gelati (at #47). At the west end of Ile St. Louis, cross Pont St. Louis to Ile de la Cité, with a view of Notre-Dame (undergoing construction). Cross the bridge to the Left Bank to stroll through the lively Latin Quarter.

SLEEPING

I've focused my recommendations on three safe, handy, and colorful neighborhoods: the village-like Rue Cler (near the Eiffel Tower); the artsy and trendy Marais (near Place de la Bastille); and the historic island of Ile St. Louis (next door to Notre-Dame).

Rue Cler Neighborhood
(7th arr., Mo: Ecole Militaire, La Tour Maubourg, Invalides)
Rue Cler is so French that when I step out of my hotel in the morning, I feel like I must have been a poodle in a previous life. This is a neighborhood of wide, tree-lined boulevards, stately apartment buildings, and lots of Americans. Hotels here are a fair value, considering the elegance of the neighborhood. And for sightseeing, you're within walking distance of the Eiffel Tower, Army Museum, Seine River, Champs-Elysées, and Orsay and Rodin museums.

In the Heart of Rue Cler
Many of my readers stay in the Rue Cler neighborhood. If you want to disappear into Paris, choose a hotel elsewhere. The following hotels are within Camembert-smelling distance of Rue Cler.

$$$ Hôtel Bosquet*** is an exceptionally good hotel in an ideal location, with comfortable public spaces and well-configured rooms that are large by local standards and feature effective darkness blinds. The staff is politely formal (RS%—use code "RSDEAL"; good but pricey breakfast buffet with eggs and sausage, 19 Rue du Champ de Mars, tel. 01 47 05 25 45, www.hotel-paris-bosquet.com, hotel@relaisbosquet.com).

$$ Hôtel du Champ de Mars*** is a top choice, brilliantly located barely 10 steps off Rue Cler. This plush little hotel has a small-town feel from top to bottom. The adorable rooms are snug but lovingly kept by hands-on owners Françoise and Stéphane, and single rooms can work as tiny doubles. It's popular, so book well ahead (continental breakfast only, 30 yards off Rue Cler at 7 Rue du Champ de Mars, tel. 01 45 51 52 30, www.hotelduchampdemars.com, hotelduchampdemars@gmail.com).

Near Ecole Militaire Métro Stop
$$$ Hôtel Duquesne Eiffel,*** a few blocks farther from the action, is handsome and hospitable. It features a welcoming lobby, a street-front terrace, comfortable rooms (some with terrific Eiffel Tower views), and connecting rooms that work well for families (RS%, big, hot breakfast—free for Rick Steves readers, 23 Avenue Duquesne, tel. 01 44 42 09 09, www.hde.fr, contact@hde.fr).

$$ Hôtel de France Invalides** is a fair midrange option run by a brother-sister team (Alain and Marie-Hélène). It has contemporary decor and 60 rooms, some with knockout views of Invalides' golden dome (but with some traffic noise and no air-con). Rooms on the courtyard are quieter, smaller, and cheaper (RS%, connecting rooms possible, first breakfast free for Rick Steves readers—maximum of two per party, 102 Boulevard de la Tour Maubourg, tel. 01 47 05 40 49,

Rue Cler Hotels & Restaurants

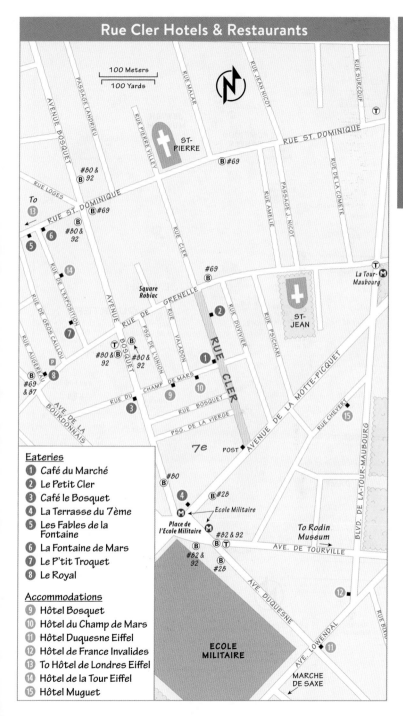

100 Meters
100 Yards

ST-PIERRE

RUE MALAR

RUE JEAN NICOT

RUE SURCOUF

AVENUE BOSQUET

PASSAGE LANDRIEU

RUE PIERRE VILLEY

#80 & 92

RUE LOGES

To ⑬

RUE ST-DOMINIQUE

Ⓑ #69

Ⓑ #80 & 92

⑤

⑥

⑭

RUE DE L'EXPOSITION

Square Robiac

AVENUE

RUE CLER

RUE DE GRENELLE

RUE ST-DOMINIQUE

Ⓑ #69

RUE AMELIE

PASSAGE J. NICOT

RUE DE LA COMETE

Ⓑ #69

La Tour-Maubourg Ⓣ Ⓜ

ST-JEAN

RUE DE GROS CAILLOU

⑦

RUE AUGEREAU

P

Ⓑ #69 & 87

⑧

Ⓣ Ⓑ #80 & 92

#80 & 92

PSG. DE L'UNION

RUE VALADON

RUE DUVIVIER

RUE PSICHARI

❷

❶

RUE CLER

RUE DU CHAMP DE MARS

⑨

⑩

RUE BOSQUET

③

AVE. DE LA BOURDONNAIS

PSG. DE LA VIERGE

AVENUE DE LA MOTTE-PICQUET

RUE CHEVERT

⑮

BLVD. DE LA-TOUR-MAUBOURG

7e   POST ◆

#80 Ⓑ

❹ Ⓑ #28

Ⓜ Ecole Militaire

Place de l'Ecole Militaire Ⓜ

Ⓑ #82 & 92

Ⓑ Ⓣ

#82 & 92 Ⓑ

Ⓑ #28

AVE. DE TOURVILLE

To Rodin Museum

AVE. DUQUESNE

⑫ ◆

ECOLE MILITAIRE

AVE. LOWENDAL

⑪ ◆

RUE BIXIO

MARCHE DE SAXE

Eateries

❶ Café du Marché
❷ Le Petit Cler
❸ Café le Bosquet
❹ La Terrasse du 7ème
❺ Les Fables de la Fontaine
❻ La Fontaine de Mars
❼ Le P'tit Troquet
❽ Le Royal

Accommodations

⑨ Hôtel Bosquet
⑩ Hôtel du Champ de Mars
⑪ Hôtel Duquesne Eiffel
⑫ Hôtel de France Invalides
⑬ To Hôtel de Londres Eiffel
⑭ Hôtel de la Tour Eiffel
⑮ Hôtel Muguet

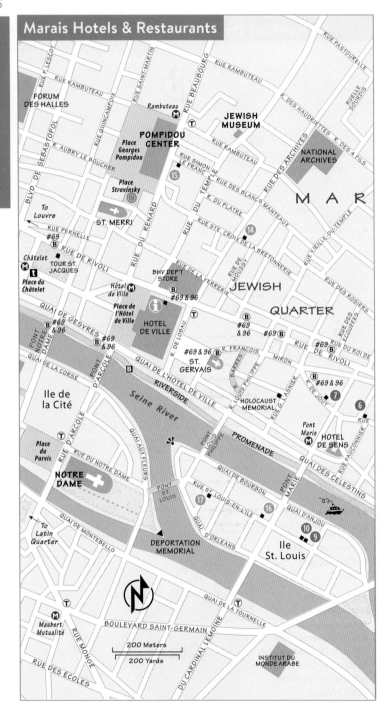

Marais Hotels & Restaurants

FORUM
DES HALLES

RUE P. LESCOT

RUE SAINT-MARTIN

RUE RAMBUTEAU

RUE RAMBUTEAU

RUE PASTOURELLE

RUE BEAUBOURG

RUE QUINCAMPOIX

Rambuteau

JEWISH
MUSEUM

R. DES HAUDRIETTES

R. DES 4 FILS

RUELLE SOURDIS

BLVD. DE SEBASTOPOL

R. AUBRY LE BOUCHER

Place
Georges
Pompidou

POMPIDOU
CENTER

RUE RAMBUTEAU

RUE DES ARCHIVES

NATIONAL
ARCHIVES

To
Louvre

Place
Stravinsky

RUE SIMON
LE FRANC

RUE DU TEMPLE

RUE DES BLANCS MANTEAUX

R. DU PLATRE

M A R

RUE PERNELLE

ST. MERRI

RUE DU RENARD

RUE STE-CROIX DE LA BRETONNERIE

RUE VIEILLE-DU-TEMPLE

#69

RUE DE RIVOLI

Châtelet

TOUR ST.
JACQUES

Place du
Châtelet

Hôtel
de Ville

BHV DEP'T
STORE

RUE DE LA VERRERIE

RUE DE
MOUSSI

JEWISH

RUE DES ROSIERS

Place de
l'Hôtel
de Ville

HOTEL
DE VILLE

#69 & 96

QUARTER

#69
& 96

#69

RUE DES ECOUFFES

QUAI DE GESVRES

#69
& 96

PONT
NOTRE
DAME

#69
& 96

R. DE LOBAU

#69 & 96

R. FRANÇOIS

ST.
GERVAIS

MIRON

RUE
DE
RIVOLI

RUE DU ROI DE

#69

QUAI DE LA CORSE

PONT
D'ARCOLE

QUAI DE L'HOTEL DE VILLE

R. DES
BARRES

LOUIS PHILIPPE

R. DE JOUY

#69 & 96

7

Ile de
la Cité

RIVERSIDE

RUE G. L'ASNIER

HOLOCAUST
MEMORIAL

6

RUE

Seine River

Pont
Marie

HOTEL
DE SENS

RUE FAUCONNIER

Place
du
Parvis

RUE D'ARCOLE

QUAI AUX FLEURS

PROMENADE

PONT
LOUIS
PHILIPPE

QUAI DES CELESTINS

NOTRE
DAME

RUE DU NOTRE DAME

PONT
ST.
LOUIS

QUAI DE BOURBON

RUE ST. LOUIS-EN-L'ILE

16

PONT
MARIE

QUAI D'ANJOU

To
Latin
Quarter

QUAI DE MONTEBELLO

17

DEPORTATION
MEMORIAL

QUAI D'ORLEANS

Ile
St. Louis

10

9

Maubert
Mutualité

RUE MONGE

200 Meters

200 Yards

BOULEVARD SAINT-GERMAIN

QUAI DE LA TOURNELLE

RUE DES ECOLES

DU CARDINAL LEMOINE

INSTITUT DU
MONDE ARABE

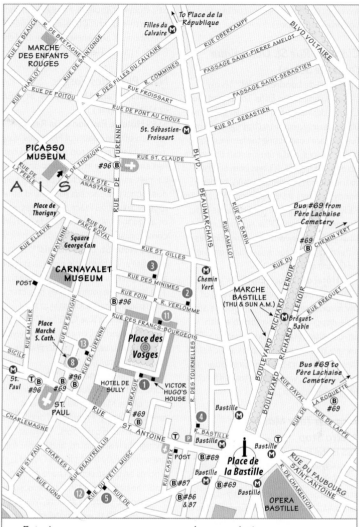

Eateries

1. La Place Royale
2. Chez Janou
3. Le Petit Marché
4. Brasserie Bofinger
5. Le Temps des Cerises
6. Chez Mademoiselle
7. Le Metropolitan
8. Place du Marché Ste. Catherine Eateries
9. L'Orangerie
10. Auberge de la Reine Blanche

Accommodations

11. Hôtel le Pavillon de la Reine
12. Hôtel St. Louis Marais
13. Hôtel Jeanne d'Arc
14. Hôtel de la Bretonnerie
15. Hôtel Beaubourg
16. Hôtel du Jeu de Paume
17. Hôtel Saint-Louis

www.hoteldefrance.com, contact@
hoteldefrance.com).

Closer to Rue St. Dominique (and the Seine)

$$$ Hôtel de Londres Eiffel*** is my closest listing to the Eiffel Tower and the Champ de Mars park. Here you get immaculate, warmly decorated but tight rooms (several are connecting for families), comfy public spaces, and a terrific staff that can't do enough to help. It's less convenient to the Métro (10-minute walk), but very handy to buses #69, #80, and #92, and to RER/Train-C: Pont de l'Alma (some Eiffel Tower view rooms, 1 Rue Augereau, tel. 01 45 51 63 02, www.hotel-paris-londres-eiffel.com, info@londres-eiffel.com, helpful Cédric and Arnaud).

$ Hôtel de la Tour Eiffel** is a solid value on a quiet street near several of my favorite restaurants. The rooms are well-designed and comfortable with air-conditioning (but no breakfast). The six sets of connecting rooms are ideal for families (RS%, 17 Rue de l'Exposition, tel. 01 47 05 14 75, www.hotel-toureiffel.com, hte7@wanadoo.fr).

Near La Tour Maubourg Métro Stop

$$$ Hôtel Muguet*** is quiet, well-located, well-run, and reasonable, with tastefully appointed rooms and a helpful staff (some view rooms, strict 7-day cancellation policy, 11 Rue Chevert, tel. 01 47 05 05 93, www.hotelparismuguet.com, contact@hotelparismuguet.com).

Marais

Those interested in a more central, diverse, and lively urban locale should make the Marais their Parisian home. This is jumbled, medieval Paris at its finest, where classy stone mansions sit alongside trendy bars, antique shops, and fashion-conscious boutiques. The streets are an intriguing parade of artists, students, tourists, immigrants, and baguette-munching babies in strollers. The Marais is also known as a hub of the Parisian gay and lesbian scene.

Near Place des Vosges
(3rd and 4th arr., Mo: Bastille, St-Paul, or Hôtel de Ville)

$$$$ Hôtel le Pavillon de la Reine,***** 15 steps off the beautiful Place des Vosges, merits its stars with top service and comfort and exquisite attention to detail, from its melt-in-your-couch lobby to its luxurious rooms (free access to spa and fitness room, parking, 28 Place des Vosges, tel. 01 40 29 19 19, www.pavillon-de-la-reine.com, contact@pavillon-de-la-reine.com).

$$$ Hôtel St. Louis Marais*** is an intimate and sharp little hotel that sits on a quiet street a few blocks from the river. The handsome rooms have character... and spacious bathrooms (skip their 3 annex rooms, 1 Rue Charles V, Mo: Sully-Morland, tel. 01 48 87 87 04, www.saintlouismarais.com, marais@saintlouis-hotels.com).

$$ Hôtel Jeanne d'Arc*** is a lovely hotel that's ideally located for connoisseurs of the Marais who don't need air-conditioning. Here, artful decor meets stone walls and oak floors, rooms are thoughtfully appointed, and corner rooms are wonderfully bright in the City of Light. Rooms on the street can have some noise until the bars close (family rooms, some view rooms, 3 Rue de Jarente, Mo: St-Paul, tel. 01 48 87 62 11, www.hoteljeannedarc.com, information@hoteljeannedarc.com).

Near the Pompidou Center
(4th arr., Mo: St-Paul, Hôtel de Ville, or Rambuteau)

$$ Hôtel de la Bretonnerie*** makes a fine Marais home. Located three blocks from the Hôtel de Ville, it has a warm, welcoming lobby and helpful staff. Its 30 good-value rooms are on the larger side with an antique, open-beam warmth (family rooms, free breakfast for Rick Steves readers who book direct, no air-con, between Rue Vieille du Temple and Rue des Archives at 22 Rue Ste. Croix de la Bretonnerie, tel. 01 48 87 77 63, www. hotelparismaraisbretonnerie.com, hotel@ bretonnerie.com).

$$ Hôtel Beaubourg*** is a top value on a small street in the shadow of the Pompidou Center. The place is surprisingly quiet, and the 28 plush and traditional rooms are well appointed (bigger doubles are worth the extra cost, 11 Rue Simon Le Franc, Mo: Rambuteau, tel. 01 42 74 34 24, www.hotelbeaubourg.com, reservation@hotelbeaubourg.com).

Ile St. Louis
(4th arr., Mo: Pont Marie)

The peaceful, residential character of this river-wrapped island, with its brilliant location and homemade ice cream, has drawn Americans for decades. There are no budget deals here—all of the hotels are three-star or more—though prices are respectable considering the level of comfort and wonderful location.

$$$$ Hôtel du Jeu de Paume**** occupies a 17th-century tennis center. Its magnificent lobby and cozy public spaces make it a fine splurge. Greet Lemon (luh-moe), *le chien,* then take a spin in the glass elevator for a half-timbered treehouse experience. The 30 rooms are carefully designed and tasteful, though not particularly spacious (you're paying for the location and public areas). Most rooms face a small garden courtyard; all are pin-drop peaceful (apartments for 4-6 people, 54 Rue St. Louis-en-l'Ile, tel. 01

43 26 14 18, www.jeudepaumehotel.com, info@jeudepaumehotel.com).

$$$ Hôtel Saint-Louis*** blends character with modern comforts. The sharp rooms come with cool stone floors and exposed beams. Rates are reasonable...for the location (some rooms with balcony, iPads available for guest use, 75 Rue St. Louis-en-l'Ile, tel. 01 46 34 04 80, www.saintlouisenlisle.com, isle@saint-louis-hotels.com).

Apartment Rentals

Consider this option if you're traveling as a family, in a group, or staying at least a few nights. Intrepid travelers around the world are accustomed to using Airbnb and VRBO when it comes to renting a vacation apartment; search for places in my recommended hotel neighborhoods. In Paris, you have many additional options among rental agencies, and I've found the following to be the most reliable. Their websites are good and essential to understanding your choices: **Paris Perfect,** www.parisperfect.com; **Adrian Leeds Group,** www.adrianleeds.com; **France Homestyle,** www.francehomestyle.com; **Home Rental Service,** www.homerental.fr; **Haven in Paris,** www.haveninparis.com; **Paris Home,** www.parishome2000.com; **Cobblestone Paris Rentals,** www.cobblestoneparis.com; **Paris for Rent,** www.parisforrent.com; and **Cross-Pollinate,** www.cross-pollinate.com.

Bed-and-Breakfasts

Several agencies can help you go local by staying in a private home in Paris. While prices and quality can range greatly, most rooms have a private bath and run from €85 to €150. Most owners won't take bookings for fewer than two nights. To limit stair-climbing, ask whether the building has an elevator. These agencies have a good selection: **Alcôve & Agapes** (www.bed-and-breakfast-in-paris.com) and **Meeting the French** (http://en.meetingthefrench.com).

EATING

Entire books (and lives) are dedicated to eating in Paris. There is no "Parisian cuisine" to speak of (only French onion soup is truly Parisian), but it draws from the best of France.

My restaurant recommendations are mostly centered on the same great neighborhoods as my hotel listings; you can come home exhausted after a busy day of sightseeing and find a good selection of eateries right around the corner. Serious eaters looking for even more suggestions should consult the always appetizing www.parisbymouth.com, an eating-and-drinking guide to Paris.

To save piles of euros, go to a bakery for takeout, or stop at a café for lunch. Cafés and brasseries are happy to serve a *plat du jour* (plate of the day, about €16-24) or a chef-like salad (about €12-16) day or night. To save even more, consider picnics (tasty takeout dishes available at charcuteries). Try eating your big meal at lunch, when many fine restaurants offer their dinnertime fixed-price *menus* at a reduced price.

Linger longer over dinner—restaurants expect you to enjoy a full meal. Most restaurants I've listed have set-price *menus* between €26 and €40. In most cases, the few extra euros you pay are well spent and open up a variety of better choices. Remember that a service charge is included in the prices (so little or no tipping is expected).

Rue Cler Neighborhood
On Rue Cler
(Mo: Ecole Militaire)
$ Café du Marché boasts the best seats on Rue Cler. The owner's philosophy: Brasserie on speed—crank out good enough food at fair prices to appreciative locals and savvy tourists. It's high-energy, with young waiters who barely have time to smile...*très* Parisian. The chalkboard lists your choices: good, hearty salads or more filling *plats du jour*. Arrive before 19:00 to avoid waiting (serves continuously, daily 11:00-23:00, no reservations, at the corner of Rue Cler and Rue du Champ de Mars, 38 Rue Cler, tel. 01 47 05 51 27).

$ Le Petit Cler is an adorable and popular little bistro with long leather booths, a vintage interior, tight ranks of tiny and cramped tables—indoors and out, and simple, tasty, inexpensive dishes such as €10 omelets and €9 soups. Eating outside here with a view of the Rue Cler action can be marvelous (delicious *pots de crème*, daily, opens early for dinner, arrive early or call in advance, 29 Rue Cler, tel. 01 45 50 17 50).

Close to Ecole Militaire
(Mo: Ecole Militaire)
$$ Café le Bosquet is a contemporary Parisian brasserie where you'll dine for a decent price inside or outside on a broad sidewalk. Come here for standard café fare—salad, French onion soup, *steak-frites*, or a *plat du jour*. Lanky owner "Jeff" offers three-course meals and *plats* (serves nonstop, closed Sun, corner of Rue du Champ de Mars at 46 Avenue Bosquet, tel. 01 45 51 38 13, www.bosquet-paris.com).

$$$ La Terrasse du 7ème is a sprawling, happening café with grand outdoor seating and a living room-like interior with comfy love seats. Chairs face the street, as a meal here is like dinner theater—and the show is slice-of-life Paris (good *salades*, French onion soup, and foie gras, nonstop service daily until at least 24:00, tel. 01 45 55 00 02).

West of Avenue Bosquet
(Mo: Ecole Militaire)
$$$$ Les Fables de la Fontaine is a fine place to relax over a gourmet dinner with appealing seating inside or out on a picturesque square. It has a Michelin star yet maintains fair prices and friendly staff. While the chef's specialty is fish, he also serves a few meat dishes (€75

tasting *menu,* less for à la carte, book ahead on weekends, daily, 131 Rue St. Dominique, tel. 01 44 18 37 55, www. lesfablesdelafontaine.net).

$$$ La Fontaine de Mars, a longtime favorite and neighborhood institution, is charmingly situated on a tiny, jumbled square with tables jammed together for the serious business of eating. Reserve in advance for a table on the ground floor or square, and pass on the upstairs room (superb foie gras and desserts, daily, 129 Rue St. Dominique, tel. 01 47 05 46 44, www.fontainedemars.com).

$$ Le P'tit Troquet is a petite eatery taking you back to the Paris of the 1920s. Anna serves while hubbie José cooks a tasty range of traditional choices. The homey charm of the tight little dining room makes this place a delight (€36 three-course dinner *menu* available for €25 at lunch, dinner service from 18:30, closed Sun, reservations smart, 28 Rue de l'Exposition, tel. 01 47 05 80 39, www.leptittroquet.fr).

$ Le Royal is a tiny neighborhood fixture offering the cheapest meals in the area. This humble time-warp place comes with prices and decor from another era.

Parisians dine here because "it's like eating at home." Gentle Guillaume is a fine host (closed Sat-Sun, 212 Rue de Grenelle, tel. 01 47 53 92 90).

Marais
On or Near Romantic Place des Vosges
(Mo: St-Paul, Bastille, or Chemin Vert)
$$$ La Place Royale offers an exceptional location on the square with comfortable seating inside or out, and is good for a relaxed lunch or dinner. The hearty cuisine is priced well and served nonstop all day, and the lengthy wine list is reasonable. The €42 dinner *menu* comes with three courses, a half-bottle of wine per person, and coffee; or just order a salad—or split one before a main course—and call it good (lunch specials, daily, reserve ahead to dine outside under the arcade, 2 bis Place des Vosges, tel. 01 42 78 58 16).

$$$ Chez Janou, a Provençal bistro, tumbles out of its corner building and fills its broad sidewalk with happy eaters. Don't let the trendy and youthful crowd

The Paris Food Scene

Food Tours

Note that several of the listings under Cooking Classes below also offer food tours.

Paris by Mouth offers well-respected yet casual small-group tours, with a maximum of seven foodies per group (€110/3 hours, includes tastings, www. parisbymouth.com, tasteparisbymouth@gmail.com).

At **Edible Paris,** friendly Canadian Rosa Jackson designs personalized itineraries based on your interests (unguided itineraries-€125-200, guided tours-€300 for 1-2 people, larger groups welcome, mobile 06 81 67 41 22, www.edible-paris. com, rosa@rosajackson.com).

Cooking Classes

At **Les Secrets Gourmands de Noémie,** charming and knowledgeable Noémie shares her culinary secrets with hands-on fun in the kitchen. Courses tackle savory and sweet dishes with the possibility of an add-on market tour (€65-130, 92 Rue Nollet, Mo: La Fourche, mobile 06 64 17 93 32, www.lessecretsgourmands denoemie.com).

Cook'n with Class gets rave reviews for its range of convivial cooking classes from breads to *macarons* to croissants to wine and cheese. There's a maximum of six students (€85-200, 6 Rue Baudelique, Mo: Jules Joffrin or Simplon, mobile 06 31 73 62 77, www.cooknwithclass.com/paris).

La Cuisine Paris has a great variety of classes in English, reasonable prices, and a beautiful space in central Paris (€70-100, €160 for 4-hour class with market tour, also offers gourmet visit to Versailles, 80 Quai de l'Hôtel de Ville, tel. 01 40 51 78 18, www.lacuisineparis.com).

REED is the creation of Catherine Reed, who also runs a restaurant with the same name a few blocks from Rue Cler. Classes are limited to eight students and focus on practical skills—from basic techniques to classic French gastronomy (€145, Sun and Wed at 10:30, 11 Rue Amelie, tel. 01 45 55 88 40, www.reedrestaurant.com).

If you're looking for an upscale demonstration course, you'll find it at **Le Cordon Bleu** (tel. 01 53 68 22 50, www.lcbparis.com) or **Ritz Escoffier Ecole de Gastronomie** (tel. 01 43 16 30 50, www.ritzparis.com).

Wine Tasting

Ô Château is decisively wine-centric, though it also has a respectable restaurant. Their team of sommeliers teach wine-tasting classes in fluent English while you sit in the 18th-century residence of Madame de Pompadour. Classes range from an introductory tasting (€59), to wine-tasting lunches (€75), or three-course dinners with wine pairings (€99). Each tasting lasts about two hours and is usually limited to 12 people; register online using code "RS2019" for a 10-percent discount, or check the website for last-minute deals (68 Rue Jean-Jacques Rousseau, Mo: Louvre-Rivoli or Etienne Marcel, tel. 01 44 73 97 80, www.o-chateau.com).

intimidate you: It's relaxed and charming, with helpful and patient service. The curbside tables are inviting, but I'd sit inside (with very tight seating) to immerse myself in the happy commotion (daily—book ahead or arrive when it opens at 19:00, 2 blocks beyond Place des Vosges at 2 Rue Roger Verlomme, tel. 01 42 72 28 41, www.chezjanou.com).

$$$ Le Petit Marché, popular with tourists, delivers a cozy bistro experience inside and out with friendly service and a tasty cuisine that blends French classics with a slight Asian influence (daily, 9 Rue du Béarn, tel. 01 42 72 06 67).

Near Place de la Bastille
(Mo: Bastille)

$$$ Brasserie Bofinger, an institution for over a century, specializes in seafood and traditional cuisine with Alsatian flair. You'll eat in a sprawling interior, surrounded by brisk, black-and-white-attired waiters. Come here for the one-of-a-kind ambience in the elaborately decorated ground-floor rooms, reminiscent of the Roaring Twenties. Reserve ahead to dine under the grand 1919 *coupole*—avoid eating upstairs—(open daily for lunch and dinner, fun kids' menu, 5 Rue de la Bastille, don't be confused by the lesser "Petite" Bofinger across the street, tel. 01 42 72 87 82, www.bofingerparis.com).

$$$ Le Temps des Cerises is a warm place with wads of character, a young and lively vibe, tight inside seating, and a couple of outdoor tables. (There are a few more upstairs that I'd avoid.) Come for a glass of wine at the small zinc bar, and stay for a very tasty dinner. Owner Ben takes good care of his guests and serves generous portions (reasonable wine list, daily, at the corner of Rue du Petit Musc and Rue de la Cerisaie, tel. 01 42 72 08 63).

In the Heart of the Marais
(Mo: St-Paul)

$$$ Chez Mademoiselle's country-elegant, candlelit decor recalls charming owner

Alexia's previous career as a French *comédienne.* Enjoy a French-paced (a.k.a. slow) dinner in a relaxing atmosphere (tables have generous spacing) inside or at a sidewalk table. Let Alexia share her enthusiasm for her seasonal dishes before you choose (good wine list, daily from 19:30, 16 Rue Charlemagne, tel. 01 42 72 14 16).

$$ Le Metropolitan is a tiny, easygoing bistro serving top-quality cuisine to those in the know. The young chef's dishes are creative and delicious. Come early (opens at 19:00) or book ahead (closed Sun, 8 Rue de Jouy, tel. 09 81 20 37 38, www.metroresto.fr).

$$ On Place du Marché Ste. Catherine: This small, romantic square, just off Rue St. Antoine, is cloaked in extremely Parisian, leafy-square ambience. It feels like the Latin Quarter but classier. On a balmy evening, this is a neighborhood favorite, with a handful of restaurants offering mediocre cuisine (you're here for the setting). It's also family-friendly: Most places serve French hamburgers, and kids can dance around the square while parents breathe. You'll find three French bistros with similar features and menus: **Le Marché, Chez Joséphine,** and **Le Bistrot de la Place** (all open daily, cheaper for lunch, tight seating on simple chairs indoors and out).

Ile St. Louis
(Mo: Pont Marie)

$$$ L'Orangerie is an inviting, rustic-yet-elegant place with soft lighting, comfortable, spacious seating, and a hushed ambience. The cuisine blends traditional with modern touches (closed Mon, 28 Rue St. Louis-en-l'Ile, tel. 01 46 33 93 98).

$$ Auberge de la Reine Blanche—woodsy, cozy, and tight—welcomes diners willing to rub elbows with their neighbors. Earnest owner Michel serves basic French cuisine at reasonable prices. Along with like-mother-made-it comfort food, he serves good dinner salads (closed Wed, 30

Rue St. Louis-en-l'Ile, tel. 01 46 33 07 87).

On the Left Bank
Near the Odéon Theater
(Mo: Odéon)

$$$ Brasserie Bouillon Racine takes you back to 1906 with an Art Nouveau carnival of carved wood, stained glass, and old-time lights reflected in beveled mirrors. It's like having dinner with Gustav Klimt and a bunch of tourists. The over-the-top decor and energetic waiters give it an inviting conviviality. Check upstairs before choosing a table (daily, serves nonstop, 3 Rue Racine, tel. 01 44 32 15 60, www.bouillon-racine.com).

$$$ La Méditerranée is all about seafood from the south served in a pastel and dressy setting...with similar clientele. The scene and the cuisine are sophisticated yet accessible, and the view of the Odéon is *formidable* (daily, reservations smart, facing the Odéon at 2 Place de l'Odéon, tel. 01 43 26 02 30, www.la-mediterranee.com).

$$ L'Avant Comptoir and **L'Avant Comptoir de la Mer** are two stand-up-only hors d'oeuvres bars sitting next door to the mothership restaurant. They serve an array of both French-Basque tapas and seafood tapas on sleek zinc counters. At the walk-up counters outside, you can get top quality sandwiches, crêpes, or seafood to go (for less and with less commotion). But step inside for the foodie bar and it's another world (daily 12:00-23:00, 3 Carrefour de l'Odéon).

$$$ Brasserie Lipp is the place to experience an unspoiled yet famous brasserie. The cool two-level interior is awash with worn leather booths and faded decor that looks like it dates to when the place opened in 1880. Come for the ambience and good-enough cuisine (daily, 151 Boulevard St. Germain, tel. 01 45 48 72 93).

Between the Panthéon and the Cluny Museum
(Mo: Cluny-La Sorbonne ; RER/Train-B: Luxembourg)

$$$ At Les Papilles, you'll dine surrounded by bottles of wine in a warm, woody bistro and eat what's offered...and you won't complain. It's one *menu,* no choices, and no regrets. Choose your wine from the shelf or ask for advice from the burly, rugby-playing owner, then relax and let the food arrive. Reserve ahead and make sure that you're OK with what he's cooking (closed Sun-Mon, 30 Rue Gay Lussac, tel. 01 43 25 20 79, www.lespapillesparis.fr).

$$ Le Pré Verre, a block from the Cluny Museum, is a welcoming wine bistro. Hands-on owner Jean-François serves imaginative, modern cuisine at fair prices (inside and out), and packs his place with locals (good wine list, closed Sun-Mon, 8 Rue Thénard, reservations necessary, tel. 01 43 54 59 47, www.lepreverre.com).

$$ Restaurant La Mosquée transports diners to Morocco with its dazzling Arabic ambience and cuisine at fair prices. It's tucked into the back of the Grande Mosquée de Paris and serves tasty baked goods, teas, and even tastier meals—including several varieties of couscous and tagine (daily 9:00-late, 39 Rue Geoffroy-Saint-Hilaire, tel. 01 43 31 38 20).

TRANSPORTATION

Getting Around Paris

Paris is easy to navigate. Your basic choices are Métro (in-city subway), suburban train (commonly called RER, rapid transit tied into the Métro system), public bus, tram, Uber, and taxi.

Métro ticket machines

Transit Basics

- The same passes are good on the Métro, RER trains (within the city), and city buses.
- Buy a Navigo Easy card or Navigo Découverte pass for ease of travel.
- Scan your pass at the turnstile to enter the Métro; on a bus, scan your pass on the purple touchpad.
- Beware of pickpockets, and don't buy fake tickets from people roaming the stations.
- Find your train by its end-of-the-line stop.
- Safeguard your belongings; avoid standing near the train doors with luggage.
- At a stop, the door may open automatically. If it doesn't, open the door by either pushing a square button (green or black) or lifting a metal latch.
- Transfers (*correspondances*) between the Métro and RER trains are free (but not between Métro/suburban trains and bus).

You can buy passes at staffed Métro stations and at many *tabacs*. Staffed ticket windows in stations are being replaced by ticket machines, so expect some stations to have only machines and an information desk. Some machines accept only credit cards and coins, though key stations always have machines that take small bills of €20 or less and chip-and-PIN cards (some American cards are accepted—try). These machines work logically with easy-to-follow instructions in English.

Information: The Métro, suburban train, and public bus systems share a helpful website: www.ratp.fr.

Public-Transit Tickets: Paper tickets on the Métro are being replaced with plastic travel cards (called Navigo Easy; see next). Single-use tickets for buses and RER/suburban trains will likely remain available.

Navigo Easy Card: This reusable travel pass can be purchased at Métro-station ticket booths for €2 (all ages), then loaded with the amount and kind of tickets you need: €1.90 for a single ride; €14.90 for 10 rides (called *Navigo avec un carnet*); or €7.50 for a day pass (*Navigo Jour*) for central Paris. There's an app (Vianavigo) for downloading tickets and passes, though it's easy to do at machines in Métro stations. Navigo Easy cards can be shared (no photo is required), but not on the same trip.

Navigo Découverte Pass: This chip-embedded card costs a one-time €5 fee (plus another €5 if you buy the required photo). The €23 weekly unlimited pass covers all forms of transit from Monday to Sunday (expires on Sunday at midnight, even if you buy it on, say, a Thursday). The pass is good for all zones in the Paris region, including to Versailles and to Charles de Gaulle and Orly airports (except on Orlyval trains). To use the Navigo pass, touch the card to the purple pad, wait for the green validation light and the "ding," and you're on your way. You can buy the pass at any staffed Métro station (for details, consult the RATP website).

By Métro

In Paris, you're never more than a 10-minute walk from a Métro station. Europe's best subway system allows you to hop from sight to sight quickly and cheaply (runs 5:30-1:00 in the morning, Fri-Sat until 2:00 in the morning). Learn to use it.

Using the Métro System: To get to your destination, determine the closest "Mo" stop and which line or lines will get you there. Lines are color-coded and numbered. You can tell their direction by the end-of-the-line stops. For example, the La Défense/Château de Vincennes line, also known as line 1 (yellow), runs between La Défense, on its west end, and

FRANCE

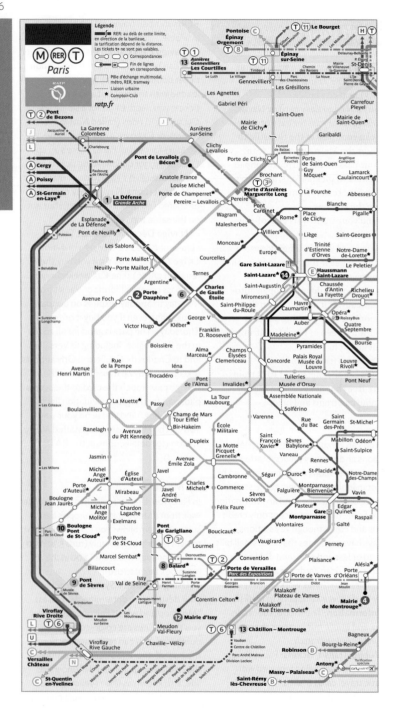

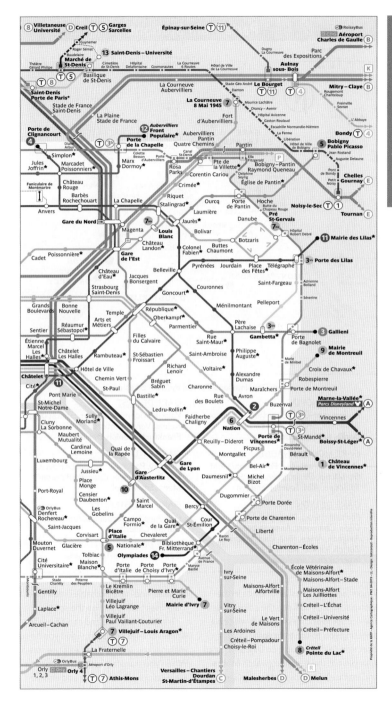

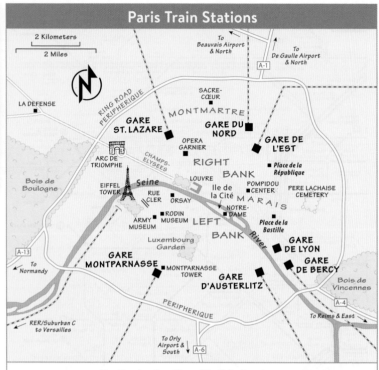

Paris Train Stations

2 Kilometers
2 Miles

To Beauvais Airport & North

To De Gaulle Airport & North

A-1

LA DEFENSE

RING ROAD PERIPHERIQUE

SACRE-CŒUR

MONTMARTRE

GARE ST. LAZARE

GARE DU NORD

OPERA GARNIER

GARE DE L'EST

ARC DE TRIOMPHE

CHAMPS-ELYSEES

RIGHT BANK

Place de la République

LOUVRE

POMPIDOU CENTER

PERE LACHAISE CEMETERY

Bois de Boulogne

EIFFEL TOWER

Seine

RUE CLER ORSAY

Ile de la Cité

MARAIS

NOTRE-DAME

RODIN MUSEUM

ARMY MUSEUM

LEFT

Place de la Bastille

Luxembourg Garden

BANK

River

GARE DE LYON

A-13

To Normandy

GARE MONTPARNASSE

Montparnasse TOWER

GARE D'AUSTERLITZ

GARE DE BERCY

Bois de Vincennes

A-4

PERIPHERIQUE

RER/Suburban C to Versailles

To Reims & East

To Orly Airport & South

A-6

Key Destinations Served by Train Stations

GARE DU NORD
Auvers-sur-Oise, Chantilly-Gouvieux, Brussels, Bruges, Amsterdam, Berlin, Koblenz, London

GARE MONTPARNASSE
Chartres, Amboise, Pontorson/Mont St-Michel, Dinan, Bordeaux, Sarlat, Toulouse, Albi, Tours, Hendaye

GARE DE LYON
Fontainebleau, Disneyland, Beaune, Dijon, Chamonix, Annecy, Lyon, Avignon, Arles, Nice, Carcassonne, Zürich, Venice, Rome, Bern, Interlaken, Barcelona

GARE DE L'EST
Vaux-le-Vicomte, Colmar, Strasbourg, Reims, Verdun, Interlaken, Zürich, Frankfurt, Munich, Berlin

GARE ST. LAZARE
Giverny, Pontoise, Rouen, Le Havre, Honfleur, Bayeux, Caen, Pontorson/Mont. St-Michel

GARE D' AUSTERLITZ
Orly Airport, Versailles, Amboise, Sarlat, Cahors

GARE DE BERCY
Southbound non-TGV trains

Vincennes on its east end. Once in the Métro station, you'll see the color-coded line numbers and/or blue-and-white signs directing you to the train going in your direction (e.g., *direction: La Défense*). Scan your pass at the turnstile (watch others and imitate). Fare inspectors regularly check for cheaters, accept absolutely no excuses, and have portable credit card machines to fine you on the spot.

Transfers are free and can be made wherever lines cross, provided you do so within 1.5 hours and don't exit the station. When you transfer, follow the appropriately colored line number and end-of-the-line stop to find your next train, or

Scenic Buses for Tourists

Of Paris' many bus routes, these are some of the most scenic. They provide a great, cheap, and convenient introduction to the city.

Bus #69 runs east-west between the Eiffel Tower and Père Lachaise Cemetery by way of Rue Cler, Quai d'Orsay, the Louvre, Ile St. Louis, and the Marais.

Bus #87 runs east-west from Invalides to Orsay Museum, St. Germain-des-Prés, St. Michel, Cluny Museum, Ile St. Louis, Bastille, Gare de Lyon, and Gare de Bercy, ending at Porte de Reuilly.

Bus #63 is another good east-west route, connecting the Marmottan Museum, Trocadéro (Eiffel Tower), Pont de l'Alma, Orsay Museum, St. Sulpice Church, Luxembourg Garden, Latin Quarter/Panthéon, and Gare de Lyon.

Bus #73 is one of Paris' most scenic lines, starting at the Orsay Museum and running westbound around Place de la Concorde, then up the Champs-Elysées, around the Arc de Triomphe, and down Avenue Charles de Gaulle to La Défense.

look for *correspondance* (connection) signs that lead to your next line.

When you reach your destination, blue-and-white *sortie* signs point you to the exit. Before leaving the station, check the helpful *plan du quartier* (map of the neighborhood) to get your bearings. At stops with several *sorties,* you can save time by choosing the best exit.

Métro Resources: Métro maps are free at Métro stations and included on freebie Paris maps at your hotel. For an interactive map of Paris' sights and Métro lines, with a trip-planning feature and information about each sight and station's history, see www.metro.paris. The free RATP mobile app can estimate Métro travel times, help you locate the best station exit, and tell you when the next bus will arrive (in English).

By Suburban Train

The suburban train is an arm of the Métro, serving outlying destinations such as Versailles, Disneyland Paris, and the airports. Traditionally called RER (which you will see on signage), it is sometimes referred to simply as "Train." These routes are indicated by thick lines on your subway map and identified by the letters A-K.

Throughout this chapter, you'll see it referred to as "RER."

Within the city center, the suburban train works like the Métro and can be speedier if it serves your destination directly, because it makes fewer stops. Métro tickets are good on the suburban train; you can transfer between the Métro and suburban train systems with the same ticket. But to travel outside the city (to Versailles or the airport, for example), you'll need a separate, more expensive ticket. The Navigo Découverte pass covers all suburban train trips, including to the airport and Versailles. Unlike the Métro, not every train stops at every station along the way; check the sign or screen over the platform to see if your

destination is listed as a stop ("*toutes les gares*" means it makes all stops along the way), or confirm with a local before you board.

By City Bus

Paris' excellent bus system is worth figuring out. Buses require less walking and fewer stairways than the Métro, and you can see Paris unfold as you travel.

Bus Stops: Stops are everywhere, and most come with a good city bus map, route maps for each bus that stops there, a frequency chart and schedule, live screens showing the time the next two buses will arrive, a *plan du quartier* map of the immediate neighborhood, and a *soirées* map explaining night service, if available (there are even phone chargers at some locations). Bus-system maps are also available in any Métro station (and in the *Paris Pratique par Arrondissement* booklet sold at newsstands).

Using the Bus System: Buses use the same passes as the Métro and RER/suburban trains. One Zone 1 ticket buys you a bus ride anywhere in central Paris within the freeway ring road (*le périphérique*). Use your Métro pass, or buy a one-use ticket on board for €2. These tickets are *sans correspondance,* which means you can't use them to transfer to another bus.

When a bus approaches, it's wise to wave to the driver to indicate that you want to be picked up. Board your bus through the front door. (Families with strollers can use any doors—the ones in the center of the bus are wider. To open the middle or back doors on long buses, push the green button located by those doors.) Buy a single-use ticket from the driver or scan your Navigo pass on the purple touchpad. Keep track of which stop is coming up next by following the onboard diagram or listening to recorded announcements. When you're ready to get off, push the red button to signal you want a stop, then exit through the central or rear door. Even if you're not certain

you've figured out the system, do some joyriding. I always check the bus stop near my hotel to see if it's convenient to my plans.

More Bus Tips: Avoid rush hour (Mon-Fri 8:00-9:30 & 17:30-19:30), when buses are jammed and traffic doesn't move. While the Métro shuts down at about 1:00 in the morning (even later Fri-Sat), some buses continue much later (called *Noctilien* lines). Not all city buses are air-conditioned, so they can become rolling greenhouses on summer days. Pass holders—but not those buying individual tickets onboard—can transfer from one bus to another on the same fare (within 1.5 hours). However, you can't do a round-trip or hop on and off the same line using the same fare. You can use the same fare to transfer between buses and trams, but you can't transfer between the bus and Métro/RER suburban train systems (it'll take two fares).

By Uber

Uber works in Paris like it does at home, and in general works better than taxis in Paris (www.uber.com). One downside is that Uber drivers can't use the taxi/bus lanes during rush hour, so your trip may take longer at busy times than it would in a cab.

By Taxi

Parisian taxis are reasonable, especially for couples and families. The meters are tamper-proof. Fares and supplements (described in English on the rear windows) are straightforward and tightly regulated. Cabbies are legally required to accept four passengers, though they don't always like it. If you have five in your group, you can book a larger taxi in advance (your hotelier can call), or try your luck at a taxi stand. A surcharge may be applied for a fifth rider.

Rates: The meter starts at €2.60 with a €7 minimum charge. A typical 20-minute ride (such as Bastille to the Eiffel Tower) costs about €25 (versus about €1.45/person using a *carnet* ticket on the Métro or bus, or about €15 via Uber). Taxis charge higher rates at rush hour, at night, all day Sunday, and for extra passengers. To tip, round up to the next euro (at least €0.50). The A, B, or C lights on a taxi's rooftop sign correspond to hourly rates, which vary with the time of day and day of the week (for example, the A rate of €32.50/hour applies Mon-Sat 10:00-17:00). Tired travelers need not bother with the subtle differences in fares—if you need a cab, take it.

How to Catch *un Taxi:* You can try waving down a taxi, but it's often easier to ask someone for the nearest taxi stand (*"Où est une station de taxi?"*; oo ay ewn stah-see-ohn duh tahk-see). Taxi stands are indicated by a circled "T" on good city maps and on many maps in this chapter. To order a taxi in English, call the reservation line for the G7 cab company (tel. 01 41 27 66 99), or ask your hotelier or waiter to call for you. When you summon a taxi by phone, a set fee of €4 is applied for an immediate booking or €7 for reserving in advance (this fee will appear on the meter when they pick you up). You can also book a taxi using the cab company's app, which provides approximate wait times (surcharge similar to booking by phone). To download an app, search for either "Taxi G7" or "Taxis Bleus" (the two major companies, both available in English; note when entering your mobile number, you must include the international access code and your country code—use "+1" before the area code for a US/Canadian phone number).

If you need to catch an early morning train or flight, book a taxi the day before (especially for weekday departures; your hotelier can help). Some taxi companies require a €5 reservation fee by credit card for weekday morning rush-hour departures (7:00-10:00) and have a limited number of reservation spots.

By Bike

Paris is surprisingly easy by bicycle. The city is flat, and riders have access to more than 370 miles of bike lanes and many of the priority lanes for buses and taxis (be careful on these). You can rent from a bike-rental shop or use a city-operated bike-share program.

Though I wouldn't use bikes to get around routinely (traffic is a bit too intense), they're perfect for a joyride away from busy streets, especially on the riverside promenades. A four-mile stretch runs from near the Eiffel Tower to below the Bastille; the round-trip ride makes a wonderful hour-or-so long experience. (It could be much longer if you succumb to the temptations of the lounge chairs, hammocks, outdoor cafés, and simple delights of riverside Parisian life.) Bike-rental shops have good route suggestions.

TIs have a helpful "Paris à Vélo" map, which shows all the dedicated bike paths. Many other versions are available for sale at newsstand kiosks, some bookstores, and department stores.

Bike About Tours is your best bet for bike rental, with good information and kid-friendly solutions such as baby seats, tandem attachments, and kid-sized bikes. Their office/coffee shop, called Le Peloton Café, offers bikes, tours, and artisan coffee (bike rental—€20/day during office hours, €25/24 hours, includes lock and helmet; Thu-Tue 9:30-17:30, closed Wed and Dec-Jan; shop/café at 17 Rue du Pont Louis Philippe, Mo: St-Paul, mobile 06 18 80 84 92, www.bikeabouttours.com).

Fat Tire Tours has a limited supply of bikes for rent, so call ahead to check availability (€4/hour, €25/24 hours, includes lock and helmet, photo ID and credit-card imprint required for deposit; RS%—€2/day rental discount with this book, 2-discount maximum; office open daily 9:00-18:30, bike rental only after 11:00 as priority is given to those taking a tour, near the Eiffel Tower at 24 Rue Edgar Faure—see the "Eiffel Tower & Nearby" map, Mo: Dupleix, tel. 01

Bike tours can be fun and informative.

82 88 80 96, www.fattiretours.com/paris).

The city's **Vélib'** bike-share program (from *vélo* + *libre* = "bike freedom") scatters bikes across town. Best for quick one-way rides, Vélib' bikes are accessible 24/7 and are free for the first half-hour. The system is being overhauled to offer lighter bikes, electric bikes, and an easier booking process; see www.velib-metropole.fr for updates.

Arriving and Departing

Budget plenty of time to reach your departure point. Paris is a big, crowded city, and getting across town or from terminal to terminal on time is a goal you'll share with millions of others. Factor in traffic delays and walking time through huge stations and vast terminals. Always keep your luggage safely near you. Thieves prey on jet-lagged and confused tourists using public transportation.

By Plane
CHARLES DE GAULLE AIRPORT

Paris' main airport (airport code: CDG, www.charlesdegaulleairport.co.uk) has three terminals: T-1, T-2, and T-3. Most flights from the US use T-1 or T-2. You can travel between terminals on the free CDGVAL shuttle train (departs every 5 minutes, 24/7) or by shuttle bus (on the arrivals level). Allow 30 minutes to travel between terminals and an hour for total travel time between your gates at T-1 and T-2. All three terminals have access to ground transportation.

When leaving Paris, make sure you know which terminal you are departing from (if it's T-2, you'll also need to know which hall you're leaving from—they're labeled A through F). Plan to arrive at the airport three hours early for an overseas flight, and two hours for flights within Europe (particularly on budget airlines, which can have especially long check-in lines). For airport and flight info, visit www.parisaeroport.fr.

Services: All terminals have Paris Tourisme information desks, where you can get city maps, buy a Paris Museum Pass, and get tickets for the RoissyBus or suburban RER/Train-B to Paris—a terrific time- and hassle-saver (to buy a Navigo Découverte card, you must go to the airport train station). You'll also find ATMs (*distributeurs*), free (but slow) Wi-Fi, shops, cafés, and bars. If you're returning home and want a VAT refund, look for tax-refund centers in the check-in area.

Getting Downtown: Buses, suburban trains, airport vans, and taxis link the airport's terminals with central Paris. Total travel time to your hotel should be around 1.5 hours by bus and Métro, one hour by train and Métro, and 50 minutes by taxi. For more information, check the "Getting There" tab at www.charlesdegaulleairport.co.uk.

Rick's Tip: *When deciding how to get from Charles de Gaulle airport into Paris, keep in mind that* **using buses and taxis requires shorter walks than taking suburban trains.** *Also remember that transfers to Métro lines often involve stairs.*

The **RoissyBus** drops you off at the Opéra Métro stop in central Paris (€12, runs 6:00-23:00, 3-4/hour, 50 minutes; buy ticket at airport Paris Tourisme desk, ticket machine, or on bus; tel. 3246, www.ratp.fr). The bus arrives on Rue Scribe; to get to the Métro entrance or nearest taxi stand, turn left as you exit the bus and walk counterclockwise around the lavish Opéra building to its front. A taxi to any of my listed hotels costs about €15 from here. **Le Bus Direct** has several routes that drop travelers at convenient points in and near the city, though it's a bit slower (€17 one-way, €30 round-trip, runs 5:45-22:30, 2/hour, Wi-Fi and power outlets, toll tel. 08 92 35 08 20, www.lebusdirect.com). You can book tickets online (must print out and bring with you), buy at ticket machines or ticket windows at stops (credit card only, availability varies by stop), or pay the driver (cash only, see www.lebusdirect.com for round-trip and group discount details).

Paris' **suburban commuter train,** RER/Train-B, is the fastest public transit option for getting between the airport and the city center (€10.50, runs 5:00-24:00, 4/hour, about 35 minutes; you may still see maps and signage referring to these trains only by their old name, "RER"). RER/Train-B runs directly to well-located RER/Train-B/Métro stations (including Gare du Nord, Châtelet-Les Halles, St. Michel, and Luxembourg); from there, you can hop the Métro to get exactly where you need to go. RER/Train-B is handy and cheap, but it can require walking with your luggage through big, crowded stations—especially at Châtelet-Les Halles, where a transfer to the Métro can take 10-15 minutes and may include stairs. For step-by-step instructions on taking RER/Train-B into Paris, see www.parisbytrain.com (see the options under "Airport").

To return to the airport on RER/Train-B from central Paris, allow plenty of time to get to your departure gate (plan for a 15-minute Métro or bus ride to the closest RER/Train-B station, a 15-minute wait for your train, a 35-minute train ride, plus walking time through the stations and airport). Your Métro or bus ticket is not valid on RER/Train-B to the airport (but a Navigo Découverte is). When you catch your train, make sure the sign over the platform shows *Aéroport Roissy-Charles de Gaulle* as a stop served. (The line splits, so not every RER/Train-B serves the airport.) If you're not clear, ask another rider, *"Air-o-por sharl duh gaul?"*

Shuttle vans carry passengers to and from their hotels, with stops along the way to drop off and pick up other riders. Shuttles require you to book a precise pickup time in advance—even though you can't know if your flight will arrive on time. For that reason, they work best for trips *from* your hotel to the airport. Though not as fast as taxis, shuttle vans are a good value for single travelers and big families (about €30 for one person, per-person price decreases the more you have in your party; have hotelier book at least a day in advance). Several companies offer shuttle service; I usually just go with the one my hotel uses. For groups of three or four, take a taxi or Uber instead.

Taxis charge a flat rate into Paris (€55

to the Left Bank, €50 to the Right Bank). Taxis can carry three people with bags comfortably, and are legally required to accept a fourth passenger (though they may not like it; beyond that, there's an extra passenger supplement). Don't take an unauthorized taxi from cabbies greeting you on arrival. Official taxi stands are well signed. For taxi trips from Paris to the airport, have your hotel arrange it. Specify that you want a real taxi (un taxi normal), not a limo service that costs €20 more (and gives your hotel a kickback). For weekday-morning departures (7:00-10:00), reserve at least a day ahead (€7 reservation fee payable by credit card). **Uber** offers Paris airport pickup and drop-off for the same rates as taxis, but since they can't use the bus-only lanes (normal taxis can), expect some added time.

The professional **Paris Webservices** car service works well from the airport because your driver meets you inside the terminal and waits if you're late (two people-€90 one-way, €5-10/extra person up to 7, tel. 01 45 56 91 67 or 09 52 06 02 59, www.pariswebservices.com). They also offer guided tours.

ORLY AIRPORT

This easy-to-navigate airport (airport code: ORY, www.airport-orly.com) feels small, but it has all the services you'd expect at a major airport. Orly is good for rental-car pickup and drop-off, as it's closer to Paris and easier to navigate than Charles de Gaulle Airport.

Orly has two terminals: Ouest (west) and Sud (south). At both terminals, arrivals are on the ground level (level 0) and departures are on level 1. You can connect the two terminals with the free Orlyval shuttle train (well signed).

Services: Both terminals have Paris Tourisme desks in the arrivals area (a good spot to buy the Paris Museum Pass and tickets for public transit into Paris) and offer free Wi-Fi.

Getting Downtown: Shuttle buses (navettes), suburban trains, airport vans, and taxis connect Paris with either terminal. Bus stops and taxis are centrally located at arrivals levels and are well signed.

Bus bays are found in the Sud terminal outside exits L and G, and in the Ouest terminal outside exit D. **Le Bus Direct** route #1 runs to Gare Montparnasse, Eiffel Tower, Trocadéro, and Arc de Triomphe/Etoile stops (all stops have connections to Métro lines). For Rue Cler hotels, take Le Bus Direct to the Eiffel Tower stop (20 Avenue de Suffren—see "Eiffel Tower & Nearby" map), then walk 15 minutes across the Champ de Mars park to your hotel. Buses depart from the arrivals level—Ouest exit B-C or Sud exit L; look for signs to navettes (€12 one-way, €20 round-trip, 4/hour, 40 minutes to the Eiffel Tower, buy ticket from driver or book online). See www.lebusdirect. com for details on round-trip and group discounts.

For the cheapest (but slow) access to central Paris (best for the Marais area), take **tram line 7** from outside the Sud terminal (direction: Villejuif-Louis Aragon) to the Villejuif station to catch Métro line 7 (you'll need one Métro ticket for the tram and one for the Métro—buy a carnet of 10 tickets at the Paris Tourisme desk in the terminal, 4/hour, 45 minutes to Villejuif Métro station, then 15-minute Métro ride to the Marais).

The next two options take you to **RER/ Train-B,** with access to the Luxembourg Garden area, Notre-Dame Cathedral, handy Métro line 1 at the Châtelet stop, Gare du Nord, and Charles de Gaulle Airport. The **Orlybus** goes directly to the Denfert-Rochereau Métro and RER/ Train-B stations (€8, 3/hour, 30 minutes). The pricier but more frequent—and more comfortable—**Orlyval shuttle train** takes you to the Antony RER/Train-B station (€12.05, 6/hour, 40 minutes, buy ticket to Paris—not just to Antony—before boarding). The Orlyval train is well signed and leaves from the departure level at both Orly terminals. Once at the RER/Train-B station, take the train in direction: Mitry-Claye or Aéroport Charles de Gaulle to reach central Paris.

For access to Left Bank neighborhoods (including Rue Cler) via **RER/Train-C,** take the bus marked *Go C Paris* five minutes to the Pont de Rungis station (€2 shuttle only, €6.25 combo-ticket includes RER/Train-C), then catch RER/Train-C to St. Michel, Musée d'Orsay, Invalides, or Pont de l'Alma (direction: Versailles Château Rive Gauche or Pontoise, 4/hour, 35 minutes).

By **airport van**, figure about €23 for one person or €30 for two (less per person for larger groups and kids).

Taxis are outside the Ouest terminal exit B, and to the far right as you leave the Sud terminal at exit M. Allow 30 minutes for a taxi ride into central Paris (fixed fare: €30 for Left Bank, €35 for Right Bank). **For Uber,** head toward exit B, following signs for *Pre-Ordered Vehicles.* Meet your Uber driver in the lot labeled *Parking Pro* (same fixed rate as taxis for central Paris).

BEAUVAIS AIRPORT

Budget airlines such as Ryanair use this small airport with two terminals (T-1 and T-2), offering dirt-cheap airfares but leaving you 50 miles north of Paris. Still, this airport has direct buses to Paris and is handy for travelers heading to Normandy or Belgium (car rental available). The airport is basic, waiting areas can be crowded, and services sparse (airport code: BVA, toll tel. 08 92 68 20 66, www.aeroportparisbeauvais.com).

Getting Downtown: Buses depart from a stop between the two terminals (€17 one-way, 2/hour, 1.5 hours to Paris, buy ticket online to save time, http://tickets.aeroportbeauvais.com). Buses arrive at Porte Maillot on the west edge of Paris (where you can connect to Métro line 1 and RER/Train-C); the closest taxi stand is next door at the Hôtel Hyatt Regency Paris Etoile. To head back to Beauvais Airport from Porte Maillot, catch the bus in the parking lot on Boulevard Pershing next to the Hyatt Regency.

Trains connect Beauvais' city center and Paris' Gare du Nord (20/day, 1.5 hours). To reach the Beauvais train station, take the Hôtel/Aéroport Navette shuttle or local bus #6 (each hourly, 25 minutes).

Taxis run from Beauvais Airport to the Beauvais train station or city center (€20), or to central Paris (allow €150 and 1.5 hours).

By Train

Paris is Europe's rail hub, with six major stations and one minor station, and trains heading in different directions: **Gare du Nord** (northbound trains); **Gare Montparnasse** (west- and southwest-bound trains); **Gare de Lyon** (southeast-bound trains); **Gare de l'Est** (eastbound trains); **Gare St. Lazare** (northwest-bound trains); **Gare d'Austerlitz** (southwest-bound trains); and **Gare de Bercy** (smaller station with non-TGV trains mostly serving cities in Burgundy).

The main train stations all have free Wi-Fi, banks or currency exchanges, ATMs, train information desks, cafés, newsstands, and clever pickpockets (pay attention in ticket lines—keep your bag firmly gripped in front of you). Not all have baggage checks. Any train station has schedule information, can make reservations, and can sell tickets for any destination, although it may be handier to buy tickets from a neighborhood SNCF office.

Each station offers two types of rail service: long distance to other cities, called Grandes Lignes (major lines, TGV—also called "InOui"—or TER trains); and commuter service to nearby areas, called Banlieue, Transilien, or suburban trains lines A-K. You also may see ticket windows identified as *Ile de France.* These are for Transilien trains serving destinations outside Paris in the Ile de France region (usually no more than an hour from Paris). When arriving by Métro, follow signs for *Grandes Lignes-SNCF* to find the main tracks. Métro and suburban train lines A–K, as well as buses and taxis, are well marked at every station.

Budget plenty of time before your departure to factor in ticket lines and making your way through large, crowded stations. Paris train stations can be intimidating, but if you slow down, take a deep breath, and ask for help, you'll find them manageable and efficient. Bring a pad of paper and a pen for clear communication at ticket/info windows. It helps to write down the ticket you want. For instance: "28/05/19 Paris-Nord→Lyon dep. 18:30."

All stations have a central information booth *(accueil);* bigger stations have roving helpers, usually wearing red or blue vests. They're capable of answering rail questions more quickly than the staff at the information desks or ticket windows. I make a habit of confirming my track number and departure time with these helpers (all rail staff speak English).

Make sure your bags have name tags attached (they're required by SNCF).

GARE DU NORD

The granddaddy of Paris' train stations serves cities in northern France and international destinations north of Paris, including Copenhagen, Amsterdam, and the Eurostar to London. The station is undergoing a €600-million renovation that won't be finished until 2024—expect changes and construction disruptions.

Key Destinations Served by Gare du Nord Banlieue/Suburban Lines: Charles de Gaulle Airport (4/hour, 35 minutes, track 41-44).

GARE MONTPARNASSE

This big, modern station covers three floors, serves lower Normandy and Brittany, and has TGV service to the Loire Valley and southwestern France, as well

as suburban service to Chartres. Trains to Chartres usually depart from tracks 18-24.

Key Destinations Served by Gare Montparnasse: Chartres (14/day, 1 hour), **Amboise** (8/day in 1.5 hours with change in St-Pierre-des-Corps, requires TGV reservation; non-TGV trains leave from Gare d'Austerlitz), **Pontorson/Mont St-Michel** (5/day, 5.5 hours, via Rennes or Caen), and **Sarlat** (4/day, 5 hours, change in Bordeaux).

GARE DE LYON

This huge, bewildering station offers TGV and regular service to southeastern France, Italy, Switzerland, and other international destinations.

Le Bus Direct coaches—to Gare Montparnasse (easy transfer to Orly Airport) and direct to Charles de Gaulle Airport—stop outside the station's main entrance. They are signed *Navette-Aéroport.*

Key Destinations Served by Gare de Lyon: Beaune (roughly hourly at rush hour but few midday, 2.5 hours, most require change in Dijon; direct trains from Paris' Bercy station take an hour longer), **Chamonix** (7/day, 5.5-7 hours, some change in Switzerland), **Avignon** (hourly direct, 2.5 hours to Avignon TGV station; 5/day in 3.5 hours to Avignon Centre-Ville Station, more connections with change—3-4 hours), **Arles** (hourly, 4 hours, transfer in Avignon or Nîmes), **Nice** (hourly, 6 hours, may require change), and **Carcassonne** (8/day, 5.5 hours, 1 change usually in Bordeaux).

GARE DE L'EST

This two-floor station (with underground Métro) serves northeastern France and international destinations east of Paris.

Key Destinations Served by Gare de l'Est: Colmar (12/day with TGV, 2.5 hours, 3 direct, others change in Strasbourg) and **Reims** Centre station (8/day by direct TGV, 45 minutes).

GARE ST. LAZARE

This compact station serves upper Normandy, including Rouen and Giverny.

Key Destinations Served by Gare St. Lazare: Giverny (train to Vernon, 8/day Mon-Sat, 6/day Sun, 45 minutes), **Honfleur** (13/day, 2-3.5 hours, via Lisieux, Deauville, or Le Havre, then bus), **Bayeux** (9/day, 2.5 hours, some change in Caen), **Pontorson/Mont St-Michel** (2/day, 4-5.5 hours, via Caen; more trains from Gare Montparnasse).

GARE D'AUSTERLITZ

This small station currently provides non-TGV service to the Loire Valley, southwestern France, and Spain.

Key Destinations Served by Gare d'Austerlitz: Orly Airport (via RER/Train-C, 4/hour, 35 minutes), **Versailles** (via RER/Train-C, 4/hour, 35 minutes), **Amboise** (3/day direct in 2 hours, more with transfer; faster TGV connection from Gare Montparnasse), and **Sarlat** (1/day, 6.5 hours, requires change to bus in Souillac, 3 more/day via Gare Montparnasse).

GARE DE BERCY

This smaller station mostly handles southbound non-TGV trains, but some TGV trains do stop here in peak season (Mo: Bercy).

By Bus

Buses generally provide the cheapest—if less comfortable and more time-consuming—transportation to major European cities. Eurolines is the old standby; two relative newcomers (Ouibus and Flixbus) are cutting prices drastically, adding more destinations, and ramping up onboard comfort with Wi-Fi and snacks. These companies provide service usually between train stations and airports within France and to many international destinations. If the schedule works for you, it's a handy and cheap way to connect Paris airports with other French destinations (Tours/Loire, Rouen, and Caen, for example) and skip central Paris train stations.

OuiBus has routes mostly within France but serves some European cities as well (central Paris stop is at Gare de Bercy, Mo: Bercy, easy online booking, toll tel. 08 92 68 00 68, www.ouibus.com). German-run **FlixBus** connects key cities within France and throughout Europe, often from secondary airports and train stations (central Paris stop is near Porte Maillot at 16 Boulevard Pershing, Mo: Porte Maillot, handy eticket system and easy-to-use app, tel. 01 76 36 04 12, www.flixbus.com). **Eurolines'** buses depart from Paris' Gare Routière du Paris-Gallieni in the suburb of Bagnolet (28 Avenue du Général de Gaulle, Mo: Gallieni, toll tel. 08 92 89 90 91; from the US, dial 011 33 1 41 86 24 21, www.eurolines.com).

NEAR PARIS

Efficient trains bring dozens of day trips within the grasp of temporary Parisians. Europe's best palace at Versailles, the awesome cathedral of Chartres, and Monet's flowery gardens at Giverny await the traveler looking for a refreshing change from urban Paris.

Versailles

Every king's dream, Versailles (vehr-"sigh") was the residence of French monarchs and the cultural heartbeat of Europe for about 100 years—until the Revolution of 1789 changed all that.

Versailles offers three blockbuster sights. The main attraction is the palace itself, the **Château.** Here you walk through dozens of lavish, chandeliered rooms once inhabited by Louis XIV and his successors. Next come the expansive **Gardens,** a landscaped wonderland crossed with footpaths and dotted with statues and fountains. The pastoral **Trianon Palaces and Domaine de Marie-Antoinette,** designed for frolicking blue bloods and featuring several small palaces, is perfect for getting away from the mobs at the Château.

Getting There

The town of Versailles is 35 minutes southwest of Paris. Take **RER/Train-C** from any of these Paris stations: Gare d'Austerlitz, St. Michel, Musée d'Orsay, Invalides, Pont de l'Alma, or Champ de Mars. Buy a round-trip ticket to "Versailles Rive Gauche/Château" (€7.10 round-trip, 4/hour). If the ticket machine doesn't immediately offer a Versailles option, try pressing "Ile de France." Insert your ticket in the turnstile to enter the system (as you would with the Métro). Then check the departure board, which will list the next train to "Versailles Rive Gauche/Château" and its track.

On all Versailles-bound trains, Versailles Rive Gauche/Château is the final stop. Once you arrive, exit through the turnstiles (you may need to insert your ticket). To reach the Château, follow the flow: Turn right out of the station, then left at the first boulevard, and walk 10

The Neptune fountain at Versailles

Louis XIV and Versailles

Around 1700, Versailles was the cultural heartbeat of Europe, and French culture was at its zenith. Throughout Europe, when you said "the king," you were referring to the French king—Louis XIV. Every king wanted a palace like Versailles. Everyone learned French. French taste in clothes, hairstyles, table manners, theater, music, art, and kissing spread across the Continent. That cultural dominance continued, to some extent, right up to the 20th century.

Louis XIV was a true Renaissance Man, a century after the Renaissance: athletic, good-looking, a musician, dancer, horseman, statesman, patron of the arts, and lover. He called himself the Sun King because he gave life and warmth to all he touched. He was also thought of as Apollo, the Greek god of the sun. For 70 years he was the perfect embodiment of the absolute monarch. He summed it up best himself with his famous expression—*"L'état, c'est moi!"*: "The state, that's me!"

Rick's Tip: Buy either a **Paris Museum Pass** or a **Versailles Le Passeport Pass,** both of which give you access to the most important parts of the complex and allow you to skip ticket-buying lines. Ideally, buy your pass (or ticket) before arriving at the palace.

Orientation

Cost: Château—€18, includes audio-guide; **Trianon Palaces and Domaine de Marie-Antoinette**—€12, no audio-guide; **Gardens**—free except when there are Spectacles (see "Spectacles in the Gardens," later). You can purchase Versailles tickets at any Paris TI, FNAC department store (small fee), or at www. chateauversailles.fr.

Passes: The Paris Museum Pass (see page 128) covers the Château and the Trianon/Domaine area and is the best solution for most. It doesn't include the Gardens on Spectacle days. The **Le Passeport** pass (€20) covers the Château and the Trianon/Domaine area (on Spectacle days, it's €27).

Hours: The **Château** is open April-Oct Tue-Sun 9:00-18:30, Nov-March Tue-Sun until 17:30, closed Mon year-round. The **Trianon Palaces and Domaine de Marie-Antoinette** are open April-Oct Tue-Sun 12:00-18:30, Nov-March until 17:30, closed Mon year-round, last entry 45 minutes before closing. The **Gardens** are open April-Oct daily 8:00-20:30, Nov-March until 18:00.

Crowd-Beating Strategies: Versailles is packed May-Sept 9:30-13:00, so come early or late. Avoid Sundays, Tuesdays, and Saturdays (in that order), when the place is jammed all day. To skip the ticket-buying line, buy a pass or ticket in advance, or book a guided tour. Everyone must go through the same two (often slow) security checkpoints: at the Château's courtyard entry and again at the Château entrance (longest lines 10:00-12:00).

minutes.

By **taxi**, the 30-minute ride (without traffic) between Versailles and Paris costs about €65.

Drivers should get on the *périphérique* freeway that circles Paris, and take the toll-free A-13 autoroute toward Rouen. Exit at Versailles, follow signs to *Versailles Château,* and avoid the hectic Garden lots by parking in the big pay lot at the foot of the Château on Place d'Armes (€4/hour).

Day Plan

Versailles merits a full sightseeing day. In general, allow 1.5 hours each for the Château, the Gardens (includes time for lunch), and the Trianon/Domaine. Add another two hours for round-trip transit, and you're looking at nearly an eight-hour day.

FRANCE

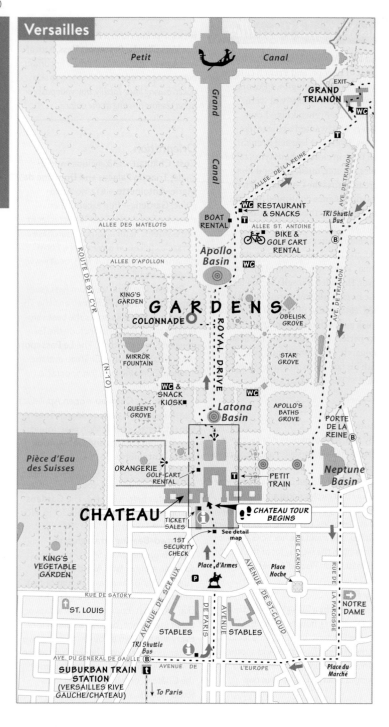

Versailles

Petit Canal

Grand Canal

GRAND TRIANON EXIT **WC**

T

ALLEE DE LA REINE

AVE. DE TRIANON

WC RESTAURANT & SNACKS

TRI Shuttle Bus **B**

T Allee St. Antoine

BOAT RENTAL

BIKE & GOLF CART RENTAL

ALLEE DES MATELOTS

Apollo Basin **WC**

ALLEE D'APOLLON

ROUTE DE ST. CYR

KING'S GARDEN

GARDENS

COLONNADE

OBELISK GROVE

ROYAL DRIVE

AVE. DE TRIANON

MIRROR FOUNTAIN

STAR GROVE

(N-10)

WC & SNACK KIOSK

WC

QUEEN'S GROVE

Latona Basin

APOLLO'S BATHS GROVE

PORTE DE LA REINE **B**

Pièce d'Eau des Suisses

ORANGERIE

GOLF-CART RENTAL

T ← PETIT TRAIN

Neptune Basin

CHATEAU

TICKET SALES

CHATEAU TOUR BEGINS

See detail map

KING'S VEGETABLE GARDEN

1ST SECURITY CHECK

Place d'Armes

P

RUE CARNOT

Place Hoche

RUE DE LA PAROISSE

RUE DE SATORY

ST. LOUIS

AVENUE DE SCEAUX

DE PARIS

AVENUE

AVENUE DE ST-CLOUD

STABLES

STABLES

NOTRE DAME

TRI Shuttle Bus

AVE. DU GENERAL DE GAULLE **B**

AVENUE DE

L'EUROPE

Place du Marché

SUBURBAN TRAIN STATION (VERSAILLES RIVE GAUCHE/CHATEAU)

↓ To Paris

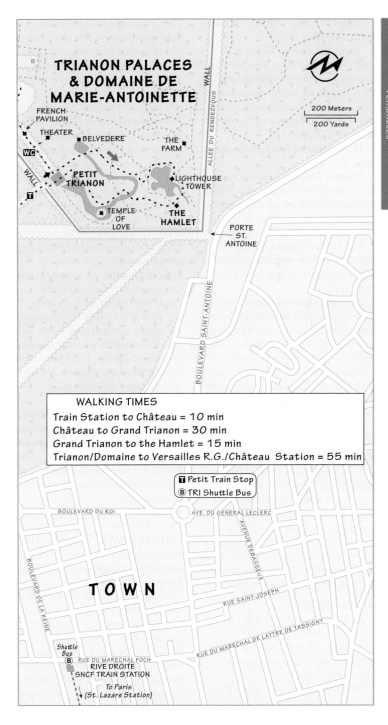

TRIANON PALACES
& DOMAINE DE
MARIE-ANTOINETTE

FRENCH
PAVILION
THEATER
BELVEDERE
THE
FARM
WC
WALL
PETIT
TRIANON
LIGHTHOUSE
TOWER
T
TEMPLE
OF
LOVE
THE
HAMLET

WALL

ALLEE DU RENDEZVOUS

200 Meters
200 Yards

PORTE
ST.
ANTOINE

BOULEVARD SAINT-ANTOINE

WALKING TIMES

Train Station to Château = 10 min
Château to Grand Trianon = 30 min
Grand Trianon to the Hamlet = 15 min
Trianon/Domaine to Versailles R.G./Château Station = 55 min

T Petit Train Stop
B TRI Shuttle Bus

BOULEVARD DU ROI
AVE. DU GENERAL LECLERC

AVENUE DE BASSEUX

BOULEVARD DE LA REINE

TOWN

RUE SAINT-JOSEPH

RUE DU MARECHAL DE LATTRE DE TASSIGNY

Shuttle
Bus
B RUE DU MARECHAL FOCH
RIVE DROITE
SNCF TRAIN STATION

To Paris
(St. Lazare Station)

Information: Tel. 01 30 83 78 00, www. chateauversailles.fr.

Tours: The 1.5-hour English **guided tour** gives you access to a few extra rooms and lets you skip the regular security line (€7). Book in advance on the palace's website, or reserve immediately upon arrival at the guided-tours office (to the right of the Château).

🎧 Download my free Versailles **audio tour.**

Baggage Check: Free and located just after Château entry security. Large bags and baby strollers are not allowed in the Château and the two Trianons.

Eating: To the left of the Château, the **$ Grand Café d'Orléans** offers good-value self-service meals. In the Gardens, you'll find several cafés and snack stands with fair prices.

Spectacles in the Gardens: The Gardens and fountains at Versailles come alive at selected times, offering a glimpse into Louis XIV's remarkable world. The Sun King had his engineers literally reroute a river to fuel his fountains and feed his plants. Even by today's standards, the fountains are impressive. Check the Versailles website for current hours and ticket prices.

➲ Self-Guided Tour

On this self-guided tour, you'll see the Château (the State Apartments of the king as well as the Hall of Mirrors), the landscaped Gardens in the "backyard," and the Trianon Palaces and Domaine de Marie-Antoinette, located at the far end of the Gardens. If your time is limited, skip the Trianon/Domaine, which is a hefty 30-minute hike from the Château.

THE CHATEAU

• *Stand in the huge courtyard and face the palace. The golden Royal Gate in the center of the courtyard—nearly 260 feet long and decorated with 100,000 gold leaves—is a replica of the original.*

The section of the palace with the clock is the original château, once a small hunting lodge where little Louis XIV spent his happiest boyhood years. Naturally, the Sun King's private bedroom (the three arched windows beneath the clock) faced the rising sun.

• *As you finally enter the Château, you'll find an information desk (get a map) and bag check. Follow the crowds directly across the courtyard, where you'll go back inside for your free (and worth-the-wait) audioguide. Now make your way to the start of our tour.*

On the way, you'll pass through a dozen ground-floor rooms. Climb the stairs and keep following the flow. You'll eventually reach a palatial golden-brown room, with a doorway that overlooks the Royal Chapel. Let the tour begin.

Royal Chapel: Every morning at 10:00, the organist and musicians struck up the music, these big golden doors opened, and Louis XIV and his family stepped onto the balcony to attend Mass. While Louis looked down on the golden altar, the lowly nobles on the ground floor knelt with their backs to the altar and looked up—worshipping Louis worshipping God.

• *Enter the next room.*

Hercules Drawing Room: Pleasure ruled. The main suppers, balls, and receptions were held in this room. Picture elegant partygoers in fine silks, wigs, rouge, lipstick, and fake moles (and that's just the men) as they dance to the strains of a string quartet.

• *From here on it's a one-way tour—getting lost is not allowed.*

The King's Wing: The names of the rooms generally come from the paintings on the ceilings. For instance, the **Venus Room** was the royal make-out space, where couples would cavort beneath the goddess of love floating on the ceiling. In the **Diana Room,** Louis and his men played pool on a table that stood in the center of the room, while ladies sat surrounding them on Persian-carpet cushions, and music wafted in from next door.

Also known as the Guard Room (as

213

NEAR PARIS
VERSAILLES

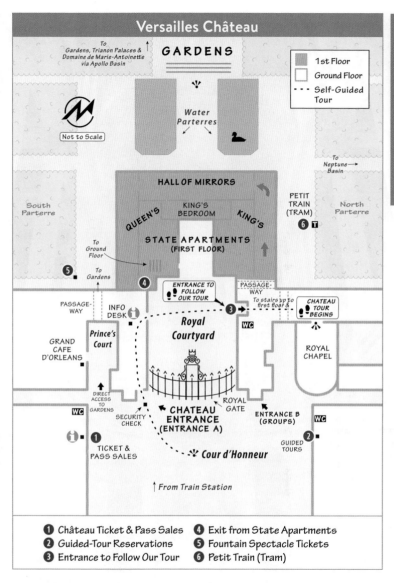

Versailles Château

GARDENS

To Gardens, Trianon Palaces & Domaine de Marie-Antoinette via Apollo Basin

1st Floor
Ground Floor
- - - Self-Guided Tour

Not to Scale

Water Parterres

To Neptune → Basin

HALL OF MIRRORS

South Parterre

QUEEN'S   **KING'S BEDROOM**   KING'S

PETIT TRAIN (TRAM)
6 T

North Parterre

STATE APARTMENTS (FIRST FLOOR)

To Ground Floor

To Gardens

5

4

ENTRANCE TO FOLLOW OUR TOUR

PASSAGE-WAY

To stairs up to first floor &

CHATEAU TOUR BEGINS

PASSAGE-WAY

INFO DESK

3

WC

Royal Courtyard

GRAND CAFE D'ORLEANS

Prince's Court

ROYAL CHAPEL

DIRECT ACCESS TO GARDENS

WC

SECURITY CHECK

ROYAL GATE

CHATEAU ENTRANCE (ENTRANCE A)

ENTRANCE B (GROUPS)

WC

GUIDED TOURS

2

1

TICKET & PASS SALES

Cour d'Honneur

↑ *From Train Station*

1 Château Ticket & Pass Sales
2 Guided-Tour Reservations
3 Entrance to Follow Our Tour
4 Exit from State Apartments
5 Fountain Spectacle Tickets
6 Petit Train (Tram)

it was the room for Louis' Swiss body-guards), the **Red Room** is decorated with a military flair. The **Mercury Room** may have served as Louis' official (not actual) bedroom, where the Sun King would ritually rise each morning to warm his subjects.

The **Apollo Room** was the grand throne room. Louis held court from a 10-foot-tall, silver-and-gold canopied throne on a raised platform placed in the center of the room. Even when the king was away, passing courtiers had to bow to the empty throne.

The final room of the King's Wing is the **War Room,** depicting Louis' victories—in

Louis XIV attended Mass in Versailles' Royal Chapel.

The vast painted ceiling of the Hercules Drawing Room

marble, gilding, stucco, and paint.

• *Next you'll visit the magnificent...*

Hall of Mirrors: No one had ever seen anything like this hall when it was opened. Mirrors were still a great luxury at the time, and the number and size of these monsters was astounding. The hall is nearly 250 feet long. There are 17 arched mirrors, matched by 17 windows letting in that breathtaking view of the Gardens. Imagine this place lit by the flames of thousands of candles, filled with ambassadors, nobles, and guests dressed in silks and powdered wigs. At the far end of the room sits the king, on the canopied throne moved in temporarily from the Apollo Room.

In another age altogether, Germany and the Allies signed the Treaty of Versailles, ending World War I (and, some say, starting World War II) right here, in the Hall of Mirrors.

• *Midway down the Hall of Mirrors, you'll be routed to the left through the heart of the palace, to the...*

King's Bedroom and Council Rooms: Louis XIV's bedroom is elaborately decorated, and the decor changed with the season. Look out the window and notice how this small room is at the exact center of the immense horseshoe-shaped building, overlooking the main courtyard and—naturally—facing the rising sun in the east. It symbolized the exact center of power in France.

• *This ends our tour of the Château. After an extensive renovation, the Queen's Wing of the Château will most likely have reopened when you visit. If it's open, you'll pass through an additional half-dozen sparkling rooms where France's queens had their apartments (described in the audioguide).*

THE GARDENS

Louis XIV was a divine-right ruler. One way he proved it was by controlling nature like a god. These lavish grounds—elaborately planned, pruned, and decorated—showed everyone that Louis was in total command. Louis loved his gardens and, until his last days, presided over their care. He personally led VIPs through them and threw his biggest parties here. With their Greco-Roman themes and incomparable beauty, the gardens illustrated his immense power.

 A *Hall of Mirrors*

B *A royal bedchamber*

C *Louis XIV, the Sun King*

D *Domaine de Marie-Antoinette*

Getting Around the Gardens

On Foot: It's a 45-minute walk from the palace, down to the Grand Canal, past the two Trianon palaces, to the far end of Domaine de Marie-Antoinette.

By Bike: A bike-rental station is by the Grand Canal. It's fun pedaling around the greatest royal park in Europe (about €8/hour or €18/half-day).

By *Petit Train*: The slow-moving hop-on, hop-off tram leaves from behind the Château (north side) and makes a one-way loop, stopping at the Petit and Grand Trianons (entry points to Domaine de Marie-Antoinette), then the Grand Canal before returning to the Château (€7.50 round-trip, €4 one-way, free for kids 10 and under, 4/hour).

By Shuttle Bus: An hourly "TRI" shuttle bus may be running between the train station (Versailles Rive Gauche/Château, leaves from curb directly in front of station) and the Trianon/Domaine (doesn't stop at the Château). It's ideal if you're visiting the Trianon/Domaine first, before the Château, or if you want to return to the station straight from the Trianon/Domaine (shuttle bus may be discontinued; check locally or look for "Ligne TRI" at www.phebus.tm.fr).

TRIANON PALACES AND DOMAINE DE MARIE-ANTOINETTE

Versailles began as an escape from the pressures of kingship. But in a short time, the Château became as busy as Paris ever was. Louis XIV needed an escape from his escape, so he built a smaller palace out in the boonies.

Delicate, pink, and set amid gardens, the **Grand Trianon** was the king's private residence away from the main palace. Louis XIV usually spent a couple of nights a week here (more in the summer) to escape the sniping politics, strict etiquette, and 24/7 scrutiny of official court life.

Nearby is the fantasy world of palaces, ponds, pavilions, and pleasure gardens called the **Domaine de Marie-Antoinette.** Here you'll find the **Hamlet**, where Marie-Antoinette built a complex of 12 thatched-roof buildings fronting a lake as her own private "Normand" village, and the Petit Trianon, her preferred home base.

Provence

This magnificent region is shaped like a giant wedge of quiche. From its sunburned crust, fanning out along the Mediterranean coast, it stretches north along the Rhône Valley. The splendid recipe *provençale* mixes pastel hills, appealing cities, bountiful vineyards, and sweet, hilltop villages.

The Romans were here in force and left many ruins—some of the finest anywhere. Over the centuries, they were followed by seven popes, who resided in a formidable palace in Avignon, and artist Vincent van Gogh, whose work celebrates Provence's sunflowers and starry nights.

The best home bases are Arles and Avignon (plus Vaison-la-Romaine for drivers exploring the Côtes du Rhône wine country). Beyond the towns, the top sights are Les Baux's medieval castle ruins and the ancient Roman aqueduct, Pont du Gard.

A car will come in handy, though towns and sights are connected by public transit. Those traveling *sans* car could take a minivan tour for time-saving efficiency.

PROVENCE IN 2 DAYS

Make Arles or Avignon your sightseeing base. While Francophiles usually pick urban Avignon, Italophiles prefer smaller Arles.

You'll want one day for sightseeing in Arles and Les Baux. Spend most of the day in Arles—try to time your arrival for Wednesday or Saturday, to enjoy the market. Then visit Les Baux in the late afternoon or early evening. On the second day, allow a half-day for Avignon and a half-day for Pont du Gard.

With another day, measure the pulse of rural Provence and spend at least

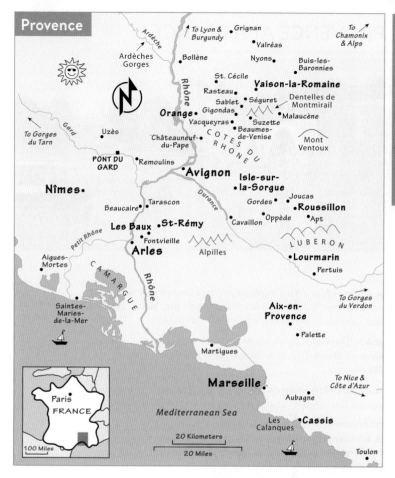

Provence

To Lyon & Burgundy
Grignan
To Chamonix & Alps
Ardèche
Valréas
Ardèches Gorges
Bollène
Nyons
Buis-les-Baronnies
Rhône
St. Cécile
Vaison-la-Romaine
Rasteau
Dentelles de Montmirail
Sablet
Séguret
Orange
Gigondas
Suzette
Malaucène
Vacqueyras
Beaumes-de-Venise
Gard
Uzès
Châteauneuf-du-Pape
CÔTES DU RHÔNE
Mont Ventoux
To Gorges du Tarn
PONT DU GARD
Remoulins
Avignon
Isle-sur-la-Sorgue
Joucas
Nîmes
Durance
Gordes
Roussillon
Beaucaire
Tarascon
Oppède
Apt
St-Rémy
Cavaillon
Les Baux
Fontvieille
LUBERON
Arles
Alpilles
Lourmarin
Aigues-Mortes
CAMARGUE
Pertuis
Petit Rhône
Rhône
To Gorges du Verdon
Saintes-Maries-de-la-Mer
Aix-en-Provence
Palette
Martigues
To Nice & Côte d'Azur
Paris
FRANCE
Marseille
Aubagne
Mediterranean Sea
Les Calanques
Cassis
100 Miles
20 Kilometers
20 Miles
Toulon

one night in a smaller town, such as Vaison-la-Romaine. Exploring the Côtes du Rhône wine country takes about a half-day, but you may want to linger.

Without a car: Explore Arles one day and take a minivan excursion the next. Or, if using public transit, visit Les Baux by bus from Arles on your first day, and on the second day, train to Avignon (for an overnight) and split your time between the town and Pont du Gard (reachable by bus).

Getting Around Provence

By Car: The region is made to order for a car, although travel time between some

Arles

▲▲**Roman Arena** A big amphitheater, once used by gladiators, that hosts summer "bullgames" and occasional bullfights. **Hours:** Daily May-Sept 9:00-19:00, shorter hours off-season. See page 232.

▲▲**St. Trophime Church** Medieval church with exquisite Romanesque entrance. **Hours:** Daily 9:00-12:00 & 14:00-18:30, until 17:00 Oct-March. See page 234.

▲▲**Arlaten Folk Museum** Leading Provencal museum for traditional culture. Due to reopen soon after renovation is complete. **Hours:** Check with TI. See page 238.

▲▲**Ancient History Museum** Filled with models and sculptures, taking you back to Arles' Roman days. **Hours:** Wed-Mon 10:00-18:00, closed Tue. See page 238.

▲**Fondation Van Gogh** Small gallery with works by major contemporary artists paying homage to Van Gogh. **Hours:** Daily 11:00-19:00, July-Aug from 10:00, shorter hours and closed Mon off-season. See page 236.

Avignon

▲▲**Palace of the Popes** A 14th-century Gothic palace built by the popes who made Avignon their home. **Hours:** Daily 9:00-19:00, July-Aug until 20:00, Nov-Feb 9:30-17:45. See page 253.

▲**St. Bénezet Bridge** The "Pont d'Avignon" of nursery-rhyme fame, once connecting the pope's territory to France. **Hours:** Daily 9:00-19:00, July-Aug until 20:00, Nov-Feb 9:30-17:45. See page 252.

▲**Jardin du Rocher des Doms** View park overlooking the Rhône River Valley and Avignon's famous broken bridge. **Hours:** Daily 7:30-20:00, June-Aug until 21:00, Oct-March until 18:00. See page 249.

Nearby

▲▲▲**Pont du Gard** Part bridge and part aqueduct, a huge stone structure heralding the greatness of Rome. **Hours:** Aqueduct—daily May 9:00-21:00, June and Sept until 22:00, July-Aug until 23:00, Feb-April and Oct until 20:00, Nov-Jan until 18:00; museum—daily April-June and Sept 9:00-19:00, July-Aug until 20:00, Oct-Nov and March until 18:00, Dec-Feb until 17:00. See page 257.

▲▲▲**Les Baux** Rock-top village sitting in the shadow of its ruined medieval citadel. **Hours:** Castle—daily 9:00-19:00, July-Aug until 20:00, March and Oct 9:30-18:30, Nov-Feb 10:00-17:00. See page 259.

▲▲**Côtes du Rhône Wine Road Drive** A self-guided drive through picturesque villages and vineyards, unfurling along a scenic wine-tasting route. See page 268.

▲**Vaison-la-Romaine** History-rich town atop a 2,000-year-old Roman site. See page 263.

sights will surprise you—thanks, in part, to narrow roads and endless roundabouts. Be wary of thieves: Park only in well-monitored spaces and leave nothing valuable in your car.

By Bus or Train: Frequent trains link Avignon and Arles. From Arles you can catch a bus to Les Baux (high season only). From Avignon, you can bus to Pont du Gard and Vaison-la-Romaine.

By Minivan Tour: Imagine Tours adapt to your interests and your guide can meet you at your hotel (€190/half-day, €315/day, prices for up to 4 people starting from near Avignon or Arles, mobile 06 89 22 19 87, www.imagine-tours.net, imagine. tours@gmail.com).

Some tour companies focus on wine, such as **Wine Safari** (www.winesafari. net), **Le Vin à la Bouche** (www.levinalabouche.com), and **Avignon Wine Tour** (www.avignon-wine-tour.com).

ARLES

In Roman times, Arles (pronounced "arl") was an important port city. With the first bridge over the Rhône River, it was a key stop on the Roman road from Italy to Spain, the Via Domitia. After reigning as the seat of an important archbishop and a trading center for centuries, Arles became a sleepy backwater of little importance in the 1700s. Vincent van Gogh settled here in the late 1800s, but left only a chunk of his ear. American bombers destroyed much of Arles in World War II as the townsfolk hid out in its underground Roman galleries. But today Arles thrives again, with its evocative Roman Arena, an eclectic assortment of museums, made-for-ice-cream pedestrian zones, and squares that play hide-and-seek with visitors.

Workaday Arles is not a wealthy city and, compared to its neighbor Avignon, it feels unpolished and even a little dirty. But to me, that's part of its charm.

Rick's Tip: *For a helpful overview to your Arles sightseeing,* **start at the Ancient History Museum,** *then head to the city-center sights, linked by my Arles City Walk. Save money by getting one of the city's* **sightseeing passes,** *which cover the ancient monuments and the Ancient History Museum.*

Orientation

Though the town is built along the Rhône, it largely ignores the river. Landmarks hide in Arles' medieval tangle of narrow, winding streets. Hotels have good, free city maps, and helpful street-corner signs point you toward sights and hotels.

Tourist Information

The TI is on the ring road Boulevard des Lices, at Esplanade Charles de Gaulle (daily 9:00-18:45; Oct-March Mon-Sat 9:00-16:45, Sun 10:00-13:00; tel. 04 90 18 41 20, www.arlestourisme.com). The TI sells worthwhile city sightseeing passes.

Roman Arena

Helpful Hints

Sightseeing Passes: The good-value **Pass Liberté** (€12) covers any four monuments and one museum of your choice (I recommend the Ancient History Museum). The **Pass Avantage** (€16) covers all monuments and museums and is worthwhile if you visit two or more museums. Both passes offer a discount at the Fondation Van Gogh. Buy your pass at the TI or any included sight.

Rick's Tip: *In Arles, the* **ancient monuments**—*Roman Arena, Classical Theater, Cryptoporticos, and St. Trophime Cloisters*—**all have the same hours** *(daily 9:00-19:00, April and Oct until 18:00, Nov-March 10:00-17:00).*

Market Days: The big markets are on Wednesdays and Saturdays.

Baggage Storage and Bike Rental: Hôtel Régence will store your bags (€3/bag, daily 7:30-22:00, closed in winter, 5 Rue Marius Jouveau). They also rent bikes (€7/half-day, €15/day, one-way rentals within Provence possible, same hours as baggage storage).

Laundry: A launderette is at 41 Rue du 4 Septembre. Another is near the bus station at 34 Boulevard Georges Clemenceau. Both are open long hours daily.

Local Guides: Charming **Agnes Barrier** offers tours covering Van Gogh and Roman history (€145/3 hours, mobile 06 11 23 03 73, agnes.barrier@hotmail.fr). **Alice Vallat** offers tours of Arles' key sights several days a week (€25/person for 1.5-hour group tour, €145 for 3-hour private tour, mobile 06 74 01 22 54, www.guidearles.com, alice.vallat13@gmail.com).

Arles City Walk

The joy of Arles is how its compact core mixes ancient sights, Van Gogh memories, and a raw and real contemporary scene that is easily covered on foot. All dimensions of the city come together in this self-guided walk. If you enter the sights described (which I recommend, even if briefly), the walk will take most of a day.

Most sights on this walk are covered by the city's sightseeing passes—sold at the TI and included sights. To better understand the ancient sites along this route, visit the Ancient History Museum on the edge of town before taking this walk (see "Sights," later).

Rick's Tip: *While only the Ancient History Museum, Roman Arena, and Arlaten Folk Museum are important to enter, a* **Pass Advantage** *lets you pop into nearly everything.*

Background

The life and artistic times of Dutch artist **Vincent van Gogh** form a big part of Arles' draw, and the city does a fine job of highlighting its Van Gogh connection: Throughout town, about a dozen steel-and-concrete panels, or "easels," provide then-and-now comparisons of the paintings versus the current view.

In the dead of winter in 1888, 35-year-old Van Gogh left big-city Paris for Provence, hoping to jump-start his floundering career and social life. He was as inspired as he was lonely. Coming from the gray skies and flat lands of the north, Vincent was bowled over by everything Provençal—the sun, bright colors, rugged landscape, and raw people. For the next two years he painted furiously, cranking out a masterpiece every few days.

Of the 200-plus paintings that Van Gogh made in the south, none permanently resides in the city that so moved him (though one is usually on loan at the Fondation Van Gogh gallery, which we'll visit on this stroll). But walking the same streets he knew and seeing the places he painted, you can understand how Arles inspired him.

At the Café Van Gogh

Van Gogh "easels" throughout Arles pair the artist's paintings with actual views.

The Rules of Boules

The game of *boules*—also called *pétanque*—is the horseshoes of France. Invented here in the early 1900s, it's a social yet serious sport, and endlessly entertaining to watch—even more so if you understand the rules.

The game is played with heavy metal balls and a small wooden target ball called a *cochonnet* (piglet). Whoever gets his *boule* closest to the *cochonnet* is awarded points. Teams commonly have specialist players: a *pointeur* and a *tireur*. The *pointeur*'s goal is to lob his balls as close to the target as he can. The *tireur*'s job is to blast away opponents' *boules*.

In teams of two, each player gets three *boules*. The starting team traces a small circle in the dirt (in which players must stand when launching their *boules*), and tosses the *cochonnet* about 30 feet to establish the target. The *boule* must be thrown underhand, and can be rolled, launched sky-high, or rocketed at its target. The first *pointeur* shoots, then the opposing *pointeur* shoots until his *boule* gets closer. Once the second team lands a *boule* nearest the *cochonnet,* the first team goes again. If the other team's *boule* is very near the *cochonnet,* the *tireur* will likely attempt to knock it away.

Once all *boules* have been launched, the tally is taken. The team with a *boule* closest to the *cochonnet* wins the round, and they receive a point for each *boule* closer to the target than their opponents' nearest *boule*. The first team to get to 13 points wins. A regulation *boules* field is 10 feet by 43 feet, but the game is played everywhere—just scratch a throwing circle in the sand, toss the *cochonnet,* and you're off.

❷ *Self-Guided Walk*

• *Start at the north gate of the city, just outside the medieval wall on Place Lamartine (100 yards in front of the medieval gate, with the big Monoprix store across the street to the right, beyond the roundabout). A four-foot-tall easel shows Van Gogh's painting.*

❶ THE YELLOW HOUSE EASEL

Vincent arrived in Arles on February 20, 1888, to a foot of snow. He rented a small house here on the north side of Place Lamartine. The house was destroyed in 1944 by an errant bridge-seeking bomb, but the four-story building behind it still stands (find it in the painting). The house had four rooms, including a small studio and the cramped trapezoid-shaped bedroom made famous in his paintings. It was painted yellow inside and out, and Vincent named it..."The Yellow House." In

the distance, the painting shows the same bridges you see today.

• *Walk to the river. You'll pass, on the right, a monument in honor of two WWII American pilots killed in action during the liberation of Arles; a post celebrating Arles' nine sister cities (left); and a big concrete high school (right).*

At the river, find the easel in the wall where ramps lead down.

❷ STARRY NIGHT OVER THE RHONE EASEL

One night, Vincent set up his easel along the river and painted the stars boiling above the city skyline. Vincent looked to the night sky for the divine and was the first to paint outside after dark, adapting his straw hat to hold candles (which must have blown the minds of locals back then). As his paintings progressed, the stars became larger and more animated (like Vincent himself). The lone couple in

FRANCE

Arles

Arles City Walk

1. The Yellow House (Easel)
2. Starry Night over the Rhône (Easel)
3. Rue Voltaire
4. Old Town
5. Arena (Easel)
6. Roman Arena
7. Alpilles Mountains View
8. L'Entrée du Jardin Public (Easel)
9. Classical Theater
10. Republic Square
11. Cryptoporticos
12. St. Trophime Church
13. St. Trophime Cloisters
14. Rue de la République
15. Espace Van Gogh (Easel)
16. Fondation Van Gogh
17. Rue du Docteur Fanton
18. Place du Forum & Café Terrace at Night (Easel)

Other

19. Bag Storage/Bike Rental
20. Launderette (2)
21. To Europcar Car Rental
22. Hertz Car Rental

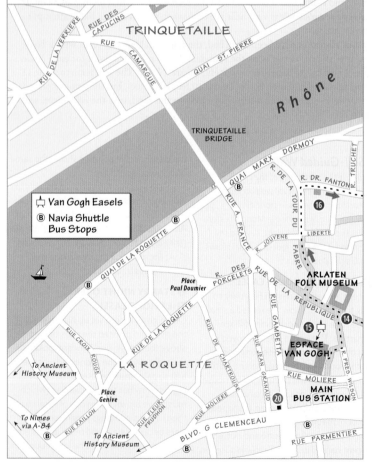

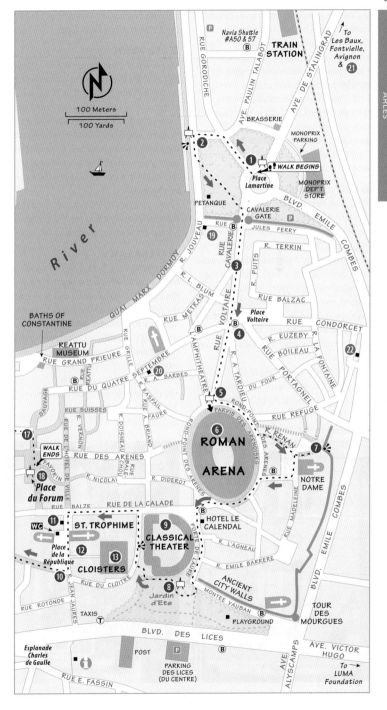

TRAIN STATION

Navia Shuttle #A50 & 57

To Les Baux, Fontvielle, Avignon & 21

RUE GORODICHE

RUE PAULIN TALABOT

AVE. DE STALINGRAD

BRASSERIE

MONOPRIX PARKING

1 WALK BEGINS

Place Lamartine

MONOPRIX DEP'T STORE

BLVD. EMILE COMBES

PETANQUE

CAVALERIE GATE

JULES FERRY

R. TERRIN

19

RUE CAVALERIE

R. PUITS

RUE BALZAC

3

Place Voltaire

RUE CONDORCET

R. JOUVEAU

RUE VOLTAIRE

4

R. EUZEBY

RUE BOILEAU

22

BATHS OF CONSTANTINE

QUAI MARX DORMOY

R. L. BLUM

RUE METRAS

R. A. TARDIEU

LA FONTAINE

RUE PORTAGNEL

River

REATTU MUSEUM

RUE GRAND PRIEURE

RUE GRILLE

L'AMPHITHEATRE

DU FOUR

RUE DU QUATRE SEPTEMBRE

20

R. R. A. BARBES

RUE REATTU

5

ROND-POINT DES ARENES

RUE REFUGE

SAUVAGE

RUE SUISSES

R. VERNON

R. DOISNEAU

R. RASPAIL

R. A. BRIAND

R. FAURE

PARVIS DES ARENES

6

ROMAN ARENA

R. RENAN

DES ARENES

7

WALK ENDS

17

R. DE L'HOTEL DE VILLE

RUE DES ARENES

R. BALZE CHOU

NOTRE DAME

18

FAVORIN RD.

Place du Forum

R. NICOLAI

R. DIDEROT

ROND-POINT DES ARENES

RUE DE LA CALADE

HOTEL LE CALENDAL

RUE MADELEINE

WC 11

ST. TROPHIME

9

CLASSICAL THEATER

R. L'AGNEAU

Place de la République

12

13

CLOISTERS

RUE EMILE BARRERE

10

RUE DU CLOITRE

PORTE DE LAURE

ANCIENT CITY WALLS

RUE ROTONDE

RUE JEAN JAURES

8

Jardin d'Ete

MONTEE VAUBAN

TOUR DES MOURGUES

TAXIS

T

PLAYGROUND

BLVD. EMILE COMBES

Esplanade Charles de Gaulle

BLVD. DES LICES

POST

PARKING DES LICES (DU CENTRE)

AVE. VICTOR HUGO

AVE. ALYSCAMPS

To LUMA Foundation

RUE E. FASSIN

the painting pops up again and again in his work. (Note: This painting is not the *Starry Night* you're probably thinking of—that one was painted later, in St-Rémy.)

• *With your back to the river, angle right through the scruffy park of plane trees (a kind of sycamore). Continue into town through the park and between the stumpy 14th-century stone towers where the city gates once stood. Walk a block up Rue de la Cavalerie to the decorative (if dry) fountain with the colorful old mosaic.*

❸ RUE VOLTAIRE

Van Gogh first walked into town down this street in 1888. When he saw this fountain, it was just a year old. Its mosaic celebrates the high culture of Provence (she's the winged woman who obviously loves music and reading). But this neighborhood was Arles' 19th-century red light district, and the far-from-home Dutchman spent many lonely nights in its bars and brothels. This street still has a certain edgy local color, with humble shops, bars, and bakeries.

• *Stay left and keep walking to Place Voltaire, a center of this working-class neighborhood (the local Communist Party headquarters is across the square on the left). Stop at the top end of the square under the plane tree in front of Brasserie le Pitchounet.*

❹ OLD TOWN

You've left the bombed-out part of town and entered the old town, with buildings predating World War II. The stony white arches of the ancient Roman Arena ahead mark your destination. As you hike up Rue Voltaire, notice the shutters, which contribute to Arles' character. The old town is strictly protected: These traditional shutters come in a variety of styles but cannot be changed.

• *Keep straight up Rue Voltaire, climb to the Roman Arena, and find the Arena easel at the top of the stairs, to the right.*

❺ ARENA EASEL

All summer long, fueled by sun and alcohol, Vincent painted the town. He loved the bullfights in the arena and sketched the colorful surge of the crowds, spending more time studying the people than watching the bullfights (notice how the bull is barely visible). Vincent had little interest in Arles' antiquity—it was people and nature that fascinated him.

• *At this point you can visit the Roman Arena.*

Arles' old town

Inside the Roman Arena

The Romans in Provence

Many scholars claim the best-preserved ancient Roman buildings are not in Italy, but in France. These ancient stones will be an important part of your sightseeing agenda.

Classical Rome endured from about 500 BC through AD 500—spending about 500 years growing, 200 years peaking, and 300 years declining. Julius Caesar conquered Gaul—which included Provence—during the Gallic Wars (58-51 BC), then crossed the Rubicon River in 49 BC to incite civil war within the Roman Republic. He erected a temple to Jupiter on the future site of Paris' Notre-Dame Cathedral.

The concept of one-man rule lived on with his grandnephew, Octavian (whom he had also adopted as his son). Octavian took the title "Augustus" and became the first in a line of emperors who would control Rome for the next 500 years. Rome morphed from a Republic into an Empire: a collection of many diverse territories ruled by a single man. At its peak (c. AD 117), the Roman Empire had 54 million people—"Rome" didn't just refer to the city, but to the entire civilized Western world.

Provence, with its strategic location, benefited greatly from Rome's global economy and grew to become an important part of its worldwide empire. After Julius Caesar conquered Gaul, Emperor Augustus Romanized it, building and renovating cities in the image of Rome.

When it came to construction, the Romans' magic building ingredient was concrete. Easier to work than stone and longer lasting than wood, concrete served as flooring, roofing, filler, glue, and support. Builders would start with a foundation of brick, then fill it in with poured concrete. They would then cover important structures, such as basilicas, in sheets of expensive marble (held on with nails), or decorate floors and walls with mosaics.

Most cities had a theater, baths, and aqueducts; the most important cities had sports arenas. A typical Roman city (such as Arles) was a garrison town, laid out on a grid plan with two main roads: one running north-south (the *cardus*), the other east-west (the *decumanus*). Approaching the city on your chariot, you'd pass by the cemetery, which was located outside of town for hygienic reasons. You'd enter the main gate and wheel past warehouses and apartment houses to the town square (forum). Facing the square were the most important temples, dedicated to the patron gods of the city. Nearby, you'd find bathhouses; like today's fitness clubs, these served the almost sacred dedication to personal vigor. Also close by were businesses that catered to the citizens' needs: the marketplace, bakeries, banks, and brothels. Aqueducts brought fresh water for drinking, filling the baths, and delighting the citizens with bubbling fountains.

❻ ROMAN ARENA (AMPHITHEATRE)

This well-preserved arena is worth ▲▲ and is still in use today. Nearly 2,000 years ago, gladiators fought wild animals to the delight of 20,000 screaming fans. Now local daredevils still fight wild animals here—"bullgame" posters around the arena advertise upcoming spectacles.

Cost and Hours: €9 combo-ticket with Classical Theater; daily 9:00-19:00, April and Oct until 18:00, Nov-March 10:00-17:00, Rond-point des Arènes, tel. 04 90 49 36 86, www.arenes-arles.com.

Visiting the Arena: After passing the ticket kiosk, find the helpful English display under the second arch, where you can read about the arena's history and renovation. Then climb up and take a seat in the theater. Thirty-four rows of stone bleachers extended all the way to the top of those vacant arches that circle the arena. All arches were numbered to help distracted fans find their seats. The many passageways you'll see (called vomitoires) allowed for rapid dispersal after the games—fights would break out among frenzied fans if they couldn't leave quickly.

Throughout medieval times and until the early 1800s, the stadium became a fortified town with towers added, arches bricked up, and 200 humble homes crammed within its circular defenses. Parts of three of the medieval **towers** survive.

To climb one of the towers and enjoy magnificent **views** over Arles and the arena, find the *"To the Tower"* sign near the ticket booth and exit.

• *Exit at street level and turn right, and after a quarter of the way around, turn left (where the metal fence ends and you hit the little street). Go up the cute stepped lane (Rue Renan). Take three steps and turn around to study the arena.*

The big stones are Roman; the little medieval stones—more like rubble—filling the two upper-level archways are a reminder of the arena's time as a fortified town in the Middle Ages. You can even see rooflines and beam holes where

The well-preserved Roman Arena

the Roman structure provided a solid foundation to lean on.

• *Hike up the pretty, stepped lane through the parking lot, keeping to the left of the stark and stony church to the highest point in Arles. Take in the countryside view.*

❼ ALPILLES MOUNTAINS VIEW

This view pretty much matches what Vincent van Gogh, an avid walker, would have seen. Imagine him hauling his easel into those fields under intense sun, leaning against a ferocious wind, struggling to keep his hat on. Vincent carried his easel as far as the medieval Abbey of Montmajour, that bulky structure on the hill in the distance. The St. Paul Hospital, where he was eventually treated in St-Rémy, is on the other side of the Alpilles mountains, several miles beyond Montmajour.

• *Cross in front of the church to return to the arena, and continue circling it clockwise. At the high point, turn left and walk out Rue de Porte de Laure. (You'll pass the ancient Classical Theater on your right, which we'll visit later.) After a couple of blocks, go right, down the curved staircase into the park. Continue toward the busy street. Take the second right (through the gate and into the park) and find the...*

❽ L'ENTREE DU JARDIN PUBLIC EASEL

Vincent spent many a sunny day painting in the leafy Jardin d'Eté. In another letter to his sister, Vincent wrote, "I don't know whether you can understand that one may make a poem by arranging colors...In a similar manner, the bizarre lines, purposely selected and multiplied, meandering all through the picture may not present a literal image of the garden, but they may present it to our minds as if in a dream."

• *Hike through the park and uphill toward the three-story surviving tower of the Classical Theater. At the ancient tower, follow the white metal fence to the left, enjoying peeks at "le jardin" of stone—a collection of carved bits of a once-grand Roman theater. Go up four steps and around to the right for a fine view of the...*

❾ CLASSICAL THEATER (THEATRE ANTIQUE)

This first-century BC Roman theater once seated 10,000. There was no hillside to provide structural support; instead, this elegant, three-level arena had 27 buttress arches radiating out behind the seats.

Cost and Hours: €9 combo-ticket with Roman Arena, same hours as Arena.

Visiting the Theater: Start with the 10-minute video, which provides background information that makes it easier to imagine the scattered stones back in place (crouch in front to make out the small English subtitles).

Then walk into the theater and pull up a stone seat in a center aisle. Imagine that for 500 years, ancient Romans gathered here for entertainment. The original structure was much higher, with 33 rows of seats covering three levels to accommodate demand. During the Middle Ages, the old theater became a convenient town quarry—much of St. Trophime Church was built from theater rubble. Precious little of the original theater survives—though it still is used for events, with seating for 2,000 spectators.

• *From the theater, walk downhill on Rue de la Calade. Take the first left into a big square.*

❿ REPUBLIC SQUARE (PLACE DE LA REPUBLIQUE)

This square used to be called "Place Royale"...until the French Revolution. The obelisk was the former centerpiece of Arles' Roman Circus (outside of town). The lions at its base are the symbol of the city, whose slogan is (roughly) "the gentle lion." Observe the age-old scene: tourists, peasants, shoppers, pilgrims, children, and street musicians. The City Hall (Hôtel

Classical Theater

de Ville) has a stately facade, built in the same generation as Versailles. Where there's a City Hall, there's always a free WC (if you win the Revolution, you can pee for free at the mayor's home). Notice the flags: The yellow-and-red of Provence is the same as the yellow-and-red of Catalunya, its linguistic cousin in Spain.

• *Today's City Hall sits upon an ancient city center. Inside, find the entrance to an ancient cryptoportico (foundation).*

⓫ CRYPTOPORTICOS (CRYPTOPORTIQUES)

This dark, drippy underworld of Roman arches was constructed to support the upper half of Forum Square. Two thousand years ago, most of this gallery of arches was at or above street level; modern Arles has buried about 20 feet of its history over the millennia. Through the tiny windows high up you would have seen the sandals of Romans on their way to the forum. Other than dark arches and broken bits of forum littering the dirt floor, there's not much down here beyond ancient memories (€4.50, same hours as Arena).

• *The highlight of Place de la République is...*

⓬ ST. TROPHIME CHURCH

Named after a third-century bishop of Arles, this church, worth ▲▲, sports the finest Romanesque main entrance I've seen anywhere. The Romanesque and Gothic interior—with tapestries, relics, and a rare painting from the French Revolution when this was a "Temple of Reason"—is worth a visit.

Cost and Hours: Free, daily 9:00-12:00 & 14:00-18:30, Oct-March until 17:00.

Exterior: Like a Roman triumphal arch, the church **facade** trumpets the promise of Judgment Day. The tympanum (the semicircular area above the door) is filled with Christian symbolism. Christ sits in majesty, surrounded by symbols of the four evangelists: Matthew (the winged man), Mark (the winged lion), Luke (the ox), and John (the eagle). The 12 apostles are lined up below Jesus. It's Judgment

Day...some are saved and others aren't. Notice the condemned (on the right)—a chain gang doing a sad bunny-hop over the fires of hell. For them, the tune trumpeted by the three angels above Christ is not a happy one. Below the chain gang, St. Stephen is being stoned to death, with his soul leaving through his mouth and instantly being welcomed by angels. Study the exquisite detail. In an illiterate world, this was colorfully painted, like a neon billboard over the town square. It's full of meaning, and a medieval pilgrim understood it all.

Interior: Just inside the door on the right, a yellow chart locates the interior highlights and helps explain the carvings you just saw on the tympanum. The tall 12th-century Romanesque nave is decorated by a set of tapestries (typical in the Middle Ages) showing scenes from the life of Mary (17th century, from the French town of Aubusson).

This church is a stop on the ancient pilgrimage route to Santiago de Compostela in northwest Spain. For 800 years pilgrims on their way to Santiago have paused here...and they still do today. Notice the modern-day pilgrimages advertised on the far right near the church's entry.

• *To reach the adjacent peaceful cloister, leave the church, turn left, then left again through a courtyard.*

⓭ ST. TROPHIME CLOISTERS

Worth seeing if you have an Arles sightseeing pass (otherwise €5.50, same hours as Arena), the cloisters' many small columns were scavenged from the ancient Roman theater and used to create an oasis of peace in Arles' center. Enjoy the delicate, sculpted capitals, the rounded Romanesque arches (12th century), and the pointed Gothic ones (14th century). The pretty vaulted hall exhibits 17th-century tapestries showing scenes from the First Crusade to the Holy Land. There's an instructive video and a chance to walk outside along an angled rooftop designed

St. Trophime Church

to catch rainwater: Notice the slanted gutter that channeled the water into a cistern and the heavy roof slabs covering the tapestry hall below.

• *From Place de la République, exit on the far corner (opposite the church and kitty-corner from where you entered) to stroll a delightful pedestrian street.*

⓪ RUE DE LA REPUBLIQUE

Rue da la République is Arles' primary shopping street. Walk downhill, enjoying the scene and popping into shops that catch your interest.

Near the start is **Maison Soulier Bakery.** Inside you'll be tempted by *fougasse* (bread studded with herbs, olives, and bacon bits), *sablés Provençal* (cookies made with honey and almonds), *tarte lavande* (a sweet almond lavender tart), and big crispy meringues. A few doors down is **Restaurant L'Atelier** (with two prized Michelin stars), **L'Occitane en Provence** (local perfumes), **Puyricard Chocolate** (with enticing €1 treats and *calisson,* a sweet almond delight), as well as local design and antique shops. The

fragile spiral columns on the left (just before the tourist-pleasing Lavender Boutique on the corner) show what 400 years of weather can do to decorative stonework. The big Arlaten Folk Museum is up on the right.

• *Take the first left onto Rue Président Wilson. Just after the butcher shop, turn right to find the* **Hôtel Dieu,** *a hospital made famous by one of its patients: Vincent van Gogh.*

⓯ ESPACE VAN GOGH EASEL

In December 1888, shortly after his famous ear-cutting incident (see *Café Terrace at Night* easel, described later), Vincent was admitted into the local hospital—today's Espace Van Gogh cultural center. It surrounds a flowery courtyard (open to the public) that the artist loved and painted when he was being treated for blood loss, hallucinations, and severe depression that left him bedridden for a month. The citizens of Arles circulated a petition demanding that the mad Dutchman be kept under medical supervision. Félix Rey, Vincent's kind doctor, worked out a compromise:

The artist could leave during the day so that he could continue painting, but he had to sleep at the hospital at night. Look through the postcards sold in the courtyard and find a painting of Vincent's ward showing nuns attending to patients in a gray hall (*Ward of Arles Hospital*).

• *Return to Rue de la République. Take a left and continue two blocks downhill. Take the second right up Rue Tour de Fabre and follow signs to Fondation Van Gogh. After a few steps, you'll pass* **La Main Qui Pense** *(The Hand That Thinks) pottery shop. A couple of blocks farther down, turn right onto Rue du Docteur Fanton. On your immediate right is the...*

⓰ FONDATION VAN GOGH

This art foundation, worth ▲, delivers a refreshing stop for modern-art lovers and Van Gogh fans, with two temporary exhibits per year in which contemporary artists pay homage to Vincent with thought-provoking interpretations of his works. You'll also see at least one original work by Van Gogh (painted during his time in the region).

Cost and Hours: €9, discount with sightseeing passes; daily 11:00-19:00, July-Aug from 10:00, Oct-March until 17:45, closed Mon off-season; audioguide-€3, 35 Rue du Docteur Fanton, tel. 04 90 49 94 04, www.fondation-vincentvangogh-arles.org.

• *Continue on Rue du Docteur Fanton.*

⓱ RUE DU DOCTEUR FANTON

A string of recommended restaurants is on the left. On the right is the **Crèche**

Municipale. Open workdays, this is a free, government-funded daycare where parents can drop off their infants up to two years old. The notion: No worker should face financial hardship in order to receive quality childcare. At the next corner is the recommended **Soleileïs,** Arles' top ice cream shop.

After the ice cream shop, turn right and step into **Bar El Paseo** at 4 Rue des Thermes, which is run by the Leal family, famous for its bullfighters. The main museum-like room is full of bull—including the mounted heads of three big ones who died in the local arena and a big black-and-white photo of Arles' arena packed to capacity. You're welcome to look around...and to buy a glass of Spanish Rioja wine or sangria.

• *A few steps farther is...*

⓲ FORUM SQUARE (PLACE DU FORUM) AND CAFE TERRACE AT NIGHT EASEL

Named for the Roman forum that once stood here, **Forum Square,** worth ▲, was the political and religious center of Roman Arles. Still lively, this café-crammed square is a local watering hole and popular for a *pastis* (anise-based aperitif). The bistros on the square can put together a passable salad or *plat du jour*—and when you sprinkle on the ambience, that's €14 well spent.

At the corner of Grand Hôtel Nord-Pinus, a plaque shows how the Romans built a foundation of galleries to make the main square level in order to compensate for Arles' slope down to the river. The two columns are all that survive from the

Fondation Van Gogh

A café on Forum Square

upper story of the entry to the forum.

The statue on the square is of **Frédéric Mistral** (1830-1914). This popular poet, who wrote in the local dialect rather than in French, was a champion of Provençal culture. After receiving the Nobel Prize in Literature in 1904, Mistral used his prize money to preserve and display the folk identity of Provence. He founded a regional folk museum (the Arlaten Folk Museum) at a time when France was rapidly centralizing and regions like Provence were losing their unique identities. (The local mistral wind has nothing to do with his name.)

• *Facing the brightly painted yellow café, find your final Van Gogh easel—***Café Terrace at Night.**

In October 1888, lonely Vincent—who dreamed of making Arles a magnet for fellow artists—persuaded his friend Paul Gauguin to come. He decorated Gauguin's room with several humble canvases of sunflowers (now some of the world's priciest paintings), knowing that Gauguin had admired a similar painting he'd done in Paris. Their plan was for Gauguin to be the "dean" of a new art school in Arles, and Vincent its instructor-in-chief. At first, the two got along well. They spent days side by side, rendering the same subjects in their two distinct styles. At night they hit the bars and brothels. Van Gogh's well-known *Café Terrace at Night* captures the glow of an absinthe buzz at Café la Nuit on Place du Forum.

After two months together, the two artists clashed over art and personality differences (Vincent was a slob around the house, whereas Gauguin was meticulous). The night of December 23, they were drinking absinthe at the café when Vincent suddenly went ballistic. He threw his glass at Gauguin. Gauguin left. Walking through Place Victor Hugo, Gauguin heard footsteps behind him and turned to see Vincent coming at him, brandishing a razor. Gauguin quickly fled town. The local paper reported what

happened next: "At 11:30 p.m., Vincent van Gogh, painter from Holland, appeared at the brothel at no. 1, asked for Rachel, and gave her his cut-off earlobe, saying, 'Treasure this precious object.' Then he vanished." He woke up the next morning at home with his head wrapped in a bloody towel and his earlobe missing.

The **bright-yellow café**—called Café la Nuit—was the subject of one of Vincent van Gogh's most famous works in Arles. Although his painting showed the café in a brilliant yellow from the glow of gas lamps, the facade was bare limestone. The café is now a tourist trap that its current owners painted to match Van Gogh's version...and to cash in on the Vincent-crazed hordes who pay too much to eat or drink here.

In spring 1889, the bipolar genius (a modern diagnosis) checked himself into the St. Paul Monastery and Hospital in St-Rémy-de-Provence. He spent a year there, thriving in the care of nurturing doctors and nuns. Painting was part of his therapy, so they gave him a studio to work in, and he produced more than 100 paintings. Alcohol-free and institutionalized, he did some of his wildest work. With thick, swirling brushstrokes and surreal colors, he made his placid surroundings throb with restless energy.

Eventually, Vincent's torment became unbearable. In the spring of 1890, he left Provence to be cared for by a sympathetic doctor in Auvers-sur-Oise, just north of Paris. On July 27, he wandered into a field and shot himself. He died two days later.

• *With this walk, you've seen most of Arles' top sights. The Arlaten Folk Museum is a short walk away; the Ancient History Museum is on the outskirts (both described next). But first, enjoy a drink on the Place du Forum and savor the joy of experiencing the essence of Provence.*

Sights

Many of Arles' city-center sights (such as the Roman Arena and St. Trophime church) are covered on my self-guided walk. Two more sights are worth your time; the first is central, the second is away from the center.

▲▲ARLATEN FOLK MUSEUM (MUSEON ARLATEN)

This is the leading museum in Provence for traditional culture and folklore. After a long closure for renovation, it should be open by the time you visit and is expected to resume its place as one of the top attractions in Arles.

Cost and Hours: Scheduled to reopen soon—check ahead for price and opening hours. Tel. 04 13 31 51 99, www.museon-arlaten.fr.

▲▲ANCIENT HISTORY MUSEUM (MUSEE DEPARTEMENTAL ARLES ANTIQUE)

This museum, just west of central Arles along the river, provides valuable background on Arles' Roman history: Visit it first, before delving into the rest of the city's sights (drivers should stop on the way into town).

Located on the site of the Roman chariot racecourse (the arc of which defines today's parking lot), this air-conditioned, all-on-one-floor museum is full of models and original sculptures that re-create the Roman city, making workaday life and culture easier to imagine.

While the museum's posted descriptions of most of its treasures are only in French, the audioguide does a fine job describing the exhibits in English. For a deeper understanding of Provence's ancient roots, read "The Romans in Provence," earlier.

Cost and Hours: €8, free first Sun of the month, Wed-Mon 10:00-18:00, closed Tue, audioguide-€2, Presqu'île du Cirque Romain, tel. 04 13 31 51 03.

Getting There: Drivers will see signs for the museum at the city's western end. To reach the museum from the city center sans car, take the €1 **Navia shuttle** (see "Getting Around Arles" under "Transportation," later). The museum is about a 20-minute **walk** from the city center; a **taxi** ride costs about €12.

Visiting the Museum: The permanent

Model of Arles' Classical Theater

collection is housed in a large hall flooded with natural light. Highlights include models of the ancient city and its major landmarks, a 2,000-year-old Roman boat, statues, mosaics, and sarcophagi. Here's what you'll see.

A wall **map** of the region during the Roman era greets visitors and shows the geographic importance of Arles: Three important Roman trade routes—vias Domitia, Grippa, and Aurelia—all converged on or near Arles.

After a small exhibit on pre-Roman Arles you'll come to fascinating **models of the Roman city** and the impressive Roman structures in (and near) Arles. These breathe life into the buildings, showing how they looked 2,000 years ago.

Start with the **model of Roman Arles** and ponder the city's splendor when Arles' population was almost double that of today. Find the forum—it's still the center of town, although only two columns survive (the smaller section of the forum is where today's Place du Forum is built). The next model shows the grandeur of the forum in greater detail.

At the museum's center stands the original **statue of Julius Caesar,** which once graced Arles' ancient theater's magnificent stage wall. To the left of Julius, find a **model of Arles' theater** and its wall, as well as models of the ancient town's other major buildings. Find the arena with its movable cover to shelter spectators from sun or rain, the floating wooden bridge over the widest, slowest part of the river—giving Arles a strategic advantage, and the hydraulic mill of Barbegal with its 16 waterwheels cascading water down a hillside.

Step down into the hall to Julius's right and find the large model of the **chariot racecourse.** Part of the original racecourse was just outside the windows, and although long gone, it likely resembled Rome's Circus Maximus. The rest of this hall is dedicated to the museum's newest and most exciting exhibit: a **Gallo-Roman vessel** and much of its cargo (English translations on panels). This almost-100-foot-long Roman barge was hauled out of the Rhône in 2010, along with some 280 amphorae and 3,000 ceramic artifacts. It was typical of flat-bottomed barges used to shuttle goods between Arles and ports along the Mediterranean (vessels were manually towed upriver). This one hauled limestone slabs and big rocks—no wonder it sank. A worthwhile 20-minute video about the barge's recovery (with English subtitles) plays continuously in a tiny theater at the end of the hall.

Elsewhere in the museum, you'll see displays of pottery, jewelry, metal, and glass artifacts. You'll also see well-crafted mosaic floors that illustrate how Roman Arles was a city of art and culture. The many **statues** are all original, except for the greatest—the *Venus of Arles,* which Louis XIV took a liking to and had moved to Versailles.

Experiences

▲▲MARKETS

Provençal market days offer France's most colorful and tantalizing outdoor shopping. On Wednesday and Saturday mornings, Arles' ring road erupts into an open-air festival of fish, flowers, produce...and everything Provençal. The main event is on Saturday, with vendors jamming the ring road from Boulevard Emile Combes to the east, along Boulevard des Lices near the TI (the heart of the market),

Wednesday and Saturday are Arles' market days.

and continuing down Boulevard Georges Clemenceau to the west. Wednesday's market runs only along Boulevard Emile Combes, between Place Lamartine and Avenue Victor Hugo; the segment nearest Place Lamartine is all about food, and the upper half features clothing, tablecloths, purses, and so on. On the first Wednesday of the month, a flea market doubles the size of the usual Wednesday market along Boulevard des Lices near the TI. Both markets are open until about 12:30.

▲▲BULLGAMES (COURSES CAMARGUAISES)

Provençal "bullgames" are held in Arles and in neighboring towns. Those in Arles occupy the same seats that fans have used for nearly 2,000 years, and deliver the city's most memorable experience—the *courses camarguaises* in the ancient arena. The nonviolent bullgames are more sporting than bloody bullfights (though traditional Spanish-style bullfights still take place on occasion). The bulls of Arles (who, locals insist, "die of old age") are promoted in posters even more boldly than their human foes. In the bullgame, a ribbon *(cocarde)* is laced between the bull's horns. The *razeteur,* dressed in white and carrying a special hook, has 15 minutes to snare the ribbon. Local businessmen encourage a *razeteur* by shouting out how much money they'll pay for the *cocarde.* If the bull pulls a good stunt, the band plays the famous "Toreador" song from *Carmen.* The following day, newspapers report on the games, including how many *Carmen*s the bull earned.

Three classes of bullgames—determined by the experience of the *razeteurs*—are advertised in posters: The *Course de Protection* is for rookies. The *Trophée de l'Avenir* comes with more experience. And the *Trophée des As* features top professionals. During Easter *(Féria de Pâques)* and the fall rice-harvest festival *(Féria du Riz),* the arena hosts traditional Spanish bullfights (look for *corrida*) with outfits, swords, spikes, and the whole gory shebang. (Nearby villages stage *courses camarguaises* in small wooden bullrings nearly every weekend; TIs have the latest schedule.)

Bulls are not harmed in Provençal-style "bullgames."

Provence's Cuisine Scene

The almost extravagant use of garlic, olive oil, herbs, and tomatoes makes Provence's cuisine France's liveliest. To sample it, order anything *à la provençale*. Among the area's spicy specialties are **ratatouille** (a mixture of vegetables in a thick, herb-flavored tomato sauce), **aioli** (a rich, garlicky mayonnaise spread over vegetables, potatoes, fish, or whatever), **tapenade** (a paste of pureed olives, capers, anchovies, herbs, and sometimes tuna), **soupe au pistou** (thin yet flavorful vegetable soup with a sauce of basil, garlic, and cheese), and **soupe à l'ail** (garlic soup, called **aigo bouido** in the local dialect). Look for **riz de Camargue** (reddish, chewy, nutty-tasting rice) and **taureau** (bull's meat). The native goat cheeses are **banon de banon** or **banon à la feuille** (dipped in brandy and wrapped in chestnut leaves) and spicy **picodon**. Don't miss the region's prized **Cavaillon melons** (cantaloupes) or its delicious cherries and apricots (often turned into jams and candied fruits).

Wines of Provence: Provence produces some of France's great wines at relatively reasonable prices. Look for wines from **Gigondas, Rasteau, Cairanne, Beaumes-de-Venise, Vacqueyras,** and **Châteauneuf-du-Pape.** For the cheapest but still tasty wines, look for labels showing **Côtes du Rhône Villages** or **Côtes de Provence.** If you like rosé, you win. **Rosés from Tavel** are considered among the best in Provence. For reds, splurge for Châteauneuf-du-Pape or Gigondas, and for a fine aperitif wine or a dessert wine, try the **Muscat** from **Beaumes-de-Venise.**

Bullgame tickets usually run €11-20; bullfights are pricier (€36-100). Schedules for bullgames vary (usually July-Aug on Wed and Fri)—ask at the TI or check www.arenes-arles.com.

BOULES

The local "*boul*ing alleys" are by the Alyscamps necropolis (a block outside the ring road and sometimes by the river on Place Lamartine). Watch the old boys congregate for a game of *pétanque* after their afternoon naps (see "The Rules of *Boules*" sidebar in the "Arles City Walk," earlier, for more on this popular local pastime).

Sleeping

Hotels are a great value here—most are air-conditioned, though few have elevators.

$$ Hôtel le Calendal*** is a service-with-a-smile place ideally located between the Roman Arena and Classical Theater. The hotel opens to the street with airy lounges and a lovely palm-shaded courtyard. You'll find snacks and drinks in the café/sandwich bar (daily 8:00-20:00). The soothing rooms show a modern flair and come in all shapes and sizes (some with balcony, family rooms, air-con, free spa for adults, ask about parking deals, 5 Rue Porte de Laure, tel. 04 90 96 11 89, www.lecalendal.com, contact@lecalendal.com).

$ Hôtel du Musée** is a quiet, affordable manor-home hideaway tucked deep in Arles (if driving, call the hotel from the street—they'll open the barrier so you can drive in to drop off your bags). This delightful place comes with 29 tasteful rooms, a flowery courtyard, and comfortable lounges. Lighthearted Claude and English-speaking Laurence are good hosts (family rooms, no elevator, pay parking garage, follow *Réattu Museum* signs to 11 Rue du Grand Prieuré, tel. 04 90 93 88 88, www.hoteldumusee.com, contact@hoteldumusee.com).

$ Hôtel de la Muette** is an intimate, good-value hotel located in a quiet corner of Arles, run by hard-working owners Brigitte and Alain. Its sharp rooms and bathrooms come with tiled floors and stone walls (RS%, family rooms, no elevator, pay private garage, 15 Rue des Suisses, tel. 04 90 96 15 39, www.hotel-muette.com, hotel.muette@wanadoo.fr).

Rick's Tip: *An international photo event* **jams hotels in Arles the second weekend of July,** *while the twice-yearly Féria* **draws crowds over Easter and in mid-September.**

$ Hôtel Régence** is a top budget deal with a riverfront location, comfortable, Provençal rooms, and easy parking. And it's just a 10-minute walk from the train station (family rooms, choose river-view or quieter courtyard rooms, no elevator; from Place Lamartine, turn right after passing between towers to reach 5 Rue Marius Jouveau; tel. 04 90 96 39 85, www.hotel-regence.com, contact@hotel-regence.com). Gentle Valérie and Eric speak English.

$ Hôtel Acacias*** sits just off Place Lamartine and inside the old city walls. It's a modern hotel with small, clean, and comfortable rooms (family rooms,

air-con, pay parking garage, 2 Rue de la Cavalerie, tel. 04 90 96 37 88, https://hotel-arles.brithotel.fr, arles@brithotel.fr).

Eating

You can dine well in Arles on a modest budget (most of my listings have *menus* for under €25). Sunday is a quiet night for restaurants, though eateries on Place du Forum are open. For a portable snack, try Maison Soulier Bakery (see "Arles City Walk," earlier), and for groceries, use the big Monoprix supermarket/department store on Place Lamartine (closed Sun).

Rick's Tip: *Cafés on the Place du Forum deliver great atmosphere and fair prices (at Le Tambourin and Mon Bar Brasserie), but* **mediocre food. Avoid the garish yellow tourist trap Café la Nuit.** *For serious cuisine, wander away from the square.*

For Lunch or a Light Dinner

$ Cuisine de Comptoir, just off Place du Forum, offers light and cheap dinners of *tartine*—a cross between pizza and bruschetta, served with soup or salad for €11—and offers a fun array of pizza-style *tartine* toppings. This Provençal answer to a pizzeria, run by Vincent, has indoor seating only (closed Sun, off lower end of square at 10 Rue de la Liberté, tel. 04 90 96 86 28).

$ Café Factory République is a youthful, creative, and fun-loving place run by jovial Gilles. He's fun to talk with and serves sandwiches, hearty salads, and a wide variety of drinks. While not really a dinner place, he takes orders until 18:00 (Mon-Sat 8:00-19:00, closed Sun, 35 Rue de la République, tel. 04 90 54 52 23, skinniest WC in France).

$ Le Comptoir du Calendal, in the recommended Hôtel le Calendal, serves light, seasonal fare either curbside overlooking the arena, in its lovely courtyard, or inside the café—order at the counter (delicious and cheap little sandwiches and salads, daily 8:00-20:00, guest computer available, 5 Rue Porte de Laure, tel. 04 90 96 11 89).

Finer Dining

One of France's most recognized chefs, Jean-Luc Rabanel, runs two very different places 50 yards from Place de la République. They sit side by side at 7 Rue des Carmes.

$$$$ L'Atelier is a top-end place with two Michelin stars (contemporary tasting menus only—around €125, closed Mon-Tue, tel. 04 90 91 07 69). And next door is **$$$ A Côté,** a place with all the quality, none of the pretense, and meals at a fraction of the price. It offers a smart wine bar/bistro ambience and fine cuisine. This is a wonderful opportunity to sample the famous chef's talents with the €32 three-course menu (limited selection of wines by the glass, closed Mon-Tue, tel. 04 90 47 61 13, www.rabanel.com).

$$ Le Criquet, possibly the best value in Arles, is a sweet little place two blocks above the arena, serving well-presented and delicious Provençal classics with joy at good prices. Sisters Lili and Charlotte serve while mama and papa run the kitchen. Their mouthwatering €25 *bourride* is the house specialty: a creamy fish soup thickened with aioli and lots of garlic and stuffed with mussels, clams, calamari, and more. They have a lovely dining room and a petite terrace (closed Sun and Wed, 21 Rue Porte de Laure, tel. 04 90 96 80 51).

On Rue du Docteur Fanton

$$$ Le Galoubet is a popular local spot, blending a warm interior, traditional French cuisine, and gregarious service, thanks to owner Frank. It's the most expensive and least flexible place on the street, serving *menus* only. If it's cold, a roaring fire keeps you toasty (closed Sun-Mon, great fries and desserts, at #18, tel. 04 90 93 18 11).

$$ Les Filles du 16 is a warm, affordable place to enjoy a good Provençal two- or three-course dinner. The choices, while tasty, are limited, so check the selection before sitting down (closed Sat-Sun, at #16, tel. 04 90 93 77 36).

$$ Le Plaza la Paillotte buzzes with happy diners enjoying delicious, well-presented Provençal cuisine. Attentive owners Stéphane and Graziela (he cooks, she serves) welcome diners with a comfortable terrace and a smart interior (open daily, at #28, tel. 04 90 96 33 15).

Ice Cream: At **Soleileïs,** Marijtje scoops up fine ice cream made with organic milk, fresh fruit, all-natural ingredients, and creative flavors that fit the season. There's also a shelf of English books for exchange (daily 14:00-18:30, closed in winter, at #9).

Transportation
Getting Around Arles

In this flat city, everything's within **walking** distance. Only the Ancient History Museum is far enough out to consider a shuttle or taxi ride. The riverside promenade provides a scenic and direct stroll to the Ancient History Museum (as well as to the train station).

The free **Navia shuttle** circles the town, stopping at the train station and along Rue du 4 Septembre, then along the river. It's useful for access to hotels and the Ancient History Museum (2/hour, Mon-Sat 7:00-19:00, none Sun).

Arles' **taxis** charge a set fee of about €12, but nothing except the Ancient History Museum is worth a taxi ride. To call a cab, dial 04 90 96 52 76.

Arriving and Departing

Compare train and bus schedules: For some nearby destinations the bus may be the better choice, and it's usually cheaper.

BY TRAIN

The train station is on the river, a 10-minute walk from the town center. For baggage storage, see "Helpful Hints," earlier

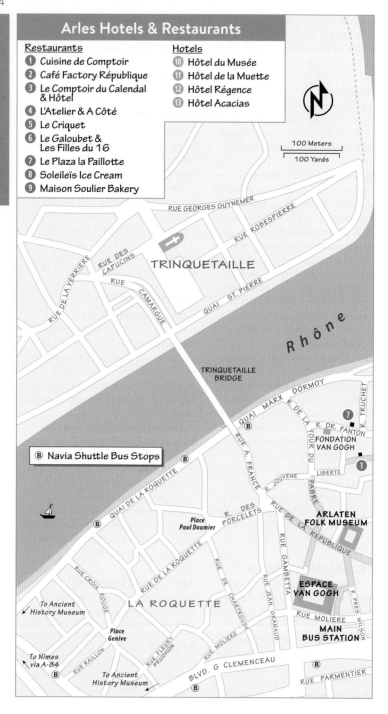

Arles Hotels & Restaurants

Restaurants
1. Cuisine de Comptoir
2. Café Factory République
3. Le Comptoir du Calendal & Hôtel
4. L'Atelier & A Côté
5. Le Criquet
6. Le Galoubet & Les Filles du 16
7. Le Plaza la Paillotte
8. Soleileïs Ice Cream
9. Maison Soulier Bakery

Hotels
10. Hôtel du Musée
11. Hôtel de la Muette
12. Hôtel Régence
13. Hôtel Acacias

100 Meters
100 Yards

RUE GEORGES GUYNEMER

RUE ROBESPIERRE

RUE DES CAPUCINS

TRINQUETAILLE

RUE DE LA VERRIERE

RUE CAMARGUE

RUE

QUAI ST. PIERRE

Rhône

TRINQUETAILLE BRIDGE

QUAI MARX DORMOY

R. DE LA TOUR DU FABRE

R. DR. FANTON

R. TRUCHET

7

FONDATION VAN GOGH

RUE A. FRANCE

R. JOUVENE

LIBERTE

1

Ⓑ Navia Shuttle Bus Stops

Ⓑ

ARLATEN FOLK MUSEUM

QUAI DE LA ROQUETTE

Ⓑ

Place Paul Doumier

R. DES PORCELETS

RUE DE LA REPUBLIQUE

RUE GAMBETTA

RUE DE LA ROQUETTE

RUE CROIX ROUGE

RUE DE CHARTROUSE

RUE JEAN GRANAUD

ESPACE VAN GOGH

R. PRES. WILSON

LA ROQUETTE

To Ancient History Museum

Place Genive

RUE MOLIERE

RUE FLEURY PRUDHON

RUE MOLIERE

MAIN BUS STATION

To Nîmes via A-84

RUE RAILLON

BLVD. G CLEMENCEAU

Ⓑ

RUE PARMENTIER

To Ancient History Museum

Ⓑ

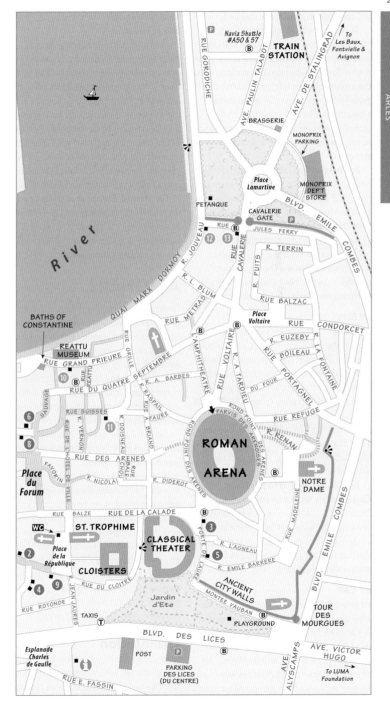

(no baggage storage at the station).

To reach the town center or Ancient History Museum from the train station, wait for the free **Navia shuttle** at the glass shelter facing away from the station (cross the street and veer left, 2/hour Mon-Sat 7:00-19:00, none Sun). The bus makes a counterclockwise loop around Arles, stopping near most of my recommended hotels. **Taxis** usually wait in front of the station.

From Arles by Train to: Paris (hourly, 4 hours, transfer in Avignon or Nîmes; or take the SNCF bus to Avignon TGV Station and train from there), **Avignon Centre-Ville** (hourly, 20 minutes), **Carcassonne** (4/day direct, 2.5 hours, more with transfer in Narbonne, direct trains may require reservations), **Beaune** (hourly, 5 hours, transfer in Lyon), **Nice** (hourly, 4 hours, most require transfer in Marseille).

BY BUS

Arles' main bus station is located on Boulevard Georges Clemenceau, a few blocks from the TI. Most buses to regional destinations depart from here, and most trips cost under €2. Get schedules at the TI or from the bus company (closed Sun, tel. 08 10 00 08 18, www.lepilote.com).

From Arles Train Station to Avignon TGV Station: The direct SNCF bus is your best option (€8, 8/day, 1 hour, included with rail pass).

From Arles by Bus to Les Baux: Cartreize bus #57 connects Arles to Les Baux (6/day, daily July-Aug, Sat-Sun only in early May-June and Sept, none in off-season; departs from the train station, not the bus station; 35 minutes to Les Baux, then runs to Avignon).

BY CAR

I'd avoid driving in old Arles. Enter on foot after stowing your car (at least temporarily) at Arles' only parking garage, **Parking des Lices,** near the TI on Boulevard des Lices (about €2/hour, €18/24 hours). All of my recommended hotels are within a 10-minute walk of this garage. Most hotels have parking deals for a nearby lot (ask before you arrive).

Lots and curbside parking spots in Arles center are metered 9:00-19:00 every day May-Sept (some limited to 2.5 hours). You'll find metered lots along the city wall at Place Lamartine (except Tue night, when it is restricted). To find these, first follow signs to *Centre-Ville,* then *Gare SNCF* (train station) until you come to the roundabout with a Monoprix department store to the right. The hotels I list are no more than a 15-minute walk from here.

Car Rental: Europcar and **Hertz** are downtown (Europcar is at 61 Avenue de Stalingrad, tel. 04 90 93 23 24; Hertz is closer to Place Voltaire at 10 Boulevard Emile Combes, tel. 04 90 96 75 23).

AVIGNON

Famous for its nursery rhyme, medieval bridge, and brooding Palace of the Popes, contemporary Avignon (ah-veen-yohn) bustles and prospers behind its mighty walls. For nearly 100 years (1309-1403) Avignon was the capital of Christendom, home to seven popes. (And, for a difficult period after that—during the Great Schism when there were two competing popes—Avignon was "the other Rome.") During this time, it grew from a quiet village into a thriving city.

Today, with its large student population and fashionable shops, Avignon is an intriguing blend of medieval history, youthful energy, and urban sophistication. Street performers entertain the international throngs who fill Avignon's ubiquitous cafés and trendy boutiques. And each July the city goes pedal to the metal during its huge theater festival (with about 2,000 performances, big crowds, higher prices, and hotels booked up long in advance).

Orientation

Cours Jean Jaurès, which turns into Rue de la République, runs straight from the Centre-Ville train station to Place de l'Horloge and the Palace of the Popes, splitting Avignon in two. The larger eastern half is where the action is. Climb to the Jardin du Rocher des Doms for the town's best view, tour the pope's immense palace, and go organic in its vibrant market hall.

Tourist Information

The TI is located on the main street linking the Centre-Ville train station to the old town (Mon-Sat 9:00-18:00 except Sat until 17:00 Nov-March, Sun 10:00-17:00 except until 12:00 Nov-March, daily until 19:00 in July, 41 Cours Jean Jaurès, tel. 04 32 74 32 74, www.avignon-tourisme.com). Pick up a map with several good (but tricky to follow) walking tours and ask about guided tours in English.

Helpful Hints

Book Ahead for July: During the July theater festival, rooms are almost impossible to come by—reserve early, or stay in Arles.

Baggage Storage: La Consigne will either be in the Centre-Ville train station or a few blocks away under the modern arcade at 1 Avenue Maréchal de Lattre de Tassigny (€6-10/day; June-Aug daily 8:00-21:00; Sept-May Mon-Sat 9:00-18:00, closed Sun, tel. 09 82 45 20 24, www.consigne-avignon.fr).

Laundry: At **La Blanchisseuse,** you can drop off your laundry and pick it up the same day (daily 7:00-21:00, several blocks west of the TI at 24 Rue Lanterne, tel. 04 90 85 58 80). The launderette at 66 Place des Corps-Saints, where Rue Agricol Perdiguier ends, is handy to most hotels (daily 7:00-20:00).

Bike Rental: Rent pedal and electric bikes and scooters near the train station at **Provence Bike** (April-Oct 9:00-18:30, 7 Avenue St. Ruf, tel. 04 90 27 92 61, www. provence-bike.com), or ask at the TI about other options. You'll enjoy riding on the Ile de la Barthelasse (the TI has bike maps), but biking is better in and around Vaison-la-Romaine.

Local Guides: Isabelle Magny is a good local guide for the city and region (€160/half-day, €330/day, no car, mobile 06 11 82 17 92, isabellemagny@sfr.fr). **Nina Seffusatti** is also good (same prices as Isabelle, mobile 06 14 80 30 37,

Place de l'Horloge

nina.seffusatti@wanadoo.fr). The **Avignon Gourmet Walking Tour** is a wonderful experience if you like to eat. Charming and passionate Aurélie meets small groups daily (except Sun and Mon) at the TI at 9:00 for a well-designed three-hour, eight-stop walk (€59/person, 2-8 people per group, mobile 06 35 32 08 96, www.avignongourmetours.com). Book in advance on her website.

Avignon Walk

This self-guided walk, worth ▲▲, offers a fine overview of the city and its major sights.

❯ Self-Guided Walk

• *Start this tour where the Romans did, on Place de l'Horloge, in front of City Hall (Hôtel de Ville).*

PLACE DE L'HORLOGE

In ancient Roman times this was the forum, and in medieval times it was the market square. The square is named for the clock tower (now hiding behind the more recently built City Hall) that, in its day, was a humanist statement. In medieval France, the only bells in town rang from the church tower to indicate not the hours but the calls to prayer. With the dawn of the modern age, secular clock towers like this rang out the hours as people organized their lives independent of the Church.

Taking humanism a step further, the City Hall, built after the French Revolution, obstructed the view of the old clock tower while celebrating a new era. The slogan "liberty, equality, and brotherhood" is a reminder that the people supersede the king and the Church. And today, judging from the square's jammed cafés and restaurants, it is indeed the people who rule.

The square's present popularity arrived with the trains in 1854. Facing City Hall, look left down the main drag, Rue de la République. When the trains came to Avignon, proud city fathers wanted a direct, impressive way to link the new

station to the heart of the city—so they destroyed existing homes to create Rue de la République and widened Place de l'Horloge.

• *Walk slightly uphill past the neo-Renaissance facade of the theater and the carousel (public WCs behind). Look back to see the late Gothic bell tower. Then veer right at the Palace of the Popes and continue into...*

PALACE SQUARE (PLACE DU PALAIS)

Pull up a concrete stump just past the café. These bollards effectively keep cars from double-parking in areas designed for people. Many of the metal ones slide up and down by remote control to let privileged cars come and go.

Now take in the scene. This grand square is lined with the Palace of the Popes, the Petit Palais, and the cathedral. In the 1300s the entire headquarters of the Roman Catholic Church was moved to Avignon. The Church purchased the city of Avignon and gave it a complete makeover. Along with clearing out vast spaces like this square and building a three-acre palace, the Church erected more than three miles of protective wall (with 39 towers), "appropriate" housing for cardinals (read: mansions), and residences for its entire bureaucracy. The city was Europe's largest construction zone. Avignon's population grew from 6,000 to 25,000 in short order. (Today, only 13,000 people live within the walls.)

Palace Square

The limits of pre-papal Avignon are outlined on your city map: Rues Joseph Vernet, Henri Fabre, des Lices, and Philonarde all follow the route of the city's earlier defensive wall (about half the diameter of today's wall).

The imposing facade behind you, across the square from the Palace of the Popes' main entry, was "the papal mint," which served as the finance department for the Holy See. The Petit Palais (Little Palace) seals the uphill end of the square and was built for a cardinal; today it houses medieval paintings.

Avignon's 12th-century Romanesque cathedral, just to the left of the Palace of the Popes, has been the seat of the local bishop for more than a thousand years.

• *You can visit the massive* **Palace of the Popes** *(described later), but it works better to visit that palace at the end of this walk.*

Now is a good time to take in the...

PETIT PALAIS MUSEUM (MUSEE DU PETIT PALAIS)

This former cardinal's palace now displays the Church's collection of (mostly) art. You'll find some English information but not a lot of detail. Still, a visit here before going to the Palace of the Popes helps furnish and populate that otherwise barren building. You'll see bits of statues and tombs—an inventory of the destruction of exquisite Church art that was wrought by the French Revolution (which tackled

Petit Palais Museum

established French society with Taliban-esque fervor). Then you'll see many rooms filled with religious Italian paintings, organized in chronological order from early Gothic to late Renaissance. Room 10 holds two paintings by Botticelli.

Cost and Hours: Free, Wed-Mon 10:00-13:00 & 14:00-18:00, closed Tue, ask about summer sound-and-light shows in main courtyard, at north end of Palace Square, tel. 04 90 86 44 58, www.petit-palais.org.

• *From Palace Square, head up to the cathedral (enjoy the viewpoint overlooking the square), and fill your water bottle just past the gate. Now climb the ramp to the top of a rocky hill to where Avignon was first settled. Atop the hill is an inviting café and pond in a park—the Jardin du Rocher des Doms. At the far side is a viewpoint from where you can see Avignon's beloved broken bridge.*

▲JARDIN DU ROCHER DES DOMS

Enjoy the view from this bluff. On a clear day, the tallest peak you see (far to the right), with its white limestone cap, is Mont Ventoux ("Windy Mountain"). Below and just to the right, you'll spot free passenger ferries shuttling across the river, and—tucked amid the trees on the far side—the recommended restaurant, Le Bercail, a local favorite. The island is the Ile de la Barthelasse, a lush nature preserve where Avignon can breathe. In the distance to the left is the TGV rail bridge.

The Rhône River marked the border of Vatican territory in medieval times. Fort St. André—across the river on the hill—was in the kingdom of France. The fort was built in 1360, shortly after the pope moved to Avignon, to counter the papal incursion into this part of Europe. Avignon's famous bridge was a key border crossing, with towers on either end—one was French, and the other was the pope's. The French one, across the river, is the Tower of Philip the Fair.

Cost and Hours: Free, park gates open daily 7:30-20:00, June-Aug until 21:00, Oct-March until 18:00.

• *Take the walkway down to the left and find*

250

FRANCE

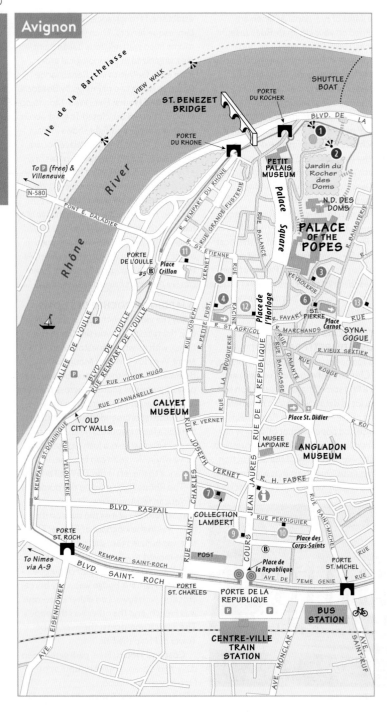

Avignon

Ile de la Barthelasse

VIEW WALK

ST. BENEZET BRIDGE

PORTE DU ROCHER

SHUTTLE BOAT

BLVD. DE LA

❶

❷

Rhône River

To 🅿 (free) & Villeneuve

N-580

PORTE DU RHONE

PETIT PALAIS MUSEUM

Jardin du Rocher des Doms

N.D. DES DOMS

PONT E. DALADIER

Rhône

PORTE DE L'OULLE
#5 🅱 Place Crillon

R. REMPART DU RHONE

R. ST. ETIENNE

RUE GRANDE FUSTERIE

RUE BALANCE

Palace Square

PALACE OF THE POPES

❸

R. BANASTERIE

R.

❶❶

VERNET

❺

❹

❶❷ Place de l'Horloge

PEYROLERIE

❻ ST. PIERRE

Place Carnot

❶❸

ALLEE DE L'OULLE

🅿

BLVD. DE L'OULLE

RUE REMPART DE L'OULLE

RUE JOSEPH

R. PETITE FUST.

R. ST. AGRICOL

LA BOUQUERIE

RUE

RACINE

R. FAVART

RUE MARCHANDS

RUE GALANTE

RUE BANCASSE

SYNA-GOGUE

R.VIEUX SEXTIER

RUE ROUGE

🅿

RUE VICTOR HUGO

RUE D'ANNANELLE

CALVET MUSEUM

R. VERNET

RUE

RUE DE LA REPUBLIQUE

Place St. Didier

R. ROI

OLD CITY WALLS

R. REMPART ST-DOMINIQUE

RUE VELOUTERIE

RUE JOSEPH VERNET

MUSEE LAPIDAIRE

RUE JEAN JAURES

ANGLADON MUSEUM

R. H. FABRE

RUE SAINT-MICHEL

BLVD. RASPAIL

RUE SAINT CHARLES

❼

COLLECTION LAMBERT

ℹ

RUE PERDIGUIER

PORTE ST. ROCH

To Nimes via A-9

RUE REMPART SAINT-ROCH

❾

POST

COURS

❶⓪

🅱

Place des Corps-Saints

PORTE ST. MICHEL

BLVD. SAINT- ROCH

PORTE ST. CHARLES

PORTE DE LA REPUBLIQUE

Place de la Republique

AVE. DE 7EME GENIE

RUE

AVE. EISENHOWER

🅿 🅿

BUS STATION

🚲

AVE. MONCLAR

CENTRE-VILLE TRAIN STATION

AVE. SAINT-RUF

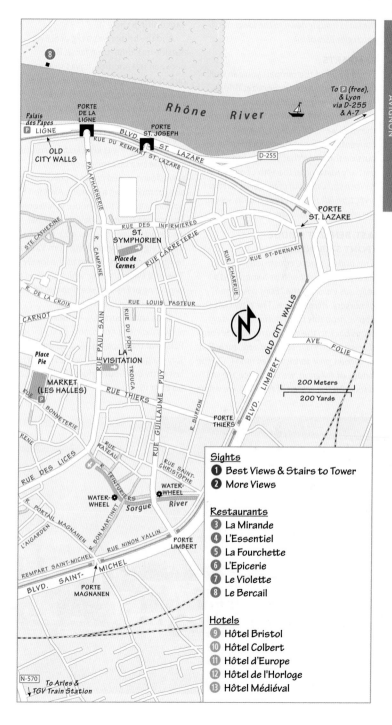

To P (free),
& Lyon
via D-255
& A-7

Rhône River

Palais des Papes P LIGNE

PORTE DE LA LIGNE

OLD CITY WALLS

PORTE ST. JOSEPH

BLVD. ST. LAZARE

RUE DU REMPART ST. LAZARE

D-255

R. PALAPHARNERIE

STE. CATHERINE

R. CAMPANE

RUE DES INFIRMIERES

ST. SYMPHORIEN

Place de Carmes

RUE CARRETERIE

RUE CHARRUE

RUE ST-BERNARD

PORTE ST. LAZARE

R. DE LA CROIX

CARNOT

RUE LOUIS PASTEUR

RUE PAUL SAIN

RUE DU PONT

Place Pie

LA VISITATION

TROUCA

OLD CITY WALLS

AVE. FOLIE

MARKET (LES HALLES) P

RUE THIERS

RUE GUILLAUME PUY

R. BUFFON

PORTE THIERS

BLVD. LIMBERT

200 Meters
200 Yards

R. BONNETERIE

RENE

RUE DES LICES

RUE RATEAU

R. TEINTURIERS

RUE SAINT-CHRISTOPHE

WATER-WHEEL

WATER-WHEEL

Sorgue River

R. PORTAIL MAGNANEN

L'AIGARDEN

R. BON MARTINET

RUE NINON VALLIN

PORTE LIMBERT

REMPART SAINT-MICHEL

BLVD. SAINT-MICHEL

PORTE MAGNANEN

PORTE MICHEL

N-570
To Arles &
TGV Train Station

Sights
1. Best Views & Stairs to Tower
2. More Views

Restaurants
3. La Mirande
4. L'Essentiel
5. La Fourchette
6. L'Epicerie
7. Le Violette
8. Le Bercail

Hotels
9. Hôtel Bristol
10. Hôtel Colbert
11. Hôtel d'Europe
12. Hôtel de l'Horloge
13. Hôtel Médiéval

*the stairs leading down to the tower. You'll
catch glimpses of the...*

RAMPARTS

The only bit of the rampart you can walk
on is accessed from St. Bénezet Bridge
(accessible with ticket, see next). Just
after the papacy took control of Avignon,
the walls were extended to take in the
convents and monasteries that had been
outside the city. What you see today was
partially restored in the 19th century.

• *When you come out of the tower on street
level, turn left to walk inside the city wall to
the entry to the old bridge.*

▲ST. BENEZET BRIDGE
(PONT ST. BENEZET)

This bridge, whose construction and
location were inspired by a shepherd's
religious vision, is the "Pont d'Avignon"
of nursery-rhyme fame. The ditty (which
you've probably been humming all day)
dates back to the 15th century: *Sur le Pont
d'Avignon, on y danse, on y danse, sur le Pont
d'Avignon, on y danse tous en rond* ("On the
bridge of Avignon, we will dance, we will
dance, on the bridge of Avignon, we will
dance all in a circle").

And the bridge was a big deal even
outside its kiddie-tune fame. Built
between 1171 and 1185, it was strategic—
one of only three bridges crossing the
mighty Rhône in the Middle Ages,
important to pilgrims, merchants, and
armies. It was damaged several times by
floods but always rebuilt. In the winter of
1668, most of it was knocked out for the
last time by a disastrous icy flood. The
townsfolk decided not to rebuild this time,
and for more than a century, Avignon had
no bridge across the Rhône. While only
four arches survive today, the original
bridge was huge: Imagine a 22-arch, half-
mile-long bridge extending from Vatican
territory across the island to the lonely
Tower of Philip the Fair, which marked the
beginning of France (see displays of the
bridge's original length).

Cost and Hours: €5, includes
audioguide, €14.50 combo-ticket includes
Palace of the Popes, daily 9:00-19:00,
July-Aug until 20:00, Nov-Feb 9:30-17:45,
last entry one hour before closing, tel. 04
90 27 51 16.

St. Bénezet Bridge

• *To get to the Palace of the Popes from here, walk away from the river and follow the signs to Palais des Papes.*

▲▲PALACE OF THE POPES (PALAIS DES PAPES)

In 1309 a French pope was elected (Pope Clément V). His Holiness decided that dangerous Italy was no place for a pope, so he moved the whole operation to Avignon for a secure rule under a supportive French king. The Catholic Church literally bought Avignon and built the Palace of the Popes, where the popes resided until 1403. Eventually, Italians demanded a Roman pope, so from 1378 on, there were twin popes—one in Rome and one in Avignon—causing a schism in the Catholic Church that wasn't fully resolved until 1417.

Cost and Hours: €12, includes multimedia Histopad; €14.50 combo-ticket includes St. Bénezet Bridge, daily 9:00-19:00, July-Aug until 20:00, Nov-Feb 9:30-17:45, last entry one hour before closing; tel. 04 90 27 50 00, www.palais-des-papes.com.

Visiting the Palace: Visitors follow a tangled one-way route through mostly massive rooms equipped with an iPad they call the "Histopad." There's a lot of history here, but artifacts are sparse and wall frescos are faint: Without guiding help, it's mostly meaningless. Your visit becomes greatly enriched if you master the included Histopad—the staff is happy to help you with it.

The palace was built stark and strong, before the popes knew how long they'd be staying (and before the affluence and fanciness of the Renaissance and Baroque ages). This was the most fortified palace of the time (remember, the pope left Rome to be more secure). With 10-foot-thick walls, it was a symbol of power.

This largest surviving Gothic palace in Europe was built to accommodate 500 people as the administrative center of the Holy See and home of the pope. Seven popes ruled from here, making this the center of Christianity for nearly 100 years. The last pope checked out in 1403, but the Church owned Avignon until the French Revolution in 1791. During this interim period, the palace still housed Church authorities. Avignon residents, many of whom had come from Rome, spoke Italian for a century after the pope left, making the town a cultural oddity within France.

The palace is pretty empty today—nothing portable survived both the pope's return to Rome and the French Revolution. Just before the gift shop exit, you can climb the tower (Tour de la Gâche) for grand views. The artillery room is now a gift shop channeling all visitors on a full tour of knickknacks for sale.

• *You'll exit at the rear of the palace. To return to Palace Square, make two rights after leaving the palace.*

Experiences

Ile de la Barthelasse Saunter

A free shuttle boat, the **Navette Fluviale,** plies back and forth across the Rhône River from near St. Bénezet Bridge to the Ile de la Barthelasse. This peaceful island offers grassy walks, bike rides, and the recommended riverside restaurant, Le Bercail. For great views, walk the riverside path to Daladier Bridge, and then cross the bridge back into town.

Cost and Hours: Free; 3 boats/hour, daily April-June and Sept 10:00-12:15 & 14:00-18:00, July-Aug 11:00-20:45; Oct-March weekends and Wed afternoons only.

Rick's Tip: *If you stay on the island to eat, check the schedule to make sure you* **don't miss the last return boat (otherwise, it's a 25-minute walk).**

Sleeping

Hotel values are better in Arles. Drivers should ask about parking discounts through hotels.

Near Centre-Ville Station

$$ Hôtel Bristol** is a big, professionally run place on the main drag, offering spacious public spaces, large rooms, big elevators, and a generous buffet breakfast (family rooms, pay parking—reserve ahead, 44 Cours Jean Jaurès, tel. 04 90 16 48 48, www.bristol-avignon.com, contact@bristol-avignon.com).

$ Hôtel Colbert** is on a quiet lane, with a dozen spacious rooms gathered on four floors around a skinny spiral staircase (no elevator). Patrice decorates each room with a colorful (occasionally erotic) flair. There are warm public spaces and a sweet little patio (some tight bathrooms, rooms off the patio can be musty, closed Nov-March, 7 Rue Agricol Perdiguier, tel. 04 90 86 20 20, www.lecolbert-hotel.com, contact@avignon-hotel-colbert.com).

Rick's Tip: During the **July theater festival,** *rooms are few in Avignon—you must book long ahead and pay inflated prices.* **It's better to stay in Arles.**

Near Place de l'Horloge

$$$$ Hôtel d'Europe,*** one of Avignon's most prestigious addresses, lets peasants sleep affordably—but only if they land one of the six reasonable *"classique"* rooms. With formal staff, spacious lounges, and a shady courtyard, the hotel is located on the handsome Place Crillon, near the river (pay garage parking, near Daladier Bridge at 12 Place Crillon, tel. 04 90 14 76 76, www.heurope.com, reservations@heurope.com).

$$$ Hôtel de l'Horloge**** is as central as it gets—on Place de l'Horloge. It offers 66 comfortable rooms, some with terraces and views of the city and the Palace of the Popes (1 Rue Félicien David, tel. 04 90 16 42 00, www.hotel-avignon-horloge.com, hotel.horloge@hotels-ocre-azur.com).

$ Hôtel Médiéval,** burrowed deep in the old center a few blocks from the Church of St. Pierre, was built as a cardinal's home. This stone mansion's grand staircase leads to 35 comfortable, pastel rooms (no elevator, kitchenettes, 5 blocks east of Place de l'Horloge, behind Church of St. Pierre at 15 Rue Petite Saunerie, tel. 04 90 86 11 06, www.hotelmedieval.com, hotel.medieval@wanadoo.fr, run by Régis).

Eating

Skip the crowd-pleasing places on Place de l'Horloge—Avignon is brimming with delightful squares and back streets lined with little restaurants eager to feed you. At the finer places, reservations are smart (especially on weekends).

Fine Dining

$$$$ La Mirande, inside Hôtel la Mirande just behind the Palace of the Popes, transports you into a historic and aristocratic world. What was once a cardinal's palace today is a romantic oasis where you'll dine in 18th-century splendor with elegant service and presentation (dine inside or in the queenly garden, closed Tue-Wed, €50 *plats,* enticing five-course €65 *menu* must be ordered by everyone in your party, 4 Place de l'Amirande, tel. 04 90 14 20 20, www.la-mirande.fr).

$$$ L'Essentiel is modern, spacious, and bright, with traditional French dishes. It has classy presentation and ambience, and seating indoors or outdoors on a romantic back terrace (€36-48 *menus,* closed Sun-Mon, reservations recommended, 2 Rue Petite Fusterie, tel. 04 90 85 87 12, www.restaurantlessentiel.com).

$$$ La Fourchette is an inviting, dressy place graced with warm colors and spacious indoor-only seating. The cuisine mixes traditional French with Provençal. Book ahead for this popular place (closed

of Avignon, all while enjoying big portions of Provençal cooking. Make a reservation before trekking out there (daily May-Oct, often closed off-season, tel. 04 90 82 20 22, www.restaurant-lebercail.fr). Take the free shuttle boat (located near St. Bénezet Bridge) to the Ile de la Barthelasse, turn right, and walk five minutes. As the boat usually stops running at about 18:00 (20:45 in July-Aug), you can either taxi back or walk 25 minutes along the pleasant riverside path and over Daladier Bridge.

Getting Around Avignon
Avignon's walled city is compact, and all the major sights can be visited on foot. The streets are cobbled, so wear comfortable shoes.

If you tire of walking, take advantage of the city's **shuttle vans.** Wave down a **Baladine** electric minivan along its loop route through Avignon, or use **City Zen** minibuses with fixed stops (€0.50, 4/hour for either). City Zen also links remote parking lots with the city center. The TI has route maps. If you want a **taxi,** dial 04 90 82 20 20.

Arriving and Departing
BY TRAIN
Avignon has two train stations: Centre-Ville and TGV (linked to downtown by shuttle trains). Some TGV trains stop at Centre-Ville—verify your station in advance.

The **Centre-Ville station** (Gare Avignon Centre-Ville) gets all non-TGV trains (and a few TGV trains). To reach the town center, cross the busy street in front of the station and walk through the city walls onto Cours Jean Jaurès. Baggage storage is close by (see "Helpful Hints," earlier).

From Avignon's Centre-Ville Station to: Arles (roughly hourly, 20 minutes, less frequent in the afternoon), **Carcassonne** (8/day, 7 with transfer in Narbonne or Nîmes, 3 hours).

The **TGV station** (Gare TGV), on the outskirts of town, has easy car rental, but no baggage storage. Car rental, buses,

Sun-Mon, 17 Rue Racine, tel. 04 90 85 20 93, www.la-fourchette.net).

Dining Well on a Moderate Budget
$$$ **L'Epicerie** sits alone under green awnings on the romantic Place St-Pierre square and is ideal for dinner outside (or in the small but cozy interior). It has an accessible menu with Mediterranean dishes and big, splittable *assiettes* (sample plates), each with a theme (daily, 10 Place St-Pierre, tel. 04 90 82 74 22, Magda speaks English).

$$ **Le Violette,** in the peaceful courtyard of the Collection Lambert modern art museum, serves fresh modern cuisine and is gorgeous when lit by the museum rooms at night (July-Aug daily, Sept-June closed Sun and Mon, 5 Rue Violette, tel. 04 90 85 36 42).

Rick's Tip: For a fun lunch spot, visit the farmers market hall Les Halles, with its handful of wonderfully characteristic and cheap places serving locals the freshest of food (on Place Pie, closes Tue-Fri at 13:30 and at 14:00 Sat-Sun; closed Mon).

Local Favorite
$$$ **Le Bercail** offers a fun opportunity to cross the Rhône River and take in the country air with a terrific riverfront view

and taxis are outside the north exit (*sortie nord*). To reach the city center, take the **shuttle train** from platform A or B to the Centre-Ville station (€1.60, included with rail pass, 2/hour, 5 minutes, buy ticket from machine on platform or at *billeterie* in main hall). A **taxi** ride between the TGV station and downtown Avignon costs about €18.

If you're connecting from the TGV station to other points, you'll find **buses** to Arles' Centre-Ville station at the second bus shelter (€7.50, 9/day, hourly, included with rail pass, schedule posted on shelter and available at TGV station info booths). If you're **driving** a rental car from the station to Arles or Les Baux, follow signs to *Avignon Sud,* then *La Rocade.* You'll soon see exits to Arles (best for Les Baux, too).

From Avignon's TGV Station to: Nice (hourly, most by TGV, 4 hours, many require transfer in Marseille), **Paris' Gare de Lyon** (hourly direct, 2.5 hours), **Paris' Charles de Gaulle airport** (7/day, 3 hours).

BY BUS

The efficient bus station (*gare routière*) is 100 yards to the right as you exit the Centre-Ville train station, beyond and below Hôtel Ibis (helpful info desk open Mon-Sat 7:00-19:30, closed Sun, tel. 04 90 82 07 35). Nearly all buses leave from this station (a few leave from the ring road outside the station—ask, buy tickets on bus or at bus station). Service is reduced or nonexistent on Sundays and holidays. Verify your destination with the driver.

From Avignon to: Pont du Gard (bus #A15, 5/day Mon-Fri, 3/day Sat-Sun, 1 hour), **Arles train station** (8/day, 1 hour, leaves from TGV station), **Vaison-la-Romaine** (bus #4, 10/day Mon-Sat, 2/day Sun, 2 hours) and **Séguret** (3-6/day; all buses pass through Orange—faster to take train to Orange, and transfer to bus there).

BY CAR

Avignon is essentially traffic-free in the old center. For the most central parking garage, follow signs to *Centre,* then to the *Centre Historique* and then **P Palais des Papes** (from where, after parking, you'll climb the stairs and arrive at the pope's doorstep, €12 half-day, €20/24 hours).

You can also park for free at the edge of town at lots with complimentary shuttle buses to the center (no shuttles on Sunday). Follow *P Gratuit* signs for **Parking de l'Ile Piot,** across Pont Daladier on Ile de la Barthelasse, with shuttles to Place Crillon; or to **Parking des Italiens,** along the river east of the Palace of the Popes, with shuttles to Place Pie (allow 30 minutes to walk from either parking lot to the center). Street parking is €1-3/hour for a maximum of four hours Mon-Sat 9:00-19:00 (free 19:00-9:00 and all day Sunday).

No matter where you park, leave nothing of value in your car.

Car Rental: The TGV station has counters for all the big companies; only Avis is at the Centre-Ville station.

NEAR ARLES AND AVIGNON

It's a short hop from Arles or Avignon to splendid scenery, Roman sights, warm stone villages, and world-class wine. See the marvelous Roman Pont du Gard aqueduct; explore the ghost town that is ancient Les Baux; and spend time in pleasant Vaison-la-Romaine, a handy hub for the sunny Côtes du Rhône wine road.

Pont du Gard

Throughout the ancient world, aqueducts were like flags of stone that heralded the greatness of Rome. A visit to this impressively preserved ▲▲▲ sight still works to proclaim the wonders of that age.

In the first century AD, the Romans built a 30-mile aqueduct that ran to Nîmes, one of ancient Europe's largest cities. While most of it ran on or below the ground, at Pont du Gard the aqueduct spans a canyon on a massive bridge over the Gardon River—one of the most remarkable surviving Roman ruins anywhere.

Allow about a full four hours for visiting Pont du Gard (including transportation time from Avignon).

Getting There: Pont du Gard is a 30-minute **drive** due west of Avignon (follow N-100 from Avignon, tracking signs to Nîmes and Remoulins, then Pont du Gard and Rive Gauche), It's 45 minutes northwest of Arles (via Tarascon on D-6113). **Buses** run to

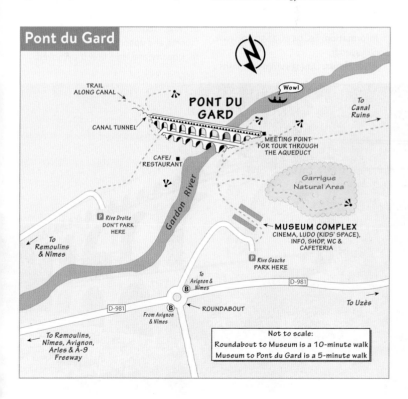

Pont du Gard

TRAIL ALONG CANAL

CANAL TUNNEL

PONT DU GARD

Wow!

To Canal Ruins

MEETING POINT FOR TOUR THROUGH THE AQUEDUCT

CAFE/ RESTAURANT

Gardon River

Garrigue Natural Area

Rive Droite DON'T PARK HERE

To Remoulins & Nîmes

MUSEUM COMPLEX
CINEMA, LUDO (KIDS' SPACE), INFO, SHOP, WC & CAFETERIA

Rive Gauche PARK HERE

To Avignon & Nîmes

From Avignon & Nîmes

D-981

ROUNDABOUT

D-981

To Uzès

To Remoulins, Nîmes, Avignon, Arles & A-9 Freeway

Not to scale:
Roundabout to Museum is a 10-minute walk
Museum to Pont du Gard is a 5-minute walk

Pont du Gard from Avignon (#A15, 5/day Mon-Fri, 3/day Sat-Sun, 1 hour).

Orientation

There are two riversides at Pont du Gard: the Left Bank (Rive Gauche) and Right Bank (Rive Droite). Park on the Rive Gauche (parking validated with ticket purchase), where you'll find the museum, ticket booth, and TI. You'll see the aqueduct in two parts: first the informative museum complex, then the actual river gorge spanned by the ancient bridge.

Cost: €8.50 Discovery Pass includes access to the aqueduct and museum; €11.50 Pass Aqueduct also includes a 30-minute tour through the top channel of the aqueduct—book online in advance. Skip the €15.50 Pass Patrimoine.

Hours: Daily from 9:00 until 21:00 or later (confirm online)—closes earlier in off-season; museum open similar hours.

Information: Tel. 04 66 37 50 99, www.pontdugard.fr.

After Hours: During summer months, the site is open late so that people can watch a light show projected on the monument. After the museum closes, you'll pay only €5/person to enter (free for kids under 17). If you don't care to see the museum, seeing Pont du Gard in the evening is dramatic (and cheap).

Rick's Tip: *Pont du Gard is perhaps best enjoyed on your back and **in the water**— bring along a swimsuit and flip-flops for the rocks. The best Pont du Gard viewpoints are up steep hills with uneven footing—**bring good shoes**, too.*

Visiting the Aqueduct

You'll enter the ▲ **state-of-the-art museum** (well presented in English) to the sound of water and understand the critical role fresh water played in the Roman "art of living." You'll see copies of lead pipes, faucets, and siphons; walk through a mock rock quarry; and learn how they moved

Pont du Gard

those huge rocks into place and how those massive arches were made.

A broad walkway from the museum complex leads in 10 minutes to the aqueduct. Before crossing the bridge, walk to a terrific riverside viewpoint by continuing under the aqueduct on a stony path, then find two staircases about 50 yards apart leading down to an unobstructed view of the world's second-highest standing Roman structure. (Rome's Colosseum is only six feet taller.)

This was the biggest bridge in the whole 30-mile-long aqueduct. The arches are twice the width of standard aqueducts, and the main arch is the largest the Romans ever built—80 feet across (the width of the river). The bridge is about 160 feet high and was originally about 1,200 feet long.

The stones that jut out—giving the aqueduct a rough, unfinished appearance—supported the original scaffolding. The protuberances were left, rather than cut off, in anticipation of future repair needs. The lips under the arches supported wooden templates that allowed the stones in the round arches to rest on something until the all-important keystone was dropped into place. Each stone weighs from two to six tons. The structure stands with no mortar (except at the very top, where the water flowed)—taking full advantage of the innovative Roman arch, made strong by gravity.

Cross to the right bank for a closer look and the best views. Soon find steps leading up a short, steep trail (marked *View Point/Bellevedere*). Follow the short-but-rugged trail with the river to your right to several superb lookouts above the aqueduct.

Back on the museum side, steps lead up to the top of the Rive Gauche side of the aqueduct, where tours meet to enter the water channel. From here you can follow the canal path along a trail (marked with red-and-white horizontal lines) to find remains of the Roman canal (spur trails off this path lead to more panoramic views).

Les Baux

Tucked between Arles and Avignon, the hilltop town of Les Baux and its medieval citadel crown the rugged Alpilles (ahl-pee) mountains. Here, you can imagine the struggles of a strong community that lived a rough-and-tumble life—thankful more for their top-notch fortifications than for their dramatic views.

Day Plan

Savor the castle, then tour—or blitz—the lower town's polished-stone gauntlet of boutiques. It's mobbed with tourists most of the day, but Les Baux rewards those who arrive by 9:00 or after 17:30. Sunsets are dramatic, and the castle is brilliantly illuminated after dark.

Getting There

Les Baux is a 20-minute **drive** from Arles. Follow signs for *Avignon,* then Les Baux. From Arles, Cartreize **bus #57** runs to Les Baux (6/day, 35 minutes, daily July-Aug, early May-June and Sept Sat-Sun only, none in off-season; timetables at www.lepilote.com). From Avignon, ride Cartreize **bus #57** to St-Rémy (12/day Mon-Fri, 6/day Sat-Sun, 45 minutes), then continue to Les Baux on the same bus (described above). Otherwise, continue to Les Baux by taxi.

A demonstration at Les Baux

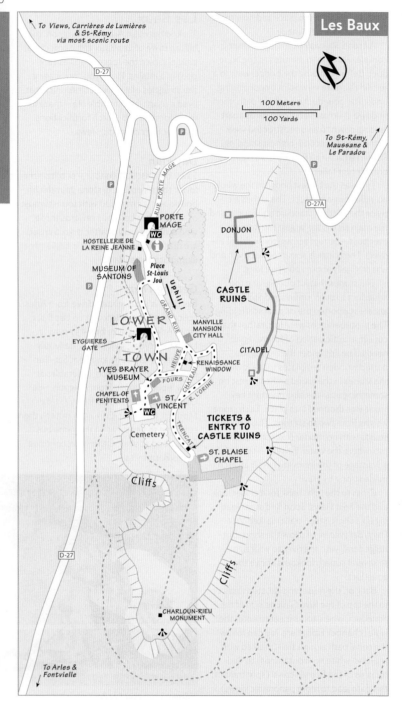

Les Baux

To Views, Carrières de Lumières & St-Rémy via most scenic route

D-27

100 Meters
100 Yards

To St-Rémy, Maussane & Le Paradou

D-27A

P

RUE PORTE MAGE

PORTE MAGE

WC

HOSTELLERIE DE LA REINE JEANNE

MUSEUM OF SANTONS

P

Place St-Louis Jou

DONJON

CASTLE RUINS

Uphill!

GRAND RUE

CITADEL

LOWER

EYGUIERES GATE

MANVILLE MANSION CITY HALL

TOWN

NEUVE

YVES BRAYER MUSEUM

RENAISSANCE WINDOW

FOURS

CHATEAU

R. L'ORME

CHAPEL OF PENITENTS

ST. VINCENT

WC

TICKETS & ENTRY TO CASTLE RUINS

TRENCAT

Cemetery

ST. BLAISE CHAPEL

Cliffs

D-27

Cliffs

CHARLOUN-RIEU MONUMENT

To Arles & Fontvieille

Orientation

Les Baux is actually two visits in one: castle ruins perched on an almost lunar landscape, and a medieval town below. The town's main drag leads directly to the castle—just keep going uphill (a 10-minute walk).

Tourist Information: The TI is immediately on the left as you enter the village (daily 9:00-18:00, shorter hours and closed Sun in off-season).

Sights

▲▲▲CASTLE RUINS (CHATEAU DES BAUX)

The sun-bleached ruins of the stone fortress of Les Baux are carved into, out of, and on top of a rock 650 feet above the valley floor. Many of the ancient walls of this striking castle still stand as a testament to the proud past of this once-feisty village.

Cost: €9, €11 if there's "entertainment" (described next), €16 Pass Provence combo-ticket with Carrières de Lumières, entry fees include excellent audioguide.

Hours: Daily 9:00-19:00 (July-Aug until 20:00), shorter hours off-season, www.chateau-baux-provence.com.

Rick's Tip: *Château des Baux closes at the end of the day, but once you're inside, you can* **stay as long as you like.** *You're welcome to bring a picnic (no food sold inside) and live out your medieval fantasies, all night long.*

Entertainment: Every weekend from April through early September and daily in summer, the castle presents medieval pageantry, tournaments, demonstrations of catapults and crossbows, and jousting matches. Pick up a schedule as you enter (or check online).

Visiting the Castle: Imagine the importance of this citadel in the Middle Ages, when the lords of Baux were notorious warriors, and Les Baux was a powerhouse in southern France, controlling about 80 towns.

View from Château des Baux

Castle ruins at Les Baux

The sight is exceptionally well presented. As you walk on the windblown spur (*baux* in French), you'll pass kid-thrilling medieval siege weaponry (go ahead, try the battering ram). Good displays in English and big paintings in key locations help reconstruct the place. Imagine 4,000 people living up here. Notice the water-catchment system (a slanted field that caught rainwater and drained it into cisterns—necessary during a siege), and find the reservoir cut into the rock below the castle's highest point. Look for post holes throughout the stone walls that reveal where beams once supported floors.

For the most sensational views, climb to the blustery top of the citadel—hold tight if the mistral wind is blowing.

▲LOWER TOWN

After your castle visit, you can shop and eat your way back through the lower town. Or, escape some of the crowds by visiting these minor but worthwhile sights as you descend: There's the **Yves Brayer Museum** (Musée Yves Brayer), with three small floors of luminous paintings (Van Gogh-like Expressionism) by Yves Brayer (1907-1990), who spent his final years in Les Baux (€8, covered by Pass Provence combo-ticket, daily 10:00-12:30 & 14:00-18:30 in season, www.yvesbrayer.com). Next door is **St. Vincent Church,** a 12th-century Romanesque church that was built short and wide to fit the terrain. Lower down, the free and fun **Museum of Santons** displays a collection of popular folk figurines that decorate local Christmas mangers.

▲CARRIERES DE LUMIERES (QUARRIES OF LIGHT)

A 15-minute walk from Les Baux, this colossal quarry-cave with immense vertical walls offers a mesmerizing multimedia experience. Enter a darkened world filled with floor-to-ceiling images and booming music. Wander through a complex of cathedral-like aisles, transepts, and choirs (no seating provided) as you experience the spectacle. The show lasts 40 minutes and runs continuously. Dress warmly, as the cave is cool.

Cost and Hours: €12.50, covered by Pass Provence combo-ticket; daily 9:30-19:30, Nov-March 10:00-18:00; tel. 04 90 54 47 37, www.carrieres-lumieres.com.

Eating

You'll find quiet cafés with views as you walk through Les Baux's lower town. **$ Hostellerie de la Reine Jeanne** offers friendly service and good-value meals indoors or out (open daily).

Vaison-la-Romaine

With quick access to vineyards, villages, and Mont Ventoux, this pleasant little ▲ town of 6,000 makes a good base for exploring the Côtes du Rhône region.

Day Plan

Explore Vaison-la-Romaine's lower Roman city (following my self-guided walk, later) and upper medieval village, then set sail along the Côtes du Rhône wine road and visit a winery or wine cooperative.

Orientation

You get two villages for the price of one: Vaison-la-Romaine's "modern" lower city (Ville-Basse) has Roman ruins, a lone pedestrian street, and a lively, café-lined main square. The car-free medieval hill town (Ville-Haute) looms above, with meandering cobbled lanes and a ruined castle. A Roman-era bridge connects the lower and upper towns.

Tourist Information: The TI is in the lower city at Place du Chanoine Sautel (daily except closed Sun mid-Oct-March; tel. 04 90 36 02 11, www.vaison-ventoux-tourisme.com).

Local Guide: Janet Henderson offers enthusiastic and educational walks of Vaison-la-Romaine (€30/person, minimum 3 people or €90, allow 2.5 hours, www.provencehistorytours.com).

FRANCE

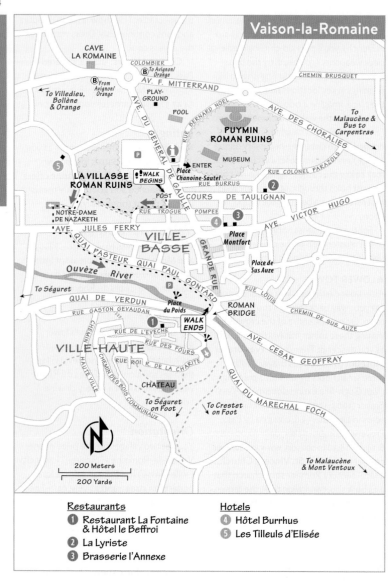

Vaison-la-Romaine

Restaurants

1 Restaurant La Fontaine & Hôtel le Beffroi

2 La Lyriste

3 Brasserie l'Annexe

Hotels

4 Hôtel Burrhus

5 Les Tilleuls d'Elisée

Cooking Classes: Charming Barbara Schuerenberg offers cooking classes from her view home (€90, cash only, includes lunch, 4-person maximum, www.cuisinedeprovence.com).

Getting There

Frequent bus (but not train) service connects Vaison-la-Romaine with Avignon (10/day Mon-Sat, 2/day Sun, 2 hours). Bus stops are near the Cave la Romaine winery on the edge of the lower town. Drivers should follow signs to *Centre-Ville,* then *Office de Tourisme,* and park in or near the big lot across from the TI. Parking is free in Vaison-la-Romaine.

Le Mistral

Provence lives with its vicious mistral winds, which blow 30-60 miles per hour, about 100 days out of the year. The mistral clears people off the streets and turns lively cities into ghost towns. You'll likely spend a few hours or days taking refuge. The winds are strongest between noon and 15:00.

When the mistral blows, it's everywhere, and you can't escape. Author Peter Mayle said it could blow the ears off a donkey (I'd include the tail). According to the natives, it ruins crops, shutters, and roofs (look for stones holding tiles in place on many homes).

The mistral starts above the Alps and Massif Central mountains and gathers steam as it heads south, gaining momentum as it screams over the Rhône Valley before exhausting itself when it hits the Mediterranean. And though this wind rattles shutters everywhere in the Riviera and Provence, it's strongest over the Rhône Valley...so Avignon, Arles, and the Côtes du Rhône villages bear its brunt. While wiping the dust from your eyes, remember the good news: The mistral brings clear skies.

Rick's Tip: *Sleep in Vaison-la-Romaine on Monday night, and you'll wake to an* **amazing Tuesday market.** *But avoid parking at market sites, or you won't find your car where you left it.*

Sights

ROMAN RUINS

A modern road splits the town's Gallo-Roman ruins into two well-presented sites, Puymin and La Villasse. The Puymin side has more to see and gives a good introduction to these ruins, thanks to its small museum offering a look at life during the Roman Empire. For helpful background about Roman civilization, read "The Romans in Provence" on page 231.

Cost and Hours: €9 ticket admits you to both sites; daily June-Sept 9:30-18:30, shorter hours off-season, closed Jan-Feb; good audioguide-€3, tel. 04 90 36 50 48, www.vaison-la-romaine.com.

Visiting the Puymin Ruins: Near the entry are the scant but worthwhile ruins of a sprawling mansion. Find the faint remains of a colorful frescoed wall and mosaic floors, as well as a few wells, used before Vaison's two aqueducts were built. Climb the short hill to the good little **museum** (pick up your audioguide here). Artifacts include lead water pipes, well-preserved mosaic floors, and a few models of ancient buildings. Be sure to see the 12-minute **film** (plays in English every other showing) that takes you inside the homes and daily life of wealthy Vaison residents some 2,000 years ago.

A five-minute walk behind the museum brings you to a largely rebuilt (but still used) 6,000-seat **theater**—just enough seats for the whole town (of yesterday and today).

❍ Walk from Roman Ruins to Roman Bridge

• *Start this self-guided walk just across from the TI, where there's a parking lot. Lean against the railing there to get a look at the...*

Villasse Ruins: The Roman town extended all the way from where you're standing to the Ouvèze River (to the left, or south). Vaison was a river port, boasting aqueducts, a big theater, baths, a forum, busy shopping streets, and the trophy homes of wealthy businessmen.

When the barbarians arrived in the fifth century AD, the Romans were forced out, and the townspeople fled from their unwalled, unprotected low neighborhoods into the hills.

Make your way to the corner of Rue Trogue Pompée, just behind the post

Vaison-la-Romaine's ancient theater

office, and turn right and stop just before reaching the tall arch. Spot the wire mesh that covers parts of a Roman sewer that was used until the 1900s. That tall arch was the centerpiece of a public Roman bath.

The stone-paved street running perpendicularly below you was lined with shops. The columns and remnants on the left side are what's left of two megahomes. You won't see the homes of poorer folks as they were built from materials that did not last.

• *Where the street curves left, continue along the pedestrian walkway that hugs the ruins; at the end of the path, turn left as you leave the ruins behind. You'll pass a lovely garden, then turn right at the first little path you come to. Stop when you reach the back of...*

Notre-Dame de Nazareth Cathedral: As you approach this medieval church, look at its base to find the stubs of Roman columns that form its foundation. The first church built over the Roman ruins was abandoned in the Middle Ages, when

residents fled to the relative safety of the upper town; the present building dates from the 11th to 12th century.

• *With your back to the church, walk out to the street and turn left on Avenue Jules Ferry, then veer right on Quai Louis Pasteur. After several blocks, angle through the parking lot and find a spot above the river.*

Medieval Hill Town: Look up to the medieval village. From the fourth century onward, Vaison-la-Romaine was ruled by a prince-bishop. When the sitting prince-bishop came under attack by the count of Toulouse in the 12th century, he built the abandoned castle you see on the top of this rocky outcrop (about 1195). Over time, the townspeople followed, vacating the lower town and building their homes behind the upper town's fortified wall—where they would remain until after the French Revolution.

• *Continue along the river until you reach the...*

Roman Bridge: The Romans cut this

sturdy, no-nonsense vault into the canyon rock 2,000 years ago, and it has survived ever since. Until the 20th century, this was the only way to cross the Ouvèze River. A vicious 1992 flood crested well above the bridge. The flood destroyed several other modern bridges downstream, but couldn't budge the 55-foot Roman arch supporting the bridge.

• *Our walk is over. From here, you have two choices:*

Upper Town (Ville-Haute): To reach the upper town, hike across the Roman bridge and up to the right (passing a WWI memorial), looping around and through the medieval gate, under the lone tower. Although there's nothing of particular importance to see in the medieval town, the cobbled lanes and enchanting fountains make you want to break out a sketchpad.

Lower Town (Ville-Basse): From the Roman bridge, do an about-face and walk up the pedestrian-only Grande Rue, Vaison's main shopping street. The modern town centers on café-friendly Place Montfort. Tables line the north side of the square, conveniently sheltered from the prevailing mistral wind while enjoying the generous shade of the ubiquitous plane trees.

▲Hiking and Biking

Stop at the TI for detailed information on hikes into the hills above Vaison-la-Romaine. It's about 1.5 hours to the quiet hill town of Crestet, and there's a five-mile trail to Séguret (allow 2 hours). For either route, consider hiking one way and taking a taxi back (best to arrange a pickup in advance in Vaison-la-Romaine—ask

your hotelier). The TI also has details on several manageable bike routes, with good directions in English, as well as information on mountain-biking trails.

Sleeping and Eating

Cozy **$$ Hôtel le Beffroi*** hides deep in the upper town (Rue de l'Evêché, www. le-beffroi.com). In the lower town, good choices are **$ Hôtel Burrhus** (1 Place Montfort, www.burrhus.com) and **$ Les Tilleuls d'Elisée** (1 Avenue Jules Mazen, www.vaisonchambres.info).

In the upper town, **$$$ Restaurant La Fontaine,** located at the recommended **Hôtel le Beffroi,** serves traditional cuisine in the lovely hotel gardens when the weather agrees (closed Wed). In the lower town, **$$ La Lyriste** is an unpretentious place to experience true Provençal cuisine (closed Sun-Mon, 45 Cours Taulignan). On Place Montfort, the popular **$$ Brasserie l'Annexe** is best (open daily).

Côtes du Rhône Wine Road

This self-guided driving tour, worth ▲▲, provides a crash course in Rhône Valley wine, an excuse to meet the locals who make the stuff, and breathtaking scenery. Allow at least a half-day for this 35-mile loop drive. Theft is a problem in this beautiful area—leave absolutely nothing in your car.

❥ Self-Guided Drive

You can start anywhere along the circular route, but I suggest beginning a bit south of Vaison-la-Romaine, in little Séguret.

❶ SEGURET

Blending into the hillside with a smattering of shops, two cafés, made-to-stroll lanes, and a natural spring, this hamlet is understandably popular. Séguret makes for a good coffee or ice cream stop and has a good café-restaurant.

Séguret's name comes from the Latin word *securitas* (meaning "security"). The town's long bulky entry arch came with a massive gate, which drilled in the message of the village's name. Walk through the arch and up a block. To appreciate how the homes' outer walls provided security in those days, drop down the first passage on your right (near the fountain). These tunnel-like exit passages, or *poternes*, were needed in periods of peace to allow the town to expand below. You will come across La Maison d'Eglantine tucked in here, serving delicious cakes, coffee, and tea in a cozy room with views.

• *Signs near Séguret's upper parking lots lead you up, up, and away to the nearby Domaine de Mourchon.*

❷ DOMAINE DE MOURCHON WINERY

This high-flying winery blends state-of-the-art technology with traditional wine-making methods (a shiny ring of stainless-steel vats holds grapes grown on land plowed by horses). Free and informative English tours of the vineyards are offered from Easter-late September on Wednesdays at 17:00, followed by a tasting (call

The village of Séguret

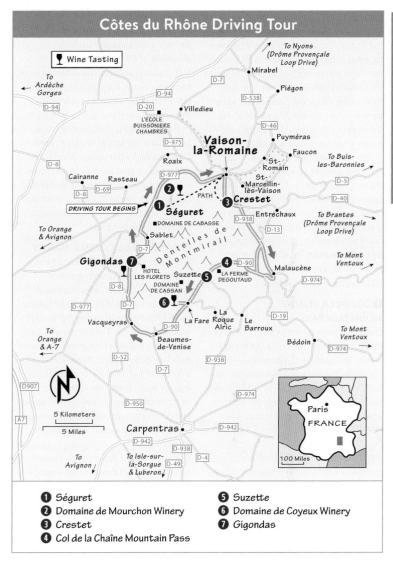

Côtes du Rhône Driving Tour

Wine Tasting

To Nyons
(Drôme Provençale
Loop Drive)

Mirabel

To
Ardèche
Gorges

D-7

D-94

Piégon

D-538

D-94

D-20

L'ECOLE
BUISSONIÈRE
CHAMBRES

Villedieu

D-46

D-975

Puyméras

Vaison-
la-Romaine

Faucon

To Buis-
les-Baronnies

D-8

Roaix

St-
Romain

D-977

St-
Marcellin-
lès-Vaison

D-5

Cairanne

Rasteau

D-69

PATH

Crestet

D-40

D-8

DRIVING TOUR BEGINS

Séguret

Entrechaux

To Brantes
(Drôme Provençale
Loop Drive)

DOMAINE DE CABASSE

D-938

To Orange
& Avignon

Sablet

Dentelles de
Montmirail

D-13

D-7

To Mont
Ventoux

Gigondas

HOTEL
LES FLORETS

Suzette

Col de la Chaîne Mountain Pass

LA FERME
DEGOUTAUD

Malaucène

D-90

D-974

D-8

DOMAINE
DE CASSAN

Domaine de Coyeux Winery

D-977

D-7

La Fare

La
Roque
Alric

Le
Barroux

D-19

To Mont
Ventoux

Vacqueyras

To
Orange
& A-7

D-90

Beaumes-
de-Venise

Bédoin

D-974

D-52

D-7

D-938

D907

A7

5 Kilometers

5 Miles

D-950

Carpentras

D-942

D-974

Paris
FRANCE

D-942

To
Avignon

To Isle-sur-
la-Sorgue
& Luberon

D-938

D-49

D-4

100 Miles

❶ Séguret
❷ Domaine de Mourchon Winery
❸ Crestet
❹ Col de la Chaîne Mountain Pass

❺ Suzette
❻ Domaine de Coyeux Winery
❼ Gigondas

to verify or to learn of times during other months). You're welcome to taste any-time they're open (winery open Mon-Sat 9:00-18:00, Sun by appointment only; tel. 04 90 46 70 30, www.domainedemourchon.com).

• Next, drop back down to Séguret, head toward Vaison-la-Romaine, and once past the city follow signs for Carpentras/Malaucène. After passing through "lower" Crestet on the main highway, look for signs for a side road leading up to Le Village. Drivers can park at the second lot on the approach to the town or keep climbing toward Place du Château at the top of town.

❸ CRESTET

This quiet village—founded after the fall of the Roman Empire, when people banded together in high places like this for protection from marauding barbarians—followed the usual hill-town evolution. The outer walls of the village did double duty as ramparts and house walls. The castle above (from about 850) provided a final safe haven when the village was attacked.

Wander the peaceful lanes and appreciate the amount of work it took to put these stones in place. The bulky Romanesque church is built into the hillside; if it's open, peek in to see the unusual stained-glass window behind the altar. The village's only business, the café-restaurant **$$ Le Panoramic,** has what must be Provence's greatest view tables (closed in bad weather and Dec-March).

❹ COL DE LA CHAINE MOUNTAIN PASS

Get out of your car at the pass (elevation: about 1,500 feet) and enjoy the breezy views. The peaks in the distance—thrusting up like the back of a stegosaurus—are the Dentelles de Montmirail, a small range running just nine miles basically north to south and reaching 2,400 feet in elevation. This region's land is constantly shifting. Those rocky tops were the result of a gradual uplifting of the land, which was then blown bald by the angry mistral wind. The village below the peaks is Suzette (you'll be there soon).

Now turn around and face Mont Ventoux. Are there clouds on the horizon? You're looking into the eyes of the Alps (behind Ventoux), and those "foothills" help keep Provence sunny.

• *Time to push on. With the medieval castle of Le Barroux topping the horizon in the distance (off to the left), drive on to little...*

❺ SUZETTE

Tiny Suzette floats on its hilltop, with a small 12th-century chapel, wine tastings, a handful of residents, and the gaggle of houses where they live. Park in Suzette's lot, then find the big orientation board above the lot. Look out to the broad shoulders of Mont Ventoux. At 6,000 feet, it always seems to have some clouds hanging around. If it's clear, the top looks like it's snow-covered; if you drive up there, you'll see it's actually white stone.

Back across the road from the orientation table is a simple tasting room for **Château Redortier** wines. Good picnic tables lie just past Suzette on our route.

• *Continue from Suzette in the direction of Beaumes-de-Venise. You'll drop down into the lush little village of La Fare. Just after leaving the village is the...*

❻ DOMAINE DE COYEUX WINERY

A private road winds up and up to this impossibly beautiful setting, with the best views of the Dentelles I've found. Le Caveau signs lead to a modern tasting room (you may need to ring the buzzer) within a big winery. The owners and staff are sincere and take your interest in their wines seriously—skip it if you only want a quick taste or are not interested in buying (generally open daily 10:00-12:00 & 14:00-18:00, except closed Sun off-season and no midday closure July-Aug; www. domainedecoyeux.com, some English spoken).

• *Drive on toward Beaumes-de-Venise. Navigate through Beaumes-de-Venise, following signs for Vacqueyras (a famous wine village with a Thursday market), and then signs for Gigondas and Vaison par la route touristique.*

❼ GIGONDAS

This upscale village produces some of the region's best reds and is ideally situated for hiking, mountain biking, and driving into the mountains. The TI has lists of wineries and tips for good hikes or drives (closed Sun, 5 Rue du Portail, www. gigondas-dm.fr). Take a short walk up through the village lanes to find a good viewing platform over the heart of the

Côtes du Rhône vineyards; you'll find even better views a little higher at the church. Several good tasting opportunities lie on the main square (Le Caveau de Gigondas is the best). The **$** restaurant at **Hôtel les Florets** is well worth the price—particularly if you dine on the magnificent terrace (closed Wed, clo sed Thu for lunch, a half-mile above Gigondas).

• *From Gigondas, follow signs to the circular wine village of Sablet (the TI and wine coopérative share a space in the town center)—then back to Séguret, where our tour ends.*

Ⓐ *Wine tasting in the Côtes du Rhône*
Ⓑ *Vineyards of Domaine de Coyeux*
Ⓒ *Côtes du Rhône vineyards*
Ⓓ *Gigondas street scene*

The French Riviera

A hundred years ago, celebrities from London to Moscow flocked to the French Riviera to socialize, gamble, and escape the dreary weather at home. Today, budget vacationers and heat-seeking Europeans fill belle époque resorts at France's most sought-after fun-in-the-sun destination.

Some of the Continent's most stunning scenery and intriguing museums lie along this strip of land—as do millions of sun-worshipping tourists. The Riviera's gateway is urban Nice, with world-class museums, a splendid beachfront promenade, a seductive old town, the best selection of hotels in all price ranges, and good nightlife options.

This sunny sliver of land is well served by public transportation, making day trips by train or bus almost effortless. If you drive here, expect traffic—although you'll be rewarded with sensational views on the coastal routes. If you head east from Nice, you'll find little Villefranche-sur-Mer staring across the bay at exclusive Cap Ferrat. Farther along, Monaco offers a royal welcome and a fairy-tale past. Wherever you choose to spend your days, evenings everywhere on the Riviera are radiant—made for a promenade and outdoor dining.

THE FRENCH RIVIERA IN 2 DAYS

My favorite home bases are Nice, Villefranche-sur-Mer, and Antibes. Nice, with convenient train and bus connections to most regional sights, is the most practical base for train travelers. Villefranche-sur-Mer is the romantic's choice, with a peaceful setting and small-town warmth, while midsize Antibes has the best beaches and works best for drivers.

Allow a full day for Nice: Spend your morning sifting through the old city (called Vieux Nice; take my Old Nice Walk) and ascend the elevator up Castle Hill for fine views. Devote the afternoon to the museums (Chagall is best, closed Tue) and strolling the Promenade des Anglais, taking my self-guided walk (best before or after dinner, but anytime is fine).

Save most of your second day for Monaco (tour Monaco-Ville, have lunch, and drop by the famous Monte Carlo casino), then consider a late afternoon or dinner in Villefranche-sur-Mer. With more time, stop by lush Cap Ferrat, filled with mansions, gardens, and beaches.

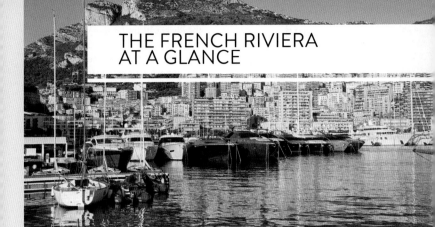

THE FRENCH RIVIERA AT A GLANCE

Nice
▲▲▲**Promenade des Anglais** Nice's sun-struck seafront promenade. See page 278.

▲▲▲**Chagall Museum** The world's largest collection of Marc Chagall's work, popular even with people who don't like modern art. **Hours:** Wed-Mon 10:00-18:00, Nov-April until 17:00, closed Tue year-round. See page 286.

▲▲**Vieux Nice** Charming old city offering enjoyable atmosphere and a look at Nice's French-Italian cultural blend. See page 283.

▲**Matisse Museum** Modest collection of Henri Matisse's paintings, sketches, and paper cutouts. **Hours:** Wed-Mon 10:00-18:00, mid-Oct-mid-June from 11:00, closed Tue year-round. See page 287.

▲**Russian Cathedral** Finest Orthodox church outside Russia. **Hours:** Daily 9:30-17:30. See page 288.

▲**Castle Hill** Site of an ancient fort boasting great views. **Hours:** Park closes at 20:00 in summer, earlier off-season. See page 288.

Nearby
▲▲▲**Villefranche-sur-Mer** Romantic pastel-orange beach village with a yacht-filled harbor and small-town ambience. See page 301.

▲▲**Cap Ferrat** Exclusive woodsy peninsula with a family-friendly beach and tourable Rothschild mansion. See page 305.

▲▲**Monaco** Tiny independent municipality known for its classy casino and Grand Prix car race. See page 306.

Getting Around the Riviera

By Bus and Train: Trains and buses do a good job of connecting places along the coast, with bonus views along many routes. Buses are often less expensive and more convenient while trains are faster and pricier.

By Car: This is France's most challenging region to drive in. Beautifully distracting vistas, loads of Sunday-driver tourists, and every hour being lush-hour in the summer make for a dangerous combination. Parking can be exasperating. Bring lots of coins and patience.

By Minivan Tour: Consider **Sylvie Di Cristo** (€600/day, €350/half-day for up to 8 people, mobile 06 09 88 83 83, http://frenchrivieraguides.com, dicristosylvie@gmail.com).

NICE

Nice (sounds like "niece"), with its spectacular Alps-meets-Mediterranean surroundings, is the big-city highlight of the Riviera. Its traffic-free Vieux Nice—the old town—blends Italian and French flavors to create a spicy Mediterranean dressing, while its big squares, broad seaside walkways, and long beaches invite lounging and people-watching. Nice may be nice, but it's jammed in May, July, and August—reserve ahead and get a room with air-conditioning.

Orientation

Focus your time on the area between the beach and the train tracks (about 15 blocks apart). The city revolves around its grand Place Masséna, where pedestrian-friendly Avenue Jean Médecin meets Vieux Nice and the Promenade du Paillon parkway (with quick access to the beaches). It's a 20-minute walk (or about €15 by taxi) from the train station to the beach, and a 20-minute stroll along the promenade from the fancy Hôtel Negresco to the heart of Vieux Nice.

Nice's historic Hôtel Negresco overlooks the Promenade des Anglais.

The French Riviera

To Digne
Entrevaux
Alpes Maritimes
To Grand Canyon du Verdon, Digne & Chamonix
ROUTE NAPOLEON
D-6085
Gorges du Loup
Tourrettes
Gourdon
Le Bar
St-Paul
Vence
Grasse
Biot
Vallauris
A-8
D-6098
Cannes
To Arles & Avignon
A-8
Massif de l'Estérel
D-559
SCENIC DRIVE
Fréjus
St-Raphaël
D-559
St-Tropez
D-6202
A-8
Venti-miglia
Menton
La Turbie
MONACO
Eze-le-Village
Nice
Villefranche-sur-Mer
Cap Ferrat
Antibes
Juan-les-Pins
ITALY
To Genoa
Mediterranean Sea
Paris
FRANCE
10 Kilometers
10 Miles
100 Miles

Tourist Information

Nice has two helpful TIs (tel. 08 92 70 74 07, www.nicetourisme.com), with branches at the **train station** and at **#5 Promenade des Anglais** (both daily 9:00-18:00, July-Aug until 19:00). Ask for day-trip information (including details on boat excursions, bus stop locations, and schedules).

Helpful Hints

Theft Alert: Nice has its share of pick-pockets (especially at the train station, on the tram, and trolling the beach). Stick to main streets in Vieux Nice after dark.

Sightseeing Tips: Mondays and Tuesdays can frustrate market lovers and museumgoers. Closed on Monday: Nice's Cours Saleya produce and flower market.

Closed on Tuesday: Chagall and Matisse museums in Nice.

A €10 **combo-ticket for Nice** covers all of the city's museums, except the Chagall Museum (sold at participating sights).

Rick's Tip: The **French Riviera Pass covers many Riviera sights and activities,** *including Nice's Chagall Museum, Monaco's Oceanography Museum (with aquarium), and Villa Ephrussi de Rothschild on Cap Ferrat (€26/24 hours, €38/48 hours, €56/72 hours, sold at TIs and online, tel. 04 92 14 46 14, http://en.frenchrivierapass.com). This pass is worthwhile if you want to do some bigger-ticket items in Nice like the included hop-on, hop-off Le Grand Tour Bus (see "Tours") or the Trans Côte d'Azur cruise (see "Experiences").*

Baggage Storage: You can store your bags inside the train station (€5-10/bag per day) or at the **Bagguys** in Vieux Nice (€8/bag per day, daily 10:00-19:00, 22 Rue Centrale, info@bagguys.fr).

Renting a Bike (and Other Wheels): **Holiday Bikes** has multiple locations, including one across from the train station, and they have electric bikes (www. loca-bike.fr). **Roller Station** is well-situated near the sea and rents bikes, rollerblades, skateboards, and Razor-style scooters (bikes–€5/hour, €10/half-day, €15/day, leave ID as deposit, open daily, 49 Quai des Etats-Unis, tel. 04 93 62 99 05).

Tours
HOP-ON, HOP-OFF BUS
Le Grand Tour Bus provides a useful 14-stop, hop-on, hop-off service on an open-deck bus with good headphone commentary (1-day pass–€23, 2-day pass–€26, buy tickets on bus, 2/hour, daily 10:00-19:00, 1.75-hour loop with Villefranche-sur-Mer, www.nicegrandtour.com).

LOCAL GUIDES AND WALKING TOURS
For a guided tour of Nice or the region (using public transit or your rental car), consider **Pascale Rucker** (€160/half-day, €260/day, mobile 06 16 24 29 52, pascalerucker@gmail.com). **Boba Vukadinovic-Millet** is an effective teacher, ideal for those wanting to dive more deeply into the region's history and art (from €250/half-day, from €350/day, mobile 06 27 45 68 39, www.yourguideboba.com, boba@yourguideboba.com). The TI on Promenade des Anglais organizes weekly walking tours of Vieux Nice in French and English (€12, Sat at 9:30, 2.5 hours, reservations necessary, departs from TI, tel. 08 92 70 74 07).

Walks in Nice
To get acquainted with Nice, combine the following two self-guided walks. "Promenade des Anglais" covers the sun-drenched seaside that made Nice famous, while "Vieux Nice" takes you through the historic old town of this engaging Franco-Italian city.

◉ *Promenade des Anglais Walk*
This leisurely, level self-guided walk, worth ▲▲▲, is a straight line along this much-strolled beachfront. It begins near the landmark Hôtel Negresco and ends just before Castle Hill. While this one-mile section is enjoyable at any time, the first half makes a great pre- or post-meal stroll (meals served at some beach cafés). If extending this stroll to Castle Hill, it's ideal to time things so you wind up on top of the hill at sunset. Allow one hour at a promenade pace to reach the elevator up to Castle Hill. To trace the route of this walk, see the "Nice" map, later.
• *Start your walk at the pink-domed...*

HOTEL NEGRESCO
Built in 1913, Nice's finest hotel is also a historic monument, offering up the city's most expensive beds and a museum-like interior. The hotel is technically off-limits if you're not a guest, but if you're decently dressed and explain to the doorman that you'd like to get a drink at Negresco's classy-cozy Le Relais bar, you'll be allowed past the registration desk. You can also explain that you want to shop at their store, which also might get you in—*bonne chance.*

If you get in, you can't miss the huge **Salon Royal** ballroom. The chandelier hanging from its dome is made of 16,000 pieces of crystal. It was built in France for the Russian czar's Moscow palace...but

Biking the promenade

thanks to the Bolshevik Revolution in 1917, he couldn't take delivery. Bronze portrait busts of Czar Alexander III and his wife, Maria Feodorovna—who returned to her native Denmark after the revolution—are to the right, facing the shops. Circle the interior of the ballroom and admire the soft light from the glass dome that Gustave Eiffel designed two decades after his more famous tower in Paris, then wander the perimeter to enjoy both historic and modern art. Fine portraits include Emperor Napoleon III and wife Empress Eugénie (who acquired Nice for France from Italy in 1860).

• Across the street from the Hôtel Negresco (to the east) is...

VILLA MASSENA

When Nice became part of France, France invested heavily in what it expected to be the country's new high society retreat—an elite resort akin to Russia's Sochi. This fine palace was built for Jean-Andre Masséna, a military hero of the Napoleonic age. Take a moment to stroll around the lovely garden (free, daily 10:00-18:00).

• From Villa Masséna, head for the beach and begin your Promenade des Anglais stroll. But first, grab a blue chair and gaze out to the...

BAY OF ANGELS (BAIE DES ANGES)

Face the water. The body of Nice's patron saint, Réparate, was supposedly escorted into this bay by angels in the fourth century. To your right is where you might have been escorted into France—Nice's airport, built on a massive landfill. The tip of land beyond the runway is Cap d'Antibes. Until 1860, Antibes and Nice were in different countries—Antibes was French, but Nice was a protectorate of the Italian kingdom of Savoy-Piedmont, a.k.a. the Kingdom of Sardinia. In 1850, the people here spoke Italian or Nissart (a local dialect) and ate pasta. As the story goes, the region was given a choice: Join newly united Italy or join France, which was enjoying prosperous times under the rule of Napoleon III. The majority voted in 1860 to go French...and voilà!

The lower green hill to your left is Castle Hill (where this walk ends). Farther left lie Villefranche-sur-Mer and Cap

The Bay of Angels epitomizes the beauty of the French Riviera.

FRANCE

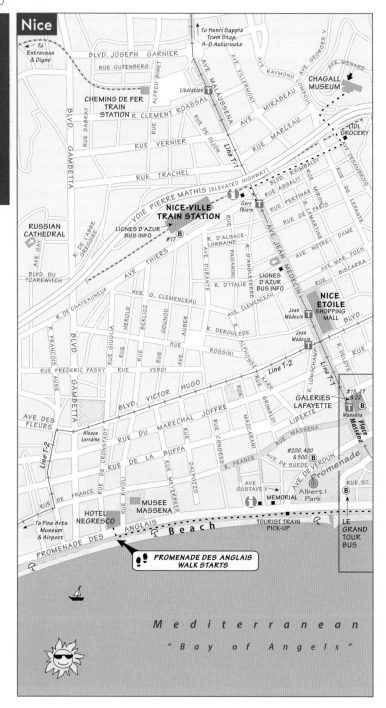

Nice

To Entrevaux & Digne

BLVD. JOSEPH GARNIER

RUE GUTENBERG

To Henri Sappia Tram Stop, A-8 Autoroute

CHEMINS DE FER TRAIN STATION

Libération

RUE DABRAY

R. CLEMENT ROASSAL

AVE. MALAUSSENA

AVE. VILLERMONT

RUE VERNIER

RUE DE DIJON

AVE. MIRABEAU

AVE. RAYMOND COMBOUL

AVE. GEORGES V

AVE. MENARD

CHAGALL MUSEUM

LIDL GROCERY

BLVD. GAMBETTA

RUE TRACHEL

Line T-1

AVE. MARCEAU

BLVD. RAINBALDI

RUE ASSALIT

AVE. D'SAMBROIS

RUE DE LEPANTE

R. DE L'ABBE GREGOIRE

VOIE PIERRE MATHIS (ELEVATED HIGHWAY)

NICE-VILLE TRAIN STATION

Gare Thiers

RUE PERTINAX

RUE MIRONS

RUSSIAN CATHEDRAL

AVE. GAY

LIGNES D'AZUR BUS INFO

#17

RUE DE PARIS

RUE DE LAMARTINE

AVE. NOTRE-DAME

BLVD. DU TZAREWITCH

AVE. THIERS

R. D'ALSACE-LORRAINE

RUE PAGANINI

R. D'ANGLETERRE

AVE. JEAN MEDECIN

AVE. MAR. FOCH

RUE BISCARRA

RUE DURANTE

R. D'ITALIE

LIGNES D'AZUR BUS INFO

NICE ETOILE SHOPPING MALL

R. DE CHATEAUNEUF

AVE. G. CLEMENCEAU

HEROLD

BERLIOZ

GOUNOD

AUBER

AVE. CLEMENCEAU

Jean Médecin

BLVD.

R. FRANCOIS

BLVD. GAMBETTA

RUE GIUGLIA

RUE

RUE DEROULEDE

Jean Médecin

R. DELOYE

RUE

ROSSINI

ALPHONSE KARR

Line T-2

Line T-1

AVE. DES FLEURS

RUE FREDERIC PASSY

RUE VERDI

BLVD. VICTOR HUGO

RUE

RUE KARR

GALERIES LAFAYETTE

#15, 17 & 22

Masséna

AUNE

Line T-2

Alsace Lorraine

RUE DU MARECHAL JOFFRE

RUE CONGRES

RUE MACCARANI

RUE GRIMALDI

LIBERTE

AVE. MASSENA

Place Masséna

RUE DE CRONSTADT

RUE DE LA BUFFA

RUE MEYERBEER

R. FRANCE

AVE. DE SUEDE

#200, 400 & 500

Promenade

RUE ST.

RUE DE FRANCE

RUE RIVOLI

MUSEE MASSENA

AVE GUSTAVE V

MEMORIAL

AVE. DE VERDUN

Albert I Park

To Fine Arts Museum & Airport

HOTEL NEGRESCO

PROMENADE DES ANGLAIS

Beach

TOURIST TRAIN PICK-UP

LE GRAND TOUR BUS

👣 PROMENADE DES ANGLAIS WALK STARTS

M e d i t e r r a n e a n

" B a y   o f   A n g e l s "

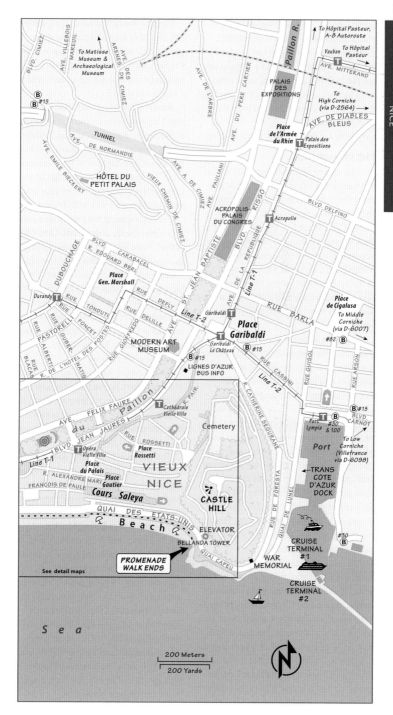

Ferrat (marked by the tower at land's end, and home to lots of millionaires), then Monaco (which you can't see, with more millionaires), then Italy. Behind you are the foothills of the Alps, which trap threatening clouds, ensuring that the Côte d'Azur enjoys sunshine more than 300 days each year.

• With the sea on your right, begin strolling.

THE PROMENADE

Nearby sit two fine belle-époque establishments: the West End and Westminster hotels, both boasting English names to help those original guests feel at home. (The West End is now part of the Best Western group...to help American guests feel at home.) These hotels symbolize Nice's arrival as a tourist mecca in the 19th century, when the combination of leisure time and a stable economy allowed visitors to find the sun even in winter.

As you walk, be careful to avoid the bike lane. Find the easel showing a painting of La Jetée Promenade—Nice's elegant pier and first casino, built in 1883. Even a hundred years ago, there was sufficient tourism in Nice to justify its construction. La Jetée Promenade stood east of those white-covered pilings just offshore, until the Germans dismantled it during World War II to salvage its copper and iron. When La Jetée was thriving, it took gamblers two full days to get to the Riviera by train from Paris. The painting shows what an event strolling the Promenade was—it was all about dressing up, being seen, and looking good.

Although La Jetée Promenade is gone, you can still see the striking 1927 Art Nouveau facade of the **Palais de la Méditerranée,** once a magnificent complex housing a casino, luxury hotel, and theater. It became one of the most famous destinations in all of Europe until it was destroyed in the 1980s to make room for a new hotel (the Hyatt Regency). The facade of the grand old building was spared the wrecking ball, but the classy interior was lost forever.

Despite the lack of sand, the pebble beaches here are still a popular draw. You can go local and rent beach gear—about €15 for a chaise longue (long chair) and a transat (mattress), €5 for an umbrella, and €5 for a towel.

Albert I Park is named after the Belgian king who defied a German ultimatum at the beginning of World War I. While the English came first, the Belgians and Russians were also big fans of 19th-century Nice. That tall statue at the edge of the park commemorates the 100-year anniversary of Nice's union with France.

Continuing along the promenade you'll soon enter the **Quai des Etats-Unis** ("Quay of the United States"). This name was given as a tip-of-the-cap to the Americans for finally entering World War I in 1917. The big, blue chair statue celebrates the inviting symbol of this venerable walk and kicks off the best stretch of beach—quieter and with less traffic. Check out the laid-back couches at the **Plage Beau Rivage** lounge and consider a beachfront drink.

Ahead on the left, the elegant back side of Nice's opera house faces the sea. The tiny bronze Statue of Liberty (right in front of you as you face the opera) reminds all that this stretch of seafront promenade is named for the USA.

The top level of the long, low galleries on the left was British tourists' preferred place for a stroll before the Promenade des Anglais was built. The ground floor served the city's fishermen. Behind the galleries bustles the **Cours Saleya Market**—long the heart and soul of Vieux Nice, with handy WCs under its arches.

Farther along, on the far-right side of the Quai des Etats-Unis (opposite Le Camboda restaurant), find the three-foot-tall white **metal winch** at the ramp to the beach. Long before tourism—and long before Nice dredged its harbor—hard-working fishing boats rather than vacationing tourists lined the beach. The boats were hauled in through the surf by winches like this and tied to the iron rings on either side.

*• Your walk is over. From here you can continue 10 minutes along the coast to the **port,** around the foot of Castle Hill (fine views of the entire promenade and a monumental war memorial carved into the hillside); hike or ride the elevator up to* **Castle Hill** *(catch the elevator next to Hôtel Suisse); or head into Vieux Nice (you can follow my "Vieux Nice Walk").*

Rick's Tip: *To make life tolerable on the rocks, swimmers should buy a pair of the cheap plastic* **beach shoes** *sold at many shops.* **Go Sport** *at #13 on Place Masséna is a good bet (open daily).*

---

❷ Vieux Nice Walk

This self-guided walk through Nice's old town, worth ▲▲, gives you a helpful introduction to the city's bicultural heritage and its most interesting neighborhoods. For the route, see the "Vieux Nice Hotels & Restaurants" map on page 292. Allow about one hour at a leisurely pace for this level walk from Place Masséna to Place Rossetti. It's best done in the morning (while the outdoor market thrives), and preferably not on a Sunday, when things are quiet. This ramble is also a joy at night, when fountains glow and pedestrians control the streets.

• Start where Avenue Jean Médecin hits the people-friendly Place Masséna—the successful result of a long, expensive city upgrade and the new center of Nice.

PLACE MASSENA

The grand Place Masséna is Nice's drawing room, where old meets new, and where the tramway bends between Vieux Nice and the train station. The square's black-and-white pavement feels like an elegant outdoor ballroom, with the sleek tram waltzing across its dance floor. While once congested with cars, the square today is crossed only by these trams, which swoosh silently by every couple of minutes. The men on pedestals sitting

high above are modern-art additions that arrived with the tram. For a mood-altering experience, return after dark and watch the illuminated figures float yoga-like above. Place Masséna is at its sophisticated best after the sun goes down.

This vast square dates from 1848 and pays tribute to Jean-André Masséna, a French military leader during the Revolutionary and Napoleonic wars. Not just another pretty face in a long lineup of French military heroes, he's considered among the greatest commanders in history—anywhere, anytime. Napoleon called him "the greatest name of my military Empire."

Avenue Jean Médecin, Nice's Champs-Elysées, cuts from here through the new town to the train station. Looking up the avenue, you'll see the tracks, the freeway, and the Alps beyond.

Appreciate the city's Italian heritage—it feels more like Venice than Paris. The portico flanking Avenue Jean Médecin is Italian, not French. The rich colors of the buildings reflect the taste of previous Italian rulers.

Now turn to the fountains and look east to see the **Promenade du Paillon,** a pedestrian-friendly parkway that extends from the sea to the Museum of Modern Art. Past the fountain stands a bronze statue of the square's namesake, Masséna.

Promenade du Paillon

The hills beyond separate Nice from Villefranche-sur-Mer.

To the right of the Promenade du Paillon lies **Vieux Nice,** with its jumbled and colorful facades below Castle Hill. Looking closer and further to the right, the **statue of Apollo** has horsey hair and holds a beach towel (in the fountain) as if to say, "It's beer o'clock, let's go."

• *Walk past Apollo into Vieux Nice (careful of those trams). A block down Rue de l'Opéra you'll see a grouping of rusted girders. Turn left onto Rue St. François de Paule.*

RUE ST. FRANÇOIS DE PAULE

This colorful street leads into the heart of Vieux Nice. On the left is the Hôtel de Ville (City Hall). Peer into the **Alziari olive oil shop** (at #14 on the right). Dating from 1868, the shop produces top-quality stone-ground olive oil. The proud and charming owner, Gilles Piot, claims that stone wheels create less acidity, since grinding with metal creates heat (see photo in back over the door). Locals fill their own containers from the huge vats.

A few awnings down, **La Couqueto** is a colorful shop filled with Provençal fabrics and crafts, including lovely folk characters (*santons*). The *boulangerie* next door is ideal for a cheap lunch and has good outdoor seating.

Next door is Nice's grand **opera house.** Imagine this opulent jewel back in the 19th century. With all the fancy big-city folks wintering here, this rough-edged town needed some high-class entertainment. And Victorians needed an alternative to those "devilish" gambling houses. (Queen Victoria, so disgusted by casinos, would actually close the drapes on her train window when passing Monte Carlo.) The four statues on top represent theater, dance, music, and party poopers.

Across the street, **Pâtisserie Auer**'s grand old storefront would love to tempt you with chocolates and candied fruits. It's changed little over the centuries. The writing on the window says, "Since 1820 from father to son." Wander in for a whiff of chocolate and a dazzling interior.

• *Continue on, sifting your way through a cluttered block of tacky souvenir shops to the big market square.*

COURS SALEYA

Named for its broad exposure to the sun (*soleil*), Cours Saleya (koor sah-lay-yuh)—a commotion of color, sights, smells, and people—has been Nice's main market square since the Middle Ages (flower market all day Tue-Sun, produce market Tue-Sun until 13:00, antiques on Mon). If you're early enough for coffee, pause for a break at **Café le Flore**'s outdoor tables in the heart of the market (a block up on the left).

The first section is devoted to the Riviera's largest **flower market.** In operation

Cours Saleya Market

A movable art gallery

since the 19th century, this market offers plants and flowers that grow effortlessly and ubiquitously in this climate, including the local favorites: carnations, roses, and jasmine. Locals know the season by what's on sale (mimosas in February, violets in March, and so on). Until the recent rise in imported flowers, this region supplied all of France with flowers.

The boisterous **produce section** trumpets the season with mushrooms, strawberries, white asparagus, zucchini flowers, and more—whatever's fresh gets top billing.

The market opens up at Place Pierre Gautier. It's also called Plassa dou Gouvernou—you'll see bilingual street signs here that include the old Niçois language, an Italian dialect. This is where farmers set up stalls to sell their produce and herbs directly.

From the steps, look up to the **hill** that dominates to the east. In the Middle Ages, a massive castle stood there with soldiers at the ready. Over time, the city sprawled down to where you are now. With the river guarding one side (running under today's Promenade du Paillon parkway) and the sea the other, this mountain fortress seemed strong—until Louis XIV leveled it in 1706. Nice's medieval seawall ran along the line of two-story buildings where you're standing.

Now, look across Place Pierre Gautier to the large "palace." The **Ducal Palace** was where the kings of Sardinia, the city's Italian rulers until 1860, resided when in Nice. (For centuries, Nice was under the rule of the Italian capital of Turin.) Today, the palace is the local police headquarters. The land upon which the Cours Saleya sits was once the duke's gardens and didn't become a market until Nice's union with France.

• *Continue down Cours Saleya. The faded golden building that seals the end of the square is where Henri Matisse spent 17 years. I imagine he was inspired by his view. The* **Café les Ponchettes** *is perfectly posi-*

tioned for you to enjoy the view, too, if you want a coffee break. At the café, turn onto...

RUE DE LA POISSONNERIE

Look up at the first floor of the first building on your right. **Adam and Eve** are squaring off, each holding a zucchini-like gourd. This scene represents the annual rapprochement in Nice to make up for the sins of a too-much-fun Carnival (Mardi Gras, the pre-Lenten festival). Residents of Nice have partied hard during Carnival for more than 700 years.

Next, check out the small **Baroque church** (Notre-Dame de l'Annonciation, closed 12:00-14:30) dedicated to St. Rita, the patron saint of desperate causes and desperate people (see display in window). She holds a special place in locals' hearts, making this the most popular church in Nice. Drop in for a peek at the dazzling Baroque decor. The first chapel on the right is dedicated to St. Erasmus, protector of mariners.

• *Turn right on the next street, where you'll pass one of Vieux Nice's most happening bars* (**Distilleries Ideales**). *Pause at the next corner and study the classic Vieux Nice scene. Now turn left on Rue Droite and enter an area that feels like Little Naples.*

RUE DROITE

In the Middle Ages, this straight, skinny street provided the most direct route from river to sea within the old walled town. Pass the recommended restaurant Acchiardo. Notice stepped lanes leading uphill to the castle. Pop into the Jesuit **Eglise St-Jacques** church (also called Eglise du Gésu) for an explosion of Baroque exuberance hidden behind that plain facade.

• *Make a left on Rue Rossetti; shortly you'll cross Rue Benoît Bunico.*

In the 18th century, this street served as a **ghetto** for Nice's Jews. At sunset, gates would seal the street at either end, locking people in until daylight. To identify Jews as non-Christians, the men were required to wear yellow stars and the women to wear yellow scarves. Wander a few steps up the street to find the white columns and archway across from #19 that mark what was the synagogue until 1848, when revolution ended the notion of ghettos in France.

• *Continue down Rue Rossetti to...*

PLACE ROSSETTI

The most Italian of Nice's piazzas, Place Rossetti comes alive after dark—in part because of the **Fenocchio gelato shop,** popular for its many innovative flavors.

Check out the **Cathedral of St. Réparate**—an unassuming building for a big-city cathedral. It was relocated here in the 1500s, when Castle Hill was temporarily converted to military use. The name comes from Nice's patron saint, a teenage virgin named Réparate, whose martyred body floated to Nice in the fourth century accompanied by angels. The beautiful interior is worth a wander.

• *This is the end of our walk. From here you can hike up* **Castle Hill** *(from Place Rossetti, take Rue Rossetti uphill). Or you can have an ice cream and browse the colorful lanes of Vieux Nice...or grab Apollo and hit the beach.*

Sights

Some of Nice's top attractions—the Promenade des Anglais, the beach, and the old town—are covered earlier in my self-guided walks. But Nice offers some additional worthwhile sights, covered here. A €10 combo-ticket (sold at participating sights) covers all of Nice's museums, except the Chagall Museum, which requires a separate admission (and is well worth it).

Rick's Tip: Visit the Chagall and Matisse museums together, *but* **not on Tuesday,** *when they're closed.*

The Chagall and Matisse museums are a long walk northeast of Nice's city center. Because they're in the same direction and served by the same bus line, try to visit them on the same trip. From Place Masséna, the Chagall Museum is a 10-minute bus ride, and the Matisse Museum is a few stops beyond that.

▲▲▲CHAGALL MUSEUM (MUSEE NATIONAL MARC CHAGALL)

Even if you don't get modern art, this museum—with the world's largest collection of Marc Chagall's work in captivity—is a delight. Between 1954 and 1967, he painted a cycle of 17 large murals designed for, and donated to, this museum. These paintings, inspired by the biblical books of Genesis, Exodus, and the Song of Songs, make up the "nave," or core, of what Chagall called the "House of Brotherhood."

Cost and Hours: €8, €2 more during frequent special exhibits; Wed-Mon 10:00-18:00, Nov-April until 17:00, closed Tue year-round; ticket includes helpful audioguide idyllic **$** garden café (salads and *plats*), tel. 04 93 53 87 20, http://en.musees-nationaux-alpesmaritimes.fr.

Getting There: The museum is located on Avenue Docteur Ménard. **Taxis** from the city center cost about €15. **Buses** connect the museum with downtown Nice. From downtown, catch bus #15 (Mon-Sat

Eglise St-Jacques

Place Rossetti

6/hour, Sun 3/hour, 10 minutes). Catch the bus from the east end of the Galeries Lafayette department store, near the Masséna tram stop, on Rue Sacha Guitry. Watch for a *Musée Chagall* sign on the bus shelter where you'll get off (on Boulevard de Cimiez).

Visiting the Museum: It takes about one hour to see this small museum.

In the **main hall** you'll find the core of the collection (Genesis and Exodus scenes). Each painting is a lighter-than-air collage of images that draws from Chagall's Russian folk-village youth, his Jewish heritage, the Bible, and his feeling that he existed somewhere between heaven and earth. He believed that the Bible was a synonym for nature, and that both color and biblical themes were key for understanding God's love for his creation. Chagall's brilliant blues and reds celebrate nature, as do his spiritual and folk themes. Notice the focus on couples. To Chagall, humans loving each other mirrored God's love of creation.

The adjacent **octagonal room** houses five more paintings. The paintings in this room were inspired by the Old Testament Song of Songs. Chagall was one of the few "serious" 20th-century artists to portray unabashed love. Where the Bible uses the metaphor of earthly, physical, sexual love to describe God's love for humans, Chagall uses unearthly colors and a mystical ambience to celebrate human love. These red-toned canvases are hard to interpret literally, but they capture the rosy spirit of a man in love with life.

Back near the entry, the wall **mosaic** (which no longer reflects in the filthy reflecting pond) evokes the prophet Elijah in his chariot of fire (from the Second Book of Kings)—with Chagall's addition of the 12 signs of the zodiac, which he used to symbolize time.

The **auditorium** is worth a peaceful moment to enjoy three Chagall stained-glass windows depicting the seven days of creation. This is also where you'll find a wonderful film (52 minutes) on Chagall, which plays at the top of each hour (not available during special exhibits).

▲MATISSE MUSEUM (MUSEE MATISSE)

This small, underachieving museum fills an old mansion in a park surrounded by scant Roman ruins, and houses a limited sampling of works from the various periods of Henri Matisse's artistic career. The museum offers an introduction to the artist's many styles and materials, both shaped by Mediterranean light and by fellow Côte d'Azur artists Picasso and Renoir.

As you tour the museum, look for Matisse's favorite motifs—including fruit, flowers, wallpaper, and sunny rooms—often with a window opening onto a sunny landscape. Another favorite subject is the *odalisque* (harem concubine), usually shown sprawled in a seductive pose and with a simplified, masklike face. You'll also see a few souvenirs from his travels, which influenced much of his work.

Chagall Museum

Chagall, Song of Songs IV

The Riviera's Art Scene

The list of artists who have painted the Riviera reads like a *Who's Who* of 20th-century art. Pierre-Auguste Renoir, Henri Matisse, Marc Chagall, Georges Braque, Raoul Dufy, Fernand Léger, and Pablo Picasso all lived and worked here—and raved about the region's wonderful light. Their simple, semi-abstract, and—most importantly—colorful works reflect the pleasurable atmosphere of the Riviera. You'll experience the same landscapes they painted in this bright, sun-drenched region, punctuated with views of the "azure sea." Try to imagine the Riviera with a fraction of the people and development you see today.

A collection of modern- and contemporary-art museums dot the Riviera, allowing art lovers to appreciate these masters' works while immersed in the same sun and culture that inspired them. Many of the museums were designed to blend pieces with the surrounding views, gardens, and fountains, thus highlighting that modern art is not only stimulating, but sometimes simply beautiful.

Cost and Hours: Covered by €10 Nice museum combo-ticket; Wed-Mon 10:00-18:00, mid-Oct-mid-June from 11:00, closed Tue year-round, 164 Avenue des Arènes de Cimiez, tel. 04 93 81 08 08, www.musee-matisse-nice.org.

Getting There: Take a cab (€20 from Promenade des Anglais). Alternatively, hop bus #15, direction: Rimiez, from the east end of Galeries Lafayette (from train station, catch #17, direction: Cimiez Hôpital). Get off at the Arènes-Matisse bus stop (look for the crumbling Roman arena that once held 10,000 spectators), then walk 50 yards into the park to find the pink villa.

▲RUSSIAN CATHEDRAL (CATHEDRALE RUSSE)

Nice's Russian Orthodox church—claimed by some to be the finest outside Russia—is worth a visit. Five hundred rich Russian families wintered in Nice in the late 19th century, and they needed a worthy Orthodox house of worship. Dowager Czarina Maria Feodorovna and her son, Nicholas II, offered the land for the construction, which began in 1903. Nicholas underwrote much of the project and gave this church to the Russian community in 1912. (A few years later, Russian comrades

who *didn't* winter on the Riviera assassinated him.) Here in the land of olives and anchovies, these proud onion domes seem odd. But, I imagine, so did those old Russians. The park around the church stays open at lunch and makes a nice setting for picnics.

Cost and Hours: Free; daily 9:30-17:30 except during services, chanted services Sat at 18:00, Sun at 10:00; no tourist visits during services, no shorts, Avenue Nicolas II, tel. 04 93 96 88 02, www.sobor.fr.

▲CASTLE HILL (COLLINE DU CHATEAU)

This hill—in an otherwise flat city center—offers sensational views over Nice, the port (to the east, created for trade

The view from Castle Hill is worth the climb.

Matisse "cutout" painting

Russian Cathedral

and military use in the 15th century), the foothills of the Alps, and the Mediterranean. The views are best early, at sunset, or whenever the weather's clear.

Nice was founded on this hill. Its residents were crammed onto the hilltop until the 12th century, as it was too risky to live in the flatlands below. Today you'll find a playground, a café, and a cemetery—but no castle—on Castle Hill.

Cost and Hours: Park is free and closes at 20:00 in summer, earlier off-season.

Getting There: You can get to the top by foot, by elevator (free, daily April-Sept 9:00-19:00, until 20:00 in summer, Oct-March 10:00-18:00, next to beachfront Hôtel Suisse).

See the "Promenade des Anglais Walk" for a pleasant stroll that ends near Castle Hill.

Experiences

MEDITERRANEAN CRUISE

To see Nice from the water, hop this one-hour ▲ **Trans Côte d'Azur cruise** in a comfortable yacht-size vessel to Cap Ferrat and past Villefranche-sur-Mer, then return to Nice with a final lap along Prom-

enade des Anglais (€18, covered by French Riviera Pass, Tue-Sun 2/day, no boats Mon or in off-season). Boats leave from Nice's port, Bassin des Amiraux, just below Castle Hill—look for the ticket booth (billeterie) on Quai de Lunel.

NIGHTLIFE

The city is a walker's delight after dark. Promenade des Anglais, Cours Saleya, Vieux Nice, Promenade du Paillon, and Place Masséna are all worth an evening wander. I can't get enough of the night scene on Place Masséna and around the adjacent fountains.

Most activity focuses on Vieux Nice. Rue de la Préfecture and Place du Palais are ground zero for bar life, though Place Rossetti and Rue Droite are also good targets. **Distilleries Ideales** is a good place to start or end your evening, with a lively international crowd, a *Pirates of the Caribbean* interior, and a *Cheers* vibe (lots of beers on tap, where Rue de la Poissonnerie and Rue Barillerie meet, happy hour 18:00-21:00). **Wayne's Bar** and others nearby are happening spots for the younger, Franco-Anglo backpacker crowd

(15 Rue Préfecture). Along the Promenade des Anglais, the classy Le Relais bar at **Hôtel Negresco** is fancy-cigar old English with frequent live jazz. To savor fine views over Nice, find **Hotel Aston La Scala**'s seventh-floor bar/terrace, which is a good spot for a drink any night, but offers jazz and blues on Thursdays and Fridays and a DJ on Saturdays (daily 17:00 to late, on Promenade du Paillon at 12 Avenue Félix Faure, tel. 04 92 17 53 00).

Sleeping

Don't look for charm in Nice. Seek out a good location and modern, reliable amenities (like air-conditioning). For parking, ask your hotelier.

In the City Center

The train station area offers Nice's cheapest sleeps, but the neighborhood feels sketchy after dark. The cheapest places are older, well-worn, and come with some street noise. Places closer to Avenue Jean Médecin are more expensive and in a more comfortable area.

Rick's Tip: *The Riviera is famous for staging major* **events.** *Stay away unless you're actually participating, as you'll only experience room shortages, higher prices, and traffic jams. The three biggies are the* **Nice Carnival** *(two weeks in Feb, www.nicecarnaval.com),* **Cannes Film Festival** *(mid-May, www. festival-cannes.com), and* **Grand Prix of Monaco** *(late May, www.acm.mc). The film festival and car race often overlap.*

$$$$ Hôtel du Petit Palais**** is a little belle-époque jewel with 25 handsome rooms tucked neatly into a residential area on the hill several blocks from the Chagall Museum. It's bird-chirping peaceful and plush, with tastefully designed rooms, a garden terrace, and small pool. You'll walk 15 minutes down to Vieux Nice (or use bus #15), free street parking is usually easy to find (17 Avenue Emile Bieckert, tel. 04 93 62 19 11, wwww.petitpalaisnice.com, reservation@petitpalaisnice.com).

$$ Hôtel Vendôme*** gives you a whiff of the belle époque, with pink pastels, high ceilings, and grand staircases in a mansion set off the street. The modern rooms come in all sizes; many have balconies (limited pay parking—book ahead, 26 Rue Pastorelli at the corner of Rue Alberti, tel. 04 93 62 00 77, www.hotel-vendome-nice.com, contact@vendome-hotel-nice.com).

$ Hôtel Durante*** rents quiet rooms in a happy orange building with rooms wrapped around a flowery courtyard. All but two rooms overlook the well-maintained patio. The rooms have adequate comfort (mostly modern decor), the price is right, and the parking is free on a first-come, first-served basis (family rooms, 16 Avenue Durante, tel. 04 93 88 84 40, www.hotel-durante.com, info@hotel-durante.com).

Near the Promenade des Anglais

$$$$ Hôtel Negresco***** owns Nice's most prestigious address on the Promenade des Anglais and knows it. Still, it's the kind of place that if you were to splurge just once in your life… Rooms are opulent and tips are expected (some view rooms, *très* classy bar, 37 Promenade des Anglais, tel. 04 93 16 64 00, www.hotel-negresco-nice.com, reservations@hotel-negresco.com).

$$$ Hôtel Splendid**** is a worthwhile splurge if you miss your Marriott. The panoramic rooftop pool, bar/restaurant, and breakfast room almost justify the cost…but throw in plush rooms, a free gym, and spa services, and you're as good as at home (pay parking, 50 Boulevard Victor Hugo, tel. 04 93 16 41 00, www.splendid-nice.com, info@splendid-nice.com).

$$ Hôtel Gounod*** is a fine value behind Hôtel Splendid. Because the two share the same owners, Gounod's guests are allowed free access to Splendid's pool, hot tub, and other amenities. Most rooms are quiet, with high ceilings and traditional decor (family rooms, pay parking, 3 Rue

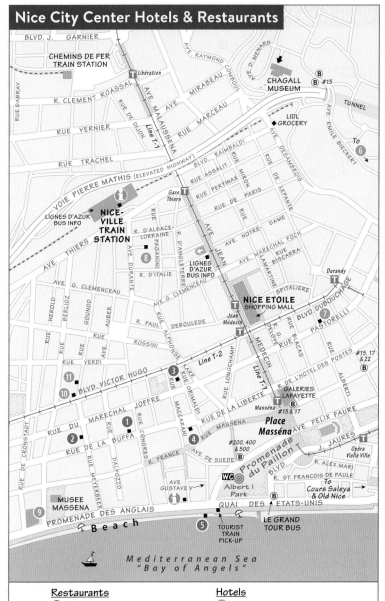

Nice City Center Hotels & Restaurants

Restaurants
1 L'Ecole de Nice
2 Le Canon
3 Mon Petit Café
4 La Voix de Son Maître
5 Restaurant Le Galet

Hotels
6 To Hôtel du Petit Palais
7 Hôtel Vendôme
8 Hôtel Durante
9 Hôtel Negresco
10 Hôtel Splendid
11 Hôtel Gounod

FRANCE

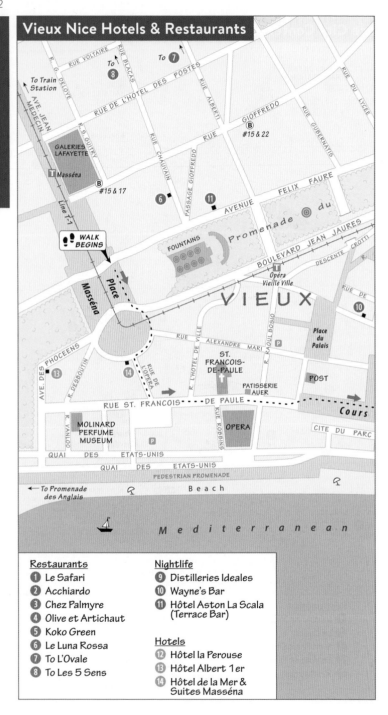

Vieux Nice Hotels & Restaurants

Map labels:

R. G. DELOYE · RUE VOLTAIRE · RUE BLACAS · To **8** · To **7** · RUE DE L'HÔTEL DES POSTES · RUE ALBERT I · RUE DU LYCEE · To Train Station · AVE. JEAN MÉDECIN · R.S GUITRY · RUE DE L'HÔTEL DES POSTES · RUE CHAUVAIN · RUE GIOFFREDO · **B** #15 & 22 · RUE GUBERNATIS · GALERIES LAFAYETTE · Masséna · **B** #15 & 17 · Line T-1 · PASSAGE GIOFFREDO · **6** · **11** · AVENUE · FELIX FAURE · Promenade · du · WALK BEGINS · FOUNTAINS · BOULEVARD JEAN JAURES · DESCENTE · CROTTI · Opéra Vieille Ville · Place · Masséna · V I E U X · RUE DE · **10** · AVE. DES PHOCEENS · R. DESBOUTIN · RUE DE L'HOTEL DE VILLE · RUE · ALEXANDRE MARI · RAOUL BOSIO · Place du Palais · **13** · **14** · RUE DE L'OPERA · ST. FRANCOIS-DE-PAULE · POST · PATISSERIE AUER · RUE ST. FRANCOIS - DE PAULE · Cours · R. YANLOO · MOLINARD PERFUME MUSEUM · RUE ROBBINS · OPERA · CITE DU PARC · QUAI DES ETATS-UNIS · QUAI DES ETATS-UNIS · PEDESTRIAN PROMENADE · To Promenade des Anglais · B e a c h · M e d i t e r r a n e a n

Restaurants
1 Le Safari
2 Acchiardo
3 Chez Palmyre
4 Olive et Artichaut
5 Koko Green
6 Le Luna Rossa
7 To L'Ovale
8 To Les 5 Sens

Nightlife
9 Distilleries Ideales
10 Wayne's Bar
11 Hôtel Aston La Scala (Terrace Bar)

Hotels
12 Hôtel la Perouse
13 Hôtel Albert 1er
14 Hôtel de la Mer & Suites Masséna

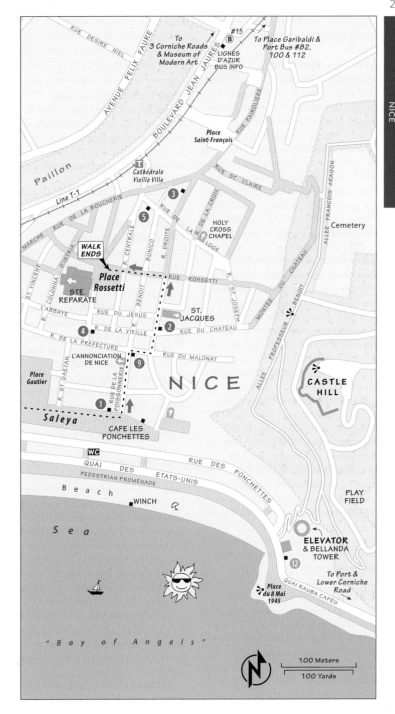

RUE DESIRE NIEL

AVENUE FELIX FAURE

BOULEVARD JEAN JAURES

To
3 Corniche Roads
& Museum of
Modern Art

#15

To Place Garibaldi &
Port Bus #82,
100 & 112

B

LIGNES
D'AZUR
BUS INFO

RUE PAIROLIERE

Place
Saint-François

Paillon

T

Cathédrale
Vieille Ville

Line T-1

RUE ST. CLAIRE

RUE DE LA BOUCHERIE

3

5

R. CENTRALE

BUNICO

R. DROITE

RUE DE LA CROIX

RUE DE LA LOGE

HOLY
CROSS
CHAPEL

Cemetery

MARCHE

COLONIA

D'ISTRIA

ST. VINCENT

WALK
ENDS

Place
Rossetti

STE.
REPARATE

L'ABBAYE

RUE DU JESUS

BENOIT

R.

RUE ROSSETTI

ST. JOSEPH

ST.
JACQUES

2

ALLEE FRANCOIS ARAGON

MONTEE DU CHATEAU

ALLEE PROFESSEUR BENOIT

4

R. DE LA VIEILLE

RUE DU CHATEAU

R. DE LA PREFECTURE

L'ANNONCIATION
DE NICE

RUE DU MALONAT

9

CASTLE
HILL

Place
Gautier

R. ST. GAETAN

RUE DE LA POISSONNERIE

N I C E

1

Saleya

CAFE LES
PONCHETTES

WC

QUAI   DES   ETATS-UNIS
PEDESTRIAN PROMENADE

RUE DES PONCHETTES

PLAY
FIELD

B e a c h

WINCH

S e a

ELEVATOR
& BELLANDA
TOWER

12

To Port &
Lower Corniche
Road

QUAI RAUBA CAPEU

Place
du 8 Mai
1945

" B a y   o f   A n g e l s "

N

100 Meters

100 Yards

Gounod, tel. 04 93 16 42 00, www.gounod-nice.com, info@gounod-nice.com).

In or near Vieux Nice

$$$$ Hôtel la Perouse,**** built into the rock of Castle Hill at the east end of the bay, is a fine splurge. This refuge-hotel is top-to-bottom flawless in every detail—from its elegant rooms (satin curtains, velour headboards) and attentive staff to its rooftop terrace with hot tub, sleek pool, and lovely **$$$$** garden restaurant. Sleep here to be spoiled and escape the big city (good family options, 11 Quai Rauba Capeu, tel. 04 93 62 34 63, www.hotel-la-perouse.com, lp@hotel-la-perouse.com).

$$$ Hôtel Albert 1er* is a fair deal in a central, busy location on Albert I Park, two blocks from the beach and Place Masséna. The staff is formal and the rooms are well-appointed and spotless, with heavy brown tones. Some have views of the bay, while others overlook the park or a quiet interior courtyard (4 Avenue des Phocéens, tel. 04 93 85 74 01, www.hotel-albert-1er.com, info@hotel-albert1er.com).

$$ Hôtel de la Mer** is an intimate, 12-room place with an enviable position overlooking Place Masséna, just steps from Vieux Nice and the beach. Rooms are modern, comfortable, and well-priced (4 Place Masséna, tel. 04 93 92 09 10, www.hoteldelamernice.com, hotel.mer@wanadoo.fr). They also run the **$$$$ Suites Masséna** in the same building, with seven huge, modern, high-ceilinged rooms—designed for two but with room for three (tel. 04 93 13 48 11, www.lessuitesmassena.com).

Eating

My favorite dining spots are in Vieux Nice. It's well worth booking ahead for these places. If Vieux Nice is too far, I've listed some great places handier to your hotel. Promenade des Anglais is ideal for picnic dinners on warm, languid evenings or a meal at a beachside restaurant. For a more romantic and peaceful meal, head for nearby Villefranche-sur-Mer. Avoid the fun-to-peruse but terribly touristy eateries lining Rue Masséna.

Rick's Tip: *Nice's **dinner scene converges on Cours Saleya,** which is entertaining enough in itself to make the generally mediocre food a good deal. It's a fun spot to compare tans and mussels—and worth wandering through even if you eat elsewhere.*

In Vieux Nice

$$$ Le Safari is a fair option for Niçois cuisine, pasta, pizza, and outdoor dining. This sprawling café-restaurant, convivial and rustic with the coolest interior on Cours Saleya, is packed with locals and tourists, and staffed with hurried waiters (daily noon to late, 1 Cours Saleya, tel. 04 93 80 18 44, www.restaurantsafari.fr).

$$ Acchiardo is a homey-but-lively eatery that mixes loyal clientele with hungry tourists. The food is delicious and copious, and the house wine is good and reasonable (Mon-Fri 19:00 until late, closed Sat-Sun and Aug, reservations smart, indoor seating only, 38 Rue Droite, tel. 04 93 85 51 16).

$ Chez Palmyre, your best budget bet in Vieux Nice, is tiny and popular, so book ahead (a week is advised). The ambience is rustic and fun, with people squeezed onto shared tables to enjoy the home-style cooking. Philippe serves everyone the same three-course, €17 *menu,* which changes every two weeks (closed Sat-Sun, 5 Rue Droite, tel. 04 93 85 72 32).

$$$ Olive et Artichaut is a sharp bistro-diner with a small counter, black-meets-white floor tiles, and a foodie vibe. It's a good choice to dine on carefully prepared Mediterranean dishes with creative twists (closed Mon-Tue, 6 Rue Ste. Réparate, tel. 04 89 14 97 51).

$$ Koko Green is a sweet little haven for vegan and raw-food types and is run by a

The Riviera's Cuisine Scene

While many of the same dishes served in Provence are available in the Riviera, there are differences, especially if you look for anything Italian or from the sea. When dining on the Riviera, I expect views and ambience more than top-quality cuisine.

A *salade niçoise* makes the perfect introduction to the Riviera's cuisine. Surprisingly, the authentic version contains no potatoes or green beans but consists of ripe tomatoes, plenty of raw vegetables (such as radishes, green peppers, celery, and perhaps artichoke or fava beans), as well as tuna (usually canned), anchovy, hard-boiled egg, and olives. This is my go-to salad for a tasty, healthy, cheap (€14), and fast lunch. I like to spend a couple of extra euros and eat it in a place with a nice ambience and view.

For lunch on the go, look for a *pan bagnat* (like a *salade niçoise* stuffed into a crusty roll drizzled with olive oil and wine vinegar). Other tasty bread treats include *pissaladière* (bread dough topped with caramelized onions, olives, and anchovies), *fougasse* (a spindly, lace-like bread sometimes flavored with nuts, herbs, olives, or ham), and *socca* (a thin chickpea-and-olive-oil crêpe, seasoned with pepper and often served in a paper cone by street vendors).

The Riviera specializes in all sorts of fish and shellfish. **Bouillabaisse** is the Riviera's most famous dish; you'll find it in seafront villages and cities. It's a spicy fish stew based on recipes handed down from sailors in Marseille. This dish often requires a minimum order of two and can cost up to €40-60 per person. Far less pricey than bouillabaisse and worth trying is the local *soupe de poissons* (fish soup). It's a creamy soup flavored like bouillabaisse, with anise and orange, and served with croutons and *rouille* sauce (but has no chunks of fish).

Other fishy options include *fruits de mer* (platters of seafood—including tiny shellfish, from which you get the edible part only by sucking really hard), herb-infused mussels, stuffed sardines, squid (slowly simmered with tomatoes and herbs), and tuna *(thon)*. The popular *loup flambé au fenouil* is grilled sea bass, flavored with fennel and torched with *pastis* prior to serving.

Do as everyone else does: Drink **wines** from Provence. **Bandol** (red) and **cassis** (white) are popular and from a region nearly on the Riviera. The only wines made in the Riviera are **Bellet** rosé and white, the latter often found in fish-shaped bottles.

Pick an outdoor table in Nice and try the socca (thin chickpea crêpe).

delightful Franco-Kiwi couple (open Thu-Sun for lunch, Sat for lunch and dinner, 1 Rue de la Loge, mobile 07 81 63 14 88).

In the City Center

$$ Le Luna Rossa is a small neighborhood place serving delicious French-Italian dishes. Owner Christine and her staff welcome diners with enthusiastic service and reasonable prices. Pasta dishes are copious and served in cast-iron pans, and the *assortiment* main course is a great sampler dish. Dine inside or outside on a sidewalk terrace (closed Sun-Mon, just north of parkway at 3 Rue Chauvain, tel. 04 93 85 55 66).

$ L'Ovale offers an unpretentious and local café-bistro experience. Owner David serves traditional dishes from southwestern France (rich and meaty). Dining is inside only. Consider the cassoulet, the hearty *salade de manchons* with duck and walnuts, or the €18-23 three-course *menus* (daily, 29 Rue Pastorelli, tel. 04 93 80 31 65).

$$$ Les 5 Sens ("The Five Senses") is a lively and dressy restaurant serving classic French fare at higher-end prices that justify the cost for discerning diners (daily, 37 Rue Pastorelli, tel. 09 81 06 57 00).

$$ L'Ecole de Nice brings wine-shop decor to a cozy-but-modern restaurant, and serves a limited selection of delicious dishes complimented by a vast selection of wines. The set-price *menu*—less than €30 for three courses—is a swinging deal (closed Sun, 16 Rue de la Buffa, tel. 04 93 81 39 30).

$$$ Le Canon is a fine-if-trendy choice, run by two friends intent on serving top-quality and inventive dishes that emphasize the region's local, fresh, and in-season ingredients (closed Sat-Sun, 23 Rue Meyerbeer, tel. 04 93 79 09 24).

$$$ Mon Petit Café delivers fine, traditional cuisine to appreciative diners in a warm, candlelit interior or on a pleasant front terrace. Book ahead for this dressy place and expect top service and mouth-watering cuisine (closed Sun-Mon, 11 bis Rue Grimaldi, tel. 04 97 20 55 36, www.monpetitcafe-nice.com).

$ La Voix de Son Maître is a handy

creperie, with seating on a broad terrace or inside (closed Sun, on Place Grimaldi, tel. 04 93 82 28 47).

On the Beach

$$$ Restaurant Le Galet is your best eat-on-the-beach option. The city vanishes as you step down to the beach. The food is nicely presented, and the tables feel elegant, even at the edge of the sand. Arrive for the sunset and you'll have an unforgettable meal (open for dinner May-mid-Sept, 3 Promenade des Anglais, tel. 04 93 88 17 23). Sunbathers can rent beach chairs and have drinks and meals served literally on the beach (lounge chairs–€16/half-day, €19/day).

Transportation
Getting Around Nice
BY PUBLIC TRANSPORTATION

Although you can walk to most attractions, smart travelers make good use of the buses and trams.

Tickets: Buses and trams are covered by the same €1.50 single-ride ticket, or you can pay €10 for a 10-ride ticket that can be shared (each use good for 74 minutes in one direction, including transfers between bus and tram). The €5 all-day pass is valid on city buses and trams, as well as buses to some nearby destinations (but not airport buses). You must validate your ticket in the machine on every trip. Buy single tickets from the bus driver or from the ticket machines on tram platforms (coins only—press the green button once to validate choice and twice at the end to get your ticket). Passes and 10-ride tickets are also available from machines at tram stops. Info: www.lignesdazur.com.

Buses: The bus is handy for reaching the Chagall and Matisse museums and the Russian Cathedral (for specifics, see listings under "Sights"). Route diagrams in the buses identify each stop.

Trams: Nice has a modern and efficient L-shaped tram line (T-1) that runs to the train station and a new line (T-2) that connects the city center to the airport (http://tramway.nice.fr). Trams to the train station run every few minutes along Avenue Jean Médecin and Boulevard Jean Jaurès, and connect the main train station with Place Masséna and Vieux Nice (Opéra stop), the port (Place Garibaldi stop), and buses east along the coast (Vauban stop). Boarding the tram in the direction of Hôpital Pasteur takes you toward the beach and Vieux Nice (direction: Henri Sappia goes the other way). The new T-2 tramway goes from the airport through the city center to Nice's Port Lympia, paralleling the Promenade des Anglais a few blocks inland.

BY TAXI OR UBER

While pricey, **cabs** are useful for getting to Nice's less-central sights (figure €8 for shortest ride, €15 from Promenade des Anglais to the Chagall Museum). Cabbies normally pick up only at taxi stands *(tête de station),* or you can call 04 93 13 78 78. **Uber** works here like it does at home (including your US app and account), though there are fewer cars here, and the price is not much cheaper than a taxi. Still, drivers are often nicer and more flexible, and you usually get a car without much delay.

Getting Around the Riviera from Nice

Nice is perfectly situated for exploring the Riviera by public transport. Trains and buses do a good job of linking towns

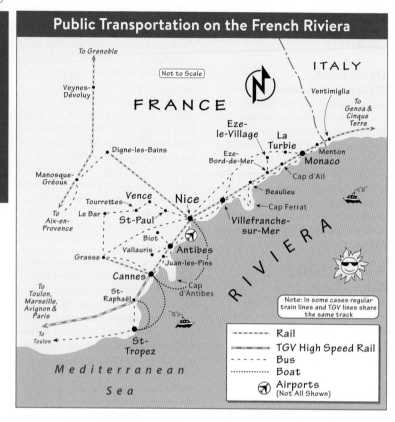

Public Transportation on the French Riviera

along the coast, with bonus views along many routes. Have coins handy. Ticket machines don't take US credit cards or euro bills; smaller train stations may be unstaffed; and bus drivers can't make change for large bills.

BY BUS

Buses are an amazing deal in the Riviera. Regardless of length, most one-way rides on regional buses (except express airport buses) cost €1.50. Tickets are good for up to 74 minutes of travel in one direction, including transfers. To connect to regional destinations, use the following bus lines and stops (see maps in this chapter for stop locations; www.lignesdazur.com).

Eastbound Buses: Due to the new T-2 tram that ends at the port, expect some

changes to stop locations for these buses. Trams T-1 and/or T-2 will get you close to these stops, and transfers are free from tram to bus for all lines but #100.

Bus #100 runs from Nice's port through **Villefranche-sur-Mer** (3-4/hour, 20 minutes), **Monaco** (1 hour). Bus #15 runs from the Promenade des Arts stop to **Villefranche-sur-Mer** (2-3/hour, 15 minutes) and around **Cap Ferrat** (30 minutes to **St-Jean-Cap-Ferrat**).

Westbound Buses: Bus #200 goes to **Antibes** (4/hour Mon-Sat, 2/hour Sun, 1.5 hours). Use the Albert I/Verdun stop on Avenue de Verdun, a 10-minute walk along the parkway west of Place Masséna. You must buy tickets before boarding these buses.

BY TRAIN

Speedy trains link the Riviera's beachfront destinations. Never board a train without a ticket or valid pass—fare inspectors accept no excuses. The minimum fine: €70. See below under "Arriving and Departing" for specific trip information.

Rick's Tip: *The Riviera is awash with* **scenic roads.** *To sample one of its most beautiful and thrilling drives, take the coastal* **Middle Corniche road** *from Nice to Monaco. You'll find breathtaking views over the Mediterranean and several scenic pullouts.*

BY CAR

This is France's most challenging region to drive in. Beautifully distracting vistas (natural and human), loads of Sunday-driver tourists, and every hour being lush-hour in the summer make for a dangerous combination. Parking can be exasperating. Bring lots of coins and patience.

BY BOAT

In summer, **Trans Côte d'Azur** offers scenic trips several days a week from Nice to Monaco (reservations required, tel. 04 92 00 42 30, www.trans-cote-azur.com). The same company also runs one-hour round-trip cruises along the coast to Cap Ferrat.

Arriving and Departing
BY TRAIN

All trains stop at Nice's main station, called Nice-Ville. The TI and bus stops are straight out the main doors. A nearby tram line zips you to the center in a few minutes (several blocks to the left as you leave the station, departs every few minutes, direction: Hôpital Pasteur). To walk to the beach, Promenade des Anglais, or many of my recommended hotels, cross Avenue Thiers in front of the station, go down the steps by Hôtel Interlaken, and continue down Avenue Durante.

Train Connections from Nice to: Antibes (2/hour, 20 minutes), **Villefranche-sur-Mer** (2/hour, 10 minutes), **Monaco** (2/hour, 20 minutes).

BY CAR

Renting a car is easiest at Nice's airport, which has offices for all the major companies. Most companies are also represented at Nice's train station and near the southwest side of Albert I Park. To reach the city center from the autoroute, take the *Nice Centre* exit and follow signs. Ask your hotelier where to park (allow €20-30/day; some hotels offer deals but space is limited—arrange ahead). The parking garage at the Nice Etoile shopping center on Avenue Jean Médecin is near many recommended hotels (ticket booth on third floor, about €28/day, 18:00-8:00). Other centrally located garages have similar rates. On-street parking is strictly metered (usually a 2-hour limit) every day but Sunday, when it is typically free.

You can avoid driving in the center—and park for free during the day (no overnight parking)—by stashing your car at a parking lot at a remote tram or bus stop. Look for blue-on-white *Parcazur* signs (find locations at www.lignesdazur.com), and ride the bus or tram into town (10/hour, 15 minutes, buy round-trip tram or bus ticket and keep it with you—you'll need it later to exit the parking lot; for tram details, see "Getting Around Nice," earlier). As lots are not guarded, don't leave anything of value in your car.

BY PLANE

Nice's easy-to-navigate airport (Aéroport de Nice Côte d'Azur, code: NCE) is literally on the Mediterranean—with landfill runways, a 30-minute drive west of the city center. The two terminals are connected by shuttle buses (navettes). Both terminals have TIs, banks, ATMs, trams, and buses to Nice (tel. 04 89 88 98 28, www.nice.aeroport.fr).

A **taxi into the city center** is expensive considering the short distance (figure €35 to Nice hotels, €60 to Villefranche-sur-Mer, about €5 more at night and on weekends, small fee for bags). Nice's airport taxis are notorious for overcharging. Before riding, confirm your fare. It's always a good idea to ask for a receipt (reçu).

The T-2 tramway runs frequently into Nice, paralleling the Promenade des Anglais and ending at Nice's Port Lympia (every 6-10 minutes, 25-minute ride). The tram is handy for those sleeping at hotels near the Promenade des Anglais and Place Masséna. Buy tickets from machines at the tram stop (€1.50, coins or credit card).

Airport shuttles work better for trips from your hotel to the airport, since they require you to book a precise pickup time in advance. Shuttle vans offer a fixed price (about €30 for one person, a little more for additional people or to Villefranche-sur-Mer). Your hotel can arrange this, and I would trust their choice of company.

Linking the Airport and Nearby Destinations: To get to **Villefranche-sur-Mer** from the airport, take the T-2 tram to the last stop (Port Lympia). There you can transfer to bus #15 to Villefranche-sur-Mer. Allow €60 for a taxi.

Express bus #110 runs from the airport directly to **Monaco** (2/hour, 50 minutes, €22).

NEAR NICE

Day-trip possibilities from Nice are easy and exciting. Villefranche-sur-Mer has a serene setting and small-town warmth. Woodsy Cap Ferrat boasts belle époque mansions and a family-friendly beach. Glitzy little Monaco offers a fancy casino and royal flair.

Quick and efficient public transportation gets you where you want to go (see "Getting Around the Riviera from Nice" on page 297).

Villefranche-sur-Mer

In the glitzy world of the Riviera, Villefranche-sur-Mer offers travelers an easygoing slice of Mediterranean life. Sand-pebble beaches and a handful of interesting sights keep visitors just busy enough.

Day Plan

My self-guided walk laces together everything of importance in town. Your biggest decision will be choosing between a beachfront meal or an ice-cream-licking village stroll.

Orientation

Tiny and easy to cover, Villefranche-sur-Mer snuggles around its harbor.

Tourist Information: The TI is located in a park (Jardin François Binon) below the Nice/Monaco Octroi bus stop (daily in season, closed Sun off-season; tel. 04 93 01 73 68, www.villefranche-sur-mer.com).

Getting There

From Nice, **trains** run to Villefranche-sur-Mer twice an hour (10 minutes); it's a level 10-minute walk from the station to the port area. Or take **bus #15** or **#100** from Nice (2-4/hour, 20 minutes); get off at the Octroi stop and walk downhill past the TI to town. From Nice's port, **drivers** should follow signs for *Menton, Monaco,* and *Basse Corniche*; pay lots are just below the TI or near the water (at Parking Wilson).

The beautiful deep-water bay at Villefranche-sur-Mer attracts every kind of boat.

FRANCE

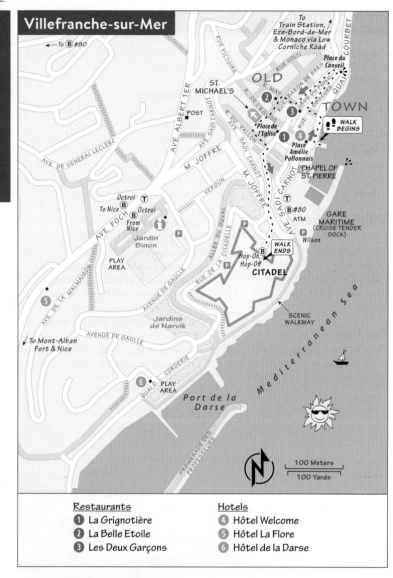

Villefranche-sur-Mer

To ⑧ #80 →

To
Train Station, ↑
Eze-Bord-de-Mer
& Monaco via Low
Corniche Road

RUE VICTOIRE

RUE VOLTI

RUE COURBET

QUAI

Place du
Conseil

OLD

R. MAY

R. DE L'EGLISE

R. DU BARON DE BRES

RUE DUPONT

RUE DE MESSORE

TOWN

ST.
MICHAEL'S

AVE. ALBERT 1ER

AVE. SADI CARNOT

POST

❷

❸

WALK
BEGINS

Place de
l'Eglise

❶

❹

R. DU VALLON

Place
Amélie
Pollonnais

AVE. DE GENERAL LECLERC

M. JOFFRE

VERDUN

ALLEE DU DUVAL

M. JOFFRE

AVE. SADI CARNOT

CHAPEL OF
ST. PIERRE

Octroi ⓣ
To Nice ⓑ
Octroi
ⓑ
From
Nice ⓑ

AVE. FOCH

Jardin
Binon

PLAY
AREA

ⓘ

P

P

⑤

AVE. DE LA MALMAISON

RUE DE LA CITADELLE

P

WALK
ENDS

Hop-On,
Hop-Off

ⓑ

CITADEL

ⓑ #80

ATM

P

Wilson

GARE
MARITIME
(CRUISE TENDER
DOCK)

SCENIC
WALKWAY

Mediterranean Sea

Jardins
de Narvik

AVENUE DE GAULLE

To Mont-Alban
Fort & Nice ↙

AVENUE DE GAULLE

QUAI DE L'CORDERIE

⑥

PLAY
AREA

Port de la
Darse

PROMENADE DES
PROFESSEURS

N

100 Meters

100 Yards

Restaurants
❶ La Grignotière
❷ La Belle Etoile
❸ Les Deux Garçons

Hotels
❹ Hôtel Welcome
❺ Hôtel La Flore
❻ Hôtel de la Darse

Rick's Tip: *A fun* **bric-a-brac market**
enlivens Villefranche-sur-Mer on **Sundays**
*on Place Amélie Pollonnais by Hôtel Wel-
come. On Saturday, Sunday, and Wednesday mornings, a market sets up in Jardin
François Binon by the TI.*

⮕ *Town Walk*

This quick self-guided walk starts at the
waterfront and finishes at the citadel.
• *Go to the end of the short pier directly in
front of Hôtel Welcome.*

The Harbor: At 2,000 feet, this is the
deepest natural harbor on the Riviera and
the region's most important port until

Nice built its own in the 18th century. Today, ships bring tourists rather than pirates. The bay is generally filled with beautiful yachts.

Up on the hill, the 16th-century citadel (where this walk ends) is marked by flags. The yellow fisherman's chapel (with the little-toe bell tower) has a special interior (more on it below). Up the skinny lane just right of the Hôtel Welcome is the baroque facade of St. Michael's Church. The waterfront, lined by fancy fish restaurants, curves to the town beach. Fifty yards above the beach stands the train station and above that, supported by arches, is the Low Corniche road, which leads to Monaco.

• *Leave the pier and walk left 30 yards to find a small bronze bust of Jean Cocteau, the artist. A few more steps take you to the...*

Chapel of St. Pierre (Chapelle Cocteau): This chapel is the town's cultural highlight. Cocteau, who decorated the place, was a Parisian transplant who adored little Villefranche-sur-Mer and whose career was distinguished by his work as an artist, poet, novelist, playwright, and filmmaker. Influenced by his pals Marcel Proust, André Gide, Edith Piaf, and Pablo Picasso, Cocteau was a leader among 20th-century avant-garde intellectuals (€3 donation, usually closed Mon-Tue, hours vary with cruise-ship traffic and season).

• *From the chapel, turn right and stroll the harbor promenade. Immediately after Restaurant La Mère Germaine, a lane leads up into the old town. Walk up a few steps, and turn right into a long tunnel-like street.*

Rue Obscure, the Old Town, and St. Michael's Church: Here, under these 13th-century vaults, you're in another age. Walk to the end of Rue Obscure (which means "dark street"), winding up to the sunlight. You'll pass a tiny fountain at Place du Conseil and, a few steps beyond that, you'll reach a viewpoint overlooking the harbor.

Turn around and stroll back past the fountain, straight down the little lane called Rue du Poilu. Notice the homes built under the heavy arches. At Place des Deux Garçons (the square with a namesake restaurant), turn right on Rue May and climb the stepped lane. Take your first left to find St. Michael's Church, facing a delightful square with a single magnolia tree (Place de l'Eglise). The deceptively large church features an 18th-century organ, a particularly engaging crucifix at the high altar, and (to the left) a fine statue of a recumbent Christ—carved, they say, from a fig tree by a galley slave in the 1600s.

• *Leaving St. Michael's, go downhill halfway to the water, where you'll rejoin Rue du Poilu. Turn right, then curve left, pass the square, and walk up to the...*

Citadel: The town's mammoth castle was built in the 1500s by the Duke of Savoy to defend against the French. When the region joined France in 1860, the castle became just a barracks.

The exterior walls slope thickly at the base, indicating that they were built in the "Age of Black Powder"—the 16th century—when the advent of gunpowder

Chapel of St. Pierre

made thicker, cannonball-deflecting walls a necessity for any effective fortification. The bastions are designed for smarter crossfire during an attack.

• *And that concludes our introductory walk.*

Experiences

▲SEAFRONT WALKS

A seaside walkway leads under the citadel and connects the old town with the work-aday harbor, Port de la Darse. At the port you'll find a few cafés, France's Institute of Oceanography, and an 18th-century dry dock. This scenic walk turns downright romantic after dark. You can also wander the other direction along Villefranche-sur-Mer's waterfront and continue beyond the train station for postcard-perfect views back to town (ideal in the morning—go before breakfast).

HIKE TO MONT-ALBAN FORT

This fort, with a remarkable setting on the high ridge that separates Nice and Ville-franche-sur-Mer, is a good destination for hikers (also accessible by car and bus; info at TI). From the TI, walk on the main road toward Nice about 500 yards past Hôtel La Flore. Look for wooden trail signs labeled *Escalier de Verre* and climb about 45 minutes up to Mont-Alban Fort (interior closed to tourists) and its sensational

view terrace. To visit with a much shorter hike, minibus #80 drops you a 15-minute walk away (by Hôtel Fiancée du Pirate).

BOAT RIDES (PROMENADES EN MER)

To view this beautiful coastline from the sea, consider taking a quick **sightseeing cruise** with AMV (€12-22, some stay in the bay, others go as far as Monaco, select days June-Sept, departs across from Hôtel Welcome, www.amv-sirenes.com).

Sleeping

Overnighters will find seaview rooms at **$$$$ Hôtel Welcome****** (3 Quai Amiral Courbet, www.welcomehotel.com), **$$ Hôtel La Flore***** (5 Boulevard Prin-cesse Grace de Monaco, www.hotel-la-flore.fr), and **$ Hôtel de la Darse**** (handy for drivers, 32 Avenue Général de Gaulle, www.hoteldeladarse.com).

Eating

$$$ La Grignotière serves generous and tasty *plats* (daily, 3 Rue du Poilu). **$$ La Belle Etoile** is the romantic's choice, a few blocks above the harbor on a small lane (closed Tue-Wed, 1 Rue Baron de Bres). **$$$ Les Deux Garçons** offers candlelit tables on a quiet square (closed Wed, 18 Rue du Poilu).

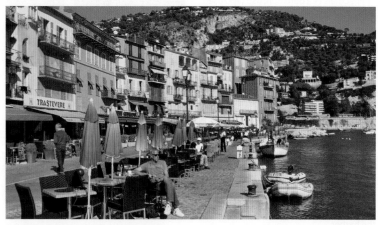

Waterfront tables line Villefranche's harbor.

Cap Ferrat

Cap Ferrat is a peaceful eddy off the busy Nice-Monaco route. You could spend a leisurely day on this peninsula, wandering the sleepy port village of St-Jean-Cap-Ferrat (usually called "St-Jean"), touring the Villa Ephrussi de Rothschild mansion and gardens, and walking on sections of the beautiful trails that follow the coast.

Tourist Information: The main TI is near the harbor in St-Jean (closed Sun; 5 Avenue Denis Séméria). A smaller TI is near the Villa Ephrussi (closed Sun, 59 Avenue Denis Séméria, www.saintjean-capferrat-tourisme.fr).

Day Plan

Visit the Villa Ephrussi de Rothschild, then walk 30 minutes, mostly downhill, to St-Jean for lunch (many options, including grocery shops for picnic supplies) and poke around the village. Take the 45-minute walk on the Plage de la Paloma trail (ideal for picnics).

Getting There

From Nice or Villefranche-sur-Mer, **bus #15** (direction: *Port de St-Jean*) runs to Cap Ferrat. For the Villa Ephrussi de Rothschild or the beach, get off at the Passable stop. The return bus (direction: *Nice*) begins in St-Jean.

In high season, late-afternoon buses can be jammed—board bus #15 on the Cap itself, before it gets crowded.

Cap Ferrat is quick by **car** (take the Low Corniche) or **taxi** (allow €30 one-way from Villefranche-sur-Mer, €65 from Nice).

Sights

▲VILLA EPHRUSSI DE ROTHSCHILD

In what seems like the ultimate in Riviera extravagance, Venice, Versailles, and the Côte d'Azur come together in the pastel-pink Villa Ephrussi. Rising above Cap Ferrat, this 1905 mansion has views west to Villefranche-sur-Mer and east to Beaulieu-sur-Mer.

Cost and Hours: Palace and gardens–€14, includes audioguide; mid-Feb-Oct daily 10:00-18:00, July-Aug until 19:00; shorter hours off-season; tel. 04 93 01 33 09, www.villa-ephrussi.com.

Visiting the Villa: Start with the well-furnished belle-époque ground floor. Upstairs, an 18-minute film (with English subtitles) explains the gardens and villa and gives you good background on the life of rich and eccentric Béatrice, Baroness de Rothschild, the French banking heiress who built and furnished the place. Don't miss the view from her private terrace.

Behind the mansion, stroll through the **seven lush gardens** re-created from locations all over the world—and with maximum sea views. An appropriately classy **$$ garden-tearoom** serves drinks and lunches with a view (12:00-17:30).

PLAGE DE PASSABLE

This pebbly little beach, located below the Villa Ephrussi, is a peaceful place, popular with families. One half is public (free, with snack bar, shower, and WC), and the other is run by a small restaurant (€30 includes changing locker, lounge chair, and shower; reserve ahead in summer or on weekends, tel. 04 93 76 06 17). If you were ever to do the French Riviera rent-a-beach ritual, this would be the place.

Getting There: Bus #15 stops a 10-minute walk uphill from the beach, near Villa Ephrussi.

Villa Ephrussi de Rothschild

Eating: $$$ Restaurant de la Plage de Passable is your chance to dine on the beach with romance and class (daily late May-early Sept, always make a reservation, tel. 04 93 76 06 17).

PLAGE DE LA PALOMA LOOP TRAIL

A few blocks east of St-Jean's port, a scenic 45-minute trail offers an easy sampling of Cap Ferrat's beauty. From the port, walk or drive about a quarter-mile east (with the port on your left, passing Hôtel La Voile d'Or); parking is available at the port or on streets near Plage de la Paloma. You'll find the trailhead where the road comes to a T—look for a *Plage Paloma* sign pointing left, but don't walk left. Cross the small gravel park (*Jardin de la Paix*) to start the trail, and do the walk counterclockwise. The trail is level and paved, yet uneven enough that good shoes are helpful. Plunk your picnic on one of the benches along the trail, or eat at the restaurant on Plage de la Paloma at the end of the walk.

Monaco

The minuscule principality of Monaco (less than a square mile) is a special place—it's home to one of the world's most famous auto races and one of its fanciest casinos. The glamorous 1956 marriage of the American actress Grace Kelly to Prince Rainier added to the mystique of this glittering little land of luxury.

Day Plan

The surgical-strike plan is to start with my self-guided walk in Monaco-Ville, then visit the aquarium or gamble away whatever you have left in the Monte Carlo Casino.

Orientation

Monaco-Ville is the oldest part of Monaco, home to the Prince's Palace and all the key sights except the casino. Monte Carlo is the area around the casino.

Tourist Information: The main TI is at the top of the park above the casino (daily, 2 Boulevard des Moulins, tel. 00-377/92 16 61 16, www.visitmonaco.com). Another TI is at the train station.

Getting Around by Local Bus: Buses #1 and #2 link all areas with frequent service (10/hour, fewer on Sun, buses run until 21:00). If you pay the driver, a single ticket is €2, 6 tickets €11, and a day pass €5.50; save by using red curbside machines, where you get 12 tickets for €11. You can split a 6- or 12-ride ticket with your travel partners. Bus tickets are good for a free transfer if used within 30 minutes.

Rick's Tip: *For a* **cheap and scenic loop ride** *through Monaco, ride bus #2 from one end to the other and back (25 minutes each way). You'll need two tickets and must get off the bus at the last stop and then get on again.*

Getting There

If coming by frequent **bus #100** from Nice (1 hour) or Villefranche-sur-Mer (40 minutes), get off at Place d'Armes (at the base of Monaco-Ville) to take my self-guided walk; use the Monte Carlo-Casino stop (in front of the TI on Boulevard des Moulins) if you're headed to the casino.

Trains from Nice (2/hour) stop at the long, entirely underground station in the center of Monaco. From here, it's a 15-minute walk to the casino or the base of the palace.

Drivers should follow *Centre-Ville* signs into Monaco, then watch for the signs to parking garages at *Le Casino* (for Monte Carlo) or *Le Palais* (for Monaco-Ville).

Rick's Tip: *For an official memento of your Monaco visit,* **get your passport stamped at the TI.**

❍ Monaco-Ville Walk

This self-guided walk connects Monaco's major sights (except the casino) in a tight little loop, starting from the palace square.

Palace Square (Place du Palais): This square is the best place to get oriented to Monaco. Facing the palace, walk to the right and look out over the city (er... principality). This rock gave birth to the little pastel Hong Kong look-alike in 1215, and it's managed to remain an independent country for most of its 800 years. Looking beyond the glitzy port, notice the faded green dome roof: It belongs to the casino that put Monaco on the map in the 1800s.

The famous Grand Prix runs along the port and then up the ramp to the casino (at top speeds of 180 mph). Italy is so close, you can almost smell the pesto. Just beyond the casino is France again (it flanks Monaco on both sides).

The odd statue of a woman with a fishing net is dedicated to the glorious reign of **Prince Albert I** (1889-1922). The son of Charles III (who built the casino), Albert I was a true Renaissance Man. He had a Jacques Cousteau-like fascination with the sea (and built Monaco's famous aquarium, the Oceanography Museum) and was a determined pacifist who made many attempts to dissuade Germany's Kaiser Wilhelm II from becoming involved in World War I.

• *Head toward the palace, and find a statue of a monk grasping a sword.*

Meet **François Grimaldi,** a renegade sword-carrying Italian dressed as a monk, who captured Monaco in 1297 and began the dynasty that still rules the principal-ity. Prince Albert is his great-great-great... grandson, which gives Monaco's royal family the distinction of being the longest-lasting dynasty in Europe.

• *Now walk to the...*

Prince's Palace (Palais Princier): A medieval castle once sat where the palace is today. Its strategic setting has had a lot to do with Monaco's ability to resist attackers. Today, Prince Albert and his wife live in the palace, while poor Princesses Stephanie and Caroline live down the street. The palace guards protect the prince 24/7 and still stage a **Changing of the Guard** ceremony with all the pageantry of an important nation (daily at 11:55 in good weather, fun to watch but jam-packed, arrive by 11:30). An audio-guide takes you through part of the prince's lavish palace in 30 minutes. The rooms are well-furnished and impressive, but interesting only if you haven't seen a château lately (€8, includes audioguide, €20.50 combo-ticket includes Oceanography Museum; generally daily 10:00-18:00, July-Aug until 19:00, closed Nov-March; www.palais.mc).

• *Head to the west end of the palace square. Below the cannonballs is the district known as...*

Fontvieille: Monaco's newest, reclaimed-from-the-sea area has seen much of the principality's post-WWII growth. Prince Rainier continued—some say, was obsessed with—Monaco's economic growth, creating landfills (topped with apartments, such as in Fontvieille), flashy ports, more beaches,

Monaco's classy port

Palace Square

FRANCE

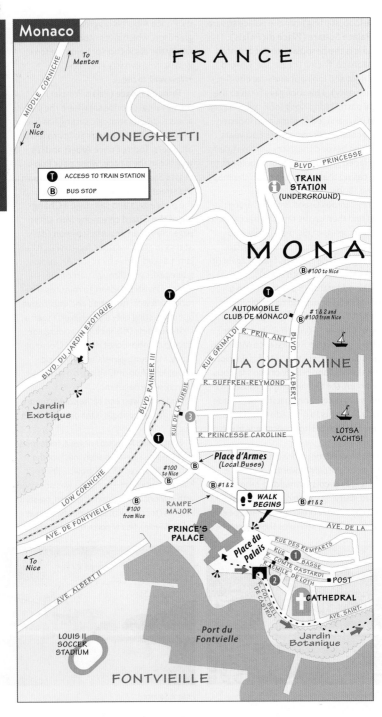

Monaco

To Menton

MIDDLE CORNICHE

To Nice

F R A N C E

MONEGHETTI

BLVD. PRINCESSE

| T | ACCESS TO TRAIN STATION |
| B | BUS STOP |

TRAIN STATION (UNDERGROUND)

M O N A

B #100 to Nice

AUTOMOBILE CLUB DE MONACO

1 & 2 and
B #100 from Nice

RUE GRIMALDI   R. PRIN. ANT.

BLVD. DU JARDIN EXOTIQUE

BLVD. RAINIER III

LA CONDAMINE

R. SUFFREN-REYMOND

Jardin Exotique

RUE DE LA TURBIE

BLVD. ALBERT I

LOTSA YACHTS!

R. PRINCESSE CAROLINE

T

Place d'Armes
(Local Buses)

LOW CORNICHE

#100 to Nice
B
B

B #1 & 2

WALK BEGINS

B #1 & 2

AVE. DE FONTVIELLE

#100 from Nice

RAMPE MAJOR

AVE. DE LA

PRINCE'S PALACE

Place du Palais

RUE DES REMPARTS

RUE BASSE

To Nice

R. COMTE GASTARDI

R. EMILE DE LOTH

POST

AVE. ALBERT II

R. COL. BEL. DE CASTRO

CATHEDRAL

AVE. SAINT-

LOUIS II SOCCER STADIUM

Port du Fontvielle

Jardin Botanique

FONTVIEILLE

BEAUSOLEIL

#112 to Eze-le-Village

🛈 #100 from Nice &
#11 to La Turbie

BLVD. DES MOULINS

BLVD. LARVOTTO

AVE. SPEL

Casino
Gardens

#1 & 2
and #100 to Nice

#1 & 2

CHARLOTTE

AVE. DE LA COSTA

Place du
Casino

AMERICAN-
STYLE
CASINO

CASINO

C O

MONTE CARLO

AVE. D'OSTENDE

PALAIS DES
CONGRES &
🅿 "Le Casino"

Port

LOTSA
YACHTS!

CRUISE
SHIP
SHUTTLE

CRUISE
TENDER
DOCK

MONACO-
VILLE

🛈

FORT
ANTOINE

AVE. QUARANTINE

PORTE NEUVE

Place de la
Visitation 🅿

Mediterranean
Sea

RUE EMILE DE LOTH

#1 & 2
Tourist Train
Stop

MARTIN

🅿 "Le Palais"

WALK
ENDS

OCEANOGRAPHY
MUSEUM

300 Meters

300 Yards

Eating & Sleeping
❶ Boulangerie
❷ U Cavagnetu Rest.
❸ Hôtel de France

a big sports stadium marked by tall arches, and a rail station.

• *With your back to the palace, leave the square through the arch at the far right (onto Rue Colonel Bellando de Castro) and find the...*

Cathedral of Monaco (Cathédrale de Monaco): The somber but beautifully lit cathedral, rebuilt in 1878, is where centuries of Grimaldis are buried, and where Princess Grace and Prince Rainier were married. Inside, circle slowly behind the altar (counterclockwise). The second tomb is that of Albert I, who did much to put Monaco on the world stage. The second-to-last tomb—inscribed *"Gratia Patricia, MCMLXXXII"* and displaying the 1956 wedding photo of Princess Grace and Prince Rainier—is where the princess was buried in 1982. Prince Rainier's tomb lies next to hers (cathedral open daily 8:30-19:15).

• *Leave the cathedral and dip into the immaculately maintained* **Jardin Botanique**. *In the gardens, turn left. Eventually you'll find the impressive building housing the...*

Rick's Tips: *If you're into stamps, drop by the* **post office** *(on Place de la Mairie), where philatelists can buy from the impressive collection of Monegasque stamps.*

A *Changing of the Guard*
B *Cathedral of Monaco*
C *Fontvieille harbor*
D *Oceanographic Museum*

Oceanography Museum (Musée Océanographique): Prince Albert I had this cliff-hanging museum built in 1910 as a monument to his enthusiasm for things from the sea. The museum's aquarium, which Jacques Cousteau captained for 32 years, has 2,000 different specimens, representing 250 species. Don't miss the elevator to the rooftop terrace view café (€11-16, €20.50 combo-ticket includes Prince's Palace; daily 10:00-19:00, longer hours July-Aug, Oct-March until 18:00; www.oceano.mc).

• *The red-brick steps across from the Oceanography Museum lead up to stops for buses #1 and #2, both of which run to the port, the casino, and the train station. To walk back to the palace and through the old city, turn left at the top of the brick steps.*

Experiences
▲MONTE CARLO CASINO (CASINO DE MONTE-CARLO)

Monte Carlo is named for Charles III, the prince who presided over Monaco's 19th-century makeover. In the mid-1800s, olive groves stood here. Then, with the construction of casino and spas, and easy road and train access, one of Europe's poorest countries was on the Grand Tour map—*the* place for the vacationing aristocracy to play. Today, Monaco has the world's highest per-capita income, and its casino is intended to make you feel comfortable while losing your retirement nest egg.

Cost and Hours: Tightwads can view the atrium entry, classy bar/café, and slot-machine room for free; daily 9:00-late. Touring the casino costs €17 (€12 off-season); daily 9:00-12:15. Gamblers pay €10; daily 14:00 until the wee hours, must be 18 and show ID; no shorts, T-shirts, hoodies, tennis shoes, or torn jeans. Expect lines at the entrance from May through September; tel. 00-377/92 16 20 00, www.montecarlocasinos.com.

Visiting the Casino: Enter through sumptuous **atrium.** This is the lobby for the 520-seat opera house (open Nov-April only for performances). The **first gambling rooms** (Salle Renaissance, Salon de l'Europe, and Salle des Amériques) offer European and English roulette, plus Trente et Quarante, Punto Banco—a version of baccarat—and slot machines. The more glamorous **game rooms** (Salons Touzet, Salle Medecin, and Terrasse Salle Blanche) have those same games and Ultimate Texas Hold 'em poker, but you play against the cashier with higher stakes.

Take the Money and Run: The stop for buses returning to Nice and Villefranche-sur-Mer, and for local buses #1 and #2, is on Avenue de la Costa, at the top of the park above the casino. To reach the train station from the casino, take bus #1 or #2 from this stop or walk 15 minutes.

Eating
You'll find massive *pan bagnat* (basically *salade niçoise* on country bread) and quiche at the yellow-bannered **$ Boulangerie** (daily, 8 Rue Basse). At **$$ U Cavagnetu,** you'll dine cheaply on pizza and such (daily, 14 Rue Comte Félix Gastaldi).

Lush gardens lead to Monte Carlo Casino.

Spain

S pain (*España*) is in Europe, but not *of* Europe—it has a unique identity and history, thanks largely to the Pyrenees Mountains that physically isolate it from the rest of the continent. Spain's seclusion contributed to the creation of distinctive customs: bullfights, flamenco dancing, and a national obsession with ham.

Spain, with 46 million people (mostly Roman Catholic), is a little bigger than California. It's been ruled by Roman emperors, Muslim sultans, hard-core Christians, conquistadors, French dandies, and a Fascist dictator; all left their mark on Spain's art, architecture, and culture.

Your best stop in Spain is trend-setting Barcelona. Nursing a glass of wine at a sidewalk table on any square gets you a front-row seat to Spain's urban scene, the best show in town.

CUISINE SCENE AT A GLANCE

Spanish cuisine is hearty, and meals are served in big, inexpensive portions. You can eat well in restaurants for about €15-20—or even more cheaply with more variety if you graze on tapas (appetizers) in bars.

The Spanish eating schedule—lunch from 13:00 to 16:00, and dinner after 21:00—frustrates many visitors. Lunch, eaten around 14:00, is the major meal of the day for most Spaniards. Because many people work until 19:30, dinner is usually served at about 21:00 or 22:00.

To satisfy your hunger nearly any time of day, it's easy to get a quick, cheap meal (see "Budget Options" below), or go to a tapas bar to build a light meal out of appetizers. Tapas are small portions of seafood, salads, meat-filled pastries, and on and on, typically costing about €4 a plate.

Eating and drinking at a bar is usually cheapest if you sit or stand at the counter (*barra*). You may pay a little more to eat sitting at a table (*mesa* or *salón*) and still more for an outdoor table (*terraza*). Traditionally, tapas are served at the bar. It's bad form to order food at the bar, then take it to a table.

When you're ready to order, be assertive or you'll never be served. *Por favor* (please) grabs the server's attention. You can often just point to what you want in the display case, and get your food. Don't worry about paying until you're ready to leave (they'll keep track of your tab).

Many bars offer larger portions called *raciones* (dinner plate-sized). But it's fine to ask for the smaller tapas portions or a *media-ración* (listed as ½ *ración* on a menu).

Most **restaurants** (like bars) serve their dishes as *raciones* and *media-raciones*. Enjoy this as an opportunity to explore the regional cuisine. Two people can fill up on four *media-raciones*.

For a budget meal in a restaurant, try a *plato combinado* (combination plate), which usually includes portions of one or two main dishes, a vegetable, and bread. Another option is the *menú del día* (menu of the day, also known as *menú turístico*), a substantial three- to four-course meal .

Tipping: Most sit-down restaurants include a service charge in the bill (*servicio incluido*). If you like to tip for good service, round up to about 5 percent. If service is not included (*servicio no incluido*), tip up to 10 percent.

Budget Options: Fast-food sandwich shops such as Pans & Company serve fresh sandwiches and salads. Many bakeries sell sandwiches and *empanadas* (pastry turnovers filled with seasoned meat and veggies). For a hearty snack any time of day, drop by a bar for a *tortilla española*—a potato omelet cooked fresh every morning and sold in wedges. Pizza shops offer slices to go. The popular El Corte Inglés department stores have a cafeteria and supermarket.

Barcelona

Barcelona may be Spain's second city, but it's undoubtedly the first city of the proud and distinct region of Catalunya. Catalan flags wave side by side with Spanish flags, and locals—while fluent in both languages—insist on speaking Catalan first. Joining hands to dance the patriotic *sardana* is a tradition that's going strong. This lively culture is on an unstoppable roll in Spain's most cosmopolitan corner.

The city itself is a work of art. Catalan architects, including Antoni Gaudí, Lluís Domènech i Montaner, and Josep Puig i Cadafalch, forged the Modernista style and remade the city's skyline into a curvy fantasy—culminating in Gaudí's over-the-top Sagrada Família, a church still under construction. Pablo Picasso lived here as a teenager, right as he was on the verge of reinventing painting; his legacy is today's Picasso Museum.

Barcelona bubbles with life—in the narrow alleys of the Barri Gòtic, along the pedestrian boulevard called the Ramblas, in the funky bohemian quarter of El Born, along the bustling beach promenade, and throughout the chic Eixample. The cafés are filled by day, and people crowd the streets at night, popping into tapas bars for a drink and a perfectly composed bite of seafood.

If you surrender to any city's charms, let it be Barcelona.

BARCELONA IN 3 DAYS

Day 1: In the cool of the morning, follow my Barri Gòtic Walk, exploring the winding lanes, unique boutiques, and historic cathedral.

Then take my Ramblas Ramble, strolling down the grand pedestrian boulevard—a festival of people-watching, street performers, and pickpockets. On the Ramblas, duck into La Boqueria Market for fresh produce and unforgettable taste treats. In the afternoon, head to the trendy El Born district to tour the Picasso Museum or Palace of Catalan Music, or both.

On any evening: Have a tapa-hopping dinner in El Born, the Barri Gòtic, or the Eixample. Take in some music (flamenco, guitar, concerts). Zip up to the hilltop of Montjuïc for the sunset, then down to the Magic Fountains (illuminated on weekends). Or stroll the long, inviting beach promenade.

Day 2: Tour the city's fanciful Modernista architecture. Marvel at the buildings on the Block of Discord and the street's masterpiece, Gaudí's La Pedrera. Tour Gaudí's soaring church, the Sagrada Família. Then head to his Park Güell, with its colorful mosaics, fountains, and stunning city views.

Day 3: Tour the museums on Montjuïc: The Catalan Art Museum displays top medieval sculptures, while Fundació Joan Miró features the hometown artist's whimsical work. The hilltop castle ramparts offer sweeping views. You could head back downtown (for museums, shopping, exploring) or take the slow, scenic cable-car from Montjuïc to the port—from here, it's easy to stroll the beach along Barceloneta, collect another sunset, and find your favorite *chiringuito* (beach bar).

Day Trips: Allot an extra day for a side trip: the holy site of Montserrat, with its dramatic mountain scenery, or Figueres, with its mind-bending Salvador Dalí museum.

Rick's Tip: *Don't miss out! To ensure you'll see Barcelona's top sights—the Picasso Museum, La Pedrera, Sagrada Família, Casa Batlló, and Park Güell—***book reserved-time tickets in advance.** *Casa Amatller and the Palace of Catalan Music require a guided tour, which also must be reserved in advance.*

ORIENTATION

Plaça de Catalunya, a large square at the center of Barcelona, divides the older and newer parts of town.

Below Plaça de Catalunya, the **Old City** (Ciutat Vella) is the compact core of Barcelona—ideal for strolling, shopping, and people-watching. It's a labyrinth of narrow streets once confined by medieval walls. The lively pedestrian drag called the **Ramblas** goes through the heart of the Old City from Plaça de Catalunya to the harbor. The Old City is divided into

thirds by the Ramblas and another major thoroughfare (running roughly parallel to the Ramblas), Via Laietana. Between the Ramblas and Via Laietana is the characteristic **Barri Gòtic** (BAH-ree GOH-teek, Gothic Quarter), with the cathedral as its navel. Locals call it "El Gòtic" for short. To the east of Via Laietana is the trendy **El Born** district (a.k.a. "La Ribera"), a shopping, dining, and nightlife mecca centered on the Picasso Museum and the Church of Santa Maria del Mar. To the west of the Ramblas is **El Raval** (rah-VAHL), enlivened by its university and modern-art museum. While rough-edged in places, it's the emerging lively, foodie zone.

The old harbor, **Port Vell,** gleams with landmark monuments and new developments. A pedestrian bridge links the Ramblas with the modern Maremagnum entertainment complex. On the peninsula across the quaint sailboat harbor is **Barceloneta,** a traditional fishing neighborhood with gritty charm and some good seafood restaurants. Beyond Barceloneta, a gorgeous man-made **beach** several miles long leads east to the commercial and convention district called the **Fòrum.**

Above the Old City, beyond the bustling hub of Plaça de Catalunya, is the elegant Eixample (eye-SHAM-plah) district, its grid plan softened by cutoff corners. Much of Barcelona's Modernista architecture is found here—especially along the swanky artery Passeig de Gràcia, in an area called **Quadrat d'Or** ("Golden Quarter"). To the east is the Sagrada Família; to the north is the **Gràcia** district and Antoni Gaudí's **Park Güell.**

The large hill overlooking the city to the southwest is **Montjuïc** (mohn-jew-EEK), home to some excellent museums (Catalan Art, Joan Miró).

Tourist Information

Barcelona's TI has several branches (central tel. 932-853-834, www.barcelonaturisme. cat). The primary TI is beneath the main square, **Plaça de Catalunya** (daily 8:30-

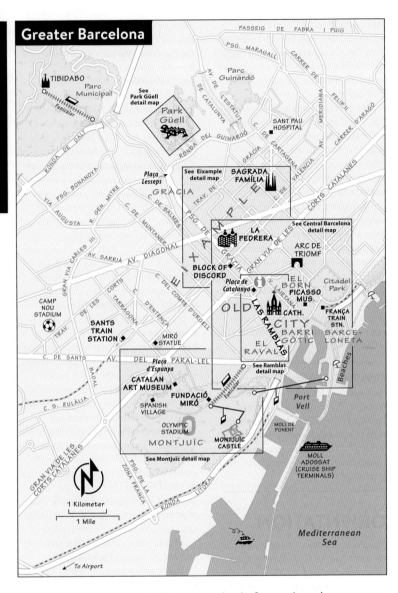

Greater Barcelona

21:00, entrance just across from El Corte Inglés department store—look for red sign and take stairs down).

Other branches include a kiosk near the top of the **Ramblas** (#115), near the cathedral (inside City Hall at Ciutat 2), inside the base of the **Columbus Monument,** at the **airport** (terminals 1 and 2B),

and at the **Sants train station.**

At any TI, pick up the monthly Visit *Barcelona* guidebook (with tips on sightseeing, shopping, events, and restaurants); *Time Out BCN Guide* (events, www.timeout.com/barcelona); *Barcelona Metropolitan* magazine (local topics and events, www.barcelona-metropolitan.

com); and *Barcelona Prestige* (upscale dining and shopping, www.bcn-guide.com).

Modernisme Route: A handy map showing all 116 Modernista buildings is available online (www.barcelonabooks.com) or at the Institut Municipal del Paisatge Urbà, inside the Edificio Colón (Mon-Fri 9:00-14:00, closed Sat-Sun, Avinguda de les Drassanes 6, 21st floor, www.rutadelmodernisme.com). They also offer a sightseeing discount package (€12) with a great guidebook.

Regional Catalunya TI: The all-Catalunya TI, inside a former palace, can help with travel and sightseeing tips for the entire region (daily 10:00-21:00, Palau Moja, midway along the Ramblas at #118, Portaferrisa 1, tel. 933-162-740, www.palaumoja.com).

Sightseeing Passes: The Articket BCN pass covers admission to six art museums including the Picasso Museum, Catalan Art Museum, and Fundació Joan Miró (€30, valid 12 months; sold online or at museums and TIs, www.articketbcn.org). If you visit three or more covered museums, this ticket can save you money and time in line—and you can visit the Picasso Museum without a reservation.

Helpful Hints

Closed Days: Many sights are closed on Monday, including the Picasso Museum, Catalan Art Museum, Palau Güell, Barcelona History Museum, Fundació Joan Miró, and Frederic Marès Museum. On Sunday, the food markets are closed, and some sights close early—check hours when planning your day.

Theft and Scam Alert: You're more likely to be pickpocketed in Barcelona—especially on the Ramblas and at the Sagrada Família—than about anywhere else in Europe. Leave valuables in your hotel and wear a money belt. Count your change carefully. Some areas of the Barri Gòtic and El Raval feel seedy and can be unsafe after dark.

Laundry: LavaXpres is near recommended Plaça de Catalunya and Ramblas hotels (self-service, English instructions, daily 8:00-22:00, Passatge d'Elisabets 3, www.lavaxpres.com).

Tours

WALKING TOURS

The **TI** at Plaça de Sant Jaume offers great guided walks through the **Barri Gòtic** (€16, daily at 9:30, 2 hours, groups limited to 35, buy online in advance—especially in summer, otherwise buy ticket 15 minutes early at the TI desk—not from the guide, tel. 932-853-832, www.barcelonaturisme.cat). The TI at Plaça de Sant Jaume also offers walks for **gourmets** (€22, Mon-Fri at 10:30, 2 hours) and fans of **Modernisme** (€16, April-Oct Wed and Fri at 18:00, off-season at 15:30, 2 hours).

The TI at Plaça de Catalunya offers a **Picasso** walk, through the streets of his youth and finishing in the Picasso Museum (€22, includes museum entry, runs Tue-Sat at 15:00, 2 hours including museum visit). It's always smart to reserve in advance and double-check departure times with the TI.

Discover Walks offers good walking tours in under two hours for €19-22. These include **Gaudí** (daily at 10:30, meet in front of KFC at Avinguda de Gaudí 2) and the **Ramblas and Barri Gòtic** (Tue, Thu, and Sat at 15:00, meet in front of Liceu Opera House on the Ramblas, tel. 931-816-810, www.discoverwalks.com).

A dozen or so companies offer "free" walks that rely on—and expect—tips to stay in business. Try **Runner Bean Tours'** 2.5-hour, English-only walks, one on the Old City and the other covering Gaudí (both depart from Plaça Reial daily at 11:00, also at 16:30 March-Sept and 15:00 Oct-Dec, mobile 636-108-776, www.runnerbeantours.com).

LOCAL GUIDES

For a private guide or group tour, try **Barcelona Guide Bureau** (check website for prices; Via Laietana 50, tel. 932-682-422,

BARCELONA AT A GLANCE

▲▲▲**Picasso Museum** Extensive collection offering insight into the brilliant Spanish artist's early years. **Hours:** Mon 10:00-17:00, Tue-Sun 9:00-20:30, Thu until 21:30, shorter hours and closed Mon in off-season. See page 346.

▲▲▲**Sagrada Família** Gaudí's remarkable, unfinished church—a masterpiece in progress. **Hours:** Daily 9:00-20:00, March and Oct until 19:00, Nov-Feb until 18:00. See page 358.

▲▲**Ramblas** Barcelona's colorful, gritty, tourist-filled pedestrian thoroughfare. See page 325.

▲▲**Palace of Catalan Music** Best Modernista interior in Barcelona. **Hours:** One-hour English tours daily 10:00-15:00, plus frequent concerts. See page 352.

▲▲**La Pedrera** (Casa Milà) Barcelona's quintessential Modernista building and Gaudí creation. **Hours:** Daily 9:00-20:00, Nov-Feb until 18:30. See page 355.

▲▲**Park Güell** Colorful Gaudí-designed park overlooking the city. **Hours:** Daily 7:30-20:30 in May-Aug, rest of year 8:00 or 8:30 until sunset. See page 365.

▲▲**Catalan Art Museum** World-class showcase of this region's art. **Hours:** Tue-Sat 10:00-20:00 (Oct-April until 18:00), Sun 10:00-15:00, closed Mon year-round. See page 368.

▲**La Boqueria Market** Colorful but touristy produce market, just off the Ramblas. **Hours:** Mon-Sat 8:00-20:00, best mornings after 9:00, closed Sun, many stalls shut down early on Mon. See page 329.

▲**Palau Güell** Exquisitely curvy Gaudí interior and fantasy rooftop. **Hours:** Tue-Sun 10:00-20:00, Nov-March until 17:30, closed Mon year-round. See page 342.

▲**Maritime Museum** A sailor's delight, housed in a medieval shipyard. **Hours:** Daily 10:00-20:00. See page 342.

▲**Barcelona Cathedral** Colossal Gothic cathedral ringed by distinctive chapels. **Hours:** Generally open to visitors Mon-Fri 8:30-19:30, Sat-Sun until 20:00. See page 343.

▲**Gaudí Exhibition Center** Fine exhibit about the man who made Barcelona what it is today. **Hours:** Daily 10:00-20:00, Nov-Feb until 18:00. See page 346.

▲**Frederic Marès Museum** Quirky museum highlighted by Marès' collection of bric-a-brac from 19th-century Barcelona. **Hours:** Tue-Sat 10:00-19:00, Sun until 20:00, closed Mon. See page 346.

▲**Barcelona History Museum** One-stop trip through town history, from Roman times to today. **Hours:** Tue-Sat 10:00-19:00, Sun until 20:00, closed Mon. See page 346.

▲**Santa Caterina Market** Fine market hall built on the site of an old monastery and updated with a wavy Gaudí-inspired roof. **Hours:** Mon-Sat 7:30-15:30, open until 20:30 on Tue and Thu-Fri, closed Sun. See page 354.

▲**Church of Santa Maria del Mar** Catalan Gothic church. **Hours:** Generally open to visitors Mon-Sat 9:00-20:30, Sun from 10:00. See page 354.

▲**Casa Batlló** Gaudí-designed home topped with fanciful dragon-inspired roof. **Hours:** Daily 9:00-21:00. See page 354.

▲**Fundació Joan Miró** World's best collection of works by Catalan modern artist Joan Miró. **Hours:** Tue-Sat 10:00-20:00 (Thu until 21:00), Sun 10:00-15:00, shorter hours in winter, closed Mon year-round. See page 368.

▲**CaixaForum** Modernista cultural center featuring good temporary art exhibits. **Hours:** Daily 10:00-20:00. See page 373.

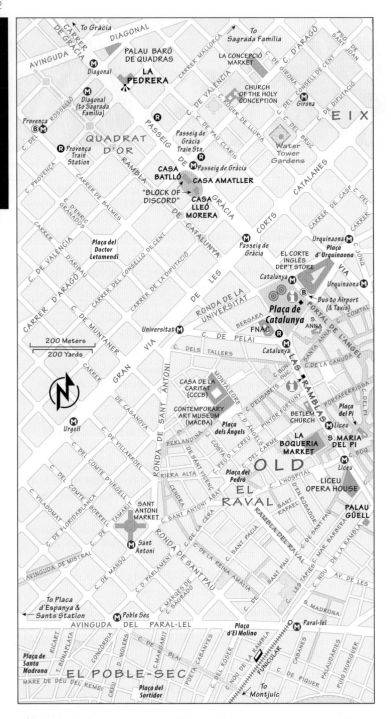

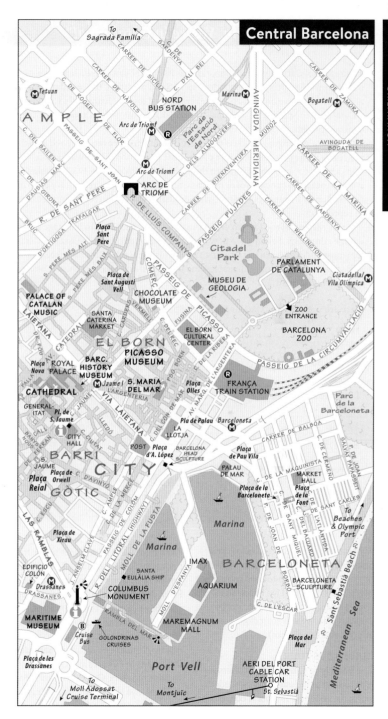

Central Barcelona

To
Sagrada Família

C. DE SARDENYA
CARRER DE SICÍLIA
C. DE NÀPOLS
C. D'ALÍ BEI

Tetuan
C. DE ROGER DE FLOR
PASSEIG DE SANT JOAN
AVINGUDA MERIDIANA
AVINGUDA MUÑOZ

AMPLE

NORD
BUS STATION

Marina
Bogatell

CARRER DE ZAMORA
CARRER DE LA MARINA

Arc de Triomf

Parc de
l'Estació
de Nord

AVINGUDA DE
BOGATELL

C. DEL BAILÉN
C. DE PAUSIAS MARC
C. DE GIRONA
D'ORTIGOSA TRAFALGAR
BRUC

Arc de Triomf

ARC DE
TRIOMF

CARRER DE LA MARINA

C. DELS ALMOGÀVERS
CARRER DE BUENAVENTURA
PASSEIG DE LLUIS COMPANYS
CARRER PUJADES
CARRER DE WELLINGTON
CARRER DE SARDENYA

R. DE SANT PERE
Plaça
Sant
Pere

Citadel
Park

PARLAMENT
DE CATALUNYA

Ciutadella/
Vila Olímpica

S. PERE MÉS ALT
S. PERE MÉS BAIX
Plaça de
Sant Augusti
Vell

MUSEU DE
GEOLOGIA

CHOCOLATE
MUSEUM

PASSEIG DE PICASSO
COMERÇ
CARRERS VERMELL
C. DEL REC

FUSINA

ZOO
ENTRANCE

PALACE OF
CATALAN
MUSIC
SANTA
CATERINA
MARKET

EL BORN
CULTURAL
CENTER

C. DE LA RIBERA

BARCELONA
ZOO

LAIETANA
AV. CATEDRAL
PG. POU

EL BORN

PICASSO
MUSEUM

PSG. BORN
C. DE LA ARGENTERIA

PASSEIG DE LA CIRCUMVALLACIÓ

Plaça
Nova
ROYAL
PALACE
BARC.
HISTORY
MUSEUM
Jaume I
S. MARIA
DEL MAR

Parc
de la
Barceloneta

CATHEDRAL

VIA LAIETANA

Plaça
Olles

FRANÇA
TRAIN STATION

C. CALL
BAIXADA DE S. JAUME
NOU S. JAUME
GENERAL-
ITAT
Pl. de
S. Jaume

CITY
HALL
C. JAUME I
L'ARGENTERIA
LLEDÓ

C. DE COMERÇ DE MAR

Pla de Palau

Barceloneta

CARRER DE BALBOA

P. DE JOAN DE BORBÓ
P. DE CERMENO
SALVAT PAPASSEIT

BARRI

CITY

POST
Plaça
d'A. López

BARCELONA
HEAD
SCULPTURE

LA
LLOTJA

Plaça
de Pau Vila

Plaça de
Orwell
C. D'AVINYÓ
C. AMPLE
Plaça
Reial

GÒTIC

C. DE LA MERÈ

PALAU
DE MAR

MARKET
HALL
Plaça
de la
Font

C. DE LA MAQUINISTA

To
Beaches
& Olympic
Port

LAS RAMBLAS
C. ESCU
C. NOU

Plaça de
Xirau

PASSEIG DE COLOM
R. DEL LITORAL (HIGHWAY)
C. ANSELM CLAVE

Plaça de la
Barceloneta

C. DE SANT CARLES
C. DE L'ATLÀNTIDA
C. DEL BALUARTE
P. DE JOAN DE BORBÓ
C. DE SANT MIQUEL

BARCELONETA

BARCELONETA
SCULPTURE

EDIFICIO
COLÓN
Drassanes
DRASSANES

Marina

IMAX

AQUARIUM

Marina

SANTA
EULÀLIA SHIP
COLUMBUS
MONUMENT

C. DE L'ESCAR

Sant Sebastià Beach

MARITIME
MUSEUM

Cruise
Bus

B

GOLONDRINAS
CRUISES

MOLL D'ESPANYA
RAMBLA DEL MAR
MOLL DE LA FUSTA

MAREMAGNUM
MALL

Plaça del
Mar

Mediterranean Sea

Plaça de les
Drassanes

To
Moll Adossat
Cruise Terminal

Port Vell

To
Montjuïc

AERI DEL PORT
CABLE CAR
STATION

St. Sebastià

"You're Not in Spain, You're in Catalunya!"

The region of Catalunya, with Barcelona as its capital, has its own language, history, culture, and proud, independent spirit (you might see the popular nationalistic refrain above on T-shirts or stickers around town). Historically, Catalunya ("Cataluña" in Spanish, "Catalonia" in English) has often been at odds with the central Spanish government in Madrid.

The Catalan language and culture were discouraged or even outlawed at various times in the past, as Catalunya often chose the wrong side in wars and rebellions against the kings in Madrid. In the Spanish Civil War (1936-1939), Catalunya was one of the last pockets of democratic resistance against the military coup of fascist dictator Francisco Franco, who punished the region with four decades of repression.

After the end of the Franco era in the mid-1970s, the Catalan language made a huge comeback. Schools are now required by law to conduct classes in Catalan; most children learn Catalan first and Spanish second. While all Barcelonans still speak Spanish, nearly all understand Catalan, three-quarters speak Catalan, and half can write it.

Here are some helpful Catalan words and phrases:

Hello	Hola (OH-lah)
Please	Si us plau (see oos plow)
Thank you	Gràcies (GRAH-see-es)
Goodbye	Adéu (ah-DAY-oo)
Long live Catalunya!	¡Visca Catalunya! (BEE-skah kah-tah-LOON-yah)
avenue	avinguda (ah-veen-GOO-dah)
boulevard	passeig (PAH-sehj)
exit	sortida (sor-TEE-dah)
square	plaça (PLAH-sah)
street	carrer (kah-REHR)

www.barcelonaguidebureau.com); **José Soler** (€250/half-day per group, mobile 615-059-326, www.pepitotours.com, info@pepitotours.com); or **Live Barcelona** (from €195/3 hours, tel. 936-327-259, mobile 609-205-844, www.livebarcelona.com, info@livebarcelona.com).

GUIDED BUS TOURS

The **Barcelona Guide Bureau** offers various tours that include most sight admissions; their Montserrat tour is convenient

if you don't want to deal with public transportation. Book tickets at a TI or online, or just show up at their departure point on Plaça de Catalunya in front of the Deutsche Bank (€35-74; tel. 933-152-261, www.barcelonaguidebureau.com). **Catalunya Bus Turístic** also runs excursions to nearby destinations, including **Salvador Dalí sights** in Figueres and Girona (€49-79, trips run April-Oct, depart from Plaça de Catalunya in front of El Corte Inglés, live trilingual commentary in Catalan, Spanish, and English; €5 extra for a more in-depth English audioguide; book at TIs, by phone, or online—10 percent web discount; tel. 932-853-832, www.catalunyabusturistic.com).

HOP-ON, HOP-OFF BUSES

The handy hop-on, hop-off **Bus Turístic,** which departs from Plaça de Catalunya, offers three multistop circuits in double-decker buses with headphone commentary. The two-hour blue route covers north Barcelona (most Gaudí sights, departs from El Corte Inglés). The two-hour red route covers south Barcelona (Barri Gòtic and Montjuïc, departs from the west—Ramblas—side of the square). The 40-minute green route covers the beaches and modern Fòrum complex from April-October (1 day-€30, 2 days-€40, buy on bus, at TI, or online, offers small discounts on major sights, daily 9:00-20:00 in summer, off-season until 19:00, buses run every 10-25 minutes, www.barcelonabusturistic.cat).

BARCELONA WALKS

These two self-guided walks take you through the old town—down the main boulevard ("Ramblas Ramble") and through the cathedral neighborhood ("Barri Gòtic Walk"). ∩ My free Barcelona City Walk audio tour covers the Ramblas (in part) and the Barri Gòtic neighborhood.

Ramblas Ramble

For more than a century, this walk down Barcelona's main boulevard has been a magnet for visitors. Raft the river of Barcelonan life, passing a grand opera house, elegant cafés, flower stands, artists, street mimes, con men, and prostitutes. This one-hour stroll goes from Plaça de Catalunya gently downhill to the waterfront, with an easy return by Metro. The word

"Ramblas" is plural; the street is actually a succession of five separately named segments. But street signs and addresses treat it as a single long street—"La Rambla," singular.

◑ Self-Guided Walk

• Start your ramble on Plaça de Catalunya, at the top of the Ramblas.

❶ Plaça de Catalunya

Dotted with fountains, statues, and pigeons, and ringed by grand buildings, this plaza is Barcelona's center. Plaça de Catalunya is the hub for the Metro, bus, airport shuttle, and Bus Turístic. Of the region's 7.4 million Catalans, more than half live in greater Barcelona. Plaça de Catalunya is their Times Square.

Geographically, the 12-acre square links the narrow streets of old Barcelona with the broad boulevards of the newer city (the Eixample). Four great thoroughfares radiate from here: The Ramblas is the popular tourist promenade. Passeig de Gràcia has fashionable shops and cafés (and noisy traffic). Rambla de Catalunya is equally fashionable but cozier and more pedestrian-friendly. Avinguda del Portal de l'Angel (shopper-friendly and traffic-free) leads to the Barri Gòtic.

At the Ramblas end of the square, the odd, inverted-staircase **monument** represents the shape of Catalunya. An inscription honors one of its former presidents, Francesc Macià i Llussà, who declared independence for the breakaway region in 1931. (It didn't quite stick.) Sculptor Josep Maria Subirachs, whose work you'll see at the Sagrada Família, designed it. These days, Catalans gather on the square by the tens of thousands to demonstrate passionately about whether Catalunya should be independent from Spain.

The giant El Corte Inglés department store towering above the square (on the northeast side) has just about anything you might need.

Plaça de Catalunya

• *Cross the street, head down about 30 yards, and pause to take in the scene.*

❷ Head of the Ramblas

The street called the Ramblas slopes gently downhill from here to the harbor. It's dotted with trees and ironwork lampposts, lined with fanciful buildings, paved with colorful mosaics, and trod upon by thousands of people both day and night.

Start with the ornate, black and gold lamppost on your right. The base is a water tap called the **Fountain of Canaletes,** which has been a local favorite for more than a century. When Barcelona tore down its medieval wall and created this elegant promenade, this fountain was one of its early attractions. Legend says that a drink from the fountain ensures that you'll come back to Barcelona one day.

As you survey the Ramblas action, get your bearings for our upcoming stroll. You'll see the following features here and all along the way:

The **wavy tile work** of the pavers underfoot represent the stream that once flowed here. *Rambla* means "stream" in Arabic, and this used to be a drainage ditch along one of the medieval walls enclosing the Barri Gòtic (to the left). Look up to see the city's characteristic shallow **balconies.** The **plane trees** lining the boulevard are known for their toughness in urban settings. These deciduous trees let in maximum sun in the winter and provide maximum shade in the summer.

Nearby, notice the **chairs** fixed to the sidewalk at jaunty angles. It used to be that you'd pay to rent a chair here to watch the parade of passersby. Enjoy these chairs while you can—you'll find virtually no public benches or other seating farther down the Ramblas, only cafés that serve beer and sangria in just one (expensive) size: *gigante*.

Along this walk are **booths** that sell lottery tickets in support of ONCE, Spain's organization for the blind. You'll see **soccer souvenirs,** especially the scarlet and blue of FC Barcelona—known as Barça.

• *Continue strolling.*

Walk 100 yards farther to #115, with an entrance flanked by two columns and a

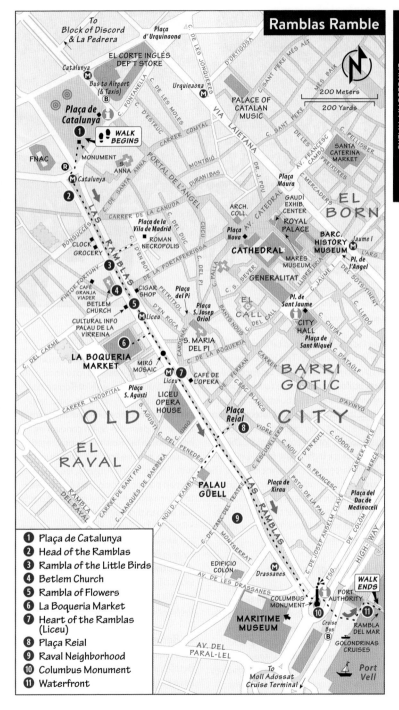

Ramblas Ramble

To Block of Discord & La Pedrera

Plaça d'Urquinaona

EL CORTE INGLÉS DEP'T STORE

Catalunya

Bus to Airport (& Taxis)

Plaça de Catalunya

1

WALK BEGINS

200 Meters

200 Yards

Urquinaona

PALACE OF CATALAN MUSIC

FNAC

MONUMENT

S. ANNA

Catalunya

2

PORTAL DE L'ANGEL

CARRER COMTAL

MONTSIÓ

DURAN I BAS

VIA LAIETANA

C. SANT PERE MÉS ALT

MÉS BAIX

SANTA CATERINA MARKET

AV. FRANCESC CAMBÓ

Plaça Maura

GAUDÍ EXHIB. CENTER

ROYAL PALACE

EL BORN

BARC. HISTORY MUSEUM

Jaume I

BONSUCCÉS

CLOCK

GROCERY

3

CARRER DE LA CANUDA

Plaça de la Vila de Madrid

ROMAN NECROPOLIS

ARCH. COLL.

Plaça Nova

CATHEDRAL

MARES MUSEUM

GENERALITAT

Pl. de l'Angel

PINTOR FORTUNY

CAFÉ GRANJA VIADER

4

BETLEM CHURCH

CIGAR SHOP

5

Liceu

CULTURAL INFO PALAU DE LA VIRREINA

6

LA BOQUERIA MARKET

C. DEL CARME

MIRÓ MOSAIC

Plaça del Pi

Plaça S. Josep Oriol

S. MARIA DEL PI

EL CALL

Pl. de Sant Jaume

CITY HALL

Plaça de Sant Miquel

BARRI GÒTIC

CARRER L'HOSPITAL

Plaça S. Agusti

7

Liceu

CAFÉ DE L'OPERA

LICEU OPERA HOUSE

Plaça Reial

8

OLD CITY

EL RAVAL

RAMBLA DEL RAVAL

PALAU GÜELL

Plaça de Xirau

9

Plaça del Duc de Medinaceli

LAS RAMBLAS

EDIFICIO COLÓN

AV. DE LES DRASSANES

Drassanes

WALK ENDS

COLUMBUS MONUMENT

10

PORT AUTHORITY

11

RAMBLA DEL MAR

MARITIME MUSEUM

Cruise Bus

GOLONDRINAS CRUISES

AV. DEL PARAL-LEL

To Moll Adossat Cruise Terminal

Port Vell

1 Plaça de Catalunya
2 Head of the Ramblas
3 Rambla of the Little Birds
4 Betlem Church
5 Rambla of Flowers
6 La Boqueria Market
7 Heart of the Ramblas (Liceu)
8 Plaça Reial
9 Raval Neighborhood
10 Columbus Monument
11 Waterfront

Leafy and broad, the Ramblas is a tourist magnet.

fine facade struggling to be noticed above the Ramblas ruckus. This marks the venerable **Royal Academy of Science and Arts building** (now home to a performing-arts theater). The building is emblematic of the city's striking architecture from the late 1900s—an industrial boom time that brought lots of construction. Look up: The clock high on the facade marks official Barcelona time—synchronize. The **Carrefour** supermarket next door has cheap groceries (at #113).

• *Remember that each of the Ramblas segments has its own name. You're now standing at what was the...*

❸ Rambla of the Little Birds (RIP)

A generation ago, kids brought their parents here to buy birds, turtles, and hamsters. Today, none of the pet kiosks survive—there's not a bird in sight.

• *At #122 (the big, modern Citadines Hotel on the left), take a 100-yard detour through a modern passageway marked with the*

hotel's name to a restored...

Roman Necropolis: Look down and imagine a 2,000-year-old road lined with tombs. Outside the walls of Roman cities, tombs typically lined the roads leading into town. Emperor Augustus spent time in modern-day Spain conquering new land, so the Romans incorporated Hispania into the empire's infrastructure. This road, Via Augusta, led into the Roman port of Barcino (today's highway to France still follows the route laid out by this Roman thoroughfare).

• *Return to the Ramblas and continue down 100 yards or so to the next cross street, Carrer de la Portaferrissa (on the left), to see the* ***decorative tile*** *over a fountain still in use by locals. The scene shows the original city wall with the gate that once stood here. Now cross the boulevard to the front of the big church.*

❹ Betlem Church

This imposing church is dedicated to Bethlehem, and for centuries locals have flocked here at Christmastime to

Canaletes fountain   *Rambla of Flowers*

see nativity scenes. Its diamond-shaped stonework is 17th-century Baroque: Check out the sloping roofline, ball-topped pinnacles, corkscrew columns, and scrolls above the entrance.

This Baroque style is unusual in Barcelona because during the Baroque and Renaissance eras (1500-1800), Barcelona was broke: New World discoveries shifted lucrative trade to the Atlantic, and the Spanish crown kept unruly Catalunya on a short leash.

For a sweet treat, head around to the narrow lane on the far side of the church (Carrer d'en Xucla) to the recommended **Café Granja Viader.**

• *Continue down the boulevard, through the stretch called the...*

❺ *Rambla of Flowers*

This colorful block is lined with flower stands. Besides admiring the blossoms on display, gardeners will covet the seeds sold here for varieties of radishes, greens, peppers, and beans seldom seen in the US—including the iconic green Padrón

pepper (if you buy seeds, you're obligated to declare them at US customs when returning home). At #99 (on the right), the **cultural center** in Palau de la Virreina sells tickets to dance and musical concerts (easier to buy here than at the main TI).

On the left, at #100, **Tabacs Gimeno** has been selling cigars since the 1920s. Step inside and appreciate the dying art of cigar boxes and hand-crafted pipes.

• *A little farther on, across the street (opposite the Erotic Museum) is the arcaded entrance to Barcelona's great covered market, La Boqueria.*

❻ *La Boqueria Market*

Since as far back as 1200, Barcelonans have brought their animal parts to this market, worth ▲. While tourists are drawn to the area around the main entry, locals know that the stalls up front pay the highest rent—and therefore inflate their prices and cater to out-of-towners. Skip the tempting but more expensive juices sold here and head to a booth farther in or along the sides (market open Mon-Sat 8:00-20:00, best mornings after 9:00, closed Sun, many stalls shut down early on Mon).

Stop in at the **Pinotxo Bar**—it's just inside the market, under the sign—and snap a photo of animated Juan giving a thumbs-up for your camera. The market and adjacent lanes are busy with tempting little eateries.

Stands show off seasonal fruits and vegetables The focus here is on Spanish specialties like olives and saffron. Full legs of *jamón* (ham) abound. Top quality *ibérico* (Iberian type) and *bellota* (acorn eaters) can cost €300 or more per hock. You'll see many types of the Catalan *botifarra* sausage. The fishmonger stalls could double as a marine biology lab. Fish is sold whole, not filleted—local shoppers like to look their dinner in the eye to be sure it's fresh.
• *After you've scoped out the market, head back to the street and continue down the Ramblas.*

You're skirting the old Barri Gòtic neighborhood. Glance left through a modern cutaway arch for a glimpse of the medieval church tower of **Santa Maria del Pi,** a popular venue for guitar concerts. This marks the Plaça del Pi and a great shopping street, Carrer Petritxol, which runs parallel to the Ramblas.

On the right side of the Ramblas (at #83), find the highly regarded **Escribà bakery,** with its appealing Modernista facade: Look for the *Antigua Casa Figueras* sign arching over the doorway, mosaics of twining plants, a stained-glass peacock, and undulating woodwork.
• *After another block, you reach the Liceu Metro station, marking the...*

❼ Heart of the Ramblas

At the Liceu Metro station's elevators, the Ramblas widens a bit into a small, lively square (Plaça de la Boqueria). Liceu marks the midpoint of the Ramblas between Plaça de Catalunya and the waterfront.

Underfoot, find the much trod-upon **Joan Miró mosaic** in red, white, yellow, and blue. The mosaic's black arrow represents an anchor, a reminder of the city's attachment to the ocean and a welcome to visitors arriving by sea. Miró's simple, colorful designs are found all over the city, from murals to mobiles to the La Caixa bank logo. The best place to see his work is in the Fundació Joan Miró at Montjuïc.

The surrounding buildings have playful ornamentation typical of the city. The **Chinese dragon** holding a lantern (at #82) decorates a former umbrella shop (notice the fun umbrellas perched high up). The dragon is an important symbol of Catalan pride for its connection to the local patron saint, St. George (Jordi).

A few steps down (on the right) is the **Liceu Opera House** (Gran Teatre del Liceu), which hosts world-class opera, dance, and theater (box office left of main entrance, open Mon-Fri 9:30-20:00). Opposite the opera house is **Café de l'Opera** (#74), an elegant stop for an expensive beverage. This bustling café, with Modernista decor and a historic atmosphere, boasts that it's been open since 1929, even during the Spanish Civil War.
• *We've seen the best stretch of the Ramblas; to cut this walk short, you could catch the Metro back to Plaça de Catalunya. Otherwise, let's continue to the port. The wide, straight street that crosses the Ramblas in another 30 feet (Carrer de Ferran) leads to Plaça de Sant Jaume, the governmental center.*

Head down the Ramblas another 50 yards (to #46), and turn left down an arcaded lane (Carrer de Colom) to the square called...

❽ Plaça Reial

Dotted with palm trees, surrounded by an arcade, and ringed by yellow buildings with white Neoclassical trim, this elegant square has a colonial ambience. It comes complete with old-fashioned taverns (*cervecerías*), modern bars with patio seating, and a Sun-

A Chinese dragon ornament

B Joan Miró's mosaic

C Plaça Reial

D La Boqueria Market

E Columbus Monument

F Palau Güell

day coin-and-stamp market. Completing the picture are Gaudí's first public works (the two colorful helmeted lampposts). The square is a lively hangout by day or by night.

• *Head back out to the Ramblas.*

Across the boulevard, a half-block detour down Carrer Nou de la Rambla brings you to **Palau Güell,** designed by Antoni Gaudí (on the left, at #3). Even from the outside, you get a sense of this innovative apartment, the first of Gaudí's Modernista buildings. As this is early Gaudí (built 1886-1890), it's darker and more Neo-Gothic than his more famous later work. The two parabolic-arch doorways and elaborate wrought-iron work signal his emerging nonlinear style. Completely restored in 2011, Palau Güell offers an informative look at a Gaudí interior (see page 342).

• *Return to the Ramblas and keep heading down.*

❾ Raval Neighborhood

The neighborhood on the right side of this stretch of the Ramblas is El Raval. In the last century, this was a rough neighborhood, home to sailors, prostitutes, and poor immigrants. Today, its new **Museum of Contemporary Art** and the massive **Sant Antoni market hall** are gentrifying the area, and it's becoming a bohemian-chic magnet for the young and trendy and the foodie crowd.

The skyscraper to the right of the Ramblas is the Edificio Colón. When built in 1970, the 28-story structure was Barcelona's first high-rise. Near the skyscraper is the Maritime Museum, housed in what were the city's giant medieval shipyards.

• *Near the bottom of the Ramblas, take note of the Drassanes Metro stop, which can take you back to Plaça de Catalunya when you're ready. Up ahead is the...*

❿ Columbus Monument

The 200-foot column honors Christopher Columbus, who came to Barcelona in 1493 after journeying to America. It was erected for the 1888 Universal Exposition,

an international fair that helped vault a surging Barcelona onto the world stage.

A tiny elevator ascends to the top of the column, lifting visitors to a covered observation area for fine panoramas over the city (entrance/ticket desk is in the TI, inside the base of the monument; elevator-€6, daily 8:30-19:30, when crowded line may close up to an hour early).

• *Scoot across the busy traffic circle and continue straight ahead to the water's edge. Turn left, walk 50 yards, and find a pedestrian bridge that juts out over the harbor for a good place from which to check out the...*

⓫ Waterfront

For more than 2,000 years, this harbor with its bustling sea trade has been the reason Barcelona is on the world map. The wooden pedestrian **bridge** you're standing on is a modern extension of the Ramblas, called La Rambla de Mar ("Rambla of the Sea"). The bridge can swing out to allow boat traffic into the marina.

As you face Columbus, take in the sights. At the foot of the Ramblas are the docks with the *golondrinas* harbor-cruise boats (€7.70, daily about 11:30-19:00, more in summer, fewer in winter, tel. 934-423-106, www.lasgolondrinas.com). To the left of Columbus is the big Maritime Museum. Farther left, in the distance, is the majestic, 570-foot bluff of parklike **Montjuïc,** with a number of sights and museums reachable by cable car (as you can see). To the right of the Columbus statue, the frilly yellow building is the fanciful Modernista-style port-authority building. Stretching to the right of that is a delightful promenade along the seawall of Barcelona's Old Port (Port Vell); it's worth a stroll. Along the promenade is a permanently moored historic schooner, the *Santa Eulàlia* (part of the Maritime Museum). Finally, over your right shoulder is Maremagnum, a modern shopping mall and entertainment complex with an

Modernista port authority building and the Old Port

IMAX cinema, a huge aquarium, restaurants, and piles of people. Late at night, it's a rollicking youth hangout.

Barri Gòtic Walk

Barcelona's Barri Gòtic (Gothic Quarter) is a bustling world of shops, bars, and nightlife packed into narrow, winding lanes and undiscovered courtyards. This is Barcelona's birthplace—where the ancient Romans built a city, where medieval Christians built their cathedral, where Jews gathered together, and where Barcelonans lived within a ring of protective walls until the 1850s, when the city expanded.

Treat this 1.5-hour self-guided walk from Plaça de Catalunya to Plaça del Rei as a historical scavenger hunt. You'll focus on the earliest chunk of Roman Barcelona, right around the cathedral, and explore some legacy sights from the city's medieval era.

◐ *Self-Guided Walk*

• *Start on Barcelona's grand main square,* *Plaça de Catalunya. From the northeast corner (between the giant El Corte Inglés department store and the Banco de España), head down the broad pedestrian boulevard called...*

❶ *Avinguda del Portal de l'Angel*

For much of Barcelona's history, this was a major city gate. A medieval wall enclosed the city, and the entrance here—the "Gate of the Angel"—gave the street its name. An angel statue atop the gate

Architectural details

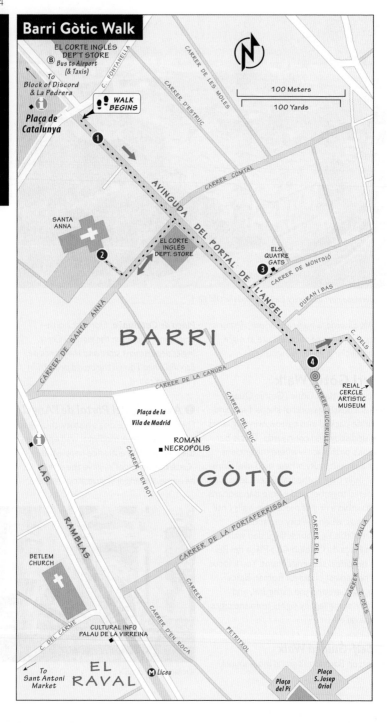

SPAIN

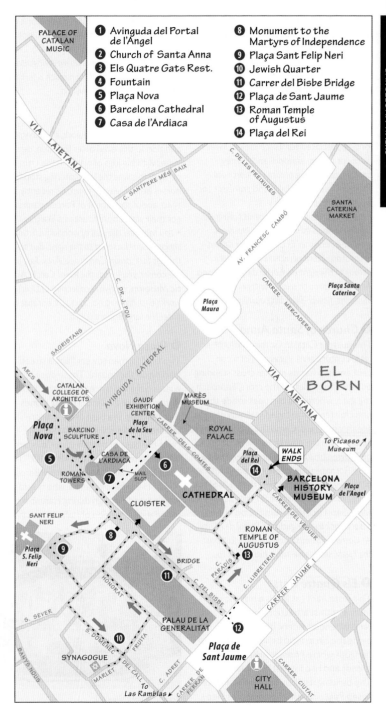

PALACE OF CATALAN MUSIC

① Avinguda del Portal de l'Angel
② Church of Santa Anna
③ Els Quatre Gats Rest.
④ Fountain
⑤ Plaça Nova
⑥ Barcelona Cathedral
⑦ Casa de l'Ardiaca
⑧ Monument to the Martyrs of Independence
⑨ Plaça Sant Felip Neri
⑩ Jewish Quarter
⑪ Carrer del Bisbe Bridge
⑫ Plaça de Sant Jaume
⑬ Roman Temple of Augustus
⑭ Plaça del Rei

VIA LAIETANA

C. SANTPERE MÈS BAIX

C. DE LES FREIXURES

SANTA CATERINA MARKET

AV. FRANCESC CAMBÓ

C. DR. J. POU

CARRER MERCADERS

Plaça Maura

Plaça Santa Caterina

SAGRISTANS

AVINGUDA CATEDRAL

VIA LAIETANA

EL BORN

ARCS

CATALAN COLLEGE OF ARCHITECTS

Plaça Nova

BARCINO SCULPTURE

GAUDÍ EXHIBITION CENTER

Plaça de la Seu

MARÈS MUSEUM

ROYAL PALACE

To Picasso Museum

⑤

CASA DE L'ARDIACA

ROMAN TOWERS

⑦

MAIL SLOT

⑥

CARRER DELS COMTES

Plaça del Rei

WALK ENDS

⑭

BARCELONA HISTORY MUSEUM

Plaça de l'Angel

CATHEDRAL

CLOISTER

SANT FELIP NERI

⑧

ROMAN TEMPLE OF AUGUSTUS

⑬

CARRER DEL VEGUER

Plaça S. Felip Neri

⑨

BRIDGE

⑪

C. PARADIS

C. LLIBRETERIA

CARRER JAUME I

HONORAT

C. DEL BISBE

S. SEVER

S. DOMÈNEC

PALAU DE LA GENERALITAT

⑩

⑫

SYNAGOGUE

DEL CALL

FRUITA

BANYS NOUS

MARLET

C. ADRET

CARRER DE FERRAN

Plaça de Sant Jaume

To Las Ramblas

CITY HALL

CARRER CIUTAT

purportedly kept Barcelonans safe from plagues and bid voyagers safe journey as they left the security of the city.

Although today this street has been globalized and sanitized, a handful of businesses with local roots survive. On the right at the first corner (at #25), a green sign and particularly appetizing display window mark **Planelles Donat**—long appreciated for its ice cream, sweet *turró* (or *turrón*, almond-and-honey candy), refreshing *orxata* (or *horchata*, almond-flavored drink), and *granissat* (or *granizado*, ice slush).

• *A block farther down, pause at Carrer de Santa Anna to admire the Art Nouveau awning at another* **El Corte Inglés** *department store. From here, take a half-block detour to the right on Carrer de Santa Anna. At #32 go through a large entryway to the pleasant, flower-fragrant courtyard of the...*

❷ Church of Santa Anna

This austere Catalan Gothic church—a 12th-century gem—was part of a convent and still has its marker cross standing outside. To the left of the cross, approach the gate, where you can peek inside the fine cloister—an arcaded walkway around a leafy courtyard. Climb the modern stairs across from the church for views of the bell tower. Inside the church you'll find a bare Romanesque interior, topped with an octagonal wooden roof. At the back of the nave, you'll find the cloister (€2, usually Mon-Sat 11:00-19:00, until 14:00 in Aug).

• *Backtrack to Avinguda del Portal de l'Angel. At Carrer de Montsió (on the left), just past the H&M store, side-trip a half-block to...*

❸ Els Quatre Gats

This restaurant (at #3) is a historic monument, tourist attraction, nightspot, and recommended eatery. It's famous for being the circa-1900 bohemian-artist hangout where Picasso nursed drinks with friends and had his first one-man show. The building itself, by prominent architect Josep Puig i Cadafalch, represents Neo-Gothic Modernisme. Even if you don't eat or drink here, you can take a quick look around (ask *"Solo mirar, por favor?"*).

• *Return to and continue down Avinguda del Portal de l'Angel. You'll soon reach a fork in the road and a building with a...*

❹ Fountain

The blue and yellow tilework, a circa-1918 addition to this even older fountain, depicts ladies with big jugs of water. In the 17th century this was the last watering stop for horses before leaving town. As recently as 1940, about 10 percent of Barcelonans still got their water from fountains like this.

• *You may feel the pull of wonderful little shops down the street to the right. But take the left fork, down Carrer dels Arcs. Just past the corner, you'll pass the* **Reial Cercle Artístic Museum,** *a private collection of Dalí's work (€10, daily 10:00-22:00). Continue and enter the large square called...*

❺ Plaça Nova

Two bold Roman towers flank a street leading off the square. These once guarded the entrance gate of the ancient Roman city of Barcino. The big stones that make up the base of the (reconstructed) towers are actually Roman. Near the base of the left tower, modern bronze letters spell out "BARCINO." The city's name may have come from Barca, one of Hannibal's generals, who is said to have passed through during Hannibal's roundabout invasion of Italy. At Barcino's

Fountain with tilework

Picasso frieze on the Catalan College building

peak, the Roman wall (see the section stretching to the left of the towers) was 25 feet high and a mile around, with 74 towers. It enclosed a population of 4,000.

One of the towers has a bit of reconstructed **Roman aqueduct** (notice the streambed on top). In ancient times, bridges of stone carried fresh water from the distant hillsides into the walled city.

Opposite the towers is the modern **Catalan College of Architects** building (Collegi d'Arquitectes de Barcelona, TI inside), which is, ironically for a city with so much great architecture, quite ugly. The frieze was designed by Picasso (1962) in his distinctive simplified style. With just a few squiggly stick-figures, Picasso captured traditional Catalan activities. If you check out all three sides of the building, you'll see scenes suggesting music, bullfighting, sea trade, and the *sardana* dance. The branch-waving kings Picasso drew are the giant puppets (*gigantes*) paraded through the streets during local festivals. Picasso spent his formative years (1895-1904, age 14-23) here in the old town. He drank with fellow bohemians at Els Quatre Gats (which we

just passed) and frequented brothels a few blocks from here on Carrer d'Avinyó ("Avignon")—which inspired his influential Cubist painting *Les Demoiselles d'Avignon*.

• *Immediately to the left as you face the Picasso frieze,* **Carrer de la Palla** *is an inviting shopping street. But let's head left through Plaça Nova to take in the mighty...*

➏ *Barcelona Cathedral*

The facade is a virtual catalog of Gothic motifs. There's the pointed arch over the entrance and the stained-glass windows with elaborate stone tracery. Statues of robed saints stand in niches, and winged angels teeter on the octagonal bell towers. And the whole thing is topped with three tall steeples. These pointy spires are meant to give the impression of a church flickering with spiritual fires. This was the Gothic style called Flamboyant—meaning "flame-like." The area in front of the cathedral is where Barcelonans dance the *sardana* on weekends (see page 344).

The cathedral's interior—with its vast space, peaceful cloister, and many ornate chapels—is worth a visit (see Barcelona Cathedral listing later). If you interrupt this tour to visit the cathedral now, you'll exit the cloister a block down Carrer del Bisbe. From there you can circle back to the right, following the wall of the cathedral to visit stop #7—or skip #7 and step directly into stop #8.

As you stand in the square facing the cathedral, look far to your left to see the multicolored, wavy canopy marking the roofline of the **Santa Caterina Market.** The busy street between here and the market—called Via Laietana—is the boundary between the Barri Gòtic and the funkier, edgier **El Born** neighborhood.

• *For now, return to the Roman towers and pass between them to head up Carrer del Bisbe. Take an immediate left, up the ramp to the entrance of...*

Barcelona Cathedral

❼ Casa de l'Ardiaca

It's free to enter this mansion, which was once the archdeacon's residence and now functions as the city archives. The elaborately carved doorway is Renaissance. To the right of the doorway is a carved mail slot by 19th-century Modernista architect Lluís Domènech i Montaner. Enter a small courtyard with a fountain, then step inside the lobby of the city archives, (often featuring free exhibits). At the left end of the lobby, go through the archway and look down into the stairwell for a peek at impressive Roman stonework. Back in the courtyard, climb to the balcony for views of the cathedral steeple, gargoyles, and the small Romanesque chapel on the right—the only surviving 13th-century bit of the cathedral.

• Return to Carrer del Bisbe and turn left. After a few steps, you reach a small square with a bronze statue ensemble.

❽ Monument to the Martyrs of Independence

Five Barcelona patriots—including two priests—calmly receive their last rites before being garroted (strangled) for resisting Napoleon's occupation of Spain in the early 19th century. They'd been outraged by French atrocities in Madrid (depicted in Goya's famous *Third of May* painting in Madrid's Prado Museum). According to the plaque marking their mortal remains, these martyrs to independence gave their lives in 1809 *"por Dios, por la Patria, y por el Rey"*—for God, country, and king.

• Exit the square down tiny Carrer de Montjuïc del Bisbe (to the right as you face the martyrs). This leads to the cute...

❾ Plaça Sant Felip Neri

This shaded square serves as the playground of an elementary school and is often bursting with energetic kids speaking Catalan (just a couple of generations ago, this would have been illegal). The Church of Sant Felip Neri, which Gaudí attended, is still pocked with bomb damage from the Spanish Civil War. As a stronghold of democratic, anti-Franco forces, Barcelona saw a lot of fighting. A plaque on the wall (left of church door) honors the 42 killed—mostly children—in that 1938 aerial bombardment.

The buildings here were paid for by the guilds that powered the local economy. The shoemakers guild (to the right of the arch where you entered the square) is decorated above the windows with reliefs depicting boots.

• Exit the square past the fun **Sabater Hermanos** artisanal soap shop, and head down Carrer de Sant Felip Neri. At the T-intersection, turn right onto Carrer de Sant Sever, then immediately left on Carrer de Salomó Ben Adret (look for the blue El Call sign). You've entered the...

❿ Jewish Quarter (El Call)

In Catalan, a Jewish quarter goes by the name El Call—literally "narrow passage," for the tight lanes where medieval Jews were forced to live, under the watchful eye of the nearby cathedral. (At its peak, some 4,000 Jews were crammed into just a few alleys in this neighborhood.)

Walk down Carrer de Salomó Ben Adret, and pass through the charming little square (a gap in the dense tangle of medieval buildings cleared by another civil war bomb), where you will find a rust-colored sign displaying a map of the Jewish Quarter. Take the next lane to the right (Carrer de Marlet). On the right is the (literally) low-profile, four-foot-high entrance to what was likely Barcelona's **main synagogue** during the Middle Ages (Antigua Sinagoga Mayor, €2.50, Mon-Fri 10:30-18:30, Sat-Sun until 15:00, shorter hours off-season). The sparse interior includes access to two small subterranean rooms with Roman walls topped by a medieval Catalan vault. Look through the glass floor to see dyeing vats used for a later shop on this site run by former

Ⓐ *Roman towers on Plaça Nova*

Ⓑ *Carrer del Bisbe Bridge*

Ⓒ *Church of Sant Felip Neri*

Ⓓ *Monument to the Martyrs of Independence*

Ⓔ *Architectural detail, Casa de l'Ardiaca*

Jews who had been forcibly converted to Christianity.

• *From the synagogue, start back the way you came but then continue straight ahead, onto Carrer de la Fruita. At the T-intersection, turn left, then right, to find your way back to the Martyrs statue. From here, we'll turn right down Carrer del Bisbe to the...*

⓫ Carrer del Bisbe Bridge

This structure connects the Catalan government building (on the right) with what was the Catalan president's ceremonial residence (on the left). Though the bridge appears to be centuries old, it was constructed in the 1920s by Catalan architect Joan Rubió (a follower of Gaudí), who also did the carved ornamentation on the buildings.

• *Continue along Carrer del Bisbe to...*

⓬ Plaça de Sant Jaume

This stately central square of the Barri Gòtic takes its name from the Church of St. James (in Catalan: Jaume, JOW-mah) that once stood here. Set at the intersection of ancient Barcino's main thoroughfares, this square was once a Roman forum. In that sense, it's been the seat of city government for 2,000 years.

For more than six centuries, the **Palau de la Generalitat** (on the uphill side of the square) has housed the offices of the autonomous government of Catalunya. It always flies the Catalan flag next to the obligatory Spanish one. Above the building's doorway is Catalunya's patron saint—St. George (Jordi), slaying the dragon. From these balconies, the nation's leaders (and soccer heroes) greet the people on momentous days. The square is often the site of festivals or demonstrations.

Facing the Generalitat across the square is the **Barcelona City Hall** (Casa de la Ciutat).

Look left and right down the main streets branching off the square; they're lined with ironwork streetlamps and bal-

conies draped with plants. Carrer de Ferran, which leads to the Ramblas, is classic Barcelona.

• *Facing the Generalitat, exit the square going up the second street to the right of the building, on tiny Carrer del Paradís. Follow this street as it turns right. When it swings left, pause at #10, the entrance to the...*

⓭ Roman Temple of Augustus (Temple Roma d'August)

You're standing at the summit of Mont Tàber, the Barri Gòtic's highest spot. A plaque on the wall by the entrance reads: "Mont Tàber, 16.9 meters" (elevation 55 feet). At your feet, a millstone inlaid in the pavement also marks a momentous spot. It was here that the ancient Romans founded the town of Barcino around 12 BC. They built a *castrum* (fort) on the hilltop, protecting the harbor, and this temple to honor their emperor, Augustus.

Go inside for a peek at the last vestiges of the imposing Roman temple (free, Tue-Sat 10:00-19:00, Sun until 20:00, Mon

Roman Temple of Augustus

until 14:00). All that's left are four columns and some fragments of the transept and its plinth (good English info on-site). The huge columns, dating from the late first century BC, are as old as Barcelona itself. They were part of the ancient town's biggest structure, dedicated to Augustus, who was worshipped as a god. These Corinthian columns (with deep fluting and topped with leafy capitals) were the back corner of a 120-foot-long temple that extended from here to Barcino's forum...Plaça de Sant Jaume, which you just visited.

• *Continue down Carrer del Paradís one block. When you bump into the back end of the cathedral, take a right, going down Carrer de la Pietat/Baixada de Santa Clara until you emerge into a square called...*

⓮ *Plaça del Rei*

The buildings enclosing this square exemplify Barcelona's medieval past. The central section (topped by a five-story addition) was the core of the **Royal Palace** (Palau Reial Major). A vast hall on its ground floor once served as the throne room and reception room. From the 13th to the 15th century, the Royal Palace housed Barcelona's counts as well as the resident kings of Aragon. In 1493, a triumphant Christopher Columbus, accompanied by six New World natives and several pure-gold statues, was welcomed home by King Ferdinand and Queen Isabel, who honored him with the title "Admiral of the Oceans."

To the right is the palace's church, the 14th-century **Chapel of Saint Agatha,** which sits atop the foundations of a Roman wall. To the left is the **Viceroy's Palace,** built in the 1500s for the right-hand man of the Spanish monarch, who was now located in far-off Castile.

SIGHTS

Near the Ramblas
▲PALAU GÜELL

This early building by Antoni Gaudí (completed in 1890) shows the architect taking his first tentative steps toward what would become his trademark curvy style. Dark and masculine, with castle-like rooms, Palau Güell (pronounced "gway") was custom built to house the Güell clan and gives an insight into Gaudí's artistic genius. The rooftop has his signature colorful tile mosaic chimneys and offers a panorama of the city. While some people will find this redundant if also visiting La Pedrera, others will appreciate this exquisite building for its delightfully loopy rooftop and far fewer crowds.

Cost and Hours: €12 timed-entry ticket includes good audioguide—buy in advance online, free first Sun of the month; open Tue-Sun 10:00-20:00, Nov-March until 17:30, closed Mon year-round; last entry one hour before closing, rooftop closes when raining; a half-block off the Ramblas at Carrer Nou de la Rambla 3, Metro: Liceu or Drassanes, tel. 934-725-775, www.palauguell.cat.

▲MARITIME MUSEUM (MUSEU MARÍTIM)

Barcelona's medieval shipyard, the best preserved in the entire Mediterranean, is home to an excellent museum near the bottom of the Ramblas. The museum's permanent collection covers the salty history of ships and navigation from the 13th to the 18th century (restoration projects on their permanent collection will eventually reveal pieces from the 18th to the 20th century). Even if you choose not to pay for a full visit, the building is worth a look; interesting free exhibits are in the lobby (inside the main entrance facing the water), where you can get a glimpse of the building's interior.

Cost and Hours: €10, free Sun from 15:00 and for kids 16 and under, ticket includes audioguide and visit to *Santa Eulàlia* boat; open daily 10:00-20:00, nice café with seating inside or out on the museum courtyard (free to enter), Avinguda de les Drassanes, Metro: Drassanes, tel. 933-429-920, www.mmb.cat.

Nearby: Your museum ticket includes entrance to the *Santa Eulàlia,* an early-20th-century schooner docked a short walk from the Columbus Monument (otherwise €3, Tue-Sun 10:00-20:30, Nov-March until 17:30, closed Mon year-round). On Saturday mornings, you can sail around the harbor on the schooner for three hours—reserve well in advance (Sat 10:00-13:00, €12 for adults, €6 for kids 6-14, tel. 933-429-920, reserves. mmaritim@diba.cat).

Barri Gòtic

▲BARCELONA CATHEDRAL (CATEDRAL DE BARCELONA)

The city's 14th-century, Gothic-style cathedral (with a Neo-Gothic facade) has played a significant role in Barcelona's history—but as far as grand cathedrals go, this one is relatively unexciting. Still, it's worth a visit to see its richly decorated chapels, finely carved choir, tomb of Santa Eulàlia, and restful cloister with gurgling fountains and resident geese.

Cost: €7 during tourist hours (Mon-Fri 12:30-19:45, Sat 12:30-17:30, Sun 14:00-17:30; covers admission to the choir, terrace, and museum). Paying the afternoon admission can be worthwhile on a crowded day.

Free Entry: The cathedral is free for worship and visits Mon-Sat before 12:30, Sun before 13:45, and Sat-Sun after 17:30—but during those times, you have to pay €3 each to visit the choir or terrace (the museum is closed during these hours). Access may be limited during church services.

Hours: Cathedral generally open Mon-Fri 8:30-19:30, Sat-Sun until 20:00. The cathedral's three minor sights are open Mon-Sat (with different hours)

and closed Sun: choir—9:00-19:00, terrace—9:00-18:00, museum—12:30-17:15. Both the choir and terrace may close earlier on slow days.

Information: Tel. 933 -428 -262, www. catedralbcn.org.

Dress Code: The dress code is strictly enforced; don't wear tank tops, shorts, or skirts above the knee.

Getting In: The main, front door entrance is open most of the time. While it can be crowded, the line generally moves fast. The entrance around the corner on Carrer del Bisbe is reserved for visitors with reduced mobility.

Visiting the Cathedral: This has been Barcelona's holiest spot for 2,000 years. The Romans built their Temple of Jupiter here. In AD 343, the pagan temple was replaced with a Christian cathedral. That building was supplanted by a Romanesque-style church (11th century). The current Gothic structure was started in 1298 and finished in 1450, during the medieval glory days of the Catalan nation. The facade was humble, so in the 19th century the proud local bourgeoisie (enjoying a second Golden Age) redid it in a more ornate, Neo-Gothic style. Construction was capped in 1913 with the central spire, 230 feet tall.

The nave is ringed with 28 **chapels.** Besides creating worship spaces, the walls defining these chapels serve as interior buttresses supporting the roof (which is why the exterior walls are smooth, without the normal Gothic buttresses outside). Barcelona honors many of the homegrown saints found in these chapels with public holidays. In the middle of the nave, the 15th-century choir (coro) features ornately carved stalls. During the standing parts of the Mass, the chairs were folded up, but VIPs still had those little wooden ledges to lean on. Each was creatively carved and—since you couldn't sit on sacred things—the artists were free to enjoy some secular and naughty fun here.

Look behind the **high altar** (beneath

Nave of Barcelona Cathedral

the crucifix) to find the bishop's chair (cathedra). As a cathedral, this church is the bishop's seat—hence its Catalan nickname of *La Seu*. To the left of the altar is the organ and the elevator up to the terrace. To the right of the altar, the wall is decorated with Catalunya's yellow-and-red coat of arms. Steps beneath the altar lead to the **crypt,** featuring the marble-and-alabaster sarcophagus (1327-1339) containing the remains of Santa Eulàlia. The cathedral is dedicated to this saint. Thirteen-year-old Eulàlia, daughter of a prominent Barcelona family, was martyred by the Romans for her faith in AD 304. Murky legends say she was subjected to 13 tortures.

The **elevator** in the left transept takes you up to the rooftop **terrace,** made of sturdy scaffolding pieces, for an expansive city view.

Exit through the right transept to enter the **cloister. Its arcaded walkway surrounds a lush** circa-1450 courtyard. Ahhhh. It's a tropical atmosphere of palm, orange, and magnolia trees; a fish pond; trickling fountains; and squawking geese. During the Corpus Christi festival in June, kids come here to watch a hollow egg

dance atop the fountain's spray. As you wander the cloister (clockwise), check out the coats of arms as well as the tombs in the pavement. These were for rich merchants who paid good money to be buried as close to the altar as possible. A few pavement stones here and there have the symbols of their trades: scissors, shoes, bakers, and so on. The resident **geese** have been here for at least 500 years. There are always 13, in memory of Eulàlia's 13 years and 13 torments.

The little **museum** (at the far end of the cloister; entry possible only during paid visiting hours) has the six-foot-tall 14th-century Great Monstrance, a ceremonial display case for the communion wafer that's paraded through the streets during the Corpus Christi festival. The next room, the Sala Capitular, has several altarpieces, including a pietà (*Desplà*, 1490) by Bartolomé Bermejo.

▲*SARDANA* DANCES

If you're in town on a weekend, you can see the *sardana*, a patriotic dance in which Barcelonans link hands and dance in a circle (Sun at 11:15, many Sat at 18:00, no

Circle Dances in Squares and Castles in the Air

From group circle dancing to human towers, Catalans have some interesting and unique traditions. A memorable Barcelona experience is watching (or participating in) the patriotic *sardana* dances. Locals of all ages seem to spontaneously appear. For some it's a highly symbolic, politically charged action representing Catalan unity—but for most it's just a fun chance to kick up their heels. All are welcome, even tourists cursed with two left feet. The dances are held in the square in front of the cathedral on Sundays at 11:15 (and many Saturdays at 18:00).

Participants gather in circles after putting their things in the center—symbolic of community and sharing (and the ever-present risk of theft). Holding hands, dancers raise their arms—slow-motion, *Zorba the Greek*-style—as they hop and sway gracefully to the music. The band *(cobla)* consists of a long flute, tenor and soprano oboes, strange-looking brass instruments, and a tiny bongo-like drum *(tambori)*. The rest of Spain mocks this lazy circle dance, but considering what it takes for a culture to survive within another culture's country, it is a stirring display of local pride and patriotism. During the 36 years of Franco dictatorship, the *sardana* was forbidden.

Another Catalan tradition is the **castell,** a tower erected solely of people. *Castells* pop up on special occasions, such as the Festa Major de Gràcia in mid-August and La Mercè festival in late September. Towers can be up to 10 humans high. Imagine balancing 50 or 60 feet in the air, with nothing but a pile of flesh and bone between you and the ground. The base is formed by burly supports called *baixos;* above them are the *manilles* ("handles"), which help haul up the people to the top. The *castell* is capped with a human steeple—usually a child—who extends four fingers into the air, representing the four red stripes of the Catalan flag. A scrum of spotters (called *pinyas*) cluster around the base in case anyone falls. *Castelleres* are judged both on how quickly they erect their human towers and how fast they can take them down. Besides during festivals, you can usually see *castells* in front of the cathedral on spring and summer Saturdays at 19:30 (as part of the Festa Catalana). If you've never seen this, it's worth searching for the spectacle on YouTube.

One thing that these two traditions have in common is their communal nature. Perhaps it's no coincidence, as Catalunya is known for its community spirit, team building, and socialistic bent.

dances in Aug, event lasts 1-2 hours, in the square in front of the cathedral; for details, see the sidebar).

▲ GAUDÍ EXHIBITION CENTER

This center fills the stony complex of ancient and medieval buildings immediately to the left of the cathedral with a beautifully lit, thoughtful, and well-described exhibit. With plenty of historic artifacts, it provides the best introduction to Antoni Gaudí—the man and the architect. You'll spend about an hour following the included audioguide through six rooms on three floors.

Cost and Hours: €15; daily 10:00-20:00, Nov-Feb until 18:00, last entry one hour before closing; Pla de la Seu 7, Metro: Jaume I, tel. 932-687-582, www.gaudiexhibitioncenter.com. While a combo-ticket sold here includes entrance to the great Modernista sights, it's impractical considering the necessity of booking those sights in advance.

▲ FREDERIC MARÈS MUSEUM (MUSEU FREDERIC MARÈS)

This delightful museum, adjacent to the cathedral, features the eclectic collection of Frederic Marès (1893-1991), a local sculptor and packrat. The museum sprawls through several old Barri Gòtic buildings around a peaceful courtyard. It offers a fascinating look at ancient Roman statues from this region and is an exquisite warehouse of Romanesque and Gothic Christian art from Catalunya.

Cost and Hours: €4.20, free first Sun of the month and all other Sun from 15:00; open Tue-Sat 10:00-19:00, Sun until 20:00, closed Mon; essential audioguide-€1, Plaça de Sant Iu 5, Metro: Jaume I, tel. 932-563-500, www.museumares.bcn.cat.

▲ BARCELONA HISTORY MUSEUM (MUSEU D'HISTÒRIA DE BARCELONA)

This museum primarily contains objects from archaeological digs around Barcelona. But the real highlight is an underground labyrinth of excavated Roman ruins.

Cost and Hours: €7; includes audioguide and other MUHBA branches; free all day first Sun of month and other Sun from 15:00—but no audioguide during free times; open Tue-Sat 10:00-19:00, Sun until 20:00, closed Mon; Plaça del Rei, enter on Carrer del Veguer, Metro: Jaume I, tel. 932-562-122.

El Born

▲▲▲ PICASSO MUSEUM (MUSEU PICASSO)

Pablo Picasso may have made his career in Paris, but the years he spent in Barcelona—from age 14 through 23—were among the most formative of his life. Here, young Pablo mastered the realistic painting style of his artistic forebears—and first felt the freedom that allowed him to leave that all behind and give in to his creative, experimental urges. When he left Barcelona, Picasso headed for Paris...and revolutionized art forever.

The pieces in this excellent museum capture that priceless moment just before this bold young thinker changed the world. While you won't find Picasso's famous later Cubist works here, you will enjoy a representative sweep of his early years, as well as works from his twilight years. It's the top collection of Picassos here in his native country and the best anywhere of his early years.

Cost and Hours: €12 for timed-entry ticket, free Thu from 18:00 and all day first Sun of month, must reserve ahead for free hours; open Mon 10:00-17:00, Tue-Sun 9:00-20:30, Thu until 21:30, shorter hours and closed Mon in off-season; audioguide-€5, Carrer de Montcada 15, tel. 932-563-000, www.museupicasso.bcn.cat.

Rick's Tip: *The* **Picasso Museum** *often sells out and there's nearly always a long line. Buy a* **timed-entry ticket** *in advance to avoid disappointment.*

Ticketing Tips: The ticketing part of the website can be temperamental—keep

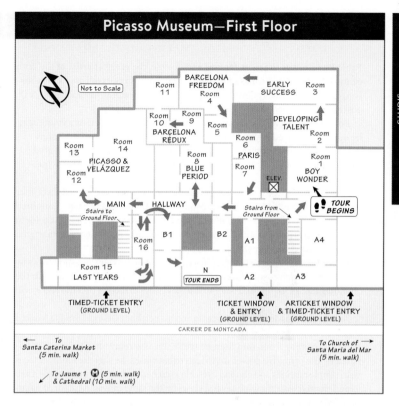

Picasso Museum—First Floor

Not to Scale

BARCELONA FREEDOM
Room 11
Room 4
EARLY SUCCESS
Room 3

Room 10
Room 9
BARCELONA REDUX
Room 5
DEVELOPING TALENT
Room 2

Room 13
Room 14
PICASSO & VELÁZQUEZ
Room 12
Room 8
BLUE PERIOD
Room 6
PARIS
Room 7
Room 1
BOY WONDER

ELEV.

MAIN HALLWAY
Stairs to Ground Floor
Stairs from Ground Floor
TOUR BEGINS

Room 16
B1
B2
A1
A4

Room 15
LAST YEARS
N
TOUR ENDS
A2
A3

TIMED-TICKET ENTRY
(GROUND LEVEL)

TICKET WINDOW & ENTRY
(GROUND LEVEL)

ARTICKET WINDOW & TIMED-TICKET ENTRY
(GROUND LEVEL)

CARRER DE MONTCADA

To Santa Caterina Market (5 min. walk)

To Church of Santa Maria del Mar (5 min. walk)

To Jaume 1 Ⓜ (5 min. walk) & Cathedral (10 min. walk)

trying. An **Articket BCN** (see page 319) allows you to enter the galleries whenever you wish (you must first obtain an admission ticket from the on-site Articket window—where you can also buy an Articket).

Day-of tickets (when available) are sold online (must purchase at least 2 hours before your visit). The museum's busiest times are mornings before 13:00, all day Tue, and during the free entry times.

Getting There: It's on Carrer de Montcada; the general ticket office is in the courtyard at #19, and the Articket BCN booth is at #23. From the Jaume I Metro stop, it's a quick five-minute walk. It's a 10-minute walk from the cathedral and many parts of the Barri Gòtic.

Services: The ground floor has a required bag check, a bookshop, and WC.

◑ SELF-GUIDED TOUR

The Picasso Museum's collection of nearly 300 paintings is presented more or less chronologically. With good text panels in every room providing context, it's easy to follow the evolution of Picasso's work. Don't be surprised if a painting described here is not on view; paintings are rotated in and out. But the themes and chronology remain constant.

BOY WONDER (ROOM 1)

Pablo's earliest art is realistic and earnest. His work quickly advanced from childish pencil drawings (from about 1890), through a series of technically skilled **art-school works** (copies of plaster feet and arms), to oil paintings of impressive technique. His **portraits** demonstrate surprising psychological insight.

Pablo Picasso (1881-1973)

Pablo Picasso was the most famous and, for me, the greatest artist of the 20th century. He became the master of many styles (Cubism, Surrealism, Expressionism) and many media (painting, sculpture, prints, ceramics, assemblages). Still, anything he touched looked unmistakably like "a Picasso."

Born in Málaga, Spain, Picasso was the son of an art teacher. At a young age, he quickly advanced beyond his teachers. Picasso's teenage works are stunningly realistic and capture the inner complexities of the people he painted. As a youth in Barcelona, he fell in with a bohemian crowd that mixed wine, women, and art.

In 1900, at age 19, Picasso started making trips to Paris and moved there four years later. When his best friend, Spanish artist Carlos Casagemas, committed suicide, Picasso plunged into a **Blue Period** (1901-1904)—the dominant color in these paintings matches their melancholy mood and subject matter (emaciated beggars, hard-eyed pimps).

In 1904, Picasso got a steady girlfriend (Fernande Olivier) and suddenly saw the world through rose-colored glasses—the **Rose Period.** He played with the "building blocks" of line and color to find new ways to reconstruct the real world on canvas.

At his studio in Montmartre, Picasso and his neighbor Georges Braque worked together, in poverty so dire they often didn't know where their next bottle of wine was coming from. And then, at age 25, Picasso reinvented painting. Fascinated by the primitive power of African tribal masks, he sketched human faces with simple outlines and almond eyes. He sketched nudes from every angle, then experimented with showing several views on the same canvas. A hundred paintings and nine months later, Picasso gave birth to a monstrous canvas of five nude, fragmented prostitutes with mask-like faces—*Les Demoiselles d'Avignon* (1907).

This bold new style was called **Cubism.** With Cubism, Picasso shattered the Old World and put it back together in a new way. The subjects are somewhat recognizable (with the help of the titles), but they're built with geometric shards (let's call them "cubes")—like viewing the world through a kaleidoscope of brown and gray.

In 1918, Picasso traveled to Rome and entered a **Classical Period** (1920s) of more realistic, full-bodied women and children, inspired by the three-dimensional sturdiness of ancient statues. While he flirted with abstraction, through-

DEVELOPING TALENT (ROOM 2)

Pablo moved to Barcelona at age 14. During a summer trip to Málaga in 1896, he experimented with a series of fresh, Impressionistic-style landscapes (relatively rare in Spain at the time). As a 15-year-old, Pablo dutifully entered art-school competitions. His first big work, *First Communion,* tackled a prescribed religious subject, but Picasso made it an excuse to paint his family. His sister Lola was the model for the communicant, and the man beside her has the face of Picasso's father. Find the portrait of his aunt Tía Pepa, painted in Málaga in 1896 (this and other family portraits are frequently rotated). Notice how ably Picasso captured the toughness of his aunt.

out his life Picasso always kept a grip on "reality." His favorite subject was people. The anatomy might be jumbled, but it's all there.

Though he lived in France and Italy, Picasso remained a Spaniard at heart, incorporating Spanish motifs into his work. Unrepentantly macho, he loved bullfights, seeing them as a metaphor for the timeless human interaction between the genders. To Picasso, the horse symbolizes the feminine, and the bull, the masculine. Spanish imagery— bulls, screaming horses, a Madonna— appears in Picasso's most famous work, *Guernica* (1937). The monumental canvas of a bombed village summed up the pain of Spain's brutal civil war (1936- 1939) and foreshadowed the onslaught of World War II.

At war's end, Picasso left Paris behind, finding fun in the **south of France.** Sun! Color! Water! Freedom! Senior citizen Pablo Picasso was reborn, enjoying worldwide fame and the love of a beautiful young painter, Françoise Gilot. Bursting with creativity, Picasso cranked out a painting a day. His Riviera works set the tone for the rest of his life: sunny, lighthearted, and childlike; filled with motifs of the sea, Greek myths, and animals. His simple drawing of a dove holding an olive branch became an international symbol of peace.

Picasso made collages, built "statues" out of wood, wire, ceramics, papier- mâché, or whatever, and even turned everyday household objects into statues (like his famous bull's head made of a bicycle seat with handlebar horns). **Multimedia** works like these have become so standard today that we forget how revolutionary they once were. His last works have the playfulness of someone much younger. As it is often said of Picasso, "When he was a child, he painted like a man. When he was old, he painted like a child."

EARLY SUCCESS (ROOM 3)

In the large, classically painted *Science and Charity* (1897), Picasso used realistic means to represent subjects of social concern—a technique typical of the social realism movement of the late 19th century. The doctor (modeled on Pablo's father) represents science. The nun represents charity and religion. From the hopeless face and lifeless hand of the sick woman, it seems that Picasso believes nothing will save her from death.

Picasso traveled to Madrid to study. At the Prado Museum, he learned by copying earlier Spanish masters, especially Diego Velázquez. An example of Picasso's impressive mimicry is sometimes displayed in this room—a nearly perfect copy of a

portrait of **Philip IV** by Velázquez.

BARCELONA FREEDOM (ROOM 4)

In 1900 Picasso returned to Barcelona, where Art Nouveau was all the rage. He fell in with an avant-garde crowd, who congregated daily at Els Quatre Gats ("The Four Cats," a popular restaurant to this day). Picasso even created the **menu cover** for this favorite hangout. He painted **portraits** of his new friends (including Jaume Sabartés, who later became Picasso's personal assistant and donated the foundational works of this museum). Still a teenager, Pablo exhibited his first one-man show at Els Quatre Gats in 1900.

PARIS (ROOMS 6-7)

In 1900 Picasso made his first trip to Paris, and began sampling the contemporary art styles around him: He painted **cancan dancers** like Toulouse-Lautrec, **still lifes** like Paul Cézanne, brightly colored **Fauvist** works like Henri Matisse, and Impressionist **landscapes** like Claude Monet. In *The Waiting (Margot),* the subject—with her bold outline and strong gaze—pops out from the vivid, mosaic-like background.

BLUE PERIOD (ROOM 8)

Picasso traveled to Paris several times before settling there permanently in 1904. The suicide of his best friend Carlos Casagemas, his own poverty, and the influence of new ideas linking color and mood led Picasso to abandon jewel-bright color for his Blue Period (1901-1904). Now the artist was painting not what he saw, but what he felt. Painting misfits and street people, Picasso revealed the beauty in ugliness.

During a visit to Barcelona, Picasso painted a nighttime view over the **rooftops** of the city. His palette is still blue, but here we see proto-Cubism...five years before the first real Cubist painting.

❶ *Picasso, Science and Charity*
❷ *Picasso, Las Meninas*
❸ *Picasso's menu design for Els Quatre Gats*

ROSE PERIOD

Picasso finally lifted out of his funk after meeting a new lady, Fernande Olivier (a bronze bust of her from 1906 may be on view). He moved out of the blue and into the happier Rose Period (1904-1907), dominated by soft pink and reddish tones. (Other than the rarely displayed **Portrait of Bernadetta Bianco,** the museum is weak on Rose Period works.)

CUBISM

Pablo's role in the invention of the groundbreaking Cubist style (with his friend Georges Braque) is well known—at least I hope so, since this museum has no true Cubist paintings. The technique of "building" a subject with "cubes" of paint simmered in Picasso's artistic stew for years. The idea was to simultaneously see several 3-D facets of the subject.

BARCELONA REDUX (ROOMS 9-10)

Picasso spent six months back in Barcelona in 1917 (yet another girlfriend, a Russian ballet dancer, had a gig in town). The paintings in these rooms demonstrate the artist's irrepressible versatility: He had already developed Cubism, but continued to play with other styles. In **Woman with Mantilla,** we see a little Post-Impressionistic Pointillism in a portrait that is as elegant as a classical statue. Nearby, **Gored Horse** has all the anguish and power of his iconic *Guernica* (painted years later).

Remember that this museum has very little from the most famous and prolific "middle" part of Picasso's career—basically, from his adoption of Cubism to his sunset years on the French Riviera. (To fill in the gaps in his middle career, see the sidebar.)

PICASSO AND VELÁZQUEZ (ROOMS 12-14)

As a mature artist, Picasso turned to the great Old Masters for inspiration, and set about making a series of work related to what many consider the greatest painting by anyone, ever: Diego Velázquez's *Las Meninas.* The 17th-century original (in Madrid's Prado Museum) depicted the young maids of honor (or *meninas*) of the Spanish royal court. Pablo painted more than **40 interpretations** of the masterwork. Picasso deconstructed Velázquez and then injected light, color, and perspective as he improvised on the earlier masterpiece. In Picasso's big, black and white canvas, he more or less re-created Velázquez's painting in its entirety. But here, the king and queen (reflected in the mirror in the back of the room) are hardly seen, while the painter—the great Velázquez—towers above everyone. In other paintings in the series, Picasso focused on details—one maid of honor or a pair of them, or he zeroed in on just their faces.

LAST YEARS (ROOM 15)

Picasso spent the last 36 years of his life living simply in the south of France. With simple black outlines and Crayola colors, Picasso painted sun-splashed nature, peaceful doves, and the joys of the beach. He enjoyed life with his second (and much younger) wife, Jacqueline Roque.

His last works have the playfulness of someone much younger. As is often said of Picasso, in his youth he was taught to see the world like an adult, and in his golden years he enjoyed seeing and portraying the world with the freedom of a child.

Nearby (in Rooms B1, N, and B2), you'll see how in his later years Picasso became a master of other media besides painting. With his **ceramics,** he made bowls and vases in fun animal shapes, decorated with simple motifs.

Picasso died in 1973 with brush in hand. Sadly, since he vowed never to set foot in fascist, Franco-ruled Spain—the artist never returned to his homeland...and never saw this museum. But to the end, Picasso continued exploring and loving life through his art.

▲▲PALACE OF CATALAN MUSIC (PALAU DE LA MÚSICA CATALANA)

This concert hall, built in just three years, features an unexceptional exterior but boasts my favorite Modernista interior in town (by Lluís Domènech i Montaner). Its inviting arches lead you into the 2,138-seat hall, which is accessible only with a tour (or by attending a concert). A kaleidoscopic skylight features a choir singing around the sun, while playful carvings and mosaics celebrate music and Catalan culture. If you're interested in Modernisme, taking this tour is one of the best experiences in town—and helps balance the hard-to-avoid focus on Gaudí as "Mr. Modernisme."

Cost and Hours: €20, daily one-hour tours in English run every hour 10:00-15:00, tour times may change based on performance schedule, about six blocks northeast of cathedral, Carrer Palau de la Música 4, Metro: Urquinaona, tel. 932-957-200, www.palaumusica.cat.

Advance Reservations Required: You must buy tickets in advance to get a spot on an English guided tour (tickets available up to four months in advance—purchase yours at least two days before, though they're sometimes available the same day or the day before—especially Oct-March). You can buy tickets in person at the concert hall box office or at its Modernista ticket window to the left of the main concert hall entrance (box office open Mon-Sat 9:30-21:00, Sun 10:00-15:00, 10-minute walk from the cathedral or Picasso Museum). You can also purchase tickets over the phone (no extra charge, tel. 902-475-485) or on the concert hall website (€1 fee).

Concerts: An excellent way to see the hall is by attending a concert (300 per year, €20-150 tickets, see website for details and to buy tickets, box office tel. 902-442-882).

Rick's Tip: *Concerts advertised as "Palace of Catalan Music" are performed in two separate concert halls. To see the Modernista main concert hall,* **be sure the show is in Sala de Concerts***—not the new Petit Palau hall.*

Palace of Catalan Music

Modernisme and the Renaixença

Modernisme is Barcelona's unique contribution to the Europe-wide Art Nouveau movement. Meaning "a taste for what is modern"—such as streetcars, electric lights, and big-wheeled bicycles—this free-flowing organic style lasted from 1888 to 1906.

Broadly speaking, there were two kinds of Modernisme (otherwise known as Catalan Art Nouveau). Early Modernisme has a Neo-Gothic flavor, clearly inspired by medieval castles and towers—logically, since architects wanted to recall the days when Barcelona was at its peak. From that starting point, Antoni Gaudí branched off on his own, adding the color and curves we most associate with the look of Barcelona's Modernisme.

Casa Amatller, with stepped roofline, and Casa Batlló, to the right

The aim was to create buildings that were both practical and decorative. To that end, Modernista architects experimented with new construction techniques. Their most important material was concrete, which they could mold to curve and ripple like a wave, and enliven with brightly colored glass and tile. Their structures were fully modern, but the decoration was a clip-art collage of natural images, exotic Moorish or Chinese themes, and fanciful Gothic crosses and knights to celebrate Catalunya's medieval glory days.

It's ironic to think that Modernisme was a response against the regimentation of the Industrial Age—and that all those organic shapes were only made possible thanks to Eiffel Tower-like iron frames. As you wander through the Eixample looking at all those fanciful facades and colorful, leafy, blooming shapes in doorways, entrances, and ceilings, remember that many of these homes were built at the same time as the first skyscrapers in Chicago and New York City.

Underpinning Modernisme was the Catalan cultural revival movement, called the Renaixença. Across Europe, it was a time of national resurgence. It was the dawn of the modern age, and downtrodden peoples—from the Basques to the Irish to the Hungarians to the Finns—were throwing off the cultural domination of other nations and celebrating what made their own culture unique. Here in Catalunya, the Renaixença encouraged everyday people to get excited about all things Catalan—from their language, patriotic dances, and inspirational art to their surprising style of architecture.

▲SANTA CATERINA MARKET (MERCAT DE SANTA CATERINA)

This eye-catching market hall's colorful, swooping roof covers a delightful shopping zone that caters more to locals than tourists. Come for the outlandish architecture, but stay for the food and the chance to picnic shop without the tourist logjam of La Boqueria. Besides fresh produce, it has many inviting eateries.

Cost and Hours: Free, Mon-Sat 7:30-15:30, until 20:30 on Tue and Thu-Fri, closed Sun, Avinguda de Francesc Cambó 16, www.mercatsantacaterina.cat.

▲CHURCH OF SANTA MARIA DEL MAR (BASÍLICA DE SANTA MARIA DEL MAR)

This "Cathedral of the Sea" was built entirely with local funds and labor, in the heart of the wealthy merchant El Born quarter. Proudly independent, the church features a purely Catalan Gothic interior that was forcibly uncluttered of its Baroque decor by civil war belligerents. On the big front doors, notice the figures of workers who donated their time and sweat to build the church. The stone they used was quarried at Montjuïc and had to be carried across town on the backs of porters called *bastaixos*.

Cost and Hours: Entry is free Mon-Sat 9:00-13:00 & 17:00-20:30, Sun 10:00-14:00 & 17:00-20:30. Entry is €5 (when the interior is illuminated and you have access to the choir and the crypt) Mon-Sat 13:00-17:00, Sun from 14:00. They offer €8 guided rooftop tours more or less on the hour during paid entry times (45 minutes, check for English tours and sign up at the door); Plaça Santa Maria, Metro: Jaume I, tel. 933-102-390, www.santamariadelmarbarcelona.org.

The Eixample
Block of Discord

At the center of this neighborhood is the Block of Discord, where three colorful Modernista facades compete for your attention: Casa Batlló, Casa Amatller, and Casa Lleó Morera (all on Passeig de Gràcia—near the Metro stop of the same name—between Carrer del Consell de Cent and Carrer d'Aragó). All were built by well-known Modernista architects at the end of the 19th century. Because the mansions look as though they are trying to outdo each other in creative twists, locals nicknamed the noisy block the "Block of Discord." Of the three houses, two are open to visitors—Casa Batlló and the less-crowded Casa Amatller.

For a tour of the Eixample, download my free 🎧 Eixample Walk audio tour.

▲CASA BATLLÓ

While the highlight of this Gaudí-designed residence is the roof, the interior is also interesting—and much more over-the-top than La Pedrera's. The house features a funky mushroom-shaped fireplace nook on the main floor, a blue-and-white-ceramic-slathered atrium, and an attic with parabolic arches. There's barely a straight line in the house. You can also get a close-up look at the dragon-inspired

Church of Santa Maria del Mar

rooftop. The ticket includes a good (if long-winded) videoguide that shows the rooms as they may have been.

Cost and Hours: €24.50 timed-entry ticket includes videoguide—purchase in advance online; daily 9:00-21:00, check website for evening wine and music visits, Passeig de Gràcia 43, tel. 932-160-306, www.casabatllo.cat.

CASA MUSEU AMATLLER

The middle residence of the Block of Discord, Casa Amatller was designed by Josep Puig I Cadafalch in the late 19th century for the Amatller chocolate-making family. Only viewable via a group tour, it features mostly original furniture, placed just as the owners had it when they lived there. Admire the home's Neo-Catalan Gothic facade, with tiles and *esgrafiado* decoration.

Rick's Tip: *If you don't want to pay for a ticket, you can step inside* **Casa Amatller's foyer (free during opening hours)** *to see the Modernist stained-glass door and ceiling, and an elaborate staircase.*

Cost and Hours: €24 for one-hour English tour at 11:00, €19 for 40-minute videoguided group tour—generally on the hour and at :30 past the hour, admission includes treat from café; open daily 10:30-18:30, advance tickets available online, Passeig de Gràcia 41, tel. 934-617-460, www.amatller.org.

CASA LLEÓ MORERA

This house was designed by Lluís Domènech i Montaner and finished in 1906. The architect demolished and rebuilt the facade, embellishing it with galleries and balconies. To create the sculptural ornamentation, he hired the city's best craftsmen. Look for the recurring references to mulberries in the decoration—an allusion to the family name, Morera (mulberry). The interior is closed to visitors.

▲▲LA PEDRERA (CASA MILÀ)

One of Gaudí's trademark works, this house—built between 1906 and 1912—is an icon of Modernisme. The wealthy industrialist Pere Milà i Camps commissioned it, and while some still call it *Casa*

La Pedrera rooftop

SPAIN

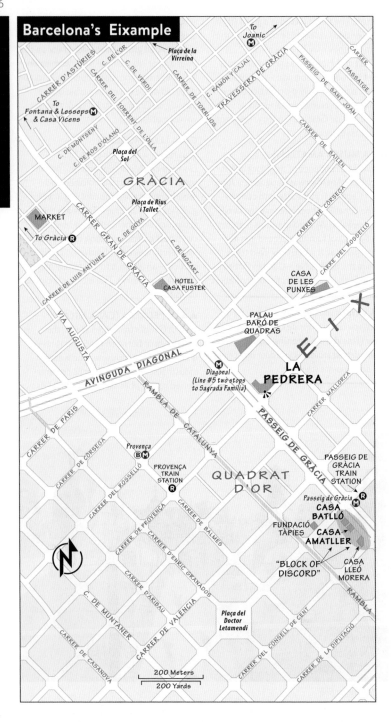

Barcelona's Eixample

To Joanic Ⓜ

Plaça de la Virreina

CARRER D'ASTÚRIES
C. DE L'OR
C. DE VERDI
CARRER DEL TORRENT DE L'OLLA
CARRER DE TORRIJOS
C. RAMÓN Y CAJAL
TRAVESSERA DE GRÀCIA
PASSEIG DE SANT JOAN
CARRER
PASSATGE

To Fontana & Lesseps Ⓜ & Casa Vicens

C. DE MONTSENY
C. DE ROS D'OLANO

CARRER DE BAILEN

Plaça del Sol

GRÀCIA

Plaça de Rius i Tallet

CARRER DE CÓRSEGA

MARKET

CARRER GRAN DE GRÀCIA

C. DE GOYA

CARRER DEL ROSSELLÓ

To Gràcia Ⓡ

C. DE MOZART

CASA DE LES PUNXES

CARRER DE LUIS ANTÚNEZ

HOTEL CASA FUSTER

PALAU BARÓ DE QUADRAS

VIA AUGUSTA

E I X

AVINGUDA DIAGONAL

Ⓜ Diagonal (Line #5 two stops to Sagrada Família)

LA PEDRERA

CARRER DE PARÍS

RAMBLA DE CATALUNYA

CARRER MALLORCA

PASSEIG DE GRÀCIA

CARRER DE CÓRSEGA

Provença Ⓑ Ⓜ

PROVENÇA TRAIN STATION Ⓡ

QUADRAT D'OR

PASSEIG DE GRÀCIA TRAIN STATION

CARRER DEL ROSSELLÓ

CARRER DE PROVENÇA

CARRER DE BALMES

Passeig de Gràcia Ⓡ

CASA BATLLÓ Ⓜ

CARRER D'ENRIC GRANADOS

FUNDACIÓ TÀPIES

CASA AMATLLER

N

CASA LLEÓ MORERA

CARRER D'ARIBAU

"BLOCK OF DISCORD"

C. DE MUNTANER

CARRER DE VALÈNCIA

RAMBLA

CARRER DE CASANOVA

Plaça del Doctor Letamendi

CARRER DEL CONSELL DE CENT

CARRER DE LA DIPUTACIÓ

200 Meters
200 Yards

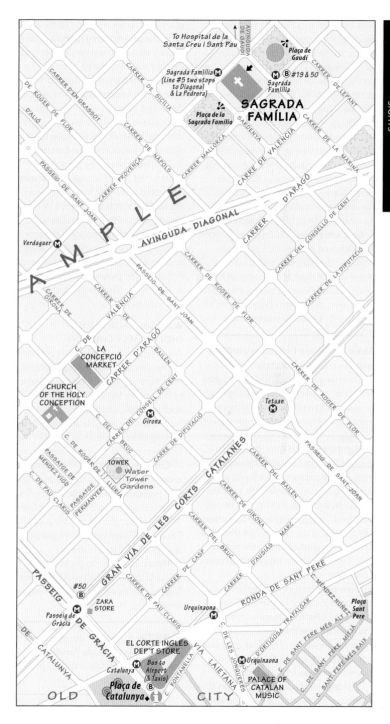

Milà, most call it *La Pedrera* (The Quarry) because of its jagged, rocky facade. While it's fun to ogle from the outside, it's also worth going inside, as it's arguably the purest Gaudí interior in Barcelona—executed at the height of his abilities (unlike his earlier Palau Güell)—and contains original furnishings. While Casa Batlló has a Gaudí facade and rooftop, these were appended to an existing building; La Pedrera, on the other hand, was built from the ground up according to Gaudí's plans. Your ticket includes entry to the interior (with the furnished apartment) and to the delightful rooftop, with its forest of tiled chimneys.

Cost and Hours: €22 timed-entry ticket includes good audioguide—purchase online in advance; open daily 9:00-20:30, Nov-Feb until 18:30; at the corner of Passeig de Gràcia and Provença (visitor entrance at Provença 261), Metro: Diagonal, info tel. 902-400-973, www.lapedrera.com.

Rick's Tip: *To enter* **La Pedrera without a wait,** *buy a €29 premium ticket, which allows you to arrive whenever you wish (no assigned entry time) and skip all lines, including those for audioguides and the elevator to the apartment and roof (sometimes a 30-minute wait).*

Nighttime Visits: After-hour visits dubbed "La Pedrera Night Experience" include a guided tour of the building (but not the apartment), along with a rooftop light show and glass of *cava* (€34; usually daily from 21:00). Another nighttime ticket (€59) includes the rooftop light show, plus dinner and a glass of *cava* at the on-site café. Options change frequently, so check online for the latest.

Concerts: On summer weekends, an evening rooftop concert series, "Summer Nights at La Pedrera," features live jazz and the chance to see the rooftop illuminated (€35, June-mid-Sept Fri-Sat at 20:15, book advance tickets online or by phone, tel. 902-101-212, www.lapedrera.com).

Visiting the House: A visit covers three sections—the rooftop, the attic, and the apartment. Enter and head up the elevator to the jaw-dropping **rooftop** to enjoy Gaudí's works and the views (note that the roof may close when it rains).

Follow the signs to go down to the **attic,** which houses a sprawling multimedia exhibit tracing the history of the architect's career, with models, photos, and videos of his work. It's all displayed under distinctive parabola-shaped arches.

Continue the visit by going downstairs to the typical bourgeois **apartment,** decorated as it might have been when the building was first occupied by middle-class urbanites (a 7-minute video explains Barcelona society at the time). Notice Gaudí's clever use of the atrium to maximize daylight in all the apartments.

Back at the **ground level** of La Pedrera, poke into the dreamily painted original entrance courtyard.

▲▲▲SAGRADA FAMÍLIA (HOLY FAMILY CHURCH)

Gaudí's grand masterpiece sits unfinished in a residential Eixample neighborhood 1.5 miles north of Plaça de Catalunya. An icon of the city, the Sagrada Família boasts bold, wildly creative, unmistakably organic architecture and decor inside and out—from its melting Glory Facade to its skull-like Passion Facade to its rainforest-esque interior.

Cost: Purchase timed-entry tickets online in advance; Basic ticket-€20 (church only, available only from 17:00), Audio Tour ticket-€26 (church and audioguide), Guided Tour ticket-€27 (church and live guide), Church and Tower ticket-€33 (church, audioguide, and tower elevator).

Hours: Daily 9:00-20:00, March and Oct until 19:00, Nov-Feb until 18:00, Metro: Sagrada Família, 932-080-414, www.sagrada familia.org.

Rick's Tip: *Buying a timed-entry ticket in advance for the* **Sagrada Família** *will save you time, money, and possibly the frustration of not getting in at all.*

Sagrada Família

Getting In: With ticket in hand (or on your phone), go through security and enter at the Nativity Facade side.

Tours: The 50-minute English tours run year-round; choose a tour time when you buy your ticket. Or rent the good 1.5-hour audioguide (€8 if purchased separately on-site, credit cards only, at desk to the right as you enter). There are often scalpers outside the gate selling admission with tours for those who don't have tickets.

Tower Elevators: Elevators on opposite sides of the church take you partway up the towers—one on the Passion Facade, and one on the Nativity Facade. The elevators go up only—to get down, you'll use a tightly wound, narrow staircase.

To ride an elevator, you must buy a Church and Tower combo-ticket. You'll choose the tower you want to visit and reserve an entry time (your entrance to the church will be assigned automatically, usually 15 minutes before your tower time). Towers can close when windy or rainy (if that happens, the tower portion of your ticket will be refunded).

The **Passion Facade elevator** takes you up a touch higher, and the stairs to come down are slightly wider than those descending from the **Nativity Facade elevator.** The facades are not joined, so it isn't possible to cross from one facade to the other, but you can cross a dizzying bridge between towers on the same facade.

BACKGROUND

Gaudí labored on Sagrada Família for 43 years, from 1883 until his death in 1926. Nearly a century on, people continue to toil to bring Gaudí's designs to life. After paying the admission price (becoming a partner in this building project), you will actually feel good. If there's any building on earth I'd like to see, it's the Basílica de la Sagrada Família...finished.

☉ SELF-GUIDED TOUR

• *Before entering the church, start on the far side of the pond in the park that faces the Nativity Facade (east side, where the entry lines for individuals are located). From there, you're back far enough to take in the entire towering facade.*

❶ VIEW OF THE EXTERIOR FROM BEYOND THE POND

Stand and imagine how grand this church will be when completed. The eight 330-foot spires topped with crosses are just a fraction of this mega-church. When finished, it will have 18 spires. Four will stand at each of the three entrances. Rising above those will be four taller towers, dedicated to the four Evangelists. A tower dedicated to Mary (expected to be completed soon) rises still higher—400 feet. And in the very center of the complex will stand the grand 560-foot Jesus tower, topped with a cross that will shine like a spiritual lighthouse, visible even from out at sea.

The Nativity Facade—where tourists enter today—is only a side entrance to the church. The grand main entry will be around to the left. To accommodate the church's planned entrance esplanade, a nine-story apartment building will have to be torn down. (This is an ongoing controversy as authorities negotiate with landowners.)

The three facades—Nativity, Passion, and Glory—will chronicle Christ's life from birth to death to resurrection. Inside and out, a goal of the church is to bring the lessons of the Bible to the world. Despite his boldly modern architectural vision, Gaudí was fundamentally traditional and deeply religious. He designed the Sagrada Família to be a bastion of solid Christian values in the midst of what was a humble workers' colony in a fast-changing city. When Gaudí died, the only section that had been completed was the Nativity Facade (with its themes of birth and new life). Notice the dove-covered Tree of Life on top, with playful little creatures carved into nooks and crannies throughout, and a white pelican at the bottom. Because it was believed that this noble bird would feed its young with its own blood, the pelican was a common symbol in the Middle Ages for the self-sacrifice of Jesus.

The Nativity Facade's four spires are dedicated to apostles, and they repeatedly bear the word "sanctus," or holy. Their colorful ceramic caps symbolize the miters (formal hats) of bishops. The shorter spires (to the left) symbolize the Eucharist (communion), alternating between a chalice with grapes and a communion host with wheat.

The rest of the church, while inspired by Gaudí's long-range vision, has been designed and executed by others. This artistic freedom was amplified in 1936, when civil war shelling burned many of Gaudí's blueprints. Supporters of the ongoing work insist that Gaudí, who enjoyed saying, "My client [God] is not in a hurry," knew he wouldn't live to complete the church and recognized that later architects and artists would rely on their own muses for inspiration.

• Now move up to the viewing plaza in front of the Nativity Facade. Check out the small **bronze model** of how the church might look when completed. Then stand as far back as you can to take it all in.

❷ NATIVITY FACADE

This is the only part of the church essentially finished in Gaudí's lifetime (although the architect had intended for this facade to be painted). The four spires decorated with his naturalistic sculpture mark this facade as unmistakably part of his original design. Mixing Gothic-era symbolism, images from nature, and Modernista asymmetry, the Nativity Facade is the best example of Gaudí's original vision, and it established the template for future architects. Cleverly, this attractive facade was built and finished first to bring in financial support for the project.

The theme of the facade, which faces the rising sun, is Christ's birth. A statue above the doorway shows Mary, Joseph, and Baby Jesus in the manger, while a curious cow and donkey peek in. It's the Holy Family—or "Sagrada Família" (literally "sacred family")—to whom this church is dedicated. Flanking the doorway are the three Magi and adoring shepherds.

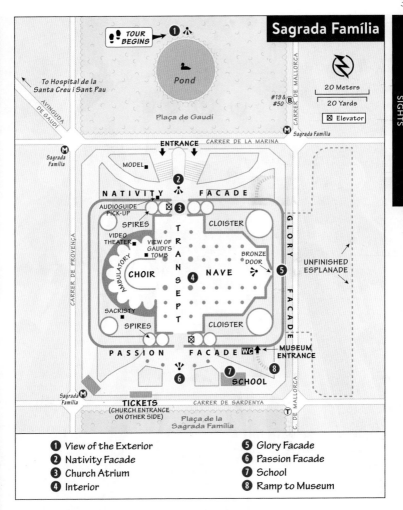

Sagrada Família

To Hospital de la
Santa Creu i Sant Pau

Pond

Plaça de Gaudí

20 Meters

20 Yards

⊠ Elevator

ENTRANCE CARRER DE LA MARINA

MODEL■

N A T I V I T Y **F A C A D E**

AUDIOGUIDE
PICK-UP

SPIRES **CLOISTER**

VIDEO
THEATER■ VIEW OF
GAUDI'S
TOMB■

CHOIR **N A V E** BRONZE
DOOR

AMBULATORY

SACRISTY

SPIRES **CLOISTER**

P A S S I O N **F A C A D E** **WC** MUSEUM
ENTRANCE

SCHOOL

TRANSEPT

GLORY FACADE

UNFINISHED
ESPLANADE

Sagrada
Família

CARRER DE PROVENÇA

CARRER DE MALLORCA

C. DE MALLORCA

TICKETS
(CHURCH ENTRANCE
ON OTHER SIDE)

CARRER DE SARDENYA

Plaça de la
Sagrada Família

1 View of the Exterior
2 Nativity Facade
3 Church Atrium
4 Interior

5 Glory Facade
6 Passion Facade
7 School
8 Ramp to Museum

Other statues at this height show Jesus as a young carpenter (right), the Holy Family fleeing to Egypt (left), and angels playing musical instruments. Much higher up, in the arched niche, Jesus crowns Mary triumphantly.

The doors in the middle of the facade (covered with small colorful bugs and leaves) were designed by head sculptor Etsuro Sotoo. Born in Japan, Sotoo visited Barcelona for the first time in 1978 and fell in love with the project. He worked hard to become a part of it and even converted to Catholicism.

• Now join the line and enter the **3** *church atrium (within your allotted window of time). If you purchased a tower ticket, a guard will direct you to your elevator. If you purchased an audioguide (or would like to rent one now), go to that desk (on the right). Continue to the center of the church, near the altar, to survey the magnificent...*

4 INTERIOR

Typical of even the most traditional Catalan and Spanish churches, the floor plan is in the shape of a Latin cross, 300 feet long

Sagrada Família nave

Nativity Facade detail

phony of colored light to encourage a contemplative mood.

At the center of the church stand four main columns, each marked with an Evangelist's symbol and name in Catalan: angel (Mateu), lion (Marc), bull (Luc), and eagle (Joan). These columns support a ceiling vault that's 200 feet high—and eventually will also support the central steeple (the Jesus tower with the shining cross).

The Holy Family is looking down from on high: Jesus is above the altar, Mary is in the left transept, and Joseph in the right transept.

Behind the high altar, peer down to see a surprisingly traditional space—the 19th-century Neo-Gothic building that Gaudí was originally hired to finish (talk about mission creep!). Today this is a **crypt** holding the tomb of Gaudí himself. A few steps away are two small theaters in adjacent side chapels. One shows a short **video** about the architect and his work.

• *Walk through the forest of massive columns to the opposite end of the church. The view from here is best for appreciating the majesty of the building's interior. (A big mirror is placed here to make admiring the ceiling easier.) Suspended high above the nave, the U-shaped* **choir** *can seat a thousand singers, who will eventually be backed by four organs. Doors here will one day open to the...*

❺ GLORY FACADE

While you can't go out what will one day be the main entrance, you can study a life-size image of the **bronze door** intended for this spot, emblazoned with the Lord's Prayer in Catalan and surrounded by "Give us this day our daily bread" in 50 languages. If you were able to exit through the actual door, you'd be face-to-face with drab, doomed apartment blocks. In the 1950s, the mayor of Barcelona, figuring this day would never really come, sold the land destined for the church project. Now the city must buy back these buildings in order to complete Gaudí's vision of a grand esplanade leading to this main entry. Four towers will rise.

and 200 feet wide. Ultimately, the church will accommodate 8,000 worshippers. The crisscross arches of the ceiling (the vaults) show off Gaudí's distinctive engineering. The church's roof and flooring were only completed in 2010—just in time for Pope Benedict XVI to arrive and consecrate the church.

Part of Gaudí's religious vision was a love for nature. He said, "Nothing is invented; it's written in nature." Like the trunks of trees, these **columns** (56 in all) blossom with life, complete with branches, leaves, and knot-like capitals. The columns vary in color and material—brown clay, gray granite, dark gray basalt.

Light filtering through the stained-glass **windows** has the dappled effect of a rainforest canopy. Notice how splashes of color breathe even more life into this amazing space. The morning light shines in through blues, greens, and other cool colors, whereas the evening light glows through reds, oranges, and warm tones. Gaudí envisioned an awe-inspiring sym-

The facade's sculpture will represent how the soul passes through death, faces the Last Judgment, avoids the pitfalls of hell, and finds its way to eternal glory with God.

• *Head back up the nave, and exit through the left transept. To the left, notice the second* **elevator** *up to the towers. Before exiting, look down at the fine porphyry floor with scenes of Jesus' entry into Jerusalem. To the right, stroll through the* **sacristy,** *where you will find benches, candelabras, and sacristy furniture designed by Gaudí. Now head outside and down the ramp. Step away to take in the...*

❻ PASSION FACADE

Judge for yourself how well Gaudí's original vision has been carried out by later artists. The Passion Facade's four spires were designed by Gaudí and completed (quite faithfully) in 1976. But the lower part was only inspired by Gaudí's designs. The sculptures intended for this facade were interpreted freely and sternly (also controversially) by Josep Maria Subirachs (1927-2014), who completed the work in 2005.

Subirachs tells the story of Christ's torture and execution. The various scenes—Last Supper, betrayal, whipping, and so on—zigzag up from bottom to top, culminating in Christ's crucifixion over the doorway. The style is severe and unadorned, quite different from Gaudí's signature naturalism. But the bone-like archways are closely based on Gaudí's original designs. And Gaudí had made it clear that this facade should be grim and terrifying.

• *Now head into the small building outside the Passion Facade. This is the...*

❼ SCHOOL

Gaudí erected this school for the children of the workers building the church. Today, it displays a replica classroom and old photos of school activities during Gaudí's time.

• *Back outside, head down the ramp, where you'll find WCs and the entrance to the...*

❽ MUSEUM

Housed in what will someday function as the church crypt, the museum takes you through the past, present, and future of Sagrada Família's development.

Upon entering, you'll see **photos** (including one of the master himself) and a **timeline** illustrating how construction work has progressed from Gaudí's day to now. Before turning into the main hall, find **three different visions** for this church.

As you wander, notice how the **plaster models,** used for the church's construction, don't always match the finished product—these are ideas, not blueprints. The Passion Facade model shows Gaudí's original vision, with which Subirachs tinkered freely (see "Passion Facade," earlier). The models also make clear the influence of nature. The columns seem light, with branches springing forth and capitals that look like palm trees.

Exploring further, you'll find a small theater showing a worthwhile 11-minute movie; the Neo-Gothic 19th-cen-

Sagrada Família Passion facade

tury crypt where Gaudí is buried—look (steeply) down at his tomb; the actual workshop where artists employ the latest technology (such as 3-D printing) to test ideas; and an intriguing "Hanging Model" for Gaudí's unfinished Church of Colònia Güell (in a suburb of Barcelona).

Beyond the Eixample
▲▲PARK GÜELL

Designed as an upscale housing develop-ment for early-20th-century urbanites, this park is home to some of Barcelona's most famous symbols, including a dragon guard-ing a whimsical staircase and a wavy bench bordering a panoramic view terrace sup-ported by a forest of columns. Gaudí used vivid tile fragments to decorate much of his work, creating a playful, pleasing effect.

Much of the park is free, but the part visitors want to see, the **Monumental Zone**—with all the iconic Gaudí features—has an admission fee and timed-entry ticket. Also in the park is the **Gaudí House Museum,** where Gaudí lived for a time—but it's not worth the entry fee for most travelers. Even without its Gaudí connec-tion, Park Güell is simply a fine place to enjoy a break from a busy city, where green space is relatively rare.

Cost: €10 for timed-entry Monumental Zone ticket (buy online), includes shut-tle to park from Alfons X Metro station (see below). It's smart to get a prepaid ticket online—while you can buy a ticket at the park, you'll likely have to wait hours to get in.

Hours: Daily 7:30-20:30 in May-Aug, rest of year 8:00 or 8:30 until sunset.

Information: Tel. 934-091-831, www.parkguell.cat.

Getting There: Park Güell is about 2.5 miles from Plaça de Catalunya. A **taxi** from downtown to the front entrance is about €15. Otherwise, take the **Metro** L4

Park Güell stairway

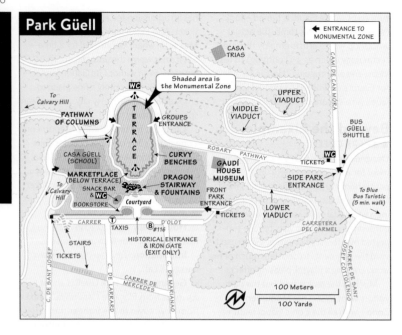

Park Güell

ENTRANCE TO MONUMENTAL ZONE

CASA TRIAS

Shaded area is the Monumental Zone

WC

To Calvary Hill

PATHWAY OF COLUMNS

T E R R A C E

GROUPS ENTRANCE

UPPER VIADUCT

MIDDLE VIADUCT

CAMÍ DE CAN MORA

BUS GÜELL SHUTTLE

CASA GÜELL (SCHOOL)

CURVY BENCHES

ROSARY PATHWAY

WC

TICKETS

MARKETPLACE (BELOW TERRACE)

To Calvary Hill

SNACK BAR & WC

BOOKSTORE

Courtyard

GAUDÍ HOUSE MUSEUM

DRAGON STAIRWAY & FOUNTAINS

FRONT PARK ENTRANCE

SIDE PARK ENTRANCE

To Blue Bus Turístic (5 min. walk)

TICKETS

LOWER VIADUCT

CARRER

TAXIS

D'OLOT

#116

CARRETERA DEL CARMEL

STAIRS

TICKETS

HISTORICAL ENTRANCE & IRON GATE (EXIT ONLY)

C. DE SANT JOSEP

C. DE LARRARD

CARRER DE MERCEDES

C. DE MARIANAO

CARRER DE SANT JOSEP COTTOLENGO

100 Meters

100 Yards

(yellow) line to the Alfons X stop and ride the **Bus Güell shuttle** to the park (allow 15 minutes transit time on shuttle bus). Or, from Plaça de Catalunya, the blue **Bus Turístic** drops you about four blocks from the side Carretera del Carmel entrance.

Getting In: The Monumental Zone has several entrances. The most practical way in for tourists arriving by taxi is on Carrer d'Olot (historical front entrance); the Bus Güell shuttle stops at the Carretera del Carmel side entrance. At either, you'll find a ticket office, WCs, and plenty of park staff to help orient you. Hang on to your ticket; you'll need to show it when you exit.

Overview: Gaudí intended this 30-acre garden to be a high-end community, with 60 upscale residences. Funded by his frequent benefactor Eusebi Güell, he began work on the project in 1900; however, the project stalled in 1914, with the outbreak of World War I, and it never resumed. Only two houses were built, neither designed by Gaudí

(one is now the Gaudí House Museum). Be thankful that the housing development faltered—as a park, this place is a delight. It offers a novel peek into Gaudí's eccentric genius in a setting that's wonderfully in keeping with the naturalism that pervades his work.

Visiting the Park: Enjoy Gaudí's **historical front entrance** (now exit only) with its palm-frond **gate** and gas lamps on either side, made of wrought iron. Gaudí's dad was a blacksmith, and he always enjoyed this medium.

Two Hansel-and-Gretel gingerbread lodges flank this former entrance, signaling to visitors that the park is a magical space. One building houses a bookshop; the other is home to the skippable **La Casa del Guarda,** a branch of the Barcelona History Museum.

Twin staircases curve upward, separated by three fountains stacked between them. The first, at the base of the steps, is rocky and leafy, typical of Gaudí's naturalism. Next is a red and gold Catalan shield, with the head of a serpent poking out. The third fountain is an icon of the park—and of Barcelona: a smiling dragon, slathered in colorful tile. The two grottos flanking the stairs were functional: One was a garage for Eusebi Güell's newfangled automobiles; the other was a cart shelter.

At the top of the dragon stairs, the **marketplace** (Hypostyle Room) was designed to house a produce market for the neighborhood's inhabitants. Eighty-six Doric columns—each lined at the base with white ceramic shards—populate the marketplace and add to its vitality. (Their main job, though, is to hold up the view terrace above.) Shards of white ceramic also cover the multiple domes of the ceiling. The four giant mosaic decorations overhead represent the four seasons.

As you continue up the left-hand staircase, look left, down the playful **Pathway of Columns.** Gaudí drew his inspiration from nature, and this arcade is like a surfer's perfect tube. Both structural and aesthetic, it is one of many clever double-decker **viaducts** that Gaudí designed for the grounds: vehicles up top, pedestrians in the portico down below.

The big pink house flanking the stairs is where Eusebi Güell lived. Now a school, this house predates the park project and was not designed by Gaudí.

At the top of the stairway, the **terrace** (Nature Square) boasts one of Barcelona's best views. (Find the Sagrada Família in the distance.) Functioning as both a seat and a balustrade, the 360-foot-long bench is designed to fit your body just so. As you wander, consider that, as a high-end housing development, Gaudí's project flopped (back then, high-society ladies didn't want to live so far from the cultural action). But a century later, as a park, it's a magnificent success.

Montjuïc

I've listed these sights by altitude, from the hill-topping castle down to the 1929 World Expo Fairgrounds at the base of Montjuïc ("Mount of the Jews"). If you're visiting them all, ride to the top by bus, funicular, or taxi, then visit them in this order so that most of your walking is downhill.

Getting to Montjuïc: You have several choices. The simplest is to take a **taxi** directly to your destination (about €12 from downtown).

Buses also take you up to Montjuïc. From Plaça de Catalunya, bus #55 goes as far as Montjuïc's cable-car station/funicular. If you want to get higher (to the castle), ride the Metro or bus #50 from Plaça de Catalunya to Plaça d'Espanya, then make the easy transfer to bus #150 to ride all the way up the hill. Alternatively, the red Bus Turístic will get you to the Montjuïc sights.

Another option is by **funicular** (covered by Metro ticket, runs every 10 minutes 9:00-22:00). To reach it, take the Metro to the Paral-lel stop, then follow signs for *Parc Montjuïc* and the (mainly underground) funicular icon—you can enter the funicular without using another ticket. (If the funicular is closed, you'll find a shuttle bus.) From the top of the funicular, turn left and walk gently downhill for the Fundació Joan Miró and Catalan Art Museum.

For a scenic (if slow) approach to Montjuïc, you can ride the fun circa-1929 Aeri del Port **cable car** (*telefèric*) from the tip of the Barceloneta peninsula (across the harbor, near the beach) to the Miramar viewpoint park in Montjuïc. The cable car is expensive, loads excruciatingly slowly, and goes between two relatively remote parts of town, so it's only worthwhile for its sweeping views over town or to head back down to Barceloneta at the end of the day, as lines are shorter if you board in Montjuïc (€11 one-way, €16.50 round-trip, 3/hour, daily 11:00-17:30, June-Sept until 20:00, closed in high wind, tel. 934-414-820, www.telefericodebarcelona.com).

If you're only visiting the Catalan Art

Fundació Joan Miró

Museum and/or CaixaForum, you can take the Metro to Plaça d'Espanya and **walk** up (primarily riding handy escalators).

Getting Around Montjuïc: Up top, it's easy and fun to walk between the sights—especially downhill. You can also connect the sights using the red Bus Turístic or one of the public buses: Bus #150 does a loop around the hilltop and is the only bus that goes to the castle; on the way up, it stops at or passes near the CaixaForum, Catalan Art Museum, Fundació Joan Miró, the lower castle cable-car station/top of the funicular, and finally, the castle. On the downhill run, it loops by Avinguda Miramar, the cable-car station for Barceloneta. Bus #55 connects only the funicular/cable-car stations, Fundació Joan Miró, and the Catalan Art Museum.

▲FUNDACIÓ JOAN MIRÓ

This museum has the best collection anywhere of works by Catalan artist Joan Miró (ZHOO-ahn mee-ROH, 1893-1983). The museum displays an overview of Miró's oeuvre (as well as generally excellent temporary exhibits of 20th- and 21st-century artists).

Cost and Hours: €12, 2-for-1 tickets Thu from 18:00; open Tue-Sat 10:00-20:00 (Thu until 21:00), Sun 10:00-15:00, shorter hours in winter, closed Mon year-round; great videoguide-€5; 200 yards from top of funicular, Parc de Montjuïc, tel. 934-439-470, www.fundaciomiro-bcn.org.

▲▲CATALAN ART MUSEUM (MUSEU NACIONAL D'ART DE CATALUNYA)

This wonderful museum showcases Catalan art from the 10th century through the mid-20th century. Often called "the Prado of Romanesque art" (and "MNAC" for short), it holds Europe's best collection of Romanesque frescoes and offers a good sweep of modern Catalan art—fitting, given Catalunya's astonishing contribution to the Modern. It's all housed in the grand Palau Nacional (National Palace), an emblematic building from the 1929 World Expo, with magnificent views over Barcelona, especially from the building's rooftop terrace.

Cost and Hours: €12, free Sat from

Catalan Art Museum

15:00 and first Sun of month; open Tue-Sat 10:00-20:00 (Oct-April until 18:00), Sun 10:00-15:00, closed Mon year-round; worthwhile videoguide-€4; above Magic Fountains near Plaça d'Espanya—take escalators up; tel. 936-220-376, www.museunacional.cat.

Rooftop Terrace: You can visit the rooftop with your museum ticket; rooftop access is €2 without a ticket. To reach the terrace from the main entrance, walk past the bathrooms on the left and show your ticket to get on the elevator. You'll ride up nearly to the viewpoint, and from there hike up a couple of flights of stairs to the terrace. To take an elevator the whole way, go to the far end of the museum, through the huge dome room, to the far-right corner.

Visiting the Museum: As you enter, pick up a map. The left wing is Romanesque, and the right wing is Gothic, Renaissance, and Baroque. Upstairs is more Baroque, plus modern art, photography, coins, and more.

The MNAC's world-class collection of **Romanesque** (Romànic) art came mostly from a handful of Catalan village churches. In **Room 1,** you're greeted by a fresco of Mary painted in a re-created apse of one of the churches. **Room 2** has lively and colorful murals. In **Room 4,** one apse features saints in halos (Peter with his keys alongside Mary with a flaming chalice) and the countess who paid for the painting (lower right). The other apse has winged angels (seraphim) who appear to the prophets Isaiah (lower left) and Ezekiel (right), alongside Ezekiel's vision of the four-wheeled flaming chariot.

Rooms 5-7 focus on one of the most popular images in the medieval world: Christ in Majesty (a.k.a. the Pantocrator, or Ruler of All). Jesus is depicted inside an almond-shaped halo, seated on a throne, with one hand raised in blessing, the other holding an open Bible. He's surrounded by either seraphim or the four symbols of the Evangelists. Christ is always easy to identify—he's the only one with a cross in his halo. Room 7 puts all the Romanesque elements together for a great in situ experience—a replica church, with Christ in Majesty in the apse and other Romanesque themes.

SPAIN

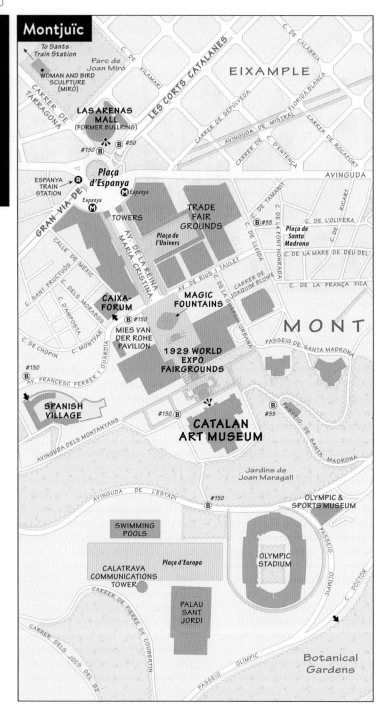

Montjuïc

To Sants
Train Station

Parc de
Joan Miró

WOMAN AND BIRD
SCULPTURE
(MIRÓ)

EIXAMPLE

C. DE VILAMARI

C. DE CALABRIA

LES CORTS CATALANES

CARRER DE TARRAGONA

LAS ARENAS
MALL
(FORMER BULLRING)

CARRER DE SEPULVEDA

FLORIDA BLANCA

CARRER DE C. D'ENTENÇA

AVINGUDA DE MISTRAL

CARRER DE ROCAFORT

#150 ⓑ ⓑ #50

Plaça
d'Espanya

AVINGUDA

ESPANYA
TRAIN
STATION ⓡ

Ⓜ Espanya

Espanya
Ⓜ

GRAN VIA DE

TOWERS

AV. DE LA REINA MARIA CRISTINA

Plaça de
l'Univers

TRADE
FAIR
GROUNDS

C. DE TAMARIT

ⓑ#55

C. DE LA FONT HONRADA

C. DE L'OLIVERA

Plaça de
Santa
Madrona

C. DE LA MARE DE DÉU DEL

C. DE LLEIDA

CALLE DE MEXIC

C. SANT FRUCTUOS

C. DELS MORABOS

C. D'AMPOSTA

CAIXA-
FORUM

ⓑ #150

AV DE RIUS I TAULET

C. DE LA GUARDIA URBANA

MAGIC
FOUNTAINS

CARRER DE JOAQUIM BLUME

C. DE LA FRANÇA XICA

MONT

MIES VAN
DER ROHE
PAVILION

C. DE CHOPIN

C. MONTFAR

1929 WORLD
EXPO
FAIRGROUNDS

PASSEIG DE SANTA MADRONA

#150
ⓑ AV. FRANCESC FERRER I GUÀRDIA

SPANISH
VILLAGE

#150 ⓑ

CATALAN
ART MUSEUM

ⓑ
#55

PASSEIG DE SANTA MADRONA

AVINGUDA DELS MONTANYANS

Jardins de
Joan Maragall

AVINGUDA DE L'ESTADI

ⓑ #150

OLYMPIC &
SPORTS MUSEUM

SWIMMING
POOLS

Plaça d'Europa

OLYMPIC
STADIUM

PASSEIG OLIMPIC

CALATRAVA
COMMUNICATIONS
TOWER

CARRER DE PIERRE DE COUBERTIN

PALAU
SANT
JORDI

C. DE DOCTOR

CARRER DELS JOCS DEL 92

PASSEIG OLIMPIC

Botanical
Gardens

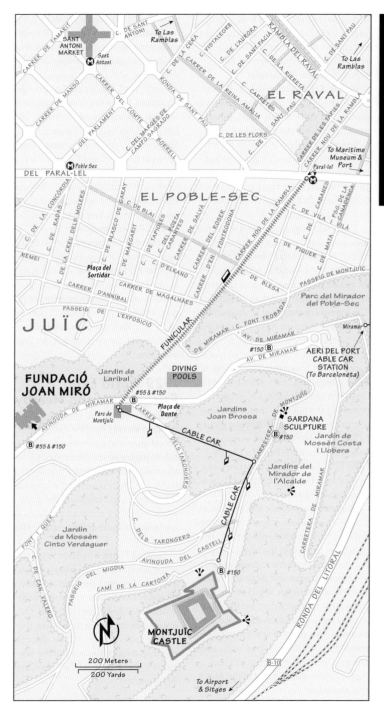

CARRER DE TAMARIT

SANT ANTONI MARKET

C. DE SANT ANTONI

To Las Ramblas

Sant Antoni

C. DE LA CERA

C. VISTALEGRE

C. DE L'AURORA

RAMBLA DEL RAVAL

C. DE SANT PAU

CARRER DE MANSO

CARRER DEL COMTE

C. DEL MARQUÈS DE CAMPO SAGRADO

C. DEL PARLAMENT

RONDA DE SANT PAU

C. DE LA CARRER DE LA REINA AMALIA

C. DE SANT PACIÀ

C. DE LA RIERETA

C. CARRETES

EL RAVAL

To Las Ramblas

C. SANT PAU

CARRER DE LES TÀPIES

CARRER NOU DE LA RAMBLA

BORRELL

C. DE LES FLORS

C. DE

To Maritime Museum & Port

Poble Sec

Paral·lel

DEL PARAL·LEL

EL POBLE-SEC

C. DE LA CONCORDIA

C. DE RADAS

C. DE BLASCO DE GARAY

C. DE BLAI

C. DE MARGARIT

C. DE TAPIOLES

C. DEL POETA CABANYES

CARRER DE SALVÀ

CARRER DEL ROSER

CARRER NOU DE LA RAMBLA

C. DE CABANES

PSG. DE LA CANADENCA

C. DE VILA I VILA

REMEI

C. DE LA CREU DELS MOLERS

C. D'ELKANO

CARRER D'EN FONTRODONA

C. DE PIQUER

C. DE MATA

Plaça del Sortidor

CARRER D'ANNÍBAL

CARRER DE MAGALHÃES

C. DE BLESA

PASSEIG DE MONTJUÏC

PASSEIG DE L'EXPOSICIÓ

JUÏC

FUNICULAR

C. FONT TROBADA

Parc del Mirador del Poble-Sec

P. DE MIRAMAR

AV. DE MIRAMAR

Miramar

#150 B

AV. DE MIRAMAR

AERI DEL PORT CABLE CAR STATION
(To Barceloneta)

FUNDACIÓ JOAN MIRÓ

Jardin de Laribal

DIVING POOLS

AVINGUDA DE MIRAMAR

#55 & #150

B

Plaça de Dante

Jardins Joan Brossa

CARRETERA DE MONTJUÏC

SARDANA SCULPTURE

Parc de Montjuïc

CARRER

CABLE CAR

#150 B

Jardin de Mossèn Costa i Llobera

B #55 & #150

DELS TARONGERS

Jardins del Mirador de l'Alcalde

CABLE CAR

FONT I QUER

Jardin de Mossèn Cinto Verdaguer

C. DELS TARONGERS

CARRETERA DE MIRAMAR

C. DE CAN VALERO

PASSEIG DEL MIGDIA

AVINGUDA DEL CASTELL

B #150

CAMÍ DE LA CARTOIXA

RONDA DEL LITORAL

MONTJUÏC CASTLE

B-10

200 Meters

200 Yards

To Airport & Sitges

Browse through **Rooms 8-16,** seeing leafy column capitals, wooden crucifixes, and statues of Mary and the saints, until you spill back out into the main hall.

• *Cross the hall to the rooms of...*

Gothic Art: Picking up where Romanesque left off (c. 1300), fresco murals give way to vivid 14th-century wood-panel paintings of Bible stories. Make your way to **Room 26** (straight in, then to the left) and find the collection's highlight: a half-dozen paintings by the Catalan master Jaume Huguet (1412-1492), particularly his Consagració de San Agustín (Consecration of Saint Augustine).

These paintings (impressive enough on their own) were once part of a huge altarpiece—an estimated 40 feet tall and 30 feet wide—with some 20 paintings, done for a church in El Born. Huguet labored on the project for more than 20 years. The theme was the life of St. Augustine. It started with the painting of young Augustine (in black robe and red cap) dropping his pagan books to the floor as he realizes the truth and converts to Christianity. In other scenes Augustine wears his golden robes and bishop's hat as he's shown preaching at a pulpit, or disputing a heretic (in green who tumbles to the ground before the power of Augie's words), or kneeling to wash the feet of a pilgrim (who turns out to be Christ in disguise), or greeting a boy (who turns out to be a vision of young Jesus).

Huguet's masterpiece was the *Consecration* scene, where Augustine becomes bishop and is crowned with the hat. The details are incredible: the bright colors and gold leaf, the sober expressive faces, the brocaded robe with pictures of saints, and the early attempt at 3-D created by the floor tiles. Notice that this isn't simply a "painting"—it has a raised surface, like a cameo. It's a sheet of wood topped with molded stucco, then covered with paints and gold leaf. Nearby is Huguet's *Last Supper,* which was also part of the Augustine altarpiece.

• *The Gothic collection leads into...*

Renaissance and Baroque: Browse several rooms, watching as Renaissance artists make altarpieces more balanced and serene, with distant realistic backgrounds. You'll see Spain's Golden Age (Zurbarán, heavy religious scenes, and Spanish royals with their endearing underbites) and examples of Romanticism (dewy-eyed Catalan landscapes). Room 32 has El Greco's *Christ Carrying the Cross* and José de Ribera's saints with wrinkled foreheads. In addition, you'll find minor works by major—if not necessarily Catalan—masters like Velázquez, Goya, Tintoretto, Rubens, and Titian.

Rest of the Museum: The Gothic/Renaissance/Baroque exit spills out by the room of the huge **dome,** which has a cafeteria. From here, you can ride the glass elevator upstairs to the **modern art** section, where a big chronological clockwise circle from Room 1 covers Symbolism, Modernisme, fin de siècle fun, Art Deco, and more.

1929 World Expo Fairgrounds and Nearby

Nearly everything you see here dates from the 1929 World Expo (the exceptions are CaixaForum and Las Arenas mall). The expo's theme was to demonstrate how electricity was about more than light-bulbs: Electricity powered the funicular, the glorious expo fountains, the many pavilion displays, and even the flame atop the fountain marking the center of Plaça d'Espanya.

Getting There: The fairgrounds sprawl at the base of Montjuïc, from the Catalan Art Museum's doorstep to Plaça d'Espanya. It's easiest to see these sights on your way down from Montjuïc. Otherwise, ride the Metro to Espanya, then use the series of stairs and escalators to climb up through the heart of the fairgrounds (eventually reaching the Catalan Art Museum).

▲MAGIC FOUNTAINS (FONT MÀGICA)

Music, colored lights, and huge amounts of water make an artistic and coordinated splash in the evening near Plaça d'Espanya.

Cost and Hours: Free, 20-minute shows start every half-hour; June-Sept Wed-Sun 21:30-22:30, April-May and Oct Thu-Sat 21:00-22:00, winter Thu-Sat 20:00-21:00 (no shows Jan-Feb); from the Espanya Metro stop, walk toward the towering National Palace.

▲CAIXAFORUM

The CaixaForum Social and Cultural Center is housed in one of Barcelona's most important Art Nouveau buildings. In 1911, Josep Puig i Cadafalch (a top architect often overshadowed by Gaudí) designed the Casaramona textile factory, using Modernista design in an industrial rather than a residential context. It functioned as a factory for less than a decade, then later served a long stint as a police station under Franco. Beautifully refurbished in 2002, the facility reopened as a great center for bringing culture and art to the people of Barcelona.

Cost and Hours: Free entrance to building, exhibits-€4, daily 10:00-20:00, Avinguda de Francesc Ferrer i Guàrdia 6, tel. 934-768-600, www.caixaforum.es/barcelona.

Visiting the Center: From the lobby, signs point to *Sala 2, 3, 4,* and *5;* each typically hosts an outstanding temporary exhibition. Ride the escalator to the first floor, which features a modest but interesting exhibit about the history and renovation of the building, including a model and photos. Then head into the appealing red-brick courtyard to access the exhibition halls. The sight features some English descriptions. Take the stairs or elevator up to the Modernista Terrace (*Planta 2,* or look for signs to *Aula 1*). This terrace, boasting a wavy floor and bristling with fanciful brick towers, offers views over the complex and to Montjuïc.

LAS ARENAS (BULLRING MALL)

The grand Neo-Moorish Modernista *plaça de toros* functioned as an arena for bullfights from around 1900 to 1977, and then reopened in 2011 as a mall. The **rooftop terrace,** with stupendous views of Plaça d'Espanya and Montjuïc, is ringed with eateries (reachable by external glass elevator for €1 or from inside escalators/elevators for free). Besides getting a bird's-eye perspective of the fairgrounds, you can gaze down at Parc de Joan Miró, which includes the giant sculpture **Woman and Bird** (*Dona i Ocell*). Miró's sense of humor is evident—if the sculpture seems phallic, keep in mind that the Catalan word for "bird" is also slang for "penis."

Cost and Hours: Free, daily 10:00-22:00, outside elevator and restaurants open until 24:00, Gran Via de les Corts Catalanes 373, Metro: Espanya, exit following Sortida Tarragona signs, www.arenasdebarcelona.com.

The Beaches and Nearby
▲BARCELONA'S BEACHES

Barcelona has created a summer tourist trade by building a huge stretch of beaches east of the town center. From Barceloneta, an uninterrupted band of sand tumbles three miles northeast to the Fòrum.

The overall scene is great for sunbathing and for an evening paseo before dinner. It's like a resort island—complete with lounge chairs, volleyball, showers,

Nova Icària beach

WCs, bike paths, and inviting beach bars called *chiringuitos*. Each beach segment has its own vibe: Sant Sebastià (closest, popular with older beachgoers and families), Barceloneta (with many seafood restaurants), Nova Icària (pleasant family beach), and Mar Bella (attracts a younger crowd, clothing-optional).

Getting There: The Barceloneta Metro stop leaves you a long walk from the sand. To get to the beaches without a hike, take the bus. From the Ramblas, bus #59 will get you as far as Barceloneta Park; bus #D20 leaves from the Columbus Monument and follows a similar route. Bus #V15 runs from Plaça de Catalunya to the tip of Barceloneta (near the W Hotel).

Rick's Tip: Biking *is a joy in Citadel Park and along the beachfront. To rent a bike near the beach, try* **Barcelona Rent-A-Bike** *(€6/2 hours, €15/day, shorter hours in winter, Passeig de Joan de Borbó 35, www.barcelonarentabike.com).*

CITADEL PARK (PARC DE LA CIUTADELLA)

In 1888, Barcelona's biggest, greenest park—originally the site of a much-hated military citadel—was transformed for a Universal Exhibition (world's fair). The stately Triumphal Arch at the top of the park, celebrating the removal of the citadel, was built as the main entrance. Inside you'll find wide pathways, plenty of trees and grass, a zoo, a museum of geology, and a castle-like former restaurant for the fair (closed to the public).

Enjoy the ornamental fountain that the young Antoni Gaudí helped design, and consider a jaunt in a rental rowboat on the lake in the center of the park. Check out the tropical Umbracle greenhouse and the Hivernacle winter garden, which has a pleasant café-bar (Mon-Sat 10:00-14:00 & 17:00-20:30, Sun 10:30-14:00, shorter hours off-season).

Cost and Hours: Park-free, daily 10:00 until dusk, north of França train station, Metro: Arc de Triomf, Barceloneta, or Ciutadella/Vila Olímpica.

EXPERIENCES

Shopping

The streets of the Barri Gòtic and El Born are bursting with characteristic hole-in-the-wall shops and delightful neighborhood boutiques, while the Eixample is the upscale "uptown" shopping district. The area around Avinguda del Portal de l'Angel (at the northern edge of the Barri Gòtic) has a number of department and chain stores.

Souvenir Items: In this artistic city, consider picking up prints, books, and posters. Museum gift shops (Picasso Museum and La Pedrera) offer a bonanza of classy souvenirs. Home decor shops sell Euro-housewares unavailable back home. Decorative tile and pottery (popularized by Moderist architects) can be a good keepsake. Foodies might bring back olive oil, wine, spices (such as saffron or sea salts), or *torró* (Catalan nougat). An *espardenya* (or *alpargata* in Spanish) is a soft-canvas, rope-soled shoe (known in the US as an espadrille). For a souvenir of Catalunyan culture, consider a Catalan flag, a dragon of St. Jordi, or a jersey or scarf from the wildly popular Barça soccer team.

Shopping Spots

BARRI GÒTIC

The wide Carrer de la Portaferrissa, between the cathedral and the Ramblas, is lined with mostly international clothing stores (H&M, Mango, etc.). For little local shops, plunge into some lanes just to the south. **Carrer de la Palla** is ideal for antiques. On **Carrer dels Banys Nous,** the sprawling **Oliver** shop sells home decor, women's clothing, and accessories. Directly across the lane, **Artesania Catalunya** is a large market-space run by the

Open-air market in the Barri Gòtic

city, featuring handmade items from Catalan artisans.

Plaça del Pi has worthwhile shops plus local food and crafts markets on many days. On **Carrer de Petritxol,** lined with art galleries and fancy jewelry shops, stop into **Granja La Pallaresa** for *churros con chocolate;* or try **Vicens,** a fancy sweets shop specializing in *torró.* **Carrer Ample** feels local but with little bursts of trendy energy (watch candy being made the old-fashioned way at **Papabubble**). Skinny **Carrer de Bonsuccés,** on the other side of the Ramblas, has fine boutiques.

EL BORN

This area is bohemian-chic, with funky shops, Santa Caterina Market, and unique boutiques. Look for interesting shops in the area around **Carrer del Rec** (boutiques), on **Carrer de l'Esparteria** (off Carrer del Rec), and the streets **between Carrer dels Banys Vells and Carrer de l'Argenteria** (artisan workshops and handmade clothing, accessories, and bags).

THE EIXAMPLE

This ritzy "uptown" district is home to some of the city's top-end shops. In general, you'll find a lot of big international names along **Passeig de Gràcia,** the main boulevard that runs from Plaça de Catalunya to the Gaudí sights—an area fittingly called the "Golden Quarter" (Quadrat d'Or). The "upper end" of Passeig de Gràcia has the fancier shops (Gucci, Luis Vuitton, and so on) while the southern part of the street is relatively "low-end" (Zara, Mango, H&M). One block to the west, **Rambla de Catalunya** holds more local (but still expensive) options: fashion, home decor, jewelry, perfume, and so on. The streets that connect Rambla de Catalunya to Passeig da Gràcia are also home to some fine shops, including some fun kitchen stores.

DEPARTMENT STORES

Plaça de Catalunya has a gigantic **El Corte Inglés** (with a supermarket in the basement and ninth-floor view cafeteria,

Mon-Sat 9:30-21:00, until 22:00 in summer, closed Sun). Across the square is **FNAC**—a French department store that sells electronics, music, books, and tickets for major concerts and events (Mon-Sat 10:00-22:00, closed Sun).

NIGHTLIFE

Barcelona is extremely lively after hours. People head out for dinner at 22:00, then bar-hop or simply wander the streets until well after midnight. Some days it seems that more people are out and about at 2:00 in the morning (party time) than at 2:00 in the afternoon (lunch time). The most "local" thing you can do here after sunset is to explore neighborhood watering holes and find your favorite place to enjoy a glass of wine.

Performing Arts

Barcelona always has a vast array of cultural events. Pick up the TI's free monthly *Time Out BCN Guide* and Visit *Barcelona* (both in English). **Palau de la Virreina,** an arts-and-culture information office, is also helpful (daily 10:00-20:30, Ramblas 99—see the "Ramblas Ramble" map, earlier, tel. 933-161-000, www.lavirreina.bcn.cat).

Tickets are available through venue websites, through TicketMaster or Telen-Trada, or through the box offices in the main El Corte Inglés department store or the giant FNAC electronics store (both on Plaça de Catalunya, extra booking fee), or at the ticket desk in Palau de la Virreina.

The **Palace of Catalan Music** offers everything from symphonic to Catalan folk songs to chamber music to flamenco (€20-150 tickets, purchase online or in person, box office open Mon-Sat 9:30-21:00, Sun 10:00-15:00, Carrer Palau de la Música 4, Metro: Urquinaona, box office tel. 902-442-882).

The **Liceu Opera House** (Gran Teatre del Liceu), right in the heart of the Ramblas, is a pre-Modernista, sumptuous venue for opera, dance, children's theater, and concerts (tickets from €10, buy tickets online up to 1.5 hours before show or in person, Ramblas 51, box office just around the corner at Carrer Sant Pau 1, Metro: Liceu, box office tel. 934-859-913, www.liceubarcelona.cat).

Some of Barcelona's top sights host good-quality concerts. On summer weekends, a classy option is the **"Summer Nights at La Pedrera"** concerts (see page 358). Also try the **Fundació Joan Miró** and **CaixaForum.**

Two famously Spanish types of music—flamenco and Spanish guitar—have little to do with Barcelona or Catalunya, but are performed to keep visitors happy. For **flamenco,** head to **Palau Dalmases** for high-quality performances (€25 includes a drink, daily at 19:30, additional shows Fri-Sun at 21:30, also hosts opera and jazz, Carrer de Montcada 20, tel. 933-100-673, www.palaudalmases.com). **Tarantos** is easy and inexpensive (€15; nightly at 19:30, 20:30, 21:30, and 22:30; Plaça Reial 17, tel. 933-191-789, go to www.masimas.com and click on "Tarantos").

Another option is the pricey (and relatively high-quality) **Tablao Cordobés** (€45 includes a drink, €80 includes mediocre buffet dinner and better seats, 3 performances/day, Ramblas 35, tel. 933-175-711, www.tablaocordobes.com).

For Spanish guitar, try **Church of Santa Maria del Pi** (€23 at the door, €4 less if you buy at least 3 hours ahead or online—look for ticket sellers in front of church and scattered around town, nightly at 21:00, Plaça del Pi 7; at Carrer de Ferran 28; tel. 647-514-513, www.maestrosdelaguitarra.com). The same company also does occasional concerts in the **Palace of Catalan Music** (€39-45). Similar guitar concerts are performed at the **Church of Santa Anna** (tel. 662-698-547, www.spanishguitarbarcelona.es).

After-Hours Hangout Neighborhoods

El Born: Passeig del Born, a broad parklike strip stretching from the Church of Santa Maria del Mar up to the old market hall, is lined with inviting bars and nightspots. Wander the side streets for more options. **Miramelindo** is a favorite for mojitos (Passeig del Born 15). **La Vinya del Senyor** is a fine place for a glass of high-quality wine on the square in front of the Church of Santa Maria del Mar.

Plaça Reial and Nearby: This elegant-feeling square bustles with popular bars and restaurants offering pleasant outdoor tables at inflated prices—perfect for nursing a drink. Try the **Bar Club Ocaña,** at #13 (open nightly, reserve a table online at www.ocana.cat).

Carrer de la Mercè: This Barri Gòtic street near the harbor is lined with salty sailors' pubs and more youthful bars. The next street up, **Carrer Ample,** has a similar scene.

Barceloneta: This broad beach is dotted with *chiringuitos*—shacks selling drinks and snacks, creating a fun, lively scene on a balmy summer evening.

Montjuïc: Take in breathtaking views and the Magic Fountains show.

SLEEPING

Despite being Spain's most expensive city, Barcelona has reasonably priced rooms. Cheap places are more crowded in summer; fancier business-class hotels fill up in winter and may offer discounts on weekends and in summer. When considering relative hotel values, in summer and on weekends you can often get modern comfort in centrally located business-class hotels for about the same price (€130) as you'll pay for ramshackle charm.

Near Plaça de Catalunya

These modern hotels are on big streets within two blocks of Barcelona's exuberant central square, where the Old City meets the Eixample. As business-class hotels, they have hard-to-pin-down prices that fluctuate with demand. In summer and on weekends, supply often far exceeds the demand, and many of these places cut prices. Some of my recommended hotels are on Carrer Pelai, a busy street; for these, request a quieter room in back.

$$$$ Hotel Catalonia Plaça Catalunya has four stars, an elegant old entryway with a modern reception area, splashy public spaces, slick marble and hardwood floors, 150 comfortable rooms, and a garden courtyard with a pool a world away from the big-city noise. It's a bit pricey for the room quality—you're paying for the posh lobby (air-con, elevator, a half-block off Plaça de Catalunya at Carrer de Bergara 11, Metro: Catalunya, tel. 933-015-151, www.hoteles-catalonia.com, catalunya@hoteles-catalonia.es).

$$$$ Hotel Midmost is an oasis a little west of Plaça de Catalunya. It has 56 rooms with luxurious, four-star style; a seaside-lounge-inspired rooftop terrace; and a mini pool to relax (family rooms, air-con, elevator, Carrer de Pelai 14, Metro: Universitat, tel. 935-051-100, www.hotel midmost.com, info@hotelmidmost.com).

$$$ Hotel Ginebra is a modern version of the old-school *pensión,* with 18 rooms in a classic, well-located building at the corner of Plaça de Catalunya (RS%—use code "HGinebra-RickSteves" and print voucher, family rooms, breakfast extra, laundry, air-con, elevator, Rambla de Catalunya 1, Metro: Catalunya, tel. 932-502-017, www.hotelginebra.com.es, info@ barcelonahotelginebra.com, Brits Alfred and Ivon).

$$$ Hotel Reding Croma, on a quiet street a 10-minute walk west of the Ramblas and the Plaça de Catalunya action, is a slick and sleek place renting 44 basic but mod rooms on color-themed floors (RS%, air-con, elevator, Carrer de Gravina 5, Metro: Universitat, tel. 934-121-097, www. hotelreding.com, recepcion@hotelreding. com).

SPAIN

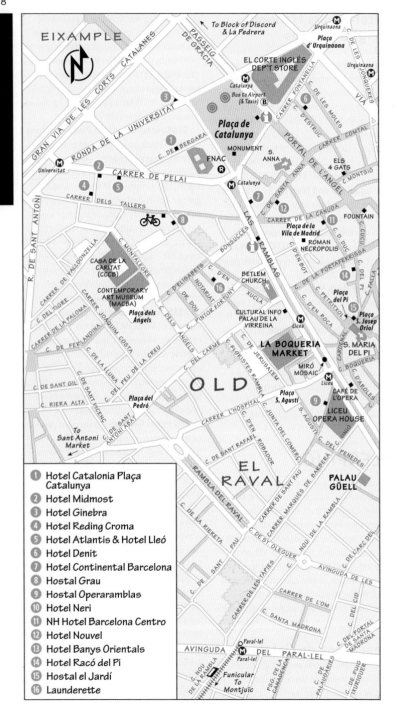

EIXAMPLE

To Block of Discord & La Pedrera

PASSEIG DE GRACIA

Urquinaona

Plaça d'Urquinaona

Urquinaona

GRAN VIA DE LES CORTS CATALANES

EL CORTE INGLÉS DEP'T STORE

Catalunya
Bus to Airport (& Taxis)

CARRER FONTANELLA

CARRER DE LES MOLES

VIA

DE LES JORQUERES

RONDA DE LA UNIVERSITAT

Plaça de Catalunya

PORTAL DE L'ANGEL

C. D'ESTRUC

CARRER COMTAL

C. DE LES CORTS CATALANES

C. DE PERGARA

MONUMENT

FNAC

S. ANNA

ELS 4 GATS

C.MONTSIÓ

Universitat

CARRER DE PELAI

Catalunya

C. DE SANTA ANNA

CARRER DELS TALLERS

CARRER DE LA CANUDA

Plaça de la Vila de Madrid

FOUNTAIN

C. D. DUC

C. DE CUCU

R. DE SANT ANTONI

C. MONTALEGRE

BONSUCCES

ROMAN NECROPOLIS

LAS RAMBLAS

C. D'EN BOT

C. DE LA PORTAFERRISSA

C. DEL PI

C. PALLA

CASA DE LA CARITAT (CCCB)

CONTEMPORARY ART MUSEUM (MACBA)

Plaça dels Àngels

C. DE VALLDONZELLA

C. DE FERLANDINA

CARRER DE LA PALOMA

CARRER JOAQUÍM COSTA

C. D'ELISABETS

NOTARIAT

DR. DOU

C. D'EN

BETLEM CHURCH

XUCLÁ

PINTOR FORTUNY

C. DE PETRITXOL

CARDENAL

Plaça del Pi

C. D'EN ROCA

CULTURAL INFO PALAU DE LA VIRREINA

Liceu

Plaça S. Josep Oriol

S. MARIA DEL PI

CARRER DEL TIGRE

C. DE LA LLUNA

C. DE SANT GIL

C. DE SANT VICENÇ

C. DEL PEU DE LA CREU

C. DELS ÁNGELS

C. DEL CARME

C. FLORISTES RAMBLA

C. DE JERUSALEM

LA BOQUERIA MARKET

C. BOQUERIA

C. DE PAROLES

RIERA ALTA

Plaça del Pedró

MIRÓ MOSAIC

Liceu

CAFÉ DE L'OPERA

To Sant Antoni Market

C. DE SANT ANTONI ABAT

CARRER L'HOSPITAL

C. D'EN RODADOR

C. JUNTA DEL COMERÇ

Plaça S. Agustí

C. AGUSTÍ

C. DEL UNIÓ

LICEU OPERA HOUSE

OLD

CARRER DE SANT RAFAEL

C. DE SANT PAU

C. DEL PENEDÉS

RAMBLA DEL RAVAL

EL RAVAL

C. DE LA RIERETA

C. DE ST. OLEGUER

NOU DE LA RAMBLA

CARRER MARQUÈS DE BARBERA

PALAU GÜELL

C. DE L'ARG DEL

AVINGUDA DE LES

C. DE SANT

CARRER DE LES TÀPIES

C. DEL CID

CARRER DE L'OM

C. SANTA MADRONA

C. DEL PORTAL DE SANTA MADRONA

C. DE PUIG I XURIGUER

AVINGUDA

Paral·lel

DEL PARAL·LEL

PSG. DE LA CABANGA

C. PALAUDÀRIES

C. NOU DE LA RAMBLA

Funicular To Montjuïc

N

1 **Hotel Catalonia Plaça Catalunya**

2 **Hotel Midmost**

3 **Hotel Ginebra**

4 **Hotel Reding Croma**

5 **Hotel Atlantis & Hotel Lleó**

6 **Hotel Denit**

7 **Hotel Continental Barcelona**

8 **Hostal Grau**

9 **Hostal Operaramblas**

10 **Hotel Neri**

11 **NH Hotel Barcelona Centro**

12 **Hotel Nouvel**

13 **Hotel Banys Orientals**

14 **Hotel Racó del Pi**

15 **Hostal el Jardí**

16 **Launderette**

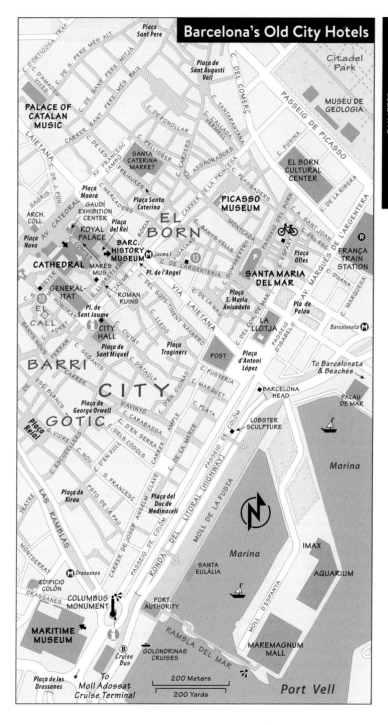

Barcelona's Old City Hotels

Plaça Sant Pere

Plaça de Sant Augustí Vell

C. D'ORTIGOSA TRAF.

C. C. DAMADEU VIVES

C. DE S. PERE MÉS ALT

C. DE SANT PERE MÉS BAIX

C. DE SANT PERE MITJA

C. DEL COMERÇ

PASSEIG DE PICASSO

Citadel Park

MUSEU DE GEOLOGIA

PALACE OF CATALAN MUSIC

CARRER SANT PERE MÉS BAIX

C. DE FONOLLAR

C. L'ALLADA VERMELL

C. TANTARANTANA

C. FUSINA

LAIETANA DE RJ POU

AV. FRANCESC CAMBÓ

C. DE LES

C. MERCADERS

C. PELLISSER

SANTA CATERINA MARKET

C. CANDERS

C. ASSAONADORS

C. FREIXURES

EL BORN CULTURAL CENTER

SAGRIS

ARCH. COLL.

Plaça Maura

GAUDÍ EXHIBITION CENTER

Plaça Santa Caterina

CARRER DE LA PRINCESA

C. FLASSADERS

C. DE LA RIBERA

AV. CATEDRAL

ROYAL PALACE

Plaça del Rei

BORIA

EL BORN

PICASSO MUSEUM

C. MONTCADA

PASSEIG DEL BORN

C. A. SANT JOAN

C. DEL REC

AV. MARQUES DE L'ARGENTERA

Plaça Nova

BARC. HISTORY MUSEUM

C. LLIGANES

C. BANYS VELLS

C. SOMBRERERS

C. ESPART

Plaça Olles

FRANÇA TRAIN STATION

CATHEDRAL

MARÈS MUS.

Jaume I

Pl. de l'Angel

C. DE L'ARGENTERIA

SANTA MARIA DEL MAR

C. DUANA

C. MARQUESA

GENERAL-ITAT

ROMAN RUINS

C. JAUME I

VIA LAIETANA

Plaça S. Maria Anisadeta

Pla de Palau

Barceloneta

EL CALL

C. S. SEVER

C. HONORAT

C. LLIBRETERI

C. DE LA NAU

AV. CONT DE MAR

LA LLOTJA

PASSEIG D'ISABEL II

Pl. de Sant Jaume

CITY HALL

C. CIUTAT

C. LLEDO

C. DEL SOTSTINENT NAVARRO

BANYS NOUS

C. ADRET

FERRAN

Plaça de Sant Miquel

C. DATAULF

Plaça Traginers

POST

Plaça d'Antoni López

To Barceloneta & Beaches

BARRI

C. GEGANTS

C. D'EN GIGNAS

C. FUSTERIA

BARCELONA HEAD

PALAU DE MAR

C. ESC. BLANCS

CITY

D'AVINYO

C. MARQUET

C. PLATA

PASSEIG DE COLOM

LOBSTER SCULPTURE

Plaça de George Orwell

C. CARABASSA

GÒTIC

Plaça Reial

C. VIDRE

C. NOU

C. D'EN SERRA

C. D'EN RULL

C. DELS CÒDOLS

C. DE LA MERCE

AMPLE

Marina

LAS RAMBLAS

C. ESCUDELLERS

S. FRANCESC

PSTG. DE LA PAU

CLAVE

RONDA DEL LITORAL (HIGHWAY)

MOLL DE LA FUSTA

IMAX

AQUARIUM

MONTSERRAT

Plaça de Xirau

Plaça del Duc de Medinaceli

PASSEIG DE COLOM

CARRER DE JOSEP ANSELM

Marina

SANTA EULÀLIA

MOLL D'ESPANYA

TEATRE

Drassanes

EDIFICIO COLÓN

DRASSANES

COLUMBUS MONUMENT

PORT AUTHORITY

MAREMAGNUM MALL

MARITIME MUSEUM

Plaça de les Drassanes

Cruise Bus

To Moll Adossat Cruise Terminal

GOLONDRINAS CRUISES

RAMBLA DEL MAR

Port Vell

200 Meters

200 Yards

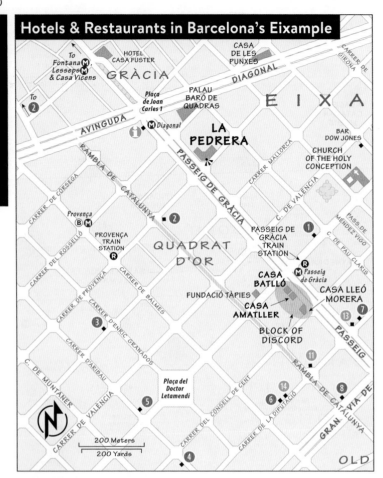

Hotels & Restaurants in Barcelona's Eixample

$$$ Hotel Lleó (YAH-oh) is well-run, with 92 big, bright, and comfortable rooms; a great breakfast room; and a generous lounge (air-con, elevator, small rooftop pool, Carrer de Pelai 22, midway between Metros: Universitat and Catalunya, tel. 933-181-312, www.hotel-lleo.com, info@hotel-lleo.com).

$$ Hotel Atlantis is solid, with 50 big, nondescript, slightly dated rooms and fair prices for the location (includes breakfast, air-con, elevator, Carrer de Pelai 20, midway between Metros: Universitat and Catalunya, tel. 933-189-012, http://hotelatlantis-atbcn.com, inf@hotelatlantis-bcn.com).

$$ Hotel Denit is a small, stylish, 36-room hotel on a pedestrian street two blocks off Plaça de Catalunya. It's chic, minimalist, and fun: Guidebook tips decorate the halls, and the rooms are sized like T-shirts, from small to extra-large (includes breakfast, air-con, elevator, Carrer d'Estruc 24, Metro: Catalunya, tel. 935-454-000, www.denit.com, info@denit.com).

On or near the Ramblas

These places are generally family-run, with ad-lib furnishings, more character, and lower prices.

$$$ Hotel Continental Barcelona, in a building overlooking the top of the

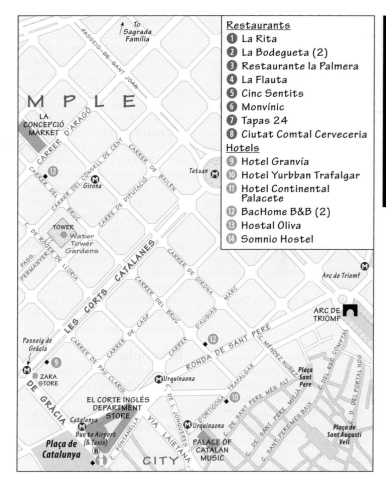

Restaurants
1 La Rita
2 La Bodegueta (2)
3 Restaurante la Palmera
4 La Flauta
5 Cinc Sentits
6 Monvínic
7 Tapas 24
8 Ciutat Comtal Cerveceria

Hotels
9 Hotel Granvía
10 Hotel Yurbban Trafalgar
11 Hotel Continental Palacete
12 BacHome B&B (2)
13 Hostal Oliva
14 Somnio Hostel

Ramblas, offers classic, tiny view-balcony opportunities if you don't mind the noise. Its 40 rooms are quite comfortable and the staff is friendly. Choose between your own little Ramblas-view balcony (where you can eat your breakfast) or a quieter back room. J. M.'s (José María's) free breakfast and all-day snack-and-drink bar are a plus (RS%, air-con, elevator, quiet terrace, Ramblas 138, Metro: Catalunya, tel. 933-012-570, www.hotelcontinental.com, barcelona@hotelcontinental.com).

$$ Hostal Grau is a homey, family-run, and extremely eco-conscious hotel with custom recycled furniture and organic bedding. It has 25 crisp, impeccable, and cheery rooms a few blocks off the Ramblas in the colorful university district. Double-glazed windows keep it quiet (some rooms with balconies, family rooms, strict cancellation policy, air-con, elevator, 200 yards up Carrer dels Tallers from the Ramblas at Ramelleres 27, Metro: Catalunya, tel. 933-018-135, www.hostalgrau.com, bookgreen@hostalgrau.com, Monica).

$$ Hostal Operaramblas, with 68 simple rooms 20 yards off the Ramblas, is clean, modern, and a great value. The street can feel a bit seedy at night, but it's safe, and the hotel is very secure (RS%—

use code "operaramblas," air-con in summer, elevator, Carrer de Sant Pau 20, Metro: Liceu, tel. 933-188-201, www.opera ramblas.com, info@operaramblas.com).

Old City

These accommodations are buried in Barcelona's Old City, mostly in the Barri Gòtic.

$$$$ Hotel Neri is posh, pretentious, and sophisticated, with 22 rooms spliced into the ancient stones of the Barri Gòtic, overlooking an overlooked square (Plaça Sant Felip Neri) a block from the cathedral. It has pricey modern art on the bedroom walls, dressed-up people in its gourmet restaurant, and high-class service (air-con, elevator, rooftop tanning deck, Carrer de Sant Sever 5, Metro: Liceu or Jaume I, tel. 933-040-655, www.hotelneri. com, info@hotelneri.com).

$$$ NH Hotel Barcelona Centro, with 156 rooms and tasteful chain-hotel predictability, is professional yet friendly, buried in the Barri Gòtic just three blocks off the Ramblas (air-con, elevator, Carrer del Duc 15, Metro: Catalunya or Liceu, tel. 932-703-410, www.nh-hotels.com, nhbarcelonacentro@nh-hotels.com).

$$$ Hotel Nouvel, in an elegant, Victorian-style building on a handy pedestrian street, is less business-oriented and offers more character than the others listed here. It boasts royal lounges and 78 comfy rooms (air-con, elevator, Carrer de Santa Anna 20, Metro: Catalunya, tel. 933-018-274, www. hotelnouvel.com, info@hotelnouvel.com).

$$$ Hotel Banys Orientals, a modern, boutique-type place, has a people-to-people ethic and refreshingly straight prices. Its 43 restful rooms are located in the El Born district on a pedestrianized street between the cathedral and Church of Santa Maria del Mar (air-con, elevator, Carrer de l'Argenteria 37, 50 yards from Metro: Jaume I, tel. 932-688-460, www.hotelbanysorientals.com, reservas@hotelbanysorientals.com).

$$$ Hotel Racó del Pi, part of the H10 hotel chain, is a quality, professional place with generous public spaces and 37 modern, bright, quiet rooms. It's located on a wonderful pedestrian street immersed in the Barri Gòtic (air-con, around the corner from Plaça del Pi at Carrer del Pi 7, three-minute walk from Metro: Liceu, tel. 933-426-190, www.h10hotels.com, h10. raco.delpi@h10hotels.com).

$ Hostal el Jardí offers 40 clean, remodeled rooms on a breezy square. Many of the tight, plain, comfy rooms come with petite balconies (for an extra charge) and enjoy an almost Parisian feel. It's a good deal only if you value the quaint-square-with-Barri-Gòtic ambience—you're definitely paying for the location. Book well in advance, as this family-run place has an avid following (air-con, elevator, some stairs, halfway between Ramblas and cathedral at Plaça Sant Josep Oriol 1, Metro: Liceu, tel. 933-015-900, www.eljardi-barcelona.com, reservations@eljardi-barcelona.com).

Eixample

For an uptown, boulevard-like neighborhood, sleep in the Eixample, a 10-minute walk from the Ramblas action. Most of these places use the Passeig de Gràcia or Catalunya Metro stops. Because these stations are so huge—especially Passeig de Gràcia, which sprawls underground for a few blocks—study the maps posted in the station to establish which exit you want before surfacing.

$$$$ Hotel Granvía, filling a palatial, brightly renovated 1870s mansion, offers a large, peaceful sun patio, several comfortable common areas, and 58 spacious, modern, business-style rooms (RS%—free breakfast with this book, family rooms, air-con, elevator, Gran Via de les Corts Catalanes 642, Metro: Passeig de Gràcia, tel. 933-181-900, www.hotelgranvia.com, hgranvia@nnhotels.com).

$$$$ Hotel Yurbban Trafalgar is a small, classy boutique hotel with 56 rooms and a masculine-minimalist decor. Their rooftop bar, tiny pool, and views alone are worth the price of your stay (air-con, free self-service laundry, gym, near the Palace of Catalan Music at Carrer de Trafalgar 30, a long block from Metro: Urquinaona, tel. 932-680-727, www.yurbban.com, trafalgar@yurbban.com).

$$$ Hotel Continental Palacete, with 22 small rooms, fills a 100-year-old chandeliered mansion. With flowery wallpaper and ornately gilded stucco, it's gaudy in the city of Gaudí, but it's also friendly, quiet, and well-located. Guests have unlimited access to the outdoor terrace and the "cruise-inspired" fruit, veggie, and drink buffet (RS%, includes breakfast, air-con, two blocks northwest of Plaça de Catalunya at corner of Rambla de Catalunya and Carrer de la Diputació, Rambla de Catalunya 30, Metro: Passeig de Gràcia, tel. 934-457-657, www.hotelcontinental.com, palacete@hotelcontinental.com).

$$ BacHome B&B has two bright and comfortable locations in traditional Eixample buildings on Carrer Bruc. BacHome Terrace (at #14) has 10 rooms and a pleasant outdoor terrace. BacHome Gallery (#96) has seven rooms and common areas with big windows looking out onto the city (includes breakfast, air-con, elevator, Metro: Urquinaona, tel. 620-657-810, www.bachomebarcelona.com, reservations@bachomebarcelona.com).

$$ Hostal Oliva, family-run with care, is a spartan, old-school place with 15 basic, bright, high-ceilinged rooms. It's on the fourth floor of a classic old Eixample building—with a beautiful mahogany elevator—in a perfect location, just a couple of blocks above Plaça de Catalunya (corner of Passeig de Gràcia and Carrer de la Diputació, Passeig de Gràcia 32, Metro: Passeig de Gràcia, tel. 934-880-162, www.hostaloliva.com, info@hostaloliva.com).

Hostels

¢ Somnio Hostel, a smaller place, has nine simple rooms (RS%, cheaper rooms with shared bath, private rooms available, air-con, Carrer de la Diputació 251, second floor, Metro: Passeig de Gràcia, tel. 932-725-308, www.somniohostels.com, info@somniohostels.com). They have a second location that's five blocks farther out.

EATING

Barcelona, the capital of Catalan cuisine, offers a tremendous variety of colorful places to eat, ranging from workaday eateries to homey Catalan bistros (cans), crowded tapas bars, and avant-garde restaurants.

Basque-style tapas places are popular and user-friendly. Just grab what looks good, order a drink, and save your toothpicks (they'll count them up at the end to tally your bill). I've listed several of these bars (including Taverna Basca Irati and Sagardi Euskal Taberna), but there are many others. Look for basca or euskal (both mean "Basque").

Budget Meals: Sandwich shops serve made-to-order bocadillos. Choose between bright (mass-produced) chains such as **Bocatta** and **Pans & Company,** or colorful hole-in-the-wall spots. **Mucci's Pizza** has good, fresh pizza slices and empanadas (just off the Ramblas, at Bonsuccés 10 and Tallers 75). **Wok to Walk** has takeaway noodle and rice dishes (branches near Plaça de Sant Jaume and Liceu Metro station). **Buenas Migas** serves quiche, salads, and pastas (locations at Baixada de Santa Clara 2, Plaça de la Sagrada Família 17, and Plaça del Bonsuccés 6). Kebab places are another standby for quick and tasty meals. For a fast, affordable lunch with a view, the ninth-floor cafeteria at **El Corte Inglés department store** on Plaça de Catalunya can't be beat. Picnickers can buy groceries at the basement supermarket in El Corte Inglés, or at **La Boqueria Market** on the Ramblas.

SPAIN

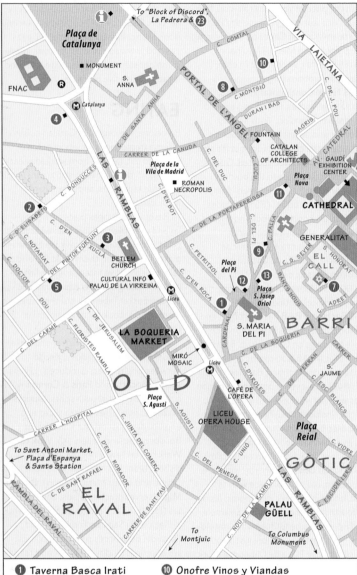

1 Taverna Basca Irati
2 Restaurant Elisabets
3 Café Granja Viader
4 Restaurante Nuria
5 Biocenter
6 Café de l'Academia
7 La Vinateria del Call
8 Els Quatre Gats
9 Xaloc
10 Onofre Vinos y Viandas
11 Bilbao Berria Pintxos & Tapas
12 Bar del Pi
13 El Drac de Sant Jordi
14 Carrer de la Mercè Tapas Bars
15 Sagardi Euskal Taberna
16 Vegetalia Vegetarian Restaurant
17 El Senyor Parellada

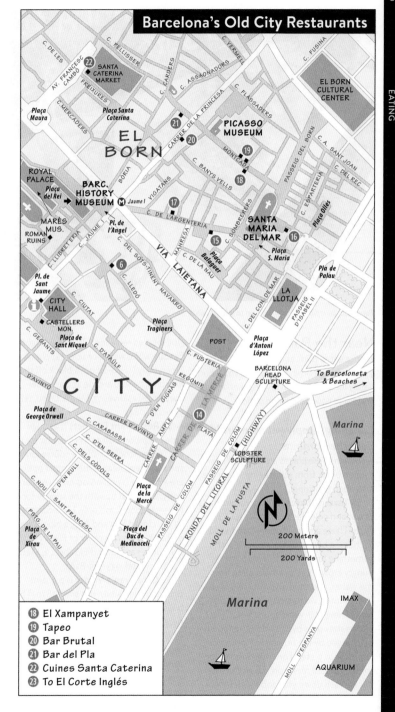

Barcelona's Old City Restaurants

18 El Xampanyet
19 Tapeo
20 Bar Brutal
21 Bar del Pla
22 Cuines Santa Caterina
23 To El Corte Inglés

Tapas can be a fun snack or add up to a light meal.

Near the Ramblas

Do not eat or drink at the tourist traps on the Ramblas. Within a few steps, you'll find handy lunch places, an inviting market hall, and some good vegetarian options.

Lunching Simply yet Memorably near the Ramblas

Although these places are enjoyable for a lunch break from sightseeing, many are also open for dinner.

$$ Taverna Basca Irati serves 40 kinds of hot and cold Basque *pintxos* for €2 each. These are small open-faced sandwiches—a baguette slice topped with something tasty. Muscle in through the hungry crowd, get an empty plate from the waiter, and then help yourself. Every few minutes, waiters circulate with platters of new, still-warm munchies. Grab one as they pass by...it's addictive (you'll be charged by the number of toothpicks left on your plate). For drink options, look for the printed menu on the wall in the back. Wash down your food with Rioja

(full-bodied red wine), Txakolí (sprightly Basque white wine), or *sidra* (apple wine). Open daily (11:00-24:00, a block off the Ramblas, behind arcade at Carrer del Cardenal Casanyes 17, Metro: Liceu, tel. 933-023-084).

$$ Restaurant Elisabets is a rough little neighborhood eatery popular for its €12 "home-cooked" three-course lunch special; even cheaper *menú rapid* options are available (13:00-16:00 only). Apparently, locals put up with the service for the tasty food (cash only, Mon-Sat 7:30-23:00, closed Sun and Aug, 2 blocks west of Ramblas on far corner of Plaça del Bonsuccés at Carrer d'Elisabets 2, Metro: Catalunya, tel. 933-175-826).

$$ Café Granja Viader is a quaint time capsule, family-run since 1870. They boast about being the first dairy business to bottle and distribute milk in Spain. This feminine-feeling place—specializing in baked and dairy treats, toasted sandwiches, and light meals—is ideal for a traditional breakfast. Or indulge your sweet tooth: Try a glass of *orxata* (or

Catalan Cuisine

Like its culture and language, Catalan food is a fusion of styles and influences. Cod, hake, tuna, squid, and anchovies appear on many menus, and you'll see Catalan favorites such as *fideuà,* a thin, flavor-infused noodle served with seafood—a kind of Catalan paella—and *arròs negre,* black rice cooked in squid ink. **Pa amb tomàquet** is the classic Catalan way to eat your bread—toasted white bread with olive oil, tomato, and a pinch of salt. It's often served with tapas and used to make sandwiches. As everywhere in Spain, Catalan cooks love garlic and olive oil—many dishes are soaked in both.

Catalan cuisine can be heavy for Americans more accustomed to salads, fruits, and grains. A few perfectly good vegetarian and lighter options exist, but you'll have to seek them out. The secret to getting your veggies at restaurants is to order two courses, because the first course generally has a green option. Resist the cheese-and-ham appetizers and instead choose first-course menu items such as creamed vegetable soup, *parrillada de verduras* (sautéed vegetables), or **ensalada mixta.** (Spaniards rarely eat only a salad, so salads tend to be small and simple—just iceberg lettuce, tomatoes, and maybe olives and tuna.)

While the famous cured *jamón* (ham) is not as typically Catalan as it is Spanish, you'll still find lots of it in Catalunya. Another popular Spanish dish is the empanada—a pastry turnover filled with seasoned meat and vegetables. The cheapest meal is a simple **bocadillo de jamón** (ham sandwich on a baguette), sold virtually everywhere.

horchata—*chufa*-nut milk, summer only), *llet mallorquina* (Majorca-style milk with cinnamon, lemon, and sugar), *crema catalana* (crème brûlée, their specialty), or *suis* ("Swiss"—hot chocolate with a snow-cap of whipped cream). *Mel i mató* is fresh cheese with honey...very Catalan (Mon-Sat 9:00-13:00 & 17:00-21:00, closed Sun, a block off the Ramblas behind Betlem Church at Xuclà 4, Metro: Liceu, tel. 933-183-486).

$$ Restaurante Nuria is a big, venerable standby that's been overlooking all the Ramblas action since 1926. It's a low-stress, hardworking place with a menu designed to please tourists: pizza, burgers, paellas, and salads (daily 24/7, Rambla de Canaletes 133, tel. 933-023-847). They have a fancier place upstairs.

$$ Biocenter, a Catalan soup-and-salad restaurant busy with local vegetarians, takes its cooking very seriously and feels

a bit more like a real restaurant than most (weekday lunch specials include soup or salad and plate of the day, Mon-Sat 13:00-23:00, Sun until 16:00, two blocks off the Ramblas at Carrer del Pintor Fortuny 25, Metro: Liceu, tel. 933-014-583).

La Boqueria Market: If you're in La Boqueria and ready for lunch, a snack, or a drink, there are several high-energy bars that would love to take your money. The Pinotxo Bar (just to the right as you enter) has a waiter beloved for his smile and his double thumbs up.

Barri Gòtic

$$$ Café de l'Academia is a delightful place on a pretty square tucked away in the heart of the Barri Gòtic—but patronized mainly by the neighbors. They serve refined cuisine with Catalan roots, using what's fresh from the market. The candlelit, air-conditioned interior is rustic yet elegant, with soft jazz, flowers, and modern art. And if you want to eat outdoors on a convivial, mellow square...this is the place. Reservations are a must, though if you show up without one, try asking to sit at the bar (lunch specials, open Mon-Fri 13:00-15:30 & 20:00-23:00, closed Sat-Sun, near the City Hall square, off Carrer de Jaume I up Carrer de la Dagueria at Carrer dels Lledó 1, Metro: Jaume I, tel. 933-198-253).

$$$ La Vinateria del Call, buried deep in the Jewish Quarter, is one of the oldest wine bars in town. It offers a romantic restaurant-style meal of tapas with fine local wines. Eating at the small bar by the entrance is discouraged, so I'd settle in at a candlelit table. They have more than 100 well-priced wines, including a decent selection of Catalan wines at €2.50 a glass. Three or four plates of their classic tapas will fill two people (daily 19:30-24:00; with back to church, leave Plaça de Sant Felip Neri and walk two short blocks to Carrer de Salomó Ben Adret 9; Metro: Jaume I, tel. 933-026-092).

$$$ Els Quatre Gats ("The Four Cats") was once the haunt of the Modernista greats—including a teenaged Picasso, and architect Josep Puig i Cadafalch, who designed the building. You can snack or drink at the bar, or go into the back for a sit-down meal after 19:00. While touristy (less so later), the food and service are good, and the prices aren't as high as you might guess (weekday lunch specials, daily 9:00-24:00, just steps off Avinguda del Portal de l'Angel at Carrer de Montsió 3, Metro: Catalunya, tel. 933-024-140).

$$$ Xaloc is a good place in the old center for nicely presented gourmet tapas. It has a woody, modern, relaxed, and spacious dining room with a fun energy, attentive service, and reasonable prices. The walls are covered with *ibérico* hamhocks and wine bottles. They focus on home-style Catalan classics—and though the food here doesn't impress locals, tourists find the place comfortable.

A bowl of gazpacho, plate of ham, *pa amb tomàquet* (comes free), and nice glass of wine make a fine light meal (daily, 13:00-17:00 & 19:00-23:00, a block toward the cathedral from Plaça de Sant Josep Oriol at Carrer de la Palla 13, Metro: Catalunya, tel. 933-011-990).

$$$ Onofre Vinos y Viandas, owned and run by Marisol and Ángel, is a tiny wine bar (20 wines by the glass) with a few simple tables behind walls of wine bottles. Foodie but without pretense, it has few tourists and a fun, creative, accessible menu—be adventurous and try the brandy foie shavings. For a gastronomic treat highlighting house favorites and seasonal specials, you can trust your hosts and order the €40-per-person "Marisol Extravaganza" (daily 10:00-16:30 & 19:30-24:00, near the Palace of Catalan Music, Carrer de les Magdalenes 19, tel. 933-176-937).

$$ Bilbao Berria Pintxos and Tapas is a hardworking tapas bar, like its Basque sisters around town. It faces the cathedral, with tables outside on the square (15 percent surcharge to sit there), and sells little open-faced sandwiches and fun bites for €2 per toothpick. Grab a plate and pick what you want, buffet-style (Plaça Nova 3, tel. 933-170-124).

On Plaça de Sant Josep Oriol: To enjoy the most inviting square in the Gothic Quarter with a meal, consider these simple eateries, both with a few tables on the square: **$$ Bar del Pi** is a hardworking bar serving salads, sandwiches, and tapas (daily 9:00-23:00). **$ El Drac de Sant Jordi** has a fun budget formula—€10 for any four tapas, a drink, and a tiny dessert (daily 12:00-22:00).

Tapas on Carrer de la Mercè

This area lets you experience a rare, unvarnished bit of old Barcelona with great tascas—colorful local tapas bars. The neighborhood's dark, the regulars are rough-edged, and you'll get a glimpse of a crusty Barcelona from before the affluence hit. Try **$ Bar Celta** (marked la pulpería, at #9); **$ La Plata** (#28); and **$ Cerveceria Vendimia,** at the north end of Carrer de la Mercè (#46).

El Born

El Born sparkles with eclectic and trendy as well as subdued and classy little restaurants hidden in the small lanes surrounding the Church of Santa Maria del Mar. Consider starting off your evening with a glass of fine wine at one of the *enotecas* on the square facing the church (such as La Vinya del Senyor). Many restaurants and shops in this area are, like the Picasso Museum, closed on Mondays. For all of these eateries, use Metro: Jaume I.

$$ Sagardi Euskal Taberna offers an array of Basque goodies—tempting *pintxos* and *montaditos* (small open-faced sandwiches) at €2 each—along its huge bar. Ask for a plate and just take whatever looks good. You can sit on the square with your plunder for about 20 percent extra. Wash it down with Txakolí, a Basque white wine poured from the spout of a huge wooden barrel into a glass as you watch. Study the two price lists— bar and terrace—posted at the bar (daily 12:00–24:00, Carrer de l'Argenteria 62, tel. 933-199-993).

$$ Vegetalia Vegetarian Restaurant, facing the Monument of Catalan Independence and the Church of Santa Maria del Mar, is a basic vegetarian diner with a cheery, healthy-feeling interior (good three-course lunch special, daily from 11:00, tel. 930-177-256).

$$$ El Senyor Parellada, filling a former cloister, is an elegant restaurant with a smart, tourist-friendly waitstaff. It serves a fun menu of Mediterranean and Catalan cuisine with a modern twist, all in a classy chandeliers-and-white-tablecloths setting (daily 13:00–15:45 & 20:30–23:30, Carrer de l'Argenteria 37, 100 yards from Jaume I Metro stop, tel. 933-105-094).

$$ El Xampanyet ("The Little Champagne Bar"), a colorful family-run bar with a fun-loving staff (Juan Carlos, his mom, and the man who may be his father). It specializes in tapas and anchovies—and their cheap homemade *cava* (Spanish champagne) goes straight to your head. Don't be put off by the seafood from a tin: Catalans like it this way. A *sortido de fumats* (assorted plate of small fish) with *pa amb tomàquet* makes for a fun meal. This place is filled with tourists during the sightseeing day, but it's jam-packed with locals after dark. The scene is great, but—especially during busy times—it's tough without Spanish skills. When I asked about the price, Juan Carlos said, "Who cares? The ATM is just across the street" (same price at bar or table, Tue-Sun 12:00–15:30 & 19:00–23:00, closed Sun evening and Mon, a half-block beyond the Picasso Museum at Carrer de Montcada 22, tel. 933-197-003).

$$ Tapeo is a mod, classy alternative to the funky Xampanyet across the street. It serves high-end tapas at a long, sit-down bar and tiny tables with stools. This small space fills quickly so go early to get a seat (Tue-Sun 12:00–16:00 & 19:00–24:00, closed Mon, Carrer de Montcada 29, tel. 933-101-607).

$$$ Bar Brutal is a creative, fun-loving, and edgy bohemian-chic place with a young, local following. It serves a mix of Spanish and Italian dishes with an emphasis on wines—especially natural wines, with plenty available by the glass (Mon-Sat 13:00–24:00, closed Sun, Carrer de Princesa 14, tel. 932-954-797).

$$$ Bar del Pla is a favorite near the Picasso Museum. This classic diner/bar— overlooking a tiny crossroads next to Barcelona's oldest church—serves traditional Catalan dishes, *raciones,* and tapas. Their *croquetas,* mushrooms with wasabi, and crispy oxtail with foie gras are highlights. They also have a local IPA on tap. Prices are the same at the bar or at a table; eating at the bar puts you in the middle of a great scene (Mon-Sat 12:00–23:00, closed Sun, reservations smart; leaving the Picasso Museum, head right two blocks past Carrer de la Princesa to Carrer de Montcada 2; tel. 932-683-003, www.bardelpla.cat).

At Santa Caterina Market

$$ Cuines Santa Caterina, bright and modern, has shared tables under the open rafters of a modern market hall. There's also a handy tapas bar and fine self-service outdoor seating on the square. Their menu—with vegetarian, international, and Mediterranean dishes, all made from market-fresh and seasonal ingredients—cross-references everything on an innovative grid (outside tables OK for both restaurant and tapas bar, daily 12:30-16:00 & 19:30-23:00, Avinguda de Francesc Cambó 16, tel. 932-689-918, no reservations).

Eixample

The people-packed boulevards of the Eixample are lined with appetizing eateries featuring breezy outdoor seating. Choose between a real restaurant or an upscale tapas bar (for the best variety, walk down Rambla de Catalunya).

Restaurants

$$ La Rita is a fresh and dressy little restaurant serving Catalan and Mediterranean cuisine near the Block of Discord. Their €11 lunch and €16 dinner *menú* specials are a great value. Arrive early...or wait (daily 13:00-15:45 & 20:00-23:00, near corner of Carrer de Pau Claris and Carrer d'Aragó at d'Aragó 279, a block from Metro: Passeig de Gràcia, tel. 934-872-376).

$$ La Bodegueta is an atmospheric below-street-level bodega serving hearty wines, homemade vermouth, *anchoas* (anchovies), tapas, and *flautas*—sandwiches made with flute-thin baguettes. On a nice day, it's great to eat outside, sitting in the median of the boulevard under shady trees. Its three-course lunch special with wine is a deal (Mon-Fri only, 13:00-16:00). A long block from Gaudí's La Pedrera, this makes a fine sightsee-

ing break (Mon-Sat 7:00-24:00, Sun from 18:00, at intersection with Carrer de Provença, Rambla de Catalunya 100, Metro: Provença, tel. 932-154-894). La Bodegueta has another location nearby—similar style and format but more comfortable and spacious (Carrer de Balmes 213).

$$$ Restaurante la Palmera serves a mix of Catalan, Mediterranean, and French cuisine in an elegant room with bottle-lined walls. This untouristy place offers great food, service, and value—for me, a very special meal in Barcelona. They have three zones: the classic main room, a more forgettable adjacent room, and a few outdoor tables. I like the classic room. Reservations are smart (creative €24 six-plate *degustation* lunch—also available at dinner Sun and Tue-Thu, open Mon-Sat 13:00-15:45 & 19:45-23:30, closed Sun, Carrer d'Enric Granados 57, at the corner with Carrer Mallorca, Metro: Provença, tel. 934-532-338, www.lapalmera.cat).

$$ La Flauta fills two floors with enthusiastic eaters (I prefer the ground floor). It's fresh and modern, with a fun, no-stress menu featuring small plates, creative *flauta* sandwiches, and a three-course lunch deal. Consider the list of *tapas del día*. Good wines by the glass are listed on the blackboard, and solo diners get great service at the bar (Mon-Sat 7:00-24:00, closed Sun, upbeat and helpful staff, no reservations, just off Carrer de la Diputació at Carrer d'Aribau 23, Metro: Universitat, tel. 933-237-038).

$$$$ Cinc Sentits ("Five Senses"), with only about 30 seats, is my gourmet recommendation for those who want to dress up and spend more money. At this chic, minimalist, slightly snooty place, all the attention goes to the fine service and beautifully presented dishes. The €55 *formula* lunch *menú* and the *quatre plats* (€90) and *sis plats* (€120) dinner menús are unforgettable extravaganzas. Each comes with a wine-pairing option (€65-70). Expect *menús* only—no à la carte. It's run by Catalans who lived in Canada (so there's no language barrier) and serve avant-garde cuisine inspired by Catalan traditions and ingredients. Reservations are essential (Tue-Sat 13:30-15:00 & 20:30-22:00, closed Sun-Mon, near Carrer d'Aragó at Carrer d'Aribau 58, between Metros: Universitat and Provença, tel. 933-239-490, www.cincsentits.com, maître d' Eric).

$$$$ Monvínic ("World of Wine")—a sleek, trendy wine bar that's evangelical about local wine culture—has an open kitchen, a passion for fine food, and little pretense. Considered one of the top wine bar/restaurants in town, their renowned chef creates Catalan and Mediterranean dishes for enjoying with the wine. Diners can use an iPad to read descriptions of the 50 open bottles. The faces of farmers—the unsung heroes of the food industry—are projected on the wall. Staff don't turn the tables and hope you'll spend the evening, so reserve in advance. For a more casual visit, they have a tapas bar (no reservations) in front where you'll also be empowered by an iPad and wine (Tue-Fri 13:00-23:00, Mon and Sat from 19:00, closed Sun, starters designed to share, creative tapas, lunch specials, Diputació 249, Metro: Passeig de Gràcia, tel. 932-726-187, www.monvinic.com).

Tapas Bars

Many trendy and touristic tapas bars in the Eixample offer a cheery welcome and slam out the appetizers. These two are particularly handy to Plaça de Catalunya and the Passeig de Gràcia artery (closest Metro stops: Catalunya and Passeig de Gràcia).

$$$ Tapas 24 makes eating fun. This local favorite, with a few street tables, fills a spot a few steps below street level with happy energy, funky decor, and good yet pricey tapas. Along with daily specials and fine breakfasts, the menu has all the typical standbys and quirky inventions. The *tapas del día* list is particularly good. The owner, Carles Abellan, is one of Barcelona's hot chefs; although his famous fare

is pricey, you can enjoy it without going broke. Prices are the same whether you dine at the bar, a table, or outside. Come early or wait; no reservations are taken (daily 9:00-24:00, just off Passeig de Gràcia at Carrer de la Diputació 269, tel. 934-880-977).

$$ Ciutat Comtal Cerveceria is an Eixample favorite, full of tourists, with an elegant bar and tables plus good seating out on the Rambla de Catalunya for all that people-watching action. It's packed after 21:00, when you'll likely need to put your name on a list and wait. While it has no restaurant-type menu, the varied list of tapas and *montaditos* is easy, fun, high-quality, and includes daily specials (daily 8:00-24:00, facing the intersection of Gran Via de les Corts Catalanes and Rambla de Catalunya at Rambla de Catalunya 18, tel. 933-181-997).

TRANSPORTATION

Getting Around Barcelona

Barcelona's Metro and bus system is run by **TMB**—Transports Metropolitans de Barcelona (tel. 902-075-027, www.tmb.cat). Ask for TMB's excellent Metro/bus map at the TI, larger stations, or the TMB information counter in the Sants train station.

By Metro

The city's Metro, among Europe's best, connects just about every place you'll visit. A single-ride ticket *(bitllet senzill)* costs €2.40. The **T-Casual** card (€11.35 for 10 rides) is for individual travelers only. The **T-Familiar** card (€10 for 8 rides) is shareable as long as you stay together the entire journey (you'll be fined for riding without a ticket). The Metro to the airport is a separate fare (the Aerobus is more convenient).

Multiride cards show how many trips you've taken, with the time and date of each ride. One "ride" covers you for 1.25 hours of unlimited use on all Metro and local bus lines, as well as local rides on the Renfe and Rodalies de Catalunya train lines (including to the train station) and suburban FGC trains. Transfers made within your 1.25-hour limit are not counted as a new ride, but you must revalidate your card when you transfer.

Multiday **"Hola BCN!"** travel cards are also available (€16.30/2 days, €23.70/3 days, €30.80/4 days, €38/5 days).

Buy tickets from machines in the Metro station. They're easy—just press "English" to start. They'll give you the whole array of tickets you can buy. Most machines accept coins, bills, and credit/debit cards.

Barcelona has several color-coded Metro lines. Most useful for tourists is the **L3 (green)** line. Handy city-center stops on this line include (in order):

Sants Estació: Main train station

Espanya: Plaça d'Espanya, with access to the lower part of Montjuïc and trains to Montserrat

Paral·lel: Funicular to the top of Montjuïc

Drassanes: Bottom of the Ramblas, near Maritime Museum and Maremagnum mall

Liceu: Middle of the Ramblas, near the heart of the Barri Gòtic and cathedral

Plaça de Catalunya: Top of the Ramblas and main square with TI, airport bus, and lots of transportation connections

Passeig de Gràcia: Classy Eixample street at the Block of Discord; also connection to L2 (purple) line to Sagrada Família and L4 (yellow) line (described below)

Diagonal: Gaudí's La Pedrera

The **L4 (yellow)** line, which crosses the L3 (green) line at Passeig de Gràcia, has a few helpful stops, including **Alfons X** (free shuttle to Park Güell), **Jaume I** (between the Barri Gòtic/cathedral and El Born/Picasso Museum), and **Barceloneta** (at the south end of El Born, near the harbor action).

By Bus

Given the excellent Metro service, it's unlikely you'll spend much time on **local buses** (also €2.20, covered by multiride cards;, insert ticket in machine behind driver). However, buses are useful for connecting the sights on Montjuïc and for getting to the beach. For information on **hop-on, hop-off bus tours,** see page 325.

By Taxi

Barcelona is one of Europe's best taxi towns. Taxis are plentiful and honest, and cab rates are reasonable (€2.10 drop charge, about €1/kilometer, figure €10 from Ramblas to Sants station; slightly more expensive *"Tarif 2"* rates are in effect weekdays 20:00-8:00 as well as holidays, *"Tarif 3"* rates apply on weekend evenings 20:00-6:00, surcharges for large suitcases, Sants train station, airport or cruise port, other fees posted in window).

Arriving and Departing
By Plane

Most flights use Barcelona's **Josep Tarradellas Barcelona-El Prat Airport;** a few budget flights use a smaller airstrip farther away, called **Girona–Costa Brava Airport.** Information on both airports can be found on the official Spanish airport website: www.aena-aeropuertos.es.

JOSEP TARRADELLAS BARCELONA-EL PRAT AIRPORT

Barcelona's primary airport is eight miles southwest of town (code: BCN, info tel. 913-211-000). It has two large terminals, linked by shuttle buses. Terminal 1 serves Air France, Air Europa, American, British Airways, Delta, Iberia, Lufthansa, United, Vueling, and others. EasyJet, Ryanair, and minor airlines use the older Terminal 2, which is divided into sections A, B, and C.

Terminal 1 and the bigger sections of Terminal 2 (A and B) each have a post office, a pharmacy, a left-luggage office, plenty of good cafeterias in the gate areas, and ATMs.

Getting Downtown: To reach central Barcelona cheaply and quickly, take the bus or train (about 30 minutes on either).

The **Aerobus** (#A1 and #A2, corresponding with Terminals 1 and 2) picks up immediately outside the arrivals lobby of both terminals and makes several stops downtown, including at Plaça de Catalunya, near many of my recommended hotels (returning from downtown, buses leave from in front of El Corte Inglés). Either way it's very easy: Buses depart about every five minutes (30-40 minutes, runs from 5:30 to 24:00, buy €6 ticket from driver, tel. 902-100-104, www.aerobusbcn.com).

The **Renfe train** (on the "R2 Nord" Rodalies line) leaves from Terminal 2 and involves more walking. Head up the escalators and down the long orange-roofed skybridge to reach the station (2/hour at about :08 and :38 past the hour, 20 minutes to Sants station, 25 minutes to Passeig de Gràcia station—near Plaça de Catalunya; €4.10 or covered by multi-ride card, which you can purchase from machines at the airport train station). If you are arriving or departing from Terminal 1, you will have to use the airport shuttle bus to connect with the train station, so allow extra time (10 buses/hour, 7-minute ride between terminals).

By **Metro,** take the L9 Sud (orange) line from either Terminal 1 or 2, to Zona Universitária, then transfer to the L3 (green) line and ride to a downtown stop (Passeig de Gràcia, Plaça de Catalunya, or Liceu). To reach the airport from downtown via Metro, take line L3 to Zona Universitária, and transfer to line L9 in the direction of Aeroport T1 (runs about every 10 minutes 5:00 until late; 20-30 minute ride; use €4.60 *Billet Aeroport* or any "Hola BCN!" travel card—multiride and single-ride Metro tickets do not work for this ride).

A **taxi** between the airport and downtown costs about €32 (including €3 airport supplement).

GIRONA–COSTA BRAVA AIRPORT

Some budget airlines use this airport, located 60 miles north of Barcelona near Girona (code: GRO, tel. 972-186-600, www.aena-aeropuertos.es). If you're arriving on a Ryanair flight, you can take a bus (#604), run by Ryanair and operated by Sagalés, to the Barcelona Nord bus station (departs airport about 20-25 minutes after each arriving flight, 1.25 hours, €16, tel. 902-361-550, www.sagales.com). You can also take a Sagalés bus (#602, about every 10 minutes, 1.5 hours, €2.75) or a taxi (€25) to the town of Girona, then catch a train to Barcelona (at least hourly, 1.5 hours, €15-20). A taxi between the Girona airport and Barcelona costs at least €130.

Rick's Tip: *Remember,* **Barcelona makes a good first or last stop for your trip.** *With the speedy AVE train, Barcelona is only three hours away from Madrid—easier than flying. If you want to rent a car, start your trip in Barcelona, take the train or fly to Madrid, and see Madrid and Toledo, all before picking up a car—cleverly saving on several days of rental fees.*

By Train

Virtually all trains end up at Barcelona's **Sants train station,** west of the Old City. AVE trains from Madrid go only to Sants station. But many other trains also pass through other stations en route, such as **França station** (between the El Born and Barceloneta neighborhoods), or the downtown **Passeig de Gràcia** or **Plaça de Catalunya** stations (which are also Metro stops—and very close to most of my recommended hotels). Figure out which stations your train stops at (ask the conductor), and get off at the one most convenient to your hotel.

SANTS TRAIN STATION

Barcelona's big white main train station offers many services. In the large lobby area, you'll find a TI, ATMs, handy shops

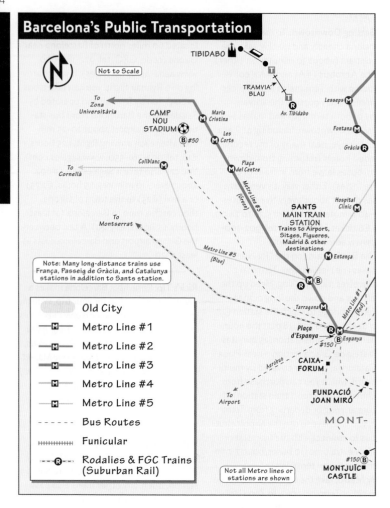

Barcelona's Public Transportation

TIBIDABO

Not to Scale

To Zona Universitària

TRAMVIA BLAU

Lesseps

CAMP NOU STADIUM

Av. Tibidabo

Maria Cristina

Fontana

B #50

Les Corts

Gràcia

To Cornellà

Collblanc

Plaça del Centre

Hospital Clínic

SANTS MAIN TRAIN STATION
Trains to Airport, Sitges, Figueres, Madrid & other destinations

To Montserrat

Metro Line #5 (Green)

Metro Line #5 (Blue)

Entença

Note: Many long-distance trains use França, Passeig de Gràcia, and Catalunya stations in addition to Sants station.

Tarragona

Metro Line #1 (Red)

Old City

—M— Metro Line #1

—M— Metro Line #2

—M— Metro Line #3

—M— Metro Line #4

—M— Metro Line #5

- - - - - Bus Routes

┉┉┉┉ Funicular

—R— Rodalies & FGC Trains (Suburban Rail)

Plaça d'Espanya

B Espanya
#150

Aerobus

CAIXA FORUM

To Airport

FUNDACIÓ JOAN MIRÓ

MONT-

Not all Metro lines or stations are shown

#150 B
MONTJUÏC CASTLE

and eateries, pay WCs, car-rental kiosks, and, in the side concourse, a classy, quiet Sala Club lounge for travelers with first-class reservations. Sants is the only Barcelona station with luggage storage (€6/ up to 2 hours, €10/day, daily 5:30-23:00, follow signs to *consigna;* go toward track 14, then exit the main building toward the parking lot and go down to level -1).

In the vast main hall is a very long wall of ticket windows. Figure out which one you need before you wait in line (all are labeled in English). Generally, win-dows 1-7 (on the left) are for local com-muter and *media distancia* trains, such as to Sitges; windows 8-21 handle advance tickets for long-distance *(larga distancia)* trains beyond Catalunya; windows 22-26 give information—go here first if you're not sure which window you want; and windows 27-31 sell tickets for long-dis-tance trains leaving today. These window assignments can shift in off-season. The information booths by windows 1 and 21 can help you find the right line and can provide some train schedules.

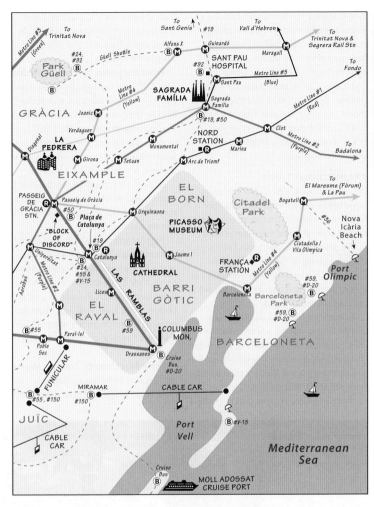

Scattered nearby are train-ticket vending machines. The red-and-gray machines sell tickets for local and *media distancia* trains within Catalunya. The purple machines are for national Renfe trains; these machines can also print out prereserved tickets if you have a confirmation code. And the orange machines sell local *Rodalies* train tickets. There are usually attendants around the machines to help you.

Getting Downtown: To reach the center of Barcelona, take a train or the Metro.

To ride the subway, follow signs for the Metro (red M), and hop on the L3 (green) or L5 (blue) line, both of which link to useful points in town. Purchase tickets for the Metro at touch-screen machines near the tracks (where you can also buy a cost-saving multiride ticket; described earlier under "By Metro").

To zip downtown even faster (just five minutes), you can take any Rodalies de Catalunya suburban train from track 8 (R1, R3, or R4) to Plaça de Catalunya (departs at least every 10 minutes). Your long-distance Renfe train ticket comes with a complimentary ride on Rodalies, as long as you use it within three hours before or after your travels. Look for a code on your ticket labeled *Combinat Rodalies* or *Combinado Cercanías.* Go to the orange commuter ticket machines, touch *Combinat Rodalies,* type in your code, and the machine will print your ticket. There is usually an attendant around to help you.

TRAIN CONNECTIONS

Unless otherwise noted, all of the trains listed below depart from Sants station; however, remember that some trains also stop at other stations more convenient to the downtown tourist zone: França station, Passeig de Gràcia, or Plaça de Catalunya. Figure out if your train stops at these stations (and board there) to save yourself the trip to Sants.

If departing from the downtown Passeig de Gràcia station, where three Metro lines converge with the rail line, you might find the underground tunnels confusing. You can't access the Renfe station directly from some of the entrances. Use the northern entrances to this station (rather than the southern "Consell de Cent" entrance, which is closest to Plaça de Catalunya). Train info: Tel. 912-320-320, www.renfe.com.

From Barcelona by Train to Madrid: The AVE train to Madrid is faster than flying (when you consider that you're zipping from downtown to downtown). The train departs at least hourly. The non-stop train is a little more expensive but faster (€130, 2.5 hours) than the train that makes a few stops (€110, 3 hours).

Look out for a new line of low-cost fast trains called ALVO. These budget bullet trains are providing service between Barcelona and Madrid.

Regular reserved AVE tickets can be prepurchased (often with a discount) at the Renfe website and printed from an email or at the station. You can also download a ticket QR code on a smartphone. If you have a rail pass, most trains require paid reservations; see the "Transportation" section of the Practicalities chapter.

From Barcelona by Train to: Montserrat (departs from Plaça d'Espanya—*not* from Sants, 1-2/hour, 1 hour, €22 round-

trip, includes cable car or rack train to monastery), **Figueres** (hourly, 1 hour via AVE or Alvia to Figueres-Vilafant; hourly, 2 hours via local trains to Figueres station), **Sevilla** (2/day direct, more with transfer in Madrid, 5.5 hours), **Granada** (2/day, 8 hours via AVE and connecting bus, transfer in Antequera), **Córdoba** (4/day direct, 5 hours, many more with transfer in Madrid), **Salamanca** (6/day, 7 hours, change in Madrid from Atocha station to Chamartín station via Metro or *cercanías* train; also 1/day with a change in Valladolid, 8.5 hours), **San Sebastián** (2/day direct, 6 hours).

By Bus

Most buses depart from the Nord bus station at Metro: Arc de Triomf, but confirm when researching schedules (www.barcelonanord.com). Destinations served by Alsa buses (www.alsa.es) include **Madrid** and **Madrid's Barajas Airport** (nearly hourly, 8 hours), and Salamanca (2/day, 12 hours). Reservations are smart for long-distance destinations, especially during the busy summer season.

One bus departs daily for the **Montserrat** monastery, leaving from Carrer de Viriat near Sants station (1.5 hours).

Italy

Stretching 850 miles long and 150 miles wide, art-drenched Italy is the cradle of European civilization. Visitors here come face to face with some of the world's most iconic images: Michelangelo's *David* in Florence, Rome's ancient Colosseum, Venice's gondolas, and the colorful, coastal villages of the Cinque Terre—Italy's Riviera.

Italy's 62 million inhabitants are more social and communal than most other Europeans. Because they're so outgoing and their language is so fun, Italians are a pleasure to communicate with. This boot-shaped country has all the elements that make travel to Europe forever fresh and rewarding: visible history, enthusiastic locals, and plenty of pasta.

CUISINE SCENE AT A GLANCE

For Italians, lunch traditionally is the largest meal of the day (between 13:00 and 15:00), and dinner is lighter and late (around 20:00-21:30). Most **restaurants** close between lunch and dinner; good restaurants don't reopen for dinner before 19:00. To bridge the gap, people drop into a bar in the late afternoon for a snack.

A full Italian meal (€15-20) consists of several courses—an appetizer (*antipasto*), a first course (*primo piatto*), and a second course (*secondo piatto*)—but no one is obliged to order all that food. To save money and avoid getting stuffed, order any two courses. For example, a couple could order and share two *antipasti* and two *primi*.

At restaurants with self-serve buffets, you can choose various cooked appetizers from a salad-type bar. Generally buffets are not all-you-can-eat; take a one-time moderate serving (watch locals and imitate).

Understand prices before ordering. Seafood and steak may be sold by weight, either priced by the kilo (just over two pounds) or by the *etto* (about a quarter-pound). The abbreviation *s.q.* (*secondo quantità*) means an item is priced "according to quantity" (such as the size of a fish). Fish is usually served whole, with the head and tail. As for steak, restaurants may require a minimum order of four or five *etti* (which diners can share). Some special dishes come in big quantities for two people (shown as "X2" on the menu), though the price listed generally indicates the cost per person.

You can save money by getting a fixed-price, multicourse meal, such as a basic *menù turistico* or often tastier *menù del giorno* (menu of the day). While fixed-price meals are convenient, galloping gourmets prefer to order à la carte for more adventurous fare.

Cover and Tipping: Familiarize yourself with two common Italian restaurant charges: *coperto* and *servizio*. The *coperto* (or *pane e coperto*) is a cover charge, added onto your bill as a flat fee (€1.50-3 per person; the amount should be clearly noted on the menu). The *servizio* (service charge) of 10-15 percent pays for the waitstaff. If *servizio incluso* is written on the menu or bill, the fee is already included in the listed prices. You don't need to tip further (many Italians don't), but for good service, you could include €1-2 for each person in your party.

Budget Options: Take advantage of bars—inexpensive cafés that quickly serve up sandwiches, mini pizzas, salads, and more. Bars have a two- or three-tiered pricing system. If you order, say, a sandwich, it's cheapest if you eat it while standing at the bar, more if you sit at an indoor table, and the most at an outdoor table.

Self-serve cafeterias are easy. Pizzerias are affordable, and takeout shops sell pizza by the slice or by weight. Or assemble a delicious picnic at a grocery or a deli (*rosticceria*).

Rome

Rome is magnificent and brutal at the same time. It's a showcase of Western civilization, with truly ancient sights and a modern vibrance. But with the wrong attitude, you'll be frustrated by the kind of chaos that only an Italian can understand. On my last visit, a cabbie struggling with the traffic said, *"Roma chaos."* I responded, *"Bella chaos."* He agreed.

Over 2,000 years ago the word "Rome" meant civilization itself. Today, Rome is Italy's political capital, the capital of Catholicism, and an open-air museum of its ancient empire, littered with evocative remains. As you peel through its fascinating and jumbled layers, you'll find Rome's buildings, cats, laundry, traffic, and 2.8 million people endlessly entertaining.

Despite Rome's rough edges, you'll fall in love with it...if you choose a comfortable hotel for a refuge, pace yourself, organize your sightseeing, and take sensible precautions to protect your valuables. Soon you'll be the one at the Trevi Fountain throwing in a coin to ensure your return.

ROME IN 3 DAYS

Rome wasn't built in a day, and you can't hope to see it all in three. Pace yourself; never regret a siesta. If you miss something, add it to your list of excuses to return.

Day 1: The Colosseum is the best place to begin your tour of ancient Rome (book an entry time in advance). Continue to the Arch of Constantine, the Roman Forum, then over Capitoline Hill (visiting the Capitoline Museums), and on to the Pantheon. Have dinner on the atmospheric Campo de' Fiori. Then take this book's Heart of Rome Walk to the Trevi Fountain and Spanish Steps.

Day 2: Tour the Vatican Museums, featuring the divine Sistine Chapel (closed Sun, except first Sun of month; reserve a museum entry time in advance), then see St. Peter's Basilica and climb its dome. With any remaining stamina, choose among these sights (or save for tomorrow afternoon): the National Museum of Rome (ancient sculpture), St. Peter-in-Chains (Michelangelo's *Moses*), and Castel Sant'Angelo (castle-museum).

Day 3: See the Borghese Gallery (reservations required, closed Mon; stroll through the park afterwards). Zip up to the top of the nearby Victor Emmanuel Monument for a grand view of the Eternal City.

Evening options: Do as the Romans do—join the Dolce Vita Stroll along the Via del Corso. Explore the Monti neighborhood; linger over dinner, or stop by an enoteca (wine bar) for a drink. Enjoy a classical concert or jazz. Or take in a sound-and-light show at the Imperial Forums.

With extra time: Take a day trip to the hill town of Orvieto or visit Naples and Pompeii in a blitz day trip: Take the early Rome-Naples express train, connect by

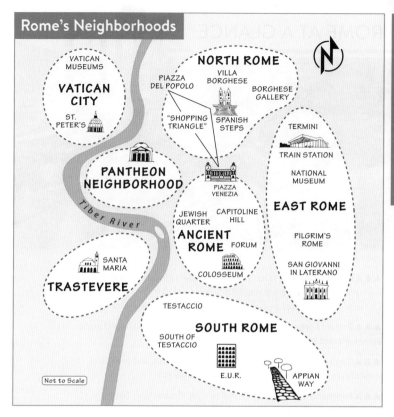

Rome's Neighborhoods

VATICAN
MUSEUMS

**VATICAN
CITY**

ST.
PETER'S

NORTH ROME

PIAZZA
DEL POPOLO

VILLA
BORGHESE

BORGHESE
GALLERY

"SHOPPING
TRIANGLE"

SPANISH
STEPS

**PANTHEON
NEIGHBORHOOD**

Tiber River

PIAZZA
VENEZIA

JEWISH
QUARTER

CAPITOLINE
HILL

**ANCIENT
ROME**

FORUM

COLOSSEUM

TERMINI

TRAIN STATION

NATIONAL
MUSEUM

EAST ROME

PILGRIM'S
ROME

SAN GIOVANNI
IN LATERANO

SANTA
MARIA

TRASTEVERE

TESTACCIO

SOUTH ROME

SOUTH OF
TESTACCIO

E.U.R.

APPIAN
WAY

Not to Scale

---

bus or train to Pompeii, return to Naples for its archaeological museum, and you'll be back in Rome around bedtime (but avoid this trip on Tue, when Naples' archaeological museum is closed). See those chapters for details.

Rick's Tip: The **siesta is the key to survival** *in summertime Rome. Lie down and contemplate the extraordinary power of gravity in the Eternal City. Drink lots of cold, refreshing water from Rome's many drinking fountains.*

ORIENTATION

Sprawling Rome actually feels manageable once you get to know it. The old core, with most of the tourist sights, sits inside a diamond formed by Termini train station (in the east), the Vatican (west), Villa Borghese Gardens (north), and the Colosseum (south). The Tiber River snakes through the diamond from north to south. At the center of the diamond is Piazza Venezia, a busy square and traffic hub. Think of Rome as a collection of neighborhoods, huddling around major landmarks.

Ancient Rome: In ancient times, this was home to the grandest buildings of a city of a million people. Today, the best of the classical sights stand in a line from the Colosseum to the ruined Roman Forum over Capitoline Hill to the Pantheon. Just north of this area, between Via Nazionale and Via Cavour, is the trendy Monti district.

Pantheon Neighborhood: The Pantheon anchors the neighborhood I like to call the "Heart of Rome," which includes

ROME AT A GLANCE

▲▲▲**Colosseum** Huge stadium where gladiators fought. **Hours:** Daily 8:30 until one hour before sunset: April-Aug until 19:15, Sept until 19:00, Oct until 18:30, off-season closes as early as 16:30. See page 420.

▲▲▲**Roman Forum** Ancient Rome's main square, with ruins and grand arches. **Hours:** Same as Colosseum. See page 425.

▲▲▲**Capitoline Museums** Ancient statues, mosaics, and expansive view of Forum. **Hours:** Daily 9:30-19:30. See page 433.

▲▲▲**Pantheon** The defining domed temple. **Hours:** Mon-Sat 8:30-19:30, Sun 9:00-18:00, holidays 9:00-13:00, closed for Mass Sat at 17:00 and Sun at 10:30. See page 437.

▲▲▲**St. Peter's Basilica** Most impressive church on earth, with Michelangelo's *Pietà* and dome. **Hours:** Church—daily April-Sept 7:00-19:00, Oct-March 7:00-18:30, often closed Wed mornings; dome—daily April-Sept 7:30-19:00, Oct-March 7:30-18:00. See page 440.

▲▲▲**Vatican Museums** Four miles of the finest art of Western civilization, culminating in Michelangelo's glorious Sistine Chapel. **Hours:** Mon-Sat 9:00-18:00. Closed on religious holidays and Sun, except last Sun of the month (open 9:00-14:00). Open Fri nights mid-April-Oct by online reservation only. See page 446.

▲▲▲**Borghese Gallery** Bernini sculptures and paintings by Caravaggio, Raphael, and Titian in a Baroque palazzo. Reservations mandatory. **Hours:** Tue-Sun 9:00-19:00, Thu until 21:00, closed Mon. See page 453.

▲▲▲**National Museum of Rome** Greatest collection of Roman sculpture anywhere. **Hours:** Tue-Sun 9:00-19:45, closed Mon. See page 456.

▲▲▲**Heart of Rome Walk** A stroll lacing the narrow lanes, intimate piazzas, fanciful fountains, and lively scenes of Rome's most colorful neighborhood. **Hours:** Anytime, but best in evening. See page 412.

▲▲**Palatine Hill** Ruins of emperors' palaces, Circus Maximus view, and museum. **Hours:** Same as Colosseum. See page 432.

▲▲**Trajan's Column, Market, and Forum** Tall column with narrative relief, forum ruins, and museum with entry to Trajan's Market. **Hours:** Forum and column always viewable; museum open daily 9:30-19:30. See page 436.

▲▲**Museo dell'Ara Pacis** Shrine marking the beginning of Rome's Golden Age. **Hours:** Daily 9:30-19:30. See page 456.

▲▲**Dolce Vita Stroll** Evening *passeggiata* where Romans strut their stuff. **Hours:** Roughly Mon-Sat 17:00-19:00 and Sun afternoons. See page 410.

▲**Arch of Constantine** Honors the emperor who legalized Christianity. **Hours:** Always viewable. See page 424.

▲**St. Peter-in-Chains** Church with Michelangelo's *Moses*. **Hours:** Daily 8:00-12:30 & 15:00-19:00, Oct-March until 18:00. See page 436.

▲**Piazza del Campidoglio** Square atop Capitoline Hill, designed by Michelangelo, with a museum, grand stairway, and Forum overlooks. See page 433.

▲**Victor Emmanuel Monument** Gigantic edifice celebrating Italian unity, with Rome from the Sky elevator ride up to 360-degree city view. **Hours:** Monument open daily 9:30-18:45 (shorter in winter), elevator until 19:00. See page 435.

▲**Trevi Fountain** Baroque hot spot into which tourists throw coins to ensure a return trip to Rome. **Hours:** Always flowing. See page 419.

▲**Castel Sant'Angelo** Hadrian's Tomb turned castle, prison, papal refuge, now museum. **Hours:** Daily 9:00-19:30. See page 453.

▲**Baths of Diocletian/Basilica S. Maria degli Angeli** Once ancient Rome's immense public baths, now a Michelangelo church. **Hours:** Daily 7:30-18:30, closes later May-Sept and Sun year-round. See page 458.

the atmospheric squares of Campo de' Fiori and Piazza Navona, the dramatic Trevi Fountain, and several historic churches.

Vatican City: Located west of the Tiber River, this is a compact world of its own, with two great, massive sights: St. Peter's Basilica and the Vatican Museums.

North Rome: This modern, classy area hosts the people-friendly Spanish Steps, an elegant grid of trendy shopping streets (between the main drag—Via del Corso—and the Spanish Steps), and the Borghese Gallery set within the fun-on-a-sunny-day Villa Borghese Gardens.

East Rome: This neighborhood around Termini Station boasts the stunning National Museum of Rome and includes Piazza della Repubblica, many recommended hotels, and convenient public-transportation connections.

Tourist Information

Rome has about a dozen small city-run tourist information offices scattered around town. The largest TIs are at Fiumicino Airport (Terminal 3, daily 8:00-21:00) and Termini train station (daily 8:00-18:45, exit by track 24 and walk 100 yards down along Via Giovanni Giolitti). Little kiosks (most open daily 9:30-19:00) are on Via Nazionale (at Palazzo delle Esposizioni), between the Trevi Fountain and Pantheon (at the corner of Via del Corso and Via Minghetti), near Piazza Navona (at Piazza delle Cinque Lune), and in Trastevere (at Piazza Sidney Sonnino).

The TI's website is www.turismoroma.it, but a better site for practical information is www.060608.it. That's also the number for Rome's **call center**—the best source of up-to-date tourist information, with English speakers on staff (answered daily 9:00-19:00, tel. 06-0608, press 2 for English).

Helpful Hints

Sightseeing Tips: Despite the crowds in Rome, you'll only find lines a problem at **St. Peter's Basilica** (go early or late to minimize), **Vatican Museums** (avoid by booking in advance online), and the **Colosseum** and **Roman Forum** (book online and go early morning or late afternoon). The **Borghese Gallery** requires a ticket with timed entry purchased in advance.

The **Roma Pass** is only worthwhile if you want a public transit pass (covers 2 or 3 days of transit, entry to 1 or 2 sights, and discounts at others—but you'll still need a Colosseum and a Borghese Gallery reservation).

Theft Alert: While violent crime is rare in the city center, petty theft is rampant. Always use your money belt. If you carry a backpack, never leave it unattended and try to keep it attached to your body in some way (even when you're seated for a meal).

Be particularly on guard in crowds, especially when boarding and leaving buses and subways. Thieves are particularly thick on the Metro and the crowded, made-for-tourists buses #40 and #64.

To report lost or stolen items, file a

Spiral staircase at the Vatican Museums

Backstreet Rome

police report (at Termini Station, with *polizia* at track 11 or with Carabinieri at track 20; offices are also at Piazza Venezia and at the corner of Via Nazionale and Via Genova).

Pedestrian Safety: Your main safety concern in Rome is crossing streets without incident. Use caution. Some streets have pedestrian-crossing signals (red means stop—or jaywalk carefully; green means go...also carefully; and yellow means go...extremely carefully, as cars may be whipping around the corner). But just as often, multilane streets have crosswalks with no signals at all.

Follow locals like a shadow when you cross a street. When you do cross alone, find a gap in the traffic and walk with confidence while making eye contact with approaching drivers—they won't hit you if they can tell where you intend to go.

Laundry: Coin launderettes are common in Rome. Your hotelier can direct you to the closest one. The **Wash & Dry Lavarapido** chain has a branch near Piazza Barberini (Mon-Sat 9:00-21:00, closed Sun, Via degli Avignonesi 17—see map on page 466, tel. 06-4201-3158).

Rick's Tip: Can't get reservations to the main sights *(or just can't stand crowds)? Rome has many magnificent attractions without the hordes. Try the Palatine Hill, National Museum of Rome, Museo dell'Ara Pacis, or Capitoline Museums. Even in peak season, you'll often be all alone with the wonders of ancient world, wondering, "Where is everyone?"*

Tours
LOCAL GUIDES
I've worked with and enjoyed each of these licensed independent local guides. Prices (roughly €60/hour) flex with the day, season, and demand: **Carla Zaia** (carlaromeguide@gmail.com); **Cristina Giannicchi** (mobile 338-111-4573, www.crisromanguide.com); **Sara Magister**

(a.magister@iol.it); **Giovanna Terzulli** (gioterzulli@gmail.com); **Alessandra Mazzoccoli** (www.romeandabout.com); and **Massimiliano Canneto** (massicanneto@gmail.com). **Francesca Caruso,** who works almost full-time with my tours when in Rome, has contributed generously to this book (www.francescacaruso.com)—if she's busy, she'll recommend one of her colleagues.

WALKING TOURS
Three-hour guided walks generally cost €25-30 per person. These companies are each well-established, creative, and competitive. Each offers a 10 percent discount with most online bookings for Rick Steves travelers: **Walks of Italy** (RS%—enter "RICKWALKSROME," US tel. 888/683-8670, tel. 06-9480-4888, www.walksofitaly.com), **Europe Odyssey** (RS%, tel. 06-8854-2416, www.europeodyssey.com), **Through Eternity** (RS%—look for "Group Tours Rome" and enter "RICKSTEVES," tel. 06-700-9336, www.througheternity.com), and **The Roman Guy** (RS%—enter "rick steves," theromanguy.com, Sean Finelli).

HOP-ON, HOP-OFF BUS TOURS
Several different agencies run hop-on, hop-off, double-decker bus tours around Rome. These tours make the same 90-minute, eight-stop loop through the traffic-congested town center with about four pickups at each stop per hour. You can join one (and pay as you board; usually around €20) at any stop; Termini Station and Piazza Venezia are handy hubs.

CAR AND DRIVER SERVICE
Autoservizi Monti Concezio, run by gentle, capable, and English-speaking Ezio (pronounced Etz-io), offers private cars or minibuses with driver/guides (car-€40/hour, minibus-€45/hour, 3-hour minimum for city sightseeing, transfers between cities are more expensive, mobile 335-636-5907 or 349-674-5643, info@tourservicemonti.it).

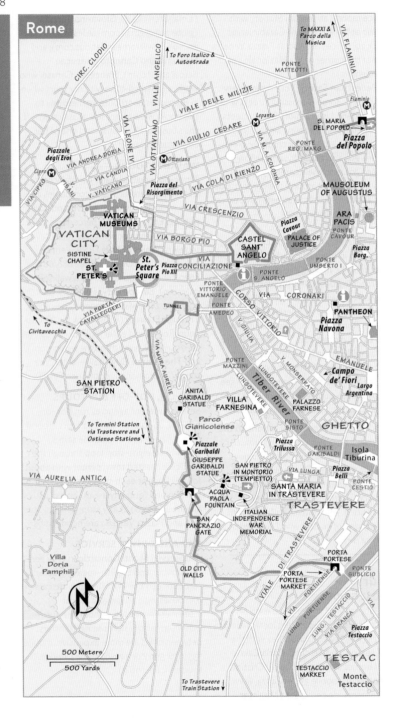

Rome

To MAXXI &
Parco della
Musica

VIA FLAMINIA

CIRC. CLODIO

VIALE ANGELICO

To Foro Italico &
Autostrada

PONTE
MATTEOTTI

VIALE DELLE MILIZIE

VIA LEONE IV

VIA OTTAVIANO

VIA GIULIO CESARE

Lepanto

VIA M. A. COLONNA

Flaminio

S. MARIA
DEL POPOLO

Piazza
del Popolo

Piazzale
degli Eroi

VIA ANDREA DORIA

PONTE
REG. MARG.

Cipro

V. PISANI

VIA CIPRO

VIA CANDIA

V. VATICANO

Ottaviano

Piazza del
Risorgimento

VIA COLA DI RIENZO

MAUSOLEUM
OF AUGUSTUS

ARA
PACIS

VIA CRESCENZIO

Piazza
Cavour

PALACE OF
JUSTICE

PONTE
CAVOUR

Piazza
Borg.

VATICAN
MUSEUMS

VIA BORGO PIO

VATICAN
CITY

CASTEL
SANT'
ANGELO

VIA
CONCILIAZIONE

SISTINE
CHAPEL

ST.
PETER'S

St.
Peter's
Square

Piazza
Pio XII

PONTE
UMBERTO I

PONTE
S. ANGELO

VIA
CORONARI

PANTHEON

VIA PORTA
CAVALLEGGERI

TUNNEL

PONTE
VITTORIO
EMANUELE

PONTE
AMEDEO

CORSO
VITTORIO

V. GIULIA

Piazza
Navona

To
Civitavecchia

SAN PIETRO
STATION

VIA MURA AURELIE

PONTE
MAZZINI

Tiber River

LUNGOTEVERE

V. MONSERRATO

EMANUELE

Campo
de' Fiori

Largo
Argentina

ANITA
GARIBALDI
STATUE

VILLA
FARNESINA

PALAZZO
FARNESE

To Termini Station
via Trastevere and
Ostiense Stations

Parco
Gianicolense

PONTE
SISTO

GHETTO

Piazzale
Garibaldi

Piazza
Trilussa

PONTE
GARIBALDI

Isola
Tiburina

VIA AURELIA ANTICA

GIUSEPPE
GARIBALDI
STATUE

SAN PIETRO
IN MONTORIO
(TEMPIETTO)

VIA LUNGA

Piazza
Belli

SANTA MARIA
IN TRASTEVERE

PONTE
CESTIO

ACQUA
PAOLA
FOUNTAIN

ITALIAN
INDEPENDENCE
WAR
MEMORIAL

TRASTEVERE

Villa
Doria
Pamphilj

SAN
PANCRAZIO
GATE

PORTA
PORTESE

N

OLD CITY
WALLS

VIALE DI TRASTEVERE

PORTA
PORTESE
MARKET

PONTE
SUBLICIO

500 Meters

500 Yards

VIA PORTUENSE

LUNG. PORTUENSE

LUNG. TESTACCIO

VIA BRANCA

VIA

Piazza
Testaccio

To Trastevere
Train Station

TESTACCIO
MARKET

TESTAC

Monte
Testaccio

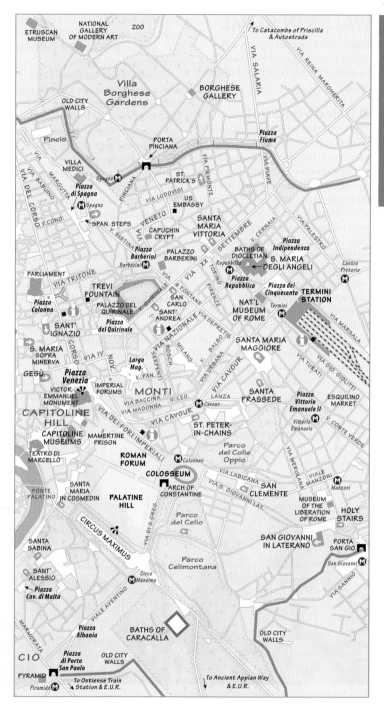

ITALY

WALKS IN ROME

Take a refreshing early evening walk (Dolce Vita Stroll) and enjoy the thriving local scene, best at night (Heart of Rome Walk).

❍ Dolce Vita Stroll

All over the Mediterranean world, people are out strolling in the early evening in a ritual known in Italy as the *passeggiata,* worth ▲▲ (see the sidebar on page 459). Rome's *passeggiata* is both elegant (with chic people enjoying fancy window shopping in the grid of streets around the Spanish Steps) and a little crude (with young people on the prowl). The major sights along this walk are covered later in this chapter.

Romans' favorite place for a chic evening stroll is along **Via del Corso.** Join in as you walk from Piazza del Popolo (Metro: Flaminio) down a wonderfully traffic-free section of Via del Corso, and up Via Condotti to the Spanish Steps. Historians can continue to Capitoline Hill. Although busy at any hour, this area really attracts crowds from around 17:00 to 19:00 each evening (Fri and Sat are best), except on Sunday, when it occurs earlier in the afternoon. Leave before 18:00 if you plan to visit the

Ara Pacis (Altar of Peace), which closes at 19:30. If you get hungry during your stroll, see page 474 for listings of neighborhood wine bars and restaurants.

To reach **Piazza del Popolo,** take Metro line A to Flaminio and walk south to the square. Delightfully car-free, Piazza del Popolo is marked by an obelisk that was brought to Rome by Augustus after he conquered Egypt. (It used to stand in the Circus Maximus.)

If starting your stroll early enough, the Baroque church of **Santa Maria del Popolo** is worth popping into (next to gate in old wall on north side of square). Inside, look for Raphael's Chigi Chapel (second on left as you face the main altar) and two paintings by Caravaggio (in the Cerasi Chapel, left of altar).

From Piazza del Popolo, stroll down **Via del Corso.** While many Italians shop online or at the mall these days, and the elegance of this street has been replaced by international chains targeting local teens, this remains a fine place to feel the pulse of Rome at twilight.

Historians can side-trip right down Via Pontefici past the fascist architecture to see the massive, round-brick **Mausoleum of Augustus,** topped with overgrown

Twin Baroque churches on bustling Piazza del Popolo

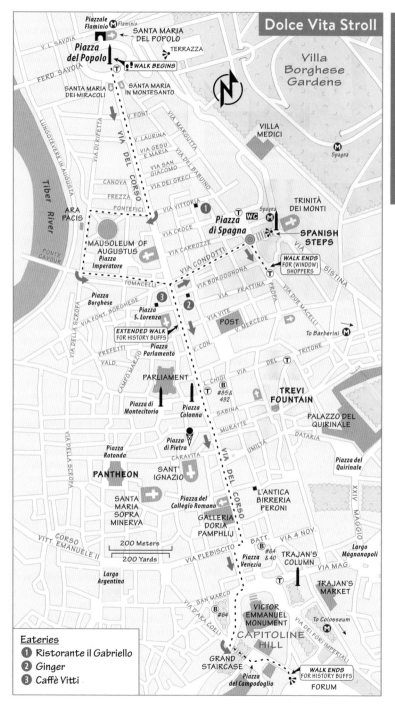

Dolce Vita Stroll

Piazzale Flaminio · Flaminio · SANTA MARIA DEL POPOLO · TERRAZZA · Piazza del Popolo · **WALK BEGINS** · Villa Borghese Gardens

SANTA MARIA DEI MIRACOLI · SANTA MARIA IN MONTESANTO · V. L. SAVOIA · FERD. SAVOIA

VILLA MEDICI · Spagna

V. FONT. · VIA MARGUTTA · VIA DI REPETTA · VIA DEL CORSO · V. LAURINA · VIA GESU E MARIA · VIA SAN GIACOMO · VIA DEL BABUINO · VIA DEI GRECI · CANOVA · FREZZA · PONTEFICI · VIA VITTORIA

Tiber River · LUNGOTEVERE IN AUGUSTA

ARA PACIS · Piazza di Spagna · TRINITÀ DEI MONTI · Spagna · WC · **SPANISH STEPS** · VIA CROCE · VIA CARROZZE · VIA CONDOTTI · VIA SISTINA

PONTE CAVOUR · MAUSOLEUM OF AUGUSTUS · Piazza Imperatore · **WALK ENDS** FOR (WINDOW) SHOPPERS

VIA DELLA SCROFA · VIA FONT. BORGHESE · TOMACELLI · Piazza Borghese · Piazza S. Lorenzo · VIA BORGOGNONA · VIA FRATTINA · PROPA. · VIA DUE MACELLI

EXTENDED WALK FOR HISTORY BUFFS · Piazza Parlamento · VIA VITE · POST · V. MERCEDE · To Barberini

PREFETTI · VALD. · CAMPO MARZIO · V. CON. · VIA DEL · TRITONE

PARLIAMENT · Piazza di Montecitorio · Piazza Colonna · L. CHIGI · #85 & 492 · SABINA · MURATTE · TREVI FOUNTAIN · PALAZZO DEL QUIRINALE · DATARIA

VIA DELLA SCROFA · Piazza Rotonda · Piazza di Pietra · CARAVITA · UMILTÀ · Piazza del Quirinale · XXIV MAGGIO

PANTHEON · SANT' IGNAZIO · SANTA MARIA SOPRA MINERVA · Piazza del Collegio Romano · VIA DEL CORSO · L'ANTICA BIRRERIA PERONI

GALLERIA DORIA PAMPHILIJ · BATT. · VIA 4 NOV. · Largo Magnanapoli

CORSO VITT. EMANUELE II · 200 Meters · 200 Yards · VIA PLEBISCITO · #64 & 40 · Piazza Venezia · TRAJAN'S COLUMN · VIA MAG. · TRAJAN'S MARKET

Largo Argentina · SAN MARCO · #64 · VICTOR EMMANUEL MONUMENT · CAPITOLINE HILL · VIA DEI FORI (IMPERIALI) · To Colosseum

VIA D'ARA COELI · GRAND STAIRCASE · Piazza del Campodoglio · **WALK ENDS** FOR HISTORY BUFFS · FORUM

Eateries
1. Ristorante il Gabriello
2. Ginger
3. Caffè Vitti

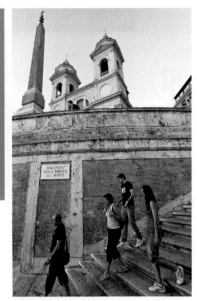

Spanish Steps

has been straight since Roman times, and walk a half-mile down to the **Victor Emmanuel Monument.** Climb Michelangelo's stairway to his glorious (especially when floodlit) square atop Capitoline Hill. Stand on the balcony (just past the mayor's palace on the right), which overlooks the Forum. As the horizon reddens and cats prowl the unclaimed rubble of ancient Rome, it's one of the finest views in the city.

◐ Heart of Rome Walk

Rome's most colorful neighborhood features narrow lanes, intimate piazzas, fanciful fountains, and some of Europe's best people-watching. During the day, this walk—worth ▲▲▲—shows off the colorful Campo de' Fiori market and trendy fashion boutiques as it meanders past major monuments such as the Pantheon and the Spanish Steps.

But the sunset brings unexpected magic. A stroll in the cool of the evening is made memorable by the romance of the Eternal City at its best. Sit so close to a bubbling fountain that traffic noise evaporates. Jostle with kids to see the gelato flavors. Watch lovers straddling more than the bench. Jaywalk past *polizia* in bullet-proof vests. And marvel at the ramshackle elegance that softens this brutal city for those who were born here and can't imagine living anywhere else. These are the flavors of Rome, best enjoyed after dark.

Allow one to three hours for this mile-long walk, depending on whether you linger and tour the Pantheon. The walk is equally pleasant in reverse order. You could ride the Metro to the Spanish Steps and finish at Campo de' Fiori, near many recommended restaurants.

🎧 Download my free Heart of Rome **audio tour,** which complements this walk.
• *Start in one of Rome's most colorful spots,* ***Campo de' Fiori.*** *It's a few blocks west of Largo Argentina, a major transportation hub.*

cypress trees. This long-neglected sight, honoring Rome's first emperor, is slated for restoration and redevelopment. Beyond it, next to the river, is the **Ara Pacis** (Altar of Peace)**,** consecrated by Augustus in 9 BC and today enclosed within a protective glass-walled museum worth ▲▲ (€10.50, or look in through huge windows for free, daily 9:30-19:30). From the mausoleum, walk down Via Tomacelli to return to Via del Corso and the 21st century.

From Via del Corso, window shoppers should take a left down **Via Condotti** to join the parade to the **Spanish Steps,** passing big-name boutiques. The streets that parallel Via Condotti to the south (Borgognona and Frattina) are also elegant and filled with high-end shops. A few streets to the north hides the narrow Via Margutta. This is where Gregory Peck's *Roman Holiday* character lived (at #51); today it has a leafy tranquility and is filled with pricey artisan and antique shops.

History Buffs: Another option is to ignore Via Condotti and forget the Spanish Steps. Stay on Via del Corso, which

❶ *Campo de' Fiori*

In the morning, this bohemian piazza hosts a fruit-and-vegetable market. In the evening, the cafés and restaurants that line the square predominate. On weekend nights, beer-drinking kids (mostly American students) pack the medieval square, transforming it into a vast Roman street party.

In ancient times, it was a pleasant meadow—literally a *campo de' fiori,* or "field of flowers." Then the Romans built a massive entertainment complex, the Theater of Pompey, right next to it. The complex covered several city blocks, stretching from here to Largo Argentina (and including the spot where Julius Caesar was stabbed to death).

Lording over the center of the square is the statue of **Giordano Bruno,** an intellectual who was burned on this spot in 1600. The pedestal shows scenes from Bruno's trial and execution, and an inscription translates, "And the flames rose up." The statue, facing a Vatican administration building, was erected in 1889, a time when the new state of Italy and the Vatican were feuding. Vatican officials protested the heretic in their midst, but they were overruled by angry neighborhood locals. This district is still known for its free spirit and antiauthoritarian demonstrations.

The square is surrounded by fun eateries and is great for people-watching. Bruno faces the bustling **Forno** (in the left corner of the square), where takeout *pizza bianca* is sold hot from the oven.

• *If Bruno did a hop, step, and jump forward, then turned left, in a block he'd reach...*

❷ *Piazza Farnese*

While the higgledy-piggledy Campo de' Fiori feels free and easy, the 16th-century Renaissance Piazza Farnese, named for the family whose palace dominates it, seems to stress order. The Farnese family hired Michelangelo to help design their palace. He created the jutting roofline (the cornice), and made the window in the very center a little wider than the others. This gave the whole facade a pleasant symmetry. The palazzo now houses the French embassy. The twin fountains decorating the square date from the third century and were made with repurposed stone tubs from the ancient Baths of Caracalla. These

Campo de' Fiori and statue of Giordano Bruno

ITALY

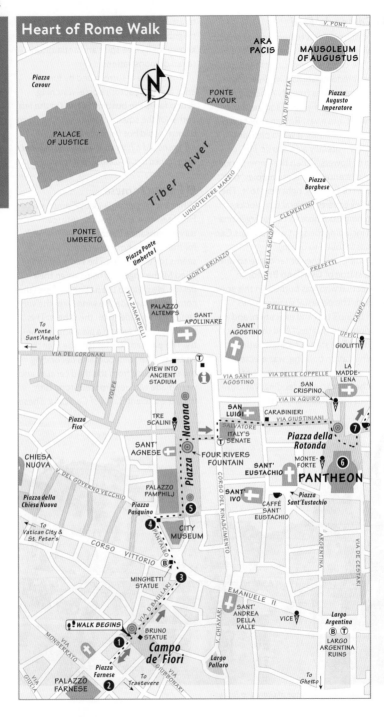

Heart of Rome Walk

ARA PACIS

MAUSOLEUM OF AUGUSTUS

Piazza Cavour

V. PONT.

PONTE CAVOUR

VIA DI RIPETTA

Piazza Augusto Imperatore

PALACE OF JUSTICE

Tiber River

Piazza Borghese

LUNGOTEVERE MARZIO

CLEMENTINO

PONTE UMBERTO

Piazza Ponte Umberto I

MONTE BRIANZO

VIA DELLA SCROFA

PREFETTI

VIA ZANARDELLI

PALAZZO ALTEMPS

SANT' APOLLINARE

SANT' AGOSTINO

STELLETTA

CAMPO

To Ponte Sant'Angelo

UFFICI

GIOLITTI

VIA DEI CORONARI

VIEW INTO ANCIENT STADIUM

VIA SANT' AGOSTINO

VIA DELLE COPPELLE

LA MADDE-LENA

VOLPE

Piazza Fico

TRE SCALINI

Piazza Navona

SAN LUIGI

SAN CRISPINO

VIA IN AQUIRO

CARABINIERI

VIA GIUSTINIANI

SALVATORE ITALY'S SENATE

Piazza della Rotonda

7

CHIESA NUOVA

SANT' AGNESE

FOUR RIVERS FOUNTAIN

SANT' EUSTACHIO

MONTE-FORTE

6

V. DEL GOVERNO VECCHIO

PALAZZO PAMPHILJ

5

SANT' IVO

CAFFÉ SANT' EUSTACHIO

Piazza Sant'Eustachio

PANTHEON

Piazza della Chiesa Nuova

Piazza Pasquino

4

CORSO DEL RINASCIMENTO

To Vatican City & St. Peter's

CORSO VITTORIO

PANTALEO

B

CITY MUSEUM

ARGENTINA

VIA DE CESTARI

MINGHETTI STATUE

3

VIA D. BAULLARI

EMANUELE II

SANT' ANDREA DELLA VALLE

VICE

Largo Argentina

B T

LARGO ARGENTINA RUINS

WALK BEGINS

1

BRUNO STATUE

Campo de' Fiori

V. CHIAVARI

VIA MONSERRATO

2

Piazza Farnese

To Trastevere

VIA GIUBBONARI

Largo Pallaro

To Ghetto

VIA GIULIA

PALAZZO FARNESE

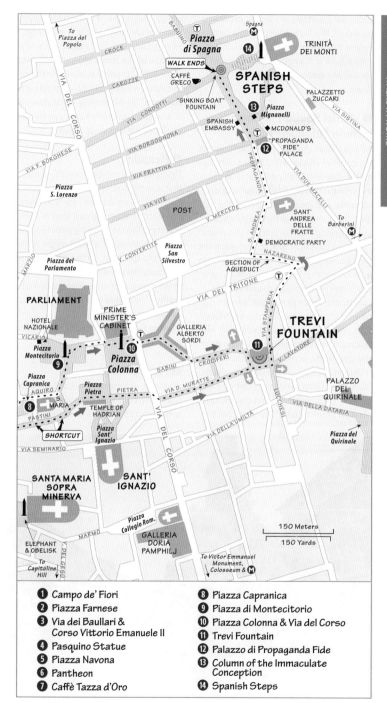

① Campo de' Fiori

② Piazza Farnese

③ Via dei Baullari &
Corso Vittorio Emanuele II

④ Pasquino Statue

⑤ Piazza Navona

⑥ Pantheon

⑦ Caffè Tazza d'Oro

⑧ Piazza Capranica

⑨ Piazza di Montecitorio

⑩ Piazza Colonna & Via del Corso

⑪ Trevi Fountain

⑫ Palazzo di Propaganda Fide

⑬ Column of the Immaculate
Conception

⑭ Spanish Steps

particular fountains are fed by an ancient aqueduct, the Acqua Vergine, the same source that feeds the Trevi Fountain.

• *Walk back to Campo de' Fiori, cross the square, and continue a couple of blocks down...*

❸ Via dei Baullari to Corso Vittorio Emanuele II

As you slalom through the crowds, notice the crush of cheap cafés, bars, and restaurants—the center of medieval Rome is morphing into a playground for tourists, students, and locals visiting from the suburbs. High rents are driving families out and changing the character of this district.

After a couple of blocks, you reach the busy boulevard, Corso Vittorio Emanuele II. In Rome, any road big enough to have city buses like this is post-unification: constructed after 1870. Look left and right down the street—the facades are mostly 19th-century neo-Renaissance, built after this main thoroughfare sliced through the city. Traffic in much of central Rome is limited to city buses, taxis, motorbikes, "dark cars" (limos and town cars of VIPs), delivery vans, residents, and disabled people with permits (a.k.a. friends of politi-

cians). This is one of the increasingly rare streets where any vehicle is welcome.

• *Cross Corso Vittorio Emanuele II, and enter a square with a statue of Marco Minghetti, an early Italian prime minister. Angle left at the statue, walking along the left side of the skippable City Museum of Rome, down Via di San Pantaleo. A block down, at the corner, you'll find a beat-up old statue.*

❹ Pasquino

Pasquino—a third-century-BC statue that was discovered near here—is one of Rome's "talking statues." For 500 years, this statue has served as a kind of community billboard, allowing people to complain anonymously when it might be dangerous to speak up. To this day, you'll see old Pasquino strewn with political posters, strike announcements, and grumbling graffiti. The statue looks worn down by centuries of bitching.

• *Facing Pasquino, veer to the left and head up Via di Pasquino to...*

❺ Piazza Navona

This long, oblong square is dotted with fountains, busy with outdoor cafés, lined with palazzos and churches, and thronged

Piazza Navona with Bernini's Four Rivers fountain

with happy visitors. By its shape you might guess that this square started out as a racetrack, part of the training grounds built here by Emperor Domitian around AD 80. That was the same year the Colosseum opened: Rome was at its peak.

But much of what we see today came in the 1600s, when the whole place got a major renovation. At the time, the popes were trying to put some big scandals behind them, and beautification projects like this were a peace offering to the public.

Three Baroque fountains decorate the piazza. The first fountain, at the southern end, features a Moor wrestling with a dolphin. In 17th-century Rome, Moors (North Africans) represented all that was exotic and mysterious. In the fountain at the northern end, Neptune slays a giant octopus.

The most famous fountain, though, is in the center: the **Four Rivers Fountain** by Gian Lorenzo Bernini, the man who in the mid-1600s remade Rome in the Baroque style. It's topped with an Egyptian-style obelisk—another of the themes we'll see along this walk. Obelisks were popular with Roman emperors because Egyptian society saw its rulers as divine—an idea Roman rulers liked to promote. Get close to admire Bernini's four enormous statues at the base. As the water of the world gushes everywhere, these four burly river gods represent the four quarters of the world.

Piazza Navona is Rome's most interesting night scene, with street music, artists, fire-eaters, local Casanovas, ice cream, and outdoor cafés that are worthy of a splurge if you've got time to sit and enjoy Italy's human river.

• Leave Piazza Navona directly across from **Tre Scalini** (famous for its tartufo, a rich, chocolate gelato concoction), and go east down Corsia Agonale, past rose peddlers and palm readers. Ahead of you (across the busy street) stands the stately Palazzo Madama, where the **Italian Senate** meets. (Hence, security is high.) Jog left around this building, and follow the brown Pantheon sign straight down Via del Salvatore.

After a block, you'll pass (on your left) the **Church of San Luigi dei Francesi,** with its très French decor and precious Caravaggio paintings. If it's open, pop in. Otherwise, continue along, following the crowd to...

Pantheon

❻ The Pantheon

Perhaps the most magnificent building surviving from ancient Rome is this temple to the "pantheon" (literally, all the gods). The 40-foot, single-piece granite columns of the Pantheon's entrance show the scale the ancient Romans built on. The columns support a triangular Greek-style roof with an inscription that proclaims, "M. Agrippa built this." In fact, the present structure was built (*fecit*) by Emperor Hadrian (AD 120), who gave credit to the builder of an earlier temple. This impressive entrance-way gives no clue that the greatest wonder of the building is inside—a domed room that inspired later domes, including Michelangelo's St. Peter's and Brunelleschi's Duomo in Florence.

If the Pantheon is open, pop in and take a look around (for details on the interior, see page 437). If the Pantheon is closed, just stand for a while under the portico, which is romantically floodlit and moonlit at night.

• *With your back to the Pantheon, veer to the right, uphill toward the yellow sign on Via Orfani that reads Casa del Caffè— you've reached the...*

❼ Caffè Tazza d'Oro

This is one of Rome's top coffee shops, dating back to the days when this area was licensed to roast coffee beans. Locals come here for a shot of espresso or, when it's hot, a refreshing *granita di caffè con panna* (coffee and crushed ice with whipped cream).

• *From here, our walk continues past some interesting landmarks to the Trevi Fountain. Bear left at the coffee shop and continue up Via degli Orfani to the next square...*

❽ Piazza Capranica

This square is home to the big, plain Florentine-Renaissance-style Palazzo Capranica (directly opposite as you enter the square). Its stubby tower was once much taller, but when a stronger government arrived, the nobles were all ordered to shorten their towers. Like so many of Rome's churches, the church on the square—Santa Maria in Aquiro—is older than its Baroque-era facade. Notice the circular little shrine on the street corner.

• *Leave the piazza to the right of the palace, heading down Via in Aquiro. The street jogs to the left and into a square called...*

❾ Piazza di Montecitorio

This square is marked by an **Egyptian obelisk** from the sixth century BC. Emperor Augustus brought it to Rome as a trophy proclaiming his victory over Mark Antony and Cleopatra. In Augustus' day, the obelisk acted as a sundial and calendar, and it still functions as a sundial today. Follow the zodiac markings in the pavement to the square's other big sight— the **Italian Parliament.**

• *One block to your right is Piazza Colonna, where we're heading next—unless you like gelato. A one-block detour to the left (past Hotel Nazionale) brings you to a famous Roman gelateria, Giolitti.*

❿ Piazza Colonna and Via del Corso

The square features a massive **column** that has stood here since the second century AD. The column's shaft is 12 feet across, almost 100 feet tall, and stands on a 30-foot base, which rests on a platform. It's 28 cylindrical blocks are stacked atop each other like a pile of 10-ton checkers. A carved frieze winds from the bottom to the top, telling the story of Emperor Marcus Aurelius heroically battling barbarians about AD 170.

Beyond Piazza Colonna runs noisy **Via del Corso,** Rome's main north-south boulevard. In ancient times, this was the Via Flaminia, the highway that stretched from the Roman Forum to the Adriatic coast. The street was renamed "corso" for a famous medieval horse race that took place here during the crazy Carnevale season leading up to Lent. Every evening, the pedestrian-only stretch of the Corso is packed with people on parade, taking to the streets for their *passeggiata*.

Before crossing the street, look left (to the obelisk marking Piazza del Popolo—the ancient north gate of the city) and right (to the Victor Emmanuel Monument).

• *Cross Via del Corso to enter a big palatial building with columns, the **Galleria Alberto Sordi** shopping mall. To the left are convenient WCs.*

Go to the right and exit out the back. (If you're here after 21:00, when the mall is closed, circle around the right side of the Galleria on Via dei Sabini.) At any time, be on guard for pickpockets, who thrive in the nearby Trevi Fountain crowds. Once out the back, the tourist kitsch builds as you head up Via de Crociferi to the roar of the water, lights, and people at the...

⓫ Trevi Fountain

The Trevi Fountain is the ultimate showcase for Rome's love affair with water. Architect Nicola Salvi conceived this liquid Baroque avalanche in 1762, cleverly incorporating the palace behind the fountain as a theatrical backdrop. Centerstage is the enormous figure known simply as the "Ocean." The statue stands in his shell-shaped chariot, surfing through his wet dream. Water gushes from 24 spouts and tumbles over 30 different kinds of plants. Winged horses represent cresting waves. They're led by Tritons who blow on their conch shells. *Drammatico!*

The square that faces the fountain has a lively atmosphere. The magic is enhanced by the fact that no streets directly approach it. You can hear the excitement as you draw near, and then—bam!—you're there. Enjoy the scene. Romantics toss a coin over their shoulder into the fountain. Legend says it will assure your return to Rome. Every year I go through this tourist ritual...and so far it's working.

• *Facing the Trevi Fountain, walk along its right side up Via della Stamperia. Cross busy*

Via del Tritone. Angle left as you continue about 30 yards up Via del Nazareno to #9, where you'll pass a fence on the left, with an exposed bit of that ancient Acqua Vergine aqueduct. At the T-intersection ahead, turn right on Via Sant'Andrea delle Fratte. The street becomes Via di Propaganda. You'll pass alongside the...

⓬ Palazzo di Propaganda Fide

At #1, on the right, the white-and-yellow entrance marks the palace from which the Catholic Church "propagated," or spread, its message to the world. Back in the 1600s, this "Propaganda Palace" was the headquarters of the Catholic Church's P.R. department—a priority after the Reformation. The building was designed by that dynamic Baroque duo, Bernini and Borromini (with his concave lines). It flies the yellow-and-white flag signifying that it is still owned by the Vatican.

• *The street opens up into a long piazza. You're approaching the Spanish Steps. But first, pause at the...*

Trevi Fountain

⑬ Column of the Immaculate Conception

Atop a tall column stands a bronze statue of Mary. She wears a diadem of stars for a halo, and stands on a crescent moon atop a globe of the earth, which is crushing a satanic serpent. To Mary's immediate left stands the Spanish embassy to the Vatican. Rome has double the embassies of a normal capital because here countries need two: one to Italy and one to the Vatican. And because of this 300-year-old embassy, the square and its famous steps are called "Spanish."

• *Just 100 yards past Mary, you reach the climax of our walk, the...*

⑭ Spanish Steps

The wide, curving staircase is one of Rome's iconic sights. Its 138 steps lead sharply up from Piazza di Spagna. Partway up, the steps fan out around a central terrace, forming a butterfly shape. The design culminates at the top in an obelisk framed between two Baroque church towers.

For decades the steps were a favorite Roman hangout, but recently the city banned anyone from sitting on them. You can walk up and down the steps, but if you sit, you'll face a €250 fine.

At the foot of the steps is the aptly named Sinking Boat Fountain. It was built by Gian Lorenzo Bernini's father, Pietro. Because the water pressure here is low, the water can't shoot high in the air. So Bernini designed the fountain to be low key—a sinking boat filled with water.

The piazza is a thriving scene both day and night. It features many of the themes we've enjoyed on this walk—fountains, obelisks, public spaces, statues, and gelato. Most of all, it's a glimpse at today's Rome—a city where friends and families live much the same kind of life as their ancient cousins.

• *Our walk is finished. To reach the top of the steps sweat-free, take the free elevator just inside the Spagna Metro stop (to the left, as you face the steps; elevator closes at 23:30).*

SIGHTS

I've clustered Rome's sights into walkable neighborhoods. When you see a 🎧 in a listing, it means the sight is also covered in a free audio tour (via my Rick Steves Audio Europe app—see page 17). Rome's good city-run information website, www.060608.it, lists current opening hours.

State museums in Italy are free to enter once or twice a month, usually on a Sunday. Free days are actually bad news—they attract crowds. In peak season, check state museum websites in advance and make a point to avoid their free days. For Rome, that means the Colosseum, Roman Forum, Palatine Hill, Borghese Gallery, National Museum of Rome, and Castel Sant'Angelo.

Ancient Rome

The core of ancient Rome, where the grandest monuments were built, is between the Colosseum and Capitoline Hill. I've listed these sights generally from south to north, starting with the biggies—the Colosseum and Forum—and continuing up to Capitoline Hill and Piazza Venezia. As a pleasant conclusion to your busy day, walk back south along the broad, parklike main drag—Via dei Fori Imperiali.

Ancient Core

▲▲▲COLOSSEUM (COLOSSEO)

This 2,000-year-old building is the classic example of Roman engineering. Used as a venue for entertaining the masses, this colossal, functional stadium is one of Europe's most recognizable landmarks. Whether you're playing gladiator or simply marveling at the remarkable ancient design and construction, the Colosseum gets a unanimous thumbs-up.

Cost and Hours: €16 combo-ticket covers the Colosseum and the Roman Forum/Palatine Hill and is valid 24 hours. Buy it online well in advance to get a

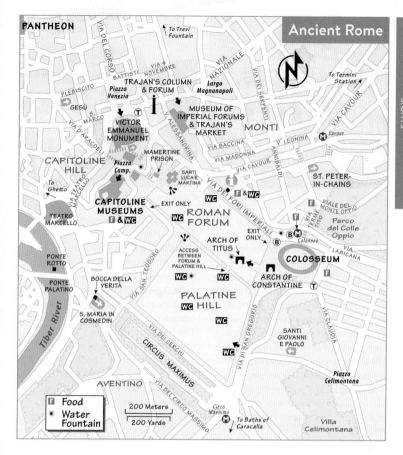

PANTHEON

Map labels include: To Trevi Fountain, VIA DEL CORSO, VIA 4 NOVEMBRE, BATTISTI, VIA NAZIONALE, VIA DEI SERPENTI, To Termini Station, PLEBISCITO, Piazza Venezia, TRAJAN'S COLUMN & FORUM, Largo Magnanapoli, GESÙ, VIA CAVOUR, VIA S. MARCO, VICTOR EMMANUEL MONUMENT, MUSEUM OF IMPERIAL FORUMS & TRAJAN'S MARKET, MONTI, VIA D. ARACOELI, VIA ALESSANDRINA, V. LEONINA, Cavour, MAMERTINE PRISON, VIA BACCINA, VIA MADONNA, ANNIBALDI, CAPITOLINE HILL, Piazza Camp., SANTI LUCA E MARTINA, VIA CAVOUR, ST. PETER-IN-CHAINS, To Ghetto, EXIT ONLY, WC, VIALE DEL MONTE OPPIO, TEATRO MARCELLO, CAPITOLINE MUSEUMS, ROMAN FORUM, WC, Parco del Colle Oppio, PONTE ROTTO, EXIT ONLY, Colosseo, VIA LABICANA, ACCESS BETWEEN FORUM & PALATINE HILL, ARCH OF TITUS, COLOSSEUM, PONTE PALATINO, BOCCA DELLA VERITÀ, WC, WC, ARCH OF CONSTANTINE, VIA SAN TEODORO, S. MARIA IN COSMEDIN, PALATINE HILL, WC, Tiber River, VIA DEI CERCHI, WC, VIA DI SAN GREGORIO, SANTI GIOVANNI E PAOLO, VIA CLAUDIA, CIRCUS MAXIMUS, AVENTINO, VIA DEL CIRCO MASSIMO, Piazza Celimontana, Circo Massimo, To Baths of Caracalla, Villa Celimontana

Legend:
🅕 Food
• Water Fountain
200 Meters
200 Yards

timed-entry reservation (€2 fee) for the Colosseum. Do not show up without a reserved entry. A Full Experience ticket costs €22, is valid for two consecutive days, and covers the Colosseum, Palatine Hill/Roman Forum, and all the minor sights at these archaeological areas. Open daily 8:30 until one hour before sunset—April-Aug until 19:15, Sept until 19:00, Oct until 18:30, off-season closes as early as 16:30; last entry one hour before closing, Metro: Colosseo, tel. 06-3996-7700, www.coopculture.it.

Reservations and Avoiding Lines: Buy your reserved-entry ticket well in advance. The official site is best (www.coopculture.it), but other sites may have more avail-

ability for a higher price (www.il-colosseo.it). Get an early morning or late afternoon time slot. Midday crowds can be so bad that even reservation-holders can face long waits. If the time slot you want is sold out, you may find availability by paying extra for an audio- or videoguide.

If you show up without a reservation you can suffer in the long ticket-buying line or, as a last resort, join one of the tours sold by hawkers outside the gate, then ditch it once you get inside. If you book a private tour in advance (see "Tours"), the guide may be able to book your ticket and reservation.

Generally, crowds are thinner (and lines shorter) in the afternoon (especially after

ITALY

Colosseum

Colosseum interior

16:00 in summer); this is also true at the Forum. A line typically has already formed at 8:30 when the Colosseum opens.

Getting There: The Colosseo Metro stop on line B is just across the street from the monument. Buses #51, #75, #85, #87, and #118 stop along Via dei Fori Imperiali near the Colosseum entrance (buses don't run on this street on Sun but still stop nearby), one of the Forum/Palatine Hill entrances, and Piazza Venezia. Tram #3 stops behind the Colosseum.

Getting In: The single entry point has two lines: one for those with reservations and another for the sorry lot without reservations.

Tours: A fact-filled **audioguide** is available just past the turnstiles (€5.50/1 hour). A handheld **videoguide** senses where you are in the site and plays related clips (€6/50 minutes) but can be hard to see in bright sunlight.

🎧 Download my free Colosseum **audio tour.**

Official **guided tours** in English depart roughly hourly between 9:45 and 15:00 (€5 plus Colosseum ticket, 45-60 minutes, purchase inside Colosseum near ticket booth marked *Visite didattiche*).

Private guides stand outside the Colosseum looking for business (€25-30/2-hour tour of the Colosseum, Forum, and Palatine Hill; includes admission). Make sure that your tour will start right away and that the ticket you receive covers all

three sights: the Colosseum, Forum, and Palatine Hill.

Visitor Services: A WC (often crowded) is inside the Colosseum, and there are also water fountains.

Background: Built when the Roman Empire was at its peak in AD 80, the Colosseum represents Rome at its grandest. The Flavian Amphitheater (the Colosseum's real name) was an arena for gladiator contests and public spectacles. When killing became a spectator sport, the Romans wanted to share the fun with as many people as possible, so they stuck two semicircular theaters together to create a freestanding amphitheater. With four oversized stories, it's 160 feet high, nearly a third of a mile around, and makes an oval-shaped footprint that covers six acres. The stadium could accommodate 50,000 roaring fans (that's 100,000 thumbs). As Romans arrived for the games, they'd be greeted outside by a huge bronze statue of the emperor Nero—100 feet tall, gleaming in the sunlight—standing where the cypress trees stand today, between the Colosseum and the Metro stop.

Rick's Tip: *While it sounds like a sacrilege, a visit to the interior of* **the Colosseum may not be worth suffering through the mob scene.** *Half the thrill of the Colosseum is seeing it from outside (free and easy at any time).*

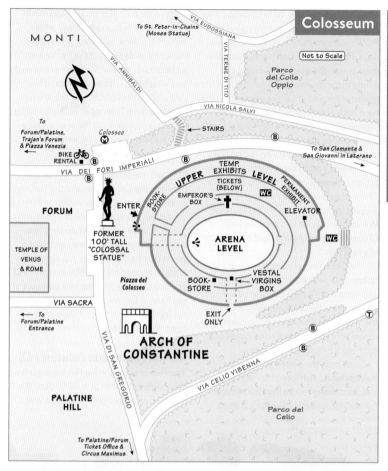

Colosseum

Visiting the Colosseum: After the turnstiles, walk directly to the arena and view it from ground level—near the Christian cross (see the "Colosseum" map). Then, climb the stairs to the permanent exhibit on the upper level. Tour the exhibit. Then step out to view the arena from that upper level. Circle the arena clockwise three-quarters of the way around. From there, enjoy a viewpoint overlooking the Arch of Constantine and Roman Forum, check out the fine bookstore, then take the stairs down to ground level and head for the exit.

The games took place in the oval-shaped **arena,** 280 feet long by 165 feet wide. When you look down into the arena, you're seeing the underground passages beneath the playing surface (which can be visited only on a private tour). The arena was originally covered with a wooden floor, then sprinkled with sand (*arena* in Latin). The bit of reconstructed floor gives you an accurate sense of the original arena level and the subterranean warren where animals and prisoners were held. Around you are the big brick masses that supported the tiers of seats.

The **games** pitted men against men, men against beasts, and beasts against beasts. First came the animals, things like watching dogs bloody themselves attacking porcupines. At lunchtime came Act Two. This was when criminals and POWs were executed, often in creative ways. Finally, in the afternoon, came the main event: the gladiators. Trumpets would blare, drums would pound, and the gladiators would enter the arena from the west end, parade around to the music, and pause at the south side. There, they'd acknowledge the Vestal Virgins sitting in their special box seats on the 50-yard line. After a nod to the Virgins, the gladiators continued on to the emperor's box. There, they'd raise their weapons, salute, and shout *"Ave, Caesar!"*—"Hail Caesar! We who are about to die salute you!" (Though some scholars doubt they actually said that.)

The Colosseum spectacles were a way to bring home the environments, animals, and people of Rome's conquered lands, parade them before the public, and make them real. Imagine never having seen an actual lion, and suddenly one jumps out to chase a prisoner in the arena.

Don't miss the upper-level **permanent exhibit,** with lots of ancient artifacts and fascinating reconstruction models (all well-described in English); it helps bring to life both the ancient and medieval scene. It features intimate details, including pulleys, pastimes, and seating hierarchy, and gives a close-up look at architectural details. Stairs are at the east and west sides, with an elevator at the east end (accessible only to those who really need it). The upper deck also offers more colossal views of the arena, plus a bookstore and temporary exhibits.

▲ARCH OF CONSTANTINE

This well-preserved arch, which stands between the Colosseum and the Forum, commemorates a military coup and, more important, the acceptance of Christianity by the Roman Empire. When the ambitious Emperor Constantine (who had a vision that he'd win under the sign of the cross) defeated his rival Maxentius in AD 312, Constantine became sole emperor of the Roman Empire and legalized Christianity. The arch is free to see—always open and viewable.

Roman Forum and Palatine Hill

The Forum and Palatine Hill are organized as a single sight with one admission. You'll need to see both sights in a single visit.

Arch of Constantine

Roman Forum looking east, down Via Sacra

Cost and Hours: €16 combo-ticket includes Colosseum (buy online in advance to secure Colosseum entry time, €2 booking fee). If you plan to skip the Colosseum, the €16 Forum Super Pass adds minor sights—the Palatine's museum, Imperial Forums, House of Augustus, and House of Livia—but doesn't cover the Colosseum. A €22 Full Experience ticket covers Forum Super Pass sights plus the Colosseum (valid 2 consecutive days). Same hours as Colosseum, tel. 06-3996-7700, www.coopculture.it.

▲▲▲ROMAN FORUM (FORO ROMANO)

This is ancient Rome's birthplace and civic center, and the common ground between Rome's famous seven hills. As just about anything important that happened in ancient Rome happened here, it's arguably the most important piece of real estate in Western civilization. While only a few fragments of that glorious past remain, history seekers find plenty to ignite their imaginations amid the half-broken columns and arches.

Avoiding Lines: Save time by buying your ticket in advance online. Generally, crowds are smaller in the afternoon, espe-cially after 16:00 in summer.

Getting There: The closest Metro stop is Colosseo. Buses #51, #75, #85, #87, and #118 stop along Via dei Fori Imperiali near the Colosseum, the Forum, and Piazza Venezia (buses don't run on this street on Sun but still stop nearby).

Getting In: There are three main entrances to the Forum/Palatine Hill sight: 1) from the Colosseum (the most crowded entry)—nearest the Arch of Titus, where this guided walk starts; 2) from Via dei Fori Imperiali; and 3) from Via di San Gregorio—at south end of Palatine Hill, which is least crowded. With a Forum Super Pass or Full Experience ticket, you can also enter near Trajan's Column.

Tours: An unexciting yet informative **audioguide** helps decipher the rubble (€5/2 hours, €7 version includes Palatine Hill and lasts 3 hours, must leave ID). You must return it to where you rented it.

🎧 Download my free Roman Forum **audio tour.**

Visitor Services: A free information center, located across from the Via dei Fori Imperiali entrance, has a bookshop, small café, food stand, and WCs (daily 9:30-19:00).

ITALY

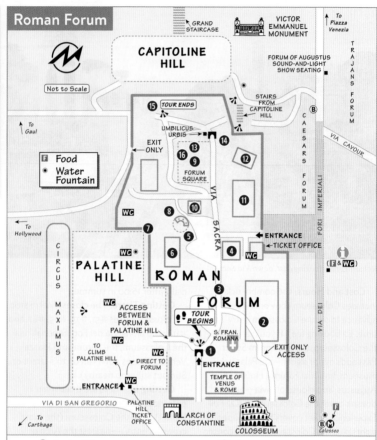

Roman Forum

- **1** Arch of Titus
- **2** Basilica of Constantine
- **3** Via Sacra
- **4** Temple of Antoninus Pius & Faustina
- **5** Temple of Vesta
- **6** House of the Vestal Virgins
- **7** Caligula's Palace
- **8** Temple of Castor & Pollux
- **9** The Forum's Main Square
- **10** Temple of Julius Caesar
- **11** Basilica Aemilia
- **12** The Curia
- **13** Rostrum
- **14** Arch of Septimius Severus
- **15** Temple of Saturn
- **16** Column of Phocas

⊙ SELF-GUIDED TOUR

As you begin this Forum tour, see things with "period eyes." We imagine the structures in ancient Rome as mostly white, but ornate buildings and monuments like the Arch of Titus were originally more colorful. Through the ages, builders scavenged stone from the Forum, and the

finest stone—the colored marble—was cannibalized first. If any was left, it was generally the white stone. Statues that filled the niches were vividly painted, but the organic paint rotted away as statues lay buried for centuries. Lettering was inset bronze and eyes were inset ivory. Even seemingly intact structures, like the

Arch of Titus, have been reassembled. Notice the columns are half smooth and half fluted. The fluted halves are original; the smooth parts are reconstructions.

• *Start at the Arch of Titus, which rises above the rubble on the Colosseum end of the Forum.*

❶ Arch of Titus (Arco di Tito): The Arch of Titus commemorated the Roman victory over the province of Judaea (Israel) in AD 70. The Romans had a reputation as benevolent conquerors who tolerated local customs and rulers. All they required was allegiance to the empire, shown by worshipping the emperor as a god. No problem for most conquered people, who already had a half-dozen gods on their prayer lists anyway. But Israelites believed in only one god, and it wasn't the emperor. Israel revolted. After a short but bitter war, the Romans defeated the rebels, took Jerusalem, destroyed their temple (leaving only a fragment of one wall's foundation—today's revered "Wailing Wall"), and brought home 50,000 Jewish slaves...who were forced to build this arch (and the Colosseum).

• *Walk down Via Sacra into the Forum. Imagine Roman sandals on these original basalt stones—perhaps the oldest street you'll ever walk. Many of the stones under your feet were walked on by Caesar Augustus 2,000 years ago. After about 50 yards, turn right and follow a path uphill to the three huge arches of the...*

❷ Basilica of Constantine (Basilica Maxentius): Yes, these are big arches. But they represent only one-third of the original Basilica of Constantine, a mammoth hall of justice. The arches were matched by a similar set along the Via Sacra side (only a few squat brick piers remain). Between them ran the central hall, which was spanned by a roof 130 feet high—about 55 feet higher than the side arches you see. (The stub of brick you see sticking up began an arch that once spanned the central hall.) The hall itself was as long as a football field, lavishly furnished (with colorful inlaid marble, a gilded bronze ceiling, and statues), and filled with strolling Romans. At the far (west) end was an enormous marble statue of Emperor Constantine on a throne. (Pieces of this statue, including a hand the size of a man, are on display in Rome's Capitoline Museums.)

This "basilica" was not a church but a Roman hall of justice. In a society that was as legal-minded as America is today, you needed a lot of lawyers—and a big place to put them. Citizens came here to work out matters like inheritances and building permits, or to sue somebody.

• *Now backtrack downhill and stroll deeper into the Forum, turning right along the...*

❸ Via Sacra: Stroll through the trees, down this main drag of the ancient city. Imagine being an out-of-town visitor during Rome's heyday—maybe from Gaul (modern France) or Londinium (modern London). You know a little Latin, but nothing would have prepared you for the bustle of Rome—a city of a million people—by far the biggest city in Europe. This street would be swarming with tribunes, slaves, and courtesans. Chariots whizzed by. Wooden stalls lined the roads, where merchants peddled their goods.

On your right, you'll pass a building with a green door still swinging on its fourth-century hinges—the original bronze door to a temple that survived because it became a church shortly after the fall of Rome. This ancient temple is still in use, sometimes hosting modern exhibits. No wonder they call Rome the Eternal City.

• *Just past the ancient temple, 10 huge columns stand in front of a much newer-looking church. This colonnade was part of the...*

❹ Temple of Antoninus Pius and Faustina: The Senate built this temple to honor Emperor Antoninus Pius (AD 138-161) and his deified wife, Faustina. The 50-foot-tall Corinthian (leafy) columns must have been awe-inspiring to out-of-towners who grew up in thatched huts.

Rome: Republic and Empire (500 B.C.–A.D. 500)

Ancient Rome lasted for a thousand years, from about 500 BC to AD 500. During that time, Rome expanded from a small tribe of barbarians to a vast empire, and then dwindled slowly to city size again. For the first 500 years, when Rome's armies made her ruler of the Italian peninsula and beyond, Rome was a republic governed by elected senators. Over the next 500 years, a time of world conquest and eventual decline, Rome was an empire ruled by a military-backed dictator.

Julius Caesar bridged the gap between republic and empire. This ambitious general and politician, popular with the people because of his military victories and charisma, suspended the Roman constitution and assumed dictatorial powers in about 50 BC. A few years later, he was assassinated by a conspiracy of senators. His adopted son, Augustus, succeeded him, and soon "Caesar" was not just a name but a title.

Emperor Augustus ushered in the Pax Romana, or Roman peace (AD 1-200), a time when Rome reached her peak and controlled an empire that stretched even beyond Eurail—from England to Egypt, Turkey to Morocco.

Although the temple has been inhabited by a church, you can still see the basic layout—a staircase led to a shaded porch (the columns), which admitted you to the main building (now a church), where the statue of the god sat.

Picture these columns supporting brightly painted statues in a triangular pediment, and the whole building capped with a gleaming bronze roof. The stately gray rubble of today's Forum is a faded black-and-white photograph of a 3-D Technicolor era.

• With your back to the colonnade, walk straight ahead—jogging a bit to the right to stay on the path. The dirt path leads to two sights associated with Rome's Vestal Virgins. Head for the three short columns, all that's left of the...

❺ **Temple of Vesta:** This is perhaps Rome's most sacred spot. Although we think of the Romans as decadent, in fact they prided themselves on their family values. People venerated their parents, grandparents, and ancestors, even keeping small statues of them in sacred shrines in their homes. This temple represented those family values on a large scale; its fire

symbolized the "hearth" of the extended family that was Rome. As long as the sacred flame burned, Rome would stand. The flame was tended by six priestesses known as the Vestal Virgins.

• Backtrack a few steps up the path, behind the Temple of Vesta. You'll find a few stairs that lead up to a big, enclosed field with two rectangular brick pools (just below the hill). This was the courtyard of the...

❻ **House of the Vestal Virgins:** The Vestal Virgins lived in a two-story building surrounding a long central courtyard with two pools at one end. Rows of statues depicting leading Vestal Virgins flanked

Temple of Antoninus Pius and Faustina

the courtyard. This place was the model—both architecturally and sexually—for medieval convents and monasteries.

Chosen from noble families before they reached the age of 10, the six Vestal Virgins each served a 30-year term. Honored and revered by the Romans, the Vestals even had their own box seats opposite the emperor in the Colosseum. The statues that line the courtyard honor dutiful Vestals.

As the name implies, a Vestal took a vow of chastity. If she served her term faithfully—abstaining for 30 years—she was given a huge dowry and allowed to marry. But if they found any Virgin who wasn't, she was strapped to a funeral car, paraded through the streets of the Forum, taken to a crypt, given a loaf of bread and a lamp...and buried alive. Many Vestals suffered the latter fate.

• *Looming just beyond this field is Palatine Hill—the corner of which may have been...*

❼ **Caligula's Palace** (Palace of Tiberius): Emperor Caligula (ruled AD 37-41) had a huge palace on Palatine Hill overlooking the Forum. It actually sprawled down the hill into the Forum (some supporting arches remain in the hillside). Caligula was not a nice person. He tortured enemies, stole senators' wives, and parked his chariot in handicap spaces. Each of Rome's luxury-loving emperors added to the glory of the Forum, trying to make his mark on history.

• *Continue downhill, passing the three short columns of the Temple of Vesta, where you'll get a view of three very tall columns just beyond.*

❽ **Temple of Castor and Pollux:** These three columns are all that remain of a once-prestigious temple—one of the city's oldest, built in the fifth century BC. It commemorated the Roman victory over the Tarquin, the notorious Etruscan king. After the battle, the legendary twin brothers Castor and Pollux watered their horses here, at the Sacred Spring of Juturna (which has been excavated nearby). As a

symbol of Rome's self-governing republic, the temple was often used as a meeting place of senators, and its front steps served as a podium for free speech.

• *The path spills into a flat, open area that stretches before you. This was the center of the ancient Forum.*

❾ **The Forum's Main Square:** The original Forum, or main square, was this flat patch about the size of a football field, stretching to the foot of Capitoline Hill. Surrounding it were temples, law courts, government buildings, and triumphal arches.

Rome was born right here. According to legend, twin brothers Romulus (Rome) and Remus were orphaned in infancy and raised by a she-wolf on top of Palatine Hill. Growing up, they found it hard to get dates. So they and their cohorts attacked the nearby Sabine tribe and kidnapped their women. After they made peace, this marshy valley became the meeting place and then the trading center for the scattered tribes on the surrounding hillsides.

Temple of Castor and Pollux

Ancient Rome's population exceeded one million, more than any city until London and Paris in the 19th century. All those Roman masses lived in tiny apartments as we would live in tents at a campsite, basically just to sleep. The public space—their Forum, today's piazza—is where they did their living. Consider how, to this day, the piazza is still such an important part of any Italian town.

The Forum is now rubble, but imagine it in its prime: blindingly brilliant marble buildings with 40-foot-high columns and shining metal roofs; rows of statues painted in realistic colors; processional chariots rattling down Via Sacra. Mentally replace tourists in T-shirts with tribunes in togas. Imagine the buildings towering and the people buzzing around you while an orator gives a rabble-rousing speech from the Rostrum. If things still look like just a pile of rocks, at least tell yourself, "But Julius Caesar once leaned against these rocks."

• And speaking of Julius Caesar, at the near end of the main square (the end closest to the Colosseum) find the foundations of a temple now sheltered by a peaked wood-and-metal roof.

🔟 **Temple of Julius Caesar** (Tempio del Divo Giulio, or Ara di Cesare): On March 15, in 44 BC, Julius Caesar (100-44 BC) was stabbed 23 times by political conspirators. After his assassination, Caesar's body was cremated on this spot (under the metal roof). Afterward, this temple was built to honor him. Peek behind the wall into the small apse area, where a mound of dirt usually has fresh flowers—given to remember the man who, more than any other, personified the greatness of Rome.

Although he was popular with the masses, not everyone liked Caesar's urban design or his politics. When he assumed dictatorial powers, he was ambushed and stabbed to death by a conspiracy of senators, including his adopted son, Brutus ("Et tu, Brute?").

The funeral was held here, facing the main square. The citizens gathered, and speeches were made. Mark Antony stood up to say (in Shakespeare's words), "Friends, Romans, countrymen, lend me your ears. I come to bury Caesar, not to praise him." When Caesar's body was burned, his adoring fans threw anything at hand on the fire, requiring the fire department to come put it out. Later, Emperor Augustus dedicated this temple in his name, making Caesar the first Roman to become a god.

• Continue past the Temple of Julius Caesar, to the open area between the columns of the Temple of Antoninus Pius and Faustina (which we passed earlier) and the boxy brick building (the Curia). You can view the ruins of the Basilica Aemilia from a ramp next to the Temple of Antoninus Pius and Faustina, or (if the path is open) walk among them.

⓫ **Basilica Aemilia:** Notice the layout. This was a long, rectangular building. The stubby columns all in a row form one long, central hall flanked by two side aisles. Medieval Christians required a larger meeting hall for their worship services than Roman temples provided, so they used the spacious Roman basilica as the model for their churches. Cathedrals from France to Spain to England, from Romanesque to Gothic to Renaissance, all have the same basic floor plan as a Roman basilica.

• Now head for the big, well-preserved brick building with the triangular roof—the Curia. It's just to the right of the big triumphal arch at the foot of Capitoline Hill. While often closed, the building is impressive even from outside.

⓬ **The Curia** (Senate House): The Curia was the most important political building in the Forum. Since the birth of the republic, this was the site of Rome's official center of government. Three hundred senators, elected by the citizens of Rome, donned their togas, tucked their scrolls under their arms, and climbed the steps into this great hall. Inside, they gave speeches, debated policy, and created the laws of the land. They sat with their backs to the walls, surrounding the big hall on three sides, in three rows of seats. At the far end sat the Senate president—and later, the emperor—on his podium. The vast room still echoes with stirring speeches and passionate debates.

The present Curia building dates from AD 283, when it replaced an earlier Senate building. It's so well-preserved because it was used as a church since early Christian times. In the 1930s, it was restored as a historic site.

• Go back down the Senate steps and find the 10-foot-high wall just to the left of the big arch, marked...

🔞 **Rostrum:** Nowhere was Roman freedom of speech more apparent than at this "Speaker's Corner." The Rostrum was a raised platform, 10 feet high and 80 feet long, decorated with statues, columns, and the prows of ships.

On a stage like this, Rome's orators, great and small, tried to draw a crowd and sway public opinion. Picture the backdrop these speakers would have had—a mountain of marble buildings piling up on Capitoline Hill. Mark Antony rose to offer Caesar the laurel-leaf crown of kingship, which Caesar publicly (and hypocritically) refused—while privately becoming a dictator. Men such as Cicero—a contemporary of Julius Caesar—railed against the corruption and decadence that came with the city's newfound wealth. (Cicero paid

the price: he was executed, and his head and hands were nailed to the Rostrum.)

In later years, when emperors ruled, it took real daring to speak out against the powers that be. Rome's democratic spirit was increasingly squelched. Eventually, the emperor and the army—not the Senate and the citizens—held ultimate power, and Rome's vast empire began to rot from within.

• In front of the Rostrum are **trees** bearing fruits that were sacred to the ancient Romans: olives (provided food, oil for light, and preservatives), figs (tasty), and wine grapes (made a popular export product). Now turn your attention to the big arch to the right of the Rostrum, the...

🔞 **Arch of Septimius Severus:** In imperial times, the Rostrum's voices of democracy would have been dwarfed by images of the empire, such as the huge six-story-high Arch of Septimius Severus (AD 203). The reliefs commemorate the African-born emperor's battles in Mesopotamia. Near ground level, see soldiers marching captured barbarians back to Rome for the victory parade.

• As we near the end of Rome's history, we're also nearing the end of our tour. Our next stop is the Temple of Saturn. You can see it from here—it's the eight big columns just up the slope of Capitol Hill. Or you could make your way to it for a closer look.

🔞 **Temple of Saturn:** These columns framed the entrance to the Forum's oldest

Arch of Septimius Severus

Temple of Saturn

temple (497 BC). Inside was a humble, very old wooden statue of the god Saturn. The statue's claim to fame was its pedestal, which held the gold bars, coins, and jewels of Rome's state treasury, the booty collected by conquering generals.

Even older than the Temple of Saturn is the **Umbilicus Urbis,** which stands nearby (next to the Arch of Septimius Severus). A humble brick ruin marks this historic "Navel of the City." The spot was considered the center of the cosmos, and all distances in the empire were measured from here.

• *Now turn your attention from the Temple of Saturn, one of the Forum's first buildings, to one of its last monuments. Find a lone, tall column standing in the Forum in front of the Rostrum. It's fluted and topped with a leafy Corinthian capital. This is the...*

🟠 **Column of Phocas:** This is the Forum's last monument (AD 608), a gift from the powerful Byzantine Empire to a fallen empire—Rome. Given to commemorate the pagan Pantheon's becoming a Christian church, it was a symbolic last nail in ancient Rome's coffin. After Rome's 1,000-year reign, the city was looted by vandals, the population of a million-plus shrank to about 10,000, and the once-grand city center—the Forum—was abandoned, slowly covered up by centuries of silt and dirt. In the 1700s, an English historian named Edward Gibbon overlooked this spot from Capitoline Hill. Hearing Christian monks singing at these pagan ruins, he looked out at the few columns poking up from the ground, pondered the decline and fall of the Roman Empire, and thought, "Hmm, that's a catchy title..."

• *Your tour is over. If you want to see Palatine Hill, don't leave the Forum complex; you won't be allowed back in without a new ticket. Instead, return to the Arch of Titus.*

If you'd rather exit the Forum, be aware that the exact ways in and out change from year to year. Refer to your map for possible exit locations. If heading for Capitoline Hill, your best escape is likely on the west side (behind #16 on the map in this chapter).

▲▲PALATINE HILL (MONTE PALATINO)

While nearly empty of tourists, Palatine Hill is jam-packed with history—"the huts of Romulus," the huge Imperial Palace, a view of the Circus Maximus—but only the barest skeleton of rubble is left to tell the story.

We get our word "palace" from this hill, where the emperors chose to live. It was once so filled with palaces that later emperors had to build out. (Looking up at it from the Forum, you see the substructure that supported these long-gone palaces.) The Palatine Museum contains statues and frescoes that help you imagine the luxury of the imperial Palatine. From the pleasant garden, you'll get an overview of the Forum. On the far side, unless excavations are blocking the viewpoint, look down into an emperor's private stadium and then beyond at the grassy Circus Maximus, once a chariot course. Imagine the cheers, jeers, and furious betting.

While many tourists consider Palatine Hill just extra credit after the Forum, it offers insight into the greatness of Rome that's well worth the effort. (And, if you're visiting the Colosseum or Forum, you've got a ticket whether you like it or not.)

Cost and Hours: Covered by same tickets and open same hours as Roman Forum, listed earlier.

Getting There: The nearest Metro stop is Colosseo. Buses #51, #75, #85, #87, and #118 stop along Via dei Fori Imperiali near the Colosseum, the Forum, and Piazza Venezia (buses don't run on this street on Sun but still stop nearby).

Getting In: There are three entrances to the combined Palatine/Forum sight; see the map on page 426. The easiest is the entrance on Via di San Gregorio, 150 yards from the Colosseum. Upon entering, follow the path to the left as it winds to the top. Alternatively, if you sightsee the Forum first, to get to Palatine Hill you must walk up from the Arch of Titus.

Capitoline Hill

Of Rome's famous seven hills, this is the smallest, tallest, and most famous—home of the ancient Temple of Jupiter and the center of city government for 2,500 years. There are several ways to get to the top of Capitoline Hill. If you're coming from the north (from Piazza Venezia), take Michelangelo's impressive stairway to the right of the big, white Victor Emmanuel Monument. Coming from the southeast (the Roman Forum), take the steep staircase near the Arch of Septimius Severus. From near Trajan's Forum along Via dei Fori Imperiali, take the winding road. All three converge at the top, in the square called Campidoglio (kahm-pee-DOHL-yoh).

▲PIAZZA DEL CAMPIDOGLIO

This square atop the hill, once the religious and political center of ancient Rome, is still the home of the city's government. In the 1530s, the pope called on Michelangelo to reestablish this square as a grand center. Michelangelo placed the ancient equestrian statue of Marcus Aurelius as its focal point—very effective. (The original statue is now in the adjacent museum.) The twin buildings on either side are the Capitoline Museums. Behind the replica of the statue is the mayoral palace (Palazzo Senatorio).

Michelangelo intended that people approach the square from his grand stairway off Piazza Venezia. From the top of the stairway, you see the new Renaissance face of Rome, with its back to the Forum. Michelangelo gave the buildings the "giant order"—huge pilasters make the existing two-story buildings feel one-storied and more harmonious with the new square. Notice how the statues atop these buildings welcome you and then draw you in.

▲▲▲CAPITOLINE MUSEUMS

Some of ancient Rome's most famous statues and art are housed in the two palaces (Palazzo dei Conservatori and Palazzo Nuovo) that flank the equestrian statue in the Campidoglio. They're connected by an underground passage that leads to the Tabularium, an ancient building with a panoramic overlook of the Forum.

Cost and Hours: €15, daily 9:30-19:30, last entry one hour before closing, video-guide-€6, good children's audioguide-€4, tel. 06-0608, www.museicapitolini.org.

Visiting the Museum: You'll enter at

Piazza del Campidoglio and statue of Marcus Aurelius

ITALY

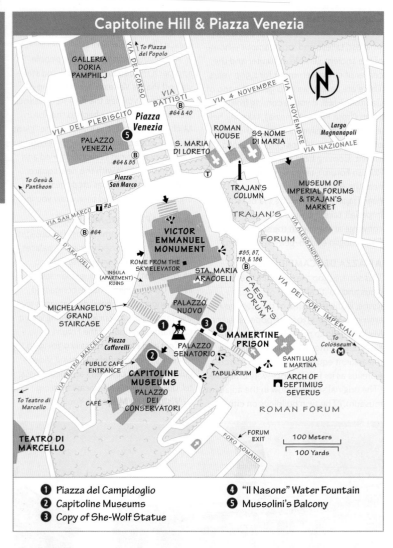

Capitoline Hill & Piazza Venezia

To Plazza del Popolo

VIA DEL CORSO

GALLERIA DORIA PAMPHILJ

VIA BATTISTI

B #64 & 40

VIA 4 NOVEMBRE

VIA 4 NOVEMBRE

VIA DEL PLEBISCITO

Piazza Venezia

5

PALAZZO VENEZIA

B #64 & 85

ROMAN HOUSE

S. MARIA DI LORETO

SS NOME DI MARIA

Largo Magnanapoli

VIA NAZIONALE

To Gesù & Pantheon

Piazza San Marco

T

TRAJAN'S COLUMN

MUSEUM OF IMPERIAL FORUMS & TRAJAN'S MARKET

VIA SAN MARCO **T** #8

B #64

VIA D'ARACOELI

VICTOR EMMANUEL MONUMENT

TRAJAN'S FORUM

VIA ALESSANDRINA

ROME FROM THE SKY ELEVATOR

INSULA (APARTMENT) RUINS

STA. MARIA ARACOELI

#85, 87, 118, & 186

B

CAESAR'S FORUM

VIA DEI FORI IMPERIALI

MICHELANGELO'S GRAND STAIRCASE

Piazza Caffarelli

PALAZZO NUOVO

1

3 **4**

MAMERTINE PRISON

To Colosseum & **M**

PUBLIC CAFÉ ENTRANCE

2

PALAZZO SENATORIO

SANTI LUCA E MARTINA

VIA TEATRO MARCELLO

CAPITOLINE MUSEUMS

PALAZZO DEI CONSERVATORI

TABULARIUM

ARCH OF SEPTIMIUS SEVERUS

To Teatro di Marcello

CAFÉ

ROMAN FORUM

TEATRO DI MARCELLO

FORUM EXIT

FORO ROMANO

100 Meters

100 Yards

1 Piazza del Campidoglio
2 Capitoline Museums
3 Copy of She-Wolf Statue

4 "Il Nasone" Water Fountain
5 Mussolini's Balcony

the **Palazzo dei Conservatori** (on your right as you face the equestrian statue), cross underneath the square (beneath the Palazzo Senatorio, the mayoral palace, not open to public), and exit from the Palazzo Nuovo (on your left). This enjoyable museum complex claims to be the world's oldest, founded in 1471 when a pope gave ancient statues to the citizens of Rome. Many of the museum's statues have become instantly recognizable

cultural icons, including the 13th-century *Capitoline She-Wolf* (the little statues of Romulus and Remus were added in the Renaissance). Don't miss the *Boy Extracting a Thorn* and the enchanting *Commodus as Hercules.* Behind Commodus is a statue of his dad, Marcus Aurelius, on a horse. The only surviving equestrian statue of a Roman emperor, this was the original centerpiece of the square (where a copy stands today). Christians in the

Dark Ages thought that the statue's hand was raised in blessing, which probably led to their misidentifying him as Constantine, the first Christian emperor. While most pagan statues were destroyed by Christians, "Constantine" was spared.

The museum's second-floor café, **Caffè Capitolino,** has a splendid patio offering city views. It's lovely at sunset (public entrance for those without a museum ticket off Piazzale Caffarelli and through door #4).

The **Tabularium,** built in the first century BC, once held the archives of ancient Rome. (The word Tabularium comes from "tablet," on which Romans wrote their laws.) You won't see any tablets, but you will see a stunning head-on view of the Forum from the windows.

The **Palazzo Nuovo** houses mostly portrait busts of forgotten emperors. But it also has two must-see statues: the *Dying Gaul* and the *Capitoline Venus* (both on the first floor up).

Piazza Venezia and Nearby

This vast square, dominated by the big, white Victor Emmanuel Monument, is a major transportation hub and the focal point of modern Rome. With your back to the monument, circle around the left side to reach two staircases leading up Capitoline Hill. One is Michelangelo's grand staircase up to the Campidoglio. The steeper of the two leads to **Santa Maria in Aracoeli,** a good example of the earliest style of Christian church. The contrast between this climb-on-your-knees ramp to God's house and Michelangelo's elegant stairs illustrates the changes Renaissance humanism brought civilization.

▲VICTOR EMMANUEL MONUMENT

This oversized monument to Italy's first king, built to celebrate the 50th anniversary of the country's unification in 1861, was part of Italy's push to overcome the new country's strong regionalism and create a national identity. Today, the mon-

Victor Emmanuel Monument

ument houses museums, and a €10 elevator to an excellent view.

The scale of the monument is over the top: 200 feet high, 500 feet wide. The 43-foot-tall statue of the king on his high horse is one of the biggest equestrian statues in the world. The king's moustache forms an arc five feet long, and a person could sit within the horse's hoof. At the base of this statue, Italy's Tomb of the Unknown Soldier (flanked by Italian flags and armed guards) is watched over by the goddess Roma (with the gold mosaic background).

With its gleaming white sheen (from a recent scrubbing) and enormous scale, the monument provides a vivid sense of what Ancient Rome looked like at its peak—imagine the Forum filled with shiny, grandiose buildings like this one.

Cost and Hours: Monument—free, daily 9:30-18:45, a few WCs scattered throughout; Rome from the Sky elevator—€10, daily until 19:00; ticket office closes 15 minutes earlier, tel. 06-0608; follow *ascensori panoramici* signs inside the Victor Emmanuel Monument (no elevator access from street level).

THE IMPERIAL FORUMS

Though the original Roman Forum is the main attraction for today's tourists, there are several more ancient forums nearby, known collectively as "The Imperial Forums." The forums stretch in a line along Via dei Fori Imperiali, from Piazza Venezia to the Colosseum. The ruins are out in the open, never crowded, and free to look down on from street level at any time, any day. (With the Forum Super Pass or Full Experience ticket—see page 425—you can access the Forum of Julius Caesar and the Forum of Trajan via a pathway that passes beneath Via dei Fori Imperiali.) If you'll be here in the evening, consider taking in a sound-and-light show (see page 460).

Trajan's Column: The world's grandest column from antiquity (rated ▲▲) anchors the first of the forums we'll see—Trajan's Forum. The 140-foot column is decorated with a spiral relief of 2,500 figures trumpeting the emperor's exploits. It has stood for centuries as a symbol of a truly cosmopolitan civilization. At one point, the ashes of Trajan and his wife were held in the base, and the sun glinted off a polished bronze statue of Trajan at the top. Since the 1500s, St. Peter has been on top.

Trajan's Forum: The dozen-plus gray columns mark one of the grandest structures in Trajan's Forum, the Basilica Ulpia, the largest law court of its day. Nearby stood two libraries that contained the world's knowledge in Greek and Latin. To

Trajan's Column

build his forum, Trajan cut away a ridge that once connected the Quirinal and Capitoline hills, creating this valley. This was the largest forum ever, and its opulence astounded even jaded Romans. But for every grand monument here, there was untold hardship and suffering in the Barbarian world.

Trajan's Market: This structure was part shopping mall, part warehouse, and part administration building and/or government offices. Shoppers could browse through goods from every corner of Rome's vast empire—exotic fruits from Africa, spices from Asia, and fish-and-chips from Londinium. Above the semicircle, the upper floors of the complex housed bureaucrats in charge of a crucial element of city life: doling out free grain to unemployed citizens, who lived off the wealth plundered from distant lands.

To walk around the market complex and see some excavated statues, you can visit the **Museum of the Imperial Forums,** which features discoveries from the forums built by the different emperors. It's well-displayed and helps put all these ruins in context (€14, daily 9:30-19:30, last entry one hour before closing).

The Forums of Augustus and Nerva: The statue captures **Emperor Augustus** in his famous hailing-a-cab pose (a copy of the original, which you can see at the Vatican Museums). This is his "commander talking to his people" pose. Behind him was the Forum of Augustus. It separated fancy "downtown Rome" from the workaday world beyond.

Farther along is a statue of **Emperor Nerva,** trying but failing to have the commanding presence of Augustus. Walk behind him for a closer look at his forum.

▲ST. PETER-IN-CHAINS CHURCH (SAN PIETRO IN VINCOLI)

A church was first built on this spot in the fifth century, to house the chains that once restrained St. Peter. Today's church, restored in the 15th century, is famous for its Michelangelo statue of Moses,

Michelangelo's Moses *dominates the tomb of Pope Julius II.*

intended for the (unfinished) tomb of Pope Julius II. Check out the chains under the high altar, then focus on mighty Moses. (Note this isn't the famous St. Peter's—that's in Vatican City.)

Pope Julius II commissioned Michelangelo to build a massive tomb, with 48 huge statues, topped with a grand statue of this egomaniacal pope. The pope had planned to have his tomb placed in the center of St. Peter's Basilica. When Julius died, the work had barely begun, and no one had the money or necessary commitment to Julius to finish the project.

In 1542, some of the remnants of the tomb project were brought to St. Peter-in-Chains and pieced together by Michelangelo's assistants. Some of the best statues ended up elsewhere, such as the *Prisoners* in Florence and the *Slaves* in the Louvre. *Moses* and the Louvre's *Slaves* are the only statues Michelangelo personally completed for the project. Flanking *Moses* are the Old Testament sister-wives of Jacob, Leah (to our right) and Rachel, both begun by Michelangelo but probably finished by pupils.

Cost and Hours: Free, daily 8:00-12:30 & 15:00-19:00, Oct-March until 18:00,

modest dress required; the church is a 10-minute uphill walk from the Colosseum, or a shorter, simpler walk (but with more steps) from the Cavour Metro stop; tel. 06-9784-4950.

Pantheon Neighborhood

Besides being home to ancient sites and historic churches, the area around the Pantheon is another part of Rome with an urban village feel. Wander narrow streets, sample the many shops and eateries, and gather with the locals in squares marked by bubbling fountains.

▲▲▲PANTHEON

For the greatest look at the splendor of Rome, antiquity's best-preserved interior is a must. Built two millennia ago, this influential domed temple served as the model for Michelangelo's dome of St. Peter's and many others.

Cost and Hours: Free, Mon-Sat 8:30-19:30, Sun 9:00-18:00, holidays 9:00-13:00, tel. 06-6830-0230, www.pantheon roma.com.

When to Go: Don't go at midday, when the Pantheon is packed. If you visit before 9:00, you'll have it all to yourself.

ITALY

Pantheon Neighborhood

To Spanish Steps
To Piazza del Popolo
To M Barberini
PONTE UMBERTO
Piazza Ponte Umberto I
VIA BRIANZO
VIA D'ORSO
VIA D. SCROFA
VIA DEL CORSO
VIA TRITONE
PARLIAMENT
UFF. VICARIO
Piazza Montecitorio
Piazza Colonna
TREVI FOUNTAIN
ANCIENT STADIUM ENTRANCE
CORONARI
SAN LUIGI
VIA D. COPPELLE
AQUIRO
Piazza di Pietra
SABINA
MURATTE
TRE SCALINI GELATERIA
SALV.
GIUST.
Piazza Rotunda
PASTINI
Piazza Sant' Ignazio
Piazza Navona
VIA DELLA SCROFA
FOUR RIVERS FOUNTAIN
S. EUST.
SEMINARIO
PANTHEON
SANT' IGNAZIO
SANT' AGNESE
Piazza S. Eust.
SANT' IGNAZIO
Piazza Pasquino
S. IVO
ELEPHANT OBELISK
Piazza Collegio Rom.
GALLERIA DORIA PAMPHILJ
CITY MUSEUM WELCOME TO ROME
CORSO VITTORIO EMANUELE II
SANTA MARIA SOPRA MINERVA
ARGENTINA
CESTARI
Campo de' Fiori
CHIAVARI
Largo Argentina
VIA PLEBISCITO
Piazza Venezia
Piazza Farnese
V. M. D. FARINA
LARGO ARGENTINA RUINS
GESÙ
To Colosseum & M
PALAZZO FARNESE
VIA GIUBBONARI
VIA D. B. OSCURE
VIA DI SAN MARCO
200 Meters
200 Yards
ARACOELI
VICTOR EMMANUEL MONUMENT
SPECCHI
VIA ARENULA
VIA DEL PORTICO D'OTTAVIA
CAPITOLINE HILL
Piazza Campidoglio

Dress Code: No visitors with skimpy shorts or bare shoulders allowed inside the Pantheon.

Tours: The Pantheon has a €6, 30-minute **audioguide** (€10/2 people). 🎧 Download my free Pantheon **audio tour.**

Visiting the Pantheon: The Pantheon was a Roman temple dedicated to all (*pan*) of the gods (*theos*). The original temple was built in 27 BC by Emperor Augustus' son-in-law, Marcus Agrippa. In fact, the inscription below the triangular **pediment** proclaims (in Latin), "Marcus Agrippa, son of Lucio, three times consul made this." But after a couple of fires, the structure we see today was completely rebuilt by Emperor Hadrian around AD 120. After the fall of Rome, the Pantheon became a Christian church (from "all the gods" to "all the martyrs"), which saved it from architectural cannibalism.

The dome is what makes this building unique—and perhaps the most influential architectural design in art history. The Pantheon's dome was the model for the Florence cathedral dome, which launched the Renaissance, and for Michelangelo's dome of St. Peter's, which capped it all off. Even the US Capitol in Washington, DC, was inspired by this dome.

Wander into the **portico** with its forest of 16 enormous **columns.** They're 40 feet tall and 15 feet around, made of red-and-gray granite. Whereas many ancient columns are a stack of cylindrical drums, these columns are each a single piece of stone.

The magnificent, soaring **dome,** the largest made until the Renaissance, is set on a circular base. The mathematical perfection of this dome-on-a-base design is a testament to Roman engineering; it's as high as it is wide—142 feet. To picture

The Pantheon's dome and oculus

it, imagine a basketball wedged inside a wastebasket so that it just touches bottom. The dome is made from concrete, a Roman invention. It gets lighter and thinner as it reaches the top. The base of the dome is 23 feet thick and made from heavy concrete mixed with travertine, while near the top, it's less than five feet thick and made with a lighter volcanic rock (pumice) mixed in.

At the top, the **oculus** is the building's only light source. It's completely open and almost 30 feet across. The 1,800-year-old **floor**—with 80 percent of its original stones surviving—has holes in it and slants toward the edges to let rainwater drain. Although some of the floor's marble has been replaced, the design—alternating circles and squares—is original.

The Pantheon's interior holds the tombs of important people from more recent centuries. The artist **Raphael** (1483-1520) lies in a stone coffin to the left of the main altar. Facing each other across the rotunda are the tombs of modern Italy's first two kings: **Victor Emmanuel II** and **Umberto I.**

▲TREVI FOUNTAIN

The bubbly Baroque fountain, worth ▲▲ by night, is a minor sight to art scholars... but a major nighttime gathering spot for teens on the make and tourists tossing coins. Those coins are collected daily to feed Rome's poor. For more on the fountain, see page 419.

Vatican City

Vatican City, the world's smallest country, contains St. Peter's Basilica (with Michelangelo's exquisite *Pietà*) and the Vatican Museums (with Michelangelo's Sistine Chapel). A helpful **TI** is just to the left of St. Peter's Basilica as you're facing it (Mon-Sat 8:30-18:15, closed Sun, tel. 06-6988-2019, www.vaticanstate.va). The entrances to St. Peter's and the Vatican Museums are a 15-minute walk apart (follow the outside of the Vatican wall, which links the two sights). The nearest Metro stop—Ottaviano—still involves a 10-minute walk to either sight. For a map of the entire district and nearby sights, see page 448.

Dress Code: Modest dress is technically required of men, women, and children

St. Peter's Square and Basilica

throughout Vatican City, even outdoors. The policy is strictly enforced in the Sistine Chapel and at St. Peter's Basilica but is more relaxed elsewhere (though always at the discretion of guards). To avoid problems, cover your shoulders; bring a light jacket or cover-up if you're wearing a tank top. Wear long pants or capris instead of shorts. Skirts or dresses should extend below your knee.

▲▲▲ST. PETER'S BASILICA

There is no doubt: This is the richest and grandest church on earth. To call it vast is like calling Einstein smart. Plaques on the floor show you where other, smaller churches would end if they were placed inside. The ornamental cherubs would dwarf a large man. Birds roost inside, and thousands of people wander about, heads craned heavenward, hardly noticing each other. Don't miss Michelangelo's *Pietà* (behind bulletproof glass) to the right of the entrance. Bernini's altar work and twisting, towering canopy are brilliant.

Cost and Hours: Free, daily April-Sept 7:00-19:00, Oct-March 7:00-18:30. The church closes on Wednesday mornings during papal audiences (until roughly 13:00). Masses occur daily throughout the day. The view from the dome is worth the climb (€10 for elevator to roof, then take stairs; €8 to climb stairs all the way, cash only, allow an hour to go up and down, daily April-Sept 7:30-19:00, Oct-March 7:30-18:00, last entry one hour before closing if you take the stairs the whole way). Tel. 06-6988-2019, www.vaticanstate.va.

Avoiding Lines: There's often a bottleneck at the security check. The checkpoint is typically on the north side of the square, but is sometimes closer to the church or tucked under the south colonnade.

Visit before 10:00 to avoid the worst crowds. Crowds are also thinner after 16:00—just as sunbeams begin working their magic on the altar. But after 16:00, the crypt is closed, and the altar area is often roped off.

Getting There: Take the Metro to Ottaviano, then walk 10 minutes south on Via Ottaviano. The #40 express bus drops off at Piazza Pio, next to Castel Sant'Angelo—a 10-minute walk from St. Peter's. The more crowded bus #64, beloved by pickpockets, stops just outside St. Peter's

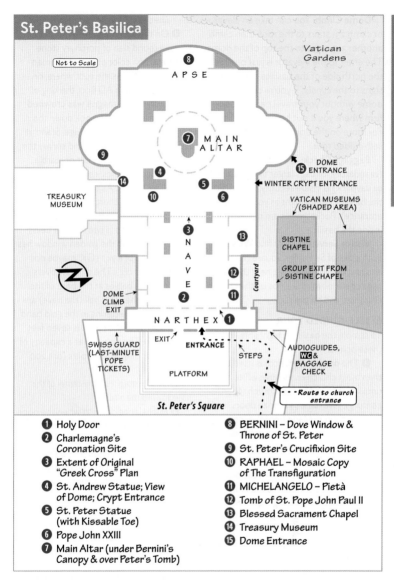

St. Peter's Basilica

1 Holy Door
2 Charlemagne's Coronation Site
3 Extent of Original "Greek Cross" Plan
4 St. Andrew Statue; View of Dome; Crypt Entrance
5 St. Peter Statue (with Kissable Toe)
6 Pope John XXIII
7 Main Altar (under Bernini's Canopy & over Peter's Tomb)
8 BERNINI – Dove Window & Throne of St. Peter
9 St. Peter's Crucifixion Site
10 RAPHAEL – Mosaic Copy of The Transfiguration
11 MICHELANGELO – Pietà
12 Tomb of St. Pope John Paul II
13 Blessed Sacrament Chapel
14 Treasury Museum
15 Dome Entrance

Square to the south. A taxi from Termini train station costs about €15.

Church Services: Mass, generally in Italian, is said varyingly in the south (left) transept, the Blessed Sacrament Chapel (on right side of nave), or at the main altar. Confirm times on the signboard as you enter. Typical schedule: Mon-Sat at 8:30, 9:00, 10:00, 11:00, 12:00, and at 17:00 (in Latin, at the main altar); Sun and holidays at 9:00, 10:30 (in Latin), 11:30, 12:15, 13:00, 16:00, 16:45 (vespers), and 17:30.

Tours: Audioguides can be rented near the baggage check (€5 plus ID, for church only, daily 8:30-17:00). 🎧 Download my free St. Peter's Basilica **audio tour.**

Dome Climb: You can take an elevator or climb 231 stairs to the roof, then climb another 323 steps to the top of the dome. The entry to the elevator is just outside the north side of the basilica—look for signs to the *cupola*. If you're climbing the dome without your travel partner, confirm where you'll exit before you split up. For more on the dome, see the end of my self-guided tour.

Baggage Check: The free bag check (mandatory for bags larger than a purse or daypack) is inside security, but outside the basilica (to the right as you face the entrance). Pocketknives are not allowed inside the basilica.

Visitor Services: You'll find **WCs** on both sides of St. Peter's Square (by the TI and just outside security), near the baggage check down the steps by the church entrance, and on the roof.

↻ SELF-GUIDED TOUR

To sample the basilica's highlights, follow these points:

① The **narthex** (portico) is itself bigger than most churches. Its huge white columns date from the first church (fourth century). Five famous bronze doors lead into the church. Made from the melted-down bronze of the original door of Old St. Peter's, the central door was the first Renaissance work in Rome (c. 1450). It's only opened on special occasions.

The far-right entrance is the **Holy Door,** opened only during Holy Years (and special "Jubilee" years designated by the pope). On Christmas Eve every 25 years, the pope knocks three times with a silver hammer and the door opens, welcoming pilgrims to pass through.

Looking down the nave, we get a sense of the splendor of ancient Rome that was carried on by the Catholic Church. The floor plan, with a central aisle (nave) flanked by two side aisles, is based on that of ancient Roman basilicas—large halls built to accommodate business and legal meetings. In fact, many of the stones used to build St. Peter's were scavenged from the ruined law courts of ancient Rome.

② On the floor near the central doorway is a round slab of porphyry stone in the maroon color of ancient Roman officialdom. This is the spot where, on Christmas night in AD 800, the king of the Franks **Charlemagne was crowned** Holy Roman Emperor. Look down the main hall—this church is huge. Stand at the very back of the nave and survey the heavenly expanse. It's a riot of marble, gold, stucco, mosaics, columns of stone, and pillars of light. As the symbol of global Catholicism, this church is appropriately big. Size before beauty: The golden window at the far end is two football fields away. The dove in the golden window has the wingspan of a 747 (OK, maybe not quite, but it *is* big). The church covers six acres. The babies at the base of the pillars along the main hall (the nave) are adult-size. The lettering in the gold band along the top of the pillars is seven feet high. Really. The church has a capacity of 60,000 standing worshippers (or 1,200 tour groups).

• *Now, walk straight up the center of the nave toward the altar.*

③ Michelangelo was 71 when the pope persuaded him to take over the church project and cap it with a dome. He agreed, intending to put the dome over Donato Bramante's original **Greek-cross floor plan.** But the Church, struggling against Protestants and its own corruption, opted for a plan designed to impress the world with its grandeur—the Latin cross of the Crucifixion, with its nave extended to accommodate the grand religious spectacles of the Baroque period.

④ Park yourself in front of the **statue of St. Andrew** to the left of the altar, the guy holding an X-shaped cross. (Note that the **entrance to the crypt** is usually here; in winter it's by the dome entrance.) Like Andrew, gaze up into the dome, and also like him, gasp.

The **dome** soars higher than a football field on end, 448 feet from the floor of

The nave of St. Peter's Basilica is two football fields long.

the cathedral to the top of the lantern. It glows with light from its windows, the blue-and-gold mosaics creating a cool, solemn atmosphere. In this majestic vision of heaven (not painted by Michelangelo), we see (above the windows) Jesus, Mary, and a ring of saints, rings of more angels above them, and, way up in the ozone, God the Father (a blur of blue and red, unless you have binoculars).

❺ Back in the nave sits a bronze **statue of St. Peter** under a canopy. This is one of a handful of pieces of art that were in the earlier church. In one hand he holds keys, the symbol of the authority given him by Christ, while with the other hand he blesses us. His big right toe has been worn smooth by the lips of pilgrims and foot fetishists. Stand in line and kiss it, or, to avoid foot-and-mouth disease, touch your hand to your lips, then rub the toe. This is simply an act of reverence with no legend attached, though you can make one up if you like.

• *Circle to the right around the statue of Peter to find the lighted glass niche.*

❻ The red-robed body is **Pope John XXIII**, whose papacy lasted from 1958 to 1963. Nicknamed "the good pope,"

he is best known for initiating the landmark Vatican II Council (1962-1965) that instituted major reforms, bringing the Church into the modern age. In 2000, Church authorities checked his body, and it was surprisingly fresh. So they moved it upstairs, put it behind glass, and now old Catholics who remember him fondly enjoy another stop on their St. Peter's visit. Pope John was canonized in 2014.

❼ Sitting over St. Peter's tomb, the **main altar** (the white marble slab with cross and candlesticks) beneath the dome and canopy is used only when the pope himself says Mass. He sometimes conducts the Sunday morning service when he's in town, a sight worth seeing.

The tiny altar would be lost in this enormous church if it weren't for Gian Lorenzo Bernini's seven-story bronze canopy (God's "four-poster bed"), which "extends" the altar upward and reduces the perceived distance between floor and ceiling. The corkscrew columns echo the marble ones that surrounded the altar/tomb in Old St. Peter's. Some of the bronze used here was taken and melted down from the ancient Pantheon.

Michelangelo, Pietà

❽ Bernini (1598-1680), the Michelangelo of the Baroque era, is the man most responsible for the interior decoration of the church.

His **dove window** shines above the smaller front altar used for everyday services. The Holy Spirit, in the form of a six-foot-high dove, pours sunlight onto the faithful through the alabaster windows, turning into artificial rays of gold and reflecting off swirling gold clouds, angels, and winged babies. During a service, real sunlight passes through real clouds of incense, mingling with Bernini's sculpture. Beneath the dove is the centerpiece of this structure, the so-called **Throne of St. Peter,** an oak chair built in medieval times for a king. Subsequently, it was encrusted with tradition and encased in bronze by Bernini as a symbol of papal authority. In the apse, Mass is said daily for pilgrims, tourists, and Roman citizens alike.

• *To the left of the main altar is the* **south transept.** *It may be roped off for worship, but anyone can step past the guard if you say you're there "for prayer." At the far end, left side, find the dark "painting" of St. Peter crucified upside down.*

❾ This marks the exact spot (according to tradition) of **Peter's crucifixion.** Peter had come to the world's greatest city to preach Jesus' message of love to the pagan, often hostile Romans. During the reign of Emperor Nero, he was arrested and brought to Nero's Circus so all of Rome could witness his execution. When the authorities told Peter he was to be crucified just like his Lord, Peter said, essentially, "I'm not worthy" and insisted they nail him on the cross upside down.

❿ Around the corner on the right (heading back toward the central nave), pause at the mosaic copy of Raphael's epic painting of **The Transfiguration.** The original is now beautifully displayed in the Pinacoteca of the Vatican Museums. This and all the other "paintings" in the church are actually mosaic copies made from thousands of colored chips the size of your little fingernail.

• *Back near the entrance of the church, in the far corner behind bulletproof glass, is the sculpture everyone has come to see, the* Pietà.

⓫ Michelangelo was 24 years old when he completed this **pietà**—a representation of Mary with the body of Christ taken from the cross. It was his first major commission, done for Holy Year 1500.

Michelangelo, with his total mastery of the real world, captures the sadness of the moment. Mary cradles her crucified son in her lap. Christ's lifeless right arm drooping down lets us know how heavy this corpse is. Mary looks at her dead son with sad tenderness. Her left hand turns upward, asking, "How could they do this to you?"

• *In the chapel to the left is the Tomb of Pope John Paul II.*

⓬ **John Paul II** (1920-2005) was one of the most beloved popes of recent times. During his papacy (1978-2005), he was the highly visible face of the Catholic Church as it labored to stay relevant in an increasingly secular world. The first non-Italian pope in four centuries, he oversaw the fall of communism in his native Poland. He survived an assassination attempt, and he publicly endured his slow decline from Parkinson's disease with great stoicism. He was sainted in April 2014, just nine years after his death.

⓭ You're welcome to step through the metalwork gates into the **Blessed Sacrament Chapel** (Capella di Santissimo Sacramento), an oasis of peace reserved for prayer and meditation (on right side of church, about midway to the altar). Mass is sometimes said here.

⓮ The **Treasury Museum** (Museo-Tesoro), on the left side of the nave near the altar, contains the room-size tomb of Sixtus IV by Antonio Pollaiuolo, a big pair of Roman pincers used to torture Christians, an original corkscrew column from Old St. Peter's, and assorted jewels, papal robes, and golden reliquaries—a marked contrast to the poverty of early Christians.

The foundations of Old St. Peter's, the **Crypt** (Grotte/Tombe), contains tombs of popes and memorial chapels. In summer, the crypt entrance is usually beside the statue of St. Andrew, to the left of the main altar (near #4 on the map); in winter, it's by the dome entrance. Stairs

The view from atop St. Peter's

lead you down to the floor level of the previous church, where you'll pass the sepulcher of Peter. This lighted niche with an icon is not Peter's actual tomb, but part of a shrine that stands atop Peter's tomb. Continue your one-way visit until it spills you out, usually near the checkroom.

⓯ For one of the best views of Rome, go up to the **dome.** The entrance is along the right (north) side of the church, but the line begins to form out front, at the church's right door (as you face the church). Look for *cupola* signs.

There are two levels: the rooftop of the church and the very top of the dome. Climb or take an elevator to the first level, on the church roof just above the facade. From the roof, you can also go inside the gallery ringing the interior of the dome and look down inside the church. To go all the way up to the top of the dome, you'll take a staircase that actually winds between the outer shell and the inner one. It's a sweaty, crowded, claustrophobic 15-minute, 323-step climb, but worth it. The view from the summit is great, the fresh air even better.

Vatican City

The tiny independent country of Vatican City is contained entirely within Rome. The Vatican has its own postal system, armed guards, beautiful gardens, helipad, mini train station, and radio station (KPOP). It also has two huge sights: St. Peter's Basilica and the Vatican Museums. Politically powerful, the Vatican is the religious capital of 1.2 billion Roman Catholics. If you're not a Catholic, become one for your visit.

The pope is both the religious and secular leader of Vatican City. For centuries, the Vatican was the capital of the Papal States, and locals referred to the pontiff as "King Pope." Because of the Vatican's territorial ambitions, it didn't always have good relations with Italy. Even though modern Italy was created in 1870, the Holy See didn't recognize it as a country until 1929.

Preparing for papal pageantry

Vatican Gardens: To walk through the manicured Vatican Gardens (with views over Rome and a good look at St. Peter's dome), book a guided tour several days in advance at www.museivaticani.va (€33, 2 hours, daily except Wed and Sun, includes entry to Vatican Museums; tours usually start at 9:30 or 11:00 at Vatican

▲▲▲VATICAN MUSEUMS (MUSEI VATICANI)

The four miles of displays in this immense museum complex—from ancient statues to Christian frescoes to modern paintings—culminate in the Raphael Rooms and Michelangelo's glorious Sistine Chapel. This is one of Europe's top three and four houses of art. It can be exhausting, so plan your visit carefully, focusing on a few themes. Allow two hours for a quick visit, three or four hours to really enjoy it.

Cost and Hours: €17, €4 online reservation fee, Mon-Sat 9:00-18:00, last entry at 16:00 (though the official closing time is 18:00, the staff starts ushering you out at 17:30), closed on religious holidays and Sun except last Sun of the month (when it's free, more crowded, and open 9:00-14:00, last entry at 12:30); open Fri nights mid-April-Oct 19:00-23:00 (last entry at 21:30) by online reservation only—check the website. Hours are subject to frequent change and holidays; look online for current times.

Closed Days: The museum is closed on many holidays (mainly religious ones). Always check the current hours and calendar on the museum website. Individual rooms may close at odd hours, especially in the afternoon. The rooms described here are usually open.

Information: Tel. 06-6988-4676, www.museivaticani.va.

Reservations: You're crazy to come without a reservation: The Vatican Muse-

Museums tour desk). A 45-minute open-bus tour through the gardens is offered in good weather (€37, includes audioguide and entry to Vatican Museums).

General Audience Tickets: For the Wednesday audience at 10:00, a (free) ticket gets you closer to the papal action. Reserve tickets (available a month or two in advance) by sending a request by mail or fax (access the form at www. vatican.va—select "Prefecture of the Papal Household"). You'll then pick up the tickets at St. Peter's Square before the audience (available Tue 15:00-19:00 and Wed 7:00-9:00; usually under Bernini's colonnade, to the right when facing the church).

Starting the Monday before the audience, Swiss Guards hand out tickets from their station near the basilica exit (see the "Vatican Museums Overview" map). Don't go through security—just march up, ask nicely, and say *"danke."* While this is perhaps easiest, I'd reserve in advance to guarantee a ticket.

General Audience Tips: On Wednesday morning, you'll need to be dressed modestly (shoulders covered, no short shorts or tank tops—long pants or knee-length skirts are safest) and clear security (no big bags). To get a seat (much less a good one), it's smart to be there a couple of hours early—there are far fewer seats than ticketholders. If you just want to see the pope, get a good photo, and don't mind standing, you can show up later (though still at least 30 minutes early) and take your place in the standing-room section in the back half of the square. The service gets underway around 9:30. Shortly thereafter, the Popemobile appears, winding through the adoring crowd (the best places—seated or standing—are near the cloth-covered wooden fences that line the Popemobile route). Around 10:00, the Pope's multilingual message begins and lasts for about an hour (you can leave at any time).

ums can be extremely crowded, with waits of up to two hours just to buy tickets. Bypass these long lines by reserving an entry time online for €21 (€17 ticket plus €4 booking fee). For sights covered by my self-guided tour, select the ticket called "Vatican Museums and Sistine Chapel." Print the emailed voucher to present at the museum (see "Getting In," later). You can also receive your reservation on your mobile phone.

When to Go: The museum is generally crowded, with shoulder-to-shoulder sightseeing through much of it. The best time to visit is a weekday after 14:00—the later the better. Another good time is during the papal audience on Wednesday morning, when many tourists are at St. Peter's Square (the drawback is that St. Peter's Basilica is closed until roughly 13:00).

The worst days are Saturdays, the last Sunday of the month (when the museum is free), Mondays, rainy days, and any day before or after a holiday closure.

More Line-Beating Tips: Booking a **guided tour** (described later, under "Tours") gets you right in—just show the guard your voucher. You can often buy **same-day timed-entry reservations** without a ticket-buying line at the Vatican TI in St. Peter's Square (to the left as you face the basilica). **Hawkers** peddling skip-the-line access swarm the Vatican area, offering guided tours—but the museum staff advises against accepting their offers

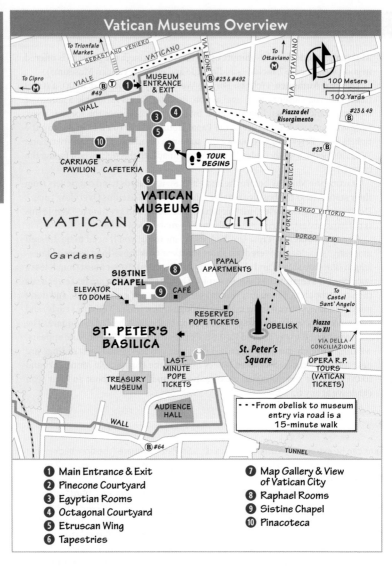

Vatican Museums Overview

1. Main Entrance & Exit
2. Pinecone Courtyard
3. Egyptian Rooms
4. Octagonal Courtyard
5. Etruscan Wing
6. Tapestries
7. Map Gallery & View of Vatican City
8. Raphael Rooms
9. Sistine Chapel
10. Pinacoteca

(while legitimate, the tour caliber is often low—use them only as a last resort).

Getting There: The Ottaviano Metro stop is a 10-minute walk from the entrance. Bus #49 from Piazza Cavour/ Castel Sant'Angelo stops right at the entrance. Bus #23 from Trastevere stops on Via Leone IV, just downhill from the entrance. Bus #492 heads from the city center and stops on Via Leone IV. Bus #64 stops on the other side of St. Peter's Square, a 15- to 20-minute walk (facing the church from the obelisk, take a right through the colonnade and follow the Vatican Wall). Or take a taxi from the city center—they are reasonable.

Getting In: Approaching the exterior entrance (the big white door), you'll see three lines: individuals without reservations (far left), individuals with reservations (usually shorter and faster), and groups (on the right).

With a reservation, show your voucher to the guard and enter via the reserved ticket-holder line. Inside, after the security check, go to any window on the left to show your voucher and pick up your ticket, then go up the steps and enter the museum. (Or, you can skip the ticket-window line by going upstairs and processing your voucher on a machine.)

Without a reservation, enter via the far left line. Once you clear security, go upstairs to buy your ticket.

Tours: An €8 **audioguide** is available at the top of the spiral ramp/escalator and can be prepaid when you book tickets online. No ID is required to rent an audioguide. Confirm the drop-off location when renting.

🎧 Download my free Vatican Museums and Sistine Chapel **audio tours.**

The Vatican offers **guided tours** in English that are easy to book on their website (€33, includes admission). Present your confirmation voucher to a guard to the right of the entrance; then, once inside, go to the Guided Tours desk (in the lobby, up a few stairs).

Visitor Services: The museum's "checkroom" (to the right after security) takes only bigger bags, not day bags.

WCs are mainly at the entrance/exit, plus a few scattered within the collection.

❷ SELF-GUIDED TOUR

Our tour starts in the large open-air "Pinecone Courtyard." This vast space sums up the Vatican's vast collection: Pinecone—ancient, a 2,000 year-old offering to Isis. Bronze sphere—modern, created in 1990. And the courtyard around it—Renaissance, designed by Bramante.

We'll begin our museum visit as civilization did, in **Egypt and Mesopotamia.** Backtrack inside and up the stairs to the right to find linen-wrapped mummies, stiff statues, and early writing on clay tablets.

Laocoön, *in the Octagonal courtyard*

After a stop at a view balcony, make your way to the **Octagonal Courtyard**, decorated with some of the best Greek and Roman statues in captivity. The *Apollo Belvedere* is a Roman copy (4th century BC) of a Hellenistic original that followed the style of the great Greek sculptor Praxiteles. It fully captures the beauty of the human form. The anatomy is perfect, his pose is natural. Instead of standing at attention, face-forward with his arms at his sides (Egyptian-style), Apollo is on the move, coming to rest with his weight on one leg.

Laocoön was sculpted some four centuries after the Golden Age (5th-4th century BC), after the scales of "balance" had been tipped. Whereas *Apollo* is a balance between stillness and motion, this is unbridled motion. *Apollo* is serene, graceful, and godlike, while *Laocoön* is powerful, emotional, and gritty. The figures (carved from four blocks of marble pieced together seamlessly) are powerful, not light and graceful. The poses are as twisted as possible, accentuating every rippling muscle and bulging vein.

The centerpiece of the next hall is the *Belvedere Torso* (just a 2,000-year-old torso, but one that had a great impact on the art of Michelangelo). Finishing off the classical statuary are two fine fourth-century porphyry sarcophagi. These royal purple tombs were made (though not used) for the Roman emperor Constantine's mother (Helena, on left) and daughter (Constanza, on right).

Raphael, School of Athens

Overachievers may first choose to pop into the **Etruscan Wing**—labeled *Museo Gregoriano Etrusco.* Otherwise, after long halls of **tapestries, old maps,** broken penises, and fig leaves, you'll come to what most people are looking for: the Raphael Rooms and Michelangelo's Sistine Chapel.

Raphael Rooms: The highlight of the Raphael Rooms, frescoed by Raphael and his assistants, is the restored *School of Athens.* It is remarkable for its blatant pre-Christian classical orientation, especially considering it originally wallpapered the apartments of Pope Julius II. Raphael honors the great pre-Christian thinkers—Aristotle, Plato, and company—who are portrayed as the leading artists of Raphael's day. There's Leonardo da Vinci, whom Raphael worshipped, in the role of Plato. Michelangelo broods in the foreground, added later. When Raphael snuck a peek at the Sistine Chapel, he decided that his arch-competitor was so good that he had to put their personal differences aside and include him in this tribute to the artists

of his generation. Today's St. Peter's was under construction as Raphael was working. In the *School of Athens,* he gives us a sneak preview of the unfinished church.

Sistine Chapel: Next is the brilliantly restored Sistine Chapel. This is the pope's personal chapel and also the place where, upon the death of the ruling pope, a new pope is elected.

The Sistine Chapel is famous for Michelangelo's pictorial culmination of the Renaissance, showing the story of creation, with a powerful God weaving in and out of each scene through that busy first week. This is an optimistic and positive expression of the High Renaissance and a stirring example of the artistic and theological maturity of the 33-year-old Michelangelo, who spent four years on this work.

The ceiling shows the history of the world before the birth of Jesus. We see God creating the world, creating man and woman, destroying the earth by flood, and so on. God himself, in his purple robe, actually appears in the first five scenes. Along the sides (where the ceiling starts

Sistine Chapel, packed with travelers marveling at Michelangelo's frescoes.

to curve), we see the Old Testament prophets and pagan Greek prophetesses who foretold the coming of Christ. Dividing these scenes and figures are fake niches (a painted 3-D illusion) decorated with nude statue-like figures with symbolic meaning.

In the central panel of the *Creation of Adam,* God and man take center stage in this Renaissance version of creation. Adam, newly formed in the image of God, lounges dreamily in perfect naked innocence. God, with his entourage, swoops in with a swirl of activity (which—with a little imagination—looks like a cross-section of a human brain...quite a strong humanist statement). Their reaching hands are the center of this work. Adam's is limp and passive; God's is strong and forceful, his finger twitching upward with energy. Here is the very moment of creation, as God passes the spark of life to man, the crowning work of his creation.

This is the spirit of the Renaissance. God is not a terrifying giant reaching down to puny and helpless man from way on high. Here they are on an equal plane, divided only by the diagonal bit of sky. God's billowing robe and the patch of green upon which Adam is lying balance each other. They are like two pieces of a jigsaw puzzle, or two long-separated continents, or like the yin and yang symbols finally coming together—uniting, complementing each other, creating wholeness. God and man work together in the divine process of Creation.

When the ceiling was finished and revealed to the public, it simply blew 'em away. It both caps the Renaissance and turns it in a new direction. In perfect Renaissance spirit, it mixes Old Testament prophets with classical figures. But the style is more dramatic, shocking, and emotional than the balanced Renaissance works before it. This is a very personal work—the Gospel according to Michelangelo—but its themes and subject matter are universal. Many art

scholars contend that the Sistine ceiling is the single greatest work of art by any one human being.

Later, as part of the Counter-Reformation, a much older Michelangelo was commissioned to paint the *Last Judgment* (behind the altar). It's Judgment Day, and Christ—the powerful figure in the center, raising his arm to spank the wicked—has come to find out who's naughty and who's nice. Beneath him, a band of angels blows its trumpets Dizzy Gillespie-style, giving a wake-up call to the sleeping dead. The dead at lower left leave their graves and prepare to be judged. The righteous, on Christ's right hand (the left side of the picture), are carried up to the glories of heaven. The wicked on the other side are hurled down to hell, where demons wait to torture them. Charon, from the underworld of Greek mythology, waits below to ferry the souls of the damned to hell.

When *The Last Judgment* was unveiled to the public in 1541, it caused a sensation. The pope is said to have dropped to his knees and cried, "Lord, charge me not with my sins when thou shalt come on the Day of Judgment."

The dramatic painting changed the course of art. The complex composition, with more than 300 figures swirling around the figure of Christ, went far beyond traditional Renaissance balance. The twisted figures shown from every imaginable angle challenged other painters to try and top this master of 3-D illusion. And the sheer terror and drama of the scene was a striking contrast to the placid optimism of, say, Raphael's *School of Athens.* Michelangelo had Baroque-en all the rules of the Renaissance, signaling a new era of art.

On the long march back to the exit, you'll find the **Pinacoteca** (paintings by Raphael, Leonardo, Caravaggio, and others), a cafeteria (long lines, uninspired food), the underrated early Christian art section, and the exit via the souvenir shop.

Castel Sant'Angelo, Hadrian's mausoleum

▲CASTEL SANT'ANGELO

Built in ancient times as a tomb for the emperor Hadrian, used through the Middle Ages as a castle, prison, and place of last refuge for popes under attack, and today a museum, this giant pile of ancient bricks is packed with history. The structure itself is striking, the opulent papal rooms are dramatic (and cool inside during the summer), and the views up top are some of the best in Rome.

Cost and Hours: €15, more with special exhibits, daily 9:00-19:30, last entry one hour before closing, near Vatican City, 10-minute walk from St. Peter's Square at Lungotevere Castello 50, Metro: Lepanto or bus #40 or #64, café, tel. 06-681-9111, www.castelsantangelo.beniculturali.it.

Visiting the Castle: Ancient Rome allowed no tombs within its walls, so Emperor Hadrian grabbed the most commanding position across the river and built this towering tomb. In the year 590, the archangel Michael appeared above the mausoleum to signal the end of a plague. The tomb became a fortified palace, renamed for the "holy angel." Castel Sant'Angelo spent the Dark Ages as a fortress and prison, but was connected to the Vatican via an elevated corridor in the 13th century (since Rome was repeatedly plundered by invaders, Castel Sant'Angelo was a handy place of last refuge for popes). In anticipation of long sieges, rooms were decorated with papal splendor.

A one-way route circulates visitors through the medieval and then the ancient parts of the monument. After the ticket booth, head upstairs to the rampart with its four bastions (named for the evangelists: Matthew, Mark, Luke, and John). Then climb a ramp and cross a bridge that traverses the sacred chamber in the center. Next, you reach a sunny courtyard with a 16th-century statue of St. Michael. Climbing to another rampart, you then pass the little 19th-century military museum and later enter medieval rooms built for the pope. The papal library was painted by followers of Raphael. Eventually you reach the rooftop terrace with the statue of the Archangel Michael sheathing his sword—and one of the best views anywhere of Rome and St. Peter's Basilica.

North Rome

▲VILLA BORGHESE GARDENS

Rome's somewhat scruffy three-square-mile "Central Park" is great for its quiet shaded paths and for people-watching plenty of modern-day Romeos and Juliets. The best entrance is at the head of Via Veneto (Metro: Barberini, then 10-minute walk—or catch a cab). You can also enter the gardens from the top of the Spanish Steps.

▲▲▲BORGHESE GALLERY (GALLERIA BORGHESE)

This plush museum, filling a cardinal's mansion in the park, offers one of Europe's most sumptuous art experiences. You'll enjoy a collection of world-class Baroque sculpture, including Bernini's *David* and his excited statue of Apollo chasing Daphne, as well as paintings by Caravaggio, Raphael, Titian, and Rubens. The museum's mandatory reservation system keeps crowds to a manageable size.

Cost and Hours: €15, covered by Roma Pass; Tue-Sun 9:00-19:00, Thu until 21:00, closed Mon; free and very crowded once or twice a month when no reservations are taken, usually on a Sun. Check in

ITALY

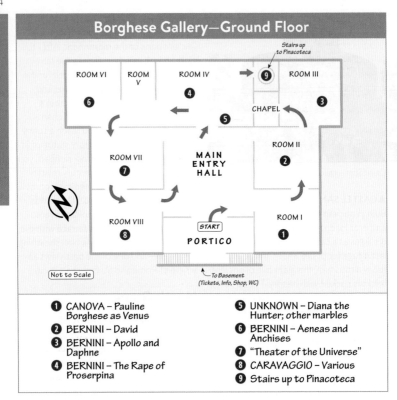

Borghese Gallery—Ground Floor

Stairs up to Pinacoteca

ROOM VI · ROOM V · ROOM IV · **9** · ROOM III

6 · **4** · CHAPEL · **3**

5

ROOM VII · MAIN ENTRY HALL · ROOM II

7 · **2**

ROOM VIII · START · ROOM I

8 · PORTICO · **1**

Not to Scale

To Basement (Tickets, Info, Shop, WC)

1 CANOVA – Pauline Borghese as Venus
2 BERNINI – David
3 BERNINI – Apollo and Daphne
4 BERNINI – The Rape of Proserpina
5 UNKNOWN – Diana the Hunter; other marbles
6 BERNINI – Aeneas and Anchises
7 "Theater of the Universe"
8 CARAVAGGIO – Various
9 Stairs up to Pinacoteca

advance and avoid going on a free day. The 1.5-hour audioguide is excellent.

Information: Tel. 06-32810, www.galleriaborghese.it.

Advance Reservations Required: Reservations are mandatory. Entry times are 9:00, 11:00, 13:00, 15:00, and 17:00 plus 19:00 on Thu. You'll get exactly two hours for your visit. The sooner you reserve, the better. It's easiest to book online at www.tosc.it (€2/person booking fee; choose to pick up tickets at venue). You can also reserve over the telephone (€2/person booking fee, tel. 06-32810, press 2 for English, phones answered Mon-Fri 9:00-18:00, Sat 9:00-13:00, closed Sat in Aug and Sun year-round). Arrive 30 minutes before your appointed time to pick up your ticket (remember to bring your reservation confirmation). Don't cut it close—arriving late can

mean forfeiting your reservation.

Getting There: The museum, at Piazzale del Museo Borghese 5, is set idyllically but inconveniently in the vast Villa Borghese Gardens. A taxi drops you 100 yards from the museum. Your destination is the Galleria Borghese, near Via Pinciana. Don't tell the cabbie "Villa Borghese," which is the park, not the museum. To go by public transit, take bus #910 from Termini train station to the Puccini stop, walk to the park, turn left, and use the first park entrance (but note that #910 runs back to Termini by a different, less convenient route). You can also go by foot (20 minutes) from the Barberini Metro stop: Walk 10 minutes up Via Veneto, enter the park, and turn right, following signs another 10 minutes to the Borghese Gallery.

Tours: Guided English tours are offered every day at 9:00 and 11:00 (€6.50;

reserve online or by phone). Or consider the museum's excellent 1.5-hour audio-guide (€5).

Baggage Check: Baggage check is free, mandatory, and strictly enforced. Even small purses must be checked.

Visiting the Museum: Two hours is all you get...and you'll want every minute. Budget most of your time for the more interesting ground floor, but set aside 30 minutes for the paintings of the Pinacoteca upstairs (highlights are marked by the audioguide icons).

The essence of the collection is the connection of the Renaissance with the classical world. As you enter, notice the second-century Roman reliefs with Michelangelo-designed panels above either end of the portico. The villa was built in the early 17th century by the great art collector Cardinal Scipione Borghese, who wanted to prove that the glories of ancient Rome were matched by the Renaissance.

Each room seems to feature a Baroque masterpiece. In Room I is **Pauline Borghese as Venus,** for which Napoleon's sister went the full monty for the sculptor Canova, scandalizing Europe. ("How could you have done such a thing?!" she was asked. She replied, "The room wasn't cold.") With the famous nose of her conqueror brother, she strikes the pose of Venus as conqueror of men's hearts. Her relaxed afterglow and slight smirk say she's already had her man. The light dent she puts in the mattress makes this goddess human.

In Room II, Gian Lorenzo Bernini's **David** twists around to put a big rock in his sling. He purses his lips, knits his brow, and winds his body like a spring as his eyes lock onto the target: Goliath, who's somewhere behind us, putting us right in the line of fire. Compared with Michelangelo's *David,* this is unvarnished realism—an unbalanced pose, bulging veins, unflattering face, and armpit hair. Michelangelo's *David* thinks, whereas Bernini's acts.

Bernini slays the pretty-boy *David*s of the Renaissance and prepares to invent Baroque.

The best one of all is in Room III: Bernini's **Apollo and Daphne.** It's the perfect Baroque subject—capturing a thrilling, action-filled moment. In the mythological story, Apollo—made stupid by Cupid's arrow of love—chases after Daphne, who has been turned off by the "arrow of disgust." Just as he's about to catch her, she calls to her father to save her. Magically, her fingers begin to sprout leaves, her toes become roots, her skin turns to bark, and she transforms into a tree. Frustrated Apollo will end up with a handful of leaves. Walk slowly around the statue. It's more air than stone.

In Room IV, admire Bernini's **The Rape of Proserpina,** proof that even at the age of 24 the sculptor was the master of marble. **Diana the Hunter** is a rare Greek original, with every limb and finger intact.

Bernini, Apollo and Daphne

Ara Pacis — Augustus' Altar of Peace

Room VII is called the "**Theater of the Universe**," with decor that sums up the eclectic nature of the villa. And in Room VIII is a fabulous collection of paintings by **Caravaggio,** who brought Christian saints down to earth with gritty realism.

Upstairs, in the **Pinacoteca** (Painting Gallery), are busts and paintings by Bernini, as well as paintings by Raphael, Titian, Correggio, and Domenichino.

▲▲MUSEO DELL'ARA PACIS (MUSEUM OF THE ALTAR OF PEACE)

On January 30, 9 BC, soon-to-be-emperor Augustus led a procession of priests up the steps and into this newly built "Altar of Peace." They sacrificed an animal on the altar and poured an offering of wine, thanking the gods for helping Augustus pacify barbarians abroad and rivals at home. This marked the dawn of the Pax Romana (c. AD 1-200), a Golden Age of good living, stability, dominance, and peace *(pax)*. The Ara Pacis (AH-rah PAH-chees) hosted annual sacrifices by the emperor until the area was flooded by the Tiber River. For an idea of how high the water could get, find the measure *(idrometro)* scaling the right side of the church closest to the entrance. Buried under silt, it was abandoned and forgotten until the 16th century, when various parts were discovered and excavated. Mussolini gathered the altar's scattered parts and reconstructed them in a building here in 1938. Today, the Altar of Peace stands in a pavilion designed by American architect Richard Meier (opened 2006).

Cost and Hours: €10.50, more with special exhibits, tightwads can look in through huge windows for free, daily 9:30-19:30, last entry one hour before closing; videoguide-€6; a long block west of Via del Corso on Via di Ara Pacis, on the east bank of the Tiber near Ponte Cavour, Metro: Spagna plus a 10-minute walk down Via dei Condotti; tel. 06-0608, www.arapacis.it.

East Rome

▲▲▲NATIONAL MUSEUM OF ROME (MUSEO NAZIONALE ROMANO PALAZZO MASSIMO ALLE TERME)

The National Museum's main branch, at Palazzo Massimo, houses the greatest collection of ancient Roman art anywhere. Think of this museum as a walk back in time. As you gaze at the same statues that the Romans swooned over, the history of Rome comes alive—from Julius Caesar's murder to Caligula's incest to Vespasian's Colosseum to the coming of Christianity.

The Discus Thrower *in the National Museum of Rome*

Cost and Hours: €10, €12 combo-ticket covers three other branches—all skippable; free and crowded once or twice a month usually on a Sun—check in advance and avoid visiting on any free days; open Tue-Sun 9:00-19:45, closed Mon, last entry one hour before closing; audioguide—€5, about 100 yards from Termini station at Largo di Villa Peretti 2, Metro: Repubblica or Termini, tel. 06-3996-7700, www. museonazionaleromano.beniculturali.it.

Visiting the Museum: The ground-floor sculptures follow Rome's history as the city changes from a republic to a dictatorial empire. The first-floor exhibits take Rome from its peak through its slow decline. The second floor houses rare frescoes and fine mosaics, and the basement presents coins and every-day objects. Take advantage of the thoughtfully written information panels throughout.

On the first floor, along with statues and busts showing such emperors as Trajan and Hadrian, you'll see the best-preserved Roman copy of the Greek *Discus Thrower*. Statues of athletes like this commonly stood in the baths, where Romans cultivated healthy bodies, minds, and social skills, hoping to lead well-rounded lives. Other statues on this floor originally stood in the pleasure gardens of the Roman rich—surrounded by greenery with the splashing sound of fountains, all painted in bright, lifelike colors. Though created by Romans, the themes are mostly Greek, with godlike humans and human-looking gods.

The second floor contains frescoes and mosaics that once decorated the walls and floors of Roman villas. They're remarkably realistic and unstuffy, featuring everyday people, animals, flowery patterns, and geometrical designs. The Villa Farnesina frescoes—in black, red, yellow, and blue—are mostly architectural designs, with fake columns, friezes, and garlands. The Villa di Livia frescoes, owned by the wily wife of Augustus, immerse you in a leafy green garden full of birds and fruit trees, symbolizing the gods.

Finally, descend into the basement to see fine gold jewelry, a mummified body, and vault doors leading into the best coin collection in Europe, with fancy magnifying glasses maneuvering you through cases of coins from ancient Rome to modern times.

Baths of Diocletian

▲BATHS OF DIOCLETIAN/CHURCH OF SANTA MARIA DEGLI ANGELI (TERME DI DIOCLEZIANO/BASILICA STA. MARIA DEGLI ANGELI)

Of all the marvelous structures built by the Romans, their public baths were arguably the grandest, and the Baths of Diocletian were the granddaddy of them all. Built by Emperor Diocletian around AD 300 and sprawling over 30 acres—roughly five times the size of the Colosseum—these baths could cleanse 3,000 Romans at once. They functioned until AD 537, when barbarians attacked and the city's aqueducts fell into disuse, plunging Rome into a thousand years of poverty, darkness, and BO. Today, tourists can visit one grand section of the baths, the former main hall. This impressive remnant of the ancient complex was later transformed (with help from Michelangelo) into the Church of Santa Maria degli Angeli.

Cost and Hours: Free, daily 7:30-18:30, closes slightly later May-Sept and Sun year-round, entrance on Piazza della Repubblica (Metro: Repubblica), www.santamariadegliangeliroma.it.

EXPERIENCES

Shopping

Rome is a wonderful city to shop in. Even if you're not aiming to buy anything, exploring popular shopping areas provides a break from stressful, clogged tourist sights and an excuse to lose yourself on a charming street. Sometimes window-shopping, rather than museum-going, is the best way to connect with the contemporary life of a city. And that's certainly true in Rome.

Department Stores

The shopping complex under Termini train station is a convenient place to peruse clothes, bags, shoes, and perfume at several major Italian chain stores (most open daily 8:00-22:00). A good upscale department store is **La Rinascente** (Via del Tritone 61). Besides deluxe brands, it has a fine design section with great and often affordable ideas for gifts, a magnificent rooftop terrace for a romantic *aperitivo*, good restaurants, free bathrooms, and a section of an ancient aqueduct in the basement. The **Galleria Alberto Sordi** is an elegant 19th-century "mall" (across from Piazza Colonna, described earlier in my "Heart of Rome Walk"). **UPIM** is a popular midrange department store (many branches, including inside Termini train station, Via Nazionale 111, and Piazza Santa Maria Maggiore).

Affordable Shopping

The shopping area all along **Via del Corso** features moderately priced goods, with prices increasing as you head toward Piazza di Spagna (by the Spanish Steps). **Via Nazionale** also features a range of reasonably priced shops, especially for clothes and shoes. Near the bottom of Via Nazionale, in the **Monti** neighborhood near the Roman Forum, Via del Boschetto and Via dei Serpenti are more unique, with a mix of clothing shops and designer bric-a-brac. **Via Cola di Rienzo,** near the Vatican, is good for midrange clothes.

The Passeggiata

Throughout Italy, early evening is time to stroll. While elsewhere in Italy this is called the *passeggiata,* in Rome it's a cruder, big-city version called the *struscio* (meaning "to rub").

Many of Italy's youth live with their parents even into their 30s. They spend a lot of time being trendy and hanging out. Like American kids once gathered at the mall, working-class suburban youth *(coatto)* converge on the old center, as there's little to keep them occupied in Rome's dreary outskirts (which lack public spaces). The hot *vroom-vroom* motor scooter is their symbol; haircuts and fashion are follow-the-leader.

In a more genteel small town, the *passeggiata* comes with sweet whispers of *"bella"* and *"bello"* ("pretty" and "handsome"). In Rome, the admiration is a little cruder and oriented toward consumption—they say *"buona"* and *"buono"*—roughly meaning "tasty."

You can be a spectator, sipping a drink at a sidewalk table, but it's more fun to stroll along with everyone else.

Boutique Shopping

The triangular-shaped area between the Spanish Steps, Piazza Venezia, and Piazza del Popolo (along Via del Corso) contains Rome's highest concentration of upscale boutiques and fashion stores. For top fashion, stroll the streets around the Spanish Steps, including **Via Condotti, Via Borgognona** (for the big-name shops), and **Via del Babuino** (more big names and a few galleries). For antiques and vintage items, wander **Via dei Coronari** (between Piazza Navona and the bend in the river), **Via Giulia** (between Campo de' Fiori and the river), **Via dei Banchi Vecchi** (parallel to Via Giulia), and the super-chic **Via Margutta,** with art galleries, too (hidden parallel to Via del Babuino and running from the Spanish Steps to Piazza del Popolo). For dozens of stores selling affordable apparel aimed mainly at a younger crowd, try **Via Giubbonari** near Campo de' Fiori.

Flea Markets

For antiques and fleas, the granddaddy of markets is the **Porta Portese** *mercato delle pulci* (flea market). While the shopping gets old (and the vendor food shouldn't be consumed), the people-watching is endlessly entertaining (6:30-13:00 Sun only, on Via Portuense and Via Ippolito Nievo; to get to the market, catch bus #75 from Termini train station or tram #8 from Piazza Venezia, get off on Viale di Trastevere, and walk toward the river—and the noise).

Nightlife

For most visitors, the best after-dark activity is simply to grab a gelato and join in the *passeggiata,* the evening stroll through the medieval lanes that connect Rome's romantic, floodlit squares and fountains. Head for Piazza Navona, the

Pantheon, Campo de' Fiori, Trevi Fountain, the Spanish Steps, Via del Corso, or the Monti area. For recommended bars and eateries in these neighborhoods, see "Eating in Rome," later).

Sound-and-Light Shows

The Imperial Forums area hosts two atmospheric and inspirational sound-and-light shows that give you a chance to fantasize about the world of the Caesars (€15, both for €25, nightly mid-April-mid-Nov—bring your warmest coat, tickets sold online and at the gate, shows can sell out on busy weekends, tel. 06-0608, www. viaggioneifori.it).

The **Caesar's Forum Stroll,** starting at Trajan's Column, leads you to eight stops along a wooden sidewalk of a few hundred yards, while an hour's narration tells the dramatic story of Julius Caesar. In the **Forum of Augustus Show,** from your perch on wooden bleachers overlooking the remains of a vast forum, you'll learn the story of Augustus.

Contemporary Music

Music lovers will seek out the mega-music complex of the Rome **Auditorium** (Auditorium Parco della Musica), hosting concerts by Italian and international artists (€20-60 tickets, check availability in advance—concerts often sell out, Viale Pietro de Coubertin 30, take Metro to Flaminio and then catch tram #2 to Apollodoro, from there it's a 5-minute walk east, just beyond the elevated road, tram/metro runs until 23:30, box office tel. 02-6006-0900, www.auditorium.com).

Classical Music and Opera

The **Teatro dell'Opera** has an active schedule of opera and classical concerts. In the summer, the productions move to the Baths of Caracalla, south of the Colosseum, where ancient ruins make an evocative backdrop (tickets from €25, online reservations encouraged, box office takes phone reservations beginning five days prior at tel. 06-4816-0255; Via Firenze 72, a block off Via Nazionale, Metro: Repubblica; www.operaroma.it).

Opera da Camera di Roma is a cute, tourist-oriented, greatest-hits-of-opera performance in the Palazzo Albertoni Spinola. Enjoy some of the most beloved works of Verdi, Rossini, Puccini, Bellini, and Vivaldi in an intimate space—much as the Italian nobility would have heard them in private concerts. There's no reason to pay for more than the cheapest seats. Book direct: Buy the cheapest tickets and request the Rick Steves upgrade (RS%, performances Tue-Sun at 19:30, none on Mon, near the Jewish quarter at Piazza Capizucchi 6; call for ticket info, mobile 320-530-7112).

Tourist-oriented musical events take place at the Episcopal **Church of St. Paul's Within the Walls.** The music ranges from orchestral concerts (usually Tue and Fri at 20:30) to full operatic performances (usually Sat at 20:30). Some Sunday evenings at 18:30, the church hosts hour-long candlelit "Luminaria" concerts. Check the church website (under "Music") to see what's on (€10-30, same-day tickets usually available, arrive 30-45 minutes early for best seat, Via Napoli 58 at corner of Via Nazionale, Metro: Repubblica, tel. 06-482-6296, www.stpaulsrome.it).

Jazz

Rome has a small but vibrant jazz scene. **Alexanderplatz** is the venerable club in town, with performances most evenings (Sun-Thu concerts at 21:45, Fri-Sat at 22:30, closed in summer, Via Ostia 9, Metro: Ottaviano, tel. 06-3972-1867, www. alexanderplatzjazzclub.com).

Il Pentagrappolo is an *enoteca* that hosts live music (usually jazz) many Friday and Saturday evenings starting at 22:00 from September to June—check under "Eventi musicali" on their website to confirm (best to reserve on weekends, three blocks east of the Colosseum at Via

Celimontana 21, www.ilpentagrappolo.
com, tel. 06-709-6301).

TramJazz, a creative venture by the
public transit company, combines dinner,
music, and a journey through the city
in a vintage cable car for a mostly local
crowd (€65, daily at 21:00, 3 hours, leaves
from Piazza di Porta Maggiore—reached
by tram #5 or #14 from Termini Station,
book at least a week in advance, www.
tramjazz.com).

SLEEPING

Choosing the right neighborhood in Rome
is as important as choosing the right hotel.
All of my recommended accommodations
are in safe areas convenient to sightseeing.

Near Ancient Rome
This area is central, so you'll find these
hotels are a short walk from the Colosseum and Roman Forum, as well as
restaurants and shopping in the Monti
district (see the next page).

$$$$ Hotel Lancelot is a 60-room hotel
with an elegant feel at a fair price. Located
in a pleasant, low-key residential neighborhood, it's quiet and safe, with a shady
courtyard, restaurant, bar, and tiny communal sixth-floor terrace (family rooms,
some view rooms, air-con, elevator, wheel-
chair-accessible, cheap parking, Via Capo
d'Africa 47, tel. 06-7045-0615, www.lance
lothotel.com, info@lancelothotel.com).

$$$$ Nerva Boutique Hotel is a
snazzy slice of tranquility with 20 small,
stylish, and often discounted rooms
(RS%—use code "RICKSTEVES," air-con,
elevator, Via Tor de' Conti 3, tel. 06-678-
1835, www.hotelnerva.com, info@hotel
nerva.com, Antonio and Paolo).

$$$ Nicolas Inn Bed & Breakfast,
a delightful little four-room place with
thoughtful touches, is spacious and bright,
and right on busy Via Cavour. Staying here
can make you feel like you have caring
friends in Rome (RS%, cash only, air-con,
Via Cavour 295, mobile 328-555-3004,

www.nicolasinn.it, info@nicolasinn.it).

$$$ Hotel Paba is homey, choco-
late-box tidy, and lovingly cared. You'll
take a vintage elevator to reach the seven
rooms (RS%, email reservations preferred,
big beds, breakfast served in room, air-
con, elevator, Via Cavour 266, second
floor, tel. 06-4782-4497, www.hotelpaba.
com, info@hotelpaba.com).

$$$ Casa Il Rosario is a peaceful, well-
run Dominican convent renting 40 rooms
with monastic simplicity to both pilgrims
and tourists in a steep but pleasant corner
of the Monti neighborhood. Doubles have
two single beds which can be pushed
together (RS%—use code "ricksteves,"
cheaper single rooms with shared bath,
reserve several months in advance, air-
con, elevator, small garden and rooftop
terrace, midnight curfew, near bottom of
Via Nazionale at Via Sant'Agata dei Goti
10, bus #40 or #170 from Termini, tel.
06-679-2346, www.casailrosarioroma.it,
info@casailrosarioroma.it).

$$ Hotel Antica Locanda is a gem on
a small street in the heart of the Monti
neighborhood. While there are four
floors and no elevator, the 15 rooms have
romantically rustic, stylish furnishings
(air-con, no elevator, Via del Boschetto
84, tel. 06-484-894, www.anticalocan-
daroma.it, anticalocandaroma@gmail.
com).

$ Hotel Rosetta, a homey and fam-
ily-run *pensione* in the same building as
Nicolas Inn, rents 15 simple rooms. It's
pretty minimal, with no lounge and no
breakfast, but its great location makes it a
fine budget option (air-con, up one flight
of stairs, Via Cavour 295, tel. 06-4782-
3069, www.rosettahotel.com, info@rosetta
hotel.com, Antonietta and Francesca).

Pantheon Neighborhood
This part of Rome still feels like a village,
and as in a real village, buses and taxis are
the only practical way to connect with
other destinations.

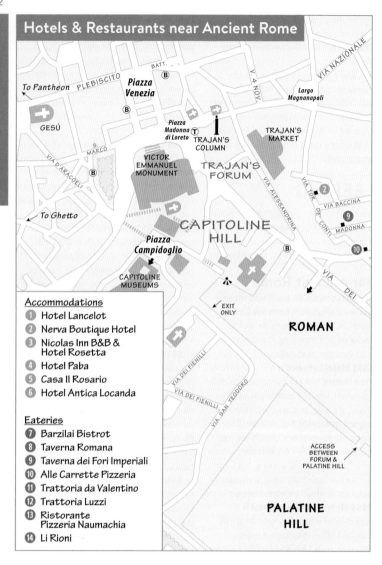

Hotels & Restaurants near Ancient Rome

Accommodations
1. Hotel Lancelot
2. Nerva Boutique Hotel
3. Nicolas Inn B&B & Hotel Rosetta
4. Hotel Paba
5. Casa Il Rosario
6. Hotel Antica Locanda

Eateries
7. Barzilai Bistrot
8. Taverna Romana
9. Taverna dei Fori Imperiali
10. Alle Carrette Pizzeria
11. Trattoria da Valentino
12. Trattoria Luzzi
13. Ristorante Pizzeria Naumachia
14. Li Rioni

Near Largo Argentina and Campo de' Fiori

$$$$ Relais Teatro Argentina, a six-room gem, is steeped in tasteful old-Rome elegance, but has all the modern comforts (air-con, 3 flights of stairs, breakfast in room or on balcony, Via del Sudario 35, tel. 06-9893-1617, www.relaisteatroargentina.com, info@relaisteatroargentina.com, kind Paolo).

$$$ Arch Rome Suites rents 12 spacious, modern, and cozy rooms—some with balconies and views (family rooms, air-con, elevator, Via dell'Arco della Ciambella 19, tel. 06-4549-8947, www.archromesuites.it, info@archromesuites.com, friendly Marika and Omar).

$$$ Casa di Santa Brigida has soft-spoken sisters gliding down polished hallways. You won't have a double bed

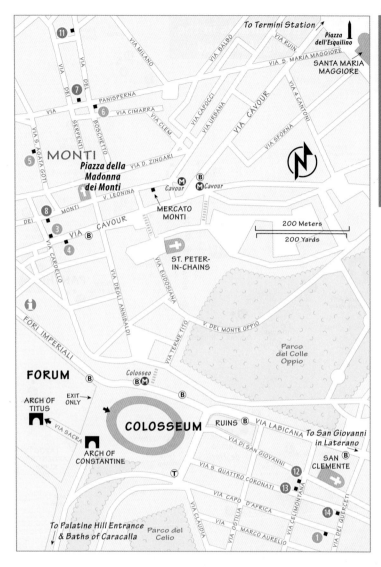

or a TV, but you can luxuriate in the inn's public spaces or on its lovely roof terrace (book well in advance, air-con, elevator, tasty €25 dinners—reserve ahead, roof garden, plush library, Via di Monserrato 54, tel. 06-6889-2596, www.brigidine.org, piazzafarnese@brigidine.org).

$$$ Hotel Smeraldo, with 66 rooms, is clean and a reasonable deal in a good location (air-con, elevator, roof terrace, midway between Campo de' Fiori and Largo Argentina at Via dei Chiavari 20, tel. 06-687-5929, www.smeraldoroma.com, info@smeraldo roma.com, Massimo and Walter).

Close to the Pantheon

$$$$ Hotel Nazionale, a four-star landmark, is a big, stuffy hotel, but it's a worthy splurge if you want security, comfort, and the heart of Rome at your doorstep

ITALY

Hotels & Restaurants in the Pantheon Neighborhood

Tiber River

Piazza Nicosia
Piazza Cardelli

21
8
7
22
Piazza delle Coppelle

To Ponte Sant'Angelo

ANCIENT STADIUM ENTRANCE

SAN LUIGI

PHARMACY

Piazza Fico
15
V. DI TOR MILLINA
V. DI SANT AGNESE
SANT' AGNESE

Piazza Navona

CHIESA NUOVA

FOUR RIVERS FOUNTAIN

19
Piazza Rotonda

PANTHEON

Piazza S. Eustachio
23 24
6

Piazza della Chiesa Nuova

16

WELCOME TO ROME
14
Piazza Pasquino
13
CITY MUSEUM

CORSO VITTORIO

9
BRUNO STATUE
Campo de' Fiori

2
Largo Argentina
B T

3

SANT' ANDREA DELLA VALLE

11
Largo Pallaro

1
LARGO ARGENTINA RUINS

Piazza Farnese

PALAZZO FARNESE

10

4
Largo Arenula FLORIDA

Tiber River

To Trastevere

12
Piazza Cairoli
T #8
GHETTO

Accommodations

1 Relais Teatro Argentina
2 Arch Rome Suites
3 Casa di Santa Brigida
4 Hotel Smeraldo
5 Hotel Nazionale
6 Albergo Santa Chiara

7 Hotel Portoghesi
8 Hotel Due Torri

Eateries

9 Forno Campo de' Fiori
10 Enoteca L'Angolo Divino
11 Trattoria der Pallaro

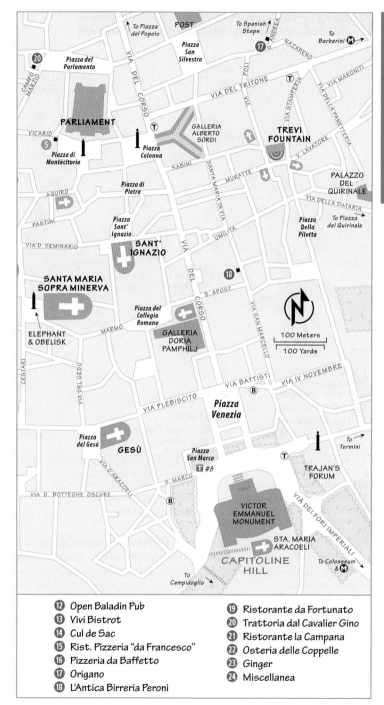

12 Open Baladin Pub
13 Vivi Bistrot
14 Cul de Sac
15 Rist. Pizzeria "da Francesco"
16 Pizzeria da Baffetto
17 Origano
18 L'Antica Birreria Peroni
19 Ristorante da Fortunato
20 Trattoria dal Cavalier Gino
21 Ristorante la Campana
22 Osteria delle Coppelle
23 Ginger
24 Miscellanea

ITALY

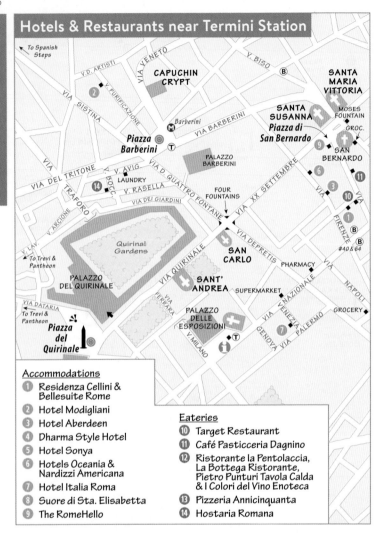

Hotels & Restaurants near Termini Station

Accommodations
1. Residenza Cellini & Bellesuite Rome
2. Hotel Modigliani
3. Hotel Aberdeen
4. Dharma Style Hotel
5. Hotel Sonya
6. Hotels Oceania & Nardizzi Americana
7. Hotel Italia Roma
8. Suore di Sta. Elisabetta
9. The RomeHello

Eateries
10. Target Restaurant
11. Café Pasticceria Dagnino
12. Ristorante la Pentolaccia, La Bottega Ristorante, Pietro Punturi Tavola Calda & I Colori del Vino Enoteca
13. Pizzeria Annicinquanta
14. Hostaria Romana

(RS%—use code "RICK," family rooms, air-con, elevator, Piazza Montecitorio 131, tel. 06-695-001, www.hotelnazionale.it, info@hotelnazionale.it).

$$$$ Albergo Santa Chiara is big, solid, and hotelesque. Its ample public lounges are dressy and professional, and its 96 rooms are quiet and spacious (RS%—use code "RICK," family rooms, air-con, elevator, Via di Santa Chiara 21, tel. 06-687-2979, www.albergosantachiara. com, info@albergosantachiara.com).

$$$$ Hotel Portoghesi is a classic hotel with 27 colorful rooms. It's peaceful, quiet, and comes with a delightful roof terrace (family rooms, breakfast on roof, air-con, elevator, Via dei Portoghesi 1, tel. 06-686-4231, www.hotelportoghesiroma. it, info@hotelportoghesiroma.it).

$$$ Hotel Due Torri feels professional yet homey, with an accommodating staff, generous public spaces, and 26 rooms (family rooms, air-con, elevator, Vicolo del Leonetto 23, tel. 06-6880-6956, www.

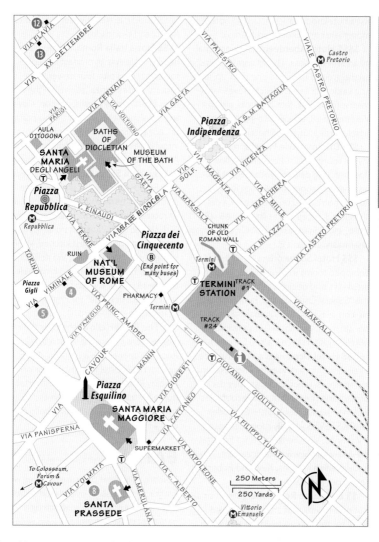

hotelduetorriroma.com, info@hoteldue
torriroma.com, Cinzia and her daughter
Giorgia).

Near Termini Station

While this neighborhood is not as atmospheric as other areas of Rome, some
hotels near Termini train station are less
expensive, and the Metro and buses link
you easily to the rest of the city.

$$$$ Residenza Cellini feels like a
gorgeous Neoclassical palace. It offers 13
rooms, four-star comforts and service,
and a small, breezy terrace (RS%, breakfast extra, air-con, elevator, Via Modena
5, third floor, tel. 06-4782-5204, www.
residenzacellini.it, info@residenzacellini.it;
Barbara, Gaetano, and Donato).

$$$$ Hotel Modigliani, a delightful
23-room place, has a vast and plush
lounge, a garden, and a newslet-
ter introducing you to each of the
staff (RS%, air-con, elevator; Via della
Purificazione 42; tel. 06-4281-5226,

ITALY

www.hotelmodigliani.com, info@hotel modigliani.com, Giulia and Marco).

$$$$ Hotel Aberdeen, combines quality and friendliness. The 37 comfy rooms, on the ground floor and one floor up, are a fine value (RS%—use "Rick Steves reader reservations" link, family rooms, air-con, Via Firenze 48, tel. 06-482-3920, www. hotelaberdeen.it, info@hotelaberdeen.it).

$$$ Dharma Style Hotel spreads its 40 stylish rooms and suites across a few floors of a big palazzo, with elegant furnishings and room to breathe (RS%, family rooms, air-con, elevator, Via del Viminale 8, reception at #10, tel. 06-482-4460, www.dharmastylehotel.it, booking@ dharmastylehotel.it).

$$$ Hotel Sonya offers 40 well-equipped rooms in varied sizes, a hearty breakfast, and decent prices (RS%—see the "Special Offers" page, family rooms, air-con, elevator, Via Viminale 58, tel. 06-481-9911, www.hotelsonya.it, info@ hotelsonya.it, Francesca and Simone).

$$$ Hotel Oceania is a peaceful slice of air-conditioned heaven. The 24 rooms are spacious, quiet, and tastefully decorated, and the elegant sitting room has a manor-house feel (RS%—use code "RICKSTEVES," family rooms, elevator, TV lounge, Via Firenze 38, third floor, tel. 06-482-4696, www.hoteloceania.it, info@ hoteloceania.it; Anna, Kira, and Roberto round out the staff).

$$ Bellesuite Rome offers seven small but nice rooms that are worth considering for the location—in the same fine building as Residenza Cellini and Target Inn (family rooms, air-con, elevator, Via Modena 5, third floor, tel. 06-9521-3049, www.bellesuiterome.com, mail@ bellesuiterome.com, Martina).

$$ Hotel Nardizzi Americana, with a small rooftop terrace, 40 standard rooms, and a laid-back atmosphere, is another decent value (RS%—email reservation for discount, family rooms, air-con, elevator, Via Firenze 38, fourth floor, tel. 06-488-0035, www.hotelnardizzi.it, info@

hotelnardizzi.it; friendly Stefano, Fabrizio, Mario, and Giancarlo).

$$ Hotel Italia Roma, in a busy and handy locale, has 35 modest but comfortable rooms plus four newer, more expensive "residenza" rooms on the third floor (RS%, family rooms, air-con, elevator, Via Venezia 18, just off Via Nazionale, tel. 06-482-8355, www.hotelitaliaroma.it, info@hotelitaliaroma.it; Andrea, Sabrina, Abdul, and Eleonora).

$ Suore di Santa Elisabetta is a heavenly Polish-run convent with a serene garden, roof terrace with grand views, and 37 rooms (family rooms, cheaper rooms with shared bath, fans but no air-con, elevator for top floors, guest kitchen, Wi-Fi in lounge only, 23:00 curfew; Via dell'Olmata 9, Metro: Termini or Vittorio Emanuele; tel. 06-488-8271, www.csse-roma.com, select "Casa per ferie" for English, ist.it.s.elisabetta@libero.it).

¢ The RomeHello hostel is, as their slogan brags, "more than just a bed." Recently opened, it's a modern, quiet, and friendly hostel run with a mission to employ locals and provide a comfortable home for travelers (Via Torino 45, tel. 06-9686-0070, www.theromehello.com, ciao@theromehello.com).

EATING

Romans take great pleasure in dining well. Embrace this passion over a multicourse meal at an outdoor table, watching a parade of passersby while you sip wine with loved ones.

sine in a snug interior that bustles with energy (Wed-Mon 12:30-15:00 & 19:30-22:30, closed Tue, reserve for dinner, Via della Madonna dei Monti 9, tel. 06-679-8643, www.latavernadeiforiimperiali.com).

$$ Alle Carrette Pizzeria—simple, rustic, and family-friendly—serves great wood-fired pizza just 200 yards from the Forum. It's cheap and fast (daily 12:00-15:30 & 19:00-24:00, Vicolo delle Carrette 14, tel. 06-679-2770).

$ Trattoria da Valentino is a classic time warp specializing in *scamorza* (grilled cheese with various toppings; about €10), pastas, and a variety of meat dishes (Mon-Sat 13:00-14:45 & 19:30-23:00, closed Sun, Via del Boschetto 37, tel. 06-488-0643).

Behind the Colosseum

$ Trattoria Luzzi is a well-worn, no-frills eatery serving simple food in a high-energy—sometimes chaotic—environment, so reserve ahead (Thu-Tue 12:00-24:00, closed Wed, Via Celimontana 1, tel. 06-709-6332).

$$ Ristorante Pizzeria Naumachia is a good second bet if Trattoria Luzzi next door is jammed up. It's a bit more upscale and serves good-quality pizza and pastas at decent prices (Via Celimontana 7, tel. 06-700-2764).

$$ Li Rioni, a pizzeria, is open only for dinner, when the busy chef plunges dough into its wood-fired oven, then pulls out crispy-crust Roman-style pizzas (Wed-Mon 19:30-24:00, closed Tue, Via dei SS. Quattro 24, tel. 06-7045-0605).

Pantheon Neighborhood
On and near Campo de' Fiori

In the evening, Campo de' Fiori offers a characteristic setting—although it can be overrun by tourists out drinking.

$$ Enoteca L'Angolo Divino is an inviting little wine bar. With tiny tables, a tiny menu, and more locals than tourists, this place can leave you with a lifelong

Eating Tips: Kitchens close at most restaurants between lunch and dinner; if it's a quality restaurant, it won't reopen before 19:00. If a smaller restaurant is booked up later in the evening (from 20:30 or so), they may accommodate walk-ins if you're willing to eat quickly.

Rome's fabled squares—most notably Piazza Navona, near the Pantheon, and Campo de' Fiori—are lined with the outdoor tables of touristy restaurants with enticing menus and formal-vested waiters. The atmosphere is super romantic. But restaurants in these areas are notorious for surprise charges, forgettable food, microwaved ravioli, and bad service. I enjoy the view by savoring just a drink or dessert on a famous square, but I dine with locals on nearby low-rent streets.

Ancient Rome

For locations, see the map on page 462.

Monti District

$$ Barzilai Bistrot, a wine bar with a kitchen under stout timbers, is family-run, with a fun menu ranging from pastas to burgers (daily, no reservations, Via Panisperna 44, tel. 06-487-4979).

$$ Taverna Romana is small, simple, and a bit chaotic. This family-run eatery's *cacio e pepe* (cheese-and-pepper pasta) is a favorite. Arrive early, as they take no reservations (daily 12:30-14:45 & 19:00-22:45, Via della Madonna dei Monti 79, tel. 06-474-5325).

$$ Taverna dei Fori Imperiali serves typical, slightly higher-priced Roman cui-

Roman Cuisine

For more on Italian food, see the "Eating" section of the Practicalities chapter.

Antipasti (Appetizers)

Antipasto misto: Marinated or grilled vegetables (eggplant, artichokes, peppers, mushrooms), cured meats, cheeses, or seafood (anchovies, octopus)

Bruschetta: Toasted bread brushed with olive oil and garlic, topped with chopped tomatoes, mushrooms, or other tidbits.

Fritti: Battered or breaded fried snacks—often olives stuffed with meat, potato croquettes, or mozzarella balls. Other classics are *supplí* (rice balls with mozzarella) and *fiori di zucca* (squash blossoms filled with mozzarella and anchovies).

Prosciutto e melone: Cantaloupe wrapped in thin-sliced ham

Primo Piatto (First Course)

Bucatini all'amatriciana: Thin pasta tubes with a sauce of tomatoes, onion, pancetta, and pecorino cheese

Gnocchi alla romana: Semolina dumplings baked with butter and cheese

Penne all'arrabbiata: Spicy tomato sauce with chili peppers (*peperoncini*) and garlic over penne

memory (daily 17:00-24:00, also Tue-Sat 11:00-14:00, Via dei Balestrari 12, tel. 06-686-4413).

$$ Trattoria der Pallaro, an eccentric and well-worn eatery that has no menu, has a slogan: "Here, you'll eat what we want to feed you." You have three menu choices: €25 for the works; €20 for appetizers, *secondi,* and dessert; or €16 for appetizers and pasta (daily 12:00-16:00 & 19:00-24:00, reserve if dining after 20:00, cash only, Largo del Pallaro 15, tel. 06-6880-1488).

$$ Open Baladin is a busy, modern, and spacious brewpub featuring a few dozen Italian craft beers and a menu of burgers, salads, and freshly cooked potato chips (daily 12:00-24:00, Via degli Specchi 5, tel. 06-683-8989).

Near Piazza Navona

$$ Vivi Bistrot is in the Museum of Rome building at the south end of Piazza Navona. This cheery and modern little restaurant serves salads, pastas, and burger plates with a focus on organic ingredients (Tue-Sun 10:00-24:00, closed Mon, Piazza Navona 2, tel. 06-683-3779).

$$ Cul de Sac, a long and skinny trattoria lined with wine bottles, is packed with an enthusiastic crowd enjoying a wide-ranging menu, from pasta to homemade pâté. They don't take reservations—come early (daily 12:00-24:00, Piazza Pasquino 73, tel. 06-6880-1094).

$$$ Ristorante Pizzeria "da Francesco," bustling and authentic, has a hardworking young waitstaff, great indoor seating, and a

Rigatoni con la pajata: Pasta topped with a stew of calf intestines
Spaghetti alla carbonara: Eggs, pancetta or *guanciale* (cured pork cheek), cheese (*pecorino romano* or *parmigiano reggiano*), and black pepper over pasta
Spaghetti alle vongole veraci: Pasta served with small clams in the shell
Stracciatella alla romana: Meat broth with whipped eggs, topped with parmesan

Secondo Piatto (Second Course)
Abbacchio alla scottadito: Baby lamb chops grilled and eaten as finger food
Anguillette in umido: Stewed baby eels from Lake Bracciano
Coda alla vaccinara: Oxtail braised with garlic, wine, tomato, and celery
Filetti di baccalà: Battered and fried salt cod fillets (like fish-and-chips minus the chips)
Involtini di vitello al sugo: Veal cutlets rolled with prosciutto, celery, and cheese in a tomato sauce
Saltimbocca alla romana: "Jump-in-the-mouth"—thinly sliced veal layered with prosciutto and sage, then lightly fried
Trippa alla romana: Tripe braised with onions, carrots, and min.

Contorni (Side Dishes)
Carciofi: Artichokes served either *alla romana* (simmered with garlic and mint) or *alla giudia* (flattened and fried)
Fave al guanciale: Fava beans simmered with cured pork cheek and onion
Misticanza: Mixed green salad of arugula (*rucola*) and curly endive (*puntarelle*)

few tables stretching along the quiet street (daily 12:00-15:30 & 19:00-24:00, Piazza del Fico 29, tel. 06-686-4009, www.dafrancesco.it). Reservations are required for evening seatings at 19:00, 20:30, or 22:00.

$ Pizzeria da Baffetto is famous and therefore generally comes with a ridiculous line. The pizzas are great, the service is surly, and the tables are tightly arranged (daily 12:00-15:30 & 18:30-late, cash only, order "M" or "D"—medium or large, Via del Governo Vecchio 114, tel. 06-686-1617).

Near the Trevi Fountain
$$$ Origano is a bustling, modern bistro located three blocks away from the Trevi Fountain. It serves well-priced traditional

Roman specialties and wood-fired pizza in an often chaotic setting (daily 12:00-24:00, Via di Sant'Andrea delle Fratte 25/26, tel. 06-699-20907).

$$ L'Antica Birreria Peroni is Rome's answer to a German beer hall, the place is a hit with Romans for a cheap night out (Mon-Sat 12:00-24:00, closed Sun, a block off Via del Corso at Via di San Marcello 19, tel. 06-679-5310).

Near the Pantheon
$$$$ Ristorante da Fortunato is an Italian classic, with white-coated, black-tie career waiters politely serving good meat and fish to politicians, foreign dignitaries, and well-heeled tourists (figure €50/person, daily 12:30-16:00 & 18:30-23:30, Via

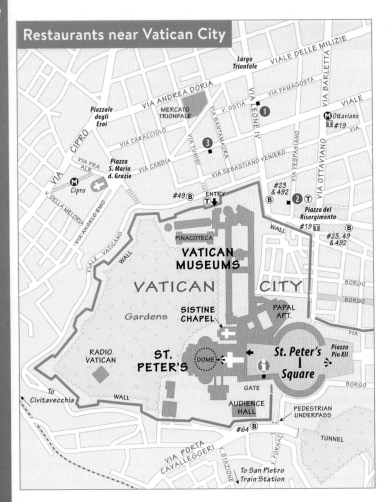

Restaurants near Vatican City

del Pantheon 55, tel. 06-679-2788, www. ristorantefortunato.it).

$$ Trattoria dal Cavalier Gino, tucked away on a tiny street behind the Parliament, has English-speaking siblings. Carla and Fabrizio serve up traditional Roman favorites. They offer four seatings a day: 13:00, 14:30, 20:00, and 22:00. Reserve ahead (Mon-Sat, closed Sun, behind Piazza del Parlamento and just off Via di Campo Marzio at Vicolo Rosini 4, tel. 06-687-3434).

$$$ Ristorante la Campana is a classic—an authentic slice of old Rome appreciated by well-dressed locals. It serves typical Roman dishes and daily specials, plus it

has a self-service *antipasti* buffet, which makes a nice €12 lunch (Tue-Sun 12:30-15:00 & 19:30-23:00, closed Mon, Vicolo della Campana 18, tel. 06-687-5273, www. ristorantelacampana.com).

$$ Osteria delle Coppelle, a slapdash, trendy place, serves traditional dishes to a local crowd and a fun selection of €3 *cicchetti*—small plates (daily 12:30-15:30 & 19:00-late, Piazza delle Coppelle 54, tel. 06-4550-2826).

$$ Ginger is a crisp, modern restaurant one block from the Pantheon, with a menu selection—pastas, *panini,* salads, and smoothies—that is healthy, organic,

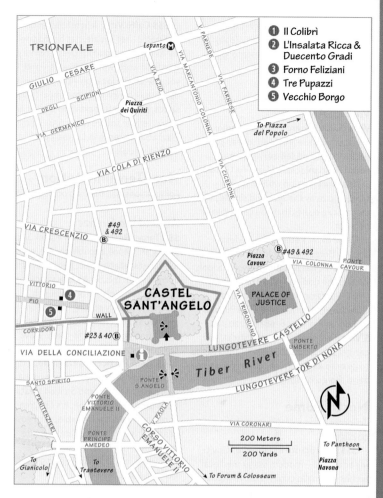

Map Legend:

1. Il Colibrì
2. L'Insalata Ricca & Duecento Gradi
3. Forno Feliziani
4. Tre Pupazzi
5. Vecchio Borgo

---

and a bit pricey (daily 8:00-23:00, Piazza di S. Eustachio 54, tel. 06-6830-8559).

$$ Miscellanea, run by much-loved Miki, offers €4 sandwiches, pizza-like bruschetta, and a long list of hearty salads, along with pasta and other staples (daily 9:00-24:00, Via della Palombella 37, tel. 06-6813-5318).

Near Vatican City

As in the Colosseum area, some eateries near the Vatican prey on exhausted tourists. Instead, tide yourself over with a slice of pizza or at any of these places, and save your euros for a better meal elsewhere.

Handy Lunch Places near Piazza Risorgimento

$$ Il Colibrì, run by the Ricci brothers, has noisy streetside seating and a quiet interior (daily 10:30-15:30 & 17:00-24:00, at corner of Via Leone IV and Via Famagosta 69, tel. 06-3751-4767).

$ L'Insalata Ricca is a branch of the popular chain that serves hearty salads and pastas (daily 12:00-23:30, across from the Vatican walls at Piazza Risorgimento 5, tel. 06-3973-0387).

$ Duecento Gradi is a good bet for fresh and creative sandwiches—though at €5-8 they're expensive by Roman standards. Munch your lunch sitting down (€1 extra) or take it away (daily 11:00-24:00, Piazza Risorgimento 3, tel. 06-3975-4239).

Other Options in the Vatican Area

Viale Giulio Cesare and **Via Candia:** These streets are lined with cheap *pizza rustica* shops and self-serve places. **$ Forno Feliziani** (closed Sun, Via Candia 61) is a fancy version with nicely presented pizza by the slice and simple cafeteria-style dishes that you can eat in or take out.

Close to St. Peter's: The pedestrian-only Borgo Pio—a block from Piazza San Pietro—has restaurants worth a look, such as the traditional **$$ Tre Pupazzi** (Mon-Sat 12:00-15:00 & 19:00-23:00, closed Sun, at corner of Via Tre Pupazzi and Borgo Pio, tel. 06-6880-3220). At **$ Vecchio Borgo,** across the street, you can get pasta, pizza by weight, and veggies to go or to eat at simple tables (daily 9:30-22:30, Borgo Pio 27a).

North Rome

To locate these restaurants, see the map on page 411.

$$$$ Ristorante il Gabriello is inviting and small—modern under medieval arches. Gabriello cooks creative Roman cuisine using fresh, organic products from his wife's farm. While you're likely to dine surrounded by my readers here, the atmosphere is fun and convivial (dinner only, Mon-Sat 19:00-23:00, closed Sun, reservations smart, air-con, dress respectfully—no shorts, 3 blocks from Spanish Steps at Via Vittoria 51, tel. 06-6994-0810, www.ilgabriello.com).

$$ Ginger, four blocks in front of the Spanish Steps, is modern and bright, with an emphasis on sustainable and healthy ingredients (daily 8:00-23:00, Via Borgognona 43, tel. 06-9603-6390). A sister location near the Pantheon is described earlier.

$$$ Caffè Vitti, delightfully set on a fine traffic-free square, has been serving its neighborhood for over a century. The food won't win any awards—and you pay for the location—but it offers a delightful chance to enjoy a meal (good salads, pizza) or a cocktail on a quiet and characteristic square (daily 6:30-24:00, Piazza San Lorenzo in Lucina 33, tel. 06-687-6304).

Near Termini Station

For locations, see the map on page 466.

Around Via Firenze

$$$ Target Restaurant has a sleek and dressy ambience, capable service, and food that's reliably good, but pricey (free *aperitivo* with this book, daily 12:00-15:30 & 19:00-24:00, closed Sun at lunch, reserve to specify seating outside or inside—avoid getting seated in basement, Via Torino 33, tel. 06-474-0066, www.targetrestaurant.it).

$$ Café Pasticceria Dagnino, a time-warp from the 1960s, is known for its fine pastry section and Sicilian treats from *arancini* to cannoli. It's fast, reasonably priced, and reliable, with good seating inside, upstairs, and outside in the mall (daily 7:00-23:00, Galleria Esedra, enter at Via Torino 95, tel. 06-481-8660).

Around Via Flavia

$$$ Ristorante la Pentolaccia, upscale and romantic, is a dressy but still tourist-friendly place with tight seating and traditional Roman cooking—reservations are smart (daily 12:00-15:00 & 18:00-23:00, a block off Via XX Settembre at Via Flavia 38, tel. 06-483-477, www.lapentolaccia-restaurant.it).

$$$ La Bottega Ristorante is a bright, contemporary, and easygoing place serving Roman and Mediterranean cuisine, and good wine by the glass (nightly from 17:00, Via Flavia 46, tel. 06-487-0391). They run the adjacent pizzeria.

$ Pietro Punturi Tavola Calda is a *rosticceria* cooking up super casual dishes sold by weight and eaten on plastic at its fast-food-type seating (Mon-Sat 8:30-20:30, closed Sun, Via Flavia 46).

$$ Pizzeria Annicinquanta, big and modern, is a neighborhood fixture serving Neapolitan-style pizzas in a calm ambience with outdoor seating (daily 12:00-15:30 & 19:30-24:00, Via Flavia 3, tel. 06-4201-0460).

$$$ I Colori del Vino Enoteca is a classy wine bar with a creative menu of *affettati* (cold cuts) and cheeses, and a great list of fine wines by the glass (Mon-Sat 12:00-15:00 & 18:00-23:00, closed Sun, Via Aureliana 15 at corner of Via Flavia, tel. 06-474-1745).

Between Piazza Barberini and Trevi Fountain

$$$ Hostaria Romana is a busy bistro with a hustling and fun-loving gang of waiters. Its menu specializes in traditional Roman dishes such as *saltimbocca alla romana* (Mon-Sat 12:30-15:00 & 19:15-23:00, closed Sun and Aug, reservations smart, Via del Boccaccio 1, tel. 06-474-5284, www.hostariaromana.it).

TRANSPORTATION

Getting Around Rome

Rome's public transportation system is cheap and efficient, but also confusing and crowded. The three Metro lines are relatively sane and straightforward, but serve a limited area. Buses are more chaotic—there are no posted timetables or maps, and stop names are announced only in the newest vehicles. But they run frequently and go everywhere. The website www.atac.roma.it has a **journey planner** in English that will help you sort through the thicket of routes.

Buying Tickets: All public transportation uses the same ticket. It costs €1.50 and is valid for one Metro ride—including

transfers underground—plus unlimited city buses and trams during a 100-minute period. Passes good on buses and the Metro are sold in increments of 24 hours (€7), 48 hours (€12.50), 72 hours (€18), one week (€24—about the cost of three taxi rides), and one month (€35, valid for a calendar month).

You can purchase tickets and passes from machines at Metro stations and a few major bus stops (cash/coins only), and from some newsstands and tobacco shops (*tabacchi,* marked by a black-and-white *T* sign). Tickets are not sold on board.

Validate your ticket by sticking it in the Metro turnstile (magnetic strip-side up, arrow-side first) or in the machine when you board the bus (magnetic strip-side down, arrow-side first)—watch others and imitate. It'll return your ticket with your expiration time printed. To get through a Metro turnstile with a transit pass, press the card to the turnstile's electronic sensor pad. On buses and trams, you need to validate your pass only your first time using it.

By Metro

The Roman subway system (Metropolitana, or "Metro") is simple, clean, cheap, and fast. The two lines you need to know—A and B—intersect at Termini Station. The Metro runs from 5:30 to 23:30 (Fri-Sat until 1:30 in the morning). The subway's first and last compartments are generally the least crowded, and the least likely to harbor pickpockets.

By Bus

The Metro is handy, but it won't get you everywhere—you often have to take the bus (or tram). Route and system maps aren't posted, but with some knowledge of major stops, you can wing it without one. (The ATAC website has a PDF bus map that you can download, bookstores sell paper transport maps, and the ATAC journey planner is helpful.) Rome's few

ITALY

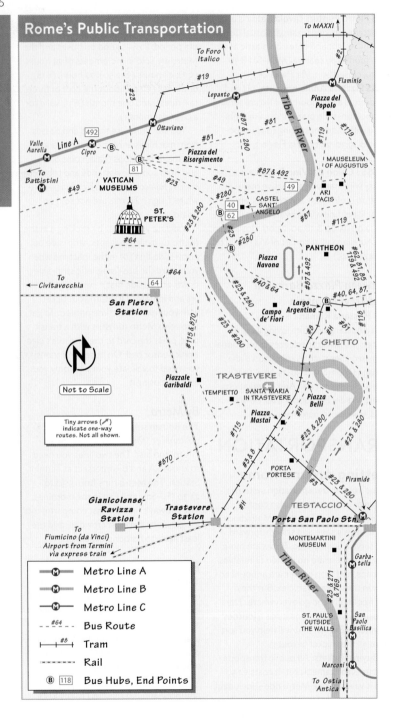

Rome's Public Transportation

To MAXXI

To Foro Italico

#19

#25

Lepanto

Flaminio

Piazza del Popolo

#87 & 280

#81

#81

#119

#119

Line A

492

Ottaviano

#81

MAUSELEUM OF AUGUSTUS

Valle Aurelia

Cipro

B

Piazza del Risorgimento

#87 & 492

49

ARA PACIS

To Battistini

81

#49

#23

#49

#280

#87

#119

VATICAN MUSEUMS

CASTEL SANT' ANGELO

ST. PETER'S

40

#23 & 280

#23

#280

PANTHEON

#62,81,85 119 & 492

62

#64

B

Piazza Navona

#87 & 492

#40, 64, 87,

To Civitacchia

#64

64

Campo de' Fiori

#40 & 64

#23 & 280

Largo Argentina

B

#8

#H

#81

#119

San Pietro Station

#23 & 280

GHETTO

#115 & 870

#23 & 280

Piazzale Garibaldi

TRASTEVERE

TEMPIETTO

SANTA MARIA IN TRASTEVERE

Piazza Belli

Not to Scale

Tiny arrows (↗) indicate one-way routes. Not all shown.

#115

Piazza Mastai

#H

#23 & 280

#23 & 280

#870

#3 & 8

PORTA PORTESE

#3

#23 & 280

Piramide

Gianicolense-Ravizza Station

Trastevere Station

#H

TESTACCIO

Porta San Paolo Stn.

To Fiumicino (da Vinci) Airport from Termini via express train

MONTEMARTINI MUSEUM

Garba-tella

Tiber River

#23, 271 & 769

San Paolo Basilica

ST. PAUL'S OUTSIDE THE WALLS

Marconi

To Ostia Antica

	Metro Line A
	Metro Line B
	Metro Line C
#64	Bus Route
#8	Tram
	Rail
B 118	Bus Hubs, End Points

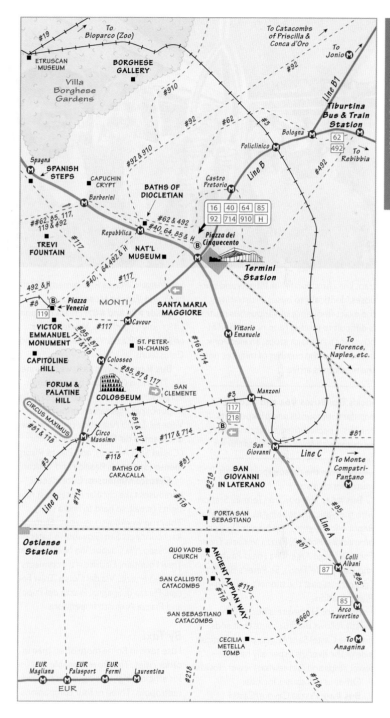

tram lines function for all intents and purposes identically to buses. Frustratingly, the exact frequency of various bus routes is difficult to predict (and not printed at bus stops). At major stops, an electronic board shows the number of minutes until the next buses arrive.

Rick's Tip: **Buses #64 and #40** *are popular with tourists and* **pickpockets.** *If one bus is packed, there's likely a second one on its tail with fewer crowds and thieves.*

These are the most important bus routes for tourists:

Bus #64: This bus links Termini Station with the Vatican, stopping at Piazza della Repubblica (sights), Via Nazionale (recommended hotels), Piazza Venezia (near Forum), Largo Argentina (near Pantheon and Campo de' Fiori), St. Peter's Basilica (get off just past the tunnel), and San Pietro Station.

Bus #40: This express bus, which mostly follows the #64 route (but ends near the Castel Sant'Angelo on the Vatican side of the river), is especially helpful—fewer stops and (somewhat) fewer crowds.

Other useful routes include:

Bus #49: Piazza Cavour/Castel Sant'Angelo, Piazza Risorgimento (Vatican), and Vatican Museums.

Buses #85 and #87: Piazza Navona (#87 only), Pantheon, Via del Corso (#85 only), Piazza Venezia, Forum, and Colosseum.

Bus #492: Travels east-west, connecting Tiburtina (train and bus stations), Largo Santa Susanna (near Piazza della Repubblica), Piazza Barberini, Piazza Venezia, Largo Argentina (near Pantheon and Campo de' Fiori), Piazza Cavour (Castel Sant'Angelo), and Piazza Risorgimento (St. Peter's Basilica and Vatican).

Elettrico **Minibuses:** Cute electric minibuses take circular routes past major sights (small, so hard to find a seat). They run weekdays 7:15-20:15. *Elettrico* #117 connects San Giovanni in Laterano, Colosseo, Via Cavour, Via Nazionale, and Trevi Fountain. *Elettrico* #119 connects Piazza Venezia, Via del Corso, Trevi Fountain, Piazza di Spagna, Piazza del Popolo, and Piazza Augusto Imperatore.

By Taxi

I use taxis in Rome more often than in other cities. They're reasonable and useful for efficient sightseeing in this big, hot metropolis. Three or four companions with more money than time should taxi almost everywhere. Taxis start at €3, then charge about €1.50 per kilometer (surcharges: €1.50 on Sun, €3.50 for nighttime hours of 22:00-6:00, one regular suitcase or bag rides free, tip by rounding up—€1 or so). Sample fares: Termini area to Vatican—€15; Termini area to Colosseum—€7; Termini area to the Borghese Gallery—€9; Colosseum to Trastevere—€12 (or look up your route at www.worldtaximeter.com).

You can hail a cab on the street, but Romans generally walk to the nearest taxi stand (many are marked on this book's maps). Or have your hotel or restaurant call a taxi for you. The meter starts when the call is received. To call a cab on your own, dial 06-3570, 06-4994, or 06-6645, or use the official city taxi line, 06-0609; they'll likely ask you for an Italian phone number (give them your mobile number or your hotel's).

You can also use the Free Now app, which orders an official white taxi at regular taxi rates, with the convenience of paying via the app.

Beware of corrupt taxis. First, only use official Rome taxis. They're white, with a taxi sign on the roof and a maroon logo on the door that reads *Roma Capitale*. When you get in, make sure the meter (*tassametro*) is turned on (you'll see the meter either on the dashboard or up by the rearview mirror). You'll rarely pay more than €12 for a ride in town. Keep an eye on the fare on the meter as you near your destination; some cabbies turn the meter off instantly when they stop and tell you a higher price.

By law, every cab must display a multilingual official price chart—usually on the back of the seat in front of you. If the fare doesn't seem right, point to the chart and ask the cabbie to explain it.

Uber works in Rome as it does in the US, but only at the more expensive Uber Black level.

Arriving and Departing
By Plane

Rome's two airports—**Fiumicino** (a.k.a. Leonardo da Vinci, code: FCO) and the small **Ciampino** (code: CIA)—share the same website (www.adr.it).

FIUMICINO AIRPORT

Rome's major airport is manageable. Terminals T1, T2, and T3 are all under one roof—walkable end to end in 20 minutes. T5 is a separate building requiring a short shuttle trip. (T4 is still being built.) The T1-2-3 complex has ground transport, a TI (in T3, daily 9:00-17:30, longer in summer), ATMs, banks, luggage storage, shops, and bars. For airport information, call 06-65951.

Getting Between Fiumicino Airport and Downtown Rome: In either direction, give yourself plenty of time to allow for traffic delays, finding your train or bus, and walking to the terminal.

By Train: Trenitalia's slick, direct, first-class-only Leonardo Express train connects the airport train station (called Fiumicino Aeroporto) and Rome's central Termini Station in 32 minutes for €14. At either station, buy your ticket from a Trenitalia machine, a ticket office (*biglietteria*), or a newsstand near the platform. You must validate your ticket before boarding by stamping it in a green-and-gray machine near the track. Be aware that people offering help are likely pickpockets: Watch your belongings. Trains run at least twice hourly in both directions from roughly 6:00 to 23:00 (up to 4/hour in busy times). Make sure the train you board is going to the central "Roma Termini" station.

Returning from Termini train station *to* the airport, trains usually depart from track 23 or 24. Check the departure boards for "Fiumicino Aeroporto" and confirm with an official or a local on the platform that the train is indeed going to the airport.

You can access most of the airport's

terminals from the airport train station. If your flight leaves from terminal T5 (where most American air carriers flying direct to the US depart), catch the T5 shuttle bus (*navetta*) on the sidewalk in front of T3—it's too far to walk with luggage.

By Bus: Four bus companies—Terravision (www.terravision.eu), SIT (www.sitbusshuttle.com), T.A.M. (www.tambus.it), and Schiaffini (www.romeairportbus.com)—connect Fiumicino and Termini train station. While cheaper than the train (about €7 one-way), buses take twice as long (about an hour, depending on traffic). At the airport, the bus station is at the far end of terminal T3.

By Airport Shuttle: Shared shuttle van services can be economical for one or two people. Consider Rome Airport Shuttle (€25 for one person, extra people-€6 each, by reservation only, tel. 06-4201-4507 or 06-4201-3469, www.airportshuttle.it).

By Taxi: A taxi between Fiumicino and downtown Rome takes 45 minutes in normal traffic and by law costs exactly €48. (Establish the price when you get in; add a €2-5 tip for good service.) From the airport, be sure to catch an official Rome city taxi at the taxi stand (see "Getting Around Rome, By Taxi," earlier).

CIAMPINO AIRPORT

Rome's smaller airport (tel. 06-6595-9515) handles charter flights and some budget airlines (including most Ryanair flights).

Getting Between Ciampino Airport and Downtown Rome: Bus companies Terravision, Schiaffini, and SIT will take you to Rome's Termini train station (about €5, 2/hour, 45 minutes). Atral runs a quicker route (25 minutes, www.atral-lazio.com) to the Anagnina Metro stop, where you can connect to the stop nearest your hotel (departs every 40 minutes). City bus #520 runs from Ciampino to the Subaugusta Metro stop for a single transit ticket. The fixed price for any official **taxi** (with the maroon *Roma Capitale* logo on

the door) is €30 to downtown (within the old city walls, including most of my recommended hotels).

Rome Airport Shuttle also offers shared van rides to and from Ciampino (€25 for one person, listed earlier).

By Train

Rome's primary train station, centrally located **Termini,** has high-speed connections to other Italian cities and fast trains to the airport. Rome's other major station is called **Tiburtina.**

TERMINI STATION

Termini, Rome's main train station (www.romatermini.com), is a buffet of tourist services. For security, entry to the train platforms themselves is restricted to ticketholders. Entrances are from the inner atrium and from the halls to the sides of the tracks. You may need to show your ticket, but there are no metal detectors and lines are generally short.

In the hall along Via Giovanni Giolitti, on the southwest side of the station (near track 24), you'll find the TI (daily 8:00-18:45), a travel agency, a car-rental desk, a medical center, and baggage storage (*deposito bagagli;* paying €12 daily rate rather than hourly allows you to skip the line; daily 6:00-23:00). The Leonardo Express train to Fiumicino Airport runs from track 23 or 24 on this side of the station (see "Getting Between Fiumicino Airport and Downtown Rome," earlier). Pay WCs are down the escalators from the inner atrium and inside the Mercato Centrale (near track 24).

The Termini Metro station, where Metro lines A and B intersect, is beneath the station. City buses leave from the square directly in front of the outer atrium. Buses to the airport leave from the streets on both sides of the station.

TRAIN CONNECTIONS

Unless otherwise specified, the following connections are for Trenitalia.

From Termini by Train to: Fiumicino

Airport (Leonardo Express; 2/hour, 32 minutes), **Venice** (hourly, 4 hours, 1 direct night train, 7 hours; Italo: 4/day, 3.5 hours), **Florence** (2-3/hour, 1.5 hours; Italo: 2/hour, 1.5 hours), **Siena** (1-2/hour, 1 change, 3-4 hours), **Orvieto** (every 1-2 hours, 1.5 hours; regional trains are half the price and only slightly slower than Intercity trains), **Assisi** (4/day direct, 2 hours; more with change in Foligno), **Pisa** (1-2/hour, 3 hours, some change in Florence), **Milan** (1-3/hour, 3.5 hours; Italo: 11/day nonstop, 3 hours, more with stops), **Naples** (1-4/hour, 1 hour on Frecciarossa, 2 hours on Intercity, 2.5 hours and much cheaper on regional trains; Italo: hourly, 70 minutes), **Sorrento** (Italo train/bus combination, 2/day, 3.5 hours).

Rick's Tip: **Shady characters** *linger around the station, especially* **near ticket machines.** *Some offer help for a "tip"; others have official-looking business cards.* **Avoid anybody selling anything** *unless they're in a legitimate shop at the station. There are no official porters;* **carry your own bags.**

TIBURTINA STATION AND AUTOSTAZIONE TIBURTINA

Tiburtina, Rome's second-largest train station (www.stazioneromatiburtina.it), sits next to the Tiburtina Metro station in the city's northeast corner. Across the road is Rome's long-distance bus station, Autostazione Tiburtina. To reach the bus station from the train station, don't follow the *Bus* signs, which lead to the city bus stop. Instead, exit the station, cross the street under the elevated freeway, and look for the fenced-in area with bus platforms. The bus station is chaotic and crowded, so buy your ticket online in advance, if possible.

From Tiburtina by Bus to: Siena (9/day, 3 hours, https://global.flixbus.com), **Sorrento** (1-2/day, 4 hours; this is a cheap and easy way to go straight to Sorrento, buy tickets at www.marozzivt.it—in Italian only, at the Tiburtina ticket office, travel agencies, or on board for a €3.50 surcharge).

Rick's Tip: *A car is a worthless headache in Rome, If Rome is the first stop of your trip,* **enjoy the city car-free,** *then take the train to Orvieto and rent a car there.*

By Car

If you absolutely must drive and park a car in Rome, there's a large underground garage at the Villa Borghese Gardens near the Spagna Metro station, just outside the restricted downtown zone (€18/day, Viale del Galoppatoio 33, www.sabait.it). Alternatively, use one of the more than two-dozen park-and-ride lots at Rome's outlying Metro stations (€5/24 hours). These vary in size and convenience; one of the largest is at the Anagnina Metro station, just inside Rome's ring expressway along the Via Tuscolana (southeast of downtown). For details, search for "park and ride" *(parcheggi di scambio)* at www.atac.roma.it.

Florence

Florence is the birthplace of the Renaissance and the modern world. It's geographically small but culturally rich—containing more artistic masterpieces per square mile than anyplace else. In a single day, you can look Michelangelo's *David* in the eyes, fall under the seductive sway of Botticelli's *Birth of Venus*, and climb the modern world's first dome, which still dominates the skyline.

A cosmopolitan vibe courses through the city's narrow lanes. You'll encounter children licking gelato, students riding Vespas, supermodels wearing Gucci fashions, and artisans sipping Chianti—Florence has long been perfecting the art of civilized living.

FLORENCE IN 2 DAYS

Compact Florence is packed with sights, but crowds and long lines can ruin your day's agenda. To maximize your time, reserve ahead for the top two sights—Accademia (Michelangelo's *David*) and Uffizi Gallery (Renaissance paintings). Avoid both sights on Monday when they're closed, and on the first Sunday of the month from October through March, when they're free but impossibly crowded. Many other sights are either closed or have shorter hours Sundays and Mondays.

Day 1: See the Accademia (*David*) with a timed reservation. Afterward, visit the nearby Museum of San Marco (Fra Angelico's art, explore the Mercato Centrale (having lunch nearby), and drop by the Church of Santa Maria Novella (art by Masaccio). To avoid heat and crowds, take my Renaissance Walk in the morning or late afternoon.

On Any Evening: Linger over dinner. Take a stroll, gelato in hand. Or take a taxi or bus to Piazzale Michelangelo for spectacular city views, and walk back into town for dinner. You can sightsee late at some sights, attend a concert at a church, or drop by a wine bar.

Day 2: See the Bargello (best statues), then either the Duomo Museum (statues by Donatello and Michelangelo) or Galileo Science Museum (if art's not your thing). Then hit the street markets for some shopping and wandering. In the afternoon, see the Uffizi with a timed reservation. Then stroll to the river and cross the historic bridge, Ponte Vecchio, to the Oltrarno neighborhood for dinner.

With extra time: See the sights on the Oltrarno side of the Arno: the Pitti Palace and its lush gardens, the Brancacci Chapel with early Renaissance artwork, or the hill-capping San Miniato Church.

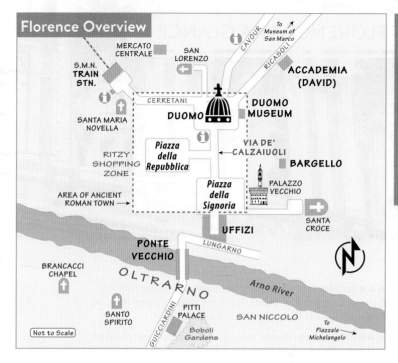

Florence Overview

MERCATO CENTRALE
SAN LORENZO
To Museum of San Marco
CAVOUR
RICASOLI
ACCADEMIA (DAVID)
S.M.N. TRAIN STN.
CERRETANI
DUOMO
DUOMO MUSEUM
SANTA MARIA NOVELLA
Piazza della Repubblica
VIA DE' CALZAIUOLI
BARGELLO
RITZY SHOPPING ZONE
Piazza della Signoria
PALAZZO VECCHIO
AREA OF ANCIENT ROMAN TOWN →
SANTA CROCE
UFFIZI
PONTE VECCHIO
LUNGARNO
BRANCACCI CHAPEL
O L T R A R N O
Arno River
N
SANTO SPIRITO
GUICCIARDINI
PITTI PALACE
SAN NICCOLO
To Piazzale Michelangelo →
Boboli Gardens
Not to Scale

ORIENTATION

Florence (pop. 380,000) is small but intense. Prepare for scorching summer heat, crowded narrow lanes and sidewalks, slick pickpockets, few WCs, steep prices, and long lines. The best of the city lies on the north bank of the Arno River. The main historical sights cluster around the venerable dome of the cathedral (Duomo). Everything is within a 20-minute walk of the train station, cathedral, or Ponte Vecchio (Old Bridge). The less famous but more characteristic Oltrarno area (south bank) is just over the bridge.

Historic Core: The Duomo—with its iconic, towering dome—is the visual, geographical, and historical center of Florence. A 10-minute walk away is the Palazzo Vecchio (City Hall), with its skyscraping medieval spire. Connecting these two landmarks is the north-south pedestrian street called Via de' Calzaiuoli. This central axis—Duomo to the Palazzo Vecchio to the Arno River—is the spine for Florentine sightseeing and the route of my self-guided Renaissance Walk. To the west of this axis is a glitzy shopping zone, and to the east is a characteristic web of narrow lanes.

Accademia/San Lorenzo (North of the Duomo): From the Duomo, Via Cavour runs north, bisecting the neighborhood. To the east lies the Accademia and the Museum of San Marco. The western part clusters around the Basilica of San Lorenzo, with its Medici Chapels. The area near San Lorenzo teems with tourists: There are the vendor stalls of San Lorenzo Market, the lively Mercato Centrale, and many hotels and trattorias.

Train Station/Santa Maria Novella (West of the Duomo): The area near the train station and Church of Santa Maria Novella has inexpensive hotels and characteristic eateries. Closer to the river (near Palazzo Strozzi) is a posh shopping zone.

Santa Croce (East of the Duomo): A 10-minute walk east from the Palazzo

FLORENCE AT A GLANCE

▲▲▲**Accademia** Michelangelo's *David* and powerful (unfinished) *Prisoners*. Reserve ahead. **Hours:** Tue-Sun 8:15-19:00, closed Mon; July-Sept open Tue and Thu 7:00-22:00. See page 506.

▲▲▲**Uffizi Gallery** Greatest collection of Italian paintings anywhere. Reserve well in advance. **Hours:** Tue-Sun 8:15-19:00, closed Mon; July-Sept Wed-Thu until 22:00. See page 508.

▲▲▲**Bargello** Underappreciated sculpture museum (Michelangelo, Donatello, Medici treasures). **Hours:** Daily 8:15-14:00 (until 17:00 for special exhibits); closed on second and fourth Sun and first, third, and fifth Mon of each month. See page 513.

▲▲▲**Duomo Museum** Freshly renovated cathedral museum with the finest in Florentine sculpture. **Hours:** Daily 9:00-19:00, closed first Tue of each month. See page 502.

▲▲▲**Pitti Palace** Several museums in lavish palace plus sprawling Boboli and Bardini Gardens. **Hours:** Palatine Gallery, Royal Apartments, Treasury, Museum of Costume and Fashion, and Gallery of Modern Art open Tue-Sun 8:15-19:00, closed Mon; Boboli and Bardini Gardens, and Porcelain Museum open daily June-Aug 8:15-19:30, April-May and Sept until 18:30, March and Oct until 17:30, Nov-Feb until 16:30, closed first and last Mon of each month. See page 514.

▲▲**Duomo** Gothic cathedral with colorful facade and the first dome built since ancient Roman times. **Hours:** Mon-Sat 10:00-16:30, Sun 13:30-16:45. See page 501.

▲▲**Museum of San Marco** Best collection anywhere of artwork by the early Renaissance master Fra Angelico. **Hours:** Tue-Fri 8:15-14:00, Sat-Sun until 17:00; also open until 14:00 on first, third, and fifth Mon of each month. See page 507.

▲▲▲**Medici Chapels** Tombs of Florence's great ruling family, designed and carved by Michelangelo. **Hours:** Tue-Sat 8:15-14:00; also open first, third, and fifth Sun and second and fourth Mon of each month. See page 507.

▲▲**Palazzo Vecchio** Fortified palace, once the home of the Medici family, wallpapered with history. **Hours:** Museum and excavations open daily 9:00-23:00 (Oct-March until 19:00), Thu until 14:00 year-round; shorter hours for tower. See page 511.

▲▲**Galileo Science Museum** Fascinating old clocks, telescopes, maps, and three of Galileo's fingers. **Hours:** Daily 9:30-18:00 except Tue until 13:00. See page 512.

▲▲**Santa Croce Church** Precious art, tombs of famous Florentines, and Brunelleschi's Pazzi Chapel in 14th-century church. **Hours:** Mon-Sat 9:30-17:00, Sun from 14:00. See page 513.

▲▲**Church of Santa Maria Novella** Thirteenth-century Dominican church with Masaccio's famous 3-D painting. **Hours:** Mon-Thu 9:00-19:00, Fri 11:00-19:00, Sat 9:00-17:30, Sun 13:00-17:30; Oct-March closes at 17:30. See page 514.

▲▲**Brancacci Chapel** Works of Masaccio, early Renaissance master who reinvented perspective. **Hours:** Wed-Mon 10:00-17:00 except Sun from 13:00, closed Tue. Reservations mandatory March-May. See page 515.

▲▲**San Miniato Church** Sumptuous Renaissance chapel and sacristy showing scenes of St. Benedict. **Hours:** Mon-Sat 9:30-13:00 & 15:00-19:30, until 19:00 off-season, Sun 8:15-19:30, closed sporadically for special occasions. See page 518.

▲**Climbing the Duomo's Dome** Grand view into the cathedral, close-up of dome architecture and, after 463 steps, a glorious city vista; reservations required. **Hours:** Mon-Fri 8:30-19:00, Sat until 17:00, Sun 13:00-16:00. See page 501.

▲**Baptistery** Bronze doors fit to be the gates of paradise. **Hours:** Doors always viewable; interior open Mon-Sat 8:15-19:30 (closed 10:15-11:15), Sun until 13:30. See page 502.

▲**Piazza Santissima Annunziata** Lovely square epitomizing Renaissance harmony, with Brunelleschi's Hospital of the Innocents, considered the first Renaissance building. See page 506.

▲**Medici-Riccardi Palace** Lorenzo the Magnificent's home, with fine art, frescoed ceilings, and Gozzoli's lovely Chapel of the Magi. **Hours:** Thu-Tue 9:00-19:00, closed Wed. See page 508.

▲**Ponte Vecchio** Famous bridge lined with gold and silver shops. See page 499.

▲**Piazzale Michelangelo** Hilltop square with stunning view of Duomo and Florence, with San Miniato Church just uphill. See page 516.

Vecchio leads to the Church of Santa Croce. Along the way is the Bargello sculpture museum. This neighborhood is congested with tourists by day and students partying by night. But the area stretching north and west from Santa Croce is increasingly authentic and workaday, offering a glimpse of untouristy Florence.

Oltrarno (South of the River): Literally the "Other Side of the Arno River," this neighborhood reveals a Florence from a time before tourism. The Oltrarno starts just across Ponte Vecchio and stretches south to the giant Pitti Palace and surrounding gardens (Boboli and Bardini). To the west is the rough-but-bohemian Piazza di Santo Spirito (with its namesake church) and the lavishly frescoed Brancacci Chapel. To the east of Pitti, perched high on the hill, is Piazzale Michelangelo, with Florence's most popular viewpoint. Tucked between there and the river is the little San Niccolò neighborhood, with its lively bars and eateries.

Tourist Information

The city TI's main branch is across the square from the **train station** (Mon-Sat 9:00-19:00; Sun until 14:00; at the back corner of the Church of Santa Maria Novella at Piazza della Stazione 4; tel. 055-212-245, www.firenzeturismo.it). A smaller branch is centrally located **across from the Duomo,** at the west corner of Via de' Calzaiuoli (inside the Loggia, same hours as train station branch, tel. 055-288-496).

A less crowded and more helpful TI (covering both the city and the greater province of Florence) is a couple of blocks **north of the Duomo,** just past the Medici-Riccardi Palace (Mon-Fri 9:00-13:00, closed Sat-Sun, Via Cavour 1 red, tel. 055-290-832). There's also a TI booth at the **airport.**

A handy little ticket booth at the Orsanmichele Church often has reservations for the Uffizi and Accademia when other sources are sold out (Mon-Sat 9:00-16:15).

Helpful Hints

Sightseeing Tips: Everyone visiting Florence wants to see the same three or four sights. Consequently, these are mobbed with long lines. While, technically, you could wait in line to get into these places, it's flat-out stupid. Don't waste your time in line—get a reservation. The process for making reservations online is clearly explained under "Sights," later.

Among Florence's many sightseeing passes, one worth considering is the **Uffizi/Pitti Palace/Boboli Gardens combo-ticket** (called "PassePartout"), which is valid for three consecutive days and offers admission to these sights at a €12 savings (€38 March-Oct, €18 Nov-Feb). Note that with this ticket, you must start your visit at the Uffizi. You can purchase it in advance at www.uffizi.it; look for "Intero Cumulativo 3 giorni" in the ticket options.

The 72-hour **Firenze Card** sold by the TI gets you into nearly all the sights in town for €85. It requires you book a time to enter the Uffizi and Accademia. It's only a savings and worth buying if you'll be sightseeing like crazy for three days. And in very busy times as a last resort, you might find you can get a reservation with a Firenze Card for the Uffizi or Accademia when you otherwise can't get in.

Some state museums in Italy (including Florence's Uffizi Gallery, Accademia, and many others) are free to enter once or twice a month, usually on a Sunday. But **free days** are bad news—they attract crowds. Check sight websites in advance.

Theft Alert: Florence has hardworking gangs of thieves who hang out near the train station, the station's underpass (especially where the tunnel surfaces), around Mercato Centrale, and at major sights. American tourists are considered easy targets. Some thieves even dress like tourists to fool you. Any crowded bus likely holds at least one thief.

Visiting Churches: Modest dress is required in some churches, including the Duomo, Santa Maria Novella, Santa Croce, Santa Maria del Carmine/Brancacci Chapel, and the Medici Chapels. Be respectful of worshippers and the paintings; don't use a flash. Many churches, though not the biggies we mention, close from 12:00 or 12:30 until 15:00 or 16:00.

Addresses: Florence has a confusing system for street addresses, with "red" numbers for businesses and "black" numbers for residences. In print, addresses are indicated with "r" (as in Via Cavour 2r) or "n" (as in Via Cavour 25n). Red and black numbers are interspersed together on the same street, but their numbers bear no connection with each other.

WCs: Public restrooms are scarce. Use them when you can, in any café or museum you patronize. Pay public WCs are typically €1. Convenient locations include: at the Baptistery ticket office (near the Duomo); near the entrance to the Church of Santa Maria Novella; inside the train station (near track 5 and in the food court); just down the street from Piazza Santa Croce (at Borgo Santa Croce 29 red); on Piazza Santo Spirito; and up near Piazzale Michelangelo.

Laundry: The **Wash & Dry Lavarapido** chain offers long hours and efficient self-service launderettes at several locations (generally daily 7:30-23:00). These locations are close to recommended hotels: Via del Sole 29 red and Via della Scala 52 red (this location is a Speed Queen, between train station and river), and Via Ghibellina 143 red (Palazzo Vecchio).

Rick's Tip: Carry a water bottle to refill at Florence's twist-the-handle **public fountains** *(around the corner from the "Piglet" at Mercato Nuovo, or in front of the Pitti Palace). Try the* fontanello *(dispenser of free cold water) on Piazza della Signoria, behind the statue of Neptune.*

Tours

Tour companies that offer a discount when you show this book are indicated in these listings with the abbreviation "RS%." In addition to the offerings mentioned here, some offer bus excursions to smaller towns in the Tuscan countryside (such as Siena, San Gimignano, Pisa, and into Chianti country for wine tasting).

WALKING (AND BIKING) TOURS

Artviva offers an intriguing variety of tours, including their popular overview tours (€33 "Original Florence" 3-hour town walk; €124 "Florence in One Glorious Day" combines town walk and tours of the Uffizi and Accademia, 6 hours total). They also have standalone Uffizi and Accademia tours, cooking classes, and more (RS%—10 percent discount, use the password "reader"). Their office is above Odeon Cinema near Piazza della

Avoid waiting in lines...

...by making advance reservations.

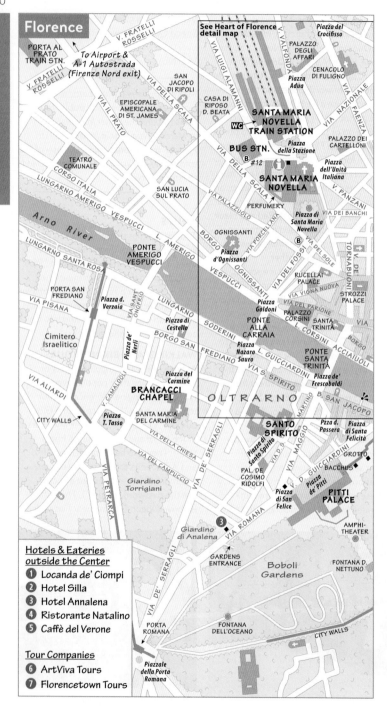

Florence

See Heart of Florence detail map

Piazza del Crocifisso

PORTA AL PRATO TRAIN STN.

To Airport & A-1 Autostrada (Firenze Nord exit)

V. FRATELLI ROSSELLI

V. FRATELLI ROSSELLI

SAN JACOPO DI RIPOLI

VIA DELLA SCALA

VIA IL PRATO

EPISCOPALE AMERICANA DI ST. JAMES

CASA DI RIPOSO D. BEATA

V. VALFONDA

PALAZZO DEGLI AFFARI

CENACOLO DI FULIGNO

VIA LUIGI ALAMANNI

Piazza Adua

VIA NAZIONALE

VIA FAENZA

SANTA MARIA NOVELLA TRAIN STATION

WC

TEATRO COMUNALE

CORSO ITALIA

LUNGARNO AMERIGO VESPUCCI

SAN LUCIA SUL PRATO

VIA DELLA SCALA

BUS STN.

B #12

i

Piazza della Stazione

PALAZZO DEI CARTELLONI

Piazza dell'Unità Italiana

SANTA MARIA NOVELLA

Arno River

VIA PALAZZUOLO

PERFUMERY

Piazza di Santa Maria Novella

VIA DEI BANCHI

V. PANZANI

LUNGARNO SANTA ROSA

PONTE AMERIGO VESPUCCI

OGNISSANTI

BORGO OGNISSANTI

VIA PORCELLANA

Piazza d'Ognissanti

B

VIA DEL SOLE

VIA DEL FOSSI

TORNABUONI

PORTA SAN FREDIANO

VIA PISANA

Piazza d. Verzaia

VIA SANT'ONOFRIO

LUNGARNO VESPUCCI

RUCELLAI PALACE

VIA VIGNA NUOVA

STROZZI PALACE

Cimitero Israelitico

Piazza de' Nerli

Piazza di Cestello

BORGO SAN FREDIANO

SODERINI

Piazza Goldoni

PONTE ALLA CARRAIA

VIA DEL PARIONE

PALAZZO CORSINI

L. CORSINI

SANTA TRINITA

VIA

BORGO ACCIAIUOLI

VIA ALIARDI

CITY WALLS

Piazza T. Tasso

V. CAMALDOLI

Piazza del Carmine

BRANCACCI CHAPEL

SANTA MARIA DEL CARMINE

L. GUICCIARDINI

Piazza Nazaro Sauro

VIA S. SPIRITO

PONTE SANTA TRINITA

Piazza de' Frescobaldi

B. SAN JACOPO

VIA MARTINO

OLTRARNO

VIA DELLA CHIESA

VIA DEL CAMPUCCIO

VIA DE' SERRAGLI

SANTO SPIRITO

Piazza di Santo Spirito

VIA D. S.

VIA MAGGIO

Pza d. Passera

D. GUICCIARDINI

Piazza di Santa Felicità

GROTTO

BACCHUS

Giardino Torrigiani

VIA PETRARCA

PAL. DE COSIMO RIDOLFI

Piazza di San Felice

Piazza de' PITTI

PITTI PALACE

AMPHI-THEATER

Giardino di Analena

VIA ROMANA

GARDENS ENTRANCE

Boboli Gardens

FONTANA D. NETTUNO

Hotels & Eateries outside the Center

1 Locanda de' Ciompi
2 Hotel Silla
3 Hotel Annalena
4 Ristorante Natalino
5 Caffè del Verone

Tour Companies

6 ArtViva Tours
7 Florencetown Tours

VIA DE' SERRAGLI

PORTA ROMANA

FONTANA DELL'OCEANO

CITY WALLS

Piazzale della Porta Romana

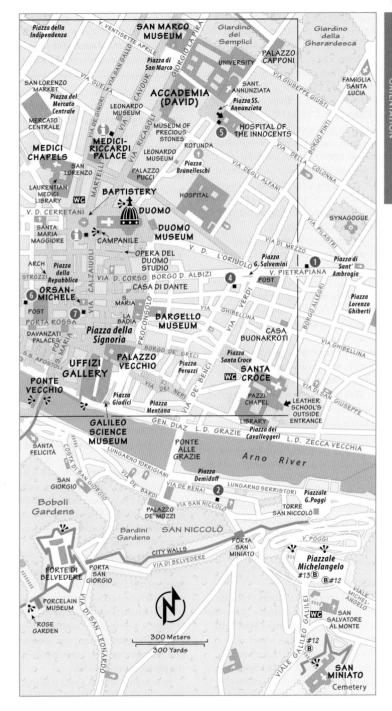

Repubblica (Mon-Sat 8:00-18:00, Sun 8:30-13:30, Via de' Sassetti 1, second floor, tel. 055-264-5033, www.artviva.com).

Florencetown runs tours on foot or by bike. Their most popular offerings are "Walk and Talk Florence" (€29, 2.5 hours, daily at 10:00, basic stops including the Oltrarno) and "I Bike Florence" (€39; 2.5 hours on one-speed bike, 15-stop blitz of town's top sights, helmets optional; in bad weather it goes as a walking tour). Their office is at Via de Lamberti 1 (facing Orsanmichele Church). They also offer cooking classes and student rates for anyone with this book (RS%, tel. 055-281-103, www.florencetown.com).

For a more scholarly approach, **Florentia**'s tours are geared for travelers with longer-than-average attention spans and range from introductory city walks and museum visits to in-depth thematic walks (from €275, includes planning assistance by email, www.florentia.org, info@florentia.org), and Context Florence's tours are led by graduate students and professors (www.contexttravel.com, info@contexttravel.com).

Walks Inside Florence, led by two art historians—Paola Barubiani and Marzia Valbonesi—provide quality private tours and a discounted rate for Rick Steves readers (RS%, €190/group for 3-hour introductory tour, up to 6 people). Their "Florence in a Day" tour gives you the essentials in four hours (€260/group, up to 6 people, museum admissions extra—they make the reservations so there's no waiting in line; Paola's mobile 335-526-6496, www.walksinsideflorence.it, paola@walksinsideflorence.it).

LOCAL GUIDES

These guides offer a variety of private tours in and around Florence (generally €60-75/hour): **Alessandra Marchetti** (mobile 347-386-9839, www.tuscany driverguide.com, alessandramarchetti tours@gmail.com); **Paola Migliorini** (mobile 347-657-2611, www.florence tour.com, info@florencetour.com);

Elena Fulceri (mobile 347-942-2054, www.florencewithflair.com, info@florence withflair.com); and **Vanessa Garau** (mobile 349-133-6894, garau.vanessa@gmail.com).

Rick's Tip: *Several tour companies (such as Florencetown or Artviva) offer* **regularly scheduled group tours** *that anyone can sign up for—usually the cheapest option for individual travelers. But families and small groups can* **book a private guide for a similar price,** *since rates are hourly for any size of group.*

RENAISSANCE WALK

This great and rich city is easily covered on foot. We'll start with the soaring church dome that stands as the proud symbol of the Renaissance spirit; just opposite, you'll find the Baptistery doors that opened the Renaissance. We'll then stroll down the city's pedestrian-only main street to the Palazzo Vecchio and the Arno River. Along the way, we'll pass elegant stores, lively eateries, and the parade of people that make up Florence today.

For more details on many of the stops on this walk, see the individual listings under "Sights," later.

Length of This Walk: The walk is less than a mile long. Allow two hours, including visits to the interiors of the Baptistery and Orsanmichele Church.

Tours: ∩ Download my free Renaissance Walk **audio tour.**

Background: The Renaissance—the "rebirth" of Greek and Roman culture that swept across Europe—started around 1400 and lasted about 150 years. In politics, the Renaissance meant democracy; in science, a renewed interest in exploring nature. The general mood was optimistic and "humanistic," with a confidence in the power of the individual.

Renaissance art was a return to the realism and balance of Greek and Roman

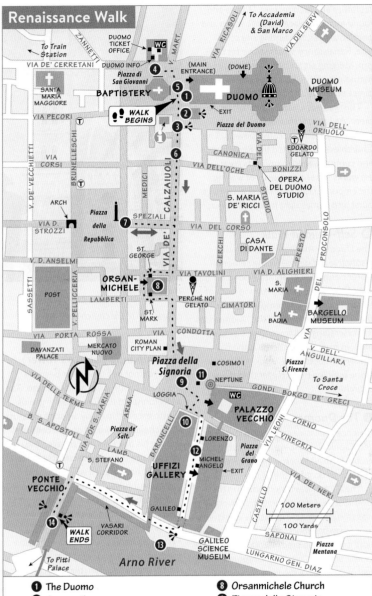

Renaissance Walk

1 The Duomo
2 Campanile
3 View of the Dome
4 Baptistery – North Doors
5 Baptistery – East Doors (Gates of Paradise)
6 Via de' Calzaiuoli
7 Piazza della Repubblica

8 Orsanmichele Church
9 Piazza della Signoria
10 Loggia dei Lanzi
11 Savonarola Plaque
12 Uffizi Courtyard Statues
13 Arno River
14 Ponte Vecchio

sculpture and architecture. Domes and round arches replaced Gothic spires and pointed arches. In painting and sculpture, Renaissance artists strove for realism. Merging art and science, they used mathematics, the laws of perspective, and direct observation of nature.

This was not an anti-Christian movement. Artists saw themselves as an extension of God's creative powers. The Church even supported the Renaissance and commissioned many of its greatest works. After 1,000 years of waiting, the embers of Europe's classical heritage burst into flames right here in Florence.

⊙ Self-Guided Walk

The Duomo—the cathedral with the distinctive red dome—is the center of Florence and the orientation point for this walk. Stroll around the piazza in front of the cathedral (the Duomo), and take in the sights. To the right of the Duomo rises its skyscraping bell tower (the Campanile). In front of the church is the Baptistery—an octagonal, black-and-white stone building that's bigger than many churches.

❶ The Duomo

Florence's massive cathedral is the city's geographical and spiritual heart. Its dome, visible from all over the city, inspired Florentines to do great things.

The church was begun in 1296 in the Gothic style. After generations of work, it was still unfinished. The facade was little more than bare brick, and it stood that way until it was completed in 1870 in the "Neo"-Gothic style. Its "retro" look captures the feel of the original medieval facade, with green, white, and pink marble sheets that cover the brick construction. This over-the-top facade is adored by many, while others call it "the cathedral in pajamas."

We won't go inside the church on this tour. It has a cavernous, bare interior with a few noteworthy sights. Entry is free, but there's often a long wait.

The Campanile

• *Now turn to the church's bell tower, to the right.*

❷ Campanile (Giotto's Tower)

The 270-foot bell tower was begun in the 1300s by the great painter Giotto. As a forerunner of the Renaissance genius, Giotto excelled in many artistic fields, just as Michelangelo would do two centuries later. In his day, Giotto was called the ugliest man to ever walk the streets of Florence, but he designed what many call the most beautiful bell tower in all of Europe.

You can climb the Campanile for great views. It doesn't require a reservation, just a Duomo combo-ticket.

• *Now take in the Duomo's star attraction: the dome. The best viewing spot is just to the right of the facade, from the corner of the pedestrian-only Via de' Calzaiuoli.*

❸ View of Brunelleschi's Dome

Though construction of the church had begun in 1296, by the 1400s there still was no suitable roof. City fathers intended to top it with a dome, but the technology to span the 140-foot-wide hole had yet to

The Renaissance and Brunelleschi's dome live on in Florence.

be invented. *Non c'è problema.* The brash Florentines knew that someday someone would come along who could handle the challenge. That man was Filippo Brunelleschi.

Brunelleschi used a dome within a dome. What you see is the outer shell, covered in terra-cotta tile. The inner dome is thicker and provides much of the structural support. The grand white skeletal ribs connect at the top, supporting each other in a way similar to a pointed arch. Hidden between them are interlocking bricks, laid in a herringbone pattern. Rather than being stacked horizontally, like traditional brickwork, the alternating vertical bricks act as "bookends." The dome grew upward like an igloo, supporting itself as it proceeded from the base. When the ribs reached the top, Brunelleschi arched them in and fixed them in place with the lantern at the top. His dome, built in only 14 years, was the largest since ancient Rome's Pantheon.

When completed in 1436, Brunelleschi's dome was the wonder of the age. It became the model for many domes to follow, from St. Peter's to the US Capitol.

You can climb the dome for Florence's best views, but it requires a reservation in advance.

• *Next up, the Baptistery.*

Baptistery and Ghiberti's Bronze Doors

Built in the 11th century, atop Roman foundations, this is Florence's oldest surviving building—a thousand years old. The spacious interior features a fine example of pre-Renaissance mosaic art (1200s-1300s) in the Byzantine style. But the Baptistery is best known for its doors. The most famous ones are the East Doors, which face the cathedral, but let's start with the North Doors—around to the right, where tourists go in—which may be even more important. (Note that the original doors are in the Duomo Museum and well worth seeing.)

Ghiberti's bronze Gates of Paradise

❹ **North Doors:** Some say that these doors actually started the Renaissance. It was the year 1401, and Florence was holding a competition to find the best artist to make some doors for the Baptistery entrance. All the greats entered the contest, including Donatello and Brunelleschi. The winner was relatively unknown 24-year-old Lorenzo Ghiberti. For the next 25 years, he worked on these North Doors.

• *Now return to the more famous doors facing the church.*

❺ **East Doors** (Gates of Paradise): Ghiberti's bronze panels for these doors added a whole new dimension to art— depth. Michelangelo said these doors were fit to be the "Gates of Paradise." Here we see how the Renaissance masters merged art and science. Realism was in, and Renaissance artists used math, illusion, and dissection to create it.

• *Head south, down the busy pedestrian-only street that runs from here toward the Arno River.*

❻ Via de' Calzaiuoli

Via de' Calzaiuoli (kahlts-ay-WOH-lee) was part of the ancient Roman grid plan that became Florence. Around the year 1400, as the Renaissance was blooming, this street connected the religious center (where we are now) with the political center (where we're heading), a five-minute walk away.

Since most vehicles were banned a few years back, this street has been transformed into a pleasant place to stroll, people-watch, window-shop, and wonder why American cities can't become more pedestrian-friendly.

• *Two blocks down from the Baptistery, turn right on Via degli Speziali toward the triumphal arch that marks...*

❼ Piazza della Repubblica

This large square sits on the site of the original Roman Forum. The lone column that still stands here once marked the intersection of the two main Roman roads (Via Corso and Via Roma). In the 1860s, the square got its magnificent arch, celebrating the unification of Italy. Venerable cafés and stores line the square. Gilli, on the northeast corner, is a favorite for its grand atmosphere and tasty sweets.

• *Return to the main street and continue walking toward the river. A block farther, at the intersection with Via Orsanmichele, is the...*

❽ Orsanmichele Church

Originally, this was an open loggia (covered porch) with a huge grain warehouse upstairs. The arches of the loggia were artfully filled in (14th century) to make walls, and the building gained a new purpose—as a church. The 14 niches in the exterior walls feature remarkable-in-their-day statues paid for by the city's rising middle class of merchants and their 21 guilds.

Circle the church exterior counterclockwise to enjoy the statues. Start on the church's right side (along Via Orsanmichele). In the third niche is **Nanni di Banco's Quattro Santi Coronati** (c. 1415-1417). These four early Christians were sculptors martyred by the Roman emperor Diocletian because they refused to sculpt pagan gods. They seem to be contemplating the consequences of the fatal decision they're about to make.

Just to the right of Banco's saints is **Donatello's St. George.** He's alert, perched on the edge of his niche, scanning the horizon for dragons. He's anxious, but he's also self-assured. Comparing this Renaissance-style *St. George* to *Quattro Santi Coronati*, you can psychoanalyze the heady changes underway. This is humanism.

Continue counterclockwise around the church (bypassing the entrance), all the way to the opposite side. The first niche features **Donatello's St. Mark** (1411-1413). The evangelist cradles his gospel in his strong, veined hand and gazes out, resting his weight on the right leg while bending the left. Though subtle, St. Mark's twisting *contrapposto* pose was the first seen since antiquity. Eighty years after young Donatello carved this statue, a teenage Michelangelo Buonarroti stood here and marveled at it.

Donatello, St. George

Donatello, St. Mark

Piazza della Signoria

Upstairs is a free museum (open Mon and Sat only) displaying most of the originals of the statues you just saw outside.
• *Continue down the mall 50 more yards, to the huge and historic square...*

❾ *Piazza della Signoria*

What a view! This piazza—the main civic center of Florence—is dominated by the massive stone facade of the Palazzo Vecchio, with a tower that reaches for the sky. The square is dotted with statues. The stately Uffizi Gallery is nearby, and the marble greatness of old Florence litters the cobbles. Piazza della Signoria still vibrates with the echoes of the city's past—executions, riots, and great celebrations. There's even Roman history: Look for the **chart** showing the ancient city (in front of Chanel). Today, it's a tourist's world with pigeons, selfie sticks, horse buggies, and tired spouses. For a little pick-me-up, stop in at **$$$ Rivoire** café to enjoy its fine desserts, pudding-thick hot chocolate, and the best view seats in town.

Before you towers the **Palazzo Vecchio,** the palatial Town Hall of the Medici—a fortress designed to contain riches and survive the many riots that

went with local politics. The windows are just beyond the reach of angry stones, and the tower was a handy lookout post. Justice was doled out sternly on this square. Until 1873, Michelangelo's **David** stood where you see the replica today.

Step through the front door into the Palazzo Vecchio's courtyard (free). This palace was Florence's symbol of civic power. You're surrounded by art for art's sake—a cherub frivolously marks the courtyard's center, and ornate stuccoes and frescoes decorate the walls and columns. Such luxury represented a big change 500 years ago.
• *Back outside, check out the arcade of three arches filled with statues.*

❿ *Loggia dei Lanzi*

The loggia, once a forum for public debate, was perfect for a city that prided itself on its democratic traditions. But later, when the Medici figured that good art was more desirable than free speech, it was turned into an outdoor sculpture gallery.

Two statues in the front deserve a closer look. At the right end of the loggia, *The Rape of the Sabine Women* (c. 1583)—with its pulse-quickening rhythm of muscles—

is from the restless Mannerist period. The sculptor, Giambologna, proved his mastery of the medium by sculpting three entangled bodies from one piece of marble. Benvenuto Cellini's **Perseus** (1545-1553), the loggia's most noteworthy piece, shows the Greek hero who decapitated the snake-headed Medusa.

• Cross the square to Bartolomeo Ammanati's big **fountain of Neptune.** Near it, the guy on the horse is Cosimo I, the post-Renaissance Medici who commissioned the Uffizi. Find the round marble plaque on the ground 10 steps in front of the fountain.

⓫ Savonarola Plaque

In the 1490s the Medici family was briefly thrown from power by an austere and charismatic monk named Savonarola, who made Florence a constitutional republic. He organized huge rallies lit by roaring bonfires here on the square where he preached. The devout brought their rich "vanities" (such as paintings, musical instruments, and playing cards) and threw them into the flames.

But not everyone wanted a return to the medieval past. Encouraged by the pope, the Florentines fought back and arrested Savonarola. For two days they tortured him. Finally, on the very spot where Savonarola's followers had built bonfires of vanities, the monk was burned, ending his theocracy. Soon after, the Medici returned to power and the Renaissance picked up where it left off.

• Stay cool, we have 200 yards to go. Follow the gaze of the fake David into the courtyard of the two-tone horseshoe-shaped building, the Uffizi.

⓬ Uffizi Courtyard Statues

The top floor of this building, known as the uffizi (offices) during Medici days, is filled with the greatest collection of Florentine painting anywhere. It's one of Europe's top art galleries. The courtyard is watched over by 19th-century statues of the great figures of the Renaissance: artists (Michelangelo, Giotto, Donatello, Leonardo), philosophers (Machiavelli), scientists (Galileo), poets (Dante and Petrarch), explorers (Vespucci), and the great patron of the Renaissance—Lorenzo "the Magnificent" de' Medici.

• At the far end of the courtyard, pause at the ⓭ **Arno River,** with a magnificent view of the Ponte Vecchio, where we'll finish this walk.

⓮ Ponte Vecchio

Since ancient times, a bridge has stood at this narrow spot in the Arno. When a flood washed away the old wooden bridge, this one was built in 1345, and is now called the Ponte Vecchio (Old Bridge).

In times past, the bridge's shops were inhabited by butchers and hide tanners—a natural fit, because they could empty their waste into the river below. In the 1500s, the Medici booted them out and installed gold- and silversmiths who

The Uffizi courtyard

Ponte Vecchio

still tempt visitors to this day. Fittingly, a famous goldsmith is honored with a fine bust at the central point of the bridge—the sculptor Benvenuto ("Perseus") Cellini.

Look up to notice the windows running across the upper part of the buildings. This is the Vasari Corridor—a protected and elevated passageway, built by the Medici. It led from the Palazzo Vecchio through the Uffizi, across Ponte Vecchio, and up to the immense Pitti Palace, four blocks beyond the bridge.

Looking upstream and down, you have timeless views of the city. The neighborhood across the river, known as the Oltrarno, is more rustic and working-class.

The Ponte Vecchio is a very romantic spot, especially in the evening. Street musicians play and lovers hold hands. The city of Florence—born in Roman times, flourishing in the medieval age, and blossoming in the Renaissance—remains a vibrant cultural capital.

• Several of the finest museums in Europe await your discovery—or perhaps it's time for a nice espresso or gelato. Enjoy.

SIGHTS

Advance Reservations for Skipping Lines

To avoid long lines, make advance reservations for the Uffizi, Accademia, and climbing the Duomo's dome. Get reservations as soon as you know when you'll be in town. Though lines are less of a problem after 16:00, and from November through March, it's always crowded from April through October and on weekends. For peace of mind, I'd reserve a spot any time of year.

Uffizi and Accademia Tickets: Book your tickets in advance at the websites for these museums (see individual sight listings next)—available time-slots for full-price tickets are marked "Intero/Full." You'll receive an email with a voucher that you take to the ticket desk a few minutes before your visit to swap for an actual ticket.

If there's no availability at the official museum sites, you can try for-profit vendors such as Florence.net or Tickitaly.com, which may have time slots available, though you'll pay about €5 more per ticket.

Uffizi and Accademia tickets are also available by phone: From a US phone, dial 011-39-055-294-883, or from an Italian phone call 055-294-883 (€4/ticket reservation fee; booking office open Mon-Fri 8:30-18:30, Sat until 12:30, closed Sun).

Various tour companies—including those listed in this chapter—sell tours that include a reserved museum admission. If you're booking a private guide well in advance, they are often happy to obtain tickets and reservations for your tour with them.

Climbing the Duomo's Dome: For reservation information, see the next page.

Rick's Tip: You can **extend your sightseeing day** into the night at a number of sights around Florence. The Uffizi, Accademia, and the Pitti Palace **stay open into the early evening** every day but Monday, and many other sights have evening hours (check individual sight listings). The stalls at the San Lorenzo Market (closed Mon in winter) and Mercato Nuovo stay open late for shoppers every night.

The Duomo and Nearby

Florence's most distinctive monuments—the Duomo, Baptistery, and Campanile—are gathered around the pedestrian-only Piazza San Giovanni and Piazza del Duomo. The Duomo Museum, just behind the cathedral, is the most important of these sights—and it never has long lines. But you must plan ahead for the dome climb (only possible with an advance reservation).

Ticketing: While the Duomo is free to enter, several associated sights are covered by a single €18 **combo-ticket,** valid for 72 hours: the Baptistery, dome, Campanile, Duomo Museum, and Santa Reparata crypt (enter inside the Duomo).

A €13 audioguide covers all of the Duomo sights.

The only way to **climb the dome** is with a reservation. Buy the combo-ticket and make a reservation at www. museumflorence.com or in person at any Duomo ticket office. Time slots can fill up days in advance, so reserve well ahead. The main ticket office, with a staffed counter and self-service machines, faces the Baptistery entrance (at #7 on the square; it may be under renovation when you visit). There are also ticket counters and self-service machines in the Duomo Museum lobby.

Themed Tours: Three themed tours are organized by the Duomo (€33 each, includes combo-ticket, 1 hour, English only). These include a Duomo visit with access to the north terrace of the church (daily at 10:30); an opportunity to watch contemporary stonemasons at work in the same workshop where Michelangelo carved *David* (Mon, Wed, and Fri at 12:00); and an up-close look at the mosaics of the Baptistery (Mon, Wed, and Fri at 16:30). To book a spot, call 055-230-2885, email commerciale@operadelduomo. firenze.it, or stop by the main ticket office.

🎧 The Duomo, dome, Campanile, and Baptistery are also covered on my free Renaissance Walk **audio tour.**

▲▲DUOMO (CATTEDRALE DI SANTA MARIA DEL FIORE)

Florence's Gothic cathedral has the third-longest nave in Christendom. The church's noisy Neo-Gothic facade (from the 1870s) is covered with pink, green, and white Tuscan marble. The cathedral's claim to artistic fame is Brunelleschi's magnificent dome—the first Renaissance dome and the model for domes to follow. While viewing it from the outside is well worth ▲▲, the massive but empty-feeling interior is lucky to rate ▲—it doesn't justify the massive crowds that line up to get inside. Much of the great art is housed in the Duomo Museum behind the church.

Cost and Hours: Free; Mon-Sat 10:00-

16:30, Sun 13:30-16:45, opening times sometimes change due to religious functions, modest dress code enforced, tel. 055-230-2885, www.museumflorence.com.

Mass: The church is open to all for Mass: English Mass on Sun at 17:00 and old-school Latin Mass with Gregorian chants on Sun at 10:30.

▲CLIMBING THE DUOMO'S DOME

For a grand view into the cathedral from the base of the dome, a chance to see Brunelleschi's "dome-within-a-dome" construction, and a glorious Florence view from the top, climb 463 steps up the dome. The claustrophobic one-way route takes you up narrow, steep staircases and walkways to the top—but it's well worth the climb.

Cost: Covered by Duomo combo-ticket; must reserve dome-climb time—best to buy combo-ticket and reserve a time either

The Duomo with Brunelleschi's dome

at the ticket office (opposite the Baptistery, at #7, open daily 8:00-19:00) or online (www.museumflorence.com).

Hours: Mon-Fri 8:30-19:00, Sat until 17:00, Sun 13:00-16:00; enter from the north side of the church (get in line about 15 minutes before your reservation time). The dome is closed during rain.

Climbing the Dome: While waiting to enter at your reserved time, spend a few minutes studying the side-entrance door, called the Porta della Mandorla ("Almond Door"). Just above the delicately carved doorframe is a colorful Annunciation mosaic by Nanni di Banco, and above that, in a sculpted almond-shaped frame, the Madonna is borne up to heaven by angels. If you look up from here you'll see an empty pedestal atop the transept. Michelangelo's *David* was originally destined to adorn one of these.

The climb is long but there are small landings where you can pull over and take a breather. Halfway up, you'll stroll on the walkway high above the altar where you can get a close-up of Vasari's *Last Judgment* ceiling (especially the ghoulish lower portion, filled with scenes of eternal torment) and a vertigo-inducing view of the nave. After a few tight, winding staircases and a steep final climb, you'll pop out of the hatch on the crowded terrace with a grand city view. If possible, visit at sunset for a romantic experience.

▲CAMPANILE (GIOTTO'S TOWER)
The 270-foot bell tower has 50-some fewer steps than the Duomo's dome (but that's still 414 steps—no elevator); offers a faster, less-intense climb (with typically short lines); and has a view of that magnificent dome to boot. On the way up, there are several intermediate levels where you can catch your breath and enjoy ever-higher views. The stairs narrow as you go, creating a mosh-pit bottleneck near the very top—but the views are worth the hassle. While the viewpoints are enclosed by cage-like bars, the gaps are big enough to snap great photos.

Last Judgment *mosaic in the Baptistery*

Cost and Hours: Covered by Duomo combo-ticket; daily 8:15-19:30, last entry 40 minutes before closing.

▲BAPTISTERY
Michelangelo said the bronze doors of this octagonal building were fit to be the gates of paradise. Check out the gleaming copies of Lorenzo Ghiberti's bronze doors facing the Duomo (the originals are in the Duomo Museum). Making a breakthrough in perspective, Ghiberti used mathematical laws to create the illusion of receding distance on a basically flat surface.

The doors on the north side of the building (around to the right) were designed by Ghiberti when he was younger; he'd won the honor and opportunity by beating Brunelleschi in a competition (the rivals' original entries are in the Bargello).

Inside, sit and savor the medieval mosaic ceiling, where it's always Judgment Day and Jesus is giving the ultimate thumbs-up or thumbs-down.

Cost and Hours: Interior covered by Duomo combo-ticket; open Mon-Sat 8:15-19:30 (closed 10:15-11:15), Sun until 13:30. The (facsimile) bronze doors on the exterior are always viewable.

▲▲▲DUOMO MUSEUM (MUSEO DELL'OPERA DEL DUOMO)
The often-overlooked but superbly presented cathedral museum is filled with some of the best sculpture of the Renaissance, including a late pieta by Michelangelo and statues from the original Baptis-

tery facade. Remarkably, it's almost never crowded. It also holds Brunelleschi's models for his dome, Donatello's emaciated *Mary Magdalene* and playful choir loft, and Ghiberti's original bronze Gates of Paradise panels (the ones on the Baptistery's doors today are copies).

Cost and Hours: Covered by Duomo combo-ticket; daily 9:00-19:00, closed first Tue of each month, last entry one hour before closing; one of the few museums in Florence always open Mon; behind the church at Via del Proconsolo 9, tel. 055-230-2885, www.museumflorence.com.

Visiting the Museum: Begin with the **model of the Duomo's facade** circa 1500, the era of Michelangelo (Room 4). Notice that only the lower third is faced with marble and statues; the rest was only bare brick. Church construction began in 1296, but after an initial burst of energy, petered out. The facade was meant to be a glorious showcase of great statues set into niches.

Now enter the **Hall of Paradise** (Sala del Paradiso, Room 6). On one wall, this room re-creates that lower third of the facade we saw on the model. The opposite wall re-creates the Baptistery facade. Both buildings were a showcase of the greatest art of Florence from roughly 1300 to 1600.

Facing the facade of the church, as they did in the Middle Ages, are the famous doors of the Baptistery. The oldest doors on the left are by Pisano (South Doors, c. 1330). The original competition doors on the right are the first ones done by Ghiberti (North Doors, 1403-1424). And in the center are the Gates of Paradise by Ghiberti (East Doors, 1425-1452).

These bronze "Gates of Paradise" revolutionized the way Renaissance people saw the world around them. They tell several Old Testament stories using perspective and realism as never before. Ghiberti poured his energy and creativity into these panels. That's him in the center of the doorframe, atop the second row of panels—the head on the left with the shiny male-pattern baldness.

Also on the ground floor are rooms dedicated to the museum's most famous statues. Donatello's **Mary Magdalene** (*Santa Maria Maddalena,* c. 1455), carved from white poplar and originally painted with realistic colors, is a Renaissance work of intense devotion (Room 8). The aging Michelangelo (1475-1564) designed his own tomb, with **Pietà** (1547-1555) as the centerpiece (Room 10). Three mourners tend the broken body of the crucified Christ. We see Mary, his mother (the shadowy figure on our right); Mary Magdalene (on the left); and Nicodemus, the converted Pharisee, whose face is that of Michelangelo himself.

Upstairs, the first floor displays original **statues and panels** from the bell tower's third story, where copies stand today, two marble **choir lofts** (*cantorie;* by Lucca della Robbia and Donatello) that once sat above the sacristy doors of the Duomo, and **Brunelleschi's model** of the dome. Don't miss the Terrazza Brunelleschiana on the third floor—an **outdoor terrace** with an up-close rooftop view of the Duomo.

Michelangelo, Pietà

ITALY

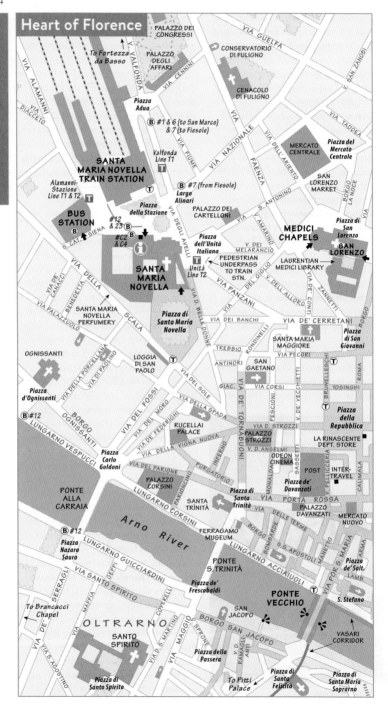

Heart of Florence

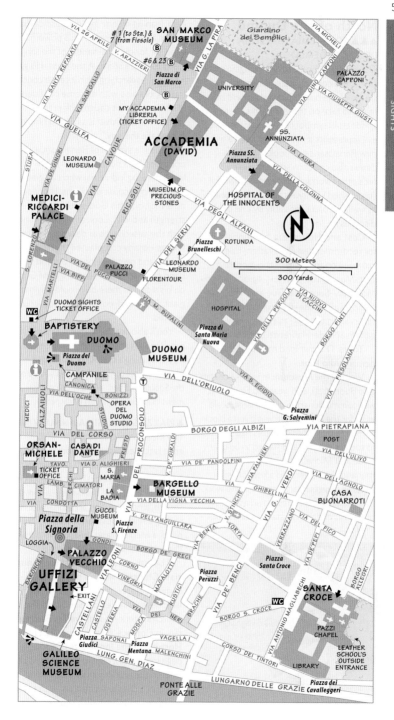

North of the Duomo

▲▲▲ACCADEMIA (GALLERIA DELL'ACCADEMIA)

This museum houses Michelangelo's *David,* the consummate Renaissance statue of the buff, biblical shepherd boy ready to take on the giant. This six-ton, 17-foot-tall symbol of divine victory over evil represents a new century and a whole new Renaissance outlook. The Accademia also contains some of the master's other works, including his powerful (unfinished) *Prisoners* and *St. Matthew,* as well as a pietà (possibly by one of his disciples).

Cost and Hours: €12, additional €4 for recommended reservation, free and crowded on first Sun of the month Oct-March; Tue-Sun 8:15-19:00, closed Mon; July-Sept open Tue and Thu 7:00-22:00; audioguide-€6, Via Ricasoli 60, reservation tel. 055-294-883, www.galleriaaccademiafirenze.beniculturali.it.

Tours: ∩ Download my free Accademia **audio tour.**

Visiting the Museum: In 1501, Michelangelo Buonarroti, a 26-year-old Florentine, was commissioned to carve a large-scale work for the Duomo. He was given a block of marble that other sculptors had rejected as too tall, shallow, and flawed to be of any value. But Michelangelo picked up his hammer and chisel, knocked a knot off what became *David*'s heart, and started to work.

The statue captures *David* as he's sizing up his enemy. He stands relaxed but alert, leaning on one leg in a classical pose known as *contrapposto.* In his powerful left hand, he fondles the handle of the sling, ready to fling a stone at the giant. His gaze is steady—searching with intense concentration, but also with extreme confidence. Michelangelo has caught the precise moment when *David* is saying to himself, "I can take this guy."

David is a symbol of Renaissance optimism. He's no brute. He's a civilized, thinking individual who can grapple with and overcome problems. He needs no armor, only his God-given physical strength and wits. Look at his right hand, with the raised veins and strong, relaxed fingers—many complained that it was too big and overdeveloped. But this is the hand of a man with the strength of God on his side. No mere boy could slay the giant. But David, powered by God, could... and did.

You'll also see some mildly interesting pre-Renaissance and Renaissance paintings, including a couple of Botticellis, the plaster model of Giambologna's *Rape of the Sabine Women,* and a musical instrument collection with an early piano.

▲PIAZZA SANTISSIMA ANNUNZIATA

The most Renaissance square in Florence is tucked just a block behind the Accademia. It's like an urban cloister (the image of the ideal city) from the 15th century, with three fine buildings—a convent church, a hospital, and an orphanage—ringing a fine equestrian statue of Ferdinand, a Medici grand duke of the then-independent state of Tuscany.

The 15th-century **Santissima Annunziata Church** is worth a peek. The welcoming cloister has early-16th-century frescoes by Andrea del Sarto, and the church's interior is slathered in Baroque—rare in Florence. Filippo Brunelleschi's **Hospital of the Innocents** (Ospedale degli Innocenti), built in the 1420s, is considered the first Renaissance building. Its graceful arches and columns, with each set of columns forming a square, embody

Michelangelo, David

the quintessence of Renaissance harmony and typified the new aesthetic of calm balance and symmetry. It's ornamented with terra-cotta medallions by Luca della Robbia—each showing a different way to wrap an infant (swaddled—meant to help babies grow straight, and practiced in Italy until about a century ago). With its mission to care for the least among society (parentless or unwanted children), this hospital was also an important symbol of the increasingly humanistic and humanitarian outlook of Renaissance Florence.

The **Museum of the Innocents** fills the hospital. A fine exhibit tells the story of these infants with artifacts that help you imagine what it was like living here. It also houses some fine art, including several iconic glazed terra-cotta medallions by the Della Robbia family (€7, daily 10:00-19:00, audioguide-€3, tel. 055-203-7301, www.museodeglinnocenti.it). **$$ Caffè del Verone,** on the museum's top terrace, offers a nice, peaceful break with rooftop views.

▲▲MUSEUM OF SAN MARCO (MUSEO DI SAN MARCO)

One block north of the Accademia, this 15th-century monastery houses the greatest collection anywhere of frescoes and paintings by the early Renaissance master Fra Angelico. Upstairs are 43 cells decorated by Fra Angelico and his assistants. Trained in the medieval religious style, he adopted Renaissance techniques to produce works that blended Christian sym-

bols and Renaissance realism. Don't miss the cell of Savonarola, the charismatic monk who threw out the Medici and sponsored "bonfires of the vanities."

Cost and Hours: €8, Tue-Fri 8:15-14:00, Sat-Sun until 17:00; also open until 14:00 on first, third, and fifth Mon of each month; reservations possible but unnecessary, on Piazza San Marco, tel. 055-238-8608.

Tours: ∩ Download my free Museum of San Marco **audio tour.**

▲▲MEDICI CHAPELS (CAPPELLE MEDICEE)

The burial site of the ruling Medici family in the Basilica of San Lorenzo includes the dusky crypt; the big, domed Chapel of Princes; and the magnificent New Sacristy, featuring architecture, tombs, and statues almost entirely by Michelangelo. The Medici made their money in textiles and banking, and patronized a dream team of Renaissance artists that put Florence on the cultural map. Michelangelo, who spent his teen years living with the Medici, was commissioned to create the family's final tribute.

Cost and Hours: €9, free first Sun of the month Oct-March; Tue-Sat 8:15-14:00, last entry 45 minutes before closing; also open second and fourth Mon and first, third, and fifth Sun of each month; audioguide-€6, modest dress required, tel. 055-238-8602, www.bargellomusei.beniculturali.it.

▲MERCATO CENTRALE (CENTRAL MARKET)

Florence's giant iron-and-glass-covered central market is a wonderland of picturesque produce. While the San Lorenzo Market that fills the surrounding streets is only a step up from a flea market, Mercato Centrale retains its Florentine elegance.

Downstairs, you'll see parts of the cow (and bull) you'd never dream of eating (no, that's not a turkey neck), enjoy free samples, watch pasta being made, and have your pick of plenty of fun eater-

Michelangelo sculptures, Medici Chapels

Mercato Centrale hosts a popular food court.

ies sloshing out cheap and tasty pasta to locals (Mon-Fri 7:00-14:00, Sat until 17:00, closed Sun).

Upstairs, the meticulously restored glass roof and steel rafters soar over a modern and extremely touristy food court (daily 10:00-24:00). For eating ideas downstairs, upstairs, and around the market, see "Eating," later.

▲MEDICI-RICCARDI PALACE (PALAZZO MEDICI-RICCARDI)

Lorenzo the Magnificent's home is worth a look for its art. The tiny Chapel of the Magi contains colorful Renaissance gems such as *The Journey of the Magi* frescoes by Benozzo Gozzoli. The former library has a Baroque ceiling fresco by Luca Giordano, a prolific artist from Naples known as "Fast Luke" (*Luca fa presto*) for his speedy workmanship. While the Medici originally occupied this 1444 house, in the 1700s it became home to the Riccardi family, who added the Baroque flourishes.

Cost and Hours: €10, Thu-Tue 9:00-19:00, closed Wed, ticket entrance is off the central courtyard, enter from Via Cavour 1 or Via de' Ginori 1, tel. 055-276-8224, www.palazzomediciriccardi.it.

On and near Piazza della Signoria

▲▲▲UFFIZI GALLERY

This greatest collection of Italian paintings anywhere features works by Giotto, Leonardo, Raphael, Caravaggio, Titian, and Michelangelo, and a roomful of Botticellis, including the *Birth of Venus*. Start with Giotto's early stabs at Renaissance-style realism, then move on through the 3-D experimentation of the early 1400s to the real thing rendered by the likes of Botticelli and Leonardo. Finish off with Michelangelo and Raphael. Because only 600 visitors are allowed inside the building at any one time, there's generally a very long wait. The good news: no Vatican-style mob scenes inside. The museum is nowhere near as big as it is great.

Cost and Hours: €20 plus €4 for recommended reservation, cheaper in winter, usually free and crowded on first Sun of the month, covered by €38 Uffizi/Pitti Palace/Boboli Gardens combo-ticket;

Botticelli's Spring *at the Uffizi Gallery*

Tue-Sun 8:15-19:00, closed Mon, July-Sept Wed-Thu until 22:00 (except for two weeks in mid-Aug), last entry one hour before closing; reservation tel. 055-294-883, www.uffizi.it.

Reservations Necessary: To skip the notoriously long ticket-buying lines, book your Uffizi entrance in advance online or by calling the reservation number above. If you don't do that, try going at lunchtime or at the end of the day, 90 minutes before closing, and see the museum in a rush.

Getting In: If you arrive with a **reservation,** go first to the courtyard door #3 to pick up your ticket (labeled *Reservation Ticket Office*). There you exchange your email voucher/confirmation number for a ticket. Tickets are available for pickup 10 minutes before your appointed time. Then, with ticket in hand, walk briskly across the courtyard to door #1. Get in the queue for "individuals," not "groups."

To **buy a ticket on the spot,** line up with everyone else at door #2, marked *Main Entrance.*

Tours: A 1.5-hour **audioguide** costs €6 (€10/2 people; must leave ID). ∩ Download my free Uffizi Gallery **audio tour.**

Visiting the Museum: The Uffizi is U-shaped, running around an exterior courtyard. The highlights are up four long flights, on the top floor. The east wing contains Florentine paintings from medieval to Renaissance times. At the far end, you pass through a short hallway filled with ancient sculpture. The west wing has the Renaissance biggies—Leonardo, Michelangelo, and Raphael. Downstairs there are many more rooms of art, showing how the Florentine Renaissance morphed into Mannerism (Parmigianino), spread to Venice (Titian), and inspired the Baroque (Caravaggio).

Medieval (1200-1400): Three similar-looking Madonna and Bambinos—all painted within a few decades of each other, in about the year 1300—show the baby steps being made from the flat Byzantine style toward Renaissance realism (Room 2). **Giotto** creates a space and fills it. Like a set designer, he builds a three-dimensional "stage"—the canopied throne—then peoples it with real beings.

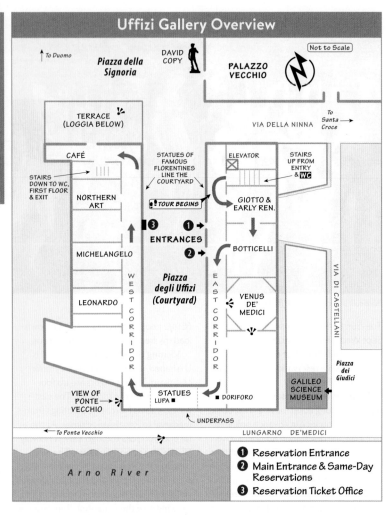

Uffizi Gallery Overview

Piazza della Signoria

To Duomo

DAVID COPY

PALAZZO VECCHIO

Not to Scale

TERRACE (LOGGIA BELOW)

To Santa Croce

VIA DELLA NINNA

CAFÉ

STATUES OF FAMOUS FLORENTINES LINE THE COURTYARD

ELEVATOR

STAIRS UP FROM ENTRY & **WC**

STAIRS DOWN TO WC, FIRST FLOOR & EXIT

NORTHERN ART

⚑ TOUR BEGINS

GIOTTO & EARLY REN.

❸ ❶ ➤
ENTRANCES
❷ ➤

MICHELANGELO

BOTTICELLI

LEONARDO

WEST CORRIDOR

Piazza degli Uffizi (Courtyard)

EAST CORRIDOR

VENUS DE' MEDICI

VIA DI CASTELLANI

Piazza dei Giudici

GALILEO SCIENCE MUSEUM

VIEW OF PONTE VECCHIO

STATUES LUPA ■

■ DORIFORO

UNDERPASS

To Ponte Vecchio

LUNGARNO DE'MEDICI

Arno River

❶ Reservation Entrance
❷ Main Entrance & Same-Day Reservations
❸ Reservation Ticket Office

The real triumph here is Mary herself—big and monumental, like a Roman statue. Beneath her robe, she has a real live body, with knees and breasts that stick out at us. This three-dimensionality was revolutionary, a taste of the Renaissance a century before it began.

Early Renaissance (mid-1400s): In the 1400s, painters worked out the problems of painting realistically, using mathematics to create the illusion of three-dimensionality. Paolo Uccello's colorful **Battle of San Romano** is not so much a piece of art as

an exercise in perspective (Room 8). The fallen horses and soldiers are experiments in "foreshortening"—creating the illusion of distance. We don't need the wispy halo over the head of Fra Filippo Lippi's **Madonna and Child with Two Angels** to tell us she's holy—she radiates sweetness and light from her divine face (Room 8). Lippi's radiant Madonnas are light years away from the generic Marys of the medieval era.

Piero della Francesca's portrait of husband and wife **Federico da Montefeltro** and **Battista Sforza** heralds the era of humanism and the new centrality of ordinary people in art.

The Renaissance (1450-1500): Florence in 1450 was in a Firenz-y of activity. There was a can-do spirit of optimism in the air, led by prosperous merchants and bankers and a strong middle class. Lorenzo de' Medici, head of the powerful Medici family, gathered Florence's best and brightest around him for evening wine and discussions of great ideas.

The Botticelli rooms (10-14) are filled with masterpieces and classical fleshiness (the famous **Birth of Venus** and **Spring**). Here is the Renaissance in its first bloom. This is a return to the pagan world of classical Greece, where things of the flesh are not sinful. Madonna is out, Venus is in.

Classical Sculpture: The foundation of the Renaissance was classical sculpture. Sculptors, painters, and poets turned for inspiration to ancient Greek and Roman works as the epitome of balance, 3-D perspective, human anatomy, and beauty.

In the Tribune Room, the highlight is the **Venus de' Medici,** a Roman copy of the lost original by the great Greek sculptor Praxiteles. Balanced, harmonious, and serene, the statue embodies the attributes of Greece's "Golden Age," when balance was admired in every aspect of life.

The **sculpture hall** has 2,000-year-old Roman copies of 2,500-year-old Greek originals... and the best view in Florence of the Arno River and Ponte Vecchio through the window, dreamy at sunset.

High Renaissance (1500-1550): A scientist, architect, engineer, musician, and painter, Leonardo da Vinci (1452-1519) was a true Renaissance Man. In his **Annunciation,** the angel Gabriel has walked up to Mary, and now kneels on one knee like an ambassador, saluting her (Room 35). Leonardo constructs a beautifully landscaped "stage" and puts his characters in it. He's taken a miraculous event—an angel appearing out of the blue—and presented it in a very human way.

Don't miss Michelangelo's **Holy Family** (a.k.a. *Doni Tondo,* Room 41), the only completed easel painting by the greatest sculptor in history. Florentine painters were sculptors with brushes; this shows it. Instead of a painting, it's more like three clusters of statues with some clothes painted on.

Nearby is Raphael's **Madonna of the Goldfinch,** with Mary and bambino brought down from heaven into the real world of trees, water, and sky.

More Art on the Lower Floor: On your way out, you'll pass a fine café, an open-air terrace, and the WC. You'll be led directly to an exit, if you're ready to go. But the first floor is worth a look. It features work from after the Renaissance: Mannerism (such as Parmigianino), Venetian (Titian), Baroque (Caravaggio), and finally Flemish and Dutch (Rubens and Rembrandt).

▲▲PALAZZO VECCHIO

This castle-like fortress with the 300-foot spire dominates Florence's main square. In Renaissance times, it was the Town Hall,

Palazzo Vecchio

where citizens pioneered the once-radical notion of self-rule. Its official name—Palazzo della Signoria—refers to the elected members of the city council. In 1540, the tyrant Cosimo I made the building his personal palace, redecorating the interior in lavish style. Today the building functions once again as the Town Hall.

Entry to the ground-floor Michelozzo courtyard is free. Paying customers can see Cosimo's (fairly) lavish royal apartments, decorated with (fairly) top-notch paintings and statues by Michelangelo and Donatello. The highlight is the 13,000-square-foot Grand Hall—lined with huge frescoes and interesting statues.

Cost and Hours: Michelozzo courtyard-free, museum-€16.50, tower climb-€12.50 (418 steps), museum plus tower-€21.50, excavations-€4, combo-ticket for all three-€23.50. Museum and excavations open daily 9:00-23:00, Oct-March until 19:00, except Thu until 14:00 year-round; tower keeps shorter hours (last entry one hour before closing) and closed in bad weather; last tickets for all sights sold one hour before closing; video-guide-€5, English tours available, Piazza della Signoria, tel. 055-276-8224, www.musefirenze.it.

▲▲GALILEO SCIENCE MUSEUM (MUSEO GALILEI)

When we think of the Florentine Renaissance, we think of visual arts: painting, mosaics, architecture, and sculpture. But when the visual arts declined in the 1600s (abused and co-opted by political powers), music and science flourished. Florence hosted many scientific breakthroughs, as you'll see in this fascinating collection of clocks, telescopes, maps, and ingenious gadgets. Trace the technical innovations as modern science emerges from 1000 to 1900. Some of the most talked about bottles in Florence are the ones here that contain Galileo's fingers. Exhibits include various tools for gauging the world, from a compass and thermometer to Galileo's telescopes. The museum is friendly, comfortably cool, never crowded, and just a block east of the Uffizi on the Arno River.

Cost and Hours: €10, daily 9:30-18:00 except Tue until 13:00, guided tours available, Piazza dei Giudici 1, tel. 055-265-311, www.museogalileo.it.

Celestial globe at Galileo Science Museum

Donatello's David *at the Bargello*

East of Piazza della Signoria

▲▲▲BARGELLO (MUSEO NAZIONALE DEL BARGELLO)

This underappreciated sculpture museum is in a former police station-turned-prison that looks like a mini Palazzo Vecchio. The Renaissance began with sculpture, and you can see the birth of this revolution of 3-D in the Bargello. It's a small, uncrowded museum and a pleasant break from the intensity of the rest of Florence. You'll see 150 years of great statues, spanning the history of Florence's heyday.

Highlights include Donatello's very influential, painfully beautiful *David* (the first male nude to be sculpted in a thousand years), multiple works by Michelangelo, and rooms of Medici treasures. Moody Donatello, who embraced realism with his lifelike statues, set the personal and artistic style for many Renaissance artists to follow. The best pieces are in the ground-floor room at the foot of the outdoor staircase (with fine works by Michelangelo, Cellini, and Giambologna) and in the "Donatello room" directly above (including his two different *David*s, plus Ghiberti and Brunelleschi's dueling competition entries for the Baptistery doors—and yet another *David* by Verrocchio).

Cost and Hours: €9, free on first Sun of the month Oct-March; daily 8:15-14:00—until 17:00 for special exhibits; closed on second and fourth Sun and first, third, and fifth Mon of each month, last entry 45 minutes before closing; reservations possible but unnecessary, audioguide-€6; Via del Proconsolo 4, tel. 055-238-8606, www.bargellomusei.beniculturali.it.

Tours: ∩ Download my free Bargello audio tour.

▲▲SANTA CROCE CHURCH

This 14th-century Franciscan church, decorated with centuries of precious art, holds the tombs of great Florentines. The loud 19th-century Victorian Gothic facade faces a huge square ringed with tempting shops and littered with tired tourists. Escape into the church and admire its sheer height and spaciousness.

Cost and Hours: €8, Mon-Sat 9:30-17:00, Sun from 14:00, multimedia guide-€6, modest dress required, 10-minute walk east of the Palazzo Vecchio along Borgo de' Greci, tel. 055-246-6105, www.

Santa Croce Church, the final resting place of Michelangelo and Galileo.

FLORENCE
SIGHTS

santacroceopera.it. The **leather school,** at the back of the church, is free and sells church tickets—handy when the church has a long line (daily 10:00-18:00, closed Sun Nov-March, has own entry behind church plus an entry within the church, www.scuoladelcuoio.com).

Visiting the Church: On the left wall (as you face the altar) is the tomb of **Galileo Galilei** (1564-1642), the Pisan who lived his last years under house arrest near Florence. His crime? Defying the Church by saying that the earth revolved around the sun. His heretical remains were only allowed in the church long after his death.

Directly opposite (on the right wall) is the tomb of **Michelangelo Buonarroti** (1475-1564). Santa Croce was Michelangelo's childhood church, as he grew up a block west of here. Farther up the nave is the tomb of **Niccolò Machiavelli** (1469-1527), a champion of democratic Florence and author of *The Prince,* a how-to manual on hardball politics—which later Medici rulers found instructive.

The first chapel to the right of the main altar features the famous *Death of St. Francis* fresco by Giotto. With simple but eloquent gestures, Francis' brothers bid him a sad farewell. The Sacristy has Cimabue's impressive *Crucifixion* (before 1288), a survivor of the devastating flood of 1966. Beyond that is the leather school.

Exit the church nave between the Rossini and Machiavelli tombs to enter a delightful cloister. On the left is the small Brunelleschi-designed Pazzi Chapel, which captures the Renaissance in miniature.

Near the Train Station
▲▲CHURCH OF SANTA MARIA NOVELLA

This 13th-century Dominican church is rich in art. Along with crucifixes by Giotto and Brunelleschi, it contains the textbook example of the early Renaissance mastery of perspective: *The Trinity* by Masaccio. The exquisite chapels trace art in Florence from medieval times to early Baroque. The outside of the church features a dash of Romanesque (horizontal stripes), Gothic (pointed arches), Renaissance (geometric shapes), and Baroque (scrolls). Step in and look down the 330-foot nave for a 14th-century optical illusion.

Next to the church are the cloisters and the **museum,** located in the old Dominican convent of Santa Maria Novella. The museum's highlight is the breathtaking Spanish Chapel, with walls covered by a series of frescoes by Andrea di Bonaiuto.

Cost and Hours: Church and museum-€7.50; Mon-Thu 9:00-19:00, Fri 11:00-19:00, Sat 9:00-17:30, Sun 13:00-17:30, church closes Oct-March at 17:30, last entry 45 minutes before closing; multimedia guide-€3, modest dress required, main entrance on Piazza Santa Maria Novella, tel. 055-219-257, www.smn.it.

The Oltrarno (South of the Arno River)
▲▲▲PITTI PALACE

The imposing Pitti Palace, several blocks southwest of Ponte Vecchio, has many separate museums and two gardens. The main reason to visit is to see the Palatine Gallery, which houses a fine painting collection that picks up where the Uffizi leaves off, with the High Renaissance. Lovers of Raphael's Madonnas and Titian's portraits will find some of the world's

Pitti Palace

best of each. If it's a nice day, take a stroll in the Boboli Gardens, a rare and inviting patch of extensive green space within old Florence.

Cost and Hours: The €16 **Pitti Palace** ticket #1 covers the Palatine Gallery, Royal Apartments, Treasury of the Grand Dukes (silver museum), Museum of Costume and Fashion, and Gallery of Modern Art; open Tue-Sun 8:15-19:00, closed Mon, last entry one hour before closing. The €10 **Boboli Garden** ticket #2 covers the Boboli and Bardini Gardens as well as the Porcelain Museum located in the garden; open daily June-Aug 8:15-19:30, April-May and Sept until 18:30, March and Oct until 17:30, Nov-Feb until 16:30, closed first and last Mon of each month, last entry one hour before closing. The place is free on the first Sun of the month Oct-March. The €8 audioguide explains the sprawling palace. Tel. 055-238-8614, www.uffizi.it.

Visiting the Museum: In the **Palatine Gallery** you'll walk through one palatial room after another, with walls sagging with masterpieces by 16th- and 17th-century masters, including Titian and Rembrandt. The Pitti's Raphael collection is the second-biggest anywhere—the Vatican beats it by one. Use the information folders in each room to help find the featured paintings.

The collection is all on one floor. To see the highlights, walk straight down the spine through a dozen or so rooms. After the Palatine Gallery, the route flows naturally into the even more lavish rooms of the Royal Apartments. These 14 rooms (of which only a few are open at any one time) are where the Pitti's rulers lived in the 18th and 19th centuries. Each room features a different color and time period. Here, you get a real feel for the splendor of the dukes' world.

The rest of Pitti Palace is skippable, unless the various sights match your interests: the **Gallery of Modern Art** (second floor; Romantic, Neoclassical, and Impressionist works by 19th- and 20th-century Tuscan painters), **Treasury of the Grand Dukes** (ground and mezzanine floors; Medici treasures from jeweled crucifixes to gilded ostrich eggs), **Museum of Costume and Fashion, Porcelain Museum,** and **Boboli and Bardini gardens** (behind the palace; enter from Pitti Palace courtyard—be prepared to climb uphill).

▲▲BRANCACCI CHAPEL

In the Brancacci Chapel, Masaccio created a world in paint that looks like the world we inhabit. For the first time in a thousand years, Man and Nature were frozen for inspection. Masaccio's painting techniques were copied by many Renaissance artists, and his people—sturdy, intelligent, and dignified, with expressions of understated astonishment—helped shape Renaissance men and women's own self-images.

Half of the chapel's frescoes are by Masaccio, and half by either Masolino or Filippino Lippi, who completed the chapel more than 50 years later. Although Masaccio is the star, the panels by his colleagues provide a good contrast in styles.

Masaccio, Expulsion from the Garden of Eden

ITALY

Oltrarno

← To Porta San Frediano

To Santa Maria Novella

Arno

BORGO SAN FREDIANO

VIA DEL LEONE

Piazza Nazaro Sauro

LUNGARNO GUICCIARDINI

VIA DI SANTO SPIRITO

GEPPI

Piazza del Carmine

BORGO STELLA

SERRAGLI

VIA SANTA MONICA

VIA DEI

MAFFIA

O L T R A R N O

VIA DE' COVERELLI

BRANCACCI CHAPEL

SANTA MARIA DEL CARMINE

VIA

VIA S. AGOSTINO

SANTO SPIRITO

VIA DE S. MARTINO

SDRUCCIOLO DE PITTI

MAGGIO

Piazza di Santo Spirito

MICH

VIA

300 Meters

300 Yards

VIA DELLE CALDAIE

BORGO TEGOLAIO

VIA MAZZETTA

PAL. DE COSIMO RIDOLFI

VIA

MARSILI

VIA DE'

Piazza di San Felice

Accommodations
1 Hotel Palazzo Guadagni

Eateries
2 Signorvino
3 Golden View Firenze & Bar Osteria
4 Gusta Osteria
5 Trattoria Sant'Agostino
6 O Munaciello Pizzeria
7 Il Santo Bevitore Ristorante & Enoteca il Santino Gastronomia
8 Trattoria 4 Leoni
9 Olio & Convivium
10 Gelateria la Carraia

VIA ROMANA

To Porta Romana

TICKET OFFICE

Nightlife & Other
11 Le Volpi e l'Uva
12 Archea Brewery
13 Supermarket
14 In Tavola Cooking School

Cost and Hours: €10 Sat-Mon (obligatory combo-ticket with Fondazione Salvatore Romano, a skippable 14th-century refectory next to the Santo Spirito Church), €8 Wed-Fri, cash only; free and easy reservations mandatory March-May and advisable through the summer and fall; Wed-Mon 10:00-17:00 except Sun from 13:00, closed Tue, last entry 45 minutes before closing; videoguide-€3, knees and shoulders must be covered, in Church of Santa Maria del Carmine on Piazza del Carmine, reservations tel. 055-276-8224 or 055-276-8558 or email info@muse.comune.fi.it, http://musefirenze.it.

▲PIAZZALE MICHELANGELO

Overlooking the city from across the river (look for the huge bronze statue of *David*), this square has a superb view of Florence and the stunning dome of the Duomo. It's worth the 25-minute hike, taxi, or bus ride.

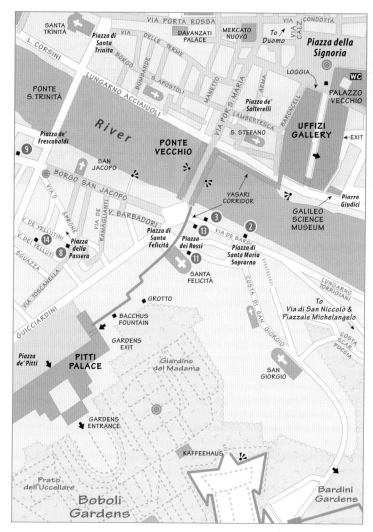

An inviting café (open seasonally) with great views is just below the overlook. The best photos are taken from the street immediately below the overlook. After dark, the square is packed with school kids licking ice cream and each other. About 200 yards beyond all the tour groups and teenagers is the stark, beautiful, crowd-free, Romanesque San Miniato Church (next listing). A WC is located just off the road, halfway between the two sights.

Getting There (and Back): While you can catch bus #12 (from near Piazza d'Ognissanti, can be a long ride) or a taxi up to the piazza, the walk up from the Oltrarno neighborhood of San Niccolò is popular—especially in the early evening—and not that challenging.

Start at the intersection of Via San Niccolò and Via San Miniato, just below Porta San Miniato. Point yourself uphill, head through the old gate, and continue until

The view from Piazzale Michelangelo

San Miniato Church

you reach a broad, terraced hill-climb to the left. Up top, Piazzale Michelangelo will be to your left, and San Miniato Church to your right.

The hike down is quick and enjoyable (or take bus #13). You can retrace your steps, or you can turn this walk into a loop: From the parking lot, take the ramp leading down toward Ponte Vecchio (near the replica *David*). At the bottom of the ramp, cross the street and continue down the pathway. You'll cross one more street, then zigzag downhill toward the river. When you draw even with the big tower (Porta San Niccolò), turn left onto Via San Niccolò and make your way back to the passel of lively cafés and restaurants where you started (for recommendations, see page 532).

▲▲SAN MINIATO CHURCH

According to legend, the martyred St. Minias—this church's namesake—was beheaded on the banks of the Arno in AD 250. He picked up his head and walked here (this was before the #12 bus), where he died and was buried in what became the first Christian cemetery in Florence. In the 11th century, this church was built to house Minias' remains.

The church's green-and-white marble facade (12th century) is classic Florentine Romanesque, one of the oldest in town. Inside you'll find some wonderful 3-D paintings, a plush ceiling of glazed terra-cotta

panels by Luca della Robbia, and an exquisite Renaissance chapel (on the left side of the nave). The highlight for me is the brilliantly preserved art in the sacristy (upstairs to right of altar, in the room on right) showing scenes from the life of St. Benedict (circa 1350, by a follower of Giotto). Drop €2 into the electronic panel in the corner to light the room for five minutes. The evening vesper service with the monks chanting in Latin offers a meditative worship experience—a peaceful way to end your visit.

Cost and Hours: Free, Mon-Sat 9:30-13:00 & 15:00-19:30, until 19:00 off-season, Sun 8:15-19:30, closed sporadically for special occasions, tel. 055-234-2731, www.sanminiatoalmonte.it.

Getting There: It's about 200 yards above Piazzale Michelangelo. Follow the walking directions in the Piazzale Michelangelo listing earlier, or take bus #12 to the San Miniato al Monte stop (hop off and hike up the grand staircase); bus #13 takes you back down the hill.

EXPERIENCES

Shopping

Florence may be one of Europe's best shopping towns—it's been known for its sense of style since the Medici days. Smaller stores are generally open about 9:00-13:00 and 15:30-19:30, usually closed on Sunday, often closed on Monday (or

San Lorenzo Market

Florence is a popular place to buy leather.

at least Monday morning), and sometimes closed for a couple of weeks around August 15. Bigger stores have similar hours, without the afternoon break.

For authentic, locally produced wares, look for shops displaying the *Esercizi Storici Fiorentini* seal, with a picture of the Palazzo Vecchio's tower. At these city-endorsed "Historical Florentine Ventures," you may pay a premium, but quality is assured (for a list of shops, see www.esercizistoricifiorentini.it).

The open-air **San Lorenzo Market** stalls, between the Basilica of San Lorenzo and Mercato Centrale, are fun to browse and bargain (just hang onto your wallet—this is pickpocket central). You'll find many of the stalls in the narrow streets around Mercato Centrale (daily 9:00-19:00, closed Mon in winter).

Originally a silk-and-straw market, **Mercato Nuovo** still functions as a rustic yet touristy market (at the intersection of Via Calimala and Via Porta Rossa; daily 9:00-18:30). It's where you'll find *Il Porcellino* (a statue of a wild boar nicknamed "The Piglet"), which people rub and give

coins to ensure their return to Florence.

Other shopping areas, mostly upscale boutiques, can be found along Via dei Calzaiuoli, Via de' Tornabuoni, and the streets in between (particularly around Piazza della Repubblica).

Running parallel to the Arno through the heart of the Oltrarno, **Via di Santo Spirito** contains a number of old *palazzi* once owned by wealthy Florentine families such as the Machiavellis (#5) and the winemaking Frescobaldis (#11). Today, the ground floors of those buildings are filled with fine local shops, with some real artisans mixed in.

Nightlife

For me, nighttime is for eating a late meal, catching a concert, strolling through the old-town pedestrian zone and piazzas with a gelato, or hitting one of the many wine bars. Get the latest on nightlife and concerts in *The Florentine* monthly (updated biweekly online, www.theflorentine.net) or *Firenze Spettacolo* (www.firenzespettacolo.it; mostly in Italian, but there's an English section).

Ponte Vecchio after dark

Strolling After Dark: The historic center has a floodlit ambience that's ideal for strolling. The pedestrian zone around the Duomo and along Via de' Calzaiuoli, between the Uffizi and the Duomo, is lively with people. Piazza della Repubblica, lined with venerable 19th-century cafés, offers good people-watching. In the evening, it's a hub of activity, with opera singers, violinists, harpists, bizarre street performers, and a cover band that plays cheesy tunes for the seating area of one of the piazza's bars. Ponte Vecchio is a popular place to enjoy river views (and kiss), and often has a street musician after dark who encourages passersby to dance.

Live Music: Orsanmichele Church regularly holds concerts under its Gothic arches. Tickets are sold on the day of the concert from the door facing Via de' Calzaiuoli or, on Sunday, from the doorway opposite the church entrance. Orchestra della Toscana presents classical concerts from November to May in Teatro Verdi (€13-20, box office open Mon-Sat 10:00-13:00 & 16:00-19:00, closed Sun, near Bargello at Via Ghibellina 97, tel. 055-210-804, www.orchestradellatoscana.it). St. Mark's English Church offers concerts and opera several nights each week from February through October (full opera performance-€35, opera concerts-€25, Via Maggio 18, mobile 340-811-9192, www.concertoclassico.info).

Dinner Theater at Teatro del Sale is a quirky place for dinner and theater (Tue-Sat at 19:30). Sometimes the show is great for non-Italian speakers (live music, for example)—and sometimes it's not (call or check their website). You'll pay a €7 membership fee to "join" the association, plus €36 for the evening, including drinks (10 blocks behind the Duomo, northeast of Santa Croce at Via dei Macci 111 red, tel. 055-200-1492, www.teatrodelsale.com).

Drinks: An *enoteca* is fun for sampling regional wines and enjoying munchies, especially before dinnertime. **Le Volpi e l'Uva,** specializing in small, often organic wine producers, has a cozy interior and romantic seating on a quiet little piazza (daily 11:00-21:00, 65 yards south of Ponte Vecchio—walk through Piazza Santa Felicità to Piazza dei Rossi 1; see map on page

516 for location, tel. 055-239-8132, run by wine experts Riccardo, Ciro, and Emilio).

Caffè del Verone, a terrace bar on the top floor of the Hospital of the Innocents, keeps late hours in summer (some nights until 23:00) so you can enjoy a spritz while taking in rooftop views. They have jazz on some weekend nights—call for details (Piazza SS. Annunziata 13, for location see map on page 490, mobile 392-498-2559).

Italy is experiencing a craft beer fad, and Florence has several places where you can join in. Handy to many recommended hotels (and near Mercato Centrale) is **Mostodolce** (daily 11:00-24:00, Via Nazionale 114 red, for location see map on page 528, tel. 055-230-2928), or head across the river to **Archea Brewery,** a small pub that brews several of their own varieties, with a few other Italian-produced beers on tap (daily 18:00-24:00, Via de'Serragli 44 red, a 5-minute walk west of Piazza di Santo Spirito, for location see map on page 516, tel. 055-219-671, Carmine).

SLEEPING

Florence is notorious for its mosquitoes. If your hotel lacks air-conditioning, request a fan and don't open your windows, especially at night. Many hotels furnish a small plug-in bulb (*zanzariere*)—usually set in the ashtray—that helps keep the bloodsuckers at bay.

Around the Duomo

$$$$ Hotel Duomo's 24 rooms are modern and comfortable enough, but you're

paying for the location and the views—the Duomo looms like a monster outside the hotel's windows. If staying here, you may as well spring the extra €20 or so for a "classic" room with a view (RS%, air-con, historic elevator, Piazza del Duomo 1, fourth floor, tel. 055-219-922, www.hotelduomofirenze.it, info@hotelduomofirenze.it; Paolo, Gilvaneide, and Federico).

$$$ Residenza Giotto B&B offers a well-priced chance to stay on Florence's upscale shopping drag, Via Roma. Occupying the top floor of a 19th-century building, this place has six bright rooms (three with Duomo views) and a terrace with knockout views of the Duomo's tower. Reception is generally open Mon-Sat 9:00-17:00 and Sun 9:00-13:00; let them know your arrival time in advance (RS%, air-con, elevator, Via Roma 6, tel. 055-214-593, www.residenzagiotto.it, info@residenzagiotto.it, helpful Giorgio).

North of the Duomo
Near the Accademia

$$$$ Hotel dei Macchiaioli offers 15 fresh and spacious rooms on one high-ceilinged, noble floor in a restored palazzo owned for generations by a well-to-do Florentine family. You'll eat breakfast under original frescoed ceilings while enjoying modern comforts (RS%, air-con, Via Cavour 21, tel. 055-213-154, www.hoteldeimacchiaioli. com, info@hoteldeimacchiaioli.com, helpful Francesca and Paolo).

$$$$ Hotel Morandi alla Crocetta, a former convent, envelops you in a 16th-century cocoon. Located on a quiet street with 12 rooms, its period furnishings, squeaky clean parquet floors, and original frescoes take you back a few centuries and up a few social classes. A few rooms come with lovely patios (family rooms, air-con, elevator, pay parking, a block off Piazza Santissima Annunziata at Via Laura 50, tel. 055-234-4748, www. hotelmorandi.it, welcome@hotelmorandi. it, well-run by Maurizio, Rolando, and Cristiano).

$$$ Residenza dei Pucci rents 13 pleasant rooms (each one different) spread over three floors (with no elevator). The appealing decor, a mix of traditional fabrics and aristocratic furniture, makes this place feel upscale for the price range (RS%—use code "RICK," family rooms, air-con, reception open 9:00-20:00, shorter hours off-season—let them know if you'll arrive late, Via dei Pucci 9, tel. 055-281-886, www.residenza deipucci.com, info@residenzadeipucci. com, friendly Rossella and Marina).

Near the Medici Chapels

$$$$ Hotel Centrale is indeed central, just a short walk from the Duomo. The 35 spacious but overpriced rooms—with a tasteful mix of old and new decor—are over a businesslike conference center (RS%, air-con, elevator, Via dei Conti 3, check in at big front desk on ground floor, tel. 055-215-761, www.hotelcentralefirenze.it, info@ hotelcentralefirenze.it, Roberto).

$$$$ Hotel Accademia has 18 quiet rooms on a pedestrianized street in a convenient location. The modern, sizeable rooms cluster around a sunny courtyard (RS%, air-con, no elevator, Via Faenza 7, tel. 055-290-993, www.hotelaccademia firenze.com, info@hotelaccademia firenze.com, Tea and Francesca).

East of the Duomo

$$$ Residenza il Villino has 10 charming rooms and a picturesque, peaceful little courtyard. The owner, Neri, has turned part of the breakfast room into a museum-like tribute to his grandfather, a pioneer of early Italian fashion. As it's in a "little villa" (as the name implies) set back from the street, this is a quiet refuge from the bustle of Florence (RS%, family rooms, air-con, parking available, just north of Via degli Alfani at Via della Pergola 53, tel. 055-200-1116, www.ilvillino.it, info@ilvillino.it, Giovanni).

$$ Locanda de' Ciompi, overlooking the inviting Piazza dei Ciompi in a lively neighborhood, is just right for travelers who want to feel like a part of the town. Alessio and daughter Lisa have five attractive rooms that are tidy, lovingly maintained, and a good value (RS%, cheaper room with private bath across the hall, includes breakfast at nearby bar, air-con, 8 blocks behind the Duomo at Via Pietrapiana 28 black—see map on page 524, tel. 055-263-8034, www.bbflorencefirenze.com, info@ bbflorencefirenze.com).

$$ Hotel Dalí has 10 cheery, worn rooms in a nice location for a great price. Samanta and Marco, who run this guesthouse with a charming passion and idealism, are a delight to know (request one of the quiet and spacious rooms facing the courtyard when you book, cheaper rooms with shared bath available, nearby apartments sleep 2-6 people, no breakfast, fans but no air-con, elevator, free parking, 2 blocks behind the Duomo at Via dell'Oriuolo 17 on the second floor, tel. 055-234-0706, www. hoteldali.com, hoteldali@tin.it).

$$ Sanctuary Firenze, run by the Oblate Sisters of the Assumption, is an institutional 35-room hotel in a Renaissance building with a dreamy garden, great public spaces, appropriately simple rooms, and a quiet, prayerful ambience (family rooms, single beds only, air-con, elevator, 23:30 curfew, limited pay parking—request when you book, Borgo Pinti 15, tel. 055-248-0582, www.sanctuary bbfirenze.com, info@sanctuarybbfirenze. com). As there's no night porter, it's best to time your arrival and departure to occur during typical business hours.

South of the Duomo
Between the Duomo and Piazza della Signoria

$$$$ In Piazza della Signoria B&B, in a stellar location overlooking Piazza della Signoria, is peaceful, refined, and homey. The service is friendly and efficient. The nine rooms are beautifully decorated; the priciest ones have genuine views of the square. Guests enjoy socializing at the big, shared breakfast table (RS%, 2 family apartments, air-con, tiny elevator, Via dei Magazzini 2, tel. 055-239-9546, mobile 348-321-0565, www.inpiazzadellasignoria.com, info@inpiazzadellasignoria.com, Sonia and Alessandro).

$$$ Hotel Maxim Axial, run by the Maoli family since 1981, has 42 straightforward rooms spread over three floors in a good location on the main pedestrian drag. Its painting-lined halls and cozy lounge have old Florentine charm. Budget travelers can choose an "economy" room on the fourth floor—which is a walk-up from the third floor (RS%—use code "RICK," family rooms, reception on third floor, air-con, elevator, Via de' Calzaiuoli 11, tel. 055-217-474, www.hotelmaximaxial.com, info@hotelmaximaxial.com, Chiara).

$$ B&B Il Bargello is a home away from home, run by friendly and helpful Canadian expat Gabriella. Hike up three long flights (no elevator) to reach six smart, relaxing rooms. Gabriella offers a cozy living room, a communal kitchenette, and an inviting rooftop terrace with close-up views of Florence's towers (RS%, fully equipped apartment across the hall sleeps up to six with one shared bathroom; air-con, 20 yards off Via Proconsolo at Via de' Pandolfini 33 black, tel. 055-215-330, mobile 339-175-3110, www.firenze-bedandbreakfast.it, info@firenze-bedandbreakfast.it).

Near Ponte Vecchio

$$$$ Hotel Davanzati, bright and shiny with artistic touches, has 25 cheerful rooms with all the comforts. The place is a family affair, thoughtfully run by friendly Tommaso and father Fabrizio, who offer drinks and snacks each evening at their candlelit happy hour, plus lots of other extras (RS%, family rooms, air-con, 20 steep steps to the elevator, handy room fridges, next to Piazza Davanzati at Via Porta Rossa 5— easy to miss so watch for low-profile sign above the door, tel. 055-286-666, www.hoteldavanzati.it, info@hoteldavanzati.it).

$$$$ Hotel Torre Guelfa has grand public spaces and is topped by a fun medieval tower with a panoramic rooftop terrace (72 stairs take you up—and back 720 years). Its 31 pricey rooms vary wildly in size and furnishings, but most come with the noise of the city center. Room 315, with a private terrace, is worth reserving several months in advance (RS%, family rooms, air-con, elevator, a couple of blocks northwest of Ponte Vecchio, Borgo SS. Apostoli 8, tel. 055-239-6338, www.hoteltorreguelfa.com, info@hoteltorreguelfa.com, Niccolo).

$$$$ Relais Uffizi is a peaceful little gem, offering a friendly welcome and tight maze of 15 classy rooms tucked away down a tiny alley off Piazza della Signoria. The lounge has a huge window overlooking the action in the piazza—a unique view (RS%, family rooms, air-con, elevator; official address is Chiasso del Buco 16—from the square, go down tiny Chiasso de Baroncelli lane—right of the loggia—and after 50 yards turn right through the arch and look for entrance on your right; tel. 055-267-6239, www.relaisuffizi.it, info@relaisuffizi.it, charming Alessandro and Elizabetta).

The Oltrarno

For locations, see the map on page 516.

$$$$ Hotel Palazzo Guadagni, perched high above Piazza Santo Spirito, is a romantic, Grand Tour retreat from modern Florence. The 15 refined rooms are spacious, with antique furnishings and frescoes. While the ample, chandeliered public spaces are pleasant, the highlight is the panoramic wraparound loggia/terrace with comfy, stay-awhile seating and lovely views (RS%, air-con, elevator, Piazza Santo Spirito 9, tel. 055-265-8376, www.palazzoguadagni.com, info@palazzoguadagni.com).

$$$ Hotel Silla is a classic three-star hotel with 36 cheery, spacious rooms. Across the river from Santa Croce Church, it has a breezy terrace and faces

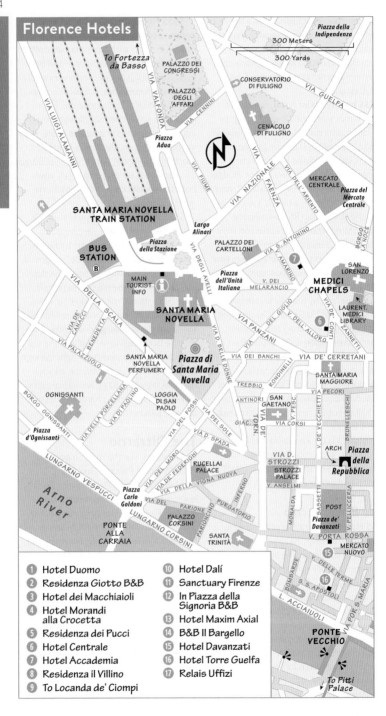

Florence Hotels

1. Hotel Duomo
2. Residenza Giotto B&B
3. Hotel dei Macchiaioli
4. Hotel Morandi alla Crocetta
5. Residenza dei Pucci
6. Hotel Centrale
7. Hotel Accademia
8. Residenza il Villino
9. To Locanda de' Ciompi
10. Hotel Dalí
11. Sanctuary Firenze
12. In Piazza della Signoria B&B
13. Hotel Maxim Axial
14. B&B Il Bargello
15. Hotel Davanzati
16. Hotel Torre Guelfa
17. Relais Uffizi

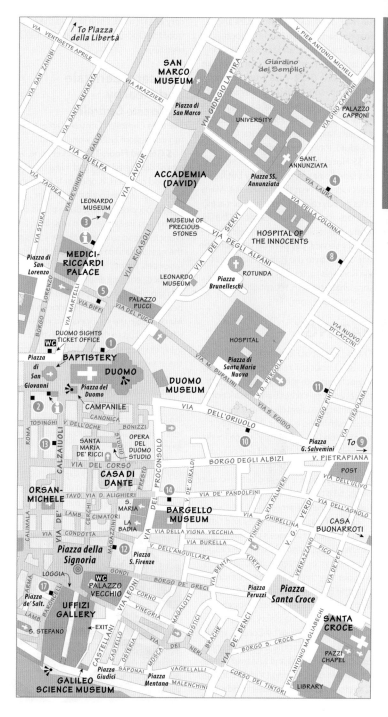

the river, overlooking a small park and near the San Niccolò neighborhood. There's free coffee and tea for guests in the late afternoon. The surroundings can be a bit noisy (RS%—use promo code "RICK," air-con, elevator, pricey self-service washing machine, pay parking, Via dei Renai 5, tel. 055-234-2888, www.hotelsilla.it, hotelsilla@hotelsilla.it; Laura, Chiara, Massimo, Ravin, and Stefano).

$$ Hotel Annalena, on the third floor of a faded palazzo, is a bit tatty but it's in a quiet location near the Pitti Palace. Many of its 20 tidy rooms (some with terraces) overlook a private park next door (family rooms, bar/lounge, air-con, no elevator, laundry service, pay parking, opposite the side entrance to the Boboli Gardens at Via Romana 34, tel. 055-222-402, www.annalenahotel.com, reception@annalenahotel.com).

EATING

The old center of Florence is dominated by tourism. Locals still keep restaurants busy at lunch, but with the city's many Airbnb guests and city-center traffic restrictions, the hometown clientele retreats away from downtown in the evening. This makes it tough to find a "nontouristy" place for dinner. Still, you'll find plenty of fine options and good values even in the tourist zone. For the best experience and better-quality meals, hike to places further out and across the river in the Oltrarno.

Eating Tips: To save money and time, lunch at one of Florence's countless sandwich shops and stands, pizzerias, or self-service cafeterias. You can picnic your way through Mercato Centrale, near the Basilica of San Lorenzo. You'll also find good *supermercati* throughout the city. I like the classy Sapori & Dintorni markets (run by Conad), which have branches near the Duomo (Borgo San Lorenzo 15 red) and just over Ponte Vecchio in the Oltrarno (Via de Bardi 45). Carrefour Express is another handy gro-

cery chain (there's one around the corner from the Duomo Museum at Via dell'Oriuolo 66).

Mercato Centrale and Nearby
In Mercato Centrale

Mercato Centrale (Central Market) is a fun-to-explore edible wonderland.

$ Ground Floor: The market zone, with lots of raw ingredients and a few humble food counters, is open only through lunchtime (Mon-Fri 7:00-14:00, Sat until 17:00, closed Sun). Buy a picnic of fresh mozzarella cheese, olives, fruit, and crunchy bread to munch on the steps of the nearby Basilica of San Lorenzo. The fancy deli, **Perini,** is famous for its quality products, enticing display, and generous samples. For a simple sit-down meal, head for the venerable **Nerbone in the Market.** Join the shoppers and workers who crowd up to the bar to grab their inexpensive plates, and then find a stool at the cramped shared tables nearby. Of the several cheap market diners, this feels the most authentic (lunch menu served Mon-Sat 12:00-14:00, cash only, on the side closest to the Basilica of San Lorenzo). Its less-famous sisters, nearby, have better seating and fewer crowds.

$$ Upstairs: The upper floor is a touristy, overcrowded and overpriced food court (daily 10:00-24:00) with counters selling pizza, pasta, fish, meat, *salumi, lampredotto,* wine, and so on.

Florentine and Tuscan Cuisine

In general, Tuscan cuisine is hearty, simple food: grilled meats, high-quality seasonal vegetables, fresh herbs, prized olive oil, and rustic bread. For more on Italian food, see the "Eating" section of the Practicalities chapter.

Antipasti (Appetizers)

Bruschetta: Toasted bread brushed with olive oil and rubbed with garlic, topped with chopped tomato, mushrooms, or whatever else sounds good

Crostini: Toasted bread rounds topped with meat or vegetable pastes. *Alla toscana* generally means with chicken liver pâté

Panzanella: Simple summer salad, made of day-old bread, chopped tomatoes, onion, and basil, tossed in a light vinaigrette

Pecorino cheese: Fresh (*fresco*) or aged (*stagionato*), from ewe's milk

Porcini mushrooms: Used as a topping for bruschetta; also served marinated or stewed

Salumi: Cold cuts, usually air- or salt-dried pork. Popular kinds include prosciutto, pancetta, *lardo* (cured pork lard), and *finocchiona* (fennel salami)

Tagliere: Selection of cold cuts and/or cheeses served on a wooden platter

Primo Piatto (First Course)

Carabaccia: Onion soup

Pappa al pomodoro: Thick stew of tomatoes, olive oil, and bread

Pappardelle al sugo di lepre: Rich wild hare sauce over long, broad noodles

Pici al ragù: Fat, spaghetti-like, hand-rolled pasta with a meat-tomato sauce

Ribollita: "Reboiled" soup, traditionally made with leftovers including white beans (*fagioli*), seasonal vegetables, and olive oil, with layers of day-old Tuscan bread

Zuppa alla volterrana: Volterra-style soup, similar to *ribollita* but with fresh bread

Secondo Piatto (Second Course)

Arrosto misto: Assortment of roasted meats, sometimes served on a skewer (*spiedino*)

Bistecca alla fiorentina: Thick T-bone steak, generally grilled very rare and lightly seasoned (often sold by weight—per *etto,* or 100 grams). The best—and most expensive—is from the white Chianina cattle you'll see grazing throughout Tuscany.

Cinghiale: Wild boar, served grilled; in soups, stews, and pasta; or made into many varieties of sausage and salami

Fegatelli: Liver meatballs

Game birds: Squab (*piccione*), pheasant (*fagiano*), and guinea hen (*faraona*) are popular.

Trippa alla fiorentina: Tripe and vegetables sautéed in tomato sauce, sometimes baked with parmesan. *Trippa* (and the similar *lampredotto*) are popular in sandwiches.

ITALY

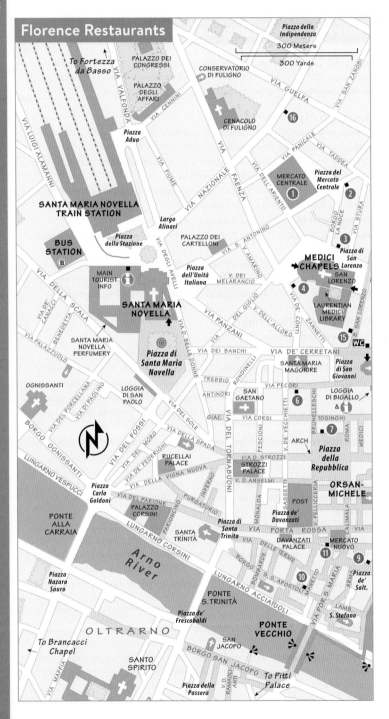

Florence Restaurants

Piazza della Indipendenza

300 Meters

300 Yards

To Fortezza da Basso

PALAZZO DEI CONGRESSI

PALAZZO DEGLI AFFARI

CONSERVATORIO DI FULIGNO

VIA GUELFA

VIA SAN ZANOBI

VIA LUIGI ALAMANNI

VIA VALFONDA

VIA GENNINI

Piazza Adua

CENACOLO DI FULIGNO

VIA PANICALE

VIA TADDEA

16

VIA NAZIONALE

VIA FIUME

VIA DELL'ARIENTO

MERCATO CENTRALE

1

Piazza del Mercato Centrale

2

VIA STURA

SANTA MARIA NOVELLA TRAIN STATION

VIA FAENZA

Largo Alinari

BORGO LA NOCE

3

BUS STATION

B

Piazza della Stazione

VIA DEGLI AVELLI

PALAZZO DEI CARTELLONI

VIA S. ANTONINO

V: V. AMARINO

Piazza di San Lorenzo

MEDICI CHAPELS

Piazza dell'Unità Italiana

V: DEI MELARANCIO

SAN LORENZO

4

LAURENTIAN MEDICI LIBRARY

VIA DE' ZANNETTI

VIA S. LORENZO

MAIN TOURIST INFO

i

SANTA MARIA NOVELLA

VIA DE' CANACCI

VIA DELLA SCALA

VIA BENEDETTA

VIA PALAZZUOLO

SANTA MARIA NOVELLA PERFUMERY

VIA DE' BELLE DONNE

VIA PANZANI

DEL GIGLIO

V: DELL'ALLORO

VIA DE' CONTI

15

WC

Piazza di Santa Maria Novella

VIA DEI BANCHI

VIA DE' CERRETANI

SANTA MARIA MAGGIORE

Piazza di San Giovanni

OGNISSANTI

VIA DEL PORCELLANA

VIA DI PAOLINO

LOGGIA DI SAN PAOLO

TREBBIO

RONDINELLI

ANTINORI

VIA PECORI

LOGGIA DI BIGALLO

&

i

BORGO OGNISSANTI

LUNGARNO VESPUCCI

VIA DEL FOSSI

VIA DEL MORO

VIA DEL SOLE

VIA DELLA SPADA

ANTINORI

SAN GAETANO

GIAC.

VIA CORSI

SAN GIOVANNI

6

V: DE' VECCHIETTI

BRUNELLESCHI

TOSINGHI

ROMA

MEDICI

7

Piazza della Repubblica

N

RUCELLAI PALACE

VIA DEI FEDERIGHI

VIA DELLA VIGNA NUOVA

VIA DEL PARIONE

INFERNO

PURGATORIO

VIA DEL TORNABUONI

PESCIONI

VIA D. STROZZI

STROZZI PALACE

V. D. ANSELMI

MONALDA

POST

SASSETTI

ORSAN-MICHELE

Piazza Carlo Goldoni

PALAZZO CORSINI

PARIONCINO

SANTA TRINITÀ

Piazza di Santa Trinita

Piazza de' Davanzati

VIA PORTA ROSSA

V. PELLICCERIA

CALIMALA

DAVANZATI PALACE

MERCATO NUOVO

9

PONTE ALLA CARRAIA

LUNGARNO CORSINI

VIA DELLE TERME

BORGO S. S. APOSTOLI

11

10

VIA POR S. MARIA

ARTE

Piazza de' Salt.

Arno River

Piazza Nazaro Sauro

PONTE S. TRINITÀ

Piazza de' Frescobaldi

LUNGARNO ACCIAIUOLI

MANETTO

PONTE VECCHIO

LAMB.

S. Stefano

OLTRARNO

To Brancacci Chapel

SANTO SPIRITO

SAN JACOPO

BORGO SAN JACOPO

V. D. RAMAGLIANTI

To Pitti Palace

VIA MAFFIA

Piazza della Passera

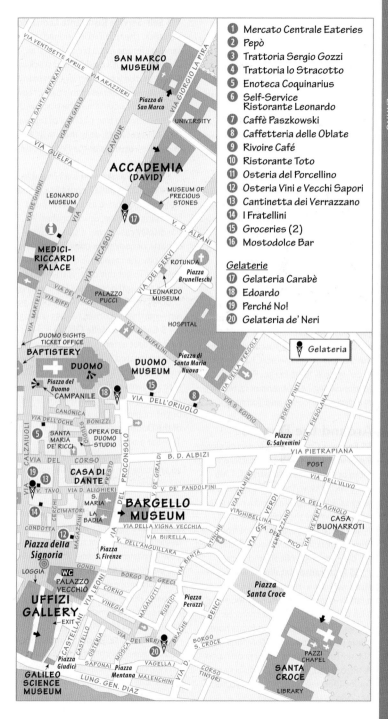

1. Mercato Centrale Eateries
2. Pepò
3. Trattoria Sergio Gozzi
4. Trattoria lo Stracotto
5. Enoteca Coquinarius
6. Self-Service Ristorante Leonardo
7. Caffè Paszkowski
8. Caffetteria delle Oblate
9. Rivoire Café
10. Ristorante Toto
11. Osteria del Porcellino
12. Osteria Vini e Vecchi Sapori
13. Cantinetta dei Verrazzano
14. I Fratellini
15. Groceries (2)
16. Mostodolce Bar

Gelaterie
17. Gelateria Carabè
18. Edoardo
19. Perché No!
20. Gelateria de' Neri

Gelateria

Near Mercato Centrale

$$ Pepò, a colorful and charmingly unpretentious space, is tucked just around the corner from the touristy glitz on Piazza del Mercato Centrale. The short menu offers simple but well-prepared Florentine classics such as *ribollita* and *pollo alla cacciatora*—chicken cacciatore (daily 12:00-14:30 & 19:00-22:30, Via Rosina 4 red, tel. 055-283-259).

$$ Trattoria Sergio Gozzi is your classic neighborhood lunch-only place, serving hearty, traditional Florentine fare to market-goers since 1915—long before the tourist crush of today. The handwritten menu is limited and changes daily, and the service can be hectic, but it remains a local favorite (Mon-Sat 12:00-15:00, closed Sun, reservations smart, Piazza di San Lorenzo 8, tel. 055-281-941).

$$ Trattoria lo Stracotto is an inviting eatery with a modern interior and good outdoor seating, where you'll enjoy good-value, standard Tuscan dishes in the shadow of the Medici Chapels (daily 12:00-15:00 & 18:00-22:30, Piazza di Madonna degli Aldobrandini 17, tel. 055-230-2062, Francesco and Tomasso).

Around the Duomo

$$ Enoteca Coquinarius feels as welcoming as someone's cool and spacious living room or library. It's an unstressful, hip place with a slow-food ethic and lots of tasty salads and pastas, and a nice selection of wines by the glass (daily 12:30-15:30 & 18:30-22:30, a few steps from the Duomo workshop at Via delle Oche 11 red, tel. 055-230-2153, Nicola and Luca).

$$ Ristorante Natalino is worth the short walk for a memorable dinner. It's a family-run fixture in its neighborhood with outdoor seating on a characteristic corner. The place is known for its homemade pasta, *bistecca alla fiorentina,* and classic Tuscan dishes (daily 12:00-14:30 & 18:30-22:30, Borgo degli Albizi 17 red, for location see map on page 490, tel. 055-289-404).

$ Self-Service Ristorante Leonardo is a quick, cheap, air-conditioned, and handy cafeteria just a block from the Duomo. While it's no-frills and stuck in the 1970s, the food is better than many table-service eateries in this part of town. Stefano and Luciano run the place with enthusiasm and free pitchers of tap water (lots of vegetables, daily 11:45-14:45 & 18:45-21:45, upstairs at Via Pecori 11, tel. 055-284-446).

$$ Caffè Paszkowski is a venerable place on Piazza della Repubblica. While famously expensive as a restaurant, it serves inexpensive, quick lunches. At the display case, order a salad or plate of pasta or cooked veggies (or half-and-half), pay the cashier, and find a seat upstairs. To get this deal, you'll need to sit where the staff designates (lunch served 12:00-15:00, Piazza della Repubblica 35 red—northwest corner, tel. 055-210-236).

$ Caffetteria delle Oblate is a laid-back budget eatery just a block from the Duomo located within a cultural center and library. You'll eat well-priced pastas with students in the top-floor cafeteria, either on an outdoor terrace or in the bright interior—with unobstructed views of the Duomo's dome (Mon 14:00-17:00, Tue-Sat 9:00-23:00, closed Sun, enter through the courtyard at Via dell'Oriuolo 26 and take the elevator to the top floor, tel. 055-263-9685).

Near Piazza della Signoria

$$$ Rivoire café is famous for its fancy desserts and thick hot chocolate (€7). A bowl of pasta or a salad—when enjoyed at the best view tables on the square—can be a worthwhile experience. Their delightful bar is perfectly affordable, and drinks often come with fine *aperitivo* munchies (daily 8:00-24:00, tel. 055-214-412).

$$ Ristorante Toto is a simple, fun, traditional eatery with a spacious dining hall serving classic Tuscan plates at decent prices. The focus is on steak and pizza (Thu-Tue 12:00-15:00 & 19:00-22:00,

Gelato

Italy's best ice cream is in Florence—many think they serve some of the world's best. But beware of scams at touristy joints on busy streets that turn a simple request for a cone into a €10 "tourist special" rip-off. To avoid this, survey the size options and specify what you want—for example, *un cono da tre euro* (a €3 cone). A rule of thumb: Stay away from places with heaping mounds of brightly (artificially) colored gelato. For more gelato tips, see the "Eating" section of the Practicalities chapter. The following places, which are a cut above the norm, are open long hours daily.

Near the Accademia: A Sicilian choice on a tourist thoroughfare, **Gelateria Carabè** is particularly famous for its pistachio and its luscious *granite*—Italian ices made with fresh fruit. A *cremolata* is a *granita* with a dollop of gelato (almond and pistachio work well together). If you'd like a real Sicilian cannoli, get it here (from the Accademia, it's a block toward the Duomo at Via Ricasoli 60 red—Simone clearly loves his work).

Near the Duomo: A favorite, **Edoardo** features organic ingredients and tasty handmade cones (facing the southwest corner of the Duomo at Piazza del Duomo 45 red).

Near Orsanmichele Church: This shop's name, **Perchè No!,** translates to "Why not!"—good advice when it comes to gelato. It feels touristy but serves one of the widest range of flavors around, and the quality's top notch (just off the busy main pedestrian drag, Via de' Calzaiuoli, at Via dei Tavolini 19).

Near the Church of Santa Croce: Florentines flock to **Gelateria de' Neri,** with an enticingly wide array of flavors (Via dei Neri 9 red).

Just Across the Carraia Bridge: On the Oltrarno side of the bridge, **Gelateria la Carraia** is a hit with locals (Piazza Nazario Sauro 25 red—see the map on page 516).

closed Wed, two blocks from the Ponte Vecchio at Borgo SS. Apostoli 6 red, tel. 055-212-096).

$$$ Osteria del Porcellino is a classic place deep in the center with a romantic ambience inside and quiet seating outside. Enzo—whose family has owned this restaurant since 1969—serves Tuscan classics. At dinner, he offers a complementary glass of bubbly when you sit down, and a vin santo with *contucci* after your meal (good €15 lunch special, daily 12:00-23:00, Via Val di Lamona 7 red, tel. 055-264-148).

$$ Osteria Vini e Vecchi Sapori is a colorful eatery—tight, tiny, and with attitude. They serve Tuscan food—like *pappardelle* with duck—from a fun, accessible menu of delicious pastas and *secondi* (Mon-Sat 12:30-14:30 & 19:30-22:30, closed Sun, reservations necessary—call ahead, Via dei Magazzini 3 red, tel. 055-293-045, run by Mario while wife Rosanna cooks and son Tommaso serves).

Sandwiches Near Piazza della Signoria

$$ Cantinetta dei Verrazzano is an elegant wine bar serving delightful sandwich plates. Their *selezione Verrazzano* is a plate of four little crostini featuring breads, cheeses, and meats from the Chianti region. The *tagliere di focacce,* a sampler of mini focaccia sandwiches, is also fun (daily 8:00-16:30, no reservations taken, off Via de' Calzaiuoli, at Via dei Tavolini 18 red, tel. 055-268-590).

$ I Fratellini is a hole-in-the-wall stand-up joint where the "little brothers" have served peasants more than 30 kinds of sandwiches and a fine selection of wine at great prices (see list on wall) since 1875. Join the local crowd to order, then sit on a nearby curb to eat, placing your glass on the wall rack before you leave. Be adventurous with the menu (order by number). It's worth ordering the most expensive wine they're selling by the glass (daily 9:00-19:30 or until the bread runs out, 20 yards in front of Orsanmichele Church on Via dei Cimatori, tel. 055-239-6096).

The Oltrarno

Dining in the Oltrarno, south of the Arno River, offers a more authentic experience. While it's just a few minutes' walk beyond Ponte Vecchio, this area sees fewer tourists. For locations, see the map on page 516.

Dining or Drinking with a Ponte Vecchio View

$$$ Signorvino is a bright and modern *enoteca* (wine shop) with a simple restaurant that has a rare terrace literally over the Arno River, with Ponte Vecchio views. Though it lacks historic charm with its stark-white IKEA vibe, it's a fun-loving place with no pretense and a passion for quality Italian ingredients. They serve regional dishes and plates of fine meats and cheeses to pair with a wonderful array of wines by the glass (food served 11:30-23:00, call to reserve, especially for terrace seating, Via dei Bardi 46 red, tel. 055-286-258, www.signorvino.com).

$$$ Golden View Firenze is two-in-one: a classy restaurant and the simpler **Bar Osteria,** both overlooking the Ponte Vecchio and Arno River. The white, minimalist interior is a dramatic contrast to atmospheric old Florence. Reservations for window tables are essential. Mixing their fine wine, river views, and live jazz makes for a wonderful evening (daily 12:00-24:00; jazz usually Mon, Fri, and Sat nights in the restaurant at 21:00; 50 yards east of Ponte Vecchio at Via dei Bardi 58, tel. 055-214-502, www.goldenviewopenbar.com, run by Paolo).

On or near Piazza di Santo Spirito

Piazza di Santo Spirito is a thriving neighborhood square, with a collection of fun eateries and bars. Several bars offer *aperitivo* buffets with their drinks during happy hour. Later in the evening, the area becomes a club scene.

Cooking Classes

The options listed below represent only a few of your many choices. As this is a fast-changing scene, it's worth doing some homework online and booking well ahead.

In Tavola is a dedicated cooking school in the heart of the Oltrarno. They feature trained, English-speaking Italian chefs who quickly demonstrate each step before setting you loose. You'll work in a functional kitchen, and then sit down to eat in the cozy wine cellar (classes range from €57-129/person, ideally book well ahead but you can try calling last-minute, between the Pitti Palace and Brancacci Chapel at Via dei Velluti 18 red, tel. 055-217-672, www.intavola.org, info@intavola.org, Fabrizio).

Both **Artviva** and **Florencetown** (see contact info under "Tours," earlier) offer cooking classes (Artviva: €59-73/person; Florencetown: from €79/person).

$$ Gusta Osteria, just around the corner from the piazza, serves big salads and predictable Tuscan fare at fun, cozy indoor seating or at outdoor tables (Tue-Sun 12:00-23:00, closed Mon, Via de' Michelozzi 13 red, tel. 055-285-033).

$$ Trattoria Sant'Agostino, a block away from the Piazza di Santo Spirito action, is charming and more relaxed with comfortable seating and a good place for traditional local cuisine (daily 12:00-23:00, Via Sant'Agostino 23 red, tel. 055-281-995).

$ O Munaciello Pizzeria, named after a ghost of Neapolitan folklore, is a kitschy, sprawling, family-friendly festival of happy eating. The menu is fun, there's a youthful energy, and the Naples-style pizza is a hit with locals (daily 12:30-15:00 & 19:00-24:00, Via Maffia 31 red, tel. 055-287-198).

Dining Well in the Oltrarno

Of the many good and colorful restaurants in the Oltrarno, these are my favorites. Reservations are a good idea in the evening.

$$$ Il Santo Bevitore Ristorante, lit like a Rembrandt painting and unusually spacious, serves creative, modern Tuscan cuisine at dressy tables. They're enthusiastic about matching quality local produce with the right wine (good wine list by the glass or bottle, daily 12:30-14:30 & 19:30-23:00, reservations smart, three tables on the sidewalk, can be noisy inside, Via di Santo Spirito 64 red, tel. 055-211-264, www.ilsantobevitore.com).

$$ Enoteca il Santino Gastronomia, Il Santo Bevitore's tiny wine bar next door, feels like the perfect after-work hangout for foodies who'd like a glass of wine and a light bite. Tight, cozy, and atmospheric, the place can be intimidating if you're shy. It has a prominent bar, where you can assemble an €8-12 *tagliere* of local cheeses and *salumi.* They also have a few affordable hot dishes (daily 12:30-23:00, Via di Santo Spirito 60 red, no reservations, tel. 055-230-2820).

$$$ Trattoria 4 Leoni creates the quintessential Oltrarno dinner scene and is understandably popular with tourists. The Tuscan-style food is made with an innovative twist and an appreciation for vegetables. Their steak and *fiocchetti* pasta are big hits (daily 12:00-24:00, dinner reservations smart; midway between Ponte Vecchio and Piazza di Santo Spirito, on Piazza della Passera at Via de' Vellutini 1; tel. 055-218-562, www.4leoni.com).

$$$$ Olio & Convivium showcases their artful, slow-food cooking in three dressy and intimate rooms that are surrounded by fine *prosciutti,* cheeses, and wine shelves. It can seem a little formal, but well-dressed foodies will appreciate this place for its romantic, exclusive atmosphere. Their list of €14-25 *gastronomia* plates offers an array of taste treats and fine wines by the glass. They also have €35-49 tasting *menus* and stylish €22 lunches with wine (Tue-Sun 12:00-14:30 & 19:00-22:30, closed Mon, Via di Santo Spirito 4, tel. 055-265-8198, www.oliorestaurant.it, chef and owner Tommaso).

TRANSPORTATION

Getting Around Florence

I organize my sightseeing geographically and do it all on foot. You likely won't need public transit, except maybe to head up to Piazzale Michelangelo and San Miniato Church for the view.

By Bus

The city's full-size buses don't cover the old center well (the whole area around the Duomo is off-limits to motorized traffic). Pick up a map of transit routes at the ATAF windows (#8 and #9) at the train station; you'll also find routes online (www.ataf.net).

Buy bus tickets at tobacco shops (*tabacchi*), newsstands, or the ATAF ticket windows (€1.50/90 minutes). Be sure to validate your ticket in the machine on board (or risk a steep fine). Follow general bus etiquette: Board at front or rear doors, exit out the center.

Of the many bus lines, I find these to be of most value for seeing outlying sights:

Bus **#12** goes from the train station, over the Carraia bridge to Porta Romana, then up to San Miniato Church and Piazzale Michelangelo (3/hour). Bus **#13** makes the return trip down the hill.

Minibuses (many of them electric) wind through the tangled old center of town and up and down the river—just €1.50 gets you a 1.5-hour joyride. They run every 10 minutes from 7:00 to 21:00 (less frequent on Sun).

Bus **#C1** stops behind the Palazzo Vecchio and Piazza Santa Croce, then heads north, passing near San Marco and the Accademia before heading up to Piazza Libertà. On its southbound route, it also stops near the train station, the Basilica of San Lorenzo, and the Duomo.

Bus **#C2** twists through the congested old center from the train station, passing near Piazza della Repubblica and Piazza della Signoria to Piazza Beccaria.

Bus **#C3** goes up and down the Arno River, with stops near Piazza Santa Croce, Ponte Vecchio, the Carraia bridge to the Oltrarno (including the Pitti Palace), and beyond.

Bus **#C4** goes from near the Duomo to the train station, crosses the Carraia bridge, and cruises through the Oltrarno (passing the Pitti Palace) before heading into the San Niccolò neighborhood.

By Tram

The T1 and T2 tram lines are cheap, easy, and frequent. For travelers, they're generally useful only for service between the tram stops in town (near the train station) and either the airport (T2) or the big park-and-ride lots at Villa Costanza (T1) near the town of Scandicci (www.gestramvia.com).

By Taxi

The minimum cost for a taxi ride is €5 (€8.30 after 22:00, €7 on Sun); rides in the town center should be charged as tariff #1. Taxi fares and supplements (e.g., €2 extra to call a cab rather than hail one) are clearly explained on signs in each taxi. Look for an official, regulated cab (white; marked with *Taxi/Comune di Firenze,* red fleur-de-lis, and one of the official phone numbers: 4390 or 4242). Before getting in a cab, ask for an approximate cost (*"Più o meno, quanto costa?"* pew oh MEH-noh, KWAHN-toh KOH-stah). If you can't get a straight answer or the price is outrageous, wait for the next one. It can be hard to find a cab on the street; to call one, dial 055-4390 or 055-4242 (or ask your waiter or hotelier to call for you).

Arriving and Departing
By Train
Florence's main train station is called **Santa Maria Novella** (*Firenze S.M.N.* on schedules and signs; Florence also has two suburban train stations: **Firenze Rifredi** and **Firenze Campo di Marte**).

Rick's Tip: Be on guard at train stations. Don't trust "porters" who want to help you find your train or carry your bags (they're not official), and **politely decline offers of help** *using the ticket machines by anyone other than uniformed staff.*

To orient yourself to Santa Maria Novella Station, stand with your back to the tracks. Look left to see the green cross of a 24-hour pharmacy (*farmacia*) and the exit to the taxi queue. **Baggage storage** (*deposito bagagli*) is also to the left, halfway down track 16 (long hours daily, passport required). **Fast-food outlets** and a **bank** are also along track 16. Directly ahead of you is the main hall (*salone biglietti*), where you can buy train and bus tickets. Pay WCs are to the right, near the head of track 5.

To reach the **TI,** walk away from the tracks and exit the station; it's straight across the square, 100 yards away, by the stone church.

Buying Tickets: For travel within Italy, it's quick and easy to buy tickets online; with the Trenitalia app, you can even

purchase them minutes before the train departs. If you decide to buy tickets at the station, take advantage of the ticket (*biglietti*) machines that display schedules, issue tickets, and even make reservations for rail-pass holders. For most international tickets, you'll need to go to a Trenitalia ticket window (in the main hall).

For Trenitalia information, use window #18 or #19 (take a number). For Italo tickets and information, use window #10 or #11, or visit their main office, opposite track 5, near the exit. To buy ATAF city bus tickets, stop at windows #8-9 in the main hall—and ask for a transit map while you're there (TIs often do not have them).

Getting to the Duomo and City Center: The Duomo and town center are to your left (with your back to the tracks). Out the doorway to the left, you'll find city buses and the taxi stand. Taxis cost about €8 to the Duomo. To walk into town (10-15 minutes), exit the station straight ahead (with your back to the tracks) through the main hall and head straight across the square outside (toward the Church of Santa Maria Novella). On the far side of the square, keep left and head down the main Via dei Panzani, which leads directly to the Duomo.

TRAIN CONNECTIONS
From Florence by Train to: Pisa (2/hour, 45-75 minutes), Siena (direct trains hourly, 1.5 hours; bus is better because Siena's train station is far from the center), La Spezia (for the Cinque Terre, 5/day direct, 2.5 hours, otherwise nearly hourly with change in Pisa), Milan (hourly, 2 hours; Italo: 2/ hour, 2 hours), Venice (hourly, 2-3 hours, may transfer in Bologna, often crowded— reserve ahead; Italo: 4/day, 2 hours, reservations required), Assisi (7/day direct, 2-3 hours), Orvieto (hourly, 2 hours, some with change in Campo di Marte or Rifredi Station), Rome (2-3/hour, 1.5 hours, most require seat reservations; Italo: 2/hour, 1.5 hours), Naples (at least hourly, 3 hours; Italo: hourly, 3 hours).

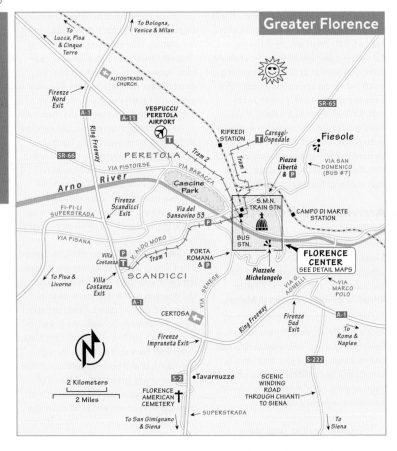

Greater Florence

By Bus

The BusItalia Station is 50 yards southwest of the train station, near the T1 tram stop. To get to the city center, exit the station through the main door, and turn left along the busy street. The train station is on your left, while downtown Florence is straight ahead and a bit to the right.

Schedules for regional trips are posted, and monitors show imminent departures. Bus service drops dramatically on Sunday. Generally it's best to buy tickets in the station, as you'll pay 30 percent more to buy tickets onboard. Bus info: Tel. 800-373-760 (Mon-Fri 9:00-15:00, closed Sat-Sun), www.fsbusitalia.it.

From Florence by Bus to: Siena (roughly 2/hour—fewer off-season, 1.5-hour *rapida/via superstrada* buses are fastest, avoid the slower *ordinaria* buses, in Siena get off at Piazza Gramsci or Via Tozzi, www.tiemmespa.it), **Montepulciano** (1-2/day, 2 hours, LFI bus, www.lfi.it; or train to Chiusi, then Tiemme/Siena Mobilità bus to Montepulciano, www.tiemmespa.it).

By Car

Don't even attempt driving into the city center. The autostrada has several exits for Florence. Get off at the Nord, Scandicci, Impruneta, or Sud exits and follow signs toward—but not into—the *Centro*. Park on the outskirts—see the next section—and take a bus, tram, or taxi in.

Florence has a traffic-reduction system that's complicated and confusing even to locals. Every car passing into the "limited traffic zone" (*Zona Traffico Limitato,* or *ZTL*) is photographed; those who haven't jumped through bureaucratic hoops to get a permit can expect a €100 ticket in the mail (and an "administrative" fee from the rental company). If you have a reservation at a hotel within the ZTL area—and it has parking—ask in advance if they can get you permission to enter town.

Parking in Florence: The city center is ringed with big, efficient parking lots (signposted with a big *P*). From these, you can ride into the center (via taxi, bus, or possibly tram). Check www.firenzeparcheggi.it for details on parking lots, availability, and prices. From the freeway, follow the signs to *Centro,* then *Stadio,* then *P.*

The huge park-and-ride lot called Villa Costanza, just outside the town of Scandicci (south of Florence), has its own dedicated freeway offramp (just north of Impruneta) and is the terminus for the T1 tram line that zips smart drivers downtown (€1.50, departing every five minutes). Just look for it as you approach Florence on the autostrada.

By Plane

Amerigo Vespucci Airport, also called Peretola Airport, is about five miles northwest of the city (code: FLR, tel. 055-306-1830, www.aeroporto.firenze.it).

On the ground floor, the **T2 tram** (to the left as you exit the arrivals hall) runs every five minutes from the airport to near the train station (Alamanni Stazione, across from the station) and Piazza dell'Unità (one stop beyond the station, slightly closer to downtown) in about 20 minutes (runs 5:00-24:00, €1.50, buy ticket from machine on platform, cash or credit card, validate onboard, good for 90 minutes and transferable to bus lines, www.gestramvia.com).

Shuttle buses (to the far right as you exit the arrivals hall) connect the airport with Florence's train and bus stations (2/hour until 22:00, 1/hour until 00:30, 30 minutes, runs 5:00-00:30, €6 one-way—buy ticket on board, €10 round-trip—buy ticket inside airport). If you're changing to a different intercity bus in Florence (for instance, one bound for Siena), stay on the bus through the first stop (at the train station); it will continue on to the bus station nearby.

Official **taxi** companies have fixed rates for the 20- to 30-minute ride between the airport and downtown: €22 during the day (6:00-22:00), €25.30 at night, and €24 on Sunday. Be sure to use an official taxi (white, marked with *Taxi/Comune di Firenze* and a red fleur-de-lis).

The airport's **rental-car** offices share one big parking lot that's a three-minute drive away (shuttle bus departs directly outside the arrivals door).

By Private Car

For small groups with more money than time, zipping to nearby towns by private car service can be a comfortable option. Consider **Transfer Chauffeur Service** (mobile 338-862-3129, www.transfercs.com, welcome@transfercs.com, Marco) or **Prestige Rent** (office at Via della Saggina 98, tel. 055-286-059, www.prestigerent.com, usa@prestigerent.com, Saverio).

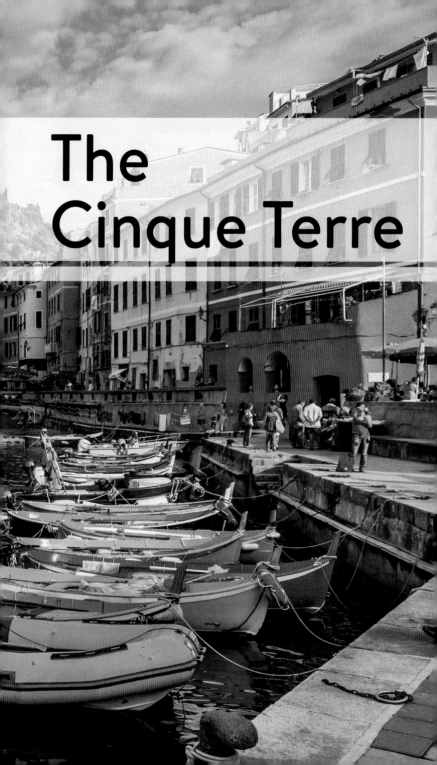

The
Cinque Terre

Along a six-mile stretch of the Riviera lies the Cinque Terre (CHINK-weh TAY-reh), gently carving a good life out of difficult terrain. With a traffic-free charm—a happy result of their natural isolation—these five (*cinque*) towns are the rugged alternative to the glitzy resorts nearby. With sun, sea, sand (well, pebbles), and wine, this is pure, unadulterated Italy.

Each addictively photogenic village fills a ravine with a lazy hive of human activity—calloused locals and sunburned travelers enjoying a unique mix of culture and nature. Enjoy swimming, hiking, and evening romance in one of God's great gifts to tourism. While the Cinque Terre is now discovered and can get jam-packed, I've never seen happier, more relaxed tourists. Most of the crowds are day-trippers, so make a point to get the most out of those cool, relaxed, and quiet hours early in the day and in the evening.

I cover the five towns in order from north to south—from Monterosso to Riomaggiore. Choose a home base according to just how cut off you'd like to be from the outer world: resorty Monterosso, cover-girl Vernazza, hilltop Corniglia, photogenic Manarola, or amiable Riomaggiore. Avoid visiting in winter, when tall, crashing waves batter the charm out of the Cinque Terre.

THE CINQUE TERRE IN 2 DAYS

This string of five villages dotting the Italian Riviera makes an idyllic escape from the obligatory museums of turnstile Italy. The ideal stay is two or three full days; my recommended minimum is two nights and an uninterrupted day. It's easiest to arrive and depart by train. Don't bring a car to the Cinque Terre; you won't need it.

Within the Cinque Terre, you can connect the towns in three ways: by train, boat, or foot. Trains are cheap, boats are more scenic, and hiking lets you enjoy more pasta. Consider supplementing the often frustratingly late trains with the sometimes more convenient boats.

Study your options, and piece together your best visit, mixing hiking, swimming, trains, boat rides, and a search for the best focaccia.

You could spend one day hiking from town to town (or take a boat or train partway, or as the return trip). For the best light, coolest temperatures, and fewest crowds,

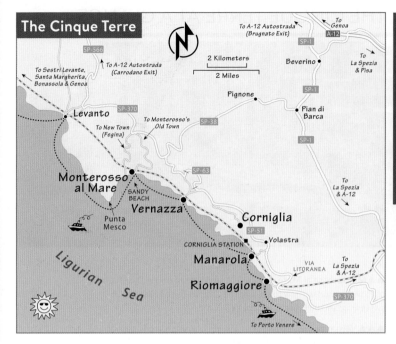

start your hike early in the morning (or late afternoon). Cool off at a beach. Spend a second day visiting any towns you've yet to see, comparing main streets, beaches, and gelato. And fit in another hike, if you like.

In the evenings, linger at a restaurant, enjoy live music at a low-key club, stroll any of the towns, or take a glass of your favorite beverage out to the breakwater to watch the sun slip into the Mediterranean.

Getting Around the Cinque Terre

Within the Cinque Terre, you can connect towns by train, boat, or foot. Trains are the cheapest, fastest, and most frequent option. In calm weather, boats connect the towns nearly as frequently—and more scenically.

By Train: The five towns are just a few minutes apart by train. You must buy a new **individual ticket** for every train ride (€4), and tickets are valid only on the day of purchase. You can buy tickets and check schedules online (www.trenitalia.

com), at train-station windows or ticket machines, or at Cinque Terre park desks. The €16 **Cinque Terre Treno Card** pays for itself if you take four rides in one day, but its value comes more from convenience than economy (https://card.parconazionale5terre.it).

In peak season, trains connecting the five towns generally run two to three times hourly in each direction, but less frequently after about 20:00. Note that some trains do not stop at all five towns. Check schedules in advance (shops, hotels, and restaurants often post the current schedule). Trains from Levanto, Monterosso, Riomaggiore, or La Spezia sometimes skip lesser stations, so confirm that the train will stop at the town you need. (Train numbers starting with 21 or 24 generally stop at all five towns.) Northbound trains (using the tracks closest to the water) are going to Levanto, Genova, or Sestri Levante; southbound trains are headed for La Spezia. Know your train's number and final destination.

THE CINQUE TERRE AT A GLANCE

▲▲**Monterosso al Mare** Resorty, flat, and spread out, with a charming old town, a modern new town, and the Cinque Terre's best beaches, swimming, and nightlife. See page 546.

▲▲▲**Vernazza** The region's gem, crowned with a ruined castle above and a lively harborfront cradling a natural harbor below. See page 557.

▲**Corniglia** Quiet hilltop village with cooler temperatures, fewer tourists, and a tradition of fine wines. See page 568.

▲▲**Manarola** Mellow, hiking-focused waterfront village wrapped in vineyards and dotted with picturesque shops and cliff-climbing houses. See page 571.

▲▲**Riomaggiore** The most workaday of the five villages, with nightlife, too. See page 575.

By Boat: From Easter through October, a daily boat service connects Monterosso, Vernazza, Manarola, Riomaggiore, Porto Venere, and beyond. Though they can be very crowded, these boats provide a scenic way to get from town to town (operated by 5 Terre-Golfo dei Poeti, tel. 0187-732-987, www.navigazionegolfodeipoeti.it). Because tourists disembark onto little more than a plank, even just a small chop can cancel some or all of the stops.

The ticket price depends on the length of the boat ride (€7-18, €27 all-day pass, €35 adds Porto Venere). Buy tickets at the little stands at each town's harbor. Boats depart about hourly; schedules are posted online and at docks, harbor bars, Cinque Terre park offices, and hotels.

Rick's Tip: *To escape the crowds—or for a scenic splurge—*hire a captain *to ferry you between towns on a* private boat. *Split the cost among a few fellow travelers, and you have an affordable water taxi. Captains offer their services at the harbors in Monterosso, Vernazza, Manarola, and Riomaggiore.*

By Shuttle Bus: ATC shuttle buses (which locals call *pulmino*) connect each Cinque Terre town with its closest parking lot and various points in the hills (but they don't connect the five towns to each other). Buy tickets and get bus schedules at park info offices or TIs, or check times posted at bus stops (also online at www.atcesercizio.it). As you board, it's smart to tell the driver where you want to go. Some shuttles go beyond the parking lots and high into the hills—often terminating at the town's sanctuary church. To soak in the scenery, you can ride up and hike down.

Helpful Hints

Book in Advance: It's essential to reserve rooms well in advance for May, June, September, October, all summer weekends, and holidays (including Easter and April 25). Many accommodations in the Cinque Terre (especially in Vernazza) are *affittacamere,* or private rooms for rent. You get a key and come and go as you like, rarely seeing your landlord. Plan on paying cash. Some places have strict cancellation policies.

Pickpocket Alert: The Cinque Terre can be notoriously crowded and pickpockets (often groups of teens, frequently dressed as tourists), aggressively and expertly work the most congested areas. Be on guard, especially in train stations, on platforms, and on trains—particularly when getting on or off with a crush of people.

Money: You'll find ATMs and banks throughout the region.

Markets: Market days perk up the Cinque Terre from around 8:00 to 13:00 on Tuesday in Vernazza and on Thursday in Monterosso.

Booking Services: Arbaspàa, based in Manarola, sets up wine tastings, cooking classes, fishing trips, and more (www.arbaspaa.com). **Cinque Terre Riviera,** based in Vernazza, books rooms and apartments throughout the region, Vernazza opera tickets, cooking classes, and more (www.cinqueterreriviera.com). **BeautifuLiguria,** run by Anna Merulla, offers various excursions (www.beautifuliguria.com).

Local Guides: These guides are knowledgeable, a delight to be with, and charge from €125/half-day and €210/day: **Andrea Bordigoni** (mobile 393-133-9409, bordigo@inwind.it) and **Marco Brizzi** (mobile 328-694-2847, marco_brizzi@yahoo.it).

Baggage Storage and Delivery: You can pay to store bags at or near the train stations in Monterosso, Vernazza, and Riomaggiore. To transfer luggage from the station to your accommodations, call ahead and arrange with **Roberto Pecunia** (mobile 370-375-7972).

HIKING THE CINQUE TERRE

The five Cinque Terre towns are connected by a main coastal trail and a web of trails higher up. The main coastal trail has four sections—two that are open (Monterosso to Vernazza, and Vernazza to Corniglia) and two that are closed due to trail conditions (Corniglia to Manarola, and Manarola to Riomaggiore—the famed "Via dell'Amore"). Also closed is the alternate Riomaggiore-Manarola trail (via "La Beccara"). Visitors hiking on the main coastal trail must buy a trail pass (see below).

Navigation: Trails are marked with red-and-white paint, white arrows, and some signs (*sentiero* means trail). The main coastal trail is variously indicated as "SVA," "the Blue Trail," or #592. Maps aren't necessary for the basic coastal hikes. But for the more challenging routes up high, pick up a good hiking map (about €5, sold everywhere).

Hiking Conditions: In general, trails are narrow, steep, rocky, and come with lots of challenging steps. I get many emails from readers who say the trails were tougher than they'd expected. The rocks and metal grates can be slippery in the rain. Don't venture up on these rocky cliffs without sun protection, water, and proper shoes (no flip-flops).

When to Go: The coastal trail can be extremely crowded and very hot at midday. For the best light, coolest temperatures, and fewer crowds, start your hike early (by 8:00) or late (16:00 or 17:00). Before setting out for an evening hike, find out when the sun will set, and leave plenty of time to arrive at your destination before then; there's no lighting on the trails.

Rick's Tip: *ATC* **shuttle buses** *can make hiking easier, connecting coastal villages to trailheads higher up.* **Locals know all the options**—*and shuttle bus schedules—so ask around. Be aware that shuttles heading into the high country only run in summer, and just once or twice a day.*

Cinque Terre Park Cards

The Cinque Terre—villages and all—is a national park. Each town's train station has a Cinque Terre national park infor-

The trail views are worth the effort.

mation office, which generally also serves as an all-purpose town TI and gift shop. They can answer questions about trails (including conditions and closures), shuttle bus schedules, and so on. Or, check the park's website, www.parconazionale5 terre.it, and the blog CinqueTerreInsider. com, written by American expat Amy Inman—it has up-to-date practicalities for visitors to this always-in-flux region.

Visitors using the main coastal trail must buy a park card. (Cards are not needed to hike on higher trails.) Cards can be purchased on the park website, above, or at train stations, TIs, and trailheads, and are good for 24 or 48 hours after validation. Some area hotels sell discounted park cards to guests.

The **Cinque Terre Trekking Card** costs €7.50 for one day of hiking or €14.50 for two days (covers trails, free use of WCs, park Wi-Fi, and ATC shuttle buses, but not trains).

The **Cinque Terre Treno Card** covers what the Trekking Card does, but also includes local trains connecting all Cinque Terre towns, plus Levanto and La Spezia (€16/24 hours, €29/48 hours, validate card at train station by punching it in the machine). Even if you're not planning to hike, this card can be worth it just to save you time on buying train tickets.

Top Three Hikes

These three hikes each give the quintessential Cinque Terre hiking experience. The first two are part of the main coastal trail (and require the national park card); the third takes you much higher (and is free).

▲▲▲**Vernazza-Monterosso** (2 hours, 2 miles): The scenic up-and-down-a-lot trek from Vernazza to Monterosso is both challenging and rewarding. The trail is narrow, steep, and crumbly in spots, with a lot of steps but easy to follow. The views just out of Vernazza, looking back at the town, are spectacular. From there you'll gradually ascend to 550 feet, passing some scenic waterfalls populated by croaking

frogs. As you approach Monterosso, you'll descend steeply through vineyards—on very deep, knee-testing stairs—and eventually follow a rivulet to the sea. The last stretch is along a pleasant, paved pathway clinging to the cliff. You'll pop out right at Monterosso's refreshing old-town beach.

▲▲▲**Corniglia-Vernazza** (1.5 hours, 2 miles): The hike from Corniglia to Vernazza—the wildest and greenest section of the coast—is very rewarding but very hilly. From the Corniglia train station, zigzag up to the town (via the steep stairs, the longer road, or the shuttle bus). From Corniglia, you'll reach the trailhead on the main road, past Villa Cecio. You'll hike through vineyards toward Vernazza. After about 10 minutes, you'll see a faded sign to Guvano beach, far beneath you (formerly a nude beach—now closed). The scenic trail continues through lots of fragrant and flowery vegetation into Vernazza. If you need a break before reaching Vernazza, stop at Bar la Torre, with a strip of amazingly scenic and delightfully shady tables perched high above the town.

▲▲**Manarola-Corniglia via Volastra** (2.5 hours, 4 miles): This challenging hike from Manarola leads up to the village of Volastra, then north through high-altitude vineyard terraces, and steeply down through a forest to Corniglia. You can shave the two steepest miles off this route by taking the ATC shuttle bus from Manarola up to Volastra (about hourly, 15-minute trip).

If you'd rather hike to Volastra, you have two options: The national park's official route (trail #506) cuts up through the valley. Locals have cleared a more scenic but rougher alternate route that begins with the vineyard hike on my self-guided walk for Manarola (page 572); partway along this walk, where you reach the wooden religious scenes scampering up the hillside, take a sharp right and walk uphill, following signs for *Panoramico Volastra (Corniglia)*. While steeper than the official route, this trail follows the ridge at the top of the vineyard, with wonderful sea views.

Either way, in Volastra (where the shuttle bus drops off), look for *Corniglia* signs. From the front door of the church, directly across the piazza, find the trailhead (marked by an iron cross) for trail #586 to Case Pianca.

Here begins one of the region's finest hikes, tightroping along narrow trails tucked between vineyard terraces, with spectacular bird's-eye views over the entire Cinque Terre. You'll cut up and down the terraces a bit—just keep following the red-and-white markings and arrows. High above Corniglia, you'll reach a fork, where you turn left to proceed downhill on trail #587 to Corniglia.

Sanctuary Trails

Each of the five towns has its own sanctuary (with a chapel or church dedicated to the Virgin Mary), hovering in the hills a mile or two above town, and accessible by a long, steep hike (quiet and uncrowded).

Villagers feel deeply connected to these spiritual retreats, where they remember lost relatives and feel part of a timeless community. A network of "sanctuary trails" (no park card required) crisscrosses the hills above the main coastal route. There's no single path, but with a good map you can link up these moderately difficult trails.

In most towns, the shuttle bus can take you from the town center to the sanctuary—you could ride up and hike down. This works particularly well from Manarola and Vernazza. Or you can ride both ways (50 minutes round-trip, covered by one ticket).

MONTEROSSO AL MARE

Monterosso al Mare—the only Cinque Terre town with some flat land—has two parts: a new town (called Fegina) with a parking lot, train station, and TI; and an old town (Centro Storico), which cradles Old World charm in its small, crooked lanes. In the old town, you'll find hole-in-the-wall shops, rustic pastel townscapes, and a new generation of creative business owners eager to keep visitors happy. A handy pedestrian tunnel connects the old with the new.

This is a resort town with a few cars and lots of hotels, rentable beach umbrellas, and crowds. Strolling the waterfront promenade, you can pick out each of the Cinque Terre towns decorating the coast. After dark, they sparkle.

Orientation

Tourist Information: The TI, called Proloco Monterosso, is on the street below the train station (daily 9:00-18:30, longer hours in summer, shorter hours off-season, baggage storage, exit station and go left a few doors, tel. 0187-817-506, www.prolocomonterosso.it). Upstairs in the station is a Cinque Terre park info desk and a ticket office near platform 1 (usually daily 8:00-20:00, shorter hours off-season).

Arrival in Monterosso: Trains arrive in the new town. To reach most of my recommended hotels in the new town, turn right from the station. To get to the old town, turn left from the station—it's a scenic, flat 10-minute stroll.

Taxis usually wait outside the train station, or you can call one (€10 from station to old town, mobile 335-616-5842, 335-616-5845, or 335-628-0933). ATC **shuttle buses** also go to the old town and are cheaper, but only run about once an hour.

For **drivers,** Monterosso is 30 minutes off the freeway (exit: Carrodano-Levanto). About three miles above Monterosso, at an intersection, you must choose either *Monterosso Centro Storico* (old town) or *Monterosso Fegina* (new town and beachfront parking). You can't drive directly between the new town and old center. Parking is easy (except July-Aug and weekends in June) in the new town in the huge beachfront guarded lot. In the old town, find the Loreto parking garage on Via Roma, from which it's a 10-minute downhill walk to the main square.

Helpful Hints

Baggage Storage: The **TI** will store bags (€6/day—confirm closing time).

Laundry: For full-service, same-day laundry in the new town, try **Wash and Dry Lavarapido**. They'll pick up at your hotel, or you can drop it at their shop. Ask your hotelier to arrange the details (daily 9:00-19:00, Via Molinelli 17, mobile 339-484-0940, Lucia and Ivano). In the old town, head to **Luètu Lavanderia,** uphill on Via Roma and across from the post office (daily 8:00-20:00, tel. 328-286-1908).

Monterosso Walks

These self-guided walks will introduce you to Monterosso. The first one, focusing on the mostly level town center, takes about 30 minutes. For the second one, you'll summit the adjacent hill—allow an hour or so.

◗ *Monterosso Harbor and Town Walk*

• *Hike out from the dock in the old town and stand atop the concrete breakwater. (If you're arriving by boat, you'll disembark here.)*

Breakwater: From this point you can survey Monterosso's old town (straight ahead) and new town (stretching to the left, with train station and parking lot). Looking to the right, you can see all *cinque* of the *terre* from one spot: Vernazza, Corniglia (above the shore), Manarola, and a few buildings of Riomaggiore beyond that.

The partial breakwater is designed to save the beach from washing away. While old-timers remember a vast beach, their grandchildren truck in sand each spring to give tourists something to bask on. (The Nazis liked the Cinque Terre, too—find two of their bomb-hardened bunkers embedded in the bluff.)

The fancy four-star Hotel Porto Roca (the pink building high on the hill, on the far right of the harbor) marks the trail to Vernazza. High above, you see an example of the costly roads built in the 1980s to connect the Cinque Terre towns with the freeway over the hills.

Monterosso al Mare

Monterosso al Mare

Accommodations
1 Hotel Villa Steno
2 Il Giardino Incantato
3 Hotel Pasquale
4 Locanda il Maestrale
5 Hotel la Colonnina
6 Albergo Marina
7 Manuel's Guesthouse
8 L'Antica Terrazza & Gastronomia "San Martino"
9 Albergo al Carugio
10 La Villa degli Argentieri
11 To Hotel Villa Adriana
12 Hotel la Spiaggia
13 Hotel Punta Mesco
14 Affittacamere Rist. Il Gabbiano
15 Le Sirene/Raggi di Sole

Eateries & Nightlife
16 Ristorante Belvedere
17 Il Casello
18 L'Ancora della Tortuga & Torre Aurora
19 Via Venti
20 L'Osteria & Emy's Way Pizzeria Friggitoria
21 Ristorante al Pozzo
22 Páe Veciu
23 La Smorfia
24 Miky
25 La Cantina di Miky
26 Il Frantoio Focacceria

The two prominent capes (Punta di Montenero to the right, and Punta Mesco to the left) define the Cinque Terre region. The closer Punta Mesco is part of a protected marine sanctuary and home to a rare sea grass that provides an ideal home for fish eggs. Buoys keep fishing boats away. The cape was once a quarry,

providing employment to locals who chipped out the stones used to build the local towns (the greenish stones making up part of the breakwater are from there).

On the far end of the new town, marking the best free beach around, you can just see the statue named *Il Gigante* (hard to spot because it blends in with the gray

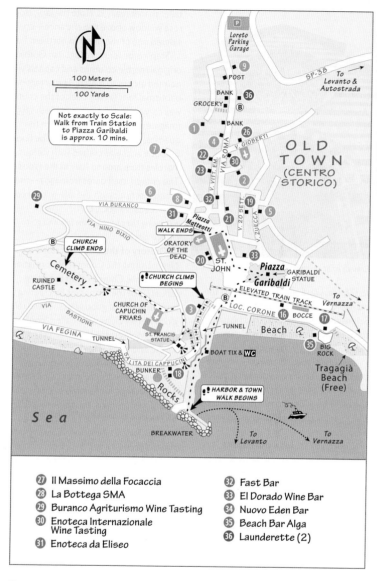

100 Meters
100 Yards

Not exactly to Scale:
Walk from Train Station
to Piazza Garibaldi
is approx. 10 mins.

Loreto
Parking
Garage

POST

BANK
GROCERY
BANK

OLD
TOWN
(CENTRO
STORICO)

To
Levanto &
Autostrada

V. ROMA
V. GIOBERTI
V. VIT. EM.
V. 20 SETT.
V. ZUECCA
VIA BURANCO
VIA NINO BIXIO

Piazza
Matteotti

WALK ENDS

ORATORY
OF THE
DEAD

CHURCH CLIMB
BEGINS

CHURCH
CLIMB ENDS

Cemetery

RUINED
CASTLE

VIA
BASTIONE

VIA FEGINA

TUNNEL

CHURCH OF
CAPUCHIN
FRIARS

ST. FRANCIS
STATUE

SALITA DEI CAPPUCCINI

BUNKER

Rocks

BOAT TIX & WC

HARBOR & TOWN
WALK BEGINS

BREAKWATER

Sea

ST.
JOHN

Piazza
Garibaldi

GARIBALDI
STATUE

ELEVATED TRAIN TRACK

LOC. CORONE
BOCCE
TUNNEL
Beach

BIG
ROCK

Tragagià
Beach
(Free)

To
Vernazza

To
Levanto

To
Vernazza

27 Il Massimo della Focaccia
28 La Bottega SMA
29 Buranco Agriturismo Wine Tasting
30 Enoteca Internazionale Wine Tasting
31 Enoteca da Eliseo

32 Fast Bar
33 El Dorado Wine Bar
34 Nuovo Eden Bar
35 Beach Bar Alga
36 Launderette (2)

rock). It's 45 feet tall and once held a trident. Made of reinforced concrete, it dates from the early 20th century, when it supported a dancing terrace for a *fin de siècle* villa. A violent storm left the giant holding nothing but memories.

• *From the breakwater, walk toward the old town and under the train tracks. Then venture right into the square and find the statue of a dandy holding what looks like a box cutter (near the big playground).*

Piazza Garibaldi: The statue honors Giuseppe Garibaldi, the dashing firebrand revolutionary who, in the 1860s, helped unite the people of Italy into a modern nation. Facing Garibaldi, with your back

Church of St. John the Baptist

taller than it really is. Note the lacy, stone rose window above the entrance—considered one of the finest in northern Italy.

Step inside for more Ligurian Gothic: original marble columns and capitals with pointed arches to match. The octagonal baptismal font (in the back of the church) was carved from Carrara marble in 1359. Imagine the job getting that from the quarries, about 40 miles away. The fine Baroque altar was crafted with various marbles from around Italy in the 1700s. The church itself dates from 1307—the proud inscription on the left-middle column reads "MilloCCCVII."

• *Leaving the church, turn left and go to church again.*

Oratory of the Dead (Oratorio dei Neri): During the Counter-Reformation, the Catholic Church offset the rising influence of the Lutherans by creating brotherhoods of good works. These religious Rotary clubs were called "confraternities." Monterosso had two, nicknamed White and Black. This building is the oratory of the Black group, whose mission—as the macabre interior indicates—was to arrange for funerals and take care of widows, orphans, the shipwrecked, and the souls of those who ignore the request for a €1 donation. It dates from the 16th century, and membership has passed from father to son for generations. Notice the fine, carved pews (c. 1700) just inside the door, and the haunted-house chandeliers. Look up at the ceiling to find the symbol of the confraternity: a skull-and-crossbones and an hourglass...death awaits us all.

• *On that cheery note, you can end your walking tour here to enjoy strolling, shopping, gelato-licking, a day at the beach...or all of the above. But if you're up for a hike, read on.*

to the sea, you'll see (on your right) the orange City Hall. You'll also see A Ca' du Sciensa restaurant, which has historic town photos inside and upstairs; you're welcome to pop in for a look.

Just under the bell tower (with your back to the sea, it's on your left), a set of covered arcades facing the sea is where the old-timers hang out. The crenellated bell tower marks the church.

• *Go to church.*

Church of St. John the Baptist (Chiesa di San Giovanni Battista): First, walk along the right side the church. Near the second side door, find the high-water mark *(altezza massima)* from an October 1966 flood—which also famously devastated Florence. Nearby, a second (higher) plaque commemorates a 2011 flood that swept through Monterosso and Vernazza, taking the lives of four villagers.

Now hook left, around the church—and appreciate its black-and-white-striped main facade. With white marble from Carrara and green marble from Punta Mesco, the church is typical of the region's Gothic style. The church's marble stripes get narrower the higher they go, creating the illusion that the church is

⮕ *Capuchin Church and Climb*

The hill that separates the old town from the new rewards anyone who climbs up with a peaceful church, a cemetery in the clouds, and a panoramic view.

St. Francis keeps an eye on Monterosso from above.

• *From the old town's beachfront, find the brick steps squeezed between Hotel Pasquale and its restaurant, and start climbing. The lane is signed* Salita dei Cappuccini *(nicknamed* Zii di Frati)*, or...*

Switchbacks of the Friars: Follow the yellow brick road (OK, it's orange...). Partway up, detour left to the terrace above the seaside castle at a statue of St. Francis and a wolf taking in a grand view. Enjoy an opportunity to see all five of the Cinque Terre towns. Then backtrack 20 yards to the switchback and continue uphill.

• *When you reach a gate marked* Convento e Chiesa Cappuccini, *you have arrived at the...*

Church of the Capuchin Friars: The former monastery is now manned by a single caretaker friar. (If you meet Father Renato, take a moment to speak with him—he's a joyful soul.) Before stepping inside, notice the church's striped Romanesque facade. It's all fake. Tap it—no marble, just cheap 18th-century stucco. Go inside and sit in the rear pew. The high altarpiece painting of St. Francis can be rolled up on special days to reveal a statue of Mary behind it.

The fine painting of the **Crucifixion (on the left)** recalls how, when Jesus died, the earth went dark. Notice the eclipsed sun in the painting, just to the right of the cross. Do the electric candles work? Pick one up, pray for peace, and plug it in. (Leave an offering, or unplug it and put it back.)

• *Leave and turn left through another gate to hike 100 yards uphill to the cemetery filling the ruined castle. Reaching the cemetery's gate, look back and enjoy the view over the town.*

Cemetery in the Ruined Castle: In the Dark Ages, the village huddled behind this castle. You're looking at the oldest part of Monterosso, tucked behind the hill, out of view of 13th-century pirates.

Respectfully explore the cemetery. On the headstones, Q.R.P. is *Qui Riposa in Pace* (a.k.a. R.I.P.). Climb to the very summit—the castle's keep, or place of last refuge. Priests are buried in a line of graves closest to the sea, but facing inland, looking toward the town's holy sanctuary high on the hillside (its triangular steeple just peeking above the trees). Each Cinque Terre town has a lofty sanctuary, dedicated to Mary and dear to the village hearts.

• *Your tour is over—any trail leads you back into town.*

Experiences
Beaches

Monterosso's **new town** has easily the Cinque Terre's best—and most crowded—

beach (immediately in front of the train station). Most of the beach is private, where (at Stella Marina) you'll pay €20 to rent two chairs and an umbrella for the day (prices get soft in the afternoon). Light lunches are served by beach cafés to sunbathers at their lounge chairs. Various outfits rent kayaks and stand-up paddleboards (look for signs at the west end of the beach). If there are no umbrellas on a stretch of beach, it's public (free). A free beach is at the far west end, near the Gigante statue.

The **old town** also has a predominantly private beach; rent umbrellas, chairs, kayaks, and paddleboats from Beach Bar Alga, which is also a scenic spot for a drink. Tucked just beyond the private beach—under the Il Casello restaurant at the east end of town—is the free public beach called Tragagià, which is gravelly and generally less crowded (showers).

Wine Tasting

Buranco Agriturismo welcomes visitors to tastings on their expansive terrace with views over the vineyards. You'll taste some of their wines plus grappa (firewater) and *limoncino,* while snacking on bruschetta, olives, and the like. Call or email ahead (€20-30/person, tastings usually daily 12:00-18:00, follow Via Buranco uphill to path, 10 minutes above town, mobile 349-434-8046, www.burancocinqueterre.it, info@buranco.it).

Enoteca Internazionale is a good place in town to sample local wines. Mario is knowledgeable and serves five wines for €20 (his bruschetta makes a fine light meal as you're sipping, open daily until late, Via Roma 62, tel. 0187-817-278).

Boat Rides

In addition to the regularly scheduled big boats (see page 543), you can hire your own captain for transfers to other towns or for a lazy sightseeing cruise. **Stefano** has two six-person boats: the *Matilde* and the *Babaah* (about €100/hour, mobile 333-821-2007, www.matildenavigazione. com). **Diego** offers half-day, daylong, and sunset excursions for up to seven on his cushy boat (group tours-€70, daily 10:30-13:30 & 17:30-20:30, best to email or call to confirm and reserve; mobile 339-233-9297, www.cinqueterreboat.com). **Sea Breeze Boat Tours** arranges day and *aperitivo* sunset tours, and will shuttle you to any of the coastal towns (€85-140/person, mobile 328-824-6889 or 338-809-9278, www.seabreezeboattours.com).

Nightlife

Enoteca da Eliseo, my favorite wine bar in town, comes with operatic ambience. Taste wine by the glass (*bicchiere*) or select a bottle, then enjoy the wine, a few included nibbles, and views of the village action. They also stock more than a hundred varieties of *grappa* (Wed-Mon 14:00-23:30, closed Tue, Piazza Matteotti 3, a block inland behind church, tel. 0187-817-308).

Fast Bar is the best bar in town for young travelers and night owls. Customers mix travel tales with big, cold beers, and the crowd (and the rock 'n' roll) gets noisier as the night rolls on (cheap *panini,* salads, and other light meals usually served until midnight, open 9:30-late, in the old town at Via Roma 13).

La Cantina di Miky, in the new town just beyond the train station, is a trendy bar-restaurant with an extensive cocktail and *grappa* menu. Try the fun "five villages" wine tasting or top-end Italian microbrews (Thu-Tue until late, closed Wed, Via Fegina 90, tel. 0187-802-525).

El Dorado Wine Bar is the old-town nighttime hangout, offering music, drinks, and people-watching (Piazza Garibaldi 22, daily 10:00-2:00 in the morning, tel. 331-475-9611).

Beach Bars: In the new town, try **Nuovo Eden Bar,** overlooking the beach by the big rock (drinks come with a light snack, good ice cream). In the old town, **Beach Bar Alga** has an island ambience (all outside, daily until 20:00).

Sleeping

Rooms in Monterosso are a better value than similar rooms in crowded Vernazza, and the proprietors seem more genuine and welcoming.

In the Old Town

$$$$ Hotel Villa Steno is lovingly managed and features great view balconies, panoramic gardens, and a roof terrace with sun beds. Of their 16 rooms, 14 have view balconies (RS%, family rooms, air-con, hearty buffet breakfast, elevator, laundry service, ask about pay parking when you reserve, hike up to their panoramic terrace, closed Nov-March, Via Roma 109, tel. 0187-817-028 or 0187-818-336, www.villasteno.com, steno@pasini.com). It's a 15-minute climb (or €10 taxi ride) from the train station to the top of the old town. My readers get a free Cinque Terre info packet and a glass of local wine at check in—ask for it.

$$$$ Il Giardino Incantato ("The Enchanted Garden") is a charming, comfortable four-room B&B with impressive attention to detail in a tastefully renovated 16th-century Ligurian home in the heart of the old town. Sip their homemade *limoncino* at *aperitivo* time, and have breakfast under lemon trees in the delightful hidden garden (air-con, free minibar and tea-and-coffee service, laundry service, Via Mazzini 18, tel. 0187-818-315, mobile 333-264-9252, www.ilgiardinoincantato.net, giardino_incantato@libero.it).

$$$$ Hotel Pasquale is modern and comfortable with 15 seaview rooms. It's just a few steps from the beach, boat dock, and tunnel to the new town. While there is some train noise, the soundtrack is mostly a lullaby of waves (RS%, family room, air-con, elevator, laundry service, closed Nov-March, Via Fegina 4, tel. 0187-817-550 or 0187-817-477, www.hotelpasquale.it, pasquale@pasini.com).

$$$ Locanda il Maestrale rents six stylish rooms in a sophisticated and peaceful little inn. Although renovated with modern comforts, it retains its centuries-old character under frescoed ceilings. The peaceful sun terrace overlooking the old town and Via Roma action is a delight. Guests enjoy complimentary drinks and snacks each afternoon (air-con, Via Roma 37, tel. 0187-817-013, mobile 338-4530-531, www.locandamaestrale.net, maestrale@monterossonet.com).

$$$ Hotel la Colonnina has 22 big rooms, generous and meticulously cared-for public spaces, a cozy garden, and an inviting shared seaview terrace with sun beds. It's buried in the town's fragrant and sleepy back streets (family rooms, all but one room has a private terrace, cash preferred but cards accepted, air-con, fridges, elevator, a block inland from main square at Via Zuecca 6, tel. 0187-817-439, www.lacolonninacinqueterre.it, info@lacolonninacinqueterre.it).

$$$ Albergo Marina has 23 pleasant rooms and a garden with lemon trees. They serve a filling breakfast buffet and host a happy hour most days on the terrace (RS%, family rooms, elevator, air-con, fridges, free kayak and snorkel equipment, Via Buranco 40, tel. 0187-817-613, www.hotelmarina5terre.com, marina@hotelmarina5terre.com).

$$$ Manuel's Guesthouse, perched high above the town among terraces, is a garden getaway with six big, artfully decorated rooms and a grand view. After climbing the killer stairs from the town center, their killer terrace is hard to leave—especially after a few drinks (cash only, air-con, up about 100 steps behind church—you can ask them to carry your bags up the hill, Via San Martino 39, mobile 333-439-0809, www.manuelsguesthouse.com, manuelsguesthouse@libero.it).

$$ L'Antica Terrazza rents four tight, classy rooms right in town. With a pretty terrace overlooking the pedestrian street, it's a good deal (single room with private bath down the hall, air-con, Vicolo San

Martino 1, mobile 347-132-6213, www.anti
caterrazza.com, post@anticaterrazza.com).

$ Albergo al Carugio has nine practical
rooms in a big apartment-style building
with a small patio at the top of the old
town. It's quiet, comfy, and a fine budget
value; one room has a private terrace (no
breakfast, air-con, fridges, Via Roma 100,
tel. 0187-817-453, www.alcarugio.it, info@
alcarugio.it).

In the New Town

$$$$ La Villa degli Argentieri offers 11
spacious rooms, many with balconies,
from a choice position at the quiet end
of the new town's beachfront street. The
inviting rooftop terrace with sunbeds has
panoramic views (air-con, elevator, Via
Fegina 120, tel. 0187-818-963, www.lavilla
degliargentieri.it, info@lavilladegli
argentieri.it).

$$$$ Hotel Villa Adriana is big, contemporary, and bright, with a peaceful garden, a pool, free parking, and a no-stress
style. They rent 55 sterile rooms—some
with terraces and/or sea views—ask for
one when you reserve (family rooms, air-
con, refrigerators, elevator, free loaner
bikes, affordable dinners, Via IV Novembre 23, tel. 0187-818-109, www.villaadriana.
info, info@villaadriana.info).

$$$$ Hotel la Spiaggia, facing the
beach, has 19 rooms (half with sea views)
and a quiet garden retreat (cash only,
air-con, elevator, free parking—reserve
in advance, Via Lungomare 96, tel. 0187-
817-567, www.laspiaggiahotel5terre.com,
laspiaggiahotel@gmail.com, Maria). They
also rent four pricey, ultra-mod rooms on
the seafront promenade.

$$$ Hotel Punta Mesco is a tidy, well-
run little haven renting 17 quiet, casual
rooms at a good price. Most rooms have
small terraces backed up to the building
next door (family room, air-con, parking, Via
Molinelli 35, tel. 0187-817-495, www.hotel
puntamesco.it, info@hotelpuntamesco.it).

**$$ Affittacamere Ristorante il Gab-
biano,** a touristy restaurant on the beach-
front road, rents five basic, dated, but
affordable rooms upstairs. Three face the
sea (two with small balconies); two have
terraces overlooking a garden. Check in
at the restaurant (big family rooms, cash
only, no breakfast, air-con, Via Fegina 84,
tel. 0187-817-578, www.affittacamere
ristorante-ilgabbiano.com, lella-v71@
hotmail.it).

$ Le Sirene/Raggi di Sole, with nine
simple rooms in two humble buildings, is a
decent budget choice in this pricey town.
It's run from a hole-in-the-wall reception
desk a block from the station. I'd request
the Le Sirene building, which has no
train noise (RS%, family rooms, fans, Via
Molinelli 1A, mobile 331-788-1088 or 329-
595-1063, www.sirenerooms.com, sirene
rooms@gmail.com).

Eating
With a Sea View

$$ Ristorante Belvedere, big and sprawl-
ing, serves good-value meals indoors or
outdoors on the harborfront. Their huge
€49 *anfora belvedere*—mixed seafood stew
dumped dramatically at the table into your
bowl—feeds four. Their *misto mare* plate
(2-person minimum, €16/person), a fishy
treat, nearly makes an entire meal (Wed-
Mon 12:00-14:30 & 18:00-22:00, closed
Tue, on the harbor in the old town, tel.
0187-817-033).

$$ Il Casello offers outdoor terrace
seating on a little bluff overlooking the old
town beach when the weather's nice. It's a
pleasant spot for pasta, seafood, or a drink
(daily 12:00-22:00, mobile 333-492-7629).

$$$ L'Ancora della Tortuga is a top
option in Monterosso for seaview ele-
gance, with gorgeous outdoor seat-
ing high on a bluff and a white-table-
cloth-and-candles interior fit for an
admiral. The food and service can be
three-star, but the setting is five-star.
Consider their €40 tasting *menu* (Tue-
Sun 12:30-15:30 & 18:30-21:30, closed Mon
and when stormy; at the tip of the point
between the old and new towns—just

Cinque Terre Cuisine

Hanging out at a seaview restaurant while sampling local specialties could become one of your favorite Cinque Terre memories. For more on Italian food, see the "Eating" section of the Practicalities chapter.

The key staple is **anchovies** (*acciughe;* ah-CHOO-gay)—ideally served the day they're caught. If you've always hated anchovies, try them fresh here. They're prepared in a dizzying variety of ways: marinated, salted, drenched in lemon juice, butterflied and deep-fried (sometimes with a tasty garlic/vinegar sauce called *giada*), and so on. ***Tegame alla vernazzana*** is the most typical main course in Vernazza: a layered, casserole-like dish of whole anchovies, potatoes, tomatoes, white wine, oil, and herbs.

Seafood is plentiful. You'll often see **muscoli ripieni** (stuffed mussels) on menus. And, while **antipasto** means cheese and salami in Tuscany, here you'll get ***antipasti frutti di mare*** (or simply *antipasti misti*): a plate of mixed "fruits of the sea." For two diners, splitting one of these and a pasta dish can be plenty.

This region is the birthplace of **pesto**. You'll see it on gnocchi or on pasta that's either *trenette* (ruffled on one side) or *trofie* (short, dense twists).

Pansotti are ravioli with ricotta and a mixture of greens, often served with a walnut sauce (*salsa di noci*).

Focaccia—pillowy, flat, salty, olive-oily bread—also originates here. Focaccia comes plain or with onions, sage, or olives. Bakeries sell it in rounds or slices by weight (a portion is about 100 grams, or *un etto*).

Farinata, a humble flatbread snack sold at pizza and focaccia places, is made from chickpea flour, water, oil, and pepper and baked on a copper tray in a wood-burning stove. It's dense, filling, and less flavorful than focaccia.

The region also loves its locally grown lemons. The popular lemon liqueur is called **limoncino** (a.k.a. *limoncello*).

Vino delle Cinque Terre flows cheap and easy throughout the region. It's a white wine—crisp, refreshing, and great with seafood. Local wines are typically blends, predominantly using the bosco grape, found only here. For a sweet but potent dessert wine, ***sciacchetrà*** (shah-keh-TRAH) is worth a try (18 percent alcohol, often served with dunkable cookies).

outside the tunnel; tel. 0187-800-065, mobile 333-240-7956).

$$$$ Torre Aurora is a top-end restaurant where you'll dine outside (wrapped in a blanket if it's cold) around the medieval tower with commanding views while enjoying simple yet creative dishes. Reservations are smart (daily in good weather, mobile 366-145-3702, www. torreaurorachinqueterre.com). They serve cocktails outside of mealtime.

In the Old Town

$$$ Via Venti is a quiet little trattoria, hidden in an alley deep in the heart of the old town, serving imaginative seafood dishes. Be tempted by their gnocchi with crab, ravioli stuffed with fresh fish, and pear-and-pecorino pasta. The outdoor seating is as humdrum as the interior—but you're here for the food (Fri-Wed 12:00-14:30 & 18:30-22:30, closed Thu, Via XX Settembre 32, tel. 0187-818-347).

$ Gastronomia "San Martino" is a tiny, humble combination of takeaway and sit-down café with surprisingly affordable, quality dishes. Eat at one of the few tables—inside or out on a pleasant street—or find a driftwood log for a feast-to-go (Tue-Sun 12:00-15:00 & 18:00-22:00, closed Mon, next to recommended L'Antica Terrazza hotel at Vicolo San Martino 3, mobile 346-109-7338).

$$ L'Osteria is a delightful little family-run place serving "cuisine with passion" at wonderful prices. Their Possa wine, from vineyards close to the sea, is the oyster of local wines (Tue-Sun lunch served 12:00-14:30, evening seatings at 19:00 and 21:00, closed Mon, Via Vittorio Emanuele 5, tel. 0187-819-224).

$$$ Ristorante al Pozzo is a favorite among locals. They have one of the best wine lists in town, serve only homemade pasta, and are known for their raw fish and wonderful seafood *antipasti misti* (Fri-Wed 12:00-15:00 & 18:30-22:30, closed Thu, Via Roma 24, tel. 0187-817-575).

$$ Páe Veciu, tucked away from the hubbub, has a short, creative menu of well-prepared seafood, pastas, and a few meat dishes. Eat inside in view of the kitchen or at one of the few streetside tables. Run by the folks from the recommended Buranco Agriturismo, it features a good selection of local wines (daily 11:30-15:00 & 18:30-22:00, Via Vittorio Emanuele 69, mobile 327-941-0430).

$ La Smorfia—a local favorite—cooks up good pizza in a sloppy setting that somehow seems to say, "Great pizza enjoyed here." Their large pizzas can feed three (Fri-Wed 11:00-24:00, closed Thu, Via Vittorio Emanuele 73, tel. 0187-818-395).

In the New Town

$$$$ Miky is packed with a well-dressed clientele who know their seafood. For elegantly presented, top-quality food that celebrates local ingredients and traditions, it's worth the steep prices. Their "pizza pasta" is served in a bowl topped with a thin pizza crust dome, then flambéed at your table (Wed-Mon 12:00-15:00 & 19:00-23:00, closed Tue, reservations wise, 100 yards from train station at Via Fegina 104, tel. 0187-817-608, www.ristorantemiky.it).

$$$ La Cantina di Miky, a few doors down from the station, is more youthful and informal than Miky, yet serves artfully crafted Ligurian specialties. Sit downstairs, in the garden, or on the promenade overlooking the sea (creative desserts, large selection of Italian microbrews, Thu-Tue 12:00-24:00, closed Wed, Via Fegina 90, tel. 0187-802-525). This place doubles as a cocktail bar in the evenings.

Light Meals and Takeout Food

In the Old Town: Lots of shops and bakeries sell pizza and focaccia to eat in or take out for an easy picnic. **$ Il Frantoio Focacceria** serves tasty pizza and focaccia (Fri-Wed 9:00-14:00 & 16:30-20:00, closed Thu, just off Via Roma at Via Gioberti 1). **$ Emy's Way Pizzeria Friggitoria** offers pasta, thick-crust pizza (whole and by the slice), and deep-fried seafood in to-go cones (daily 11:00-20:00, later in summer, along the skinny street next to the church, tel. 331-788-1088, Emiliano).

In the New Town: For a quick bite right at the train station (or on the beach), try **$ Il Massimo della Focaccia** for quiche-like tortes, sandwiches, focaccia pizzas, and desserts with a sea view (Thu-Tue 9:00-19:00, closed Wed except June-Aug, Via Fegina 50 at the station). **La Bottega SMA** is a smart minimart with fresh produce, *antipasti,* deli items, pay-by-the-weight sandwiches, and other picnic fare (daily 8:00-13:00 & 16:30-19:30 except closed Sun afternoon, shorter hours off-season, near Lavarapido at Vittoria Gianni 21).

VERNAZZA

With the closest thing to a natural harbor—overseen by a ruined castle, a stout stone church, and a pastel canyon of fisherfolk homes—Vernazza is the jewel of the Cinque Terre. Only the regular, noisy train reminds you of the modern world.

Proud of their Vernazzan heritage, the town's 500 residents like to brag: "Vernazza is locally owned. Portofino has sold out." Fearing change, proponents of keeping Vernazza small stopped the construction of a major road into the town and region. Families are tight and go back centuries; you'll notice certain surnames (such as Basso and Moggia) everywhere.

The action is at the harbor, where you'll find outdoor eateries ringing a humble piazza, a restaurant hanging on the edge of the castle, and a breakwater with a promenade, corralled by a natural amphitheater of terraced hills. Join (or watch) the locals devoting their leisure time to the *passeggiata*—strolling lazily together up and down the main street. Learn—and live—the phrase *"la vita pigra di Vernazza"* (the lazy life of Vernazza).

Orientation

Tourist Information: At the train station, you can get answers to basic questions at the gift shop/park office (daily 8:00-20:00, closed in winter, tel. 0187-812-533, WCs just down the track; see "Helpful Hints," later, for baggage storage).

Boats are a way of life in Vernazza.

ITALY

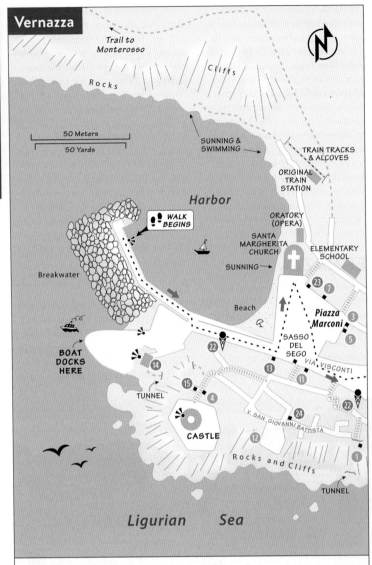

Accommodations

1. La Malà & La Marina Rooms
2. Vernazza sul Mare
3. Nicolina Rooms Reception & Ristorante Pizzeria Vulnetia
4. Monica Lercari Rooms
5. Francamaria Reception & Albergo Barbara Rooms
6. Vernazza Rooms Reception
7. Martina Callo Rooms & Trattoria del Capitano
8. Casa Cato
9. Giuliano Basso Rooms
10. Camere Fontanavecchia
11. Gianni Franzi Reception/Ristorante
12. Gianni Franzi Rooms

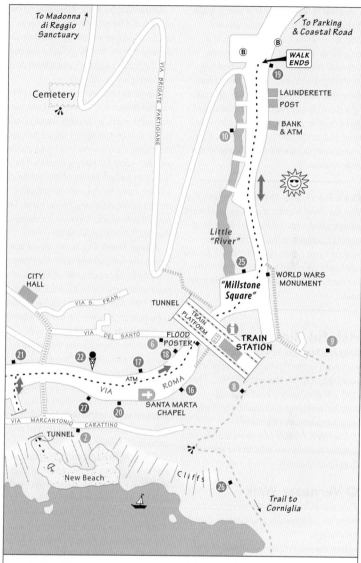

Eateries & Other

⑬ Gambero Rosso
⑭ Ristorante Belforte
⑮ Ristorante al Castello
⑯ Trattoria da Sandro
⑰ Antica Osteria il Baretto
⑱ Blue Marlin Bar
⑲ Il Pirata delle Cinque Terre Café
⑳ Lunch Box
㉑ Grocery
㉒ Gelateria (3)
㉓ Ananasso Bar
㉔ Vernazza Wine Experience
㉕ Cinque Sensi Wine Tastings
㉖ Bar la Torre
㉗ Cinque Terre Riviera Agency
(Room Rental; Opera Tickets)

Arrival in Vernazza: The town's **train station** is only about three train cars long, so most cars come to a stop in a long, dimly lit tunnel. Get out anyway, and walk through the tunnel—heading for the light—to reach the station. From there the main street flows through town right down to the harbor. If you're sleeping here, many locals who rent rooms will meet you at the station and walk you to your place (call ahead to tell them which train you're on).

Rick's Tip: *A steep 10-minute hike in either direction from Vernazza gives you a* **classic village photo op.** *For the best light, head toward Corniglia in the morning—best views are just before the ticket booth for the national park—and toward Monterosso in the evening—best views are after the ticket booth.*

Helpful Hints

Baggage Storage: You can pay to leave your bags at the train station TI/gift shop (daily 9:00-19:00, closed in winter). The staff will also happily haul your luggage between the train station and your accommodations (€4/piece).

Laundry: A small self-serve launderette is at the top of town next to the post office (daily 9:00-22:00).

❷ Vernazza Walk

This self-guided walk gives you a quick overview of the town and starts out on its breakwater.

• *From the train station, walk downhill and all the way out onto the breakwater. Find a comfortable and safe place to sit and get to know Vernazza.*

The Town: Before the 11th century, pirates made this coast uninhabitable, so the first Vernazzans lived in the hills above. The town's towers, fortified walls, and hillside terracing date mostly from the 12th through 15th century.

In the Middle Ages, there was no beach or square. The water went right up to the buildings, where boats would tie up, Venetian-style. Buildings had a water gate (facing today's square) and a front door on the higher inland side.

Vernazza has two halves. *Sciuiu* (Vernazzan dialect for "flowery") is the sunny side on the left, and *luvegu* (dank) is the shady side on the right. Houses below the castle were connected by an interior arcade—ideal for fleeing attacks. The "Ligurian pastel" colors of the buildings are regulated by the regional government's commissioner of good taste. The square before you is known for some of the area's finest restaurants.

Above Town: The small, **round tower** above the red building is another part of the city fortifications, reminding us of the town's importance in the Middle Ages. Back then, Genoa's enemies (rival maritime republics) were Vernazza's enemies.

Vineyards fill the mountainside beyond the town. Notice the many terraces. For six centuries, the economy was based on wine and olive oil. Then came the 1980s—and the tourists. Locals turned to tourism to make a living, and stopped tending the land, though many still maintain their small plots and proudly serve their family wines.

Church, School, and City Hall: Vernazza's Ligurian Gothic **church,** built with black stones quarried from Punta Mesco (the distant point between Monterosso and Levanto), dates from 1318. Note the gray stone (on the left) that marks the church's 16th-century expansion. The gray-and-red house above the spire is the **elementary school** (about 25 children attend). Older students go to the "big city," La Spezia. The red building on the hill to the right of the schoolhouse is the **City Hall.** Finally, on the top of the hill, is the **town cemetery.** It's only fair that hardworking Vernazzans—who spend their lives climbing up and down the hillsides—are rewarded with a world-class view from their eternal resting place.

• *Look high on your right to the castle.*

Castle (Castello Doria): The castle, which is now just stones and a grassy park with super views, still guards the town (€1.50, daily 10:00-20:00, summer until 21:00, closed Nov-March; from harbor, take stairs by Trattoria Gianni and follow *Ristorante al Castello* signs, the tower is a few steps beyond). This was the town's watchtower back in pirate days.

Ristorante Belforte, in the squat tower below the castle overlooking the water, is a great spot for a glass of wine or a meal. From the breakwater, you could follow the rope to the restaurant and pop inside, past an actual submarine door. A photo of a major storm showing the entire tower under a wave (not uncommon in the winter) hangs near the bar.

Harbor: In a moderate storm, you'd get soaked, as waves routinely crash over the *molo* (breakwater, built in 1972). Waves can rearrange the huge rocks—depositing them from the breakwater onto the piazza and its benches. Freak waves have even washed away tourists squinting excitedly into their cameras.

Vernazza's **fishing fleet** is down to just a few boats with net spools, but Vernazzans are still more likely to own a boat than a car. Boats are moored on buoys, except in winter or when the red storm flag indicates rough seas (see the pole at

the start of the breakwater). When the red flag flies, boat owners are permitted to pull them up onto the square—which is usually reserved for restaurant tables.

• *Stroll from the breakwater to the harbor square. Look for a small historic stone just before the narrow stairway on the right.*

Harbor Square (Piazza Marconi): Vernazza, with the Cinque Terre's only natural harbor, was established as the sole place boats could pick up the fine local wine. The two-foot-high square **stone** at the foot of the stairs is marked *Sasso del Sego* (stone of tallow). Workers crushed animal flesh and fat in its basin to make tallow, which drained out from the tiny hole below. The tallow was then used to waterproof boats or wine barrels.

Take some time to appreciate the medieval stonework and chestnut timbers of the restaurant interiors facing the harbor. From here steps lead to your right up to the castle.

Towns along this coast were designed as what's called a "Ligurian Palazzata"—an interlinked series of buildings intended to provide protection from seaborne attacks. Vernazza's harborfront retains its thousand-year-old "stockade" of buildings, connected with tiny and easy-to-defend staircases leading from the vulnerable harbor higher into the community.

• *Cross to the church side of the harbor, and peek into the tiny street leading away from the water with its commotion of arches.*

Vernazza's harbor and breakwater

Castle at Vernazza

Vernazza's most characteristic side streets (caruggi) lead up from here.

Vernazza's Church: Vernazza's harborfront church sits on the tiny piazza, decorated with a river-rock mosaic. This popular hangout spot is where the town's older ladies soak up the last bit of sun, and kids enjoy a patch of level ball field. The church, nestled awkwardly into the rocks, is unusual for its east-facing (rather than the standard west-facing) entryway. With relative peace and prosperity in the 16th century, the townspeople doubled the size of their church, extending it west over what was the little piazza that faced it.

• Now walk back across the harbor square and head left into town. After the lane opens up on the right, hike through the cave to the...

"New Beach": This is where the town's stream used to hit the sea back in the 1970s. When a massive flood hit in 2011, it deposited landslide material here from the hills above. In the flood's aftermath, Vernazza's main drag and harbor were filled with mud and silt. Workers used the debris to fill in even more of this beach. But as time goes on, the forces of nature are once again taking it away.

• Back on the main drag, continue uphill to...

Vernazza's "Main Street": You're now strolling through Vernazza's "commercial center": souvenir shops, wine shops, the Blue Marlin Bar (a good nightspot), and so on. The small stone chapel with iron grillwork over the window (on the right) is the tiny **Chapel of Santa Marta,** where Mass is celebrated on special Sundays. You'll walk by a *gelateria,* bakery, pharmacy, grocery, and another *gelateria.* There are plenty of fun and cheap food-to-go options here. While it's easy to get distracted by all the tourists, try to see through them to notice locals going about their business.

On the right, just before the train tracks, study the big **poster,** which shows photos of the 2011 flood (*alluvione*) and the shops it devastated. Imagine this street from here to the harbor buried under 13 feet of mud.

• Hike a few steps under and above the tracks to the little square.

"Millstone Square": The **millstones** set on the square are a reminder that the town stream (which goes underground here and which you've been walking over ever since leaving the harbor area) once powered Vernazza's water mill. (You can still see its tiny "river" if you follow this road up a few steps.) Until the 1950s, the river ran openly through the center of town. Old-timers recall the days before the breakwater, when the river cascaded down, charming bridges spanned the ravine, and the surf sent waves rolling up Vernazza's main drag.

On the wall ahead at the bend in the road, notice the **World Wars Monument**—dedicated to those killed in World Wars I and II. Not a family in Vernazza was spared. Listed on the left are soldiers *morti*

Santa Margherita Church

Sunbathing in Vernazza

in combattimento who died in World War
I; on the right is the WWII section. Some
were deported to Germania; others—
labeled Part (for partigiani, or partisans)—
were killed while fighting Mussolini.

The path to Corniglia begins here
(behind and above the monument). Even
if you don't plan to hike its entire length,
you don't have to go far to find fine views
over Vernazza's stony peninsula.

• To see a more workaday part of Vernazza,
head a couple of minutes uphill from here
to the...

Top of Town; First you'll pass the
ambulance barn (on the left, at #7, with
big brown garage doors and a croce verde
Vernazza sign), where a group of volunteers is always on call for a dash to the
hospital, 40 minutes away in La Spezia.
Farther up, you'll come to a functional
strip of modern apartment blocks facing
the river. In this practical zone—the only
place in town that allows cars—are a
bank, the post office, a launderette, and
the popular bar/café called Il Pirata delle
Cinque Terre. The parking lot fills a square
called **Fontana Vecchia,** named for an
"old fountain" that's so old, it's long gone.
Shuttle buses run from here to hamlets
and sanctuaries in the hills above. (Check
the schedule post if you want to enjoy the
scenic shuttle bus up to the sanctuary,
described next.)

Experiences
Sanctuary Shuttle Bus
Joyride and Hike

For a cheap and scenic joyride to the
Madonna di Reggio sanctuary, worth
▲▲, hop on an ATC shuttle bus that
loops from the top of Vernazza to sanctuaries and hamlets high in the hills—
including the Madonna di Reggio and
San Bernardino sanctuaries—and back
again (50 minutes, €1.50; for times, check
schedule posted at the bus stop, ask at
the TI, or check online at www.atceser-
cizio.it). Look for the bus to Madonna di
Reggio via Fornacchi.

The bus ride is absolutely stunning. I
prefer to stay on for three-quarters of the
loop (to Madonna di Reggio, then hike
back to Vernazza from there; see below),
or you can ride all the way to complete
the scenic circle. You'll see tiny settlements that predate the Cinque Terre villages, built back when people were afraid
to live on the coast for fear of pirates.
These hamlets and their terraces go back
a thousand years.

For a delightful (if steep) half-hour
hike into Vernazza, ask the driver to let
you out at the stop for Santuario Nostra
Signora di Reggio.

First, walk two minutes below the bus
stop to the sanctuary, which dates from
1248 and has a Romanesque facade.
Inside, interesting votives fill the rear
corner—gifts from sailors who survived
storms and soldiers who survived wars. A
volunteer staffs the church selling coffee,
water, and snacks.

From here signs direct you to trail
#508. You'll be walking on thousand-
year-old cobbles through abandoned
olive groves and past the Stations of the
Cross, which have inspired generations of
processions trudging up from Vernazza.
You'll descend through the cemetery,
then either take the stairs down to the
train station, or continue to the left down
the lane to the square called Fontana Vecchia, where you caught the shuttle bus.

Beaches

The harbor's sandy cove has sunning
rocks and showers by the breakwater.
The sunbathing lane directly under the
church has a shower. A ladder on the seaside of the breakwater aids deep-water
swimmers. Vernazza's "new beach" can be
accessed through a hole halfway along the
town's main drag.

Boat Rides

In addition to the regularly scheduled big
boats that depart from Vernazza's harbor
(see page 543), hiring your own boat can

be handy for intertown transport. From Vernazza, figure around €50 one-way to boat to the other towns (for up to six passengers in an outboard). At Vernazza's breakwater you'll find **Nord Est,** run by Vincenzo, the best-established trip (mobile 338-700-0436, info@nordest-vernazza.com). **Vernazza Water Taxi,** run by Pietro, is another choice (mobile 338-911-3869, info@vernazzawatertaxi.it).

Wine Tasting

Vernazza Wine Experience hides out at the top of town just under the castle. Run by Alessandro, a sommelier, it's romantic, with mellow music and a hardwood, ship-deck ambience. Tastings start at €15/person and can be matched up with meat-and-cheese small plates. While the bill can add up, the quality is excellent and the view is unforgettable (cash only, daily 17:00-20:00, hike from harborfront and turn left before castle, Via S. Giovanni Battista 31, tel. 331-343-3801). Or, drop by his place behind the train station called **Cinque Sensi** (similar prices, Via Roma 71, daily 12:00-24:00).

A Little Taste of Opera

A favorite Cinque Terre evening memory for many is Vernazza's summer opera. A big-name maestro from Lucca brings talented singers to town twice weekly. Performances fill the small oratory, a medieval building with fine acoustics that was beautifully restored for this purpose (just up the steps from the church). Performances begin at 19:00 and last just over an hour (€18 in advance, €20 at the door, May-Oct Wed and Fri at 19:00, book tickets at Cinque Terre Riviera office at #24 on the main street, tel. 0187-812-123, info@cinqueterreriviera.com).

Nightlife

The town's nightlife centers on the bars on its waterfront piazza. The **Blue Marlin Bar** dominates the late-night scene with a mix of locals and tourists, good drinks,

and an open piano (for more, see "Eating," later). **Ananasso Bar** offers early evening happy-hour fun and cocktails (*aperitivi*). Its harborfront tables get the last sunshine of the day (Fri-Wed 8:00-late, closed Thu, on Piazza Marconi).

Sleeping

Vernazza lacks any real hotels, and almost all of my listings are *affittacamere* (private rooms for rent). I favor hosts who rent multiple rooms and speak just enough English, have email, and are reliable. Most places accept only cash, promise free Wi-Fi (often spotty), and don't include breakfast unless noted. Some have killer views, and some come with lots of stairs. Expect noise at night: trains, church bells (7:00-22:00), crashing waves, cars in the upper town. Communicate your arrival time to your host and get clear instructions on where to meet and pick up the keys. They'll usually offer to meet you at the train station if they know when you're coming.

Rooms for Rent (Affittacamere)

The **Cinque Terre Riviera** agency, based in Vernazza, rents rooms here and throughout the region (www.cinqueterreriviera.com).

$$$$ La Malà is the town's jet-setter pad. Four crisp, pristine white rooms boast fancy-hotel-type extras and a shared seaview terrace. It's a climb—way up to the top of town—but they'll carry your bags to and from the station. Book early; this place fills up quickly (includes breakfast at a bar, family rooms, air-con, mobile 334-287-5718, www.lamala.it, info@lamala.it). They also rent two rooms at the simpler **$ "Armanda's Room"** nearby—a great value, since you get their attention to detail and amenities without paying for a big view (includes simple breakfast, air-con).

$$$$ Vernazza sul Mare rents two view, luxury apartments (one- and two-bedroom, sleeping 4-6) that overlook the sea and town from private, spacious terraces. The light-filled, airy units come with sea breezes and a crashing-waves soundtrack. These are great for families and can be connected (both with air-con, fully equipped kitchens, climb steps up to Via Carattino 12, mobile 345-363-6118, www.vernazzasulmare.com, info@vernazzasulmare.com).

$$$ Nicolina Rooms consists of seven rooms and one apartment in three buildings. Two cheaper rooms are in the center over the pharmacy, up a few steep steps; another, pricier studio with a terrace is on a twisty lane above the harbor; and four more rooms are in a building beyond the church, with great views and church bells (all include breakfast, Piazza Marconi 29—check in at Pizzeria Vulnetia, tel. 0187-821-193, mobile 333-842-6879, www.camerenicolina.it, info@camerenicolina.it).

$$$ La Marina Rooms is run by hardworking Christian, who speaks English and happily meets guests at the station to carry bags. There are five well-tended, airy, and renovated units, most high above the main street: One single works as a (very) tight double, and three doubles have fine oceanview terraces; he also has two apartments—one with terrace and sea views, and the other on the harborfront square (rooms have fridges, mobile 338-476-7472, www.lamarinarooms.com, mapcri@yahoo.it).

$$$ Monica Lercari rents several rooms with modern comforts, perched at the top of town (more for seaview terrace, includes breakfast, air-con, tel. 0187-812-296, mobile 320-025-4515, monimarimax@gmail.com). Monica and her husband, Massimo, run the recommended Ristorante al Castello, in the old castle tower that overlooks the town.

$$ Francamaria and her husband Andrea rent 10 sharp, comfortable, and creatively renovated rooms. Their reception desk is on the harbor square (on the ground floor at Piazza Marconi 30), but the rooms are all over town (family rooms, some with air-con, mobile 328-711-9728, www.francamaria.com, francamariareservation@gmail.com). They also rent a room in Manarola.

$$ Vernazza Rooms rents 14 rooms: Four are above the Blue Marlin Bar looking down on the main street; another seven are a steep climb higher up, just under the City Hall (big family apartments, a few with air-con and others with fans, refrigerators, arrange check-in time in advance and meet your host at Via del Santo 9, mobile 351-918-3164, www.vernazzarooms.com, info@vernazzarooms.com).

$$ Martina Callo's four old-fashioned, spartan rooms overlook the harbor square; they're up plenty of steps near the silent-at-night church tower. While the rooms are simple, guests pay for and appreciate the views (family rooms, cheaper nonview room, air-con, ring bell at Piazza Marconi 26, tel. 0187-812-365, mobile 329-435-5344, www.roomartina.it, roomartina@roomartina.it).

$ Albergo Barbara rents nine tidy, Ikea-chic top-floor rooms overlooking the square with an attic communal lounge. Most have small windows and small views; view rooms are more expensive. It's a good value in a nice location (cheaper rooms with shared bathroom, lots of stairs, reserve online with credit card but pay cash, Piazza Marconi 30, tel. 0187-812-398, www.albergobarbara.it, info@albergobarbara.it).

Above the Train Station: $$$$ Casa Cato offers six modern, tight but well-outfitted rooms, some with private balconies and all with access to an inviting shared terrace overlooking the sea and town (RS%, air-con, fridge, expect some train noise, mobile 334-123-8579, www.casacatocinqueterre.com, info@casacatocinqueterre.com, Lisa). They also rent an apartment in the center of town.

$$$ Giuliano Basso's four carefully crafted, well-appointed rooms form a cozy little compound with a common lounge and view terrace, straddling a ravine among orange trees. Giuliano—the town's last stone-layer—proudly built the place himself (2 rooms have air-con, more train noise than others; follow the main road up above the station, take the ramp up toward Corniglia just before Pensione Sorriso, follow the path, and watch for a sharp left turn—or ask Giuliano to meet you at the station; mobile 333-341-4792, www. cameregiuliano.com, giuliano@cdh.it).

$$ Camere Fontanavecchia, at the top of the town, is run by Annamaria, with eight bright and cheery rooms (three with terraces) overlooking a ravine and its rushing river (Via Gavino 15, tel. 0187-821-130, mobile 333-454-9371, www.cinque terrecamere.com, m.annamaria@libero. it). She also rents an apartment.

Guesthouse (Pensione)

$$$ Gianni Franzi, a busy restaurant on the harbor square, runs the closest thing to a big hotel in Vernazza. There are 25 small rooms scattered across three buildings a hundred tight, winding stairs above the harbor square. Some rooms are funky and decorated à la shipwreck, with tiny balconies and grand sea views. The comfy, newer rooms lack views. All guests have access to a super-scenic cliff-hanging garden and panoramic terrace (where breakfast is served in season). Steely Marisa requires check-in before 16:00 or a phone call to explain when you're coming (RS%, closed Jan-Feb, Piazza Marconi 1, tel. 0187-812-228, mobile 393-9008-155, www.giannifranzi.it, info@giannifranzi.it). Pick up your keys at the restaurant, but on Wed, when the restaurant is closed, call ahead to make other arrangements.

Eating

Vernazza's restaurants work hard to win your business. Wander around at about 20:00 and compare the ambience. To get an outdoor table on summer weekends, reserve ahead. Harborside restaurants and bars are easygoing. You're welcome to grab a cup of coffee or glass of wine and disappear somewhere on the breakwater, returning your glass when you're done.

Rick's Tip: *If you dine in Vernazza but are staying in another town, be sure to* **check train schedules before sitting down to eat,** *as trains run less frequently in the evening.*

Harborside

$$$ Gianni Franzi is an old standby for well-prepared seafood and pastas and friendly service. The outdoor seating is under an arcade, while the indoor setting is big and classy (check their *menù cucina tipica Vernazza,* Thu-Tue 12:00-15:00 & 19:00-22:00, closed Wed except in Aug, tel. 0187-812-228).

$$$ Trattoria del Capitano feels unpretentious and serves breakfast and a short menu of straightforward local dishes, including *spaghetti allo scoglio*—pasta entangled with various types of seafood (Wed-Mon 8:00-22:00, closed Tue except in Aug, on Piazza Marconi, tel. 0187-812-201).

$$$ Ristorante Pizzeria Vulnetia has a jovial atmosphere and serves regional specialties and thin-crust pizzas—making this a good choice for those on a budget and families (Tue-Sun 12:00-22:00, closed Mon, Piazza Marconi 29, tel. 0187-821-193).

$$$$ Gambero Rosso is reliably good, and has a fine interior and great outdoor tables on the piazza (Fri-Wed 12:00-15:00 & 19:00-22:00, closed Thu and Dec-Feb, Piazza Marconi 7, tel. 0187-812-265).

By the Castle

$$$$ Ristorante Belforte is a cut above the rest, serving traditional and creative cuisine at tables embedded in four levels of the old castle. For the ultimate seaside perch, reserve a table on the *terrazza con vista* (view terrace) or request the "lovers'

table" on its own little terrace (Wed-Mon 12:00-15:00 & 19:00-22:00, closed Tue and Nov-March, tel. 0187-812-222).

$$$ Ristorante al Castello is just below the castle and offers commanding views. Reserve one of the dozen romantic cliffside seaview tables for two—where you'll feel like you're eating all alone with the Mediterranean. With this book get a free *sciacchetrà* or *limoncello* with biscotti by request (Thu-Tue 12:00–15:00 & 19:00–22:00, closed Wed and Nov–April, tel. 0187-812-296).

On or near the Main Street

$$ Trattoria da Sandro, on the main drag, mixes quality Genovese and Ligurian cuisine—including award-winning stuffed mussels—with friendly service (Wed-Mon 12:00-15:00 & 18:30-22:00, closed Tue, Via Roma 62, tel. 0187-812-223).

$$ Antica Osteria il Baretto is a solid bet for homey, reasonably priced traditional cuisine that's favored by locals (Tue-Sun 12:00-22:00, closed Mon, indoor and outdoor seating in summer, Via Roma 31, tel. 0187-812-381).

$$ Blue Marlin Bar, on the main street, busts out a short, creative menu of more casual dishes (pizzas, salads). It's a good choice if you want to grab something basic (Italian breakfast from 7:30, eggs and bacon 8:30-11:30). If you're awaiting a train, enjoy the outdoor seating with a prepaid drink in view of the tracks (Thu-Tue 7:30-23:00, closed Wed).

$$ Il Pirata delle Cinque Terre, a huge hit for breakfast, also attracts travelers

for lunch and dinner. While you're eating at the parking lot at the top of town, the food, service, and energy are great. And many are charmed by the Cannoli twins, who entertain while they serve. The menu is aimed squarely at American taste buds (reserve ahead for dinner from 18:00, daily 7:00-24:00, Via Gavino 36, tel. 0187-812-047).

$ Lunch Box serves *panini,* salads, and fresh fruit juices from a clever and flexible menu, with a couple of tables overlooking the main drag (daily 7:00-22:00, Via Roma 34, mobile 338-908-2841).

Rick's Tip: *Drop by one of Vernazza's many little bakeries, focaccia shops, or grocery stores to assemble a* **picnic breakfast** *to eat on the breakwater. Top it off with a coffee in a nearby bar.*

Pizzerias, Sandwiches, and Groceries: Vernazza's main-street eateries offer a fine range of quick meals. Several bakeries and creative little takeaway joints sell sandwiches and pizza by the slice. **Pino's grocery store** at #19 makes inexpensive sandwiches to order (generally Mon-Sat 8:00-13:00 & 17:00-19:30, closed Sun).

Gelato

Gelateria Il Porticciolo uses fresh ingredients to create intense flavors (try their *cannella*—cinnamon, or *nocciola*—hazelnut). **Gelateria Vernazza,** near the top of the main street, also takes its gelato seriously. **Gelateria Amore Mio** (midtown) has great people-watching tables.

CORNIGLIA

If you think of the Cinque Terre as The Beatles, Corniglia is Ringo. This tiny, sleepy town is the only one of the five not directly on the water. Locals claim that its ancient Roman residents produced a wine so widely exported that vases have been found at Pompeii stamped with the town name. Wine remains Corniglia's lifeblood today.

Corniglia has fewer tourists, cooler temperatures, a laid-back main square, a few restaurants, a windy overlook on its promontory, and plenty of private rooms for rent. From the town center, signs for *al mare* or *Marina* point to where a stepped path leads steeply down to sunning rocks by the water.

Orientation

Hill-capping Corniglia is connected with its train station far below by a long set of stairs (385 zigzagging steps), and much easier, by a hardworking little shuttle bus (schedule posted at the station and in town; buy ticket at station).

Tourist Information: A TI/park information office is down at the train station (likely daily 8:00-20:00, shorter hours off-season). A kiosk may also be open up in town on Ciappà square.

Hiking: From Corniglia, you can hike on the coastal trail to **Vernazza**. Also consider the challenging but rewarding "high road" to **Manarola via Volastra**. For details, see "Hiking the Cinque Terre" on page 544.

◯ Corniglia Walk

This self-guided walk might take 30 minutes...but only if you let yourself browse, sample the wine, or lick a gelato cone.
• *Begin near the shuttle bus stop located at a...*

Town Square: The gateway to this community is Ciappà square, with an ATM, old wine press, bus stop, and sometimes a TI kiosk in summer.
• *Look for the arrow pointing to the* centro. *Stroll along Via Fieschi, the spine of Corniglia. In the fall, the smell of grapes becoming wine wafts from busy cellars. Along this main street, you'll see...*

Corniglia's little lanes invite exploration.

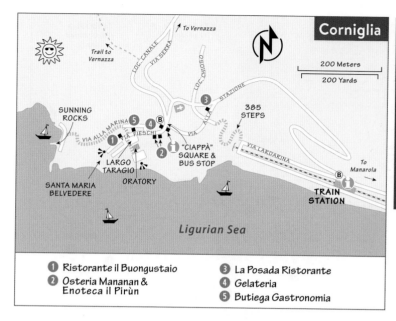

Corniglia

1. Ristorante il Buongustaio
2. Osteria Mananan & Enoteca il Pirùn
3. La Posada Ristorante
4. Gelateria
5. Butiega Gastronomia

Corniglia's Enticing Shops: As you enter Via Fieschi, a trio of neighboring gelato shops jockeys for your business. My favorite is the last one you come to (at #74, on the right), **Alberto's Gelateria** (open late). Before ordering, get a free taste of Alberto's *miele di Corniglia,* made from local honey.

Farther along, on the left, **Enoteca il Pirùn**—named for an oddly shaped wine pitcher designed to give the alcohol more kick as you squirt it into your mouth—is in a cool cantina at Via Fieschi 115. Try some local wines (small tastes generally free, €3/glass). If you order wine to drink from the *pirùn,* Mario will give you a bib (rookies tend to dribble).

Butiega Gastronomia (#142) is an old-fashioned grocery store/deli where Vincenzo sells organic local specialties (daily 8:00-19:30). For picnickers, they offer €5 made-to-order ham-and-cheese sandwiches and a fun *antipasti misti* (priced by weight). You'll find good places to picnic along on this walk.

• *Following Via Fieschi, you'll end up at the mellow...*

Main Square (Largo Taragio): On the square, tables from two bars and a trattoria spill around a WWI memorial and the town's old well. What looks like a church is the **Oratory of Santa Caterina**—a kind of spiritual clubhouse for a service group doing social work in the name of the Catholic Church. Up the stairs and behind the oratory, you'll find a terrace that children have made into a soccer field. The stone benches and viewpoint make this a peaceful place for a picnic.

• *Opposite the oratory, notice how steps lead steeply down on Via alla Marina to sunning rocks and a small deck. From the square, continue up Via Fieschi to the...*

End-of-Town Viewpoint: The Santa Maria Belvedere, named for a church that once stood here, marks the scenic end of Corniglia. This is a super picnic spot. From here, look high to the west (right), where the village and sanctuary of San Bernardino straddle a ridge. Way down below are the local swimming hole and huge sunning rocks.

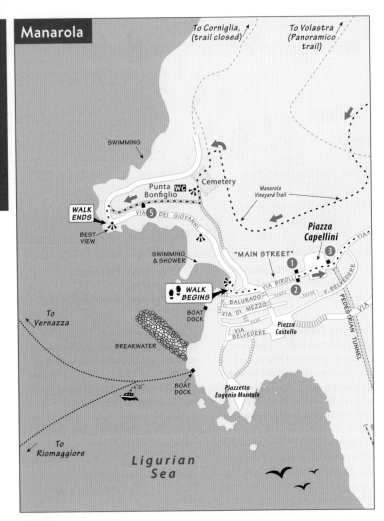

Manarola

To Corniglia,
(trail closed)

To Volastra
(Panoramico
trail)

SWIMMING

Punta **WC** Cemetery
Bonfiglio

Manarola
Vineyard Trail

**WALK
ENDS**

VIA **5** DEI GIOVANNI

BEST
VIEW

*Piazza
Capellini*

VIA

3

SWIMMING
& SHOWER

"MAIN STREET"

1

VIA BELVEDERE

SWIMMING
& SHOWER

**WALK
BEGINS**

VIA BIROLI

2

V. BELVEDERE

BALURADO

To
Vernazza

VIA DI MEZZO

BOAT
DOCK

PEDESTRIAN TUNNEL

VIA

VIA
BELVEDERE

*Piazza
Castello*

BREAKWATER

BOAT
DOCK

*Piazzetta
Eugenio Montale*

To
Riomaggiore

*Ligurian
Sea*

Eating

$$$ Ristorante il Buongustaio is a good bet for dinner on the square, serving *cucina casalinga* (home cooking) and good seafood pasta and risotto (nice tables on the square, daily 12:00-21:15, Via Fieschi 164, tel. 0187-821-424).

$$ Osteria Mananan—between the Ciappà bus stop and the main square at Via Fieschi 117—has tasty dishes and a small, elegant interior (Tue-Sun 12:30-14:30 & 19:30-22:00, closed Mon, no out-

door seating, tel. 0187-821-166).

$$ Enoteca il Pirùn, on Via Fieschi, has a small restaurant above the wine bar serving typical local dishes (Fri-Wed 12:00-16:00 & 19:00-23:30, closed Thu, tel. 0187-812-315).

$$ La Posada Ristorante offers dinner in a garden under trees, overlooking the Ligurian Sea. To get here, stroll out of town to the top of the stairs that lead down to the station (daily 12:00-16:00 & 19:00-23:00, closed Nov-March, tel. 0187-821-174, mobile 338-232-5734).

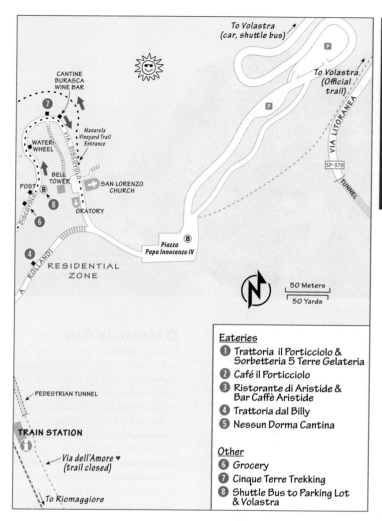

To Volastra
(car, shuttle bus)

To Volastra
(Official
trail)

VIA LITORANEA

SP-370

TUNNEL

CANTINE
BURASCA
WINE BAR

7

VIA DISCOVOLO

Manarola
Vineyard Trail
Entrance

WATER
WHEEL

BELL
TOWER

POST **B**

8

ORATORY

SAN LORENZO
CHURCH

DISCOVOLO

6

A ROLLANDI

4

RESIDENTIAL
ZONE

Piazza
Papa Innocenzo IV **B**

N

50 Meters

50 Yards

PEDESTRIAN TUNNEL

TRAIN STATION

Via dell'Amore ♥
(trail closed)

To Riomaggiore

Eateries
1 Trattoria il Porticciolo &
Sorbetteria 5 Terre Gelateria
2 Café il Porticciolo
3 Ristorante di Aristide &
Bar Caffè Aristide
4 Trattoria dal Billy
5 Nessun Dorma Cantina

Other
6 Grocery
7 Cinque Terre Trekking
8 Shuttle Bus to Parking Lot
& Volastra

MANAROLA

Mellow Manarola fills a ravine, bookended by its wild little harbor to the west and a diminutive hilltop church square inland to the east. The village hits a fine balance, giving it the "just right" combination of Cinque Terre qualities. The touristy zone squeezed between the train tracks and the harbor can be stressfully congested, but head just a few steps uphill and you can breathe again.

Manarola, which has hillsides that are blanketed with vineyards, also provides the easiest access to the Cinque Terre's remarkable dry-stone terraces. The trail ringing the town's cemetery peninsula, adjacent to the main harbor, provides some of the most strikingly beautiful town views anywhere in the region.

Orientation

Tourist Information: The TI/national park information office is in the train station (likely daily 8:00-20:00, shorter hours off-season).

Manarola

Arrival in Manarola: From the **train station,** walk through a 200-yard-long tunnel that's lined with interesting photos. To reach the busy harbor—with touristy restaurants, boat dock, and the start of my self-guided walk, head left (downhill) when you come out of the tunnel.

The ATC **shuttle bus** runs from near the old waterwheel (halfway up Manarola's main street), stopping at the parking lots above town, and then going all the way up to Volastra (about 2/hour except for afternoon breaks).

Drivers are better off parking in La Spezia. Or, park your car in one of the two pay lots just before town, then walk down the road to the church, and downhill to the main piazza.

Rick's Tip: *To get to the **boats that connect Manarola** with the other Cinque Terre towns, find the steps to the left of the harbor view—they lead down to the ticket kiosk. Continue around the left side of the cliff (as you face the water) to the dock.*

◐ Manarola Walk

From the harbor, this 45-minute self-guided walk shows you the town and surrounding vineyards and ends at a fantastic viewpoint.
• *Start down at the waterfront. Belly up to the wooden banister overlooking the rocky harbor, between the two restaurants.*

Harbor: Manarola is tiny and picturesque, a tumble of buildings bunny-hopping down its ravine to the fun-loving waterfront. The **breakwater**—which attempts to make this jagged harbor a bit less dangerous—was built (with reject marble from Carrara) just over a decade ago.

Facing the water, look up to the right, at the hillside Punta Bonfiglio **cemetery** and park. The trail running around the base of the point—where this walk ends—offers magnificent views back on this part of town.

The town's **swimming hole** is just below you. Manarola has no sand, but offers the best deep-water swimming in the area. The first "beach" has a shower, ladder, and wonderful rocks. The second has tougher access and no shower, but feels more remote and pristine (follow the paved path toward Corniglia, just around the point).

• *Go inland up the town's main drag—you'll climb a steep ramp that leads to Manarola's "new" square, which covers the train tracks.*

Piazza Capellini: Built in 2004, this square is an all-around great idea, giving the town a safe, fun zone for kids. Locals living near the tracks also enjoy a little less train noise. The mosaic in the middle of the square depicts the varieties of local fish in colorful enamel.

• *Go down the stairs at the upper end of the square. On your right, notice the tunnel that leads to Manarola's train station (and the closed Via dell'Amore trailhead). Head up...*

Via Discovolo: Manarola's main street twists up through town, lined by modest shops and filled with pooped hikers. About 100 yards up, just before the road bends sharply right, watch (on the right) for a **waterwheel.** Mills like this once powered the local industry. As you continue up, you'll hear the rushing waters of Manarola's stream. The rivulet was covered over after World War II. Before that time, romantic bridges arched over its ravine. You can peek below the concrete street in several places to see the stream surging below your feet.

Across the street from the waterwheel and a bit farther up, notice the **Cinque Terre Trekking** shop on your left, which outfits hikers. Around the corner is **Cantine Burasca** wine bar, a good place for a little wine tasting (closed Wed, Via Discovolo 86, mobile 339-807-1261).

• *Keep climbing until you come to the square at the...*

Top of Manarola: The square is faced by a church, an oratory—now a religious and community meeting place—and a bell tower, which served as a watchtower when pirates raided the town. To the right of the oratory, a stepped lane leads to the town's tourist-free residential zone.

The **Parish Church of St. Lawrence**

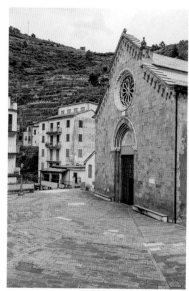

Church of St. Lawrence, Manarola

(San Lorenzo) dates from "MCCCXXX-VIII" (1338). Step inside to see two altarpiece paintings from the unnamed Master of the Cinque Terre, the only painter of any note from this region (left wall and above main altar). Note the humble painted stone ceiling, which features Lawrence, patron saint of the Cinque Terre, with his grill—the symbol of his martyrdom (he was roasted on it).

• *With the bell tower on your left, head about 20 yards back down the main street below the church and find a wooden railing on the right. It marks the start of a delightful stroll around the high side of town, and back to the seafront. This is the beginning of the...*

Manarola Vineyard Trail: Don't miss this experience. Simply follow the wooden railing, enjoying lemon groves and great views. Along the path, which is primarily flat, you'll get a close-up look at the region's famous dry-stone walls and finely crafted vineyards (with dried-heather thatches to protect the grapes from southwest winds). Smell the rosemary. Pick out the scant remains of an old fort.

Vineyards above Manarola

Manarola's cemetery

Notice the S-shape of the Manarola's main road—once a riverbed. The town's roofs are traditionally made of locally quarried slate and held down by rocks during windstorms.

Halfway along the lip of the ravine, a path marked *Panoramico Volastra (Corniglia)* leads steeply up into the vineyards (a challenging route that leads to the tiny hamlet of Volastra and then to Corniglia—see page 568).

Stick with your level path, passing a variety of simple wooden religious scenes, the work of local resident Mario Andreoli. Before his father died, Mario promised him he'd replace the old cross on the family's vineyard. Mario has been adding figures ever since. High above, notice ancient terraces that line the terrain like a topographic map.
• *Continue down to the cemetery (closed to the public). Stop by the gate for a peek inside.*

Cemetery: Ever since Napoleon—who was king of Italy in the early 1800s—decreed that cemeteries were health risks, Cinque Terre's burial spots have been located outside the towns. The result: The dearly departed generally get first-class sea views. Each cemetery—with evocative photos and finely carved Carrara marble memorial reliefs—is worth a look.
• *From the cemetery follow the steep and narrow stairs (through the green gate immediately below) and walk out onto the bluff.*

Punta Bonfiglio: This point offers some of the most commanding **views** of the entire region. For the best vantage point, walk out toward the water through a park. An inviting and recommended bar, **Nessun Dorma,** fills a long narrow terrace with people enjoying the vista.

Your Manarola finale is the bench at the tip of the point. Pause and take in the view.
• *From here steps go down and the path winds scenically back to the harbor, where we started.*

Experiences
Hikes

One of my favorite easy hikes is to head up into the **vineyards above Manarola,** then drop down into the town cemetery, enjoying great views on the way. This route is outlined in my "Manarola Walk," earlier.

For a longer hike, consider taking the **high route to Corniglia via Volastra** (much easier if you ride the shuttle bus, rather than hike, up to Volastra). For details, see "Hiking the Cinque Terre" on page 544.

Hiking Gear and Tips: A wonderful resource for hikers, **Cinque Terre Trekking** is near the top of the main street (halfway up to the church). If you're serious about hiking, stop in here to confirm your plans and gear up (daily 11:00-13:00 & 14:00-19:00, shorter hours off-season, Via Discovolo 108, tel. 0187-920-834, www.cinqueterretrekking.com).

Pesto Making

Entrepreneurial Simone at the Nessun Dorma cantina (perched next to the cemetery at the most scenic edge of Manarola) leads a pesto-making workshop for up to 30 people at 10:30, followed by lunch at noon. The setting is unforgettable, and you get to eat what you make (€50/person, includes wine, no class on Tue, reserve ahead at www.nessundormacinqueterre.com or call mobile 340-888-4133, class cancelled in bad weather).

Eating

Via Discovolo, the main street climbing up through town from Piazza Capellini to the church, is lined with simple places and some small grocery stores. **Bar Caffè Aristide** is the busiest for breakfast. And the most enticing *gelateria* in town is **Sorbetteria 5 Terre Gelateria** (a couple of doors away).

Touristy restaurants are concentrated between Piazza Capellini and the harbor. The Scorza family works hard at **$$ Trattoria il Porticciolo** (Thu-Tue 12:00-21:30, closed Wed, Via Birolli 92, tel. 0187-920-083) and at their contemporary **cafè,** cheap and fast, across the way.

$$$ Ristorante di Aristide, right on Piazza Capellini, offers a trendy atmosphere and a pleasant outdoor setting (Fri-Wed 12:00-22:30, closed Thu, Via Discovolo 290, tel. 0187-920-000).

$$ Bar Caffè Aristide, next door, has indoor and streetside seating and a lighter menu (Fri-Wed 8:00-11:30 & 12:00-16:00, closed Thu).

$$$ Trattoria dal Billy, in the residential zone high above the touristy action, is top-notch. It's worth the climb for homemade black pasta with seafood and squid ink, green pasta with artichokes, and homemade desserts. Outdoor terraces offer commanding views over Manarola, while across the street an elegant, glassy dining room is carved into the rock. Reservations are a must (Fri-Wed 12:00-15:00 & 18:00-22:00, closed Thu, Via Aldo Rollandi 122, tel. 0187-920-628, www.trattoriabilly.com).

$$ Nessun Dorma Cantina is scenically perched under the cemetery and above the harbor, keeping the masses happy with bruschetta, cold cuts, salads, and lots of drinks (Wed-Mon 12:00-21:00, closed Tue, Localita Punta Bonfiglio, mobile 340-888-4133).

RIOMAGGIORE

Riomaggiore is a more real and laid-back town than its more touristy neighbors. The main drag, while traffic-free, feels more urban than "village," and surrounding the harbor is a fascinating tangle of pastel homes leaning on each other like drunken sailors. The views back on its harbor from the breakwater—especially at sunset—are some of the region's prettiest.

Orientation

Tourist Information: The **info point** in the station is for train info and tickets. The adjacent striped building, with a **national park shop** and info desk, is best for visitor information (both open daily 8:00-20:00, shorter hours off-season).

Arrival in Riomaggiore: The **train station** is separated from the town center by a bluff. To get to the center, take the pedestrian tunnel that parallels the rail

Jumping for joy in Riomaggiore

ITALY

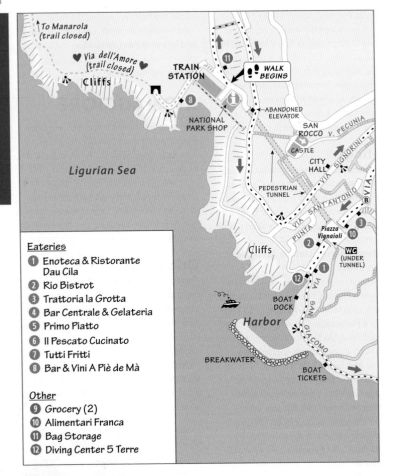

Eateries
1. Enoteca & Ristorante Dau Cila
2. Rio Bistrot
3. Trattoria la Grotta
4. Bar Centrale & Gelateria
5. Primo Piatto
6. Il Pescato Cucinato
7. Tutti Fritti
8. Bar & Vini A Piè de Mà

Other
9. Grocery (2)
10. Alimentari Franca
11. Bag Storage
12. Diving Center 5 Terre

tunnel. You'll exit at the bottom of Via Colombo. For a scenic route into town (for those not carrying luggage), take my "Riomaggiore Walk," later.

Drivers can park for the day at the two-story pay-and-display lot above town (€5/hour, €35/day). It is easier to park at La Spezia's train station and ride the train in.

Helpful Hints

Baggage Storage: You can check your bag at the casually run *deposito bagagli office*—it's behind the café/bar that's straight ahead as you exit the station (daily 9:00-12:00 & 14:00-19:00—confirm times, closed in winter).

Laundry: A self-service launderette is on the main street (daily in summer 8:00-20:00, shorter hours off-season, Via Colombo 107).

⬆ Riomaggiore Walk

This easy self-guided walk loops up and over, taking the long and scenic way from the station into town. You'll enjoy some fine views before strolling down the main street to the harbor.

• *Start at the train station. (If you arrive by boat, cross beneath the tracks and take a left, then hike through the tunnel along the tracks to reach the station.)*

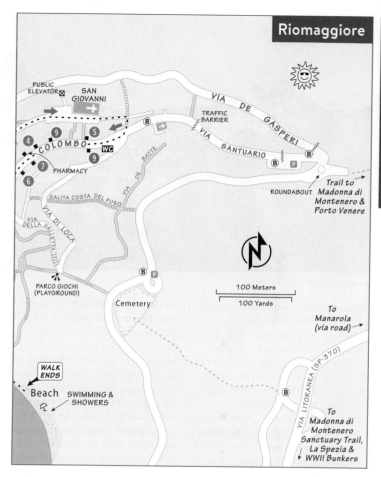

Riomaggiore

PUBLIC ELEVATOR
SAN GIOVANNI
TRAFFIC BARRIER
VIA DE GASPERI
VIA SANTUARIO
WC
COLOMBO
VIA DE BATTE
PHARMACY
SALITA COSTA DEL FUSO
VIA DELLA VALLETTA
VIA DI LOCA
ROUNDABOUT
Trail to Madonna di Montenero & Porto Venere
PARCO GIOCHI (PLAYGROUND)
Cemetery
100 Meters
100 Yards
To Manarola (via road)
VIA LITORANEA (SP-370)
WALK ENDS
Beach SWIMMING & SHOWERS
To Madonna di Montenero Sanctuary Trail, La Spezia & WWII Bunkers

Climb to the Top of Town: Hike up the main street. Listen to the paved-over creek under your feet and at the first turn see the waterfall (and turtles in the cage). Farther along is a close-up look at dry-stone rockery work. Look down on the historic train line. A bit farther, you'll arrive at a fine **viewpoint,** with spectacular sea views.

• *When you're ready to move on, hook left around the bluff; rounding the bend, ignore the steps marked* marina seacoast *(which lead to the harbor) and continue another five minutes along the main (level) path toward the church. Along the way, consider a steep little side trip to the castle.*

Riomaggiore Castle: A steep stepped lane on the left leads to the castle (€2, daily 10:30-13:30). Taking this five-minute side trip, you'll find a humble art and heritage exhibit, the town's only well-preserved mural by Argentinian artist Silvio Benedetto, great sea views, and the tiny church of San Rocco (built for plague victims, and therefore outside of the town walls). More of Benedetto's murals are near the City Hall.

Town Views and Church of San Giovanni Battista (St. John the Baptist): Back down on the smooth and level lane, you'll go by the **City Hall** and several decaying **murals** (also by Silvio

Riomaggiore's harbor

Benedetto), celebrating the heroic grape-pickers and fishermen of the region.

Pause at the big **terrace** to enjoy the views of town and perhaps lots of local kids (the preschool is nearby). The major river of this region once ran through this valley, as implied by the name Riomaggiore (local dialect for "river" and "major"). As in the other Cinque Terre towns, the main street covers its *rio maggiore,* which carved the canyon now filled by the town's pastel high-rises.

The **church,** while rebuilt in 1870, was first established in 1340. It's dedicated to St. John the Baptist, the patron saint of Genoa, the maritime republic that once dominated the region.

• *Continue straight past the church and along the narrow lane leading down to the town's main street...*

Via Colombo: Heading down the hill on Via Colombo, you'll pass several handy fast-food joints. Farther along, the big covered terrace on the right belongs to the recommended **Bar Centrale,** a popular hangout day or night.

As you round the bend to the left, notice the old-timey pharmacy just above (on the right, with a good bakery under-

neath). On your left, at #199, peek into the **Il Pescato Cucinato** shop, where Laura fries up her husband Edoardo's fresh catch; grab a paper cone of deep-fried seafood as a snack. Where the road bends sharply right, notice the bench on your left (just before La Zorza Café)—the hangout for the town's old-timers, who keep a running commentary on the steady flow of people. Straight ahead, you can already see where this street will dead-end. The last shop on the left, **Alimentari Franca** (at #251), is a well-stocked grocery where you can gather the makings for a perfect picnic out on the harbor.

Rick's Tip: *With a youthful spirit and lively evening bustle, Riomaggiore has an enjoyable* **night scene.** *Stroll the main drag, Via Colombo, to scope out fun spots to enjoy €6-8 cocktails.*

Where Via Colombo dead-ends, look right to see the tunnel leading back to the station. Look left to see two sets of stairs. Climb the "up" stairs to a parklike **square** built over the train tracks, which provides the children of the town a bit of level land on which to kick their soccer balls and to learn to ride bikes. The murals above, marking the town's middle school, celebrate the great-grandparents of these very children—the salt-of-the-earth locals who earned a humble living before the age of tourism.

• Take the "down" stairs to the...

Harbor: This most picturesque corner of Riomaggiore features a tight cluster of buildings huddling nervously around a tiny square and harbor. Because Riomaggiore lacks the naturally protected harbor of Vernazza, when bad weather is expected, fishermen pull their boats up to the safety of the little square. Sometimes the fishermen are busy beaching their boats even on a bright, sunny day—an indication that they know something you don't.

A couple of recommended restaurants—with high prices and memorable seating—look down over the action. Head past them and up the walkway along the left side of the harbor, and enjoy the **views** back at the town's colorful pastel buildings, with the craggy coastline just beyond. The best views are from up top, at the edge of the bluff. Below you, the breakwater curves out to sea. These rocks are popular with sunbathers by day and romantics and photographers at sunset.

For a peek at Riomaggiore's **beach,** continue around the bluff on this trail toward Punta di Montenero, the cape that defines the southern end of the Cinque Terre. You'll pass the rugged boat landing and eventually run into Riomaggiore's rocky but still inviting beach (*spiaggia*). Ponder how Europeans manage to look relaxed when lounging on football-sized "pebbles."

Experiences
Hike

A scenic one-hour trail rises from Riomaggiore to the 14th-century **Madonna di Montenero sanctuary,** high above the town. Take the main road inland until you see signs at the roundabout at the top of town; or ride the shuttle bus 12 minutes from the town center to the sanctuary trail, then walk uphill another 20 minutes (great picnic spot up top).

Beach

Riomaggiore's tiny "beach" is rocky, but it's clean and peaceful. To find it, see the end of my self-guided walk, above. There's a shower here in the summer, and another

Sunbathers and kayakers flock to Riomaggiore.

by the boat landing—where many enjoy sunning on and jumping from the rocks.

Kayaks and Water Sports
Diving Center 5 Terre rents kayaks and snorkeling and scuba equipment; they also lead guided dives of the protected marine waters nearby (daily May-Sept 9:00-18:00, open only in good weather, likely weekends only in shoulder season, office down the stairs and under the tracks on Via San Giacomo, tel. 0187-920-011, www.5terrediving.it).

Eating
On the Harbor
$$$$ Enoteca & Ristorante Dau Cila (pronounced "dow CHEE-lah") is decked out like a black-and-white movie set in an old boat shed with extra tables outside on a rustic deck over dinghies. Try their anti-pasto specialty of several seafood appetizers (dinner only) and listen to the waves (cheaper lunch menu, daily 12:00-24:00, Via San Giacomo 65, tel. 0187-760-032).

$$$$ Rio Bistrot, small and intimate at the top of the harbor, tries to jazz up its Ligurian cuisine with international influ-ences. You can order à la carte from the short but well-designed menu, or try their €39 tasting *menu* (cheaper lunch menu, daily 12:00-16:00 & 18:00-22:00, Via San Giacomo 46, tel. 0187-920-616).

On the Main Street, Via Colombo
$$ Trattoria la Grotta, right in the town center, has a passion for anchovies and mussels. You'll enjoy reliably good food surrounded by historical photos and won-derful stonework in a dramatic, dressy, cave-like setting (daily 12:00-14:30 & 17:30-22:30, closed Wed in winter, Via Colombo 247, tel. 0187-920-187).

$$ Bar Centrale is a casual, fami-ly-friendly place for hamburgers, salads, and pesto. They also serve breakfast, have a *gelateria* on site, and make great mojitos (daily 7:30-late, Via Colombo 144).

Light Meals: $ Primo Piatto, at the top of town, offers takeaway handmade pastas and sauces, cooked to order on the spot. It's cheap and delicious (Wed-Mon 10:30-19:30 or later, closed Tue, Via Colombo 72). For deep-fried seafood in a paper cone, **$ Il Pescato Cucinato** is where Edoardo fishes and his wife, Laura,

The catch of the day

Boats connect Cinque Terre towns.

Vernazza's train platform

fries (daily 11:20-20:30, near the bottom of Via Colombo at #199). A few doors away, **$ Tutti Fritti** serves only fried nibbles, including fish (daily 10:00-21:00, Via Colombo 161).

Picnics: Groceries and delis lining Via Colombo sell food to go for a picnic at the harbor or beach. **Co-op** grocery stores (several on the main drag) have the best prices. For a more appetizing selection, head to **Alimentari Franca** on the main street by the train-station tunnel (daily 8:00-20:00, Via Colombo 251).

Near the Train Station

$$ Bar & Vini A Piè de Mà, at the trailhead on the Manarola end of town, is good for a scenic light bite or quiet drink at night (daily 10:00-20:00, June-Sept until 24:00, closed Mon-Tue off-season, tel. 0187-921-037). Enjoy a meal on its dramatically situated terrace for an indelible Cinque Terre memory.

TRANSPORTATION

Arriving and Departing
By Train

The five towns of the Cinque Terre are on a milk-run line, with trains coming through about every 30 minutes; most trains connect to the Cinque Terre from La Spezia or Genoa. Big, fast trains usually speed right past the Cinque Terre, although a few IC trains connect Monterosso to Milan or Pisa.

Unless you're coming from another Cinque Terre town, you'll change trains at least once to reach Manarola, Corniglia, or Vernazza. From the south or east, you'll probably transfer at La Spezia's Centrale station. From the north, you'll transfer at Genoa's Piazza Principe station, Sestri Levante, Levanto, or Monterosso.

By Train After Parking Your Car

Given the narrow roads and parking headache, the only Cinque Terre town I'd drive to is Monterosso (and only if my hotel had parking). Otherwise, park your car in the nearest big city and take the train in—it's safer, cheaper, faster, and smarter. Parking is easy at the stations in Levanto or La Spezia.

TRAIN CONNECTIONS

Of the five Cinque Terre towns, Monterosso has the most direct train connections with towns outside the Cinque Terre.

From Monterosso by Train to: Levanto (3-4/hour, 4 minutes), **Sestri Levante** (hourly, 30 minutes, most trains to Genoa stop here), **Santa Margherita Ligure** (at least hourly, 45 minutes), **Genoa** (hourly, 1.5 hours; for destinations in France, you'll change trains here), **Milan** (8/day direct, otherwise hourly with change in Genoa, 3 hours), **Venice** (5/day, 6 hours, change in Milan), **La Spezia** (2-3/hour, 15-30 minutes), **Pisa** (hourly, 1-1.5 hours), **Rome** (hourly, 4.5 hours, change in La Spezia).

Venice

Venice is a world apart. Built on a hundred islands, its exotic-looking palaces are laced together by graceful bridges over sun-speckled canals. Romantics revel in the city's atmosphere of elegant decay, seeing the peeling plaster as a metaphor for beauty in decline. And first-time visitors are often stirred deeply, waking from their ordinary lives to a fantasy world unlike anything they've ever seen.

Those are strong reactions, considering that Venice today, frankly, can also be an overcrowded tourist trap. While there are about 270,000 people in greater Venice (counting the mainland, not counting tourists), the old town has a small-town feel. To see Venice away from the touristic flak, escape the Rialto-San Marco tourist zone and savor the town early and late. At night, when the hordes of day-trippers have gone, another Venice appears. Glide in a gondola through quiet canals. Dance across a floodlit square. Pretend it's Carnevale, don a mask—or just a clean shirt—and become someone else for a night.

VENICE IN 2 DAYS

Venice's greatest sight is the city itself, easily worth two days. It can be Europe's best medieval wander if you make time to stroll and explore.

Day 1: In the morning, take the slow vaporetto #1 from the train station down the Grand Canal to St. Mark's Square. Stop off midway at the Rialto market (Rialto Mercato) to grab an early lunch. Resume your ride down the Grand Canal to St. Mark's Square. Spend the afternoon on the square, visiting your choice of St. Mark's Basilica, Doge's Palace, Bridge of Sighs, the Correr Museum, and Campanile bell tower (open late in summer).

On any evening: Do a *cicchetti* (appetizer) crawl for dinner (except on Sun, when most bars are closed), or dine later at a restaurant. Enjoy a gondola ride (or, the

budget version, a moonlit vaporetto. Catch a Vivaldi concert. Hum along with the dueling orchestras on St. Mark's Square, whether you get a drink or just stroll.

Day 2: Spend the morning shopping and exploring as you make your way over the Rialto Bridge to the Frari Church for the art. Afterward, head to the Dorsoduro neighborhood for lunch, then devote the afternoon to more art—select from the Accademia (Venetian art), Peggy Guggenheim Collection (modern art), and Ca' Rezzonico (18th-century palace).

Too many museums? Go on a photo safari through back streets and canals. Or take a short vaporetto trip to the San Giorgio Maggiore island for a sublime skyline view of Venice.

With extra time: Visit the lagoon islands of Murano, Burano, and Torcello. For beach time, it's the Lido (across the

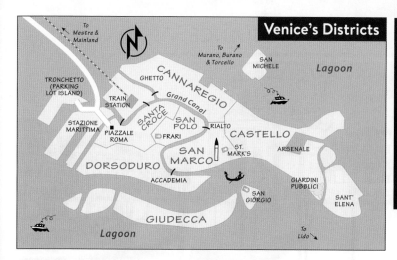

lagoon via vaporetto). The nearby towns of Padua (with Giotto's frescoed Scrovegni Chapel—reserve ahead) and Verona (with a Roman amphitheater) make great day trips or stops to or from Venice.

ORIENTATION

The island city of Venice is shaped like a fish. Its major thoroughfares are canals. The Grand Canal winds through the middle of the fish, starting at the mouth where all the people and food enter, passing under the Rialto Bridge, and ending at St. Mark's Square (Piazza San Marco). Park your 21st-century perspective at the mouth and let Venice swallow you whole.

Venice has six districts known as *sestieri*: San Marco (from St. Mark's Square to the Accademia Bridge), Castello (the area east of St. Mark's Square—the "tail" of the fish), Dorsoduro (the "belly," on the far side of the Accademia Bridge), Cannaregio (between the train station and the Rialto Bridge), San Polo (west of the Rialto Bridge), and Santa Croce (the "eye" of the fish, across the canal from the train station).

The easiest way to navigate is by landmarks. Many street corners have a sign pointing you to (*per*) the nearest major landmark, such as San Marco, Accademia,

Rialto, and Ferrovia (train station). Obedient visitors stick to the main thoroughfares as directed by these signs...and miss the charm of back-street Venice.

Beyond the city's core there are several other islands, including San Giorgio (with great views of Venice), Giudecca (more views), San Michele (old cemetery), Murano (famous for glass), Burano (lace-making), Torcello (old church), and the skinny Lido (with Venice's beach).

Rick's Tip: *Don't worry about* **getting lost**—*in fact, get as lost as possible. When it comes time to find your way,* **follow the arrows** *on building corners or simply ask a local, "Dov'è San Marco?" ("Where is St. Mark's?") Or, if you're lost, pop into a hotel and ask for their business card—it probably comes with a map and a prominent "You are here."*

Tourist Information

With this chapter, a city map, and the events schedule on the TI's website, there's little need to make an in-person visit to a Venice TI. To check or confirm something, try phoning the TI information line at 041-2424 or visit VeneziaUnica.it.

If you must visit a TI, you'll find four convenient branches (all are open daily):

VENICE AT A GLANCE

▲▲▲**St. Mark's Square** Venice's grand main square. See page 602.

▲▲▲**St. Mark's Basilica** Cathedral with mosaics, saint's bones, treasury, museum, and viewpoint of square. **Hours:** Mon-Sat 9:30-17:00, Sun 14:00-17:00 (Sun until 16:30 Nov-Easter). See page 604.

▲▲▲**Doge's Palace** Art-splashed palace of former rulers, with prison accessible through Bridge of Sighs. **Hours:** Sun-Thu 8:30-21:00, Fri-Sat until 23:00, Nov-March daily until 19:00. See page 608.

▲▲▲**Rialto Bridge** Distinctive bridge spanning the Grand Canal, with a market nearby. **Hours:** Market—souvenir stalls open daily, produce market closed Sun, fish market closed Sun-Mon. See page 613.

▲▲**Correr Museum** Venetian history and art. **Hours:** Daily 10:00-19:00, Nov-March 10:30-17:00. See page 609.

▲▲**Accademia** Venice's top art museum. **Hours:** Tue-Sun 8:15-19:15, Mon until 14:00. See page 611.

▲▲**Peggy Guggenheim Collection** Popular display of 20th-century art. **Hours:** Wed-Mon 10:00-18:00, closed Tue. See page 612.

▲▲**Frari Church** Franciscan church featuring Renaissance masters. **Hours:** Mon-Sat 9:00-18:00, Sun from 13:00. See page 613.

▲▲**Scuola San Rocco** Tintoretto's "Sistine Chapel." **Hours:** Daily 9:30-17:30. See page 614.

▲▲**Ca' Rezzonico** Posh Grand Canal palazzo with 18th-century Venetian art. **Hours:** Wed-Mon 10:00-18:00, Nov-March until 17:00, closed Tue year-round. See page 613.

▲**Campanile** Dramatic bell tower on St. Mark's Square with elevator to the top. **Hours:** Daily 8:30-21:00, Sept-mid-Oct until sunset, mid-Oct-April 9:30-17:30. See page 610.

▲**Bridge of Sighs** Famous enclosed bridge, part of Doge's Palace, near St. Mark's Square. **Hours:** Always viewable. See page 610.

▲**La Salute Church** Striking church dedicated to the Virgin Mary. **Hours:** Daily 9:30-12:00 & 15:00-17:30. See page 612.

▲**T Fondaco dei Tedeschi View Terrace** Rooftop terrace atop luxury mall, with views over the Grand Canal. **Hours:** Daily 10:15-19:30, June-Aug until 20:15, Nov-March until 19:15. See page 613.

Nearby Islands

▲▲**Burano** Sleepy island known for lacemaking and lace museum. **Hours:** Museum open Tue-Sun 10:30-17:00, Nov-March until 16:30, closed Mon year-round. See page 616.

▲**San Giorgio Maggiore** Island facing St. Mark's Square, featuring dreamy church and fine views back on Venice. **Hours:** Daily 9:00-19:00, Nov-March 8:30-18:00. See page 611.

▲**Murano** Island famous for glass factories and glassmaking museum. **Hours:** Glass Museum open daily 10:30-18:30, Nov-March until 16:30. See page 615.

▲**Torcello** Near-deserted island with old church, bell tower, and museum. **Hours:** Church open daily 10:30-18:00, Nov-Feb 10:00-17:00, museum closed Mon. See page 616.

St. Mark's Square (in the far-left corner with your back to the basilica), airport, bus station (inside the huge white Autorimessa Comunale parking garage), and train station (across from track 2).

Maps: Venice demands a good map. Hotels give away freebies. TIs and vaporetto ticket booths sell decent maps—but you can find a wider range at bookshops, newsstands, and postcard stands. If you spend €5, you'll get a map that shows all the tiny alleys. It may be the best money you spend in Venice. But know you'll still spend some time "exploring" (read: lost). Also consider a mapping app for your mobile phone. (City Maps 2Go and Google Maps cover Venice well.)

Helpful Hints

Sightseeing Tips: Venice offers plenty of sightseeing passes, but only a few—like the Doge's Palace and Correr Museum combo-ticket—are worth the money. For more on passes and other sightseeing advice, see page 602.

Theft Alert: The dark, late-night streets of Venice are generally safe. Even so, pickpockets (often elegantly dressed) work the crowded main streets, docks, and vaporetti. Your biggest risk of pickpockets is inside St. Mark's Basilica, near the Accademia or Rialto bridges, or on a tightly packed vaporetto.

Dress Modestly: When visiting St. Mark's Basilica or other major churches, men, women, and even children must cover their shoulders and knees. Remove hats when entering a church.

Public Toilets: Handy pay WCs are near major landmarks, including St. Mark's Square (behind the Correr Museum and at the waterfront park, Giardinetti Reali), Rialto, and the Accademia Bridge.

Laundry: These laundry places are near St. Mark's Square (see page 624 for locations): Self-service **Effe Erre** is off Campo Santa Maria Formosa (daily 6:30-23:30, on Ruga Giuffa, Castello 4826, mobile 349-058-3881). **Lavanderia Gabriella** offers

full-service laundry, a few streets north of St. Mark's Square (drop off Mon-Fri 8:00-12:30, closed Sat-Sun; pick up 2 hours later or next working day, on Rio Terà de le Colonne, San Marco 985, tel. 041-522-1758, friendly Elisabetta).

Tours
WALKING TOURS
Avventure Bellissime Venice Tours offers small-group tours, including a basic two-hour St. Mark's Square introduction (€25, includes church entry) and a 65-minute boat tour of the Grand Canal (€48, RS%—10 percent discount, contact before booking for promo code, www.tours-italy.com, tel. 041-970-499, info@tours-italy.com).

Alessandro's Classic Venice Bars Backstreets Tours introduce Venetian *bacari*—classic old bars serving wine and traditional *cicchetti* snacks in two-hour evening tours (€40/person). His 1.5-hour Backstreets Tour gets you into offbeat Venice (€20/person, book via email at alessandro@schezzini.it or by phone at 335-530-9024; www.schezzini.it).

Venice Bites Food Tours is run by two expats who enjoy sharing their love for *cicchetti* culture. Their 3.5-hour food tours include lots of walking, noshing, and fun insights (€105-112/person, RS%—€15 off if you book online with discount code "RICKSTEVES"; tel. 800-656-0713, www.venicebitesfoodtours.com).

Venicescapes offers private, themed tours of Venice that are intellectually demanding, intertwining history, art, politics, economics, culture, and religion (2 people—$280-320 or the euro equivalent, $60/person after that, admissions and transport extra, tel. 041-850-5742, mobile 349-479-7406, www.venicescapes.org, info@venicescapes.org).

LOCAL GUIDES
Figure about €75/hour with a 2-hour minimum for most local guides: **Walks Inside Venice** is enthusiastic about

Is Venice Sinking?

Venice has battled rising water levels since the fifth century. Several factors, both natural and man-made, cause Venice to flood dozens of times a year—usually from October until late winter—a phenomenon called the *acqua alta*.

Venice sits atop sediments deposited at the ancient mouth of the Po River. Early industrial projects, such as offshore piers and the railroad bridge to the mainland, affected the sea floor and tidal cycles in ways that made the city more vulnerable to flooding. Twentieth-century industry worsened things by pumping massive amounts of groundwater out of the aquifer beneath the lagoon for nearly 50 years before the government stopped the practice in the 1970s. In the last century, Venice has sunk by about nine inches.

Meanwhile, the waters around Venice are rising. The notorious *acqua alta* happens when an unusually high tide combines with strong sirocco winds and a storm, causing a surging storm tide. Add to that the worldwide sea-level rise caused by climate change, and a high sea gets much higher.

If the *acqua alta* appears during your visit, you'll see the first puddles in the center of paved squares, pooling around the limestone grates at the square's lowest point. These grates cover cisterns that long held Venice's only source of drinking water. For centuries, residents carried water from the mainland with much effort and risk. In the ninth century, they devised a way to collect rainwater by using paved, sloped squares as catchment systems, with limestone filters covering underground clay tubs. Hundreds of cisterns provided the city with drinking water until 1884, when an aqueduct was built to bring in water from nearby mountains. Now the wells are capped, the clay tubs are rotted out, and rain drains from squares into the lagoon—or up from it.

So, what is Venice doing about the flooding? In 2003, engineers began construction on the MOSE Project. Underwater "mobile" gates are being installed on the sea floor at the three inlets where the open sea enters Venice's lagoon. When the seawater rises above a certain level, air will be pumped into the gates, causing them to rise and shut out the Adriatic. The first gates are already installed. But, a corruption scandal has stranded the entire project for the foreseeable future.

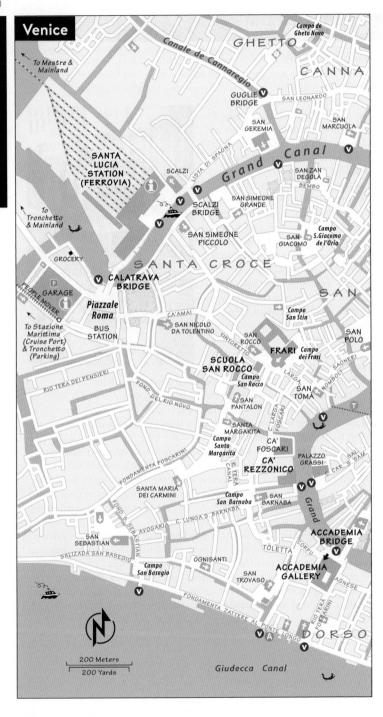

Venice

To Mestre & Mainland

Canale de Cannaregio

GHETTO

Campo de Gheto Novo

CANNA

GUGLIE BRIDGE

SAN LEONARDO

SAN GEREMIA

SAN MARCUOLA

SANTA LUCIA STATION (FERROVIA)

SCALZI

LISTA DI SPAGNA

Grand Canal

SAN ZAN DEGOLÀ

BEMBO

SCALZI BRIDGE

SAN SIMEONE GRANDE

To Tronchetto & Mainland

SAN SIMEONE PICCOLO

SAN GIACOMO

Campo S.Giacomo de l'Orio

GROCERY

SANTA CROCE

SAN

CALATRAVA BRIDGE

PEOPLE MOVER

GARAGE

Piazzale Roma

BUS STATION

CA'AMAI

SAN NICOLO DA TOLENTINO

TINTORETTO

Campo San Stin

SAN ROCCO

FRARI

Campo dei Frari

SAN POLO

To Stazione Marittima (Cruise Port) & Tronchetto (Parking)

RIO TERA DEI PENSIERI

FOND. DEL RIO NOVO

SCUOLA SAN ROCCO

Campo San Rocco

SAN PANTALON

C. LARGA FOSCARI

LARGA

NOMBOLI

SAGNERI

SAN TOMA

SANTA MARGARITA

Campo Santa Margarita

FONDAMENTA FOSCARINI

R. TERA CANAL

CA' FOSCARI

CA' REZZONICO

PALAZZO GRASSI

CA. CAR. S. SAM

GAL.

SANTA MARIA DEI CARMINI

Campo San Barnaba

SAN BARNABA

Grand

AVOGARIA

C. LUNGA S. BARNABA

SAN SEBASTIAN

FOND. S. SEBASTIAN

SALIZADA SAN BASEGIO

Campo San Basegio

OGNISANTI

TOLETTA

CORFU

ACCADEMIA BRIDGE

ACCADEMIA GALLERY

SAN TROVASO

AGNESE

RIO TERA FOSCARINI

FONDAMENTA ZATTERE AL PONTE LONGO

DORSO

N

200 Meters

200 Yards

Giudecca Canal

591

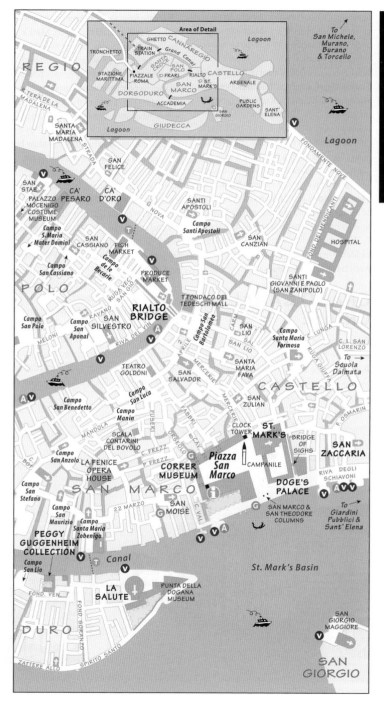

VENICE
ORIENTATION

teaching (€280/3 hours per group of up to 6, RS%; Roberta: mobile 347-253-0560; Sara: mobile 335-522-9714; www.walksinsidevenice.com, info@walksinsidevenice.com). **Elisabetta Morelli** and **Corine Govi,** who run **2Guides4Venice,** are informative and reliable (Elisabetta: mobile 328-753-5220, bettamorelli@inwind.it; Corine: mobile 347-966-8346, corine_g@libero.it; www.2guides4venice.com). **Venice with a Guide** is a co-op of eight good Venetian guides (€75/hour, www.venicewithaguide.com). **Best VeniceGuides.it** offers an online catalog of about 100 local guides, with information to help you pick the right one (family-friendly guides, shared group tours available, most guides about €75/hour, www.bestveniceguides.it).

GRAND CANAL CRUISE

Take a joyride and introduce yourself to Venice by boat, an experience worth ▲▲▲. Cruise the Canal Grande all the way to St. Mark's Square, starting at the train station (Ferrovia) or the bus station (Piazzale Roma). Consider topping it off with my self-guided tour of St. Mark's Basilica (later, under "Sights in Venice"). Or, to avoid daytime vaporetto crowds, ride at night. With nearly empty boats and chandelier-lit palace interiors viewable from the Grand Canal, this cruise can be a highlight of your Venetian experience.

This 45-minute tour, organized by boat stop, is designed to be done on **slow boat #1.** Express boat #2 travels the same route, but skips many stops, making this tour hard to follow and hop-on/hop-off sightseeing impossible.

You can break up the tour by hopping on and off at various sights—but remember, a single-fare vaporetto ticket is good for just 75 minutes (passes let you hop on and off all day).

Tours: ∩ Download my free Grand Canal Cruise **audio tour.**

Seating Strategies: As the vaporetti can be jammed, strategize about where to sit—then, when the boat pulls up, make a beeline for your preference. You're more likely to find an empty seat if you catch the vaporetto at Piazzale Roma—the stop *before* Ferrovia.

Grand Canal

Vaporetto stop at the train station

Calatrava Bridge

A few remaining older vaporetti have seats in the bow (in front of the captain's bridge), the perfect vantage point for spotting sights left, right, and forward. With a standard boat and normal crowds, I'd head for the open-air section in the stern and grab the middle seat. If it's not crowded, you can hang out in the middle (loading zone) and bop from side to side (especially easy after dark). Your worst option is sitting inside and trying to look out the window.

Overview

The Grand Canal is Venice's "Main Street." At more than two miles long, nearly 150 feet wide, and nearly 15 feet deep, it's the city's largest canal. It's the remnant of a river that once spilled from the mainland into the Adriatic. The sediment it carried formed barrier islands that cut Venice off from the sea, forming a lagoon.

Venice was built on the marshy islands of the former delta, sitting on wood pilings driven nearly 15 feet into the clay. About 25 miles of canals drain the city, dumping like streams into the Grand Canal. Technically, Venice has only three canals: Grand, Giudecca, and Cannaregio. The 45 small waterways that dump into the Grand Canal are referred to as rivers (e.g., Rio Novo).

Venice is a city of palaces, dating from the days when the city was the world's richest. The most lavish palaces formed a grand architectural cancan along the Grand Canal. Once frescoed in reds and blues, with black-and-white borders and gold-leaf trim, they made Venice a city of dazzling color. This cruise is the only way to truly appreciate the palaces, approaching them at water level, where their main entrances were located. Today, strict laws prohibit any changes in these buildings, so while landowners gnash their teeth, we can enjoy Europe's best-preserved medieval/Renaissance city—slowly rotting.

● Self-Guided Cruise

Start at the Ferrovia vaporetto stop (at **Santa Lucia train station**). The #1 boat to San Marco generally leaves from dock E (far to the right).

❶ Ferrovia

This site has been the gateway into Venice since 1860, when the first train station was built. The Santa Lucia station, one of the few modern buildings in town, was built in 1954. The "F.S." logo above the entry stands for "Ferrovie dello Stato," the Italian state railway system. Consider that before the causeway was built in the mid-1800s, Venice was an island with no road or train access and no water system. With the causeway the city got a train line, an aqueduct, and a highway.

More than 20,000 people a day commute in from the mainland, making this the busiest part of Venice during rush hour. The nearby **Calatrava Bridge,** spanning the Grand Canal between the train station and Piazzale Roma upstream,

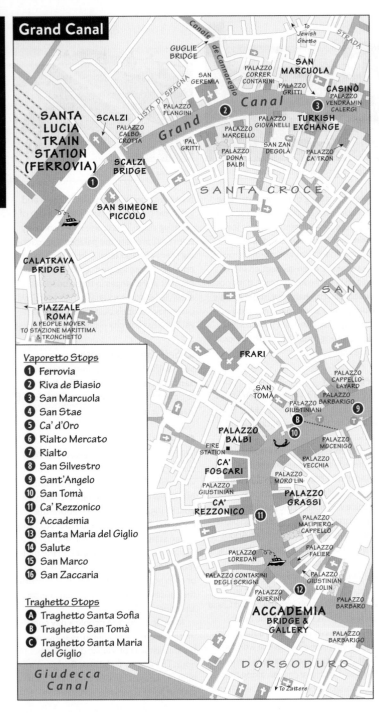

Grand Canal

Canale di Cannaregio

GUGLIE BRIDGE

PALAZZO CORRER CONTARINI

SAN GEREMIA

SAN MARCUOLA

PALAZZO GRITTI

CASINÒ

PALAZZO VENDRAMIN CALERGI

To Jewish Ghetto

STRADA

Canal

LISTA DI SPAGNA

PALAZZO FLANGINI

SCALZI

PALAZZO CALBO-CROTTA

SANTA LUCIA TRAIN STATION (FERROVIA)

SCALZI BRIDGE

PAL. GRITTI

Grand

PALAZZO MARCELLO

PALAZZO GIOVANELLI

TURKISH EXCHANGE

PALAZZO DONÀ BALBI

SAN ZAN DEGOLÀ

PALAZZO CA' TRON

SAN SIMEONE PICCOLO

SANTA CROCE

CALATRAVA BRIDGE

PIAZZALE ROMA
& PEOPLE MOVER
TO STAZIONE MARITTIMA
& TRONCHETTO

FRARI

SAN

SAN TOMÀ

PALAZZO CAPPELLO-LAYARD

PALAZZO BARBARIGO

PALAZZO GIUSTINIANI

PALAZZO BALBI

FIRE STATION

CA' FOSCARI

PALAZZO MOCENIGO

PALAZZO VECCHIA

PALAZZO MORO LIN

PALAZZO GRASSI

PALAZZO GIUSTINIAN

CA' REZZONICO

PALAZZO MALIPIERO-CAPPELLO

PALAZZO FALIER

PALAZZO LOREDAN

PALAZZO CONTARINI DEGLI SCRIGNI

PALAZZO QUERINI

PALAZZO GIUSTINIAN LOLIN

ACCADEMIA BRIDGE & GALLERY

PALAZZO BARBARO

PALAZZO BARBARIGO

DORSODURO

Giudecca Canal

To Zattere

Vaporetto Stops

1. Ferrovia
2. Riva de Biasio
3. San Marcuola
4. San Stae
5. Ca' d'Oro
6. Rialto Mercato
7. Rialto
8. San Silvestro
9. Sant'Angelo
10. San Tomà
11. Ca' Rezzonico
12. Accademia
13. Santa Maria del Giglio
14. Salute
15. San Marco
16. San Zaccaria

Traghetto Stops

A. Traghetto Santa Sofia
B. Traghetto San Tomà
C. Traghetto Santa Maria del Giglio

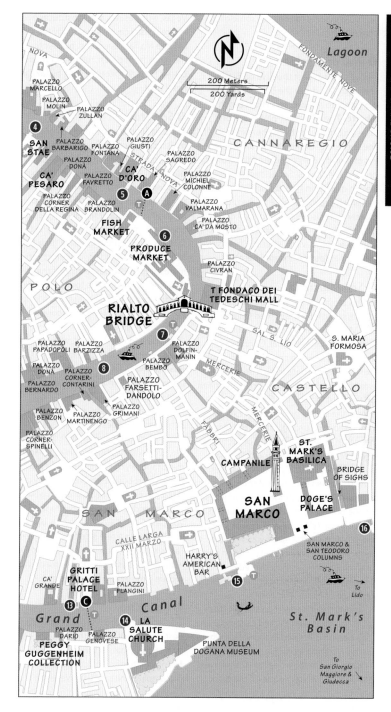

was built in 2008 to alleviate some of the congestion.

❷ Riva de Biasio

About 25 yards past the Riva de Biasio stop, look left down the broad **Cannaregio Canal** to see what was the **Jewish Ghetto.** The twin, pale-pink, six-story "skyscrapers"—the tallest buildings you'll see at this end of the canal—are reminders of how densely populated the world's original ghetto was. Set aside as the local Jewish quarter in 1516, this area became extremely crowded—one of the most closely knit business and cultural quarters of all the Jewish communities in Italy— and gave us our word "ghetto" (from *geto*, the copper foundry located here).

❸ San Marcuola

At this stop, facing a tiny square just ahead, stands the unfinished Church of San Marcuola, one of only five churches fronting the Grand Canal. Centuries ago, this canal was a commercial drag of expensive real estate in high demand by wealthy merchants. About 20 yards ahead on the right (across the Grand Canal) stands the stately gray **Turkish Exchange (Fondaco dei Turchi),** one of the oldest houses in Venice. Its horseshoe arches and roofline of triangles and dingle balls are reminders of its Byzantine heritage. Turkish traders in turbans docked here, unloaded their goods into the warehouse on the bottom story, then went upstairs for a home-style meal and a place to sleep. Venice in the 1500s was very cosmopolitan, welcoming every religion and ethnicity, so long as they carried cash. (Today the building contains the city's Museum of Natural History.)

Just 100 yards ahead on the left (the tallest building with the red canopy), Venice's **Casinò** is housed in the palace where German composer Richard (*The Ring*) Wagner died in 1883. See his strong-jawed profile in the white plaque on the brick wall. In the 1700s, Venice was Europe's Vegas, with casinos and prostitutes everywhere. Today casinos are run by the state to keep Mafia influence at bay. Notice the fancy front porch, rolling out the red carpet for high rollers arriving by taxi or hotel boat.

❹ San Stae

The San Stae Church sports a delightful Baroque facade. Opposite the San Stae stop is a little canal opening—on the second building to the right of that opening, look for the peeling plaster that once made up **frescoes** (you can barely distinguish the scant remains of little angels on the lower floors). Imagine the facades of the Grand Canal at their finest. Most of them would have been covered in frescoes by the best artists of the day. As colorful as the city is today, it's still only a faded, sepia-toned remnant of a long-gone era, a time of lavishly decorated, brilliantly colored palaces.

Just ahead (on the right, with blue posts) is the ornate white facade of **Ca' Pesaro** (which houses the International Gallery of Modern Art). "*Ca'*" is short for *casa* (house).

In this city of masks, notice how the rich marble facades along the Grand Canal mask what are generally just simple, no-nonsense brick buildings. Most merchants enjoyed showing off. However, being smart businessmen, they only decorated the sides of the buildings that would be seen and appreciated. But look back as you pass Ca' Pesaro. It's the only building you'll see with a fine side facade. Ahead (about 100 yards on the left) is Ca' d'Oro, with its glorious triple-decker medieval arcade (just before the next stop).

❺ Ca' d'Oro

The lacy **Ca' d'Oro** (House of Gold) is the best example of Venetian Gothic architecture on the canal. Its three stories offer different variations on balcony design, topped with a spiny white roofline. Venetian Gothic mixes traditional Gothic (pointed arches and round medallions stamped with a four-leaf clover) with Byzantine styles (tall, narrow arches atop thin columns), filled in with Islamic frills. Like all the palaces, this was originally painted and gilded to make it even more glorious than it is now. Today the Ca' d'Oro is an art gallery.

Look at the Venetian chorus line of palaces in front of the boat. On the right is the arcade of the covered **fish market,** with the open-air **produce market** just beyond. It bustles in the morning but is quiet the rest of the day. This is a great scene to wander through—even though European Union hygiene standards have made it cleaner and less colorful than it once was.

Find the **traghetto** gondola ferrying shoppers—standing like Washington crossing the Delaware—back and forth. While once much more numerable, today only three *traghetto* crossings survive along the Grand Canal, each one marked by a classy low-key green-and-black sign. Piloting a *traghetto* isn't the normal day job of these gondoliers. As a public service, all gondoliers are obliged to row a *traghetto* a few days a month. Make a point to use them. At €2 a ride, *traghetti* offer the cheapest gondola ride in Venice (but at this price, don't expect them to sing to you).

❻ Rialto Mercato

This stop serves the busy market. The long, official-looking building at the

stop is the Venice courthouse. Directly ahead (on the left), is the **T Fondaco dei Tedeschi**—the former German Exchange (a trading center for German merchants in the 16th century). Later the central post office, it's now a luxury shopping mall with great rooftop views. Rising above it is the tip of the Campanile (bell tower), crowned by its golden-angel weathervane at St. Mark's Square, where this tour will end.

You'll cruise by some trendy and beautifully situated wine bars on the right, but look ahead as you round the corner and see the impressive Rialto Bridge come into view.

A major landmark, the **Rialto Bridge** is lined with shops and tourists. Constructed in 1588, it's the third bridge built on this spot. Until the 1850s, this was the only bridge crossing the Grand Canal. With a span of 160 feet and foundations stretching 650 feet on either side, the Rialto was an impressive engineering feat in its day. Earlier bridges here could open to let big ships in, but not this one. By the time it was completed in the 16th century, Venetian trading power was ebbing. After that, much of the Grand Canal was closed to shipping and became a canal of palaces.

When gondoliers pass under the fat arch of the Rialto Bridge, they take full advantage of its acoustics: *"Volare, oh, oh..."*

Ca' d'Oro—the House of Gold

The lively Rialto market

Rialto Bridge

❼ *Rialto*

A separate town in the early days of Venice, Rialto has always been the commercial district, while San Marco was the religious and governmental center. Today, a winding street called the Mercerie connects the two, providing travelers with human traffic jams and shopping temptations. Boats unloaded the city's basic necessities here: oil, wine, charcoal, iron. Today, the quay is lined with tourist-trap restaurants.

Venice's sleek, black, graceful **gondolas** are a symbol of the city. With about 500 gondoliers joyriding amid the churning vaporetti, there's a lot of congestion on the Grand Canal. Pay attention—this is where most of the gondola and vaporetto accidents take place. While the Rialto is the highlight of many gondola rides, gondoliers understandably prefer the quieter small canals. Watch your vaporetto driver curse the better-paid gondoliers.

❽ *San Silvestro*

We now enter a long stretch of important **merchants' palaces,** each with proud and different facades. Because ships couldn't navigate beyond the Rialto Bridge, the biggest palaces—with the major shipping needs—line this last stretch of the navigable Grand Canal.

Palaces like these were multifunctional: ground floor for the warehouse, offices and showrooms upstairs, and living quarters above, on the "noble floors" (with big windows to allow in maximum light). Servants lived and worked on the very top floors (with the smallest windows). For fire-safety reasons, kitchens were also located on the top floors. Peek into the noble floors to catch a glimpse of their still-glorious chandeliers of Murano glass.

The **Palazzo Grimani** (across from the San Silvestro dock) sports a heavy white Roman-style facade—a reminder that the Grimani family included a cardinal and had strong Roman connections. The **Palazzo Papadopoli,** with the two obelisks on its roof (50 yards beyond the San Silvestro stop on the right, with the blue posts), is the very fancy Aman Hotel where George and Amal Clooney were married in 2014.

❾ *Sant'Angelo*

Notice how many buildings have a foundation of waterproof white stone (*pietra* d'Istria) upon which the bricks sit high and dry. Many canal-level floors are abandoned as the rising water level takes its toll.

The **posts**—historically painted gaily with the equivalent of family coats of arms—don't rot underwater. But the wood at the waterline, where it's exposed to oxygen, does. On the smallest canals, little "no motorboats" signs indicate that these canals are for gondolas only (no motorized craft, 5 kph speed limit, no wake).

⑩ San Tomà

Fifty yards ahead, on the right side (with twin obelisks on the rooftop) stands **Palazzo Balbi,** the palace of an early-17th-century captain general of the sea. This palace, like so many in the city, flies three flags: Italy (green-white-red), the European Union (blue with ring of stars), and Venice (a lion on a field of red and gold). Today it houses the administrative headquarters of the regional government.

Just past the admiral's palace, look immediately to the right, down a side canal. On the right side of that canal, before the bridge, see the traffic light and the **fire station** (the 1930s Mussolini-era building with four arches hiding fireboats parked and ready to go).

The impressive **Ca' Foscari,** with a classic Venetian facade (on the corner, across from the fire station), dominates the bend in the canal. This is the main building of the University of Venice, which has about 25,000 students. Notice the elegant lamp

on the corner—needed in the old days to light this intersection.

The grand, heavy, white **Ca' Rezzonico,** just before the stop of the same name, houses the Museum of 18th-Century Venice. Across the canal is the cleaner and leaner **Palazzo Grassi,** the last major palace built on the canal, erected in the late 1700s. It was purchased by a French tycoon and now displays part of Punta della Dogana's contemporary art collection.

⑪ Ca' Rezzonico

Up ahead, the Accademia Bridge leads over the Grand Canal to the **Accademia Gallery** (right side), filled with the best Venetian paintings. There was no bridge here until 1854, when a cast-iron one was built. It was replaced with this wooden bridge in 1933.

⑫ Accademia

From here, look through the graceful bridge and way ahead to enjoy a classic view of **La Salute Church,** topped by a crown-shaped dome supported by scrolls. This Church of St. Mary of Good Health was built to ask God to deliver Venetians from the devastating plague of 1630 (which had killed about a third of the city's population).

The low, white building among greenery (100 yards ahead, on the right, between the Accademia Bridge and the church) is the **Peggy Guggenheim Collection.** The

A Venetian water taxi

Ca' Foscari

Best Views in Venice

- A slow vaporetto ride down the **Grand Canal**—ideally very early or just before sunset—is a shutterbug's delight.
- On St. Mark's Square, enjoy views from the soaring **Campanile** or the **balcony of St. Mark's Basilica** (both require admission).
- The **Rialto and Accademia bridges** provide expansive views of the Grand Canal, along with a cooling breeze.
- The luxury mall **T Fondaco dei Tedeschi,** just north of the Rialto Bridge, has even better views, especially around sunset (free but book a reservation; see details on page 613).
- Get off the main island for a view of the Venetian skyline: Ascend **San Giorgio Maggiore's bell tower** (admission fee), or venture to Giudecca Island to visit the swanky bar of the **Molino Stucky Hilton Hotel** (the free-to-"customers" shuttle boat leaves from near the San Zaccaria-B vaporetto dock).

American heiress "retired" here, sprucing up a palace that had been abandoned in mid-construction. Peggy willed the city her fine collection of modern art.

Two doors past the Guggenheim, Palazzo Dario has a great set of characteristic **funnel-shaped chimneys.** These forced embers through a loop-the-loop channel until they were dead—required in the days when stone palaces were surrounded by humble wooden buildings, and a live spark could make a merchant's workforce homeless. Three doors later is the **Salviati building,** which once served as a glassworks. Its fine Art Nouveau mosaic, done in the early 20th century, features Venice as a queen being appreciated by the big shots of society.

⓭ Santa Maria del Giglio

Back on the left stands the fancy **Gritti Palace hotel.** Hemingway and Woody Allen both stayed here.

Take a deep whiff of Venice. What's all this nonsense about stinky canals? All I smell is my shirt.

⓮ Salute

The huge **La Salute Church** towers overhead as if squirted from a can of Catholic Reddi-wip.

As the Grand Canal opens up into the lagoon, the last building on the right with the golden ball is the 17th-century **Customs House,** which now houses the Punta della Dogana contemporary art museum. Its two bronze Atlases hold a statue of Fortune riding the ball. Arriving ships stopped here to pay their tolls.

⓯ San Marco

Up ahead on the left, the green pointed tip of the Campanile marks **St. Mark's**

La Salute Church

The Campanile and Doge's Palace dominate the view of Venice from San Giorgio Maggiore.

Square, the political and religious center of Venice...and the final destination of this tour. You could get off at the San Marco stop and go straight to St. Mark's Square. But I'm staying on the boat for one more stop, just past St. Mark's Square (it's a quick walk back).

Survey the lagoon. Opposite St. Mark's Square, across the water, the ghostly white church with the pointy bell tower is **San Giorgio Maggiore,** with great views of Venice. Next to it is the residential island Giudecca, stretching from close to San Giorgio Maggiore past the Venice youth hostel (with a nice view, directly across) to the Hilton Hotel (good nighttime view, far right end of island).

Still on board? If you are, as we leave the San Marco stop look left and prepare for a drive-by view of St. Mark's Square. First comes the bold white facade of the old mint (in front of the bell tower) marked by a tiny cupola, where Venice's golden ducat, the "dollar" of the Venetian Republic, was made. Then come the twin columns topped by St. Theodore standing on a crocodile and the winged lion of St. Mark, who've welcomed visitors since

the 15th century. Between the columns, catch a glimpse of two giant figures atop the **Clock Tower**—they've been whacking their clappers every hour since 1499. The domes of **St. Mark's Basilica** are soon eclipsed by the lacy facade of the **Doge's Palace.** Next you'll see many gondolas with their green breakwater buoys, the **Bridge of Sighs** (leading from the palace to the prison—check out the maximum-security bars), and finally the grand harborside promenade—the **Riva.**

Follow the Riva with your eye, past elegant hotels to the green area in the distance. This is the largest of Venice's few **parks,** which hosts the annual Biennale festival. Much farther in the distance is the **Lido,** the island with Venice's beach. Its sand and casinos are tempting, though given its car traffic, it lacks the medieval charm of Venice.

⑯ *San Zaccaria*

OK, you're at your last stop. Quick—muscle your way off this boat! (If you don't, you'll eventually end up at the Lido.)

At San Zaccaria, you're right in the thick of the action. A number of other vaporetti depart from here (see page 641). Otherwise, it's a short walk back along the Riva to St. Mark's Square. Ahoy!

SIGHTS

Sightseeing Strategies
Avoiding Lines and Crowds
The city is inundated with cruise-ship passengers and tours from mainland hotels daily from 10:00 to about 16:00. Major sights are busiest in the late morning, making this a smart time to explore the back lanes.

To avoid the worst of the crowds at St. Mark's Basilica, go early or late. To bypass the ticket line, reserve a time online—or if you have a large day bag, you can usually avoid the line by checking it (see the St. Mark's Basilica listing). For the Doge's Palace, purchase your ticket at the Correr Museum across St. Mark's Square (see next). You can also visit later in the day, when crowds thin out. For the Campanile, ascend first thing in the morning or go late, or skip it entirely if you're going to the similar San Giorgio Maggiore bell tower.

Free Days: Some state museums in Italy (including Venice's Accademia) are free to enter once or twice a month, usually on a Sunday. Free days are actually bad news—they attract crowds. Check sight websites in advance.

Sightseeing Passes
Venice offers a dizzying array of combo-tickets and sightseeing passes. For most people, the two best options are the combo-ticket for the Doge's Palace and Correr Museum or the Museum Pass (which covers those two plus more). Note that many of the most visit-worthy sights in town (the Accademia, Peggy Guggenheim Collection, Scuola San Rocco, Campanile, and the three sights within St. Mark's Basilica that charge admission) are not covered by any pass.

All the passes described here are sold at the TI (except for the combo-ticket). Most are also available at participating sights.

Doge's Palace/Correr Museum Combo-Ticket: A €25 combo-ticket covers both of these sights. To bypass the long line at the Doge's Palace, buy your combo-ticket at the never-crowded Correr Museum (or online—€1 surcharge). The two sights are also covered by the Museum Pass.

Museum Pass: Busy sightseers may prefer this more expensive pass, which covers these city-run museums: the Doge's Palace; Correr Museum; Ca' Rezzonico (Museum of 18th-Century Venice); Palazzo Mocenigo Costume Museum; Casa Goldoni (home of the Italian playwright); Ca' Pesaro (modern art); Museum of Natural History in the Santa Croce district; the Glass Museum on the island of Murano; and the Lace Museum on the island of Burano. At €35, this pass is the best value if you plan to see the Doge's Palace, Correr Museum, and one or two of the other covered museums. You can buy it at any participating museum or via their websites (€1 surcharge).

Rolling Venice: If you're under 30, this youth pass offers discounts at dozens of sights and shops, but its best deal is for transit. It lets you buy a 72-hour transit pass for just €22—about half price (€6 pass for ages 14-29; sold at TIs, vaporetto ticket offices, and VèneziaUnica shops).

San Marco District
▲▲▲ST. MARK'S SQUARE (PIAZZA SAN MARCO)
This grand square is surrounded by splashy, historic buildings and sights: St. Mark's Basilica, the Doge's Palace, the Campanile bell tower, the Clock Tower, and the Correr Museum. It's your private rendezvous with the Venetian past late at night, when it becomes Europe's most magnificent dance floor.

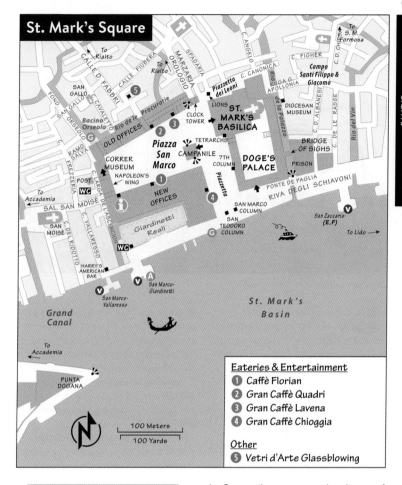

St. Mark's Square

Eateries & Entertainment
1 Caffè Florian
2 Gran Caffè Quadri
3 Gran Caffè Lavena
4 Gran Caffè Chioggia

Other
5 Vetri d'Arte Glassblowing

100 Meters
100 Yards

Rick's Tip: If you're **bombed by a pigeon,** *resist the initial response to wipe it off immediately—it'll just smear into your hair. Wait until it dries, and it should flake off cleanly. But if the poop splatters on your clothes, wipe it off immediately to avoid a stain.*

St. Mark's Basilica dominates the square with its Eastern-style onion domes and glowing mosaics. Mark Twain said it looked like "a vast warty bug taking a meditative walk." To the right of the basilica is its 325-foot-tall Campanile. Behind the Campanile, you can catch a glimpse of the pale pink Doge's Palace.

With your back to the church, survey one of Europe's great urban spaces. Lining the square are the former government offices (procuratie) that administered the Venetian empire's vast network of trading outposts, which stretched all the way to Turkey. On the right are the "old offices" (16th-century Renaissance). At left are the "new offices" (17th-century High Renaissance). Napoleon called the piazza "the most beautiful drawing room in Europe," and added to the intimacy by building the final wing, opposite the

The ornate exterior of St. Mark's Basilica

basilica, that encloses the square.

🎧 For more on the square, the Clock Tower, the Campanile, and other sights on the square, download my free St. Mark's Square **audio tour.**

▲▲▲ST. MARK'S BASILICA (BASILICA DI SAN MARCO)

Built in the 11th century, this basilica's distinctly Eastern-style architecture underlines Venice's connection with Byzantium (which protected it from the ambition of Charlemagne and his Holy Roman Empire). It's decorated with booty from returning sea captains—a Venetian trophy chest. The interior glows mysteriously with gold mosaics and colored marble. Since about AD 830, the saint's bones have been housed on this site. The San Marco Museum within holds the original bronze horses (copies of these overlook the square), and a balcony offering a remarkable view over St. Mark's Square.

Cost and Hours: Basilica entry is free, though you can pay €3 for an online reservation that lets you skip the line (see next). Three separate exhibits within the church charge admission: **Treasury**-€3, **Golden Altarpiece**-€2, and **San Marco Museum**-€5. Church and all exhibits open Mon-Sat 9:30-17:00, Sun 14:00-17:00 (Sun until 16:30 Nov-Easter), interior brilliantly lit Mon-Sat 11:30-12:45. Tel. 041-270-8311, www.basilicasanmarco.it.

Avoiding Lines: There's almost always a long line to get into St. Mark's, but you can avoid it by reserving an entry time online, even for the same day (€3, April-Oct only, book at www.venetoinside.com). Or, if you have a large day bag (bigger than a purse), you can check it and skip the line (larger bags and backpacks are not allowed inside the church). Check above-limit bags for free for up to one hour at Ateneo San Basso church, 30 yards to the left of the basilica, down narrow Calle San Basso (see the map; daily 9:30-17:00). Take your claim tag to the basilica's tourist entrance. Keep to the left of the railing where the line forms and show your tag to the gatekeeper.

Tours: Free, hour-long English **tours** (heavy on the mosaics' religious symbolism) are offered many days at 11:00 (meet in atrium, schedule varies, see schedule board just inside entrance). Audioguides are on sale as you enter.

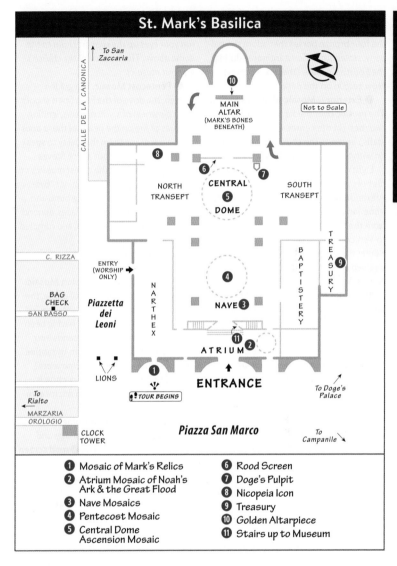

St. Mark's Basilica

Not to Scale

10 MAIN ALTAR (MARK'S BONES BENEATH)

8 NICOPEIA ICON

6 ROOD SCREEN

7 DOGE'S PULPIT

NORTH TRANSEPT

5 CENTRAL DOME

SOUTH TRANSEPT

9 TREASURY

BAPTISTERY

ENTRY (WORSHIP ONLY)

4 PENTECOST

NARTHEX

3 NAVE

C. RIZZA

BAG CHECK
SAN BASSO

Piazzetta dei Leoni

CALLE DE LA CANONICA

To San Zaccaria

11 Stairs up to Museum

2 ATRIUM

LIONS

1

TOUR BEGINS

ENTRANCE

To Doge's Palace

To Rialto

MARZARIA OROLOGIO

CLOCK TOWER

Piazza San Marco

To Campanile

1 Mosaic of Mark's Relics
2 Atrium Mosaic of Noah's Ark & the Great Flood
3 Nave Mosaics
4 Pentecost Mosaic
5 Central Dome Ascension Mosaic
6 Rood Screen
7 Doge's Pulpit
8 Nicopeia Icon
9 Treasury
10 Golden Altarpiece
11 Stairs up to Museum

🎧 Download my free St. Mark's Basilica **audio tour.**

⊙ SELF-GUIDED TOUR

Start outside in the square, far enough back to take in the whole facade. It's a riot of domes, columns, and statues, completely unlike the towering Gothic churches of northern Europe or the heavy Baroque of much of the rest of Italy.

Inside is a decor of mosaics, colored marbles, and oriental treasures that's rarely seen elsewhere. The Christian symbolism is unfamiliar to Western eyes, done in the style of Byzantine icons and even Islamic designs. Older than most of Europe's churches, St. Mark's feels like a remnant of a lost world.

The church is encrusted with materi-

ITALY

als looted from buildings throughout the Venetian empire. Their prize booty was the four bronze horses that adorn the balcony, stolen from Constantinople during the Fourth Crusade (these are copies). Now zero in on the details.

❶ Exterior—Mosaic of Mark's Relics: The mosaic over the far left door shows two men (in the center, with crooked staffs) entering the church bearing a coffin with the body of St. Mark.

Eight centuries after Mark's death, his holy body was in Muslim-occupied Alexandria, Egypt. In AD 829, two visiting Venetian merchants "rescued" the body from the "infidels" and spirited it away to Venice.

• *Enter the atrium of the basilica and find a golden arch overhead with scenes of Noah's Ark.*

❷ Atrium Mosaic of Noah's Ark and the Great Flood: Of all the famous mosaics of St. Mark's, this is one of the oldest (13th century) and finest. The scenes show Noah and his sons sawing logs to build the Ark. Below that are scenes of Noah putting all species of animals into the Ark. Then the Flood hits in full force, drowning the wicked. Noah sends out a dove twice to see whether there's any dry land where he can dock. He finds it, leaves the Ark with a gorgeous rainbow overhead, and offers a sacrifice of thanks to God.

• *Climb a few steps, and into church. Just inside the door, step out of the flow and survey the church.*

❸ The Nave—Mosaics Above and Below: These golden mosaics are in the Byzantine style, though many were designed by artists from the Italian Renaissance and later. The often-overlooked lower walls are covered with green-, yellow-, purple-, and rose-colored marble slabs, cut to expose the grain, and laid out in geometric patterns. Even the floor is mosaic, with mostly geometrical designs. It rolls like the sea. Venice is sinking and shifting, creating these cresting waves of stone.

• *Find the chandelier in the nave (in the shape of a cathedral space station) and run your eyes up the support chain to the dome above. This has one of the church's greatest mosaics.*

❹ Pentecost Mosaic: In a golden heaven, the dove of the Holy Spirit shoots out a pinwheel of spiritual lasers, igniting tongues of fire on the heads of the 12 apostles below, giving them the ability to speak other languages without a Rick Steves phrase book. One of the oldest mosaics in the church (c. 1125), it has distinct "Byzantine" features: a gold background and apostles with halos, solemn faces, almond eyes, delicate blessing hands, and rumpled robes, all facing forward.

• *Shuffle along with the crowds up to the center of the church.*

❺ Central Dome Ascension Mosaic: Gape upward into the central dome, the very heart of the church. Christ—having lived his miraculous life and having been crucified for man's sins—ascends into the starry sky on a rainbow. In Byzantine churches, the window-lit dome represented heaven, while the dark church below represented earth—a microcosm of the hierarchical universe.

Under the Ascension Dome: Look around at the church's furnishings and imagine a service here. The ❻ rood screen (like the iconostasis in a Greek church), topped with 14 saints, separates the congregation from the high altar, heightening the "mystery" of the Mass. The ❼ pulpit (the purple one on the right) was reserved for the doge, who led prayers and made important announcements.

• *In the north transept (left of the altar), is an area usually reserved for prayer. The worshippers are facing a big stone canopy, which houses a small painting of the Virgin Mary.*

❽ Nicopeia (North Transept): Venetians then and now pray to a painted wooden icon of Mary and Baby Jesus known as Nicopeia, or Our Lady of Victory. For centuries, Nicopeia was venerated by the Byzantines, who asked

Ⓐ *The altar and tomb of St. Mark*

Ⓑ *Mosaic showing St. Mark's body being carried into the church*

Ⓒ *Noah's Ark mosaic*

Ⓓ *Central dome and the Ascension mosaic*

Mary to protect them in battle. When Venetian Crusaders captured it, the icon came to protect Venice.

Additional Sights: The **❾ Treasury** (Tesoro) and **❿ Golden Altarpiece** (Pala d'Oro) are the easiest ways to see the glories of the Byzantine Empire outside of Istanbul or Ravenna. The treasury is a beautiful collection of chalices, reliquaries, and jewels, most of them stolen from Constantinople. As you view these treasures, remember that some are nearly 2,000 years old. Beneath the high altar lies the body of St. Mark ("Marce") and the Golden Altarpiece, made of 250 blue-backed enamels with religious scenes, all set in a gold frame and studded with 15 hefty rubies, 300 emeralds, 1,500 pearls, and assorted sapphires, amethysts, and topaz.

Upstairs, in the **⓫ San Marco Museum** (Museo di San Marco) you can see an up-close mosaic exhibition, more religious objects that once adorned the church, a fine view of the church interior, a view of the square from the balcony with bronze horses, and (inside, in their own room)

the original horses. The staircase up to the museum is in the atrium, near the basilica's main entrance.

▲▲▲DOGE'S PALACE (PALAZZO DUCALE)

The seat of the Venetian government and home of its ruling duke, or doge, this was the most powerful half-acre in Europe for 400 years. The Doge's Palace was built to show off the power and wealth of the Republic. The doge lived with his family on the first floor up, near the halls of power. From his once-lavish (now sparse) quarters, you'll follow the one-way tour through the public rooms of the top floor, finishing with the Bridge of Sighs and the prison. The place is wallpapered with masterpieces by Veronese and Tintoretto.

Cost and Hours: €25 combo-ticket includes Correr Museum, also covered by Museum Pass; Sun-Thu 8:30-21:00, Fri-Sat until 23:00, Nov-March daily until 19:00; café, next to St. Mark's Basilica, just off St. Mark's Square, vaporetto stops: San Marco or San Zaccaria, tel. 041-271-5911, http://palazzoducale.visitmuve.it.

Doge's Palace

Avoiding Lines: If the line is long at the Doge's Palace, buy your combo-ticket at the Correr Museum across the square; then you can go directly through the Doge's turnstile without waiting in line. Or, you can buy your ticket online. Crowds tend to diminish after 16:00.

Tours: The fine **Secret Itineraries Tour** follows the doge's footsteps through rooms not included in the general admission ticket. Though the tour skips the palace's main hall, you're welcome to visit the hall afterward on your own. Three 75-minute English-language tours run each morning. Reserve ahead, as tours can fill up several weeks in advance—although you can try just showing up at the information desk (€28, includes Doge's Palace admission but not Correr Museum, €15 with combo-ticket; reserve over the phone or online: tel. 041-4273-0892, http://palazzoducale.visitmuve.it, €1 online surcharge). Don't confuse this with the Doge's Hidden Treasures Tour, which isn't worth its fee.

The **audioguide** is dry but informative (€5, 1.5 hours, need ID for deposit).

Visiting the Doge's Palace: You'll see the restored facades from the **courtyard.** Notice a grand staircase (with nearly naked Moses and Paul Newman at the top). Even the most powerful visitors climbed this to meet the doge. This was the beginning of an architectural power trip.

In the **Senate Hall,** the 120 senators met, debated, and passed laws. Tintoretto's large *Triumph of Venice* on the ceiling (central painting, best viewed from the top) is an allegory of the city in all her glory. Lady Venice is up in heaven with the Greek gods, while barbaric lesser nations swirl up to give her gifts and tribute.

The **Armory**—a dazzling display originally assembled to intimidate potential adversaries—shows remnants of the military might that the empire employed to keep the East-West trade lines open (and the local economy booming).

The giant **Hall of the Grand Council** (175 feet by 80 feet, capacity 2,600) is

Tintoretto, Triumph of Venice

where the entire nobility met to elect the senate and doge. It took a room this size to contain the grandeur of the Most Serene Republic. Ringing the top of the room are portraits of the first 76 doges (in chronological order). The one at the far end that's blacked out (in the left corner) is the notorious Doge Marin Falier, who opposed the will of the Grand Council in 1355. He was tried for treason, beheaded, and airbrushed from history.

On the wall over the doge's throne is Tintoretto's monsterpiece, ***Paradise,*** the largest oil painting in the world. Christ and Mary are surrounded by a heavenly host of 500 saints. The painting leaves you feeling that you get to heaven not by being a good Christian, but by being a good Venetian.

Cross the covered **Bridge of Sighs** over the canal to the **prisons.** Circle the cells. Notice the carvings made by prisoners—from olden days up until 1930—on some of the stone windowsills of the cells, especially in the far corner of the building.

Cross back over the Bridge of Sighs, pausing to look through the marble-trel-lised windows at all the tourists.

More Sights on the Square
▲▲CORRER MUSEUM (MUSEO CORRER)
This uncrowded museum gives you a good overview of Venetian history and art. The doge memorabilia, armor, banners, statues (by Canova), and paintings (by

Canova, Daedalus and Icarus

the Bellini family and others) re-create the festive days of the Venetian Republic. And it's all accompanied—throughout the museum—by English descriptions and views of St. Mark's Square. But the Correr Museum has one more thing to offer, and that's a quiet refuge—an elegant Neoclassical space—in which to rise above St. Mark's Square when the piazza is too hot, too rainy, or too overrun with tourists.

Cost and Hours: €25 combo-ticket includes Doge's Palace, also covered by Museum Pass; daily 10:00-19:00, Nov-March 10:30-17:00; bag check free and mandatory for bags bigger than a large purse, elegant café, enter at far end of square directly opposite basilica, tel. 041-240-5211, http://correr.visitmuve.it.

▲CAMPANILE (CAMPANILE DI SAN MARCO)

This dramatic bell tower replaced a shorter tower, part of the original fortress that guarded the entry of the Grand Canal. That tower crumbled into a pile of bricks in 1902, a thousand years after it was built. Ride the elevator 325 feet to the top of the bell tower for one of the best views in Venice (especially at sunset). For an ear-shattering experience, be on top when the bells ring. The golden archangel Gabriel at the top always faces into the wind. Beat the crowds and enjoy the crisp morning air at 9:00 or the cool evening breeze at 18:00. Go inside to buy tickets; the kiosk in front rents audioguides and is operated by a private company.

Rick's Tip: *Lines at the Campanile can be long. For* **shorter lines and a view** *that's just as impressive, head across the lagoon to the similar San Giorgio Maggiore bell tower.*

Cost and Hours: €8; daily 8:30-21:00, Sept-mid-Oct until sunset, mid-Oct-April 9:30-17:30, last entry 45 minutes before closing; may close during thunderstorms, audioguide-€3, tel. 041-522-4064, www.basilicasanmarco.it.

Behind St. Mark's Basilica
▲BRIDGE OF SIGHS

This much-photographed bridge connects the Doge's Palace with the prison. Travelers popularized this bridge in the Romantic 19th century. Supposedly, a condemned man would be led over this bridge on his way to the prison, take one last look at the glory of Venice, and sigh. Though overhyped, the Bridge of Sighs is undeniably tingle-worthy—especially after dark, when the crowds have dispersed and it's just you and floodlit Venice. In the middle of the day, however, being immersed in the pandemonium of global tourism (and selfie sticks) can be a fascinating experience in itself.

Getting There: The Bridge of Sighs is around the corner from the Doge's Palace. Walk toward the waterfront, turn left along the water, and look up the first canal on your left. You can walk across the bridge (from the inside) by visiting the Doge's Palace.

Bridge of Sighs

San Giorgio Maggiore

Across the Lagoon from St. Mark's Square

▲SAN GIORGIO MAGGIORE

This is the dreamy church-topped island you can see from the waterfront by St. Mark's Square. The striking church, designed by Palladio, features art by Tintoretto, a bell tower, and good views of Venice.

Cost and Hours: Church—free, open daily 9:00-19:00, Nov-March 8:30-18:00; bell tower elevator—€6, runs until 20 minutes before the church closes, does not run during Sun services; tel. 041-522-7827.

Getting There: To reach the island from St. Mark's Square, take the one-stop, five-minute ride on vaporetto #2 from San Zaccaria (€5 special vaporetto ticket, runs every 12 minutes from dock B, direction: Piazza Roma).

Dorsoduro District

▲▲ACCADEMIA
(GALLERIA DELL'ACCADEMIA)

Venice's top art museum, packed with highlights of the Venetian Renaissance, features paintings by the Bellini family, Titian, Tintoretto, Veronese, Tiepolo, Giorgione, Canaletto, and Testosterone. It's just over the wooden Accademia

Bridge from the San Marco action.

Cost and Hours: €15; Tue-Sun 8:15-19:15, Mon until 14:00, last entry one hour before closing; dull audioguide-€6, vaporetto: Accademia, tel. 041-522-2247, www.gallerieaccademia.it.

Avoiding Lines: Just 400 people are allowed into the gallery at one time, so you may have to wait. It's most crowded on Tue mornings and whenever it rains; it's least crowded Wed, Thu, and Sun mornings (before 10:00) and late afternoons (after 17:00). While it's possible to book tickets in advance (€2/ticket surcharge; either book online or call 041-520-0345), it's generally not necessary if you avoid the busiest times.

Renovation: The museum is nearing the end of a major expansion and renovation. If you can't find paintings in the rooms listed below, ask a museum guard to point you in the right direction.

Visiting the Accademia: The Accademia offers a good overview of painters whose works you'll see all over town. Venetian art is underrated and, I think, misunderstood. It's nowhere near as famous today as the work of the florescent Florentines, but—with historical slices of Venice, ravishing nudes, and very

ITALY

Veronese, Feast in the House of Levi, *at the Accademia*

human Madonnas—it's livelier, more colorful, and simply more fun. The Venetian love of luxury shines through in this collection, which starts in the Middle Ages and runs to the 1700s.

Medieval highlights include elaborate altarpieces and golden-haloed Madonnas, all painted at a time when realism, depth of field, and emotion were considered beside the point. Medieval Venetians, with their close ties to the East, borrowed techniques such as gold-leafing, frontal poses, and "iconic" faces from the religious icons of Byzantium (modern-day Istanbul).

Among early masterpieces of the Renaissance is Mantegna's studly *St. George* (Room 4). As the Renaissance reaches its heights, so do the paintings, such as Titian's magnificent *Presentation of the Virgin* (Room 24). It's a religious scene, yes, but it's really just an excuse to display secular splendor (Titian was the most famous painter of his day—perhaps even more famous than Michelangelo). Veronese's sumptuous *Feast in the House of Levi* (Room 10), pictured below, also has an ostensibly religious theme (in the middle, find Jesus eating his final meal)—but it's outdone by the luxury and optimism of Renaissance Venice. Life was a good thing and beauty was to be enjoyed. (Veronese was hauled before the Inquisition for painting such a bawdy Last Supper...so he fine-tuned the title.)

End your tour in the largest room in the museum, Room 23. This giant hall is the upper half of an old Gothic church. The nave was divided under Napoleon's rule, and this became the fine arts academy—the Accademia. It's now home to fine temporary exhibitions, and where art displaced by the gallery's ongoing renovation often ends up.

▲▲PEGGY GUGGENHEIM COLLECTION

The popular museum of far-out art, housed in the American heiress' former retirement palazzo, offers one of Europe's best reviews of the art of the first half of the 20th century. Stroll through styles represented by artists whom Peggy knew personally—Cubism (Picasso, Braque), Surrealism (Dalí, Ernst), Futurism (Boccioni), American Abstract Expressionism (Pollock), and a sprinkling of Klee, Calder, and Chagall.

Cost and Hours: €15; Wed-Mon 10:00-18:00, closed Tue; audioguide-€7, pricey café, 5-minute walk from the Accademia Bridge, vaporetto: Accademia or Salute, tel. 041-240-5411, www.guggenheim-venice.it.

▲LA SALUTE CHURCH (SANTA MARIA DELLA SALUTE)

This impressive church with a crown-shaped dome was built and dedicated to the Virgin Mary by grateful survivors of the 1630 plague.

Cost and Hours: Church-free; Sacristy-€4; both open daily 9:30-12:00 & 15:00-17:30; 10-minute walk from the Accademia Bridge, at vaporetto: Salute, tel. 041-274-3928, www.seminariovenezia.it.

▲▲CA' REZZONICO (MUSEUM OF 18TH-CENTURY VENICE)

This Grand Canal palazzo offers the most insightful look at the life of Venice's rich and famous in the 1700s. Wander under ceilings by Tiepolo, among furnishings from that most decadent century, enjoying views of the canal and paintings by Guardi, Canaletto, and Longhi.

Cost and Hours: €10; Wed-Mon 10:00-18:00, Nov-March until 17:00, closed Tue year-round; ticket office closes one hour before museum, audioguide-€5 or €6/2 people, café, at vaporetto: Ca' Rezzonico, tel. 041-241-0100, http://carezzonico.visitmuve.it.

San Polo District

▲▲▲RIALTO BRIDGE

One of the world's most famous bridges, this distinctive and dramatic stone structure crosses the Grand Canal with a single confident span. The arcades along the top of the bridge help reinforce the structure... and offer some enjoyable shopping diversions, as does the market surrounding the bridge (produce market closed Sun, fish market closed Sun-Mon).

▲T FONDACO DEI TEDESCHI (GERMAN EXCHANGE) VIEW TERRACE

In the Middle Ages, Venice was the world's trading center, hosting scores of nationalities, each with its own caravanserai-like center. The most famous is the home of the Tedeschi (German) traders, just off the Rialto Bridge. It was recently purchased by the Benetton family and turned into a luxury mall. The ground floor features gourmet food shops and ritzy cafés.

The mall's top floor terrace offers a unique perspective over the roofs of Venice and an unforgettable view of the big bend in the Grand Canal. Four times an hour, 80 people are allowed onto the roof for 15 minutes. As you ride the red-carpet elevator to the top floor, notice how the old architectural bones of the structure survive.

Cost and Hours: The terrace is free but access requires a reservation (15-minute timeslots, book online at www.dfs.com/en/info/t-fondaco-rooftop-terrace; you can attempt to show up and reserve, but no guarantees). Terrace open daily 10:15-19:30, June-Aug until 20:15; east side of Rialto Bridge, tel. 041-314-2000.

▲▲FRARI CHURCH (BASILICA DI SANTA MARIA GLORIOSA DEI FRARI)

My favorite art experience in Venice is seeing art in the setting for which it was designed—as it is at the Frari Church. The Franciscan "Church of the Brothers" and the art that decorates it are warmed by the spirit of St. Francis. It features the work of three great Renaissance masters: Donatello, Giovanni Bellini, and Titian—each showing worshippers the glory of God in human terms.

Cost and Hours: €3; Mon-Sat 9:00-18:00, Sun from 13:00; audioguide-€2, modest dress recommended, on Campo dei Frari, near San Tomà vaporetto and *traghetto* stops, tel. 041-272-8611, www.basilicadeifrari.it.

Tours: You can rent an **audioguide** for €2, or download my free 🎧 Frari Church **audio tour.**

Visiting the Church: In **Donatello's wood statue of St. John the Baptist** (in the first chapel to the right of the high altar), the prophet of the desert—emaciated from his breakfast of bugs 'n' honey and dressed in animal skins—announces the coming of the Messiah. Donatello was a Florentine working at the dawn of the Renaissance.

Bellini's *Madonna and Child with Saints and Angels* painting (in the sacristy farther to the right) came later, done by a Venetian in a more Venetian style—soft

Frari Church

Titian, Assumption of the Virgin

focus without Donatello's harsh realism. While Renaissance humanism demanded Madonnas and saints that were accessible and human, Bellini places them in a physical setting so beautiful that it creates its own mood of serene holiness. The genius of Bellini, perhaps the greatest Venetian painter, is obvious in the pristine clarity, rich colors (notice Mary's clothing), believable depth, and reassuring calm of this three-paneled altarpiece.

Finally, glowing red and gold like a stained-glass window over the high altar, **Titian's** *Assumption of the Virgin* sets the tone of exuberant beauty found in the otherwise sparse church. Titian the Venetian—a student of Bellini—painted steadily for 60 years...you'll see a lot of his art. As stunned apostles look up past the swirl of arms and legs, the complex composition of this painting draws you right to the radiant face of the once-dying, now-triumphant Mary as she joins God in heaven.

▲▲SCUOLA SAN ROCCO

Sometimes called "Tintoretto's Sistine Chapel," this lavish meeting hall (next to the Frari Church) has some 50 large, colorful Tintoretto paintings plastered to the walls and ceilings. The best paintings are upstairs in the grand Chapter Room and especially in an adjacent smaller room, with Tintoretto's *Crucifixion*. View the neck-breaking splendor with the mirrors available in the Chapter Room.

Cost and Hours: €10, daily 9:30-17:30, tel. 041-523-4864, www.scuolagrandesan rocco.org.

Venice's Lagoon

With more time, venture to some nearby islands in Venice's lagoon. While still touristy, they offer an escape from the crowds, a chance to get out on a boat, and some enjoyable diversions for fans of glassmaking, lace, and sunbathing.

LAGOON TOUR

The islands of San Michele (cemetery), Murano (glass), Burano (lace), and Torcello (oldest church in Venice) make a good, varied, and long day trip that you can do on your own.

The Plan: You can travel to any of the

four islands by vaporetto. Since single vaporetto tickets (€7.50) are only valid for 75 minutes, getting a vaporetto pass for a lagoon excursion makes more sense (for details on tickets and passes, see page 639). Confirm vaporetto times by downloading the latest schedule from www.actv.it.

Start your journey at the **Fondamente Nove** vaporetto stop, on Venice's north shore (the "back" of the fish). Fondamente Nove is a pleasant 15-minute walk from Rialto or St. Mark's. Alternatively, you could reach Fondamente Nove by vaporetto: From San Zaccaria (near St. Mark's), take the #4.1 (35 minutes). From the train or bus station, take #4.2 (30 minutes).

From Fondamente Nove, take the #4.1 or #4.2 vaporetto for Murano (about every 10 minutes). On the way, get off at the Cimitero stop on the island of San Michele to see the cemetery (6-minute ride). Continue on to Murano, arriving at the Murano-Colonna stop (3-minute ride). Sightsee Murano as you make your way to the Murano-Faro stop, where you board vaporetto #12 for the trip to Burano (30-40 minutes). From Burano, you can side-trip to Torcello (on the #12, 5-minute trip each way). To return to Venice from Burano, take vaporetto #12 all the way back to Fondamente Nove (45 minutes). For a longer, more scenic return past even more lagoon islands, take the #14 from Burano to the San Zaccaria dock near St.

Mark's Square (70 minutes).

Note that during summer, slightly faster express vaporetti go directly to Murano-Colonna (if you're OK with skipping the cemetery on San Michele): From San Zaccaria, catch the #7, or from the train/bus stations catch the #3.

SAN MICHELE (A.K.A. CIMITERO)

This island is the final resting place of Venetians and a few foreign VIPs, from poet Ezra Pound to composer Igor Stravinsky. It's also full of flowers, trees, scurrying lizards, and birdsong, and has an intriguing chapel (cemetery open daily 7:30-18:00, Oct-March until 16:30).

▲MURANO

Famous for its glassmaking, this island is home to several glass factories and the Glass Museum. From the Colonna vaporetto stop, skip the glass shops in front of you, walk to the right, and wander up the street along the canal, **Fondamenta dei Vetrai** (Glassmakers' Embankment). The Faro district of Murano, on the other side of the canal, is packed with factories (*fabriche*) and their furnaces (*fornaci*). You'll pass dozens more glass shops, including the high-class **Venini** shop, with glass that's a cut above much of what else is on offer here, and with an interior showing off the ultimate in modern Venetian glass design (at #47, closed Sun). Murano's **Glass Museum** (Museo del Vetro)

Murano's Fondamenta dei Vetrai

Firing up the glass furnace on Murano

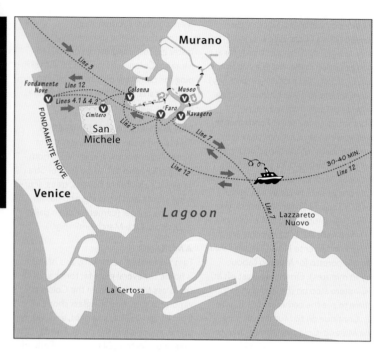

traces the history of this delicate art (€14, daily 10:30-18:30, Nov-March until 16:30, tel. 041-739-586, http://museovetro.visit muve.it).

▲▲BURANO

This island's claim to fame is lacemaking, and (along with countless lace shops) it offers a delightful pastel village alternative to big, bustling Venice. The tight main drag is packed with tourists and lined with shops, some of which sell Burano's locally

produced white wine. Its **Lace Museum** (*Museo del Merletto di Burano*) shows the island's lace heritage (€5, Tue-Sun 10:30-17:00, Nov-March until 16:30, closed Mon year-round, tel. 041-730-034, http://museomerletto.visitmuve.it).

▲TORCELLO

The birthplace of Venice, Torcello is where the first mainland refugees settled, escaping the barbarian hordes. Yet today, it's the least-developed island (pop.

Colorful Burano

Burano lace is prized.

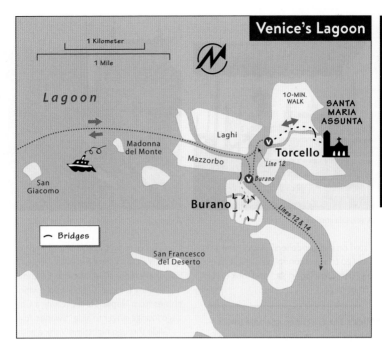

20) in the most natural state, marshy and shrub-covered. There's little for tourists to see except the **Santa Maria Assunta Church,** the oldest in Venice, which still sports some impressive mosaics, a climbable bell tower, and a modest museum of Roman sculpture and medieval sculpture and manuscripts (10-minute walk from dock, €12 combo-ticket covers museum, church, and bell tower; museum only–€3; church and bell tower–€5 each; church open daily 10:30-18:00, Nov-Feb 10:00-17:00, museum and bell tower close 30 minutes earlier, museum closed Mon year-round; museum tel. 041-730-761).

LIDO BEACH

Venice's nearest beach is across the lagoon on an island connected to the mainland (which means car traffic). The sandy beach is pleasant, family-friendly, and good for swimming. You can rent an umbrella, buy beach gear at the shop, get food at the self-service café, or have a drink at the bar. Everything is affordable

and in the same building (vaporetto: Lido S.M.E., walk 10 minutes on Gran Viale S. Maria Elisabetta to beach entry).

EXPERIENCES

Gondola Rides

Riding a gondola in Venice is simple, expensive, and one of the great experiences in Europe. Gondoliers hanging out all over town are eager to have you hop in for a ride. While this is a rip-off for some, it's a traditional must for romantics.

The price for a gondola starts at €80 for a 35-minute ride during the day. You can divide the cost—and the romance—among up to six people per boat, but only two get the love seat. Prices jump to €100 after 19:00—when it's most romantic and relaxing. Adding a singer and an accordionist will cost an additional €120. If you value budget over romance, you can save money by recruiting fellow travelers to split a gondola. Prices are standard and

A gondola station

A gondola ride at night is worth the price.

listed on the gondoliers' association website (go to www.gondolavenezia.it, click on "Using the Gondola," and look under "charterage").

Rick's Tip: *For* **cheap gondola thrills** *during the day, stick to the one-minute ferry ride on a Grand Canal traghetto. At night, vaporetti are nearly empty, and it's a great time to cruise the Grand Canal on the slow boat #1.*

Dozens of gondola stations (*servizio gondole*) are set up along canals all over town. Because your gondolier may offer narration or conversation during your ride, talk with several and choose one you like. You're welcome to review the map and discuss the route. Doing so is also a good way to see if you enjoy the gondolier's personality and language skills. Establish the price, route, and duration of the trip before boarding, enjoy your ride, and pay only when you're finished. Most gondoliers honor the official prices, but a few might try to scam you out of some extra euros, particularly by insisting on a tip. (While not required or even expected, if your gondolier does the full 35 minutes and entertains you en route, a 5-10 percent tip is appreciated; if he's surly or rushes through the trip, skip it.)

If you've hired musicians and want to hear a Venetian song (*un canto Veneziano*), try requesting "Venezia La Luna e Tu." Asking to hear "O Sole Mio" (which comes from Naples) is like asking a Chicago lounge singer to sing "Swanee River."

Glide through nighttime Venice with your head on someone's shoulder. Follow the moon as it sails past otherwise unseen buildings. Silhouettes gaze down from bridges while window glitter spills onto the black water. You're anonymous in the city of masks, as the rhythmic thrust of your striped-shirted gondolier turns old crows into songbirds. This is extremely relaxing (and, I think, worth the extra cost to experience at night).

Festivals

Venice's most famous festival is **Carnevale,** the celebration Americans call Mardi Gras (February; www.carnevale.venezia. it). In Carnevale's heyday—the 1600s and 1700s—you could do pretty much anything with anybody from any social class if you were wearing a mask. These days, tourists and Venetians gather for 18 days of parades, parties, and masquerade balls.

Every year, the city hosts the Venice **Biennale International Art Exhibition,** alternating between art in odd years (the main event) and architecture in even years (much smaller). The exhibition

Carnevale is a masked extravaganza.

spreads over the Arsenale and Giardini park (take vaporetto #1 or #2 to Giardini-Biennale; for details and an events calendar, see www.labiennale.org). The actual exhibition usually runs from June through November, but other events loosely connected with the Biennale—film, dance, theater—are held throughout the year in various venues on the island.

Shopping

Popular souvenirs and gifts include Murano glass, Burano lace, Carnevale masks, prints of Venetian scenes, traditional stationery (pens and marbled paper products of all kinds), calendars with Venetian scenes (and sexy gondoliers), and plenty of goofy knickknacks.

In touristy areas, shops are typically open from 9:00 to 19:30 (sometimes with a break at midday), and some stores are open on Sunday. If you're buying at a market, bargain—it's accepted and almost expected. In shops, you may save by offering to pay cash.

Popular **Venetian glass** is available in many forms: vases, tea sets, decanters, glasses, jewelry, lamps, mod sculptures, and on and on. Shops will ship your glass home for you, but it's expensive, and you may have to pay duty on larger purchases. Make sure the shop insures its merchandise (*assicurazione*), or you're out of luck if it breaks.

You'll want to avoid the cheap glass you'll see—most of it is imported. Genuine, high-end Venetian glass comes with the signature of the artist etched directly into the glass, along with a number if it's a limited edition piece (for example, 14/30—number 14 of a total of 30 pieces made).

If you're serious about glass, visit the island of Murano, its glass museum, and its many shops—you'll find greater variety on the island. Or, consider a free glass-blowing demo at the **Vetri d'Arte** showroom in Palazzo Rota. From Gran Caffè Quadri on St. Mark's Square, Sottoportico dei Dai leads over a bridge and, 30 yards later, directly into a lobby (it's unsigned, look for the ATM) where stairs lead up to the showroom (RS%—20 percent dis-

A Dying City?

Venice's population (fewer than 55,000 in the historic city) is half what it was just 30 years ago, and a thousand people leave every year. Of those who stay, 25 percent are 65 or older.

Sad, yes, but imagine raising a family here: Apartments are small and expensive. Humidity and occasional flooding make basic maintenance a pain. Home-improvement projects require navigating miles of red tape, and you must follow regulations intended to preserve the historical ambience. Everything is expensive because it must be shipped in from the mainland. Running errands involves lots of walking and stairs—imagine crossing over arched bridges while pushing a child in a stroller and carrying a day's worth of groceries.

With millions of visitors a year (150,000 a day at peak times), on any given day Venetians are likely outnumbered by tourists. Despite government efforts to subsidize rents and build cheap housing, the city is losing its residents. The economy itself is thriving, thanks to tourist dollars and rich foreigners buying second homes. But the culture is dying.

Locals happily rent apartments to tourists a few times a month rather than affordably to local families, and shopkeepers sell trinkets to tourists before pots and pans to the local population. Even the most hopeful city planners worry that in a few decades Venice will not be a city at all, but a museum, a cultural theme park, a decaying Disneyland for adults.

count on glass with this book, daily 8:30-17:00, San Marco 834—see the map on page 603 for location, tel. 041-241-2664).

Nightlife

You must experience Venice after dark. The city is quiet at night, as many tour groups (not mine) stay in the cheaper hotels of Mestre on the mainland, and the masses of day-trippers return to their beach resorts and cruise ships.

Check at the TI or the TI's website (www.veneziaunica.it) for listings of events, church concerts, festivals, and entertainment. The free monthly *Un Ospite di Venezia* lists all the latest happenings in English (free at fancy hotels, or check www.unospitedivenezia.it).

Concerts

Venice is a city of the powdered-wig Baroque era. For about €25, you can take your pick of traditional Vivaldi concerts in churches throughout town. You'll find frilly young Vivaldis hawking concert tickets on many corners. Most shows start at 20:30 and generally last 1.5 hours. Hotels sell tickets at face value. Tickets can usually be bought the same day as the concert, so don't bother with websites that sell tickets with a surcharge. Musicians in wigs and tights offer better spectacle; musicians in black-and-white suits are better performers.

The **Interpreti Veneziani orchestra,** considered the best group in town, generally performs 1.5-hour concerts nightly at 21:00 inside the sumptuous San Vidal Church (€28, church ticket booth open daily 9:30-21:00, north end of Accademia Bridge, tel. 041-277-0561, www.interpreti veneziani.com).

Musica a Palazzo is a unique evening of opera at a Venetian palace on the Grand Canal. You'll spend about 45 delightful minutes in each of three sumptuous rooms (about 2.25 hours total) as seven musicians (generally three instruments

The evening café scene on St. Mark's Square

and four singers) perform. With these kinds of surroundings, and under Tiepolo frescoes, you'll be glad you dressed up. As there are only 70 seats, you must book by phone or online in advance (€85, nightly at 20:30, Palazzo Barbarigo Minotto, Fondamenta Duodo o Barbarigo, vaporetto: Santa Maria del Giglio, San Marco 2504, mobile 340-971-7272, www.musicapalazzo.com).

St. Mark's Square

Streetlamp halos, live music, floodlit history, and a ceiling of stars make St. Mark's magic at midnight. Just being here after dark is a thrill, as **dueling café orchestras** entertain.

You can wander around the square listening to the different orchestras, or take a seat at a café. At any place with live music, it's perfectly acceptable to nurse a drink for an hour—you're paying for the music with the cover charge. The prices are clearly posted. If you sit outside and get just an espresso (your cheapest option), expect to pay €12.50—€6.50 for the coffee and a €6 cover charge when the orchestra is playing (which is most of the day). Service is included (no need to tip).

Caffè Florian (on the right as you face the church) is the most famous Venetian café and was one of the first places in Europe to serve coffee. The outside tables are the main action, but walk inside through the richly decorated, old-time rooms where Casanova, Lord Byron, Charles Dickens, and Woody Allen have all paid too much for a drink. The café's orchestra—the most serious on the square—plays daily from 10:00 to 24:00. Each hour comes with a musical theme (operetta, Latin, Romantic, jazz, Venetian, and so on—you can ask for the program; open daily 9:00-24:00, shorter hours in winter, www.caffeflorian.com).

Gran Caffè Quadri, opposite the Florian and established in 1780, has another illustrious roster of famous clientele.

Gran Caffè Lavena, near the Clock Tower, is less storied—although it dates from 1750 and counts composer Richard Wagner as a former regular—so it's less intimidating than the more formal cafés here. Drop in to check out its dazzling but politically incorrect chandelier.

Gran Caffè Chioggia, on the Piazzetta facing the Doge's Palace, charges no cover and has one or two musicians playing—usually a pianist (€7 cocktails, music from 10:30 to 23:00—jazz after 21:00).

Rick's Tip: *You'll hear about the famous* **Harry's American Bar,** *which sells overpriced food and cocktails, but* **it's a tourist trap**...*and the last place Hemingway would drink today. It's cheaper to get a drink at any of the hole-in-the-wall bars just off St. Mark's Square.*

SLEEPING

I've listed rooms in these areas: St. Mark's bustle, the Rialto action, the quiet Dorsoduro area behind the Accademia art museum, and near the train station.

Hotels in Venice can be tricky to locate. The website Venicexplorer.net allows you to search using a hotel's address number and district, which I've included in my listings (click "Venice Civic Number" on the website to open the search window).

Near St. Mark's Square

To get here from the train station or Piazzale Roma bus station, ride the slow vaporetto #1 to San Zaccaria or the fast #2 (which also leaves from Tronchetto parking lot) to San Marco.

East of St. Mark's Square

Located near the Bridge of Sighs, just off the Riva degli Schiavoni waterfront promenade, these places rub drainpipes with Venice's most palatial five-star hotels.

$$$ **Hotel Campiello,** lacy and bright, was once part of a 19th-century convent. Ideally located 50 yards off the waterfront on a tiny square, its 16 rooms offer a tranquil, friendly refuge (RS%, air-con, elevator, just steps from the San Zaccaria vaporetto stop, Castello 4647; tel. 041-520-5764, www.hcampiello.it, campiello@hcampiello.it; family-run for four generations, currently by Thomas, Nicoletta, and Monica). They also rent three modern, upscale, and quiet family apartments for up to six people, under rustic timbers just steps away from the hotel.

$$$$ **Hotel Fontana,** two bridges behind St. Mark's Square, is a pleasant family-run place with 15 sparse but classic-feeling rooms overlooking a lively square (RS%, several rooms with terraces, family rooms, air-con, elevator, closed Jan, on Campo San Provolo at Castello 4701, tel. 041-522-0533, www.hotelfontana.it, info@hotelfontana.it, cousins Diego and Gabriele).

$$$ **Locanda al Leon,** which feels a little like a medieval tower house, is conscientiously run and rents 12 rooms just off Campo Santi Filippo e Giacomo (RS%, some view rooms, family rooms, air-con, one- and two-bedroom apartments, Campo Santi Filippo e Giacomo, Castello 4270, tel. 041-277-0393, www.hotelalleon.com, leon@hotelalleon.com, Giuliano and Marcella). Their annex down the street,

B&B Ca' Marcella, has three newer, classy, and spacious rooms for the same rates (check in at main hotel).

$$ **Albergo Doni,** situated along a quiet canal, is dark and quiet. This time-warp—with creaky floors and 13 well-worn, once-classy rooms—is run by friendly Tessa and her two brothers, Barnaba and (now "retired") Italian stallion Nikos (RS%, cheaper rooms with shared bath, family rooms, ceiling fans, a few rooms have air-con, Wi-Fi in common areas, on Fondamenta del Vin at Castello 4656, tel. 041-522-4267, albergodoni@hotmail.it). The hotel also has three nice overflow apartments at the same prices (but without breakfast).

North of St. Mark's Square

$$$$ **Hotel Orion** rents 21 simple, welcoming, pricey rooms in the center of the action (you're paying a premium for the location). Steep stairs (there's no elevator) take you from the touristy street into a peaceful world high above (RS%—use code RSTEVES, air-con, 2 minutes inland from St. Mark's Square, 10 steps toward St. Mark's from San Zulian Church at Calle Spadaria 700a, tel. 041-522-3053, www.hotelorion.it, info@hotelorion.it).

$$$ **Hotel al Piave,** with 25 rooms above a bright, tight lobby and breakfast room, is comfortable and cheery, and you'll enjoy the neighborhood (RS%, family rooms, lots of narrow stairs, air-con, on Ruga Giuffa at Castello 4838, tel. 041-528-5174, www.hotelalpiave.com, info@hotelalpiave.com; Mirella, Paolo, Ilaria, and Federico).

$$$ **Locanda Silva** is a well-located hotel with a functional 1960s feel and a small terrace. It rents 23 simple rooms with small bathrooms (RS%, a few cheaper rooms with shared bathrooms, closed Dec-Jan, family rooms, air-con, lots of stairs, on Fondamenta del Remedio at Castello 4423, tel. 041-522-7643, www.locandasilva.it, info@locandasilva.it; Sandra and Katia).

Near Campo Santa Maria Formosa

Farther north, the quiet Castello area lies beyond inviting Campo Santa Maria Formosa.

$$$ Locanda la Corte is perfumed with elegance without being snooty. Its 14 attractive, high-ceilinged, wood-beamed rooms—Venetian-style, done in earthy pastels—circle a small, sun-drenched courtyard and a ground-level restaurant (RS%, family rooms, air-con, on Calle Bressana at Castello 6317, tel. 041-241-1300, www.locandalacorte.it, info@locandalacorte.it).

West of St. Mark's Square

These more expensive hotels are solid choices in a more elegant neighborhood.

$$$$ Hotel Flora sits buried in a sea of fancy designer boutiques and elegant hotels almost on the Grand Canal. It's formal, with uniformed staff and grand public spaces, yet the 40 rooms have a homey warmth and the garden oasis is a sanctuary for well-heeled, foot-weary guests (RS%, air-con, elevator, great family-size apartment, on Calle Bergamaschi at San Marco 2283a, tel. 041-520-5844, www.hotelflora.it, info@hotelflora.it).

$$$$ Hotel Bel Sito offers pleasing Old World character, 34 smallish rooms, generous public spaces, a peaceful courtyard, and a picturesque location—facing a church on a small square between St. Mark's Square and the Accademia (RS%, some view rooms, air-con, elevator; near Santa Maria del Giglio vaporetto stop—line #1, on Campo Santa Maria Zobenigo/del Giglio at San Marco 2517, tel. 041-522-3365, www.hotelbelsitovenezia.it, info@hotelbelsitovenezia.it, graceful Rossella).

Near the Rialto Bridge

These places are on opposite sides of the Grand Canal, within a short walk of the Rialto Bridge. Express vaporetto #2 brings you to the Rialto quickly from the train station, the Piazzale Roma bus station, and the parking-lot island of Tronchetto, but you'll need to take the "local" vaporetto #1 to reach the minor stops closer to the last two listings.

$$$$ Hotel al Ponte Antico is exquisite, professional, and small. With nine plush rooms, a velvety royal living/breakfast room, and its own dock for water taxi arrivals, it's perfect for a romantic anniversary. Because its wonderful terrace overlooks the Grand Canal, Rialto Bridge, and market action, its rooms without a canal view may be a better value (air-con, 100 yards from Rialto Bridge at Cannaregio 5768, use Rialto vaporetto stop, tel. 041-241-1944, www.alponteantico.com, info@alponteantico.com, Matteo).

$$$ Pensione Guerrato, right above the colorful Rialto produce market and just two minutes from the Rialto Bridge, is run by friendly, creative, and hardworking Roberto, Piero, Monica, and Matilde. Their 800-year-old building—with 22 spacious, charming rooms—is simple, airy, and wonderfully characteristic. It's a great value considering the location and charm (RS%, cheaper rooms with shared bath, family rooms, air-con, on Calle drio la Scimia at San Polo 240a, take vaporetto #1 to Rialto Mercato stop to save walk over bridge, tel. 041-528-5927, www.hotelguerrato.com, info@hotelguerrato.com). They also rent family apartments in the old center (great for groups of 4-8).

$$$ Hotel al Ponte Mocenigo is off the beaten path—a 10-minute walk northwest of the Rialto Bridge—but it's a great value. This 16th-century Venetian palazzo has a garden terrace and 15 comfy, beautifully appointed, and tranquil rooms (RS%, air-con, take vaporetto #1 to San Stae stop, head inland along right side of church and find Santa Croce 1985, tel. 041-524-4797, www.alpontemocenigo.com, info@alpontemocenigo.com, Sandro and Valter).

Near the Accademia Bridge

As you step over the Accademia Bridge, the commotion of touristy Venice is

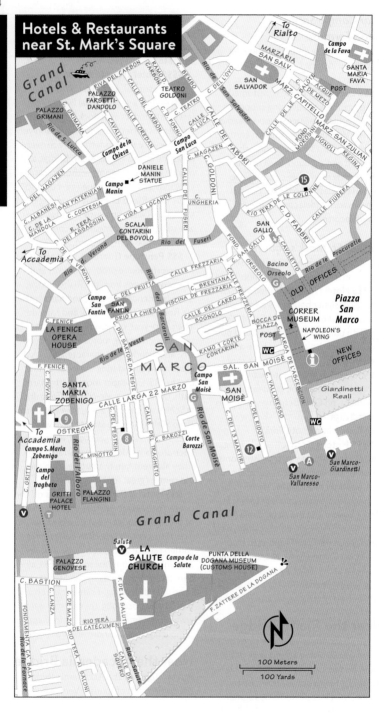

Hotels & Restaurants near St. Mark's Square

Grand Canal

To Rialto

Campo de la Fava

SANTA MARIA FAVA

MARZARIA SAN SALV.

SAN SALVADOR

MARZ. CAPITELLO

POST

PALAZZO GRIMANI

PALAZZO FARSETTI-DANDOLO

RIVA DEL CARBON

RAMO DEL CARBON

C. BEMBO

TEATRO GOLDONI

C. DELL'OVO

C. DE LE ACQUE

C. DE MEZO

MARZ. SAN ZULIAN

FOND. MOROSINI PIGNOLI REGINA

Rio de S. Lucca

Rio del Loyo

CALLE DEL CARBON

CALLE TOREDAN

CAVALLI

C. D. FORNO

CALLE DEL TEATRO

C. TEATRO

CALLE S. LUCA

CALLE DEI FABBRI

Campo San Luca

C. MAGAZEN

Campo de la Chiesa

DANIELE MANIN STATUE

Campo Manin

C. MAGAZEN

C. GOLDONI

C. DE LE COLONNE

CALLE FIUBERA

15

C. DEL MAGAZEN

SAN PATERNIAN

C. VIDA E LOCANDE

CALLE DEI FUSERI

C. UNGHERIA

RIO TERA DE LE COLONNE

C. D. FABBRI

SAN GALLO

C. CAVALETO

C. ALBANESI

C. CORTESIA

SCALA CONTARINI DEL BOVOLO

C. DE LA MANDOLA

R. TERA DEI ASSASSINI

Rio del Fuseri

C. SAN GALLO

Bacino Orseolo

G

Rio de le Procuratie

OLD OFFICES

To Accademia

Rio d. Verona

CALLE FREZZARIA

Piazza San Marco

Campo San Fantin

C. DEL FRUTTA

C. BRENTANA

Rio del Barcaroli

PISCINA DE FREZZARIA

CALLE FREZZARIA

Bacino Orseolo

CORRER MUSEUM

NAPOLEON'S WING

SAN FANTIN

ORIO LA CHIESA

CALLE DEL CARRO BOGNOLO

Bocca de PIAZZA

POST

NEW OFFICES

LA FENICE OPERA HOUSE

C. FENICE

SAN MARCO

RAMO 1 CORTE CONTARINA

WC

i

Rio de le Sartor da Veste

Giardinetti Reali

F. FENICE

C. PIOVAN

SANTA MARIA ZOBENIGO

CALLE LARGA 22 MARZO

SAL. SAN MOISÈ

Campo San Moisè

C. VALLARESSO

CARGA DE L'ASCENSION

9

OSTREGHE

C. DEL PESTRIN

G

SAN MOISÈ

C. DEL RIDOTTO

WC

To Accademia

Campo S. Maria Zobenigo

8

Rio del l'Alboro

G. MINOTTO

CALLE DEL C. BAROZZI

Corte Barozzi

C. DEI 13 MARTIRI

12

V A

San Marco-Giardinetti

Campo del Tragheto

C. GRITTI

GRITTI PALACE HOTEL

PALAZZO FLANGINI

Rio de San Moisè

CALLE DEL TRAGHETO

V

San Marco-Vallaresso

V

T

Grand Canal

PALAZZO GENOVESE

Salute

V

LA SALUTE CHURCH

Campo de la Salute

PUNTA DELLA DOGANA MUSEUM (CUSTOMS HOUSE)

C. BASTION

C. LANZA

C. DE MAZO

F. DE LA SALUTE

F. ZATTERE DE LA DOGANA

FONDAMENTA CA' BALA

Rio de la Fornace

RIO TERA DEI CATECUMENI

RIO TERA AI SALONI

CALLE DEL SQUERO

Rio d. Salute

N

100 Meters

100 Yards

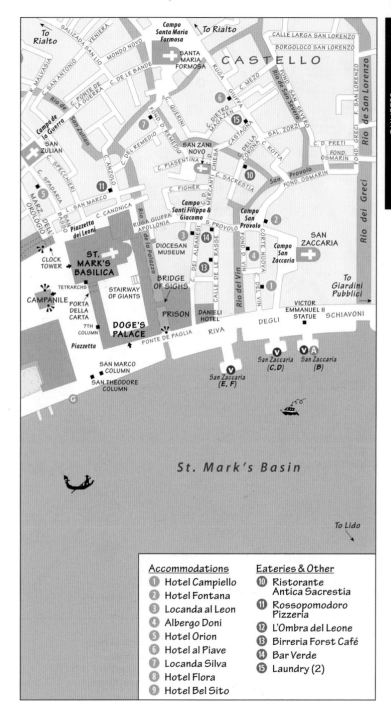

Accommodations
1. Hotel Campiello
2. Hotel Fontana
3. Locanda al Leon
4. Albergo Doni
5. Hotel Orion
6. Hotel al Piave
7. Locanda Silva
8. Hotel Flora
9. Hotel Bel Sito

Eateries & Other
10. Ristorante Antica Sacrestia
11. Rossopomodoro Pizzeria
12. L'Ombra del Leone
13. Birreria Forst Café
14. Bar Verde
15. Laundry (2)

ITALY

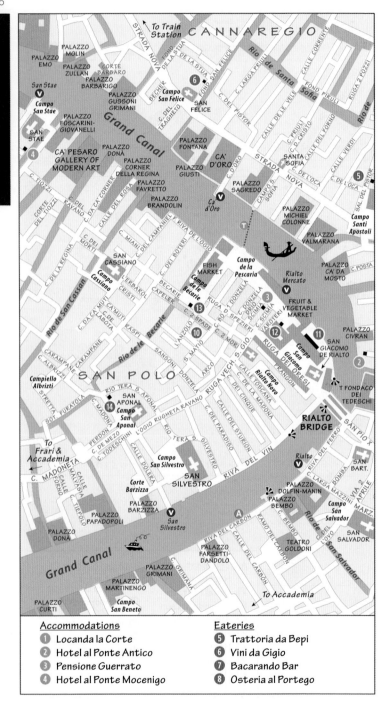

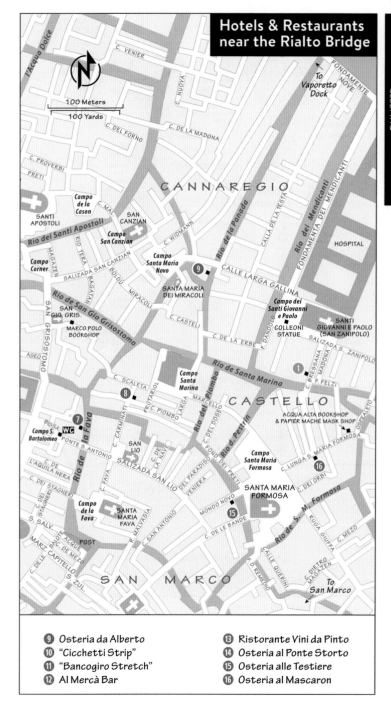

Hotels & Restaurants near the Rialto Bridge

9 Osteria da Alberto

10 "Cicchetti Strip"

11 "Bancogiro Stretch"

12 Al Mercà Bar

13 Ristorante Vini da Pinto

14 Osteria al Ponte Storto

15 Osteria alle Testiere

16 Osteria al Mascaron

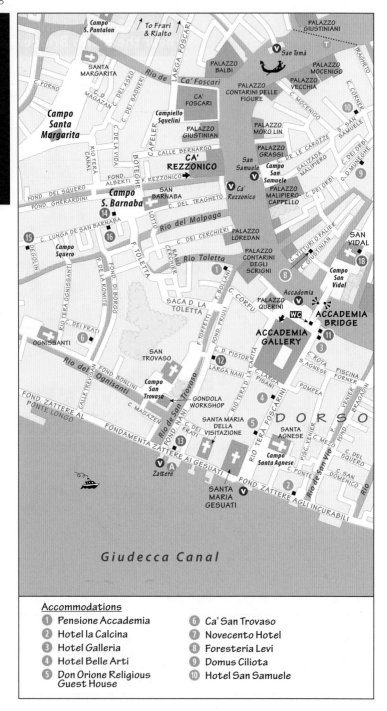

Accommodations

1. Pensione Accademia
2. Hotel la Calcina
3. Hotel Galleria
4. Hotel Belle Arti
5. Don Orione Religious Guest House
6. Ca' San Trovaso
7. Novecento Hotel
8. Foresteria Levi
9. Domus Ciliota
10. Hotel San Samuele

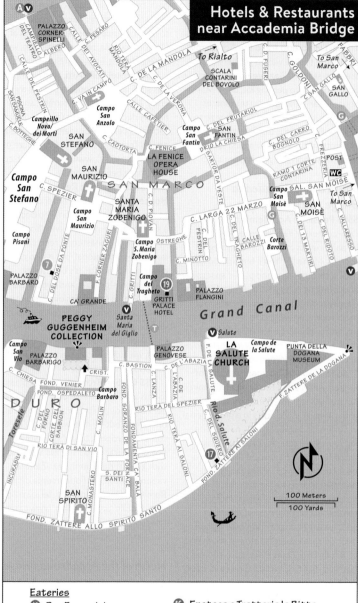

Hotels & Restaurants near Accademia Bridge

Eateries

11 Bar Foscarini

12 Enoteca Cantine del Vino Già Schiavi

13 Terrazza dei Nobili

14 Ristoteca Oniga

15 Pizzeria al Profeta

16 Enoteca e Trattoria la Bitta

17 Ristorante Lineadombra

Nightlife

18 Interpreti Veneziani Concerts

19 Musica a Palazzo

replaced by a sleepy village laced with canals. This quiet area, is a 15-minute walk from the Rialto or St. Mark's Square. The fast vaporetto #2 to the Accademia stop is the typical way to get here from the train station, Piazzale Roma bus station, Tronchetto parking lot, or St. Mark's Square (early and late, #2 terminates at the Rialto stop, where you change to #1). For hotels near the Zattere stop, vaporetto #5.1 or the Alilaguna speedboat from the airport are good options.

South of the Accademia Bridge, in Dorsoduro

$$$$ Pensione Accademia fills the 17th-century Villa Maravege like a Bellini painting. Its 27 comfortable, elegant rooms gild the lily. You'll feel aristocratic gliding through its grand public spaces and lounging in its wistful, breezy gardens (family rooms, air-con, no elevator but most rooms on ground floor or one floor up, on Fondamenta Bollani at Dorsoduro 1058, tel. 041-521-0188, www.pensione accademia.it, info@pensioneaccademia.it).

$$$$ Hotel la Calcina, the home of English writer John Ruskin in 1876, maintains a 19th-century formality. It comes with three-star comforts in a professional yet intimate package. Its 25 nautical-feeling rooms are squeaky clean, with nice wood furniture, hardwood floors, and a peaceful waterside setting facing Giudecca Island (some view rooms, air-con, no elevator and lots of stairs, rooftop terrace, buffet breakfast outdoors in good weather on platform over lagoon, near Zattere vaporetto stop at south end of Rio de San Vio at Dorsoduro 780, tel. 041-520-6466, www.lacalcina.com, info@ lacalcina.com).

$$$$ Hotel Galleria has nine old-fashioned and velvety rooms, half with views of the Grand Canal. Some rooms are quite narrow, but you can open your window to watch boats pass by at any time. It's run with a family feel by Luciano (one cheaper room with detached private bath, breakfast in room, ceiling fans, 30 yards from Accademia art museum, next to recommended Foscarini pizzeria at Dorsoduro 878a, tel. 041-523-2489, www. hotelgalleria.it, info@hotelgalleria.it).

$$$$ Hotel Belle Arti, with a stiff, serious staff, lacks personality but has a grand entry, an inviting garden terrace, and 67 heavily decorated rooms (air-con, elevator, 100 yards behind Accademia art museum on Rio Terà A. Foscarini at Dorsoduro 912a, tel. 041-522-6230, www.hotelbellearti.com, info@hotelbellearti.com).

$$$$ Don Orione Religious Guest House is a big cultural center dedicated to the work of a local man who became a saint in modern times. With 80 rooms filling an old monastery, it feels cookie-cutter-institutional, but is also classy, clean, and peaceful. It's beautifully located, comfortable, and supports a fine cause: Profits go to mission work in the developing world (family rooms, groups welcome, air-con, elevator, on Rio Terà A. Foscarini, Dorsoduro 909a, tel. 041-522-4077, www.donorione-venezia.it, info@ donorione-venezia.it).

$$$ Ca' San Trovaso rents six pleasant rooms in a little three-floor, formerly residential building. The location is peaceful, on a small, out-of-the-way canal (RS%, some view rooms, breakfast in your room, tiny roof terrace, apartments available with 3-night minimum, near Zattere vaporetto stop, off Fondamenta de le Romite at Dorsoduro 1350, tel. 041-241-2215, mobile 349-125-3890, www.casan trovaso.com, info@casantrovaso.com, Anna and Alessandra).

North of the Accademia Bridge

These places are between the Accademia Bridge and St. Mark's Square.

$$$$ Novecento Hotel rents nine plush rooms on three floors, complemented by a big, welcoming lounge, an elegant living room, and a small breakfast garden. This boutique hotel is nicely located and has a tasteful sense of style, mingling Art Deco with North African and Turkish decor (air-con, lots of stairs, on Calle del Dose, off Campo San Maurizio at San Marco 2684, tel. 041-241-3765, www.novecento.biz, info@novecento.biz).

$$$$ Foresteria Levi, run by a foundation that promotes research on Venetian music, offers 32 quiet, institutional yet comfortable and spacious rooms—some are loft quads, a good deal for families (RS%, air-con, elevator, on Calle Giustinian at San Marco 2893, tel. 041-277-0542, www.foresterialevi.it, info@foresterialevi.it). From the base of the Accademia Bridge, it's just over the tiny Ponte Giustinian.

$$$ Domus Ciliota is a big, efficient, and sparkling-clean place—well-run, well-located, church-owned, and plainly furnished—with 30 dorm-like rooms and a peaceful courtyard. If you want industrial-strength comfort with no stress and little character, this is a fine value. During the school year, half the rooms are used by students (air-con, elevator; just off Campo San Stefano at San Marco 2976; tel. 041-520-4888, www.ciliota.it, info@ciliota.it).

$$$ Hotel San Samuele rents 10 tidy rooms in an old *palazzo* near Campo San Stefano. Antique furniture and restored original floors give this place a homey feel. It's in a great locale, and the rooms with shared bath can be a good deal (RS%, no breakfast, fans, some stairs, on Salizada San Samuele at San Marco 3358, tel. 041-520-5165, www.hotelsansamuele.com, info@hotelsansamuele.com, Judith).

EATING

While touristy restaurants are the norm in Venice, my recommended places are popular with locals and respect the tourists who happen by. First trick: Walk away from triple-language menus or laminated pictures of food. Second trick: For freshness, eat fish. Many seafood dishes are the catch-of-the-day. Third trick: Eat later. A place may feel touristy at 19:00, but if you come back at 21:00, it can be filled with locals...or, at least, Italian visitors.

Eating Tips: Unique to Venice, *cicchetti* bars specialize in finger foods and appetizers that combine to make a speedy and tasty meal. *Cicchetti* (the Venetian version of tapas) was designed as a quick meal for working people. The selection and ambience are best on workdays—Monday

Cicchetti *bars in Venice offer tasty snacks.*

through Saturday for lunch or early dinner (see "The Stand-Up Progressive Venetian Pub-Crawl Dinner" sidebar, later).

Sandwiches are sold fast and cheaply at bars everywhere (order a *panini, piadini,* or *tramezzini*). You can eat your sandwich at the bar or take it with you.

A favorite Italian tradition is the *aperitivo* (predinner drink). The dominant *aperitivo* among Venetians is the *spritz* (white wine, soda, and ice with a liquor of your choice). When you order, you'll be asked if you'd like your *spritz con Campari* (bitter) or *con Aperol* (sweeter). Another popular drink is the Bellini—a cocktail of prosecco and white-peach puree, invented at the pricey Harry's American Bar near St. Mark's Square.

Near the Rialto Bridge
North of the Bridge

These restaurants and wine bars are located near or beyond Campo Santi Apostoli, on or near the Strada Nova, the main drag going from Rialto toward the train station.

$$$ Trattoria da Bepi, bright and alpine-paneled, feels like a classic, where Loris carries on his mother's passion for good, traditional Venetian cuisine. Ask for the seasonal specialties: The seafood appetizer plate and crab dishes are excellent. There's good seating inside and out (Fri-Wed 12:00-14:30 & 19:00-22:00, closed Thu, reservations recommended, a half-block off Campo Santi Apostoli on Salizada Pistor, Cannaregio 4550, tel. 041-528-5031, www.dabepi.it).

$$$$ Vini da Gigio, a more expensive option, has a traditional Venetian menu and a classy but unsnooty setting that's a pleasant mix of traditional and contemporary (Wed-Sun 12:00-14:30 & 19:00-22:30, closed Mon-Tue, 4 blocks from Ca' d'Oro vaporetto stop on Fondamenta San Felice, behind the church on Campo San Felice, Cannaregio 3628a, tel. 041-528-5140, www.vinidagigio.com).

East of the Rialto Bridge

The next few places hide away in the twisty lanes between the Rialto Bridge and Campo Santa Maria Formosa. Osteria da Alberto is a tad farther north of the others.

$ Bacarando Bar has a youthful feel, with clearly marked and priced little dishes at the counter and table seating (daily 11:00-24:00, tel. 342-800-3823). It's behind Campo San Bartolomeo (if the statue turned around, walked to the far right-hand corner, and explored the back lanes there, he'd find Bacarando in Corte dell'Orso).

$$ Osteria al Portego is a small and popular neighborhood eatery near Campo San Lio. Carlo serves good meals, bargain-priced house wine, and excellent €1-3 cicchetti—best enjoyed around 18:00 (picked over by 21:00). The *cicchetti* here can make a great meal, but consider sitting down for a dinner from their menu. From 12:00-14:30 & 17:30-21:30, their six tables are reserved for those ordering from the menu; reserve ahead if you want a table (daily 11:30-15:00 & 17:30-22:00, on Calle de la Malvasia, Castello 6015, tel. 041-522-9038, Federica). From Campo San Bartolomeo, continue over a bridge to Campo San Lio, turn left, and follow Calle Carminati straight 50 yards over another bridge.

$$ Osteria da Alberto, up near Campo Santa Maria Novo, is one of my standbys, with locals at lunch and tourists at dinner. They offer up excellent daily specials: seafood dishes, pastas, and a good house wine in a woody and characteristic interior. It's smart to reserve at night—I'd request a table in front (daily 12:00-15:00 & 18:30-22:00; on Calle Larga Giacinto Gallina, midway between Campo Santi Apostoli and Campo San Zanipolo/Santi Giovanni e Paolo, and next to Ponte de la Panada bridge, Cannaregio 5401; tel. 041-523-8153, www.osteriadaalberto.it, run by Graziano and Giovanni).

The Stand-Up Progressive Venetian Pub-Crawl Dinner

My favorite Venetian dinner is a pub crawl (*giro d'ombra*)—a tradition unique to Venice. (*Giro* means stroll, and *ombra*—slang for a glass of wine—means shade, from the old days when a portable wine bar scooted with the shadow of the Campanile bell tower across St. Mark's Square.)

Venice's residential back streets hide plenty of characteristic bars (*bacari*), with countless trays of interesting toothpick munchies (*cicchetti*) and wines served by the glass. The *cicchetti* selection is best early, so start your evening by 18:00. Many bars are closed on Sunday. For a guided pub crawl, consider a tour with charming Alessandro Schezzini (see page 588).

Cicchetti bars have a social stand-up zone and a cozy gaggle of tables where you can generally sit down with your *cicchetti* or order from a simple menu. Look for a place that's more "bar" than "restaurant." Make sure they have *cicchetti* on display. Bar-hopping Venetians enjoy an *aperitivo*, a before-dinner drink (try a Bellini, a *spritz con Aperol,* or a prosecco).

While you can order a plate, Venetians prefer going one-by-one...sipping their wine and trying this...then one of those...and so on. Try deep-fried mozzarella cheese, gorgonzola, calamari, artichoke hearts, and anything ugly on a toothpick. Crostini (small toasted bread with a topping) are popular, as are marinated seafood, olives, and prosciutto with melon. Meat and fish (*pesce;* PESH-ay) munchies can be expensive; veggies (*verdure*) are cheap, at about €3 for a meal-sized plate. There's usually a set price per food item (e.g., €1.50). To get a plate of assorted appetizers for €8, ask for "*Un piatto classico di cicchetti misti da €8*" (oon pee-AH-toh KLAH-see-koh dee chee-KET-tee MEE-stee dah OH-toh eh-OO-roh). Bread sticks (*grissini*) are free.

An *ombra rosso* (red) or *ombra bianco* (white), or a small beer (*birrino*) costs about €1. *Vin bon,* Venetian for fine wine, is €2-6 per little glass. A good last drink is *fragolino,* the local sweet wine—*bianco* or *rosso.* It often comes with a little cookie (*biscotto*) for dipping.

Rialto Market Area

The north end of the Rialto Bridge is a great area for menu browsing, bar-hopping, drinks, and snacks; it also has fine sit-down restaurants. You'll find lots of hard-working holes-in-the-wall with a line on the freshest of ingredients and catering to local shoppers needing a quick, affordable, and tasty bite. It's crowded by day, nearly empty early in the evening, and packed with trendy Venetians later.

My listings include a stretch of dark and rustic pubs serving *cicchetti* (Venetian tapas), a strip of trendy places fronting the Grand Canal, and several places at the market and nearby.

The Cicchetti Strip: The 100-yard-long stretch starting two blocks inland from the Rialto Market (along Sotoportego dei Do Mori and Calle de le Do Spade) is beloved for its delightful bar munchies, good wine by the glass, and fun stand-up conviviality. These four **$** places serve food all day, but the spread is best at around noon (unless otherwise noted, generally open daily 12:00-15:00 & 18:00-20:00 or 21:00). Scout these places in advance (listed in the order you'll reach

Venetian Cuisine

Even more so than the rest of Italy, Venetian cuisine relies heavily on fish, shellfish, risotto, and polenta. For more on Italian food, see the "Eating" section of the Practicalities chapter.

Antipasti (Appetizers)

Venetians often start a meal with some *cicchetti*—finger-food appetizers. For tips on eating in Venice's *cicchetti* bars, see page 631.

Antipasto di mare: Marinated mix of chilled fish and shellfish

Asiago cheese: Cow's-milk cheese that's either *mezzano* (young, creamy) or *stravecchio* (aged, pungent)

Sarde in saor: Sardines marinated with onions

Rice, Pasta, and Polenta

Bigoli in salsa: Long, fat, whole-wheat noodle in anchovy sauce

Pasta alla buzzara: Pasta in a seafood-tomato sauce, generally with shrimp

Pasta al pomodoro: Pasta in a simple tomato sauce

Pasta al vongole: Pasta with clams

Pasta e fagioli: Bean-and-pasta soup

Polenta: Thick cornmeal porridge served soft or cut into firm slabs and grilled

Risi e bisi: Rice and peas

them, if coming from the Rialto Bridge) to help decide which ambience is right for the experience you have in mind.

At each place, look for the list of snacks (around €2) and wine by the glass (€1-3) at the bar or on the wall. **Bar all'Arco,** a bustling one-room joint, is particularly enjoyable for its *cicchetti* (Mon-Sat 10:00-17:00, closed Sun, San Polo 436; Francesco, Anna, Matteo). **Cantina Do Mori** has been famous with locals (since 1462) and savvy travelers (since 1982) as a convivial place for wine and *francobolli* (a spicy selection of 20 tiny, mayo-soaked sandwiches nicknamed "stamps"). Go here to be abused in

a fine atmosphere—the frowns are part of the shtick—and be aware that prices can add up quickly (closed Sun, can be shoulder-to-shoulder, San Polo 430).

Osteria ai Storti is more of a sit-down place (tables inside and on street). It's run by Alessandro, who speaks English and enjoys helping educate travelers (around the corner from Cantina Do Mori on Calle San Matio, San Polo 819). **Cantina Do Spade** is run by Francesco and is also good for sit-down restaurant-style meals (30 yards down Calle de le Do Spade from Osteria ai Storti at San Polo 860, tel. 041-521-0583).

Risotto: Short-grain rice simmered in broth with seafood, meat, or veggies. *Risotto al nero*—black risotto—is made with squid ink.

Frutti di Mare (Seafood)

Baccalà: Preserved Atlantic salt cod that's rehydrated and served with polenta; also mixed with mayonnaise as a *cicchetti* topping called *baccalà mantecato*

Branzino: Sea bass, grilled and served whole

Calamari: Squid, often cut into rings and deep-fried or marinated

Cozze: Mussels, often steamed in an herb broth with tomato

Gamberi: Shrimp—*gamberetti* are small, and *gamberoni* are large.

Moleche col pien: Fried soft-shell crabs

Orata: Sea bream, a white fish

Pesce fritto misto: Deep-fried seafood, often calamari and prawns

Pesce spada: Swordfish

Rombo: Turbot, a flatfish similar to flounder

Rospo: Frogfish, a small fish that's often grilled

Salmone: Salmon

Seppia: Cuttlefish, a squid-like creature. *Nero di seppia* is the squid served in its own ink, often over spaghetti.

Sogliola: Sole, served poached or oven-roasted

Vitello di mare: "Sea veal," like swordfish—firm, mild, and grilled

Vongole: Clams, often steamed with fresh herbs and wine, or served as *spaghetti alle vongole*

Zuppa di pesce: Seafood stew

Canalside Seating: What I call the "Bancogiro Stretch," just past the Rialto Bridge, between Campo San Giacomo and the Grand Canal, has some of the best canalside seating in Venice. Unless otherwise noted, all are open daily and serve drinks, *cicchetti,* and somewhat pricey sit-down meals. But between mealtimes you can enjoy a drink or a snack at fine prices. After dinner hours, the Bancogiro Stretch—especially in the surrounding alleys that house low-rent bars—becomes a trendy nightspot. Here's the rundown (in the order you'll reach them from the Rialto Bridge): **$$$ Bar Naranzaria** serves Italian dishes with a few Japanese options. **$$ Caffè Vergnano** is your cheapest option (vegetarian dishes and a busy microwave oven). **$$$ Osteria al Pesador** has a friendly staff and serves local specialties. **$$$ Osteria Bancogiro** has the best reputation for dinner, a passion for the best cheese, and good *cicchetti* options at the bar (nice cheese plate, closed Mon, tel. 041-523-2061). The more modern **$$ Bar Ancòra** seems to be most popular with the local bar crowd, with a live piano player crooning lounge music during busy times (*cicchetti* at the bar).

At the Market: A few steps away and off the canal, **$ Al Mercà Bar** ("At the Market") is a lively little nook with a happy crowd. The price list is clear, and the youthful crowd seems to enjoy connecting with curious tourists (stand at bar or in square—there are no tables and no interior, Mon-Sat 10:00-14:30 & 18:00-21:00, closed Sun, on Campo Cesare Battisti, San Polo 213).

$$ Ristorante Vini da Pinto is a tourist-friendly eatery facing the fish market, with a large menu and relaxing outdoor seating (and easily confused with the restaurant next door). Owner Giorgio visits the market each morning to select the day's best catch. Enjoy the lunch-only, fixed-price, three-course seafood meal for €18, including a pasta, seafood sampler plate, veggies, and dessert. Rick Steves readers receive a welcoming prosecco and a farewell *limoncello* and homemade cookie (daily 11:00-23:00, Campo de le Becarie, San Polo 367a, tel. 041-522-4599).

Farther Inland, off Campo San Aponal: A little family-run place, **$$ Osteria al Ponte Storto** is on a quiet canalside corner a block off the main drag and worth seeking out for its good-value main dishes, daily specials, and peaceful location (Tue-Sun 12:00-15:00 & 18:00-21:45, closed Mon, down Calle Bianca from San Aponal church, San Polo 1278, tel. 041-528-2144, Nicola is the chef/owner).

Near St. Mark's Square

$$$$ Ristorante Antica Sacrestia is a classic restaurant where the owner, Pino, greets you personally. His staff serves creative fixed-price meals (€35, €55, or €80), a humdrum *menù del giorno,* and wonderful pizzas. You can also order à la carte; their antipasto spread looks like a lagoon aquarium spread out on a plate. My readers are welcome to a free *sgroppino* (lemon vodka after-dinner drink) upon request (Tue-Sun 11:30-15:00 & 18:00-23:00, closed Mon, behind San Zaninovo/Giovanni Novo Church on Calle Corona, Castello 4463, tel. 041-523-0749, www.anticasacrestia.it). There's no wine by the glass. Order carefully. Pizza is your only budget escape.

$$ Rossopomodoro Pizzeria is a big, fun, and practical pizzeria offering top quality, good prices, and a very handy location. They cook Naples-style pizzas in their wood oven and offer a selection of hearty salads and pastas (long hours daily, Calle Larga San Marco 404, tel. 041-243-8949).

$$$ L'Ombra del Leone is a modern and classy bar (with attached restaurant) featuring an outdoor terrace right on the Grand Canal. It's in the Biennale offices and is popular with gondoliers. Its bar menu of salads and sandwiches has reasonable prices for the elegance and location (long hours daily, in Ca' Giustinian, behind San Moisè Church at the end of Calle Ridotto, tel. 041-241-3519).

Sandwich Row: On Calle de le Rasse, just steps away from the tourist intensity at St. Mark's Square, is a handy strip lined with several **$ sandwich bars.** It's the closest place to St. Mark's to get a decent sandwich at an affordable price with a place to sit down (most places open long hours daily, about €1 extra per item to sit; from the Bridge of Sighs, head down the Riva and take the second lane on the left). They all sell the *tramezzino* local-style sandwiches. Try **Birreria Forst** (daily 9:30-23:00, air-con, rustic wood tables, Castello 4540, tel. 041-523-0557) or **Bar Verde** (also splittable salads, fresh pastries, at the end of Calle de le Rasse facing Campo Santi Filippo e Giacomo, Castello 4526).

Rick's Tip: *Though you* **can't picnic on St. Mark's Square,** *you can take your snacks to the* **nearby Giardinetti Reali,** *the small park along the waterfront west of the Piazzetta.*

North of St. Mark's Square, near Campo Santa Maria Formosa

For a (marginally) less touristy scene, walk a few blocks north to the inviting Campo Santa Maria Formosa.

$$$$ Osteria alle Testiere is my top dining splurge in Venice. Hugely respected, Luca and his staff are dedicated to quality, serving up creative, artfully presented market-fresh seafood (there's no meat on the menu), homemade pastas, and fine wine. With only 22 seats, it's tight and homey, with the focus on food and service. They have daily specials, 10 wines by the glass, and one agenda: a great dining experience. They're open for lunch (12:00-15:00), and reservations made via email only are a must for their two dinner seatings: 19:00 and 21:30 (plan on spending €60 for dinner, closed Sun-Mon, on Calle del Mondo Novo, just off Campo Santa Maria Formosa, Castello 5801, tel. 041-522-7220, www.osterialletestiere.it, info@osterialletestiere.it

$$$ Osteria al Mascaron is a rustic little bar-turned-restaurant where Gigi, Momi, and their food-loving band of ruffians dish up rustic-yet-sumptuous pastas with steamy seafood. The *antipasto misto* fish-and-vegetable plate and two glasses of wine make a terrific light meal (Mon-Sat 12:00-15:00 & 18:00-23:00, closed Sun, reservations smart Fri-Sat; on Calle Lunga Santa Maria Formosa, a block past Campo Santa Maria Formosa, Castello 5225; tel. 041-522-5995, www.osteriamascaron.it).

Dorsoduro

These recommendations are within a 10-minute walk of the Accademia Bridge and well worth the walk.

Near the Accademia Bridge

$$ Bar Foscarini, next to the Accademia Bridge and Galleria, offers decent pizzas and *panini* in a memorable Grand Canal-view setting. The food is forgettable and drinks are pricey. But you're paying a premium for this premium location. They also serve breakfast (daily 8:00-23:00, Nov-April until 20:30, on Rio Terà A. Foscarini, Dorsoduro 878c, tel. 041-522-7281, Paolo and Simone).

$ Enoteca Cantine del Vino Già Schiavi, with a wonderfully characteristic *cicchetti*-bar ambience, is much loved for its inexpensive *cicchetti,* sandwiches (order from list on board), and wine. You're welcome to enjoy your wine and finger food at the bar, in the back room surrounded by wine bottles, or out on the sidewalk (specify *"fuori"* to sit outside and they'll provide plastic cups; please don't sit on the bridge). This is primarily a wine shop with great prices for bottles to go (Mon-Sat 8:30-20:30, closed Sun, 100 yards from Accademia art museum on San Trovaso canal; facing the Accademia, take a right and then a forced left at the canal to the second bridge—it's at Dorsoduro 992, tel. 041-523-0034; they have no WC).

Zattere

The far south side of Dorsoduro has a wide promenade along the canal that, on warm summer evenings, has a special charm.

$$$ Terrazza dei Nobili takes full advantage of the warm, romantic evening sun. They serve regional specialties and pizza at tolerable prices. The breezy and beautiful seaside seating comes with formal service and the rumble of vaporetti from the nearby stop. The interior is bright and hip (daily 12:00-24:00; at the Zattere vaporetto stop, turn left to Dorsoduro 924; tel. 041-520-6895).

On or near Campo San Barnaba

This small square is a delight—especially in the evening. Reservations may be necessary to dine later in the evening.

$$$ Ristoteca Oniga has an eclectic yet cozy interior, great tables on the square, and is run by the enthusiastic Raffaele. The menu has a few vegetarian and meat dishes but focuses on fresh fish and other

ITALY

Splurging on a Great View

A meal with a view generally comes with lower quality and/or higher prices. But if you're determined to take home a canalside memory, these places are worth the splurge.

Overlooking the Giudecca Canal: Immediately behind La Salute Church, **$$$$ Ristorante Lineadombra** has commanding lagoon views of the Giudecca Canal. The gorgeously presented dishes are both local and modern. Reserve ahead and choose seating inside or on their terrace (daily 12:00-15:00 & 19:00-22:00, closed Tue off-season, directly across the island from the Salute vaporetto stop, Dorsoduro 19, tel. 041-241-1881, www.ristorantelineadombra.com).

On Fondamente Nove, with a Lagoon View: $$$$ Ristorante Algiubagiò is a good place for quality, creative Venetian cuisine with a view over the northern lagoon. Reserve a waterside table or sit in their classy dining room (daily 12:00-15:00 & 19:00-22:30, between the two sets of vaporetto docks on Fondamente Nove, Cannaregio 5039, tel. 041-523-6084, www.algiubagio.net).

On St. Mark's Square: At **$$$$ Gran Caffè Quadri** (a.k.a. Bistro ABC Quadri), you'll enjoy a traditional and accessible menu and prices that won't ruin your appetite. While its 15 tables are all inside, the orchestra is just out the window (daily 12:00-15:00 & 19:00-22:30, reservations smart, San Marco 121, tel. 041-522-2105, www.alajmo.it/grancaffe-quadri).

sea creatures, highlighted by their specialty, *bucintoro*—a pan full of mussels, clams, prawns, calamari, and spaghetti (daily 12:00-14:30 & 19:00-22:30, reservations smart, Campo San Barnaba, Dorsoduro 2852, tel. 041-522-4410, www.oniga.it).

$$ Pizzeria al Profeta is a casual place popular with tourists for great pizza. Its sprawling interior seems to stoke conviviality, as does its leafy garden out back (daily 12:00-14:30 & 19:00-23:30; from Campo San Barnaba, a long walk down Calle Lunga San Barnaba to #2671; tel. 041-523-7466).

$$$ Enoteca e Trattoria la Bitta is dark and woody, with a soft-jazz bistro feel, tight seating, and a small back patio. They serve beautifully presented, traditional Venetian food with—proudly—no fish. Their helpful wait staff and small, handwritten daily menu are focused on local ingredients (including rabbit) and a "slow food" ethic. They offer two dinner seatings (19:00 and 21:00) and require res-

ervations (dinner only, closed Sun, cash only, just off Campo San Barnaba on Calle Lunga San Barnaba, Dorsoduro 2753a, tel. 041-523-0531, Debora and Marcellino).

TRANSPORTATION

Getting Around Venice

Narrow pedestrian walkways connect Venice's docks, squares, bridges, and courtyards. To navigate, look for signs on street corners pointing you to (*per*) the nearest major landmark. Determine whether your destination is in the direction of a major, signposted landmark, then follow the signs through the maze.

Every building in Venice has a house number. The numbers relate to the district (each with about 6,000 address numbers), not the street. If you need to find a specific address, it helps to know its district, street, house number, and nearby landmarks.

Some helpful street terminology:

Campo means square, a campiello is a small square, calle (pronounced "KAH-lay" with an "L" sound) means "street," and a ponte is a bridge. A fondamenta is the embankment along a canal or the lagoon. A rio terà is a street that was once a canal and has been filled in. A sotoportego is a covered passageway. Salizzada literally means a paved area (usually a wide street). The abbreviations S. and SS. mean "saint" and "saints" respectively. Don't get hung up on the exact spelling of street and square names, which may sometimes appear in Venetian dialect (which uses de la, novo, and vechio) and other times in standard Italian (which uses della, nuovo, and vecchio).

By Vaporetto

These motorized bus-boats work like city buses except that they never get a flat, the stops are docks, and if you jump off between stops, you might drown. You can purchase tickets and passes at docks and from ACTV affiliate VèneziaUnica (ACTV—tel. 041-2424, www.actv.it; VèneziaUnica—www.veneziaunica.it).

TICKETS AND PASSES

Individual Vaporetto Tickets: A single ticket costs €7.50 (kids under 6 travel free). Tickets are good for 75 minutes; you can hop on and off at stops and change boats during that time. Your ticket (a paper ticket embedded with a chip) is refillable—you can put more money on it at the kiosks and avoid waiting in line at the ticket window. It's also smart to keep your receipt (in case you're checked and your ticket is faulty).

Vaporetto Passes: You can buy a pass for unlimited use of vaporetti: €20/24 hours, €30/48 hours, €40/72 hours, €60/7-day pass (the clock starts ticking the first time you use it). Because single tickets are pricey, these passes pay for themselves in a hurry. Think through your Venice itinerary before you step up to the ticket booth to pay for your first vaporetto trip. The 48-hour pass pays for itself with five rides (for example: to your hotel on your arrival, on a Grand Canal joyride, into the lagoon and back, to the train station...and that spur-of-the-moment moonlight cruise). Some smaller and outlying stops are

Helpful signs direct you toward (per) your destination in maze-like Venice.

unstaffed—another reason to buy a pass.

Travelers between ages 14-29 can get a 72-hour pass for €22 if they also buy a **Rolling Venice** discount card for €6 (see page 602).

Passes are also valid on some of ACTV's mainland buses, including bus #2 to Mestre (but not the #5 to the airport nor the airport buses run by ATVO, a separate company). Pass holders get a discounted fare for all ACTV buses that originate or terminate at Marco Polo Airport (see page 645).

Buying and Validating Tickets and Passes: Purchase tickets and passes from the machines at most stops (English-language option, major credit cards accepted), from ticket windows (at larger stops), or from the VèneziaUnica offices at the train station, bus station, and Tronchetto parking lot.

Before you board, validate your ticket or pass by touching it to the small white pad on the dock until you hear a pinging sound. With passes, you need to touch the pass each time you board. The machine readout shows how long your ticket is valid—and inspectors often check tickets. If you're unable to purchase a ticket before boarding, seek out the conductor immediately to buy a single ticket (or risk a €60 fine).

IMPORTANT VAPORETTO LINES

For most travelers, only two vaporetto lines matter: **line #1** and **line #2**. These lines leave every 10 minutes or so and go up and down the Grand Canal, between the "mouth" of the fish at one end and St. Mark's Square at the other. Line #1 is the slow boat, taking 45 minutes and making every stop along the way. Line #2 is the fast boat that zips down the Grand Canal in 25 minutes, stopping only at Tronchetto (parking lot), Piazzale Roma (bus station), Ferrovia (train station), Rialto Bridge, San Tomà (Frari Church), San Samuele (opposite Ca' Rezzonico), Accademia Bridge, and San Marco (west end of St. Mark's Square, end of the line).

Study the maps at docks before you board. Some boats run on circular routes, in one direction only (for example, lines #5.1 and #5.2, plus the non-Murano sections of lines #4.1 and #4.2). Line #2 runs in both directions and is almost, but not quite, a full loop. The #2 boat leaving from the San Marco stop goes in one direction (up the Grand Canal), while from the San Zaccaria stop—just a five-minute walk away—it goes in the opposite direction (around the tail of the "fish").

To clear up any confusion, ask a ticket-seller or conductor for help (sometimes they're stationed on the dock). Get a copy of the most current ACTV map and timetable (download from www.actv.it, theoretically free at ticket booths but often unavailable). System maps are posted at stops, but it's smart to print out your own copy of the map from the ACTV website before your trip.

BOARDING AND RIDING

Many stops have more than one departure platform. At these larger stops, check the electronic departure board to see which boats are coming next, when, where they're going, and from which platform they leave (for example, "Line 2 to San Marco, from platform B"). At smaller stops without electronic displays, signs on each platform show the vaporetto lines that stop there and the direction they are headed. Be aware that other boats may

A traghetto *crossing*

Handy Vaporetti from San Zaccaria, near St. Mark's Square

Several vaporetti leave from the San Zaccaria docks, located 150 yards east of St. Mark's Square. The four docks are spaced about 70 yards apart, with six different berths, lettered A to F. Check the big electronic board (next to the C/D dock), which indicates the departure time, line number, destination, and berth letter of upcoming vaporetti. Once you've figured out which boat you want, go to that letter berth and hop on.

• **Line #1:** This vaporetto goes up the Grand Canal, making all the stops, including San Marco, Rialto, Ferrovia (train station), and Piazzale Roma (but it does not go as far as Tronchetto). In the other direction, it goes from San Zaccaria to Arsenale and Giardini before ending on the Lido (dock E).

• **Line #2:** This vaporetto zips over to San Giorgio Maggiore, the island church across from St. Mark's Square (5 minutes, €5 ride). From there, it continues on to stops on the island of Giudecca, the parking lot at Tronchetto, and then down the Grand Canal (dock B). Note: You cannot ride the #2 up the Grand Canal (for example, to Rialto or the train station) directly from this stop—you'll need to walk five minutes along the waterfront, past St. Mark's Square, to the San Marco-Giardinetti dock and hop the #2 from there.

• **Line #4.1:** This boat goes to San Michele and Murano (45 minutes, dock D).

• **Line #7:** This is the summertime express boat to Murano (25 minutes, dock D).

• **Molino Stucky Shuttle Boat:** This takes even non-guests to the Hilton Hotel, with its popular view bar (20-minute ride, 3/hour, from its own dock near the San Zaccaria-B dock).

• **Lines #5.1 and #5.2:** These are the *circulare* (cheer-koo-LAH-ray) lines, making a loop around the perimeter of the island, with a stop at the Lido—perfect if you just like riding boats. Line #5.1 goes counterclockwise, and #5.2 goes clockwise. Both run less frequently in the evenings (#5.1 leaves from dock D, #5.2 from dock C).

• **Alilaguna Shuttle Boat:** This runs to and from the airport (dock D).

also be leaving from your same platform. When your boat arrives, confirm the direction posted on the bow ("Line 2, San Marco"). To double-check, ask the conductor when you board ("San Marco?").

By Traghetto

Only four bridges cross the Grand Canal, but *traghetti* (shuttle gondolas) ferry locals and in-the-know tourists across the Grand Canal at three additional locations. Just step in, hand the gondolier €2, and enjoy the ride. Some *traghetti* are seasonal, some stop running as early as 12:30,

and all stop by 18:00. *Traghetti* are not covered by any transit pass.

By Water Taxi

Venetian taxis hang out at busy points along the Grand Canal. Prices are regulated: €15 for pickup, then €2 per minute; €5 per person for more than four passengers (boats can carry around 10 people); and €10 between 22:00 and 6:00. If you have more bags than passengers, the extra ones cost €5 apiece. Despite regulation, prices can be soft; negotiate before stepping in. For travelers with lots of luggage or small

Vaporettos ply the busy Grand Canal.

groups who can split the cost, taxi boat rides can be a worthwhile and time-saving convenience—and skipping across the lagoon in a classic wooden motorboat is a cool indulgence. For about €120 an hour, you can have a private, unguided taxi-boat tour. You may find more competitive rates if you prebook through the Consorzio Motoscafi water taxi association (tel. 041-522-2303, www.motoscafivenezia.it).

Arriving and Departing

A two-mile-long causeway (with highway and train lines) connects Venice to the mainland.

By Train

All trains to "Venice" stop at Venezia Mestre (on the mainland). Most continue on to **Santa Lucia Station** (a.k.a. Venezia S.L.) on the island of Venice itself. If your train happens to terminate at Mestre, you'll need to buy a €1.25 Mestre-Santa Lucia ticket and validate it before hopping any nonexpress, regional train (with an R or RV prefix) for the ride across the

causeway to Venice (6/hour, 10 minutes).

Santa Lucia train station is right on the Grand Canal, an easy vaporetto ride or fascinating 45-minute walk (with a number of bridges and steps) to St. Mark's Square.

The station has a **baggage check** (daily 6:00-23:00, no lockers; along track 1). Pay **WCs** are at track 1 and in the back of the big bar/cafeteria area inside the station. You'll find the **TI** across from track 2.

Getting from the Train Station to Central Venice: It's best by **vaporetto.** Walk straight out of the station to the canal, where you'll see five vaporetto docks (A, B, C, D, and E), each serving different boats. Electronic signboards show which boats are leaving when and from which dock (for example, boat #2 to San Marco, from dock B). Most tourists want the fast boat #2 down the Grand Canal to Rialto and San Marco (generally from dock B) or the slow boat #1 down the Grand Canal, making every stop all the way to Rialto and San Marco. A **water taxi** from the train station to central Venice costs about €60-80 (the taxi dock is straight ahead).

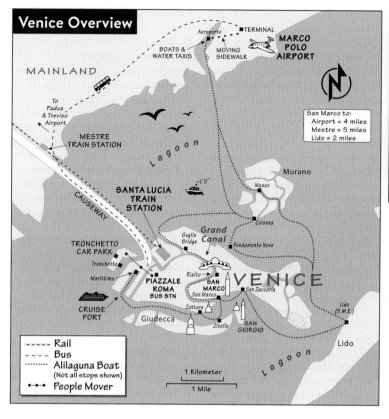

Map labels: Venice Overview · MARCO POLO AIRPORT · TERMINAL · Aeroporto · BOATS & WATER TAXIS · MOVING SIDEWALK · MAINLAND · To Padua & Treviso Airport · MESTRE TRAIN STATION · Lagoon · SANTA LUCIA TRAIN STATION · CAUSEWAY · Murano · Museo · Colonna · Fondamente Nove · Guglie Bridge · Grand Canal · TRONCHETTO CAR PARK · Tronchetto · Marittima · PIAZZALE ROMA BUS STN · Rialto · SAN MARCO · San Marco · VENICE · San Zaccaria · CRUISE PORT · Zattere · Giudecca · Zitelle · SAN GIORGIO · Lido (S.M.E.) · Lido

San Marco to:
Airport = 4 miles
Mestre = 5 miles
Lido = 2 miles

Legend:
Rail
Bus
Alilaguna Boat (Not all stops shown)
People Mover

1 Kilometer
1 Mile

TRAIN CONNECTIONS

From Venice by Train to: Padua (30 minutes, Trenitalia: 2/hour, Italo: hourly), **Verona** (1.5 hours, Trenitalia: 2/hour, Italo: 7/day), **Florence** (Trenitalia: hourly, 2-3 hours, may transfer in Bologna, often crowded—reserve ahead; Italo: 4/day, 2 hours, reservations required), **Milan** (Trenitalia: 2/hour, most direct on high-speed ES trains, 2.5 hours; Italo: 7/day, 2.5 hours), **Cinque Terre/Monterosso** (5/day, 6 hours, change in Milan), **Rome** (Trenitalia: hourly, 4 hours; direct night train, 7 hours, reserve ahead; Italo: 4/day, 3.5 hours, reservations required), **Naples** (Trenitalia: almost hourly, 5.5 hours, some change in Bologna or Rome, reserve ahead; Italo: 3/day, 5.5 hours, reservations required).

By Bus

Venice's "bus station" is an open-air parking lot called **Piazzale Roma.** The square itself is a jumble of different operators, platforms, and crosswalks over busy lanes of traffic. But bus stops are well-signed. The ticket windows for ACTV (including #5 to Marco Polo Airport) are in a building near the modern Calatrava Bridge and the vaporetto stop. The ATVO ticket office (express buses to Marco Polo and Treviso airports and to Padua) is at #497g in the big, white building, on the right side of the square as you face away from the canal (office open daily 6:45-19:30).

Piazzale Roma also has two big **parking garages** and the **People Mover monorail** (€1.50, links to the cruise port and then the parking-lot island of Tronchetto).

Baggage storage is next to the monorail at #497m (€7/24 hours, daily 6:00-21:00).

Getting from the Bus Station to Central Venice: Find the vaporetto docks (just left of the modern bridge) and take #1 or the faster #2 down the Grand Canal to reach the Rialto, Accademia, or San Marco (St. Mark's Square) stops.

By Car

The freeway dead-ends after crossing the causeway to Venice. At the end of the road you have two parking-garage choices: Tronchetto or Piazzale Roma. As you drive into the city, signboards with green and red lights indicate which lots are full.

Parking at Tronchetto: This big garage is a bit farther out, but it's a little cheaper and well-connected by vaporetto (€3-5/hour, €21/24 hours, tel. 041-520-7555, www.veniceparking.it).

From the garage, cross the street to the brick building and go right to the vaporetto dock (not well-signed, look for *ACTV*), where you can catch vaporetto #2 in one of two directions: via the Grand Canal (more scenic, stops at Rialto, 40 minutes to San Marco), or via Giudecca (around the city, faster, no Rialto stop, 30 minutes to San Marco).

If you're staying near the bus or train station, you can take the €1.50 **People Mover** monorail, which brings you from Tronchetto to the bus station at Piazzale Roma. From there, it's a five-minute walk across the Calatrava Bridge to the train station (buy tickets with cash or credit card from machine, 3-minute trip).

Parking at Piazzale Roma: The two garages here are more convenient but a bit more expensive and likelier to be full. Both face the busy Piazzale Roma, where the road ends. The big white building on your right is the **Autorimessa Comunale** city garage (€26/24 hours, TI office in payment lobby open daily 7:30-19:30, tel. 041-272-7211, www.avmspa.it). In a back corner of the square is the private **Garage San Marco** (€32/24 hours, tel. 041-523-

2213, www.garagesanmarco.it).

By Plane

MARCO POLO AIRPORT

Venice's surprisingly large, modern airport is on the mainland shore of the lagoon, six miles north of the city (code: VCE, tel. 041-260-9260, www.veniceairport.it). There's one sleek terminal, with a TI (daily 9:00-20:00), car-rental agencies, ATMs, a bank, and plenty of shops and eateries.

Getting Between the Airport and Venice: You can get between the airport and central Venice in any of four ways: by Alilaguna boat, water taxi, airport bus, or land taxi.

Alilaguna boats reach most of my recommended hotels very simply, with no changes. Both Alilaguna boats and water taxis leave from the airport's boat dock, an eight-minute walk from the terminal, following signs along a sleek series of (indoor) moving sidewalks. Ticket offices are at the docks.

When flying out of Venice, allow plenty of time to get to the airport. From your hotel to the airport can take two hours.

Alilaguna Airport Boats: These boats shuttle across the lagoon between the airport and the island of Venice (€15, €27 round-trip, €1 surcharge if bought on boat, includes 1 suitcase and 1 piece of hand luggage, additional bags-€3 each, roughly 2/hour, 1-1.5-hour trip depending on destination). Alilaguna boats are not covered by city transit passes, but they do use the same docks and ticket windows as the regular vaporetti. You can buy Alilaguna tickets online for a slight discount, but it does not ensure a reservation as you must still exchange the voucher for a ticket (www.alilaguna.it or www.venicelink.com).

There are three key Alilaguna lines for reaching St. Mark's Square. From the airport, the **orange line** *(linea arancio)* runs down the Grand Canal, reaching Guglie (handy for Cannaregio hotels, roughly 2/hour, 45 minutes), Rialto (1 hour), and San

Transport	Speed	Cost	Notes
Alilaguna boat	Slow	Moderate	No transfer
Water taxi	Fast	Expensive	No transfer
Airport bus to Piazzale Roma	Medium	Cheap	Transfer to vaporetto
Land taxi to Piazzale Roma	Medium	Moderate	Transfer to vaporetto

Marco (1.25 hours). The **blue line** *(linea blu)* heads first to Fondamente Nove (40 minutes), then loops around to San Zaccaria and San Marco (roughly 2/hour, about 1.5 hours) before continuing to Zattere and the cruise terminal (almost 2 hours). In high season, the **red line** *(linea rossa)* runs to St. Mark's (1/hour, just over an hour). It circumnavigates Murano and then runs parallel to the blue line, ending at Giudecca Zitelle. For a full schedule, see www.alilaguna.it.

Water Taxis: Luxury taxi speedboats zip directly between the airport and the closest dock to your hotel in about 30 minutes. The official price is €110 for up to four people; add €10 for every extra person (10-passenger limit). You may get a higher quote—politely talk it down.

From the airport, arrange your ride at the water-taxi desk or with the boat captains at the dock. From Venice, book your taxi trip the day before your departure, either through your hotel or directly with the Consorzio Motoscafi water taxi association (tel. 041-522-2303, www.motoscafivenezia.it).

Airport Shuttle Buses: Buses between the airport and Venice are fast, frequent, and cheap. They drop you at Venice's bus station, at the square called Piazzale Roma. From there, you can catch a vaporetto down the Grand Canal—convenient for hotels near the Rialto Bridge and St. Mark's Square.

Two bus companies serve this route: ACTV and ATVO. ATVO buses take 20 minutes and go nonstop. ACTV buses make a few stops en route and take

slightly longer (30 minutes), but you get a discount if you buy a Venice vaporetto pass at the same time (see page 639). The service is equally good (either bus: €8 one-way, €15 round-trip; ACTV bus with transit-pass discount: €6 one-way, €12 round-trip; runs about 5:00-24:00, 2/hour, drops to 1/hour early and late, check schedules at www.atvo.it or www.actv.it). Double-check the destination; you want Piazzale Roma. If taking ACTV, you want bus #5.

Land Taxi or Private Minivan: A **land taxi** can get you from the airport to Piazzale Roma for about €50 (20 minutes). To reserve a private minivan, contact **Treviso Car Service** (minivan—€55, seats up to 8; car—€50, seats up to 3; mobile 338-204-4390 or 333-411-2840, www.trevisocarservice.com).

TREVISO AIRPORT

Several budget airlines use Treviso Airport, 12 miles northwest of Venice (code: TSF, tel. 042-231-5111, www.trevisoairport.it). The fastest option into Venice is on the **Barzi express bus,** which does the trip in just 40 minutes (€12, buy tickets on board, every 1-2 hours, www.barzi service.com). **ATVO buses** are a bit more frequent and drop you right at Piazzale Roma, but take nearly twice as long (€12 one-way, €22 round-trip, about 2/hour, 70 minutes, www.atvo.it; buy tickets at the ATVO desk in the airport and stamp them on the bus). **Treviso Car Service** offers minivan service to Piazzale Roma (minivan-€75, seats up to 8; car-€65, seats up to 3; for contact info, see listing earlier).

Switzerland

Mountainous, efficient Switzerland is one of Europe's most appealing destinations. A tiny country (about twice the size of New Jersey), it's wedged neatly between Germany, Austria, France, and Italy.

Switzerland melds the best of all worlds—and adds a healthy dose of chocolate, cowbells, and cable cars. Fiercely independent and decidedly high-tech, the Swiss (at 8 million strong) stubbornly hold on to their quaint traditions, too. Join cheesemakers in a high valley, try to call the shepherds on an alphorn, and hike through some of the world's most stunning mountain scenery to find the perfect perch for a picnic.

CUISINE SCENE AT A GLANCE

The Swiss eat when we do and enjoy a straightforward, no-nonsense cuisine. Specialties include delicious fondue, a melted cheese dish called raclette, *Rösti* (hash browns), and 100 varieties of cheese.

The high prices at Swiss restaurants are up to double what you'd pay in neighboring Germany. If you're on a budget, think of restaurants as a luxury for special occasions, and self-service cafeterias and supermarkets as everyday options.

At **restaurants,** the cheapest main courses (about 20 CHF) are typically starchy dishes topped with meat or cheese (pasta, pizza, and potato dishes) or sausages with kraut or potato salad. Meat courses will cost you more (25-45 CHF). Many, but not all, restaurants offer a daily special at lunch, and sometimes weekends and evenings, too.

Different kinds of restaurants offer different experiences. Hotels often serve fine food. A *Gaststätte* is a simple, less expensive restaurant. A *Weinstübli* (wine bar) or *Bierstübli* (tavern) usually serves food.

Most restaurants tack a menu onto their door for browsers and have an English menu inside. If you're not too hungry, order from the *kleine Hunger* (small hunger) section of the menu. Many restaurants offer half-portions, which is a great relief on your budget (although two people save even more by sharing one full portion).

Tipping: If you buy your food at a counter, don't tip. Service is included at restaurants with table service, but it's customary to round up the bill (no more than 5-10 percent). Give the tip directly to your server.

Budget Options: Grocery stores, such as the midrange Migros and Co-op, are the hungry hiker's best budget bet. The larger stores have a great selection of prepared foods and picnic fixings. These include a variety of salads (green, potato, pasta, or meat), hard-boiled eggs, sandwiches, cheese, single portions of cake and ice cream, chocolate bars, and sometimes a hot-meal counter. By law, most supermarkets are required to close on Sunday, with a few exceptions, such as stores in train stations.

Self-service cafeterias have good food at much lower prices than restaurants. You'll find them in bigger cities, usually at downtown branches of Co-op, Migros, and Manor supermarkets. While cafeteria food may not be inventive, it is typical, fresh, and high-quality.

Tempting bakeries sell sandwiches, quiches, and pastries—enough to make a filling meal.

The Berner Oberland

Of all the famous Swiss mountains and resorts, I savor one region: the Alps of the Berner Oberland. With alpine lakes, snow-capped mountains, little villages, hiking trails, and more, this is just the place to recharge your touristic batteries. The clang of cowbells, the whistle of marmots, and the crunchy footsteps of happy hikers are the dominant sounds.

Your gateway to the rugged Berner Oberland is the old resort town of Interlaken, a transportation hub. Use it as a springboard for alpine thrills.

Head deep into the heart of the Alps by train and cable car, riding to stops just this side of heaven—the villages in the Lauterbrunnen Valley. The cliff-hangers are Gimmelwald and Mürren, while Lauterbrunnen is on the valley floor. Use any of these as a base to explore alpine whitecaps at higher elevations, including the 9,748-foot Schilthorn peak.

What are you waiting for? The sun's coming out and the Alps beckon.

THE BERNER OBERLAND IN 2 DAYS

If the weather's decent, explore the two areas that tower above either side of the Lauterbrunnen Valley: On one side is the summit of Jungfrau (and beneath it, the tiny settlement of Kleine Scheidegg), and on the other is Schilthorn (overlooking the villages of Gimmelwald and Mürren).

Ideally, spend three nights in the region, with a day exploring each side of the valley. On one day, you could zip up to the Schilthorn in the morning for panoramic views, then tackle a hike or two (on the Schilthorn side) in the afternoon.

On the other day, explore the Jung-frau side. My favorite hike is the gentle downhill trail from Männlichen to Kleine Scheidegg, facing a panoramic mountain view the entire way if the weather's good. From there, you could take a pricey train up up up to the Jungfraujoch (for the highest viewpoint in the region), or simply train (or hike) down to the village of Wengen (which is connected by train to Lauterbrunnen).

With another day, you could take more hikes, explore all the towns, or even relax. For an overview of the panoramic train rides, lifts, and spectacular hikes in the region, see the "Scenic Lifts and Trains" and "Hiking" sections later in this chapter.

Home Bases: For accommodations without the expense and headache of mountain lifts—and equally handy to both sides of the valley—consider the valley-floor village of Lauterbrunnen. But for the best overnight options, I'd stay on the scenic ridge high above the valley, in the rustic hamlet of Gimmelwald or the resort town of Mürren.

Rick's Tip: *In* **bad weather,** *take a low-altitude hike (see recommendations on page 682), hang out at Mürren's Sportzentrum (sauna, steam bath, pool), visit the Lauterbrunnen Valley Folk Museum, or tour the Swiss Open-Air Museum at Ballenberg.*

Weather: The highest-altitude lifts are very expensive, and it only makes sense to splurge if you have a good chance of seeing an alpine panorama instead of fog or clouds. Let your plans flex with the weather. If it's good—go! Ask at your hotel or the TI for the latest info or check www.jungfrau.ch, www.schilthorn.ch, or www.meteo.search.ch. Webcams showing live video from the famous (and most expensive-to-reach) peaks play just about wherever you go in the area.

Getting Around the Berner Oberland

For more than a century, this region has been the target of nature-worshipping pilgrims. And Swiss engineers and visionaries have made the most exciting alpine perches accessible.

By Lift and Train

Part of the fun here—and most of the expense—is riding the many mountain trains and lifts (gondolas, cable cars, and funiculars).

Trains connect Interlaken to Wilderswil, Lauterbrunnen, Wengen, Kleine Scheidegg, and the Jungfraujoch. Lifts connect Wengen to Männlichen and Grund (near Grindelwald); Grindelwald to First and Männlichen (it will eventually reach Eigergletscher); Lauterbrunnen to Grütschalp (where a train connects to Mürren); and the cable-car station near Stechelberg to Gimmelwald, Mürren, and the Schilthorn.

For an overview of your many options, study the "Berner Oberland Transport Time/Cost" map and the "Berner Oberland at a Glance" sidebar in this chapter. Lifts generally go at least twice hourly (sneak preview: www.jungfrau.ch or www.schilthorn.ch). While train and bus schedules are stable, lift schedules flex with demand, doubling their scheduled departures when necessary.

Passes and Deals: If you have a **Eurail Global Pass,** trains and lifts beyond Interlaken are 25 percent off (doesn't require a flexi-day); with the **Swiss Travel Pass,** they're covered up to Wengen (above Wengen, pass holders get 25-50 percent off) and up to Mürren (ascending from there to the Schilthorn is 50 percent off). While those two passes are the best option for most Swiss trips using public transportation, there are a few others to consider: The **Berner Oberland Regional Pass** covers most trains, buses, and lifts in

Rustic Gimmelwald

A gondola makes its way to Männlichen above Grindelwald.

BERNER OBERLAND AT A GLANCE

Towns, Villages, and Resorts

▲▲▲ **Gimmelwald** Wonderfully rustic time-warp village—and a good home-base option—overlooking the Lauterbrunnen Valley. See page 665.

▲▲ **Mürren** Pleasant resort town near Gimmelwald, midway up the Schilthorn cable-car line; a good high-mountain home base for those who find Gimmelwald too small and rustic. See page 671.

▲ **Lauterbrunnen** Small town in the middle of the Lauterbrunnen Valley. From here, a cable car goes up to Grütschalp (with connections to Mürren and Gimmelwald), a train runs up to Wengen (with connections to Kleine Scheidegg and the Jungfraujoch), and the PostBus goes to Stechelberg (near the Schilthornbahn lift). See page 661.

▲ **Interlaken** Big town between Lake Brienz and Lake Thun, at the "entrance" to the Berner Oberland. See page 655.

Top Lifts and Trains

▲▲▲ **Schilthornbahn** Cable car soaring from Stechelberg in the Lauterbrunnen Valley to the 9,748-foot Schilthorn peak, with Piz Gloria revolving restaurant, James Bond exhibit, and stupendous views. Stops at Gimmelwald, Mürren, and Birg along the way. See page 678.

▲▲▲ **Jungfraubahn** Train running from Kleine Scheidegg station and through tunnel inside Eiger and Mönch mountains to 11,333-foot Jungfraujoch saddle, with observation deck, shops, tip-top views, and snow activities. See page 679.

Walks and Hikes

▲▲▲ **Männlichen-Kleine Scheidegg** Easy, mostly downhill ridge hike from cable-car station at Männlichen to Kleine Scheidegg, with spectacular views of Eiger and more. See page 686.

▲▲ **Cloudy-Day Lauterbrunnen Valley Walk** Easy trails and pleasant walks along valley floor, plus short trail to Staubbach Falls at upper end of town. See page 682.

▲▲ **North Face Trail** Relatively easy, view-filled hike from top of Allmendhubel funicular to villages of Mürren and/or Gimmelwald, passing farms with food service, Sprutz waterfall, mountain huts, and meadows. See page 684.

▲▲ **Birg to Gimmelwald via Bryndli** High, scenic, difficult hike from Birg cable-car station below Schilthorn summit to Gimmelwald. Trail winds past knobby summit of Bryndli, with nonstop views. See page 688.

▲▲ **Schynige Platte to First** Demanding, all-day ridge walk from Schynige Platte train station to gondola station at First. Fabulous views of Jungfrau-area peaks and Lake Brienz. See page 689.

▲ **Allmendhubel to Grütschalp** Fairly easy walk from Allmendhubel down to Grütschalp, with views of the Jungfrau. See page 686.

▲ **Grütschalp to Mürren** Super-easy, family-friendly stroll along the ridge with grand views of the Eiger, Mönch, and Jungfrau. See page 686.

More Sightseeing Options

▲▲ **Swiss Open-Air Museum at Ballenberg** Fine collection of traditional buildings near Interlaken, on Lake Brienz. See page 656.

▲ **Trümmelbach Falls** Lauterbrunnen Valley's most powerful falls, accessed via elevator ride up into the mountain and dramatic walk through several wet caves. See page 663.

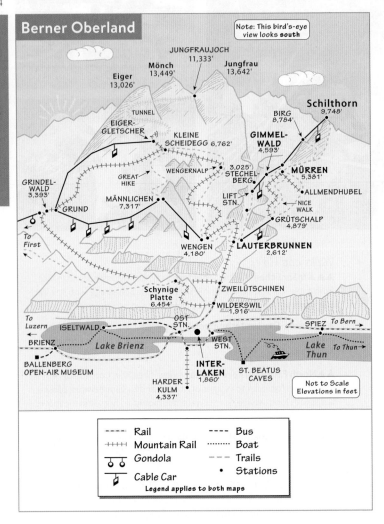

Berner Oberland

Note: This bird's-eye view looks **south**

JUNGFRAUJOCH 11,333'

Mönch 13,449'

Jungfrau 13,642'

Eiger 13,026'

Schilthorn 9,748'

BIRG 8,784'

TUNNEL

EIGER-GLETSCHER

KLEINE SCHEIDEGG 6,762'

GIMMEL-WALD 4,593'

MÜRREN 5,381'

WENGERNALP

3,025' STECHEL-BERG

GREAT HIKE

GRINDEL-WALD 3,393'

ALLMENDHUBEL

LIFT STN.

NICE WALK

MÄNNLICHEN 7,317'

GRUND

GRÜTSCHALP 4,879'

WENGEN 4,180'

LAUTERBRUNNEN 2,612'

To First

Schynige Platte 6,454'

ZWEILÜTSCHINEN

WILDERSWIL 1,916'

To Luzern

OST STN.

ISELTWALD

SPIEZ To Bern

BRIENZ

Lake Brienz

WEST STN.

Lake Thun

To Thun

BALLENBERG OPEN-AIR MUSEUM

INTER-LAKEN 1,860'

ST. BEATUS CAVES

Not to Scale Elevations in feet

HARDER KULM 4,337'

- - - Rail
+++++ Mountain Rail
Gondola
Cable Car

- - - - Bus
· · · · · Boat
– – – Trails
• Stations

Legend applies to both maps

this area (and all the way to Bern, Luzern, Gstaad, and Brig) but costs about the same as the more versatile Swiss Travel Pass (www.regionalpass-berneroberland. ch).

The **Jungfrau Travel Pass** is worth considering only if you're focusing exclusively on the Wengen-Kleine Scheidegg-Jungfraujoch area (3-8 day versions available, from 180 CHF, www.jungfrau.ch). And the **Junior Travelcard,** valid across Switzerland for families traveling with children,

lets kids ages 5-16 travel free with at least one parent (children under age 5 already travel free; 30 CHF/one child, 60 CHF/ two or more children, buy at Swiss train stations).

By Car

Interlaken, Lauterbrunnen, and Stechelberg are accessible by car. You can't drive to Gimmelwald, Mürren, Wengen, or Kleine Scheidegg. Instead, you'll need to park your car and zip up on a lift. For the

Berner Oberland Transport Time/Cost

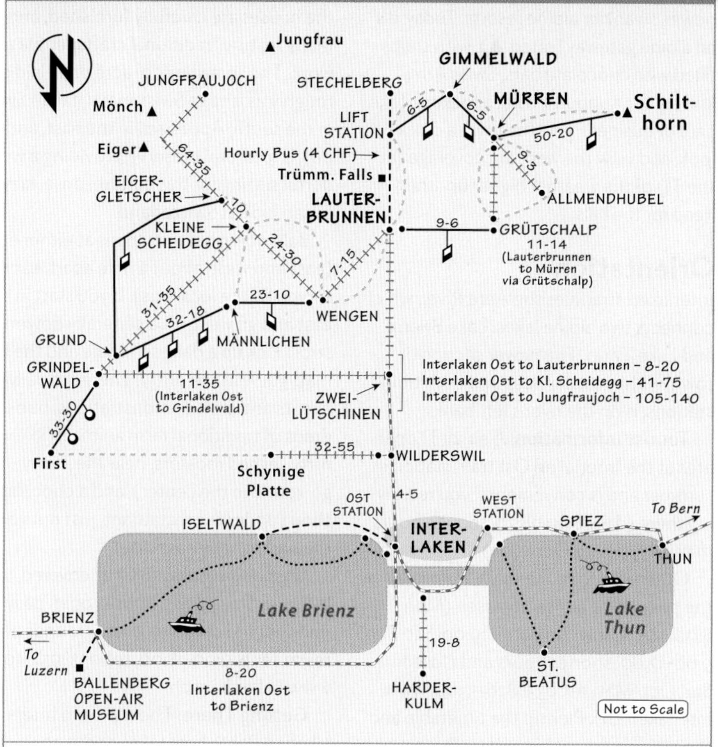

Jungfrau

JUNGFRAUJOCH   STECHELBERG   GIMMELWALD

Mönch   MÜRREN   Schilt-horn

Eiger   LIFT STATION   6-5   6-5   50-20

EIGER-GLETSCHER   Hourly Bus (4 CHF)→   9-3
Trümm. Falls   ÄLLMENDHUBEL

KLEINE SCHEIDEGG   LAUTER-BRUNNEN   9-6   GRÜTSCHALP
11-14
(Lauterbrunnen to Mürren via Grütschalp)

24-30   7-15

23-10   WENGEN

GRUND   MÄNNLICHEN

GRINDEL-WALD   Interlaken Ost to Lauterbrunnen – 8-20
11-35
(Interlaken Ost to Grindelwald)   Interlaken Ost to Kl. Scheidegg – 41-75
ZWEI-LÜTSCHINEN   Interlaken Ost to Jungfraujoch – 105-140

33-30

First   32-55   WILDERSWIL

Schynige Platte   OST STATION   4-5   WEST STATION   To Bern

ISELTWALD   INTER-LAKEN   SPIEZ   THUN

Lake Brienz   Lake Thun

BRIENZ   19-8

To Luzern   ST. BEATUS

BALLENBERG OPEN-AIR MUSEUM   8-20
Interlaken Ost to Brienz   HARDER-KULM   Not to Scale

Code:
1st # = Approx. 2nd class one-way cost in Swiss francs (CHF)
2nd # = Duration of trip in minutes

Notes:
Confirm prices locally.
Round-trip fares can be cheaper.
Most lifts run twice hourly.

Swiss Passes cover travel to Wengen and Mürren; Eurail/other int'l passes cover travel only to Interlaken. (Passes offer discounts beyond these points.)

lift to Gimmelwald, Mürren, and the Schilthorn, use the pay parking lot at the cable-car station near Stechelberg. For the train to Wengen or Kleine Scheidegg, use the pay parking garage behind the train station in Lauterbrunnen.

By Bus

The handy PostBus connects points along the valley, from Lauterbrunnen to Trümmelbach Falls to the Schilthornbahn cable-car station at Stechelberg (4.40

CHF, 2/hour, about 20 minutes from Lauterbrunnen to the cable car, covered by many transit passes, www.postauto.ch).

INTERLAKEN

When the 19th-century Romantics redefined mountains as something more than cold and troublesome obstacles, Interlaken became the original alpine resort. Ever since, tourists have flocked to the Alps "because they're there." Interlaken's glory days are long gone, its elegant old hotels eclipsed by newer, swankier alpine resorts. Today, it's an alpine gateway (rated ▲), with shops filled with chocolate bars, Swiss Army knives, and sunburned backpackers. Take care of business, give the town a quick look, and view the webcam coverage (at the TI) of the weather higher up...then head for the hills.

Orientation

Interlaken straddles the Aare River, which connects two alpine lakes: Lake Brienz and Lake Thun. The newer section of town, with most services and both train stations, is on the river's left bank.

Tourist Information: A small TI operates at the Interlaken Ost train station in summer and is convenient if you're arriving there (daily 8:30-18:30, though hours may vary; closed Oct-May).

Otherwise, visit the main TI, located by the post office at Marktgasse 1 (Mon-Fri 8:00-18:00, July-Aug until 19:00, Sat-Sun 9:00-17:00; shorter hours and closed Sun Oct-May; tel. 033-826-5300, www.interlaken.ch). Pick up the timetable and the hiking guide published by the Jungfraubahn mountain railway (both include a good map of the area). The TI sells tickets for the Swiss rail system, the various mountain trains and lifts, and adventure sports.

Rick's Tip: *On* **Sundays and holidays,** *hotels are open, and lifts and trains run, but many stores are closed. At higher altitudes* **many businesses close off-season** *from late April until late May, and again from mid-October to mid-December.*

Sights

▲▲▲SWISS OPEN-AIR MUSEUM AT BALLENBERG

At the far end of Lake Brienz from Interlaken, the Ballenberg open-air museum is a rich collection of more than 100 traditional and historic buildings brought here from every region of the country. All the houses are carefully furnished, and many feature traditional craftspeople at work. The sprawling 50-acre park, laid out roughly as a huge Swiss map (Italian Swiss in the south, Appenzell in the east, and so on), is a natural preserve providing a wonderful setting for this culture-on-a-lazy-Susan look at Switzerland.

Ballenberg has entrances at either end (east and west, about a mile apart, each served by the local bus). If you start in the east and go west, it's a generally downhill stroll. Pick up a daily schedule and the free map/guide at the entry. There are daily events and craft demonstrations, hundreds of traditional farm animals (like very furry-legged roosters, near the merry-go-round in the center), and a chocolate shop (under the restaurant, just outside the park, on the east side).

Cost and Hours: 28 CHF, covered by Swiss Travel Pass, houses open daily mid-April-Oct 10:00-17:00, grounds and restaurants 9:00-18:00, tel. 033-952-1030, www.ballenberg.ch.

Getting There: The trip from Interlaken to Ballenberg takes about 20 minutes by car (pay parking at either entrance), 50 minutes by train and bus, or 2 hours by boat and bus. By public transport, you'll first go to Brienz by train or boat, then from Brienz to Ballenberg by local bus. Trains for Brienz leave from the Interlaken Ost train station (2/hour, 15-20 minutes). Boats to Brienz leave from a dock just behind the Ost train station (every 1-2 hours, 1.25 hours, early April-late Oct only, tel. 058-327-4811, www.bls.ch). From the Brienz station or boat dock, catch local bus #151 to either museum entrance (hourly, 20 minutes). Use the online timetables at www.sbb.ch to plan your trip, and check bus return times carefully—after 18:00, buses back to Brienz leave only from the park's west entrance. Without a rail pass, ask for the Ballenberg combo-ticket when buying your train or boat tickets: This covers the complete round-trip from Interlaken (or beyond), and saves about 10 percent off your fare and park entry.

Experiences

For hikes and walks in the Berner Oberland, see the "Hiking" section, later.

BIKE TOURS AND RENTAL

Flying Wheels offers bike tours of varying length and difficulty, including a tour of the Lauterbrunnen Valley (189 CHF, 6 hours, includes picnic and Trümmelbach Falls visit). A short walk from the Ost train station, this well-organized, family-friendly outfit also rents bikes (electric, too). Its English-speaking staff give tips on where to go and can help you pick the right bike (bikes-35 CHF/half-day, 40 CHF/day; electric bikes-45 CHF/half-day, 55 CHF/day; includes helmet, daily May-Sept 9:30-20:00, shorter hours off-season, across street from northeast corner of Höhematte Park at Höheweg 133, tel. 033-557-8838, www.flyingwheels.ch).

HIGH-ADRENALINE TRIPS

For the thrill-seeker with money, several companies offer trips such as rafting, canyoning (rappelling down watery gorges), bungee jumping, and paragliding. Costs range from roughly 150 CHF to 200 CHF—higher for skydiving and hot-air balloon rides. Interlaken's two dominant companies are **Alpin Raft** (tel. 033-823-4100, www.alpinraft.ch) and **Outdoor Interlaken** (tel. 033-826-7719, www.outdoor-interlaken.ch). Other compa-

nies are generally just booking agents for these two outfits. For an overview of your options, study the racks of brochures at most TIs and hotels.

Sleeping

$$ Hotel Lötschberg has a sun terrace and 18 rooms just a three-minute walk from the West train station, but it's still residential and quiet. They have a lounge with microwave, fridge, and free tea and coffee (closed Jan-mid-April; from the West train station turn right, after Migros at the circle go left to General-Guisan-Strasse 31; tel. 033-822-2545, www.lotschberg.ch, hotel@lotschberg.ch).

Rick's Tip: *Hotels issue free* **Visitor Cards** *(Gästekarten) that include small discounts on some sights (paid for by your room tax).*

$$ The Aarburg offers nine plain, peaceful rooms over a restaurant in a traditional, beautifully located building just steps from the charming main square of Unterseen, a 10-minute walk from the West train station. Rooms are small, but guests can enjoy the shared lounge (check-in 16:00-21:00—make arrangements for other times, Beatenbergstrasse 1, tel. 033-820-4460, www.theaarburg.ch, well-run by Tim and Kat).

$$ Hotel Rössli, across the river from the West train station in Unterseen, is nicely located, if a bit dated. Their 35 rooms include "economy" rooms with a private bath down the hall and "budget" rooms with shared facilities (closed Dec-mid-Jan, elevator, comfy lounge, Hauptstrasse 10, tel. 033-822-7816, www.roessli-interlaken.ch, info@roessli-interlaken.ch).

$ Adventure Guesthouse, owned by a nearby hostel, is a cheery, family-friendly, nine-room place in a quiet residential neighborhood (family rooms, patio; from West train station exit left and take first bridge to your left, after crossing two bridges turn left on Helvetiastrasse and go 3 blocks to #29; mobile 077-456-2338,

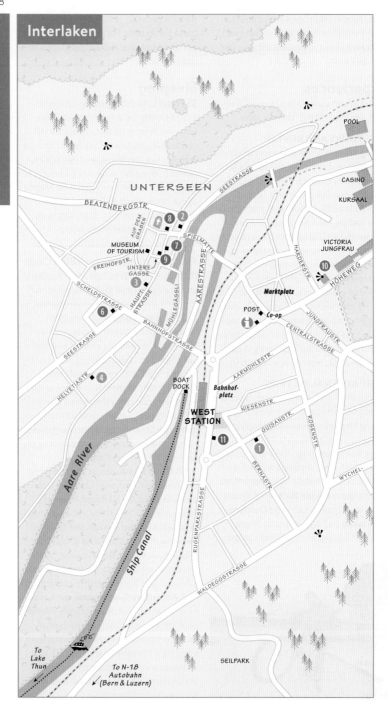

Interlaken

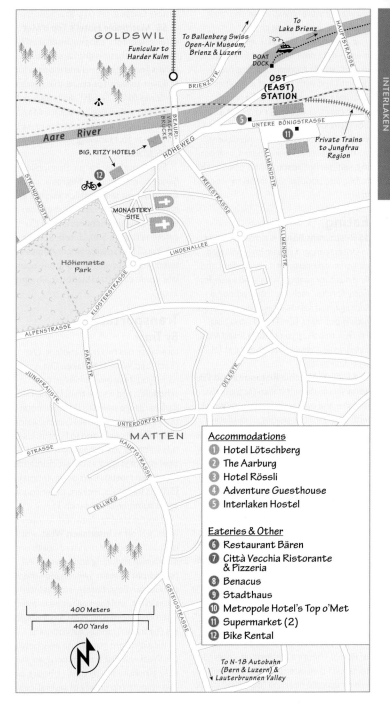

GOLDSWIL

Funicular to
Harder Kulm

To Ballenberg Swiss
Open-Air Museum,
Brienz & Luzern

To
Lake Brienz

BOAT
DOCK

OST
(EAST)
STATION

BRIENZSTR.

HAUPTSTRASSE

Aare River

BIG, RITZY HOTELS

Private Trains
to Jungfrau
Region

UNTERE BÖNIGSTRASSE

HÖHEWEG

BEAURI-
VAGER-
BRÜCKE

STRANDBADSTR.

ALLMENDSTR.

FREIESTRASSE

MONASTERY
SITE

LINDENALLEE

ALLMENDSTR.

Höhematte
Park

KLOSTERSTRASSE

ALPENSTRASSE

PARKSTR.

OELESTR.

JUNGFRAUSTR.

UNTERDORFSTR.

MATTEN

HAUPTSTRASSE

STRASSE

TELLWEG

GSTEIGSTRASSE

Accommodations
1 Hotel Lötschberg
2 The Aarburg
3 Hotel Rössli
4 Adventure Guesthouse
5 Interlaken Hostel

Eateries & Other
6 Restaurant Bären
7 Città Vecchia Ristorante
  & Pizzeria
8 Benacus
9 Stadthaus
10 Metropole Hotel's Top o'Met
11 Supermarket (2)
12 Bike Rental

400 Meters

400 Yards

N

To N-18 Autobahn
(Bern & Luzern) &
Lauterbrunnen Valley

www.adventure-guesthouse.ch, info@adventure-guesthouse.ch).

¢ **Interlaken Hostel** is very convenient—right next to the Ost train station in a big, sterile modern building, full of daylight and with plenty of amenities (private rooms available, bike rental, game room, check-in 15:00-24:00, Untere Bönigstrasse 3, tel. 033-826-1090, www.youthhostel.ch/interlaken, interlaken@youthhostel.ch). Their modern, welcoming, self-service **restaurant** is open to the public and popular with locals for its good value.

Eating

$$ Restaurant Bären is across the river in Unterseen, in a classic low-ceilinged gingerbread house with cozy indoor and fine outdoor seating. It's a solid value for *Rösti,* fondue, raclette, fish, traditional sausage, and salads. Their chicken cordon bleu is popular (Tue-Thu 17:00-23:00, Fri-Sun 10:00-23:30 or later, closed Mon, Seestrasse 2, reserve in advance at tel. 033-822-7526).

$$ Città Vecchia Ristorante and Pizzeria serves decent Italian (actually, Sardinian—the operating family's heritage) with classy indoor seating or outdoors on Unterseen's leafy main square (lunch specials, daily 12:00-14:00 & 18:30-22:00, Untere Gasse 5, tel. 033-822-1754).

$$$ Benacus, run by Wilderswil-born celebrity chef René Schudel, has a seasonal menu of quality international fare in an upscale atmosphere (plus a few tables out on the square). This is the place to splurge with class (Tue-Sat 17:00-24:00, closed Sun-Mon, Kirchgasse 15, tel. 033-821-2020).

$$ Stadthaus, a big, high-energy eatery just across the square, is also owned by René Schudel. The concept here is classic Swiss dishes done in a quality way, but without pretense (for example, a variety of *Rösti*). There's a big, inviting, covered terrace and an interior space that feels like an upscale beer hall (daily 9:00-24:00,

Untere Gasse 2, tel. 033-822-8689).

$$ Metropole Hotel's Top o'Met café/restaurant, capping Interlaken's 18-story aesthetic nightmare, actually serves good traditional and modern food at down-to-earth prices, with no gouging on drinks (daily 25-CHF deals for lunch or dinner; daily 8:00-23:00, Oct-May 10:00-22:00; hot food served 11:30-14:00 & 18:00-21:30, Höheweg 37, tel. 033-828-6666, Marco).

Supermarkets: For picnic supplies, handy options include **Migros** and a big **Co-op** supermarket, which also has a good cafeteria, across the street from the Ost station (similar hours except Co-Op cafeteria is open Sun, Untere Bönigstrasse 10). You'll find smaller grocery stores scattered around town, including one open late inside each train station (daily until 21:00).

Transportation
By Train

Interlaken has two train stations: Ost (East) and West. **Interlaken Ost** is the name you'll see most often on train schedules, and it's the transfer point for narrow-gauge trains to the high mountains (to Lauterbrunnen, Gimmelwald, Jungfraujoch, etc.) and to Luzern. Use this station if you're headed to those destinations or staying at the recommended Interlaken Hostel (next door). Interlaken Ost has free WCs, lockers, ticket counters, and a summer-only branch TI.

If you're staying elsewhere in Interlaken, get off at **Interlaken West**, which is closer to most of my listed hotels and downtown shopping and services. All trains from western Switzerland—Bern, the Golden Pass, Basel—stop at Interlaken West, and then continue to Interlaken Ost. Interlaken West has WCs, lockers (by track 1), and ticket counters.

It's a pleasant 30-minute walk between the West and Ost train stations; an easy 3-minute trip by train (3/hour); or a 10-minute trip on any of several local buses (free with Visitor Card; #21, #102, #103, or #104).

TRAIN CONNECTIONS

Interlaken, Bern, Basel, and Frankfurt are linked by an express train, but for most other destinations you'll change in Bern. Train info: www.sbb.ch.

From Interlaken Ost by Train to: **Lauterbrunnen** (1-2/hour, 20 minutes), **Bern** (2-3/hour, 1 hour), **Zürich** (2-3/hour, 2 hours, 1-2 changes), **Zürich Airport** (2-3/hour, 2.5 hours, 1-3 changes), **Luzern** (3-4/hour, 2.5 hours, 1-3 changes), **Zermatt** (1-2/hour, 2 hours, change in Spiez and Visp).

LAUTERBRUNNEN

Lauterbrunnen is the valley's commercial center and transportation hub. Sitting under sheer cliffs at the base of its namesake valley, with its signature waterfall spurting mightily out from the cliff (floodlit at night), Lauterbrunnen (rated ▲) is a fine springboard for Jungfrau and Schilthorn adventures.

Orientation

In addition to its train station and cable car, the town is just big enough to have all the essential services (grocery, bank, bike rental, launderette, and so on)—plus several hotels and hostels. It's idyllic, in spite of the busy road that slices it in two.

Tourist Information: Stop by the friendly TI to check the weather forecast, find out about guided walks and events, and buy hiking maps or regional train or lift tickets (daily 8:30-12:00 & 14:00-18:30; Oct-May Tue-Sat 9:00-12:00 & 13:30-17:00, closed Sun-Mon; on the main street a few houses up from the train station, tel. 033-856-8568, www.lauterbrunnen.swiss).

Arrival in Lauterbrunnen: The small, modern **train station** has a ticket office, a few small lockers (hiding just to the right of ticket office; check larger bags at ticket desks), and free WCs. Across the main street is the cable-car station. Go left as you exit the station to head up the main drag (toward the gushing waterfall) and find the TI. **Drivers** can pay to park in the large multistory lot behind the station.

Laundry: The **Valley Hostel** has coin-op machines (daily 9:00-21:00,

Traditional cow culture thrives in the Berner Oberland.

SWITZERLAND

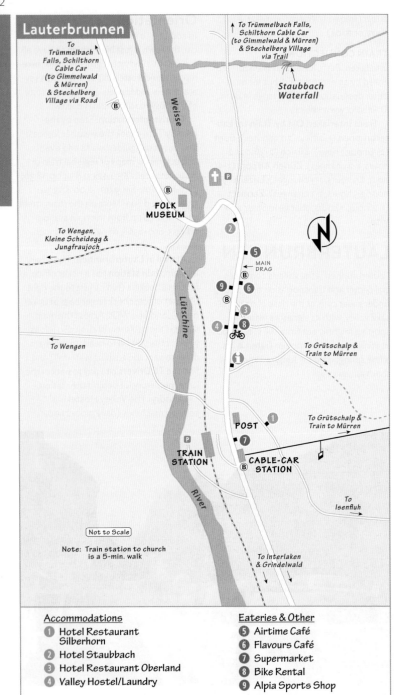

Lauterbrunnen

To Trümmelbach Falls, Schilthorn Cable Car (to Gimmelwald & Mürren) & Stechelberg Village via Road

To Trümmelbach Falls, Schilthorn Cable Car (to Gimmelwald & Mürren) & Stechelberg Village via Trail

Staubbach Waterfall

Weisse

FOLK MUSEUM

To Wengen, Kleine Scheidegg & Jungfraujoch

MAIN DRAG

Lütschine

To Wengen

To Grütschalp & Train to Mürren

To Grütschalp & Train to Mürren

POST

TRAIN STATION

CABLE-CAR STATION

To Isenfluh

River

To Interlaken & Grindelwald

Not to Scale

Note: Train station to church is a 5-min. walk

Accommodations
1 Hotel Restaurant Silberhorn
2 Hotel Staubbach
3 Hotel Restaurant Oberland
4 Valley Hostel/Laundry

Eateries & Other
5 Airtime Café
6 Flavours Café
7 Supermarket
8 Bike Rental
9 Alpia Sports Shop

Wi-Fi, tel. 033-855-2008).

Bike Rental: You can rent mountain bikes at **Imboden Bike** on the main street (bikes-28 CHF/4 hours, 38 CHF/day; electric bikes-38 CHF/4 hours, 50 CHF/day; RS%, includes helmet, Mon-Fri 8:30-18:30, Sat-Sun 9:00-17:00—until 18:30 June-mid-Sept, tel. 033-855-2114, www.imboden-bike.ch).

Sports Gear: Rent hiking boots, skis, and snowboards at the **Alpia Sports/Intersport** shop (daily 8:00-12:30 & 14:00-18:30, longer hours in winter, closed during Easter holiday, at Hotel Crystal, tel. 033-855-3292, www.alpiasport.ch).

Sights

For hikes and walks from Lauterbrunnen, including the "Cloudy-Day Lauterbrunnen Valley Walk" that links Lauterbrunnen to Staubbach and Trümmelbach falls, see page 682.

STAUBBACH FALLS

The second highest waterfall in Switzerland (nearly 900 feet) is literally in Lauterbrunnen's backyard—just follow the trail past the church toward the sound of rushing water. Its spray looks like falling dust—*Staub*—hence the name. A trail cut into the cliff takes visitors up "behind" the falls (in winter, it's closed due to the danger of rockslides).

▲TRÜMMELBACH FALLS

Sneak a behind-the-scenes look at the valley's most powerful waterfall, Trümmelbach Falls. Ride the elevator up through the mountain, climb up to the upper falls, and then hike down through several caves (wet, with lots of stairs, and claustrophobic for some). You'll see the melt from the Eiger, Mönch, and Jungfrau grinding like God's band saw through the mountain at the rate of up to 5,000 gallons a second. The upper area is the best; if your legs ache, skip the lower falls and ride down on the elevator. A café (with WC) is directly across from the bus stop. The falls ticket kiosk is a short walk beyond the café.

Cost and Hours: 11 CHF, daily 9:00-17:00, July-Aug until 18:00, closed Nov-March, opening date varies with ice conditions, tel. 033-855-3232, www.truemmelbachfaelle.ch.

Getting There: The falls are about halfway between Lauterbrunnen and the Schilthornbahn cable-car station; from either, it's a short ride on the PostBus or a 45-minute walk. Or combine a visit to Trümmelbach with a walk on the valley floor; see page 682.

LAUTERBRUNNEN VALLEY FOLK MUSEUM (TALMUSEUM LAUTERBRUNNEN)

This interesting museum shows off the region's folk culture and two centuries of mountaineering from all the towns of this valley. You'll see lace, old tools, exhibits on cheese and woodworking, cowbells, and classic old photos. Request an English translation booklet.

Cost and Hours: 5 CHF, free with hotel

Staubbach Falls is in Lauterbrunnen's backyard.   *Lauterbrunnen Valley Folk Museum*

Visitor Card, mid-June-early Oct Tue and Fri-Sun 14:00-17:30, closed Mon and Wed-Thu year-round, closed off-season, over bridge and below church at the far end of Lauterbrunnen town, tel. 033-855-3586, www.talmuseum-sagenwelt-lauterbrunnen.ch.

Sleeping

$$ Hotel Silberhorn is a family-run, formal, 40-room hotel. It's in a very convenient location—a hundred yards uphill from the train station on a quiet side street. Almost every double room comes with a fine view and balcony (closed late Oct-mid-Dec, lots of stairs, dinner available, tel. 033-856-2210, www.silberhorn.com, info@silberhorn.com).

$$ Hotel Staubbach is one of the oldest hotels in the valley (1890), with 33 simple rooms. Rooms that face up the valley have fabulous waterfall views (closed mid-Nov-March, elevator, 10-minute walk up from station on the left, tel. 033-855-5454, www.staubbach.com, hotel@staubbach.com).

$$ Hotel Oberland is in the center of town, with 28 tidy rooms, most with balconies and views of the Staubbach waterfall or Jungfrau (closed mid-Oct-mid-Dec, family rooms and apartments

available, 5 rooms are in nearby Crystal Hotel annex, popular with my tour groups, 5-minute walk up from station on the right, free parking, tel. 033-855-1241, www.hoteloberland.ch, info@hoteloberland.ch, Bev works the front desk).

¢ Valley Hostel is practical and comfortable, offering inexpensive beds for quieter travelers of all ages, with a pleasant garden (private rooms, family rooms, reception open 8:00-12:00 & 15:00-22:00—shorter hours off-season, 5-minute walk up from train station, tel. 033-855-2008, www.valleyhostel.ch, info@valleyhostel.ch, Abegglen family: Stefan and Fränzi).

Eating

$$ Hotel Restaurant Oberland, along the main drag a few minutes up from the station, serves good-value meals including traditional Swiss dishes and pizzas. It's a high-energy place with lots of tourists and a huge front porch good for lingering into the evening. Reservations should be considered required (daily 11:30-21:00, dinner seatings at 18:00 and 20:00, tel. 033-855-1241, www.hoteloberland.ch).

$$ Hotel Restaurant Silberhorn, with an elegant dining room, is the local choice for a fancy dinner out. Prices are reasonable, and they have all of the Swiss standards, plus good wood-fired pizzas. Call to reserve a view table (daily 18:00-21:00, classy indoor and outdoor seating, above the cable-car station, tel. 033-856-2210).

$ Airtime Café feels like a hipster alpine Starbucks with hot drinks, homemade treats, breakfast, and simple lunches. They can help you book adventure-sport activities (daily 8:30-18:00, kitchen until 16:00, closed Nov, tel. 033-855-1515).

$ Flavours, a café without a hint of yodeling or cowbells, serves up full breakfasts, burgers, focaccia sandwiches, fresh-squeezed juices, and gelato (takeaway available, daily 9:00-18:00, kitchen until

15:00, shorter hours off-season, closed Nov-April, tel. 033-855-3652).

Supermarket: The small but well-stocked **Co-op** is on the main street across from the station (Mon-Fri 8:00-18:30, Sat until 17:00, closed Sun).

Transportation

The valley-floor towns of Lauterbrunnen and Stechelberg have connections by mountain train, bus, and cable car to the traffic-free villages, peaks, and hikes high above. Prices and trip durations given are one-way and per leg unless otherwise noted.

From Lauterbrunnen

By Train to: Interlaken Ost (1-2/hour, 20 minutes, covered by Swiss Travel Pass, 25 percent discount with Eurail Global Pass), **Wengen** (2/hour, 15 minutes), **Kleine Scheidegg** (2/hour, 45 minutes), **Jungfraujoch** (2/hour, 1.5 hours, change in Kleine Scheidegg, see details on page 679).

By Cable Car and Train to: Männlichen (for the hike to Kleine Scheidegg—take train to Wengen and change to cable car), **Grütschalp** and **Mürren** (ride cable car to Grütschalp then train to Mürren; total trip time 20 minutes, www.jungfrau.ch).

By PostBus to: Schilthornbahn cable-car station (2/hour, 20 minutes, 4.40 CHF, covered by Swiss Travel Pass), continues to the hamlet of **Stechelberg.**

By Car to: Schilthornbahn cable-car station (10-minute drive, pay parking lot).

From Schilthornbahn Cable-Car Station near Stechelberg

By Cable Car to: Gimmelwald (2/hour, 5 minutes), **Mürren** (2/hour, 10 minutes, change in Gimmelwald), **Schilthorn** (2/hour, 35 minutes, change in Gimmelwald, Mürren, and Birg). From Stechelberg, cable cars run at :25 and :55 past the hour (Mon-Fri until 23:45, Sat-Sun until 24:55; after 20:00 it's just once hourly).

GIMMELWALD

Saved from developers by its "avalanche zone" classification, Gimmelwald was (before modern tourism) one of the poorest places in Switzerland. Its traditional economy was stuck in the hay, and its farmers—unable to make it in their disadvantaged trade—survived only on a trickle of visitors and Swiss government subsidies (and working the ski lifts in winter). Although Gimmelwald's population dropped in the last century to about 100 residents, traditions survive. Raising hay in this rugged terrain is labor-intensive. Tough and proud, local families harvest enough to feed only about 15 cows each. But they'd have it no other way. Don't confuse Gimmelwald (rated ▲▲▲) and touristy Grindelwald—they couldn't be more different.

Rick's Tip: Gimmelwald has a **helpful website** *(www.gimmelwald.ch) where you can check out photos, get directions for the best hikes, and see the latest on activities and rooms for rent.*

Take a walk through the town. The huge, sheer cliff face that dominates your mountain views is the Schwarzmönch (Black Monk). The three peaks above (or behind) it are, left to right, the Eiger, Mönch, and Jungfrau.

For some travelers, there's little to see

Gimmelwald's farmers raise just enough hay for their cows.

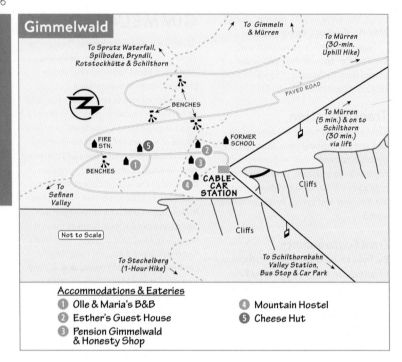

Gimmelwald

Accommodations & Eateries

1. Olle & Maria's B&B
2. Esther's Guest House
3. Pension Gimmelwald & Honesty Shop
4. Mountain Hostel
5. Cheese Hut

in the village. Others (like me) enjoy a fascinating day sitting on a bench and learning why they say, "If heaven isn't what it's cracked up to be, send me back to Gimmelwald."

⊙ Gimmelwald Walk

Gimmelwald, though tiny, with one zigzag street, offers a fine look at a traditional Swiss mountain community.

• *Start this quick self-guided walk at the...*

Cable-Car Station: When the lift came in the 1960s, the village's back end became its front door. As you walk out of the station, pause at the big Infopoint map to orient yourself. Then turn right (uphill).

Gimmelwald was, and still is, a farm village. As you start up the street, you'll see a sweet little hut on the right. Set on stilts to keep out mice, the hut was used for storing cheese (the rocks on the rooftop here and throughout the town are not decorative—they keep the shingles on

through wild storms). Behind the cheese hut stands the former village schoolhouse, long the largest structure in town. (In Catholic Swiss towns, the biggest building is the church; in Protestant towns, it's the school.) Gimmelwald's students now go to school in Lauterbrunnen, and the building is used as a chapel when the Protestant pastor makes his monthly visit. The little gray tower-like structure on the roof is the town fire siren. Now turn around: On the other side of the street, next to the little playground, is a bench with a nice view, and just beyond it is the recommended Mountain Hostel.

• *Walk up the lane 50 yards to Gimmelwald's...*

"Times Square": The yellow alpine "street sign" shows where you are, the altitude (1,370 meters, or 4,470 feet), how many hours and minutes it takes to walk to nearby points, and which tracks are serious hiking paths (marked with red and white, and further indicated along the way

Swiss Cow Culture

In a good year, farmers produce enough cheese to break even—they support their families on government subsidies of about $5,000 per cow. (Throughout the Alps, various governments support traditional farming as much for the tourism as for the cheese.) But these farmers have made a lifestyle choice to keep tradition alive and live high in the mountains.

The cows' grazing ground can range in elevation by as much as 5,000 feet throughout the year. In the summer (usually mid-June), the farmer straps elaborate ceremonial bells on his cows and takes them up to a hut at high elevation. The cows hate these big bells, which weigh upward of 10 pounds and can cost more than 2,000 CHF apiece—a proud investment for a humble farmer. When the cows arrive at their summer home, the ornamental bells are hung under the eaves and the cows get more practical bells.

These high-elevation summer stables are called "alps." The cows stay at the alps for about 100 days (roughly from June 10 to September 21). The farmers hire a team of cheesemakers to work at each alp—mostly hippies, students, and city slickers eager to spend three summer months in mountainous solitude. Each morning, the hired hands get up at 5:00 to milk the cows; take them to pasture; and make the cheese, milking the cows again when they come home in the evening. In the summer, all the milk is turned into alp cheese (it's too difficult to get it down to the market in liquid form). In the winter, with the cows at lower altitudes, the fresh milk is sold as milk.

Meanwhile, the farmers, free of their bovine responsibilities in summer, turn their attention to making hay. The average farmer has a few huts at various altitudes, each surrounded by small hay fields. The farmer follows the seasons up into the mountains, making hay and storing it above the huts. In the fall, the cows come down from the alps and spend the winter in the village, eating the hay the farmer spent the summer preparing for them.

Throughout the year you'll see farmers moving their herds to various elevations. If snow is in the way, farmers sometimes use tourist cable cars to move their cows.

---

with red and white patches of paint on stones). You're surrounded by buildings that were built as duplexes, divided vertically right down the middle to house two separate families. Look for the Honesty Shop at Pension Gimmelwald, which features local crafts and little edibles for sale (summer only).

Behind the street sign, the lettering

high up on the post office building is a folksy blessing: "Summer brings green, winter brings snow. The sun greets the day, the stars greet the night. This house will protect you from rain, cold, and wind. May God give us his blessings." Small as Gimmelwald is, it still has daily mail service. The postman comes down from Mürren each day to deliver and pick up mail. The date on this building indicates when it was built or rebuilt (1911). Gimmelwald has a strict building code: For instance, shutters must be of wood and can only be painted certain colors.

• *From this tiny intersection, walk away from the cable-car station and follow the town's...*

Main Street: Walk up the road past the garden-gnome greeting committee on the right. On the left, notice the announcement board, with notifications such as deals on chainsaw sharpening, upcoming shooting competitions, and news on community projects. Cross the street and admire the big barn, dated 1995. At the far front corner is a cow-scratcher. Swiss cows have legal rights (for example, in the winter they must be taken out for exercise at least three times a week). This big barn is built in a modern style. Traditionally, barns were small (like those on the hillside high above) and closer to the hay. But with trucks and paved roads, hay can be moved more easily, and farm businesses need more cows to be viable. Still, even a well-run big farm hopes just to break even. The industry survives only with government subsidies (see sidebar, previous page).

• *Go just beyond the next big barn. On your right is a...*

Water Fountain/Trough: This is the site of the town's historic water supply—still perfectly drinkable. Village kids love to bathe and wage water wars here when the cows aren't drinking from it.

• *Detour left down a gravel path (along a wooden fence). First you'll pass (on your left) the lovingly tended pea-patch gardens of the woman with the best green thumb in the village. Continue along the path, which ends after 50 yards at another water trough in front of a house called...*

Husmättli: This is the oldest building in town, from 1658. (There are more 17th-century buildings on the road that zigzags down from Gimmelwald into the Sefinen Valley.) Study the log-cabin construction. Many old houses were built without nails. The wood was logged up the valley and cut on the water-powered village mill (also in the Sefinen Valley). Gimmelwald heats with wood, and since the wood needs to age a couple of years to burn well, it's stacked everywhere.

• *Return up the gravel path to the main paved road, turn left, and continue.*

Twenty yards along, on the left, look for the house with the *Self Service* sign. Climb the ramp, open the door, and you'll find a refrigerator with local cheese sold on the honor system by the Rubin family. (Villagers generally see no need to lock their doors.) Just outside the door, in the summer months, you may see a bunch of scythes hanging above a sharpening stone. Farmers pound, rather than grind, the blade to get it razor-sharp for efficient mowing on slopes too rocky or steep for machines or grazing animals. Feel a blade...carefully.

A few steps farther, notice the cute **cheese hut** on the right. This is where the cheese you saw on sale was produced (thousands of pounds turned and salted). The hut's front wall is an alpine art gallery with nail-shoes used as flower pots. Nail shoes grip the steep, wet fields—this is critical for a farmer's safety, especially when carrying a sharp scythe. Even today, farmers buy metal tacks and fasten them to boots. The hut is full of strong cheese—up to three years old.

Look up. In the summer, a few goats are kept here behind the hut (rather than at a high alp) to provide families with

"Main Street" in Gimmelwald

Gimmelwald offers a fine look at traditional Swiss mountain life.

fresh milk (about a half-gallon per day per goat). The farmers fence the goats in so they eat only this difficult-to-harvest grass.

On the left (at the *B&B* sign) is Olle and Maria's home. Proprietors of a popular B&B, they ran the local school until it closed in 2010; now they both commute to teach at schools in other villages.

• *Fifty yards farther along on the right is the house called...*

Alpenrose: This is the old village school building, in use from about 1810 to 1930. Now it's a family home. You might see big ceremonial cowbells hanging under the eaves on the uphill side. These swing from the necks of cows during the procession from town to the high Alps (mid-June) and back down (mid-Sept).

• *At the end of town, pause at the tiny viewpoint just before where a lane branches off to the left, leading into the dramatic...*

Sefinen Valley: At the bottom of this wild valley is a stream that rushes down toward Stechelberg. All the old homes in town are made from wood cut from the left-hand side of this valley (shady side,

slow-growing, better timber) and milled on the valley floor.

• *A few steps ahead, the road switches back at the...*

Gimmelwald Fire Station (*Feuerwehrmagazin*): Peer through the windows in the bottom-floor door at the tractor-like engines. Then walk up around the hairpin bend to the notice board on the side of the building. The Föhnwacht-*Reglement* sheet explains rules to keep the village from burning down during the Föhn season, a period of fierce dry winds. During this time, there's a 24-hour fire watch, and even smoking cigarettes outdoors is forbidden.

Check out the other posted notices. This year's Swiss Army calendar tells reservists when and where to go (in all four official Swiss languages). Every Swiss male does a 22-week stint in the military, then serves three weeks a year in the reserves until age 34. The *Schiessübungen* poster details the shooting exercises required this year.

• *Unless you're really pooped, continue uphill along the road.*

High Road to More Views: The resort town of Mürren hovers in the distance. And high on the left, notice the hay field. This field is a festival of alpine flowers in season (best at this altitude in May and June).

• *In a couple of minutes, you'll reach a peaceful set of benches, off the lane on the downhill side (just before the now-closed Hotel Mittaghorn and just steps from where you started). Grab a bench. Take a moment to relax and savor the view. For three decades, this has been a favorite place of mine to sit quietly, appreciate the Alps, and be thankful that I can travel and experience such wonders.*

Sleeping and Eating

Gimmelwald is my home base in the Berner Oberland. Poor and pleasantly stuck in the past, the village has only a few accommodations options—all of them quirky and memorable—and one restaurant. Prices don't include breakfast (except for the hostel) but do include the local tax, which gives you free entry to the public swimming pool in nearby Mürren (at the Sportzentrum).

$$ Olle and Maria's B&B rents Gimmelwald's most expensive and comfortable rooms. Two rooms with shared bath are upstairs, while the "double" with private bath is a ground-level studio apartment with a kitchenette and a private entrance (family room available, breakfast extra, 3-night minimum, cash or PayPal only, non-refundable 50 percent deposit via PayPal required, pay laundry service; from cable car, continue straight for 200 yards along the town's only road, look for *B&B* sign on left; tel. 033-855-3575, www.olleandmarias.ch, oeggimann@bluewin.ch).

$$ Esther's Guest House, overlooking the village's main intersection, rents seven clean, basic, and comfortable rooms. Three rooms have private bathrooms, and all share a generous lounge and kitchen (10 percent cheaper for 3 nights or more, family rooms available—

one sleeps up to 6, breakfast extra, sack lunches available, low ceilings, tel. 033-855-5488, www.esthersguesthouse.ch, info@esthersguesthouse.ch). Tobias and Franziska also rent two five-person apartments with kitchenettes next door.

$ Pension Gimmelwald is an old, low-ceilinged farmhouse converted into a family-style inn, with 10 simple shared-bath rooms, 2 rooms with private bath, a six-bed family room, a restaurant, and a cozy bar. Its generous restaurant terrace, overlooking the Mountain Hostel, has gorgeous views across the valley (breakfast extra, dinner available, open late May-mid-Oct and late Dec-March, 2-minute walk up from cable-car station, tel. 033-855-1730, www.hotel-pensiongimmelwald.ch, welcome@hotel-pensiongimmelwald.ch, Englishman David and Sabine).

¢ Mountain Hostel is a beehive of activity, as clean as its guests, cheap, respectable, and friendly. The 40-bed hostel has low ceilings, bar, pool table, and healthy plumbing. It's mostly a college-age crowd; families and older travelers will probably feel more comfortable elsewhere (closed Nov, from the lift station it's 20 yards up the path to the left, tel. 033-855-1704, www.mountainhostel.com, info@mountainhostel.com).

Rick's Tip: Consider bringing a **picnic meal to Gimmelwald** *from Lauterbrunnen or Mürren, which have grocery stores and cafés selling sandwiches to go.*

$$ Pension Gimmelwald Restaurant is the only place to eat in town. Each night at 19:00 they serve a maximum of 30 people one 30-CHF three-course meal (you have no choices). During the day they serve drinks, soup, and simple meat-and-cheese board-type dishes. You can eat in their rustic indoor dining room or on a jaw-dropping view terrace. David proudly serves their award-winning, very smooth Schwarzmönch dark beer (reservations required for dinner, daily late May–mid-Oct and late Dec–March 12:00–15:00 & 18:00–21:00, bar open until 22:00, closed off-season, tel. 033-855-1730, www.hotel-pensiongimmelwald.ch).

MÜRREN

Pleasant as an alpine resort can be, Mürren is traffic-free and filled with cafés, souvenirs, old-timers with walking sticks, and snap-happy tourists. Its chalets are prefab-rustic. With help from a cliffside train, a funicular, and a cable car, hiking options are endless from Mürren (rated ▲▲). Sitting on a ledge more than 2,000 feet above the Lauterbrunnen Valley, surrounded by a fortissimo chorus of mountains, the town has all the comforts of home without the pretense of more famous resorts.

Mürren dates from 1384, but its historic character has been overwhelmed by development (unlike Gimmelwald). Still, it's a peaceful town, with 400 permanent residents. Depending on the time of year, Mürren is either lively (winter and summer, when the population swells to 4,000) or completely dead (spring and fall).

Orientation

Mürren perches high on a ledge, overlooking the Lauterbrunnen Valley. You can walk from one end of town to the other in about 15 minutes.

Tourist Information: Mürren's TI, inconveniently located in the sports center at the top end of town, is a wealth of information (June-Oct and mid-Dec-April daily 8:30-19:30, off-season 8:30-12:00 & 13:00-17:00, free WCs and Wi-Fi, follow signs to *Sportzentrum* on the upper road—behind the giant old Hotel Alpin Palace, tel. 033-856-8686, www.muerren.swiss, Sam). Pick up the flier that lists weekly activities, including a town walking tour (1/week June-Oct and Dec-April, free with your hotel's Visitor Card, otherwise 20 CHF).

Laundry: Hotel Bellevue has a little self-service launderette in a shed on the side of the hotel (open 24/7, but you must buy tokens at the bar inside).

Bike Rental: You can rent mountain bikes at **Stäger Sport** (30 CHF/half-day, 40 CHF/day, includes helmet, daily 9:00-18:00, closed late Oct-mid-May, in middle of town, tel. 033-855-2355, www.staegersport.ch). There's a bigger bike-rental place in Lauterbrunnen (Imboden Bike).

Sports Center: The slick **Sportzentrum** that houses the TI offers a world of indoor activities, including table tennis, a fitness room, sauna, hot tub, and steam bath (each with its own charge; most services open same hours as TI—see above). A **$ café** offers a reasonably priced, basic menu, with indoor and outdoor seating (daily 8:00-18:00). The indoor pool is free with the Visitor Card given out by hotels and hostels (otherwise 12 CHF, daily 13:00-20:00, until 21:00 in winter, tel. 033-856-8686, www.sportzentrum-muerren.ch). In July and August, you can enjoy occasional folkloric evenings at Sportzentrum.

Skiing and Snowboarding: The Mürren-Schilthorn ski area is the Berner Oberland's best place for experts, especially those eager to tackle the famous, nearly 10-mile-long Inferno run. The runs on top, especially the Kanonenrohr, are quite steep and have predictably good snow; lower areas cater to all levels, but can be icier. For rental gear, try the

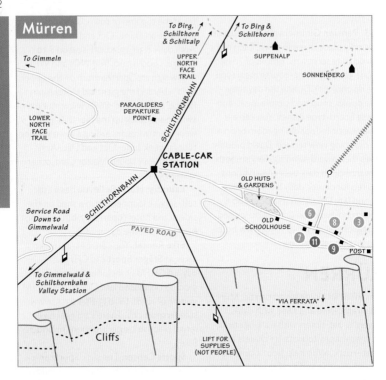

Mürren

To Birg,
Schilthorn
& Schiltalp

To Birg &
Schilthorn

To Gimmeln

UPPER
NORTH
FACE
TRAIL

SUPPENALP

SONNENBERG

PARAGLIDERS
DEPARTURE
POINT

LOWER
NORTH
FACE
TRAIL

SCHILTHORNBAHN

CABLE-CAR
STATION

OLD HUTS
& GARDENS

Service Road
Down to
Gimmelwald

SCHILTHORNBAHN

PAVED ROAD

OLD
SCHOOLHOUSE

6

8

3

7

11

9

POST

To Gimmelwald &
Schilthornbahn
Valley Station

"VIA FERRATA"

Cliffs

LIFT FOR
SUPPLIES
(NOT PEOPLE)

friendly, convenient **Ed Abegglen** shop (best prices, next to recommended Chalet Fontana, tel. 033-855-1245), **Alfred's Sporthaus** (good selection and decent prices, between ski school and Sportzentrum, tel. 033-855-3030), or **Stäger Sport** (in the town center, tel. 033-855-2330).

⊙ Mürren Walk

Mürren has long been a top ski resort, but a walk across town offers a glimpse into a time before ski lifts. This stroll takes you through town on the main drag, from the train station (where you'll arrive if coming from Lauterbrunnen) to the cable-car station.

• Start at the...

Train Station: The first trains pulled into Mürren in 1891. A case inside the station displays an original car from the narrow-gauge, horse-powered line that rolled fancy visitors from here into town. The current station, built in 1964, comes with

impressive engineering for heavy cargo.

• Wander into town along the main road (take the lower, left fork) for a stroll under the...

Alpin Palace Hotel: This towering place was the "Grand Palace Hotel" until it burned in 1928. Today they're planning an ambitious renovation (in the meantime, it houses a "pop-up lodge," described later). The green meadow below the station on the left is a popular hangout for wild mountain goats and chamois (the animals, not the rags).

• Carry on past the hotel for a...

Cliffside Stroll: Just ahead, the small wooden platform cantilevered over the cliff is where snow-removal trucks dump their loads in the winter. Just beyond, on the right (across from Hotel Alpina), you can fill your water bottle with sweet spring water from the Alps high above. Farther down, Hotel Edelweiss' restaurant terrace comes with breathtaking views (over-

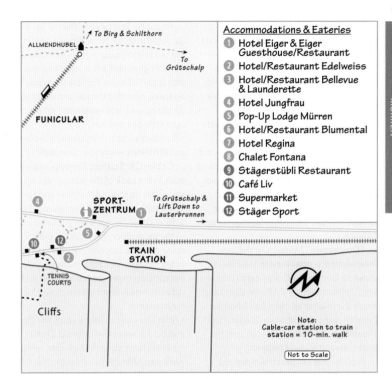

Accommodations & Eateries

1. Hotel Eiger & Eiger Guesthouse/Restaurant
2. Hotel/Restaurant Edelweiss
3. Hotel/Restaurant Bellevue & Launderette
4. Hotel Jungfrau
5. Pop-Up Lodge Mürren
6. Hotel/Restaurant Blumental
7. Hotel Regina
8. Chalet Fontana
9. Stägerstübli Restaurant
10. Café Liv
11. Supermarket
12. Stäger Sport

Note: Cable-car station to train station = 10-min. walk

Not to Scale

hanging a sheer cliff).

A few houses beyond, the vacant lot offers the same views stretching from the big three: Eiger, Mönch, and Jungfrau—plus the Schwarzmönch looming in the foreground. Panning right, you'll see waterfalls gushing from the cliffsides (especially after a good rain), and eventually a cattle farm in the high alp. There

were plans for a big apartment-hotel to be built here, but the community said no. Now the lonely tree stump is a popular place for Instagram photos.

• *Just after the café, detour from the main street out to the cliff-hanging tennis court. Pause at the far corner of the first court, step up to the small arch, and look down.*

Via Ferrata: Directly below, at the base

You'll have many hiking options from Mürren.

of the modern wall, is the start of the 1.5-mile *via ferrata,* a "trail" with a steel-cable guide that mountaineers use to venture safely along the cliff all the way to Gimmelwald. The steel cable disappears over the cliff and ends at the Gimmelwald lift station (which you can see in the distance). Farther to the right, the Allmendhubel funicular trundles visitors up to some of the best views in the region—and the start of some glorious hikes (described later). Listen for the river, waterfalls, and avalanches on the far side.

• *Backtrack the way you came, then turn left at the Stäger Sport onto the main street to reach...*

"Downtown" Mürren: At the main intersection, a small service road leads down to Gimmelwald. Stay right (following *Schilthornbahn* and *Mürren* signs) and enter the main drag. Here you'll find my favorite restaurant in town (Stägerstübli), the only grocery store (Co-op), and the best souvenir shop (Abegglen).

A bit farther on, past the faded old Hotel Regina, the tiny fire barn on the right (labeled *Feuerwehr*) has a list showing the leaders of the volunteer force and their responsibilities.

About 60 feet beyond the fire barn (across the street from and just before the old schoolhouse—*Altes Schulhaus*), detour right uphill a few steps into the oldest part of town. Explore the windy little lanes, admiring the ancient woodwork on the houses, 400-year-old timbers, and cute little pea patches.

• *Back on the main drag, continue to the far end of Mürren, where you come to the...*

Cable-Car Station: The larger cars that dock in the back of the station take hikers and skiers up to the Schilthorn and run down to the valley via Gimmelwald. The smaller cable car out front goes directly to the valley floor. This was the main route down to Stechelberg until 1987, but today it is only for cargo, garbage, and backup passenger service in spring and fall when the newer cars are closed for maintenance.

• *From here you can hike or catch the lift (5 minutes) down to Gimmelwald. Or, hike back into town along the high road, where you'll pass Mürren's two churches, the Allmendhubel funicular station, and the Sportzentrum (with swimming pool and TI).*

Mürren's cute town center

Experiences

For hikes from Mürren, see page 684.

ALLMENDHUBEL FUNICULAR (ALLMENDHUBELBAHN)

A surprisingly rewarding funicular (built in 1912, renovated in 1999) carries nature lovers in less than four minutes from Mürren up to Allmendhubel, a 6,257-foot perch offering a Jungfrau view that, though much lower, rivals the Schilthorn. Consider mixing a mountain lift, grand views, and a hike with your meal by eating at the restaurant on Allmendhubel (good chef, open daily until 17:00).

Allmendhubel is particularly good for families. This is also the departure point for the North Face hike and walks to Grütschalp (see page 684). While at Allmendhubel, consider its Flower trail, a 20-minute loop with nice mountain views and (from July through Sept) a chance to see more than 150 different types of alpine flowers in bloom. At a minimum, simply climb the steep hill behind the playground to reach a stunning viewpoint, with benches looking out over the little restaurant facing all that big scenery.

Cost and Hours: 8.80 CHF one-way, 14 CHF round-trip, half-price with Swiss Travel Pass, early June-mid-Oct daily 9:00-17:00, runs every 20 minutes, tel. 033-855-2042 or 033-856-2141, www. schilthorn.ch.

TANDEM PARAGLIDING

If you've ever wondered what it's like to soar like an eagle, a tandem paragliding flight will give you a pretty good idea. Two companies offer guided flights that take off just above the Mürren cable-car station and end near the Stechelberg cable-car station. Flights last around 15 to 20 minutes...God willing.

Cost: 180 CHF for Mürren-Stechelberg flight, transport to Mürren not included. Airtime Paragliding is based at the recommended Airtime Café in Lauterbrunnen (tel. 079-247-8463, https://airtime-paragliding.ch). Paragliding

Jungfrau offers similar tandem flights at similar prices (tel. 079-779-9000, www. paragliding-jungfrau.ch).

Sleeping

Half-board, if available, can be a good idea in Mürren.

$$$ Hotel Eiger, a four-star hotel dramatically and conveniently situated just across from the tiny train station, is a good but expensive bet. Family-run for four generations, it offers all the services you'd expect in a big-city hotel (plush lounge, elegant dining rooms, indoor swimming pool, exercise room, and saunas) while maintaining an Old World, woody elegance in its 50 business-class yet charming rooms (grand breakfast, discounts for stays of 3 nights or more, email for best deals, elevator, tel. 033-856-5454, www. hoteleiger.com, info@hoteleiger.com).

$$ Hotel Edelweiss is all about the location—convenient and literally hanging on the cliff with devastating views. It's a big, modern building with 30 straightforward rooms (some with balconies) and a busy, recommended restaurant (closed Nov-mid-Dec, elevator, piano in lounge, self-serve pay laundry, tel. 033-856-5600, www.edelweiss-muerren.ch, info@ edelweiss-muerren.ch).

$$ Hotel Bellevue feels country-upscale and authentically Swiss, with a homey lounge, solid woodsy furniture, a great view terrace, the recommended hunter-themed Jägerstübli restaurant, and 19 comfortable rooms—most with balconies and views. It may be under new management in the near future, so some details could change (discount if staying 2 nights or more in June or Oct, self-serve pay laundry, tel. 033-855-1401, www. bellevuemuerren.ch, bellevue@muerren. ch, Ruth and Othmar Suter).

$$ Hotel Jungfrau has a classic exterior and a modern interior—with 29 rooms plus two apartments for up to six people (email for best deals, elevator, pay laundry service, close to TI/Sportzentrum on the upper road, tel. 033-856-6464, www. hoteljungfrau.ch, mail@hoteljungfrau.ch, Martin and Connie).

$$ Pop-Up Lodge Mürren is a fun concept: The giant, hulking Hotel Alpin Palace looms at the train-station end of town, awaiting a massive renovation. In the meantime, they're renting dated, charmless, but clean and well-equipped rooms to travelers. It's attached by a long walkway to the Sportzentrum and the TI, which is where you'll check in (includes full access to Sportzentrum, tel. 033-856-8686, www.popuplodge.ch, info@popuplodge.ch). For budget travelers, they're also renting basic rooms with shared bathrooms inside the old **$ Sport Lodge** by the tennis courts (the former hotel staff house)—book and check in through the TI.

$$ Hotel Blumental has 14 rooms with woody accents and down comforters, a recommended restaurant in the main building, plus six modern rooms of equal quality in the chalet out back (half-board available, tel. 033-855-1826, www. blumental-muerren.ch, blumental@muerren.ch).

$ Eiger Guesthouse offers 12 good, small, budget rooms—including some great bunk-bed family rooms—across from the train station, above an easygoing ground-floor pub. Four of the rooms share three sets of bathroom facilities, while the rest are en suite (RS%, closed Nov, lots of stairs, game room, view terrace, tel. 033-856-5460, www.eigerguesthouse.com, info@eigerguesthouse.com).

$ Hotel Regina has 50 basic rooms (most with shared toilets and showers) and is conveniently located at the cable-car end of town. For solo travelers, the single rooms are a decent value (family deals, tel. 033-855-4242, www.reginamuerren.ch, info@reginamuerren.ch).

$ Chalet Fontana, run by charming Englishwoman Denise Fussell, is a fine budget option, with five simple, crispy-clean, and comfortable rooms (cash only, closed late Oct-April, fridge in common kitchen, across street from Stäger-stübli restaurant in town center, mobile 078-642-3485, www.chaletfontana.ch, chaletfontana@gmail.com). Denise also rents a family apartment with kitchen, bathroom, and breakfast (in a separate building with a mountain view).

Eating

$$ Hotel Edelweiss offers lunch and dinner with the most cliff-hanging dining in town, with Swiss specialties, burgers, pizzas, salads, and daily specials. It's family-friendly, the views are incredible, and the prices are good (daily 11:00-20:30, tel. 033-856-5600).

$$ Eiger Guesthouse Restaurant, a busy local hangout with a relaxed pub atmosphere, has long hours and a mostly Italian menu. They also serve fondue, raclette, *Rösti,* inexpensive house wine, and proudly local beers (daily 8:00-22:00, closed Nov, tel. 033-856-5460).

$$$ Stägerstübli, serving big portions of *Rösti* and meat dishes in the town center, is in a 1902 building that was once a tearoom for rich tourists. Sitting on its terrace, you know just who's out and about in town (Thu-Mon 11:30-20:30, closed Tue-Wed, tel. 033-855-1316).

$$ Hotel Blumental's restaurant (called **La Grotte**) specializes in typical Swiss cuisine, but also serves fish, international, and vegetarian dishes in a stony and woody dining area. It's one of Mürren's most elegant, romantic settings (cheese fondue served for one or more,

daily from 14:00, tel. 033-855-1826).

$$$ Hotel Bellevue's restaurant is atmospheric, with three dining zones: a spectacular view terrace, a sophisticated indoor area, and the *Jägerstübli*—a cozy, well-antlered hunters' room (meatless dishes available, daily 11:30-14:00 & 18:00-21:00, tel. 033-855-1401).

$ Café Liv is a mod, hip, and youthful coffee shop with light lunch plates, smoothies, pastries, and quality coffee, including takeaway (Mon-Thu 12:00-18:00, Fri-Sun from 10:00, in town center on the main street, across from tennis courts, tel. 076-213-7305).

Supermarket: The **Co-op** has good picnic fixings and sandwiches (Mon-Fri 8:00-18:30, Sat until 18:00, Sun 11:00-17:00, can be closed Tue-Thu afternoons off-season). Given restaurant prices, this place is a godsend for those on a tight budget.

SCENIC LIFTS AND TRAINS

The Berner Oberland is famous for its high-altitude thrill rides. I've described the best of them here.

The Schilthornbahn cable car leaves the Gimmelwald station.

▲▲▲SCHILTHORNBAHN CABLE CAR

The Schilthornbahn cable car carries skiers, hikers, and sightseers effortlessly to the nearly 10,000-foot summit of the Schilthorn, where the Piz Gloria cable-car station awaits, with its solar-powered revolving restaurant, shop, and panorama terrace. At the top, you have a spectacular panoramic view of over 100 peaks—starring the Eiger, Mönch, and Jungfrau mountains, all lined up on the horizon.

Getting There: You can ride to the Schilthorn and back from several points—the cable-car station near Stechelberg on the valley floor (105 CHF), cliff-hanging Gimmelwald (94.60 CHF), or the higher Mürren (82.60 CHF).

Starting from Stechelberg, the ride requires three changes on the way up: at Gimmelwald (5 minutes), Mürren (5 minutes), and Birg; the entire ride, from valley floor to mountaintop, takes about 35 minutes (or about 25 minutes from Mürren). Lifts run all year, except during maintenance closures (a week in April and three weeks in Nov-Dec)—check online for current operating hours.

Discounts: With a Swiss Travel Pass, you ride free to Mürren, then pay half-price to the top; if you have a Eurail Global Pass, you get 25 percent off any ride. Special promotions can save you even more (including a good-value early-morning breakfast deal)—check the website or ask when buying tickets.

Information: See www.schilthorn.ch or call 033-826-0007 for more details and current weather conditions.

Avoiding Crowds: Crowds are a big problem in peak season, especially on weekends (the worst bottleneck is in Mürren). Groups have priority access. Beat the hordes by catching an early lift—preferably before 9:30. It can also make sense to ascend later—it's quieter after about 14:30 (and the mountains across the valley are bathed in late-day sunlight). You can also reserve a specific lift departure time online 24 hours in advance (5 CHF extra).

Ascending the Schilthorn: As the cable car floats up the first stage of the ascent, from Stechelberg to Gimmelwald, you'll see sweet little farms dotting the valley, the paved trail along the river, a line of tour buses foretelling how many groups are above you, and the treacherous metal bridge marking the end of the *via ferrata* cableway hike. On stage

Viewing platform at the top of the Schilthorn

two—Gimmelwald to Mürren—you'll see fields of wooden tripods, which serve two purposes: They stop avalanches and shelter newly planted trees. Made of wood, they're designed to eventually rot when the tree they protect is strong enough to survive the winter snowpack.

You'll change cable cars at Birg. While Birg has the thrilling Skyline Walk (described next), if the weather is good, continue directly to the summit—you'll come back down through Birg later anyway.

Birg Station and Skyline Walk: The Birg station (8,784 feet) has a handy **$ café** with basic food (bratwurst, soup) and glorious outdoor seating; nearby is the breezy (and free) **Skyline Walk** viewing platform that juts out over the cliff face. With more time, it's worth hiking down to the **Thrill Walk**—a free 600-foot-long catwalk bolted to the cliffside. If walking the see-through metal catwalk seems tame to you, you can choose to tightrope across a cable bridge (there's a net below), cross a section of glass flooring, and crawl through a chain-link tube—all with airy views to the valley far below (both experiences are free with cable-car ticket).

At the Top: Head up two escalators to the **Skyline View Platform** (or go to the right out of the lift to zip up on the elevator). Outside, information boards identify the peaks, and directional signs point hikers toward some seriously steep downhill climbs. The big, round viewing scopes identify each peak as you survey the panorama; the pink scopes magnify. Note that the classic "Eiger, Mönch, Jungfrau" panorama is on the opposite side from the big platform. Watch paragliders set up, psych up, take off, and fly with the birds.

Find the stairs near the big platform to walk along the ridge out back—the **007 Walk of Fame,** where cast and crew members from the film have left their handprints and personal messages. At the end of this is the Piz Gloria view platform, offering great views back at the revolving

restaurant with the mountains beyond. If you dare, let yourself through the gate by the platform and walk carefully along a gravelly, vertiginous trail (with no railings)—to leave the crowds behind and really feel rugged. This is a great place for a photo of the mountain-climber you.

Back inside, consider a drink or a bite at the revolving **$$ 360° Restaurant** (up the stairs; if you're heading up for an early breakfast, mention it when you buy your ticket down below to save 11 CHF on the buffet before 9:00). There's a cheaper **$ snack bar** on the main level.

Then head down the stairs and follow the maze that leads to the **Bond World 007** exhibit and cinema. This interactive exhibit, well-signed in English, is worth a few minutes for even non-Bond fans.

Finished? You can hike down from the Schilthorn, but it's tough. (Hiking *up* is easier on your knees...if you don't mind a 5,000-foot altitude gain.) For information on hikes from lift stations along the Schilthorn cable-car line, see "Hiking," later. My favorite "hike" from the Schilthorn is simply along the ridge out back, to get away from the station and be all alone on top of an Alp.

▲▲▲JUNGFRAUBAHN TRAIN

A literal high point of any trip to the Swiss Alps is the Jungfraubahn train ride through the Eiger mountain to the Jungfraujoch (the saddle between the Mönch and Jungfrau mountains). At 11,333 feet, it's Europe's highest train station. (If you have a heart or lung condition, you may want to check with your doctor before making this ascent.) Keep in mind that you can enjoy the Berner Oberland without taking this trip—it's long, slow, expensive, crowded, and cold. But if the weather's perfect and you have a spare day and spare cash, the views are exhilarating and it's fun to be up on a snowy glacier in midsummer.

Getting There: Round-trip fares are 211 CHF from Interlaken Ost, 190 CHF

Enjoy a sky-high breakfast at the top of the Schilthorn.

Ride the Jungfraubahn to Europe's highest train station.

from Lauterbrunnen, 176 CHF from Wengen, and 128 CHF from Kleine Scheidegg. The train runs about twice hourly year-round—check online for current schedule.

Discounts: From May to late October, a "Good Morning Ticket" saves you 25 percent on early departures from Interlaken Ost, Lauterbrunnen, and Kleine Scheidegg. To get the discount you must leave the top by 13:00. Eurail Global pass holders get 25 percent off and can't combine discounts, so they should go whenever they want. The same goes for Swiss Travel Pass holders, who travel free as far as Wengen (with a 25 percent discount beyond)—buy your supplementary ticket before boarding, or pay a 10-CHF surcharge to buy it on board.

Information: Visit www.jungfrau.ch or call 033-828-7233.

Crowd-Beating Tips: At peak periods (especially July-Aug), trains are standing-room only. During peak times, reserve a seat at a fixed time the day before (5 CHF extra for each leg—up and down; allow about two hours up top). Without a reservation, you may have to wait up to an hour in line both to get up and back down.

Weather: Be aware that even when it's socked in down in the valleys, it can still be gloriously sunny up top—check the webcams and weather forecast at www.jungfrau.ch before committing.

Planning Your Trip: Visiting the Jungfraujoch takes most of a day. The trip up

from Lauterbrunnen takes a little under two hours each way, with a change of trains halfway at Kleine Scheidegg. If you're coming from Interlaken, Gimmelwald, or Mürren, add another half-hour. You'll want at least 1.5 hours at the top—more if you eat, hike, or sled. Expect outdoor temperatures to be around freezing in summer—so if you plan to go outside, bring a hat and gloves, shoes with good traction, sunglasses, and sunscreen. Even if you stay inside, the train is chilly, and you'll need a jacket. To minimize altitude sickness, local guides recommend drinking a half-liter of water as you ascend on the train. Eateries at the top are overpriced; consider bringing a picnic.

Rick's Tip: For a thrilling day of alpine scenery, *try this plan: Ride the* **train** *to Wengen, take the* **cable car** *up to Männlichen,* **hike** *from there to Kleine Scheidegg (about 1.5 hours, easy), then catch the* **train** *up to the Jungfraujoch.*

Ascending the Jungfraujoch: From Lauterbrunnen or Wengen, you'll board a characteristic little yellow-and-green Wengernalpbahn train to get as far as Kleine Scheidegg. There, you'll transfer to the Jungfraujoch train. Find your way to the end of the correct line: green if you've reserved, yellow if you haven't.

The 35-minute ride from Kleine Scheidegg to the top is mostly in a tunnel, with just a couple of stops. The first one,

Jungfraujoch overlooks the longest glacial flow in the Alps.

after 5 minutes, is at **Eigergletscher**—stay on the train, and you'll soon enter the tunnel in which you'll travel through the Eiger to the Jungfraujoch. After 11 more minutes, you'll stop for 5 minutes at **Eismeer,** where you can enjoy glacier and mountain views from an amazing perch (10,368 feet). From there, you'll ride up through darkness—watching video screens explaining all your sightseeing options up top—to the **Jungfraujoch.**

At the Top: Once you reach the top, breathe deep, take it easy, and move slowly—you're way high up and your body isn't used to such altitudes. Big, blue *TOUR* signs lead you on a loosely one-way route through the complex, with several optional stops and shortcuts.

To get ahead of the crowds, upon arrival, muscle your way through the congested shopping zone, bearing left for the *TOUR* signs. You'll follow a tunnel to the Jungfrau Panorama, a 360-degree video that's pleasantly distracting while you wait in line for the elevator that rockets you up to the **Sphinx observation deck** (with a tiny snack bar). At 11,782 feet, the views are truly astounding.

Use the orientation panels to get your bearings: You're between the Mönch and the Jungfrau (the Eiger is hidden, behind the Mönch). Looking left, you're gazing (north) down on the Lauterbrunnen Valley area: Kleine Scheidegg, Gimmelwald, and in the distance, Interlaken. Farther to the left looms the giant Jungfrau. And left of that spreads the Aletsch Glacier—Europe's longest, at nearly 11 miles (or a bit less, by the time you read this).

Back downstairs and outside, you'll find a **Snow Fun Park** set up on the Aletsch Glacier, offering skiing and snowboarding (35 CHF), sledding (20 CHF), and a zip line (25 CHF—prices include equipment; 45 CHF for all three activities, mid-May–mid-Oct). The ticket desk also sells hot, cold, and hard drinks to enjoy in a sling-backed chair on the snow. To get away from the Jungfraujoch crowds, you can hike an hour across the ice to **Mönchs-jochhütte** (a mountain hut with a small restaurant). While this can be a highlight,

SWITZERLAND

Gimmelwald Area Hikes

❶ North Face Trail
❷ Allmendhubel to Grütschalp
❸ Allmendhubel to Grütschalp via Winteregg
❹ Grütschalp to Mürren
❺ Birg to Gimmelwald via Bryndli

you need good shoes—when it's slushy, you'll end up with wet feet.

Another outdoor experience is the **Plateau**, where you can walk out on the snow toward the Jungfrau, and look back at the classic Jungfraujoch view—with the Sphinx's glittering silver dome capping a sheer cliff.

HIKING

This area offers days of possible hikes. Many are a fun combination of trails, mountain trains, and cable-car rides. The information below can help you decide which hike to tackle, but isn't intended as a turn-by-turn guide. Good hiking maps

and more detailed trail descriptions are essential and available from area TIs and hotels. Before setting out on any hike, check locally to be sure you've made the best match between your skills, gear, and trail conditions (snow can persist on trails even into summer).

▲▲CLOUDY-DAY LAUTERBRUNNEN VALLEY WALK

Try the easy trails along the floor of the Lauterbrunnen Valley. You don't ever need to (and shouldn't) walk along the main road, which parallels the river. A fine, paved, mostly vehicle-free farm lane (great for walkers, runners, bikers, and people with strollers) goes all the way

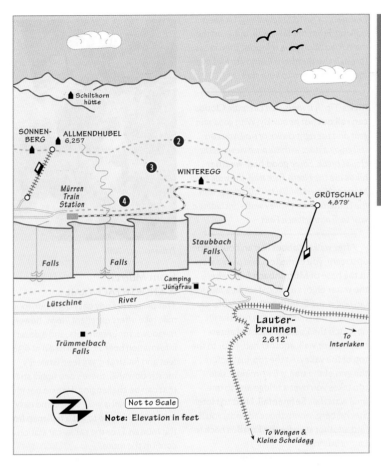

Schilthorn hütte

SONNEN-BERG
ALLMENDHUBEL 6,257

❷

❸

WINTEREGG

GRÜTSCHALP 4,879'

Mürren Train Station

❹

Staubbach Falls

Falls   Falls

Camping Jüngfrau

Lütschine   River

Lauter-brunnen 2,612'

To Interlaken

Trümmelbach Falls

Not to Scale
Note: Elevation in feet

To Wengen & Kleine Scheidegg

along the valley on the opposite side of the river from the main road, from the town of Lauterbrunnen to the top of the valley (Stechelberg). Small bridges let you cross from the lane to the main road at various points. The local PostBus runs the entire length, with stops along the way, twice an hour.

For a smell-the-cows-and-flowers lowland walk—ideal for a cloudy day, weary body, or tight budget—try this three-mile, basically level ramble from Lauterbrunnen to Stechelberg. While you could go either way, I'd go upstream (very gradually uphill) to walk toward the grandest mountain views.

At the edge of Lauterbrunnen town is the Horner Pub. Just beyond that, hike up the (free and slippery) gallery for a close-up view of mighty **Staubbach Falls.** Staubbach is one of 72 waterfalls in this "Valley of Loud Fountains" (as *lauter Brunnen* means).

Follow the river up the valley. Along the way, you may see **BASE jumpers**—parachutists who leap from cliffs (or helicopters looking for their bodies).

About 45 minutes after leaving town, you can cross the river for an optional side trip to **Trümmelbach Falls.** After seeing the falls, you can catch the PostBus in either direction—back to Lauterbrunnen, or on to Stechelberg. Or keep walking: From the falls, walk uphill on the main road about five minutes, then cross through the Breithorn Campsite and over the river to return to your trail.

Rick's Tip: *If it rains, don't despair.* **Clouds can roll out** *just as quickly. With good rain gear and the right choice of trail, you can still enjoy a hike, with surprise views as the clouds break. Some* **good bad-weather hikes** *are the North Face trail, the walk from Mürren/Allmendhubel to Grütschalp, and the Lauterbrunnen Valley walks, including a visit to Trümmelbach Falls.*

After walking about half an hour farther upstream, you come to a fine picnic stop at the base of **Mürrenbach falls,** where the water enjoys a 1,400-foot free fall. Just beyond is the **Schilthornbahn cable-car station.** From here you can ride the lift up; catch the PostBus back to Lauterbrunnen; or walk another half-hour to the top of the valley. At the top, just before the end of the trail, a five-minute side trip takes you over a bridge and to one final waterfall, **Sefinenfall.** Next to Hotel Stechelberg, where the road ends, you'll find another stop for the PostBus back to Lauterbrunnen.

Alternate Route via Gimmelwald: If you're staying in Gimmelwald, try this plan: Take the Schilthornbahn lift down to the station near Stechelberg (5 minutes), then walk 1.5 hours along the river to Lauterbrunnen (side-tripping to Trümmelbach Falls about halfway). To return to Gimmelwald from Lauterbrunnen, take the cable car up to Grütschalp (10 minutes), then either walk to Gimmelwald (1.5 hours) or take the train to Mürren (10 minutes). From Mürren, it's a downhill walk (30 minutes) to Gimmelwald. (This loop trip can be reversed or started at any point along the way—such as Lauterbrunnen or Mürren.)

Trümmelbach Falls

From Mürren
▲▲▲NORTH FACE TRAIL

This pleasant, fairly easy, 2.5-hour, four-mile hike offers excellent views, flowery meadows, mountain huts, and a dozen information boards. You'll begin at 6,385 feet and finish at 5,375 feet; while it's mostly downhill, there's one uphill stretch that can be challenging if you're not in shape. The trail is well-signed and easy to follow, but it's wise to get a trail map from the Mürren TI or the cable-car station and confirm the route.

To begin the hike, ride the Allmendhubel funicular up from Mürren (good restaurant at top). Leaving the funicular, look for the children's play area and a blue *North Face Trail* sign. Follow the path uphill, skirting to the right around the play area, passing through small cattle gates, and past the chairlift station. From here, follow the blue signs down into the valley toward Sonnenberg. (Along the way, you'll see yellow directional signs pointing toward *Sonnenberg, Suppenalp,* and *Schiltalp,* as well as blue *North Face Trail* signs.)

You'll head over a little ridge and drop into lovely **Blumental** ("Flower Valley," under the Schilthornbahn cable-car line), which is hopping with marmots.

Following the trail down into the valley,

Hiking in the Berner Oberland

To do any serious hiking, invest in a good hiking map at any TI, and ask about current weather and trail conditions. For easy hikes, it's usually enough to use the 3-D maps in the free brochures (called *Wandern/Hiking*) published by the Schilthornbahn (for the west side of the valley) and the Jungfraubahn (for the east side); they're available at stations, hotels, and TIs. These overview maps of the mountainsides also make attractive souvenirs.

Don't forget a water bottle and some munchies. In addition to a good map, for serious hikes it's wise to carry sun protection, an extra layer of clothing, and basic first-aid supplies. Know when the last lifts run in the afternoon. Trails are well-marked, with yellow signs listing destinations and the estimated time it'll take you to walk there.

Weather Concerns: Snow can curtail your hiking plans, even in July. The high trails (Männlichen to Kleine Scheidegg, Schynige Platte to First, and anything from Schilthorn or Birg) are typically passable only from June into October.

Locals always seem to know the weather report (as much of their income depends on it). Clouds can roll in anytime, but on warm summer days, skies are usually clearest in the morning. All over the region, TV sets are tuned to the local weather station, with real-time views from all the famous peaks. You can also check weather reports and view live webcams at www.jungfrau.ch and www.schilthorn.ch. For more detailed weather reports in English, visit www.meteoswiss.admin.ch.

you can make a brief detour to the left to the remote and quirky pension/restaurant **Sonnenberg;** they were allowed to break the all-wood building code with concrete for protection against avalanches.

From here, follow the paved trail across the meadow, then hook left to the quainter **Suppenalp.** Lean against the house with a salad, soup, or sandwich, and enjoy the view (closed Mon-Tue). Notice how older huts are built into the protected side of rocks and outcroppings, in anticipation of avalanches.

From here, you'll head uphill on the gravel path—directly toward the looming, craggy Schwarzmönch peak. You'll gain altitude as you curve around the ridge (called **Schiltgrat**), directly under

the tourists gliding in cable cars up to the Schilthorn. In spots where the path is not clearly defined, look for white-and-red stripes painted on rocks. Watch on your left for great views down over Mürren. Going through a small alpine forest, more peaks come into view. You'll emerge at a broad, grassy **meadow** high over Gimmelwald, where the views open up. Look high on the right for both the Birg and Piz Gloria stations on the Schilthornbahn.

After strolling blissfully through high alpine meadows, you'll finally come to a group of huts called **Schiltalp** (with a romantic farm setting and good self-service food and drink). At Schiltalp, if the poles under the eaves have bells, the cows are up here. If not, the cows are at the

The family-friendly North Face trail takes you past flowery meadows and mountain huts.

Hiking from Männlichen to Kleine Scheidegg: Wow!

lower farms. In July, August, and September, you can watch cheese being made.

From Schiltalp, the trail winds gracefully downhill, where you'll cross the bridge to pick up the trail to Spilboden—another rustic alp settlement. To finish the North Face trail, head left through meadows and the hamlet of Gimmeln, then back to Mürren.

▲ALLMENDHUBEL TO GRÜTSCHALP (A.K.A. MOUNTAIN VIEW TRAIL)

For a not-too-tough two-hour walk with great Jungfrau views, ride the funicular from Mürren to Allmendhubel and walk to Grütschalp (a drop of about 1,500 feet), where you can catch the train back to Mürren. You'll see this route clearly marked as the "Mountain View trail" on maps and brochures.

▲GRÜTSCHALP TO MÜRREN

For a family-friendly, super-easy panorama stroll with grand views, walk either direction between Mürren (5,381 feet) and Grütschalp (4,879 feet)—roughly following the scenic train line between the same points. You'll enjoy the best

Jungfrau views walking from Grütschalp to Mürren. The trail from the tiny station at Grütschalp to Winteregg (5,177 feet) is a 30-minute scenic walk mostly through cow country with an accompaniment of tinkling bells on a gravelly lane. The trail between Winteregg and Mürren mostly parallels the train track—also scenic and gravelly, but less interesting. The highlight, along with the dramatic views of the Eiger, Mönch, and Jungfrau, is the wonderful restaurant/playground/cheese farm midway at Winteregg. (The Grütschalp-Mürren train also stops here.) The Alpkäserei Staubbach offers windows to peer into the cheese-making action (before 11:00), and sells fresh yogurt and cheese. The Winteregg Restaurant has a dramatic view terrace and an extensive alp-happy playground.

From Lauterbrunnen/Wengen
▲▲▲MÄNNLICHEN-KLEINE SCHEIDEGG HIKE

This is my favorite easy alpine hike (2.5 miles, about 1.5 hours, 900-foot altitude drop to Kleine Scheidegg). It's entertain-

Cow bells on a herder's hut

Easy trail between Mürren and Grütschalp

ing all the way, with glorious mountain views. If you missed the plot, it's the Monk (Mönch) protecting the Young Maiden (Jungfrau) from the Ogre (Eiger). The trail usually opens sometime in June and closes due to snow in October. Ask about conditions and get a map at the lift stations or at TIs; there are also useful webcams at www.maennlichen.ch and www.jungfrau.ch.

Ascending to Männlichen: If the weather's good, start off bright and early. From the Lauterbrunnen train station, take the little mountain train up to **Wengen.** Sit on the right side of the train for great valley and waterfall views. In Wengen, buy a picnic at the Co-op grocery across the square from the station, walk a couple of blocks into town, and catch the lift to Männlichen, located on top of the ridge high above you (23 CHF one-way, half-price with Swiss Travel Pass, 3/hour, 6-minute trip, mid-May–mid-Oct first ascent at 8:30, at 8:10 July–mid-Sept, last ascent at 16:50, somewhat shorter hours off-season, tel. 033-855-2933, www.maennlichen.ch).

Riding the gondola from Wengen to **Männlichen,** you'll go over the old lift station—built in 1978, then inundated by a 1999 avalanche that buried a good part of Wengen (notice there's no development in the "red zone" above the tennis courts). Farms are built with earthen ramps on the uphill side in anticipation of the next slide. The forest of avalanche fences near the top was reinforced after that 1999

avalanche.

When you get to the station at the top of the Wengen-Männlichen lift (7,313 feet, WCs), check inside to see if they have any free "king for a day" Männlichen Experience envelopes; these fun souvenirs open up to make a panoramic crown that names the mountains you're seeing.

Männlichen Gipfel Detour ("The Royal Walk"): Before your easy hike, consider a steeper detour that'll give you an easy king- or queen-of-the-day feeling: Turn left from the Wengen-Männlichen lift station, and hike uphill to the little peak you see up ahead, topped with a crown-shaped viewpoint (Männlichen Gipfel, 7,687 feet). Marked as "The Royal Walk," this path gains more than 350 feet of elevation; if you're in decent shape, it takes about 20 minutes up, then 10 minutes back down. The last stretch is thin-air-sucking steep, with ropes you can grab onto for added confidence; even Coloradans get a bit winded. But once at the **summit,** you're rewarded with 360-degree views. Beneath you, look for avalanche barriers—both directly below the viewpoint, and striping the cliffs across the valley.

Easy Hike to Kleine Scheidegg: Back at the lift station, enjoy the walk—facing spectacular alpine panorama views—to Kleine Scheidegg for a picnic or restaurant lunch. To start the hike, leave the Wengen-Männlichen lift station to the right. Ahead of you in the distance, left to right, are the north faces of the Eiger, Mönch, and Jungfrau; in the foreground is the Tschuggen peak, and just behind it, the Lauberhorn. This hike takes you around the left (east) side of this ridge. Simply follow the signs for *Kleine Scheidegg,* and you'll be there in about 1.5 hours—allowing extra time for gawkers, picnickers, and photographers. (Speed walkers can make it in an hour.)

Walk a few minutes to the second Männlichen lift station (with free WCs; these lifts go to Grindelwald, the touristy town in the valley to your left). Nearby is the Berghaus Männlichen restaurant (wait for better options later), a great kids' play area, and a landing pad for helicopter sightseeing flights.

From here, carry on along the path as it curls around the left (Grindelwald-facing) side of the ridge. From time to time, you might have to tiptoe through streams of melted snow—or some small snow banks (with ropes to hang onto for safety), even well into the summer—but the path is well-marked, well-maintained, and mostly level all the way to Kleine Scheidegg.

About two-thirds of the way through the hike, you'll curve around the bend and arrive at a cluster of benches and a shelter with incredible unobstructed views of all three peaks—the perfect picnic spot.

About 15 minutes later, you'll reach the first sign of civilization: the **Restaurant Grindelwaldblick** (the best lunch stop up here—less crowded, more Swiss and friendly than Kleine Scheidegg options). Hike to the restaurant's fun mountain lookout to survey the Eiger and look down on the Kleine Scheidegg (rated ▲▲ for its spectacular panoramic mountain view).

From the Grindelwaldblick, it's a steep 10-minute hike down to the Kleine Scheidegg train station, with plenty of lesser lunch options.

Optional Add-Ons: From Kleine Scheidegg, you can catch the train up to "the top of Europe" (see Jungfraujoch listing, earlier), take the train back down to Wengen (note that your Swiss Travel Pass

doesn't cover you until Wengen; buy a supplementary ticket before boarding, or pay a 10-CHF surcharge to buy on board), or hike downhill (gorgeous 30-minute hike to the Wengernalp station, a little farther to the Allmend stop; 60 more steep minutes from there into Wengen—not dangerous, but requires a good set of knees). The alpine views might be accompanied by the valley-filling mellow sound of cow bells, alphorns, and distant avalanches. If the weather turns bad or you run out of steam, catch the train at any of the stations along the way. The boring final descent from Wengen to Lauterbrunnen is knee-killer steep—catch the train instead.

More Difficult Hikes
Above Interlaken

Several tough trails lead down from the Schilthorn (there's a reason that virtually all visitors take the cable car down). Only a serious, experienced hiker should consider walking all or part of the way back into Gimmelwald. Proper shoes and clothing (weather can change quickly) and good knees are required. Don't attempt to hike down unless you've confirmed that the trail is clear of snow. While it's possible to make the steep descent directly from the top of the Schilthorn, I prefer the less strenuous (but still challenging) hike from the intermediate cable-car station at Birg.

▲▲BIRG TO GIMMELWALD VIA BRYNDLI

You can combine this difficult downhill hike (4-5 hours) from the Birg cable-car station with a visit to the Schilthorn by buying the round-trip excursion early-bird fare (it's cheaper than the Gimmelwald-Schilthorn-Birg ticket). Visit the summit first, then descend to Birg to hike down.

The most interesting trail from Birg to Gimmelwald is the high one via Grauseeli lake and Wasenegg Ridge to **Bryndli,** then down to Spilboden and the Sprutz waterfall. **Warning:** This trail drops 4,500 feet, is quite steep and slippery in places, and can take over four hours. Locals take their kindergarteners on this hike, but Americans not accustomed to to alpine hikes shouldn't attempt it.

From the **Birg lift station,** hike toward the Schilthorn, taking your first left down and passing along the left side of the little Grauseeli lake. From the lake, a gravelly trail leads down rough switchbacks (including a stretch where the path narrows and you can hang onto a guide cable against the cliff face) until it levels out. When you see a rock painted with arrows pointing to Mürren and Rotstockhütte, follow the path to **Rotstockhütte** (traditional old farm with light meals and drinks), traversing the cow-grazed mountainside.

The safer, well-signposted approach to Bryndli is to drop down to Rotstockhütte, then climb back up to Bryndli. Thrill-seekers instead follow **Wasenegg Ridge.** It's more scary than dangerous if you're sure-footed and can handle the 50-foot-long "tightrope-with-handrail" section along an extremely narrow ledge with a thousand-foot drop. This trail gets you to Bryndli with the least altitude change. A barbed-wire fence leads you to Bryndli's knobby little summit, where you'll enjoy an incredible 360-degree view and a chance to sign your name on the register stored in the little wooden box.

From **Bryndli,** a steep trail winds directly down toward Gimmelwald and soon hits a bigger, easier trail. The trail bends right (just before the farm/restaurant at Spilboden), leading to Sprutz. Walk under the Sprutz waterfall, then follow a steep, wooded trail that deposits you in a meadow of flowers at the top side of Gimmelwald.

▲▲SCHYNIGE PLATTE TO FIRST

The best day I've had hiking in the Berner Oberland was on this demanding seven-hour ridge walk, with Lake Brienz on one side and all that Jungfrau beauty on the other. Start at the Wilderswil train station (just outside Interlaken), and catch the little train up to Schynige Platte (6,454 feet; 32 CHF one-way, goes every 40 minutes and takes about an hour, runs late May-late Oct). Catch the early 8:05 train to have time for Faulhorn and get to First before it closes. The high point on the trail is Faulhorn (8,790 feet, with a famous mountaintop hotel from 1832). From here, hike on to First (7,110 feet), where you ride a small gondola down to Grindelwald (33 CHF; runs continuously—until at least 17:00 in summer) and catch a train back via Zweilutschinen to wherever you're staying.

You can also do this hike in reverse, which means less climbing, from First (7,113 feet) to Schynige Platte (last train down at 17:53). The TI produces a great Schynige Platte map/guide narrating the train ride up and describing various hiking options from there (available at Wilderswil train station).

Easier Options at Schynige Platte: For a shorter (3-hour) ridge walk, consider the well-signposted Panoramaweg, a loop from Schynige Platte to Daub Peak.

The alpine flower park at the Schynige Platte station offers a delightful stroll through several hundred alpine flowers (free, late May-late Oct daily 8:30-18:00, www.alpengarten.ch), including a chance to see edelweiss growing in the wild.

Germany

Germany (Deutschland) is energetic and organized. The European Union's most populous country and biggest economy, Germany is home to 82 million people—one-third Catholic and one-third Protestant. It's 138,000 square miles (about half the size of Texas) and bordered by nine countries. Germany is young compared with most of its European neighbors ("born" in 1871) but was a founding member of the EU.

Germany offers travelers an intriguing mix: rollicking Munich, the little medieval-walled town of Rothenburg, the sleepy villages lining the mighty Rhine, and the surprising city of Berlin, with monuments that embody the country's past turbulence and modern resurgence.

CUISINE SCENE AT A GLANCE

Germanic food is filling, meaty, and—by European standards—inexpensive. Each region has its specialties, which are often good values. Be adventurous.

Traditional **restaurants** go by many names. At a beer hall *(Brauhaus)* or a beer garden *(Biergarten)*, you can get big, basic, stick-to-the-ribs meals and huge liter beers (called *ein Mass* in German, or *"ein* pitcher" in English). Many beer halls have a cafeteria system; the food is usually *selbstdienst* (self-service). Any real beer garden will keep a few tables (those without tablecloths) available for customers who buy only beer and bring their own food.

Gasthaus, Gasthof, and *Gaststube* all loosely describe an informal, inn-type eatery. A *Kneipe* is a bar, and a *Keller* (or *Ratskeller*) is a restaurant or tavern located in a cellar. A *Weinstube* serves wine and usually traditional (that is, meaty) food as well.

Most eateries have menus tacked onto their front doors, with an English menu inside. Some restaurants offer inexpensive €7-10 weekday hot-lunch specials that aren't listed on the regular menu (look for the *Tageskarte* or *Tagesangebot*, or just ask—may be offered at dinner, too). For smaller portions, order from the *kleine Hunger* (small hunger) section of the menu. Vegetarians can opt for big dinner-size salads.

At any restaurant, a *Stammtisch* sign hanging over or on a table means that it's reserved for regulars.

Tipping: If you order your food at a counter, don't tip. At restaurants that have table service, it's standard to leave about 10 percent for good service.

Rather than leaving coins behind on the table (considered slightly rude), Germans usually pay directly: When the server comes by with the bill, simply hand over paper money, stating the total you'd like to pay. For example, if paying for a €10 meal with a €20 bill, while handing your money to the server, say "Eleven, please" (or *"Elf, bitte"* if you've got your German numbers down). The server will keep a €1 tip and give you €9 in change.

Budget Options: It's easy to get a meal in Germany for €10 or less. Bakeries sell cheap sandwiches and often have tables. Department stores usually have self-service cafeterias. A *Schnellimbiss* is a small fast-food takeaway stand that sells bratwurst and other grilled sausage. Some stands and shops sell Turkish-style *döner kebab* (gyro-like, pita-wrapped rotisserie meat).

Munich

Munich ("München" in German), often called Germany's most livable city, is also one of its most historic, artistic, and entertaining. Also known as "Germany's biggest village," Munich is big and growing, with a population of 1.5 million.

Until 1871, it was the capital of an independent Bavaria. Its royal palaces, jewels, and grand boulevards remind visitors that Munich has long been a political and cultural powerhouse. Meanwhile, the concentration camp memorial in nearby Dachau reminds us that eight decades ago, Munich provided a springboard for Nazism.

Orient yourself in Munich's old center, with its colorful pedestrian zones. Immerse yourself in the city's art and history—crown jewels, Baroque theater, Wittelsbach palaces, great paintings, and beautiful parks. Spend your Munich evenings in a frothy beer hall or outdoor *Biergarten*, prying big pretzels from buxom, no-nonsense beer maids amid an oompah, bunny-hopping, and belching Bavarian atmosphere.

MUNICH IN 3 DAYS

Day 1: Follow the "Munich City Walk" laid out in this chapter, visiting sights along the way. After lunch, tour the Residenz.

On any evening: Try a beer hall one night and a beer garden on another. Stroll through Marienplatz and the core pedestrian streets. Have a dinner picnic at the English Garden.

Day 2: Visit the Dachau Memorial in the morning. Later, if the weather's fine, rent a bike to enjoy the English Garden. Or tour the top art museum, the Alte Pinakothek.

Day 3: Take your pick of these fine sights: Egyptian Museum, Lenbachhaus (German art), Nazi Documentation Center, Munich City Museum, or—away from the center—the Nymphenburg Palace and BMW-Welt and Museum.

With extra time: Day-trip options include a day-long bus tour to see "Mad" King Ludwig's Castles (covered in the Bavarian Alps chapter) or even a visit to Salzburg, Austria (1.5 hours one-way by fast train).

ORIENTATION

The tourist's Munich is circled by a ring road (site of the old town wall) marked by four old gates: Karlstor (near the main train station—the Hauptbahnhof), Sendlinger Tor, Isartor (near the river), and Odeonsplatz (no surviving gate, near the palace). Marienplatz marks the city's center. A great pedestrian-only zone (Kaufingerstrasse and Neuhauser Strasse) cuts this circle in half, running neatly from the Karlstor and the train station through Marienplatz to the Isartor. Orient yourself along this east-west axis. Most of the sights and hotels I recommend are within a 20-minute walk of Marienplatz and each other.

Tourist Information

Munich has two helpful city-run TIs (www.muenchen.de): in front of the **main train station** (may be closed when you visit while station undergoes renovations; Mon-Sat 9:00-20:00, Sun 10:00-18:00, tel. 089/2339-6500—answered Mon-Fri 9:00-17:00), and on Munich's main square, **Marienplatz,** below the glocken-spiel (Mon-Sat 9:30-19:30, Sun 10:00-18:00; sometimes closed Sun off-season). Pick up the *Discovering Munich* brochure, which describes transportation options, and the free, twice-monthly magazine *In München,* which lists movies and enter-tainment (in German, organized by date).

EurAide Train Assistance: At counter #1 in the train station's main *Reisezen-trum* (travel center, opposite track 21), the eager-to-help EurAide desk is a godsend for Eurailers and budget travelers. EurAide makes reservations and sells tickets and sleepers for the train at the same price you'd pay at the other counters (May-Oct Mon-Fri 8:30-20:00, Sat until 14:00, closed Sun; Nov-April Mon-Fri 10:00-19:00—except Jan-Feb 8:00-13:00, Sat 10:00-12:00, closed Sun; www.euraide.com). A line can form at this popular service; do your home-work and have a list of questions ready.

Rick's Tip: Supposedly **"free" walking tours are advertised all over town.** *Tip-ping is expected, and the guides actually have to pay the company for each person who takes the tour—so unless you tip more than they owe the company, they don't make a penny. Expect a sales pitch for the company's other, paid tours.*

Helpful Hints

Museum Tips: Museums closed on Mon-day include the Alte Pinakothek, Egyptian Museum, Lenbachhaus, Munich City Museum, Nazi Documentation Center, and the BMW Museum. The art museums are generally open late one night a week.

Your ticket to the Jewish History Museum, Munich City Museum, or Len-bachhaus gets you half-price admission to any of the others up to two days later (e.g., show your Munich City Museum ticket to get €5 off your €10 Lenbachhaus ticket).

Laundry: Waschcenter is a 10-minute walk from the train station (self-service daily 7:00-23:00; drop-off Mon-Fri 7:00-19:00, Sat 9:00-16:00; English instructions; Paul-Heyse-Strasse 21, near intersection with Landwehrstrasse; U-Bahn: There-sienwiese, mobile 0171-734-2094).

Taxi: Call 089/21610 for a taxi.

Private Driver: Reliable **Johann Fay-oumi** speaks English (€70/hour, mobile 0174-183-8473, www.firstclasslimousines.de, johannfayoumi@gmail.com).

TOURS

🎧 To sightsee on your own, download my free **Munich City Walk audio tour** (see sidebar on page 17 for details).

WALKING AND BIKE TOURS

Munich's two largest conventional tour companies, Radius Tours and Munich Walk, run comparable walking and bike tours in Munich, and day trips to Dachau, Neuschwanstein Castle, and other places. Both offer RS% discounts to my read-ers. Just show your book and ask at the time of booking (online reservations not required).

Radius Tours has a convenient office and meeting point in the main train sta-tion, in front of track 32 (tel. 089/543-487-7740, www.radiustours.com). Consider their city walking tour (€15, at 10:15, 2.5 hours), "Birthplace of the Third Reich"

GERMANY

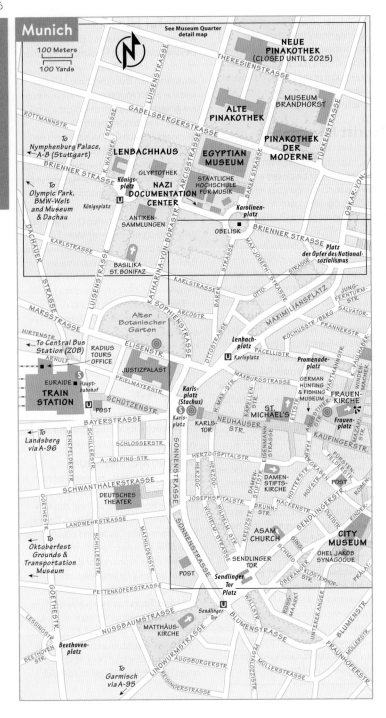

Munich

100 Meters
100 Yards

NEUE PINAKOTHEK (CLOSED UNTIL 2025)

See Museum Quarter detail map

THERESIENSTRASSE

ROTTMANNSTR.

GABELSBERGERSTRASSE

MUSEUM BRANDHORST

ALTE PINAKOTHEK

To Nymphenburg Palace, A-8 (Stuttgart)

LENBACHHAUS

BRIENNER STRASSE

WAGNER STRASSE

LUISENSTRASSE

GLYPTOTHEK

EGYPTIAN MUSEUM

PINAKOTHEK DER MODERNE

TÜRKENSTRASSE

Königs-platz

NAZI DOCUMENTATION CENTER

STAATLICHE HOCHSCHULE FÜR MUSIK

BARER STRASSE

ARCISSTRASSE

KATHARINA-VON-BORA-STR.

OSKAR-VON-

To Olympic Park, BMW-Welt and Museum & Dachau

Königsplatz

ANTIKEN-SAMMLUNGEN

Karolinen-platz

OBELISK

BRIENNER STRASSE

Platz der Opfer des National-sozialismus

DACHAUER STRASSE

KARLSTRASSE

MAX-JOSEPH-STRASSE

LUISENSTRASSE

BASILIKA ST. BONIFAZ

KARLSTRASSE

BAKER STR.

OTTOSTR.

MARSSTRASSE

K.-SOPHIENSTRASSE

ARCOSTR.

JUNG-FERNTURM-STR.

MAXIMILIANSPLATZ

SALVATOR.

Alter Botanischer Garten

Lenbach-platz

ROCHUSSTR./BERG

PRANNERSTR.

HIRTENSTR.

To Central Bus Station (ZOB)

RADIUS TOURS OFFICE

ELISENSTR.

Karlsplatz

PACELLISTR.

Promenade-platz

MAX-FAULHABER-

ARNULF

JUSTIZPALAST

PRIELMAYERSTR.

OTTOSTRASSE

MAXBURGSTRASSE

GERMAN HUNTING & FISHING MUSEUM

HARTMANNSTR.

WINDEN-MACHER-

EURAIDE

Haupt-bahnhof

TRAIN STATION

POST

SCHÜTZENSTR.

Karls-platz (Stachus)

H.-MAX-STR.

KAPELLEN-STR.

FRAUEN-KIRCHE

BAYERSTRASSE

Karls-platz

KARLS-TOR

NEUHAUSER STR.

EISENMANN-STRASSE

ST. MICHAEL'S

AUGUSTINER.

ETTSTR.

Frauen-platz

KAUFINGERSTR.

MAZARI-STR.

To Landsberg via A-96

SENEFELDERSTR.

SCHLOSSERSTR.

A.-KOLPING-STR.

HERZOGSPITALSTR.

HERZOG-STR.

DAMEN-STIFTS-STR.

DAMEN-STIFTS-KIRCHE

HOTTERSTR.

HACKENSTR.

ROSENTAL

FÜRSTEN-FELDBR.

SCHWANTHALERSTRASSE

GOETHESTR.

DEUTSCHES THEATER

LANDWEHRSTRASSE

SONNENSTRASSE

JOSEPHSPITALSTR.

WILHELM-STRASSE

BRUNN-STR.

SENDLINGERSTR.

POST

SINGLSTR.

DULTSTR.

RINDER-

To Oktoberfest Grounds & Transportation Museum

SCHILLERSTR.

MATHILDENSTR.

KREUZSTR.

ASAM CHURCH

SCHMID

CITY MUSEUM

POST

SENDLINGER TOR

OHEL JAKOB SYNAGOGUE

OBERANGER

KLOSTERHOF-STR.

PRÄLAT-

PETTENKOFERSTRASSE

Sendlinger Tor Platz

WALLSTR.

ROSS-MARKT

UNTERER ANGER

BLUMENSTRASSE

LESSINGSTR.

NUSSBAUMSTRASSE

Sendlinger Tor

LINDWURMSTRASSE

BLUMENSTRASSE

MÜLLERSTR.

FRAUNHOFERSTR.

Beethoven-platz

BEETHOVEN-STR.

MATTHÄUS-KIRCHE

AUGSBURGERSTR.

REISINGERSTRASSE

PESTALOZZISTR.

To Garmisch via A-95

GOETHESTR.

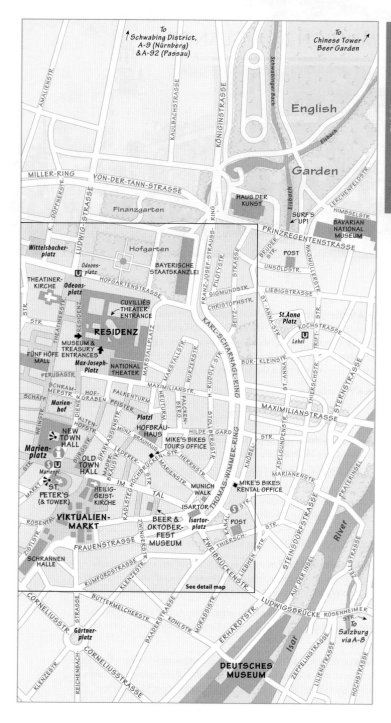

MUNICH AT A GLANCE

In the Center

▲▲**Marienplatz** Munich's main square, at the heart of a lively pedestrian zone, watched over by New Town Hall (and its glockenspiel show). **Hours:** Glockenspiel jousts daily at 11:00 and 12:00, plus 17:00 March-Oct; New Town Hall tower elevator runs daily 10:00-19:00; Oct-April Mon-Fri 10:00-17:00, closed Sat-Sun. See page 701.

▲▲**Viktualienmarkt** Munich's "small-town" open-air market, perfect for a quick snack or meal. **Hours:** Market closed Sun; beer garden open daily 10:00-22:00 (weather permitting). See page 706.

▲▲**Hofbräuhaus** World-famous beer hall, worth a visit even if you're not chugging. **Hours:** Daily 9:00-23:30. See page 713.

▲▲**The Residenz** Elegant palace awash in Bavarian opulence. Complex includes the Residenz Museum (lavish apartments), Residenz Treasury (Wittelsbach family crowns and royal knickknacks), and the impressive, heavily restored Cuvilliés Theater. **Hours:** Museum and treasury—daily 9:00-18:00, mid-Oct-mid-March 10:00-17:00; theater—generally Mon-Sat 14:00-18:00, Sun from 9:00, longer hours Aug-mid-Sept. See page 717.

▲▲**Alte Pinakothek** Bavaria's best painting gallery, with a wonderful collection of European masters from the 14th through the 19th century. **Hours:** Wed-Sun 10:00-18:00, Tue until 20:00, closed Mon. See page 726.

▲▲**Egyptian Museum** Easy-to-enjoy collection of ancient Egyptian treasures. **Hours:** Wed-Sun 10:00-18:00, Tue until 20:00, closed Mon. See page 729.

▲▲**Lenbachhaus** Three stages of German art: 19th-century, Blue Rider, and post-WWI—most important for its Blue Rider collection. **Hours:** Wed-Sun 10:00-18:00, Tue until 20:00, closed Mon.

▲▲**Nazi Documentation Center** Thoughtful look at Munich's role in the rise of Nazism. **Hours:** Tue-Sun 10:00-19:00, closed Mon. See page 730.

▲**Munich City Museum** The city's history in five floors. **Hours:** Tue-Sun 10:00-18:00, closed Mon. See page 724.

▲**Asam Church** Asam brothers' private church, dripping with Baroque. **Hours:** Sat-Thu 9:00-18:00, Fri from 13:00. See page 709.

▲**English Garden** The largest city park on the Continent, packed with locals, tourists, surfers, and nude sunbathers. (On a bike, I'd rate this ▲▲.) See page 731.

▲**Deutsches Museum** Germany's version of our Smithsonian Institution, with 10 miles of science and technology exhibits (main branch). **Hours:** Daily 9:00-17:00. See page 732.

Outside the City Center

▲▲▲**Dachau Concentration Camp Memorial** Notorious Nazi camp, now a powerful museum and memorial. **Hours:** Daily 9:00-17:00. See page 758.

▲▲**Nymphenburg Palace** Impressive summer palace, featuring a hunting lodge, coach museum, fine royal porcelain collection, and vast park. **Hours:** Park—daily 6:00-dusk; palace buildings—daily April-mid-Oct 9:00-18:00, mid-Oct-March 10:00-16:00. See page 733.

▲**BMW-Welt and Museum** The carmaker's futuristic museum and floating-cloud showroom, highlighting BMW past, present, and future. **Hours:** BMW-Welt showroom exhibits—daily 9:00-18:00; museum—Tue-Sun 10:00-18:00, closed Mon. See page 739.

tour (€17.50, April-mid-Oct daily at 15:00, off-season daily at 11:30; 2.5 hours), "Bavarian Beer and Food" tour (€36; April-mid-Oct Mon-Sat 18:00, off-season Tue, Thu, and Sat at 18:00; 3.5 hours), or 3-hour bike tour (€29.50, April-mid-Oct daily at 10:00).

Munich Walk uses Marienplatz as its meeting point (tel. 089/2423-1767, www.munichwalktours.de). Check out their city walking tour (€14, year-round at 10:45, May-Oct also daily at 14:45, 2 hours), "Third Reich in Munich" tour (€16, daily year-round at 10:15, 2.5 hours), "Beer and Brewery" tour (€30, May-mid-Sept Mon, Wed, and Fri-Sat at 18:15, less frequent off-season, 3.5 hours), or 3.5-hour bike tour (€25, daily 10:45, no tours Nov-March).

HOP-ON, HOP-OFF BUS TOUR

Gray Line Tours has hop-on, hop-off bus tours that leave from in front of the Karstadt department store at Bahnhofplatz, directly across from the train station. Choose from a basic, one-hour "Express Circle" that heads past the Pinakotheks, Marienplatz, and Karlsplatz; or the more extensive "Grand Circle" that lasts 2.5 hours and also includes Nymphenburg Palace and BMW-Welt and Museum—a very efficient way to visit these two sights (both tours depart 3/hour, 9:40-18:00). Just show up and pay the driver (€17 Express tour—valid 24 hours, €22/€27 Grand tour—valid 24/48 hours, daily in season, tel. 089/5490-7560, www.stadtrundfahrten-muenchen.de).

Rick's Tip: *If you're interested in a* **Gray Line bus tour** *of the city or to nearby castles, such as Neuschwanstein,* **get discounted tickets at EurAide** *(cash only). They also sell* **Munich Walk** *tour tickets.*

LOCAL GUIDES

I've had great days with two good guides: **Georg Reichlmayr**, who has helped me generously with this chapter (€200/3

hours, mobile 0170-341-6384, www.muenchen-stadtfuehrung.de, and **Birgit Stempfle** (€180/3 hours, mobile 0171-718-1465, www.sightseeing-munich.de).

TOURS TO NEUSCHWANSTEIN

While you can do many **day trips from Munich** on your own by train, going as part of an organized group can be convenient. **Gray Line Tours** offers rushed all-day bus tours of Neuschwanstein that also include Ludwig's Linderhof Castle and 30 minutes in Oberammergau (€54, does not include castle admissions, RS% at EurAide, daily, www.stadtrundfahrten-muenchen.de). **Radius Tours** runs all-day tours to Neuschwanstein using public transportation (€49, €42 with rail pass, RS%—use "student rate" when you book online, does not include castle admission; daily April-Dec, Jan-March tours run Mon, Wed, and Fri-Sun; reserve ahead online, www.radiustours.com). Of these options, I prefer the guided private bus tours because you're guaranteed a seat (public transport to Neuschwanstein is routinely standing-room only in summer).

MUNICH CITY WALK

Munich is big and modern, but, with its pedestrian-friendly historic core, it feels a lot like an easygoing Bavarian town. On this self-guided walk, rated ▲▲▲, we'll start in the central square, see its famous glockenspiel, stroll through a thriving open-air market, and visit historic churches with lavish Baroque decor. We'll sample edibles at a venerable gourmet deli and take a spin through the world's most famous beer hall.

Length of This Tour: Allow two to three hours for this walk through a thousand years of Munich's history. Allow extra time if you want to tour the museums along the way—details in "Sights," later.

🎧 Download my free Munich City Walk audio tour.

◯ Self-Guided Walk

• *Begin at the heart of the old city, with a stroll through...*

❶ *Marienplatz*

Riding the escalator out of the subway into sunlit Marienplatz (mah-REE-en-platz, "Mary's Square," rated ▲▲) gives you a fine first look at the glory of Munich: great buildings, outdoor cafés, and people bustling and lingering like the birds and breeze with which they share this square.

The square is both old and new: For a thousand years, it's been the center of Munich. It was the town's marketplace and public forum, standing at a crossroads along the Salt Road, which ran between Salzburg and Augsburg.

Lining one entire side of the square is the impressive facade of the **New Town Hall** (Neues Rathaus), with its soaring 280-foot spire. The structure looks medieval, but it was actually built in the late 1800s (1867-1908). The style is "Neo"-Gothic—pointed arches over the doorways and a roofline bristling with prickly spires. The 40 statues look like medieval saints, but they're from around 1900, depicting more recent Bavarian kings and

nobles. This medieval style was all the rage in the 19th century as Germans were rediscovering their historical roots and uniting as a modern nation.

The New Town Hall is famous for its **glockenspiel.** A carillon in the tower chimes a tune while colorful figurines come out on the balcony to spin and dance. It happens daily at 11:00 and 12:00 all year (also at 17:00 March-Oct) and lasts about 10 minutes. The *Spiel* of the glockenspiel tells the story of a noble wedding that took place on the market square in 1568. You see the wedding procession and the friendly joust of knights on horseback. The duke and his bride watch the action as the groom's Bavarian family (in Bavarian white and blue) joyfully jousts with the bride's French family (in red and white). Below, the barrel makers—famous for being the first to dance in the streets after a deadly plague lifted—do their popular jig. Finally, the solitary cock crows.

At the very top of the New Town Hall is a statue of a child with outstretched arms, dressed in monk's garb and holding a book in its left hand. This is the **Münchner Kindl,** the symbol of Munich. The town got its name from the people who

New Town Hall

Glockenspiel

GERMANY

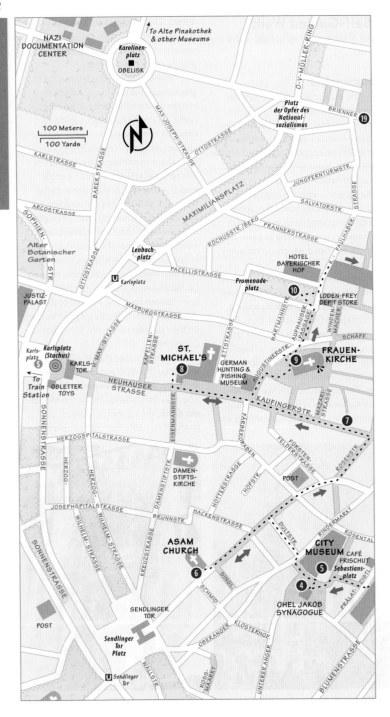

NAZI DOCUMENTATION CENTER

To Alte Pinakothek & other Museums

Karolinen-platz
OBELISK

100 Meters
100 Yards

Platz der Opfer des National-sozialismus

19

KARLSTRASSE

BARER STRASSE

MAX-JOSEPH-STRASSE

OTTOSTRASSE

O-V-MÜLLER-RING

BRIENNER

JUNGFERNTURMSTR.

STRASSE

ARCOSTRASSE

SOPHIEN-STR.

OTTOSTRASSE

Alter Botanischer Garten

Lenbach-platz

MAXIMILIANSPLATZ

SALVATORSTR.

KOCHUSSTR./BERG

PRANNERSTRASSE

K.-FAULHABER-STRASSE

JUSTIZ-PALAST

Karlsplatz

PACELLISTRASSE

HOTEL BAYERISCHER HOF

Karlsplatz

MAXBURGSTRASSE

Promenade-platz

10

LODEN-FREY DEP'T STORE

WINDEN-MACHER.

SCHÄFF.

Karls-platz
KARLSPLATZ (Stachus)
KARLS-TOR

To Train Station

OBLETTER TOYS

NEUHAUSER STRASSE

KAPELLEN-STRASSE

H-MAX-STRASSE

ST. MICHAEL'S
8

GERMAN HUNTING & FISHING MUSEUM

ETTSTRASSE

AUGUSTINERSTR.

9

HARTMANNSTR.

AUFHAUSER PASSAGE

FRAUEN-KIRCHE

MAZARI-STRASSE

KAUFINGERSTR.

7

SONNENSTRASSE

HERZOGSPITALSTRASSE

HERZOG-

EISENMANNSTR.

FARBERGRABEN

FÜRSTEN-FELDERSTRASSE

ROSENSTR.

DAMEN-STIFTS-KIRCHE

DAMENSTIFTSTR.

HOTTERSTRASSE

HOFSTR.

POST

JOSEPHSPITALSTRASSE

BRUNNSTR.

HACKENSTRASSE

ROSENTAL

RINDERMARKT

SONNENSTRASSE

WILHELM-STRASSE

KREUZSTRASSE

ASAM CHURCH
6

SINGL-

DULTSTR.

CITY MUSEUM
5

CAFÉ FRISCHUT

Sebastians-platz

4

SENDLINGER TOR

SCHMID-

OHEL JAKOB SYNAGOGUE

PRALAT-ZIST-L.

POST

Sendlinger Tor Platz

WALLSTR.

OBERANGER

KLOSTERHOF

UNTERERANGER

BLUMENSTRASSE

Sendlinger Tor

ROSS-MARKT

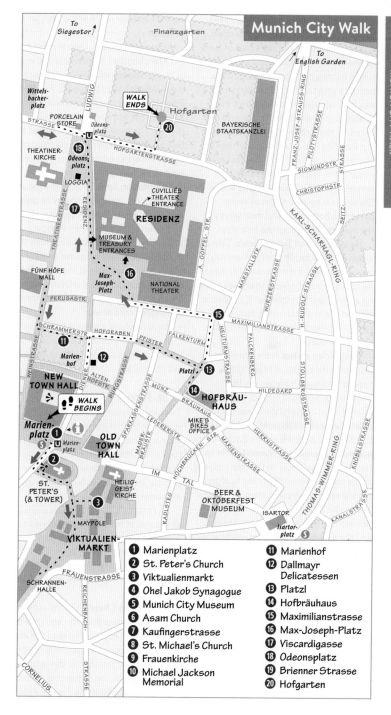

Munich City Walk

To
Siegestor

Finanzgarten

To
English Garden

WALK
ENDS

Hofgarten

20

BAYERISCHE
STAATSKANZLEI

Wittels-
bacher-
platz

PORCELAIN
STORE

Odeons-
platz

18

THEATINER-
KIRCHE

Odeons-
platz

LOGGIA

17

CUVILLIÉS
THEATER
ENTRANCE

RESIDENZ

FÜNF HÖFE
MALL

MUSEUM &
TREASURY
ENTRANCES

16

Max-
Joseph-
Platz

NATIONAL
THEATER

PERUSASTR.

SCHRAMMERSTR.

HOFGRABEN

PFISTER.

FALKENTURM

15

MAXIMILIANSTRASSE

11

Marien-
hof

12

Platzl

13

NEW
TOWN HALL

WALK
BEGINS

14

HOFBRÄU-
HAUS

HILDEGARD

Marien-
platz

1

Marien-
platz

OLD
TOWN
HALL

MIKE'S
BIKES
OFFICE

2

ST.
PETER'S
(& TOWER)

HEILIG-
GEIST-
KIRCHE

IM   TAL

BEER &
OKTOBERFEST
MUSEUM

ISARTOR

3

MAYPOLE

RADLSTEG

Isartor-
platz

VIKTUALIEN-
MARKT

FRAUENSTRASSE

SCHRANNEN-
HALLE

CORNELIUS

❶ Marienplatz
❷ St. Peter's Church
❸ Viktualienmarkt
❹ Ohel Jakob Synagogue
❺ Munich City Museum
❻ Asam Church
❼ Kaufingerstrasse
❽ St. Michael's Church
❾ Frauenkirche
❿ Michael Jackson
   Memorial

⓫ Marienhof
⓬ Dallmayr
   Delicatessen
⓭ Platzl
⓮ Hofbräuhaus
⓯ Maximilianstrasse
⓰ Max-Joseph-Platz
⓱ Viscardigasse
⓲ Odeonsplatz
⓳ Brienner Strasse
⓴ Hofgarten

first settled here: the monks (Mönchen). You'll spot this mini monk all over town, on everything from the city's coat of arms to souvenir shot glasses to ad campaigns (often holding not a book, but maybe a beer or a smartphone). The city symbol was originally depicted as a grown man, wearing a gold-lined black cloak and red shoes. By the 19th century, artists were representing him as a young boy, then a gender-neutral child, and, more recently, a young girl. These days, a teenage girl dressed as the Kindl kicks off the annual Oktoberfest by leading the opening parade on horseback, and then serves as the mascot throughout the festivities.

New Town Hall Tower Views: Take an elevator to the fourth floor (where you buy your ticket), then ride another elevator to the top of the New Town Hall tower for a commanding city view (€3, elevator located under glockenspiel; daily 10:00-19:00; Oct-April Mon-Fri 10:00-17:00, closed Sat-Sun).

The **golden statue** at the top of the column in the center of Marienplatz honors the square's namesake, the Virgin Mary. Sculpted in 1590, it was a rallying point in the religious wars of the Reformation. Back then, Munich was a bastion of southern-German Catholicism against the heresies of Martin Luther to the north. Notice how, at the four corners of the statue, cherubs fight the four great biblical enemies of civilization: the dragon of war, the lion of hunger, the rooster-headed monster of plague and disease, and the serpent. The serpent represents heresy—namely, Protestants. Bavaria is still Catholic country, and Protestants weren't allowed to worship openly here until about 1800.

To the right of the New Town Hall, the gray pointy building with the green spires is the **Old Town Hall** (Altes Rathaus). On its adjoining bell tower, find the city seal. It has the Münchner Kindl (symbolizing the first monks), a castle (representing the first fortifications), and a lion (represent-ing the first ruler—Henry the Lion, who built them).

As you look around, keep in mind that the Allies bombed Marienplatz and much of Munich during World War II. Most of the buildings had to be rebuilt. The Old Town Hall looks newer now because it was destroyed by bombs and rebuilt after the war. The New Town Hall survived the bombs, and it served as the US military headquarters after the Americans occupied Munich in 1945.

Orientation Spin: Back on the ground, face the New Town Hall one more time and get oriented. Straight ahead is north. To the left is the pedestrian shopping street called Kaufingerstrasse, which leads to the old gate called Karlstor and the train station. To the right, the street leads to the Isartor gate and the Deutsches Museum. This east-west axis cuts through the historic core of Munich.

• *Turn around and notice the small street to the left leading a short block to St. Peter's Church, with its steeple poking up above a row of buildings.*

❷ St. Peter's Church

The oldest church in town, St. Peter's stands on the hill where Munich's original monks probably settled—perhaps as far back as the ninth century (though the city marks its official birthday as 1158). Today's church (from 1368) replaced the original monastery church.

St. Peter's ("Old Peter" to locals) is part of the soul of the city. There's even a popular song about it that goes, "Munich is not Munich without St. Peter's."

Cost and Hours: Church-free, tower climb-€3, Mon-Fri 9:00-18:30, Sat-Sun from 10:00.

Visiting the Church: On the outside of the church, notice the 16th- and 17th-century tombstones plastered onto the wall. Originally, people were buried in the holy ground around the church. But in the Napoleonic age, the cemeteries were dug up and relocated outside the city walls for

Old Town Hall

Climb the tower of St. Peter's Church for great views.

hygienic and space reasons. They kept a few tombstones here as a reminder.

Step inside. (If there's a Mass in progress, visitors are welcome, but stay in the back. If there's no Mass, feel free to explore.) Typical of so many Bavarian churches, it's whitewashed and light-filled, with highlights in pastel pinks and blues framed by gold curlicues. The ceiling painting opens up to the heavens, where Peter is crucified upside down.

Photos (on a pillar near the entrance) show how St. Peter's was badly damaged in World War II—the roof caved in, and the tower was demolished during an air raid. But the beloved church was rebuilt and restored, thanks to donations—half from the Augustiner brewery, the rest from private donors. (The accuracy of the restoration was possible thanks to Nazi catalog photos.) For decades after World War II, the bells played a popular tune that stopped just before the last note, reminding locals that the church still needed money to rebuild.

Explore further. The nave is lined with bronze statues of the apostles, and the altar shows a statue of St. Peter being adored by four Church fathers. The finely crafted, gray iron fences that line the nave were donated after World War II by the local blacksmiths of the national railway. The precious and fragile sandstone Gothic chapel altar (to the left of the main altar) survived the war only because it was buried in sandbags.

Find the second chapel from the back on the left side. Now there's something you don't see every day: a skeleton in a box. As the red Latin inscription says, this is St. Munditia. In the fourth century, she was beheaded by the Romans for her Christian faith. Munich has more relics of saints than any city outside Rome. That's because it was the pope's Catholic bastion against the rising tide of Protestantism in northern Europe during the Reformation. In 1675, St. Munditia's remains were given to Munich by the pope as thanks for the city's devoted service. It was also a vivid reminder to the faithful that those who die for the cause of the Roman Church go directly to heaven without waiting for Judgment Day.

The History of Munich

Born from Salt and Beer (1100-1500): Munich began in the 12th century, when Henry the Lion (Heinrich der Löwe) established a lucrative salt trade near a monastery of monks—München. After Henry's death, an ambitious merchant family, the Wittelsbachs, took over. By the 1400s, Munich's maypole-studded market bustled with trade in salt and beer, the twin-domed Frauenkirche drew pilgrims, and the Wittelsbachs made their home in the Residenz. When the various regions of Bavaria united in 1506, Munich (pop. 14,000) was the natural capital.

Religious Wars, Plagues, Decline (1500-1800): While Martin Luther and the Protestant Reformation raged in northern Germany, Munich became the ultra-Catholic heart of the Counter-Reformation, decorated in the ornate Baroque and Rococo style of its Italian Catholic allies. The religious wars and periodic plagues left the city weakened. While the rest of Europe modernized, Munich remained behind the times.

The Golden Age of Kings (1806-1886): When Napoleon invaded, the Wittelsbach dukes surrendered and were rewarded with a grander title: King of Bavaria. Munich boomed. **Maximilian I** (r. 1806-1825), a.k.a. Max Joseph, rebuilt in Neoclassical style—grand columned buildings connected by broad boulevards. **Ludwig I** (r. 1825-1848) turned Munich into a modern railroad hub, budding industrial city. His son **Maximilian II** (r. 1848-1864) continued Ludwig's modernization program. In 1864, 18-year-old **Ludwig II** (r. 1864-1886) became king. Ludwig didn't much like Munich, preferring to build castles in the Bavarian countryside.

• Leave St. Peter's out the door opposite the one you entered. Then, head to the right to the tower entrance. It's a long climb to the top of the **tower** (306 steps, no elevator)—but the view is dynamite. Try to be two flights from the top when the bells ring at the top of the hour. When your friends back home ask you about your trip, you'll say, "What?" Afterward, head downhill to join the busy commotion of the...

❸ Viktualienmarkt

The market (rated ▲▲, closed Sun) is a lively world of produce stands and budget eateries. Browse your way through the stalls and pavilions, as you make your way to the market's main landmark, the blue-and-white striped maypole. Early in

Viktualienmarkt

End of the Wittelsbachs (1886-1918): When Bavaria became part of the newly united Germany, Berlin overtook Munich as Germany's power center. Then World War I devastated Munich. After the war, mobs of poor, angry Münchners roamed the streets. In 1918, they drove the last Bavarian king out, ending 700 years of Wittelsbach rule.

Nazis, World War II, and Munich Bombed (1918-1945): In the power vacuum, a fringe group emerged—the Nazi party, headed by Adolf Hitler. Hitler rallied the Nazis in a Munich beer hall, leading a failed coup d'état known as the Beer Hall Putsch (1923). When the Nazis eventually took power in Berlin, they remembered their roots, dubbing Munich "Capital of the Movement." In World War II, nearly half the city was leveled by Allied air raids.

Munich Rebuilds (1945-Present): After the war, with generous American aid, Münchners rebuilt. Nazi authorities had created a photo archive of historic sights, which now came in handy. Munich chose to preserve the low-rise, medieval feel, but with a modern infrastructure. For the 1972 Olympic Games, they built a futuristic stadium, a sleek new subway system, and one of Europe's first pedestrian-only zones—Kaufingerstrasse. In 1990, when Germany reunited, Berlin once again became the country's focal point, relegating Munich to the role of sleepy Second City.

These days, Munich seems to be comfortable just being itself rather than trying to keep up with Berlin. Though rich and modern—home to BMW and Siemens, and a producer of software, books, movies, and the latest fashions—it remains safe, clean, and cultured. It's a university town, built on a human scale, and close to the beauties of nature.

the morning, you can still feel small-town Munich here. Remember, Munich has been a market town since its earliest days as a stop on the salt-trade crossroads. By the 1400s, the market bustled, most likely beneath a traditional maypole, just like you see today.

Besides salt, Munich gained a reputation for beer. By the 15th century, more than 30 breweries pumped out the golden liquid, brewed by monks, who were licensed to sell it. They stored their beer in cellars under courtyards kept cool by the shade of bushy chestnut trees—a tradition Munich's breweries still follow.

The market's centerpiece seems to be its **beer garden** (daily 10:00-22:00, weather permitting). Its picnic tables are filled with hungry and thirsty locals, all in the shade of the traditional chestnut trees. Shoppers often pause here for a late-morning snack of *Weisswurst*—white sausage—served with mustard, a pretzel, and a beer. Here, you can order just a half-liter—unlike some other beer gardens that only sell by the full liter. This is handy for shoppers who want just a quick sip. As is the tradition at all the city's beer gardens, some tables—those without tablecloths—are set aside for patrons who bring their own food; they're welcome here as long as they buy a drink. The Viktualienmarkt is ideal for a light meal (see page 752).

Now make your way to the towering **maypole.** Throughout Bavaria, colorfully

Viktualienmarkt's maypole

ornamented maypoles decorate town squares. Many are painted, like this one, in Bavaria's colors, white and blue. The decorations are festively replaced every year on the first of May. Traditionally, rival communities try to steal each other's maypole. Locals guard their new pole day and night as May Day approaches. Stolen poles are ransomed only with lots of beer for the clever thieves.

The decorations that line each side of the pole explain which merchants are doing business in the market. Munich's maypole gives prominence (on the bottom level) to a horse-drawn wagon bringing in beer barrels. And you can't have a kegger without coopers—find the merry barrel makers, the four cute guys dancing. Today, traditional barrel making is enjoying a comeback as top breweries like to have real wooden kegs.

The bottom of the pole celebrates the world's oldest food law. The German Beer Purity Law *(Reinheitsgebot)* of 1487 actually originated here in Munich. It stipulated that beer could consist only of three ingredients: barley, hops, and water. (Later they realized that a fourth ingredient, yeast, is always present in fermentation.) Why was beer so treasured? Back in the Middle Ages, it was considered liquid food.

From the maypole, take in the bustling scene around you. The market was modernized in the 1800s as the city grew. Old buildings were torn down, replaced with stalls and modern market halls. Now, in the 21st century, this traditional market (sitting on the city's most expensive real estate) survives thanks to a ban on fast-food chains and city laws that favor small-time merchants with low taxes. This keeps the market classy and authentic.

• *At the far end of the Viktualienmarkt, spot* **Café Frischhut** *with its colorful old-time sign hanging out front (at Prälat-Zistl-Strasse 8). This is Munich's favorite place to stop for a fresh* Schmalznudel—*a traditional fried-dough treat (best enjoyed warm, with a sprinkling of sugar).*

Continue straight to a modern glass-and-iron building.

The **Schrannenhalle,** an 1800s grain exchange, has been renovated into a high-end paradise for foodies, especially those seeking Italian edibles. Stroll through Eataly, past enticing bottles of olive oil. Pause to watch bakers tending to the day's bread, and make your way to the far end, where wine connoisseurs could detour downstairs for a vast wine collection (and a WC).

• *When you're ready to move on, exit the Schrannenhalle midway down on the right-hand side. You'll spill out into* **Sebastiansplatz,** *a small square lined with healthy eateries. Continue through Sebastiansplatz and veer left, where you'll see a cube-shaped building, the...*

❹ Ohel Jakob Synagogue

This modern synagogue anchors a revitalized Jewish quarter. In the 1930s, about 10,000 Jews lived in Munich, and the main synagogue stood near here. Then, in 1938,

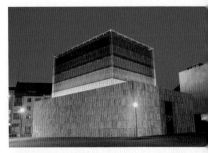

Ohel Jakob Synagogue

Hitler demanded that the synagogue be torn down. By the end of World War II, Munich's Jewish community was gone. But thanks to Germany's acceptance of religious refugees from former Soviet states, the Jewish population has now reached its prewar size. The new synagogue was built in 2006. There's also a kindergarten and day school, playground, fine kosher restaurant (at #18), and bookstore. Notice the low-key but efficient security.

While the synagogue is shut tight to nonworshippers, its architecture is striking from the outside. Lower stones of travertine evoke the Wailing Wall in Jerusalem, while an upper section represents the tent that held important religious wares during the 40 years of wandering through the desert. The synagogue's door features the first 10 letters of the Hebrew alphabet, symbolizing the Ten Commandments.

The cube-shaped **Jewish History Museum** (behind the cube-shaped synagogue) is stark and windowless. While the museum's small permanent collection is disappointing, good temporary exhibits might justify the entry fee (€6; ticket gets you half-price admission to Munich City Museum and Lenbachhaus; Tue-Sun 10:00-18:00, closed Mon, St.-Jakobs-Platz 16, tel. 089/2339-6096, www.juedisches-museum-muenchen.de).

• *Facing the synagogue, on the same square, is the...*

❺ Munich City Museum (Münchner Stadtmuseum)

The highs and lows of Munich's history are covered in this surprisingly honest municipal museum (rated ▲). It covers the cultural upheavals of the early 1900s, Munich's role as the birthplace of the Nazis, and the city's renaissance during Germany's postwar "economic miracle." There's scant information posted in English, but an included audioguide can fill in the gaps.

• *You can stop and tour the museum now (see page 724). Otherwise, continue through the synagogue's square, past the fountain, across the street, and one block farther to the pedestrianized Sendlinger Strasse. Take a left and walk 100 yards until you see a fancy facade on your right (at #32), which marks the...*

❻ Asam Church (Asamkirche)

This tiny church (rated ▲) is a slice of heaven on earth—a gooey, drippy Baroque-concentrate masterpiece by Bavaria's top two Rococonuts, the Asam brothers. Just 30 feet wide, it was built in 1740 to fit within this row of homes. Originally, it was a private chapel where these two brother-architects could show off their work (on their own land, next to their home and business headquarters, to the left), but it's now a public place of worship.

Cost and Hours: Free, Sat-Thu 9:00-18:00, Fri from 13:00, tel. 089/2368-7989. The church is small, so visitors are asked not to enter during Mass.

Visiting the Church: This place of worship served as a promotional brochure to woo clients, and is packed with every architectural trick in the book. Imagine approaching the church not as a worshipper, but as a shopper representing your church's building committee. First stand outside: Hmmm, the look of those foundation stones really packs a punch. And the legs hanging over the portico... nice effect. Those starbursts on the door would be a hit back home, too.

Asam Church

Then step inside: I'll take a set of those over-the-top golden capitals, please. We'd also like to order the gilded garlands draping the church in jubilation, and the twin cupids capping the confessional. And how about some fancy stucco work, too? (Molded-and-painted plaster was clearly an Asam brothers specialty.) Check out the illusion of a dome painted on the flat ceiling—that'll save us lots of money. The yellow glass above the altar has the effect of the thin-sliced alabaster at St. Peter's in Rome, but it's within our budget! And, tapping the "marble" pilasters to determine that they are just painted fakes, we decide to take that, too. Crammed between two buildings, light inside this narrow church is limited, so there's a big, clear window in the back for maximum illumination—we'll order one to cut back on our electricity bill.

On the way out, say goodbye to the gilded grim reaper in the narthex (left side as you're leaving) as he cuts the thread of life—reminding all who visit of our mortality...and, by the way, that shrouds have no pockets.
• *Leaving the church, look to your right, noticing the Sendlinger Tor at the end of the street—part of the fortified town wall that circled Munich in the 14th century. Then turn left and walk straight up Sendlinger Strasse. Walk toward the Münchner Kindl, still capping the spire of the New Town Hall in the distance, and then up (pedestrian-only) Rosenstrasse, until you hit Marienplatz and the big, busy...*

❼ Kaufingerstrasse

This car-free street leads you through a great shopping district, past cheap department stores, carnivals of street entertainers, and good old-fashioned slicers and dicers. As far back as the 12th century, this was the town's main commercial street. Traders from Salzburg and Augsburg would enter the town through the fortified Karlstor. This street led past the Augustiner beer hall (opposite St. Michael's Church to this day), right to the main square and cathedral.

Up until the 1970s, the street was jammed with car traffic. Then, for the 1972 Olympics, it was turned into one of Europe's first pedestrian zones. At first, shopkeepers were afraid that would ruin business. Now it's Munich's living room. Nearly 9,000 shoppers pass through it each hour. Merchants nearby are begging for their streets to become traffic-free, too.

The 1972 Olympics transformed this part of Munich—the whole area around Marienplatz was pedestrianized and the transit system expanded. Since then, Munich has become one of the globe's greenest cities. Skyscrapers have been banished to the suburbs, and the nearby Frauenkirche is still the tallest building in the center.
• *Stroll a few blocks away from Marienplatz toward the Karlstor, until you arrive at the imposing church on the right.*

❽ St. Michael's Church (Michaelskirche)

This is one of the first great Renaissance buildings north of the Alps. The ornate facade, with its sloped roofline, was inspired by the Gesù Church in Rome—

St. Michael's Church

home of the Jesuit order. Jesuits saw themselves as the intellectual defenders of Catholicism. St. Michael's was built in the late 1500s—at the height of the Protestant Reformation—to serve as the northern outpost of the Jesuits. Appropriately, the facade features a statue of Michael fighting a Protestant demon.

Cost and Hours: Church-free, generally daily 8:00-19:00, until later on Sun and summer evenings; crypt-€2, Mon-Fri 9:30-16:30, Sat until 14:30, closed Sun; frequent concerts—check schedule posted outside; tel. 089/231-7060.

Visiting the Church: Inside, admire the ornate Baroque interior, topped with a barrel vault, the largest of its day. Stroll up the nave to the ornate pulpit, where Jesuit priests would hammer away at Reformation heresy. The church's acoustics are spectacular, and the choir—famous in Munich—sounds heavenly singing from the organ loft high in the rear.

The **crypt** (*Fürstengruft,* down the stairs to the right by the altar) contains 40 stark, somewhat forlorn tombs of Bavaria's ruling family, the Wittelsbachs.

The most ornate tomb (center of back wall, facing altar) holds the illustrious Ludwig II, known for his fairy-tale castle at Neuschwanstein. Ludwig didn't care much for Munich. He escaped to the Bavarian countryside where he spent his days building castles, listening to music, and dreaming about knights of old. His excesses earned him the nickname "Mad" King Ludwig. But of all the Wittelsbachs, it's his tomb that's decorated with flowers—placed here by romantics still mad about their "mad" king.

Also on the back wall is the tomb of Wilhelm V, who built this church, and Maximilian I, who saved Munich from Swedish invaders during the Thirty Years' War. Finally there's Otto, who went insane and was deposed in 1916, virtually bringing the Wittelsbachs' seven-century reign to an end.

• *Our next stop, the Frauenkirche, is a few hundred yards away. Backtrack a couple of blocks up Kaufingerstrasse to the wild boar statue, which marks the German Hunting and Fishing Museum. This place has outdoorsy regalia, kid-friendly exhibits, and the infamous Wolpertinger—a German "jackalope" created by very creative local taxidermists. At the boar statue, turn left on Augustinerstrasse, which leads to Munich's towering, twin-domed cathedral.*

❾ *Frauenkirche*

These twin onion domes are the symbol of the city. They're unusual in that most Gothic churches have either pointed steeples or square towers. Some say Crusaders, inspired by the Dome of the Rock in Jerusalem, brought home the idea. Or it may be that, due to money problems, the towers weren't completed until Renaissance times, when domes were popular. Whatever the reason, the Frauenkirche's domes may be the inspiration for the characteristic domed church spires that mark villages all over Bavaria.

Cost and Hours: Free, generally open daily 7:00-20:30, tel. 089/290-0820.

Restorations: The church towers are

Frauenkirche

under restoration and may not be open for climbing during your visit.

Rick's Tip: *If the* **Frauenkirche** *towers are closed for renovation during your visit, you can enjoy great* **city views** *from* **New Town Hall** *(elevator) or the towers of* **St. Peter's Church** *(stairs only).*

Visiting the Church: The church was built in just 22 years, from 1466 to 1488. It's made of brick—easy to make locally, and cheaper and faster to build with than stone. Construction was partly funded with the sale of indulgences (which let sinners bypass purgatory on the way to heaven). It's dedicated to the Virgin—Our Lady *(Frau)*—and has been the city's cathedral since 1821.

Step inside, and remember that much of this church was destroyed during World War II. The towers survived, and the rest was rebuilt essentially from scratch.

Near the entrance is a big, black, ornate, tomb-like monument honoring Ludwig IV the Bavarian (1282-1347), who was elected Holy Roman Emperor—a big deal. The Frauenkirche was built a century later with the express purpose of honoring his memory. His monument was originally situated in front at the high altar, right near Christ. Those Wittelsbachs—always trying to be associated with God. This alliance was instilled in people through the prayers they were forced to recite: "Virgin Mary, mother of our duke, please protect us."

Nearby, a relief (over the back pew on the left) honors one of Munich's more recent citizens. Joseph Ratzinger was born in Bavaria in 1927, became archbishop of the Frauenkirche (1977-1982), then moved to the Vatican where he later served as Pope Benedict XVI (2005-2013).

Now walk slowly up the main aisle, enjoying stained glass right and left. This glass is obviously modern, having replaced the original glass that was shattered in World War II. Ahead is the high altar, under a huge hanging crucifix. Find the throne—the ceremonial seat of the local bishop. From here, look up to the tops of the columns, and notice the tiny painted portraits. They're the craftsmen from five centuries ago who helped build the church.

Walk behind the altar to the apse, where the three tall windows still have their original 15th-century glass. To survive the bombs of 1944, each pane was lovingly removed and stored safely away.

• *Our next stop is on Promenadeplatz, just 400 yards north of here. Facing the altar, take the left side exit and walk straight 50 yards until you see a tiny but well-signed passageway (on the left) called the Aufhauser Passage. Follow it through a modern building, where you'll emerge at a little park called* **Promenadeplatz.** *Detour a few steps left into the park, where you'll find a colorful modern memorial. (If the passage is closed, circle around the block to the next stop.)*

🔟 *Michael Jackson Memorial*

When Michael Jackson was in town, he'd stay at the Hotel Bayerischer Hof, like many VIPs. Fans would gather in the park waiting for him to appear at his window. He'd sometimes oblige (but his infamous baby-dangling incident happened in Berlin, not here). When Jackson died in 2009, devotees created this memorial by taking over a statue of Renaissance composer Orlando di Lasso. They still visit daily, leave a memento, and keep it tidy.

• *Now exit the park at the end with the giant silver statue and turn left down Kardinal-Faulhaber-Strasse, lined with former 18th-century mansions that have since become offices and bank buildings. At #11, turn right and enter a modern shopping mall called the Fünf Höfe Passage. The place takes your basic shopping mall and gives it more class. It's divided into five connecting courtyards ("fünf Höfe"), spruced up with bubbling fountains, exotic plants, and a hanging garden.*

Emerging on a busy pedestrian street, turn right, and head down the street (noticing the Münchner Kindl again high above) to a big green square: Marienhof, with the most aristocratic grocery store in all of Germany.

⓫ Marienhof

This square, tucked behind the New Town Hall, was left as a green island after the 1945 bombings. For now, the square's all dug up while Munich builds an additional subway tunnel here. With virtually the entire underground system converging on nearby Marienplatz, this new tunnel will provide a huge relief to the city's congested subterranean infrastructure.

• *On the far side of Marienhof, the stately yellow building is...*

⓬ Dallmayr Delicatessen

When the king called out for dinner, he called Alois Dallmayr. This place became famous for its exotic and luxurious food items: tropical fruits, seafood, chocolates, fine wines, and coffee (there are meat and cheese counters, too). As you enter, read the black plaque with the royal seal by the door: *Königlich Bayerischer Hof-Lieferant* ("Deliverer for the King of Bavaria and his Court"). Catering to royal and aristocratic tastes (and budgets) since 1700, it's still the choice of Munich's old rich (closed Sun, www.dallmayr.com).

• *Leaving Dallmayr, turn right and then right again to continue along Hofgraben. Walk straight three blocks, gently downhill, to Platzl—"small square." (If you get turned around, ask any local to point you toward the Hofbräuhaus.)*

Marienhof

⓭ Platzl

As you stand here—admiring classic facades in the heart of medieval Munich—recall that everything around you was flattened in World War II. Here on Platzl, reconstruction happened in stages: From 1945 to 1950, they removed 12 million tons of bricks and replaced roofs to make buildings weather-tight. From 1950 to 1972, they redid the exteriors. From 1972 to 2000, they refurbished the interiors. Today, the rebuilt Platzl sports new—but old-looking—facades.

Officials estimate that hundreds of unexploded bombs still lie buried under Munich. As recently as 2012, a 550-pound bomb was found in Schwabing, a neighborhood just north of the old city center. They had to evacuate the neighborhood and detonate the bomb.

Today's Platzl hosts a lively mix of places to eat and drink—chains like Starbucks and Hard Rock Café alongside local spots like Schuhbecks Eissalon, a favorite for ice cream (Pfisterstrasse 11).

• *At the bottom of the square (#9), you can experience the venerable...*

⓮ Hofbräuhaus

The world's most famous beer hall (rated ▲▲) is a trip. Whether or not you slide your lederhosen on its polished benches, it's a great experience just to walk through the place in all its rowdy glory (with its own gift shop).

Cost and Hours: Free to enter, daily 9:00-23:30, live oompah music at lunch and dinner; tel. 089/2901-3610, www.hofbraeuhaus.de. For details on eating here, see page 747.

Visiting the Hofbräuhaus: Before going in, check out the huge arches at the entrance and the crown logo. The original brewery was built here in 1589. As the crown suggests, it was the Wittelsbachs' personal brewery, to make the "court brew" (*Hof Brau*). In 1880, the brewery moved out, and this 5,000-seat food-and-beer palace was built in its place.

Hofbräuhaus

After being bombed in World War II, the Hofbräuhaus was one of the first places to be rebuilt (German priorities).

Now, dive headlong into the sudsy Hofbräu mosh pit. Don't be shy. Everyone's drunk anyway. The atmosphere is thick with the sounds of oompah music, played here every night of the year.

You'll see locals stuffed into lederhosen and dirndls, giant gingerbread cookies that sport romantic messages, and kiosks selling postcards of the German (and apparently beer-drinking) ex-pope. Notice the quirky 1950s-style painted ceiling, with Bavarian colors, grapes, chestnuts, and fun "eat, drink, and be merry" themes. You'll see signs on some tables reading *Stammtisch,* meaning they're reserved for regulars, and their racks of old beer steins made of pottery and pewter. Beer halls like the Hofbräuhaus sell beer only by the liter mug, called a *Mass* (mahs). You can get it light *(helles)* or dark *(dunkles).* A slogan on the ceiling above the band reads: *Durst ist schlimmer als Heimweh*—"Thirst is worse than homesickness."

• *Leaving the Hofbräuhaus, turn right and walk two blocks, then turn left when you reach the street called...*

⓯ *Maximilianstrasse*

This broad east-west boulevard, lined with grand buildings and exclusive shops, introduces us to Munich's Golden Age of the 1800s. In that period, Bavaria was ruled by three important kings: Max

Joseph, Ludwig I, and Ludwig II. They transformed Munich from a cluster of medieval lanes to a modern city of spacious squares, Neoclassical monuments, and wide boulevards. At the east end of this boulevard is the palatial home of the Bavarian parliament.

The street was purposely designed for people and for shopping, not military parades. And to this day, Maximilianstrasse is busy with shoppers browsing Munich's most exclusive shops.

• *Maximilianstrasse leads to a big square—Max-Joseph-Platz.*

⓰ *Max-Joseph-Platz*

The square is fronted by two big buildings: the National Theater (with its columns) and the Residenz (with its intimidating stone facade).

The **Residenz,** the former "residence" of the royal Wittelsbach family, started as a crude castle (c. 1385). Over the centuries, it evolved into one of Europe's most opulent palaces (see "Sights," later).

The centerpiece of the square is a grand statue of **Maximilian I**—a.k.a. Max Joseph. In 1806, Max was the city's duke, serving in the long tradition of his Wittelsbach family... until Napoleon invaded and deposed the duke. But then Napoleon—eager to marry into the aristocracy—agreed to reinstate Max, with one condition: that his daughter marry Napoleon's stepson. Max Joseph agreed, and was quickly crowned not duke but king of Bavaria.

Max Joseph and his heirs ruled as constitutional monarchs. Now a king, Max Joseph was popular; he emancipated Protestants and Jews, revamped the Viktualienmarkt, and graced Munich with grand buildings like the **National Theater.** This Neoclassical building, opened in 1818, celebrated Bavaria's strong culture, deep roots, and legitimacy as a nation; four of Richard Wagner's operas were first performed here. It's now where the Bavarian State Opera and the Bavarian State Orchestra perform. (The Roman

Max-Joseph-Platz

came to power, he made a memorial at Odeonsplatz to honor the "first martyrs of the Third Reich." Germans were required to raise their arms in a *Sieg Heil* salute as they entered the square. The only way to avoid the indignity of saluting Nazism was to turn left down Viscardigasse instead. That stream of shiny cobbles marks the detour taken by those brave dissenters.
• *But now that Hitler's odious memorial is long gone, you can continue to...*

⑱ Odeonsplatz

This square links Munich's illustrious past with the Munich of today. It was laid out by the Wittelsbach kings in the 1800s. They incorporated the much older (yellow) church that was already on the square, the Theatinerkirche. This church contains about half of the Wittelsbach tombs. The church's twin towers and 230-foot-high dome are classic Italian Baroque, reflecting Munich's strong Catholic bent in the 1600s.

Overlooking the square from the south is an arcaded loggia filled with statues. In the 1800s the Wittelsbachs commissioned this Hall of Heroes to honor Bavarian generals. It was modeled after the famous Renaissance loggia in Florence. Odeonsplatz was part of the Wittelsbachs' grand vision of modern urban planning.

At the far end of the square, several wide boulevards lead away from here. Look west (left) down ⑲ **Brienner Strasse** (watch out for bikes). In the distance, and just out of sight, a black obelisk commemorates the 30,000 Bavarians who marched with Napoleon to Moscow and never returned. Beyond the obelisk is the grand Königsplatz, or "King's Square," with its Neoclassical buildings. Back in the 1930s, Königsplatz was the center of the Nazi party. Today, the Nazi shadow has largely lifted from that square (only two buildings from that era remain) and Königsplatz is home to Munich's cluster of great art museums. A few miles beyond Königsplatz is the Wittelsbachs' impressive summer home, Nymphenburg Palace.

numerals MCMLXIII in the frieze mark the year the theater reopened after WWII bombing restoration—1963.)
• *Leave Max-Joseph-Platz opposite where you entered, walking alongside the Residenz on Residenzstrasse for about 100 yards to the next grand square. But before you get to Odeonsplatz, pause at the first corner on the left and look down Viscardigasse at the gold-cobbled swoosh in the pavement.*

⑰ Viscardigasse

The cobbles in Viscardigasse recall one of Munich's most dramatic moments: It was 1923, and Munich was in chaos. World War I had left Germany in shambles. Angry mobs roamed the streets. Out of the fury rose a new and frightening movement—Adolf Hitler and the Nazi Party. On November 8, Hitler launched a coup, later known as the Beer Hall Putsch, to try to topple the German government. It started with a fiery speech by Hitler in a beer hall a few blocks from here (the beer hall no longer exists). The next day, Hitler and his mob of Nazis marched up Residenzstrasse. A block ahead, where Residenzstrasse spills into Odeonsplatz, stood a hundred government police. Shots were fired. Hitler was injured, and 16 Nazis were killed, along with four policemen. The coup was put down, and Hitler was sent to a prison outside Munich. During his nine months there, he wrote down his twisted ideas in his book *Mein Kampf.*

Ten years later, when Hitler finally

Odeonsplatz and Theatinerkirche

Now turn your attention 90 degrees to the right. The boulevard heading north from Odeonsplatz is **Ludwigstrasse.** It stretches a full mile, flanked by an impressive line of uniform 60-foot-tall buildings in the Neo-Gothic style. In the far distance is the city's Triumphal Arch, the Siegestor, capped with a figure of Bavaria, a goddess riding a lion-drawn chariot. The street is named for the great Wittelsbach builder-king Ludwig I, who truly made Munich into a grand capital. ("I won't rest," he famously swore, "until Munich looks like Athens.") Ludwigstrasse was used for big parades and processions, as it leads to that Roman-style arch.

Beyond the arch—and beyond what you can see—lie the suburbs of modern Munich, including the city's modern skyscrapers, Olympic Park, and the famous BMW headquarters.

Yes, Munich is a major metropolis, but you'd hardly know it by walking through its pleasant streets and parks.

• *We'll finish our walk in the pleasant Hofgarten. Its formal gate is to your right as you're facing up Ludwigstrasse. Step through the gate and enter the...*

⑳ *Hofgarten*

The elegant "garden of the royal court" is a delight. Built by the Wittelsbachs as their own private backyard to the Residenz palace, it's now open to everyone. Just inside the gate is an arcade decorated with murals commissioned by Ludwig I in the early 1800s. While faded, they still tell the glorious story of Bavaria from 1155 until 1688. The garden's 400-year-old centerpiece is a Renaissance-style temple with great acoustics. (There's often a musician performing here for tips.) It's decorated with the same shell decor as was popular inside the Residenz.

• *This walk is done. Where to go next? You're near the English Garden (just a few blocks away—see the map on page 696; people surf in the rapids created as the small river tumbles underground beneath the bridge east of Haus der Kunst), the Residenz complex, and the Odeonsplatz U-Bahn stop for points elsewhere.*

SIGHTS

Most of the top sights in the city center are covered on my self-guided walk. But there's much more to see in this city.

*Rick's Tip: If you're unsure about which of Munich's top two palaces to visit, the **Residenz** is more central and has the best interior, while **Nymphenburg** has the finest garden and outdoor views.*

▲▲The Residenz Complex

For 500 years, this was the palatial "residence" and seat of power of the ruling Wittelsbach family. It began (1385) as a crude castle with a moat around it. The main building was built from 1550 to 1650, and decorated in Rococo style during the 18th century. The final touch (under Ludwig I) was the grand south facade modeled after Florence's Pitti Palace. In March 1944, Allied air raids left the Residenz in shambles, so much of what we see today is a reconstruction.

The vast Residenz complex is divided into three sections: The **Residenz Museum** is a long hike through 90 lavishly decorated rooms. The **Residenz Treasury** shows off the Wittelsbach crown jewels. The **Cuvilliés Theater** is an ornate Rococo opera house. While each has its own admission, I'd just get the combo-ticket and see them all.

*Rick's Tip: The Bavarian Palace Department offers a **14-day ticket** (called the **Mehrtagesticket**) that covers admission to Munich's Residenz and Nymphenburg Palace complexes, as well as the Neuschwanstein and Linderhof castles in Bavaria. If you're planning to visit at least three of these sights within a two-week period, the pass will likely pay for itself (€24, €44 family/partner pass, purchase at participating sights or online at www.schloesser.bayern.de).*

Planning Your Time: Start your visit with the Residenz Treasury—small, manageable, and dazzling. Then hike through the sprawling palace called the Residenz Museum. The Cuvilliés Theater is a quick dollop of architectural whipped cream at the end. If you run out of time or energy, you can reenter with the same ticket on another day to visit anything you missed. The entrances on Max-Joseph-Platz and Residenzstrasse both lead to the ticket office, gift shop, and start of the treasury and Residenz Museum tours.

The Residenz—the "residence" of Bavaria's rulers

Cost and Hours: Residenz Museum-€7, Residenz Treasury-€7 (both include essential audioguides), Cuvilliés Theater-€3.50; €11 combo-ticket covers museum and treasury; €13 version covers all three; treasury and museum open daily 9:00-18:00, mid-Oct-mid-March 10:00-17:00; theater generally open Mon-Sat 14:00-18:00, Sun from 9:00, longer hours Aug-mid-Sept; last entry one hour before closing for all three sights, mandatory bag check, tel. 089/290-671, www.residenz-muenchen.de.

RESIDENZ TREASURY (SCHATZKAMMER)

The treasury shows off a thousand years of Wittelsbach crowns and knickknacks. You'll see the regalia used in Bavaria's coronation ceremonies, the revered sacred objects that gave the Wittelsbachs divine legitimacy, and miscellaneous wonders that dazzled their European relatives. It's the best treasury in Bavaria, with fine 13th- and 14th-century crowns and delicately carved ivory and glass.

Visiting the Treasury: In **Room 1,** the oldest jewels are 200 years older than Munich. Treasures of particular interest line the left wall. The gem-studded Crown of Kunigunde is associated with the saintly Bavarian queen, who was crowned Holy Roman Empress in 1014 by the pope in St. Peter's Basilica in Rome. The pearl-studded prayer book of Charles the Bald (Charlemagne's grandson) allowed the book's owner to claim royal roots dating all the way back to that first Holy Roman Emperor crowned in 800. The spiky Crown of an English Queen (c. 1370) is actually England's oldest crown, brought to Munich by an English princess who married a Wittelsbach duke. The angel and gilt-embellished Crown of Henry II (c. 1270-1280) dates from Munich's roots, when the town was emerging as a regional capital.

Along the right side of the room are religious objects such as reliquaries and portable altars. The tiny mobile altar allowed a Carolingian king to pack light in 890—and still have a little Mass while on the road. Many of the precious and very old objects in this room came from various prince-bishops' collections when their realms came under Bavarian rule in the Napoleonic era (c. 1800).

Room 3: Study the reliquary with St. George killing the dragon—sparkling with more than 2,000 precious stones. Get up close (it's OK to walk around the rope posts)...you can almost hear the dragon hissing. A gold-armored St. George, seated atop a ruby-studded ivory horse, tramples an emerald-green dragon. The golden box below contained the supposed relics of St. George, who was the patron saint of the Wittelsbachs. If you could lift the minuscule visor, you'd see that the carved ivory face of St. George is actually the Wittelsbach Duke Wilhelm V—the great champion of the Catholic Counter-

Crown of Henry II

St. George reliquary

Reformation—slaying the dragon of Protestantism.

Room 4: The incredibly realistic carved ivory crucifixes from 1630 were done by local artist Georg Petel. Look at the flesh of Jesus' wrist pulling around the nails. In the center of the room is the intricate portable altarpiece (1573-74) of Duke Albrecht V, the Wittelsbach ruler who (as we'll see in the Residenz Museum) made a big mark on the Residenz.

Room 5: The freestanding glass case (#245) holds the impressive royal regalia of the 19th-century Wittelsbach kings—the crown, scepter, orb, and sword that were given to the king during the coronation ceremony. (The smaller pearl crown was for the queen.) They date from the early 1800s when Bavaria had been conquered by Napoleon. The Wittelsbachs struck a deal that allowed them to stay in power, under the elevated title of "king" (not just "duke" or "prince-elector" or "prince-archbishop"). These objects were made in France by the same craftsmen who created Napoleon's crown.

Rooms 6-10: The rest of the treasury has objects that are more beautiful than historic. Admire the dinnerware made of rock crystal (Room 6), stone (Room 7), and gold and enamel (Room 8). Room 9 has a silver-gilt-and-marble replica of Trajan's Column. Finally, explore the "Exotica" of Room 10, including an ancient green Olmec figure encased in a Baroque niche and a Chinese rhino-horn bowl with a teeny-tiny Neptune inside.

• *From the micro-detail of the treasury, it's time to visit the expansive Residenz Museum. Stop by the audioguide desk to have your wand reprogrammed for the museum, cross the hall, and enter the...*

RESIDENZ MUSEUM (RESIDENZMUSEUM)

Though called a "museum," what's really on display here are the 90 rooms of the Residenz itself: the palace's spectacular banquet and reception halls, and the Wittelsbachs' lavish private apartments.

The rooms are decorated with period (but generally not original) furniture: chandeliers, canopied beds, Louis XIV-style chairs, old clocks, tapestries, and dinnerware of porcelain and silver. It's the best place to glimpse the opulent lifestyle of Bavaria's late, great royal family.

(Whatever happened to the Wittelsbachs, the longest continuously ruling family in European history? They're still around, but they're no longer royalty, so most of them have real jobs now—you may well have passed one on the street.)

➔ **Self-Guided Tour:** The place is big. Follow the museum's prescribed route, using this section to hit the highlights and supplementing it with the audioguide. Grab a free museum floor plan as you enter to help locate specific room numbers mentioned here. Be flexible. The route can vary because rooms are occasionally closed off.

• *One of the first "rooms" you encounter (it's actually part of an outdoor courtyard) is the...*

❶ **Shell Grotto** (Room 6): This artificial grotto is made of volcanic tuff and covered completely in Bavarian freshwater shells. In its day, it was an exercise in man controlling nature—a celebration of the Renaissance humanism that flourished in the 1550s. Mercury—the pre-Christian god of trade and business—oversees the action. Check out the statue in the courtyard—in the Wittelsbachs' heyday, red wine would have flowed from the mermaid's breasts and dripped from Medusa's severed head.

• *Before moving on, note the door marked OO, leading to handy WCs. Now continue into the next room, the...*

❷ **Antiquarium** (Room 7): This long, low, arched hall stretches 220 feet end to end. It's the oldest room in the Residenz, built around 1550. The room was, and still is, a festival banquet hall. The ruler presided from the raised dais at the near end (warmed by the fireplace). Two hundred dignitaries can dine here, surrounded by

The Antiquarium, the palace's banquet hall

allegories of the goodness of just rule on the ceiling.

The hall is lined with busts of Roman emperors. In the mid-16th century, Europe's royal families (such as the Wittelsbachs) collected and displayed such busts, implying a connection between themselves and the enlightened ancient Roman rulers. There was such huge demand for these classical statues in the courts of Europe that many of the "ancient busts" were fakes cranked out by crooked Romans. Still, a third of the statuary you see here is original.

The small paintings around the room show 120 Bavarian villages as they looked in 1550. Even today, when a Bavarian historian wants a record of how his village once looked, he comes here. Notice the town of Dachau in 1550 (in the archway closest to the entrance door).

• *Follow the red arrows through a few more rooms, then up a stairway to the upper floor. Pause in the* **Black Hall** *(Room 13) to admire the head-spinning trompe l'oeil ceiling, which makes the nearly flat roof appear to be* *a much grander arched vault. From here, the prescribed route winds through a number of rooms surrounding a large courtyard.*

❸ **Upper Floor Apartments** (Rooms 14-45): In this series of rooms we get the first glimpse of the Residenz Museum's forte: chandeliered rooms decorated with ceiling paintings, stucco work, tapestries, parquet floors, and period furniture.

Rooms to the left of the Black Hall are the **Electoral Apartments** (Rooms 22-31), the private apartments of the monarch and his consort.

The door from the Black Hall that's opposite the staircase leads to the long **All Saints' Corridor** (Room 32), where you can glance into the adjoining All Saints' Chapel. This early 19th-century chapel, commissioned by Ludwig I, was severely damaged in World War II and didn't reopen until 2003.

From the All Saints' Corridor you can reach the **Charlotte Chambers/Court Garden Rooms,** a long row of impressive rooms across the courtyard from the Electoral Apartments, first used to house

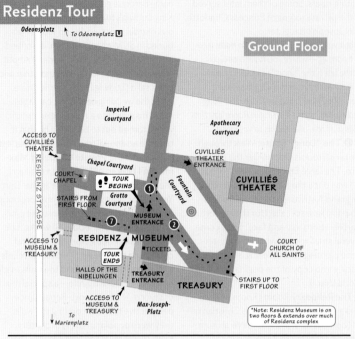

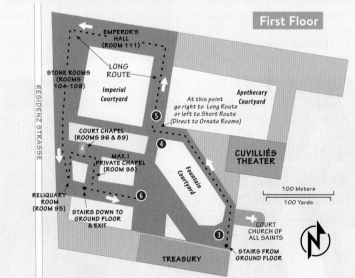

Residenz Tour

Ground Floor

Odeonsplatz

↑ To Odeonsplatz

Imperial Courtyard

Apothecary Courtyard

ACCESS TO CUVILLIÉS THEATER

CUVILLIÉS THEATER ENTRANCE

RESIDENZ STRASSE

Chapel Courtyard

COURT CHAPEL

❶ TOUR BEGINS

STAIRS FROM FIRST FLOOR

Grotto Courtyard

Fountain Courtyard

CUVILLIÉS THEATER

❼

MUSEUM ENTRANCE

❷

ACCESS TO MUSEUM & TREASURY

RESIDENZ MUSEUM*

TICKETS

COURT CHURCH OF ALL SAINTS

TOUR ENDS

HALLS OF THE NIBELUNGEN

TREASURY ENTRANCE

TREASURY

STAIRS UP TO FIRST FLOOR

ACCESS TO MUSEUM & TREASURY

Max-Joseph-Platz

To Marienplatz

*Note: Residenz Museum is on two floors & extends over much of Residenz complex

First Floor

EMPEROR'S HALL (ROOM 111)

LONG ROUTE

RESIDENZ STRASSE

STONE ROOMS (ROOMS 104-109)

Imperial Courtyard

Apothecary Courtyard

At this point go right to Long Route or left to Short Route (Direct to Ornate Rooms)

❺

COURT CHAPEL (ROOMS 96 & 89)

❹

MAX. I PRIVATE CHAPEL (ROOM 98)

CUVILLIÉS THEATER

Fountain Courtyard

RELIQUARY ROOM (ROOM 95)

❻

STAIRS DOWN TO GROUND FLOOR & EXIT

100 Meters
100 Yards

COURT CHURCH OF ALL SAINTS

N

❸

STAIRS FROM GROUND FLOOR

TREASURY

❶ Shell Grotto
❷ Antiquarium
❸ Upper Floor Apartments
❹ Room 45
❺ "Long" Route
❻ Ornate Rooms
❼ Porcelain Cabinet & Ancestral Gallery

visiting rulers. Some of them later served as the private rooms of Princess Charlotte, Max Joseph's daughter.

• *Your visit eventually reaches a hallway—* ❹ *Room 45—where you have a choice: To the left is the "short" route that heads directly to the stunning Ornate Rooms (described later). But we'll take the "long" route to the right (starting in Room 47) that adds a dozen-plus rooms to your visit.*

❺ **The "Long" Route:** Walk through the lavish rooms that border the courtyard. The large **Emperor's Hall** (Room 111) was once the most important room for grand festivities; the **Stone Rooms** (104-109) are so-called for their colorful marble—both real and fake. Then come several small rooms, where the centerpiece painting on the ceiling is just blank black, as no copy of the original survived World War II.

The **Reliquary Room** (Room 95) harbors a collection of gruesome Christian relics (bones, skulls, and even several mummified hands) in ornate golden cases.

• *A few more steps brings you to the balcony of the...*

Court Chapel (Rooms 96/89): Dedicated to Mary, this late-Renaissance/ early-Baroque gem was the site of "Mad" King Ludwig's funeral after his mysterious murder—or suicide—in 1886. (He's buried in St. Michael's Church, described in my "Munich City Walk," earlier.) About 75 years earlier, in 1810, his grandfather and namesake (Ludwig I) was married here. After the wedding ceremony, carriages rolled his guests to a rollicking reception, which turned out to be such a hit that it became an annual tradition—Oktoberfest.

Ahead is the **Private Chapel of Maximilian I** (Room 98). Duke Maximilian I, the dominant Bavarian figure in the Thirty Years' War, built one of the most precious rooms in the palace. The miniature pipe organ (from about 1600) still works. The room is sumptuous, from the gold leaf ceiling and the fine altar with silver reliefs to the miniature dome and the walls made of *scagliola*—fake marble—a special mix of stucco. Note the post-Renaissance perspective tricks decorating the walls; they were popular in the 17th century.

• *Whichever route you take—long or short— you'll eventually reach a set of rooms known as the...*

❻ **Ornate Rooms** (Rooms 55-62): As the name implies, these are some of the

Every Residenz room is unique and ornate.

richest rooms in the palace. The Wittelsbachs were always trying to keep up with the Habsburgs, and this long string of ceremonial rooms—used for official business—was designed to impress. The decor and furniture are Rococo—over-the-top Baroque. The family art collection, now in the Alte Pinakothek, once decorated these walls.

The rooms were designed in the 1730s by François de Cuvilliés. The Belgian-born Cuvilliés first attracted notice as the clever court dwarf for the Bavarian ruler. He was sent to Paris to study art and returned to become the court architect. Besides the Residenz, he went on to also design the Cuvilliés Theater and Amalienburg at Nymphenburg Palace. Cuvilliés' style, featuring incredibly intricate stucco tracery twisted into unusual shapes, defined Bavarian Rococo. As you glide through this section of the palace, be sure to appreciate the gilded stucco ceilings above you.

The **Green Gallery** (Room 58)—named for its green silk damask wallpaper—was the ballroom. Imagine the parties they had here—aristocrats in powdered wigs, a string quartet playing Baroque tunes, a card game going on, while everyone admired the paintings on the walls or themselves reflected in the mirrors.

The **State Bedroom** (Room 60), though furnished with a canopy bed, wasn't an actual bedroom—it was just for show. Rulers invited their subjects to come at morning and evening to stand at the railing and watch their boss ceremonially rise from his slumber to symbolically start and end the working day.

Perhaps the most ornate of these Ornate Rooms is the **Cabinet of Mirrors** (Room 61) and the adjoining **Cabinet of Miniatures** (Room 62) from 1740. In the Cabinet of Mirrors, notice the fun visual effects of the mirrors around you—the corner mirrors make things go on forever. Then peek inside the coral red

room and imagine visiting the duke and having him take you here to ogle miniature copies of the most famous paintings of the day, composed with one-haired brushes.

• *After exploring the Ornate Rooms (and the many other elaborate rooms here on the upper floor), find the staircase (past Room 69) that heads back downstairs. On the ground floor, you emerge in the long Ancestral Gallery (Room 4). Before walking down it, detour to the right, into Room 5.*

❼ **Porcelain Cabinet** (Room 5) and **Ancestral Gallery** (Room 4): In the 18th century, the royal family bolstered their status with an in-house porcelain works: Nymphenburg porcelain. See how the mirrors enhance the porcelain vases, creating the effect of infinite pedestals. If this inspires you to acquire some pieces of your own, head to the Nymphenburg Porcelain Store at Odeonsplatz.

The Ancestral Gallery (Room 4) was built in the 1740s to display portraits of the Wittelsbachs. All official guests had to pass through here to meet the duke (and his 100 Wittelsbach relatives). The room's symbolism reinforced the Wittelsbachs' claims to being as powerful as the Habsburgs of Vienna.

Midway down the hall, find the family tree labeled (in Latin) "genealogy of an imperial family." The tree is shown being planted by Hercules, to boost their royal street cred. Opposite the tree are two notable portraits: Charlemagne, the first Holy Roman Emperor, and to his right, Louis IV (wearing the same crown), the first Wittelsbach H.R.E., crowned in 1328. For the next 500 years, this lineage was used to substantiate the family's claim to power as they competed with the Habsburgs. (After failing to sort out their differences through strategic weddings, the two families eventually went to war.)

Allied bombs took their toll on this hall. The central ceiling painting has been restored, but since there were no photos documenting the other two ceiling paintings, those spots remain empty. Looking carefully at the walls, you can see how each painting was hastily cut out of its frame. That's because—though most of Munich's museums were closed during World War II—the Residenz remained open to instill confidence in local people. It wasn't until 1944, when bombs were imminent, that the last-minute order was given to hide the paintings away.

Also on the ground floor are the **Halls of the Nibelungen** (*Nibelungensäle*, Rooms 74-79), which feature mythological scenes that were the basis of Wagner's *Der Ring des Nibelungen*. Wagner and "Mad" King Ludwig were friends and spent time hanging out here (c. 1864). The images in this hall could well have inspired Wagner to write his Ring and Ludwig to build his "fairy-tale castle," Neuschwanstein.

• *Your Residenz Museum tour is over. The doorway at the end of the hall leads back to the museum entrance. If you're visiting the Cuvilliés Theater, exit the museum and return to Residenzstrasse. Enter the Chapel Courtyard by passing between the green lions standing guard. Walk to the far end of the lane until you reach a fountain. Just above a doorway to the left you'll see a nondescript sign that says* Cuvilliés Theater.

CUVILLIÉS THEATER
In 1751, this was Germany's ultimate Rococo theater. Mozart conducted here several times. Designed by the same brilliant architect who did the Amalienburg, this theater is dazzling enough to send you back to the days of divine monarchs.

It's an intimate, horseshoe-shaped performance venue, seating fewer than 400. The four tiers of box seats were for the four classes of society: city burghers on bottom, royalty next up (in the most elaborate seats), and lesser courtiers in the two highest tiers. The ruler occupied the large Royal Box directly opposite the stage. "Mad" King Ludwig II occasionally bought out the entire theater to watch performances here by himself.

François Cuvilliés' interior is exquisite. Red, white, and gold hues dominate. Most of the decoration is painted wood, even parts that look like marble. Even the proscenium above the stage—seemingly draped with a red-velvet "curtain"—is actually made of carved wood. Also above the stage is an elaborate Wittelsbach coat of arms. The balconies seem to be supported by statues of the four seasons and are adorned with gold garlands. Cuvilliés achieved the Rococo ideal of giving theater-goers a multimedia experience— uniting the beauty of his creation with the beautiful performance on stage. It's still a working theater.

WWII bombs completely obliterated the old Cuvilliés Theater, which originally stood at a different location a short distance from here. Fortunately, much of the carved wooden interior had been removed from the walls and stored away for safekeeping. After the war, this entirely new building was constructed near the ruins of the old theater and paneled with the original decor.

Near the Residenz
▲MUNICH CITY MUSEUM (MÜNCHNER STADTMUSEUM)
The museum's permanent exhibit on Munich's history (called "Typically Munich!") is interesting, but it's an exhaustive and confusing maze, and there's no posted English information. Use the following mini tour for an overview, then supplement it with the audioguide and English booklet.

Cuvilliés Theater

Cost and Hours: €4, includes good audioguide, €7 includes temporary exhibits; ticket gets you half-price admission to Jewish History Museum and Lenbachhaus; Tue-Sun 10:00-18:00, closed Mon; St.-Jakobs-Platz 1, tel. 089/2332-2370, www.muenchner-stadtmuseum.de. The humorous Servus Heimat souvenir shop in the courtyard is worth a stop.

Eating: The museum's recommended Stadt Café is handy for a light meal.

Visiting the Museum: Start in the ticketing hall with the wooden model showing Munich today. Find the Frauenkirche, Isar River, New Town Hall, Residenz...and no skyscrapers. The city looks remarkably similar in scale to the model (in the next room) from 1570.

Ground Floor (Medieval): An imposing gray statue of Henry the Lion introduces us to the city's 12th-century founder. The eight statues of Morris dancers (1480) became a symbol of the vibrant market town (and the tradition continued with the New Town Hall glockenspiel's dancing coopers). On the rest of the ground floor, paintings, swords, and cherubs clad in armor capture more medieval ambience.

First Floor (1800s): The "New Munich" was created when the city was expanded beyond the old medieval walls (see the illuminated view of the city from 1761 in the "Canaletto-Blick" opposite the top of the stairs). The city was prosperous, as evidenced by the furniture and paintings on display. In the center of the room, find big paintings ("Effigies") of the century's magnificent kings—Maximilian I, Maximilian II, and Ludwig I.

Second Floor (Munich 1900): As Munich approached its 700th birthday, it was becoming aware of itself as a major capital. The Münchner Kindl logo was born. It was a city of artists (Wagner operas, Lenbach portraits, Von Stuck soirées), *Jugendstil* furniture, beer, and a cosmopolitan outlook (see the "Kaiser Panorama," the big barrel-shaped 3-D peep show of Indian/Asian peoples). But after the destruction of World War I, Munich became a hotbed of discontent. The "revue" room shows the city's clash of ideas: communists, capitalists, Nazis, and the anarchic theater of comedian Karl Valentin and early works by playwright Bertolt Brecht. A nearby display gives some background on Munich's role as the birthplace of Nazism (thoroughly covered in the museum's National Socialism wing).

Third Floor (Puppetry and Fairground Art): Consider a trip to the third floor to see the puppetry exhibit (worthwhile and included with your ticket). The collection of objects from the 19th century onward highlights Germany's long tradition of puppetry. Fair and Oktoberfest items may attract children, but beware that horror-house displays may scare the daylights out of them.

Video Finish: End your visit back on the first floor with a kaleidoscope of video images capturing contemporary Munich—rock music, World Cup triumphs, beer gardens, and other things "typically Munich."

National Socialism Wing: This small but worthwhile exhibit (in a building across the courtyard) of photos and uniforms takes you chronologically through the Nazi years: the post-WWI struggles, Hitler's 1923 Beer Hall Putsch, his writing of *Mein Kampf,* the mass rallies in Königsplatz and Odeonsplatz, the Dachau concentration camp, the destruction rained on Munich in World War II, and postwar reconstruction.

Munich City Museum

GERMANY

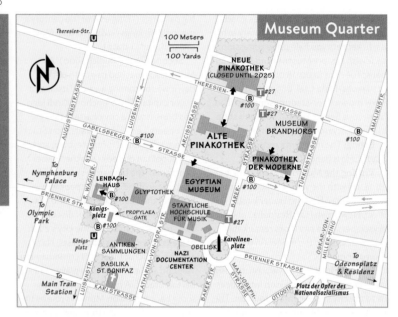

Museum Quarter (Kunstareal)

This quarter's impressive cluster of fine museums displays art from 3000 BC right up to the present. We'll focus on the Egyptian Museum, Alte Pinakothek, and Lenbachhaus. Most people don't come to Munich for the art, but this group makes a case for the city's world-class status.

Getting There: Handy tram #27 whisks you right to the Pinakothek stop from Karlsplatz (between the train station and Marienplatz). You can also take bus #100 from the train station, or walk 10 minutes from the Theresienstrasse or Königsplatz stops on the U-2 line.

▲▲ALTE PINAKOTHEK

The Alte Pinakothek ("Old Art Gallery," pronounced ALL-teh pee-nah-koh-TEHK) shows off a world-class collection of European masterpieces from the 14th to 19th century, starring the two tumultuous centuries (1450-1650) when Europe went from medieval to modern. See paintings from the Italian Renaissance (Raphael, Leonardo, Botticelli, Titian)

and the German Renaissance it inspired (Albrecht Dürer). Through the art displayed here, you can follow along as the Reformation of Martin Luther eventually split Europe into two subcultures—Protestant and Catholic—with their two distinct art styles (exemplified by Rembrandt and Rubens, respectively). You may also see some top-notch paintings (from 1800 to 1920, including Impressionism) belonging to the museum's younger sister across the street—the Neue Pinakothek—which is closed for renovations until 2025.

Cost and Hours: €7, €1 on Sun, covered by day pass and combo-ticket; Wed-Sun 10:00-18:00, Tue until 20:00, closed Mon; excellent audioguide (free, but €4.50 on Sun), pleasant Café Klenze; U-2: Theresienstrasse, tram #27, or bus #100; Barer Strasse 27, tel. 089/2380-5216, www.pinakothek.de/alte-pinakothek.

Visiting the Museum: All the paintings we'll see are on the upper floor, which is laid out like a barbell. Start at one fat end and work your way through the "handle" to the other end. From the ticket counter, head up the stairway to the left to reach

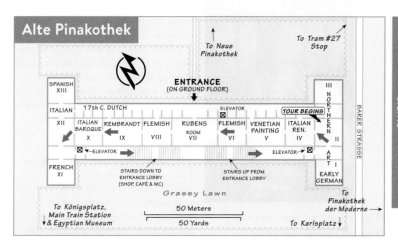

the first rooms.

German Renaissance (Room II): Albrecht Altdorfer's *The Battle of Issus* (*Schlacht bei Issus*) shows a world at war. Masses of soldiers are swept along in the currents and tides of a battle completely beyond their control, their confused motion reflected in the swirling sky. Though the painting depicts Alexander the Great's history-changing victory over the Persians (find the Persian king Darius turning and fleeing), it could as easily have been Germany in the 1520s. Christians were fighting Muslims, peasants battled masters, and Catholics and Protestants were squaring off for a century of conflict. The armies melt into a huge landscape, leaving the impression that the battle goes on forever.

Albrecht Dürer's larger-than-life *Four Apostles* (*Johannes und Petrus* and *Paulus und Marcus*) are saints of a radical new religion: Martin Luther's Protestantism. Just as Luther challenged Church authority, Dürer—a friend of Luther's—strips these saints of any rich clothes, halos, or trappings of power and gives them down-to-earth human features: receding hairlines, wrinkles, and suspicious eyes. The inscription warns German rulers to follow the Bible rather than Catholic Church leaders. The figure of Mark—a Bible in

one hand and a sword in the other—is a fitting symbol of the dangerous times.

Dürer's *Self-Portrait in Fur Coat* (*Selbstbildnis im Pelzrock*) looks like Jesus Christ but is actually 28-year-old Dürer himself, gazing out, with his right hand solemnly giving a blessing. This is the ultimate image of humanism: the artist as an instrument of God's continued creation.

Italian Renaissance (Room IV): With the Italian Renaissance—the "rebirth" of interest in the art and learning of ancient Greece and Rome—artists captured the realism, three-dimensionality, and sym-

Dürer, Self-Portrait in Fur Coat

A *Leonardo da Vinci,* Virgin and Child

B *Raphael,* Canigiani Holy Family

C *Rubens,* Rubens and Isabella Brant

metry found in classical statues. Twenty-one-year-old Leonardo da Vinci's *Virgin and Child (Maria mit dem Kinde)* need no halos—they radiate purity. Mary is a solid pyramid of maternal love, flanked by Renaissance-arch windows that look out on the hazy distance. Baby Jesus reaches out to play innocently with a carnation, the blood-colored symbol of his eventual death.

Raphael's *Holy Family at the Canigiani House (Die hl. Familie aus dem Hause Canigiani)* takes Leonardo's pyramid form and runs with it. Father Joseph forms the peak, with his staff as the strong central axis. Mary and Jesus (on the right) form a pyramid-within-the-pyramid, as do Elizabeth and baby John the Baptist on the left.

In Botticelli's *Lamentation over Christ (Die Beweinung Christi),* the Renaissance "pyramid" implodes, as the weight of the dead Christ drags everyone down, and the tomb grins darkly behind them.

Venetian Painting (Room V): In Titian's *Christ Crowned with Thorns (Die Dornenkrönung),* a powerfully built Christ sits silently enduring torture by prison guards. The painting is by Venice's greatest Renaissance painter, but there's no symmetry, no pyramid form, and the brushwork is intentionally messy and Impressionistic. By the way, this is the first painting we've seen done on canvas rather than wood, as artists experimented with vegetable oil-based paints.

Rubens and Baroque (Room VII): Europe's religious wars split the Continent in two—Protestants in the northern countries, Catholics in the south. (Germany itself was divided, with Bavaria remaining Catholic.) The Baroque style, popular in Catholic countries, featured large canvases, bright colors, lots of flesh, rippling motion, wild emotions, grand themes... and pudgy winged babies, the sure sign of Baroque. This room holds several canvases by the great Flemish painter Peter Paul Rubens.

In Rubens' 300-square-foot *Great Last Judgment (Das Grosse Jüngste Gericht),*

Christ raises the righteous up to heaven (left side) and damns the sinners to hell (on the right). This swirling cycle of nudes was considered risqué and kept under wraps by the very monks who'd commissioned it.

Rubens and Isabella Brant in the Honeysuckle Bower shows the artist with his first wife, both of them the very picture of health, wealth, and success. They lean together unconsciously, as people in love will do, with their hands clasped in mutual affection. When his first wife died, 53-year-old Rubens found a replacement—16-year-old Hélène Fourment, shown in an adjacent painting (just to the left) in her wedding dress. You may recognize Hélène's face in other Rubens paintings.

The Rape of the Daughters of Leucippus (Der Raub der Töchter des Leukippos) has many of Rubens' most typical elements—fleshy, emotional, rippling motion; bright colors; and a classical subject. The legendary twins Castor and Pollux crash a wedding and steal the brides as their own. The chaos of flailing limbs and rearing horses is all held together in a subtle X-shaped composition. Like the weaving counterpoint in a Baroque fugue, Rubens balances opposites.

Rembrandt and Dutch (Room IX): From Holland, Rembrandt van Rijn's *Six Paintings from the Life of Christ* are a down-to-earth look at supernatural events. *The Holy Family (Die Heilige Familie)* is set in a carpenter's workshop (with tools on the wall). The canvases are dark brown, lit by strong light. The *Holy Family*'s light source is the Baby Jesus himself—literally the "light of the world." In the *Raising of the Cross (Kreuzaufrichtung),* a man dressed in blue is looking on—a self-portrait of Rembrandt.

In the *Deposition (Kreuzabnahme),* the light bounces off Christ's pale body onto his mother Mary, who has fainted in the shadows, showing how his death also hurts her. The drama is underplayed, with subdued emotions.

▲▲EGYPTIAN MUSEUM (STAATLICHES MUSEUM ÄGYPTISCHER KUNST)

To enjoy this museum, you don't need a strong interest in ancient Egypt (but you may have one by the time you leave). This modern space was custom-made to evoke the feeling of being deep in an ancient tomb, from the wide, easy-to-miss staircase outside that descends to the narrow entry, to the twisty interior rooms that grow narrower and more catacomb-like as you progress. The museum's clever design creates a low-stress visit (just follow the one-way route marked by brass arrows in the floor).

Cost and Hours: €7, €1 on Sun, Wed-Sun 10:00-18:00, Tue until 20:00, closed Mon, audioguide is usually free (€1 on Sun); U-2 or U-8 to Königsplatz, tram #27 to Karolinenplatz, or bus #100 to Pinakothek stop; 10-minute walk from main train station, Gabelsbergerstrasse 35, tel. 089/2892-7630, www.smaek.de.

▲▲LENBACHHAUS

Locals like to say, "Berlin had generals, Munich had artists." And that was particularly true in the decades before World War I. A bunch of art-school cronies got fed up with being told how and what to paint, and together, as the revolutionary "Blue Rider" *(Blaue Reiter)* group, they galloped toward a brand-new horizon—abstract art. In the Lenbachhaus' pleasant galleries you can witness the birth of Modernist nonrepresentational art, with paintings by Kandinsky, Klee, and Marc, then stroll the rest of the building's offerings (including the apartments of painter Franz von Lenbach).

Cost and Hours: €10, includes well-done audioguide; ticket gets you half-price admission to Jewish History Museum and Munich City Museum (or use any of those tickets to get half-price admission here); Wed-Sun 10:00-18:00, Tue until 20:00, closed Mon; Luisenstrasse 33, tel. 089/2333-2000, www.lenbachhaus.de.

Lenbachhaus

Visiting the Museum: The collection includes three distinct sections: 19th century (conservative, colorful, optimistic); Blue Rider (emotional, inspired, modern); and Post-1945 (abstract). The Blue Rider revolution begins on the second floor, with seemingly innocuous paintings of the cute Bavarian town of Murnau. It was here in 1908 that two Munich couples—Wassily Kandinsky, Alexej Jawlensky, and their artist girl-friends—came for vacation. The four painted together, employing intense colors, thick paint, and bold black outlines. Over the next few years (c. 1911-1914), they'd gather together into a group of Munich-based artists calling themselves the Blue Rider, which included Paul Klee and Franz Marc. They were all devoted to expressing spiritual truths by using intense colors and geometric shapes.

The Blue Rider School was blown apart by World War I: The artists who survived went on to pioneer abstract art.

Kandinsky's "Improvisations" eventually became the art world's first purely abstract canvases. Soon his style spread everywhere. Jawlensky and Klee also went on to develop a simpler and more abstract style.

One floor down, in the "Art After 1945" section, you'll see big, empty canvases by the Abstract Expressionists who tried to "express" deep truths through "abstract" color and line alone. Finally, across the entry hall from the ticket desk and up one floor, enter the luxe villa of Franz von Lenbach, who made portraits of 19th-century notables. His paintings fill the walls of ornate rooms accentuated by fine 15th- to 19th-century furnishings.

▲▲NAZI DOCUMENTATION CENTER (NS-DOKUMENTATIONSZENTRUM MÜNCHEN)

This center—housed in a stark, light-filled, cube-shaped building—documents the rise and fall of Nazism with a focus on Munich's role and the reasons behind it, as this city, like the rest of Germany, is determined to learn from its 20th-century nightmare. While there are no actual artifacts here, the learning experience is moving and a worthwhile companion to the Dachau Concentration Camp Memorial.

Cost and Hours: Free, with well-done and techie audioguide; Tue-Sun 10:00-19:00, closed Mon, U-2: Königsplatz, Brienner Strasse 34, tel. 089/2336-7001, www.ns-dokumentationszentrum-muenchen.de.

Visiting the Museum: The museum is arranged chronologically and begins on the top floor. (Take the elevator to avoid confusion.) The top floor covers the end of World War I and the beginning of Hitler's movement in Munich (1918-1933). It includes gripping biographies of the early opponents of the Nazi Party.

The third floor (covering 1933-1939) documents the establishment of the racially pure *Volksgemeinschaft* ("people's community") and the effect of Nazi domination on everyday life, including a timeline that illustrates the restrictions and ordinances that worsened Jewish isolation. Look out onto Königsplatz and envision Hitler's rise to power, which started right here.

The second floor (1939-1945) covers the horrors of war, the Holocaust, and the "denazification" period after the end of Nazi rule. Find the video showing Munich in ruins immediately following the war and compare the footage to what you see today.

The first floor (after 1945) examines the faith people put in the Nazi regime and the difficulty in coming to terms with the past. The Learning Center, in the basement, encourages reflection, with a collection of books banned during Nazi rule and research stations where you can delve into topics of interest.

Near the River

▲ENGLISH GARDEN (ENGLISCHER GARTEN)

Munich's "Central Park," the largest urban park on the Continent, was laid out in 1789 by an American. More than 100,000 locals commune with nature here on sunny summer days (including lots of students from the nearby university). The park stretches three miles from the center, past the university and the trendy Schwabing quarter. For the best quick visit, take bus #100 or tram #18 to the National-museum/Haus der Kunst stop. Under the bridge, you'll see surfers. (The surf's always up here—even through the night; surfers bring their own lights.) Follow the path, to the right of the surfing spot, downstream until you reach the big lawn. The Chinese Tower beer garden is just beyond the tree-covered hill to the right. Follow the oompah music and walk to the hilltop temple, with a postcard view of the city on your way. Afterward, instead of retracing your steps, you can walk (or take bus #54 a couple of stops) to the Giselas-trasse U-Bahn station and return to town on the U-3 or U-6.

A rewarding respite from the city, the park is especially fun—and worth ▲▲—on a bike under the summer sun and on

English Garden

GERMANY

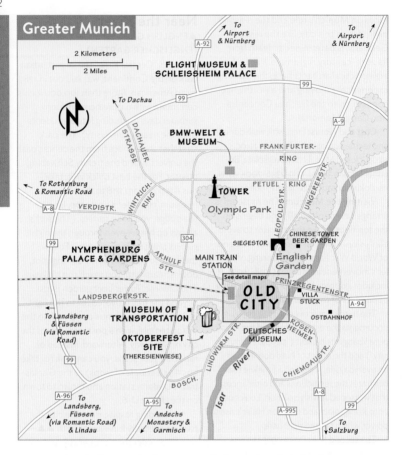

Greater Munich

2 Kilometers

2 Miles

To Airport & Nürnberg

To Airport & Nürnberg

A-92

FLIGHT MUSEUM & SCHLEISSHEIM PALACE

99

99

To Dachau

A-9

DACHAUER STRASSE

BMW-WELT & MUSEUM

FRANK FURTER-RING

TOWER

PETUEL - RING

WINTRICH-RING

To Rothenburg & Romantic Road

Olympic Park

UNGERERSTR.

A-8

VERDISTR.

LEOPOLDSTR.

99

NYMPHENBURG PALACE & GARDENS

ARNULF STR.

SIEGESTOR

CHINESE TOWER BEER GARDEN

304

MAIN TRAIN STATION

English Garden

See detail maps

PRINZREGENTENSTR

LANDSBERGERSTR.

OLD CITY

VILLA STUCK

A-94

To Landsberg & Füssen (via Romantic Road)

MUSEUM OF TRANSPORTATION

OKTOBERFEST SITE (THERESIENWIESE)

LINDWURM STR.

DEUTSCHES MUSEUM

ROSEN-HEIMER

OSTBAHNHOF

CHIEMGAUSTR.

BOSCH.

Isar River

99

A-96 To Landsberg, Füssen (via Romantic Road) & Lindau

A-95 To Andechs Monastery & Garmisch

A-8

A-995

99

To Salzburg

warm evenings (unfortunately, there are no bike-rental agencies in or near the park; to rent some wheels, see page 755). Caution: While local law requires sun worshippers to wear clothes on the tram, the park is sprinkled with buck-naked sunbathers—quite a shock to prudish Americans (they're the ones riding their bikes into the river and trees).

▲DEUTSCHES MUSEUM (MAIN BRANCH)

Germany's answer to our Smithsonian Institution, the Deutsches Museum traces the evolution of science and technology. Enjoy wandering through rooms of historic airplanes, spaceships, mining,

the harnessing of wind and water power, hydraulics, musical instruments, printing, chemistry, computers, astronomy, and nanotechnology. The museum feels a bit dated, and not all the displays have English descriptions—but major renovations are under way. Though about a third of the collection may be closed during your visit, even those on roller skates will still need to be selective. Use my mini tour to get oriented.

Cost and Hours: €12, daily 9:00-17:00, English map available, several small cafés in the museum, tel. 089/217-9333, www. deutsches-museum.de.

Getting There: Take tram #17 to the

Deutsches Museum stop. Or, take the S-Bahn or tram #18 to Isartor, then walk 300 yards over the river and turn right, following the signs. The entrance is near the far end of the building along the riverside.

Visiting the Museum: After buying your ticket, head inside and stop by the information desk to ask about the day's schedule of demonstrations (for example, electric power or glass-blowing). Pick up a floor plan (you'll get lost without it) and walk toward the vast high-ceilinged room dominated by a tall-masted ship.

Ground Floor: Get oriented and locate the handy elevator behind you—it's one of the few elevators in this labyrinthine building that goes to all six floors. Now, let's explore.

The exhibit on **marine navigation** is anchored by the 60-foot sailing ship *Maria*. Take the staircase down, where you can look inside her cut-away hull and imagine life below decks. Before heading back upstairs, find the bisected U1 submarine (on the wall farthest from the entrance)—the first German *U-Boot* (undersea boat), dating from 1906.

Now make your way to several technology exhibits—DNA and nanotechnology (downstairs). Children will enjoy the "Kinderreich" (past the cloakroom to the left as you enter) and the exciting twice-daily high-voltage demonstrations (ground floor) creating a five-foot bolt of lightning.

First Floor: The **historic aviation** collection occupies the center of the first floor. You'll see early attempts at flight—gliders, hot-air balloons, and a model of the airship pioneered by Germany's Count Zeppelin. The highlight is a Wright Brothers double-decker airplane from 1909—six years after their famous first flight, when they began to manufacture multiple copies of their prototype. By World War I, airplanes were becoming a formidable force. The Fokker triplane was made famous by Germany's war ace the Red Baron (Manfred von Richthofen).

Second Floor: Gathered together near the main elevator, you'll find a replica of prehistoric **cave paintings** and daily **glass-blowing** demonstrations. Don't miss the flight simulator—a training device that is almost identical to flying a real airplane.

Third Floor: The third floor traces the history of **measurement,** including time (from a 16th-century sundial and an 18th-century clock to a scary Black Forest wall clock complete with grim reaper), weights, and geodesy (surveying and mapping). In the **computer** section, you go from the ancient abacus to a 1956 Univac computer—as big as a room, with a million components, costing a million dollars, and with less computing power than your smartphone.

Floors 4-6: The focus here is on **astronomy.** A light-show exhibit traces the evolution of the universe. The **planetarium** lecture is in German, but might be worthwhile if you love the stars. Finally, you emerge on the museum rooftop—the **"sundial garden"**—with great views. On a clear day, you can see the Alps.

▲▲Nymphenburg Palace Complex

For 200 years, this oasis of palaces and gardens was the Wittelsbach rulers' summer vacation home, a getaway from the sniping politics of court life in the city. Their kids could play, picnic, ride horses, and frolic in the ponds and gardens, while the adults played cards, listened to music, and sipped coffee on the veranda. It was at Nymphenburg that a seven-year-old Mozart gave a widely heralded concert, that 60-year-old Ludwig I courted the femme fatale Lola Montez, and that "Mad" King Ludwig II (Ludwig I's grandson) was born and baptized.

Today, Nymphenburg Palace and the surrounding one-square-mile park are a great place for a royal stroll or discreet picnic. Indoors, you can tour the Bavarian royal family's summer quarters and visit the Royal Stables Museum (carriages, sleighs, and porcelain). If you have time, check out playful extras such as a hunting lodge (Amalienburg), bathhouse (Badenburg), pagoda (Pagodenburg), and fake ruins (Magdalenenklause). The complex also houses a humble natural history museum and Baroque chapel. Allow at least three hours (including travel time) to see the palace complex at a leisurely pace.

Cost and Hours: Palace-€6; combo-ticket-€11.50 (€8.50 off-season) covers the palace, Royal Stables Museum, and outlying sights. All of these sights are open daily 9:00-18:00, mid-Oct-March 10:00-16:00—except for Amalienburg and the other small palaces in the park, which are closed in winter; park open daily 6:00-dusk and free to enter; audioguide-€3.50, tel. 089/179-080, www.schloss-nymphenburg.de.

Getting There: The palace is three miles northwest of central Munich. Take tram #17 (direction: Amalienburgstrasse) from the train station or Karlsplatz. In 15 minutes you reach the Schloss Nymphen-burg stop. From the bridge by the tram stop, you'll see the palace—a 10-minute walk away. The palace is a pleasant 30-minute bike ride from the main train station (either follow Arnulfstrasse all the way to Nymphenburg, or turn up Landshuter Allee—at Donersburgerbrücke—then follow Nymphenburger Strasse until you hit the canal that stretches to the palace). Be aware that biking in the palace grounds is not permitted.

Eating: A $$ café serves lunch and snacks in a winter garden or on a nice terrace, a five-minute walk behind and to the right of the palace (open year-round). More eating options are near the tram stop.

NYMPHENBURG PALACE

In 1662, after 10 years of trying, the Bavarian ruler Ferdinand Maria and his wife, Henriette Adelaide of Savoy, finally had a son, Max Emanuel. In gratitude for a male heir, Ferdinand gave this land to his Italian wife, who proceeded to build an Italian-style Baroque palace as their summer residence. Their son expanded the palace to its current size. (Today's Wittelsbachs, who still refer to themselves as "princes"

Nymphenburg Palace

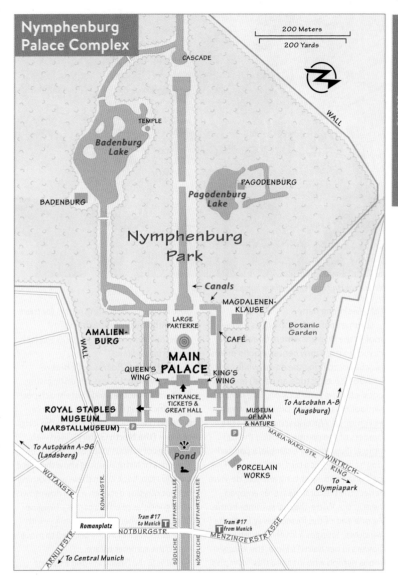

Nymphenburg
Palace Complex

200 Meters
200 Yards

CASCADE

WALL

TEMPLE

Badenburg
Lake

PAGODENBURG

Pagodenburg
Lake

BADENBURG

Nymphenburg
Park

← Canals

MAGDALENEN-
KLAUSE

LARGE
PARTERRE

Botanic
Garden

AMALIEN-
BURG

WALL

CAFÉ

MAIN
PALACE

QUEEN'S
WING

KING'S
WING

To Autobahn A-8
(Augsburg)

ROYAL STABLES
MUSEUM
(MARSTALLMUSEUM)

ENTRANCE,
TICKETS &
GREAT HALL

MUSEUM
OF MAN
& NATURE

MARIA-WARD-STR.

To Autobahn A-96
(Landsberg)

Pond

PORCELAIN
WORKS

WINTRICH-
RING

To →
Olympiapark

WOTANSTR.

ROMANSTR.

SÜDLICHE AUFFAHRTSALLEE

NÖRDLICHE AUFFAHRTSALLEE

Tram #17
to Munich

Tram #17
from Munich

MENZINGERSTRASSE

Romanplatz

NOTBURGSTR.

ARNULFSTR.

← To Central Munich

or "dukes," live in one wing of the palace.)

The palace interior, while interesting, is much less extensive than Munich's Residenz. The place is stingy on free information; you'll need the serviceable audioguide if you'd like more info than what I've provided below.

⊙ **Self-Guided Tour:** Your visit starts in the **Great Hall** (a.k.a. **Stone Hall**). As the central room of the palace, this light and airy space was the dining hall, site of big Wittelsbach family festivals. One of the grandest and best-preserved Rococo rooms in Bavaria (from about 1760), it sports elaborate stucco work and a ceiling fresco by Johann Baptist Zimmermann

The Great Hall has remained unchanged since 1758.

(of Wieskirche fame).

Zimmermann's fresco opens a sun-roof to the heavens, where Greek gods cavort. In the sunny center, Apollo drives his chariot to bring the dawn, while bearded Zeus (astride an eagle) and pea-cock-carrying Juno look on. The rainbow symbolizes the peace brought by the enlightened Wittelsbachs. Around the borders of the painting, notice the fun optical illusions: For example, a painted dog holds a stucco bird in its mouth. The painting's natural setting and joie de vivre reflect the pastoral pleasures enjoyed here at the Wittelsbachs' summer home. At one end of the fresco (away from the windows) lounges a lovely maiden with flowers in her hair: It's Flora, the epony-mous nymph who inspired this "nymph's castle"—Nymphenburg.

From here, two wings stretch to the left and right. They're mirror images of one another: antechamber, audience cham-ber, bedchamber, and private living quar-ters. Guests would arrive here in the Great Hall for an awe-inspiring first impression, then make their way through a series of (also-impressive) waiting rooms for their date with the Wittelsbach nobility.

• *The tour continues to the left (as you look out the big windows).*

North Wing (Rooms 2-9): Breeze quickly through this less interesting wing, filled with tapestries and Wittelsbach por-traits (including curly-haired Max Eman-uel, who built this wing). Pause in the long corridor **(the North Gallery)** lined with paintings of various Wittelsbach palaces. The ones of Nymphenburg show the place around 1720, back when there was nothing but countryside between it and downtown (and gondolas plied the canals). Imagine the logistics when the royal family—with their entourage of 200—decided to move out to the summer palace.

• *Return to the Great Hall and enter the other wing.*

South Wing (Rooms 10-20): Pass through the gold-and-white Room 10 and turn right into the red-walled **South Apartment Antechamber.** The room calls up the exuberant time of Nymphen-burg's founding couple, Ferdinand and Henriette. A portrait on the wall shows them posing together in their rich courtly dress. The large painting on the left depicts the family in a Greek myth: Henriette (as the moon goddess) leads her youngest son Joseph Clemens by the hand, while her first son Max Emanuel (as Hercules) receives the gift of a sword. On the right side of the room, Ferdinand is represented as Endymion, a mortal loved by the moon goddess.

After admiring the Queen's Bedroom and Chinese lacquer cabinet, head back down the long hall to **King Ludwig I's Gallery of Beauties.** The room is decorated top to bottom with portraits of 36 beautiful women (all painted by Joseph Stieler between 1826 and 1850). Ludwig I was a consummate girl-watcher.

Ludwig prided himself on his ability to appreciate beauty regardless of social rank. He enjoyed picking out the prettiest women from the general public and, with one of the most effective pickup lines of all time, inviting them to the palace for a portrait. Who could refuse? The portraits were on public display in the Residenz, and catapulted their subjects to stardom. The women range from commoners to princesses, but notice that they share one physical trait—Ludwig obviously preferred brunettes. The portraits are done in the modest and slightly sentimental Biedermeier style popular in central Europe, as opposed to the more flamboyant Romanticism (so beloved of Ludwig's "mad" grandson) also thriving at that time.

Most of these portraits have rich stories behind them, none more than Lola Montez, the king's most notorious mistress, who led him to his downfall. The portrait shows her the year she met Ludwig (she was 29, he was 60), wearing the black-lace mantilla and red flowers of a Spanish dancer. Lola became his mistress, and he fawned over her in public, scandalizing Munich. The Münchners resented her spending their tax money and dominating their king. In 1848, as Europe was swept by a tide of revolution, the citizens rose up and forced Ludwig to abdicate.

Pass through the blue Audience Room (with elaborate curtain rods and mahogany furniture in the French-inspired Empire style) and into the (other) **Queen's Bedroom.** The room has much the same furniture it had on August 25, 1845, when Princess Marie gave birth to the future King Ludwig II. Little Ludwig (see his bust, next to brother Otto's) was greatly inspired by Nymphenburg—riding horses in summer, taking sleigh rides in winter, reading poetry at Amalienburg. The love of nature and solitude he absorbed at Nymphenburg eventually led Ludwig to abandon Munich for his castles in the remote Bavarian countryside. By the way, note the mirror in this bedroom. Royal births were carefully witnessed, and the mirror allowed for a better view. While Ludwig's birth was well-documented, his death was shrouded in mystery.

PALACE GROUNDS
The wooded grounds extend far back beyond the formal gardens and are popular with joggers and walkers. Find a bench for

Stieler, Lola Montez *(detail)*

a low-profile picnic. The park is laced with canals and small lakes, where court guests once rode on Venetian-style gondolas.

ROYAL STABLES MUSEUM (MARSTALLMUSEUM)

These former stables (to the left of the main palace as you approach the complex) are full of gilded coaches that will make you think of Cinderella's journey to the king's ball. Upstairs, a porcelain exhibit shows off some of the famous Nymphenburg finery. If you don't want to visit the main palace, you can buy a €4.50 ticket just for this museum (no audioguide available).

Visiting the Museum: Wandering through the collection, you can trace the evolution of 300 years of coaches—getting lighter and with better suspension as they were harnessed to faster horses. In the big entrance hall is a golden carriage drawn by eight fake white horses. In 1742, it carried Karl Albrecht Wittelsbach to Frankfurt to be crowned Holy Roman Emperor. As emperor, he got eight horses—kings got only six. The event is depicted in a frieze on the museum wall; Karl's carriage is #159.

Other objects bear witness to the good times of the relaxed Nymphenburg lifestyle and are a window into the pomp and circumstance surrounding the royals.

Next up are some over-the-top objects—sleighs, golden carriages, and (in the glass cases) harnesses—owned by Ludwig II. Ludwig's over-the-top coaches were Baroque. But this was 1870. The coaches,

Royal Stables Museum

like the king, were in the wrong century.

Head upstairs to a collection of **Nymphenburg porcelain.** Historically, royal families such as the Wittelsbachs liked to have their own porcelain factories to make fit-for-a-king plates, vases, and so on. The Nymphenburg Palace porcelain works is still in operation (the factory store on Odeonsplatz is happy to see you). Find the large room with copies of 17th-century Old Masters' paintings from the Wittelsbach art collection (now at the Alte Pinakothek). Ludwig I had these paintings copied onto porcelain for safekeeping into the distant future. Take a close look—they're exquisite.

AMALIENBURG

Three hundred yards from Nymphenburg Palace, hiding in the park (head into the sculpted garden and veer to the left, following signs), you'll find a fine little Rococo hunting lodge, which takes just a few minutes to tour. In 1734, Prince-Elector Karl Albrecht had it built for his wife, Maria Amalia. Amalienburg was designed by François de Cuvilliés (of Residenz fame) and decorated by Johann Baptist Zimmermann. It's the most worthwhile of the four small "extra" palaces buried in the park that are included on the combo-ticket. The others are the Pagodenburg, a Chinese-inspired pavilion; Badenburg, an opulent bathing house and banquet hall; and the Magdalenenklause, a mini palace that looks like a ruin from the outside but has an elaborate altar and woody apartments inside.

Visiting Amalienburg: As you approach, circle around and notice the facade. Above the pink-and-white grand entryway, Diana, goddess of the chase, is surrounded by themes of the hunt and flanked by busts of satyrs. The queen would shoot from the perch atop the roof. Behind a wall in the garden, dogs would scare nonflying pheasants. When they jumped up in the air above the wall, the sporting queen—as if shooting skeet—

Amalienburg

would pick the birds off.

Tourists now enter this tiny getaway through the back door. Doghouses under gun cupboards fill the first room. In the fine yellow-and-silver bedroom, the bed is flanked by portraits of Karl Albrecht and Maria Amalia—decked out in hunting attire. She liked her dogs. The door under her portrait leads to stairs to the rooftop pheasant-shooting perch.

The mini Hall of Mirrors is a blue-and-silver commotion of Rococo nymphs designed by Cuvilliés. In the next room, paintings depict court festivities, formal hunting parties, and no-contest kills (where the animal is put at an impossible disadvantage—like shooting fish in a barrel). Finally, the sparse kitchen is decorated with Chinese-style drawings on Dutch tile.

Outside the Center

▲BMW-WELT AND MUSEUM

At the headquarters of BMW ("beh-em-VEH" to Germans), Beamer dreamers can visit two space-age buildings to learn more about this brand's storied heritage (worth ▲▲ to enthusiasts). The renowned *Autos* and *Motorräder* are beautifully displayed (perhaps even fetishized by car enthusiasts). This vast complex—built on the site of Munich's first airstrip and home to the BMW factory since 1920—has four com-

ponents: the headquarters (in the building nicknamed "the Four Cylinders"—not open to the public), the factory (tourable with advance reservations), the showroom (called BMW-Welt—"BMW World"), and the BMW Museum.

Cost and Hours: Museum-€10; Tue-Sun 10:00-18:00, closed Mon; BMW-Welt showroom-free, building open daily until 24:00, exhibits staffed 9:00-18:00; tel. 089/125-016-001, www.bmw-welt.com.

Tours: English tours are offered of both the museum (€13, 1 hour, call or email ahead for times) and BMW-Welt (€7.50, 1 hour, Mon-Wed and Sat at 15:30). Factory tours must be booked at least two months in advance (€9, 2.5 hours, Mon-Fri only, ages 6 and up, reservations tel. 089/125-016-001, infowelt@bmw-welt.com).

Getting There: From the city center, ride the U-3 to Olympia-Zentrum. Follow *Ausgang* signs to BMW-Welt/BMW Museum. Leaving the station, climb the stairs and get oriented: Ahead is the BMW-Welt (showroom) entry, and the BMW Museum is marked by the gray "soup bowl." To reach the BMW Museum, head down Lerchenauer Strasse, staying parallel to the factory on your left, and cross at the stoplight just before the bridge.

Visiting BMW: The futuristic, bowl-shaped **museum** encloses a world of

The futuristic BMW-Welt is a one-of-a-kind auto showroom.

floating walkways linking exhibits highlighting BMW motorcycle and car design and technology through the years. The museum traces the Bavarian Motor Works' history since 1917, when the company began making airplane engines. Motorcycles came next, followed by the first BMW sedan in 1929. You'll see how design was celebrated here from the start. Exhibits showcase motorsports, roadsters, and luxury cars. Stand on an *E* for English to hear the chief designer talk about his favorite cars in the "treasury." And the 1956 BMW 507 is enough to rev almost anyone's engine.

After the museum, cross over the swoopy bridge to enter **BMW-Welt** on the first floor. The building itself—a cloud-shaped, glass-and-steel architectural masterpiece—is reason enough to visit. It's free and filled with exhibits designed to enthuse car lovers so they'll find a way to afford a Beemer. While the adjacent museum reviews the BMW past, BMW-Welt shows you the present and gives you a breathtaking look at the future. This is where customers come to pick up their new Beemers (stand on the sky bridge viewpoint to watch in envy), and where hopeful customers-to-be come to nurture their automotive dreams.

EXPERIENCES

Oktoberfest

The 1810 marriage reception of King Ludwig I was such a success that it turned into an annual bash. These days, Oktoberfest lasts just over two weeks, starting on a Saturday in September and usually ending on the first Sunday in October (www.oktoberfest.de). It's held at the Theresienwiese fairground south of the main train station, in a meadow known as the "Wies'n" (VEE-zen), where huge tents seat nearly 120,000 beer drinkers. The festivities kick off with an opening parade and then, for the next two weeks, it's a frenzy of drinking, dancing, music, and

food. Total strangers stroll arm-in-arm down rows of picnic tables amid a carnival of beer, pretzels, and wurst, drawing visitors from all over the globe. A million gallons of beer later, they roast the last ox.

If you'll be here during the festivities, it's best to reserve a room early. During the fair, the city functions even better than normal, but is admittedly more expensive and crowded. It's a good time to sightsee, even if beer-hall rowdiness isn't your cup of tea.

The enormous beer tents are often full, especially on weekends—if possible, avoid going on a Friday or Saturday night. For some cultural background, consider hiring a local guide or going with a group (Radius Tours, for example, offers a €140 tour that includes two beers, half a chicken, and guaranteed seating, Sun-Fri at 10:00, none on Sat, reserve ahead, www.radiustours.com; Size Matters Beer Tour runs options for €129-209 that include breakfast, lunch, four beers, and reserved seating, www.sizemattersbeertour.de).

In the city center, the humble **Beer and Oktoberfest Museum** (Bier- und Okto-berfestmuseum) offers a low-tech and underwhelming take on beer history (€4, Tue-Sat 13:00-18:00, closed Sun-Mon, Sterneckerstrasse 2, tel. 089/2423-1607, www.bier-und-oktoberfestmuseum.de).

Rick's Tip: *Along with Oktoberfest, the Theresienwiese fairground also hosts a* **Spring Festival** *(Frühlingsfest, two weeks in late April-early May, www.fruehlingsfest-muenchen.de) and* **Tollwood,** *an artsy, multicultural event held twice a year—once in summer (late June-July) and in winter (alternative Christmas market, late Nov-Dec, www.tollwood.de).*

Shopping

While the whole city is great for shopping, the most glamorous area is around Marienplatz. It's fun to window shop, even if you have no plans to buy. Stroll from Marienplatz down the pedestrianized Weinstrasse (to the left as you face the New Town Hall). Look for **Fünf Höfe** on your left, a delightful indoor/outdoor mall

filled with Germany's top shops (Mon-Fri 10:00-19:00, Sat until 18:00, closed Sun).

Bavarian Souvenirs: Servus Heimat's amusing shops are a good source for unusual gifts (City Museum store, between Munich City Museum and Stadt Café: daily 10:00-18:00, St.-Jakobs-Platz 1, tel. 089/2370-2380; also at Im Tal 20—between Marienplatz and the Isartor—and at Brunnstrasse 3—near Asam Church, Mon-Sat 10:00-19:00, closed Sun; www.servusheimat.com).

For that beer stein you promised your uncle, try the shops on the pedestrian zone by St. Michael's Church and the gift shops that surround the Hofbräuhaus.

Dirndls and Lederhosen: For fine-quality (and very expensive) traditional clothing (*Trachten*), head to the third floor of **Loden-Frey Verkaufshaus** (Mon-Sat 10:00-20:00, closed Sun, a block west of Marienplatz at Maffeistrasse 7, tel. 089/210-390, www.loden-frey.com). For less expensive (but still good quality) gear, visit **Angermaier Trachten**, near the Viktualienmarkt (Mon-Fri 10:00-19:00, Sat until 18:00, closed Sun; Rosental 10, tel. 089/2300-0199, www.trachten-angermaier.de).

Department Stores: Ludwig Beck, an upscale department store at Marienplatz, has been a local institution since 1861 (Mon-Sat 10:00-20:00, closed Sun). For more reasonable prices near Marienplatz,

try **C&A** (cheap yet respected; sells only clothing) and **Galeria Kaufhof** (midrange; sells everything).

Nightlife

Here are a few nightlife alternatives to the beer-and-oompah scene. Ballet and opera fans can check the schedule at the **Bayerisch Staatsoper,** centrally located next door to the Residenz. Book at least two months ahead—seats range from reasonable to very pricey (Max-Joseph-Platz 2, tel. 089/2185-1920, www.bayerische.staatsoper.de). The **Hotel Bayerischerhof**'s posh nightclub has major jazz acts plus pop, soul, and disco (Promenadeplatz 2, tel. 089/212-0994, www.bayerischerhof.de). For familiar Broadway-style musicals (usually in German), try the **Deutsches Theatre,** located near the train station (Schwanthalerstrasse 13, tel. 089/5523-4444, www.deutsches-theater.de).

SLEEPING

I've listed accommodations in two main neighborhoods: within a few blocks of the central train station (Hauptbahnhof), and in the old center, between Marienplatz and Sendlinger Tor.

Near the Train Station

Good-value hotels cluster in the multicultural area immediately south of the station. To some this is a colorful neighborhood, for others it feels seedy after dark, but it's sketchy only for those in search of trouble.

$$$$ Hotel Deutsches Theater, filled with brass and marble, has 27 well-worn, three-star rooms. The back rooms face the courtyard of a neighboring theater—when there's a show, there can be some noise (breakfast extra, elevator, Landwehrstrasse 18, tel. 089/545-8525, www.hoteldeutschestheater.de, info@hoteldeutschestheater.de).

$$$$ Hotel Uhland is a stately mansion that rents 29 rooms with modern bathrooms in a genteel residential neighborhood a slightly longer walk from the station than other places listed here (toward the Theresienwiese Oktoberfest grounds). It's been in the Hauzenberger and Reim families for 60 years (family rooms, some waterbeds, limited parking, Uhlandstrasse 1, tel. 089/543-350, www.hotel-uhland.de, info@hotel-uhland.de). From the station, take bus #58 (direction: Silberhornstrasse) to Georg-Hirth-Platz, or walk 15 minutes: Out the station's south exit, cross Bayerstrasse, take Paul-Heyse-Strasse three blocks to Georg-Hirth-Platz, then take a soft right on Uhlandstrasse.

$$$ Hotel Monaco is a delightful and welcoming little hideaway, tucked inside three floors of a giant, nondescript building two blocks from the station (breakfast extra, cash preferred, cheaper rooms with shared bath, family rooms, pay parking nearby, Schillerstrasse 9, entrance on Adolf-Kolping-Strasse, reception on fifth floor, tel. 089/545-9940, www.hotel-monaco.de, info@hotel-monaco.de).

$$$ Marc München—polished, modern, and with 80 rooms—is a good option if you need a little more luxury than the other listings here and are willing to pay the price. It's just a half-block from the station, and has a refined lobby and classy breakfast spread (RS%, air-con, pay parking, Senefelderstrasse 12, tel. 089/559-820, www.hotel-marc.de, info@hotel-marc.de).

$$ Hotel Belle Blue, three blocks from the station, has 30 brightly colored rooms and air-conditioning. Run by Irmgard, this hotel has been in the family for 90 years and offers a good value. The breakfast is tops, and several stylish apartments with kitchenettes are perfect for families (elevator, pay parking, Schillerstrasse 21, tel. 089/550-6260, www.hotel-belleblue.de, info@hotel-belleblue.com).

$$ Hotel Europäischer Hof, across the street from the station, is a huge, impersonal hotel with 150 decent rooms. During cool weather, when you can keep the windows shut, the street-facing rooms are an accept-able option. The quieter, courtyard-facing rooms are more expensive and a lesser value (RS%, includes breakfast when you book directly, cheaper rooms with shared bath, elevator, pay parking, Bayerstrasse 31, tel. 089/551-510, www.heh.de, info@heh.de).

$$ Hotel Royal is one of the best values in the neighborhood (if you can ignore the strip joints flanking the entry). While a bit institutional, it's plenty comfortable and clean. Most importantly, it's energetically run by Pasha and Christiane. Each of its 40 rooms is sharp and bright (RS%, family rooms, comfort rooms on the quiet side cost extra—worth it in summer when you'll want the window open, elevator, Schillerstrasse 11a, tel. 089/5998-8160, www.hotel-royal.de, info@hotel-royal.de).

$$ Hotel Cocoon Hauptbahnhof is part of a trendy chain but it's a good value. This location has a rustic countryside/alpine theme. Ride the elevator like a personal gondola up to one of their 103 rooms (breakfast extra, air-con, bike rental, pay parking, Mittererstrasse 9, tel. 089/5999-3905, www.hotel-cocoon.de, info@hotel-cocoon.de).

$ Litty's Hotel is a basic place offering 42 small rooms with little personality (breakfast extra, cheaper rooms with shared bath, elevator, pay parking, Landwehrstrasse 32c, tel. 089/5434-4211, www.littyshotel.de, info@littyshotel.de, Verena and Bernd Litty).

¢ The CVJM (YMCA), open to all ages, rents 87 beds in clean, slick, and simple rooms, each with its own bathroom. Doubles are head-to-head; triples are like doubles with a bunk over one of the beds (family rooms available, reserve at least 6 months ahead for Oktoberfest weekdays, a year ahead for Oktoberfest weekends; Landwehrstrasse 13, tel. 089/552-1410, www.cvjm-muenchen.org/hotel, hotel@cvjm-muenchen.org).

Hostels near the Station

The following hostels are casual and well-run, with friendly and creative manage-

GERMANY

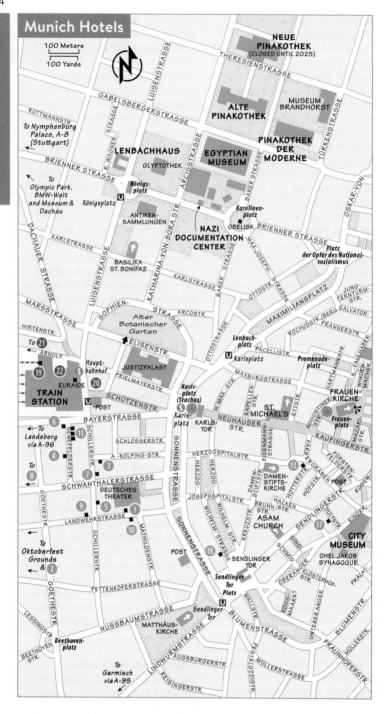

Munich Hotels

100 Meters
100 Yards

THERESIENSTRASSE

NEUE PINAKOTHEK
(CLOSED UNTIL 2025)

ALTE PINAKOTHEK

MUSEUM BRANDHORST

GABELSBERGERSTRASSE

LUISENSTRASSE

ROTTMANNSTR.
To Nymphenburg Palace, A-8 (Stuttgart)

LENBACHHAUS

GLYPTOTHEK

EGYPTIAN MUSEUM

PINAKOTHEK DER MODERNE

R. WAGNER STRASSE

BARER STRASSE

TÜRKENSTRASSE

OSKAR-VON-

BRIENNER STRASSE

To Olympic Park, BMW-Welt and Museum & Dachau

Königs-platz

Königsplatz

ARCISSTRASSE

Karolinen-platz
OBELISK

BRIENNER STRASSE

Platz der Opfer des National-sozialismus

ANTIKEN-SAMMLUNGEN

NAZI DOCUMENTATION CENTER

KATHARINA-VON-BORA-STR.

BAKER STRASSE

MAX-JOSEPH-STRASSE

DACHAUER STRASSE

KARLSTRASSE

LUISENSTRASSE

BASILIKA ST. BONIFAZ

KARLSTRASSE

OTTOSTRASSE

MAXIMILIANSPLATZ

JUNG-FERNTURM-STR.

MARSSTRASSE

SOPHIEN-STRASSE

ARCOSTR.

MAXIMILIANSPLATZ

RÖCHUSSTR. BERG SALVATOR-

PRANNERSTR.

HIRTENSTR.

Alter Botanischer Garten

ELISENSTR.

OTTOSTRASSE

Lenbach-platz

PACELLISTR.

Promenade-platz

K.-FAULHABER-

To 21

ARNULF.

Haupt-bahnhof

JUSTIZPALAST

Karlsplatz

Karls-platz (Stachus)

MAXBURGSTRASSE

HARTMANNSTR.

WINDEN-MACHER

19 22
EURAIDE
TRAIN STATION 20

S

PRIELMAYERSTR.

SCHÜTZENSTR.

POST

Karls-platz

KARLS-TOR

NEUHAUSER-STR.

ST. MICHAEL'S

FRAUEN-KIRCHE

AUGUSTINER-STR.

EISENMANN-STRASSE

ETTSTR.

Frauen-platz

BAYERSTRASSE

6

SCHILLERSTR.

SENEFELDERSTR.

11

SCHLOSSERSTR.

SONNENSTRASSE

HERZOGSPITALSTR.

HERZOG-

DAMEN-STIFTSTR.

FRAUEN-KIRCHE

ROTTERGRABEN

HOFSTR.

MAZARI-STR.

KAUFINGERSTR.

FÜRSTEN-FELDERSTR.

POST

To Landsberg via A-96

4

A.-KOLPING-STR.

3

7

13

ROGEN-

SCHWANTHALERSTRASSE

DEUTSCHES THEATER

JOSEPHSPITALSTR.

HACKEN-STR.

BRUNN-STR.

DUTSTR.

SENDLINGERSTR.

17

To 8

9 5 1

LANDWEHRSTRASSE

10

MATHILDENSTR.

KREUZSTR.

WILHELM-STR.

ASAM CHURCH

SINGL-

SCHMID-

CITY MUSEUM

GOETHESTR.

SCHILLERSTR.

POST

18

SENDLINGER TOR

OHEL JAKOB SYNAGOGUE

OBERANGER

KLOSTERHOF-

PRÄLAT-

To Oktoberfest Grounds & 2

PETTENKOFERSTRASSE

Sendlinger Tor Platz

WALLSTR.

ROSS-MARKT

UNTERER ANGER

BLUMENSTRASSE

NUSSBAUMSTRASSE

Sendlinger Tor

BLUMENSTRASSE

FRAUNHOFERSTR.

LESSINGSTR.

MATTHÄUS-KIRCHE

LINDWURMSTRASSE

AUGSBURGERSTR.

PESTALOZZISTR.

MÜLLERSTR.

Beethoven-platz

BEETHOVEN-STR.

To Garmisch via A-95

NUSSBAUMSTRASSE

REISINGERSTR.

GOETHESTR.

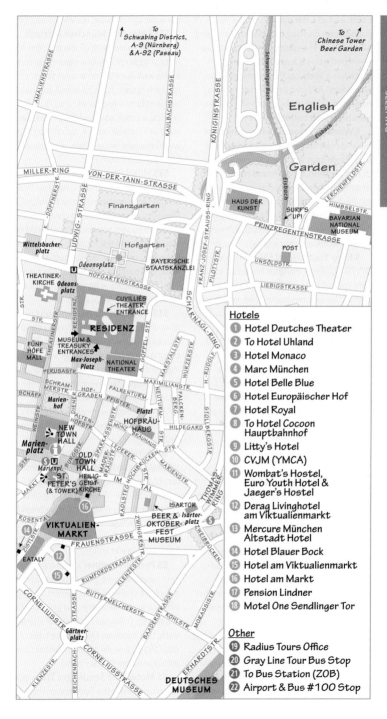

Hotels

1. Hotel Deutches Theater
2. To Hotel Uhland
3. Hotel Monaco
4. Marc München
5. Hotel Belle Blue
6. Hotel Europäischer Hof
7. Hotel Royal
8. To Hotel Cocoon Hauptbahnhof
9. Litty's Hotel
10. CVJM (YMCA)
11. Wombat's Hostel, Euro Youth Hotel & Jaeger's Hostel
12. Derag Livinghotel am Viktualienmarkt
13. Mercure München Altstadt Hotel
14. Hotel Blauer Bock
15. Hotel am Viktualienmarkt
16. Hotel am Markt
17. Pension Lindner
18. Motel One Sendlinger Tor

Other

19. Radius Tours Office
20. Gray Line Tour Bus Stop
21. To Bus Station (ZOB)
22. Airport & Bus #100 Stop

ment, and all cater expertly to the needs of young beer-drinking backpackers enjoying Munich on a shoestring. With 900 cheap dorm beds, this is a spirited street. Each place has a lively bar that rages until the wee hours. All have 24-hour receptions, none has a kitchen, but each offers a reasonably priced buffet breakfast.

¢ **Wombat's Hostel,** perhaps the most hip and colorful, rents cheap doubles and dorm beds, plus some private rooms. The dorms are fresh, modern, and contain bathrooms. The bright rooms facing the winter garden have huge windows (family room available, Senefelderstrasse 1, tel. 089/5998-9180, www.wombats-hostels.com/munich, office@wombats-munich.de).

¢ **Euro Youth Hotel** fills a rare pre-WWII building (includes breakfast for private rooms, bar with live music and game nights, Senefelderstrasse 5, tel. 089/5990-8811, www.euro-youth-hotel.de, info@euro-youth-hotel.de).

¢ **Jaeger's Hostel** has all the fun and efficiency you'd hope for in a hostel—plus the only air-conditioning on the street. Popular with backpackers and business travelers, this is the quietest hostel of the group (family rooms available, Senefelderstrasse 3, tel. 089/555-281, www.jaegershostel.de, office@jaegershostel.de).

In the Old Center

A few good deals remain in the area south of Marienplatz, going toward the Sendlinger Tor. This neighborhood feels more genteel and is convenient for sightseeing.

$$$$ **Derag Livinghotel am Viktualienmarkt** rents 83 rooms in two connected buildings. One is elegant and tech-savvy, with great views of the Viktualienmarkt. The other has stylish rooms with kitchenettes but no views. Both buildings share the same homey breakfast room (breakfast extra, complimentary minibar, air-con, elevator, laundry facilities, pay parking, entrance facing the market on Frauenstrasse 4, tel. 089/885-6560,

www.deraghotels.de, res.vik@derag.de).

$$$$ **Mercure München Altstadt Hotel** is reliable, with all the modern comforts in its 80 pricey business-class rooms, and is well-located on a quiet street close to Marienplatz. It's a bit bland, but has fine service (family rooms, air-con, laundry service, a block south of the pedestrian zone at Hotterstrasse 4, tel. 089/232-590, www.mercure-muenchen-altstadt.de, h3709@accor.com).

$$$ **Hotel Blauer Bock,** formerly a dormitory for Benedictine monks, has been on the same corner near the Munich City Museum since 1841. Its 69 contemporary Bavarian rooms are classy, the breakfast is top-notch, and the location is great (family rooms, elevator, guest iPads at front desk, pay parking, Sebastiansplatz 9, tel. 089/231-780, www.hotelblauerbock.de, info@hotelblauerbock.de).

$$$ **Hotel am Viktualienmarkt** rents 26 rooms on a small side street a couple of blocks from the Viktualienmarkt. Everything is small but well-designed—including the elevator and three good-value, tiny single rooms (family rooms, apartment, Utzschneiderstrasse 14, tel. 089/231-1090, www.hotel-am-viktualienmarkt.de, reservierung@hotel-am-viktualienmarkt.de).

$$ **Hotel am Markt,** right next to the Viktualienmarkt, has 32 simple rooms with lots of wainscoting. Light sleepers may need earplugs—the neighboring church's bells ring hourly (skip expensive breakfast, elevator, Heiliggeiststrasse 6, tel. 089/225-014, www.hotel-am-markt.eu, service@hotel-am-markt.eu).

$$ **Pension Lindner** is clean and quiet, with nine pleasant, pastel-bouquet rooms off a bare stairway. Frau Marion Sinzinger offers a warm welcome and good buffet breakfasts (cheaper rooms with shared bath, tiny elevator, Dultstrasse 1, tel. 089/263-413, www.pension-lindner.com, info@pension-lindner.com).

$$ **Motel One Sendlinger Tor,** around the corner from the Sendlinger Tor tram

and U-Bahn stop, is a posh-feeling, 241-room, inexpensive chain hotel in a fine location. The stylish, modern rooms are fairly tight and lack some basic amenities (phones, minibars), but otherwise are a good value—and tend to sell out a few weeks in advance. Streetside rooms on upper floors have great views for a little extra. When booking on their website, make sure to choose the Sendlinger Tor location (breakfast extra, air-con, guest iPad at front desk, pay parking, Herzog-Wilhelm-Strasse 28, tel. 089/5177-7250, www.motel-one.com, muenchen-sendlingertor@motel-one.com).

EATING

Munich's cuisine is traditionally seasoned with beer. In beer halls, beer gardens, or at the Viktualienmarkt, try the most typical meal in town: *Weisswurst* (white-colored veal sausage—peel off the skin before eating, often available only until noon) with *süsser Senf* (sweet mustard), a salty *Brezel* (pretzel), and *Weissbier* ("white" wheat beer). Another traditional favorite is *Obatzter,* a mix of soft cheeses, butter, paprika, and often garlic or onions that's spread on bread. *Brotzeit,* literally "bread time," gets you a wooden platter of cold cuts, cheese, and pickles and is a good option for a light dinner.

Rick's Tip: *By law,* **any place serving beer** *must admit the public (whether or not they're customers)* to **use the WCs.**

Beer Halls and Gardens

Nothing beats the Hofbräuhaus (the only beer hall in town where you'll find oompah music) for those in search of the boisterous, clichéd image of the beer hall. Locals prefer the innumerable beer gardens. On a warm day, when you're looking for the authentic outdoor beer-garden experience, your best options are the Augustiner (near the train station), the small beer garden at the Viktualienmarkt (near Marienplatz), or the sea of tables in the English Garden (near the Chinese Tower).

Near Marienplatz
$$ The **Hofbräuhaus** (HOAF-broy-

GERMANY

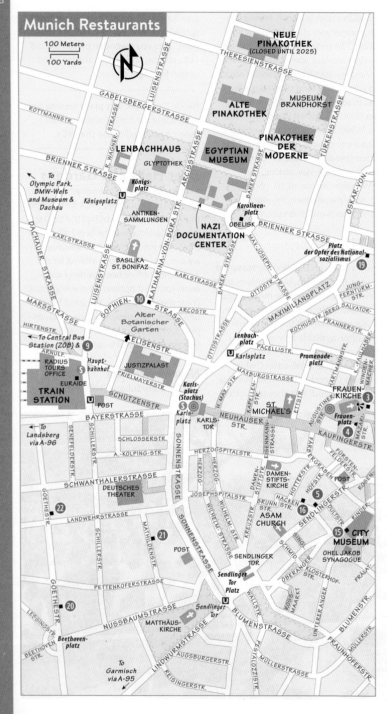

Munich Restaurants

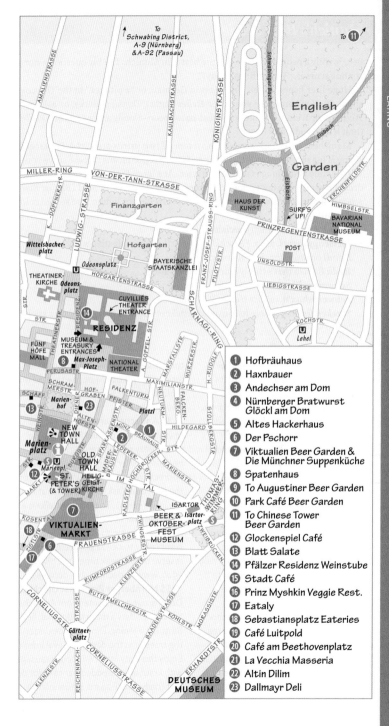

1 Hofbräuhaus
2 Haxnbauer
3 Andechser am Dom
4 Nürnberger Bratwurst Glöckl am Dom
5 Altes Hackerhaus
6 Der Pschorr
7 Viktualien Beer Garden & Die Münchner Suppenküche
8 Spatenhaus
9 To Augustiner Beer Garden
10 Park Café Beer Garden
11 To Chinese Tower Beer Garden
12 Glockenspiel Café
13 Blatt Salate
14 Pfälzer Residenz Weinstube
15 Stadt Café
16 Prinz Myshkin Veggie Rest.
17 Eataly
18 Sebastiansplatz Eateries
19 Café Luitpold
20 Café am Beethovenplatz
21 La Vecchia Masseria
22 Altin Dilim
23 Dallmayr Deli

Munich's Beer Scene

Beer is truly a people's drink—and the best is in Munich. The big question among connoisseurs is, "Which brew today?"

Huge liter beers (called *eine Mass* in German, or "a pitcher" in the US) cost about €8. You can order your beer *Helles* (light), *Dunkles* (dark), or ask for a *Weissbier* or *Weizen* ("white" or wheat-based beer—cloudy and sweet) or a *Radler* (half lemon soda, half beer).

Many beer halls have a cafeteria system. If two prices are listed, *Selbstbedienung* is for self-service (*Bitte bedienen Sie sich selbst* means "please serve yourself"), while *Bedienung* is for table service. At a large *Biergarten*, assemble your dream feast by visiting various counters, marked by type of food (*Bier* or *Bierschänke* for beer, *Bratwürste* for sausages, *Brotzeiten* for lighter fare served cold, and so on).

Look for these Munich specialties:

Fleischpfanzerl, a.k.a. *Fleischklösse* or *Frikadellen:* Meatballs

Hendl or *Brathähnchen:* Roasted chicken

Radi: Radish that's thinly spiral-cut and salted

Schweinrollbraten: Pork belly

Schweinshax'n, or just **Hax'n:** Pork knuckle

Steckerlfisch: A whole fish, usually mackerel, herbed and grilled on a stick

---

howz) is the world's most famous beer hall. While it's grotesquely touristy, it's a Munich must. You can drop by anytime for a large or light meal, or just for a drink. Except for *Weissbier,* the Hofbräuhaus sells beer only by the *Mass* (one-liter mug) after 18:00—and they claim to sell 10,000 of these liters every day. Choose from four zones: the rowdy main hall on the ground floor, a quieter courtyard under the stars, a dainty restaurant with mellow music the first floor up, or the giant festival hall under a big barrel vault on the top floor. Live oompah music plays at lunch and dinner in the main hall/restaurant (daily 9:00-23:30, 5-minute walk from Marienplatz at Platzl 9, tel. 089/2901-3610).

$$$ Haxnbauer, stark and old-school, is a hit with German tourists for one reason: the best pork knuckle in town (half *Schweinshaxe*—€19, slightly less if you just get some slices). It's clearly the place for what looks like a pork knee—notice

the rotisserie window luring customers inside (daily 11:00-24:00, two blocks from Hofbräuhaus at Sparkassenstrasse 6, tel. 089/216-6540).

$$ Andechser am Dom sits at the rear of the twin-domed Frauenkirche on a breezy square, serving Andechs beer brewed by monks and great food to appreciative regulars. Münchners favor the dark beer (ask for *dunkles*), but I love the light *(helles)*. The *Gourmetteller* is a great sampler of their specialties, but you can't go wrong with *Rostbratwurst* with kraut (daily 10:00-24:00, Weinstrasse 7a, reserve during peak times, tel. 089/2429-2920, www.andechser-am-dom.de).

$$ Nürnberger Bratwurst Glöckl am Dom, around the corner from Andechser am Dom, offers a more traditional, fiercely Bavarian evening. Dine outside under the trees or in the dark, medieval interior. Enjoy the tasty little *Nürnberger* sausages with kraut and shredded pancake for dessert (daily 10:00-24:00, Frauenplatz 9, tel.

089/291-9450).

$$$ Altes Hackerhaus is popular for its traditional *Bayerisch* (Bavarian) fare served with a slightly fancier feel in one of the oldest buildings in town. It offers a small courtyard and a fun forest of characteristic nooks. Naturally, Hacker-Pschorr beer is popular, especially the *Weisse* ("small appetite" menu available, daily 10:30-24:00, Sendlinger Strasse 14, tel. 089/260-5026).

$$$ Der Pschorr, an upscale beer hall occupying a former slaughterhouse, has a terrace overlooking the Viktualienmarkt and serves what many consider Munich's finest beer. With organic "slow food" including vegan and vegetarian options, this place mixes modern concepts with traditional dishes. The sound of the hammer tapping wooden kegs lets patrons know their beer is good and fresh (seasonal specials, daily 10:00-24:00, Viktualienmarkt 15, at end of Schrannenhalle, tel. 089/442-383-940).

$ Viktualien Beer Garden, at the center of the Viktualienmarkt, has about the best budget eating in town. It's just steps from Marienplatz (daily 10:00-22:00 in good weather). There's table service wherever you see a tablecloth; to picnic, choose a table without one—but you must buy a drink from the counter. Countless stalls surround the beer garden and sell wurst, sandwiches, produce, and more.

$$$ Spatenhaus is the opera-goers' classy beer hall, serving elegant food in a rustic, traditional setting since 1896—maybe it's not even right to call it a "beer hall." You can also eat outside, on the square facing the opera and palace. It's pricey, but you won't find better quality Bavarian cuisine. The upstairs restaurant is more formal—reservations recommended (daily 9:30-23:00, on Max-Joseph-Platz opposite opera, Residenzstrasse 12, tel. 089/290-7060, www.spatenhaus.de).

Near the Train Station

$$ Augustiner Beer Garden, a true under-the-leaves beer garden packed with Münchners, is a delight. In fact, most Münchners consider Augustiner the best beer garden in town—which may be why it has 6,000 seats. There's no music, it's away from the tourist hordes, and it serves up great beer, good traditional food, huge portions, reasonable prices, and perfect conviviality. The outdoor self-service (at the opposite end from the entrance) is best on a nice summer evening. Parents with kids can sit at tables adjoining a sizable playground. There's also indoor and outdoor seating at a more expensive **$$$** restaurant with table service by the entrance (daily 11:30-24:00, Arnulfstrasse 52, 3 looooong blocks from station going away from the center—or take tram #16/#17 one stop to Hopfenstrasse, tel. 089/594-393).

$$ Park Café Beer Garden is a nice hideaway in good weather, tucked inside the Alter Botanischer Garden, just north of the train station. Order Bavarian food from self-service counters (don't forget to reclaim your deposit at the counter for your plate and mug). The indoor **$$$** restaurant is a modern and cozy pricier option, and often features DJs or live music in the late evening (daily 11:00-24:00, beer garden open until 19:00 in nice weather, Sophienstrasse 7, tel. 089/5161-7980).

In the English Garden

$$ The Chinese Tower beer garden
(*Chinesischer Turm Biergarten*), deep in
the English Garden, is famed for outdoor
ambience and a cheap meal; it's a great
place for a balmy, relaxed evening. You're
welcome to B.Y.O. food and grab a table,
or buy from the cafeteria-style food stalls.
Don't bother to phone ahead—they have
6,000 seats. This is a fine opportunity to
try a *Steckerlfisch,* sold at a separate kiosk.
Take your blue token and your beer mug
around back to redeem your refund (daily,
long hours in good weather, usually live
music, playground, tel. 089/383-8730; take
tram #18 from main train station or Send-
linger Tor to Tivolistrasse, or U-3 or U-6
to Giselastrasse and then bus #54 or #154
two stops).

Restaurants

Man does not live by beer alone. Well,
maybe some do. But for the rest of us, I
recommend the following alternatives.

On and near Marienplatz

$$$ Glockenspiel Café is good for a cof-
fee or a meal with a bird's-eye view down
on the Marienplatz action—I'd come
for the view more than the Italian food.
Regardless of the weather, I grab a seat
overlooking Marienplatz—but after 18:00,
you must order dinner for view seating
(Mon-Sat 9:00-24:00, Sun 10:00-19:00,
ride elevator from Rosenstrasse entrance,
opposite glockenspiel at Marienplatz 28,
tel. 089/264-256).

   $$ Blatt Salate is a self-serve salad bar
on a side street between the Frauenkirche
and the New Town Hall; it's a great little
hideaway for a healthy, quick lunch (veg-
etarian and meat salads and soups, Mon-
Sat 11:00-19:00, closed Sun, Schäffler-
strasse 7, tel. 089/2102-0281).

   $$ Pfälzer Residenz Weinstube,
a very traditional German dining hall
actually in the Residenz complex, is
dedicated to food and wine from the
Rhineland (Palatine)—which was ruled

Chinese Tower beer garden

by the Wittelsbach family. Serving small
wine-friendly dishes and a big variety of
German wines by the tiny glass, it's ideal
for wine lovers needing a break from beer
(daily 10:30-24:00, Residenzstrasse 1, tel.
089/225-628).

Around the Viktualienmarkt

$ Die Münchner Suppenküche ("Munich
Soup Kitchen"), a soup tent at the Viktualienmarkt, is a fine place for a small,
cozy sit-down lunch at picnic tables under
a closed-in awning. The red sign lists
the soups of the day—I go for the gou-
lash or Bavarian potato soup (Mon-Sat
10:00-18:00, closed Sun, near corner of
Reichenbachstrasse and Frauenstrasse,
tel. 089/260-9599).

   $$ Stadt Café is a lively café serving
a selection of sandwiches, with a nice
wine list and cakes. This informal, no-frills
restaurant draws newspaper readers,
stroller moms, and locals meeting for a
drink after work. Dine in the quiet cobbled
courtyard, inside, or outside facing the
new synagogue (open daily 10:00-24:00,
in same building as Munich City Museum,

St.-Jakobs-Platz 1, tel. 089/266-949).

$$$ Prinz Myshkin Vegetarian Restaurant is an upscale vegetarian eatery in the old center. Don't miss the enticing appetizer selection on display as you enter (they do a fine €14 mixed-appetizer plate). They also have vegetarian sushi, pastas, Indian dishes, and their own baker, so they're proud of their sweets (lunch specials, seasonal menu, daily 11:00-late, Hackenstrasse 2, tel. 089/265-596).

$$ Eataly at Schrannenhalle, the former grain exchange just off Viktualienmarkt, is a sparkling, pricey food court full of Italian taste treats. It's a festival of food fun with great seating inside the old market hall and outside overlooking the square (café open Mon-Sat 8:00-20:00, Sun 10:00-19:00; restaurants open Mon-Sat 11:30-22:30, Sun until 21:30, Viktualienmarkt 15, tel. 089/248-817-711).

Eateries on Sebastiansplatz: Looking for a no-schnitzel-or-dumplings alternative? Sebastiansplatz is a long, pedestrianized square across from Eataly, between the Viktualienmarkt and the synagogue, lined with **$$ bistros** handy for a healthy and quick lunch. Options range from French to Italian to Asian to salads. You can eat out on the busy cobbled square or inside.

Near Odeonsplatz

$$ Café Luitpold is where Munich's high society comes to sip its coffee and nibble on exquisite cakes. The café is proudly home to the original *Luitpoldtorte* (sponge cake with layers of marzipan and buttercream, covered in dark chocolate). I prefer their strawberry-cream cake (Tue-Sat 8:00-23:00, Sun-Mon 9:00-19:00, Brienner Strasse 11, tel. 089/242-8750).

Near the Train Station

$$$ Café am Beethovenplatz feels like an old Vienna café with its inviting, woody interior and charming garden. While just a 10-minute walk from the station, it's in a leafy and quiet residential neighborhood.

They serve a mix of Italian, Bavarian, and vegetarian fare, offer cheap lunch specials and homemade cakes, and have live music almost nightly (daily 9:00-24:00, at Mariandl Hotel, Goethestrasse 51, tel. 089/552-9100).

$$$ La Vecchia Masseria, between Sendlinger Tor and the train station hotels, serves Italian food in a cozy Tuscan farmhouse-style interior, or outside in a beautiful flowery courtyard. Pasta, pizzas, and seasonal, more expensive main courses are served. Can't decide which pasta to get? Ask for a *bis,* half-portions of two pastas (daily 11:30-23:30, garden dining until 21:30, reservations smart, Mathildenstrasse 3, tel. 089/550-9090, www.lavecchiamasseria.de).

$$ Altin Dilim, a cafeteria-style Turkish restaurant, is a standout among the many hole-in-the-wall Middle Eastern places in the ethnic area near the station. A handy pictorial menu helps you order (cheap *döner kebabs,* daily 6:00-24:00, Goethestrasse 17, tel. 089/9734-0869).

Picnics

For a truly elegant (and pricey) picnic, **Dallmayr's** is the place to shop. The crown in their emblem reflects that even the royal family assembled its picnics at this historic delicatessen. Put together a royal spread to munch in the nearby Hofgarten or visit the classy café that serves light meals on the first floor (Mon-Sat 9:30-19:00, closed Sun, behind New Town Hall, Dienerstrasse 14, tel. 089/213-5110).

Budget Picnic: To save money, buy at a **supermarket** (generally open Mon-Sat until 20:00, closed Sun). The ones in the basements of department stores are on the upscale side: **Galeria Kaufhof** stores at Marienplatz and Karlsplatz, or **Karstadt** across from the train station. Cheaper stores include the **REWE** in the basement at Fünf Höfe (entrance is in Viscardihof), **Lidl** at Schwanthalerstrasse 31 (near train-station hotels), or **Yorma's** (several at the train station).

TRANSPORTATION

Getting Around Munich

Much of Munich is walkable. But given that the city is laced by many trams, buses, and subways, it's worth learning the system and considering getting a day pass. Public transit also makes it easy to access sights outside the historic core, such as Dachau or Nymphenburg Palace. Taxis are honest and professional, but expensive (about €12 between the Hauptbahnhof and Marienplatz) and generally unnecessary.

By Public Transit

Munich's transit system uses the same ticket for its subway/trains, buses, and trams. There are two types of trains: The U-Bahn, like a subway, and the S-Bahn, light rail that stops only at major stations. Transit lines are numbered (for example, S-3 or U-5). U-Bahn lines mainly run north-south, while S-Bahn lines are generally east-west. There are seven concentric transit zones, but you'll spend most of your time in Zone M (central Munich).

Information: Pick up a transit map at the TI or station, use the journey planner at www.mvv-muenchen.de, or download the MVV app. You can also head straight to an **MVG customer service center** underground at the train station (open daily) and at Marienplatz (closed Sun; kiosks outside open long hours daily; tel. 0800-344-226-600, www.mvg.de.

TICKET OPTIONS

Transit tickets are sold at booths in the subway and at any ticket machine that has an MVG (blue machines) or DB (red machines) logo. Though operated by different companies, the machines work much the same way (and accept coins, bills, and credit cards).

A **regular ticket** (*Einzelfahrkarte*) costs €3.30 and is good for three hours in one direction, including changes and stops.

For short rides (four stops max, only two of which can be on the subway lines), buy the €1.50 **short-stretch ticket** (*Kurzstrecke*), good for one ride. The €7.80 **day pass** (*Single-Tageskarte*) for Zone M is a great deal for a single traveler.

All-day small-group passes (*Partner-Tageskarte*) are an even better deal—they cover all public transportation for up to five adults (or up to two adults and six kids). A *Partner-Tageskarte* for Zone M costs €12.80. The M-1 version, which includes Dachau, costs €16.10; and the **airport-city day ticket** (*Flughafen*) costs €24.30. These partner tickets are a real steal. The only catch is that you've got to stay together.

USING THE SYSTEM

To find the right platform, look for the name of the last station in the direction (*Richtung*) you want to travel. For example, *Richtung: Marienplatz* means that that particular subway, bus, or tram is traveling in the direction of Marienplatz. Know where you're going relative to Marienplatz, the Hauptbahnhof, and Ostbahnhof, as these are often referred to as end points.

You must stamp tickets with the date and time prior to using them (for an all-day or multiday pass, stamp it only the first time you use it; some tickets bought at a machine come prestamped). For the subway, punch your ticket in the blue machine *before* going down to the platform. For buses and trams, stamp your ticket once on board. Plainclothes ticket checkers enforce this honor system, rewarding freeloaders with stiff €60 fines.

USEFUL TRANSIT LINES

Several subway lines, trams, and buses are especially convenient for tourists. All the main S-Bahn lines (S-1 through S-8) run east-west along the main tourist axis between the Hauptbahnhof, Marienplatz, and the Ostbahnhof. For travel within the city center, just find the platform for lines S-1 through S-8. One track (*Gleis*)

Arriving and Departing
By Plane
Munich's airport is an easy 40-minute ride on the S-1 or S-8 **subway** (both run every 20 minutes from 4:00 to after midnight). The S-8 is a bit quicker and easier; the S-1 line has two branches and some trains split—if you ride the S-1 to the airport, be certain your train is going to the *Flughafen* (airport). A single **airport ticket** costs €11.20, but the all-day pass (€12.80) is worth getting if you'll be making even one more public transport trip that day. The trip is free with a validated and dated rail pass.

The **Lufthansa airport bus** links the airport with the main train station (€10.50, €17 round-trip, 4/hour, 45 minutes, buses depart airport 6:30-22:30, depart train station 5:15-20:00, buy tickets on bus; from inside the station, exit near track 26 and look for yellow *Airport Bus* signs; www.airportbus-muenchen.de). Avoid taking a **taxi** from the airport—it's a long, expensive drive (roughly €65). Airport info: Tel. 089/97500, www.munich-airport.de.

will be headed east to the Ostbahnhof, the other west to the Hauptbahnhof. Hop on any train going your direction. The U-3 goes to the BMW sights, and the S-2 goes to Dachau. Bus #100 is useful for getting to the English Garden (from the train station) and to the Museum Quarter (from Odeonsplatz). Tram #17 goes to Nymphenburg Palace (from the train station and the Sendlinger Tor).

By Bike
Level, compact, and with plenty of bike paths, Munich feels made for those on two wheels. You can take your bike on the subway, but not during rush hour (Mon-Fri 6:00-9:00 & 16:00-18:00) and only if you buy a €2.60 bike day pass.

Rick's Tip: The **strip of pathway closest to the street is usually reserved for bikes.** *Signs painted on the sidewalk or blue-and-white street signs show which part of the sidewalk is designated for pedestrians and which is for cyclists.*

You can **rent bikes** quickly and easily from **Radius Tours** in the train station in front of track 32 (RS%—ask, daily 8:30-19:00, May-Aug until 20:00, closed Nov-March, tel. 089/543-487-7730, www.radiustours.com).

By Train
For quick help at the main train station (München Hauptbahnhof), stop by the service counter in front of track 18. For better English and more patience, drop by the EurAide desk in the *Reisezentrum* (see page 695). Train info: www.bahn.com.

A complete renovation of Munich's main train station is in progress as the city builds a new S-Bahn tunnel (the locations of some services may change as construction progresses).

The Hauptbahnhof is a hive of activity, with a vast **shopping mall** stretching for blocks underground (open daily). Clean, high-tech, pay **WCs** are downstairs near tracks 11 and 26. Check out the bright and modern **food court** or the Dean & David kiosk opposite track 14. For prepared meals to bring on board, I shop at **Yorma's** (four branches: by track 26, by track 32, at street level next to the TI, and in Bahnhofplatz, the underground passage-

GERMANY

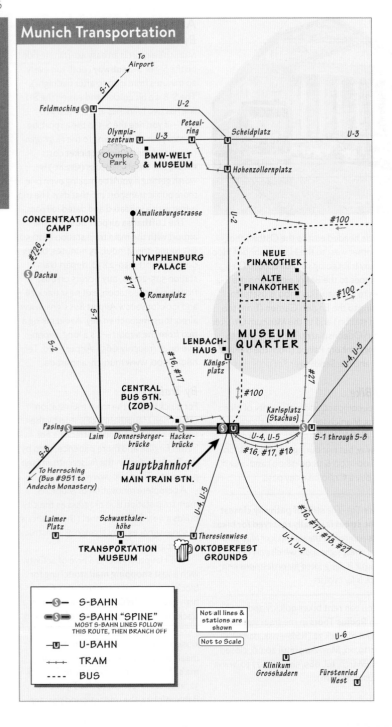

Munich Transportation

To Airport

S-1

Feldmoching Ⓢ Ⓤ

U-2

Olympia-zentrum Ⓤ   U-3   Peteul-ring Ⓤ   Scheidplatz Ⓤ   U-3

Olympic Park

■ BMW-WELT & MUSEUM

Hohenzollernplatz Ⓤ

CONCENTRATION CAMP

#726

Ⓢ Dachau

S-1

S-2

● Amalienburgstrasse

NYMPHENBURG PALACE

#17

● Romanplatz

#16, #17

#100

NEUE PINAKOTHEK ■

U-2

ALTE PINAKOTHEK ■

#100

LENBACH-HAUS ■

MUSEUM QUARTER

Königs-platz

U-4, U-5

#27

CENTRAL BUS STN. (ZOB) ■

↕ #100

Karlsplatz (Stachus)

Pasing Ⓢ   Laim Ⓢ   Donnersberger-brücke Ⓢ   Hacker-brücke Ⓢ   Ⓢ Ⓤ   Ⓤ   S-1 through S-8

S-8   U-4, U-5   #16, #17, #18

To Herrsching (Bus #951 to Andechs Monastery)

Hauptbahnhof MAIN TRAIN STN.

Laimer Platz Ⓤ   Schwanthaler-höhe Ⓤ   Ⓤ Theresienwiese   U-4, U-5

TRANSPORTATION MUSEUM   🍺 OKTOBERFEST GROUNDS

U-1, U-2

#16, #17, #18, #27

U-6

—Ⓢ—   S-BAHN

═Ⓢ═   S-BAHN "SPINE"
MOST S-BAHN LINES FOLLOW THIS ROUTE, THEN BRANCH OFF

—Ⓤ—   U-BAHN

+++   TRAM

----   BUS

Not all lines & stations are shown

Not to Scale

Klinikum Grosshadern Ⓤ   Fürstenried West Ⓤ

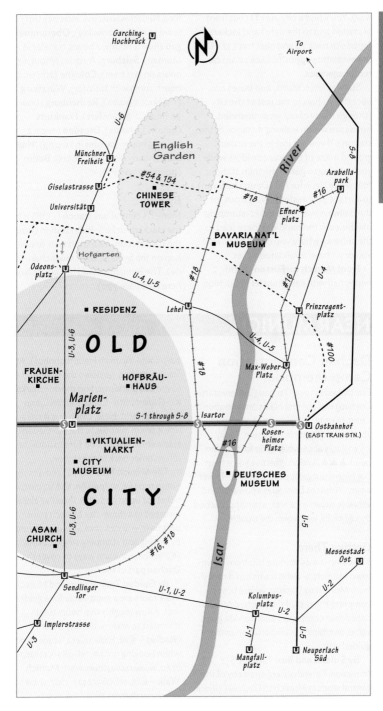

way). You'll find a city-run **TI** (out front of station and to the right) and **lockers** (opposite track 26 and near track 17). Up the escalators opposite track 22 are **car-rental agencies.**

Subway lines, trams, and buses connect the station to the rest of the city (though many of my recommended hotels are within walking distance of the station). If you get lost in the underground maze of subway corridors while you're trying to get to the train station, follow the signs for *DB* (Deutsche Bahn) to surface successfully. Watch out for the hallways with blue ticket-stamping machines in the middle—these lead to the subway, where you could be fined if you don't have a validated ticket.

From Munich to: Füssen (hourly, 2 hours, half with easy transfer in Buchloe; for a Neuschwanstein Castle day trip, leave as early as possible), **Oberammergau** (nearly hourly, 2 hours, transfer in Murnau), **Salzburg,** Austria (2/hour, 1.5 hours on fast train), **Cologne** (2/hour, 4.5 hours, some with transfer), **Würzburg** (1-2/hour, 2 hours), **Rothenburg** (hourly, 3.5 hours, 2-3 transfers), **Frankfurt** (hourly, 3.5 hours), **Dresden** (every 2 hours, 5 hours, transfer in Leipzig), **Hamburg** (hourly direct, 6.5 hours), **Berlin** (hourly, 4-5 hours).

By Bus

Munich's central bus station (ZOB) is by the Hackerbrücke S-Bahn station (from the train station, it's a short walk or one hop on the S-Bahn; www.muenchen-zob.de). The Romantic Road bus leaves from here (see page 790).

NEAR MUNICH

Dachau Concentration Camp Memorial

Established in 1933, Dachau (Gedenkstätte Dachau) was the first Nazi concentration camp. In its 12 dismal years of operation, about 40,000 people died here. Today, it's an easily accessible camp for travelers, rated ▲▲▲, and an effective voice from our recent but grisly past, pleading, "Never again." A visit to Dachau is a powerful and valuable experience and, when approached thoughtfully, well worth the trouble.

Getting There

The camp is a 45-minute trip from downtown Munich. S-Bahn trains run directly from Munich to Dachau, where buses complete the rest of the journey. Munich-based tour companies also provide good value, combining transportation and a guided visit.

By S-Bahn and Bus: Take the S-2 (direction: Petershausen) from any of the central stops in Munich to Dachau (3/hour, 20-minute trip from Hauptbahnhof). At Dachau station, go down the stairs and out to the bus platforms; find the one marked *KZ-Gedenkstätte-Concentration Camp Memorial Sight.* Here, catch bus #726 and ride it seven minutes to the KZ-Gedenkstätte stop (3/hour). Be sure to note the return times back to the station.

The Munich XXL day pass covers the entire trip (€8.90/person, €16.10/partner ticket for up to 5 adults). If you've already invested in a three-day Munich transport pass, you can save a couple of euros by buying and stamping single tickets (€2.90/person each way) to cover the Dachau part of the trip.

By Guided Tour: Radius and Munich Walk tours are a great value for a guided visit. Allow roughly five hours total. It's smart to reserve the day before (**Radius**—€28, RS%-select "student rate" when booking online; tel. 089/543-487-7740, www.radiustours.com; **Munich Walk**—€25, tel. 089/2423-1767, www.munichwalktours.de).

Powerful art at the Memorial

Orientation

Cost and Hours: Free, daily 9:00-17:00. Some areas of the camp may begin to close before 17:00. The museum discourages parents from bringing children under age 14.

The Town: The town of Dachau—quiet, tree-lined, and residential—is more pleasant than its unfortunate association with the camp on its outskirts, and it tries hard to encourage you to visit its old town and castle (www.dachau.de).

Visitors Center: Coming from the bus stop or parking lot, you'll first see the visitors center, outside the camp wall. It lacks exhibits, but does have a small cafeteria, a bookstore with English-language books, and a WC (more WCs inside the camp). At the information desk, pick up the English pamphlet, rent an audioguide (€4, cash only, leave ID; not essential), or sign up for a tour. Two different **guided walks** in English start from the visitors center (€3, daily at 11:00 and 13:00, 2.5 hours; limited to 30 people so show up early—especially in summer, 11:00 walk fills up first; call or visit website to confirm times, tel.

08131/669-970, www.kz-gedenkstaette-dachau.de).

● Self-Guided Tour

You enter, like the inmates did, through the infamous **iron gate** that held the taunting slogan *Arbeit macht frei* ("Work makes you free"). Inside are the four key experiences: the museum, the bunker behind the museum, the restored barracks, and a pensive walk across the huge but now-empty camp to the memorials and crematorium at the far end.

Museum: Enter the museum, housed in a former camp maintenance building. Immediately to the right, check show times for the museum's powerful 22-minute documentary film (usually shown in English at 10:00, 11:30, 12:30. 14:00, and 15:00). The museum is organized chronologically, everything is thoughtfully described in English, and touch-screens let you watch early newsreels.

Rooms 1-2 cover the founding of the camp and give an overview of the Nazi camp system. Some were concentra-

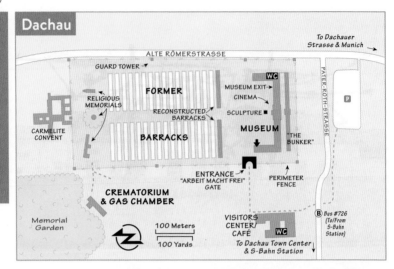

Dachau

tion camps (like Dachau), and others were extermination camps, built with the express purpose of executing people on a mass scale. Photos and posters chronicle the rise of Hitler in the 1920s.

Rooms 3-7 are devoted to the early years of the camp. Besides political activists, prisoners included homosexuals, Jehovah's Witnesses, Roma, and Jews. The camp was run by the SS, the organization charged with Germany's internal security. Dachau was a work camp, where inmates were expected to pay for their "crimes" with slave labor. The camp was strictly regimented: a wake-up call at 4:00, an 11-hour workday, roll call at 5:15 and 19:00, lights out at 21:00. The work was hard, whether quarrying or hauling loads or constructing the very buildings you see today. The rations were meager, rule-breakers were punished severely, and all manner of torture took place here.

Rooms 8-15 document the war years and their immediate aftermath. Once the war began, conditions at Dachau deteriorated. The original camp had been designed to hold just under 3,000 inmates. In 1937 and 1938, the camp was expanded, with barracks intended to hold 6,000 prisoners. With the war, the pris-

oner population swelled, and the Nazis found other purposes for the camp. It was less a concentration camp for German dissidents and more a dumping ground for foreigners, POWs, and even 2,000 Catholic priests. From Dachau, Jewish prisoners were sent east to the gas chambers. Inmates were used as slave labor for the German war machine—many were shipped to nearby camps to make armaments. Prisoners were used as human guinea pigs for war-related medical experiments of human tolerance for air pressure, hypothermia, and biological agents like malaria; the photos of these victims may be the most painful to view.

As the Allies closed in on both fronts, Dachau was bursting with more than 30,000 prisoners jammed into its 34 barracks. In the winter of 1944-1945, disease broke out and food ran short. With coal for the crematorium running low, those who died were buried in mass graves outside the camp site. The Allies arrived on April 29. After 12 years of existence, Dachau was finally liberated.

Bunker: This was a cellblock for prominent "special prisoners," such as failed Hitler assassins, German religious leaders, and politicians who challenged Nazism. Most

Memorials throughout Dachau remind visitors: Never Again.

of the 136 cells are empty, but exhibits in a few of them (near the entrance) profile the inmates and the SS guards who worked at Dachau, and allow you to listen to some inmates' testimonies. Cell #2 was the interrogation room. Cell #9 was a "standing cell"—inmates were tortured here by being forced to stay on their feet for days at a time.

Barracks: Take a quick look inside to get an idea of what sleeping and living conditions were like in the camp. There were 34 barracks, each measuring about 10 yards by 100 yards. When the camp was at its fullest, there was only about one square yard of living space per inmate.

Religious Remembrance Sites: At the far end of the camp, there are now three places of meditation and worship (Jewish to your right, Catholic straight ahead, and Protestant to your left).

Camp Crematorium: A memorial garden surrounds the two camp crematorium buildings, which were used to burn the bodies of prisoners who had died or been killed. The newer, larger concrete crematorium was built to replace the smaller wooden one. One of its rooms is a **gas chamber,** which worked on the same principles as the much larger one at Auschwitz, and was originally disguised as a shower room (the fittings are gone now). It was never put to use at Dachau for mass murder, but survivors have testified that small groups were killed in it "experimentally." In the garden near the buildings is a Russian Orthodox shrine.

Rothenburg
& the
Romantic Road

The Romantic Road takes you through Bavaria's medieval heartland, a route strewn with picturesque villages, farmhouses, onion-domed churches, Baroque palaces, and walled cities. The route, which runs from Würzburg to Füssen, is the most scenic way to connect Frankfurt with Munich. No trains run along the full length of the Romantic Road, but Rothenburg (ROH-tehn-burg), the most interesting town along the way, is easy to reach by rail. Drivers can either zero in on Rothenburg or meander from town to town on the way. For nondrivers, a tour bus travels a portion of the Romantic Road several days a week in summer.

Countless travelers have searched for the elusive "untouristy Rothenburg." There are many contenders (such as Michelstadt, Miltenberg, Bamberg, Bad Windsheim, and Dinkelsbühl), but none holds a candle to the king of medieval German cuteness. Even with crowds, overpriced souvenirs, and, yes, even *Schneeballen*, Rothenburg is best. Save time and mileage and be satisfied with the winner.

ROTHENBURG & THE ROMANTIC ROAD IN 2 DAYS

I'd spend one full day in Rothenburg this way: Start with my self-guided town walk, including a visit to St. Jakob's Church (for the carved altarpiece) and the Rothenburg Museum (historic artifacts). Spend the afternoon visiting the Medieval Crime and Punishment Museum and taking my "Schmiedgasse-Spitalgasse Shopping Stroll," followed by a walk on the wall (from Spitaltor to Klingentor).

Cap your day with the entertaining Night Watchman's Tour at 20:00. Locals love *"die blaue Stunde"* (the blue hour)—the time just before dark when city lamps and the sky hold hands. Be sure to be out enjoying the magic of the city at this time.

Other evening options include beer-garden fun (at Gasthof Rödertor) if the weather's good, or the English Conversation Club (at Altfränkische Weinstube am Klosterhof) if it's Wednesday.

With extra time in Rothenburg, spread out your sightseeing and add the Old Town Historic Walk (offered by the TI), the Town Hall Tower climb, and the German Christmas Museum.

If you're driving, take in the top Romantic Road highlights en route, devoting a half-day to the sights on your way to Rothenburg and another half-day after leaving it.

ROTHENBURG OB DER TAUBER

In the Middle Ages, when Berlin and Munich were just wide spots on the road, Rothenburg ob der Tauber was a "free imperial city" beholden only to the Holy Roman Emperor. From 1150 to 1400, because of its strategic location on the trade routes, along with the abundant resources of its surrounding farmlands, Rothenburg thrived, with a whopping population of 6,000. But the Thirty Years' War and a plague that followed did the town in. With no money to fix up its antiquated, severely leaning buildings, the town was left to languish in this state. Today, it's the country's best-preserved medieval walled town, enjoying tremendous tourist popularity without losing its charm.

Rick's Tip: *Germany has several towns named Rothenburg.* **Make sure you're going to Rothenburg ob der Tauber** *(not "ob der" any other river). People really do sometimes drive or ride the train to the wrong Rothenburg by accident.*

Rothenburg's great trade these days is tourism: Two-thirds of the 2,500 people who live within its walls are employed to serve you. While roughly 2 million people visit each year, most come only on day trips. Rothenburg is yours after dark, when the groups vacate and the town's floodlit cobbles wring some romance out of any travel partner.

ORIENTATION

Think of the town map as a human head. Its nose—the castle garden—sticks out to the left, and the skinny lower part forms a neck, with the youth hostel and a recommended hotel being the Adam's apple. The town is a delight on foot. No sights or hotels are more than a 15-minute walk from the train station or each other.

Most of the buildings you'll see were in place by 1400. The city was born around its long-gone castle fortress—built in 1142, destroyed in 1356—which was located where the castle garden is now. You can see the shadow of the first town wall, which defines the oldest part of Rothenburg, in its contemporary street plan.

Picturesque Rothenburg ob der Tauber

GERMANY

To Detwang

To Detwang

To Romantic Road North to Creglingen & Würzburg

ST. WOLFGANG'S KLINGENTOR

WC

Tauber River

Note: Not possible to walk on wall from Klingentor to Kohlturm

KLINGEN-

KREBENG-

100 Meters

100 Yards

PLAY-GROUND

ROTHENBURG MUSEUM

KLOSTERHOF

WALKABLE PORTION OF TOWN WALLS

ACCESS STAIRS TO WALLS

Convent Garden

KLOSTER-

TOPPLER CASTLE

BURG-TOR

WC

7

HERRN-

Castle Garden

5

2

FRANCISCAN CHURCH

Restaurants

1 Reichsküchenmeister
2 Hotel Rest. Kloster-Stüble
3 Gasthof Goldener Greifen
4 Altfränkische Weinstube am Klosterhof
5 Zum Pulverer
6 Alter Keller
7 Hotel Rest. Herrnschlösschen
8 Pizzeria Roma
9 TobinGo
10 Brot & Zeit
11 Metzgerei Trumpp
12 Gasthof Rödertor
13 Eis Café D' Isep
14 Allegra Schokolade

Hotels

15 Hotel Spitzweg
16 Hotel Gerberhaus
17 Pension Elke
18 Gästehaus Raidel
19 Gasthof zum Breiterle
20 Kreuzerhof Hotel
21 To Wildbad

TAUBERTALWEG

DOUBLE BRIDGE

Tauber River

TAUBERTALWEG

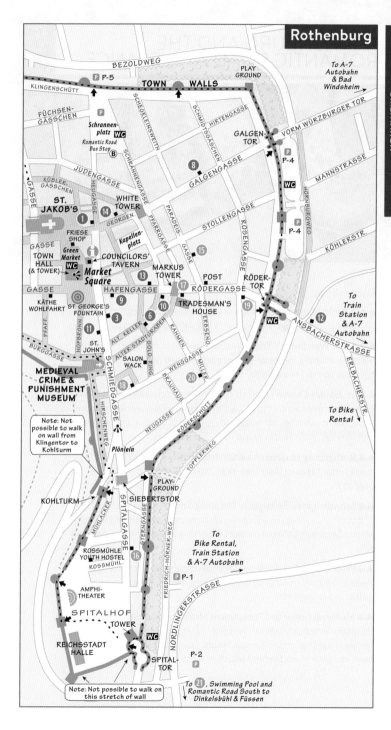

Rothenburg

ROTHENBURG AND THE ROMANTIC ROAD AT A GLANCE

Rothenburg

▲▲▲ **Rothenburg Town Walk** A self-guided loop, starting and ending on Market Square, covering the town's top sights. See page 772.

▲▲ **Night Watchman's Tour** Germany's best hour of medieval wonder, led by an amusing, medieval-garbed guide. **Hours:** Mid-March-Dec nightly at 20:00. See page 770.

▲▲ **St. Jakob's Church** Home to Tilman Riemenschneider's breathtaking, wood-carved Altar of the Holy Blood. **Hours:** Daily April-Oct 9:00-17:00, Dec 10:00-16:45, off-season 10:00-12:00 & 14:00-16:00, on Sun wait to enter until services end at 10:45. See page 775.

▲▲ **Rothenburg Museum** An artifact-filled sweep through Rothenburg's history. **Hours:** Daily 9:30-17:30, Nov-March 13:00-16:00. See page 777.

▲▲ **Schmiedgasse-Spitalgasse Shopping Stroll** A fun look at crafts and family-run shops, on a (mostly) picturesque street running between Market Square and the town's most impressive tower, Spitaltor. See page 780.

▲▲ **Walk the Wall** A strollable wall encircling the town, providing great views and a good orientation to Rothenburg. **Hours:** Always open and walkable. See page 781.

▲▲ **Medieval Crime and Punishment Museum** Specializing in everything connected to medieval justice, this exhibit is a cut above the tacky torture museums around Europe. **Hours:** Daily 10:00-18:00, Nov and Jan-Feb 14:00-16:00, Dec and March 13:00-16:00. See page 782.

▲**Old Town Historic Walk** Covers the serious side of Rothenburg's history and the town's architecture. **Hours:** Easter-Oct and Dec daily at 14:00. See page 772.

▲**Historical Town Hall Vaults** An insightful look at Rothenburg during the Catholics-vs.-Protestants Thirty Years' War. **Hours:** Daily 9:30-17:30, shorter hours Nov-April, closed Jan, weekends only Feb. See page 774.

▲**Town Hall Tower** Rothenburg's tallest perch, with a commanding view. **Hours:** Daily in season 9:30-12:30 & 13:00-17:00. See page 782.

▲**German Christmas Museum** Tells the interesting history of Christmas decorations. **Hours:** Daily 10:00-17:30, shorter and irregular hours Jan-March. See page 783.

Along the Romantic Road

▲▲**Wieskirche** Lovely Baroque-Rococo church set in a meadow. **Hours:** Daily 8:00-20:00. See page 793.

▲**Creglingen's Herrgottskirche** Church featuring Riemenschneider's greatest carved altarpiece. See page 790.

▲**Weikersheim** Picturesque town with an impressive palace, Baroque gardens, and a quaint town square. See page 791.

▲**Dinkelsbühl** A town like Rothenburg's little sister, cute enough to merit a short stop. See page 792.

▲**Nördlingen** Workaday town with one of the best walls in Germany and a crater left by an ancient meteor. See page 792.

Two gates from this wall still survive: the Markus Tower and the White Tower. The richest and biggest houses were in this central part. The commoners built higgle-dy-piggledy (read: picturesque) houses farther from the center but still inside the present walls.

Although Rothenburg is technically in Bavaria, the region around the town is called—and strongly identifies itself as—"Franken," one of Germany's many medieval dukedoms ("Franconia" in English).

Rick's Tip: A **fun pictorial town map,** *which also helpfully indicates some walking paths in the countryside beyond the town walls, is available for free with this book at the* **Friese shop** *(see page 784).*

Tourist Information: The TI is on Market Square (May-Oct and Dec Mon-Fri 9:00-18:00, Sat-Sun 10:00-17:00; off-season Mon-Fri until 17:00, Sat until 13:00, closed Sun; Marktplatz 2, tel. 09861/404-800, www.rothenburg.de/tourismus, run by Jörg Christöphler). The free city map comes with a walking guide to the town.

The *Events* booklet covers the basics in English. They offer a variety of themed tours; ask when you arrive or check their website in advance.

Bike Rental: A ride through the nearby countryside is enjoyable on nice days (get route suggestions from rental shop). **Rad & Tat** rents bikes for €14 for a 24-hour day (otherwise €10/6 hours, electric bike-€28/day; Mon-Fri 9:00-18:00, Sat until 13:00, closed Sun; Bensenstrasse 17, tel. 09861/87984, www.mietraeder.de). To reach it, leave the old town toward the train station, take a right on Erlbacher Strasse, cross the tracks, and look across the street from the Lidl supermarket.

Taxi: For a taxi, call 09861/2000 or 09861/7227.

TOURS

▲▲NIGHT WATCHMAN'S TOUR

This tour is flat-out the most entertaining hour of medieval wonder anywhere in Germany and the best evening activity in town. The Night Watchman (a.k.a. Hans-Georg Baumgartner) jokes like a medieval John Cleese as he lights his lamp and takes tourists on his rounds, telling slice-

Rothenburg's Night Watchman

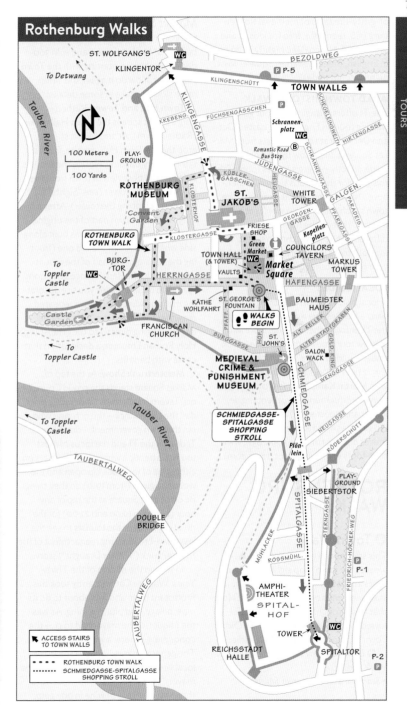

Rothenburg Walks

To Detwang

ST. WOLFGANG'S WC

KLINGENTOR

P P-5

BEZOLDWEG

KLINGENSCHÜTT

TOWN WALLS

N

100 Meters

100 Yards

Tauber River

KREBENG

KLINGENGASSE

FÜCHSENGÄSSCHEN

Schrannen-
platz WC

SCHEGELENSWETH

HIRTENGASSE

Romantic Road
Bus Stop B

SCHRANNENGASSE

GALGEN.

PLAY-
GROUND

ROTHENBURG
MUSEUM

KLOSTERHOF

KÜBLER-
GÄSSCHEN

ST.
JAKOB'S

JUDENGASSE

HEUGASSE

WHITE
TOWER

GEORGEN-
GASSE

PFARRG.

PARADEIS

Convent
Garden

ROTHENBURG
TOWN WALK

KLOSTERGASSE

FRIESE
SHOP

Green
Market

Kapellen-
platz

COUNCILORS'
TAVERN

To
Toppler
Castle

BURG-
TOR

WC

HERRNGASSE

TOWN HALL
(& TOWER)

VAULTS

i

Market
Square

WC

HAFENGASSE

MARKUS
TOWER

Castle
Garden

KÄTHE
WOHLFAHRT

PFAFF.

ST. GEORGE'S
FOUNTAIN

WALKS
BEGIN

BAUMEISTER
HAUS

ALT. KELLER

ALTER STADTGRABEN

GOLD. RING.

SALON
WACK

To
Toppler Castle

FRANCISCAN
CHURCH

BURGGASSE

HOF

ST.
JOHN'S

SCHMIEDGASSE

WENGGASSE

NEUGASSE

MEDIEVAL
CRIME &
PUNISHMENT
MUSEUM

Tauber River

SCHMIEDGASSE-
SPITALGASSE
SHOPPING
STROLL

Plön-
lein

RÖDERSCHÜTT

To Toppler
Castle

TAUBERTALWEG

SIEBERTSTOR

PLAY-
GROUND

STERNGASSE

SPITALGASSE

FRIEDRICH-HÖRNER-WEG

P P-1

DOUBLE
BRIDGE

MÜHLACKER

ROSSMÜHL.

TAUBERTALWEG

AMPHI-
THEATER

SPITAL-
HOF

TOWER WC

REICHSSTADT
HALLE

SPITALTOR P-2
P

ACCESS STAIRS
TO TOWN WALLS

ROTHENBURG TOWN WALK

SCHMIEDGASSE-SPITALGASSE
SHOPPING STROLL

of-gritty-life tales of medieval Rothenburg (€8, teens-€4, free for kids 12 and under, mid-March-Dec nightly at 20:00, in English, meet at Market Square, www.nightwatchman.de).

▲OLD TOWN HISTORIC WALK

The TI offers engaging 1.5-hour guided walking tours in English (€8, Easter-Oct and Dec daily at 14:00, departs from Market Square). Just show up and pay the guide directly—there's always room. Take this tour for the serious side of Rothenburg's history, and to make sense of the town's architecture; you won't get as much of that on the fun—and completely different—Night Watchman's Tour. Taking both tours is a smart way to round out your overall Rothenburg experience.

LOCAL GUIDES

A local historian can really bring the ramparts alive. Reserve a guide by emailing the TI (info@rothenburg.de; more info at www.tourismus.rothenburg.de—look under "Guided Tours"; €75/1.5 hours, €95/2 hours). I've had good experiences with **Martin Kamphans** (tel. 09861/7941, www.stadtfuehrungen-rothenburg.de, kamphans@posteo.de) and **Daniel Weber** (to get rates listed above ask for Rick Steves discount, mobile 0795-8311, www.toot-tours.com, mail@toot-tours.com).

ROTHENBURG WALKS

❺ Town Walk

This self-guided loop, worth ▲▲▲, weaves the town's top sights together, takes about an hour without stops, and starts and ends on Market Square. (Note that this is roughly the same route followed by city guides on their daily Old Town Historic Walk, described earlier.)

🎧 Download my free Rothenburg Town Walk audio tour.

• *Start the walk on Market Square.*

Market Square Spin-Tour

Stand in front of the fountain at the bottom of Market Square and spin 360 degrees clockwise, starting with the Town Hall tower. Now do it again, this time more slowly to take in some details:

Town Hall and Tower: Rothenburg's tallest spire is the Town Hall tower (Rathausturm). At 200 feet, it stands atop the old Town Hall, a white, Gothic, 13th-century building. Notice the tourists enjoying the best view in town from the black top of the tower (see "Sights" for details on climbing the tower). After a fire in 1501 burned down part of the original building, a new Town Hall was built alongside what survived of the old one (fronting the square). This half of the rebuilt complex is in the Renaissance style from 1570. The double eagles you see decorating many buildings here are a repeated reminder that this was a "free imperial city" belonging directly to the (Habsburg) Holy Roman Emperor, a designation that came with benefits.

Meistertrunk Show: At the top of Market Square stands the proud Councilors' Tavern (clock tower from 1466). In its day, the city council—the rich guys who ran the town government—drank here. Today, it's the **TI** and the focus of most tourists' attention when the little doors on either side of the clock flip open and the wooden figures (from 1910) do their thing. Be on Market Square at the top of any hour (between 10:00 and 22:00) for the ritual gathering of the tourists to see the less-than-breathtaking reenactment of the Meistertrunk ("Master Draught") story:

In 1631, in the middle of the Thirty Years' War, the Catholic army took this Protestant town and was about to do its rape, pillage, and plunder thing. As was the etiquette, the mayor had to give the conquering general a welcoming drink. The general enjoyed a huge tankard of local wine. Feeling really good, he told the mayor, "Hey, if you can drink this entire three-liter tankard of wine in one gulp,

Rothenburg's Town Hall and Tower

I'll spare your town." The mayor amazed everyone by drinking the entire thing, and Rothenburg was saved. (While this is a nice story, it was dreamed up in the late 1800s for a theatrical play designed—effectively—to promote a romantic image of the town. In actuality, if Rothenburg was spared, it had likely bribed its way out of the jam.) The city was occupied and ransacked several times in the Thirty Years' War, and it never recovered—which is why it's such a well-preserved time capsule today.

Bottom of Market Square: As this was the most prestigious address in town, it's ringed by big homes with big carriage gates. One of the finest is just downhill from the bottom end of the square—the **Baumeister** ("master builder") **Haus,** where the man who designed and built the Town Hall lived. It features a famous Renaissance facade with statues of the seven virtues and the seven vices. The statues are copies; the originals are in the Rothenburg Museum (described later). While "Gluttony" is easy to find, see if you can figure out what his companions represent.

Behind you, take in the big 17th-century **St. George's fountain.** Its long metal gutters could slide to deposit the water into villagers' buckets. It's part of Rothenburg's ingenious water system: Built on a rock, the town had one real source above, which was plumbed to serve a series of fountains; water flowed from high to low through Rothenburg. Its many fountains had practical functions beyond providing drinking water—some were stocked with fish on market days and during times of siege, and their water was useful for fighting fire. Because of its plentiful water supply—and its policy of requiring relatively wide lanes as fire breaks—the town never burned entirely, as so many neighboring villages did.

Two fine half-timbered buildings behind the fountain show the old-time lofts with warehouse doors and pulleys on top for hoisting. All over town, lofts like these were filled with grain. A year's supply was required by the city so it could survive any siege. The building behind the fountain is an art gallery showing off work by members of the local artists' association. To the right is Marien Apotheke, an old-time pharmacy mixing old and new in typical Rothenburg style.

The broad street running under the

Herrngasse

Town Hall tower is **Herrngasse.** The town originated with its castle fortress (built in 1142 but now long gone; a lovely garden now fills that space). Herrngasse connected the castle to Market Square. The last leg of this circular walking tour will take you from the castle garden up Herrngasse and back here.

For now, walk a few steps down Herrngasse and stop by the arch under the Town Hall tower (between the new and old town halls). On the wall to the left of the gate are the town's measuring rods—a reminder that medieval Germany was made of 300 independent little countries, many with their own weights and measures. Merchants and shoppers knew that these were the local standards: the rod (4.3 yards), the *Schuh* ("shoe," roughly a foot), and the *Ell* (from elbow to fingertip—four inches longer than mine...climb up and try it). The protruding cornerstone you're standing on is one of many all over town—intended to protect buildings from careening horse carts. In German, going recklessly fast is called "scratching the cornerstone."

• *Careen around that stone and under the arch to find the...*

Historical Town Hall Vaults

The vaults (Historiengewölbe, worth ▲) house an eclectic and grade-school-ish little museum that gives a waxy but interesting look at Rothenburg during the Catholics-vs.-Protestants Thirty Years' War. Popping in here can help prep your imagination to filter out the tourists and picture ye olde Rothenburg along the rest of this walk. With helpful English descriptions, it offers a look at "the fateful year 1631," a replica of the mythical Meistertrunk tankard, an alchemist's workshop, and a dungeon—used as a bomb shelter during World War II—complete with three dank cells and some torture lore.

Cost and Hours: €3.50, daily 9:30-17:30, shorter hours Nov-April, closed Jan, weekends only Feb, tel. 09861/86751, www.meistertrunk.de.

• *Leaving the museum, turn left (past a venerable and much-sketched-and-photographed door) and find a posted copy of a centuries-old map showing the territory of Rothenburg.*

Map of Rothenburg City Territory

In 1537 Rothenburg actually ruled a little country—one of about 300 petty dukedoms like this that made up what is today's Germany. The territory spanned a 12-by-12-mile area, encompassing 180 villages—a good example of the fragmentation of feudal Germany. While not to scale (Rothenburg is actually less than a mile wide), the map is fun to study. In the 1380s, Mayor Toppler purchased much of this territory. In 1562 the city sold off some of its land to neighboring dukes, which gave it the money for all the fine Renaissance buildings that embellish the town to this day.

• *Continue through the courtyard and into a square called...*

Green Market (Grüner Markt)

Once a produce market, this parking lot fills with Christmas stands during December. Notice the clay-tile roofs. These "beaver tail" tiles became standard after thatched roofs were outlawed to prevent fires. Today, all the town's roofs are made of these. The little fences stop heaps of snow from falling off the roof and onto people below. A free public WC is on your left, and the recommended Friese gift shop (see "Shopping," later) is on your right.

• *Continue straight ahead to St. Jakob's Church. Study the exterior first, then pay to go inside.*

St. Jakob's Church (St. Jakobskirche)

Rothenburg's main church, worth ▲▲ is home to Tilman Riemenschneider's breathtaking, wood-carved *Altar of the Holy Blood.*

Cost and Hours: €2.50, daily April-Oct 9:00-17:00, Dec 10:00-16:45, off-season 10:00-12:00 & 14:00-16:00, on Sun wait to enter until services end at 10:45.

Tours and Information: A free, helpful English info sheet is available. Guided tours in English run on Sat at 15:30 (April-Oct) for no extra charge. Or get the worthwhile audioguide (€2, 45 minutes) for a handful of important stops in the church.

Visiting the Church: Start by viewing the exterior. Then, enter the church, where you'll see the main nave first, then climb above the pipe organ (in the back) to finish with the famous carved altar.

Exterior: Outside the church, under the little roof at the base of the tower, you'll see 14th-century statues (mostly original) showing Jesus praying at Gethsemane, a common feature of Gothic churches. The sculptor is anonymous—in the Gothic age (pre-Albrecht Dürer), artists were nameless craftspeople working only for the glory of God. Five yards to the left (on the wall), notice the nub of a sandstone statue—a rare original, looking pretty bad after 500 years of weather and, more recently, pollution. Most original statues are now in the city museum. The better-preserved statues you see on the church are copies. Also outside the church is a bronze model of the city. Look closely to appreciate the detail, including descriptions in braille.

Before entering, notice how the church was extended to the west and actually built over the street. The newer chapel was built to accommodate pilgrims and to contain the sumptuous Riemenschneider carved altarpiece.

If it's your wedding day, take the first entrance—marked by a very fertile Eve and, around the corner, Adam showing off an impressive six-pack. Otherwise, head toward the church's second (downhill) door. Before going inside, notice the modern statue at the base of the stairs. This is **St. James** (a.k.a. Sankt Jakob in German, Santiago in Spanish, and Saint-Jacques in French). You can tell this important saint by his big, floppy hat, his walking stick, the gourd on his hip (used by pilgrims to carry water), and—most importantly—the scallop shell in his hand. St. James' remains are entombed in the grand cathedral of Santiago de Compostela, in the northwestern corner of Spain. The medieval pilgrimage route called the Camino de

Map of Old Rothenburg

St. Jakob's Church

Santiago passed through here on its way to that distant corner of Europe. Pilgrims would wear the scallop shell as a symbol of their destination (where that type of marine life was abundant). To this day, the word for "scallop" in many languages carries the name of this saint: *Jakobsmuschel* in German, *coquille Saint-Jacques* in French, and so on.

Inside the Church: Built in the 14th century, this church has been Lutheran since 1544. The interior was "purified" by Romantics in the 19th century—cleaned of everything Baroque or not original and refitted in the Neo-Gothic style. (For example, the baptismal font—in the middle of the choir—and the pulpit above the second pew *look* Gothic but are actually Neo-Gothic.) The stained-glass windows behind the altar, which are most colorful in the morning light, are originals from the 1330s. Admiring this church, consider what it says about the priorities of a town of just a few thousand people, who decided to use their collective wealth to build such a place. The size of a church is a good indication of the town's wealth when it was built. Medallions and portraits of Rothenburg's leading families and church leaders line the walls above the choir in the front of the church.

The **main altar,** from 1466, is by Friedrich Herlin. Below Christ are statues of six saints—including St. James (a.k.a. Jakob), with the telltale shell on his floppy hat. Study the painted panels—ever see Peter with spectacles (below the carved saints)? Go around the back of the altarpiece to look at the doors. In the upper left, you'll see a painting of Rothenburg's Market Square in the 15th century, looking much like it does today, with the exception of the full-Gothic Town Hall (as it was before the big fire of 1501). Notice Christ's face on the white "veil of Veronica" (center of back side, bottom edge). It follows you as you walk from side to side—this must have given the faithful the religious heebie-jeebies four centuries ago.

The **Tabernacle of the Holy Eucharist** (just left of the main altar—on your right as you walk back around) is a century older. It stored the wine and bread used for Holy Communion. Before the Reformation this was a Roman Catholic church, which meant that the bread and wine were considered to be the actual body and blood of Jesus (and therefore needed a worthy repository). Notice the unusual Trinity: The Father and Son are bridged by a dove, which represents the Holy Spirit. Stepping back, you can see that Jesus is standing on a skull—clearly "overcoming death."

Now, as pilgrims did centuries ago, climb the stairs at the back of the church that lead up behind the pipe organ to a loft-like chapel. Here you'll find the artistic highlight of Rothenburg and perhaps the most wonderful wood carving in all of Germany: the glorious 500-year-old, 35-foot-high **Altar of the Holy Blood.** Tilman Riemenschneider, the Michelangelo of German woodcarvers, carved this from 1499 to 1504 (at the same time Michelangelo was working on his own masterpieces). The altarpiece was designed to hold a rock-crystal capsule—set in the cross you see high above—that contains a precious scrap of tablecloth stained in the shape of a cross by a drop of communion wine considered to be the actual blood of Christ.

The altar is a realistic commotion, showing that Riemenschneider—a High

Altar of the Holy Blood

Gothic artist—was ahead of his time. Below, in the scene of the Last Supper, Jesus gives Judas a piece of bread, marking him as the traitor, while John lays his head on Christ's lap. Judas, with his big bag of cash, could be removed from the scene (illustrated by photos on the wall nearby), as was the tradition for the four days leading up to Easter.

Everything is portrayed exactly as described in the Bible. In the relief panel on the left, Jesus enters the walled city of Jerusalem. Notice the exacting attention to detail—down to the nails on the horseshoe. In the relief panel on the right, Jesus prays in the Garden of Gethsemane.

Take a moment to simply linger over the lovingly executed details: the curly locks of the apostles' hair and beards, and the folds of their garments; the delicate vines intertwining above their heads; Jesus' expression, at once tender and accusing.
• After leaving the church, walk around the corner to the right and under the chapel (built over the road). Go two blocks down Klingengasse and stop at the corner of the street called Klosterhof. Looking farther ahead of you down Klingengasse, you see the...

Klingentor

This cliff tower was Rothenburg's water reservoir. From 1595 until 1910, a 900-liter (240-gallon) copper tank high in the tower provided clean spring water—pumped up by river power—to the privileged. To the right of the Klingentor is a good stretch of wall rampart to walk. To the left, the wall is low and simple, lacking a rampart because it guards only a cliff.

Now find the shell decorating a building on the street corner next to you. That's once again the symbol of St. James, indicating that this building is associated with the church.
• Turn left down Klosterhof, passing the shell and, on your right, the colorful, recommended Altfränkische Weinstube am Klosterhof pub. As you approach the next stop, notice the lazy Susan embedded in the wall

(to the right of the museum door), which allowed cloistered nuns to give food to the poor without being seen.

Rothenburg Museum

You'll get a vivid and artifact-filled sweep through Rothenburg's history at this excellent ▲▲ museum, housed in a former Dominican convent. The highlight for many is the painted glass mug said to have prompted the myth of the Meistertrunk.

Cost and Hours: €6; daily 9:30-17:30, Nov-March generally 13:00-16:00; pick up English info sheet at entrance, Klosterhof 5, tel. 09861/939-043, www.reichsstadtmuseum.rothenburg.de.

Visiting the Museum: As you follow the Rundgang/Tour signs to the left, watch for these highlights:

Immediately inside, a glass case displays the 1616 Prince Elector's colorful glass tankard (which inspired the famous legend of the Meistertrunk) and a set of golden Rothenburg coins. Down the hall, find a modern city model and trace the city's growth, its walls expanding like rings on a big tree. Before going upstairs, you'll see medieval and Renaissance sculptures, including original sandstone statues from St. Jakob's Church and original statues that once decorated the Baumeister Haus near Market Square. Upstairs in the nuns' dormitory are craftsmen's signs that once hung outside shops (see if you can guess the craft before reading the museum's

Rothenburg Museum

label), ornate locks, tools for various professions, and a collection of armor and weapons. You'll then go through two levels of rooms showcasing old furniture, housewares, and the Baroque statues that decorated the organ loft in St. Jakob's Church from 1669 until the 19th century, when they were cleared out to achieve "Gothic purity." Take time to enjoy the several rooms and shop fronts outfitted as they would have been centuries ago.

The painting gallery is lined with Romantic paintings of Rothenburg, which served as the first tourist promotion and depict the city as it appeared in centuries past. Look for the large, gloomy work by Englishman Arthur Wasse (labeled *"Es spukt"*)—does that door look familiar?

Back downstairs near where you entered, circle left around the cloister to see a 14th-century convent kitchen (*Klosterküche*) with a working model of a lazy Susan (the kind that nuns used to share food with the poor outside the convent) and a massive chimney (step inside and look up). Continue around to an exhibit of Jewish culture in Rothenburg through the ages (*Judaika*), then see the grand finale (in the *Konventsaal*), the *Rothenburger Passion*. This 12-panel series of paintings showing scenes leading up to Christ's Crucifixion—originally intended for the town's Franciscan church (which we'll pass later)—dates from 1492.

• *Leaving the museum, go around to the right and into the Convent Garden (when locked at night, continue straight to the T-intersection and turn right).*

Convent Garden

This spot is a peaceful place to work on your tan...or mix a poisoned potion. Monks and nuns—who were responsible for concocting herbal cures in the olden days, finding disinfectants, and coming up with ways to disguise the taste of rotten food—often tended herb gardens. Smell (but don't pick) the *Pfefferminze* (peppermint), *Heidewacholder* (juniper/gin), *Rosmarin*

Convent Garden

(rosemary), *Lavandel* (lavender), and the tallest plant, *Hopfen* (hops...monks were the great medieval brewers). Don't smell the plants that are poisonous (potency indicated by the number of crosses). Appreciate the setting, taking in the fine architecture and expansive garden—all within the city walls, where land was at such a premium. It's a reminder of the power of the pre-Reformation Church.

• *Exit opposite from where you entered, angling left through the nuns' garden, leaving via an arch along the far wall. Then turn right and go downhill to the...*

Town Wall

This part of the wall takes advantage of the natural fortification provided by the cliff (view through bars, look to far right) and is therefore much shorter than the ramparts.

• *Angle left along the wall. Cross the big street (Herrngasse, with the Burgtor tower on your right—which we'll enter from outside soon) and continue downhill on Burggasse until you hit another section of the town wall. Turn right, go through a small tower gate, and park yourself at the town's finest viewpoint.*

Castle Garden Viewpoint

From here enjoy a fine view of fortified Rothenburg. You're looking at the Spital-tor end of town (with the most interesting gate and the former hospital). After this walk, you can continue with my "Schmiedgasse-Spitalgasse Shopping Stroll," which leads from Market Square down to this end of town, known as Plönlein, and then enter the city walls and walk the ramparts 180 degrees to the Klingentor tower (which we saw earlier, in the distance just after St. Jakob's Church). The droopy-eyed building at the far end of town (today's youth hostel) was the horse mill—which provided grinding power when the water mill in the valley below was not working (during drought or siege). Stretching below you is the fine parklike land around the Tauber River, nicknamed the "Tauber Riviera."

• *Now explore deeper into the park.*

Castle Garden and the Burgtor Gate

The park *(Burggarten)* before you was a castle fortress until it was destroyed in the 14th century. The chapel (50 yards straight into the park, on the left) is the only surviving bit of the original castle. In front of the chapel is a memorial to local Jews killed in a 1298 slaughter. A few steps beyond that is a flowery trellis that provides a fine picnic spot. If you walk all the way out to the garden's far end, you'll find another great viewpoint.

When you're ready to leave the park, approach the Burgtor, the ornate fortified gate flanked by twin stubby towers, and imagine being locked out in the year 1400. (There's a WC on the left.) The tall tower behind the gate was accessed by a wooden drawbridge—see the chain slits above the inner gate, and between them the "pitch" mask with holes designed to allow defenders to pour boiling Nutella on attackers. High above is the town coat of arms: a red *(roten)* castle *(Burg)*.

As you go through the gate, study the big wooden door with the tiny "eye of the needle" door cut into it. If you were trying to enter town after curfew, you could have bribed the guard to let you through this door, which was small enough to keep out any fully armed attackers. Note also the square hole on the right and imagine the massive timber that once barricaded the gate.

• *Now climb up the big street, Herrngasse, as you return to your starting point.*

Herrngasse

Many towns have a Herrngasse, where the richest patricians and merchants (the *Herren*) lived. Predictably, it's your best chance to see the town's finest old mansions. Strolling back to Market Square, you'll pass, on the right, the **Franciscan Church** (from 1285—the oldest in town). Across the street, the mint-green house at #18 is the biggest patrician house on this main drag. The front door was big enough to allow a carriage to drive through it; a human-sized door cut into it was used by those on foot. The gift shop at #11 (Hornburghaus, on the right) offers a chance to poke into one of these big landowners' homes and appreciate their structure: living quarters in front above carriage-sized doors, courtyard out back functioning as a garage, stables, warehouse, servants' quarters, and a private well.

Farther up, also on the right, is Hotel Eisenhut, Rothenburg's fanciest hotel and worth a peek inside. Finally, passing the Käthe Wohlfahrt Christmas headquarters/ shop (described under "Shopping," later), you'll be back at Market Square, where you started this walk.

• *From here, you can continue walking by following my "Schmiedgasse-Spitalgasse Shopping Stroll," next. This stroll ends at the city gate called Spitaltor, a good access point for a walk on the town walls.*

Burgtor Gate

Schmiedgasse-Spitalgasse Shopping Stroll

After doing the basic town walk and visiting the town's three essential interior sights (Rothenburg Museum, Medieval Crime and Punishment Museum, and St. Jakob's Church), your next priority might be Rothenburg's shops and its town wall. This fun walk, worth ▲▲, goes from Market Square in a straight line south (past the best selection of characteristic family-run shops) to the city's most impressive fortification (Spitaltor).

Standing on Market Square, with your back to the TI, you'll see a street sloping downward toward the south end of town. That's where you're headed. This street changes names as you walk, from **Obere Schmiedgasse** (upper blacksmith street) to **Spitalgasse** (hospital street), and runs directly to the **Spitaltor** tower and gate. From Spitaltor you can access the town wall and walk the ramparts 180 degrees around the city to the Klingentor tower.

As you stroll down this delightful lane, pop in and explore shops along this cultural and historical scavenger hunt. I've provided the street number and "left" or "right" to indicate the side of the street (see the "Rothenburg Walks" map).

The facade of the fine Renaissance **Baumeister Haus** at #3 (left) celebrates a secular morality, with statues representing the seven virtues and the seven vices.

At #5 (left), **Gasthof Goldener Greifen** was once the home of the illustrious Mayor Toppler (d. 1408). By the looks of its door (right of the main entrance), the mayor must have had an impressive wine cellar. Note the fine hanging sign of a gilded griffin. Business signs in a mostly illiterate medieval world needed to be easy for all to read. The entire street is ornamented with fun signs like this one. Nearby, a pretzel marks the bakery, and the crossed swords advertise the weaponmaker.

Shops on both sides of the street at #7 display examples of *Schneeballen* gone wild. These "snowballs," once a humble way to bake extra flour into a simple treat, are now iced and dolled up a million ways.

Waffenkammer, at #9 (left), is "the weapons chamber," where Johannes Wittmann works hard to make a wonderland in which young-at-heart tourists can shop for (and try out) medieval weapons, armor, and clothing. Fun photo ops abound, especially downstairs (ask about Rick Steves discount).

At #18 (right), **Metzgerei Trumpp,** a top-end butcher, is a carnivore's heaven. Check out the endless wurst offerings in the window—a reminder that in the unrefrigerated Middle Ages meat needed to be smoked or salted. Locals who love bacon opt for fat slices of pork with crackling skins. At the next corner, with **Burggasse,** find the Catholic St. John's Church. The Medieval Crime and Punishment Museum (just down the lane to the right) marks the site of Rothenburg's first town wall.

The **Jutta Korn** shop, on the right at #4, showcases the work of a local artisan who has designed her own jewelry here for more than 30 years. At #6 (right), **Leyk** sells "lighthouses" made in town, many modeled after local buildings. The **Kleiderey,** an offbeat clothing store at #7 (left), is run by Tina, the Night Watchman's wife. The clothing is inspired by their southeast Asian travels.

At #13 (left), look opposite to find a narrow lane **(Ander Eich)** that leads to a little viewpoint in the town wall. Overlooking the "Tauber Riviera," it's a popular romantic perch in the evening.

At #17 (left), the **Lebe Gesund Vegetarian** shop is all about healthy living. This charming little place (run by tasty-sample-dealing Universalist Christians who like to think of Jesus as a vegan) seems designed to offer forgiveness to those who loved the butcher's shop but are ready to repent.

The **Käthe Wohlfahrt** shop at #19 (left) is one of the six Wohlfahrt stores around town, all owned by a local family and selling German clichés with gusto. Also on the left, at #21, the **An Ra** shop is where Annett Perner designs and sells her flowery clothes. (There's more of An Ra across the street at #26.) Annett was behind a recent initiative, called "Hand-made in Rothenburg," that formed a coalition between 10 local business owners who make everything from chocolate to jewelry to ceramics—an example of the special bond of Rothenburg's town members.

At #29 (left), **Glocke Weinladen am Plönlein** is an inviting shop of wine glasses and related accessories. The **Gasthof Glocke,** next door, with its wine-barrel-sized cellar door just waiting for some action, is a respected restaurant and home to the town's last vintner—a wonderful place to try local wines. The picturesque corner immediately to your right is dubbed **Plönlein,** named for the carpenter's plumb line—a string that dangles exactly straight down when anchored by a plumb (a lead weight). The line helps carpenters build things straight, but of course, here, nothing is made "to plumb." If this scene feels nostalgic, that's because Rothenburg was the inspiration for the village in the 1940 Disney animated film *Pinocchio.*

Walk a few more yards and look far up the lane **(Neugasse)** to the left. You'll see some cute pastel buildings with uniform windows and rooflines—clues that the buildings were rebuilt after WWII

bombings. Straight ahead, the **Siebertstor Tower** marks the next layer of expansion to the town wall. Continue through the tower. The former tannery is now a pub featuring **Landwehr Bräu,** the local brew.

Farther along, at #14 (right), **Antiq & Trödel,** which smells like an antique shop should, is fun to browse through.

Still farther down, on the left at #25, **Hotel-Café Gerberhaus** is a fine stop for a coffee and cake, with a delicate dining room and a peaceful courtyard hiding out back under the town wall.

From here, the town runs out of energy. This is Spitalhof—the former Hospital Quarter—with some nice architecture and the town's retirement home. Continue a few blocks to Spitaltor, the gate with the tall tower marking the end of town (and a good place to begin a ramparts ramble).

Outside the fortified gate is the ditch that kept artillery at a distance (most medieval moats were dry like this one; water and alligators were mostly added by Hollywood). Standing outside the wall, ponder this sight as if approaching the city 400 years ago. The wealth of a city was shown by its walls and towers. (Stone was costly—in fact, the German saying for "filthy rich" is "stone rich.")

Circle around to the right. Look up at the formidable tower. The guardhouse atop it, one of several in the wall, was manned 24/7. Above the entry gate, notice the emblem: Angels bless the double eagle of the Holy Roman Emperor, which blesses the town (symbolized by the two red towers).

⊘ Walk the Wall

Just longer than a mile and a half, providing great views and a good orientation, this ▲▲ walk can be done by those under six feet tall in less than an hour. Much of the walk is covered and is a great option in the rain. Photographers will stay very busy, especially before breakfast or at sunset, when the lighting is best and the crowds

The city ramparts

are gone. You can enter or exit the ramparts at nearly every tower.

While the ramparts circle the city, some stretches aren't walkable per se: Along much of the western side of town, you can't walk atop the wall, but you can walk alongside it and peek over or through it for great views outward from street level. Refer to my "Rothenburg Walks" map, earlier, to see which portions of the wall are walkable.

If you want to make a full town circuit, Spitaltor—at the south end of town, with the best fortifications—is a good starting place. From here it's a counterclockwise walk along the eastern and northern ramparts. After exiting at Klingentor you can follow the wall for a bit, but you'll have to cut away from the wall when you hit the Rothenburg Museum and again near the Medieval Crime and Punishment Museum. At the Kohlturm tower, at the southern end of town, you can climb the stairs and walk atop the remaining stretch of wall to the Spitalhof quarter, where you'll need to exit again. Spitaltor, where you started, is just a *Schneeball*'s toss away.

The TI has installed a helpful series of English-language plaques at about 20 stops along the route. The names you see along the way belong to people who donated money to rebuild the wall after World War II, and those who've more recently donated for the maintenance of Rothenburg's heritage.

SIGHTS

Note that a number of sights (including St. Jakob's Church and the Rothenburg Museum) have already been covered in the Rothenburg Town Walk.

On and Near Market Square

▲TOWN HALL TOWER

From Market Square you can see tourists on the crow's nest capping the Town Hall's tower. For a commanding view from the town's tallest perch, climb the steps of the tower. It's a rigorous but interesting 214-step climb that gets narrow and steep near the top—watch your head. Be here during the first or last hour of the day to avoid day-tripping crowds.

Cost and Hours: €2.50, pay at top, daily in season 9:30-12:30 & 13:00-17:00, enter from the grand steps overlooking Market Square.

▲▲MEDIEVAL CRIME AND PUNISHMENT MUSEUM (MITTELALTERLICHES KRIMINALMUSEUM)

Specializing in everything connected to medieval criminal justice, this exhibit (well described in English) is a cut above all the tacky torture museums around Europe. Nearly everything on display here is an actual medieval artifact. In addition to ogling spiked chairs, thumbscrews, and shame masks, you'll learn about medieval police and criminal law. The museum is more eclectic than its name and includes exhibits on general history, superstition, witchcraft, biblical art, and so on. The museum is undergoing renovations in 2019, which may affect some areas. A thoughtfully curated **Luther and the Witches** exhibit, created for the 500th anniversary of the Protestant Reformation, should still be on display when you visit.

Cost and Hours: €7, includes Luther exhibit; daily 10:00-18:00, Nov and Jan-

Feb 14:00-16:00, Dec and March 13:00-16:00; last entry 45 minutes before closing, fun cards and posters, Burggasse 3-5, tel. 09861/5359, www.kriminalmuseum.eu.

Visiting the Museum: It's a one-way route—just follow the yellow arrows. Keep an eye out for several well-done interactive media stations that provide extra background on the museum's highlights.

From the entrance, head downstairs to the **cellar** to see some enhanced-interrogation devices. Torture was common in the Middle Ages—not to punish, but to extract a confession (medieval "justice" required a confession). Just the sight of these tools was often enough to make an innocent man confess. You'll see the rack, "stretching ladder," thumb screws, spiked leg screws, and other items that would make Dick Cheney proud. Medieval torturers also employed a waterboarding-like technique—but here, the special ingredient was holy water.

Upstairs, on the **first and second floors,** the walls are lined with various legal documents of the age, while the dusty glass cases show off law-enforcement tools—many of them quite creative. Shame was a big tool back then. The town could publicly humiliate those who ran afoul of the law by tying them to a pillory in the main square and covering their faces in an iron mask of shame. Fanciful mask decorations indicated the crime: Chicken feathers meant promiscuity, horns indicated that a man's wife slept around (i.e., cuckold), and a snout

suggested that the person had acted piggishly. The infamous "iron maiden" started out as more of a "shame barrel"; the internal spikes were added to play up popular lore when it went on display for 18th-century tourists. For more serious offenses, criminals were branded—so that even if they left town, they'd take that shame with them for the rest of their lives. When all else failed, those in charge could always turn to the executioner's sword.

To safely capture potential witches, lawmen used a device resembling a metal collar—with spikes pointing in—that was easy to get into but nearly impossible to escape. A neck violin—like a portable version of a stock—kept the accused under control. The chastity belts were used to ensure a wife's loyalty and/or to protect women from rape, then a commonplace crime.

The exit routes you through a courtyard garden to a **last building** with temporary exhibits and a café. If you must buy a *Schneeball,* consider doing it here. A recent blind taste test among the town's tour guides deemed these the best.

▲GERMAN CHRISTMAS MUSEUM (DEUTSCHES WEIHNACHTSMUSEUM)

This excellent museum, in a Disney-esque space upstairs in the giant Käthe Wohlfahrt Christmas Village shop, tells the history of Christmas decorations. There's a unique and thoughtfully described collection of tree stands, mini trees sent in boxes to WWI soldiers at the front, early Advent calendars, old-time Christmas cards, and a look at the evolution of Father Christmas as well as tree decorations through the ages. The museum is not just a ploy to get shoppers to spend more money but a serious collection managed by professional curator Felicitas Höptner.

Cost and Hours: €4 most of the year, €2.50 low-season rate available to my readers year-round with this book; daily 10:00-17:30, shorter and irregular hours Jan-March; Herrngasse 1, tel. 09861/409-365, www.christmasmuseum.com.

EXPERIENCES

Shopping

Rothenburg is one of Germany's best shopping towns. Lovely prints, carvings, wine glasses, Christmas-tree ornaments, and beer steins are popular. Rödergasse is the old town's everyday shopping street. There's also a modern shopping center across the street from the train station.

To find local artisans, pick up the *Handmade in Rothenburg* pamphlet at the TI or visit the group's website (www. rothenburg-handmade.com).

For an appealing string of family-run shops, follow my "Schmiedgasse-Spital-gasse Shopping Stroll" (described earlier, under "Rothenburg Walks"). Below are two shops not on that walk:

KÄTHE WOHLFAHRT CHRISTMAS HEADQUARTERS

Rothenburg is the headquarters of the Käthe Wohlfahrt Christmas trinkets empire, which has spread across the half-timbered reaches of Europe. Rothenburg has six Wohlfahrts. Tourists flock to the two biggest, just below Market Square (Herrngasse 1 and 2). Start with the **Christmas Village** (Weihnachtsdorf) at Herrngasse 1. This Christmas wonderland is filled with enough twinkling lights (196,000—mostly LEDs) to require a special electrical hookup. You're greeted by instant Christmas mood music and tourists hungrily filling little woven shopping baskets with goodies (items handmade in Germany are the most expensive). With this book, you'll get 10 percent off official wooden KW products (look for the *Käthes Original* tag; must show book to receive discount).

Let the spinning, flocked tree whisk you in, and pause at the wall of Steiff stuffed animals. Then head downstairs to find the sprawling "made in Germany" section, surrounding a slowly spinning 15-foot tree decorated with a thousand glass balls. The fascinating **Christmas Museum** upstairs

is described earlier, under "Sights." The smaller shop (across the street at Herrngasse 2) specializes in finely crafted wooden ornaments. Käthe opened her first storefront here in Rothenburg in 1977. The company is now run by her son Harald (Christmas Village open Mon-Sat 9:00-18:00, Sun from 10:00 beginning in late April; shorter hours at other locations).

FRIESE SHOP

Cuckoo with friendliness, trinkets, and reasonably priced souvenirs, the Friese shop has been open for more than 90 years—and they've been welcoming my readers for more than 30. They give shoppers with this book tremendous service: a 10 percent discount off all items and a free pictorial map. Run for many years by Anneliese Friese, it's now lovingly run by her son, Bernie. They let tired travelers leave their bags in the back room for free (Mon-Sat 9:00-17:00, Sun from 10:00, 20 steps off Market Square at Grüner Markt 8—around the corner from TI and across from free public WC, tel. 09861/7166).

Festivals

For one weekend each spring (during Pentecost), beer gardens spill out into the street and Rothenburgers dress up in medieval costumes to celebrate Mayor Nusch's **Meistertrunk** victory (www. meistertrunk.de). The **Reichsstadt festival** every September celebrates Rothenburg's history, and the town's **Weindorf festival** celebrates its wine (mid-Aug). Check the TI website for specifics.

In winter, Rothenburg is quiet except for its **Christmas Market** in December, when the entire town cranks up the medieval cuteness with concerts and costumes, shops with schnapps, stalls filling squares, hot spiced wine, and mobs of ear-muffed Germans. Try to avoid Saturdays and Sundays, when big-city day-trippers really clog the grog.

SLEEPING

Rothenburg is crowded with visitors, but most are day-trippers. Except for the rare Saturday night and during festivals (see page 784), finding a room is easy. Competition keeps quality high. If you want to splurge, you'll snare the best value by paying extra for the biggest and best rooms at the hotels I recommend. In the off-season (Nov and Jan-March), hoteliers may be willing to discount.

Train travelers save steps by staying in the Rödertor area (east end of town). Hotels and guesthouses will sometimes pick up tired heavy-packers at the station. If you're driving, call ahead to get directions and parking tips. Save some energy to climb the stairs: Only one of my recommended hotels (Wildbad) has an elevator.

Keep your key when out late. As Rothenburg's hotels are small and mostly family-run, they often lock up early (at about 22:00) and take one day a week off, so you'll need to let yourself in at those times.

In the Old Town

$$$$ Hotel Herrnschlösschen prides itself on being the smallest (8 rooms) and most exclusive hotel in Rothenburg. If you're looking for a splurge, this 1,000-year-old building has a beautiful Baroque garden and every amenity you'd ever want (including a sauna), but you'll pay for them (Herrngasse 20, tel. 09861/873-890, www.herrnschloesschen.de, info@herrnschloesschen.de).

$$$ Gasthof Goldener Greifen, once Mayor Toppler's home, is a big, traditional, 650-year-old place with 14 spacious rooms and all the comforts. It's run by a helpful family staff and creaks with rustic splendor (family rooms, free loaner bikes for guests, free and easy parking, half a block downhill from Market Square at Obere Schmiedgasse 5, tel. 09861/2281, www.gasthof-greifen-rothenburg.de, info@gasthof-greifen-rothenburg.de; Brigitte, daughter Ursula, and Klingler family). The family also runs a good restaurant, serving meals in the back garden or dining room.

$$ Hotel Kloster-Stüble, deep in the old town near the castle garden, is one of my classiest listings. Twenty-one rooms, plus two apartments, each with its own special touches, fill two medieval buildings connected by a modern atrium (family rooms, just off Herrngasse at Heringsbronnengasse 5, tel. 09861/938-890, www.klosterstueble.de, hotel@klosterstueble.de, energetic Erika).

$$ Hotel Spitzweg is a rustic-yet-elegant 1536 mansion (never bombed or burned) with 10 big rooms, new bathrooms, open beams, and endearing hand-painted antique furniture. It's run by gentle Herr Hocher, whom I suspect is the former Wizard of Oz—now retired and in a very good mood (apartment, inviting old-fashioned breakfast room, free but limited parking, Paradeisgasse 2, tel. 09861/94290, www.hotel-spitzweg.de, info@hotel-spitzweg.de).

$$ Hotel Gerberhaus mixes modern comforts into 20 bright and airy rooms—some with four-poster *Himmel* beds—that maintain a sense of half-timbered elegance. Enjoy the pleasant garden in back and the delightful breakfast buffet. It's just inside the town wall, a five-minute walk to the main square (family rooms, apartment, pay parking, pay laundry, Spitalgasse 25, tel. 09861/94900, www.gerberhaus.rothenburg.de, info@hotelgerberhaus.com, Inge).

$$ Hotel Altfränkische Weinstube am Klosterhof is *the* place for well-heeled bohemians. Mario and Hanne rent eight cozy rooms above their dark and evocative pub in a 650-year-old building. It's an upscale *Lord of the Rings* atmosphere, with modern plumbing, open-beam ceilings, and some canopied four-poster beds (off Klingengasse at Klosterhof 7, tel. 09861/6404, www.altfraenkische.de, altfraenkische-weinstube@web.de). Their pub is a candlelit classic—and a favorite with locals, serving hot food to Hobbits (see listing later, under "Eating").

$ Pension Elke, run by spry Erich Endress and his son Klaus, rents 12 comfy rooms above the family grocery store. Guests who jog are welcome to join Klaus on his half-hour run around the city every evening at 19:30 (RS%, cheaper rooms with shared bath, cash only; reception in grocery store until 19:00, otherwise go around back and ring bell at top of stairs; near Markus Tower at Rödergasse 6, tel. 09861/2331, www.pension-elke-rothenburg.de, info@pension-elke-rothenburg.de).

$ Gästehaus Raidel rents eight rooms in a 500-year-old house filled with furniture all handmade by friendly, soft-spoken Norry Raidel. The ramshackle ambience makes me want to sing the *Addams Family* theme song, but the place has a rare, time-passed family charm. Norry, who plays in a Dixieland band, invented a fascinating hybrid saxophone/trombone called the Norryphone...and loves to jam (family rooms, cash only, pleasant terrace with small garden, Wenggasse 3, tel. 09861/3115, Norry asks you to use the reservations form at www.romanticroad.com/raidel).

$ Gasthof zum Breiterle offers 23 comfortable rooms with wooden accents above their spacious breakfast room near the Rödertor. Because the inn sits on a busy street, light sleepers may want to request a room not facing Wenggasse (apartment, reception in restaurant, pay parking, Rödergasse 30, tel. 09861/6730, www.breiterle.de, info@breiterle.de, Mike and Nicole).

$ Kreuzerhof Hotel offers 11 decent rooms surrounding a courtyard on a quiet side street near the Rödertor (family rooms, pay parking in courtyard, Millergasse 2, tel. 09861/3424, www.kreuzerhof.eu, info@kreuzerhof.eu, Heike and Walter Maltz).

Outside the Wall

$$ Wildbad provides a tranquil escape on the edge of the Tauber River. Offering 58 stylish rooms, this historic building occupies the site of a former 10th-century spa. The vast park surrounding the hotel, replete with walking trails, offers free summer concerts and Sunday *Kaffee und Kuchen* on the terrace. There's even a covered *Kegeln* lane where you can rent 19th-century wooden pins and try your hand at ninepin bowling. An elevator covers the first seven floors, but you'll have to walk to the eighth, where there's a tiny chapel and library (family rooms, free parking, Taubertalweg 42, tel. 09861/9770, www.wildbad.de, info@wildbad.de). While it's walkable to town, those arriving by train can take a taxi for around €7.

EATING

My recommendations are all within a five-minute walk of Market Square. While all survive on tourism, many still feel like local hangouts. Your choices are typical German or ethnic. You'll see regional Franconian (*fränkische*) specialties advertised, such as the German ravioli called *Maultaschen* and Franconian bratwurst (similar to other brats, but a bit more coarsely ground, with less fat, and liberally seasoned with marjoram). Many restaurants take a midafternoon break and stop serving lunch at 14:00; dinner may end as early as 20:00.

Traditional German Restaurants

$$$ Reichsküchenmeister's interior is like any forgettable big-hotel restaurant's, but on a balmy evening, its pleasant tree-shaded terrace overlooking St. Jakob's Church and reliably good dishes are hard to beat, including the *Flammkuchen*—southern German flatbread (daily 11:30-22:30, reservations smart, Kirchplatz 8, tel. 09861/9700, www.hotel-reichskuechenmeister-rothenburg.de).

$$$ Hotel Restaurant Kloster-Stüble, on a small street off Herrngasse near the castle garden, is a classy place for delicious and beautifully presented traditional cuisine, including homemade

English Conversation Club

Maultaschen (German ravioli). Choose from their shaded terrace, sleek-and-stony modern dining room, or woody traditional dining room (daily 18:00-20:30, Sat-Sun also 12:00-14:30, Heringsbronnengasse 5, tel. 09861/938-890).

Rick's Tip: *For a rare chance to* **meet the locals,** *bring your favorite slang and tongue-twisters to the* **English Conversation Club** *at* **Altfränkische Weinstube am Klosterhof.** *Hermann the German and his sidekick Wolfgang are regulars. A big table is reserved from 18:30 on Wednesday evenings. Consider arriving early for dinner, or after 21:00, when the beer starts to sink in and everyone speaks that second language more easily.*

\$\$ Gasthof Goldener Greifen, in a historic building with a peaceful garden out back, is just off the main square. The Klingler family serves quality Franconian food at a good price...and with a smile. The wood is ancient and polished from generations of happy use, and the ambi-ence is practical rather than posh (affordable kids' meals, Wed-Mon 11:30-21:00, closed Tue, Obere Schmiedgasse 5, tel. 09861/2281, Ursula).

\$\$ Altfränkische Weinstube am Klosterhof seems designed for gnomes to celebrate their anniversaries. At this very dark pub, classically candlelit in a 650-year-old building, Mario whips up gourmet pub grub (hot food served Wed-Mon 18:00-21:30, closed Tue, off Klingengasse at Klosterhof 7, tel. 09861/6404).

\$\$ Zum Pulverer ("The Powderer") is a very traditional *Weinstube* (wine bar) just inside the Burgtor gate that serves a menu of affordable and well-executed regional fare, some with modern flourishes. The interior is a cozy wood-hewn place that oozes history, with chairs carved in the shape of past senators of Rothenburg (daily 17:00-23:00 except Sat-Sun from 12:00, closed Tue, Herrengasse 31, tel. 09861/976-182).

\$\$ Alter Keller is a modest, tourist-friendly restaurant with an extremely characteristic interior and outdoor tables on a peaceful square just a couple blocks off Market Square. The menu has German classics at reasonable prices—*Spätzle,* schnitzel, and roasts—as well as steak (Wed-Sun 11:30-15:00 & 17:30-21:00, closed Mon-Tue, Alter Keller 8, tel. 09861/2268, Markus and Miriam).

Non-Franconian Fare

$$$$ Hotel Restaurant Herrnschlösschen offers a small menu of international and seasonal dishes. There's always a serious vegetarian option and a €50 fixed-price meal with wine pairing. It's perhaps the most elegant dining in town, whether in the classy dining hall or in the shaded Baroque garden out back. Reservations are a must (Herrngasse 20, tel. 09861/873-890, Ulrika, www.hotel-rothenburg.de).

$$ Pizzeria Roma is the locals' favorite for Italian. The Magrini family moved here from Tuscany in 1968, and they've been cooking pasta for Rothenburg ever since (Thu-Tue 11:30-23:00, closed Wed and mid-Aug-mid-Sept, Galgengasse 19, tel. 09861/4540, Riccardo).

$ TobinGo, just off Market Square, serves cheap and tasty Turkish food to eat in or take away. Their *döner kebab* must be the best €4.20 hot meal in Rothenburg. For about €1 more, try a less-bready *dürüm döner*—same ingredients but in a warm tortilla (daily 10:00-22:00, Hafengasse 2).

Sandwiches and Snacks

$ Brot & Zeit (a pun on *Brotzeit,* "bread time," the German term for snacking), conveniently located a block off Market Square, is like a German bakery dressed up as a Starbucks. In a bright, modern atmosphere just inside the super-picturesque Markus Tower gate, they sell take-away coffee, sandwiches, and a few hot dishes, making it a good one-stop shop (Mon-Sat 6:00-18:30, Sun 7:30-18:00, Hafengasse 24, tel. 09861/936-8701).

Bakery and Butcher Sandwiches: While any bakery in town can sell you a sandwich for a couple of euros, I like to pop into **$ Metzgerei Trumpp,** a high-quality butcher shop serving up cheap and tasty sausages on a bun with kraut to go (Mon-Fri 7:30-18:00, Sat until 16:00, usually closed Sun, a block off Market Square at Schmiedgasse 18).

Beer Garden

$$ Gasthof Rödertor, just outside the wall through the Rödertor, runs a backyard *Biergarten* that's popular with locals. It's great for a rowdy crowd looking for classic beer garden fare and good beer. Try a plate of *Schupfnudeln*—potato noodles with sauerkraut and bacon (May-Sept Tue-Sat 17:30-22:00, Sun until 21:00, closed Mon and in bad weather, table service only—no ordering at counter, Ansbacher Strasse 7, look for wooden gate, tel. 09861/2022). If the *Biergarten* is closed, their indoor restaurant, with a more extensive menu, is a good value (Tue-Sun 11:30-14:00 & 17:30-21:00, closed Mon).

Dessert

Eis Café D'Isep, with a pleasant "Venetian minimalist" interior, has been making gelato in Rothenburg since 1960, using family recipes that span four generations. Their sidewalk tables are great for lazy people-watching (daily 10:00-22:00, closed early Oct-mid-Feb, one block off Market Square at Hafengasse 17, run by Paolo and Paola D'Isep and son Enrico).

The **Allegra Schokolade** chocolate shop is run by delightful Alex, a pastry chef-turned-chocolatier who trained in Switzerland. He makes artisan chocolates with local ingredients and can arrange group workshops (Tue-Sat 10:00-18:00, Sun from 11:00, closed Mon; workshops from €10, minimum 4 people, 1.5 hours, arrange in advance; Georgengasse 9, tel. 9861/688-0293, www.allegra-schokolade.de, info@allegra-schokolade.de).

Rothenburg's **bakeries** (*Bäckereien*) offer succulent pastries, pies, and cakes... but skip the bad-tasting *Rothenburger Schneeballen.* Unworthy of the heavy promotion they receive, *Schneeballen* are bland pie crusts crumpled into a ball and dusted with powdered sugar or frosted with sticky-sweet glop. There's little reason to waste your appetite on a *Schneeball* when you can enjoy a curvy *Mandelhörnchen* (almond crescent cookie), a triangular *Nussecke* ("nut corner"), a round *Florentiner* cookie, a couple of fresh *Krapfen* (like jelly dough-nuts), or a soft, warm German pretzel.

TRANSPORTATION

Arriving and Departing
BY TRAIN

Arriving in Rothenburg: It's a 10-minute walk from the station to Rothenburg's Market Square (following the brown *Altstadt* signs, exit left from station, walk a block down Bahnhofstrasse, turn right on Ansbacher Strasse, and head straight into the Middle Ages). Taxis wait at the station (€10 to any hotel). Day-trippers can leave luggage in lockers on the platform. Free WCs are behind the Speedy snack bar on track 1.

The Rothenburg station has ticket machines for fare and schedule information and ticket sales. For extra help, visit the combined ticket office/travel agency in the station (€1-3 surcharge for most tickets, Mon-Fri 10:00-18:00, Sat 9:00-13:00, closed Sun, tel. 09861/7711). The station at Steinach is entirely unstaffed but has ticket machines. Train info: www.bahn.com.

Getting to/from Rothenburg via Steinach: If you take the train to or from Rothenburg, you'll transfer at Steinach. A tiny branch train line shuttles back and forth hourly between Steinach and Rothenburg (15 minutes, generally departs Steinach at :35 and Rothenburg at :06). Train connections in Steinach are usually quick and efficient (trains to and from Rothenburg generally use track 5; use the conveyor belts to haul your bags smartly up and down the stairs).

Note that the last train from Steinach to Rothenburg departs at about 22:30. But all is not lost if you arrive in Steinach after the last train: A subsidized taxi service runs to Rothenburg (cheaper for the government than running an almost-empty train). To use this handy service, called AST (*Anruf-sammeltaxi*), make an appointment with a participating taxi service (call 09861/2000 or 09861/7227) at least an hour in advance (2 hours ahead is better), and they'll drive you from Steinach to Rothenburg for the cost of train fare (€4.70/person) rather than the regular €30 taxi fare.

From Rothenburg (via Steinach) by Train to: Würzburg (hourly, 70 minutes), **Nürnberg** (hourly, 1.5 hours, change in Ansbach), **Munich** (hourly, 3.5 hours, 2-3 changes), **Füssen** (hourly, 5 hours, often with changes in Treuchtlingen and Augsburg), **Frankfurt** (hourly, 3 hours, change in Würzburg), **Frankfurt Airport** (hourly, 3.5 hours, change in Würzburg), **Berlin** (hourly, 5.5 hours, 3 changes).

BY CAR

Driving and parking rules in Rothenburg change constantly—ask your hotelier for advice. In general, you're allowed to drive into the old town to get to your hotel. Otherwise, driving within the old walled center is discouraged. Some hotels offer private parking (either free or paid). To keep things simple, park in one of the lots—numbered P-1 through P-5—that line the outside of the town walls (€5/day, buy ticket from *Parkscheinautomat* machines and display, 5- to 10-minute walk to Market Square).

Driving from Frankfurt Airport: The three-hour autobahn drive from **Frankfurt Airport** to Rothenburg is something even a jet-lagged zombie can handle. It's a 75-mile straight shot to Würzburg on the A-3 autobahn; just follow the blue autobahn signs toward *Würzburg*. Then turn south on A-7 and take the *Rothenburg o.d.T.* exit (#108).

NEAR ROTHENBURG

The Romantic Road

The countryside between Frankfurt and Munich is Germany's medieval heartland. Walls and towers ring half-timbered towns, flowers spill over the windowsills of well-kept houses, and glockenspiels dance from town halls. Many travelers bypass these small towns by fast train or autobahn. But, especially if you're driving, consider an extra day or two to take in the slow pace of small-town German life.

Getting There

BY CAR

Wander through quaint hills and rolling villages along the 220-mile scenic driving route called the Romantic Road (*Romantische Strasse,* www.romantischestrasse. de), stopping wherever the cows look friendly or a town fountain beckons. If your goal is to meander and explore, skip the GPS, get a good map, and follow the brown *Romantische Strasse* signs. If you're driving north of Rothenburg, good stops are Creglingen and Weikersheim. Driving south of Rothenburg (whether heading toward it or leaving it), stop at the Wieskirche and the towns of Nördlingen and Dinkelsbühl.

BY BUS

The Romantic Road bus runs Wednesday and Sunday from April through October, with a third departure on Saturday from mid-May to early September. One bus goes north to south (Frankfurt to Munich), and another follows the reverse route south to north (Munich to Frankfurt). Check the full timetable at www. romantischestrasse.de (choose "Bus & Train," then "Romantic Road Bus").

North of Rothenburg

CREGLINGEN

While Creglingen itself isn't worth much fuss (www.creglingen.de), two quick and rewarding sights sit across the road from each other a mile south of town.

The peaceful 14th-century **Herr-**

The palace at Weikersheim has fine gardens.

gottskirche Church, worth ▲, is graced with Tilman Riemenschneider's greatest carved altarpiece, completed sometime between 1505 and 1510, and nearly 30 feet high—tall enough that its tip pokes up between the rafters. The church's other, colorful (non-Riemenschneider) altars are also worth a peek (www.herrgottskirche.de).

The **Fingerhut Museum,** showing off thimbles (literally, "finger hats"), is far more interesting than it sounds. You'll step from case to case to squint at the collection, which numbers about 4,000 (but still fits in a single room) and comes from all over the world; some pieces are centuries old (www.fingerhutmuseum.de).

▲WEIKERSHEIM

This picturesquely set town, nestled between hills, has a charming little main square offering easy access to a fine park and an impressive palace.

Weikersheim's **palace** (Schloss Weikersheim), across a moat-turned-park from the main square, was built in the late 16th century as the Renaissance country estate of a local count. With its bucolic location and glowing sandstone texture, it gives off a *Downton Abbey* vibe. The palace interior is only viewable by a guided tour in German (www.schloss-weikersheim.de)—skip the tour and instead focus on exploring the palace's fine Baroque **gardens.**

If you have time after your garden visit, Weikersheim's pleasant **town square** and cobbled old town are worth exploring. The **city park** (*Stadtpark,* enter off town square) is a fine picnic spot, and from it you can peer over the hedge into the palace gardens.

South of Rothenburg
▲DINKELSBÜHL

Rothenburg's little sister is cute enough to merit a short stop. A moat, towers, gates, and a beautifully preserved medieval wall surround this town. Park at one of the free lots outside the town walls, which are well signed from the main road.

To orient yourself, head for the tower of **St. Georg's Cathedral,** at the center of town. This 15th-century church has a surprisingly light, airy interior and fine carved altarpieces. On good-weather summer weekends, you can climb to the top of the tower.

Outside the church, follow signs around the corner (to the **TI** (www.dinkelsbuehl.de), which doubles as the ticket office for the fine **City History Museum** (Haus der Geschichte) in the same building.

Sleeping in Dinkelsbühl: Dinkelsbühl has a good selection of hotels. Options include: **$$$ Hezelhof Hotel** (modern rooms in an old shell at Segringer Strasse 7, www.hezelhof.com), **$$$ Weisses Ross** ("White Horse," attached to a historic restaurant at Steingasse 12, www.hotel-weisses-ross.de), and Dinkelsbühl's unique **¢ youth hostel** (in a medieval granary at Koppengasse 10, www.dinkelsbuehl.jugendherberge.de).

▲NÖRDLINGEN

Nördlingen is a real workaday town that has one of the best city walls in Germany, not to mention a surprising geological history. For centuries, Nördlingen's residents puzzled over the local terrain, a flattish plain called the Ries, which rises to a low circular ridge that surrounds the town in the distance. In the 1960s, geologists

Dinkelsbühl

St. Georg's Church dominates Nördlingen.

figured out that Nördlingen lies in the middle of an impact crater blasted out 15 million years ago by a meteor.

Park in one of the big, free lots at the Delninger Tor and the Baldinger Tor, then head into the center of town by zeroing in on the tower of **St. Georg's Church.** The rickety 350-step climb up the church tower rewards you with the very best view of the city walls and crater. With more time, walk all the way around on the top of the **town wall,** which is even better preserved than Rothenburg's or Dinkelsbühl's. It's more than a mile and a half long, has 16 towers and 5 gates, and offers great views of backyards and garden furniture.

Sleeping in Nördlingen: Several small hotels surrounding St. Georg's Church offer mediocre but reasonably priced rooms. Try **$$ Hotel Altreuter** (over an inviting bakery/café at Marktplatz 11, www. hotel-altreuter.de).

▲▲Wieskirche

Germany's most glorious Baroque-Rococo church is beautifully restored and set in a sweet meadow. Bright and bursting with beauty, the church is worth the pilgrimage (open daily 8:00-20:00, shorter hours in winter, www.wieskirche. de).

Rhine Valley

The Rhine Valley is storybook Germany, a fairy-tale world of legends and "robber-baron" castles. Cruise the most turret-studded stretch of the romantic Rhine as you listen for the song of the treacherous Loreley. For hands-on thrills, climb through the Rhineland's greatest castle, Rheinfels, above the town of St. Goar. Castle connoisseurs enjoy the fine interiors of Marksburg Castle near Koblenz and Burg Eltz on the Mosel River.

Spend your nights in a castle-crowned village, either Bacharach or St. Goar. They're 10 miles apart, connected by milk-run trains, riverboats, and a riverside bike path. Bacharach is a more interesting town, but St. Goar has the famous Rheinfels Castle.

Marvel at the Rhine's ever-changing parade. Ever since Roman times, when this was the empire's northern boundary, the Rhine has been one of the world's busiest shipping rivers. Traveling along the river today, you'll see a steady flow of barges with 1,000- to 2,000-ton loads. Cars, buses, and trains rush along highways and tracks lining both banks as cruiseboats glide by, making it easy to get around.

If possible, visit the Rhine between April and October, when it's at its touristic best. In winter, some sights close, along with some hotels and restaurants, and only one riverboat runs.

THE RHINE VALLEY IN 1 OR 2 DAYS

With one day and two nights, stay in Bacharach. Cruise the best and most scenic stretch of the river (the hour from Bacharach to St. Goar), and tour Rheinfels Castle. Enjoy dinner in Bacharach, and maybe a wine tasting, too.

For a busier day, take a longer cruise, following all or part of my Rhine Blitz Tour. For example, you could cruise from Bacharach to Braubach (to tour Marksburg Castle), before returning by train to Bacharach.

With a second day, visit Burg Eltz on the Mosel as a day trip. Or bike or hike along the Rhine. This is a fun place to relax and explore.

If you're traveling by car, park it at your hotel, cruise the Rhine by boat, and visit Burg Eltz and/or Cologne on your drive in or out.

RHINE VALLEY AT A GLANCE

On the Rhine

▲▲▲**Rhine Blitz Tour** One of Europe's great joys—touring the Rhine River by boat, train, bike, or car. See page 798.

▲▲▲**Rheinfels Castle** The best opportunity to explore a ruined castle on the river. **Hours:** Daily 9:00-18:00, Nov-mid-March possibly Sat-Sun only 11:00-17:00 (call ahead). See page 820.

▲▲**Marksburg Castle in Braubach** The best-preserved medieval castle on the Rhine. **Hours:** Daily 10:00-17:00, Nov-mid-March 11:00-16:00, last tour departs one hour before closing. See page 826.

Near the Rhine Valley

▲▲▲**Burg Eltz, on the Mosel** My favorite castle in Europe, set deep in a forest, with a rare furnished interior—take the required guided tour. **Hours:** Daily from 9:30, last tour departs at 17:30, closed Nov-March. See page 830.

GERMANY

Rhine Overview

Düsseldorf

Rhine

Cologne

UNROMANTIC
RHINE

Aachen

Bonn

Remagen

BEST OF
THE RHINE
See detail map

GERMANY
Berlin

BELG.

BURG
ELTZ

Koblenz

Frankfurt

Cochem

St.
Goar

Wies-
baden

Main R.

Beilstein

Oberwesel

Bingen

Frankfurt

Bacharach

Mainz

Mosel R.

Neckar R.

LUX.

Trier

Hahn

Heidelberg

Lux.
City

GERMANY

Rhine

50 Kilometers

50 Miles

FRANCE

Rick's Tip: *Rhine Valley* **guesthouses and hotels often have similar names.** *When reserving, double-check that you're contacting the one in your planned destination.*

RHINE BLITZ TOUR

One of Europe's great train thrills is zipping along the Rhine enjoying this self-guided blitz tour, worth ▲▲▲. For short distances, cruising is best because it's slower. A cruise going upstream (heading south, toward Bingen) takes longer than the same cruise going downstream (north, toward Koblenz). If you want to draw out a short cruise, go upstream (for instance, from St. Goar to Bacharach).

To cover long distances (e.g., Koblenz to Bingen), consider the train. Or take the

boat one way and the train back. See page 805 for specifics on traveling the Rhine.

⊖ Self-Guided Tour

This quick and easy tour (you can cut in anywhere) skips most of the syrupy myths filling normal Rhine guides. You can follow along on a train, boat, bike, or car. By train or boat, sit on the left (river) side going south from Koblenz.

You'll notice large black-and-white kilometer markers along the riverbank. I erected these years ago to make this tour easier to follow. They tell the distance from the Rhine Falls, where the Rhine leaves Switzerland and becomes navigable. (Today, river-barge pilots also use these markers to navigate.)

We're tackling just 36 miles (58 km) of the 820-mile-long (1,320-km) Rhine. This "Best of the Rhine" tour starts at Koblenz

Castles of the Rhine

Many of the castles of the Rhine were "robber-baron" castles, put there by petty rulers (there were 300 independent little countries in medieval Germany) to levy tolls on passing river traffic. A robber baron would put his castle on, or even in, the river. Then, often with the help of chains and a tower on the opposite bank, he'd stop each ship and get his toll. There were 10 customs stops in the 60-mile stretch between Mainz and Koblenz alone.

Some castles were built to control and protect settlements, and others were the residences of kings. As times changed, so did the lifestyles of the rich and feudal. Many castles were abandoned for more comfortable mansions in the towns.

Most Rhine castles date from the 11th, 12th, and 13th centuries. When the pope successfully asserted his power over the German emperor in 1076, local princes ran wild over the rule of their emperor. The castles saw military action in the 1300s and 1400s, as emperors began reasserting their control over Germany's many silly kingdoms.

The castles were also involved in the Reformation wars, in which Europe's Catholic and Protestant dynasties fought it out using a fragmented Germany as their battleground. The Thirty Years' War (1618-1648) devastated Germany. The outcome: Each ruler got the freedom to decide if his people would be Catholic or Protestant, and one-third of Germans died. (Production of Gummi Bears ceased entirely.)

The French—who feared a strong Germany and felt the Rhine was the logical border between them and Germany—destroyed most of the castles as a preventive measure (Louis XIV in the 1680s, the Revolutionary army in the 1790s, and Napoleon in 1806). Many were rebuilt in the Neo-Gothic style in the Romantic Age—the late 1800s—and today are enjoyed as restaurants, hotels, hostels, and museums.

and heads upstream to Bingen. If you're going the other direction, it still works. Just hold the book upside-down.

🎧 Download my free Best of the Rhine audio tour—it works in either direction.

Koblenz to Bingen

Many of these sights are described in greater detail later in this chapter.

Km 590—Koblenz: This Rhine blitz starts with Romantic Rhine thrills, at Koblenz. Koblenz isn't terribly attractive (it was hit hard in World War II), but its place at the historic Deutsches Eck ("German Corner")—the tip of land where the Mosel River joins the Rhine—gives it a certain patriotic charm. A cable car links the Deutsches Eck with the yellow Ehren-

Little Bacharach's dock and boat ramp

breitstein Fortress across the river.

Km 586—Lahneck Castle: Above the modern autobahn bridge over the Lahn River, this castle *(Burg)* was built in 1240 to defend local silver mines. The castle was ruined by the French in 1688 and rebuilt in the 1850s in Neo-Gothic style. Burg Lahneck faces another Romantic rebuild, the yellow Schloss Stolzenfels (€5, out of view above the train, Tue-Sun 10:00-18:00, closed Mon, Sat-Sun only and shorter hours off-season, closed Dec-Jan, a 10-minute climb from tiny parking lot, www.schloss-stolzenfels.de). Note that a *Burg* is a defensive fortress, while a *Schloss* is mainly a showy palace.

Km 580—Marksburg Castle: This castle stands bold and white—restored to look like most Rhine castles once did, with their slate stonework covered with stucco to look as if made from a richer stone. You'll spot Marksburg with the three modern smokestacks behind it (these vent Europe's biggest car-battery recycling plant just up the valley), just before the town of Spay. This is the best-looking of all the Rhine castles and the only surviving medieval castle on the Rhine. Because of its commanding position, it was never attacked in the Middle Ages (though it was captured

Boppard

by the US Army in March 1945). It's now a museum with a medieval interior second only to the Mosel Valley's Burg Eltz.

Km 570—Boppard: Once a Roman town, Boppard has some impressive remains of fourth-century walls. Look for the Roman towers and the substantial chunk of Roman wall near the train station, just above the main square.

If you visit Boppard, head to the fascinating Church of St. Severus below the main square. Find the carved Romanesque crazies at the doorway. Inside, to the right of the entrance, you'll see Christian symbols from Roman times. Also

Maus Castle

notice the painted arches and vaults (originally, most Romanesque churches were painted this way). Down by the river, look for the high-water (*Hochwasser*) marks on the arches from various flood years. You'll find these flood marks throughout the Rhine and Mosel valleys.

Km 567—Sterrenberg Castle and Liebenstein Castle: These neighboring castles, across from the town of Bad Salzig, are known as the "Hostile Brothers." Notice how they're isolated from each other by a low-slung wall. The wall was built to improve defenses from both castles, but this is the *romantic* Rhine so there has to be a legend: Take one wall between castles, add two greedy and jealous brothers and a fair maiden, and create your own legend. **$$$ Burg Liebenstein** is now a fun, friendly, and reasonably affordable family-run hotel (9 rooms, giant king-and-the-family room, easy parking, tel. 06773/251, www.castle-liebenstein.com, info@burg-liebenstein.de, Nickenig family).

Km 559—Maus Castle: The Maus (mouse) got its name because the next castle was owned by the Katzenelnbogen family. (*Katz* means "cat.") In the 1300s, it was considered a state-of-the-art fortification...until 1806, when Napoleon

Bonaparte had it blown apart with then-state-of-the-art explosives. It was rebuilt true to its original plans in about 1900. Today, Burg Maus is open for concerts, weddings, and guided tours in German (20-minute walk up, weekends only, reservations required, tel. 06771/2303, www.burg-maus.de).

St. Goar to Bacharach: The Best of the Rhine

Km 557—St. Goar and Rheinfels Castle: Cross to the other side of the train. The pleasant town of St. Goar was named for a sixth-century hometown monk. It originated in Celtic times as a place where sailors would stop, catch their breath, send home a postcard, and give thanks after surviving the seductive and treacherous Loreley crossing. St. Goar is worth a stop to explore its mighty Rheinfels Castle.

Km 556—Katz Castle: Burg Katz (Katzenelnbogen) faces St. Goar from across the river. Together, Burg Katz (built in 1371) and Rheinfels Castle had a clear view up and down the river, effectively controlling traffic (there was absolutely no duty-free shopping on the medieval Rhine). Katz got Napoleoned in 1806 and rebuilt in about 1900.

The scenic cliffs of the Rhine, steeped in history

GERMANY

The Rhine River Trade and Barge-Watching

The Rhine is great for barge-watching. There's a constant parade of action, and each boat is different. Since ancient times, this has been a highway for trade. Today, Europe's biggest port (Rotterdam) waits at the mouth of the river.

Barge workers are almost a subculture. Many own their own ships. The captain lives in the stern, with his family. The family car is often parked on the stern. Workers live in the bow.

The flag of the boat's home country flies in the stern (Dutch—horizontal red, white, and blue; Belgian—vertical black, yellow, and red; Swiss—white cross on a red field; German—horizontal black, red, and yellow; French—vertical red, white, and blue). Logically, imports go upstream (Japanese cars, coal, and oil) and exports go downstream (German cars, chemicals, and pharmaceuticals). A clever captain ships goods in each direction. Recently, giant Dutch container ships (which transport five times the cargo) have been driving many of the traditional barges out of business, presenting the German economy with another challenge.

Going downstream, tugs can push a floating train of up to five barges at once, but upstream, as the slope gets steeper (and the stream gradient gets higher), they can push only one at a time. Before modern shipping, horses dragged boats upstream. From 1873 to 1900, workers laid a chain from Bonn to Bingen, and boats with cogwheels and steam engines hoisted themselves upstream. Today, 265 million tons travel each year along the 530 miles from Basel on the German-Swiss border to the Dutch city of Rotterdam on the Atlantic.

Riverside navigational aids are vital. Boats pass on the right unless they clearly signal otherwise with a large blue sign. Since ships heading downstream can't stop or maneuver as freely, boats heading upstream are expected to do the tricky do-si-do work. Cameras monitor traffic all along and relay warnings of oncoming ships by posting large triangular signals before narrow and troublesome bends in the river. Each triangle tells whether there's a ship in that sector. When the bottom side of a triangle is lit, that sector is empty. When the left side is lit, an oncoming ship is in that sector.

About Km 555: A statue of the Loreley, the beautiful-but-deadly nymph, combs her hair at the end of a long spit—built to give barges protection from vicious ice floes that until recent years raged down the river in the winter. The actual Loreley, a landmark cliff, is just ahead.

Km 554—The Loreley: Steep a big slate rock in centuries of legend and it becomes a tourist attraction—the ulti-

mate Rhinestone. The Loreley (name painted near shoreline), rising 450 feet over the narrowest and deepest point of the Rhine, has long been important. It was a holy site in pre-Roman days. The fine echoes here—thought to be ghostly voices—fertilized legend-tellers' imaginations.

Because of the reefs just upstream (at km 552), many ships never made it to

St. Goar. Sailors (after days on the river) blamed their misfortune on a *wunderbare Fräulein,* whose long, blond hair almost covered her body. Heinrich Heine's *Song of Loreley* tells the story of a count sending his men to kill or capture this siren after she distracted his horny son, who forgot to watch where he was sailing and drowned. When the soldiers cornered the nymph in her cave, she called her father (Father Rhine) for help. Huge waves, the likes of which you'll never see today, rose from the river and carried Loreley to safety. And she has never been seen since.

Pfalz Castle (left) and Gutenfels Castle (on hillside)

But alas, when the moon shines brightly and the tour buses are parked, a soft, playful Rhine whine can still be heard from the Loreley. As you pass, listen carefully ("Sailors...sailors...over my bounding mane"). Today a visitors center keeps the story alive; if you visit you can hike to the top of the cliff.

Km 552—The Seven Maidens: Killer reefs, marked by red-and-green buoys, are called the "Seven Maidens." OK, one more goofy legend: The prince of Schönburg Castle (über Oberwesel—described next) had seven spoiled daughters who always dumped men because of their shortcomings. Fed up, he invited seven of his knights to the castle and demanded that his daughters each choose one to marry. But they complained that each man had too big a nose, was too fat, too stupid, and so on. The rude and teasing girls escaped into a riverboat. Just downstream, God turned them into the seven rocks that form this reef. While this story probably isn't entirely true, there is a lesson in it for medieval children: Don't be hard-hearted.

Km 550—Oberwesel: Cross to the other side of the train. The town of Oberwesel, topped by the commanding Schönburg Castle (now a hotel), boasts some of the best medieval wall and tower remains on the Rhine.

Notice how many of the train tunnels along here have entrances designed like medieval turrets—they were actually built in the Romantic 19th century. OK, back to the riverside.

Km 547—Gutenfels Castle and Pfalz Castle, the Classic Rhine View: Burg Gutenfels (now a privately owned hotel) and the shipshape Pfalz Castle (built in the river in the 1300s) worked effectively to tax medieval river traffic. The town of Kaub grew rich as Pfalz raised its chains when boats came, and lowered them only when the merchants had paid their duty. Those who didn't pay spent time touring its prison, on a raft at the bottom of its well. In 1504, a pope called for the destruction of Pfalz, but the locals withstood a six-week siege, and the castle still stands. Notice the overhanging outhouse (tiny white room between two wooden ones). Pfalz (also known as Pfalzgrafenstein) is tourable but bare and dull (€2.50 ferry from Kaub, €3 entry, Tue-Sun 10:00-18:00, closed Mon; shorter hours in March; Nov and Jan-Feb Sat-Sun only, closed Dec; last entry one hour before closing, mobile 0172-262-2800, www.burg-pfalzgrafenstein.de).

In Kaub, on the riverfront directly below the castles, a green statue (near the waving flags) honors the German general Gebhard von Blücher. He was Napoleon's nemesis. In 1813, as Napoleon fought his way back to Paris after his disastrous Russian campaign, he stopped at Mainz—

hoping to fend off the Germans and Russians pursuing him by controlling that strategic bridge. Blücher tricked Napoleon. By building the first major pontoon bridge of its kind here at the Pfalz Castle, he crossed the Rhine and outflanked the French. Two years later, Blücher and Wellington teamed up to defeat Napoleon once and for all at Waterloo.

Immediately opposite Kaub (where the ferry lands, marked by blue roadside flags) is a gaping hole in the mountainside. This marks the last working slate mine on the Rhine.

Km 544—"The Raft Busters": Just before Bacharach, at the top of the island, buoys mark a gang of rocks notorious for busting up rafts. The Black Forest, upstream from here, was once poor, and wood was its best export. Black Foresters would ride log booms down the Rhine to the Ruhr (where their timber fortified coal-mine shafts) or to Holland (where logs were sold to shipbuilders). If they could navigate the sweeping bend just before Bacharach and then survive these "raft busters," they'd come home reckless and horny—the German folkloric equivalent of American cowboys after payday.

Km 543—Bacharach and Stahleck Castle: Cross to the other side of the train. The town of Bacharach is a great stop. Some of the Rhine's best wine is from this town, whose name likely derives from "altar to Bacchus" (the Roman god of wine). Local vintners brag that the medieval Pope Pius II ordered Bacharach wine by the cartload. Perched above the town, the 13th-century Burg Stahleck is now a hostel. Return to the riverside.

Km 541—Lorch: This stub of a castle is barely visible from the road. The hillside vineyards once blanketed four times as much land as they do today, but modern economics have driven most of them out of business. The vineyards that do survive require government subsidies. Notice the small car ferry, one of several along the bridgeless stretch between Mainz and Koblenz.

Km 538—Sooneck Castle: Cross back to the other side of the train. Built in the 11th century, this castle was twice destroyed by people sick and tired of robber barons.

Km 534—Reichenstein Castle and **Km 533—Rheinstein Castle:** Stay on the other side of the train to see two of the first castles to be rebuilt in the Romantic

Stahleck Castle

Sooneck Castle

Ehrenfels Castle's little "mouse tower" keeps guard on the river.

Rhein in Flammen

During the annual "Rhine in Flames" festival, spectacular displays of fireworks take place along the most scenic stretches of the Rhine, while beautifully illuminated ships ply the river, offering up-close views of the fireworks above. Held on five separate days between May and September, the festival rotates between several Rhine towns. Traditional wine festivals and other local celebrations are often timed to coincide with the Rhein in Flammen (www.rhein-in-flammen.com).

era. Both are privately owned, tourable, and connected by a pleasant trail. Go back to the river side.

Km 530—Ehrenfels Castle: Opposite Bingerbrück and the Bingen station, you'll see the ghostly Ehrenfels Castle (clobbered by the Swedes in 1636 and by the French in 1689). Since it had no view of the river traffic to the north, the owner built the cute little *Mäuseturm* (mouse tower) on an island (the yellow tower you'll see near the train station today). Rebuilt in the 1800s in Neo-Gothic style, it's now used as a Rhine navigation signal station.

Km 528—Niederwald Monument: Across from the Bingen station on a hilltop is the 120-foot-high Niederwald monument, a memorial built with 32 tons of bronze in 1877 to commemorate "the re-establishment of the German Empire." A lift takes tourists to this statue from the famous and extremely touristy wine town of Rüdesheim.

From here, the Romantic Rhine becomes the industrial Rhine, and our tour is over.

Transportation
Getting Around the Rhine

The Rhine flows north from Switzerland to Holland, but the scenic stretch from Mainz to Koblenz hoards all the touristic charm. Studded with the crenellated cream of Germany's castles, it bustles with boats, trains, and highway traffic. Have fun exploring with a mix of big steamers, tiny ferries *(Fähre)*, trains, and bikes.

BY BOAT

While some travelers do the whole Mainz-Koblenz trip by boat (5.5 hours downstream, 8.5 hours up), I'd just focus on the most scenic hour—from Bacharach to St. Goar. Sit on the boat's top deck with your handy Rhine map-guide (or the kilometer-keyed tour in this chapter) and enjoy the parade of castles, towns, boats, and vineyards.

Two boat companies take travelers along this stretch of the Rhine. Boats run daily in both directions from early April through October, with only one boat running off-season.

Most travelers sail on the bigger, more expensive, and romantic **Köln-Düsseldorfer (K-D) Line** (recommended Bacharach-St. Goar trip: €14.80 one-

K-D Line Rhine Cruise Schedule

This schedule is approximate; check www.k-d.com for the latest. Boats run from early April through October (usually 5/day, but 3-4/day in early April and most of Oct). From November through March, one boat runs daily for groups, but you can tag along if they know you're coming—call the boat directly (tel. 0172/1360-335) or the main office in Cologne (tel. 0221/2088-318).

Koblenz	Boppard	St. Goar	Bacharach
—	9:00	10:20	11:30
*9:00	*11:00	*12:20	*13:30
—	13:00	14:20	15:30
—	14:00	15:20	16:30
14:00	16:00	17:20	18:30
13:10	11:50	10:55	10:15
—	12:50	11:55	11:15
—	13:50	12:55	12:15
18:10	16:50	15:55	15:15
*20:10	*18:50	*17:55	*17:15

These sailings are generally on the 1913 paddle-wheeler Goethe.

way, €16.80 round-trip, bikes-€2.80/day; discounts: up to 30 percent if over 60, 20 percent with connecting train ticket, 20 percent with rail passes and does not count as a flexipass day; tel. 06741/1634 in St. Goar, tel. 06743/1322 in Bacharach, www.k-d.com). I've included an abridged K-D cruise schedule in this chapter. Complete, up-to-date schedules are posted at any Rhineland station, hotel, TI, and www.k-d.com. (Confirm times at your hotel the night before.) Purchase tickets at the dock up to five minutes before departure. The boat is never full. Romantics will enjoy the old-time paddle-wheeler *Goethe*, which sails each direction once a day (noted on schedule, confirm time locally).

The smaller **Bingen-Rüdesheimer Line** is slightly cheaper than the K-D, doesn't offer any rail pass deals, and makes three trips in each direction daily from mid-March through October (Bacharach-St. Goar: €13.40 one-way, €15.40 round-trip, bikes-€2/day, buy tickets at ticket booth or on boat, ticket booth opens just before boat departs, 30 percent discount if over 60; departs Bacharach at 10:10, 12:00, and 15:15; departs St. Goar at 11:00, 14:00, and 16:15; tel. 06721/308-0810, www.bingen-ruedesheimer.de).

BY CAR

Drivers have these options: 1) skip the boat; 2) take a round-trip cruise from St. Goar or Bacharach; 3) draw pretzels and let the loser drive, prepare the picnic, and meet the boat; 4) rent a bike, bring it on the boat, and bike back; or 5) take the boat one-way and return to your car by train. When exploring by car, don't hesitate to pop onto one of the many little ferries that shuttle across the bridge-less-around-here river.

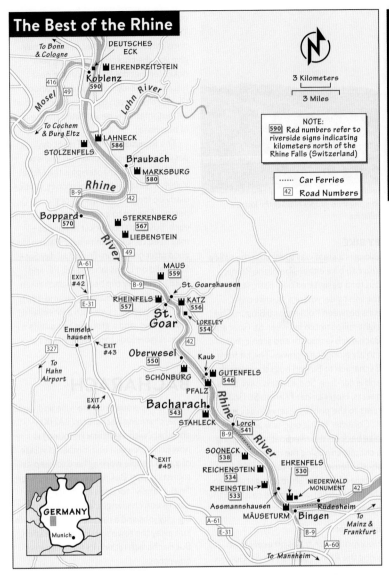

The Best of the Rhine

To Bonn & Cologne

DEUTSCHES ECK

EHRENBREITSTEIN

Koblenz
590

416
49

Mosel

Lahn River

To Cochem & Burg Eltz

LAHNECK
586

STOLZENFELS

Braubach

MARKSBURG
580

Rhine

B-9

42

River

Boppard
570

STERRENBERG
567

LIEBENSTEIN

49

A-61

EXIT #42

MAUS
559

B-9

St. Goarshausen

E-31

RHEINFELS
557

KATZ
556

St. Goar

LORELEY
554

Emmels-hausen

EXIT #43

327

To Hahn Airport

Oberwesel
550

42

Kaub

SCHÖNBURG

GUTENFELS
546

PFALZ

EXIT #44

Bacharach
543

STAHLECK

Lorch
541

B-9

River

EXIT #45

SOONECK
538

REICHENSTEIN
534

EHRENFELS
530

RHEINSTEIN
533

NIEDERWALD MONUMENT

42

Assmannshausen

MÄUSETURM

Rüdesheim

Bingen

A-61

E-31

B-9

To Mainz & Frankfurt

A-60

To Mannheim

GERMANY

Munich

NOTE:
590 Red numbers refer to riverside signs indicating kilometers north of the Rhine Falls (Switzerland)

...... Car Ferries
42 Road Numbers

3 Kilometers

3 Miles

BY FERRY

As there are no bridges between Koblenz and Mainz, you'll see car-and-passenger ferries (usually family-run for generations) about every three miles. Bingen-Rüdesheim, Lorch-Niederheimbach, Engelsburg-Kaub, and St. Goar-St. Goarshausen are some of the most useful routes (times vary; St. Goar-St. Goarshausen ferry departs each side every 20 minutes daily until 22:30, less frequently Sun; one-way fares: adult–€1.80, car and driver–€4.50, pay on boat; www.faehreloreley.de). For a fun little jaunt, take a quick round-trip with some time to explore the other side.

Riesling wine grapes blanket the Rhine's hillsides.

BY BIKE

Biking is a great way to explore the valley. You can bike either side of the Rhine, but for a designated bike path, stay on the west side, where a 35-mile path runs between Koblenz and Bingen. The eight-mile stretch between St. Goar and Bacharach is smooth and scenic, but mostly along the highway. The bit from Bacharach to Bingen hugs the riverside and is car-free. Some hotels have bikes for guests; Hotel an der Fähre in St. Goar also rents to the public (reserve in advance).

Consider biking one-way and taking the bike back on the riverboat, or designing a circular trip using the fun and frequent shuttle ferries. A good target is Kaub (where a tiny boat shuttles sightseers to the better-from-a-distance castle on the island) or Rheinstein Castle.

BY TRAIN

Hourly milk-run trains hit every town along the Rhine (Bacharach-St. Goar in both directions about :50 after the hour, 10 minutes; Mainz-Bacharach, 40 minutes; Mainz-Koblenz, 1 hour). Express trains speed past the small towns, taking only 50 minutes nonstop between Mainz and Koblenz. Tiny stations are unstaffed—buy tickets at machines. Though generally user-friendly, some ticket machines only take exact change; others may not accept US credit cards. When buying a ticket, follow the instructions carefully. The ticket machine may give you the choice of validating your ticket for that day or a day in the near future—but only for some destinations (if you're not given this option, your ticket will automatically be validated for the day of purchase).

The **Rheinland-Pfalz-Ticket** day pass covers travel on milk-run trains to anywhere in this chapter, plus the Mosel Valley. It can save heaps of money, particularly on longer day trips or for groups (1 person-€24, up to 4 additional people-€5/ each, buy at station ticket machines— may need to select Rhineland-Palatinate, good after 9:00 Mon-Fri and all day Sat-Sun, valid on trains labeled *RB, RE,* and *MRB*). For a day trip between Bacharach and Burg Eltz (normally €35 round-trip), even one person saves with a Rheinland-Pfalz-Ticket, and a group of five adults saves €130—look for travel partners at breakfast.

BACHARACH

Once prosperous from the wine and wood trade, charming Bacharach (BAHKH-ah-rahkh, with a guttural *kh* sound) is now just a pleasant half-timbered village of 2,000 people working hard to keep its tourists happy. Businesses that have been "in the family" for eons are dealing with succession challenges, as the allure of big-city jobs and a more cosmopolitan life lure away the town's younger generation. But Bacharach retains its time-capsule quaintness.

Orientation

Bacharach cuddles, long and narrow, along the Rhine. The village is easily strollable—you can walk from one end of town to the other along its main drag, Oberstrasse, in about 10 minutes. Bacharach widens at its stream, where more houses trickle up its small valley (along

Blücherstrasse) away from the Rhine. The hillsides above town are occupied by vineyards, scant remains of the former town walls, and a castle-turned-hostel.

Tourist Information: The bright and well-stocked TI, on the main street a block-and-a-half from the train station, will store bags and bikes for day-trippers (April-Oct Mon-Fri 9:00-17:00, Sat-Sun 10:00-15:00; Nov-March Mon-Fri 9:00-13:00, closed Sat-Sun; from the train station, exit right and walk down the main street with the castle high on your left—the TI will be on your right at Oberstrasse 10; tel. 06743/919-303, www.bacharach.de or www.rhein-nahe-touristik.de, Herr Kuhn and his team).

Rick's Tip: *Although more places are accepting credit cards,* **come prepared to pay cash** *for most things in the Rhine Valley.*

Bike Rental: Some hotels loan bikes to guests. For bike rental in town, head to **Rent-a-Bike Weber** (€10/day, Koblenzer Strasse 35, tel. 06743-1898, mobile 0175-168073, heidi100450@aol.com).

Parking: It's simple to park along the highway next to the train tracks or, better, in the big public lot by the boat dock (€4 from 9:00 to 18:00, pay with coins at *Parkscheinautomat,* display ticket on dash, free overnight).

Local Guides: Thomas Gundlach happily gives 1.5-hour town walks to individuals or small groups for €35. History buffs will enjoy his "war tour," which focuses on the town's survival from 1864 through World War II. He also offers 4- to 10-hour hiking or biking tours for the more ambitious (mobile 0179-353-6004, thomas_gundlach@gmx.de). Also good is **Birgit Wessels** (€45/1.5-hour walk, tel. 06743/937-514, wessels.birgit@t-online.de). The **TI** offers 1.5-hour tours in English with various themes, including a night tour (prices vary, gather a group).

❂ Bacharach Town Walk

• *Start this self-guided walk at the Köln-Düsseldorfer ferry dock (next to a fine picnic park).*

Riverfront: View the town from the parking lot—a modern landfill. The Rhine

Classic and quaint Bacharach

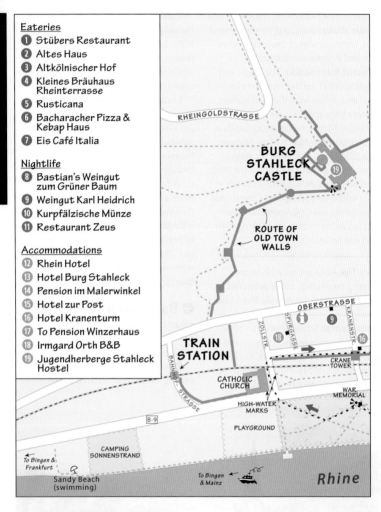

Eateries
1 Stübers Restaurant
2 Altes Haus
3 Altkölnischer Hof
4 Kleines Bräuhaus Rheinterrasse
5 Rusticana
6 Bacharacher Pizza & Kebap Haus
7 Eis Café Italia

Nightlife
8 Bastian's Weingut zum Grüner Baum
9 Weingut Karl Heidrich
10 Kurpfälzische Münze
11 Restaurant Zeus

Accommodations
12 Rhein Hotel
13 Hotel Burg Stahleck
14 Pension im Malerwinkel
15 Hotel zur Post
16 Hotel Kranenturm
17 To Pension Winzerhaus
18 Irmgard Orth B&B
19 Jugendherberge Stahleck Hostel

used to lap against Bacharach's town wall, just over the present-day highway. Every few years the river floods, covering the highway with several feet of water. Flat land like this is rare in the Rhine Valley, where towns are often shaped like the letter "T," stretching thin along the riverfront and up a crease in the hills beyond.

Reefs farther upstream forced boats to unload upriver and reload here. Consequently, in the Middle Ages, Bacharach was the biggest wine-trading town on the Rhine. A riverfront crane hoisted huge kegs of prestigious "Bacharach" wine (which, in practice, was from anywhere in the region). Today, the economy is based on tourism.

Look above town. The **castle** on the hill is now a hostel. Two of the town's original 16 towers are visible from here (up to five if you look really hard). The bluff on the right, with the yellow flag, is the **Heinrich Heine Viewpoint** (the end-point of a popular hike). Old-timers remember when, rather than the flag marking the town as a World Heritage site, a swastika sculpture 30 feet

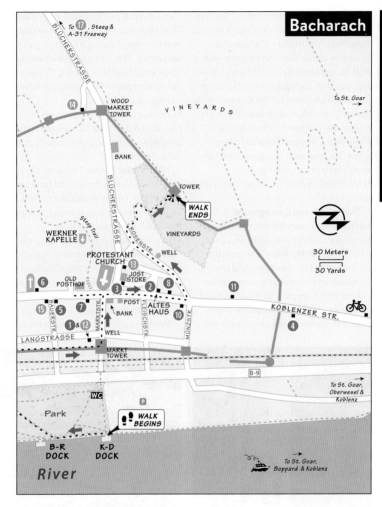

Bacharach

wide and tall stood there. Realizing that it could be an enticing target for Allied planes in the last months of World War II, locals tore it down even before Hitler fell.

Nearby, a stone column in the park describes the Bingen to Koblenz stretch of the Rhine gorge.

• *Before entering the town, walk upstream through the...*

Riverside Park: The park was originally laid out in 1910 in the English style: Notice how the trees were planted to frame fine town views, highlighting the most picturesque bits of architecture. Erected in 2016, a Picasso-esque sculpture by Bacharach artist Liesel Metten—of three figures sharing a bottle of wine (a Riesling, perhaps?)—celebrates three men who brought fame to the area through poetry and prose: Victor Hugo, Clemens Brentano, and Heinrich Heine.

The dark, sad-looking monument— its "eternal" flame long snuffed out— is a **war memorial.** The German psyche is permanently scarred by war memories. Today, many Germans would rather avoid monuments like this, which recall the dark periods before Germany became a nation of pacifists. The military Maltese cross—flanked by classic German helmets—has a W at its center, for Kaiser Wilhelm. On the opposite side, each panel honors sons of Bacharach who died for the Kaiser: in 1864 against Denmark, in 1866 against Austria, in 1870 against France, in 1914 during World War I. Review the family names below: You may later recognize them on today's restaurants and hotels.

• *Look upstream from here to see (in the distance) the...*

Trailer Park and Campground: In Germany, trailer vacationers and campers are two distinct subcultures. Folks who travel in motorhomes, like many retirees in the US, are a nomadic bunch, cruising around the countryside and paying a few euros a night to park. Campers, on the other hand, tend to set up camp in one place—complete with comfortable lounge chairs and

TVs—and stay put for weeks, even months. They often come back to the same spot year after year, treating it like their own private estate. These camping devotees have made a science out of relaxing. Tourists are welcome to pop in for a drink or meal at the campground café.

• *Continue to where the park meets the playground, and then cross the highway to the fortified riverside wall of the Catholic church, decorated with...*

High-Water Marks: These recall various floods. Before the 1910 reclamation project, the river extended out to here, and boats would tie up at mooring rings that used to be in this wall.

• *From the church, go under the 1858 train tracks (and past more high-water marks) and hook right up the stairs at the yellow floodwater yardstick to reach the town wall. Atop the wall, turn left and walk under the long arcade. After 30 yards, on your left, notice a...*

Well: Rebuilt as it appeared in the 17th

High-water marks indicate the heights reached by floodwaters.

A facsimile of a 17th-century well

century, this is one of seven such wells that brought water to the townsfolk until 1900. Each neighborhood's well also provided a social gathering place and the communal laundry. Walk 50 yards past the well along the wall to an alcove in the medieval tower with a view of the war memorial in the park. You're under the crane tower (*Kranenturm*). After barrels of wine were moved overland from Bingen, avoiding dangerous stretches of river, the precious cargo could be lowered by cranes from here into ships to continue more safely down the river. The Rhine has long been a major shipping route through Germany. In modern times, it's a bottleneck in Germany's train system. The train company gives hotels and residents along the tracks money for soundproof windows.

• *Continue walking along the town wall. Pass the recommended Rhein Hotel just before the...*

Markt Tower: This marks one of the town's 15 original 14th-century gates and is a reminder that in that century there was a big wine market here.

• *Descend the stairs closest to the Rhein Hotel, pass another well, and follow Marktstrasse away from the river toward the town center, the two-tone church, and the town's...*

Main Intersection: From here, Bacharach's main street (Oberstrasse) goes right to the half-timbered red-and-white Altes Haus (which we'll visit later) and left 400 yards to the train station. Spin around to enjoy the higgledy-piggledy building styles. The town has a case of the doldrums: The younger generation is moving to the big cities and many long-established family businesses have no one to take over for their aging owners. In the winter the town is particularly dead.

• *To the left (south) of the church, a golden horn hangs over the old...*

Posthof: Throughout Europe, the postal horn is the symbol of the postal service. In olden days, when the postman blew this, traffic stopped and the mail sped through. This post station dates from 1724, when stagecoaches ran from

Cologne to Frankfurt and would change horses here, Pony Express-style. Notice the cornerstones at the Posthof entrance, protecting the venerable building from reckless carriage wheels. If it's open, inside the old oak doors (on the left) is the actual door to the post office that served Bacharach for 200 years. Find the mark on the wall labeled *Rheinhöhe 30/1-4/2 1850*. This recalls a historic flood caused by an ice jam at the Loreley just downstream. Notice also the fascist eagle in the alcove on the right (from 1936; a swastika once filled its center). The courtyard was once a carriage house and inn that accommodated Bacharach's first VIP visitors.

Two hundred years ago, Bacharach's main drag was the only road along the Rhine. Napoleon widened it to fit his cannon wagons. The steps alongside the church lead to the ruins of the 15th-century Werner Chapel and the castle.

• *Return to the church, passing the recommended Italian ice-cream café (**Eis Café Italia**), where friendly Mimo serves his special invention: Riesling wine-flavored gelato.*

Protestant Church: Inside the church (daily 10:00-18:00, closed Nov-March), you'll find grotesque capitals, brightly painted in medieval style, and a mix of round Romanesque and pointed Gothic arches. The church was fancier before the Reformation wars, when it (and the region) was Catholic. Bacharach lies on the religious border of Germany and, like the country as a whole, is split between Catholics and Protestants. To the left

Altes Haus is the oldest dwelling (1368) in Bacharach.

of the altar, some medieval (pre-Reformation) frescoes survive where an older Romanesque arch was cut by a pointed Gothic one.

If you're considering bombing the town, take note: A blue-and-white plaque just outside the church's door warns that, according to the Hague Convention, this historic building shouldn't be targeted in times of war.

• *Continue down Oberstrasse to the...*

Altes Haus: Dating from 1389, this is the oldest house in town. Notice the 14th-century building style—the first floor is made of stone, while upper floors are half-timbered (in the ornate style common in the Rhine Valley). Some of its windows still look medieval, with small, flattened circles as panes, pieced together with molten lead (like medieval stained glass in churches). Frau Weber welcomes visitors to enjoy the fascinating ground floor of the recommended Altes Haus restaurant, with its evocative old photos and etchings (consider eating here later).

• *Keep going down Oberstrasse to the...*

Old Mint (Münze): The old mint is marked by a crude coin in its sign. As a practicality, any great trading town needed coinage, and since 1356, Bacharach minted theirs here. Now, it's a restaurant and bar, **Kurpfälzische Münze,** with occasional live music. Across from the mint, the recommended **Bastian** family's wine garden is another lively place in the evening. Above you in the vineyards stands a lonely white-and-red tower—your final destination.

• *At the next street, look right and see the mint tower, painted in the medieval style, and then turn left. Wander 30 yards up Rosenstrasse to the **well**. Notice the sundial and the wall painting of 1632 Bacharach with its walls intact. Study the fine slate roof over the well: The town's roof tiles were quarried and split right here in the Rhineland. Continue another 30 yards up Rosenstrasse to find the tiny-stepped lane on the right leading up into the vineyard and to the...*

Tall Tower: The slate steps lead to a small path through the vineyard that deposits you at a viewpoint atop the stubby remains of the medieval wall and a tower. The town's towers jutted out from the wall and had only three sides, with the "open" side facing the town. Towers were covered with stucco to make them look more impressive, as if they were made of a finer white stone. If this tower's open, hike up to climb the stairs for the best view. (The top floor has been closed to give nesting falcons some privacy.)

Romantic Rhine View: Looking south, a grand medieval town spreads before you. For 300 years (1300-1600), Bacharach was big (population 4,000), rich, and politically powerful.

From this perch, you can see the ruins of a 15th-century chapel and six surviving **city towers.** Visually trace the wall to the Stahleck Castle. The castle was actually the capital of Germany for a couple of years in the 1200s. When Holy Roman Emperor Frederick Barbarossa went away to fight the Crusades, he left his brother (who lived here) in charge of his vast realm. Bacharach was home to one of the seven electors who voted for the Holy Roman Emperor in 1275. To protect their own power, these prince electors did their best to choose the weakest guy on the ballot. The elector from Bacharach helped select a two-bit prince named Rudolf von Habsburg (from a no-name castle in Switzerland). However, the underestimated Rudolf brutally silenced the robber barons along the Rhine and established the mightiest dynasty in European history. His family line, the Habsburgs, ruled much of Central and Eastern Europe from Vienna until 1918.

Plagues, fires, and the Thirty Years' War (1618-1648) finally did in Bacharach. The town has slumbered for several centuries. Today, the castle houses commoners—40,000 overnights annually by hostelers.

In the mid-19th century, painters such as J. M. W. Turner and writers such as Victor Hugo were charmed by the Rhineland's romantic mix of past glory, present poverty, and rich legend. They put this part of the Rhine on the old Grand Tour map as the "Romantic Rhine." Hugo pondered the chapel ruins that you see under the castle: In his 1842 travel book, *Excursions Along the Banks of the Rhine,* he wrote, "No doors, no roof or windows, a magnificent skeleton puts its silhouette against the sky. Above it, the ivy-covered castle ruins provide a fitting crown. This is Bacharach, land of fairy tales, covered with legends and sagas." If you're enjoying the Romantic Rhine, thank Victor Hugo and company.

• *Our walk is done. To get back into town, just retrace your steps. Or, to extend this walk, take the level path away from the river that leads along the once-mighty wall up the valley to the next tower, the...*

Wood Market Tower: Timber was gathered here in Bacharach and lashed together into vast log booms known as "Holland rafts" (as big as a soccer field) that were floated downstream. Two weeks later the lumber would reach Amsterdam, where it was in high demand as foundation posts for buildings and for the great Dutch shipbuilders. Notice the four stones above the arch on the uphill side of the tower—these guided the gate as it was hoisted up and down.

• *From here, cross the street and go downhill into the parking lot. Pass the recommended **Pension im Malerwinkel** on your right, being careful not to damage the old arch with your head. Follow the creek past a delightful little series of half-timbered homes and cheery gardens known as **"Painters' Corner"** (Malerwinkel). Resist looking into some weirdo's peep show (on the right) and continue downhill back to the village center.*

Experiences
Wine Tasting

Bacharach is proud of its wine. Two places in town offer an inexpensive tasting alongside light plates of food.

At **$$ Bastian's Weingut zum Grüner Baum,** pay €29.50 for a wine carousel of

12 glasses—nine different white wines, two reds, and one lonely rosé—and a basket of bread. Spin the Lazy Susan, share a common cup, and discuss the taste. The Bastian family insists: "After each wine, you must talk to each other" (daily 12:00-22:00, Nov-Dec closed Mon-Wed, closed Jan-Feb, just past Altes Haus, tel. 06743/1208).

$$ Weingut Karl Heidrich is a fun family-run wine shop and *Stube* in the town center, where Markus and daughters Magdalena and Katharina proudly share their family's centuries-old wine tradition, explaining its fine points. They offer a variety of €14.50 carousels with six wines, English descriptions, and bread—ideal for the more sophisticated wine taster—plus light meals and a meat-and-cheese plate (Thu-Mon 12:00-22:00, kitchen closes at 21:00, closed Tue-Wed and Nov-mid-April, Oberstrasse 16, will ship to the US, tel. 06743/93060, info@weingut-karl-heidrich.de).

Rick's Tip: *Bacharach goes to bed early, so if you're looking for* **nightlife,** *head to one of the* **wine-tasting places.** *Or try* **Kurpfälzische Münze,** *which often hosts live music.* **Restaurant Zeus** *has outdoor seating that adds a spark to the town center after dark (daily 17:30-24:00, Koblenzer Strasse 11, tel. 06743/909-7171). The hilltop youth hostel,* **Jugendherberge Stahleck,** *serves cheap wine with priceless views until late in summer.*

Shopping

The **Jost** German gift store, across from the main square from the church, carries most everything a souvenir shopper could want—from beer steins to cuckoo clocks—and can ship purchases to the US (RS% with €10 minimum purchase: 10 percent with cash, 5 percent with credit card; open daily 9:00-18:00, closed Nov-Feb; Blücherstrasse 4, tel. 06743/909-7214).

Walk Along the Old Town Walls

A steep and rocky but clearly marked walking path follows the remains of Bacharach's old town walls and makes for a good hour's workout. There are benches along the way where you can pause and take in views of the Rhine and Bacharach's slate roofs. The TI has maps that show the entire route. The path starts near the train station, climbs up to the hostel in what was Stahleck Castle (serves lunch from 12:00-13:30), descends into the side valley, and then continues up the other side to the tower in the vineyards before returning to town. To start the walk at the train station, find the house at Oberstrasse 2 and climb up the stairway to its left. Then follow the *Stadtmauer-Rundweg* signs. Good bilingual signposts tell the history of each of the towers along the wall—some are intact, one is a private residence, and others are now only stubs.

Sleeping

The only listings with parking are Pension im Malerwinkel and Pension Winzerhaus. For the others, you can drive in to unload your bags and then park in the public lot (see "Orientation," earlier). If you'll arrive after 20:00, let your hotel know in advance (many hotels with restaurants stay open late, but none have 24-hour reception desks).

$$ Rhein Hotel, overlooking the river with 14 spacious and comfortable rooms, is classy, well-run, and decorated with modern flair. This place has been in the Stüber family for six generations and is decorated with works of art by the current owner's siblings. The large family room downstairs is über stylish, while the quaint "hiker room" on the top floor features terrific views of both the town and river. You can sip local wines in the renovated room where owner Andreas was born (river- and train-side rooms come with quadruple-paned windows and air-con, in-room sauna, packages available including big three-course dinner, ask about "picnic bags" when you check in, free loaner bikes, directly inland from the K-D boat dock at Langstrasse 50, tel. 06743/1243, www.rhein-hotel-bacharach. de, info@rhein-hotel-bacharach.de). Their recommended Stübers Restaurant is considered the best in town.

$$ Hotel Burg Stahleck, above a cozy café in the town center, rents five big, bright rooms, more chic than shabby. Birgit treats guests to homemade cakes at breakfast (family rooms, view room, free parking, cheaper rooms in guesthouse around the corner, Blücherstrasse 6, tel. 06743/1388, www.urlaub-bacharach.de, info@urlaub-bacharach.de).

$ Pension im Malerwinkel sits like a grand gingerbread house that straddles the town wall in a quiet little neighborhood so charming it's called "Painters' Corner" (Malerwinkel). The Vollmer family's super-quiet 20-room place is a short stroll from the town center. Here guests can sit in a picturesque garden on a brook and enjoy views of the vineyards (cash only, family rooms, elevator, no train noise, bike rentals, easy parking; from Oberstrasse, turn left at the church, walkers can follow the path to the left just before the town gate but drivers must pass through the gate to find the hotel parking lot, Blücherstrasse 41; tel. 06743/1239, www.im-malerwinkel.de, pension@ im-malerwinkel.de, Armin and Daniela).

$ Hotel zur Post, refreshingly clean and quiet, is conveniently located right in the town center with no train noise. Its 12 rooms are a good value. Run by friendly and efficient Ute, the hotel offers more solid comfort than old-fashioned character, though the lovely wood-paneled breakfast room has a rustic feel (family room, Oberstrasse 38, tel. 06743/1277, www.hotel-zur-post-bacharach.de, h.zurpost@t-online.de).

$ Hotel Kranenturm, part of the medieval town wall, has 16 rooms with rustic castle ambience and Privatzimmer funkiness right downtown. The rooms in its former Kranenturm (crane tower) have the best views. While just 15 feet from the train tracks, a combination of medieval sturdiness and triple-paned windows makes the riverside rooms sleepable (RS%, family rooms, Rhine views come with train noise—earplugs on request, back rooms are quieter, closed Jan-Feb, Langstrasse 30, tel. 06743/1308, mobile 0176-8056-3863, www.kranenturm.com, hotel.kranenturm@gmail.com).

$ Pension Winzerhaus, a 10-room place run by friendly Sybille and Stefan, is just outside the town walls, directly under the vineyards. The rooms are simple, clean, and modern, and parking is a breeze (cash only, family room, laundry service, parking, nondrivers may be able to arrange a pickup at the train station—ask in advance, Blücherstrasse 60, tel. 06743/1294, www.pension-winzerhaus.de, winzerhaus@gmx.de).

¢ Irmgard Orth B&B rents three bright rooms, two of which share a small bathroom on the hall. Charming Irmgard speaks almost no English, but is exuberantly cheery and serves homemade honey with breakfast (cash only, Spurgasse 2, tel. 06743/1553—speak slowly; she prefers email: orth.irmgard@gmail.com).

Eating
Restaurants

Bacharach has several reasonably priced, atmospheric restaurants offering fine indoor and outdoor dining. Most places don't take credit cards.

The recommended Rhein Hotel's **$$$ Stübers Restaurant** is Bacharach's best top-end choice. Andreas Stüber, his family's sixth-generation chef, creates regional plates prepared with a slow-food ethic. Consider the William Turner pâté starter plate, named after the British painter who liked Bacharach. Book in advance for the special Tuesday slow-food menu (discount for hotel guests, always good vegetarian and vegan options, daily 17:00-21:30 plus Sun 11:30-14:15, closed mid-Dec-Feb, call or email to reserve on weekends or for an outdoor table when balmy, family-friendly with a play area, Langstrasse 50, tel. 06743/1243, info@rhein-hotel-bacharach.de). Their Posten Riesling is well worth the splurge and pairs well with both the food and the atmosphere.

$$$ Altes Haus, the oldest building in town (see "Bacharach Town Walk," earlier), serves classic German dishes with Bacharach's most romantic atmosphere. Find the cozy dining room with photos of the opera singer who sang about Bacharach, adding to its fame (Thu-Tue 12:00-14:30 & 18:00-21:30, Mon dinner only, limited menu and closes at 18:00 on weekends, closed Wed and Dec-Easter, dead center by the Protestant church, tel. 06743/1209).

$$$ Altkölnischer Hof is a family-run place with outdoor seating right on the main square, serving Rhine specialties that burst with flavor. This restored 18th-century banquet hall feels sophisticated inside, with high ceilings and oil paintings depicting the building's history. Reserve an outdoor table for a more relaxed meal, especially on weekends when locals pack the place (Tue-Sun 12:00-14:30 & 17:30-21:00, closed Mon and Nov-Easter, Blücherstrasse 2, tel. 06743/947-780, www.altkoelnischer-hof.de).

Casual Options

$$ Kleines Brauhaus Rheinterrasse is a funky microbrewery serving hearty meals, fresh-baked bread, and homemade beer under a 1958 circus carousel that overlooks the town and river. For a sweet finish, try the "beer-liquor," which tastes like Christmas (Tue-Sun 13:00-22:00, closed Mon, at the downstream end of town, Koblenzer Strasse 14, tel. 06743/919-179). The little flea market in the attached shed seems to fit right in.

$$ Rusticana, draped in greenery, is an inviting place serving homestyle German food and apple strudel that locals swear by. Sit on the delightful patio or at cozy tables inside (daily 11:00-20:00, credit cards accepted, Oberstrasse 40, tel. 06743/1741).

$ Bacharacher Pizza and Kebap Haus, on the main drag, is the town favorite for *döner kebabs,* cheap pizzas, and salads (daily 11:00-22:00, Oberstrasse 43, tel. 06743/3127).

Gelato: Right on the main street, **Eis Café Italia** is known for its refreshing, not-too-sweet Riesling-flavored gelato (no tastes offered, homemade, Waldmeister flavor is made with forest herbs—top secret, daily 13:00-19:00, closed mid-Oct-March, Oberstrasse 48).

Transportation
Arriving and Departing
BY TRAIN

Milk-run trains stop at Rhine towns each hour starting as early as 6:00, connecting at Mainz and Koblenz to trains farther afield. Trains between St. Goar and Bacharach depart at about :50 after the hour in each direction (buy tickets from the machine in the unstaffed stations, carry cash since some machines won't accept US credit cards).

The durations listed below are calculated from Bacharach; for St. Goar, the difference is only 10 minutes. From Bacharach (or St. Goar), to go anywhere distant, you'll need to change trains in Koblenz for points north, or in Mainz for points south. Milk-run connections to these towns depart hourly, at about :50 past the hour for northbound trains, and at about :05 past the hour for southbound trains (with a few more on the half hour). Train info: www.bahn.com.

From Bacharach by Train to: St. Goar (hourly, 10 minutes), **Moselkern** near Burg Eltz (hourly, 1.5 hours, change in Koblenz), **Cologne** (hourly, 2 hours with change in Koblenz, 2.5 hours direct), **Frankfurt Airport** (hourly, 1 hour, change in Mainz or Bingen), **Frankfurt** (hourly, 1.5 hours, change in Mainz or Bingen), **Rothenburg ob der Tauber** (every 2 hours, 4.5 hours, 3-4 changes),

Munich (hourly, 5 hours, 2 changes), **Berlin** (every 2 hours with a transfer in Frankfurt, 5.5 hours; more with 2-3 changes).

BY CAR

This region, with its small towns, can make an easygoing first (or last) stop in Germany. If you're using Frankfurt Airport, here are some tips.

Frankfurt Airport to the Rhine: Driving from Frankfurt to the Rhine or Mosel takes about an hour (follow blue autobahn signs from airport—major cities are signposted).

The Rhine to Frankfurt: From St. Goar or Bacharach, follow the river to Bingen, then autobahn signs to *Mainz,* then *Frankfurt.* From there, head for the airport *(Flughafen)* or downtown (signs to *Messe,* then *Hauptbahnhof,* to find the parking under Frankfurt's main train station).

ST. GOAR

St. Goar (sahnkt gwahr) is a classic Rhine tourist town. Its hulk of a castle overlooks a half-timbered shopping street and leafy riverside park, busy with sightseeing ships and contented strollers. Rheinfels Castle, once the mightiest on the river, is the single best Rhineland ruin to explore. While the town of St. Goar itself is less interesting than Bacharach, be sure to explore beyond the shops: Thoughtful little placards scattered around town explain factoids (in English) about each street, lane, and square. St. Goar also makes a good base for hiking or biking the region. A tiny car ferry will shuttle you back and forth across the busy Rhine from here.

Orientation

St. Goar is dominated by its mighty castle, Rheinfels. The village—basically a wide spot in the road at the foot of Rheinfels' hill—isn't much more than a few hotels and restaurants. From the riverboat docks, the main drag—Heerstrasse, a dull pedestrian mall without history—cuts through town before ending at the road up to the castle.

Tourist Information: The helpful St. Goar TI, which stores bags for free, is on the main pedestrian street (Mon-Fri 9:00-13:00 & 14:00-18:00, Sat-Sun 10:00-13:00; shorter hours and closed Sat-Sun off-season; from train station, go downhill around church and turn left after the recommended Hotel Am Markt, Heerstrasse 127; tel. 06741/383, www.st-goar.de).

Bike Rental: Call ahead to reserve

St. Goar on the Rhine

a bike at Hotel an der Fähre, which rents wheels to the public (€10/day, pickup after 10:00, Heerstrasse 47, tel. 06741/980-577).

Parking: A free lot is at the downstream end of town, by the harbor. For on-street parking by the K-D boat dock and recommended hotels, get a ticket from the machine (Parkscheinautomat) and put it on the dashboard (€4/day, daily 9:00-18:00, coins only, free overnight). Make sure you press the button for a day ticket.

Sights

▲▲▲RHEINFELS CASTLE (BURG RHEINFELS)

Perched proudly atop the hill above St. Goar, the ruins of this once mightiest of Rhine River castles still exude a hint of menace. Built in the 13th century, Rheinfels ruled the river for more than 500 years. The castle you see today, though impressive and evocative sight to visit, is but a shadow of its former sprawling self.

Cost and Hours: €5, family card-€10, daily 9:00-18:00, Nov-mid-March possibly Sat-Sun only 11:00-17:00 (call ahead),

last entry one hour before closing—weather permitting.

Information: Tel. 06741/7753, in winter 06741/383, www.st-goar.de.

Tours: Due to a multiyear restoration, parts of the castle grounds can only be seen with a guided tour. Tours are run in both German and English but determined on the day by who shows up; to arrange an English tour for a group, call 1-2 days in advance.

Services: A handy WC is immediately across from the ticket booth (men take note of the guillotine urinals—stand back when you pull to flush). There are also WCs in the hotel across from the entrance.

Rick's Tip: *To explore* **the castle tunnels at Rheinfels, bring a flashlight**—*or buy one at the ticket office. For real medieval atmosphere, they also sell candles with matches.*

Getting to the Castle: A **taxi** up from town costs €5 (tel. 06741/7011). Or take the shuttle bus (€2 one-way, generally April-Oct daily 10:55-16:55, departs roughly every 30 minutes or when full).

Rheinfels' inner courtyard

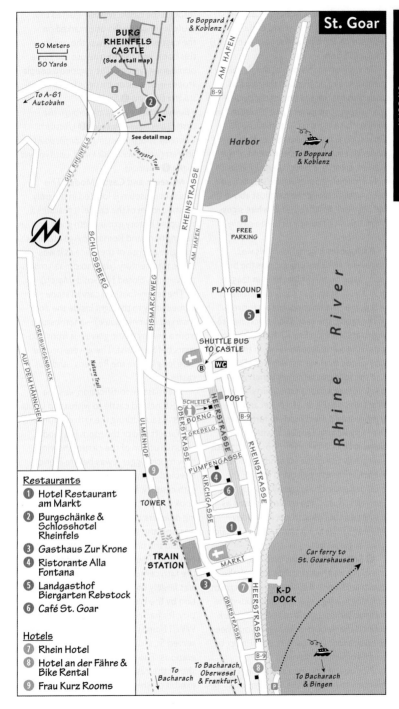

St. Goar

Restaurants

1. Hotel Restaurant am Markt
2. Burgschänke & Schlosshotel Rheinfels
3. Gasthaus Zur Krone
4. Ristorante Alla Fontana
5. Landgasthof Biergarten Rebstock
6. Café St. Goar

Hotels

7. Rhein Hotel
8. Hotel an der Fähre & Bike Rental
9. Frau Kurz Rooms

BURG RHEINFELS CASTLE (See detail map)

50 Meters
50 Yards

To A-61 Autobahn

See detail map

Vineyard Trail

To Boppard & Koblenz

AM HAFEN

B-9

Harbor

To Boppard & Koblenz

RHEINSTRASSE

AM HAFEN

FREE PARKING

PLAYGROUND

SHUTTLE BUS TO CASTLE

WC

SCHLOSSBERG

BISMARCKWEG

Nature Trail

DREIBURGENBLICK

AUF DEM HÄHNCHEN

GUT RHEINFELS

ULMENHOF

SCHLEIE.

OBERSTRASSE

BORNG.

GREBELG.

POST

B-9

Rhine River

PUMPENGASSE

KIRCHGASSE

HEERSTRASSE

RHEINSTRASSE

TOWER

TRAIN STATION

MARKT

Car ferry to St. Goarshausen

K-D DOCK

HEERSTRASSE

OBERSTRASSE

To Bacharach

To Bacharach, Oberwesel & Frankfurt

B-9

To Bacharach & Bingen

The shuttle departs from the Catholic church just past the top end of the pedestrian street. **Parking** at the castle costs €1/hour, cash only.

To **walk** up to the castle, simply follow the main road up through the railroad underpass at the top end of the pedestrian street (5 minutes). But it's more fun to **hike** the nature trail: Start at the St. Goar train station. Take the underpass under the tracks at the north end of the station, climb the steep stairs uphill, turn right (following *Burg Rheinfels* signs), and keep straight along the path just above the old city wall. Small red-and-white signs show the way, taking you to the castle in 15 minutes.

Background: Burg Rheinfels *was* huge—for five centuries, it was the biggest castle on the Rhine. Built in 1245 to guard a toll station, it soon earned the nickname "the unconquerable fortress." In the 1400s, the castle was thickened to withstand cannon fire. Rheinfels became a thriving cultural center and, in the 1520s, was visited by the artist Albrecht Dürer and the religious reformer Ulrich Zwingli. It saw lots of action in the Thirty Years' War (1618-1648), and later became the strongest and most modern fortress in the Holy Roman Empire. It withstood a siege of 28,000 French troops in 1692. But eventually the castle surrendered to the French without a fight, and in 1797, the French Revolutionary army destroyed it. For years, the ruined castle was used as a source of building stone, and today—while still mighty—it's only a small fraction of its original size.

◉ Self-Guided Tour: We'll start at the museum, then circulate through the courtyards, up to the highest lookout point, finishing in a big cellar. To walk around the fortified ramparts, and to access the dark tunnels that require a flashlight, you'll need to book a tour (see earlier). If it's damp, be careful of slippery stones.

Pick up the free map and use its commentary to navigate the red signposts

through the castle. My self-guided tour route is similar to the one marked on the castle map. That map, the one in this book, and this tour all use the same numbering system. (I've skipped a couple stops—just walk on by signs for ❷ *Darmstädter Bau* and ❺ *Stables*.)

• *Buy your ticket and walk through the castle's clock tower, labeled* ❶ *Uhrturm. Continue straight, passing a couple points of interest (which we'll visit later), until you get to the* ❸ *museum.*

Museum and Castle Model: The pleasant museum is located in the only finished room of the castle. It features a sweeping history exhibit with good English descriptions and Romantic Age etchings that give a sense of the place as it was in the 19th century (daily 10:00-12:30 & 13:00-17:30, closed Nov-mid-March).

The seven-foot-tall carved stone immediately to the right inside the door (marked *Flammensäule*)—a tombstone from a nearby Celtic grave—is from 400 years before Christ. There were people here long before the Romans...and this castle.

The massive fortification was the only Rhineland castle to withstand Louis XIV's assault during the 17th century. At the far left end of the room is a model reconstruction of the castle, showing how much bigger it was before French Revolutionary troops destroyed it in the 18th century. Find where you are. (Hint: Look for the tall tower.) This was the living quarters of the original castle, which was only the smallest ring of buildings around the tiny central courtyard (13th century). The ramparts were added in the 14th century. By 1650, the fortress was largely complete. Since its destruction by the French in the late 18th century, it's had no military value. While no WWII bombs were wasted on this ruin, it served St. Goar as a stone quarry for generations. The basement of the museum shows the castle pharmacy and an exhibit of Rhine-region odds and ends,

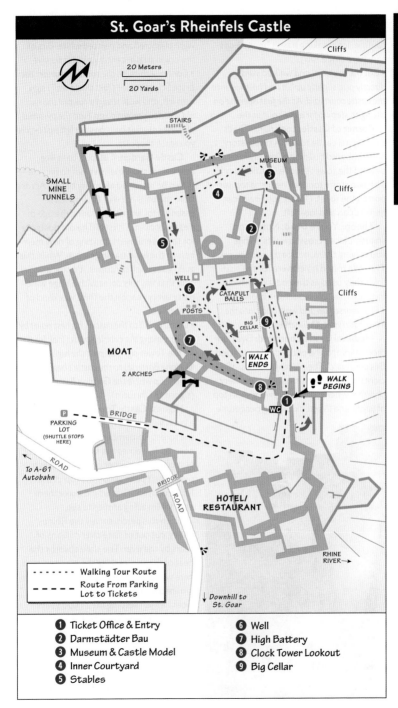

St. Goar's Rheinfels Castle

20 Meters
20 Yards

Cliffs

Cliffs

Cliffs

STAIRS

MUSEUM **3**

4

SMALL MINE TUNNELS

2

5

WELL

6

CATAPULT BALLS

POSTS

BIG CELLAR

9

MOAT

7

2 ARCHES

WALK ENDS

8

1 WALK BEGINS

WC

BRIDGE

P PARKING LOT (SHUTTLE STOPS HERE)

ROAD

To A-61 Autobahn

BRIDGE ROAD

HOTEL/ RESTAURANT

RHINE RIVER →

↓ Downhill to St. Goar

- - - - - - Walking Tour Route
- - - - Route From Parking Lot to Tickets

1 Ticket Office & Entry
2 Darmstädter Bau
3 Museum & Castle Model
4 Inner Courtyard
5 Stables

6 Well
7 High Battery
8 Clock Tower Lookout
9 Big Cellar

including tools, an 1830 loom, and photos of icebreaking on the Rhine. While once routine, icebreaking hasn't been necessary here since 1963.

• *Exit the museum and walk 20 yards directly out, slightly uphill and halfway into the castle courtyard. At the first opening on the right, step up for a peek out at the...*

Corner of Castle: Look right. That's the original castle tower. A three-story, half-timbered building originally rose beyond the tower's stone fortification. The two stone tongues near the top supported the toilet. (Insert your own joke here.) Lean and look left.

Thoop...You're Dead: Notice the smartly placed crossbow slits. While you're lying there, notice the stonework. The little round holes were for the scaffolds they used as they built up, which indicate that this stonework is original.

• *Pick yourself up and walk back into the inner courtyard, ❹ Innenhof.*

Medieval Castle Courtyard: Five hundred years ago, the entire castle encircled this courtyard. The place was self-sufficient and ready for a siege, with a bakery, pharmacy, herb garden, brewery, well (top of yard), and livestock. During peacetime,

300-600 people lived here; during a siege, there would be as many as 4,000. The walls were plastered and painted white. Bits of the original 13th-century plaster survive.

• *Continue through the courtyard under the Erste Schildmauer (first shield wall) sign, turn left, and walk straight toward the two old wooden upright posts. Find the pyramid of stone catapult balls on your left just before you reach the posts.*

Castle Garden: Catapult balls like these were too expensive not to recycle— they'd be retrieved after any battle. Across from the balls is a well ❻ *Brunnen)*— essential for any castle during the age of sieges. Look in. Thirsty? The old posts are for the ceremonial baptizing of new members of the local trading league. While this guild goes back centuries, it's now a social club that fills this court with a huge wine party every year on the third weekend of September.

• *Climb uphill to the castle's highest point by walking along the cobbled path (look for the To the Tower sign) up past the high battery ❼ Hohe Batterie) to the castle's best viewpoint—up where the German flag waves (signed ❽ Uhrturm).*

Highest Castle Tower Lookout: Enjoy a great view of the river, the castle, and the forest. Remember, the fortress once covered five times the land it does today. Notice how the other castles (across the river) don't poke above the top of the Rhine canyon. That would make them easy for invading armies to see.

From this perch, survey the Rhine Valley, cut out of slate over millions of years by the river. The slate absorbs the heat of the sun, making the grapes grown here well-suited for wine. Today the slate is mined to provide roofing. Imagine St. Goar himself settling here 1,500 years ago, establishing a place where sailors— thankful to have survived the treacherous Loreley—would stop and pray. Imagine the frozen river of years past, when the ice would break up and boats would huddle in man-made harbors like the one below for protection. Consider the history of trade on this busy river—from the days when castles levied tolls on ships, to the days when boats would be hauled upstream with the help of riverside towpaths, to the 21st century when 300 ships a day move their cargo past St. Goar. And imagine this castle before the French destroyed it... when it was the mightiest structure on the river, filled with people and inspiring awe among all who passed.

• *Return to the catapult balls, walk downhill and through the tunnel, and pause to look back up and see the original 13th-century core of the castle. Now go right toward the entrance, first veering down to see the...*

Big Cellar: This ❾ *Grosser Keller* was a big pantry. When the castle was smaller, this was the original moat—you can see the rough lower parts of the wall. The original floor was 13 feet deeper. The drawbridge rested upon the stone nubs on the left. When the castle expanded, the moat became this cellar. Halfway up the walls on the entrance side of the room, square holes mark spots where timbers made a storage loft, perhaps filled with grain. In the back, an arch leads to the wine cellar (probably blocked off) where finer wine was kept. Part of a soldier's pay was wine...table wine. This wine was kept in a single 180,000-liter stone barrel (that's 47,550 gallons), which generally lasted about 18 months.

The count owned the surrounding farmland. Farmers got to keep 20 percent of their production. Later, in more liberal feudal times, the nobility let them keep 40 percent. Today, the German government leaves the workers with 60 percent...and provides a few more services.

• *You're free. Climb out, turn right, and leave. For coffee on a terrace with a great view, visit Schlosshotel Rheinfels, opposite the entrance.*

Shopping

The Montag family runs two shops (one specializes in steins and the other in cuckoo clocks), both at the base of the

castle hill road. The stein shop under Hotel Montag has Rhine guides and fine steins. The other shop boasts "the largest free-hanging cuckoo clock in the world" (RS%—10 percent discount, €10 minimum purchase; both locations open daily 9:00-18:00, shorter hours Nov-April). They'll ship your souvenirs home—or give you a VAT form to claim your tax refund at the airport if you're carrying your items with you. A couple of other souvenir shops are across from the K-D boat dock.

Sleeping

$ Hotel am Markt, run by Herr and Frau Marx, is a decent value with modern comforts. It features 15 rustic rooms in the main building (think antlers with a pastel flair), 10 classier rooms right next door, and a good restaurant. It's a stone's throw from the boat dock and train station (family rooms, some rooms with river view, two apartments also available, closed Nov-Feb, pay parking, Markt 1, tel. 06741/1689, http://hotel-sankt-goar.de, dashotel@t-online.de).

$ Rhein Hotel, on the other side of the church from Hotel am Markt and run with enthusiasm by young and energetic Gil Velich, has 10 bright and stylish rooms in a spacious building (some rooms with river view and balconies, family rooms, pay laundry, closed mid-Nov-March, Heerstrasse 71, tel. 06741/981-240, www.rheinhotel-st-goar.de, info@rheinhotel-st-goar.de).

$ Hotel an der Fähre is a simple place

on the busy road at the end of town, immediately across from the ferry dock. It rents 12 cheap and colorful rooms (cash only, some view rooms, cheapest rooms with shared bath, street noise but double-glazed windows, parking, closed Nov-Feb, Heerstrasse 47, tel. 06741/980-577, www.hotel-stgoar.de, info@hotel-stgoar.de, friendly Alessya). They also offer rental bikes by reservation.

$ Frau Kurz has been housing my readers since 1988 in St. Goar's best B&B, renting three delightful rooms (sharing 2.5 bathrooms) with a breakfast terrace with castle views, a garden, and homemade marmalade (cash only, free and easy parking, ask about apartment with kitchen, Ulmenhof 11, tel. 06741/459, www.gaestehaus-kurz.de, fewo-kurz@kabelmail.de). If you're not driving, it's a steep five-minute hike from the train station: Exit left from the station, take an immediate left under the tracks, and go partway up the zigzag stairs, turning right through an archway onto Ulmenhof; #11 is just past the tower.

Eating

$$ Hotel Restaurant am Markt serves tasty traditional meals with plenty of game and fish (specialties include marinated roast beef and homemade cheesecake) at fair prices with good atmosphere and service. Choose cozy indoor seating, or dine outside with a river and castle view (daily 9:00-21:00, closed Nov-Feb, Markt 1, tel. 06741/1689).

$$$ Burgschänke is easy to miss on the ground floor of Schlosshotel Rheinfels (the hotel across from the castle entrance—enter through the souvenir shop). It offers the only reasonably priced lunches up at Rheinfels Castle, is family-friendly, and has a Rhine view from its fabulous outdoor terrace (*Flammkuchen* and regional dishes, Sun-Thu 11:00-21:00, Fri-Sat until 21:30, tel. 06741/802-806).

The **$$$$ Schlosshotel Rheinfels** dining room is your Rhine splurge, with an incredible indoor view terrace in an elegant, dressy setting. Call to reserve for weekends or if you want a window table (daily 7:00-11:00, 12:00-14:00 & 18:00-21:00, tel. 06741/8020, www.schloss-rheinfels.de).

$$ Gasthaus Zur Krone is the local choice for traditional German food in a restaurant off the main drag. There's no river view, but it's cozy and offers some outdoor seating on weekends (Thu-Tue 11:00-14:30 & 18:00-21:00, closed Wed, cash only, next to the train station and church at Oberstrasse 38, tel. 06741/1515).

$$ Ristorante Alla Fontana, tucked away on a back lane and busy with locals, serves the best Italian food in town at great prices in a lovely dining room or on a leafy patio (Tue-Sun 11:30-14:00 & 17:30-21:30, closed Mon, cash only, dinner reservations smart, Pumpengasse 5, 06741/96117).

$$ Landgasthof Biergarten Rebstock is hidden on the far end of town on the banks of the Rhine. They serve schnitzel and plenty of beer and wine. A nice playground and minigolf course on either side keeps the kids busy (April-Oct long hours daily—weather permitting, Am Hafen 1, tel. 06741/980-0337).

$ Café St. Goar is the perfect spot for a quick lunch or *Kaffee und Kuchen.* They sell open-face sandwiches, strudel, tiny cookies, and a variety of cakes to satisfy any appetite. Grab something for a picnic or enjoy seating on the pedestrian-only street out front (Mon-Sat 9:00-18:00, Sun from 10:00, Heerstrasse 95, tel. 06741/1635).

MARKSBURG CASTLE IN BRAUBACH

Medieval invaders decided to give ▲▲ Marksburg a miss, thanks to its formidable defenses. This best-preserved castle on the Rhine can be toured only with a guide on a 50-minute tour. In summer, tours in English normally run daily at 13:00 and 16:00. Otherwise, you can join a German tour (3/hour in summer, hourly in winter) that's almost as good—there are no explanations in English in the castle itself, but your ticket includes an English handout. It's an awesome castle, and between the handout and my commentary below, you'll feel fully informed, so don't worry about being on time for the English tours.

Orientation

Cost and Hours: €7, family card-€16, daily 10:00-17:00, Nov-mid-March 11:00-16:00, last tour departs one hour before closing, tel. 02627/206, www.marksburg.de.

Getting There: Marksburg caps a hill above the village of Braubach, on the east bank of the Rhine. By **train,** it's a 10-minute trip from Koblenz to Braubach (1-2/hour); from Bacharach or St. Goar, it can take up to two hours, depending on the length of the layover in Koblenz. The train is quicker than the **boat** (downstream from Bacharach to Braubach-2 hours, upstream return-3.5 hours; €30.40 one-way, €36.40 round-trip). Consider taking the downstream boat to Braubach, and

the train back. If traveling with luggage, store it in the convenient lockers in the underground passage at the Koblenz train station (Braubach has no enclosed station—just platforms—and no lockers).

Once you reach Braubach, **walk** into the old town (follow *Altstadt* signs—coming out of tunnel from train platforms, it's to your right); then follow the *Zur Burg* signs to the path up to the castle. Allow 25 minutes for the climb up. Scarce **taxis** charge at least €10 from the train platforms to the castle. A green **tourist train** circles up to the castle, but there's no fixed schedule (Easter-mid-Oct Tue-Sun, no trains Mon or off-season, €3 one-way, €5 round-trip, leaves from Barbarastrasse, confirm departure times by calling 06773/587, www.ruckes-reisen.de). Even if you take the tourist train, you'll still have to climb the last five minutes up to the castle from its parking lot.

❷ Visiting the Castle

Your guided tour starts inside the castle's first gate.

Inside the First Gate: While the dramatic castles lining the Rhine are generally

Marksburg Castle was built originally as a fortress, not a royal residence.

Romantic rebuilds, Marksburg is the real McCoy—nearly all original construction. It's littered with bits of its medieval past, like the big stone ball that was swung on a rope to be used as a battering ram. Ahead, notice how the inner gate—originally tall enough for knights on horseback to gallop through—was made smaller to deter enemies on horseback. Climb the Knights' Stairway, carved out of slate, and pass under the murder hole—handy for pouring boiling pitch on invaders. (Germans still say someone with bad luck "has pitch on his head.")

Coats of Arms: Colorful coats of arms line the wall just inside the gate. These are from the noble families who have owned the castle since 1283. In that year, financial troubles drove the first family to sell to the powerful and wealthy Katzenelnbogen family (who made the castle into what you see today). When Napoleon took this region in 1803, an Austrian family who sided with the French got the keys. When Prussia took the region in 1866, control passed to a friend of the Prussians who had a passion for medieval things—typical of this Romantic period. Then it was sold to the German Castles Association in 1900. Its offices are in the main palace at the top of the stairs.

Romanesque Palace: White outlines mark where the larger original windows were located, before they were replaced by easier-to-defend smaller ones. On the far right, a bit of the original plaster survives. Slate, which is vulnerable to the elements, needs to be covered—in this case, by plaster. Because this is a protected historic building, restorers can use only the traditional plaster methods...but no one knows how to make plaster that works as well as the 800-year-old surviving bits.

Cannons: The oldest cannon here—from 1500—was back-loaded. This was advantageous because many cartridges could be preloaded. But since the seal was leaky, it wasn't very powerful. The bigger, more modern cannons—from 1640—

were one piece and therefore airtight, but had to be front-loaded. They could easily hit targets across the river from here. Stone balls were rough, so they let the explosive force leak out. The best cannonballs were stones covered in smooth lead—airtight and therefore more powerful and more accurate.

Gothic Garden: Walking along an outer wall, you'll see 160 plants from the Middle Ages—used for cooking, medicine, and witchcraft. Schierling (hemlock, in the first corner) is the same poison that killed Socrates.

Inland Rampart: This most vulnerable part of the castle had a triangular construction to better deflect attacks. Notice the factory in the valley. In the 14th century, this was a lead, copper, and silver mine. Today's factory—Europe's largest car-battery recycling plant—uses the old mine shafts as vents (see the three modern smokestacks).

Wine Cellar: Since Roman times, wine has been the traditional Rhineland drink. Because castle water was impure, wine—less alcoholic than today's beer—was the way knights got their fluids. The pitchers on the wall were their daily allotment. The bellows were part of the barrel's filtering system. Stairs lead to the...

Gothic Hall: This hall is set up as a kitchen, with an oven designed to roast an ox whole. The arms holding the pots have notches to control the heat. To this day, when Germans want someone to hurry up, they say, "give it one tooth more." Medieval windows were made of thin sheets of translucent alabaster or animal skins. A nearby wall is peeled away to show the wattle-and-daub construction (sticks, straw, clay, mud, then plaster) of a castle's inner walls. The iron plate to the left of the next door enabled servants to stoke the heater without being seen by the noble family.

Bedroom: This was the only heated room in the castle. The canopy kept in heat and kept out critters. In medieval times, it was impolite for a lady to argue with her lord in public. She would wait for him in bed to give him what Germans still call "a curtain lecture." The deep window seat caught maximum light for needlework and reading. Women would sit here and chat (or "spin a yarn") while working the spinning wheel.

Hall of the Knights: This was the dining hall. The long table is an unattached plank. After each course, servants could replace it with another pre-set plank. Even today, when a meal is over and Germans are ready for the action to begin, they say, "Let's lift up the table." The action back then consisted of traveling minstrels who sang and told of news gleaned from their travels.

Notice the outhouse—made of wood—hanging over thin air. When not in use, its door was locked from the outside (the castle side) to prevent any invaders from entering this weak point in the castle's defenses.

Chapel: This chapel is still painted in Gothic style with the castle's namesake, St. Mark, and his lion. Even the chapel was designed with defense in mind. The small doorway kept out heavily armed attackers. The staircase spirals clockwise, favoring the sword-wielding defender (assuming he was right-handed).

Linen Room: About the year 1800, the castle—with diminished military value—housed disabled soldiers. They'd earn a little extra money working raw flax into linen.

Two Thousand Years of Armor: Follow the evolution of armor since Celtic times.

Because helmets covered the entire head, soldiers identified themselves as friendly by tipping their visor up with their right hand. This evolved into the military salute that is still used around the world today. Armor and the close-range weapons along the back were made obsolete by the invention of the rifle. Armor was replaced with breastplates—pointed (like the castle itself) to deflect enemy fire. This design was used as late as the start of World War I. A medieval lady's armor hangs over the door. While popular fiction has men locking up their women before heading off to battle, chastity belts were actually used by women as protection against rape when traveling.

The Keep: This served as an observation tower, a dungeon (with a 22-square-foot cell in the bottom), and a place of last refuge. When all was nearly lost, the defenders would bundle into the keep and burn the wooden bridge, hoping to outwait their enemies.

Horse Stable: The stable shows off bits of medieval crime and punishment. Cheaters were attached to stones or pillories. Shame masks punished gossipmongers. A mask with a heavy ball had its victim crawling around with his nose in the mud. The handcuffs with a neck hole were for the transport of prisoners. The pictures on the wall show various medieval capital punishments. Many times the accused was simply taken into a torture dungeon to see all these tools, and, guilty or not, confessions spilled out of him. On that cheery note, your tour is over.

GERMANY

While you're in the region, two stops worth considering are Burg Eltz, a beautiful castle on the Mosel River, and the city of Cologne, with its knockout cathedral. If you're using public transit, Burg Eltz makes a fine day trip from the Rhine, but Cologne (2 hours by train) works better as a stop en route to or from the Rhine.

Burg Eltz

My favorite castle in all of Europe—worth ▲▲▲—lurks in a mysterious forest. It's been left intact for 700 years and is decorated and furnished throughout much as it was 500 years ago. Thanks to smart diplomacy, clever marriages, and lots of luck, Burg Eltz (pronounced "boorg elts") was never destroyed. It's been in the Eltz family for 850 years.

Day Plan

Drivers can figure on a half-day to storm the castle. Day-trippers from the Rhine should allow all day (including the scenic 1.5-hour walk up the Elz Valley to the castle).

Getting There

The pleasant 1.5-hour **walk** from the nearest train station, in the little village of Moselkern, is not only easy, it's the most fun and scenic way to visit the castle. Alternatively, you can take a **taxi** (or, on summer weekends only, the **bus**) to the castle from the village of Karden (see "By Bus from the Treis-Karden Station," later).

Hiking to the Castle from Moselkern: You can do the hike in 75 minutes at a steady clip, but allow an extra 20 minutes or so to enjoy the scenery. The overall elevation gain from the river to the castle is less than 400 feet (you can reach Moselkern from towns on the Rhine, including Cologne and Bacharach).

To find the path up to the castle, turn right from the station along Oberstrasse and continue to the village church. Just past the church, turn right through the underpass. On your left is the Elzbach stream, which you'll follow all the way up to the castle. Just before the road crosses the stream on a stone bridge, take either the footpath (stay right) or the bridge—they join up again later.

When the road ends at the parking lot of the Hotel Ringelsteiner Mühle, stay to the right of the hotel and continue upstream along the easy-to-follow trail, which starts out paved but soon changes to dirt. From here, it's another 45 minutes through the forest to the castle.

By Bus from the Treis-Karden Station: From May through October on Saturdays and Sundays only, bus #330 runs to Burg Eltz from the Treis-Karden railway station (4/day, 40 minutes; check schedule with bus operator at tel. 02671/8976, or at www.burg-eltz.de).

By Taxi: You can taxi to the castle from **Moselkern** (€28 one-way, taxi tel. 02672/1407) or **Karden** (€30 one-way, taxi tel. 02672/1407). If you're planning to taxi from Moselkern, call ahead and ask the taxi to meet your train at Moselkern station. Consider taxiing up to Burg Eltz and then enjoying the hike downhill back to the train station in Moselkern.

By Car: Cars (and taxis) park in a lot near, but not quite at, Burg Eltz. From the lot, hike 15 minutes downhill to the castle or wait (10 minutes at most) for the red castle shuttle bus (€2 each way).

Drive/Hike Combo: If you're driving but would enjoy walking part of the path up to the castle, drive to Moselkern, follow the *Burg Eltz* signs up the Elz Valley, park at Hotel Ringelsteiner Mühle (buy ticket from machine), and hike about 45 minutes up the trail to the castle.

Orientation

Cost and Hours: €10 castle entry includes required guided tour and treasury, daily

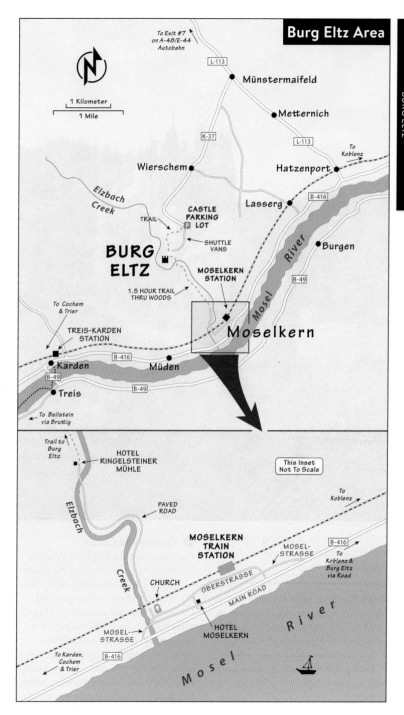

from 9:30, last tour departs at 17:30, closed Nov-March. Tel. 02672/950-500, www.burg-eltz.de.

Rick's Tip: Bring cash! *The castle (including the parking lot and café) doesn't accept credit cards (unless you spend at least €30 at the ticket desk), and there's no ATM.*

Eating: The $ castle café serves lunch, with soups and bratwurst-and-fries cuisine.

🡆 Visiting the Castle

The first record of a *Burg* (castle) on the Elz is from 1157. By about 1490, the castle looked like it does today, with the homes of three big landlord families gathered around a tiny courtyard within one formidable fortification. Today, the excellent tour winds you through two of those homes, while the third is still the residence of the castellan (the man who maintains the castle). This is where members of the **Eltz family** stay when they're not at one of their other feudal holdings.

It was a comfortable castle for its day: 80 rooms made cozy by 40 fireplaces and wall-hanging tapestries. Many of its 20 toilets were automatically flushed by a rain drain. The delightful **chapel** is on a lower floor. Even though "no one should live above God," this chapel's placement was acceptable because it filled a bay window, which flooded the delicate Gothic space with light. The three families met—working out common problems as if sharing a condo complex—in the large "conference room." A carved jester and a rose look down on the big table, reminding those who gathered that they were free to discuss anything ("fool's freedom"—jesters could say anything to the king), but nothing discussed could leave the room (the "rose of silence"). In the **bedroom,** have fun with the suggestive decor: the jousting relief carved into the canopy, and the fertile and phallic figures hiding in the lusty green wall paintings.

Near the exit, the **treasury** fills the four higgledy-piggledy floors of a cellar with the precious, eccentric, and historic mementos of this family that once helped elect the Holy Roman Emperor.

Berlin

Berlin is a city of leafy boulevards, grand Neoclassical buildings, world-class art, glitzy shopping arcades, and funky graffitied neighborhoods with gourmet street food. It's big and bombastic—the showcase city of kings and kaisers, of the Führer and 21st-century commerce.

Berlin is still largely defined by its WWII years, and the Cold War. The East-West division was set in stone in 1961, when the East German government surrounded West Berlin with the Berlin Wall. Since the fall of the Wall in 1989, Berlin has been a constant construction zone. Standing on ripped-up streets and under a canopy of cranes, visitors have witnessed the city's reunification and rebirth. Today Berlin is a world capital once again.

In the city's top-notch museums, you can walk through an enormous Babylonian gate amid rough-and-tumble ancient statuary, fondle a chunk of the Berlin Wall, and peruse canvases by Dürer and Rembrandt. A series of thought-provoking memorials confront Germany's difficult past. And some of the best history exhibits anywhere—covering everything from Prussian princes to Nazi atrocities to life under communism—can turn even those who claim to hate history into armchair experts.

Berlin is simply a pleasurable place—captivating, lively, fun-loving, and easy on the budget. Grab a drink from a sidewalk vendor, find a bench along the river, watch the sun set over a skyline of domes and cranes...and simply bask in Berlin.

BERLIN IN 3 DAYS

Day 1: Begin your day getting oriented to this huge city. For a quick and relaxing once-over-lightly tour, jump on one of the many hop-on, hop-off buses that make orientation loops through the city.

Then take Part 1 of my self-guided "Berlin City Walk," starting at the Reichstag (reservations and passport required to climb its dome), going through the Brandenburg Gate, and down the boulevard, Unter den Linden. Visit the charming Gendarmenmarkt square. Then tour the German History Museum.

On any evening: Any of these neighborhoods (all near each other) are worth exploring: Hackescher Markt, the old Jewish quarter, and Prenzlauer Berg. Take in live music or cabaret. Linger at a beer garden or stroll the banks of the Spree River. Or even continue your sightseeing—a number of sights stay open late, including the Reichstag and its view dome.

Day 2: Start your morning at Bebelplatz with Part 2 of my "Berlin City Walk." Along the way, visit any museum that interests you on Museum Island or nearby: Pergamon, Neues, Old National Gallery, or the DDR.

In the afternoon, catch a one-hour boat tour (or pedal a rented bike) along the parklike banks of the Spree River. Explore the Hackescher Markt's shops and nearby Hackesche Höfe (connected shopping courtyards), and stay into the evening.

Day 3: Tour the sights of the Third Reich and Cold War: the Topography of Terror exhibit and Museum of the Wall at Checkpoint Charlie. The Jewish Museum Berlin is also nearby.

In the afternoon, visit the Gemäldegalerie art museum.

Head to Prenzlauer Berg to visit the Berlin Wall Memorial, then stay for the café and nightlife scene.

ORIENTATION

Berlin is huge and spread out—a series of colorful neighborhoods, with broad boulevards, pleasant parks, long blocks, and low five-story buildings.

Historic Core: Berlin's 1.5-mile sightseeing axis runs west-to-east along **Unter den Linden** boulevard. At the western edge, you'll find the **Reichstag** (parliament), the historic **Brandenburg Gate,** and poignant memorials. It runs past the grand squares of Gendarmenmarkt and Bebelplatz before ending at **Museum Island**—home to the Pergamon, Neues, German History, and DDR museums, among others.

Northern Berlin: The trendy **old Jewish quarter,** near the Hackescher Markt transit hub, has eateries, shopping, and Jewish history. Farther out is the even hipper **Prenzlauer Berg,** with recommended hotels, restaurants, and shopping. Also in this zone are the **Berlin Wall Memorial**—the best place in town to learn more about the Wall—and the **Hauptbahnhof** (main train station).

Southern Berlin: South of Unter den Linden, **fascism and Cold War sights** dominate, anchored by Checkpoint Charlie (former Wall crossing point) and the Topography of Terror (documenting Nazi atrocities). The Jewish Museum Berlin is also here.

Eastern Berlin: East of Museum Island, Unter den Linden changes its name to Karl-Liebknecht-Strasse and leads to **Alexanderplatz**—formerly the hub of communist East Berlin, still marinated in brutal architecture, and marked by its impossible-to-miss TV Tower.

The Brandenburg Gate—historic and grand

GERMANY

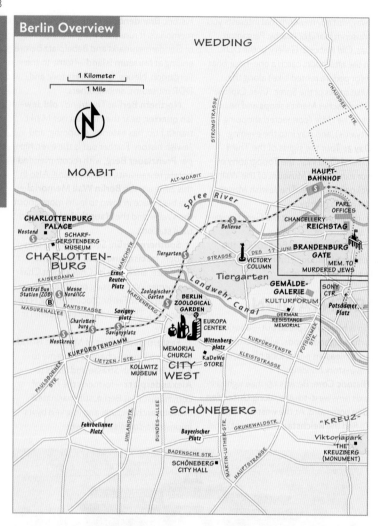

Berlin Overview

Rick's Tip: *What Americans called* **"East Germany"** *was technically the German Democratic Republic—the Deutsche Demokratische Republik, or* **DDR** *(pronounced day-day-AIR). You'll still see those initials around what was once East Germany. The name for what was "West Germany"—the Federal Republic of Germany (Bundesrepublik Deutschland, or* **BRD**)—is now the name shared by all of Germany.*

Western Berlin: Just west of the Brandenburg Gate is Berlin's huge central park, **Tiergarten.** South of the gate, **Potsdamer Platz** is home to Berlin's 21st-century glitz, with skyscrapers and shopping plazas. Down the street, the **Kulturforum** is a cluster of museums, including the impressive Gemäldegalerie (starring Rembrandt, Dürer, and others).

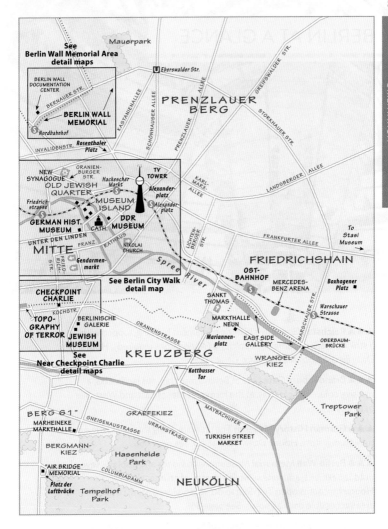

Tourist Information

Berlin's TIs are for-profit agencies that are only marginally helpful (tel. 030/250-025, www.visitberlin.de). You'll find one at the **Hauptbahnhof** (daily 8:00-21:00, by main entrance on Europaplatz), and "info box" kiosks at the **Brandenburg Gate** (daily 9:30-19:00, Nov-March until 18:00) and **Tegel Airport** (daily 8:00-21:00).

Sightseeing Passes

The €29 **Museum Pass Berlin** is best for serious museumgoers—it covers nearly all the city sights for three consecutive days (see details at www.visitberlin.de). It gets you into more than 35 museums, including the national museums and most of the recommended biggies. Covered sights include the Museum Island museums, German History Museum, and the Gemäldegalerie. Buy it at any participating museum or a TI. The pass generally lets

BERLIN AT A GLANCE

▲▲▲**Reichstag** Germany's historic parliament building, topped with a striking modern dome you can climb (reservations required). **Hours:** Daily 8:00-24:00. See page 857.

▲▲▲**Brandenburg Gate** One of Berlin's most famous landmarks, a massive columned gateway, at the former border of East and West. See page 859.

▲▲▲**German History Museum** The ultimate swing through Germany's tumultuous story. **Hours:** Daily 10:00-18:00. See page 866.

▲▲▲**Berlin Wall Memorial** Museums with videos and displays, several outdoor exhibits, and lone surviving stretch of an intact Wall section. **Hours:** Museums open Tue-Sun 10:00-18:00, closed Mon; outdoor areas accessible daily 24 hours. See page 868.

▲▲**Memorial to the Murdered Jews of Europe** Holocaust memorial with almost 3,000 symbolic pillars, plus an exhibition about Hitler's Jewish victims. **Hours:** Memorial always open; information center Tue-Sun 10:00-20:00, Oct-March until 19:00, closed Mon year-round. See page 859.

▲▲**Unter den Linden** Leafy boulevard in the heart of former East Berlin, lined with some of the city's top sights. See page 859.

▲▲**Memorials near the Reichstag** Tributes to Nazi victims, including Jews, Roma, homosexuals, and opposing politicians. See page 858.

▲▲**Pergamon Museum** World-class museum of classical antiquities on Museum Island (Pergamon Altar closed through 2025). **Hours:** Daily 10:00-18:00, Thu until 20:00. See page 862.

▲▲Neues Museum Egyptian antiquities collection and proud home of the exquisite 3,000-year-old bust of Queen Nefertiti. **Hours:** Daily 10:00-18:00, Thu until 20:00. See page 864.

▲▲Old National Gallery German paintings, mostly from the Romantic Age. **Hours:** Tue-Sun 10:00-18:00, Thu until 20:00, closed Mon. See page 865.

▲▲DDR Museum Quirky collection of communist-era artifacts. **Hours:** Daily 10:00-20:00, Sat until 22:00. See page 867.

▲▲Courtyards *(Höfe)* Interconnected courtyards with shops, eateries, and museums, best explored in the old Jewish quarter. See page 867.

▲▲Prenzlauer Berg Lively, colorful neighborhood with hip cafés, restaurants, boutiques, and street life. See page 868.

▲▲Topography of Terror Chilling exhibit documenting the Nazi perpetrators, built on the site of the former Gestapo/SS headquarters. **Hours:** Daily 10:00-20:00. See page 875.

▲▲Gemäldegalerie Germany's top collection of 13th- through 18th-century European paintings, featuring Holbein, Dürer, Cranach, Van der Weyden, Rubens, Hals, Rembrandt, Vermeer, Raphael, and more. **Hours:** Tue-Fri 10:00-18:00, Thu until 20:00, Sat-Sun 11:00-18:00, closed Mon. See page 877.

▲Museum of the Wall at Checkpoint Charlie Stories of brave Cold War escapes, near the site of the famous former East-West border checkpoint; the surrounding street scene is almost as interesting. **Hours:** Daily 9:00-22:00. See page 873.

you skip the line and go directly into the museum—except at the Pergamon and Neues, where you should prebook a time slot on their websites.

The €18 **Museum Island Pass** (not sold at TIs; see www.smb.museum) covers all sights on Museum Island and is a fine value (though for just €11 more, the three-day Museum Pass Berlin described above gives you triple the days and many more entries).

TIs sell the **WelcomeCard,** a transportation pass that includes discounts for many sights; it's a good value if you'll be using public transit frequently (see page 894).

Helpful Hints

Closures: Many museums are closed on Monday, including the Berlin Wall Memorial Visitors Center and Documentation Center, and the Gemäldegalerie, but many also stay open late on Thursdays.

Laundry: You'll find several self-service launderettes near my recommended hotels (generally daily 6:00-22:00). In Prenzlauer Berg, try **Eco-Express Waschsalon** (Danziger Strasse 7) or **Schnell & Sauber Waschcenter** (Oderberger Strasse 1). In the old Jewish quarter, there are two launderettes around the corner from Rosenthaler Platz: **Waschsalon 115** (Wi-Fi, Torstrasse 115) and **Eco-Express Waschsalon** (Torstrasse 109).

Tours

▲▲HOP-ON, HOP-OFF BUSES

Several companies offer a circuit of the city with unlimited, all-day hop-on, hop-

off privileges for around €25. Buses make about a dozen stops at the city's major tourist spots (Museum Island, Brandenburg Gate, and so on). Look for brochures in your hotel lobby or at the TI, or check the websites for **CitySightseeing Berlin,** a.k.a. Berlin City Tour (www.berlin-city-tour.de) and **City Circle Sightseeing,** a.k.a. BEX (www.berlinerstadtrundfahrten.de). Try to catch a bus with a live guide, not recorded narration (buses generally run daily 10:00-18:00, 4/hour, last departure from all stops around 16:00, 2-hour loop; Nov-March 2/hour, last departure 15:00).

▲▲▲SPREE RIVER CRUISES

Several boat companies offer €15 trips up and down the river in one relaxing hour. Boats leave from docks clustered near the bridge behind the Berlin Cathedral (just off Unter den Linden, near the DDR Museum). For better views, go for a two-story boat with open-deck seating. I enjoyed the Historical Sightseeing Cruise from **Stern und Kreisschiffahrt** (departures on the half-hour, mid-March-Nov daily 10:30-17:30, leaves from Nikolaiviertel Dock—cross bridge from Berlin Cathedral toward Alexanderplatz and look right; RS%—show this book for free English audioguide, otherwise €2; tel. 030/536-3600, www.sternundkreis.de).

▲▲▲WALKING TOURS

Berlin's fascinating and complex history can be challenging to appreciate on your own, but a good Berlin tour guide and walking tour makes the city's dynamic

story come to life. Germany has no regulations controlling who can give city tours, so guide quality is hit-or-miss. To improve your odds of landing a great guide, try one of my recommendations. Most tours cost about €12-15 and last 3-4 hours.

Original Berlin Walks' "Discover Berlin" walk offers a solid overview with a smart itinerary in four hours (daily, RS%—€2 less with this book). Tours depart from opposite the Hackescher Markt S-Bahn station (tel. 030/301-9194, www.berlinwalks.de).

Insider Tour runs the full gamut of itineraries, as well as a day trip to Dresden. Their tours meet outside the Friedrichstrasse train station, on the square beside the Palace of Tears, or "Tränenpalast" (tel. 030/692-3149, www.insidertour.com).

Rick's Tip: *Supposedly* **"free" tours are advertised all over town.** *English-speaking students deliver a memorized script and expect to be "tipped in paper" (€5 minimum per person is encouraged). While the guides can be highly entertaining, when it comes to walking tours, you get what you pay for.*

LOCAL GUIDES
Most licensed guides charge €65/hour or €200-300/day. Guides can get booked up—especially in summer—so reserve ahead. I've personally worked with and can strongly recommend archaeologist **Nick Jackson** (mobile 0171-537-8768, www.jacksonsberlintours.com).

Lee Evans (makes 20th-century Germany a thriller, mobile 0176-6335-5565, lee.evans@berlin.de); **Torben Brown** (a walking Berlin encyclopedia, mobile 0176-5004-2572, www.berlinperspectives.com); and **Holger Zimmer** (a cultural connoisseur and public radio journalist, mobile 0163-345-4427, explore@berlin.de).

BERLIN CITY WALK

Trace Germany's turbulent 20th-century history on this two-mile self-guided walk, worth ▲▲▲. We'll start in front of the Reichstag, pass through the Brandenburg Gate, walk down Unter den Linden, and finish on Alexanderplatz, near the TV Tower. If you have just one day in Berlin, or want a good orientation to the city, simply follow this walk (allow 2-3 hours at a brisk pace, not counting museum visits). If you have more time and want to use this walk as a spine for your sightseeing, entering sights and museums as you go, consider doing Part 1 and Part 2 on different days.

Part 1 goes from the Reichstag and partway down Unter den Linden, with stops at the Brandenburg Gate, Memorial to the Murdered Jews of Europe, and Friedrichstrasse, the glitzy shopping street. Part 2 continues down Unter den Linden, from Bebelplatz to Alexanderplatz, visiting Museum Island and the Spree River, the Berlin Cathedral, and the iconic TV Tower.

Tours: ⌂ Download my free Berlin City Walk audio tour.

❷ Self-Guided Walk
Part 1: The Reichstag to Unter den Linden
• *Start in Platz der Republik and take in your surroundings. Dominating this park is a giant domed building.*

❶ REICHSTAG
The Reichstag is the heart of Germany's government. It's where the Bundestag—the lower house of parliament—meets to govern the nation (similar to the US House of Representatives).

When the building was inaugurated in 1895, Germany was still a kingdom. Back then, the real center of power was a mile east of here, at the royal palace. But after the emperor was deposed in World War I, the German Republic was proclaimed. Meanwhile, the storm of

The Reichstag is the symbolic heart of German democracy.

National Socialism was growing—the Nazis. Soon the Reichstag had dozens of duly elected National Socialists, and Adolf Hitler seized power. In 1933, the Reichstag building nearly burned down. Many believe that Hitler planned the fire as an excuse to frame the communists and grab power for himself.

With Hitler as Führer and real democracy a thing of the past, the Reichstag was hardly used. But it remained a powerful symbol and was a prime target for Allied bombers during World War II. As the war wound down and Soviet troops advanced on the city, it was here at the Reichstag that 1,500 German troops made their last stand. After the war, Berlin was divided and the Berlin Wall ran right behind the Reichstag. The building fell into disuse, and the West German capital was moved from Berlin to the remote city of Bonn.

After the Berlin Wall fell, the Reichstag again became the focus of the new nation. It was renovated by British architect Norman Foster, who added the glass dome. In 1999, the new Reichstag reopened, and the parliament reconvened. To many Germans, the proud resurrection of their Reichstag symbolizes the end of a terrible chapter in their country's history.

Look now at the Reichstag's modern **dome.** The cupola rises 155 feet above the ground. Inside the dome, a cone of 360 mirrors reflects natural light into the legislative chamber below, and an opening at the top allows air to circulate. Lit from inside after dark, it gives Berlin a memorable nightlight. If you make a reservation to visit the interior, you can climb the spiral ramp all the way to the top of the dome for a grand city view (for details on visiting, see the Reichstag listing under "Sights," later).

Facing the Reichstag, do a 360-degree spin to find some other big landmarks. To the left of the Reichstag, at the Bundestag U-Bahn stop, the long, partly transparent building houses parliamentary offices. Beyond that, in the distance, is the tower of the huge main train station, the Hauptbahnhof (marked *DB* for Deutsche Bahn, the German rail company). Farther left is the mammoth, white, concrete-and-glass Chancellery (nicknamed "the Washing Machine"). This is the office of Germany's most powerful person, the chancellor. To remind the chancellor who he or she works for, Germany's Reichstag (housing the parliament) is about six feet taller than the Chancellery.

• *Approach the Reichstag, turn right, walk nearly to the street, and find a small memo-*

rial next to the shipping container-like entrance buildings. It's a row of slate stones sticking out of the ground—it looks like a bike rack. This is the...

❷ MEMORIAL TO POLITICIANS WHO OPPOSED HITLER

These 96 slabs honor the 96 Reichstag members who spoke out against Adolf Hitler and the rising tide of fascism. When Hitler became chancellor, these critics were persecuted and murdered. On each slab, you'll see a name and political party—most are KPD (Communists) and SPD (Social Democrats)—and the date and location of death (*KZ* denotes those who died in concentration camps).

• Walk east, along the right side of the Reichstag, on busy Scheidemannstrasse, toward the rear of the building. At the intersection at the back of the Reichstag, turn right and cross the street to a humble row of white crosses that predate the fall of the wall.

❸ BERLIN WALL VICTIMS MEMORIAL

The Berlin Wall once stood right here, running north-south down what is now busy Ebertstrasse, dividing the city in two. The row of white crosses commemorates a few of the many brave East Berliners who died trying to cross the Wall to freedom. (For more on the Wall, see page 874.) The last person killed was 20-year-old Chris Gueffroy. He died nine months before the Wall fell, shot through the heart just a few steps away

from here.

Several other memorials dedicated to groups targeted by the Nazis (from Sinti/Roma to homosexuals) are in the vicinity. For details and where to find them, see page 858.

• Continue south down Ebertstrasse toward the Brandenburg Gate, tracing the former course of the Berlin Wall. A thin strip of memorial bricks embedded in the street pavement indicates where it once stood. Ebertstrasse spills into a busy intersection dominated by the imposing Brandenburg Gate. To take in this scene, cross the Berlin Wall bricks to the piazza in front of the...

❹ BRANDENBURG GATE

This massive classical-looking monument is the grandest—and last survivor—of the 14 original gates in Berlin's old city wall. (This one led to the neighboring city of Brandenburg.) The majestic four-horse chariot on top is driven by the Goddess of Peace. When Napoleon conquered Prussia in 1806, he took this statue to the Louvre in Paris. Then, after the Prussians defeated Napoleon, they got it back (in 1813)...and the Goddess of Peace was renamed the "Goddess of Victory."

The gate straddles the major east-west axis of the city. The western segment—behind you—stretches four miles, running through Tiergarten Park to the Olympic Stadium. To the east—on the other side of the gate—the street is called Unter den

Memorial to Politicians Who Opposed Hitler

Berlin Wall Victims Memorial

GERMANY

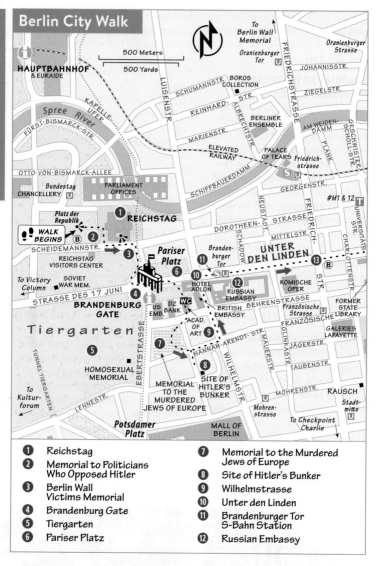

Berlin City Walk

- **1** Reichstag
- **2** Memorial to Politicians Who Opposed Hitler
- **3** Berlin Wall Victims Memorial
- **4** Brandenburg Gate
- **5** Tiergarten
- **6** Pariser Platz
- **7** Memorial to the Murdered Jews of Europe
- **8** Site of Hitler's Bunker
- **9** Wilhelmstrasse
- **10** Unter den Linden
- **11** Brandenburger Tor S-Bahn Station
- **12** Russian Embassy

Linden. That's where we're headed.

Historically, the Brandenburg Gate was just another of this city's many stately Prussian landmarks. But in our lifetime, it became *the* symbol of Berlin—of its Cold War division and its reunification. That's because, from 1961 to 1989, the gate was stranded in the no-man's land between East and West. For an entire generation, scores of

German families were divided—some on this side of the Wall, some on the other. This landmark stood tantalizingly close to both East and West...but was off-limits to all.

By the 1980s, the once-mighty Soviet empire was slowly crumbling from within. Finally, on November 9, 1989, the East German government opened the border. The world rejoiced at the sight of happy

13	Friedrichstrasse	**19**	Karl-Liebknecht-Strasse & Plattenbau
14	Bebelplatz		
15	Neue Wache	**20**	Martin Luther Statue & Marien Church
16	Museum Island & Former City Palace		
17	Spree River	**21**	TV Tower
18	Marx & Engels Statues	**22**	Alexanderplatz

Berliners standing atop the Wall. They chipped away at it with hammers, passed beers to their long-lost cousins on the other side, and adorned the Brandenburg Gate with flowers like a parade float.

• *Turn 180 degrees and take in the vast, green expanse of the park called...*

❺ TIERGARTEN

Look down the long boulevard (Strasse des 17. Juni) that bisects the 500-acre park called Tiergarten ("Animal Garden"). The boulevard's name comes from the 17th of June, 1953, when brave East Germans rose up against their communist leaders. The rebellion was crushed, and East Berliners had to wait another 36 years for the freedom to walk through the Brandenburg Gate. In the distance is the 220-foot **Victory Column,** topped with a golden statue that commemorates the three big military victories that established Prussia as a world power in the late 1800s—over France, Denmark, and Austria—and kicked off Berlin's golden age.

• *Walk through the Brandenburg Gate, entering what for years was forbidden territory. Just past the gate, there's a small TI on the right, and on the left is the Room of Silence, dedicated to meditation. As you cross through this historic but long forbidden gate, you enter a grand square known as…*

➏ PARISER PLATZ

Pariser Platz marks the start of Unter den Linden, the broad boulevard that stretches before you. "Parisian Square" was so named after the Prussians defeated France and Napoleon in 1813. The square was once filled with important government buildings, but all were bombed to smithereens in World War II. For decades, it was an unrecognizable, deserted no-man's-land, cut off from both East and West by the Wall. But now it's rebuilt, and the banks and hotels that were here before the bombing have reclaimed their original places, with a few modern additions. And the winners of World War II—the US, France, Great Britain, and Russia—continue to enjoy this prime real estate: Their embassies are all on or near this square.

The **US Embassy** (on the right as you come through the gate) reopened here in its original location on July 4, 2008. To the left of the US Embassy is the **DZ Bank Building,** built as a conference center in 2001 by Canadian-American architect Frank Gehry (its low-profile exterior was designed so as not to draw attention away from the Brandenburg Gate). To get your fix of wild and colorful Gehry, step into the building's lobby. The undulating interior is like a big, slithery fish.

Two doors past the bank is the ritzy **Hotel Adlon.** Over the years, this place has hosted celebrities and VIPs from Charlie Chaplin to Albert Einstein. And yes, this was where pop star Michael Jackson shocked millions by dangling his infant son over the railing (from the second balcony up).

• *The most direct route to our next stop is by cutting through the **Academy of Arts** (Akademie der Künst) building—it's between Hotel Adlon and the DZ Bank, at Pariser Platz 4. (If the Academy of Arts is closed, loop to the left around the Hotel Adlon to Behrenstrasse.)*

Enter the glassy Academy of Arts (WC in basement) and head toward the back. Just past the ground-floor café (an oasis of calm) is the former office of Albert Speer, Hitler's architect. Continue on, passing Speer's favorite statue, Prometheus (from around 1900). This is the kind of art that turned on Hitler: a strong, soldierly, vital man, defending the homeland.

• *As you exit out the back of the building, veer right on Behrenstrasse and cross the street. You'll wind up at our next stop, a sprawling field of stubby concrete pillars.*

➐ MEMORIAL TO THE MURDERED JEWS OF EUROPE

This memorial consists of 2,711 coffin-shaped pillars covering an entire city block. More than 160,000 Jewish people lived in Berlin when Hitler took power. Tens of thousands fled, and many more were arrested, sent to nearby Sachsenhausen concentration camp and eventually murdered. The memorial remembers them and the other six million Jews who were killed by the Nazis during World War II. Completed in 2005 by the Jewish-American architect Peter Eisenman, this was the first formal, German government-sponsored Holocaust memorial. Using the word "murdered" in the title was intentional, and a big deal. Germany, as a nation, was admitting to a crime.

Inside the **information center** (in the far-left corner), exhibits trace the rise of Nazism and tell the victims' stories (for

Memorial to the Murdered Jews of Europe

details on visiting the information center, see page 859).

• *At the far-left corner, a little beyond the information center, you eventually emerge on the street corner. Our next stop is about a block farther. Carefully jaywalk across Hannah-Arendt-Strasse and continue straight (south) down Gertrud-Kolmar-Strasse. On the left side of the street, you'll reach a rough parking lot. At the far end of the lot is an information plaque labeled* Führerbunker. *This marks the...*

❽ SITE OF HITLER'S BUNKER

You're standing atop the buried remains of the *Führerbunker*. In early 1945, as Allied armies advanced on Berlin and Nazi Germany lay in ruins, Hitler and his staff retreated to this bunker complex behind the former Reich Chancellery. He stayed here for two months.

It was here, on April 30, 1945—as the Soviet army tightened its noose on the Nazi capital—that Hitler and Eva Braun, his wife of less than 48 hours, committed suicide. A week later, the war in Europe was over. The information board here

explains the rest of the story. Though the site of Hitler's bunker is part of history, there really isn't much to see here. And that's on purpose. No one wants to turn Hitler's final stronghold into a tourist attraction.

• *Backtrack up Gertrud-Kolmar-Strasse, and turn right on Hannah-Arendt-Strasse. Take your first left (at the traffic light) on...*

❾ WILHELMSTRASSE

This street was the traditional center of the German power, beginning back when Germany first became a nation in the 19th century. It was lined with stately palaces housing foreign embassies and government offices. This was the home of the Reich Chancellery, where the nation's chief executive presided. When the Nazis took control, this street was where Hitler waved to his adoring fans, and where Joseph Goebbels had his Ministry of Propaganda.

During World War II, Wilhelmstrasse was the nerve center of the German war command. From here, Hitler directed the war and ordered the Blitz (the air raids that destroyed much of London). As the war turned to the Allies' side, Wilhelmstrasse and the neighborhood around it were heavily bombed. Most of the stately palaces were destroyed, and virtually nothing historic survives today.

• *The pedestrianized part of the street is home to the* **British Embassy.** *The fun purple color of its wall represents the colors of the Union Jack mixed together. Wilhelmstrasse spills out onto Berlin's main artery, the tree-lined Unter den Linden, next to the Hotel Adlon.*

⑩ UNTER DEN LINDEN

This boulevard, worth ▲▲, is the heart of imperial Germany. During Berlin's Golden Age in the late 1800s, this was one of Europe's grand boulevards—the Champs-Elysées of Berlin, a city of nearly two million people. It was lined with linden trees, so as you promenaded down, you'd be walking *"unter den Linden."* The street got its start in the 15th century as a way to connect the royal palace (a half-mile down the road, at the end of this walk) with the king's hunting grounds (today's Tiergarten Park). Over the centuries, aristocrats moved into this area so their palaces could be close to their king's.

Many of the grandest landmarks we'll pass along here are thanks to Frederick the Great, who ruled from 1740 to 1786, and put his kingdom (Prussia) and his capital (Berlin) on the map. After World War II, this part of Berlin fell under Soviet influence, and Unter den Linden was the main street of communist East Berlin.

• *Turn your attention to the subway stop in front of the Hotel Adlon (labeled Brandenburger Tor). We'll enter the station and reemerge a block or so farther down the boulevard.*

⑪ BRANDENBURGER TOR S-BAHN STATION

For a time-travel experience back to DDR days, head down the stairs into this station (no ticket necessary). Keep to the right as you descend (toward the S-Bahn, not the U-Bahn) to the subway tracks. As you walk along the platform about 200 yards, survey the historic black-and-white photos on the walls and feel the 1950s vibe of the station.

For decades, the Brandenburger Tor S-Bahn station was unused—one of Berlin's "ghost stations." There's the original 1930s green tilework on the walls, and harsh fluorescent lighting. Some old signs (on the central kiosks) still have *Unter den Linden* (the original name of this stop) written in old Gothic lettering. During the Cold War, the zigzag line dividing East and West Berlin meant that some existing train lines crossed the border underground. To make a little hard Western cash, the East German government allowed a few trains to cut under East Berlin (without stopping) on their way between Western destinations. For 28 years, as Western trains slowly passed through, passengers saw only East German guards...and lots of cobwebs. Then,

Unter den Linden

Brandenburger Tor ghost subway station

in 1989, within days of the fall of the Wall, these stations were reopened.

• *At the far end of the platform, ascend the escalator, bear right, and head up the stairs to exit. You'll emerge on the right side of Unter den Linden. Belly up to the bars and look in at the...*

⑫ RUSSIAN EMBASSY

Built from the ashes of World War II, this imposing building made it clear to East Berliners who was now in charge: the Soviet Union. It was the first big postwar building project in East Berlin, built in the powerful, simplified Neoclassical style that Stalin liked. After the fall of the Soviet Union in 1991, this building became the Russian Embassy, flying the white, blue, and red flag. Find the hammer-and-sickle motif decorating the window frames—a reminder of the days when Russia was part of the USSR.

• *Keep walking down the boulevard for two blocks. You'll pass blocks of dull banks, tacky trinket shops, and a few high-end boutiques, eventually reaching cultural buildings—the university, the opera, and so on. That's intentional: The Prussian kings wanted to have culture closer to their palace. Pause when you reach the intersection with...*

⑬ FRIEDRICHSTRASSE

You're standing at perhaps the most central crossroads in Berlin—named for, you guessed it, Frederick the Great. Before World War II, Friedrichstrasse was the heart of cultural Berlin. In the Roaring Twenties, it was home to anything-goes nightlife and cabarets where entertainers like Marlene Dietrich, Bertolt Brecht, and Josephine Baker performed. And since the fall of the Wall, it's become home to supersized department stores and big-time hotels.

Consider popping into the grand **Galeries Lafayette** department store (two blocks down to your right). Inside, you can ogle a huge glass-domed atrium—a miniature version of the Reichstag cupola. There's a WC and a handy designer food

court in the basement—which you can see below the cupola viewpoint. Note: If you were to continue down Friedrichstrasse from here, you'd wind up at **Checkpoint Charlie** in about 10 minutes.

• *We've reached the end of Part 1. This is a good place to take a break, if you'd like, and tackle Part 2 another time. But if you're up for ambling on, head down Unter den Linden a few more blocks, past the large equestrian statue of Frederick the Great. Frederick is pointing east, toward the epicenter of Prussian imperial power, where his royal palace once stood. We're now entering the stretch of Unter den Linden that best represents Frederick's legacy.*

Turn right into Bebelplatz.

Part 2: Bebelplatz to Alexanderplatz

• *Head to the center of the square, and find the square of glass window set into the pavement. We'll begin with some history and a spin tour, then consider the memorial below our feet.*

⑭ BEBELPLATZ: SQUARE OF THE BOOKS

Frederick the Great built this square to show off Prussian ideals: education, the arts, improvement of the individual, and a tolerance for different groups—provided they were committed to the betterment of society. This square was the cultural center of Frederick's capital. In many ways, it still is. Spin counterclockwise to take in the cultural sights, some of which date back to Frederick's time.

Start by looking across Unter den Linden. That's **Humboldt University,** one of Europe's greatest. Continue panning left. Fronting Bebelplatz is the **former state library**—which was funded by Frederick the Great. After the library was damaged in World War II, communist authorities decided to rebuild it in the original style...but only because Lenin studied here during much of his exile from Russia. The square's far end is marked by one of

A plaque and memorial on Bebelplatz mark the site of a Nazi book burning.

Berlin's swankiest lodgings—**Hotel de Rome,** housed in a historic bank building. Their trendy rooftop bar is a treat in good weather.

Next, the green-domed structure is **St. Hedwig's Church** (nicknamed the "Upside-Down Teacup"). It stands as a symbol of Frederick the Great's religious and cultural tolerance. The pragmatic king wanted to encourage the integration of Catholic Silesians into Protestant Prussia.

Up next is the **Berlin State Opera** (*Staatsoper*)—originally established in Frederick the Great's time. Frederick believed that the arts were essential to having a well-rounded populace. He moved the opera house from inside the castle to this showcase square.

Look down through the glass window in the pavement at what appears to be a room of empty bookshelves. This **book-burning memorial** commemorates a notorious event that took place here during the Nazi years. It was on this square in 1933 that staff and students from the university built a bonfire. Into the flames they threw 20,000 newly forbidden books—authored by the likes of Einstein, Hemingway, Freud, and T.S. Eliot.

Overseeing it all was the Nazi propaganda minister, Joseph Goebbels. Hitler purposely chose this square—built by Frederick the Great to embody culture and enlightenment—to symbolically demonstrate that the era of tolerance and openness was over.

• *Leave Bebelplatz toward Unter den Linden, cross to the university side, and continue heading east down Unter den Linden. You'll pass in front of Humboldt University's main gate. Immediately in front of the gate, embedded in the cobbles, notice the row of square, bronze plaques—each one bearing the name of a university student who was executed by the Nazis. You'll see similar* **Stolpersteine** *("stumbling stones") all over Berlin. Just beyond the university on the left, head for a building that looks like a Greek temple set in a small park filled with chestnut trees.*

⓯ NEUE WACHE

The "New Guardhouse" was built in 1816 as just that—a fancy barracks for the bodyguards assigned to the Hohenzollern palace just ahead (it's the Neoclassical building across the street, with four tall columns marking the doorway). Over the

Memorial at the Neue Wache

years, the Neue Wache has been transformed into a memorial for fallen warriors.

In 1993, the austere interior was fitted with the statue we see today—a replica of *Mother with Her Dead Son,* by Käthe Kollwitz, a Berlin artist who lived through both world wars. It marks the tombs of Germany's unknown soldier and an unknown concentration camp victim. The memorial, open to the sky, incorporates the elements—sunshine, rain, snow—falling on this modern-day pietà.

• *Continue down Unter den Linden, passing by the pink yet formidable Zeughaus (early 1700s), the oldest building on the boulevard. Built in the Baroque style as the royal arsenal, it later became a military museum, and today houses the excellent **German History Museum** (see page 866). When you reach the bridge, cross the Spree and step onto Museum Island.*

⑯ MUSEUM ISLAND AND FORMER CITY PALACE

This island, sitting in the middle of the Spree River, is Berlin's historic birthplace. As the city grew, the island remained the site of the ruler's castle and residence. At its peak under Prussian rulers (1701-1918),

it was a splendid and sprawling Baroque palace called the Stadtschloss, topped at one end with a dome (as you see on the right side of Unter den Linden). The palace was gutted in a 1945 air raid in the last days of World War II. In 1950, the East Germans erected in its place the Palace of the Republic—a massive, blocky parliament building. In the early 21st century, that communist building was demolished, and for years this entire city block was just a big grassy park.

Now, at great expense, Germany has rebuilt a palace on the site, creating the **Humboldt Forum,** a huge public space for business, a celebration of diverse cultures, and a place of higher education. The open "piazza" courtyard inside helps give it a community feel. This "palace for all" (which may be open by 2020) complements the cultural offerings on Museum Island, rounding out what this central place brings to Berlin.

• *Now, turn your attention to the left side of Unter den Linden. There's a spacious garden, bordered on two sides by impressive buildings.*

The elegant Berlin Cathedral (flanked by the DDR-era TV Tower)

MUSEUM ISLAND SIGHTS

For 300 years, the **Lustgarten** has flip-flopped between being a military parade ground and a people-friendly park. In the Nazi era, Hitler enjoyed giving speeches from the top of the museum steps overlooking this square. At the far end of the Lustgarten stand grandiose museum buildings that represent the can-do German spirit of the 1800s, when city leaders envisioned the island as an oasis of culture and learning. Today, these impressive buildings host five grand museums: the **Altes Museum** (classical antiquities), **Neues Museum** (Egyptian, prehistoric, and classical antiquities), **Pergamon Museum** (classical antiquities), **Old National Gallery** (German Romantic painting), and **Bode Museum** (Byzantine art and mosaics).

Dominating the island is the towering, green-domed **Berlin Cathedral** (Berliner Dom). This is only a century old, built during the reign of Kaiser Wilhelm II—who led Europe into World War I. The Wilhelmian style is over the top: a garish mix of Neoclassical, Neo-Baroque, and Neo-Renaissance, with rippling stucco and gold-tiled mosaics. The church is at its most impressive from the outside.

• *Continue down Unter den Linden past the cathedral, and pause on the bridge over the Spree. Look left, past the cathedral.*

⓱ SPREE RIVER

The Spree River is people-friendly and welcoming. A parklike promenade leads all the way from here to the Hauptbahnhof. Along it, you'll find impromptu "beachside" beer gardens with imported sand, barbecues in pocket parks, and lots of locals walking their dogs, taking a lazy bike ride, or jogging. Spree River boat tours depart from near here (for details, see page 842).

• *From here you could return to Museum Island to see the sights there or backtrack to the German History Museum. But we'll continue toward the TV Tower and Alexanderplatz (where this walk ends). Cross the bridge and find the statues of Marx and Engels, at the river-end of the big park. Note that as the boulevard crosses the river, Unter den Linden becomes Karl-Liebknecht-Strasse.*

Spree River sightseeing boats

⑱ STATUES OF KARL MARX AND FRIEDRICH ENGELS

These statues of the founders of communism mark the Marx-Engels-Forum, a park dedicated in 1986 by the East German government. During the heady days before the Berlin Wall and the Iron Curtain fell, a half-million Berliners gathered here to call for freedom and an end to the economic and social experiment preached by these two philosophers.

• *From here, with your back to the river, angle through the park veering left, in the direction of the TV Tower. As you emerge from the park and hit Spandauer Strasse, look right to see the red-brick* **city hall,** *where Berlin's mayor has an office. It was built after the revolutions of 1848 and was arguably the first democratic building in the city. At the intersection, a cute DDR-era Ampelmännchen ("little traffic-light man") street light will tell you to stop or walk.*

Cross Spandauer Strasse. To your left is...

⑲ KARL-LIEBKNECHT-STRASSE AND *PLATTENBAU*

This street is named for a founder of Germany's communist party: Karl Liebknecht. As you continue walking toward the TV

Tower, notice the uniformity of the high-rise concrete buildings lining the boulevard to your left. These are *Plattenbau* ("panel buildings"). While the DDR government maintained a few token historic landmarks (like the Rotes Rathaus), their real architectural forte was prefabricated, high-capacity, low-aesthetics housing.

But residents prided themselves on creating cozy and welcoming little nests inside, and being invited to dinner at one of these apartments showed you the stark contrast between cold, paranoid public life and colorful, gregarious private life.

• *Head for the old church up on the right.*

⑳ MARTIN LUTHER STATUE AND MARIEN CHURCH

Approaching the church, you see a bold statue of **Martin Luther.** Marien Church, like the rest of Europe, was Roman Catholic until about 500 years ago when this solitary German monk rocked European history by kicking off the Protestant Reformation.

The **Marien Church,** with its prominent steeple, dates from 1270. Just inside the church, an artist's rendering helps you follow the interesting but very faded old "Dance of Death" mural that wraps around the narthex (dating from before Luther). In true Protestant style, the interior is dominated by the pulpit (for Protestants, it's all about the word of God) and the pipe organ (Luther said, "When you sing, you pray double").

• *Across the street and a half-block down is another Berlin memorial that's worth a detour—the* **Women's Protest Memorial.** *It commemorates a courageous—and unusually successful—protest by the Gentile wives of Jewish men who were arrested by the Nazis. Remarkably, these brave women actually won the freedom of their husbands.*

Otherwise, gaze up at the 1,200-foot-tall...

㉑ TV TOWER (FERNSEHTURM)

The communist regime is long gone, but it left this enduring legacy. The TV Tower—built in 1969 to celebrate the 20th anniversary of communist East Germany—was meant to show the power of the atheistic state at a time when DDR leaders were removing crosses from the country's church domes and spires. But when the sun hit the tower, the reflected light created a huge, bright cross on the mirrored ball. Cynics called it "The Pope's Revenge." East Berliners joked that if the TV tower fell over, they'd have an elevator to freedom in the West. (For a steep price you can ride to the top for a grand view.)

• *Return to the church side of the boulevard and continue walking east down Karl-Liebknecht-Strasse, passing the TV Tower on your right. You'll cross under a railway overpass, then walk alongside a mall called Galeria Kaufhof. Just past the mall, turn right onto a broad pedestrian street. It leads through a low tunnel and into a big square...*

㉒ ALEXANDERPLATZ

Alexanderplatz was built in 1805, during the Prussian Golden Age. Because this was a gateway for trade to Eastern Europe, it was named for a Russian czar, Alexander. In the Industrial Age, it became a transportation hub. In the roaring 1920s, it was a center of cabaret nightlife to rival Friedrichstrasse. And under the DDR, it was transformed into a commercial center. This was the pride and joy of East Berlin shoppers. And then, on November 4, 1989, more than a half-million East Berliners gathered on Alexanderplatz to demand their freedom; a week later, the Berlin Wall was history.

Stand just beyond the first U-Bahn station entrance and take a clockwise spin-tour—starting with Galeria Kaufhof, to the right of the TV Tower. In communist times, the Kaufhof department store was the ultimate shopping mecca... which wasn't saying much. In front is an abstract-sculpture fountain ringed with a colorful base that attracts sitters. Next, the tall, glassy skyscraper is a DDR-era hotel, now called the Park Inn. Continuing clockwise past the Saturn electronics store and the colorful Kandinsky-esque Alexa building, notice the once-futuristic **World Time Clock,** a nostalgic favorite installed in 1969 that remains a popular meeting point.

The TV Tower punctuates Berlin's skyline.

• From here, you can hike back a bit to catch the Spree riverboat tour, visit Museum Island or the German History Museum, or venture into the colorful Prenzlauer Berg neighborhood. Or you can take bus #100 or #300 back along Karl-Liebknecht-Strasse and on to Unter den Linden.

SIGHTS

Reichstag and Brandenburg Gate Area

The Reichstag's original facade

Much of Berlin's sightseeing is concentrated in this area, which is covered in more detail in my "Berlin City Walk" (earlier; also available as a free 🎧 audio tour).

▲▲▲REICHSTAG

Germany's historic parliament building—completed in 1894, burned in 1933, sad and lonely in a no-man's-land throughout the Cold War, and finally rebuilt and topped with a glittering glass cupola in 1999—is a symbol of a proudly reunited nation. Visit here to spiral up the remarkable dome and gaze across Berlin's rooftops, and to watch today's parliament in action. Because of security concerns, you'll need a reservation and your passport to enter.

Cost and Hours: Free, reservations required—see below, daily 8:00-24:00, last entry at 22:00, metal detectors, no big luggage allowed, Platz der Republik 1; S- or U-Bahn: Friedrichstrasse, Brandenburger Tor, or Bundestag.

Information: Tel. 030/2273-2152, www.bundestag.de.

Advance Tickets: You must make a free reservation. It's easy to do online, but book early—spots often fill up several days in advance. Go to www.bundestag.de, and from the "Visit the Bundestag" menu, select "Online registration." You have two choices: "Visit to the dome" includes a good audioguide and is plenty for most; or, the 90-minute guided tour provides more in-depth information. You'll be sent an email link to a website where you'll enter details for each person in your party. A final email will contain your reservation (with a letter you must print out or download to your mobile device).

Another option is to have lunch or dinner at the pricey rooftop restaurant, **$$$$ Käfer Dachgarten** (daily 12:00-16:30 & 18:30-24:00, last access at 22:00, reserve well in advance at tel. 030/2262-9933 or www.feinkost-kaefer.de/berlin).

Getting In: Report 15 minutes before your appointed time to the temporary-looking entrance facility in front of the Reichstag, and be ready to show your passport and confirmation letter. After passing through a security check, you'll wait with other visitors for a guard to take you to the Reichstag entrance.

Visiting the Reichstag: The open, airy **lobby** towers 100 feet high, with 65-foot-tall colors of the German flag. See-through glass doors show the central legislative chamber. The message: There will be no secrets in this government. Look inside. Spreading his wings behind the podium is a stylized German eagle, the *Bundestagsadler* (affectionately nicknamed the "Fat Hen"), representing the Bundestag (each branch of government has its own symbolic eagle). Notice the doors marked *Ja* (Yes), *Nein* (No), and *Enthalten* (Abstain)...an homage to the Bundestag's traditional "sheep jump" way of counting votes by exiting the chamber through the corresponding door. (For critical votes, however, they vote with

GERMANY

Inside the Reichstag's glass dome

electronic cards.)

Germany's Bundestag (comparable to the US House of Representatives) meets here. Its 631 members are elected to four-year terms. They in turn elect the chancellor. Unlike America's two-party system, Germany has a handful of significant parties, so they must form coalitions to govern effectively. Bundestag members have offices in the building to the left of the Reichstag.

Ride the elevator to the base of the **glass dome** (where you'll pick up the ***Berlin Panorama*** flier and your audioguide). The dome is 80 feet high, 130 feet across, and weighs a quarter of a million pounds. It uses about 33,000 square feet of glass, or nearly enough to cover a football field.

Study the photos and read the circle of captions (around the base of the central funnel) telling the Reichstag story. Then study the surrounding architecture: a broken collage of new on old, torn between antiquity and modernity, like Germany's history. Notice the dome's giant and unobtrusive sunscreen that moves as necessary with the sun. Peer down through the skylight to look over the shoulders of the elected representatives at work. For Germans, the best view from here is down—keeping a close eye on their government.

Walking up the ramp, you'll spiral past 360-degree views of the city, including the Tiergarten, the "green lungs of Berlin"; the Teufelsberg ("Devil's Hill"; famous during the Cold War as a powerful ear of the West—notice the telecommunications tower on top); Potsdamer Platz; the Brandenburg Gate; Frank Gehry's fish-like roof of the DZ Bank building; the Memorial to the Murdered Jews of Europe; the former East Berlin, with a forest of 300-foot-tall skyscrapers in the works; Berlin's huge main train station; and the blocky, postmodern Chancellery, the federal government's headquarters (the audioguide explains what you're seeing as you walk).

▲▲MEMORIALS NEAR THE REICHSTAG
The area immediately surrounding the Reichstag is rich with memorials. Within a few steps, you'll find monuments to politicians who opposed Hitler and victims of the Berlin Wall (both described earlier, on

the "Berlin City Walk").

In the park just behind the Berlin Wall Victims Memorial is the **Monument to the Murdered Sinti and Roma of Europe,** an opaque glass wall, with a timeline in English and German, commemorating the roughly 500,000 Holocaust victims who identified as "Sinti" and "Roma"—the main tribes and politically correct terms for the group often called "Gypsies."

Also in the park (toward the Victory Column) is the **Soviet War Memorial.** It honors the Soviet army soldiers who died in the bitter battle for Berlin, which brought World War II to a decisive conclusion.

Across the street from the Memorial to the Murdered Jews of Europe, tucked into a corner of the park, is the **Memorial to the Homosexuals Persecuted Under the National Socialist Regime.** Access it from the Jewish memorial's southwest corner, across Ebertstrasse from Hannah-Arendt-Strasse. Through a small window, you can watch a film loop of same-sex couples kissing—a reminder that life and love are precious.

▲▲▲**BRANDENBURG GATE**

The icon of Berlin, this majestic gateway has seen more than its share of history. Armies from Napoleon to Hitler have marched under its gilded statues, and for more than 25 years, it sat forlorn in the Berlin Wall's death strip. Today it's a symbol of Berlin's rejuvenated capital.

Just inside (east of) the Brandenburg gate is the tidy "Parisian Square"—Pariser Platz. This prime real estate is ringed by governmental buildings, banks, historic plush hotels, the Academy of Arts, and the heavily fortified US Embassy.

▲▲**MEMORIAL TO THE MURDERED JEWS OF EUROPE (DENKMAL FÜR DIE ERMORDETEN JUDEN EUROPAS)**

This labyrinth of 2,711 irregularly shaped pillars memorializes the six million Jewish people who were executed by the Nazis. Loaded with symbolism, it's designed to encourage a pensive moment in the heart of a big city. Inside the **information center** (far-left corner), exhibits trace the rise of Nazism and how it led to World War II. Six portraits, representing the six million Jewish victims, put a human face on the numbers, as do diaries, letters, and final farewells penned by Holocaust victims. You'll learn about 15 Jewish families from very different backgrounds, who all met the same fate. A continually running soundtrack recites victims' names. To read them all aloud would take more than six and a half years.

Cost and Hours: Memorial—free and always open; information center—free, open Tue-Sun 10:00-20:00, Oct-March until 19:00, closed Mon year-round, last entry 45 minutes before closing, security screening at entry, audioguide-€3; S-Bahn: Brandenburger Tor or Potsdamer Platz, tel. 030/2639-4336, www.stiftung-denkmal.de.

Unter Den Linden

▲▲**STROLLING UNTER DEN LINDEN**
Berlin's main boulevard—"Under the Linden Trees"—has been the city's artery since the 15th century. Today, it's a well-tended place to stroll. This main drag and its sights are covered in my "Berlin City Walk" earlier (and also available as a free 🎧 audio tour).

GENDARMENMARKT
Berlin's finest square sits two blocks south of Unter den Linden (and one block south of Bebelplatz). The square, like its name ("Square of the Gens d'Armes," Frederick the Great's French guard), is a hybrid of Prussia and France. The square is bookended by two matching churches: the **German Cathedral** (with a free exhibit on the German parliamentary system) and the **French Cathedral** (dedicated to the French Huguenots who found refuge in Prussia). Gendarmenmarkt's centerpiece is the Concert Hall (Konzerthaus), commissioned by Frederick the Great and built by his favorite architect, Karl Friedrich

GERMANY

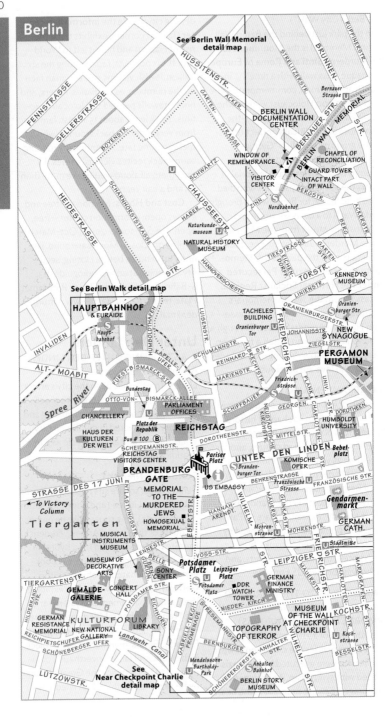

Berlin

See Berlin Wall Memorial detail map

FENNSTRASSE

SELLERSTRASSE

HEIDESTRASSE

BOYENSTR.

SCHARNHORSTRASSE

HUSSITENSTR.

ACKER

GARTEN-STRASSE

SCHWARTZ

HABER-STR.

CHAUSSEESTR.

BERNAUER-STR.

RUPPINERSTR.

STRELITZERSTR.

BRUNNEN

Bernauer Strasse

BERLIN WALL DOCUMENTATION CENTER

WINDOW OF REMEMBRANCE

VISITOR CENTER

CHAPEL OF RECONCILIATION

GUARD TOWER

INTACT PART OF WALL

BERLIN WALL MEMORIAL

ZINN-STR.

BERGSTR.

Nordbahnhof

BERG

ACKERSTR.

Naturkunde-museum

NATURAL HISTORY MUSEUM

STR.

HANNOVERSCHESTR.

TIEKSTRASSE

EICHEN-DORFF

GARTEN-STR.

TORSTR.

KENNEDYS MUSEUM

See Berlin Walk detail map

HAUPTBAHNHOF & EURAIDE

Haupt-bahnhof

INVALIDEN

ALT-MOABIT

Spree River

HUMBOLDTHAFEN

KAPELLE-UFER

LUISENSTR.

SCHUMANNSTR.

REINHARDT STR.

MARIENSTR.

LINIENSTR.

ORANIENBURGERSTR.

TACHELES BUILDING

Oranienburger Tor

FRIEDRICHSTR.

JOHANNISSTR.

ZIEGELSTR.

ALBRECHTSTR.

SCHIFFBAUER

Oranien-burger Str.

NEW SYNAGOGUE

PERGAMON MUSEUM

Friedrich-strasse

UNIV.

FÜRST-BISMARCK-STR.

Bundestag

OTTO-VON-BISMARCK-ALLEE

CHANCELLERY

PARLIAMENT OFFICES

HAUS DER KULTUREN DER WELT

Platz der Republik

Bus #100 B

SCHEIDEMANNSTR.

REICHSTAG VISITORS CENTER

REICHSTAG

DOROTHEENSTR.

NEUSTÄDTISCHE KIRCHSTR.

GEORGEN.

MITTELSTR.

CHARLOTTEN-STR.

DOROTHEEN

HUMBOLDT UNIVERSITY

UNTER DEN LINDEN

KOMISCHE OPER

Bebel-platz

STRASSE DES 17 JUNI

←To Victory Column

Tiergarten

ENTLASTUNGSSTR.

BRANDENBURG GATE

MEMORIAL TO THE MURDERED JEWS

Pariser Platz

Brandenburger Tor

US EMBASSY

BEHRENSTRASSE

Französische Strasse

MAUERSTR.

GLINKASTR.

EBERTSTR.

HANNAH-ARENDT-

WILHELM-

FRANZÖSISCHE STR.

Gendarmen-markt

GERMAN CATH.

HOMOSEXUAL MEMORIAL

Mohren-strasse

MOHRENSTR.

FRIEDRICHSTR.

Stadtmitte

MUSICAL INSTRUMENTS MUSEUM

LENNÉSTR.

BELLE

GÜRTEL

VOSS-STR.

Potsdamer Platz

Leipziger Platz

LEIPZIGER STR.

MUSEUM OF DECORATIVE ARTS

TIERGARTENSTR.

GEMÄLDE-GALERIE

CONCERT HALL

SONY CENTER

EICHHORN

POTSDAMER STR.

Potsdamer Platz

DDR WATCH-TOWER

GERMAN FINANCE MINISTRY

NIEDER-KIRCH

STRESEMANN STR.

MARGRAFEN-STR.

CHARLOTTEN-STR.

KOCHSTR.

MUSEUM OF THE WALL AT CHECKPOINT CHARLIE

Koch-strasse

HILDEBRAND STR.

GERMAN RESISTANCE MEMORIAL

NEW NATIONAL GALLERY

KULTURFORUM LIBRARY

Landwehr Canal

GABRIELE-TERGIT-PROMENADE

BERNBURGER

ANHALTER STR.

TOPOGRAPHY OF TERROR

WILHELM-STR.

BESSELSTR.

REICHPIETSCHUFER

SCHÖNEBERGER UFER

LÜTZOWSTR.

Mendelssohn-Bartholdy-Park

SCHÖNEBERGERSTR.

Anhalter Bahnhof

BERLIN STORY MUSEUM

See Near Checkpoint Charlie detail map

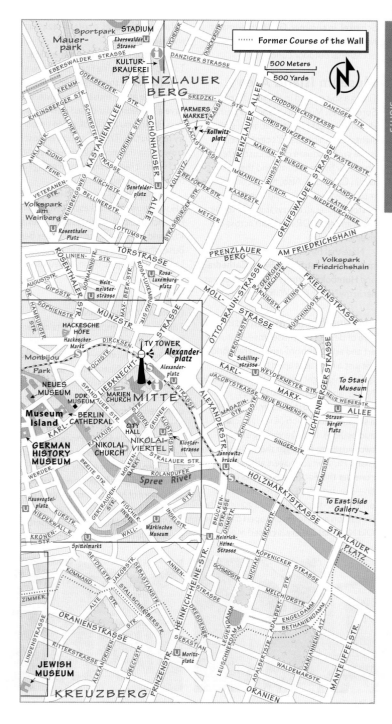

..... Former Course of the Wall

500 Meters
500 Yards

Schinkel. In summer, Gendarmenmarkt hosts outdoor cafés, *Biergartens,* and occasional outdoor concerts.

Museum Island Area

Filling a spit of land in the middle of the Spree River, Museum Island has perhaps Berlin's highest concentration of serious sightseeing. The island's centerpiece is the grassy square called Lustgarten, ringed by five museums and the hulking Berlin Cathedral. Also, two recommended museums flank the island: the German History Museum across the river to the west, and the DDR Museum across the river to the east.

Note that three Museum Island landmarks—the **Lustgarten, Berlin Cathedral,** and **Humboldt Forum**—are described earlier in my "Berlin City Walk"; see page 853.

Museum Island (Museumsinsel)

Five of Berlin's top museums—featuring art and artifacts from around the world—are just a few steps apart on Museum Island. I highlight the top three: Pergamon, Neues, and Old National Gallery.

Cost and Hours: Each museum has a separate admission (€10-12, includes audioguide). If you're visiting at least two museums here, get the €18 Museum Island Pass (which covers all 5; also consider the €29 Museum Pass Berlin—see page 839). The museums are open 10:00-18:00 (Thu until 20:00). The Pergamon and Neues are open daily; the Old National Gallery is closed Mon.

Information: Tel. 030/266-424-242, www.smb.museum.

Advance Tickets Recommended: To skip ticket-buying lines, purchase a timed ticket for the Pergamon Museum in advance at the museum website. If you have a Museum Island Pass or Museum Pass Berlin, you can book a free timed-entry reservation. The Pergamon is most crowded in the morning, on weekends, and when it rains; Thursday evenings are the least crowded.

Getting There: The island is a 10-minute walk from the Hackescher Markt or Friedrichstrasse S-Bahn stations. Trams #M1 and #12 connect to Prenzlauer Berg. Buses #100 and #300 run along Unter den Linden, stopping near the museums at the Lustgarten stop.

▲▲PERGAMON MUSEUM (PERGAMONMUSEUM)

This world-class museum contains Berlin's Collection of Classical Antiquities (Antikensammlung)—full-sized buildings from the most illustrious civilizations of the ancient world. Its namesake and highlight—the gigantic Pergamon Altar—is under renovation and off-limits to visitors until 2025. But there's still plenty to see: the massive Babylonian Processional Way and Ishtar Gate (slathered with glazed blue tiles, from the sixth century BC); the full-sized market gate from the ancient Roman settlement of Miletus (first century BC); and, treasures from the Islamic world.

Visiting the Museum: The superb audioguide (included) helps broaden your

Ishtar Gate

Market Gate of Miletus

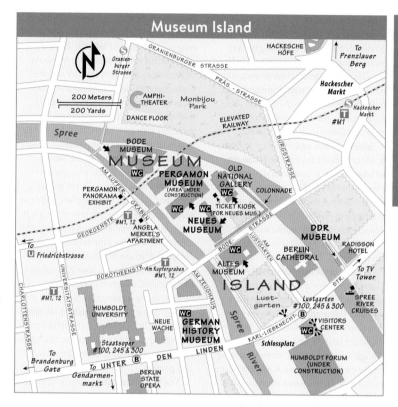

Museum Island

experience. From the entry hall, head up to floor 1 and all the way back to 575 BC and Mesopotamia.

Processional Way and Ishtar Gate: The ruler Nebuchadnezzar II made sure that all who approached his city got a grand first impression. His massive blue Ishtar Gate stands 46 feet tall and 100 feet wide. This was the grandest of Babylon's gates, one of eight in the 11-mile wall that encompassed this city of 200,000. The Gate was one of the original Seven Wonders of the World. All the pieces in this hall—the Gate, Processional Way, and Throne Room panels—are made of decorative brick, glazed and fired in the ancient Egyptian faience technique. Decorations like the lions, which project outward from the surface, were carved or molded before the painted glaze went on.

The museum's Babylonian treasures are meticulous reconstructions. A Berlin archaeologist discovered the ruins in modern-day Iraq in 1900. What was recovered was little more than piles of shattered shards of brick. It's since been augmented with modern tilework and pieced together like a 2,500-year-old Babylonian jigsaw puzzle. (You could peek into Room 6—if it's open—to see a model of Babylon.)

Market Gate of Miletus: You've flashed forward 700 years to ancient Miletus—the wealthy, cosmopolitan, Roman-ruled, and Greek-speaking city on the southwest coast of Asia Minor (modern Turkey). Dominating this room is the huge Market Gate of Miletus. This served as the entrance to the town's agora, or marketplace. Traders from across the Mediterranean and Middle East passed through the three arched doorways into a football-field-sized courtyard surrounded by arcades.

Miletus was destroyed by an earthquake centuries ago and the gate was painstakingly reconstructed here in Berlin. This room also displays an exquisite mosaic floor of colored stone and glass from the dining room of a Roman villa in Miletus, c. AD 200, and features the mythical Greek musician Orpheus.

Islamic Treasures: Head up to **floor 2,** which is dedicated to the **Museum of Islamic Art.** It demonstrates how—after Rome fell and Europe was mired in medievalism—the Islamic world carried the torch of civilization. The impressive Aleppo Room is illustrated with motifs from Christian, Arabic, Persian, and Jewish traditions.

What About the Pergamon Altar?

During the museum's restoration, a special exhibit called *Pergamonmuseum-Das Panorama* is in a pavilion on Am Kupfergraben (directly across from Museum Island). The main attraction is a huge, wraparound panorama painting of the city of Pergamon in AD 129. Some of the original sculpture from the altar, the largest piece of the altar frieze, and digital 3D models help visitors fill in the details (€19 combo-ticket with Pergamon Museum, €6 with Museum Island Pass or Museum Pass Berlin, open same hours as the museum).

▲▲NEUES (NEW) MUSEUM

This beautiful museum, featuring objects from the prehistoric world, contains three collections. Most visitors focus on the Egyptian Collection, with the stunning bust of Queen Nefertiti. But it's also worth a walk through the Museum of Prehistory and Early History and the Collection of Classical Antiquities (artifacts from ancient Troy). Everything is well-described in English (fine audioguide included with admission; for more on the museum, see www.neues-museum.de).

Visiting the Museum: The Neues Museum ticket desk is across the courtyard from the entrance. Ticket in hand, enter and pick up the floor plan. The main reason to visit is to enjoy one of the great thrills in art appreciation—gazing into the still young and beautiful face of Queen Nefertiti. If you're in a pinch for time, make a beeline to her (floor 2, far corner of Egyptian Collection in Room 210).

To tour the whole collection, start at the top (floor 3), the **prehistory section.** The entire floor is filled with Stone Age, Ice Age, and Bronze Age items. You'll see early human remains, tools, spearheads, and pottery.

The most interesting item on this floor (in corner of Room 305)—the tall, conehead-like **Golden Hat,** made of paper-thin gold leaf—was likely worn by the priest of a sun cult popular among the Celtic people of central Europe around 1,000 BC. Admire the incredible workmanship of these prehistoric people. The hat, 30 inches tall, was hammered from a pound of gold into a single sheet of gold leaf less than a millimeter thick.

Neues Museum

Queen Nefertiti

On floor 2, in a room all her own (Room 210), is the 3,000-year-old bust of **Queen Nefertiti**, wife of Akhenaton—the most famous piece of Egyptian art in Europe. Nefertiti has all the right beauty marks: long slender neck, perfect lips, almond eyes, symmetrical eyebrows, pronounced cheekbones, and a perfect spray-on tan. And yet, despite her seemingly perfect beauty, Nefertiti has a touch of humanity. Notice the fine wrinkles around the eyes—these only enhance her beauty. She has a slight Mona Lisa smile, pursed at the corners.

The bust never left its studio, but served as a master model for all other portraits of the queen. (That's probably why the artist didn't bother putting the quartz inlay in the left eye.) Stare at her long enough, and you may get the sensation that she's winking at you.

▲▲OLD NATIONAL GALLERY (ALTE NATIONALGALERIE)

Of Berlin's many top-notch art collections, this is the best for *German* art—mostly paintings from the 19th century, the era in which "German culture" first came to mean something. For a concise visit, focus on the Romantic German paintings (top floor), where Caspar David Friedrich's hauntingly beautiful canvases offer an insightful glimpse into German landscapes...and the German psyche. With more time, peruse the French and German Impressionists and German Realists on the first and second floors.

Visiting the Museum: Start on the third floor and work your way down.

Casa Bartholdy Murals (Room 3.02): These frescoes tell the biblical story of Joseph. They were done by idealistic artists of the artistic brotherhood called the Nazarenes. It was the early 1800s, and the German people were searching for their unique national identity. In art, the Nazarenes were seeking a purer form of expression that was uniquely German. This almost religious fervor would inspire the next generation of German artists—the Romantics.

Karl Friedrich Schinkel (Room 3.05): Schinkel is best known as the Neoclassical architect who remade Berlin in the 1820s. But as a painter, Gothic cathedrals and castles dominate his scenes. Where puny humans do appear, they are dwarfed by the landscape and buildings. Scenes are lit by a dramatic, eerie light, as though the world is charged from within by the power of God. Welcome to Romanticism.

Caspar David Friedrich (Room 3.06): The greatest German artist of the Romantic era was Caspar David Friedrich (1774-1840). A quick glance around this room gives you a sense of Friedrich's subjects: craggy mountains, twisted trees, ominous clouds, burning sunsets, and lone figures in the gloom. The few people he painted are tiny and solitary, pondering the vastness of their surroundings.

Biedermeier Style (Rooms 3.08-3.13): These rooms feature paintings in the so-called Biedermeier style (c. 1815-1848). Biedermeier landscapes are pretty, not dramatic. The style is soft-focus, hypersensitive, super-sweet, and sentimental. The poor are happy, the middle class are happy, and the world they inhabit is perfectly lit.

French Impressionists (Room 2.03): Unlike the carefully composed, turbulent, and highly symbolic paintings of the German Romantics, these scenes appear like simple unposed "snapshots" of everyday life. Pan the room to see Renoir's pink-cheeked girls, Degas' working girls, Cézanne's fruit bowls, and Gauguin's Tahitian girls.

Rest of the Museum: In Room 2.14 are two well-known **portraits by Franz von Lenbach** of world-changing Germans: Otto von Bismarck (Germany's first prime minister) and the composer Richard Wagner.

Near Museum Island

The German History Museum is on Unter den Linden, immediately west of Museum Island; and the DDR Museum is (fittingly) just east of Museum Island, on the riverbank facing the back of the Berlin Cathedral.

▲▲▲GERMAN HISTORY MUSEUM (DEUTSCHES HISTORISCHES MUSEUM)

This impressive museum offers the best look at German history under one roof, anywhere. The permanent collection packs 9,000 artifacts into two huge rectangular floors of the old arsenal building. You'll stroll through insightfully described historical objects, paintings, photographs, and models—all intermingled with multimedia stations. The 20th-century section—on the ground floor—is far better than any of the many price-gouging historical Nazi or Cold War "museums" all over town. A thoughtful visit here provides valuable context for your explorations of Berlin (and Germany).

Cost and Hours: €8, covered by Museum Pass Berlin, daily 10:00-18:00, worthwhile €3 audioguide, Unter den Linden 2.

Information: Tel. 030/2030-4751, www.dhm.de.

Getting There: It's at Unter den Linden 2. Buses #100, #245, and #300 stop right in front (Staatsoper stop). By tram, the Am Kupfergraben stop (for trams #M1 and #12) is a block behind the museum. The nearest S-Bahn stops are Friedrichstrasse and Hackescher Markt, each about a 10-minute walk away.

Visiting the Museum: As you tour the collection, stay on track by locating the museum's historic chapters (pillars along the way marked with a date span) then browse the exhibits nearby.

First Floor (500-1918): This floor weaves its way through the centuries, with exhibits on early cultures, the Middle Ages, the Reformation, the Thirty Years' War, and the German Empire.

Several rooms are dedicated to the German monk Martin Luther, who in the 16th century shocked Europe with new and radical ideas, sparking the Protestant Reformation. You'll find a number of Luther artifacts, including the Edict of Worms (next to the portrait of Charles V), where Charles V condemned the Protestant heretic, and a Bible translated by Luther into everyday German.

Frederick the Great made Prussia (an area of northern Germany) a European power and Berlin a cultural capital. Science flourished (see scientific instruments) as did music (see early keyboards and a picture of the Mozart family). In the 1800s, Prussia took over Germany's destiny when Wilhelm I and his shrewd prime minister, Otto von Bismarck (see their busts), forged Germany's principalities and dukedoms together. In 1871, the German people united, and they waved an eagle flag (on display) of a new nation: Germany.

Ground Floor (20th Century): World War I pit Germany against France, England, and others. Photos show the grim reality of a war fought from defensive trenches, while posters (and a poignant woodcut by Berlin artist Käthe Kollwitz) capture the bitter and cynical mood that descended over Germany.

Europe's victors dealt harshly with

Exhibits at the German History Museum are comprehensive and thought-provoking.

Germany, sowing enormous resentment. In 1933, the Nazis took control of Germany under Adolf Hitler, who appealed to Germans' sense of national and ethnic pride. Hitler made plans to turn Berlin into "Welthaupstadt Germania," the "world capital" of his far-reaching Third Reich. The centerpiece would be the impossibly huge domed Volkshalle—950 feet high and able to accommodate 180,000 people. It would squat over the Spree River, just north of the Reichstag.

Exhibits document the atrocities at Hitler's concentration camps, including registration photos of prisoners and a model of a crematorium at Auschwitz (in Nazi-occupied Poland), which were designed to exterminate Jews. By the end of the war, more than 60 million were dead, including 6 million Jews and 6 million non-Jewish Germans.

After losing the war, Berlin and Germany were divided between the Soviet-leaning East and the US-leaning West. Exhibits juxtapose slices of life in the two Germanys. By the 1980s, the Soviet empire was cracking, and in 1989 the Berlin Wall began crumbling.

For architecture buffs, the big attraction is the modern annex behind the history museum, designed by American architect **I. M. Pei**, who is famous for his glass pyramid at Paris' Louvre. (To get there, cross through the courtyard, admiring the Pei glass canopy overhead.) This annex complements the museum with temporary exhibits. A striking glassed-in spiral staircase unites four floors with surprising views and lots of light.

▲▲DDR MUSEUM

This museum has a knack for helping outsiders understand life in communist East Germany (the *Deutsche Demokratische Republik*, or DDR). It's well-stocked with kitschy everyday items from the DDR period, plus photos, video clips, and concise English explanations. You can crawl through a Trabant car (known as a "Trabi"; take it for a virtual test drive) and pick

up some DDR-era black humor ("East Germany had 39 newspapers, four radio stations, two TV channels...and one opinion"). The highlight is a tourable reconstructed communist-era home.

Cost and Hours: €8.50, buy online in advance to avoid waiting in a long line at the entrance; daily 10:00-20:00, Sat until 22:00; just across the Spree from Museum Island at Karl-Liebknecht-Strasse 1, tel. 030/847-123-731, www.ddr-museum.de.

Old Jewish Quarter

Immediately northeast of the Spree River is the old Jewish quarter which, in addition to being packed with intriguing shops and fun eateries, is one of the most important areas for Berlin's historic Jewish community—offering insights into a culture that thrived here until the 1940s.

▲▲COURTYARDS (HÖFE)

The old Jewish quarter is a particularly handy place to explore Berlin's unique *Höfe*—interconnected courtyards that burrow through city blocks, today often filled with trendy shops and eateries. Two starkly different examples are nearly next door, and just steps from the Hackescher Markt transit hub: the upscale, *Jugendstil* Hackesche Höfe (Rosenthaler Strasse 40), with eye-pleasing architectural flourishes and upscale shops; and the funky Haus Schwarzenberg (Rosenthaler Strasse 39), with a museum honoring Otto Weidt—a Berliner who defied the Nazis and saved many lived by employing blind and deaf Jews in his workshop.

NEW SYNAGOGUE (NEUE SYNAGOGUE)

Marked by its beautiful golden dome, this large, mid-19th-century synagogue is now a museum memorializing the Berlin Jewish community that was decimated by the Nazis. Berlin was long the center of German Jewry and this small but moving exhibit (with good English descriptions) tells the story of this community through the centuries. You'll enter through a low-profile door

New Synagogue

in the modern building to the right of the synagogue facade and go through very tight security. A cutaway model shows the entire synagogue that once housed 3,200 worshippers. The upper floor personalizes the Nazi terror with individual stories.

Cost and Hours: €7; Sun-Fri 10:00-18:00, closed Sat; audioguide-€3, Oranienburger Strasse 28, S-Bahn: Oranienburger Strasse, tel. 030/8802-8300, www.centrumjudaicum.de.

▲PALACE OF TEARS (*TRÄNENPALAST*) AT FRIEDRICHSTRASSE STATION

Just south of the old Jewish quarter (cross the river on Friedrichstrasse at Weidendammer Brücke and bear right) stands this impactful Cold War site. The Friedrichstrasse train station was one of the few places where Westerners were allowed to cross into East Berlin. And when crossing back into the free world, this was where they'd take leave of their East German loved ones. The scene of so many sad farewells, it earned the nickname *"Tränenpalast"* (palace of tears). The boxy structure that was once attached to the station is now a museum about everyday life in a divided Germany, with a fascinating peek into the paranoid border-control world of the DDR.

Cost and Hours: Free, includes excellent audioguide, Tue-Fri 9:00-19:00, Sat-Sun 10:00-18:00, closed Mon, on the river side of the Friedrichstrasse station—look for the building with large glass windows and blue trim, Reichstagufer 17, tel. 030/4677-7790, www.hdg.de/traenenpalast.

Berlin Wall Memorial near Prenzlauer Berg

The thriving Prenzlauer Berg district, worth ▲▲, offers an ideal opportunity to see a corner of today's "real Berlin," just beyond the core tourist zone but still easily accessible. Prenzlauer Berg (PRENTS-low-er behrk) was largely untouched by WWII bombs, fell into disrepair during DDR days, and has since been completely rejuvenated. Prenzlauer Berg is also a great place to sleep, eat, shop, and enjoy nightlife.

▲▲▲BERLIN WALL MEMORIAL (GEDENKSTÄTTE BERLINER MAUER)

This is Berlin's most substantial and educational sight relating to its gone-but-not-forgotten Wall. As you visit the park, you'll

Fragments of the Berlin Wall in the memorial area

learn about how the Wall went up, the brutal methods used to keep Easterners in, and the stories of brave people who risked everything to be free.

Exhibits line up along several blocks of Bernauer Strasse, stretching more than a mile northeast from the Nordbahnhof S-Bahn station (one of the DDR's "ghost stations") to Schwedter Strasse and the Mauerpark. For a targeted visit, focus on the engaging sights clustered near the Nordbahnhof: two museums (the Visitors Center and the Documentation Center)—with films, photos, and harrowing personal stories; various open-air exhibits and memorials; original Wall fragments; and observation tower views into the only preserved, complete stretch of the Wall system (with "death strip").

Cost and Hours: Free; outdoor areas accessible daily 24 hours; Visitors Center and Documentation Center both open Tue-Sun 10:00-18:00, closed Mon, memorial chapel closes at 17:00; on Bernauer Strasse at #119 (Visitors Center) and #111 (Documentation Center).

Information: Tel. 030/4679-86666, www.berliner-mauer-gedenkstaette.de.

Getting There: Take the S-Bahn (line S1, S2, or S25) to Nordbahnhof. Exit by following signs for *Bernauer Strasse*—you'll pop out at the memorial. You can also get there on tram #12 or #M10 (from near Prenzlauer Berg hotels).

Overview: Begin at the Nordbahnhof and pick up an informational pamphlet from the Visitors Center. Head up Bernauer Strasse, visit the exhibits and memorials, then ride home from the Bernauer Strasse U-Bahn station. For a longer visit, walk several more blocks to the Mauerpark. The entire stretch is lined with informational posts and larger-than-life images from the Wall on the sides of buildings.

◉ SELF-GUIDED WALK
• *Start your visit at the...*

Visitors Center (Bezucherzentrum): Check the next showtimes for the two 15-minute introductory films in English. The film titled **The Berlin Wall** covers the four-decade history of the Wall. The other film—**Walled In!**—features a 3-D re-creation of the former death strip, helping you visualize what it is you're about to walk through.

• *Exit the Visitors Center, cross Bernauer Strasse, and enter the Memorial park. Find*

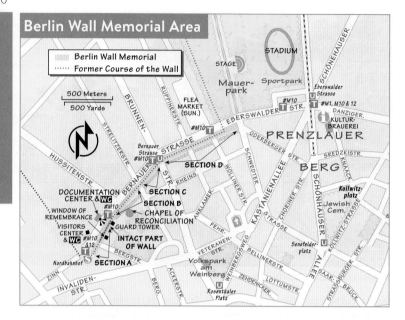

Berlin Wall Memorial Area

Legend:
- Berlin Wall Memorial
- Former Course of the Wall

500 Meters
500 Yards

STADIUM
STAGE
Mauer-park
Sportpark
FLEA MARKET (SUN.)
Eberswalder Strasse
#M10
#M1, M10 & 12
DANZIGER
KULTUR-BRAUEREI
EBERSWALDER STR.
ODERBERGER STR.
PRENZLAUER
BRUNNEN-
STREITZERSTR.
RUPPINERSTR.
Bernauer Strasse #M10
SREDZKISTR.
BERG
HUSSITENSTR.
BERNAUER STRASSE
RHEINS.
SCHWEDTER STR.
SECTION D
KASTANIENALLEE
CHORINER STR.
SCHÖNHAUSER
Kollwitz-platz
Jewish Cem.
DOCUMENTATION CENTER & WC
SECTION C
SECTION B
CHAPEL OF RECONCILIATION
WINDOW OF REMEMBRANCE
#M10
ANKLAMER
FEHR.
STRASSE
VISITORS CENTER & WC
#M10
GUARD TOWER
INTACT PART OF WALL
Senefelder-platz
KOLLWITZSTR.
ALLEE
Nordbahnhof
SECTION A
BERGSTR.
VETERANEN-STR.
BELLINERSTR.
ZINN
INVALIDEN-STR.
BERG
ACKERSTR.
Volkspark am Weinberg
WEINBERGSWEG
ZEHDENICKER
LOTTUMSTR.
STRASSBURGER
SAAR-SBURGER STR.
Rosenthaler Platz

the rusty rectangular monument with a 3-D map.

3-D Map of the Former Neighborhood: The map shows what this neighborhood looked like back in the Wall's heyday. Fifty years ago, you'd be right at the division between East and West Berlin—in the narrow strip between two sets of walls. One of those walls is still standing—there it is, stretching along Bernauer Strasse. As you gaze down the long park, West Berlin would be to your left (on the north side of Bernauer Strasse), and East Berlin to your right.

Now find the Nordbahnhof, across the street on your left. While the Wall stood, the Nordbahnhof station straddled both East and West—one of the "ghost stations" of Cold War Berlin (inside the station, photos compare 1989 with 2009).
• *Stroll along the path through this first section of the park ("Section A"). Along the way are small sights, remembrances, and exhibits. As you stroll, you're walking through the...*

"Death Strip" (Section A): Today's grassy park, with a pleasant path through it, was once the notorious "death strip"

(*Todesstreifen*). If someone was trying to escape from the East, they'd have to scale one wall (a smaller one, to your right), cross this narrow strip of land, and climb the main Wall (to your left, along Bernauer Strasse). The death strip was an obstacle course of barbed wire, tire-spike strips to stop cars, and other diabolical devices. Armed guards looked down from watchtowers, with orders to shoot to kill.
• *About midway through this section of the park, find the freestanding rusted-iron wall filled with photos.*

Window of Remembrance: Find **Otfried Reck,** just 17 years old (eighth from the left, top row). On November 27, 1962, he and a friend pried open a ventilation shaft at the boarded-up Nordbahnhof, and descended to the tracks, where they hoped to flag down a passing westbound train. The police discovered them, and Reck was shot in the back.

Continue walking through Section A. You're now walking along the original, preserved asphalt patrol path.
• *Now, walk across the grass and find a place to get a good close-up look at...*

The Wall: The Wall here is typical of the whole system: about 12 feet tall, made of concrete and rebar, and capped by a rounded pipe that made it tough for escapees to get a grip. This was part of a 96-mile-long Wall that encircled West Berlin, making it an island of democracy in communist East Germany. The West Berlin side of the Wall was typically covered with colorful graffiti by free-spirited West Berliners.

• *Now, exit the park through the hole in the Wall, turn right along Bernauer Strasse, and make your way a short distance to the crosswalk. Across Bernauer Strasse is a modern gray building at #119 (labeled* Gedenkstätte Berliner Mauer). *This is the...*

Documentation Center (Dokumentationszentrum Berliner Mauer): This excellent museum is geared to a new generation of Berliners who can hardly imagine their hometown split so brutally in two. The two floors of exhibits have photos and displays to explain the logistics of the city's division and its effects. Listen to the riveting personal accounts of escapees—and of the border guards armed with machine guns and tasked with stopping them.

On the second floor, be sure to watch the poignant seven-minute film, ***Peaceful Revolution.*** The video highlights the power of the people and traces the events that led to the Wall's collapse. From this floor, stairs lead to the rooftop **Tower** (*Turm*) where you're rewarded with a view. You can look across Bernauer Strasse and down at Berlin's last preserved stretch of the death strip with an original guard tower. More than 100 sentry towers like this one kept a close eye on the Wall.

• *Exit and continue on. Cross Bernauer Strasse (where it intersects with Ackerstrasse) and enter the next section of the Memorial park.*

Escapes from Border-Strip Buildings (Section B): Ahead, you'll see a group of information panels. The panels tell the story of what happened here: On August 13, 1961, the East German government officially closed the border. People began fleeing to the parts of Berlin controlled by other European powers.

Over the next few months, the border hardened. Ackerstrasse was closed as East German soldiers laid down rows of barbed wire. People were suddenly separated from their West Berlin neighbors just across the street. During this brief window of time (summer of '61 to early '62), there were many escape attempts.

• *Keep going up the path through Section B, to the round building up ahead.*

Chapel of Reconciliation (Kapelle der Versöhnung): This modern chapel stands on the site of the old Church of Reconciliation. Built in 1894, the old church served the neighborhood parish. When the Wall went up, the church found itself stranded in the death strip. It became famous in the West as a symbol of how the godless commies had driven out religion. The church was finally blown up by the East Germans in 1985.

Intact part of the Wall

Chapel of Reconciliation

After the Wall came down, this chapel was built. The carved wooden altarpiece inside was saved from the original structure. The chapel hosts daily prayer services for the victims of the Wall.

• Continue past the chapel into the second portion of Section B.

Tunnels and More: Walk uphill then bear left to a large open-air display under a canopy (amid the ruins of a destroyed Bernauer Strasse home). Photos, info boards, and press-the-button audio clips explain what it was like to live here, so close to the front line of the Cold War. Head back up to the main path, turn left, and continue. You'll pass two parallel rows of metal slabs, labeled *Fluchttunnel 1964.* This marks the route of the most famous tunnel of all: **Tunnel 57** (named after the 57 people who escaped through it).

• The main part of our walk is done. To experience more of the Memorial, you could continue through more open-air exhibits. **Section C** focuses on the building of the Wall. **Section D**—nearly as long as the first three sections combined—covers everyday life in the shadow of the Berlin Wall.

If you're ready to leave, the Bernauer Strasse U-Bahn station is just a block farther up Bernauer Strasse. Or you can backtrack to the Nordbahnhof. And tram #M10 follows Bernauer Strasse all the way to Eberswalder Strasse, in the heart of Prenzlauer Berg.

Fascism and Cold War Sites near Checkpoint Charlie

▲CHECKPOINT CHARLIE

Famous as the place where many visiting Westerners crossed into East Berlin during the Cold War, the original Checkpoint Charlie is long gone. But today a reconstructed guard station—with big posters of American and Soviet guards, and a chilling *You are leaving the American sector* sign—attracts curious tourists for a photo op. Nothing here is original (except

Checkpoint Charlie

for the nearby museum—described next), and the whole area feels like a Cold War theme park, with kitschy communist-themed attractions, hucksters, and sleazy vendors who charge through the nose for a DDR stamp in your passport. The replica checkpoint is free to view and always open (but you'll pay to take photos with the "guards").

For nearly three decades (1961-1989), this was a border crossing between East and West Berlin. It became known worldwide and stood as a symbol of the Cold War itself. The name "Charlie" came about because it was the third checkpoint in a series. Checkpoint A (Alpha) was at the East-West German border. Checkpoint B (Bravo) was where people left East Germany and entered the Allied sector of Berlin. And this was Checkpoint C (Charlie), on the border between the US-occupied neighborhood and the Soviet zone. Checkpoint Charlie was a humble shack for document-checking GIs. It sat on a traffic island in the middle of Friedrichstrasse, fortified with a few piles of sandbags.

Today you see a **mock-up,** with a guard station, sandbags, and a US flag. Larger-than-life posters show an American soldier facing east and a young Soviet soldier facing west—look at these portraits and consider the decades of armed standoffs here.

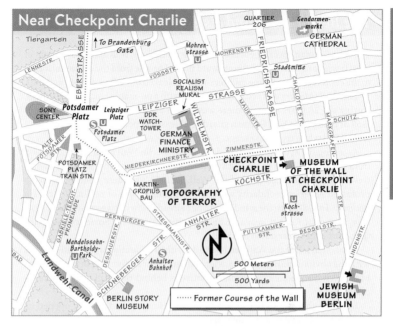

Near Checkpoint Charlie

QUARTIER 206

Gendarmen-markt

GERMAN CATHEDRAL

Tiergarten

To Brandenburg Gate

Mohren-strasse

MOHRENSTR.

Stadtmitte

VOSSSTR.

SOCIALIST REALISM MURAL

LEIPZIGER STRASSE

MAUERSTR.

CHARLOTTE STR.

SCHÜTZ.

MARKGRAFEN-

Potsdamer Platz

Leipziger Platz

DDR WATCH-TOWER

GERMAN FINANCE MINISTRY

WILHELMSTR.

SONY CENTER

Potsdamer Platz

NIEDERKIRCHNERSTR.

ZIMMERSTR.

CHECKPOINT CHARLIE

MUSEUM OF THE WALL AT CHECKPOINT CHARLIE

POTSDAMER PLATZ TRAIN STN.

MARTIN-GROPIUS BAU

TOPOGRAPHY OF TERROR

KOCHSTR.

Koch-strasse

GABRIELE TERGIT PROMENADE

BERNBURGER

STRESEMANNSTR.

ANHALTER STR.

PUTTKAMMER STR.

BESSELSTR.

LINDENSTR.

Mendelssohn-Bartholdy-Park

Anhalter Bahnhof

500 Meters

500 Yards

Landwehr Canal

SCHÖNEBERGER STR.

DESSAUERSTR.

BERLIN STORY MUSEUM

······ Former Course of the Wall

JEWISH MUSEUM BERLIN

BERLIN SIGHTS

▲MUSEUM OF THE WALL AT CHECKPOINT CHARLIE (MAUERMUSEUM HAUS AM CHECKPOINT CHARLIE)

This ragtag but riveting celebration of the many ways desperate East Germans managed to slip through the Wall to freedom has stood here since 1963... taunting DDR authorities. Today East Germany and its Wall are long gone, but the museum is still going strong. Some of the displays have yellowed, the place is cramped and confusing, and the ticket price is way too high, but the museum retains a special sense of history. Visiting here, you'll learn about the creation of the Wall and the many escape attempts (including several of the actual items used by clever escapees). If you're pressed for time, visit after dinner, when most other museums are closed. Compared to the soberly academic official Berlin Wall Memorial near the Nordbahnhof, this museum has more personality, buoyed by a still-defiant spirit.

Cost and Hours: €14.50, daily 9:00-

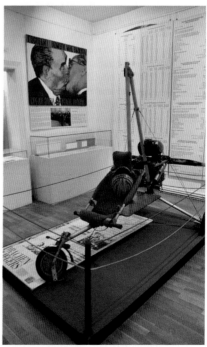

Museum of the Wall at Checkpoint Charlie

The Berlin Wall (and Its Fall)

The East German government erected the 96-mile-long Wall almost overnight in 1961. It was intended to stop the outward flow of people from the communist East to the capitalist West: Three million souls had leaked out between 1949 and 1961.

The Wall (*Mauer*) was actually two walls, with a no-man's-land between them. During the 28 years it stood, there were 5,043 documented successful escapes (565 of these were East German guards). At least 138 people died or were killed at the Wall while trying to escape.

As a tangible symbol for the Cold War, the Berlin Wall got a lot of attention from politicians. Two of the 20th century's most repeated presidential quotes were uttered within earshot of the Wall. In 1963, President John F. Kennedy professed American solidarity with the struggling people of Berlin: *"Ich bin ein Berliner."* In 1987, with the winds of change already blowing westward from Moscow, President Ronald Reagan issued an ultimatum to his Soviet counterpart: "Mr. Gorbachev, tear down this wall."

The actual fall of the Wall had less to do with presidential proclamations than with the obvious failings of the Soviet system, a general thawing in Moscow, the brave civil disobedience of ordinary citizens behind the Wall—and a bureaucratic snafu.

By November 1989, change was in the air. Hungary had already opened its borders to the West that summer, making it impossible for East German authorities to keep people in. Anti-regime protests swept nearby Leipzig, attracting hundreds of thousands of supporters. A rally in East Berlin's Alexanderplatz on November 4—with a half-million protesters chanting, *"Wir wollen raus!"* (We want out!)—persuaded the East German politburo to begin gradually relaxing travel restrictions.

The DDR intended to crack the door to the West, but an unknowing spokesman inadvertently threw it wide open. In back-room meetings early on November 9, officials decided they would allow a few more Easterners to cross into the West. The politburo members then left town for a long weekend. The announcement of the decision was left to Günter Schabowski, who knew only what was on a piece of paper handed to him moments before a routine press conference. At 18:54, Schabowski read the statement on live TV, with little emotion: "exit via border crossings...possible for every citizen." Reporters, unable to believe what they were hearing, prodded him about when the borders would open. Schabowski shrugged and offered his best guess: *"Ab sofort, unverzüglich."* ("Immediately, without delay.")

Schabowski's words spread like wildfire. East Berliners showed up at Wall checkpoints, demanding that border guards let them pass. Finally, around 23:30, a border guard at the Bornholmer Strasse crossing decided to open the gates. Easterners flooded into the West, embracing their long-separated cousins, unable to believe their good fortune. Once open, the Wall could never be closed again. After that wild night, Berlin faced a fitful transition to reunification. Two cities—and countries—became one at a staggering pace.

22:00, last entry one hour before closing, audioguide-€5, U6 to Kochstrasse or U2 to Stadtmitte, Friedrichstrasse 43, tel. 030/253-7250, www.mauermuseum.de.

▲▲TOPOGRAPHY OF TERROR (TOPOGRAPHIE DES TERRORS)

A rare undeveloped patch of land in central Berlin, right next to a surviving stretch of Wall, was once the nerve center for the Gestapo and the SS—the most despicable elements of the Nazi government. Today this site hosts a modern documentation center, along with an outdoor exhibit in the Gestapo headquarters' excavated foundations. While there isn't much in the way of original artifacts, the exhibit does a good job of telling this powerful story, in the place where it happened. The information is a bit dense, but WWII historians (even armchair ones) find it fascinating.

Cost and Hours: Free, includes audioguide, daily 10:00-20:00, outdoor exhibit closes at dusk and closed entirely Dec-Jan, Niederkirchnerstrasse 8, U-Bahn: Potsdamer Platz or Kochstrasse, S-Bahn:

Anhalter Bahnhof or Potsdamer Platz.

Information: Tel. 030/254-5090, www.topographie.de.

Visiting the Museum: Start in the lobby and study a **model** of the neighborhood showing the home of the German government at the outbreak of World War II. (We're standing at #20.) Back in the 1930s and '40s, this was just one of many governmental office buildings along Wilhelmstrasse. Seeing this sprawling bureaucratic quarter gives you a sense of how much mundane paperwork was involved in administering Hitler's reign of terror in an efficient, rational way. In the small theater nearby, the six-minute film provides context for the exhibit (and can be shown in English upon request).

The **ground floor** houses the permanent collection. Stepping in, you begin a chronological journey (with a timeline of events, old photographs, documents, and newspaper clippings) through the evolution of Nazism, the reign of terror, the start of World War II, and the Holocaust.

The displays illustrate how Hitler,

Some exhibits at the Topography of Terror are incorporated into a surviving stretch of the Berlin Wall.

Himmler, and their team expertly manipulated the German people to build a broadly supported "dictatorship of consent." You'll learn about the Gestapo and SS *(Schutzstaffel)*, and their brutal methods—including their chillingly systematic implementation of the Holocaust.

Some images here are indelible. Gleeful SS soldiers, stationed at Auschwitz, yuk it up on a retreat in the countryside (as their helpless prisoners were being gassed and burned a few miles away). Graphic images show executions—by hanging, firing squad, and so on.

The exhibits end with the conclusion of the war in 1945. While the Nazi leadership was captured and prosecuted at the Nürnberg trials, the majority of midlevel bureaucrats who routinely facilitated genocide with the flick of a pen...were never brought to justice.

With more time, use the audioguide and posted signs to explore the grounds surrounding the blocky building. Around the corner (to the right facing the museum entrance) are the scant remains of the **House Prison** outlined in cement. The building was equipped with dungeons, where the Gestapo detained and tortured prisoners.

Nearby: Immediately next door is an unusually long surviving stretch of the Berlin Wall. A block beyond that is the looming, fascist-style former Air Ministry for Hitler's Luftwaffe (air force), today the German Finance Ministry, though still adorned with cheery 1950s communist propaganda. A short walk away is a surviving DDR watchtower.

▲JEWISH MUSEUM BERLIN (JÜDISCHES MUSEUM BERLIN)

Combining a remarkable building with a thoughtful permanent exhibit, this is the most educational Jewish-themed sight in Berlin. Designed by American architect Daniel Libeskind (the master planner for the redeveloped World Trade Center in New York), the zinc-walled building has a zigzag shape pierced by voids symbolic of the irreplaceable cultural loss caused by the Holocaust.

Enter the 18th-century Baroque building next door to reach three memorial spaces. Follow the **Axis of Exile**—lined with the names of cities where the Jew-

The Jewish Museum's fractured facade suggests the dislocation of the Holocaust.

ish diaspora settled—to a disorienting slanted garden with 49 pillars. Next, the **Axis of Holocaust**—lined with names of concentration camps and artifacts from Jews imprisoned and murdered by the Nazis—leads to an eerily empty tower shut off from the outside world. Finally, the **Axis of Continuity** takes you to stairs and the main exhibit (if the extensive renovation has been completed).

Cost and Hours: €8, daily 10:00-20:00, closed on Jewish holidays; tight security includes bag check and metal detectors; tel. 030/2599-3300, www.jmberlin.de.

Getting There: Take the U1/U6 to Hallesches Tor, find the exit marked *Jüdisches Museum,* exit straight ahead, then turn right onto Franz-Klühs-Strasse at the first corner. The museum is a five-minute walk ahead on your left, at Lindenstrasse 9.

Eating: The museum's $$ restaurant offers good Jewish-style meals, albeit not kosher.

Kulturforum Complex

The Kulturforum, off the southeast corner of Tiergarten park, hosts Berlin's concert hall and several sprawling museums, but only the Gemäldegalerie is a must for art lovers.

▲▲GEMÄLDEGALERIE

This "Painting Gallery" is one of Germany's top collections of great works by European masters. The Gemäldegalerie shows off fine works from the 13th through 18th century. While there's no one famous piece of art, you'll get an enticing taste of just about all the big names. In the North Wing are painters from Germany (Albrecht Dürer, Hans Holbein, Lucas Cranach), the Low Countries (Jan van Eyck, Pieter Brueghel, Peter Paul Rubens, Anthony van Dyck, Frans Hals, Johannes Vermeer), Britain (Thomas Gainsborough), France (Antoine Watteau), and an impressive hall of Rembrandts. The South Wing is the terrain of Italian greats, including Giotto,

Botticelli, Titian, Raphael, and Caravaggio.

Cost and Hours: €10, includes audioguide; Tue-Fri 10:00-18:00, Thu until 20:00, Sat-Sun 11:00-18:00, closed Mon; clever little loaner stools, great salad bar in cafeteria upstairs, Matthäikirchplatz 4.

Information: Tel. 030/266-424-242, www.smb.museum.

Getting There: Ride the S-Bahn or U-Bahn to Potsdamer Platz, then walk along Potsdamer Platz.

Visiting the Museum: When you buy your ticket, pick up the current museum map for help locating specific paintings (artwork locations may change). Northern Art is on one side (where we'll begin) and Italian art is on the other (where we'll end). Note that inner rooms have Roman numerals (I, II, III), while adjacent outer rooms use Arabic numerals (1, 2, 3). We'll work counterclockwise (and roughly chronologically) through the collection.

Hans Holbein the Younger, 1497-1543 (Room 1): Holbein's portrait *Merchant Georg Gisze* (*Der Kaufmann Georg Gisze,* 1532) depicts a wealthy 34-year-old German businessman. His black beret and immaculate clothes mark him as a suc-

Holbein the Younger, The Merchant Georg Gisze

Ⓐ *Van der Weyden,* Portrait of a Woman

Ⓑ *Rubens,* Jesus Giving Peter the Keys to Heaven

Ⓒ *Rembrandt,* Self-Portrait with a Velvet Beret

Ⓓ *Vermeer,* The Glass of Wine

cessful dealer in cloth. Around him are the tools of his trade—logbooks, business letters with wax seals, signet rings, scales, and coins. Typical of detail-rich Northern European art, the canvas is bursting with highly symbolic tidbits. The clock (on the table, inside the small gold canister) reminds the viewer that time passes and worldly success fades. The unbalanced scales suggest that wealth is fleeting. Those negative symbols are counterbalanced by the carnations and herbs in the vase, representing Gisze's upcoming marriage.

Albrecht Dürer, 1471-1528 (Room 2): In 1494, the young Dürer traveled from Germany to Italy, where he soaked up the technique and spirit of the burgeoning Renaissance movement. In his portrait *Hieronymus Holzschuher* (1526), Dürer captured the personality of a white-bearded friend from Nürnberg, right down to the sly twinkle in his sidelong glance. Dürer does not gloss over the 57-year-old's unflattering features like the wrinkles or receding hairline (with the clever comb-over).

Lucas Cranach the Elder, 1472-1553 (Room III): Cranach's *Fountain of Youth* (*Der Jungbrunnen,* 1546) depicts the perennial human pursuit of eternal youth. Ladies flock to bathe in the swimming pool of youth. They arrive (on the left) as old women—by wagon, on horseback, carried by men, even in a wheelbarrow. They strip and enter with sagging breasts, frolic awhile in the pool, rinse and repeat, then emerge (on the right) young again. Newly nubile, the women go into a tent to dress up, snog with noblemen in the bushes (right foreground), dance merrily beneath the trees, and dine grandly beneath a landscape of mountains and towers.

Rogier van der Weyden, 1400-1464 (Room IV): Dutch painters were early adopters of oil paint, and Van der Weyden was a virtuoso of the new medium. In *Portrait of a Young Woman* (*Bildnis einer jungen Frau,* 1440-1445), the subject wears

a typical winged bonnet, addressing the viewer directly with her fetching blue eyes. In the same room is a remarkable, rare trio of three-panel altarpieces by Van der Weyden showing the life of the Virgin Mary, the life of John the Baptist, and the story of the Nativity. Savor the fine details in each panel.

Peter Paul Rubens, 1577-1640 (Room VIII): We've fast-forwarded a hundred years, and it's apparent how much the Protestant Reformation changed the tenor of Northern European art. Rubens' paintings represent the Catholic response, the Counter-Reformation. You'll see huge, brightly-colored canvases of Mary, alongside angels, bishops, and venerated saints (like the arrow-pierced martyr, St. Sebastian). This exuberant Baroque style trumpeted the greatness of the Catholic Church.

You'll also catch glimpses of Rubens' second wife, Helene Fourment, in mythological scenes such as *Andromeda* (1638). Helene, the amply-figured nymph with a sweetly smiling face, came to define the phrase "Ruben-esque."

Frans Hals, c. 1582-1666 (Room 13): Hals' *Portrait of Catharina Hooft with Her Nurse* (*Bildnis der Catharina Hooft mit ihrer Amme,* 1619-1620) presents a startlingly self-possessed baby (the newest member of a wealthy merchant family), dressed in the lacy, jeweled finery of a queen and clutching a golden rattle. At the other end of the social spectrum is Hals' *Malle Babbe* (1633-1635). The subject, a notorious barfly nicknamed "Crazy" Babbe, was well known in Hals' hometown. Hals captures her hefting her pewter beer stein and turning to laugh at a joke. The messy brushstrokes that define her collar and cap are as wild and lively as her over-the-top personality.

Rembrandt van Rijn, 1606-1669 (Room X): The ultimate Dutch master, Rembrandt was propelled to fame in his lifetime by his powers of perception and invention. Browse Room X and the adjoining galleries to get a taste of the range of Rembrandt's work. There are storytelling scenes, taut with pulse-racing emotion (*The Rape of Persephone,* 1631, Room 16). There are Bible scenes (*Samson and Delilah,* 1628-1629, Room 16; *Samson Threatens His Father-in-Law,* 1635, Room X).

And there are expressive portraits. In Room X, a *Self-Portrait* (1634) shows Rembrandt wearing a beret. The 28-year-old genius was already famous. He soon married the beautiful Saskia (*Portrait of Saskia,* 1643, Room 16), and seemed to have it all. But then Saskia died, Rembrandt declared bankruptcy, and his painting style went out of fashion...all of which contributed to his brooding, dark canvases.

Johannes Vermeer, 1632-1675 (Room 18): Vermeer was a master at conveying a complicated story through a deceptively simple scene with a few significant details. *Young Woman with a Pearl Necklace* (1664) is classic Vermeer. He lets us glimpse an intimate, unguarded moment in the life of an everyday woman. She wears a beautiful yellow coat with an ermine fur lining, ribbons in her hair, and pearl earrings. Vermeer tells us a bit about the woman with objects on the table: her comb, make-up brush, and water bowl.

Caravaggio, 1573-1610 (Room XIV): In the year 1600, living in Rome, Caravaggio burst onto the scene with a new and shocking art style. Even religious and allegorical subjects got his uncompromising, gritty, ultrarealistic treatment. In Caravaggio's *Amor Vincit Omnia* (1601-1602), "Love Conquers All." Cupid stands victorious over all the vain accomplishments of ambitious men: Military triumphs (symbolized by the fallen armor), Art (the discarded musical instruments), Literature (paper and pen), Science (a globe), Grand Architecture (compass and square), and Power (the crown). Cupid—a young, naked boy—mocks those grown-up ambitions. He laughs derisively and splays his genitals over the fallen symbols.

Now turn your attention to a painting in Room XIV by a different artist—**Giovanni Baglione**'s *Sacred and Profane Love* (1602-1603). Baglione was hired by a conservative cardinal to paint a moralizing response to Caravaggio. Here, the main figure is a more upright incarnation of love—Sacred Love—embodied by a radiant angel. He corners his rascally counterpart, the cowering and "Profane" little Cupid (lower right).

EXPERIENCES

Shopping

One big draw is **communist kitsch.** Gift shops at museums (such as the DDR Museum or Museum of the Wall at Checkpoint Charlie) sell a variety of "East Berlin" paraphernalia. Maybe *the* top communist-kitsch souvenir is anything with the image of the *Ampelmännchen* (traffic-light man), the DDR-era crossing-guard symbol that's become Berlin's unofficial mascot. The best selection is at the local chain of Ampelmann shops; the flagship store—with a hunk of Berlin Wall autographed by David Hasselhoff (no joke)—is along Unter den Linden at #35 (at the corner with Friedrichstrasse).

Flea Markets (Flohmarkt)

Virtually every Berlin neighborhood hosts a regular flea market. In **Prenzlauer Berg,** the Sunday rummage market in the **Mauerpark** isn't just about buying and selling—it's an excuse for a big, weekly, community-wide party. You'll find lots of inventive snack stalls and, in the afternoon, karaoke in the park's amphitheater (Sun 10:00-18:00, U2: Eberswalder Strasse, www.flohmarktimmauerpark.de). On Sundays there's also a lively "junk market" (*Trödelmarkt*) several blocks south on **Arkonaplatz** (10:00-16:00, U8: Bernauer Strasse or a 10-minute walk from Mauerpark). **Hackescher Markt** hosts a twice-weekly market with an odd variety of produce, clothes, trinkets, jewelry, hats, and food stalls; less funky than the best Berlin markets, it's conveniently located (Thu 9:00-18:00, Sat from 10:00). One of Berlin's largest flea markets is right next to the Tiergarten park on **Strasse des 17 Juni,** with great antiques, more than 200 stalls, collector-savvy merchants, and fun German fast-food stands (Sat-Sun 10:00-17:00, S-Bahn: Tiergarten, www.berlinertroedelmarkt.com).

Hackesche Höfe

This delightfully restored old series of eight interlocking shopping courtyards sits in the heart of the old Jewish quarter. It's a convenient place to window-shop for everything from locally made porcelain to fashion (typically open Mon-Sat from 10:00 or 11:00 until 19:00, closed Sun, Rosenthaler Strasse 40, www.hackesche-hoefe.com).

Chocolate Shops on Gendarmenmarkt

This delightful square has two very different chocolate shops: one bourgeois, the other proletarian.

Rausch claims to be Europe's biggest chocolate store and proudly displays its sweet delights—250 kinds—on a 55-foot-long buffet. Upstairs is an elegant café with fine views (Mon-Sat 10:00-20:00, Sun from 11:00, corner of Mohrenstrasse at Charlottenstrasse 60, tel. 030/757-882-440). If you're a choco-populist, head to the Volkswagen of candy, **Rittersport Bunte Schokowelt**—the flagship store of Rittersport. This is basically Germany's answer to the M&M's store (daily 10:00-19:00, Französische Strasse 24, tel. 030/200-950-810).

Big, Glitzy Department Stores

Unter den Linden is lined with some high-end shops, but for a wider selection, head a few blocks south. The French department store **Galeries Lafayette** has several floors of high-end goods under a glass dome (top-quality basement food court; Mon-Sat 10:00-20:00, closed Sun, Französische Strasse 23). Several blocks west is the massive, state-of-the-art **Mall of Berlin,** with 270 shops surrounding a cavernous glass-covered passageway (Mon-Sat 10:00-21:00, closed Sun, Vossstrasse 35, www.mallofberlin.de). Nearby, **Potsdamer Platz** and **Sony Center** have additional shops.

Nightlife

Berlin is a happening place for nightlife—whether it's clubs, pubs, jazz, cabaret, concerts, or even sightseeing.

For good **live music** listings, see www.askhelmut.com or shell out a few euros for a Berlin magazine (sold at kiosks): *Zitty* (www.zitty.de) and *Tip* (www.tip-berlin.de) are the top guides to alternative culture (mostly in German); *Exberliner Magazine* is colorfully written in English (www.exberliner.com).

Berlin's ticket clearinghouse, **Hekticket,** offers advance tickets and deeply discounted last-minute tickets (daily after 14:00, up to half off. Call or go online (tel. 030/230-9930, www.hekticket.de), or visit their booth near Alexanderplatz (cash only) to see what's on the push list for that evening (Mon-Fri 10:30-19:00, closed Sat-Sun, Alexanderstrasse 1—see map on page 889).

Rick's Tip: Stretch your sightseeing day into the night. These museums are **open late** *every day:* **Reichstag** *(last entry at 22:00),* **Museum of the Wall at Checkpoint Charlie** *(until 22:00), and* **Topography of Terror** *(until 20:00).* **Museum Island** *museums are open until 20:00 on Thursdays. Outdoor monuments such as the* **Berlin Wall Memorial** *and the* **Memorial to the Murdered Jews of Europe** *are safe and well-lit late into the night, even though their visitor centers close earlier.*

Jazz

Berlin has a lively jazz scene (for schedules, see www.jazzclubsinberlin.com). Near the TV Tower, **B-Flat Acoustic**

Festivals keep Berlin lively year-round.

Music and Jazz Club has live shows and jam sessions (from free to €15, nightly from 21:00, in Alexanderplatz at Dircksenstrasse 40, tel. 030/283-3123, www.b-flat-berlin.de).

Theater

Berliner Ensemble—made famous under the direction of Bertolt Brecht—stages a dozen or so productions ranging from classic to contemporary in the majestic Theater am Schiffbauerdamm, across from the Friedrichstrasse Bahnhof (€12-50, generally daily at 19:30 or 20:00, box office open Mon-Sat 10:00-18:30, Bertolt-Brecht-Platz 1, tel. 030/2840-8155, www.berliner-ensemble.de).

Live Music

Berlin has a staggering array of smaller music venues. Here are two: **Frannz Club,** in Prenzlauer Berg's Kulturbrauerei, attracts talented rock and alternative bands (www.frannz.com). **Aufsturz,** the recommended pub in the old Jewish quarter, hosts jazz and other music (www.aufsturz.de).

Big concerts are often held at **Olympic Stadium, Mercedes-Benz Arena** in Friedrichshain, the **Spandau Citadel,** and the outdoor **Waldbühne** ("Forest Stage").

Al Fresco Summer Fun

Berlin's emerging **beach bar** scene—where people grab a drink along the Spree riverfront and watch the excursion boats go by—is a great way to wind down from a day of sightseeing. The classic spot is the **Strandbar Mitte** in **Monbijoupark,** with a breezy and scenic setting overlooking the Bode Museum on Museum Island.

SLEEPING

Prenzlauer Berg

My favorite Berlin neighborhood to call home, Prenzlauer Berg offers easy transit connections to sightseeing; diverse eateries, coffeehouses, and nightspots; and a welcoming personality (think of all that graffiti as just some people's way of saying they care).

The area's transit hub is the Eberswalder Strasse U-Bahn station (U2 line). Trams #M1 and #12 run up and down Kastanienallee, connecting to the Rosenthaler Platz U-Bahn (#M1 continues all the way to the Hackescher Markt S-Bahn station).

$$$ Hotel Jurine is a pleasant and well-run 53-room business-style hotel on a peaceful street. If you want calm atmosphere, your own peaceful back garden, and a very friendly staff, this is my choice (mention Rick Steves when you book for a free upgraded room, breakfast extra, elevator, pay parking—reserve ahead, Schwedter Strasse 15, 5-minute walk to #M1: Zionskirchplatz or U2: Senefelderplatz, tel. 030/443-2990, www.hotel-jurine.de, mail@hotel-jurine.de).

$$$ Hotel Oderberger has 70 modern rooms filling part of a Neo-Renaissance bathhouse complex (originally opened in 1902, renovated in 2016). From the reception, you can peek into the elegant old swimming pool area. It's a fine choice, with its understated elegance, historic aura, and good location, tucked away on a quiet side street near the most happening stretch of Kastanienallee (elevator, guest discount for swimming pool, Oderberger Strasse 57, tel. 030/780-089-760, www.hotel-oderberger.de, info@hotel-oderberger.berlin).

$$ Myer's Hotel rents 50 comfortable rooms decorated with lots of bold colors. Located on a tranquil, tree-lined street, you'll find it hard to believe you're in the heart of a capital city. The gorgeous public spaces, including an art-filled patio and garden, host frequent cultural events (air-con, elevator, sauna, Metzer Strasse 26—midway between U2: Senefelderplatz and #M2 tram: Prenzlauer Allee/Metzer Strasse, #M2 goes to/from Alexanderplatz, tel. 030/440-140, www.myershotel.de, info@myershotel.de).

$$ Hotel Kastanienhof feels like a traditional small-town German hotel. It's on the #M1 tram line, with easy access to the Prenzlauer Berg bustle (so ask for a quiet room in the back). Its 44 rooms come with helpful service (breakfast extra, deluxe top-floor rooms offer air-con and/or balcony, elevator, wheelchair-accessible room, pay parking, 20 yards from #M1: Zionskirchplatz at Kastanienallee 65, tel. 030/443-050, www.kastanienhof.berlin, info@kastanienhof.berlin).

¢ EastSeven Hostel rents 100 of the best cheap beds in Prenzlauer Berg. Modern and conscientiously run, it offers all the hostel services plus an inviting lounge, guest kitchen, backyard terrace, and bike rental. Children are welcome (private rooms available, no curfew, 100 yards from U2: Senefelderplatz at Schwedter Strasse 7, tel. 030/9362-2240, www.eastseven.de, info@eastseven.de).

Old Jewish Quarter

The old Jewish quarter is closer to the historic core than Prenzlauer Berg but feels less residential, and the hotels here are bigger and less personable.

Near Rosenthaler Platz

Though bustling and congested, Rosenthaler Platz makes a good base for getting around the city thanks to its U-Bahn (U8: Rosenthaler Platz) and tram service (#M1 and #M8).

$$ The Circus Hotel is fun, entirely comfortable, and a great value. The achingly hip lobby has a café serving delicious (optional) breakfasts, and the 60 rooms are straightforward and colorful. As the hotel overlooks a busy intersection, ask for a quieter back room (breakfast extra, elevator, Rosenthaler Strasse 1, tel. 030/2000-3939, www.circus-berlin.de, info@circus-berlin.de). The Circus also offers spacious, modern **$$$ apartments** within the hotel and two blocks away at Choriner Strasse 84.

$ EasyHotel Berlin Hackescher Markt is part of an unapologetically cheap, Europe-wide chain where you pay for exactly what you use—nothing more, nothing less. The 125 orange-and-gray rooms are very small, basic, and feel popped out of a plastic mold (no breakfast, elevator, call to request a quieter back room after booking online, Rosenthaler Strasse 69, tel. 030/4000-6550, www.easyhotel-berlin.de, enquiries@berlinhm.easyhotel.com).

¢ The Circus Hostel is a brightly colored, well-run place with 250 beds, and a trendy lounge and microbrewery. It has typical hostel dorms as well as some hotel-like private rooms; for a few big steps up in comfort, consider the Circus Hotel, listed earlier (no curfew, elevator, Weinbergsweg 1A, tel. 030/2000-3939, www.circus-berlin.de, info@circus-berlin.de).

By Hackescher Markt

Lively Hackescher Markt is brimming with people, eateries, and on some days, an open-air market. It has an S-Bahn station and is connected to Prenzlauer Berg by tram #M1.

$$$ Adina Apartment Hotel Berlin Hackescher Markt has 134 studio and one-bedroom apartments with kitchenettes, though breakfast is available for an extra fee (air-con, elevator, pay parking, An der Spandauer Brücke 11, tel. 030/209-6980, www.adinahotels.com, berlinhm@adina.eu).

$$$ Monbijou Hotel's 101 rooms are small, but they make up for it with pleasing public spaces, a postcard-worthy rooftop terrace (with views of the cathedral and TV Tower), and a flair for design—from antique furnishings to plenty of natural light (breakfast extra, family rooms, air-con, elevator, pay parking, Monbijouplatz 1, tel. 030/6162-0300, www.monbijouhotel.com, info@monbijouhotel.com).

$$ Hotel Hackescher Markt, with 32 rooms, offers an inviting lounge and modern decor without being predictable or pretentious (breakfast extra, family

GERMANY

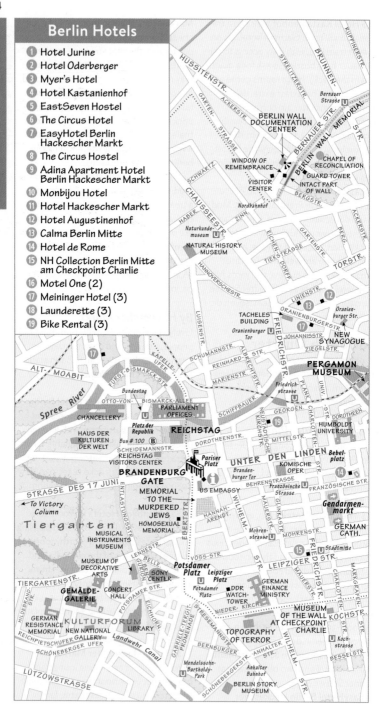

Berlin Hotels

1. Hotel Jurine
2. Hotel Oderberger
3. Myer's Hotel
4. Hotel Kastanienhof
5. EastSeven Hostel
6. The Circus Hotel
7. EasyHotel Berlin Hackescher Markt
8. The Circus Hostel
9. Adina Apartment Hotel Berlin Hackescher Markt
10. Monbijou Hotel
11. Hotel Hackescher Markt
12. Hotel Augustinenhof
13. Calma Berlin Mitte
14. Hotel de Rome
15. NH Collection Berlin Mitte am Checkpoint Charlie
16. Motel One (2)
17. Meininger Hotel (3)
18. Launderette (3)
19. Bike Rental (3)

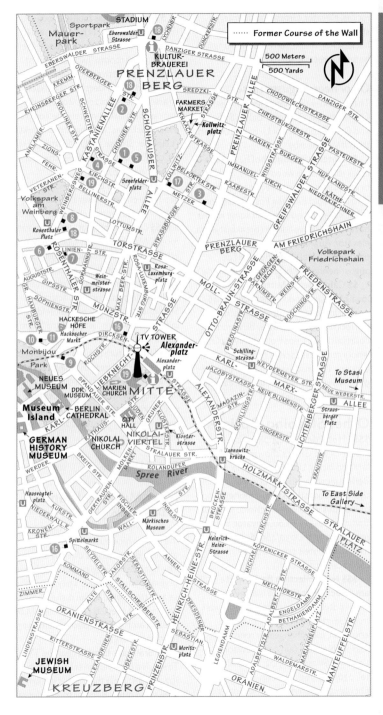

rooms, elevator, Grosse Präsidenten-strasse 8, tel. 030/280 030, www.hotel-hackescher-markt.com, reservierung@hotel-hackescher-markt.com).

On or near Auguststrasse

These good-value hotels are between the Oranienburger Strasse S-Bahn (S1/S2) and Oranienburger Tor U-Bahn (U6), and tram #M1 is nearby.

$$ Hotel Augustinenhof has 66 spacious rooms, nice woody floors, and firm beds. Rooms in front overlook the courtyard of the old Imperial Post Office, rooms in back are a bit quieter, and some rooms have older, thin windows (breakfast extra, elevator, Auguststrasse 82, tel. 030/3088-6710, www.hotel-augustinenhof.de, augustinenhof@albrechtshof-hotels.de).

$$ Calma Berlin Mitte, part of a small local chain, is a good budget bet. Its 46 straightforward but comfortable, modern rooms are tucked away on a tranquil courtyard, just steps from the lively Oranienburger Strasse scene (breakfast extra, elevator, Linienstrasse 139, tel. 030/9153-9333, www.lindemannhotels.de, calma@lindemannhotels.de).

Other Sleeping Options

$$$$ Hotel de Rome, holding court on Frederick the Great's showpiece Bebelplatz and facing Unter den Linden, is *the* Berlin splurge, with 108 rooms and all the luxurious little extras. If money is no object, this is a tempting choice for your Berlin address (air-con, elevator, Behrenstrasse 37, tel. 030/460-6090, www.roccofortehotels.com, info.derome@roccofortehotels.com).

$$$ NH Collection Berlin Mitte am Checkpoint Charlie is an elegant chain hotel on a busy street a short walk from Gendarmenmarkt, with nearly 400 fresh, interchangeable rooms at reasonable rates (air-con, elevator, Leipziger Strasse 106, U2: Stadtmitte, tel. 030/203-760, www.nh-hotels.com, nhcollectionberlinmitte@nh-hotels.com).

$ Motel One has multiple locations across Berlin; all have the same aqua-and-brown decor and posh-feeling but small rooms. Two convenient locations are between Hackescher Markt and Alexanderplatz (Dircksenstrasse 36, tel. 030/2005-4080, berlin-hackeschermarkt@motel-one.com) and a few blocks east of Gendarmenmarkt (Leipziger Strasse 50, U2: Spittelmarkt, tel. 030/2014-3630, berlin-spittelmarkt@motel-one.com).

Meininger is a Europe-wide budget-hotel chain with several locations in Berlin. With both ¢ cheap dorm beds and $$ comfortable, hotelesque private rooms, Meininger is basic but lively, modern, and generally a solid budget option, even for nonhostelers. They have three well-located branches: in Prenzlauer Berg ("Alexanderplatz" branch, actually at Schönhauser Allee 19 on Senefelderplatz); in the old Jewish quarter (Mitte "Humboldthaus" branch, next to the recommended Aufsturz pub at Oranienburger Strasse 67); and near the Hauptbahnhof at Ella-Trebe-Strasse 9 (all locations have elevator and 24-hour reception, pay parking at some, tel. 030/666-36100, www.meininger-hostels.com, welcome@meininger-hostels.com).

EATING

Near Museum Island

$$ Deponie No. 3 is a rustic if touristy Berlin *Kneipe* (pub). Garden seating in the back is nice but comes with the noise of the S-Bahn passing directly above. The bar interior is cozy and woody with several inviting spaces. They serve basic salads, traditional Berlin dishes, and hearty daily specials (daily 10:00-24:00, S-Bahn arch #187 at Georgenstrasse 5, tel. 030/2016-5740).

$$ Brauhaus Lemke, near the TV Tower, is a big, lively beer hall (still in its 1970s DDR shell) that makes its own brews and offers Berliner specialties and

Bavarian dishes. They have decent salads and serve a six-beer sampler board (daily 12:00-24:00, across from the TV Tower and tucked a bit back from the street at Karl-Liebknecht-Strasse 13, tel. 030/3087-8989).

Near Gendarmenmarkt

South of Unter den Linden, Gendarmenmarkt, with its twin churches, is a delightful place for an al fresco meal.

$$$$ Lutter & Wegner Restaurant is respected for its Austrian cuisine (*Schnitzel* and *Sauerbraten*). It's dressy, with fun sidewalk seating or a dark and elegant interior. Weekday €9 lunch specials are an affordable way to sample their cooking (daily 12:00-24:00, Charlottenstrasse 56, tel. 030/202-9515, www.l-w-berlin.de).

$ Dom Curry, behind the German Cathedral, is a *Currywurst* stand that works for a quick bite out on the square (daily 12:00-20:00).

$$ Galeries Lafayette Food Circus is a French festival of fun eateries in the basement of the landmark department store. You'll find sandwiches, savory crêpes, quiches, sushi bar, *les macarons,* and so on (Mon-Sat 10:00-20:00, closed Sun, Friedrichstrasse 76, U6: Französische Strasse, tel. 030/209-480).

Prenzlauer Berg

$ Prater Biergarten is Berlin's oldest beer garden. It's mellow, shaded, and supercheap—with a family-friendly outdoor area, including a playground (no table service, order food at one counter, beer at the other). Prater's rustic indoor restaurant (more expensive, with table service) serves well-executed German classics (restaurant open Mon-Sat 18:00-24:00, Sun from 12:00; beer garden open daily in good weather 12:00-24:00, closed in winter; Kastanienallee 7, tel. 030/448-5688).

$$ Zum Schusterjungen ("The Cobbler's Apprentice") is a classic, German-with-attitude eatery that retains its circa-1986 DDR decor. Famous for its filling meals (including schnitzel and pork knuckle), it's a no-frills place with quality ingredients and a strong local following (small 40-seat dining hall plus outdoor tables, daily 12:00-24:00, corner of

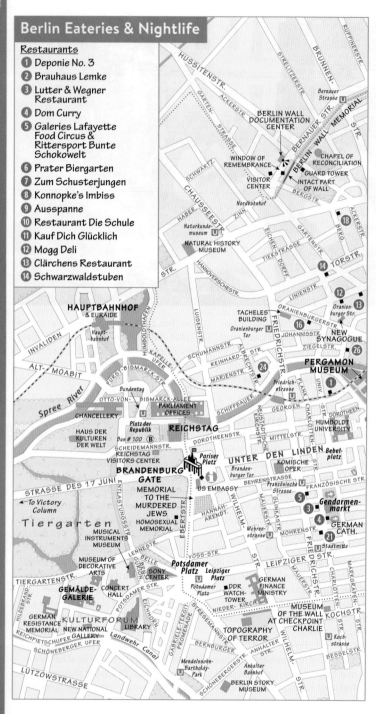

Berlin Eateries & Nightlife

Restaurants

1. Deponie No. 3
2. Brauhaus Lemke
3. Lutter & Wegner Restaurant
4. Dom Curry
5. Galeries Lafayette Food Circus & Rittersport Bunte Schokowelt
6. Prater Biergarten
7. Zum Schusterjungen
8. Konnopke's Imbiss
9. Ausspanne
10. Restaurant Die Schule
11. Kauf Dich Glücklich
12. Mogg Deli
13. Clärchens Restaurant
14. Schwarzwaldstuben

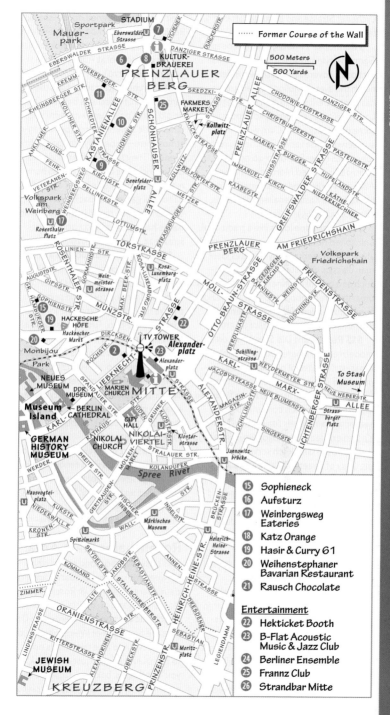

...... Former Course of the Wall

500 Meters
500 Yards

N

15 Sophieneck
16 Aufsturz
17 Weinbergsweg Eateries
18 Katz Orange
19 Hasir & Curry 61
20 Weihenstephaner Bavarian Restaurant
21 Rausch Chocolate

Entertainment

22 Hekticket Booth
23 B-Flat Acoustic Music & Jazz Club
24 Berliner Ensemble
25 Frannz Club
26 Strandbar Mitte

Lychener Strasse and Danziger Strasse 9, tel. 030/442-7654).

$ Konnopke's Imbiss, a super-cheap German-style sausage stand with a small section of covered picnic tables underneath the ever-rumbling U2 train tracks, has been a Berlin institution since 1930. Loyal Berliners say Konnopke's cooks up some of the city's best *Currywurst;* they also serve a wide variety of other wurst specialties (Tue-Sat 10:00-20:00, Sun 12:00-18:00, closed Mon; Schönhauser Allee 44A—underneath elevated train tracks where Kastanienallee dead-ends, tel. 030/442-7765).

$$$ Ausspanne looks like a traditional, uninspired hotel restaurant. But the small, always fresh menu boldly elevates German classics with surprising flourishes— such as a puff of habanero foam with duck breast and red cabbage (daily 17:00-22:00, in recommended Hotel Kastanienhof at Kastanienallee 65, tel. 030/4430-5199).

$$$ Restaurant Die Schule is a dressy, modern eatery where you can sample €3 tapas-style plates of old-fashioned German food. They have several varieties of *Flammkuchen* (German pizza—a flatbread dish from the French borderlands) and seasonal main dishes (daily 11:00-22:00, Kastanienallee 82, tel. 030/780-089-550).

Kauf Dich Glücklich serves an enticing array of sweet Belgian waffles and homemade ice cream in an inviting candy-sprinkled, bohemian lounge and a garden-like front terrace on a great street (or get your dessert to go, daily 10:00-23:00, Oderberger Strasse 44, tel. 030/4862-3292).

Old Jewish Quarter

Most of these places are a reasonable walk from Unter den Linden and within 10 minutes of the Hackescher Markt S-Bahn station.

$$ Mogg Deli is a foodie favorite, serving a short but thoughtful menu of soups, salads, and sandwiches. They're known for their home-cured pastrami, especially their monster, designed-to-be-shared Reuben (Mon-Sat 11:00-22:00, Sun until 20:00; inside the huge red-brick former Jewish girls school at Auguststrasse 11, tel. 030/330-060-770).

$$ Clärchens Restaurant fills the courtyard in front of Clärchens Ballhaus (a classic old Berlin ballroom) with twinkle lights, ramshackle furniture, and a bohemian-chic atmosphere—especially nice on a balmy evening. They serve German and Italian dishes, including brats, pizza, and homemade cakes. You can also eat in the dance hall or in a garden out back. After 21:00, the DJ cranks up the music in the ground floor dance hall (daily 12:00-22:00, Auguststrasse 24, tel. 030/282-9295).

$$$ Schwarzwaldstuben is a Black Forest-themed pub—which explains the antlers and cuckoo clocks. It's friendly, with good service, food, and prices. If they're full, you can eat at the long bar (daily 12:00-23:00, Tucholskystrasse 48, tel. 030/2809-8084).

$$ Sophieneck upholds its *Kneipe* roots as the neighborhood's ersatz living room, serving hearty Berliner specialties like *Buletten* and *Eisbein* on a breezy corner to a happy mix of locals and tourists (daily 12:00-22:30, Grosse Hamburger Strasse 37, tel. 030/283-4065).

$$ Aufsturz is a lively pub that's more for serious drinkers than serious eaters. It has a huge selection of beer and whisky and dishes up traditional Berliner pub grub to a young crowd (daily 12:00-24:00, Oranienburger Strasse 67, tel. 030/2804-7407).

Rosenthaler Platz Area

This busy neighborhood sits roughly between the old Jewish quarter and Prenzlauer Berg, near the U8: Rosenthaler Platz station and on the tram #M1 line.

Eclectic Eats on Weinbergsweg: Don't miss the first block of Weinbergsweg, the tram track-lined lane that heads north to Prenzlauer Berg. In just one block, you'll find cafés, bakeries, superfoods and organic juice, *Gemüse kebab, döner kebab,*

Berliner Street Food

Sausage stands are everywhere. You may even see portable human hot-dog stands—cooks in clever harnesses that let them grill and sell hot dogs from under an umbrella.

Most sausage stands specialize in **Currywurst,** created in Berlin after World War II when a fast-food cook got her hands on some curry and Worcestershire sauce from British troops stationed here. It's basically a grilled pork sausage smothered with curry sauce. *Currywurst* comes either *mit Darm* (with casing) or *ohne Darm* (without casing). If the casing is left on to grill, it gives the sausage a smokier flavor. (*Berliner Art*—"Berlin-style"—means that the sausage is boiled *ohne Darm,* then grilled.) Either way, the grilled sausage is then chopped into small pieces or cut in half (East Berlin style) and topped with sauce. While some places simply use ketchup and sprinkle on some curry powder, real *Currywurst* joints use a proper *Currysauce:* tomato paste, Worcestershire sauce, and curry. With your wurst comes either a toothpick or small wooden fork; you'll usually get a plate of fries as well.

The other big Berlin street food is fast Turkish and Middle Eastern food. Schwarma and falafel joints are cheap and tasty. And the kebab—either **döner kebab** (Turkish-style skewered meat slow-roasted and served in pita bread) or the vegetarian alternative, **Gemüse kebab** (with lots of veggies, and sometimes falafel)—is a quick way to fill up for a couple euros.

an Italian deli, Mexican street food, Russian, Korean barbecue, a French bistro, Chinese dumplings, and gelato.

$$$$ Katz Orange is a mecca for foodies and feels regal from the moment you enter its intimate courtyard. It's surprisingly affordable and known for its "candy on the bone" slow-cooked meat (daily 18:00-23:00, reservations recommended, Bergstrasse 22, tel. 030/9832-08430, www.katzorange.com).

Hackescher Markt Area

$$$ Hasir is a popular, somewhat stuffy opportunity to splurge on Turkish and Anatolian specialties amid candles and hardwood floors. While a bit past its prime and with hit-or-miss service, Hasir enjoys a handy location (large and split-table portions, daily 16:00-24:00, a block from the Hackescher Markt S-Bahn station at Oranienburger Strasse 4, tel. 030/2804-1616).

$$ Weihenstephaner Bavarian Restaurant serves traditional Bavarian food in an atmospheric cellar, on an inner courtyard, or on a busy people-watching terrace facing the delightful Hackescher Markt square; and, of course, it has excellent beer (daily 11:00-24:00, Neue Promenade 5 at Hackescher Markt, tel. 030/8471-0760).

$ Curry 61 serves, for many, the best *Currywurst* in Berlin; vegetarians and vegans appreciate good options, too. Eat in or grab a €5 meal to eat on a bench at the fine Monbijoupark across the street (daily, long hours, Oranienburger Strasse 6).

TRANSPORTATION

Getting Around Berlin
By Public Transit

Berlin's transit system uses the same ticket for its buses, trams *(Strassenbahn)*, and trains. There are two types of trains: The

GERMANY

Berlin Public Transportation

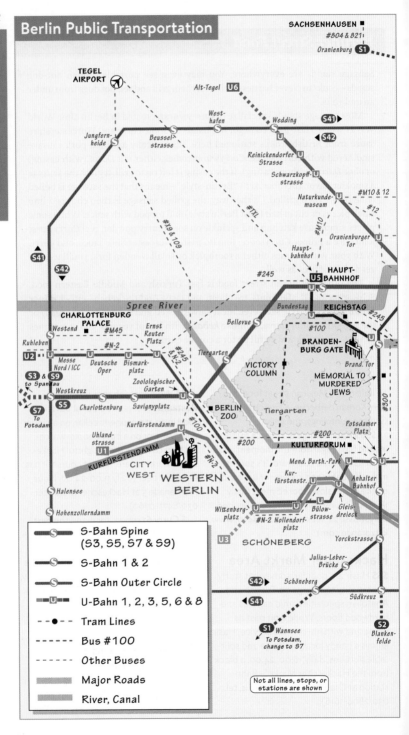

SACHSENHAUSEN ■
#804 & 821
Oranienburg **S1**

TEGEL AIRPORT ✈
Alt-Tegel **U6**
West-hafen
Wedding
S41▶
◀**S42**
Jungfern-heide **S**
Beussel-strasse
Reinickendorfer Strasse **U**
Schwarzkopff-strasse **U**
#M10 & 12
Naturkunde-museum **U**
#12
#TXL
#19 & 109
#M10
Oranienburger Tor **U**
S41▲
S42▼
Haupt-bahnhof
#245
U5 HAUPT-BAHNHOF
U
Spree River
Bundestag
REICHSTAG ■
#245
Bellevue **S**
CHARLOTTENBURG PALACE ■
Westend ■ #M45
Ernst Reuter Platz
#100
BRANDEN-BURG GATE 🏛
Ruhleben **U**
#N-2
Tiergarten **S**
Brand. Tor **U** **S**
U2 **U**
Messe Nord / ICC
Deutsche Oper
Bismark-platz
VICTORY COLUMN
MEMORIAL TO MURDERED JEWS ■
S3 & **S9** to Spandau
#245 & N2
Zoolologischer Garten **U**
U
#500
Westkreuz **S**
S7 To Potsdam
S5 Charlottenburg
Savignyplatz **S**
■ BERLIN ZOO
Tiergarten
Potsdamer Platz
Kurfürstendamm
#100
#200
KULTURFORUM ■
Uhland-strasse
#200
Mend. Barth-Park **U**
U1
KURFÜRSTENDAMM
CITY WEST
WESTERN BERLIN
#N-2
Kur-fürstenstr.
Anhalter Bahnhof **U**
U
S Halensee
Wittenberg-platz **U**
Bülow-strasse **U**
Gleis-dreieck
S Hohenzollerndamm
#N-2 Nollendorf-platz
U3
SCHÖNEBERG
Yorckstrasse **S**
Julius-Leber-Brücke **S**
S42▶ Schöneberg
Südkreuz **S**
◀**S41**
S1 Wannsee → To Potsdam, change to S7
S2 Blanken-felde

S	S-Bahn Spine (S3, S5, S7 & S9)
S	S-Bahn 1 & 2
S	S-Bahn Outer Circle
U	U-Bahn 1, 2, 3, 5, 6 & 8
– ● –	Tram Lines
– – –	Bus #100
– – –	Other Buses
	Major Roads
	River, Canal

Not all lines, stops, or stations are shown

Not to Scale

Note: Express trains RB & RE run along the "S-Bahn Spine" stopping at Hauptbahnhof and other select destinations

U-Bahn—like a subway, making lots of short hops around town—is run by transit authority BVG; the S-Bahn, a fast light rail that stops only at major stations, is operated by Deutsche Bahn. For all types of transit, there are three lettered zones: A, B, and C. Most of your sightseeing will be in zones A and B (in the city proper).

Timetables, prices, and trip planning are available on two helpful websites: BVG (www.bvg.de) or VBB (www.vbb.de).

TICKET OPTIONS

The €2.80 **basic single** ticket (*Einzelfahrschein*) covers two hours of travel in one direction. It's easy to make this ticket stretch to cover several rides...if they're in the same direction.

The €1.70 **short-ride** ticket (*Kurzstrecke Fahrschein*) covers a single ride of up to six bus/tram stops or three subway stations (one transfer allowed on subway). You can save on short-ride tickets by buying them in groups of four (€5.60).

The €9 **four-trip** ticket (*4-Fahrten-Karte*) is the same as four basic single tickets at a small discount.

The **day pass** (*Tageskarte*) is good until 3:00 the morning after you buy it (€7 for zones AB, €7.70 for zones ABC). For longer stays, consider a seven-day pass (*Sieben-Tage-Karte*; €30 for zones AB, €37.50 for zones ABC), or the **WelcomeCard** (available at TIs and U-Bahn/S-Bahn ticket machines; www.visitberlin.de/welcomecard).

Buying Tickets: You can buy U-Bahn/S-Bahn tickets from machines at stations (coins and bills accepted). Tickets are also sold at BVG pavilions at train stations and at the TI, from machines onboard trams (coins only), and on buses from drivers, who give change. Select the zone and type of ticket you want, then pay. Most travelers want the AB ticket—either single or all-day ticket.

Boarding Transit: As you board the bus or tram or enter the subway, validate your ticket in a clock machine (or risk a €60 fine; with a pass, stamp it only the first time you ride). Tickets are checked periodically, often by plainclothes inspectors. You may be asked to show your ticket when boarding the bus.

By Taxi and Uber

Cabs are easy to flag down, and taxi stands are common. A typical ride within town costs around €10, and a crosstown trip will run about €20.

Tariff 1 is for a *Kurzstrecke* ticket (short-stretch ride). This ticket can save you several euros for any ride of less than two kilometers (about a mile). To get this rate, you must flag down the cab on the street—not at a taxi stand—and ask for the *Kurzstrecke* rate as soon as you hop in. Confidently say *"Kurzstrecke, bitte"* (KOORTS-shtreh-keh, BIT-teh); your driver will grumble and flip the meter to a fixed €5 rate (for a ride that would otherwise cost €8). All other rides are **tariff 2** (€3.90 drop plus €2/km for the first seven kilometers, then €1.50/km after that). If possible, use cash: Credit card payment comes with a surcharge.

Uber works in Berlin like it does in the US (but rates are tied to taxi fares, so you don't really save any money).

By Bike

Fat Tire Bikes rents good bikes at the base of the TV Tower near Alexanderplatz (€14/day, cheaper for 2 or more days, trekking bikes available, free luggage storage, daily 9:30-20:00, shorter hours off-season, tel. 030/2404-7991, www.berlinbikerental.com).

Take a Bike—near the Friedrichstrasse S-Bahn station—is owned by a knowledgeable Dutch-German with a huge inventory (3-gear bikes: €8/4 hours, €12.50/day, €19/2 days, slightly cheaper for longer rentals, more for better bikes, includes helmets, daily 9:30-19:00, Nov-March closed Tue-Thu, Neustädtische Kirchstrasse 8, tel. 030/2065-4730, www.takeabike.de). To find it, leave the S-Bahn station via the Friedrichstrasse exit, turn right, go through a triangle-shaped square, and hang a left on Neustädtische Kirchstrasse.

Bike Rental Berlin is a good option in Prenzlauer Berg (€10/day, helmets–€1, kids' bikes and child seats available, daily 10:00-18:00, often closed off-season—call ahead, Kastanienallee 55, tel. 030/7153-3020, http://bike-rental-berlin.de).

Arriving and Departing
By Plane
The state-of-the-art **Willy Brandt Berlin-Brandenburg International Airport** (airport code: BER), 11 miles south of central Berlin, has been under construction since 2006 and may be in service by late 2020. **Tegel Airport** (airport code: TXL), four miles northwest of the center, serves as Berlin's "main airport" until Willy Brandt opens. To reach the city center, hop on **bus #TXL**, which stops at the Hauptbahnhof and then ends at Robert-Koch-Platz.

Most flights from the east and many discount airlines arrive at **Schönefeld Airport** (airport code: SXF), 11 miles south of downtown. From the arrivals hall, it's a three-minute walk to the train station, where you can catch a regional express train into the city. Airport Express RE and RB trains go directly to Ostbahnhof, Alexanderplatz, Friedrichstrasse, and Hauptbahnhof (€3.40, 2/hour, direction: Nauen or Dessau, covered by ABC transit ticket). A taxi to the city center costs about €45.

By Train
Virtually all long-distance trains pass through the **Berlin Hauptbahnhof** ("Berlin Hbf" on schedules)—a massive temple of railroad travel in the heart of the city. This mostly underground train station is where the national train system meets Berlin's S-Bahn.

Services: On the main floor (EG),

you'll find the **TI** and the **"Rail & Fresh WC"** facility (public pay toilets, near the food court). Up one level (OG1) are the Deutsche Bahn *Reisezentrum* information center, a 24-hour **pharmacy**, and **lockers** (directly under track 14). **Car rental** offices are down one level (UG1), near platforms 7-8.

Getting into Town: Taxis and buses wait outside the station on the Washingtonplatz side, but the S-Bahn is probably your best bet for connecting to most hotels. It's simple: S-Bahn trains are on tracks 15 and 16 at the top of the station (level OG2). Trains on track 15 go east, stopping at Friedrichstrasse, Hackescher Markt, Alexanderplatz, and Ostbahnhof; trains on track 16 go west, toward Zoologischer Garten and beyond.

To reach most hotels in the **Prenzlauer Berg** neighborhood, it's fastest to take any train on track 15 two stops to Hackescher Markt. Once there, follow signs to *Hackescher Markt* down the stairs, then exit to Spandauer Strasse and cross the tracks to the tram stop. Here you'll catch tram #M1 north (direction: Schillerstrasse).

From Berlin by Train to: Dresden (direct every 2 hours, 2 hours), **Hamburg** (1-2/hour, 2 hours), **Frankfurt** (at least hourly, 4 hours), **Bacharach** (every 2 hours with transfer in Frankfurt, 5.5 hours), **Würzburg** (hourly, 4 hours, transfer points vary), **Rothenburg** (hourly, 5.5 hours, 3 changes), **Nürnberg** (hourly, 3.5 hours), **Munich** (hourly, 4-5 hours), **Cologne** (hourly, 4.5 hours, night train possible).

By Bus
The city's bus station, **ZOB** (Zentraler Omnibusbahnhof), is in Charlottenburg (Masurenallee 4, U2: Kaiserdamm or S41/S42: Messe Nord, www.zob.berlin). **FlixBus, MeinFern,** and **Eurolines** all operate from here to locations around Germany and Europe.

The Netherlands

The Netherlands—commonly referred to as "Holland"—is one of Europe's most densely populated, wealthiest, and best-organized countries. Occupying a delta near the mouth of three large rivers, the Netherlands has battled the sea for centuries, reclaiming low-lying land and converting it into fertile farmland.

The Netherlands has 17 million people: 80 percent are Dutch, and half have no religious affiliation. Despite its small size (16,000 square miles—about twice the size of New Jersey), the Netherlands boasts the planet's 28th-largest economy. It also has one of Europe's lowest unemployment rates, relying heavily on foreign trade through its port at Rotterdam, Europe's largest.

Amsterdam, laced with grand canals and crisscrossed by bikes, has the powerhouse sights, while the nearby town of Haarlem is wonderfully *gezellig*—the much-prized Dutch atmosphere of relaxed coziness.

Treat yourself to new taste experiences in the Netherlands: Try pickled herring at an outdoor stand, enjoy a sweet "syrup waffle" (*stroopwafel*), and sip an old *jenever* with a new friend. It's *gezellig*.

CUISINE SCENE AT A GLANCE

Traditional Dutch food is basic and hearty, with lots of bread, soup, and fish. Lunch and dinner are served at typical American times (roughly 12:00-14:00 and 18:00-21:00). Dutch treats include cheese, pancakes (*pannenkoeken*), and "syrup waffles" (*stroopwafels*). Popular drinks are light, pilsner-type beer and gin (*jenever*).

The tastiest "Dutch" cuisine comes from the former colony of Indonesia. Seek out an *Indisch* restaurant to experience a *rijsttafel* ("rice table"). The spread usually includes many dishes, ranging from small sides to entrée-sized plates (some are spicy) and a big bowl of rice. A *rijsttafel* can be split (when restaurants allow it) and still fill two hungry tourists. Vegetarian versions are always available. For a smaller version, order *nasi rames* (several portions on one plate). Or try *bami goreng* (stir-fried noodles) or *nasi goreng* (fried rice), served with *rijsttafel* items.

A *café* or *eetcafé* serves simple fare in a generally comfortable but no-nonsense setting.

Pancake restaurants serve sweet and savory pancakes (*pannenkoeken*) all day. Dutch pancakes are halfway between a fluffy American-style pancake and a thin French crêpe.

Bruin cafés ("brown cafés") are named for their nicotine-stained walls, though smoking indoors was banned years ago. They serve drinks and Dutch food in a dimly lit bar-like setting.

A *salon de thé* serves tea, coffee, sandwiches, and pastries. In contrast, a "coffeeshop" is the code word for an establishment where marijuana is sold and consumed, though most offer drinks and munchies, too.

Tipping: At Dutch restaurants with waitstaff, 15 percent service is included in the menu price, although it's common to round up the bill after a good meal (usually 5-10 percent). If you order food at a counter, don't tip. In bars, rounding up to the next euro ("keep the change") is appropriate if you get table service, rather than ordering at the bar.

Budget Options: Takeout places serve fast food and sandwiches (*broodjes*). Small stands sell *friets* (french fries, served with mayonnaise), pickled herring, falafels (fried chickpea balls in pita bread), *shoarmas* (lamb in pita bread), or *döner kebabs* (a Turkish kebab). And it's easy to forage for picnic fare at delis and groceries.

Amsterdam

In Amsterdam, you'll enjoy good living, cozy cafés, street-corner jazz, great art, stately history, and a spirit of live and let live. The city still looks much like it did in the 1600s—the Dutch Golden Age—when it was the cradle of capitalism. Wealthy, democratic burghers built a wonderland of canals lined with trees and townhouses topped with fancy gables. Immigrants, outcasts, and political rebels were drawn here by its open-minded atmosphere, while painters such as young Rembrandt captured that atmosphere on canvas.

For centuries, the city has advocated tolerance for things other places try to forbid. Its international sea-trading port has always attracted sailors and businessmen, so it was profitable to allow them to have a little fun. In the 1960s, Amsterdam became a magnet for Europe's hippies. Since then, it's become a world capital of alternative lifestyles. This bold experiment in freedom may box your Puritan ears. Prostitution is allowed in the Red Light District, while "smartshops" sell psychedelic drugs, and marijuana is openly sold and smoked in "coffeeshops."

Take in all of the city's charms, then pause to watch the clouds blow past its stately old gables—and see the Golden Age reflected in its quiet canals.

AMSTERDAM IN 2 DAYS

Day 1: In the morning, follow my self-guided Amsterdam City Walk, leading from the train station to Leidseplein, via the Amsterdam Museum (which you could tour now) and the flower market. Stop for lunch along the walk.

From Leidseplein, take a one-hour canal boat tour (unless you'd rather save it for an evening activity).

Later in the day, tour the Anne Frank House (advance reservations essential).

On any evening: Have an Indonesian *rijsttafel* dinner, wander through Vondelpark (rent a bike?), or stroll the eye-opening Red Light District (but not after 22:30, when it's sketchy). Visit late-night sights: The Van Gogh Museum is open late on Fridays and some Saturdays (until 21:00), and the Anne Frank Museum is open until 22:00 on many nights. Nurse a drink at a traditional "brown" café or take a canal boat ride. Get high at a coffeeshop if you want; it's legal!

Day 2: Visit two top museums—Rijksmuseum and Van Gogh—next to each other on Museumplein (it's smart to reserve both museums online in

Amsterdam Neighborhoods

advance). If you want to minimize crowds (which are heaviest at midday), start with the Van Gogh Museum when it opens at 9:00. Visit the Rijksmuseum after lunch (crowds begin to subside after 14:00). In between visiting these two major museums, have lunch (cafés are at the museums and nearby), hang out at lively Museumplein, tour the Stedelijk (modern art), or visit Vondelpark.

With extra time: You could easily spend another day or two in Amsterdam, visiting anything else that appeals, such as the Dutch Resistance Museum, Rembrandt's House, Our Lord in the Attic Museum, the Netherlands Maritime Museum, or the Albert Cuyp street market. You could also day-trip to the cozy town of Haarlem.

ORIENTATION

Amsterdam's Centraal Station, on the north edge of the city, is your starting point, with the TI, bike rental, and trams branching out to all points. Damrak is the main north-south axis, connecting Centraal Station with Dam Square (people-watching and hangout center) and its Royal Palace. From this main street, the city spreads out like a fan, with 90 islands, hundreds of bridges, and a series of concentric canals that were laid out in the 17th century, Holland's Golden Age. Amsterdam's major sights are all within walking distance of Dam Square.

To the east of Damrak is the oldest part of the city (today's Red Light District), and to the west is the newer part, where you'll find the Anne Frank House and the peaceful Jordaan neighborhood. Museums and Leidseplein nightlife cluster at the southern edge of the city center.

AMSTERDAM AT A GLANCE

▲▲▲ **Rijksmuseum** Best collection anywhere of the Dutch Masters—Rembrandt, Hals, Vermeer, and Steen—in a spectacular setting. **Hours:** Daily 9:00-17:00. See page 920.

▲▲▲ **Van Gogh Museum** More than 200 paintings by the angst-ridden artist. **Hours:** Daily April-Aug 9:00-19:00, Fri until 21:00, Sat until 18:00 (April-June) and 21:00 (July-Aug); Sept-Oct 9:00-18:00, Fri until 21:00; Nov-March 9:00-17:00, Fri until 21:00. See page 926.

▲▲▲ **Anne Frank House** Young Anne's hideaway during the Nazi occupation. **Hours:** Daily 9:00-22:00; Nov-March Mon-Fri 9:00-20:00, Sat until 22:00, Sun until 19:00. See page 930.

▲▲ **Stedelijk Museum** The Netherlands' top modern-art museum. **Hours:** Daily 10:00-18:00, Fri until 22:00. See page 929.

▲▲ **Amsterdam Museum** City's growth from fishing village to trading capital to today, including some Rembrandts and a playable carillon. **Hours:** Daily 10:00-17:00. See page 932.

▲▲ **Our Lord in the Attic Museum** Catholic church hidden in the attic of a 17th-century merchant's house. **Hours:** Mon-Sat 10:00-18:00, Sun from 13:00. See page 933.

▲▲ **Netherlands Maritime Museum** Rich seafaring story of the Netherlands, told with vivid artifacts. **Hours:** Daily 9:00-17:00. See page 933.

▲▲ **Dutch Resistance Museum** History of the Dutch struggle against the Nazis. **Hours:** Mon-Fri 10:00-17:00, Sat-Sun from 11:00. See page 934.

▲**Begijnhof** Quiet courtyard lined with picturesque houses. **Hours:** Daily 8:00-17:30. See page 917.

▲**Hash, Marijuana, and Hemp Museum** All the dope, from history and science to memorabilia. **Hours:** Daily 10:00-22:00. See page 934.

▲**Rembrandt's House** The master's reconstructed house, displaying his etchings. **Hours:** Daily 10:00-18:00. See page 933.

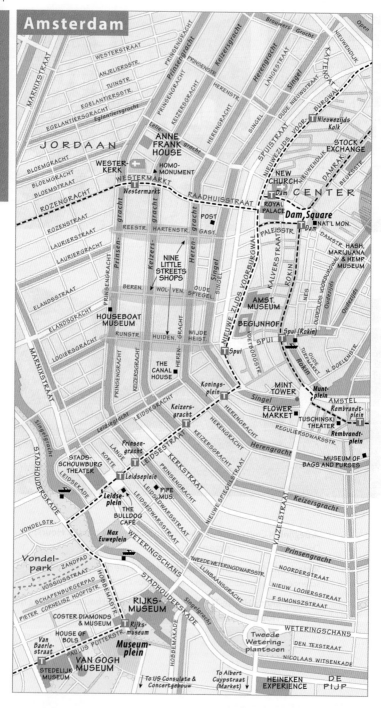

Amsterdam

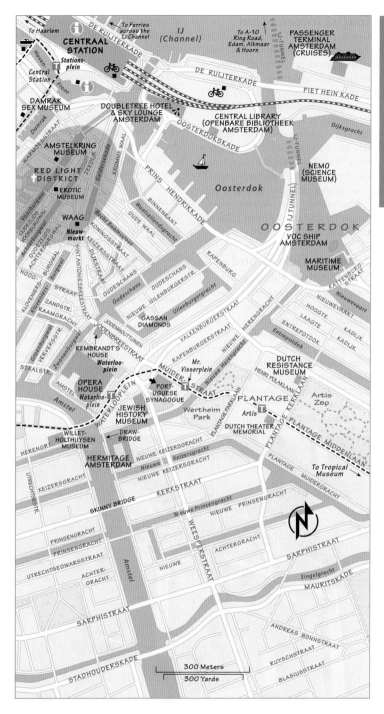

To Haarlem

DE RUIJTERKADE

To Ferries
across the
IJ Channel

IJ
(Channel)

To A-10
Ring Road,
Edam, Alkmaar
& Hoorn

PASSENGER
TERMINAL
AMSTERDAM
(CRUISES)

CENTRAAL
STATION

Stations-
plein

Central
Station

Haven-
Front

DE RUIJTERKADE

PIET HEIN KADE

Damrak

DAMRAK
SEX MUSEUM

WARMOESSTRAAT

DOUBLETREE HOTEL
& SKY LOUNGE
AMSTERDAM

KROMME WAAL

GELDERSEKADE

OOSTERDOKSKADE

CENTRAL LIBRARY
(OPENBARE BIBLIOTHEEK
AMSTERDAM)

Dijksgracht

IJ-TUNNEL

IJ-TUNNEL

AMSTELKRING
MUSEUM

ZEEDIJK

RED LIGHT
DISTRICT

EROTIC
MUSEUM

PRINS HENDRIKKADE

Oosterdok

NEMO
(SCIENCE
MUSEUM)

VOORBURGWAL

OUDEZIJDS
VOORBURGWAL

ACHTERBURGWAL

OUDEZIJDS
ACHTERBURGWAL

WAAG

Nieuw-
markt

Recht Boomssloot

KONINGSSTRAAT

BINNENKANT

Waalseilandsgracht

OUDE WAAL

O O S T E R D O K

VOC SHIP
AMSTERDAM

IJ TUNNEL

KATTENBURG-
STRAAT

HOOG-

BURGWAL

KLOVENIERS-

BURGWAL

SINT ANTONIESBREESTRAAT

KEIZERSSTRAAT

DIJKSTRAAT

Oudeschans

Oudeschans

OUDESCHANS

UILENBURGERSTR.

Uilenburgergracht

RAPENBURG

MARITIME
MUSEUM

NIEUWEVAART

Nieuwevaart

STRAAT

ZANDSTR.

NIEUWE

GASSAN
DIAMONDS

HOOGTE

LAAGTE

ENTREPOTDOK

KADIJK

KADIJK

RAAMGRACHT

JODENHOUTTUINEN

VALKENBURGERSTRAAT

Entrepotdok

Groenburgwal

VERVERSSTR.

Zwanenburgwal

JODENBREESTRAAT

REMBRANDT'S
HOUSE

Waterloo-
plein

RAPENBURGERSTRAAT

NIEUWE HERENGRACHT

HERENGRACHT

DUTCH
RESISTANCE
MUSEUM

HENRI POLAKLAAN

STAALSTR.

Amstel

OPERA
HOUSE

Waterloo-
plein

WATERLOOPLEIN

MUIDERSTRAAT

Mr.
Visserplein

PORT-
UGUESE
SYNAGOGUE

Nieuwe Herengracht

PLANTAGE

Artis
Zoo

PLANTAGE KERKLAAN

PLANTAGE MIDDENLAAN

HERENGR.

JEWISH
HISTORY
MUSEUM

Wertheim
Park

PLANTAGE PARKLAAN

Artis

WILLET-
HOLTHUYSEN
MUSEUM

DRAW-
BRIDGE

DUTCH THEATER
MEMORIAL

PLANTAGE

To Tropical
Museum

UTRECHTSESTR.

HERMITAGE
AMSTERDAM

NIEUWE KEIZERSGRACHT

Nieuwe Keizersgracht

NIEUWE KEIZERSGRACHT

MUIDERGRACHT

KEIZERSGRACHT

SKINNY BRIDGE

KERKSTRAAT

Nieuwe Prinsengracht

NIEUWE PRINSENGRACHT

WEESPERSTRAAT

PRINSENGRACHT

PRINSENGRACHT

Amstel

ACHTERGRACHT

SARPHISTRAAT

UTRECHTSEDWARSSTRAAT

ACHTER-
GRACHT

NIEUWE

Singelgracht

MAURITSKADE

SARPHISTRAAT

ANDREAS BONNSTRAAT

300 Meters

300 Yards

RUYSCHSTRAAT

STADHOUDERSKADE

BLASIUSSTRAAT

Tourist Information

Amsterdam's main TI, located across the street from Centraal Station, is centrally located, but it's crowded and sometimes inefficient (Mon-Sat 9:00-17:00, Sun 10:00-16:00, tel. 020/702-6000). The TI sells a good city map and the *I Amsterdam* magazine. A second Centraal Station TI is in the new section on the north side. While it's labeled the "I Amsterdam Store," it really is an official TI and is much less crowded (Mon-Wed 8:00-19:00, Thu-Sat until 20:00, Sun 9:00-18:00).

Also helpful and possibly less crowded are the TIs at Schiphol Airport (daily 7:00-22:00) and in the town of Haarlem.

Advance Tickets and Sightseeing Passes

You should buy advance tickets online for the Anne Frank House, Van Gogh Museum, and Rijksmuseum. Alternatively, a sightseeing pass lets you skip some ticket lines, though you still need to reserve an entrance time for the Anne Frank House and Van Gogh Museum. Entry to most sights is free with a sightseeing pass.

Advance Tickets: It's smart to buy tickets online for the three major museums through each museum's website, generally with no extra booking fee. Just print out your ticket and bring it to the ticket-holder's line for a quick entry. You can also buy advance tickets at TIs (though lines there can be long). Reservations for the Anne Frank House are extremely limited: Buy your ticket starting two months prior to the date of your visit (see page 930).

Sightseeing Passes: If you'll be visiting many museums, a pass can save you money (and time in line). The €60 **Museumkaart** sightseeing pass gives you five admissions which can be used at around 400 museums throughout the Netherlands for 31 days. If you visit the Rijksmuseum, Van Gogh Museum, Anne Frank House, and Amsterdam Museum, the pass almost pays for itself. Tourists can buy it, but only in person at a covered sight; don't be confused by the Dutch-only website, which doesn't even mention this option (www.museumkaart.nl).

The widely advertised **I Amsterdam City Card** covers many Amsterdam sights (including a canal boat ride) and includes a transportation pass, but it doesn't cover the Anne Frank House or muse-

ums outside of Amsterdam. It only lets you skip lines at the Van Gogh Museum when online reservations are not required (€59/24 hours, €74/48 hours, €87/72 hours, www.iamsterdamcard.com).

Rick's Tip: For a brief visit, **skip all the sightseeing passes and buy advance tickets** *online instead.*

Without Advance Tickets or a Pass: If you end up visiting the Anne Frank House without a reservation, trim your time in line by showing up late in the day; this works better in early spring and fall than in summer, when even after-dinner lines can be long. You can visit the Van Gogh Museum on weekend evenings until 21:00 on Fridays year-round, and some Saturdays (July-Aug).

Helpful Hints

Theft Alert: Tourists are considered green and rich, and the city has more than its share of hungry thieves—especially in the train station, on trams, in and near crowded museums, at places of drunkenness, and at the many hostels. Wear your money belt.

Street Smarts: Beware of silent transportation—trams, electric mopeds, and bicycles—when walking around town. Don't walk on tram tracks or pink/maroon bicycle paths. Before you step off a sidewalk, double-check both directions to make sure all's clear.

Maps: Given the city's maze of streets and canals, I'd definitely get a good city map (available at Centraal Station TI). I also like the *Carto Studio Centrumkaart Amsterdam* map.

Laundry: Try **Clean Brothers Wasserij** in the Jordaan (self-service daily 8:00-20:00; drop-off available Mon-Fri 9:00-17:00, Sat until 18:00, ready in an hour, no drop-off Sun; Westerstraat 26, one block from Prinsengracht, tel. 020/627-9888) or **Powders,** near Leidseplein (self-service daily 8:00-22:00; drop-off available Mon-

Fri 8:00-17:00, Sat 9:00-15:00, no drop-off Sun; Kerkstraat 56, one block south of Leidsestraat, mobile 06-5741-2403).

Tours
▲▲TRADITIONAL CANAL BOAT TOURS

These long, low, tourist-laden boats leave continually from several docks around town for a relaxing, if uninspiring, one-hour introduction to the city (with recorded headphone commentary). Select a boat tour based on your proximity to its starting point, or whether it's included with your I Amsterdam City Card.

Rederij P. Kooij is cheapest (€11; boats docking opposite Centraal Station go 2-3/hour daily 10:00-16:00; boats docking off Rokin 125 go 3/hour in summer 10:00-22:00, 2/hour in winter 10:00-17:00; tel. 020/623-3810, www.rederijkooij.nl).

Rick's Tip: Boats leave only when full, so jump on a full boat to avoid waiting at the dock.

Blue Boat Company's boats depart from near Leidseplein (€18, €16 if you book online; daily 10:00-18:00, every half-hour March-Oct, hourly Nov-Feb 10:00-18:00; 1.25 hours, Stadhouderskade 30, tel. 020/679-1370, www.blueboat.nl). Their evening cruise includes the Red Light District (€21, €19 online, nightly at 20:00, 1.5 hours, March-Oct also at 21:00 and 22:00, reservations required).

Gray Line-Stromma offers a standard one-hour trip and a variety of longer tours from the docks opposite Centraal Station (€18, €15 online, 1-hour "100 Highlights" tour with recorded commentary, daily 2-4/hour 9:00-21:00; Prins Hendrikkade 33a, tel. 020/217-0500, www.stromma.nl).

WALKING TOURS
New Europe Tours "employs" native English-speaking students to give irreverent and entertaining three-hour walks.

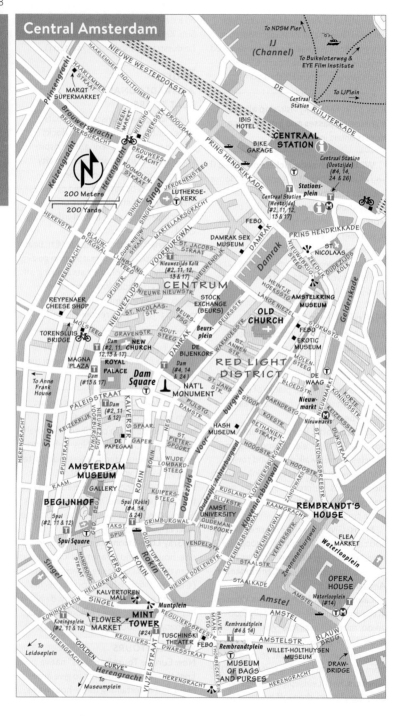

Central Amsterdam

200 Meters

200 Yards

To NDSM Pier

IJ
(Channel)

To Buiksloterweg &
EYE Film Institute

To IJPlein

DE

Centraal
Station

RUIJTERKADE

PRINS HENDRIKKADE

IBIS
HOTEL

BIKE
GARAGE

**CENTRAAL
STATION**

Centraal Station
(Oostzijde)
(#4, 14,
24 & 26)

Stations-
plein

Centraal Station
(Westzijde)
(#2, 11, 12,
13 & 17)

HAARLEMMER-
STRAAT

HAARLEMMER

NIEUWE WESTERDOKSTR.

HOUTTUINEN

DROOGBAK

FRINS HENDRIKKADE

MARQT
SUPERMARKET

Prinsengracht

Brouwersgracht

BROUWERS-
GRACHT

Keizersgracht

Herengracht

BROUWERS-
GRACHT

ROOMEN-
STRAAT

HEREN-
MARKT

WIERINGST.

VISSERSSTR.

Singel

Singel

JEROENENSTEEG

LUTHERSE-
KERK

MARTELAARSGRACHT

FEBO

PRINS HENDRIKKADE

ST.
NICOLAAS

ZEEDIJK

HERENSTR.

BLAUW-
BURGWAL

HERENGRACHT

LIJNBAANS-
STEEG

OUDE NIEUW-
STRAAT

VOORBURGWAL

ST. JACOBS-
STRAAT

NIEUWENDIJK

DAMRAK SEX
MUSEUM

Nieuwezijds Kolk
(#2, 11, 12,
13 & 17)

DAMRAK

NIEUWEZIJDS

Damrak

NIEUWEBRUG-
STEEG

OUDEZIJDS
KOLK

GELDERSKADE

REYPENAER
CHEESE SHOP

SPUISTR.

NIEUWE NIEUWSTR.

CENTRUM

STOCK
EXCHANGE
(BEURS)

HEINTJE
HOEKSSTG.

LANGE NIEZEL

AMSTELKRING
MUSEUM

MOLSTEEG

ST. NICOLAAS-
STR.

GRAVENSTR.

ZOUT-
STEEG

BEURS
PSG.

*Beurs-
plein*

WARMOESSTR.

**OLD
CHURCH**

FEBO

STORMSTG.

EROTIC
MUSEUM

TORENSLUIS
BRIDGE

Dam
(#2, 11,
12,15 & 17)

**NEW
CHURCH**

DAMRAK

DE
BIJENKORF

ST.
ANNEN
STR.

WARMOESSTR.

**RED LIGHT
DISTRICT**

MOLEN-
STEEG

DE
WAAG

KORTE
KONINGSTR.

MAGNA
PLAZA

**ROYAL
PALACE**

Dam
(#13 & 17)

**Dam
Square**

Dam
(#4, 14
& 24)

**NAT'L
MONUMENT**

ST. JANS
STR.

Nieuwmarkt

KEIZERSTR.

NIEUWMARKT

To Anne
Frank
House

PALEISSTRAAT

KEIZERRIJK

NIEUWEZIJDS
VOORBURGWAL

SPUISTRAAT

KALVERSTR.

SPAAR

GAPER

PIJLSTG.

DAMSTR.

burgwal

HASH
MUSEUM

BARNDESJG.

STOOF

KOESTR.

BETHANIEN-
STRAAT

BLOEDSTR.

ST. ANTONIESBREESTR.

DIJKSTR.

HERENGRACHT

Singel

Dam
(#2, 11
& 12)

DE
PAPEGAAI

NES

ST.
PIETER-
SPOORT

WIJDE
LOMBARD-
STEEG

ROKIN

OUDEZIJDS

VOOR

Oudezijds Achterburgwal

RUSLAND

KLOVENIERSBURGWAL

N. HOOGSTR.

ZANDSTR.

**AMSTERDAM
MUSEUM**

GALLERY

BEGIJNHOF

Spui
(#2, 11 & 12)

*Spui
Square*

Spui (Rokin)
(#4, 14,
& 24)

KUIPERS-
STEEG

ROKIN

AMST.
UNIVERSITY

SLIJKSTR.

OUDEMAN-
HUISPOORT

GROENBURGWAL

RAAMGRACHT

VERVERSSTR.

**REMBRANDT'S
HOUSE**

FLEA
MARKET

Waterlooplein

GED. BEG.

RAAM

TAKST.

GRIMBURGWAL

Spui

OUDE TURFMARKT

VENDELSTR.

NIEUWE DOELENSTR.

STAALSTR.

KLOVENIERSBURGWAL

Zwanenburgwal

**OPERA
HOUSE**

Waterlooplein
(#14)

Singel

HEILIGEWEG

HANDBOOG-
STRAAT

KALVERSTR.

Rokin

STAALKADE

AMSTEL

Amstel

AMSTEL

BLAUW
BRUG

DRAW-
BRIDGE

**KALVERTOREN
MALL**

Muntplein

**MINT
TOWER**

(#24)

REGULIERSBREESTR.

HALVE-
MAAN-
STG.

Rembrandtplein
(#4 & 14)

AMSTELSTR.

Koningsplein
(#2, 11 & 12)

**FLOWER
MARKET**

REGULIERS

TUSCHINSKI
THEATER

FEBO

Rembrandtplein

WILLET-HOLTHUYSEN
MUSEUM

HERENGRACHT

To
Leidseplein

"GOLDEN

CURVE"

Herengracht

REGULIERS

VIJZELSTRAAT

DWARSSTRAAT

VIJZELSTRAAT

HERENGRACHT

NOORDERKERK

**MUSEUM
OF BAGS
AND PURSES**

HERENGRACHT

To
Museumplein

While most guides lack a local's deep understanding of Dutch culture, not to mention professional training, they're certainly high energy. This long walk covers a lot of the city with an enthusiasm for the contemporary pot-and-prostitution scene (free but tips expected, 5/day, www.neweuropetours.eu). They also offer paid tours (coffeeshop scene–€14, daily at 15:00; Amsterdam by bike–€20, includes bike, daily at 10:00; food tour–€26, daily at 15:00). All tours leave from the National Monument on Dam Square.

Amsterdam has many competing food tours. I enjoyed the **Eating Amsterdam** tour, which takes 8-12 people on an eight-stop, four-hour food tour of the Jordaan neighborhood. You'll sample cheese, cider, pancakes, *bitterballen,* herring, apple pie, and more. They also offer a tour that includes a one-hour boat ride (Jordaan tour–€79, Tue–Sat at 11:00; food tour with canal boat–€106, March-Dec Tue–Sat at 10:30; book online or by phone, tel. 020/808-3099, www.eatingamsterdamtours.com, Camilla Lundberg).

PRIVATE GUIDES

Larae Malooly and her team of guides offer lively cultural and historic tours (€35 small group tours up to 10 people,

€175 private tours for up to four people, www.amsterdamsel.com).

Albert Walet is a knowledgeable local guide who enjoys personalizing tours for Americans interested in getting to know his city (€70/2 hours, €120/4 hours, up to 4 people, on foot or by bike, mobile 06-2069-7882, abwalet2@yahoo.nl). Al also takes travelers to nearby Haarlem, Leiden, and Delft.

Dennis from Love My City Tours offers a customized introduction to the city's neighborhoods with great tips for places to eat like a local and experiences you won't find on the tourist route (from €25/person for small groups up to 10, private tours from €100, mobile 06-3840-2919, www.lovemycitytours.com, support@lovemycitytours.com).

BIKE TOURS

Yellow Bike Guided Tours offers city bike tours of either two hours (€24.50, daily at 10:30, in winter at 13:30) or three hours (€27.50, daily at 13:30), which both include a 20-minute break. All tours leave from Nieuwezijds Kolk 29, three blocks from Centraal Station (reservations smart, tel. 020/620-6940, www.yellowbike.nl).

Joy Ride Bike Tours pedal through the pastoral polder land in 4.5 hours (€40, €35 online, April-Sept Sat, Mon, and Thu, meet at 10:15 and depart precisely at 10:30, no kids under age 13). Helmets, rain gear, and saddlebags are included. Tours meet behind the Rijksmuseum next to Cobra Café; private tours must be booked in advance (mobile 06-4361-1798, www.joyridetours.nl).

AMSTERDAM CITY WALK

Take a Dutch sampler walk from one end of the old center to the other, tasting all that Amsterdam has to offer along the way. It's your best single stroll through quintessentially Dutch scenes, hidden churches, surprising shops, thriving hap-

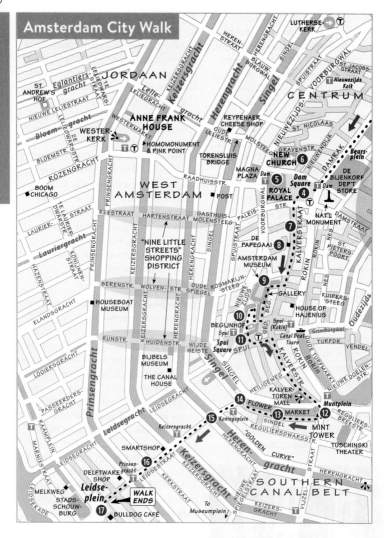

Amsterdam City Walk

py-hour hangouts, and eight centuries of history.

This three-mile walk starts at Centraal Station and ends at Leidseplein, near the Rijksmuseum. Allow three hours; this walk is best during the day, when churches and sights are open.

➋ Self-Guided Walk
➊ *Centraal Station*
Centraal Station, built in the late 1800s,

sits on reclaimed land at what was once the harbor mouth. With warm red brick and prickly spires, the station is the first of several Neo-Gothic buildings we'll see from the late 19th century, the era of Amsterdam's economic revival. One of the station's towers has a clock dial; the other tower's dial is a weather vane.

Let's get oriented: *nord, zuid, ost,* and *vest.* Facing the station, you're facing north. Farther north, on the other side of

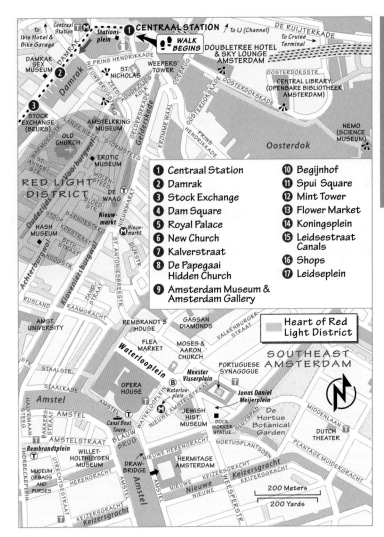

Walk Map Legend:

1. Centraal Station
2. Damrak
3. Stock Exchange
4. Dam Square
5. Royal Palace
6. New Church
7. Kalverstraat
8. De Papegaai Hidden Church
9. Amsterdam Museum & Amsterdam Gallery
10. Begijnhof
11. Spui Square
12. Mint Tower
13. Flower Market
14. Koningsplein
15. Leidsestraat Canals
16. Shops
17. Leidseplein

Heart of Red Light District

the station, is the IJ (pronounced "eye"), the body of water that gives Amsterdam access to the open sea.

Now turn your back to the station and face the city, looking south. The city spreads out before you like a fan, in a series of concentric canals. Ahead of you stretches the street called Damrak, which leads—like a red carpet for guests entering Amsterdam—to Dam Square a half-mile away. That's where we're headed.

To the left of Damrak is the city's old (oude) town. More recently, that historic quarter has become the Red Light District. Closer to you, towering above the old part of town, is the domed St. Nicholas Church. It was built in the 1880s, when Catholics—after about three centuries of oppression—were finally free to worship in public. To your far left is the Double-Tree by Hilton Hotel, with the city's best viewpoint.

The Neo-Gothic central train station borders the Old Town.

To the right of Damrak is the new (*nieuwe*) part of town, where you'll find the Anne Frank House and the peaceful Jordaan neighborhood.

Rick's Tip: *Although sea-level Amsterdam is notoriously horizontal, you can get the big picture at the rooftop* **Sky Lounge Amsterdam,** *on the 11th floor of the DoubleTree by Hilton Hotel, a five-minute walk east of the train station.*

On your far right, in front of Ibis Hotel, is a huge, multistory parking garage—for bikes only. Biking in Holland is the way to go—the land is flat, distances are short, and there are designated bike paths everywhere. The bike parking garage is free, courtesy of the government, and intended to encourage this green and ultra-efficient mode of transportation.
• *With your back to the station, walk to the head of Damrak. Be aware of trams and bikes as you cross the street. Keep going south straight along the right side of the street, following the crowds on...*

❷ *Damrak*

This street was once a riverbed. It's where the Amstel River flowed north into the IJ, which led to a vast inlet of the North Sea called the Zuiderzee. It's this unique geography that turned Amsterdam into a center of trade. Boats could sail up the Amstel into the interior of Europe, or out to the North Sea, to reach the rest of the world.

As you stroll along Damrak, look left. There's a marina, lined with old brick buildings. Though they aren't terribly historic, the scene still captures a bit of Golden Age Amsterdam. Think of it: Back in the 1600s, this area was the harbor, and those buildings warehoused exotic goods from all over the world.

All along Damrak, you'll pass a veritable gauntlet of touristy shops. These seem to cover every Dutch cliché. You'll see wooden shoes, which the Dutch used to wear to get around easily in the marshy soil, and all manner of tulips; the real ones come from Holland's famed fresh-flower industry. Heineken fridge magnets advertise one of the world's most popular pilsner beers. There are wheels of cheese,

Souvenir Scene

Stock Exchange

marijuana-leaf hats, team jerseys for the Ajax football (soccer) club, and memorabilia with the city's "XXX" logo. You'll likely hear a hand-cranked barrel organ and see windmill-shaped saltshakers. And everything seems to be available in bright orange—because that's the official color of the Dutch royal family.

At the **Damrak Sex Museum** at Damrak 18, you'll find the city's most notorious commodity on display. As a port town catering to sailors and businessmen away from home, Amsterdam has always accommodated the sex trade.

Continue up Damrak (noting the **canal boats** on your right) for more touristy delectables. You'll pass places selling the popular local fast food: french fries. Here they're called **Vlaamse friets** (Flemish fries). The stand at Damrak 41 is a favorite, where plenty of locals stop to dip their fries in mayonnaise (not ketchup). As you pass Damrak's many restaurants, you'll see many offering international cuisine. *Rijsttafel*, a sampler of assorted Indonesian dishes, is especially popular, thanks to the days when the Dutch East Indies were a colony.

• *The long brick building with the square clock tower, along the left side of Damrak, is the...*

❸ *Stock Exchange (Beurs van Berlage)*

This impressive structure, a symbol of the city's long tradition as a trading town,

was built with nine million bricks. Like so many buildings in this once-marshy city, it was constructed on a foundation of pilings—some 5,000 tree trunks hammered vertically into the soil. When the Beurs opened in 1903, it was one of the world's first modernist buildings, with a geometric, minimal, no-frills style. Emphasizing function over looks, it helped set the architectural tone for many 20th-century buildings.

Make your way to the end of the long, century-old building. Amsterdammers have gathered in this neighborhood to trade since medieval times. Back then, "trading stock" meant buying and selling any kind of goods that could be loaded and unloaded onto a boat—goats, chickens, or kegs of beer. Over time, they began exchanging slips of paper, or "futures," rather than actual goods. Traders needed moneychangers, who needed bankers, who made money by lending money. By the 1600s, Amsterdam had become one of the world's first great capitalist cities, loaning money to free-spending kings, dukes, and bishops.

• *Continue south along Damrak until it opens into Dam Square. Make your way—carefully—across the street to the cobblestone pavement. Now, stand in the middle of the square and take it all in.*

❹ *Dam Square*

This is the historic heart of Amsterdam. The city got its start right here in about the year 1250, when fishermen in this marshy delta settled along the built-up banks of the Amstel River. They built a *damme,* blocking the Amstel River, and creating a small village called "Amstel-damme." To the north was the *damrak* (meaning "outer harbor"), a waterway that eventually led to the sea. That's the street we just walked. To the south was the *rokin* ("inner harbor"), for river traffic—and nowadays also a main street. With access to the sea, fishermen were soon trading with German riverboats traveling downstream and with seafaring boats from Stockholm, Hamburg, and London. Land trade routes converged here as well, and a customs house stood in this spot. Dam Square was the center of it all.

Today, Dam Square is still the center of Dutch life, at least symbolically. The Royal Palace and major department stores face the square. Mimes, jugglers, and human statues mingle with locals and tourists. As Holland's most recognizable place, Dam Square is where political demonstrations begin and end.

Circling the Square: Pan the square clockwise, and take in the sights, starting with the Royal Palace—the large domed building on the west side. To its right

stands the New Church (Nieuwe Kerk); it's located on the pedestrian-only shopping street called Nieuwendijk, which runs parallel to Damrak and stretches all the way to Centraal Station. Panning past Damrak, see the proud old De Bijenkorf ("The Beehive") department store.

Farther right, the Grand Hotel Krasnapolsky has a lovely circa-1900 glass-roofed "winter garden." The white obelisk is the National Monument, built in 1956 to honor WWII casualties.

A few blocks behind the hotel is the edge of the Red Light District. To the right of the hotel stretches the street called the Nes, lined with some of Amsterdam's edgy live-theater venues. Panning farther right, find Rokin street—Damrak's southern counterpart, continuing past the square. Next, just to the right of the touristy Madame Tussauds, is Kalverstraat, a busy pedestrian-only shopping mall (look for *Rabobank* sign).

❺ Royal Palace (Koninklijk Huis)

Despite the name, this is really the former City Hall—and Amsterdam is one of the cradles of modern democracy. In medieval times, this was where the city council and mayor met. In about 1650, the old medieval Town Hall was replaced with

Dam Square is the historic heart of Amsterdam.

this one. Its style is appropriately Classical, recalling the democratic Greeks. The triangular pediment features denizens of the sea cavorting with Neptune and his gilded copper trident—all appropriate imagery for sea-trading Amsterdam. The small balcony (just above the entry doors) is where city leaders have long appeared for major speeches, pronouncements, executions, and (these days) for newly married royalty to blow kisses to the crowds. Today, the palace remains one of the four official residences of King Willem-Alexander.

• *A few paces away, to the right as you're facing the Royal Palace, is the...*

❻ New Church (Nieuwe Kerk)

Though called the "New" Church, this building is actually 600 years old—a mere 100 years newer than the "Old" Church (in the Red Light District). The sundial above the entrance once served as the city's official timepiece.

While it's pricey to enter the church (which offers little besides the temporary exhibits), cheapskates can see much of it for free. Enter through the "Museumshop" door to the left of the main entrance, then climb the stairs to a balcony with a small free museum and great views of the nave.

Take in the church's main highlights. At the far left end is an organ from 1655, still played for midday concerts. Opposite the entrance, a stained-glass window shows Count William IV giving the city its "XXX" coat of arms. And the window over the entrance portrays the inauguration of Queen Wilhelmina (1880-1962), who became the steadfast center of the Dutch resistance during World War II. The choir, once used by the monks, was turned into a mausoleum for a great Dutch admiral after the Reformation. This church is where many of the Netherlands' monarchs are married, and all are "inaugurated." (Dutch royals never actually wear the official crown.)

Back outside, look at the **monument** standing tall in the middle of Dam Square, built in 1956 as a WWII memorial. When the Nazis occupied Holland from 1940 to 1945, they deported some 60,000 Jewish Amsterdammers, driving many—including young Anne Frank and her family—into hiding. The "Hunger Winter" of 1944-1945 killed thousands of Dutch and forced many to survive on little more than tulip bulbs. This obelisk remembers the suffering of that grim time and is also considered a monument for peace.

• *From Dam Square, head south (at the*

The Royal Palace got its start as Amsterdam's City Hall.

Rabobank sign) on ❼ *Kalverstraat. This pedestrian-only strip has been a shopping street for centuries, although today it's mostly a noisy, soulless string of chain stores.*

For smaller and more elegant stores, try the adjacent district called De Negen Straatjes ("The Nine Little Streets"). About four blocks west of Kalverstraat, it's where 200 or so shops and cafés mingle along tranquil canals.

About 100 yards along, keep a sharp eye out for the next sight: It's on the right, just before and across from the McDonald's, at #58. Now pop into...

❽ De Papegaai Hidden Church (Petrus en Paulus Kerk)

This Catholic church—with a simple white interior, carved wood, and Stations of the Cross paintings—is an oasis of peace amid crass 21st-century commercialism. It's not exactly a hidden church (after all, you've found it), but it still keeps a low profile. That's because it dates from an era when Catholics in Amsterdam were forced to worship in secret. While technically illegal, Catholicism was tolerated

(kind of like marijuana is, these days). Catholics could worship so long as they practiced in humble, unadvertised places, like this church. The church gets its nickname from a parrot *(papegaai)* carved over the entrance of the house that formerly stood on this site. Now, a stuffed parrot hangs in the nave to remember that original *papegaai*.

• Return to Kalverstraat and continue south for about 100 yards. At #92, where Kalverstraat crosses Wijde Kapel Steeg, look to the right at an archway that leads to the entrance and courtyard of the Amsterdam Museum.

❾ Amsterdam Museum and Amsterdam Gallery

Pause at the entrance to the museum complex to view the archway. On the slumping arch is Amsterdam's coat of arms—a red shield with three Xs and a crown. The X-shaped crosses represent the crucifixion of St. Andrew, the patron saint of fishermen. They also represent the three virtues of heroism, determination, and mercy—symbolism that was

The New Church is 600 years old.

WWII obelisk-memorial on Dam Square

declared by the queen after the Dutch experience in World War II. (Before that, they likely symbolized the three great medieval threats: fire, flood, and plague.) The crown dates from 1489, when Maximilian I—a Habsburg emperor—also ruled the Low Countries. He paid off a big loan with help from Amsterdam's city bankers and, as thanks for the cash, gave the city permission to use his prestigious trademark, the Habsburg crown, atop its shield.

The courtyard leads to the best city history museum in town, the **Amsterdam Museum** (described under "Sights," later). Next to the museum's entrance is a free, glassed-in passageway lined with paintings. If it's closed, you'll need to backtrack to Kalverstraat to continue our walk (continue south, then turn right on Begijnensteeg, then look for the gate leading to the Begijnhof). Otherwise, step into the **Amsterdam Gallery** (formerly known as the "Civic Guards Gallery").

This hall features group portraits of Amsterdam's citizens from the Golden Age to modern times. Giant statues of Goliath and a knee-high David (from 1650) watch over the whole thing. Civic Guard paintings from the 1600s (featuring men and their weapons) established a tradition of group portraits that continues today. Stroll around and gaze into the eyes of the hardworking men and women who made tiny Holland so prosperous and powerful.

Don't miss the colorful patchwork carpet. Dutch society has long been a melting pot society and this—with a patch representing each country from where Dutch immigrants originated—celebrates today's multicultural reality. (A chart locates the various countries.)

• *The Amsterdam Gallery offers a shortcut to our next stop, a hidden and peaceful little courtyard. To get there, exit out the far end of the gallery. Once in the light of day, continue ahead one block farther south and find the humble gate on the right, which leads to the...*

⑩ *Begijnhof*

This quiet courtyard, lined with houses around a church, has sheltered women since 1346 (and is worth ▲). For centuries this was the home of a community of Beguines—pious and simple women who removed themselves from the world at large to dedicate their lives to God. When it was first established, it literally was a "woman's island"—a circle of houses facing a peaceful courtyard, surrounded by water. As you enter, keep in mind that this spot isn't just a tourist attraction; it's also a place where people live. Be considerate.

Begin your visit at the **statue** of one of these charitable sisters. You'll find it just beyond the church. The Beguines' ranks swelled during the Crusades, when so many men took off, never to return, leaving society with an abundance of single women. Later, women widowed by the hazards of overseas trade lived out their days as Beguines. They spent their days

Kalverstraat

Dove relief at the Amsterdam Museum

Begijnhof courtyard

Mint Tower

deep in prayer and busy with daily tasks—spinning wool, making lace, teaching, and caring for the sick.

Now turn your attention to the brick-faced **English Reformed church** (Engelse Kerk). The church was built in 1420 to serve the Beguine community. But then, in 1578, Catholicism was outlawed, and the Dutch Reformed Church took over many Catholic monasteries. Still, the Begijnhof survived; in 1607, this church became Anglican. The church served as a refuge for English traders and religious separatists fleeing persecution in England, including the Pilgrims, who prayed here before boarding the Mayflower.

A **Catholic church** faces the English Reformed Church. Because Catholics were being persecuted when it was built, this had to be a low-profile, "hidden" church—notice the painted-out windows on the second and third floors. This church served Amsterdam's oppressed 17th-century Catholics, who refused to worship as Protestants.

The last Beguine died in 1971, but this Begijnhof still thrives, providing subsidized housing to about 100 single women (mostly Catholic seniors). The statue of the Beguine faces a black **wooden house,** at #34. This structure dates from 1528 and is the city's oldest. Originally, the whole city consisted of wooden houses like this one. They were eventually replaced with brick houses to minimize the fire danger of so many homes packed together.

• *Near the wooden house, find a little corridor leading you back into the modern world. Head up a few steps to emerge into the lively...*

⓫ *Spui Square*

Lined with cafés and bars, this square is one of the city's more popular spots for nightlife and sunny afternoon people-watching. Its name, Spui (rhymes with "now" and means "spew"), recalls the days when water was moved over dikes to keep the place dry.

Rick's Tip: *For a* **city view** *(rare in flat Amsterdam), enter the Kalvertoren mall and take the slanting glass elevator to the recommended top-floor* **Blue Amsterdam Restaurant** *for a coffee or light lunch.*

Head two blocks to the left, crossing busy Kalverstraat, to the bustling street called the **Rokin.** A small black statue of Queen Wilhelmina on the Rokin shows her daintily riding sidesaddle. Remember that in real life, she was the iron-willed inspiration for the Dutch resistance against the Nazis.

Continue south on Kalverstraat. Just before the end of this shopping boulevard, on the right, you'll see the modern **Kalvertoren** shopping mall.

• *At the center of the square stands the...*

⓬ *Mint Tower (Munttoren)*

This tower marked the limit of the medieval walled city and served as one of its original gates. In the Middle Ages, the city walls were girdled by a moat—the Singel canal. Until about 1500, the area beyond here was nothing but marshy fields and a few farms on reclaimed land. The Mint Tower's steeple was added later—in the year 1620, as you can see written below the clock face. Today, the tower is a favorite within Amsterdam's marijuana culture. Stoners love to take a photo of the clock and its 1620 sign at exactly 4:20 p.m.—the traditional time to quit work and light one up. (On the 24-hour clock, 4:20 p.m. is 16:20...Du-u-u-ude!)

• *Continue past the Mint Tower, first walking a few yards south along busy Vijzelstraat (keep an eye out for trams). Then turn right and walk west along the south bank of the Singel canal. It's lined with the greenhouse shops of the...*

⑬ Flower Market (Bloemenmarkt)

Browse your way along while heading for the end of the block. The Netherlands is by far the largest flower exporter in Europe, and a major flower power worldwide. If you're looking for a souvenir, note that certain seeds are marked as OK to bring back through customs into the US (the marijuana starter-kit-in-a-can is probably...not).

• *The long Flower Market ends at the next bridge, where you'll see a square named...*

Flower Market

⑭ Koningsplein

This pleasant square, with a popular outdoor *haringhandel* (herring shop), is a great place to choke down a raw herring—a fish that has a special place in every Dutch heart. After all, herring was the commodity that first put Amsterdam on the trading map. Locals eat it chopped up with onions and pickles, using the Dutch-flag toothpick as a utensil.

• *Turn left, heading straight south to Leidseplein along Koningsplein, which changes its name to Leidsestraat.*

⑮ Leidsestraat Canals and ⑯ Shops

As you walk along, you'll reach Herengracht, the first of several grand canals. Look left down Herengracht to see the so-called **Golden Curve** of the canal. It's lined with townhouses sporting especially nice gables. Amsterdam has many different types of gable—bell-shaped, step-shaped, and so on. This stretch is best known for its "cornice" gables (straight across); these topped the Classical-looking facades belonging to rich merchants—the *heren*.

Cross over the next canal (Keizersgracht) and find the little **smartshop** on the right-hand corner (at Keisersgracht 508). While "smartshops" like this one are all just as above-board as any other in the city, they sell drugs—some of them quite strong, most of them illegal back home, and not all of them harmless. But since all these products are found in nature, the Dutch government considers them legal. You can check out the window displays or go on in and browse.

Just over the next bridge, where Leidsestraat crosses Prinsengracht, you'll find a **Delftware shop** (to the right, at Prinsengracht 440), which sells the distinctive ceramics known as Delftware. In the early 1600s, Dutch traders brought home blue-and-white porcelain from China, which became so popular that Dutch potters scrambled to come up with their

Leidseplein bustles with action day and night.

Bulldog Café and Coffeeshop

own version.

• *Follow Leidsestraat down to the big, busy square, called...*

⓱ *Leidseplein*

This is Amsterdam's liveliest square, worth ▲: filled with outdoor tables under trees; ringed with cafés, theaters, and nightclubs; bustling with tourists, diners, trams, mimes, and fire eaters.

Leidseplein's south side is bordered by a gray Neoclassical building that houses a huge Apple Store. Nearby is the city's main serious theater, the **Stadsschouwburg.** The theater company dates back to the 17th-century Golden Age, and the present building is from 1890. Does the building look familiar, with its red brick and fanciful turrets? That's because it, along with Centraal Station and the Rijksmuseum, were built by the same architect, Pierre Cuypers, who helped rebuild the city during its late-19th-century revival.

The neighborhood beyond Burger King is Amsterdam's **"Restaurant Row,"** featuring countless Thai, Brazilian, Indian, Italian, Indonesian—and even a few Dutch—eateries. Next, on the east end of Leidseplein, is the flagship **Bulldog Café and Coffeeshop.** (Notice the sign above the door: It once housed the police bureau.) A small green-and-white decal on the window indicates that it's a city-licensed "coffeeshop," where marijuana

is sold and smoked legally.

• *Our walk is over. But those with more energy could get out their maps and make their way to Vondelpark or the Rijksmuseum (one stop away on tram #2 or #12). To return to Centraal Station (or to nearly any place along this walk), catch tram #2, #11, or #12 from Leidseplein.*

SIGHTS

One of Amsterdam's delights is that it has perhaps more small specialty museums than any other city its size. From houseboats to sex, from marijuana to Old Masters, you can find a museum to suit your interests.

For tips on how to save time otherwise spent in the long ticket-buying lines of the big three museums—the Anne Frank House, Van Gogh Museum, and Rijksmuseum—see "Advance Tickets and Sightseeing Passes" on page 906. The following sights are arranged by neighborhood for handy sightseeing.

On Museumplein

The park-like Museumplein is conveniently bordered by the Rijks, Van Gogh, and Stedelijk museums as well as the Concertgebouw (classical music hall).

▲▲▲RIJKSMUSEUM

At Amsterdam's Rijksmuseum ("Rijks" rhymes with "bikes"), Holland's Golden Age shines with the best collection any-

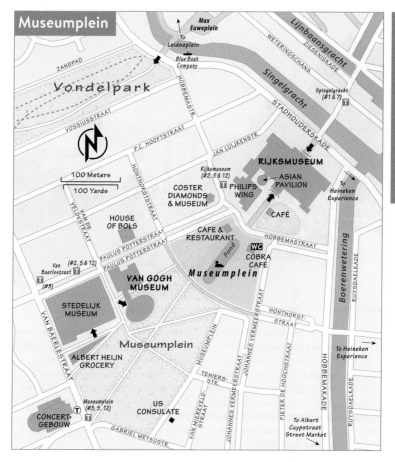

Museumplein

Max Euweplein

To Leidseplein

Blue Boat Company

Lijnbaansgracht

WETERINGSCHANS
ZIESENISKADE

ZANDPAD

Vondelpark

Singelgracht

Spiegelgracht (#1 & 7)

STADHOUDERSKADE

VOSSIUSSTRAAT

HOBBEMASTR.

P.C. HOOFTSTRAAT

JAN LUIJKENSTR.

RIJKSMUSEUM

100 Meters

100 Yards

HONTHORSTSTRAAT

Rijksmuseum (#2, 5 & 12)

COSTER DIAMONDS & MUSEUM

PHILIPS WING

ASIAN PAVILION

To Heineken Experience

VAN DE VELDESTRAAT

HOUSE OF BOLS

CAFÉ

CAFE & RESTAURANT

HOBBEMASTRAAT

PAULUS POTTERSTRAAT

PAULUS POTTERSTRAAT

Pond

WC

COBRA CAFÉ

Boerenwetering

RUYSDAELKADE

Van Baerlestraat (#2, 5 & 12)

(#3)

VAN GOGH MUSEUM

Museumplein

HONTHORST-STRAAT

JOHANNES VERMEERSTRAAT

VAN BAERLESTRAAT

STEDELIJK MUSEUM

Museumplein

MUSEUMPLEIN

To Heineken Experience

ALBERT HEIJN GROCERY

VAN MIEREVELD-STRAAT

TENIERS-STR.

JOHANNES VERMEERSTRAAT

PIETER DE HOOCHSTRAAT

HOBBEMAKADE

RUYSDAELKADE

Museumplein (#3, 5, 12)

CONCERT-GEBOUW

US CONSULATE

GABRIEL METSUSTR.

To Albert Cuypstraat Street Market

where of the Dutch Masters—from Vermeer's quiet domestic scenes and Steen's raucous family meals to Hals' snapshot portraits and Rembrandt's moody brilliance.

The 17th century saw the Netherlands at the pinnacle of its power. The Dutch had won their independence from Spain, trade and shipping boomed, wealth poured in, the people were understandably proud, and the arts flourished. This era was later dubbed the Dutch Golden Age. With no church bigwigs or royalty around to commission big canvases in the Protestant Dutch Republic, artists had to find different patrons—and they discov-

ered the upper-middle-class businessmen who fueled Holland's capitalist economy. Artists painted their portraits and decorated their homes with pretty still lifes and unpreachy, slice-of-life art.

This delightful museum offers one of the most exciting and enjoyable art experiences in Europe. As if in homage to Dutch art and history, the Rijksmuseum lets you linger over a vast array of objects and paintings, appreciating the beauty of everyday things.

Cost and Hours: €17.50, daily 9:00-17:00.

Information: Info tel. 020/674-7047, www.rijksmuseum.nl.

The Rijksmuseum's collections pay homage to Dutch art and history.

Avoiding Crowds/Lines: The museum is most crowded on weekends and holidays, and there's always a midday crush between 11:00 and 14:00. Plan your visit for either first thing in the morning or later in the day (it's least crowded after 15:00). Those with an advance ticket or Museumkaart can use a less-crowded entrance and skip the ticket-buying lines.

Getting There: From Centraal Station, catch tram #2 or #12 to the Rijksmuseum stop. The museum entrance is inside the arched passage that cuts under the building at its center.

Tours: The museum's free app offers tours, maps, and other useful info (download in advance or use the museum's free Wi-Fi). Guided tours are often offered at 11:00, 13:00, and 15:00 (€5). A multimedia videoguide (€5) provides both a 45-minute highlights tour and an in-depth version.

Eating: The Rijksmuseum Café, in the Atrium, is outside the ticket entry, so you don't need a museum ticket to eat here. On the south side of the building, there's a restaurant in the Philips Wing and a pleasant coffee-and-pastry café in the garden to the right. Nearby on Museumplein, you'll find the Cobra Café, a number of take-out stands, and (at the far end, near the Stedelijk Museum), an Albert Heijn grocery. Museumplein and nearby Vondelpark are both perfect for a picnic.

◑ SELF-GUIDED TOUR

Dutch art is meant to be enjoyed, not studied. It's straightforward, meat-and-potatoes art for the common man. The Dutch love the beauty of mundane things painted realistically and with exquisite detail. So set your cerebral cortex on "low" and let this art pass straight from the eyes to the heart, with minimal detours.

Follow the crowds up the stairway to the top (second) floor, where you emerge into the **Great Hall.** With its stained-glass windows depicting great artists and thinkers, vaulted ceiling, and murals of Golden Age explorers, it feels like a cathedral to Holland's middle-class merchants. Gaze down the long adjoining hall to the far end, with the "altarpiece" of this cathe-

dral—Rembrandt's *The Night Watch*.
• *Follow the flow of the crowds toward it, into the...*

Gallery of Honor: This grand space was purpose-built to hold the Greatest Hits of the Golden Age by the era's biggest rock stars: Hals, Vermeer, Steen, and Rembrandt.
• *In the first alcove to the right is the work of...*

Frans Hals (c. 1582-1666): Hals was the premier Golden Age portrait painter. Merchants hired him the way we'd hire a wedding photographer. With a few quick strokes, Hals captured not only the features, but also the personality. In *A Militiaman Holding a Berkemeyer,* a.k.a. *The Merry Drinker* (c. 1628-1630), you're greeted by a jovial man in a black hat, capturing the earthy, exuberant spirit of the Dutch Golden Age. Notice the details— the happy red face of the man offering us a *berkemeyer* drinking glass, the sparkle in his eyes, the lacy collar, the decorative belt buckle, and so on. Hals often painted common people, fishermen, and barflies such as this one. He used a stop-action technique, freezing the man in mid-gesture, with the rough brushwork creating a blur that suggests the man is still moving.
• *A little farther along are the small-scale canvases of...*

Johannes Vermeer (1632-1675): Vermeer is the master of tranquility and stillness. He creates a clear and silent pool that is a world in itself. Most of his canvases show interiors of Dutch homes, where Dutch women engage in everyday activities, lit by a side window.

The Rijksmuseum has the best collection of Vermeers in the world—four of them. (There are only some 34 in captivity.) But each is a small jewel worth lingering over. Vermeer's *The Milkmaid* (c. 1660) brings out the beauty in everyday things. The subject is ordinary—a kitchen maid—but you could look for hours at the tiny details and rich color tones. These are everyday objects, but they glow in a dif-

🅐 *Hals,* The Merry Drinker
🅑 *Vermeer,* The Milkmaid
🅒 *Steen,* The Merry Family

fused light: the crunchy crust, the hanging basket, even the rusty nail in the wall with its tiny shadow.

In paintings such as *Woman Reading a Letter* (c. 1663), notice how Vermeer's placid scenes often have an air of mystery. The woman is reading a letter. From whom? A lover? A father on a two-year business trip to the East Indies? Not even taking time to sit down, she reads intently, with parted lips and a bowed head. It must be important. Again, Vermeer has framed a moment of everyday life. But within this small world are hints of a wider, wilder world—the light coming from the left is obviously from a large window, giving us a whiff of the life going on outside.

• *In an alcove nearby are some rollicking paintings by...*

Jan Steen (c. 1625-1679): The Norman Rockwell of his day, Jan Steen (pronounced "yahn stain") painted humorous scenes from the lives of the lower classes. As a tavern owner, he observed society firsthand.

Find the painting *The Merry Family* (1668). This family is eating, drinking, and singing like there's no tomorrow. The broken eggshells and scattered cookware symbolize waste and extravagance. The neglected proverb tacked to the fireplace reminds us that children will follow in the footsteps of their parents. Dutch Golden Age families were notoriously lenient with their kids. Even today, the Dutch describe a rowdy family as a "Jan Steen household."

In *Adolf and Catharina Croeser*, a.k.a. *The Burgomaster of Delft and His Daughter* (1655), a well-dressed burgher sits on his front porch, when a poor woman and child approach to beg, putting him squarely between the horns of a moral dilemma. On the one hand, we see his rich home, well-dressed daughter, and a vase of flowers—a symbol that his money came from morally suspect capitalism. On the other hand, there are his poor fellow citizens and the church steeple, reminding him of his Christian duty.

• *You're getting closer to the iconic Night*

Rembrandt, The Night Watch

Watch, but first you'll find other works by...

Rembrandt van Rijn (1606-1669): Rembrandt was the greatest of all Dutch painters. Whereas most painters specialized in one field—portraits, landscapes, still lifes—Rembrandt excelled in them all.

The son of a Leiden miller who owned a waterwheel on the Rhine ("van Rijn"), Rembrandt took Amsterdam by storm with his famous painting *The Anatomy Lesson of Dr. Nicolaes Tulp* (1632). The commissions poured in for official portraits, and he was soon wealthy and married. Holland's war with England (1652-1654) devastated the art market, and Rembrandt's free-spending ways forced him to declare bankruptcy (1656)—the ultimate humiliation in success-oriented Amsterdam. His bitter losses added a new wisdom to his work. In his last years, Rembrandt's greatest works were his self-portraits, showing a tired, wrinkled man stoically enduring life's misfortunes. His death effectively marked the end of the Dutch Golden Age.

At the far end of the Gallery of Honor is the museum's star masterpiece—*The Night Watch*, a.k.a. *The Militia Company of Captain Frans Banninck Cocq* (1642). This is Rembrandt's most famous—though not necessarily greatest—painting. Created in 1642, when he was 36, it was one of his most important commissions: a group portrait of a company of Amsterdam's Civic Guards to hang in their meeting hall.

It's an action shot. With flags waving and drums beating, the guardsmen (who, by the 1640s, were really only an honorary militia of rich bigwigs) spill onto the street from under an arch in the back. These guardsmen on the move epitomize the proud, independent, upwardly mobile Dutch.

Why is *The Night Watch* so famous? Compare it with other, less famous group portraits nearby, where every face is visible and everyone is well-lit, flat, and flash-bulb-perfect. By contrast, Rembrandt rousted the Civic Guards off their fat duffs. By adding movement and depth to an otherwise static scene, he took posers and turned them into warriors. He turned a simple portrait into great art.

Now backtrack a few steps to the Gallery of Honor's last alcove to find Rembrandt's *Self-Portrait as the Apostle Paul* (1661).

Rembrandt's many self-portraits show us the evolution of a great painter's style, as well as the progress of a genius's life. For Rembrandt, the two were intertwined. With a lined forehead, a bulbous nose, and messy hair, he peers out from under several coats of glazing, holding old, wrinkled pages. His look is...skeptical? Weary? Resigned to life's misfortunes? Or amused?

This man has seen it all—success, love, money, fatherhood, loss, poverty, death. He took these experiences and wove them into his art. Rembrandt died poor and misunderstood, but he remained very much his own man to the end.

The Rest of the Rijks: The Rijks is dedicated to detailing Dutch history from 1200 until the present, with upward of 8,000 works on display. There's everything from an airplane (third floor, in the 20th-century exhibit) to women's fashion and Delftware (lower level). The Asian

Rembrandt, Self-Portrait

Art Pavilion shows off 365 objects from the East Indies—a former Dutch colony—as well as items from India, Japan, Korea, and China.

The **Philips Wing** hosts temporary exhibits upstairs (with themes that complement the Rijksmuseum's strengths) and a rotating photography collection downstairs (admission covered by Rijksmuseum ticket).

▲▲▲VAN GOGH MUSEUM

Located near the Rijksmuseum, this remarkable museum features works by the troubled Dutch artist whose art seemed to mirror his life. Vincent, who killed himself in 1890 at age 37, is best known for expressive canvases that pulse with vitality. The museum's 200 paintings—which offer a virtual stroll through the artist's work and life—were owned by Theo, Vincent's art-dealer brother. Highlights include *Sunflowers, The Bedroom, The Potato Eaters,* and many brooding self-portraits. The museum also includes works that influenced Vincent, from Monet and Pissarro to Gauguin, Cézanne, and Toulouse-Lautrec. The worthwhile audioguide includes insightful commentaries and quotes from Vincent himself. Temporary exhibits fill the new wing, down the escalator from the ground-floor lobby.

Cost and Hours: €18; daily April-Aug 9:00-19:00, Fri until 21:00, Sat until 18:00 (April-June) and 21:00 (July-Aug); Sept-Oct 9:00-18:00, Fri until 21:00; Nov-March 9:00-17:00, Fri until 21:00. Confirm evening hours before you visit.

Information: Tel. 020/570-5200, www.vangoghmuseum.com.

Avoiding Lines: To get in without a wait, buy timed-entry tickets online at www.vangoghmuseum.com (tickets go on sale about four months in advance). If you have a Museumkaart, you're required to reserve a time slot when it's busy (check website for updates); outside of those times pass holders queue up in a shorter line than same-day ticket buyers.

Getting There: Paulus Potterstraat7; from Centraal Station, tram #2 or #12 to the Rijksmuseum or Van Baerlestraat stop.

Tours: The €5 multimedia guide gives insightful commentaries about Van Gogh's paintings and his technique, along with related quotations from Vincent himself. There's also a kids' multimedia guide (€3).

➲ SELF-GUIDED TOUR

The collection is laid out roughly chronologically, through the changes in Vincent van Gogh's life (1853-1890) and styles. But you'll need to be flexible—the paintings are spread over three floors, and every few months there's a different array of paintings from the museum's large collection. You start on level 0, where self-portraits introduce you to the artist. Level 1 has his early paintings; level 2 focuses on the man and his contemporaries; and level 3 has his final works.

You could see Vincent van Gogh's can-

Van Gogh Museum

Van Gogh, The Potato Eaters

Van Gogh, The Yellow House

Van Gogh, Red Cabbages and Onions

vases as a series of suicide notes—or as the record of a life full of beauty...perhaps too full of beauty. He attacked life with a passion, experiencing highs and lows more intensely than the average person. The beauty of the world overwhelmed him; its ugliness struck him as only another dimension of beauty. He tried to absorb the full spectrum of experience, good and bad, and channel it onto a canvas. The frustration of this overwhelming task drove him to madness. If all this is a bit overstated—and I guess it is—it's an attempt to show the emotional impact that Van Gogh's works have had on many people, me included.

• *Pass through security and the ticket booth into the glass-pavilion reception hall. Here you'll find an info desk (pick up a free floor plan), bag check, multimedia-guide rental, and WCs. There's also a bookstore (with several good, basic "Vincent" guidebooks and lots of posters with mailing tubes) and an excellent temporary exhibit gallery (generally free).*

Ascend to level 1. Work clockwise around the floor and follow the stages of Vincent's life.

The Netherlands (1880-1885): Start with his stark, dark early work. These dark, gray-brown canvases show us the hard, plain existence of the people and town of Nuenen in the rural southern Netherlands. The style is crude—Van Gogh couldn't draw very well and would

never become a great technician. The paint is laid on thick, as though painted with Nuenen mud. The main subject is almost always dead center, with little or no background, so there's a claustrophobic feeling. We are unable to see anything but the immediate surroundings. For example, *The Potato Eaters* (1885) is set in a dark, cramped room lit only by a dim lamp, where poor workers help themselves to a steaming plate of potatoes. They've earned it. Their hands are gnarly, their faces kind. Vincent deliberately wanted the canvas to be potato-colored.

• *Continue to the room with work he did in...*

Paris (March 1886-Feb 1888): After his father's death, Vincent moved from rural, religious, poor Holland to the City of Light. There his younger brother Theo, an art dealer, provided the financial and emotional support that allowed Vincent to spend the rest of his short life painting.

The sun begins to break through, lighting up everything he paints. His canvases are more colorful and the landscapes more spacious, with plenty of open sky, giving a feeling of exhilaration after the closed, dark world of Nuenen. In the cafés and bars of Paris' bohemian Montmartre district, Vincent met the revolutionary Impressionists. At first, Vincent copied from the Impressionist masters. He painted garden scenes like Claude Monet, café snapshots like Edgar Degas, "block prints" like the Japanese masters, and

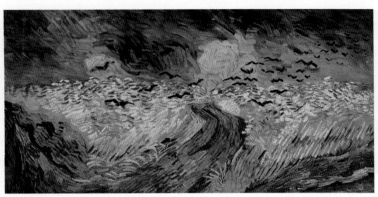

Van Gogh, Wheat Field with Crows

self-portraits like...nobody else.

In his *Self Portrait as a Painter* (1887-1888), the budding young artist proudly displays his new palette full of bright new colors, trying his hand at the Impressionist technique of building a scene using dabs of different-colored paint. In *Red Cabbages and Onions* (1887), Vincent quickly developed his own style: thicker paint; broad, swirling brushstrokes; and brighter, clashing colors that make even inanimate objects seem to pulsate with life. Despite his new sociability, Vincent never quite fit in with his Impressionist friends. He wanted peace and quiet, a place where he could throw himself into his work completely. He headed for the sunny south of France.

• *Travel to the next room to reach...*

Arles (Feb 1888-May 1889): After the dreary Paris winter, the colors of springtime overwhelmed Vincent. The blossoming trees and colorful fields inspired him to paint canvas after canvas, drenched in sunlight. One fine example is *The Yellow House*, a.k.a. *The Street* (1888). Vincent rented this house with the green shutters. (He ate at the pink café next door.) Look at that blue sky! He painted in a frenzy, working feverishly to try and take it all in. His unique style evolved beyond Impressionism—thicker paint, stronger outlines, brighter colors (often applied right from

the paint tube), and swirling brushwork that makes inanimate objects pulse and vibrate with life.

He invited his friend Paul Gauguin to join him, envisioning a sort of artists' colony in Arles. He spent months preparing a room upstairs for Gauguin's arrival. He painted *Sunflowers* (1889) to brighten up the place. At first, Gaugin and Vincent got along great. But then things went sour. They clashed over art, life, and their prickly personalities. On Christmas Eve 1888, Vincent went ballistic. Enraged during an alcohol-fueled argument, he pulled out a razor and waved it in Gauguin's face. Gauguin took the hint and quickly left town. Vincent was horrified at himself. In a fit of remorse and madness, he mutilated his own ear and presented it to a prostitute.

The people of Arles realized they had a madman on their hands. A doctor diagnosed "acute mania with hallucinations," and the local vicar talked Vincent into admitting himself to a peaceful mental hospital.

• *Ascend to **level 2**, where you may see displays about Van Gogh's contemporaries— Gauguin, his brother Theo—as well as more Van Gogh paintings. The visit concludes on level 3, with Vincent's final paintings.*

St-Remy (May 1889-May 1890): In the mental hospital, Vincent kept painting whenever he was well enough. At St-Remy, we see a change from bright, happy landscapes to more introspective subjects. The colors are less bright and more surreal, the brushwork even more furious. The strong outlines of figures are twisted and tortured, such as in *The Garden of Saint Paul's Hospital,* a.k.a. *Leaf Fall* (1889). A solitary figure (Vincent?) winds along a narrow, snaky path as the wind blows leaves on him. The colors are surreal—blue, green, and red tree trunks with heavy black outlines. A road runs away from us, heading nowhere.

Vincent moved north to Auvers-sur-Oise (May-July 1890), a small town near Paris where he could stay under a doctor-friend's supervision. *Wheat Field with Crows* (1890) is one of the last paintings Vincent finished. We can try to search the wreckage of his life for the black box explaining what happened, but there's not much there. His life was sad and tragic, but the record he left is one not of sadness, but of beauty—intense beauty.

The windblown wheat field is a nest of restless energy. Scenes like this must have overwhelmed Vincent with their incredible beauty—too much, too fast, with no release. The sky is stormy and dark blue, almost nighttime, barely lit by two suns boiling through the deep ocean of blue. The road starts nowhere, leads nowhere, disappearing into the burning wheat field. Above all of this swirling beauty fly the crows, the dark ghosts that had hov-

ered over his life since the cemetery in Nuenen. On July 27, 1890, Vincent left his room, walked out to a nearby field, and put a bullet through his chest. He stumbled back to his room, where he died two days later, with Theo by his side.

Art Beyond Van Gogh: Scattered throughout the museum are works by those who influenced Van Gogh and those who were influenced by him: Academy painters and their smooth-surfaced canvases, Impressionists Claude Monet and Camille Pissarro, and fellow Post-Impressionists Paul Gauguin, Paul Cézanne, and Henri de Toulouse-Lautrec.

Rick's Tip: **Vondelpark**, *a huge city park popular with the Dutch, is a joy to* **explore by bike**. *MacBike has a rental shop nearby at Leidseplein (listed under "Transportation," later).*

▲▲STEDELIJK MUSEUM

The Netherlands' top modern-art museum, the Stedelijk (STAYD-eh-lik), is filled with a fun, far-out, and refreshing collection of 20th-century modern classics as well as cutting-edge contemporary works. Before entering, notice the architecture of the modern entrance—aptly nicknamed "the bathtub." The layout is always changing, so once inside, pick up the current map. There are always temporary exhibits, and even the "permanent" collection rotates frequently. Don't try to

Vondelpark

Modern art fills the Stedelijk Museum.

do a painting-by-painting tour—this is a museum for exploring, so let yourself go. Each room comes with thoughtful English descriptions. (And if you're into marijuana, I can't think of a better space than the Stedelijk in which to enjoy its effects.)

Cost and Hours: €17.50, includes good audioguide, daily 10:00-18:00, Fri until 22:00, top-notch gift shop, Paulus Potterstraat 13, tram #2 or #12 from Centraal Station to Van Baerlestraat, tel. 020/573-2911, www.stedelijk.nl.

West Amsterdam
▲▲▲Anne Frank House

A pilgrimage for many, this house offers a fascinating look at the hideaway of young Anne during the Nazi occupation of the Netherlands. Anne, her parents, an older sister, and four others spent a little more than two years in a "Secret Annex" behind her father's business. While in hiding, 13-year-old Anne kept a diary chronicling her extraordinary experience. The thoughtfully designed exhibit offers thorough coverage of the Frank family, the diary, the stories of others who hid, and the Holocaust.

Cost and Hours: €9.50—buy online in advance, includes audioguide; daily 9:00-22:00; Nov-March Mon-Fri 9:00-20:00, Sat until 22:00, Sun until 19:00; only advance-ticket holders are admitted 9:00-15:30, same-day tickets sold only after 15:30; cloakroom for coats and small bags, no large bags allowed inside; tram

#13 or #17 from Centraal Station to Westerkerk, then a one-block walk to Prinsengracht 267; tel. 020/556-7105, www.annefrank.org.

Reservations: Online timed-entry tickets go on sale two months in advance. The tickets are not released all at once—they become available gradually over a two-month period between the on-sale date and the visit date. There is no science to the timing of their release: If no tickets for your preferred date are available initially, keep checking back.

Museumkaart holders get in free but must also reserve an entry time online for €0.50 (reservations available beginning two months in advance). You can make this reservation even if you haven't purchased a card yet—but be sure to buy the pass at another sight before your Anne Frank House visit.

Visiting the Museum: Begin in the **first floor** offices, where Otto Frank ran a successful business called Opekta, selling spices and pectin for making jelly. Photos and displays (typewriters, balance sheets) bring to life the business concerns of Otto and his colleagues. During the Nazi occupation, while the Frank family hid in the back of the building, these brave people kept Otto's business running, secretly bringing supplies to the Franks. Upstairs in the second-floor **storeroom,** models show the two floors where Anne, her family, and four fellow Jews lived. All told, eight people lived in a tiny apartment

Anne Frank House

The secret bookcase

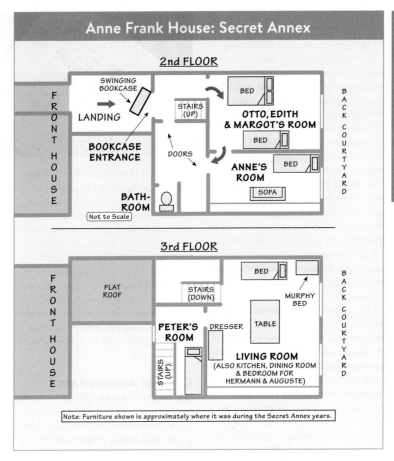

Anne Frank House: Secret Annex

2nd FLOOR

FRONT HOUSE

SWINGING BOOKCASE

LANDING

BOOKCASE ENTRANCE

DOORS

STAIRS (UP)

BATH-ROOM

Not to Scale

BED

OTTO, EDITH & MARGOT'S ROOM

BED

ANNE'S ROOM

BED

SOFA

BACK COURTYARD

3rd FLOOR

FRONT HOUSE

FLAT ROOF

STAIRS (DOWN)

PETER'S ROOM

STAIRS (UP)

DRESSER

TABLE

BED

MURPHY BED

LIVING ROOM
(ALSO KITCHEN, DINING ROOM & BEDROOM FOR HERMANN & AUGUSTE)

BACK COURTYARD

Note: Furniture shown is approximately where it was during the Secret Annex years.

smaller than 1,000 square feet.

In July 1942, they went into hiding. Otto handed over the keys to the business to his "Aryan" colleagues, sent a final postcard to relatives, gave the family cat to a neighbor, spread rumors that they were fleeing to Switzerland, and prepared his family to "dive under" (*onderduik,* as it was called).

At the back of the second floor storeroom is the clever hidden passageway into the **Secret Annex**. Though not exactly a secret (since it's hard to hide an entire building), the annex was a typical backhouse (*achterhuis*), a common feature in Amsterdam buildings, and the Nazis

had no reason to suspect anything on the premises of the legitimate Opekta business. Pass through the bookcase entrance into Otto, Edith, and Margot's room. The room is very small, even without the furniture. Imagine yourself and two fellow tourists confined here for two years. Pencil lines on the wall track Margot's and Anne's heights, marking the point at which these growing lives were cut short.

Next is **Anne Frank's room**. Pan the room clockwise to see some of the young girl's idols in photos and clippings she pasted there herself. Photos of flowers and landscapes gave Anne a window on the outside world she was forbidden to see. Out the window (which had to be blacked out) is the back courtyard, which had a chestnut tree and a few buildings. These things, along with the Westerkerk bell chiming every 15 minutes, represented the borders of Anne's "outside world." Imagine Anne sitting here at a small desk, writing in her diary.

Ascend the steep staircase—silently—to the **Common Living Room**. This was the kitchen (note the remains of the stove and sink) and dining room. Otto Frank was well off, and early on, the annex was well-stocked with food. Later, as war and German restrictions plunged Holland into poverty and famine, they survived on canned foods and dried kidney beans. The inhabitants spent their days reading and studying in this room. At night, it became sleeping quarters for Hermann and Auguste van Pels.

The next space is **Peter van Pels' room**. Initially, Anne was cool toward Peter, but after two years together, a courtship developed, and their flirtation culminated in a kiss. The **staircase** (no visitor access) leads up to where the inhabitants stored their food. Anne loved to steal away here for a bit of privacy. At night they'd open a hatch to let in fresh air. From here we leave the Secret Annex, returning to the Opekta storeroom and offices in the front house.

On August 4, 1944, a German policeman accompanied by three Dutch Nazis pulled up in a car, politely entered the Opekta office, and went straight to the bookcase entrance. No one knows who tipped them off. The Franks were sent to Auschwitz, a Nazi extermination camp in Poland. On the platform at Auschwitz, they were "forcibly separated from each other" (as Otto later reported) and sent to different camps. Anne and Margot were sent to Bergen-Belsen. They both died of typhus in March 1945, only weeks before the camp was liberated. The other Secret Annex residents—except Otto—were gassed or died of disease.

The Rest of the Museum: The **Otto Frank Room** has a 1967 video, in which Anne's father talks about his reaction as he read the diaries. (You may see one, two, or all three of them, as well as individual pages.) Other exhibits display memorabilia of the Franks and their friends.

It was Otto Frank's dream that visitors come away from the Anne Frank House with hope for a better world. He wrote: "The task that Anne entrusted to me continually gives me new strength to strive for reconciliation and for human rights all over the world."

Central Amsterdam
▲▲AMSTERDAM MUSEUM

Housed in a 500-year-old former orphanage, this creative museum traces the city's growth from fishing village to world trade center to hippie haven. The museum does a good job of making it engaging and fun. Try not to get lost somewhere in the 17th century as you navigate the meandering maze of rooms.

Start with the easy-to-follow "DNA" section, which hits the historic highlights from 1000-2000. In the first (long) room, you learn how the city was built atop pilings in marshy soil; by 1500, they'd built a ring of canals and established the sea trade. As you pass into the next room, the Golden Age (1600s) comes alive in fine paintings of citizens. Cross the skybridge into rooms covering the 1700s and 1800s, which brought modernization and new technologies like the bicycle. Then, after the gloom of World War II, Amsterdam emerged to become the "Capital of Freedom."

Cost and Hours: €13.50, free for kids 17 and under, includes audioguide, daily 10:00-17:00, pleasant restaurant in courtyard before entrance, mandatory and free bag check, next to Begijnhof at Kalverstraat 92, tel. 020/523-1822, www.amsterdammuseum.nl. This museum is a fine place to buy the Museumkaart.

▲▲OUR LORD IN THE ATTIC MUSEUM

Although Amsterdam has long been known for its tolerant attitudes, 16th-century politics forced Dutch Catholics to worship discreetly for a few hundred years. At this museum (formerly known as the Amstelkring) near Centraal Station, you'll find a fascinating, hidden Catholic church filling the attic of three 17th-century merchants' houses. Seek out the silver collection and other exhibits of daily life from 300 years ago.

Cost and Hours: €11, includes audioguide, Mon-Sat 10:00-18:00, Sun from 13:00, Oudezijds Voorburgwal 38, tel. 020/624-6604, www.opsolder.nl.

East Amsterdam

▲▲NETHERLANDS MARITIME MUSEUM (NEDERLANDS SCHEEPVAARTMUSEUM)

This huge, kid-friendly collection of model ships, maps, and sea-battle paintings fills the 300-year-old Dutch Navy Arsenal (cleverly located a little way from the city

center, as this was where they stored the gunpowder). The east building holds the core collection: globes, an exhibit on the city's busy shipping port, original navigational tools, displays of ship ornamentation, and paintings of dramatic 17th-century naval battles against the British. The west building has exhibits on whaling and of seafaring in the Dutch Golden Age. The finale is a chance to explore below the decks of an old tall-masted ship and gaze at a royal barge. Given the Dutch seafaring heritage, this is an appropriately important and impressive place.

Cost and Hours: €16, €7.50 for kids 5-17, includes audioguide, daily 9:00-17:00, bus #22 or #48 from Centraal Station to Kattenburgerplein 1, tel. 020/523-2222, www.scheepvaartmuseum.nl.

▲REMBRANDT'S HOUSE (MUSEUM HET REMBRANDTHUIS)

A middle-aged Rembrandt lived here from 1639 to 1658 after his wife's death, as his popularity and wealth dwindled down to obscurity and bankruptcy. As you enter, ask when the next etching or painting demonstration is scheduled and pick up the excellent audioguide. In the large studio, imagine Rembrandt at work here in the well-lit room where he created *The Night Watch, The Portrait of Maria Trip,* and numerous self-portraits (seen at the Rijksmuseum).

Cost and Hours: €13, includes audioguide, daily 10:00-18:00, etch-

Amsterdam Museum

Our Lord in the Attic Museum

Netherlands Maritime Museum

Dutch Resistance Museum

ing and paint-making demonstrations almost hourly between 11:00 and 15:00, fewer crowds (but fewer demos) early and late in the day, Jodenbreestraat 4, tel. 020/520-0400, www.rembrandthuis.nl.

▲▲DUTCH RESISTANCE MUSEUM (VERZETSMUSEUM)
This is an impressive look at how the Dutch resisted (or collaborated with) their Nazi occupiers from 1940 to 1945. You'll see propaganda movie clips, study forged ID cards under a magnifying glass, and read about ingenious and courageous efforts—big and small—to hide local Jews from the Germans and undermine the Nazi regime. This museum presents a timeless moral dilemma: Is it better to collaborate with a wicked system to effect small-scale change—or to resist outright, even if your efforts are doomed to fail? You'll learn why some opted for the former, and others for the latter.

Cost and Hours: €11, €6 for kids 7-15, family tickets available, includes audioguide; Mon-Fri 10:00-17:00, Sat-Sun from 11:00, mandatory and free bag check, tram #14 from the train station or Dam Square, Plantage Kerklaan 61, tel. 020/620-2535, www.verzetsmuseum.org.

EXPERIENCES

Red Light District
Europe's most popular ladies of the night tease and tempt here, as they have for centuries, in several hundred display-case windows around Oudezijds Achterburgwal and Oudezijds Voorburgwal, surrounding the Old Church (Oude Kerk). Drunks and druggies make the streets uncomfortable late at night after the gawking tour groups leave (about 22:30), but it's a fascinating walk earlier in the evening.

The neighborhood, one of Amsterdam's oldest, has hosted prostitutes since 1200. Prostitution is entirely legal here, and the prostitutes are generally entrepreneurs, renting space and running their own businesses, as well as filling out tax returns and even paying union dues. Popular prostitutes net about €500 a day (charging €30-50 per customer).

Marijuana Sights in the Red Light District: Three related establishments cluster together along a canal in the Red Light District. The Hash, Marijuana, and Hemp Museum, worth ▲, is the most worthwhile of the three; it shares a ticket with the less substantial Hemp Gallery. Right nearby is Cannabis College, a free non-profit center that's "dedicated to ending the global war against the cannabis plant through public education" (museum and gallery-€9, daily 10:00-22:00, Oudezijds

Red Light District

Achterburgwal 148, tel. 020/624-8926, www.hashmuseum.com; college-free to enter, daily 11:00-19:00, Oudezijds Achterburgwal 124, tel. 020/423-4420, www.cannabiscollege.com).

Smoking

For tourists from lands where you can do hard time for lighting up, the open use of marijuana here can feel either somewhat disturbing, or exhilaratingly liberating...or maybe just normal. Several decades after being decriminalized in the Netherlands, marijuana causes about as much excitement here as a bottle of beer. Throughout the Netherlands, you'll see "coffeeshops"—cafés selling marijuana, with display cases showing various joints or baggies for sale.

Rules and Regulations: The retail sale of marijuana is strictly regulated, and proceeds are taxed. The minimum age for purchase is 18, and coffeeshops can sell up to five grams of marijuana per person per day. It's also illegal for these shops (or anyone) to advertise marijuana. In fact, in many places, the prospective customer must take the initiative and ask to see the menu.

Shops sell marijuana and hashish both in pre-rolled joints and in little baggies. Joints are generally sold individually (€4-5, depending on whether it's hash with tobacco, marijuana with tobacco, or pure marijuana), though some places sell only small packs of three or four joints. Baggies generally contain a gram and go for €8-15. The better pot, though costlier, can actually be a better value, as it takes less to get high—and it's a better high. But if you want to take it easy, as a general rule, cheaper is milder.

Smoking Tips: Shops have loaner bongs and inhalers, and dispense rolling papers like toothpicks. While it's good style to ask first, if you're a paying customer (e.g., you buy a cup of coffee), you can generally pop into any coffeeshop and light up, even if you didn't buy your pot there.

Tourists who haven't smoked pot since their college days are famous for overindulging in Amsterdam. Coffeeshop baristas warn Americans (who aren't used to the strength of the local stuff) to try a lighter leaf. If you do overdo it, the key is to eat or drink something sweet to avoid getting sick.

Don't ever buy pot on the street in Amsterdam. Well-established coffeeshops are considered much safer, and coffeeshop owners have an interest in keeping their trade safe and healthy. They're also generally very patient in explaining the varieties available.

Coffeeshops

Most of downtown Amsterdam's coffeeshops feel grungy and foreboding to American travelers who aren't part of the youth-hostel crowd. I've listed a few places with a more pub-like ambience for Americans wanting to go local, but within reason. Most purchases are in cash.

Paradox is the most *gezellig* (cozy) coffeeshop I found—a mellow, graceful place. The managers, Ludo and Wiljan, and their staff are happy to walk you through all your options. The music is easy and the neighborhood is charming (daily 10:00-20:00, loaner bongs, games, two blocks from Anne Frank House at Eerste Bloemdwarsstraat 2, tel. 020/623-5639).

The Grey Area—a hole-in-the-wall spot with three tiny tables—is a cool, welcoming, and smoky place appreciated among local aficionados as a perennial winner at Amsterdam's Cannabis Cup Awards. You're welcome to just nurse a bottomless cup of coffee (daily 12:00-

20:00, between Dam Square and Anne Frank House at Oude Leliestraat 2, tel. 020/420-4301).

Siberië Coffeeshop is a short walk from Centraal Station, but feels cozy, with a friendly canalside ambience. Clean, big, and bright, this place has the vibe of a mellow Starbucks, hosts the occasional astrology reading, and is proud that all their pot is "lab tested" (daily 10:00-23:00, Fri-Sat until 24:00, helpful staff, English menu, Brouwersgracht 11, tel. 020/623-5909).

The Bulldog Café is the high-profile, leading touristy chain of coffeeshops. These establishments are young but welcoming, with reliable selections. They're comfortable for green tourists wanting to just hang out for a while. The flagship branch, in a former police station right on Leidseplein, is very handy, offering alcohol upstairs, pot downstairs, and fun outdoor seating on a heated patio (daily 10:00-24:00, later on weekends, Leidseplein 17, tel. 020/625-6278). Their original café still sits on the canal near the Old Church in the Red Light District.

Nightlife

On summer evenings, people flock to the main squares for drinks at outdoor tables. Leidseplein is the liveliest square, surrounded by theaters, restaurants, and nightclubs. The slightly quieter Rembrandtplein (with adjoining Thorbeckeplein and nearby Reguliersdwarsstraat) is

Window-shopping   *At a marijuana coffeeshop*

the center of gay clubs and nightlife. Spui features a full city block of bars.

The Red Light District (particularly Oudezijds Achterburgwal) is less sleazy in the early evening, and almost carnival-like as the neon lights come on. But it starts to feel scuzzy after about 22:30. The **brown cafés** recommended in the "Eating" section of this chapter are ideal after-hours hangouts. Peruse those listings for pre- or post-dinner drink ideas.

For entertainment and nightlife information, the TI's website, www. iamsterdam.com, has good English listings for upcoming events (select "See and do," then "What's on"). Newsstands sell the *I Amsterdam* entertainment guide and Dutch newspapers (Thu editions generally list events).

Shopping

Amsterdam has lots of one-of-a-kind specialty stores, street markets, and streets and neighborhoods worthy of a browse.

Top shopping zones include the Nine Little Streets (touristy, tidy, and central); Haarlemmerstraat/Haarlemmerdijk (emerging, borderline-edgy neighborhood of creative, unpretentious shops); and Staalstraat (postcard-cute, tucked just away from the tourist crowds). Of these, the **Nine Little Streets** (De Negen Straatjes) is a handy central zone. Hemmed in by a grid plan between Dam Square and the Jordaan, it's home to a diverse array of shops and trendy cafés. Walking west from the Amsterdam Museum/Spui Square or south from the Anne Frank House puts you right in the thick of things. For a preview, see www. theninestreets.com.

Souvenir Ideas: Good consumable souvenirs include cheese, chocolates, or a bottle of *jenever* (traditional Dutch gin). If you're seeking Dutch clichés (wooden shoes, flower seeds, or bulbs, and so on), visit any souvenir stand or the shops at the airport. Just make sure bulbs are cer-

tified to bring into the United States. Look for a paper certificate in the package.

Department Stores: Hema is handy for everything from inexpensive clothes and notebooks to cosmetics. Stores are at Kalverstraat 212, in the Kalvertoren shopping mall (Mon-Sat 9:00-19:00, Thu until 21:00, Sun 11:00-18:30) and at Centraal Station (similar hours).

The **De Bijenkorf** department store, towering high above Dam Square, is Amsterdam's top-end option and worth a look even if you're not shopping. The entire fifth floor is a ritzy self-service cafeteria with a rooftop terrace (store open daily 10:00-20:00).

Albert Cuyp Market: Amsterdam's biggest open-air market, stretching for several blocks along Albert Cuypstraat, bustles daily (roughly 9:00-17:00) except Sunday. You'll find fish, exotic vegetables, bolts of fabric, bargain clothes, native Dutch and ethnic food stands (especially *stroopwafels* and Surinamese *rotis*), and great people-watching. It's located a 10-minute walk east of Museumplein and a block south of the Heineken Experience (tram #24).

Flower Market (Bloemenmarkt): While flower shops are scattered around the city, the most enjoyable browsing is at the **Flower Market,** which stretches luxuriously along the Singel canal between the Mint Tower and Koningsplein. Actually situated on a row of barges, this floating market boasts a well-stocked cornucopia

of pretty petals tucked under tents. Stock up on seeds and bulbs to bring home—look for ones that are packed with a seal or certificate that promises they are US Customs-friendly.

Delftware Galleries: Ceramic plates, vases, and tiles decorated with a fake Chinese blue-and-white design were all the rage in the 1600s. Only a few licensed places sell the real stuff (expensive) and antiques (very expensive). Reputable vendors include **Heinen Delfts Blauw,** with one store between the museum neighborhood and Rokin (at Prinsengracht 440, www.jorritheinen.com) and another at the Mint Tower; and **Galleria D'Arte Rinascimento,** in the Jordaan (Prinsengracht 170, www.delft-art-gallery.com).

Diamond Shops: Diamonds have been a big Dutch commodity ever since Golden Age traders first exploited the mines of Africa. In Amsterdam, you can get them cut or uncut, expensive or really expensive. Diamond dealers offer free cutting and polishing demos at their shops. **Gassan Diamonds,** near Rembrandt's House, is best; **Coster** is on Potterstraat, behind the Rijksmuseum .

SLEEPING

Greeting a new day by descending steep stairs and stepping into a leafy canalside scene—graceful bridges, historic gables, and bikes clattering on cobbles—is a fun part of experiencing Amsterdam. But Amsterdam is a tough city for budget accommodations, and any hotel room under €150 (or B&B room under €125) will have rough edges. Still, you can sleep well and safely in a great location for around €100 per double.

Hotel Tips: Some national holidays merit making reservations far in advance. Amsterdam is jammed during tulip season (late March-mid-May), conventions, festivals, and on summer weekends. During peak season, some places won't take weekend bookings for those staying fewer than two or three nights.

Downtown Amsterdam is a sea of construction, and canalside rooms can come with great views—and early-morning construction-crew noise. Light sleepers should ask for a quiet room in the back. Parking in Amsterdam is even worse than driving—if you must park a car, ask your hotelier for advice. If you'd rather trade away big-city action for small-town coziness, consider sleeping in Haarlem, 20 minutes away by train.

Canal houses were built tight. They have steep stairs with narrow treads, and only some have elevators. If that's a problem, look for a hotel with an elevator—and confirm that it reaches your room.

Canalside Hotels

$$$$ The Toren is a smartly renovated, chandeliered mansion with a pleasant canalside setting and a peaceful garden for guests out back. This romantic hotel is classy yet friendly, with 40 rooms in a great location on a quiet street two blocks northeast of the Anne Frank House. The capable staff is a good source of local advice. The gilt-frame, velvet-curtained rooms are an opulent splurge (RS%, breakfast extra, air-con, elevator, some stairs, Keizersgracht 164, tel. 020/622-6033, www.thetoren.nl, info@thetoren.nl).

$$$$ Hotel Ambassade is elegant, traditional, and modern all at once, lacing together 56 rooms in a maze of connected houses. The staff is top-notch, and the library of books signed by authors who've slept here was designed by Rijksmuseum architects (RS%, breakfast extra, air-con, elevator, some stairs, Herengracht 341, tel. 020/555-0222, www.ambassade-hotel.nl, info@ambassade-hotel.nl).

$$$ The Times Hotel is a business-comfort hotel in a scenic canal setting. The 33 modern rooms are tight, but a handful have a real bathtub instead of just a shower. Each room features a wall mural of a Dutch masterpiece—if you majored in art history, you might love a blown-up version of Vermeer—or you might hate it (breakfast extra, air-con, elevator, Herengracht 135, tel. 020/330-6030, www. thetimeshotel.com, info@thetimeshotel. com, Glenn at the front desk).

$$$ **Wiechmann Hotel**'s 37 rooms are worn and sparsely furnished with just the dark-wood essentials, but they're spacious, and the *gezellig* (cozy) public areas are chock-full of Old World charm. Expect lots of stairs and no elevator in this historic building (some canal views, back rooms are quiet, nicely located at Prinsengracht 328, tel. 020/626-3321, www.hotelwiechmann.nl, info@ hotelwiechmann.nl, John).

$$$ **Hotel Hegra** is cozy, with nine rooms filling a 17th-century merchant's house overlooking the canal. While some rooms are small, everything is clean, modern, and functional (some canal views, breakfast extra, just north of Wolvenstraat at Herengracht 269, tel. 020/623-7877, www.hotelhegra.nl, info@hotelhegra.nl, Robert).

$$$ **Max Brown Hotel,** the flagship hotel of a boutique-style chain, has a trendy urban design geared toward a hipster clientele. Located in a quiet neighborhood near Centraal Station, it offers 34 modern rooms and public areas with funky-chic details. Rooms with canal views are pricier and breezier (continental breakfast, tangled floor plan connects three canalside buildings, Herengracht 13, tel. 020/522-2345, www.maxbrownhotels. com, hello.cd@maxbrownamsterdam. com). Another location is near Vondelpark and the Rijksmuseum.

$$$ **Mr. Jordaan Hotel,** in the heart of this Greenwich Village-like neighborhood, offers 34 rooms with funky-but-stylish touches—*Twin Peaks* meets Brooklyn Heights. Some are very tight, but they warn you in advance it's a "cozy" double. Hotel manager Eko will charm you as he shares neighborhood secrets (RS%, use

"enjoyjordaan" when booking, family rooms available, breakfast extra, elevator, Eko can arrange local guides and canal boat rides, Bloemgracht 102, tel. 020/626 5801, www.mrjordaan.nl, stay@mrjordaan. nl).

$$$ **Linden Hotel** is Mr. Jordaan's sister hotel, similar in its décor, tight rooms, and friendly staff, but with slightly cheaper rates. While it's on the edge of the Jordaan neighborhood, some of its 25 rooms have canal views (RS%, use "enjoylinden" when booking, family rooms, fans, breakfast extra, Lindengracht 251, 020/622-1460, www.lindenhotel.nl, info@lindenhotel.nl).

$$ **Hotel Hoksbergen** is your budget option for a canalside setting, so expect cramped rooms and a decidedly lived-in feel. The new owners promise to renovate all 14 rooms eventually—and the bathrooms are already up to snuff—but there are lots of steep stairs and ho-hum hallways. Avoid Room 4, which is sold as a double but should be a single (ask about apartments, fans, all-day coffee and tea in the common room, Singel 301, tel. 020/626-6043, www.hotelhoksbergen. com, info@hotelhoksbergen.nl).

B&Bs and Private Rooms

$$$ **Herengracht 21 B&B** lies between the Anne Frank House and Centraal Station, with two stylish, intimate rooms in a canal house filled with art and run by lovely Loes Olden, who also offers private tours in his family's 1920s-era canal boat (air-con, Herengracht 21; tours-€150/4 people, 1.5 hours, weather permitting; tel. 020/625-6305, mobile 06-2812-0962, www.herengracht21.nl, loes@ herengracht21.nl).

$$ With **Truelove Guesthouse,** a room-rental service, you'll feel like you're staying at your Dutch friends' house while they're out of town. René and Ingrid—whose jewelry store and bike-rental shop on Prinsenstraat doubles as the reception desk for their rental service—have eight rooms and apartments in houses sprin-

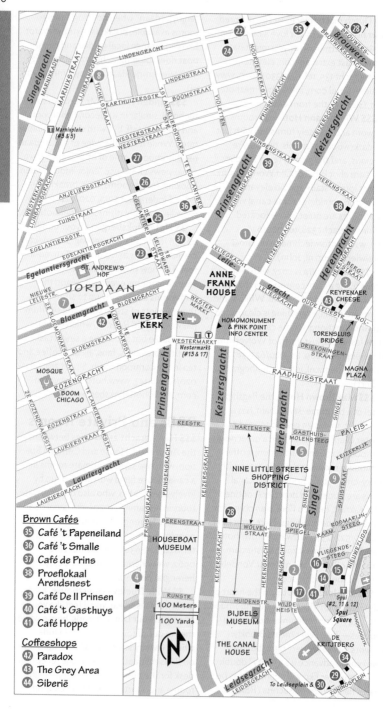

Brown Cafés
- 35 Café 't Papeneiland
- 36 Café 't Smalle
- 37 Café de Prins
- 38 Proeflokaal Arendsnest
- 39 Café De Il Prinsen
- 40 Café 't Gasthuys
- 41 Café Hoppe

Coffeeshops
- 42 Paradox
- 43 The Grey Area
- 44 Siberië

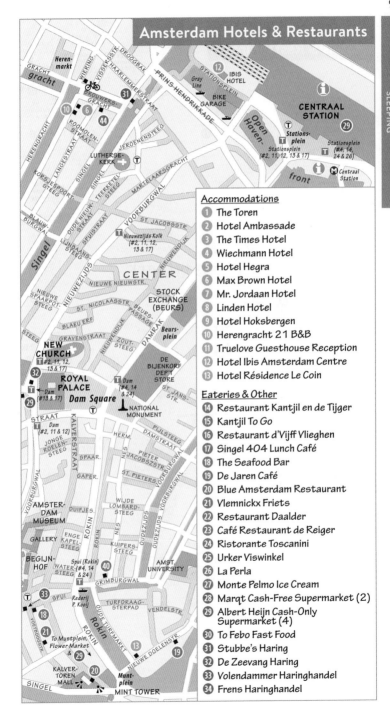

Amsterdam Hotels & Restaurants

Accommodations

1. The Toren
2. Hotel Ambassade
3. The Times Hotel
4. Wiechmann Hotel
5. Hotel Hegra
6. Max Brown Hotel
7. Mr. Jordaan Hotel
8. Linden Hotel
9. Hotel Hoksbergen
10. Herengracht 21 B&B
11. Truelove Guesthouse Reception
12. Hotel Ibis Amsterdam Centre
13. Hotel Résidence Le Coin

Eateries & Other

14. Restaurant Kantjil en de Tijger
15. Kantjil To Go
16. Restaurant d'Vijff Vlieghen
17. Singel 404 Lunch Café
18. The Seafood Bar
19. De Jaren Café
20. Blue Amsterdam Restaurant
21. Vlemnickx Friets
22. Restaurant Daalder
23. Café Restaurant de Reiger
24. Ristorante Toscanini
25. Urker Viswinkel
26. La Perla
27. Monte Pelmo Ice Cream
28. Marqt Cash-Free Supermarket (2)
29. Albert Heijn Cash-Only Supermarket (4)
30. To Febo Fast Food
31. Stubbe's Haring
32. De Zeevang Haring
33. Volendammer Haringhandel
34. Frens Haringhandel

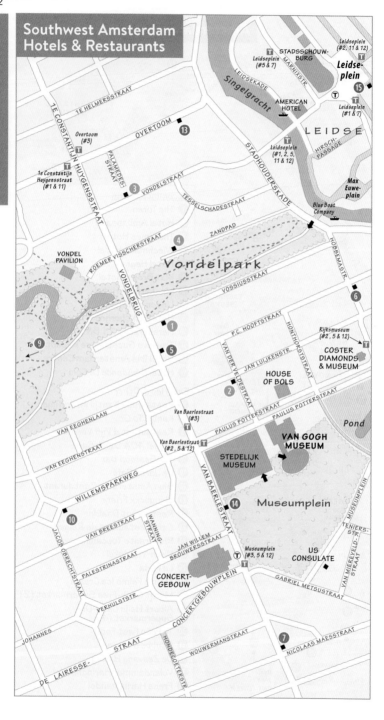

Southwest Amsterdam Hotels & Restaurants

Leidseplein (#2, 11 & 12)

STADSSCHOUW-BURG

Leidseplein (#5 & 7)

Leidse-plein

Singelgracht

15

AMERICAN HOTEL

Leidseplein (#1 & 7)

LEIDSE

1E HELMERSSTRAAT

Overtoom (#3)

OVERTOOM

13

Leidseplein (#1, 2, 5, 11 & 12)

HIRSCH-PASSAGE

1E CONSTANTIJN HUYGENSSTRAAT

1e Constantijn Huygensstraat (#1 & 11)

3

VONDELSTRAAT

PALAMEDES-STRAAT

STADHOUDERSKADE

Max Euwe-plein

TESSELSCHADESTRAAT

Blue Boat Company

ROEMER VISSCHERSTRAAT

ZANDPAD

4

Vondelpark

VONDEL PAVILION

VONDELBRUG

VOSSIUSSTRAAT

HOBBEMASTR.

6

To 9

1

P.C. HOOFTSTRAAT

5

VAN DER VELDESTRAAT

JAN LUIJKENSTR.

HONTHORSTSTRAAT

Rijksmuseum (#2, 5 & 12)

COSTER DIAMONDS & MUSEUM

HOUSE OF BOLS

2

Van Baerlestraat (#3)

PAULUS POTTERSTRAAT

PAULUS POTTERSTRAAT

VAN GOGH MUSEUM

Pond

VAN EEGHENLAAN

Van Baerlestraat (#2, 5 & 12)

STEDELIJK MUSEUM

VAN EEGHENSTRAAT

WILLEMSPARKWEG

10

VAN BAERLESTRAAT

14

Museumplein

MUSEUMPLEIN

TENIERS-STR.

JACOB OBRECHTSTRAAT

VAN BREESTRAAT

WANNING-STRAAT

JAN WILLEM BROUWERSSTRAAT

Museumplein (#3, 5 & 12)

US CONSULATE

VAN MIEREVELD-STRAAT

PALESTRINASTRAAT

CONCERT-GEBOUW

CONCERTGEBOUWPLEIN

GABRIEL METSUSTRAAT

VERHULSTSTR.

JOHANNES

STRAAT

HONDECOETERSTR.

WOUWERMANSTRAAT

7

NICOLAAS MAESSTRAAT

DE LAIRESSE-

Accommodations
1 Hotel Piet Hein
2 Hotel Fita
3 Hotel Alexander
4 Stayokay Vondelpark Hostel

Eateries & Other
5 The Seafood Bar
6 Sama Sebo Indonesian Restaurant
7 Renzo's

8 Café Loetje
9 To 'T Blauwe Theehuis
10 Café Gruter
11 Febo Fast Food
12 Cobra Café
13 Marqt Cash-Free Supermarket
14 Albert Heijn Cash-Only Supermarket
15 The Bulldog Café Coffeeshop
16 Launderette

kled throughout the northern end of the Jordaan neighborhood. The apartments are stylish and come with kitchens and pull-out beds (2-night minimum on weekends, no breakfast, pick up keys in store at Prinsenstraat 4, mobile 06-5334-0866, info@trueloveguesthouse.com).

$$$ **Hotel de Leydsche Hof,** a hidden gem located on a canal, doesn't charge extra for its views. Its four large rooms are a symphony in white—some overlooking a tree-filled backyard, others a canal—but be prepared for lots of stairs. Frits and Loes give their big, elegant, old building a stylish air (2-night minimum, closed Dec and sometimes Jan, Leidsegracht 14, tel. 020/638-2327, mobile 06-3099-2744, www.hoteldeleydschehof.com, loespiller@planet.nl).

$$$ **Wildervanck B&B,** run by Helene and Sjoerd Wildervanck with the help of their three kids, offers two tastefully decorated rooms in an elegant 17th-century canal house. If you want to meet a friendly Dutch family, this is the place (2-night minimum, cash only, breakfast in their pleasant dining room, just west of Leidsestraat at Keizersgracht 498, tel. 020/623-3846, www.wildervanck.com, info@wildervanck.com).

Near Vondelpark and Museumplein

For locations, see map on page 492.

$$$ **Hotel Piet Hein** offers 84 stylishly sleek yet comfortable rooms as well as a swanky lounge, good breakfast, and a peaceful garden, all on a quiet street. Be aware that the "economy double" is so tight, you'll have to climb over your partner to get to the other side of the bed (breakfast extra, air-con, Vossiusstraat 51, tel. 020/662-7205, www.hotelpiethein.nl, info@hotelpiethein.nl).

$$$ **Hotel Fita** has 20 bright rooms in a great location—100 yards from the Van Gogh Museum, an even shorter hop from the tram stop, and on a pleasant corner with a grade school's lively recess yard filling a traffic-free street. The style is modern yet rustic, with minimalist plywood furniture and nice extras, including espresso machines in every room. It's well-run by Roel, who offers a friendly welcome and generous advice (air-con on upper floors, elevator, stairs to breakfast room, free laundry service, Jan Luijkenstraat 37, tel. 020/679-0976, www.fita.nl, info@fita.nl).

$$ **Hotel Alexander** is a modern 34-room hotel on a quiet street. Some of the rooms overlook the garden patio out back. If you're looking for a smart, clean, relaxed place, this is it (breakfast extra, elevator, some stairs, tel. 020/589-4020, Vondelstraat 44, www.hotelalexander.nl, info@hotelalexander.nl).

¢ **Stayokay Vondelpark (IYHF),** is one of Amsterdam's top hostels for the under-25 set—but over-25s will feel comfortable here too (family rooms, lots of school groups, bike rental, right on Vondelpark at Zandpad 5, tel. 020/589-8996, www.stayokay.com, vondelpark@stayokay.com).

No-Nonsense Central Hotels

You won't get a warm welcome, but if you're looking for a hotel that's convenient to plenty of tram lines, these fit the bill.

$$$ **Hotel Ibis Amsterdam Centre,** next door to Centraal Station, is a modern, efficient, 363-room place. It offers a central location, comfort, and good value, without a hint of charm (pricier Sept-Oct, breakfast extra, book long in advance—especially for Sept-Oct, air-con, elevators; facing Centraal Station, go left toward the multistory bicycle garage to Stationsplein 49; tel. 020/721-9172, www.ibishotel.com, h1556@accor.com).

$$$ **Hotel Résidence Le Coin** has 42 larger-than-average rooms complete with small kitchenettes. The bathrooms have been updated, while the rooms have a slightly dated look. Located near the Mint

Tower, this hotel is a two-minute walk to the Flower Market and a five-minute walk to Rembrandtplein (breakfast extra, elevator, by the university at Nieuwe Doelenstraat 5, tel. 020/524-6800, www.lecoin.nl, hotel@lecoin.nl).

EATING

Amsterdam has a thriving and ever-changing restaurant scene. While I've listed options, one good strategy is simply to pick an area and wander. Note that many of my listings are lunch-only (usually termed "café" rather than "restaurant")—good for a handy bite near major sights. Similarly, many top restaurants serve only dinner. Before trekking across town to any of my listings, check the hours.

Central Amsterdam

You'll likely have lunch at some point at one of these places in the city's core (for locations, see map on page 940), but you'll find a better range of dinner choices in the Jordaan area of West Amsterdam (described later).

$$$ Restaurant Kantjil en de Tijger is a lively, modern place serving Indonesian food; the waiters are happy to explain your many enticing options. Their four *rijsttafels* (traditional "rice tables" with about a dozen small courses) are designed for two, but three people can make a meal by getting a *rijsttafel* for two plus a soup or light dish (daily 12:00-23:00, reservations smart, mostly indoor with a little outdoor seating, Spuistraat 291, tel. 020/620-0994, www.kantjil.nl).

$ Kantjil To Go is a tiny Indonesian take-out bar. Their printed menu explains the mix-and-match plan (daily 12:00-21:00, a half-block off Spui Square at Nieuwezijds Voorburgwal 342, behind the restaurant listed above, tel. 020/620-3074). Split a large box, grab a bench on the charming Spui Square around the corner, and you've got perhaps the best cheap, hot meal in town.

$$$$ Restaurant d'Vijff Vlieghen has an interior right out of a Rembrandt painting. It's a huge, dressy, and romantic place offering Dutch and international cuisine, professional service, and a multi-course tasting menu with matching wines (nightly 18:00-22:00, Spuistraat 294, tel. 020/530-4060).

$ Singel 404 Lunch Café, just across the Singel canal from Spui and near the

Nine Little Streets, is a popular café serving sandwiches on bread, bagels, and flatbread (daily 10:30-19:00, Singel 404, tel. 020/428-0154).

$$$ The Seafood Bar focuses on fresh and fishy, and is understandably popular—reserve ahead for lunch or dinner (daily 12:00-22:00, Spui 15, tel. 020/233-7452, www.theseafoodbar.nl). Another branch is near the Rijksmuseum (listed later).

Near the Mint Tower

$$$ De Jaren Café ("The Years") is chic yet inviting, and clearly a favorite with locals. Upstairs is a minimalist restaurant with a top-notch salad bar and canal-view deck (dinners after 17:30, meals include salad bar). Downstairs is a modern, less-expensive café, great for light lunches (soups, salads, and sandwiches served all day and evening). On a sunny day, the café's canalside patio is a fine spot to savor a drink (daily 9:30-24:00, a long block up from Muntplein at Nieuwe Doelenstraat 20, tel. 020/625-5771).

$$ Blue Amsterdam Restaurant, high above the Kalvertoren shopping mall, serves light lunches with one of the best views in town (just ride up the slanted elevator, daily 11:00-18:30, tel. 020/427-3901).

Fries: While Amsterdam has no shortage of *Vlaamse friets* ("Flemish fries") stands, locals and in-the-know visitors head for **$ Vlemnickx,** an unpretentious hole-in-the-wall *friets* counter hiding just off the main Kalverstraat shopping street. They sell only fries, with a wide variety of sauces—they call themselves *"de sausmeesters"* (Sun-Mon 12:00-19:00, Tue-Sat 11:00-19:00, Thu until 20:00, Voetboogstraat 31).

Jordaan District

Nearly all of these places are within a few scenic blocks of the Anne Frank House, providing handy lunches and atmospheric dinners in the city's most charming neighborhood.

$$$$ Restaurant Daalder is all about quality, fun, and the chef's surprise. There's no menu. Your waiter will discuss your interests with you and then you must sit back, relax, and dine on a multi-course meal. The dishes are French/Italian/Asian/Dutch and playful, and reservations are a must (options range from 4 courses for €45 to 7 courses for €68, daily 12:00-14:00 & 18:00-22:00, Lindengracht 90, tel. 020/624-8864, http://daalderamsterdam.nl/en).

$$$ Café Restaurant de Reiger must serve up the best cooking of any *eetcafé* in the Jordaan. Famous for its fresh ingredients, ribs, good beer on tap, and delightful bistro ambience, it's part of the classic Jordaan scene. They're proud of their fresh fish and French-Dutch cuisine. The café, which is crowded late and on weekends, takes no reservations. Come early and have a drink at the bar while you wait (daily 17:00-24:00, Nieuwe Leliestraat 34, tel. 020/624-7426).

$$$ Ristorante Toscanini is an upmarket Italian place that's always packed. With a lively, spacious ambience and

great cuisine, this place is a treat—if you can get a seat. Reservations are essentially required (Mon-Sat 18:00-22:30, closed Sun, deep in the Jordaan at Lindengracht 75, tel. 020/623-2813, http://restauranttoscanini.nl).

Jordaan's "Restaurant Row" is located along Jordaan's trendiest street. Tweede ("2nd") Egelantiersdwarsstraat, which turns into Tweede Anjeliersdwarsstraat, is home to a variety of tempting places to eat. This is a youthful and exuberant scene, with high-energy eateries that spill out into lively brick-sidewalk seating. Stroll its length from Egelantiers Canal to Westerstraat to survey your options. My favorites include **$ Urker Viswinkel,** a classic fish-and-chips joint; **$$ La Perla**, a big, busy wood-fired pizza oven surrounded by a few humble tables; and for dessert, **Monte Pelmo Ice Cream**.

Southwest Amsterdam

While a few eateries are within just a few steps of the big museums, my less-touristy picks are generally within a 10-minute walk and have better food and service—but none is worth going

out of your way for.

$$$ The Seafood Bar—modern, slick, and extremely popular—features a tasty array of seafood. The decor is white-sub-way-tile trendy, and the food focuses on fresh and sustainable dishes with a Burgundian flair. You can try dropping by, but it's best to reserve during mealtimes (daily 12:00-22:00, Van Baerlestraat 5, between the Rijksmuseum and Vondelpark, tel. 020/670-8355, www.theseafoodbar.nl).

$$$ Sama Sebo Indonesian Restaurant is considered one of the best Indonesian restaurants in town. It's a venerable local favorite for *rijsttafel*. I prefer the energy in the casual "bodega" to the more formal restaurant (and only in the bodega will they serve the smaller lunch plate for dinner). Their 17-dish, classic *rijsttafel* spread is as good as any. At lunch the *bami goreng* or *nasi goreng* (fried noodles or rice) is a feast of its own (Mon-Sat 12:00-15:00 & 17:00-22:00, closed Sun, reservations smart for dinner, P. C. Hooft-straat 27, between the Rijksmuseum and Vondelpark, tel. 020/662-81460, http://samasebo.nl).

$$ Renzo's is a tempting Italian delicatessen where you can buy good sandwiches or prepared pasta dishes and *antipasti* (priced by weight, can be heated up). Get your food to go, or pay a bit more to sit at one of the tables in the tiny interior, with more seating upstairs (house wine by the glass, or buy a bottle for the takeaway price to enjoy with your meal, daily 10:00-21:00, Van Baerlestraat 67, tel. 020/763-1673).

$$ Café Loetje has a rollicking, neighborhood beer-hall feel. Of the three dining zones, the interior is least interesting; head instead for the glassed-in winter garden (in bad weather) or the sprawling outdoor tables (in good weather). In addition to beer, they slam out good, affordable pub grub (daily 11:00 until late, several blocks southeast of Museumplein at Johannes Vermeerstraat 52, tel. 020/662-8173).

traditional rijsttafel *("rice table")*

In and Near Vondelpark: A venerable meeting point since the 1930s, **$$ 'T Blauwe Theehuis** ("The Blue Tea House") welcomes all generations for drinks and light meals. The setting, deep in Vondelpark, is like a Monet painting. Sandwiches are served at tables outside, inside, and on the rooftop from 11:00 to 17:00, drinks and apple pie are served all day, and pot smoking—while discreet—is as natural here as the falling leaves (daily 9:00-22:00 in summer, Vondelpark 5, tel. 020/662-0254).

$$ Café Gruter is just outside a gateway to Vondelpark. With a classic brown café interior and great seating on a little square, it's a neighborhood hangout—away from the center's tourism in a ritzy residential zone with fashion boutiques and leafy squares (lunch daily 11:00-16:00, also serves dinner, open very late, Willemsparkweg 73, tel. 020/679-6252). Ride tram #2 to the Jacob Obrechtstraat stop—one stop beyond the Van Gogh Museum.

Cheap and Fast Eats

To dine cheaply yet memorably alongside the big spenders, grab a meal to go, then find a bench on a lively neighborhood square or along a canal. Sandwiches (*broodjes*) of delicious cheese on fresh bread are cheap at snack bars, delis, and *broodje* shops. Ethnic restaurants—many of them Indonesian or Surinamese, and seemingly all named with varying puns on "wok"—serve inexpensive, splittable carryout meals. Middle Eastern fast-food stands and diners abound, offering a variety of meats wrapped in pita bread.

Supermarkets: Marqt Cash-Free Supermarket is the picnicking hipster's dream, with the freshest organic produce and plenty of prepared foods (credit cards only). **Albert Heijn** grocery stores are more traditional, cheaper, and have great deli sections with picnic-perfect takeaway salads and sandwiches. They take cash, but no US credit cards (don't get in the checkout lines marked *PIN alleen*).

Dutch Fried Fast Food: $ Febo caters mainly to late-night drinkers looking for greasy fried foods to soak up the booze. A wall of self-service, coin-op windows provides piping-hot fried cheese, burgers, croquettes, and so on (change machine on wall). You'll find branches all over town, including Leidsestraat 94, just north of Leidseplein.

Traditional Herring Stands

Amsterdam's old-fashioned fish stands (*haringhandel*) sell cheap herring sandwiches and other salty and fishy treats, usually from easy photo menus. The easiest order for novices is the sandwich (**broodje,** tucked into a soft roll with pickles and raw onions), while purists prefer their herring unadulterated.

Most of these handy outposts (all **$**, listed from north to south) are open until 17:00 or 18:00.

Near Centraal Station, on Singel Canal: A few blocks from Centraal Station, the well-established **Stubbe's Haring** has been selling herring for 100 years (closed Sun-Mon, at the locks on Singel canal).

Near Dam Square: Just behind the Royal Palace, **De Zeevang** sits at a busy tram-and-traffic intersection (closed Sun-Mon, corner of Nieuwezijds Voorburgwal and Raadhuisstraat).

On Spui Square: Central **Volendammer Haringhandel** is at the Rokin end of Spui Square (daily).

Near the Flower Market and Mint Tower: With an especially good location, **Frens Haringhandel** sits right along my "Amsterdam City Walk" (daily, Singel 468 at Koningsplein).

"Brown" Cafés

Be sure to experience the Dutch institution of the *bruin* café (brown café)—so called for the typically hardwood decor and nicotine-stained walls. (While cigarette smoking was banned several years ago—making these places even more inviting to nonsmokers—the prior pigmentation persists.) Exemplifying the *gezellig* (cozy) quality that the Dutch hold dear, these are convivial hangouts. Some brown cafés specialize in beer, while others focus on the Dutch gin, *jenever;* some offer light meals, but any food menu is usually very short—often limited to bar snacks called *hapjes* (mostly deep-fried goodies).

Admittedly, the line separating a brown café from a plain old bar is blurry, but here I've recommended my favorites. While some brown cafés are jammed with noisy drinkers, others are a bit more sleepy and mellow.

In the Jordaan: A classic brown café, **$ Café 't Papeneiland** has Delft tiles, an evocative old stove, and a stay-awhile perch overlooking a canal with welcoming benches (daily 10:00-24:00, drinks but almost no food—cheese or liverwurst sandwiches, overlooking northwest end of Prinsengracht at #2, tel. 020/624-1989).

$ Café 't Smalle serves simple meals of soups, salads, and sandwiches from 11:00 to 17:30 (bar snacks only after 17:30, plenty of fine Belgian beers on tap, interesting wines by the glass; at Egelantiersgracht 12—where it hits Prinsengracht, tel. 020/623-9617). **$$ Café de Prins** is a fine spot for *poffertjes*—those beloved tiny Dutch pancakes—as well as bar food, steaks, and fries (daily 10:00-late, Prinsengracht 124, tel. 020/624-9382).

Between Centraal Station and the Jordaan: Beer lovers will find the ideal brown café experience at **$ Proeflokaal Arendsnest.** Awash in wonderful old-fashioned decor, it displays 52 rotating Dutch beers "on tap/on draft" on a big chalkboard. The only food is Dutch bar snacks but the place is inviting, with seating inside and on the canal (daily 12:00-24:00, Herengracht 90, tel. 020/421-2057).

$ Café De II Prinsen, dating from 1910, feels more local. It's relaxed and convivial, with a few outdoor tables facing a particularly pretty canal and a lively shopping street (Dutch beers on tap, daily 12:00-24:00, Prinsenstraat 27, tel. 020/428-4488).

Near Rokin: With a lovely secluded back room and peaceful canalside seating, **$$ Café 't Gasthuys** cranks out light lunches, sandwiches, and reasonably priced basic dinners (cheeseburgers are a favorite, daily 12:00-16:30 & 17:30-22:00, Grimburgwal 7—from the Rondvaart Kooij boat dock, head down Langebrugsteeg, and it's one block down on the left, tel. 020/624-8230).

On Spui Square: A classic drinking bar, **$ Café Hoppe** is a good choice if you want to hang out with locals. "Hoppe" is their house brew, but there are many beers on tap, a good selection of traditional drinks, sandwiches at lunch, very simple bar food, a packed interior, and fun stools outside to oversee the action on Spui (Mon-Thu 14:00-24:00, Fri-Sun from 12:00, Spui 18, tel. 020/420-4420).

TRANSPORTATION

Getting Around Amsterdam

Amsterdam is big, and you'll find the trams handy. The longest walk a tourist would make is an hour from Centraal Station to the Rijksmuseum.

By Tram, Bus, and Metro

Amsterdam's public transit system includes trams, buses, and an underground Metro. Of these, trams are most useful for most tourists.

Information: The helpful GVB public-transit information office is in front of Centraal Station (Mon-Fri 7:00-21:00, Sat-Sun from 8:00, www.gvb.nl). The official **GVB app** offers route-planning features and real-time updates on buses, trams, Metro, trains, and ferries.

Single Tickets and Day Passes: Within Amsterdam, a **single transit ticket** costs

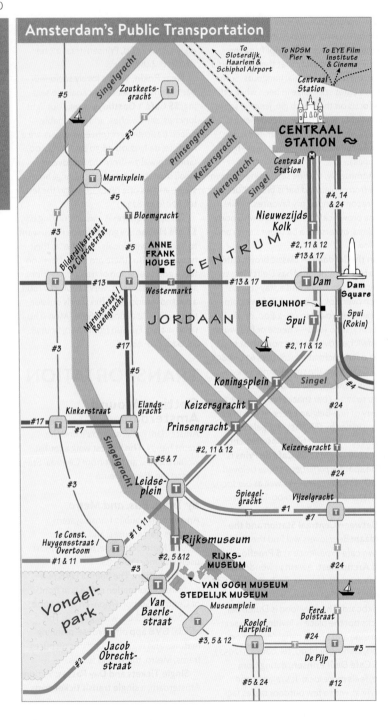

Amsterdam's Public Transportation

To Sloterdijk, Haarlem & Schiphol Airport

To NDSM Pier

To EYE Film Institute & Cinema

Centraal Station

CENTRAAL STATION

Zoutkeets-gracht

#5

#3

Singelgracht

Prinsengracht

Keizersgracht

Herengracht

Singel

Marnixplein

#5

Bloemgracht

#3

Bilderdijkstraat / De Clercqstraat

#5

ANNE FRANK HOUSE

CENTRUM

Centraal Station

#4, 14 & 24

Nieuwezijds Kolk

#2, 11 & 12
#13 & 17

Dam

Dam Square

#13

Marnixstraat / Rozengracht

#13 & 17

Westermarkt

JORDAAN

BEGIJNHOF

Spui

Spui (Rokin)

#2, 11 & 12

#17

#3

#5

Koningsplein

Singel

#4

Kinkerstraat

Elands-gracht

Keizersgracht

#24

#17

#7

Prinsengracht

Singelgracht

#5 & 7

#2, 11 & 12

Keizersgracht

#24

#3

Leidse-plein

Spiegel-gracht

Vijzelgracht

#1

#7

#24

1e Const. Huygensstraat / Overtoom

#1 & 11

#1 & 11

Rijksmuseum

#2, 5 &12

RIJKS-MUSEUM

VAN GOGH MUSEUM
STEDELIJK MUSEUM

Vondel-park

#3

Van Baerle-straat

Museumplein

Roelof Hartplein

Ferd. Bolstraat

#2

Jacob Obrecht-straat

#3, 5 & 12

#24

De Pijp

#3

#5 & 24

#12

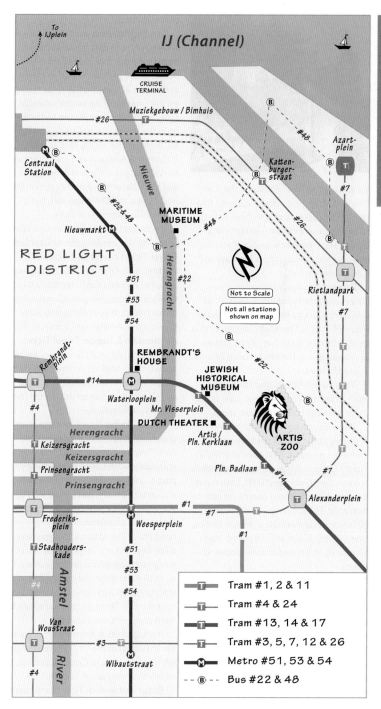

€3 and is good for one hour on the tram, bus, and Metro, including transfers. I find these "OV paper card" one-hour tickets to be the easiest option for short visits. But a pass is more economical if you're staying in Amsterdam for a few days and riding a lot of trams.

Passes good for unlimited city transit are available for 24 hours (€7.50), 48 hours (€12.50), 72 hours (€17.50), and 96 hours (€22.50). There are also passes that cover both the tram-bus-Metro system and train rides in the Netherlands (discussed below).

You can buy tickets and day passes from ticket machines at most tram stops, or on board all buses and most trams.

If you buy on board, the ticket booth is usually at the rear of the tram or bus. (If there's no conductor, pay the driver in front.) On board, you can only pay with a credit card (may need PIN); cash is not accepted, and 96-hour passes are not available. The full range of tickets and passes are also available at Metro-station vending machines, at GVB public-transit offices, at TIs, and at some souvenir shops.

The **I Amsterdam City Card,** a sightseeing pass, also covers all tram, bus, and Metro travel within Amsterdam (see "Advance Tickets and Sightseeing Passes" on page 906).

Transit Passes That Include Trains: If you're staying longer than three or four days or plan to use Dutch trains as well as trams and buses, consider a pass that covers them all.

The **TripKey Pass** is a pay-as-you-go system, with the cost automatically deducted from your credit card. The details of the pass are in flux, so check at the TI or at www.tripkey.nl for the latest information. If passes are available, order in advance from home and pick it up in the Netherlands. Convenient spots are the Hertz car rental desk at Schipol Airport, the Amsterdam Ticket Shop at Kerkstraat 155a in Central Amsterdam, and the Haarlem TI. Another option you might see is the **OV-chipkaart**, but it's not as useful for short-term visits.

If you don't get the TripKey, and plan to stick to Amsterdam, the **Amsterdam Travel Ticket** covers trams, buses, and the Metro plus the train ride to and from Schipol Airport (€16/1 day, €21/2 days, €26/3 days, http://en.gvb.nl/amsterdam-travel-ticket). If you plan to make day trips outside Amsterdam, consider the **Amsterdam & Region Travel Ticket** (€26/2 days, €33.50/3 days; one-day pass not worth it); sold at I Amsterdam TIs and stores, and ticket machines at Schipol and Centraal Station on the IJ-Hall (north side); www.iamsterdam.com.

Riding Trams: Board the tram at any door not marked with a red/white "do not enter" sticker. Once aboard, you must immediately "check in" by touching your pass or paper ticket to one of the pink-and-gray scanners. Just before exiting, you must "check out" by scanning it again. Occasionally controllers fine people who don't check in and out, and if you have a TripKey pass and forget to check out, you'll be charged for a longer journey. To open the rear door when you reach your stop, press a button on one of the poles near the exit. Don't try to exit through the front door—it's not allowed.

If you get lost in Amsterdam, remember that most of the city's trams eventually take you back to Centraal Station, and nearly all drivers speak English.

Buses and Metro: Tickets and passes

see their bright-red bikes everywhere. It has a huge and efficient outlet at Centraal Station (€7.50/3 hours, €9.75/24 hours, €6/extra day, more for 3 gears and optional insurance, 25 percent discount with I Amsterdam City Card; leave €50 deposit plus a copy of your passport, or provide credit-card number; free helmets, also rents electric bikes, daily 9:00-17:45; at east end of station—on the left as you exit; tel. 020/624-8391, www.macbike.nl). They have a smaller satellite at Leidseplein (Weteringschans 2). Return your bike to the station where you rented it. MacBike sells several €1-2 pamphlets outlining bike tours with a variety of themes in and around Amsterdam.

work on buses and the Metro as they do on the trams—pay with a credit card (may need PIN; no cash), and scan your ticket or pass as you enter and again when you leave. The Metro system is limited and used mostly for commuting to the suburbs—but it does loosely connect Centraal Station with some sights to the south (Rokin-Vijzelgracht-De Pijp) and east (Nieuwmarkt-Waterlooplein-Weesperplein) of Damrak.

By Bike

Everyone uses this mode of transport. It's by far the smartest way to travel in a city where 40 percent of all traffic rolls on two wheels. You'll get around town by bike faster than you can by taxi. One-speed bikes, with *"brrringing"* bells and foot brakes, rent for about €10 per day (cheaper for longer periods) at any number of places—hotels can send you to the nearest spot.

Rental Shops: Star Bikes Rental has cheap rates, long hours, and inconspicuous black bikes (€5/3 hours, €7/day, €9/24 hours, €12/2 days, €17/3 days, Mon-Fri 8:00-19:00, Sat-Sun from 9:00, shorter hours in winter, requires ID but no monetary deposit, 5-minute walk from east end of Centraal Station—walk underneath tracks near DoubleTree by Hilton Hotel and then turn right, De Ruyterkade 143, tel. 020/620-3215, www.starbikesrental.com).

MacBike, with thousands of bikes, is the city's bike-rental powerhouse—you'll

Lock Your Bike: Bike thieves are bold and brazen. Bikes come with two locks and stern instructions to use both. The wimpy ones go through the spokes, whereas the industrial-strength chains are meant to be wrapped around the body of the bike and through the front wheel, and connected to something stronger than any human. (Note the steel bike-hitching racks sticking up all around town, called "staples.") Follow your rental agency's locking directions diligently. If you're sloppy, it's an expensive mistake and one that any "included" theft insurance won't cover.

Biking Tips: As the Dutch believe in fashion over safety, no one here wears a helmet. They do, however, ride cautiously, and so should you: Use arm signals, follow the bike-only traffic signals, stay in the obvious and omnipresent bike lanes, and yield to traffic on the right. Fear oncoming trams and tram tracks. Carefully cross tram tracks at a perpendicular angle to avoid catching your tire in the rut. Police ticket cyclists just as they do drivers: Obey all traffic signals, and walk your bike through pedestrian zones (fines are reportedly €30-50). Google Maps helpfully includes bicycles as a mode of transportation for the Netherlands.

By Boat

While the city is great on foot, bike, or tram, you can also get around Amsterdam by hop-on, hop-off boat. **Lovers** boat lines shuttle tourists on two routes covering different combinations of the city's top sights. Their Green Line stops near the Hermitage, Rijksmuseum/Van Gogh Museum, and Centraal Station (€27.50/24-hour pass, roughly every 20 minutes, 2 hours). Sales booths in front of Centraal Station (and the boats) offer free brochures listing museum hours and admission prices. Most routes come with recorded narration (departures daily 9:30-18:15, tel. 020/530-1090, www.lovers.nl).

The similar **Stromma** is another hop-on, hop-off boat, offering nine stops on two different boat routes (€24.50/24-hour pass, online discounts, departures daily 9:30-19:00, until 20:00 July-Aug, leaves near Centraal Station at the Gray Line dock, tel. 020/217-0500, www.stromma.nl).

If you're simply looking for a floating, nonstop tour, the regular canal tour boats (without the stops) give more information, cover more ground, and cost less (see "Tours," earlier in the chapter).

For do-it-yourself canal tours and lots of exercise, Stromma also rents "canal bikes" (a.k.a. paddleboats) at several locations: near the Anne Frank House, near the Rijksmuseum, near Leidseplein, and where Leidsestraat meets Keizersgracht (€10/1 hour, €15/1.5 hours, prices are per person, €20 deposit, mid-March-Oct 10:00-18:00, may be open as late as 21:00 depending on weather).

By Taxi and Uber

For short rides, Amsterdam is a bad town for **taxis**. They're expensive and have to take circuitous routes through winding, traffic-filled streets. You can wave them down, find a rare taxi stand, call one (tel. 020/777-7777), or download their app (Taxi Amsterdam "TaxiTCA"). **Uber** works in Amsterdam like in the US.

You'll also see **bike taxis,** particularly near Dam Square and Leidseplein. Negotiate a rate for the trip before you board (no meter), and they'll wheel you wherever you want to go (sample fare from Leidseplein to Anne Frank House: about €6).

By Car

If you must bring a car to Amsterdam, it's best to leave it at one of the city's supervised suburban park-and-ride lots (follow *P&R* signs from freeway, €8/24 hours, includes round-trip transit into city center for up to five people, 4-day maximum).

Arriving and Departing

The Netherlands is so small, level, and well covered by trains and buses that transportation is a snap. Bus stations and bike-rental shops cluster around train stations. The easy-to-navigate airport is well connected to Amsterdam and other destinations by bus and train. Use the comprehensive transit website www.9292.nl to plan connections inside the Netherlands by train, bus, or both.

By Train

Amsterdam is the country's hub, but all major cities are linked by speedy trains that come and go every 15 minutes or so. Dutch rail schedules are online at www.ns.nl (domestic) and www.nshispeed.nl (international). Google Maps also does a good job of giving you real-time schedules, including departures, transfers, and

which track (spoor) your train will use.

The portal connecting Amsterdam to the world is its aptly named Amsterdam Centraal. The station's train-information center can require a long wait. Save lots of time by getting international train tickets and information at a small-town station (such as Haarlem), the airport upon arrival, or online.

TRAIN CONNECTIONS
From Amsterdam to: Schiphol Airport (4-6/hour, 20 minutes, buy from a machine to avoid lines), **Haarlem** (8/hour, 20 minutes), **London** (by Eurostar—2-3/day direct, 4 hours; more with transfer in Brussels, 5 hours, www.eurostar.com), **Bacharach/St. Goar** (roughly every 2 hours, 5.5 hours), **Frankfurt** (every 2 hours, 5 hours direct), **Berlin** (5/day, 6.5 hours), **Munich** (roughly hourly, 9 hours with 1-2 transfers), **Paris** (nearly hourly, 3.25 hours direct on fast Thalys train or 4.75 hours with change to Thalys train in Brussels, www.thalys.com). When booking Thalys trains, even rail-pass holders need to buy a seat reservation.

By Bus

Without a rail pass, the cheapest way to get to Paris is on a Eurolines or Flixbus bus (about 12/day including night buses, 8 hours, check online for deals; Eurolines leaves from Amsterdam Duivendrecht station, 8 stops by Metro from Centraal station, French tel. 33-141-862-421, www.eurolines.eu; Flixbus leaves from Amster-

dam Sloterdijk station, UK tel. 44-178-829-8784, www.flixbus.com).

By Plane

Schiphol (SKIP-pol) Airport is located about 10 miles southwest of Amsterdam's city center (code: AMS, www.schiphol.nl). Though Schiphol officially has four terminals, it's really just one big building. All terminals have ATMs, banks, shops, bars, and Wi-Fi.

Baggage-claim areas for all terminals empty into the same central zone, officially called Schiphol Plaza but generally signed simply *Arrivals Hall*. It's a big atrium of shops, tourist services, a busy TI (near Terminal 2, daily 7:00-22:00), and all your transportation options for getting into the city: train, bus, taxi, and Uber.

To get train information, buy a ticket, or validate your rail pass, take advantage of the **"Train Tickets and Services" counter** (Schiphol Plaza ground level, across from Burger King). They have an easy info desk and generally short lines.

Getting from Schiphol Airport to Amsterdam: Direct **trains** to Amsterdam's Centraal Station run frequently from Schiphol Plaza (4-6/hour, 20 minutes, €5.30, shortest lines at ticket machines near baggage claim). The Connexxion **shuttle bus** departs from lane A7, outside the main doors of Schiphol Plaza, and takes you directly to most hotels (2/hour, 20-45 minutes depending on hotel, €17 one-way, €28 round-trip, pay inside at Connexxion desk with credit card, tel. 088-339-4741, www.airporthotelshuttle.nl).

Public bus #397 is handy for those going to the Leidseplein district (€5, buy ticket from driver—credit card only, departs from lane B9 in front of the airport).

By **taxi**, allow about €50 to downtown Amsterdam. **Uber** also serves the airport.

NEAR AMSTERDAM

Haarlem

A Golden Age kind of town, cute and cozy Haarlem is quintessentially Dutch. With small-town warmth and easy access to Amsterdam or Schiphol Airport (20-30 minutes by train), it makes a good day trip or even a home base.

The Gothic Grote Kerk, or Great Church, towers over the market square (Grote Markt). Enjoy the market on Monday (clothing) or Saturday (general), when the atmospheric square bustles like a Brueghel painting, with cheese, fish, flowers, and families.

Haarlem's top museum features the work of its most famous son, portrait artist Frans Hals. The Corrie ten Boom House relates the inspirational story of a family that courageously hid Jews from the Nazis. If it's a sunny day and you need a beach, head to nearby Zandvoort.

Orientation

The town gate, no longer needed as part of its fortification, welcomes all into Haarlem's old center. For centuries Haarlem has been a market town, buzzing with shoppers heading home with fresh bouquets.

Tourist Information: Haarlem's TI (VVV), in the Town Hall building on Grote Markt, is friendlier, more helpful, and less crowded than Amsterdam's, so you could ask your Amsterdam questions here (closed Sun, tel. 023/531-7325, www. haarlem.nl, info@vvvhaarlem.nl).

Bike Rental: You can rent bikes from **Pieters Fietsverhuur** inside the train station (fixed-gear bike—€7.50/day, 3-speed bike—€10/day, €50 deposit and passport number required, long hours daily, Stationsplein 1, tel. 023/531-7066, www. rijwielshoppieters.nl). They often run out of bikes by midmorning—especially when

Haarlem has a small-town feel.

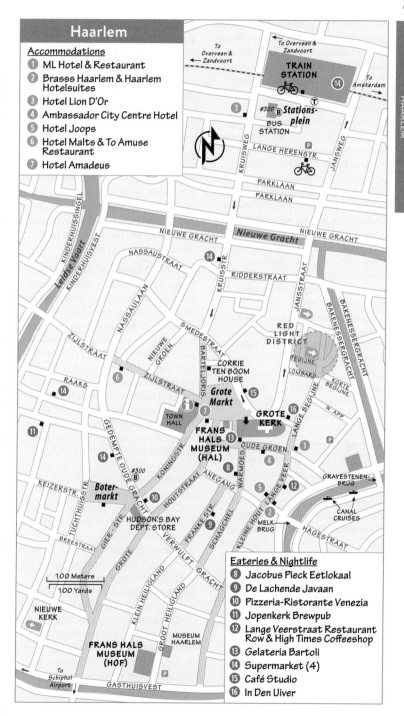

Haarlem

Accommodations

1. ML Hotel & Restaurant
2. Brasss Haarlem & Haarlem Hotelsuites
3. Hotel Lion D'Or
4. Ambassador City Centre Hotel
5. Hotel Joops
6. Hotel Malts & To Amuse Restaurant
7. Hotel Amadeus

Eateries & Nightlife

8. Jacobus Pieck Eetlokaal
9. De Lachende Javaan
10. Pizzeria-Ristorante Venezia
11. Jopenkerk Brewpub
12. Lange Veerstraat Restaurant Row & High Times Coffeeshop
13. Gelateria Bartoli
14. Supermarket (4)
15. Café Studio
16. In Den Uiver

the weather's good. **Rent a Bike Haarlem** charges more, but is friendly and efficient, and carries plenty of new, good-quality bikes (fixed-gear bike-€10/day, 3-speed bike-€13.50/day, mountain and electric bikes available, leave ID or €150 cash deposit; daily 9:00-18:00, closed Sun Nov-March; near station at Lange Herenstraat 36, tel. 023/542-1195, www.rentabikehaarlem.nl).

Canal Cruises: Making a scenic 50-minute loop through and around Haarlem with a live guide who speaks Dutch and sometimes English, **Smidtje Cruise**'s little trips are more relaxing than informative (€13.50; April-Oct departs daily at the top of the hour 12:00-16:00; reservations smart; also evening cruises, across canal from Teylers Museum at Spaarne 11a, tel. 023/535-7723, www.smidtjecanalcruises.nl).

Haarlem Canal Tours runs similar but longer tours in an open 12-person boat. You'll find them farther down Spaarne, across from #17 (€13.50; 70 minutes, every 1.5 hours daily 10:00-19:00, may not run in bad weather and off-season; online reservations smart at www.haarlemcanaltours.com).

Getting There

Direct trains run frequently from Amsterdam Centraal Station (8/hour, 20 minutes). From Schiphol Airport, your best option is the **bus** (4-10/hour, 40 minutes, €5—buy ticket from driver, bus #300).

Arrival in Haarlem: If you arrive at the train station, you'll see that two parallel streets flank the station (Kruisweg and Jansweg). Head up either one, and you'll reach the town square and church within 10 minutes. Buses from Schiphol Airport stop both in the center (Centrum/Verwulft stop, a short walk from Grote Markt) and at the train station.

Sights

▲▲GROTE MARKT (MARKET SQUARE)

Haarlem's Grote Markt, where 10 streets converge, is the town's delightful centerpiece...as it has been for 700 years. Enjoy a coffee or beer here, simmering in Dutch good living. Observe. Sit and gaze at the church, appreciating essentially the same scene that Dutch artists captured centuries ago in oil paintings that now hang in museums. Until the 1990s, trolleys ran through the square, and cars were parked everywhere. But now it's a pedestrian zone, with market stalls filling the square on Mondays and Saturdays, and café tables dominating on other days.

▲ST. BAVO CHURCH (GROTE KERK)

Haarlem's impressive St. Bavo Church is better known here as the Grote Kerk—the Great Church. One of the best-known landmarks in the Netherlands, it's visible from miles around, rising above the flat plain that surrounds it. This 15th-century Gothic church is worth a look, if only to see Holland's greatest pipe organ (from 1738, 100 feet high). Its more than 5,000 pipes impressed both Handel and Mozart. Note how the organ, which fills the west end, seems to steal the show from the altar. Quirky highlights of the church include a replica of Foucault's pendulum, the "Dog-Whipper's Chapel," and a 400-year-old cannonball.

Cost and Hours: €2.50, not covered by Museumkaart; Mon-Sat 10:00-17:00, closed Sun to tourists except July-Aug, Sun service at 10:00 (May-Oct) and 19:00 (June-Sept); tours offered by request Sat at 14:00 and 14:30, at 14:00 only off-season (€5, includes church entry); Grote Markt 22, tel. 023/553-2040, www.bavo.nl.

Concerts: Consider attending even just part of a concert to hear Holland's greatest pipe organ (regular free concerts Tue at 20:15 mid-May-mid-Oct, additional concerts Thu at 16:00 July-Aug; bring a sweater—the church isn't heated; enter

Haarlem's main square is perfect for people-watching.

through south transept, around the back).

▲▲CORRIE TEN BOOM HOUSE

Haarlem was home to the Ten Boom family, who, from this house, created a safe haven for Jews during World War II. This museum gives the other half of the Anne Frank story—the point of view of those who risked their lives to hide Dutch Jews during the Nazi occupation. The family's story was popularized by Corrie ten Boom's inspirational 1971 book (and 1975 movie), *The Hiding Place.*

Access to the Ten Boom House is by tour only and reservations can be smart. The gentle and loving one-hour tour comes with evangelizing that some may find objectionable.

Cost and Hours: Free, but donations accepted; Tue-Sat first English tour at 10:00, last at 15:00; Nov-March first English tour at 11:00, last at 14:30; closed Sun-Mon year-round; 50 yards north of Grote Markt at Barteljorisstraat 19; the clock-shop people get all wound up if you go inside—wait in the little side street at the door, where tour times are posted; tel. 023/531-0823, www.corrietenboom.com.

Reservations: Tours are limited to 20 people and often fill up. You can reserve a spot only on morning tours—sign up at least 10 days in advance on their website or via email at tours@corrietenboom.com. A donation of €2.50/person is requested if you reserve in advance. Without a reservation, go in the morning to check the sign on the door for openings, then line up about 30-60 minutes before the tour begins. Tuesdays tend to be busiest.

▲TEYLERS MUSEUM

Famous as the oldest museum in the Netherlands, Teylers is a time-warp experience, filled with all sorts of fun curios for science buffs: fossils, minerals, primitive electronic gadgetry, and examples of 18th- and 19th-century technology (it also has two lovely painting galleries and hosts good temporary exhibits).

Cost and Hours: €12.50, €21 combo-ticket with Frans Hals Museum (purchase at TI); includes excellent (and

I'd say, essential) audioguide; Tue-Fri 10:00-17:00, Sat-Sun from 11:00, closed Mon; Spaarne 16, tel. 023/531-9010, www.teylersmuseum.eu. The museum's modern café has good prices and faces a delightful garden.

▲▲FRANS HALS MUSEUM (FRANS HALSMUSEUM)

Haarlem is the hometown of Frans Hals (c. 1582-1666), the foremost Dutch portrait painter of the 17th-century Golden Age. This bold humanist painted everyday people in their warts-and-all glory. He was a forerunner of Impressionist brushwork, a master of composition, and an articulate visual spokesman for his generation.

Your ticket covers the museum's two locations: the main building ("Hof") described here, and the smaller building ("Hal") a short walk away. The refreshing main museum displays many of Hals' greatest paintings and works by other Dutch masters. You'll stand eye-to-eye with life-size, lifelike portraits of Haarlem's citizens—brewers, preachers, workers, bureaucrats, and housewives. Take a close look at the people who built the Dutch Golden Age, and then watched it start to fade.

Cost and Hours: €15 covers both Frans Hals buildings, includes audioguide, €21 combo-ticket with Teylers Museum (purchase at TI); both Frans Hals locations open Tue-Sat 11:00-17:00, Sun from 12:00, closed Mon; main building ("Hof") is a five-minute walk from Grote Markt at Groot Heiligland 62, secondary building ("Hal") is at Grote Markt 16; tel. 023/511-5775, www.franshalsmuseum.nl.

▲RED LIGHT DISTRICT

Wander through a precious little Red Light District, legal since the 1980s (2 blocks northeast of Grote Markt, off Lange Begijnestraat, no senior or student discounts). Don't miss the mall on Begijnesteeg marked by the red neon sign reading 't Steegje ("free"). Just beyond that, the nearby 't Poortje ("office park") costs €6 to enter. Jog to the right to pop into the much more inviting "Red Lantern" (window-shopping welcome, at Korte Begijnestraat 27). As you wander through this area, remember that the people here don't condone prostitution any more than your own community back home probably does; they just find it practical not to criminalize it and drive it underground, but instead to regulate it and keep the practice as safe as possible.

▲DE ADRIAAN WINDMILL

Haarlem's old-time windmill, located just a 10-minute walk from the station, welcomes visitors with a short video, a little museum, and fine town views. The windmill may look old, but it's a replica from 2002 (the original windmill burned down in 1932). Be prepared for steep stairs that are more like ladders—if you get vertigo, skip it.

Cost and Hours: €3.50, €1 for ages

Haarlem's Red Light District

The beach at Zandvoort

5-12, not covered by Museumkaart;
Mon-Fri 13:00-17:00, Sat-Sun from 10:30;
Nov-Feb Mon and Fri 13:00-16:30, Sat-
Sun from 10:30, closed Tue-Thu; Papen-
torenvest 1, tel. 023/545-0259, www.
molenadriaan.nl.

ZANDVOORT

For a quick and easy look at the windy
coastline in a shell lover's Shangri-la,
visit the beach burg of Zandvoort, just 10
minutes away from Haarlem. This pretty,
manicured resort has plenty of cafés,
ice-cream parlors, *Vlaamse friet* stands,
restaurants, and boutiques. Just beyond
the town is the vast and sandy beach,
lined with cafés and rentable chairs.
Above it all is a pedestrian promenade
and a line of high-rise hotels. South of the
main beach, sunbathers work on all-over
tans.

Tourist Information: The helpful TI is
on Bakkerstraat 2 (Mon-Fri 9:00-17:00,
Sat from 10:00, closed Sun, tel. 023/571-
7947, www.vvvzandvoort.nl).

Getting There: It's easy to reach by
train (2/hour from Haarlem, 10 minutes;
2/hour from Amsterdam, 30 minutes).
By bike, it's a breezy 45-minute ride from
Haarlem, heading west and following road
signs for *Bloemendaal,* then *Zandvoort.*

Experiences
SMOKING

Haarlem is a laid-back place for observing
the Dutch approach to recreational marijuana. The town is dotted with about a
dozen coffeeshops, where pot is sold and
smoked by relaxed, noncriminal types.
These easygoing coffeeshops are more
welcoming than they may initially seem—
bartenders understand that Yankee travelers might feel a bit out of their element
and are happy to answer questions.

If you don't like the smell of pot, avoid
places sporting wildly painted walls; plants
in the windows; or Rastafarian yellow, red,
and green. **High Times,** with a living-room
ambience and loaner bongs, is inviting and

Ⓐ *Grote Kerk nave*

Ⓑ *Pew decoration, Grote Kerk*

Ⓒ *Frans Hals Museum*

Ⓓ *Corrie Ten Boom House*

particularly friendly to American visitors. Smokers choose from 14 varieties of joints in racks behind the bar (neatly prepacked in trademarked "Joint Packs," €2-5, open long hours daily, Lange Veerstraat 47, www.coffeeshophightimes.nl).

NIGHTLIFE

Grote Markt is lined with trendy bars that seem made for nursing a drink—**Café Studio** is generally the hot spot for a drink here (at Grote Markt 25); I'd also duck into the dark interior of **In Den Uiver** (near the Grote Kerk entry at Riviervisch-markt 13, live jazz on Tue twice a month). Lange Veerstraat (behind the Grote Kerk) is colorful and bordered with lively spots. Botermarkt (connected to Grote Markt by Koningstraat street) is more convivial and local, as it's less central and away from the tourists—or try the nearby **Jopenkerk** brewpub (described later, under "Eating").

Sleeping

$$$$ ML Hotel, modern yet elegant, is located in a renovated 300-year-old building with a grand staircase, bare floors, comfy high-quality beds, and minimalist touches in its 17 rooms. It's just a block east of Grote Markt, with a bustling brasse-rie and bar, and the recommended ML Restaurant downstairs (family rooms, suites available, breakfast extra, elevator, Klokhuisplein 9, tel. 023/512-3910, www.mlinhaarlem.nl, welkom@mlinhaarlem.nl).

$$$$ Brasss Haarlem rents 14 upscale suites in a turn-of-the-century building once home to Haarlem's first department store. Each cushy room is named after a fish and has an open-floor plan with a see-through bathroom (in-room espresso machine, air-con, Korte Veerstraat 40, tel. 023/542-7804, www.brassshaarlem.nl, info@brassshaarlem.nl).

$$$ Haarlem Hotelsuites, nearby and run by Brasss Haarlem, offers 16 cozy apartment-style units with kitchens (check-in at Brasss Haar-lem, www.haarlem-hotelsuites.nl, haarlemhotelsuites@gmail.com).

$$ Hotel Lion D'Or, across from the train station, is a classy 43-room business hotel with all the professional comforts and pleasingly posh decor (RS%, air-con, elevator, Kruisweg 34, tel. 023/532-1750, www.hotelliondor.nl, reservations@hotelliondor.nl, friendly Dirk Pauw).

$$ Ambassador City Centre Hotel, with 99 comfortable if tight rooms in a big plain hotel, is located just behind the Grote Kerk. If you're willing to trade some street noise for amazing church views, ask for a room in the front (elevator, some stairs, breakfast buffet extra, Oude Groenmarkt 20, tel. 023/512-5300, www.acc-hotel.nl, info@acc-hotel.nl). They also run **$$ Hotel Joops,** with 32 rooms, a block away (studios and apartments with kitchenettes, breakfast extra).

$$ Hotel Malts rents 14 modern, bright, and fresh rooms in a central location for a good price. Owners Henk and Annemarie

Grote Markt cafés are lively by day—and night

Tranquil winter scene in Haarlem

have a wealth of Haarlem knowledge and sit with each guest over coffee to share the town's secrets (honor bar; coffee, tea, and fruit all day; steep stairs and no elevator; Zijlstraat 58, tel. 023/551-2385, www.maltshotel.nl, info@maltshotel.nl).

$ Hotel Amadeus, on Grote Markt, is charming and has 15 small, bright, and basic rooms. Front rooms with views of the square are noisy, while the back rooms are relatively quiet. Breakfast is served in a trendy restaurant overlooking the main square (RS%, use code "RS1516," Grote Markt 10—from the square it's a steep climb to the lounge, check-in at ground-floor restaurant where there's an elevator accessible during open hours, otherwise expect lots of stairs, tel. 023/532-4530, www.amadeus-hotel.com, info@amadeus-hotel.com).

Eating

$$ Jacobus Pieck Eetlokaal is popular with locals for its fine-value "global cuisine," good salads, and unpretentious flair. Sit in the peaceful garden courtyard, at a sidewalk table, or in the romantically cozy interior. The Oriental Peak Salad is a perennial favorite, and the dish of the day (*dagschotel,* €12.50) always sells out (great sandwiches at lunch, Tue-Sat 11:00-16:00 & 17:30-22:00, closed Sun-Mon, cash only, Warmoesstraat 18, behind church, tel. 023/532-6144).

$$$$ De Lachende Javaan ("The Laughing Javanese") is a long-established Indonesian place serving a memorable *rijsttafel* that can be ordered for single diners—a rare option in the Netherlands (Tue-Sun 17:00-22:00, closed Mon, Frankestraat 27, tel. 023/532-8792).

$$$ To Amuse serves creative meals in a modern, unpretentious setting. Their multi-course meals and a la carte dishes impress with interesting ingredients and appealing presentation (Tue-Thu 18:00-22:00, Fri-Sat 12:00-15:00 & 18:00-22:00, closed Sun-Mon; Zijlstraat 56, tel. 023/531-0070).

$$ Pizzeria-Ristorante Venezia, run for 25 years by the same Italian family from Bari, is Haarlem's default place for pizza or pasta (daily 13:00-23:00, Verwulft 7, tel. 023/531-7753). Sit outdoors for quality people-watching, or indoors at a well-worn table.

Dressy Splurge: At **$$$$ Restaurant ML,** expert chef Mark Gratama serves chichi French-fusion cuisine in an elegant and modern dining room below the ML Hotel. This Michelin-rated restaurant offers four- to seven-course tasting menus starting at about €54 (reservations necessary, Tue-Sat 18:00-22:00, closed Sun-Mon, Klokhuisplein 9, tel. 023/534-5343, www.restaurant-ml.nl).

Trendy Brewpub: The Jopen brewery has converted a church into a flashy, popular gastropub called **$ Jopenkerk.** With 18 brews on tap, including a *Hoppenbier* from a 1501 recipe, this is a beer lover's mecca. Budget pub grub—burgers, salads, and quiche—is served on the ground floor; the pricey upstairs restaurant offers more elegant fare (brewpub daily 10:00-24:00; restaurant Tue-Sat 17:30-22:00, closed Sun-Mon; Gedempte Voldersgracht 2, tel. 023/533-4114).

Restaurant Row: If you don't know what you want to eat, stroll the delightful Lange Veerstraat behind the church and survey a fun range of restaurants (from cheap falafels to Cuban, and much more).

Best Ice Cream: Gelateria Bartoli, on the south side of the church, is the local favorite (daily, closed Jan-Feb).

Supermarkets: Albert Heijn has three convenient locations; all are cash only and open daily. One is in the train station, another is at Kruisstraat 10, and their largest store is near the river and recommended Jopenkerk pub at Drossestraat 11. The **DekaMarkt** is a few blocks west of Grote Markt (daily, Gedempte Oudegracht 54, near Hudson's Bay department store).

Practicalities

HELP!

Travel Advisories

For updated health and safety conditions, including any restrictions for your destination, consult the US State Department's international travel website (travel.state. gov).

Emergency and Medical Help

In any of the countries covered in this book, dial 112 for any emergency service—ambulance, police, or fire. You can also ask at your hotel for help—they'll know the nearest medical and emergency services. If you get a minor ailment, do as the locals do and go to a pharmacist for advice.

ETIAS Registration

The European Union may soon require US and Canadian citizens to register online with the European Travel Information and Authorization System (ETIAS) before entering Schengen Zone countries. For the latest, check www.etiasvisa.com.

Theft or Loss

To replace a passport, you'll need to go in person to an embassy (listed later). If your credit and debit cards disappear, cancel and replace them. If your things are lost or stolen, file a police report, either on the spot or within a day or two; you'll need it to submit an insurance claim for lost or stolen rail passes or electronics, and it can help with replacing your passport or credit and debit cards. For more information, see RickSteves.com/help.

Damage Control for Lost Cards

If you lose your credit or debit card, report the loss immediately to your card company. Visa's and MasterCard's websites list European toll-free numbers by country. You can generally receive a temporary replacement card within two or three business days in Europe.

Avoiding Theft

Anywhere in Europe, thieves target tourists, especially in bigger cities and towns. Pickpockets often stage a commotion or a fight to enable them to work unnoticed. Someone in a small group pushing you as you enter or exit a crowded subway car may slip a hand in your pocket or day bag. Thieves snatch purses and break into cars.

Be on guard, and treat any disturbance around you as a smoke screen for theft. Remember to wear a money belt (tucked under your clothes) to keep your cash, credit cards, and passport secure; carry only the money you need for the day in your front pocket. Pickpockets are common in crowded, touristy places, but fortunately, violent crime is rare. Thieves don't want to hurt you; they just want your money and gadgets.

US Embassies and Consulates

ENGLAND
In London: Tel. 020/7499-9000 (all services), no walk-in passport services, 24 Grosvenor Square, http://uk.usembassy.gov/

FRANCE
In Paris: Tel. 01 43 12 22 22, 2 Avenue Gabriel, http://fr.usembassy.gov

GERMANY
In Berlin: Tel. 030/83050, by appointment only, closed Sat-Sun and last Thu of month, Clayallee 170; http://de.usembassy.gov

ITALY
In Rome: 24-hour emergency tel. 06-46741, nonemergency tel. 06-4674-2420, Via Vittorio Veneto 121, http://it.usembassy.gov

In Florence: Tel. 055-266-951, Lungarno Vespucci 38, http://it.usembassy.gov

NETHERLANDS
In Amsterdam: Tel. 020/575-5309, after-hours emergency tel. 070/310-2209, Museumplein 19, services by appointment only, http://nl.usembassy.gov.

SPAIN
In Barcelona: Tel. 932-802-227, after-hours emergency tel. 915-872-200, Paseo Reina Elisenda de Montcada 23, http://es.usembassy.gov

SWITZERLAND
In Bern: Tel. 031-357-7011, after-hours tel. 031-357-7777, Sulgeneckstrasse 19, services by appointment only, closed Sat-Sun, http://ch.usembassy.gov

MONEY

Here's my basic strategy for using money in Europe:
- Upon arrival, head for a cash machine (ATM) at the airport and withdraw some local currency, using a debit card with low international transaction fees.
- In general, pay for bigger expenses with a credit card and use cash for smaller purchases and tips. Use a debit card only for cash withdrawals.
- Keep your cards and cash safe in a money belt.

What to Bring

I pack the following and keep it all safe in my money belt.

Debit Card: Use at ATMs to withdraw cash.

Credit Card: Handy for bigger transactions (at hotels, shops, restaurants, car-rental agencies, and so on), payment machines, and online purchases.

Backup Card: Some travelers carry a third card (debit or credit; ideally from a different bank), in case one gets lost, demagnetized, eaten by a temperamental machine, or simply doesn't work.

A Stash of Cash: I carry US $100-200 as a cash backup, which comes in handy in an emergency (such as if your ATM card gets eaten by the machine).

What NOT to Bring: Resist the urge to buy the local currency before your trip or you'll pay the price in bad stateside exchange rates. I've yet to see a European airport that doesn't have plenty of ATMs.

Before You Go

Report your travel dates. Let your bank know that you'll be using your debit and credit cards in Europe, and when and where you're headed.

Know your PIN. Make sure you know the numeric, four-digit PIN for all your cards, both debit and credit. Request it if you don't have one, as it may be required for some purchases in Europe.

Adjust your ATM withdrawal limit. Find out how much you can take out daily and ask for a higher daily withdrawal limit if you want to get more cash at once. Note that European ATMs will withdraw funds only from checking accounts; you're unlikely to have access to your savings account.

Ask about fees. For any purchase or withdrawal made with a card, you may be charged a currency conversion fee (1-3 percent) and a Visa or MasterCard international transaction fee (less than 1 percent).

Rick's Tip: *Looking to upgrade your European travel skills? You'll find plenty of practical info at* **RickSteves.com/travel-tips.**

In Europe

Using Cash Machines: European cash machines have English-language instructions and work just like they do at home—except they spit out local currency instead of dollars, calculated at the day's standard bank-to-bank rate.

In most places, ATMs are easy to locate. When possible, withdraw cash

Exchange Rates

1 euro (€1) = about $1.20. To convert prices in euros to dollars, add 20 percent: €20 is about $24.

1 British pound (£1) = about $1.30. To convert prices in pounds to dollars, add 30 percent: £20 = about $26.

1 Swiss franc (1 CHF) = about $1.

Check Oanda.com for the latest exchange rates.

---

from a bank-run ATM located just outside that bank. If your debit card doesn't work, try a lower amount—your request may have exceeded your withdrawal limit or the ATM's limit.

Avoid "independent" ATMs, such as Travelex, Euronet, Moneybox, Your Cash, Cardpoint, and Cashzone. These have high fees, can be less secure than a bank ATM, and may try to trick users with "dynamic currency conversion" (see later).

Exchanging Cash: Avoid exchanging money in Europe; it's a big rip-off. In a pinch you can always find exchange desks at major train stations or airports—convenient but with crummy rates. Banks generally do not exchange money unless you have an account with them.

Using Credit Cards**:** Despite some differences between European and US cards, there's little to worry about. US credit cards generally work fine in Europe. I've been inconvenienced a few times by unattended payment machines (transit-ticket kiosks, parking, self-service gas stations, toll booths) where US cards may not work. Always carry cash as a backup.

Dynamic Currency Conversion: Some European merchants and hoteliers cheerfully charge you for converting your purchase price into dollars (called dynamic currency conversion, or DCC). If it's offered, refuse this "service." You'll pay

extra for the expensive convenience of
seeing your charge in dollars.

Tipping

Tipping in Europe isn't as automatic and
generous as it is in the US. For special
service, tips are appreciated, but not
expected. As in the US, the right amount
depends on your resources and the cir-
cumstances, but some general guidelines
apply.

Restaurants: You don't need to tip
if you order your food at a counter. At
restaurants, check the menu to see if service is included; if it isn't, generally a tip
of 5-10 percent is normal. France is the
exception, where tipping isn't necessary
or expected.

Taxis: For a typical ride, round up your
fare a bit (for instance, if your fare is €13,
pay €14).

Customs for American Shoppers

You can take home $800 worth of items
per person duty-free, once every 31 days.
Many processed and packaged foods
are allowed, including vacuum-packed
cheeses, dried herbs, jams, baked goods,
candy, chocolate, oil, vinegar, mustard,
and honey. Fresh fruits and vegetables and
most meats are not allowed, with exceptions for some canned items. As for alcohol, you can bring in one liter duty-free.

For details on allowable goods, customs
rules, and duty rates, visit http://help.cbp.
gov.

SIGHTSEEING

This book offers tips on the best times
to see specific sights. Try visiting popular
sights very early or very late. Evening visits
(when possible) are usually peaceful, with
fewer crowds. Late morning is usually the
worst time to visit a popular sight.

Reservations and Advance Tickets

Given how precious your vacation time is,
I recommend getting reservations for any
must-see sight that offers them.

To deal with lines, many popular sights
sell advance tickets that guarantee admission at a certain time of day and allow
you to skip entry lines. It's worth giving
up some spontaneity to book in advance.
While hundreds of tourists sweat in long
ticket-buying lines—or arrive to find the
sight sold out—those who've booked
ahead are assured of getting in. In some
cases, getting a ticket in advance simply
means buying your ticket earlier on the
same day. But for other sights, you may
need to book weeks or even months in
advance. As soon as you're ready to com-
mit to a certain date, book it.

SLEEPING

Extensive and opinionated listings of
good-value rooms are a major feature of
this book's Sleeping sections. Rather than
list accommodations scattered throughout a town, I choose hotels in my favorite
neighborhoods that are convenient to
your sightseeing.

Accommodations
Hotels

Europe offers a wide variety of hotels:
homey guesthouses, traditional old hotels,
impersonal business-class chains, and
chic boutiques.

In this book, the price for a double
room in a hotel ranges from €60 (very
basic) to €200-plus (maximum plumbing and the works). You'll pay more for
accommodations in bigger cities. While I
favor family-run hotels, I also recommend
chain hotels when they're a good value.

If you arrive at your hotel in the
morning, your room probably won't be
ready. Check your bag safely at the hotel
and dive right into sightseeing.

Sleep Code

Hotels in this book are classified based on the average price of a standard double room in high season:

Code	England	France	Spain, Italy, Germany & Netherlands	Switzerland
$$$$ Splurge	Over £160	Over €250	Over €170	Over 220 CHF
$$$ Pricier	£120-160	€190-250	€130-170	180-220 CHF
$$ Moderate	£80-120	€130-190	€90-130	120-180 CHF
$ Budget	£40-80	€70-130	€50-90	80-120 CHF
¢ Backpacker	Under £40	Under €70	Under €50	Under 80 CHF

Unless otherwise noted, credit cards are accepted, and free Wi-Fi is available. Comparison-shop by checking prices at several hotels (on each hotel's own website, on a booking site, or by email). For the best deal, book directly with the hotel. Ask for a discount if paying in cash; if the listing includes **RS%**, request a Rick Steves discount.

Note that the French have a simple hotel rating system based on amenities and rated by stars, indicated in this book by asterisks, from basic hotels (*) up to the most luxurious (*****).

Some cities require hoteliers to charge a **tourist tax** (about €1-5/person, per night, often payable only in cash).

Hoteliers can be a great help and source of advice. Most know their city well and can assist you with everything from public transit and airport connections to finding a good restaurant, the nearest launderette, or a late-night pharmacy.

The EU requires that hotels collect your name, nationality, and ID number. When you check in, the receptionist will normally ask for your passport and may keep it for anywhere from a couple of minutes to a couple of hours.

Bed-and-Breakfasts

B&Bs can offer good-value accommodations in excellent locations. Usually converted family homes or apartments, they can range from humble rooms with communal kitchens to high-end boutique accommodations with extra amenities. Because the B&B scene is constantly changing, it's smart to supplement this book's recommendations with your own research.

Short-Term Rentals

A short-term rental is an increasingly popular alternative, especially if you plan to settle in one location for several nights. Websites such as Airbnb, FlipKey, Booking.com, and the HomeAway family of sites (HomeAway, VRBO, and VacationRentals) let you browse a wide range of properties. Alternatively, rental agencies such as InterhomeUSA.com or RentaVilla.com can provide more personalized service.

Hostels

A hostel provides cheap beds in dorms where you sleep alongside strangers for about €25-30 per night. Travelers of any age are welcome if they don't mind dorm-style accommodations and meeting

Making Hotel Reservations

Requesting a Reservation: For family-run hotels, it's generally best to book your room directly via email or phone. For business-class hotels, or if you'd rather book online, reserve directly through the hotel's official website (not a booking website).

Here's what the hotelier wants to know:
- Type(s) of rooms you want and size of your party
- Number of nights you'll stay
- Your arrival and departure dates, written European-style as day/month/year (18/06/22 or 18 June 2022)
- Special requests (en suite bathroom, cheapest room, twin beds vs. double bed, quiet room)
- Applicable discounts (such as a Rick Steves reader discount, cash discount, or promotional rate)

Confirming a Reservation: Most places will request a credit-card number to hold your room. If you're using an online reservation form, look for the *https* or a lock icon at the top of your browser. If the website isn't secure, it's best to share that confidential info via a phone call.

Canceling a Reservation: If you must cancel, do so with as much notice as possible, especially for smaller family-run places. Cancellation policies can be strict; read the fine print before you book. Many discount deals require prepayment, with no cancellation refunds.

Reconfirming a Reservation: Always call or email to reconfirm your room reservation a few days in advance. For B&Bs or very small hotels, I call again on my day of arrival to tell my host what time to expect me (especially important if arriving late—after 17:00).

Phoning: For tips on calling hotels overseas, see page 973.

other travelers. Most hostels offer kitchen facilities, guest computers, Wi-Fi, and a self-service laundry. Family and private rooms are often available.

Independent hostels tend to be easygoing, colorful, and informal (no membership required; www.hostelworld.com). You may pay slightly less by booking directly with the hostel. **Official hostels** are part of Hostelling International (HI) and share a booking site (www.hihostels.com). HI hostels typically require that you be a member or else pay a bit more per night.

EATING

Each country has its own cuisine, specialties, deals, and unique quirks. See the "Cuisine Scene at a Glance" sidebars at the beginning of every country section for my best advice.

In any country, you'll find that the most authentic eateries are family-run and located in lower-rent spots a few blocks off the main square. A posted menu in the native language is a good tip-off they have a loyal, local following. As you travel, make it a point to try regional specialties. Enjoy salade niçoise in Nice, paella in Barcelona, and the best Wurst in Germany.

Using Online Services to Your Advantage

From booking services to user reviews, online businesses play a greater role in travelers' planning than ever before. Take advantage of their pluses—and be wise to their downsides.

Booking Sites

Booking websites Booking.com and Hotels.com offer one-stop shopping for hotels. To be listed, a hotel must pay a sizable commission. When you use an online booking service, you're adding a middleman. To support small, family-run hotels whose world is more difficult than ever, book direct.

Short-Term Rental Sites

Rental juggernaut Airbnb and other short-term rental sites allow travelers to rent rooms and apartments directly from locals. Airbnb fans appreciate feeling part of a real neighborhood as "temporary Europeans."

Critics view Airbnb as creating unfair competition for established guesthouse owners. As a lover of Europe, I share the worry of those who see residents nudged aside by tourists. But as an advocate for travelers, I appreciate the value and cultural intimacy Airbnb provides.

User Reviews

User-generated review sites and apps such as Yelp and TripAdvisor can give you a consensus of opinions about everything from hotels and restaurants to sights and nightlife. But a user-generated review is based on the limited experience of one person, while a guidebook is the work of a trained researcher who visits many restaurants and hotels year after year.

Both types of information have their place, and in many ways, they're complementary. If something is well reviewed in a guidebook and it also gets good online reviews, it's likely a winner.

I like to order family-style so I can eat my way through more of the menu. Sometimes, rather than getting two main courses, my travel partner and I share a little buffet of appetizers or first courses—they're filling and less expensive. These small plates go by different names throughout Europe: tapas in Spain and antipasti in Italy.

To save money, mix picnics and quick, budget eats with atmospheric restaurant meals. If you splurge one day, go cheap the next; you can find a satisfying dinner for the equivalent of $25 or less anywhere in Europe. If you have more money, of course, it's delightful to spend it dining well.

STAYING CONNECTED

One of the most common questions I hear from travelers is, "How can I stay connected in Europe?" The short answer is: more easily and cheaply than you might think. The simplest solution is to bring your own device—mobile phone, tablet, or laptop—and use it just as you would at home (following the money-saving tips below). For more details, see RickSteves.com/phoning. For a very practical one-hour talk covering tech issues for travelers, see RickSteves.com/mobile-travel-skills.

Restaurant Code

Eateries in this book are categorized (using dollar signs) according to the average cost of a typical main course. Drinks, desserts, and splurge items can raise the price considerably.

Code	England	France	Spain, Italy, Germany & Netherlands	Switzerland
$$$$ Splurge	Over £120	Over €30	Over €25	Over 30 CHF
$$$ Pricier	£15-20	€25-30	€18-25	20-30 CHF
$$ Moderate	£10-15	€15-25	€12-18	10-20 CHF
$ Budget	Under £10	Under €15	Under €12	Under 10 CHF

Using a Mobile Phone in Europe

Sign up for an international plan. To stay connected at a lower cost, sign up for an international service plan through your carrier. Most providers offer a simple bundle that includes calling, messaging, and data. Your normal plan may already include international coverage (T-Mobile's does).

Use free Wi-Fi whenever possible. Unless you have an unlimited-data plan, you're best off saving most of your online tasks for Wi-Fi. You can access the Internet, send texts, and even make voice calls over Wi-Fi.

Minimize the use of your cellular network. The best way to make sure you're not accidentally burning through data is to put your device in "airplane" mode (which also disables phone calls and texts), turn your Wi-Fi back on, and connect to networks as needed. When you need to get online but can't find Wi-Fi, simply turn on your cellular network (or turn off airplane mode) just long enough for the task at hand. Disable automatic updates so your apps will update only when you're on Wi-Fi.

Use Wi-Fi calling and messaging apps. Skype, WhatsApp, FaceTime, and Google Hangouts are great for making free or low-cost calls or sending texts over Wi-Fi worldwide. Just log on to a Wi-Fi network, then connect with any of your friends or family members who use the same service.

Buy a European SIM Card. If you anticipate making a lot of local calls or need a local phone number, , consider buying a SIM card in Europe to replace the one in your (unlocked) US phone or tablet.

TRANSPORTATION

This section covers the basics on trains, buses, rental cars, and flights.

Trains

Considering the efficiency of Europe's trains (and buses), you'd never need to use a car. You can buy point-to-point tickets (either in advance or as you travel) or buy a rail pass.

High-speed, long-distance, international, and overnight trains are more likely to require reservations. If so, you automatically get reservations when you buy point-to-point tickets, but if you're using a rail pass, you'll need to make any required reservations yourself. You can reserve the more critical journeys from home (through RickSteves.com/rail); otherwise you can make them all at one time at any staffed station in Europe.

To check train schedules online, see Bahn.com (Germany's excellent Europe-wide timetable).

Tips on Internet Security

Make sure that your device is running the latest versions of its operating system, security software, and apps. Next, ensure that your device and key programs (like email) are password-protected. On the road, use only secure, password-protected Wi-Fi. Ask the hotel or café staff for the specific name of their network, and make sure you log on to that exact one.

If you must access your financial info online, use a banking app rather than accessing your account via a browser, and use a cellular connection, not Wi-Fi. Never log on to personal finance sites on a public computer. If you're very concerned, consider subscribing to a VPN (virtual private network).

Tickets

Point-to-point tickets are just that: tickets bought individually to get you from Point A to Point B.

First Class vs. Second Class: On most trains in most countries, tickets in second class cost about a third less than those in first class. First-class cars are more spacious and less crowded than second class, but riding in second class gets you there at the same time, and with the same scenery.

Discount Fares: If you reserve a ticket on a fast train in advance and are comfortable committing to particular departure times, you can usually enjoy substantial savings over full-fare tickets. Discounted fares go on sale several months in advance and remain available until one day before departure—unless all the cheap seats sell out early (which often happens). Rules vary per country.

Savings on Slow Trains: You can save money on point-to-point tickets if you're willing to limit yourself to regional trains.

Buying Tickets: You can buy tickets online, with a smartphone app, at train station ticket windows, from ticket machines, or at travel agencies. For long-haul runs or travel on a busy weekend or holiday, it can be cheaper to buy tickets in advance **online** from the train company's website (NationalRail.co.uk for Britain, Eurostar.com for the Chunnel linking England with France, Belgium, and the Netherlands, Sncf.com for France, Bahn.com for Germany, Trenitalia.com for Italy, Ns.nl for the Netherlands, Sbb.ch for Switzerland, and Renfe.com for Spain).

If you must board a train without a ticket, find the conductor before they find (and fine) you; ask to buy a ticket (you'll pay extra for this service).

Rail Passes

A rail pass covers train travel in one or more countries for a certain number of days (either a continuous span of days or a number of days spread over a wider window of time). Depending on how many trips you take, passes can offer a savings over regular point-to-point tickets.

Pass prices vary depending on the number of days and type of pass you choose, and discounts are offered for two or more people traveling together.

For a multicountry trip, a Eurail pass generally offers the best deal. For instance, the Global Pass covers virtually all European countries, and allows for travel on 4 to 15 travel days spread out (4, 5, or 7 days within one month, 10 or 15 days within two months), or for continuous periods lasting between 15 days and three months. For advice on figuring out the smartest options for your train trip, visit RickSteves.com/rail.

How to Dial

To make an international call, follow the dialing instructions below. Drop an initial zero, if present, when dialing a European phone number—except when calling Italy. I've used the telephone number of one of my recommended Paris hotels as an example (tel. 01 45 51 63 02).

From a Mobile Phone

It's easy to dial with a mobile phone. Whether calling from the US to Europe, country to country within Europe, or from Europe to the US—it's all the same. Press zero until you get a + sign, enter the country code (33 for France), then dial the phone number.

→ To call the Paris hotel from any location, dial +33 1 45 51 63 02.

From a US Landline to Europe

Dial 011 (US/Canada access code), country code (33 for France), and phone number.

→ To call the Paris hotel from home, dial 011 33 1 45 51 63 02.

From a European Landline to the US or Europe

Dial 00 (Europe access code), country code (1 for the US, 33 for France), and phone number.

→ To call my US office from France, dial 00 1 425 771 8303.

→ To call the Paris hotel from Germany, dial 00 33 1 45 51 63 02.

For a complete list of European country codes and more phoning help, see www.howtocallabroad.com.

Long-Distance Buses

While buses don't offer as extensive a network as trains, they do cover the most popular cities for travelers, quite often with direct connections. Bus tickets are sold on the spot (on board and/or at kiosks at some bus terminals), but because the cheapest fares often sell out, it's best to book online as soon as you're sure of your plans (at a minimum, book a few days ahead to nab the best prices).

Renting a Car

It's cheaper to arrange most car rentals from the US, so research and compare rates before you go. Most of the major US rental agencies (including Avis, Budget, Enterprise, Hertz, and Thrifty) have offices throughout Europe. Also consider the two major Europe-based agencies, Europcar and Sixt. Consolidators such as Auto Europe (www.autoeurope.com—or the sometimes cheaper www.autoeurope.eu) compare rates at several companies to get you the best deal.

Figure on paying roughly $250 for a one-week rental for a basic compact car. Allow extra for supplemental insurance, fuel, tolls, and parking.

Manual vs. Automatic: Almost all rental cars in Europe are manual by default—and cars with a stick shift are generally cheaper. If you need an automatic, request one in advance.

Picking Up Your Car: Always check the hours of the location you choose: Many rental offices close from midday Saturday until Monday morning and, in

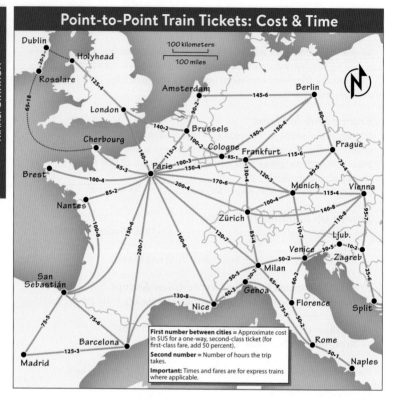

Point-to-Point Train Tickets: Cost & Time

First number between cities = Approximate cost in $US for a one-way, second-class ticket (for first-class fare, add 50 percent).

Second number = Number of hours the trip takes.

Important: Times and fares are for express trains where applicable.

smaller towns, at lunchtime. When you pick up the car, check it thoroughly. Rental agencies in Europe are very strict when it comes to charging for even minor dings, so make sure any damage is noted on your rental agreement. Before driving off, find out how your car's gearshift, lights, turn signals, wipers, radio, and fuel cap function, and know what kind of fuel the car takes (diesel vs. unleaded). When you return the car, make sure the agent verifies its condition with you. Some drivers take pictures of the returned vehicle as proof of its condition.

Car Insurance Options

When you rent a car in Europe, the price typically includes liability insurance, which covers harm to other cars or motorists—but not the rental car itself. To limit your financial risk in case of damage to the

rental, choose one of these options: Buy a Collision Damage Waiver (CDW) with a low or zero deductible from the car-rental company (roughly 30-40 percent extra), get coverage through your credit card (free, but more complicated), or get collision insurance as part of a larger travel-insurance policy. For more on car-rental insurance, see RickSteves.com/cdw.

Driving

Be aware of typical European road rules; for example, many countries require headlights to be turned on at all times, and you're not allowed to turn right on a red light, unless a sign or signal specifically authorizes it.

Be warned that driving is restricted in many Italian city centers. If you drive in an area marked Zona Traffico Limitato (ZTL, often shown above a red circle),

Resources from Rick Steves

Begin Your Trip at RickSteves.com

My mobile-friendly **website** is *the* place to explore Europe in preparation for your trip. You'll find thousands of fun articles, videos, and radio interviews; a wealth of money-saving tips for planning your dream trip; travel news dispatches; a video library of my travel talks; my travel blog; and my latest guidebook updates (www.ricksteves.com/update).

Our **Travel Forum** is a well-groomed collection of message boards where our travel-savvy community answers questions and shares personal travel experiences—and our well-traveled staff chimes in when they can be helpful.

Our **online Travel Store** offers bags and accessories that I've designed to help you travel smarter and lighter. These include my popular carry-on bags (which I live out of four months a year), money belts, totes, toiletries kits, adapters, guidebooks, and planning maps.

Our website can also help you find the perfect **rail pass** for your itinerary and your budget.

Rick Steves' Tours, Guidebooks, TV Shows, and More

Small Group Tours: Want to travel with greater efficiency and less stress? We offer more than 40 itineraries reaching the best destinations in this book...and beyond. You'll enjoy both great guides and a fun bunch of travel partners. For all the details, and to get our tour catalog, visit RickSteves.com/tours or call us at 425/608-4217.

Books: This book is just one of many in my series on European travel, which includes country and city guidebooks, Snapshots (excerpted chapters from bigger guides), Pocket guides (full-color little books on big cities), and my budget-travel skills handbook, *Rick Steves Europe Through the Back Door.* A complete list of my titles—including phrase books; cruising guides; and travelogues on European art, history, and culture—appears near the end of this book.

TV Shows and Travel Talks: My public television series, *Rick Steves' Europe,* covers Europe from top to bottom with over 100 half-hour episodes (watch full episodes at my website). My free online video library, Rick Steves Classroom Europe, offers a searchable database of short video clips on European history and culture. And, to raise your travel I.Q., check out the video versions of our popular classes (covering most European countries as well as travel skills).

Radio: My weekly public radio show, *Travel with Rick Steves,* features interviews with travel experts from around the world. It airs on 400 public radio stations across the US, or you can hear it as a podcast. A complete archive of programs is available on my website.

Audio Tours on My Free App: I've produced dozens of free, self-guided audio tours of the top sights in Europe. For those tours and other audio content, get my free **Rick Steves Audio Europe app,** an extensive online library organized by destination. For more on the app, see page 17.

your license plate can be photographed and a hefty (€80-plus) fine mailed to your home without you ever being stopped by a cop.

You'll pay to use tollways in Italy, France, and Spain, and will need to buy a toll sticker if you enter Switzerland.

At self-service gas pumps and automated parking garages, your US credit and debit cards might not work. Carry cash to fuel your trip.

If you have questions about road rules, ask your car-rental company or check the US State Department website (Travel. State.gov, search for your country in the "Country Information" box, then click "Travel & Transportation").

Flights

To compare flight costs and times, begin with an online travel search engine: **Kayak** is the top site for flights to and within Europe, easy-to-use **Google Flights** has price alerts, and **Skyscanner** includes many inexpensive flights within Europe.

Flights to Europe: Start looking for international flights about four to six months before your trip, especially for peak-season travel. Depending on your itinerary, it can be efficient and no more expensive to fly into one city and out of another.

Flights within Europe: Flying between European cities is surprisingly affordable. Before buying a long-distance train or bus ticket, check the cost of a flight on one of Europe's airlines, whether a major carrier or a no-frills outfit like **Easyjet** or **Ryanair.**

Be aware that flying with a discount airline can have drawbacks, such as minimal customer service and time-consuming treks to secondary airports.

CONVERSIONS

Numbers and Stumblers

- Europeans write a few of their numbers differently than we do: 1 = 1, 4 = 4, 7 = 7.
- In Europe, dates appear as day/month/year; Christmas 2022 is 25/12/22.
- What Americans call the second floor of a building is the first floor in Europe.
- On escalators and moving sidewalks, Europeans keep the left "lane" open for passing. Keep to the right.

Clothing and Shoe Sizes

Women: For clothing or shoe sizes, add 30-32 (US shirt size 10 = European size 40 or 42, depending on the country; US shoe size 8 = European size 38-39).

Men: For shirts, multiply by 2 and add about 8 (US size 15 = European size 38). For jackets and suits, add 10. For shoes, add 32-34.

Children: Clothing is sized in centimeters by height (2.5 cm = 1 inch), so a US size 8 roughly equates to 132-140. For shoes up to size 13, add 16-18, and for sizes 1 and up, add 30-32.

Metric Conversions

A kilogram equals 1,000 grams and about 2.2 pounds. One hundred **grams** (a common unit at markets) is about a quarter-pound. A kilometer is six-tenths of a mile. One meter is 39 inches—just over a yard.

Packing Checklist

Whether you're traveling for five days or five weeks, you won't need more than this. Pack light to enjoy the sweet freedom of true mobility.

Clothing

- ❏ 5 shirts: long- & short-sleeve
- ❏ 2 pairs pants (or skirts/capris)
- ❏ 1 pair shorts
- ❏ 5 pairs underwear & socks
- ❏ 1 pair walking shoes
- ❏ Sweater or warm layer
- ❏ Rainproof jacket with hood
- ❏ Tie, scarf, belt, and/or hat
- ❏ Swimsuit
- ❏ Sleepwear/loungewear

Money

- ❏ Debit card(s)
- ❏ Credit card(s)
- ❏ Hard cash (US $100-200)
- ❏ Money belt

Documents

- ❏ Passport
- ❏ Tickets & confirmations: flights, hotels, trains, rail pass, car rental, sight entries
- ❏ Driver's license
- ❏ Student ID, hostel card, etc.
- ❏ Photocopies of important documents
- ❏ Insurance details
- ❏ Guidebooks & maps

Toiletries Kit

- ❏ Basics: soap, shampoo, toothbrush, toothpaste, floss, deodorant, sunscreen, brush/comb, etc.
- ❏ Medicines & vitamins
- ❏ First-aid kit
- ❏ Glasses/contacts/sunglasses
- ❏ Sewing kit
- ❏ Packet of tissues (for WC)
- ❏ Earplugs

Electronics

- ❏ Mobile phone
- ❏ Camera & related gear
- ❏ Tablet/ebook reader/laptop
- ❏ Headphones/earbuds
- ❏ Chargers & batteries
- ❏ Phone car charger & mount (or GPS device)
- ❏ Plug adapters

Miscellaneous

- ❏ Daypack
- ❏ Sealable plastic baggies
- ❏ Laundry supplies: soap, laundry bag, clothesline, spot remover
- ❏ Small umbrella
- ❏ Travel alarm/watch
- ❏ Notepad & pen
- ❏ Journal

Optional Extras

- ❏ Second pair of shoes (flip-flops, sandals, tennis shoes, boots)
- ❏ Travel hairdryer
- ❏ Picnic supplies
- ❏ Water bottle
- ❏ Fold-up tote bag
- ❏ Small flashlight
- ❏ Mini binoculars
- ❏ Small towel or washcloth
- ❏ Inflatable pillow/neck rest
- ❏ Tiny lock
- ❏ Address list (to mail postcards)
- ❏ Extra passport photos

French Survival Phrases

When using the phonetics, try to nasalize the <u>n</u> sound.

English	French	Pronunciation
Good day.	Bonjour.	bohn-zhoor
Mrs. / Mr.	Madame / Monsieur	mah-dahm / muhs-yur
Do you speak English?	Parlez-vous anglais?	par-lay-voo ah<u>n</u>-glay
Yes. / No.	Oui. / Non.	wee / noh<u>n</u>
I understand.	Je comprends.	zhuh koh<u>n</u>-prah<u>n</u>
I don't understand.	Je ne comprends pas.	zhuh nuh koh<u>n</u>-prah<u>n</u> pah
Please.	S'il vous plaît.	see voo play
Thank you.	Merci.	mehr-see
I'm sorry.	Désolé.	day-zoh-lay
Excuse me.	Pardon.	par-doh<u>n</u>
(No) problem.	(Pas de) problème.	(pah duh) proh-blehm
It's good.	C'est bon.	say boh<u>n</u>
Goodbye.	Au revoir.	oh vwahr
one / two	un / deux	uh<u>n</u> / duh
three / four	trois / quatre	twah / kah-truh
five / six	cinq / six	sa<u>n</u>k / sees
seven / eight	sept / huit	seht / weet
nine / ten	neuf / dix	nuhf / dees
How much is it?	Combien?	koh<u>n</u>-bee-a<u>n</u>
Write it?	Ecrivez?	ay-kree-vay
Is it free?	C'est gratuit?	say grah-twee
Included?	Inclus?	a<u>n</u>-klew
Where can I buy / find...?	Où puis-je acheter / trouver...?	oo pwee-zhuh ah-shuh-tay / troo-vay
I'd like / We'd like...	Je voudrais / Nous voudrions...	zhuh voo-dray / noo voo-dree-oh<u>n</u>
...a room.	...une chambre.	ewn shah<u>n</u>-bruh
...a ticket to _____.	...un billet pour _____.	uh<u>n</u> bee-yay poor _____
Is it possible?	C'est possible?	say poh-see-bluh
Where is...?	Où est...?	oo ay
...the train station	...la gare	lah gar
...the bus station	...la gare routière	lah gar root-yehr
...tourist information	...l'office du tourisme	loh-fees dew too-reez-muh
Where are the toilets?	Où sont les toilettes?	oo soh<u>n</u> lay twah-leht
men	hommes	ohm
women	dames	dahm
left / right	à gauche / à droite	ah gohsh / ah dwaht
straight	tout droit	too dwah
When does this open / close?	Ça ouvre / ferme à quelle heure?	sah oo-vruh / fehrm ah kehl ur
At what time?	À quelle heure?	ah kehl ur
Just a moment.	Un moment.	uh<u>n</u> moh-mah<u>n</u>
now / soon / later	maintenant / bientôt / plus tard	ma<u>n</u>-tuh-nah<u>n</u> / bee-a<u>n</u>-toh / plew tar
today / tomorrow	aujourd'hui / demain	oh-zhoor-dwee / duh-ma<u>n</u>

For more user-friendly French phrases, check out *Rick Steves French Phrase Book* or *Rick Steves French, Italian & German Phrase Book*.

In a French Restaurant

English	French	Pronunciation
I'd like / We'd like...	Je voudrais / Nous voudrions...	zhuh voo-dray / noo voo-dree-oh<u>n</u>
...to reserve...	...réserver...	ray-zehr-vay
...a table for one / two.	...une table pour un / deux.	ewn tah-bluh poor uh<u>n</u> / duh
Is this seat free?	C'est libre?	say lee-bruh
The menu (in English), please.	La carte (en anglais), s'il vous plaît.	lah kart (ah<u>n</u> ah<u>n</u>-glay) see voo play
service (not) included	service (non) compris	sehr-vees (noh<u>n</u>) koh<u>n</u>-pree
to go	à emporter	ah ah<u>n</u>-por-tay
with / without	avec / sans	ah-vehk / sah<u>n</u>
and / or	et / ou	ay / oo
special of the day	plat du jour	plah dew zhoor
specialty of the house	spécialité de la maison	spay-see-ah-lee-tay duh lah may-zoh<u>n</u>
appetizers	hors d'oeuvre	or duh-vruh
first course (soup, salad)	entrée	ah<u>n</u>-tray
main course (meat, fish)	plat principal	plah pra<u>n</u>-see-pahl
bread	pain	pa<u>n</u>
cheese	fromage	froh-mahzh
sandwich	sandwich	sah<u>n</u>d-weech
soup	soupe	soop
salad	salade	sah-lahd
meat	viande	vee-ah<u>n</u>d
chicken	poulet	poo-lay
fish	poisson	pwah-soh<u>n</u>
seafood	fruits de mer	frwee duh mehr
fruit	fruit	frwee
vegetables	légumes	lay-gewm
dessert	dessert	day-sehr
mineral water	eau minérale	oh mee-nay-rahl
tap water	l'eau du robinet	loh dew roh-bee-nay
milk	lait	lay
(orange) juice	jus (d'orange)	zhew (doh-rah<u>n</u>zh)
coffee / tea	café / thé	kah-fay / tay
wine	vin	va<u>n</u>
red / white	rouge / blanc	roozh / blah<u>n</u>
glass / bottle	verre / bouteille	vehr / boo-tay
beer	bière	bee-her
Cheers!	Santé!	sah<u>n</u>-tay
More. / Another.	Plus. / Un autre.	plew / uh<u>n</u> oh-truh
The same.	La même chose.	lah mehm shohz
The bill, please.	L'addition, s'il vous plaît.	lah-dee-see-oh<u>n</u> see voo play
Do you accept credit cards?	Vous prenez les cartes?	voo pruh-nay lay kart
tip	pourboire	poor-bwahr
Delicious!	Délicieux!	day-lee-see-uh

Spanish Survival Phrases

In Spanish, the letter *j* is aspirated, similar to the *j* in "Baja California." In the phonetics, the symbol for this clearing-your-throat sound is the italicized *h*.

English	Spanish	Pronunciation
Good day.	*Buenos días.*	**bweh**-nohs **dee**-ahs
Do you speak English?	*¿Habla Usted inglés?*	**ah**-blah oo-**stehd** een-**glays**
Yes. / No.	*Sí. / No.*	see / noh
I (don't) understand.	*(No) comprendo.*	(noh) kohm-**prehn**-doh
Please.	*Por favor.*	por fah-**bor**
Thank you.	*Gracias.*	**grah**-thee-ahs
I'm sorry.	*Lo siento.*	loh see-**ehn**-toh
Excuse me.	*Perdóne.*	pehr-**doh**-nay
(No) problem.	*(No) problema.*	(noh) proh-**bleh**-mah
Good.	*Bueno.*	**bweh**-noh
Goodbye.	*Adiós.*	ah-dee-**ohs**
one / two	*uno / dos*	**oo**-noh / dohs
three / four	*tres / cuatro*	trehs / **kwah**-troh
five / six	*cinco / seis*	**theen**-koh / says
seven / eight	*siete / ocho*	see-**eh**-tay / **oh**-choh
nine / ten	*nueve / diez*	**nweh**-bay / dee-**ehth**
How much is it?	*¿Cuánto cuesta?*	**kwahn**-toh kweh-stah
Write it?	*¿Me lo escribe?*	may loh eh-**skree**-bay
Is it free?	*¿Es gratis?*	ehs **grah**-tees
Is it included?	*¿Está incluido?*	eh-**stah** een-kloo-**ee**-doh
Where can I buy / find...?	*¿Dónde puedo comprar / encontrar...?*	**dohn**-day **pweh**-doh kohm-**prar** / ehn-kohn-**trar**
I'd like / We'd like...	*Quiero / Queremos...*	kee-**ehr**-oh / kehr-**eh**-mohs
...a room.	*...una habitación.*	**oo**-nah ah-bee-tah-thee-**ohn**
...a ticket to ____.	*...un billete para ____.*	oon bee-**yeh**-tay **pah**-rah ____
Is it possible?	*¿Es posible?*	ays poh-**see**-blay
Where is...?	*¿Dónde está...?*	**dohn**-day eh-**stah**
...the train station	*...la estación de trenes*	lah eh-stah-thee-**ohn** day **treh**-nehs
...the bus station	*...la estación de autobuses*	lah eh-stah-thee-**ohn** day ow-toh-**boo**-sehs
...the tourist information office	*...la oficina de turismo*	lah oh-fee-**thee**-nah day too-**rees**-moh
Where are the toilets?	*¿Dónde están los servicios?*	**dohn**-day eh-**stahn** lohs sehr-**bee**-thee-ohs
men	*hombres, caballeros*	**ohm**-brehs, kah-bah-**yeh**-rohs
women	*mujeres, damas*	moo-**heh**-rehs, **dah**-mahs
left / right	*izquierda / derecha*	eeth-kee-**ehr**-dah / deh-**reh**-chah
straight	*derecho*	deh-**reh**-choh
When do you open / close?	*¿A qué hora abren / cierran?*	ah kay **oh**-rah **ah**-brehn / thee-**ehr**-ahn
At what time?	*¿A qué hora?*	ah kay **oh**-rah
Just a moment.	*Un momento.*	oon moh-**mehn**-toh
now / soon / later	*ahora / pronto / más tarde*	ah-**oh**-rah / **prohn**-toh / mahs **tar**-day
today / tomorrow	*hoy / mañana*	oy / mahn-**yah**-nah

For more user-friendly Spanish phrases, check out *Rick Steves Spanish Phrase Book*.

In a Spanish Restaurant

English	Spanish	Pronunciation
I'd like / We'd like...	Quiero / Queremos...	kee-**ehr**-oh / kehr-**ay**-mohs
...to reserve...	...reservar...	ray-sehr-**bar**
...a table for one / two.	...una mesa para uno / dos.	**oo**-nah **may**-sah **pah**-rah **oo**-noh / dohs
Nonsmoking.	No fumador.	noh foo-mah-**dohr**
Is this table free?	¿Está esta mesa libre?	ay-**stah** ay-stah may-sah **lee**-bray
The menu (in English), please.	La carta (en inglés), por favor.	lah **kar**-tah (ayn een-**glays**) por fah-**bor**
service (not) included	servicio (no) incluido	sehr-**bee**-thee-oh (noh) een-kloo-**ee**-doh
cover charge	precio de entrada	**pray**-thee-oh day ayn-**trah**-dah
to go	para llevar	**pah**-rah yay-**bar**
with / without	con / sin	kohn / seen
and / or	y / o	ee / oh
menu (of the day)	menú (del día)	may-**noo** (dayl **dee**-ah)
specialty of the house	especialidad de la casa	ay-spay-thee-ah-lee-**dahd** day lah **kah**-sah
tourist menu	menú turístico	meh-**noo** too-**ree**-stee-koh
combination plate	plato combinado	**plah**-toh kohm-bee-**nah**-doh
appetizers	tapas	**tah**-pahs
bread	pan	pahn
cheese	queso	**kay**-soh
sandwich	bocadillo	boh-kah-**dee**-yoh
soup	sopa	**soh**-pah
salad	ensalada	ayn-sah-**lah**-dah
meat	carne	**kar**-nay
poultry	aves	**ah**-bays
fish	pescado	pay-**skah**-doh
seafood	marisco	mah-**ree**-skoh
fruit	fruta	**froo**-tah
vegetables	verduras	behr-**doo**-rahs
dessert	postres	**poh**-strays
tap water	agua del grifo	**ah**-gwah dayl **gree**-foh
mineral water	agua mineral	**ah**-gwah mee-nay-**rahl**
milk	leche	**lay**-chay
(orange) juice	zumo (de naranja)	**thoo**-moh (day nah-**rahn**-hah)
coffee	café	kah-**feh**
tea	té	tay
wine	vino	**bee**-noh
red / white	tinto / blanco	**teen**-toh / **blahn**-koh
glass / bottle	vaso / botella	**bah**-soh / boh-**tay**-yah
beer	cerveza	thehr-**bay**-thah
Cheers!	¡Salud!	sah-**lood**
More. / Another.	Más. / Otro.	mahs / **oh**-troh
The same.	El mismo.	ehl **mees**-moh
The bill, please.	La cuenta, por favor.	lah **kwayn**-tah por fah-**bor**
tip	propina	proh-**pee**-nah
Delicious!	¡Delicioso!	day-lee-thee-**oh**-soh

Italian Survival Phrases

English	Italian	Pronunciation
Good day.	Buon giorno.	bwohn **jor**-noh
Do you speak English?	Parla inglese?	**par**-lah een-**gleh**-zay
Yes. / No.	Sì. / No.	see / noh
I (don't) understand.	(Non) capisco.	(nohn) kah-**pees**-koh
Please.	Per favore.	pehr fah-**voh**-ray
Thank you.	Grazie.	**graht**-see-ay
You're welcome.	Prego.	**preh**-go
I'm sorry.	Mi dispiace.	mee dee-spee-**ah**-chay
Excuse me.	Mi scusi.	mee **skoo**-zee
(No) problem.	(Non) c'è un problema.	(nohn) cheh oon proh-**bleh**-mah
Good.	Va bene.	vah **beh**-nay
Goodbye.	Arrivederci.	ah-ree-veh-**dehr**-chee
one / two	uno / due	**oo**-noh / **doo**-ay
three / four	tre / quattro	tray / **kwah**-troh
five / six	cinque / sei	**cheeng**-kway / **seh**-ee
seven / eight	sette / otto	**seh**-tay / **oh**-toh
nine / ten	nove / dieci	**noh**-vay / dee-**ay**-chee
How much is it?	Quanto costa?	**kwahn**-toh **koh**-stah
Write it?	Me lo scrive?	may loh **skree**-vay
Is it free?	È gratis?	eh **grah**-tees
Is it included?	È incluso?	eh een-**kloo**-zoh
Where can I buy / find...?	Dove posso comprare / trovare...?	**doh**-vay **poh**-soh kohm-**prah**-ray / troh-**vah**-ray
I'd like / We'd like...	Vorrei / Vorremmo...	voh-**reh**-ee / voh-**reh**-moh
...a room.	...una camera.	**oo**-nah **kah**-meh-rah
...a ticket to _____.	...un biglietto per _____.	oon beel-**yeh**-toh pehr _____
Is it possible?	È possibile?	eh poh-**see**-bee-lay
Where is...?	Dov'è...?	doh-**veh**
...the train station	...la stazione	lah staht-see-**oh**-nay
...the bus station	...la stazione degli autobus	lah staht-see-**oh**-nay **dehl**-yee ow-toh-boos
...tourist information	...informazioni per turisti	een-for-maht-see-**oh**-nee pehr too-**ree**-stee
...the toilet	...la toilette	lah twah-**leh**-tay
men	uomini / signori	**woh**-mee-nee / seen-**yoh**-ree
women	donne / signore	**doh**-nay / seen-**yoh**-ray
left / right	sinistra / destra	see-**nee**-strah / **deh**-strah
straight	sempre dritto	**sehm**-pray **dree**-toh
What time does this open / close?	A che ora apre / chiude?	ah kay **oh**-rah ah-**pray** / kee-**oo**-day
At what time?	A che ora?	ah kay **oh**-rah
Just a moment.	Un momento.	oon moh-**mehn**-toh
now / soon / later	adesso / presto / tardi	ah-**deh**-soh / **preh**-stoh / **tar**-dee
today / tomorrow	oggi / domani	**oh**-jee / doh-**mah**-nee

For more user-friendly Italian phrases, check out *Rick Steves Italian Phrase Book* or *Rick Steves French, Italian, and German Phrase Book*.

In an Italian Restaurant

English	Italian	Pronunciation
I'd like...	*Vorrei...*	voh-**reh**-ee
We'd like...	*Vorremmo...*	vor-**reh**-moh
...to reserve...	*...prenotare...*	preh-noh-**tah**-ray
...a table for one / two.	*...un tavolo per uno / due.*	oon **tah**-voh-loh pehr **oo**-noh / **doo**-ay
Is this seat free?	*È libero questo posto?*	eh **lee**-beh-roh **kweh**-stoh **poh**-stoh
The menu (in English), please.	*Il menù (in inglese), per favore.*	eel meh-**noo** (een een-**gleh**-zay) pehr fah-**voh**-ray
service (not) included	*servizio (non) incluso*	sehr-**veet**-see-oh (nohn) een-**kloo**-zoh
cover charge	*pane e coperto*	**pah**-nay ay koh-**pehr**-toh
to go	*da portar via*	dah **por**-tar **vee**-ah
with / without	*con / senza*	kohn / **sehnt**-sah
and / or	*e / o*	ay / oh
menu (of the day)	*menù (del giorno)*	meh-**noo** (dehl **jor**-noh)
specialty of the house	*specialità della casa*	speh-chah-lee-**tah** deh-lah **kah**-zah
first course (pasta, soup)	*primo piatto*	**pree**-moh pee-**ah**-toh
main course (meat, fish)	*secondo piatto*	seh-**kohn**-doh pee-**ah**-toh
side dishes	*contorni*	kohn-**tor**-nee
bread	*pane*	**pah**-nay
cheese	*formaggio*	for-**mah**-joh
sandwich	*panino*	pah-**nee**-noh
soup	*zuppa*	**tsoo**-pah
salad	*insalata*	een-sah-**lah**-tah
meat	*carne*	**kar**-nay
chicken	*pollo*	**poh**-loh
fish	*pesce*	**peh**-shay
seafood	*frutti di mare*	**froo**-tee dee **mah**-ray
fruit / vegetables	*frutta / legumi*	**froo**-tah / lay-**goo**-mee
dessert	*dolce*	**dohl**-chay
tap water	*acqua del rubinetto*	**ah**-kwah dehl roo-bee-**neh**-toh
mineral water	*acqua minerale*	**ah**-kwah mee-neh-**rah**-lay
milk	*latte*	**lah**-tay
(orange) juice	*succo (d'arancia)*	**soo**-koh (dah-**rahn**-chah)
coffee / tea	*caffè / tè*	kah-**feh** / teh
wine	*vino*	**vee**-noh
red / white	*rosso / bianco*	**roh**-soh / bee-**ahn**-koh
glass / bottle	*bicchiere / bottiglia*	bee-kee-**eh**-ray / boh-**teel**-yah
beer	*birra*	**bee**-rah
Cheers!	*Cin cin!*	cheen cheen
More. / Another.	*Di più. / Un altro.*	dee pew / oon **ahl**-troh
The same.	*Lo stesso.*	loh **steh**-soh
The bill, please.	*Il conto, per favore.*	eel **kohn**-toh pehr fah-**voh**-ray
Do you accept credit cards?	*Accettate carte di credito?*	ah-cheh-**tah**-tay **kar**-tay dee **kreh**-dee-toh
tip	*mancia*	**mahn**-chah
Delicious!	*Delizioso!*	day-leet-see-**oh**-zoh

German Survival Phrases

When using the phonetics, pronounce ī like the long i in "light." Bolded syllables are stressed.

English	German	Pronunciation
Good day.	Guten Tag.	**goo**-tehn tahg
Do you speak English?	Sprechen Sie Englisch?	**shprehkh**-ehn zee **ehgn**-lish
Yes. / No.	Ja. / Nein.	yah / nīn
I (don't) understand.	Ich verstehe (nicht).	ikh fehr-**shtay**-heh (nikht)
Please.	Bitte.	**bit**-teh
Thank you.	Danke.	**dahng**-keh
I'm sorry.	Es tut mir leid.	ehs toot meer līt
Excuse me.	Entschuldigung.	ehnt-**shool**-dig-oong
(No) problem.	(Kein) Problem.	(kīn) proh-**blaym**
(Very) good.	(Sehr) gut.	(zehr) goot
Goodbye.	Auf Wiedersehen.	owf **vee**-der-zayn
one / two	eins / zwei	īns / tsvī
three / four	drei / vier	drī / feer
five / six	fünf / sechs	fewnf / zehkhs
seven / eight	sieben / acht	**zee**-behn / ahkht
nine / ten	neun / zehn	noyn / tsayn
How much is it?	Wieviel kostet das?	**vee**-feel **kohs**-teht dahs
Write it?	Schreiben?	**shrī**-behn
Is it free?	Ist es umsonst?	ist ehs oom-**zohnst**
Included?	Inklusive?	in-kloo-**zee**-veh
Where can I buy / find...?	Wo kann ich kaufen / finden...?	voh kahn ikh **kow**-fehn / **fin**-dehn
I'd like / We'd like...	Ich hätte gern / Wir hätten gern...	ikh **heh**-teh gehrn / veer **heh**-tehn gehrn
...a room.	...ein Zimmer.	īn **tsim**-mer
...a ticket to _____ .	...eine Fahrkarte nach _____ .	**ī**-neh **far**-kar-teh nahkh
Is it possible?	Ist es möglich?	ist ehs **mur**-glikh
Where is...?	Wo ist...?	voh ist
...the train station	...der Bahnhof	dehr **bahn**-hohf
...the bus station	...der Busbahnhof	dehr **boos**-bahn-hohf
...the tourist information office	...das Touristen-informations-büro	dahs too-**ris**-tehn-in-for-maht-see-**ohns**-**bew**-roh
...the toilet	...die Toilette	dee toh-**leh**-teh
men	Herren	**hehr**-rehn
women	Damen	**dah**-mehn
left / right	links / rechts	links / rehkhts
straight	geradeaus	geh-**rah**-deh-**ows**
What time does this open / close?	Um wieviel Uhr wird hier geöffnet / geschlossen?	oom **vee**-feel oor veerd heer geh-**urf**-neht / geh-**shloh**-sehn
At what time?	Um wieviel Uhr?	oom **vee**-feel oor
Just a moment.	Moment.	moh-**mehnt**
now / soon / later	jetzt / bald / später	yehtst / bahld / **shpay**-ter
today / tomorrow	heute / morgen	**hoy**-teh / **mor**-gehn

For more user-friendly German phrases, check out *Rick Steves German Phrase Book* or *Rick Steves French, Italian & German Phrase Book*.

In a German Restaurant

English	German	Pronunciation
I'd like / We'd like...	Ich hätte gern / Wir hätten gern...	ikh **heh**-teh gehrn / veer **heh**-tehn gehrn
...a reservation for...	...eine Reservierung für...	**ī**-neh reh-zer-**feer**-oong fewr
...a table for one / two.	...einen Tisch für eine Person / zwei Personen.	**ī**-nehn tish fewr **ī**-neh pehr-zohn / tsvī pehr-**zoh**-nehn
Nonsmoking.	Nichtraucher.	**nikht**-rowkh-er
Is this seat free?	Ist hier frei?	ist heer frī
Menu (in English), please.	Speisekarte (auf Englisch), bitte.	**shpī**-zeh-kar-teh (owf **ehng**-lish) **bit**-teh
service (not) included	Trinkgeld (nicht) inklusive	**trink**-gehlt (nikht) in-kloo-**zee**-veh
cover charge	Eintritt	**īn**-trit
to go	zum Mitnehmen	tsoom **mit**-nay-mehn
with / without	mit / ohne	mit / **oh**-neh
and / or	und / oder	oont / **oh**-der
menu (of the day)	(Tages-) Karte	(**tah**-gehs-) **kar**-teh
set meal for tourists	Touristenmenü	too-**ris**-tehn-meh-**new**
specialty of the house	Spezialität des Hauses	**shpayt**-see-ah-lee-**tayt** dehs **how**-zehs
appetizers	Vorspeise	**for**-shpī-zeh
bread / cheese	Brot / Käse	broht / **kay**-zeh
sandwich	Sandwich	**zahnd**-vich
soup	Suppe	**zup**-peh
salad	Salat	zah-**laht**
meat	Fleisch	flīsh
poultry	Geflügel	geh-**flew**-gehl
fish	Fisch	fish
seafood	Meeresfrüchte	**meh**-rehs-**frewkh**-teh
fruit	Obst	ohpst
vegetables	Gemüse	geh-**mew**-zeh
dessert	Nachspeise	**nahkh**-shpī-zeh
mineral water	Mineralwasser	min-eh-**rahl**-vah-ser
tap water	Leitungswasser	**lī**-toongs-vah-ser
milk	Milch	milkh
(orange) juice	(Orangen-) Saft	(oh-**rahn**-zhehn-) zahft
coffee / tea	Kaffee / Tee	kah-**fay** / tay
wine	Wein	vīn
red / white	rot / weiß	roht / vīs
glass / bottle	Glas / Flasche	glahs / **flah**-sheh
beer	Bier	beer
Cheers!	Prost!	prohst
More. / Another.	Mehr. / Noch eins.	mehr / nohkh īns
The same.	Das gleiche.	dahs **glīkh**-eh
Bill, please.	Rechnung, bitte.	**rehkh**-noong **bit**-teh
tip	Trinkgeld	**trink**-gehlt
Delicious!	Lecker!	**lehk**-er

Dutch Survival Phrases

Most people speak English, but if you learn the pleasantries and key phrases, you'll connect better with the locals. To pronounce the guttural Dutch "g" (indicated in phonetics by *h*), make a clear-your-throat sound, similar to the "ch" in the Scottish word "loch."

English	Dutch	Pronunciation
Hello.	Hallo.	**hah**-loh
Good day.	Dag.	dah
Good morning.	Goedemorgen.	**hoo**-deh-mor-hehn
Good afternoon.	Goedemiddag.	**hoo**-deh-mid-dah
Good evening.	Goedenavond.	**hoo**-dehn-ah-fohnd
Do you speak English?	Spreekt u Engels?	shpraykt oo **eng**-ehls
Yes. / No.	Ja. / Nee.	yah / nay
I (don't) understand.	Ik begrijp (het niet).	ik beh-**hripe** (heht neet)
Please. (can also mean "You're welcome")	Alstublieft.	**ahl**-stoo-bleeft
Thank you.	Dank u wel.	dahnk oo vehl
I'm sorry.	Het spijt me.	heht spite meh
Excuse me.	Pardon.	**par**-dohn
(No) problem.	(Geen) probleem.	(hayn) **proh**-blaym
Good.	Goede.	**hoo**-deh
Goodbye.	Tot ziens.	toht zeens
one / two	een / twee	ayn / t'vay
three / four	drie / vier	dree / feer
five / six	vijf / zes	fife / zehs
seven / eight	zeven / acht	**zay**-fehn / aht
nine / ten	negen / tien	**nay**-hehn / teen
What does it cost?	Wat kost het?	vaht kohst heht
Is it free?	Is het vrij?	is heht fry
Is it included?	Is het inclusief?	is heht in-**kloo**-seev
Can you please help me?	Kunt u alstublieft helpen?	koont oo **ahl**-stoo-bleeft **hehl**-pehn
Where can I buy / find...?	Waar kan ik kopen / vinden...?	var kahn ik **koh**-pehn / **fin**-dehn
I'd like / We'd like...	Ik wil graag / Wij willen graag...	ik vil *hrah* / vy **vil**-lehn *hrah*
...a room.	...een kamer.	ayn **kah**-mer
...a train / bus ticket to	...een trein / bus kaartje naar	ayn trayn / boos **kart**-yeh nar
...to rent a bike.	...een fiets huren.	ayn feets **hoo**-rehn
Where is...?	Waar is...?	var is
...the train / bus station	...het trein / bus station	heht trayn / boos **staht**-see-ohn
...the tourist info office	...de VVV	deh fay fay fay
...the toilet	...het toilet	heht **twah**-leht
men / women	mannen / vrouwen	**mah**-nehn / **frow**-ehn
left / right	links / rechts	links / rehts
straight ahead	rechtdoor	**reht**-dor
What time does it open / close?	Hoe laat gaat het open / dicht?	hoo laht haht heht **oh**-pehn / di*h*t
now / soon / later	nu / straks / later	noo / strahks / **lah**-ter
today / tomorrow	vandaag / morgen	**fahn**-dah / **mor**-hehn

In a Dutch Restaurant

The all-purpose Dutch word *alstublieft* (ahl-stoo-bleeft) means "please," but it can also mean "here you are" (when the server hands you something), "thanks" (when taking payment from you), or "you're welcome" (when handing you change). Here are other words that might come in handy at restaurants:

English	Dutch	Pronunciation
I'd like / We'd like...	Ik wil graag / Wij willen graag...	ik vil hrah / vy **vil**-lehn hrah
...a table for one / two.	...een tafel voor een / twee.	ayn **tah**-fehl for ayn / t'vay
...to reserve a table.	...een tafel reserveren.	ayn **tah**-fehl **ray**-zehr-feh-rehn
...the menu (in English).	...het menu (in het Engels).	heht meh-**noo** (in heht **eng**-ehls)
Is this table free?	Is deze tafel vrij?	is **day**-zeh **tah**-fehl fry
to go	om mee te nemen	ohm may teh **nay**-mehn
with / without	met / zonder	meht / **zohn**-der
and / or	en / of	ehn / of
special of the day	dagschotel	**dahs**-hoh-tehl
specialty of the house	huisspecialiteit	**hows**-shpeh-shah-lee-tite
breakfast	ontbijt	**ohnt**-bite
lunch	middagmaal	**mid**-dah-mahl
dinner	avondmaal	**ah**-fohnd-mahl
appetizers	hapjes	**hahp**-yehs
main courses	hoofdgerechten	**hohfd**-heh-reh-tehn
side dishes	bijgerechten	**bye**-heh-reh-tehn
bread / cheese	brood / kaas	brohd / kahs
sandwich	sandwich	**sand**-vich
soup / salad	soep / sla	soop / slah
meat / chicken / fish	vlees / kip / vis	flays / kip / fis
fruit / vegetables	vrucht / groenten	fruht / **hroon**-tehn
dessert / pastries	gebak	heh-**bahk**
I am vegetarian.	Ik ben vegetarisch.	ik behn vay-heh-**tah**-rish
mineral water / tap water	mineraalwater / kraanwater	min-eh-rahl-**vah**-ter / **krahn**-vah-ter
milk / (orange) juice	melk / (sinaasappel) sap	mehlk / **see**-nahs-ah-pehl (sahp)
coffee / tea	koffie / thee	**koh**-fee / tay
wine / beer	wijn / bier	vine / beer
red / white	rode / witte	**roh**-deh / **vit**-teh
glass / bottle	glas / fles	hlahs / flehs
Cheers!	Proost!	prohst
More. / Another.	Meer. / Nog een.	mayr / noh ayn
The same.	Het zelfde.	heht **zehlf**-deh
The bill, please.	De rekening, alstublieft.	deh **ray**-keh-neeng **ahl**-stoo-bleeft
Do you accept credit cards?	Accepteert u kredietkaarten?	**ahk**-shehp-tayrt oo kray-deet-**kar**-tehn
Is service included?	Is bediening inbegrepen?	is beh-**dee**-neeng in-beh-**hray**-pehn
tip	fooi	foy
Tasty.	Lekker.	**leh**-ker
Enjoy!	Smakelijk!	**smah**-keh-like

INDEX

MAP INDEX

Start your trip at

Explore Europe

At ricksteves.com you can browse through thousands of articles, videos, photos and radio interviews, plus find a wealth of money-saving travel tips for planning your dream trip. And with our mobile-friendly website, you can easily access all this great travel information anywhere you go.

TV Shows

Preview the places you'll visit by watching entire half-hour episodes of *Rick Steves' Europe* (choose from all 100 shows) on-demand, for free.

ricksteves.com

your travel dreams into affordable reality

Radio Interviews

Enjoy ready access to Rick's vast library of radio interviews covering travel tips and cultural insights that relate specifically to your Europe travel plans.

Travel Forums

Learn, ask, share! Our online community of savvy travelers is a great resource for first-time travelers to Europe, as well as seasoned pros.

Travel News

Subscribe to our free Travel News e-newsletter, and get monthly updates from Rick on what's happening in Europe.

Classroom Europe

Check out our free resource for educators with 400+ short video clips from the *Rick Steves' Europe* TV show.

Audio Europe™

Rick's Free Travel App

Get your FREE Rick Steves Audio Europe™ app to enjoy...

- Dozens of self-guided tours of Europe's top museums, sights and historic walks
- Hundreds of tracks filled with cultural insights and sightseeing tips from Rick's radio interviews
- All organized into handy geographic playlists
- For Apple and Android

With Rick whispering in your ear, Europe gets even better.

Find out more at ricksteves.com

Pack Light and Right

Gear up for your next adventure at ricksteves.com

Light Luggage

Pack light and right with Rick Steves' affordable, custom-designed rolling carry-on bags, backpacks, day packs and shoulder bags.

Accessories

From packing cubes to moneybelts and beyond, Rick has personally selected the travel goodies that will help your trip go smoother.

Shop at **ricksteves.com**

Rick Steves has

great tours, too!

with minimum stress

interesting places with great guides and small groups. We follow Rick's favorite itineraries, ride in comfy buses, stay in family-run hotels, and bring you intimately close to the Europe you've traveled so far to see. Most importantly, we take away the logistical headaches so you can focus on the fun.

travelers—nearly half of them repeat customers—along with us on four dozen different itineraries, from Ireland to Italy to Athens.

Is a Rick Steves tour the right fit for your travel dreams? Find out at ricksteves.com, where you can also check seat availability and sign up.

Join the fun

This year we'll take thousands of free-spirited

Europe is best experienced with happy travel partners. We hope you can join us.

See our itineraries at ricksteves.com

A Guide for Every Trip

BEST OF GUIDES

Full color easy-to-scan format, focusing on Europe's most popular destinations and sights

Best of England
Best of Europe
Best of France
Best of Germany
Best of Ireland
Best of Italy
Best of Scotland
Best of Spain

COMPREHENSIVE GUIDES

City, country, and regional guides with detailed coverage for a multi-week trip exploring the most iconic sights and venturing off the beaten track

Amsterdam & the Netherlands
Barcelona
Belgium: Bruges, Brussels,
   Antwerp & Ghent
Berlin
Budapest
Croatia & Slovenia
Eastern Europe
England
Florence & Tuscany
France
Germany
Great Britain
Greece: Athens & the Peloponnese
Iceland
Ireland
Istanbul
Italy
London
Paris
Portugal
Prague & the Czech Republic
Provence & the French Riviera
Rome
Scandinavia
Scotland
Sicily
Spain
Switzerland
Venice
Vienna, Salzburg & Tirol

THE BEST OF ROME

...ome, Italy's capital, is studded with ...ncient ruins and floodlit-fountain ...quares. From the Vatican to the Col-...seum, with crazy traffic in between, ...me is wonderful, huge, and exhaust-... The crowds, the heat, and the

weighty history of the Eternal City where Caesars walked can make tourists wilt. Recharge by taking siestas, gelato breaks, and after-dark walks, strolling from one atmospheric square to another in the refreshing evening air.

...mired **Pantheon**—which
...rgest dome until the
...early 2,000 years old
... day over 1,500).

...ol of Athens in
...ums embodies the
...f the Renaissance.

...m, gladiators fought
...e another, entertaining
...00.

...his Rome **ristora**...

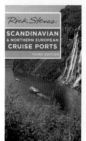

POCKET GUIDES

Compact, full color city guides with the essentials for shorter trips

Amsterdam	Munich & Salzburg
Athens	Paris
Barcelona	Prague
Florence	Rome
Italy's Cinque Terre	Venice
London	Vienna

SNAPSHOT GUIDES

Focused single-destination coverage

Basque Country: Spain & France
Copenhagen & the Best of Denmark
Dublin
Dubrovnik
Edinburgh
Hill Towns of Central Italy
Krakow, Warsaw & Gdansk
Lisbon
Loire Valley
Madrid & Toledo
Milan & the Italian Lakes District
Naples & the Amalfi Coast
Nice & the French Riviera
Normandy
Northern Ireland
Norway
Reykjavík
Rothenburg & the Rhine
Sevilla, Granada & Southern Spain
St. Petersburg, Helsinki & Tallinn
Stockholm

CRUISE PORTS GUIDES

Reference for cruise ports of call

Mediterranean Cruise Ports
Scandinavian & Northern European Cruise Ports

Complete your library with...

TRAVEL SKILLS & CULTURE

Europe 101
Europe Through the Back Door
European Christmas
European Easter
European Festivals
Europe's Top 100 Masterpieces
For the Love of Europe
Postcards from Europe
Travel as a Political Act

PHRASE BOOKS & DICTIONARIES

French
French, Italian & German
German
Italian
Portuguese
Spanish

PLANNING MAPS

Britain, Ireland & London
Europe
France & Paris
Germany, Austria & Switzerland
Iceland
Ireland
Italy
Spain & Portugal

PHOTO CREDITS

Avalon Travel
Hachette Book Group
1700 Fourth Street
Berkeley, CA 94710

Printed in China by RR Donnelley

Third Edition. First printing April 2021.

ISBN 978-1-64171-308-5

For the latest on Rick's talks, guidebooks, tours, public television series, and public radio show, contact Rick Steves' Europe, 130 Fourth Avenue North, Edmonds, WA 98020, 425/771-8303, RickSteves.com, rick@ricksteves.com.

RICK STEVES' EUROPE
Managing Editor: Jennifer Madison Davis
Assistant Managing Editor: Cathy Lu
Special Publications Manager: Risa Laib
Editors: Glenn Eriksen, Suzanne Kotz, Rosie Leutzinger, Teresa Nemeth, Jessica Shaw, Carrie Shepherd, Meg Sneeringer
Editorial & Production Assistant: Megan Simms
Graphic Content Director: Sandra Hundacker
Maps & Graphics: David C. Hoerlein, Lauren Mills, Mary Rostad
Digital Asset Coordinator: Orin Dubrow

AVALON TRAVEL
Editorial Director: Kevin McLain
Senior Editor and Series Manager: Madhu Prasher
Associate Managing Editors: Jamie Andrade, Sierra Machado
Indexer: Stephen Callahan
Interior Design: McGuire Barber Design
Production: Rue Flaherty, Jane Musser, Tabitha Lahr
Cover Design: Kimberly Glyder Design
Maps & Graphics: Kat Bennett, Mike Morgenfeld

Let's Keep on Travelin'

Your trip doesn't need to end.

Follow Rick on social media!